W.F. Finlason

Reeves´ History of the English Law
Volume II

Salzwasser

W.F. Finlason

Reeves´ History of the English Law Volume II

1. Auflage | ISBN: 978-3-75250-004-2

Erscheinungsort: Frankfurt, Deutschland

Erscheinungsjahr: 2020

Salzwasser Verlag GmbH

Reprint of the original, first published in 1869.

REEVES'

HISTORY OF THE ENGLISH LAW.

EDITED BY

W. F. FINLASON.

VOL. II.

REEVES'
HISTORY OF THE ENGLISH LAW,

FROM THE

TIME OF THE ROMANS,

TO THE

END OF THE REIGN OF ELIZABETH.

A NEW EDITION, IN THREE VOLUMES.

WITH NUMEROUS NOTES, AND

AN INTRODUCTORY DISSERTATION

ON

THE NATURE AND USE OF LEGAL HISTORY, THE RISE AND PROGRESS OF OUR LAWS, AND THE INFLUENCE OF THE ROMAN LAW IN THE FORMATION OF OUR OWN.

BY W. F. FINLASON, ESQ.,

BARRISTER-AT-LAW.

VOL. II.

FROM THE REIGN OF EDWARD I. TO THE REIGN OF EDWARD IV.

LONDON:

REEVES & TURNER, CHANCERY LANE.

1869.

CONTENTS OF THE SECOND VOLUME.

PAGE

CHAPTER XIII.

EDWARD III.

CHAPTER XIV.

EDWARD III.

CHAPTER XV.

EDWARD III.

CHAPTER XVI.

EDWARD III.

CHAPTER XVII.

RICHARD II.

CHAPTER XVIII.

HENRY IV.

PAGE

CHAPTER XIX.

HENRY V.

CHAPTER XX.

HENRY VI.

CHAPTER XXI.

HENRY VI. AND EDWARD IV.

CHAPTER XXII.

HENRY VI.

CHAPTER XXIII.

HENRY VI. AND EDWARD IV.

HISTORY OF THE ENGLISH LAW.

CHAPTER IX.

EDWARD I.

Statutum Walliæ—Ordinatio pro Statu Hiberniæ—Confirmations of the Charters—De Tallagio non Concedendo—Ordinatio Forestæ—Of Wreck—Wards—Of Aids—Distresses—Assizes—Of Attaints—Vouching to Warranty—Attachment—Of Rape—Extortion of Officers—Spreaders of False Reports—Of Replevying Prisoners—Of Clergy—Peine Forte et Dure—The Office of Coroners—Warranty of Tenant per Legem Angliæ—Waste—Feigned Recoveries—Homicide se Defendendo—Statute of Mortmain—Statute of Acton Burnell.

We now enter upon a period when the law made a very great and sudden advancement. It is generally agreed that this is, in no small degree, to be ascribed to the wisdom and activity of the prince on the throne, who, through his whole reign, and indeed within the first thirteen years of it, laboured more than any of his predecessors to improve our judicial polity in all its parts. So successful were his endeavours, and so permanent have been their effects, that Edward I. has obtained with posterity the distinguished title of the English Justinian.

Sir Matthew Hale is very full and significant in the eulogium he bestows on this monarch. "It appears," says he, "that the very scheme, mould, and model of the common law, especially in relation to the administration of the common justice between party and party, as it was highly rectified, and set in a much better light and order by this king than his predecessors left it to him; so in a very great measure it was continued the same in all succeeding ages to this day; so that the mark or epocha we are to take for the true stating of the law of England, *What it is*, is to be considered, stated, and estimated, from what it was when this king left it" (*a*).[1] The justness of this representation will be seen in the sequel.

(*a*) Our author considered the reign of Edward I. as marking a great era or epoch in the history of our law; and there can be no doubt that, in the opinion of all our legal authorities, it does so; and it fitly, therefore, makes the commencement of a book or volume in this history. And it may be convenient here to present something like a general view of the policy and legal history of the reign. In order to

[1] Hale's *Hist. Com. Law*, 163.

The reader who has gone through the last reign is sufficiently apprised of the then state of the law to comprehend the effect of the numerous alterations which it will receive in this. These

understand the subject, it is necessary to bear in mind the state of things at the accession of this king.

During the long and turbulent reign of Henry III., there had been a long struggle between the rising spirit of liberty and regal tyranny; and as law had not yet attained supremacy, and there was therefore no guarantee of its observance but civil war, the country for nearly half a century had suffered all the misery of constant intestine strife, in which the struggle between the spirit of liberty and of tyranny necessarily assumed the aspect of a contest between the principles of anarchy and authority. During this period, on the one hand, the nation had become so wearied of the strife, and so sensible of the necessity for the supremacy of law in order for the security of liberty, that it was prepared to acquiesce in any fair exercise of royal authority necessary to the attainment of that end, and even any exercise of it short of actual tyranny; and, on the other hand, the royal resources were so crippled, that it was not prepared for any extension of that authority beyond what would be sanctioned by law. In a word, the crown and the people were alike weary of contest, and *the treasury was empty*. Hence a mutual sense of the necessity of peace, and a desire on the part of the crown to replenish the treasury as much as possible by means not contrary to law; and a disposition, on the part of the people, to submit to any exactions which could be reconciled with law and any fair degree of liberty. The king, in short, was prepared to administer justice between his subjects if they would pay for it; and they were quite willing to pay a reasonable price for the blessings of peace and order. Hence the whole policy of the internal legislation of the reign may be summed upthus: the making law and justice profitable to the crown, and thus deriving a revenue, with advantage to the subject, from the administration of justice and the supremacy of law.

It also was a necessary consequence of the principle that the crown is charged with the duty of seeing that justice is administered, and that thus allegiance and protection are correlative. Where there is the duty and responsibility, there must be the power. And, again, as the crown alone can enforce the execution of the sentences of courts, of necessity their power or jurisdiction must be derived therefrom. And, again, as jurisdiction, civil or criminal, is coercive, it is a necessary attribute of the executive power of government, as Guizot points out. Thus Rayneval lays it down that "le pouvoir judiciaire est une émanation du pouvoir exécutif" (*Droits de la Nature*, ch. xii.) Thus, our most ancient authorities of law lay it down that all jurisdiction is from the crown. Thus Fleta: "Sine warranto jurisdictionem non habent neque coercionem" (c. xxxiv.) So, in the *Mirror of Justice*, it is said that jurisdiction is the power to *declare* the law, and that it rests with the king, because he alone can enforce and execute it (c. i.) The county courts were in theory the courts of the king, but *only* in theory: in reality, they were mere popular assemblies. *Practically*, a king's judge made a king's court; and the object was to establish the supremacy of the king's courts on the basis of the supremacy of the royal authority. This was done indirectly by getting parliaments to grant subsidies, in consideration of the remedy of abuses, (which belongs more to political than legal history), and, in a more direct manner, by improving and extending the administration of justice in the king's courts, and thus bringing litigation thereto, and then deriving, by means of fees, or fines, or forfeitures, a revenue therefrom. Such was the policy of the reign, and with this latter part of it legal history has to deal. The acquisition of a revenue from the administration of justice, was not indeed entirely a novelty, or a discovery of this particular king. The discovery had been made and acted upon by one of our worst sovereigns, John, who, however, had acted upon it according to his nature, in a crude and arbitrary way, by the infliction of fines or exaction of bribes; and hence the clause in the Great Charter against selling justice. Edward I., however, was a far more wise and astute prince, and, having been disciplined in adversity, and instructed by experience and observation, pursued a far more wise and politic course. This policy was to improve the administration of justice between his subjects, by means of a more regular procedure, and to make them pay for it in a regular and proper manner. Hence so much of the legislation of his reign relates to procedure. This was a policy naturally appreciated by lawyers. From the age immediately following that of Edward I., his reign has

alterations were principally made by parliamentary interposition. The statutes of this reign present a new scene to the reader, very different from that which he has passed in the preceding. We

always been spoken of as that of a singularly wise and sagacious prince, and as the era of very useful and valuable legislation, especially as to the administration of justice. Thus, in the Year-books of his grandson Edward III., an eminent judge, Sir William Herle, Lord-Chief Justice of the Common Pleas, described him from the bench as the wisest king that ever had reigned: "Fuit le pluis sage roy que unques fuit" (*Year-book*, 5 Edward III., 14). And the very terms of the preamble of the first great statute of his reign, the first great statute of Westminster (anno 3 Edward I.), marks a great era in the history of law: "Ceux sont les establishments le roi Eduard faits a Westminster a son primer parliament-general apres son coronement; per son counsell et per l'assentments des archievesques, evesques, abbes, priors, countes, barons, et tout le commonalty de la terre, ellonques summones. Pur ceo que nostre seignior le roy ad graund volunt et desire del estate de son realme redresser en les choses ou mestier est d'amendment; et ceo pur le common profit de saint eglise et de son realme; et pur ceo que l'estate de son realme et de saint eglise ad este malement garde; et les prelates et religious de la terre en mults des manners grieves; et le people autrement treit que estre duist; et la peace meines garde et les leyes meins uses, et les misfesants meins punies, que estre duissent; que quoy les gents de la terre doubteront meins a misfaire; ey ad le roy ordeine et establie les choses souscripts; les queux il entende destre profitables et covenables a tout le realme." There is no reason to doubt that this really expressed the views with which this wise and sagacious sovereign ascended the throne and assumed the government of the realm; and that, after the experience of half a century of turbulence and discord, in which civil war had been the only remedy against tyranny, he and his councillors were really impressed with the necessity of establishing the supremacy of law, and for that purpose of asserting the supremacy of the royal power, and basing upon it the supreme and sovereign jurisdiction of the king's courts. And to that end certainly the legislation of the reign was constantly and consistently directed. But it is not less manifest that this wise policy of the king was dictated by an enlightened sense of self interest rather than by any regard for justice in the abstract, or for the rights or interests of his subjects. For there never was a sovereign more rapacious or unscrupulous, nor one who, while zealous for justice as between his subjects, was more utterly regardless of it as between his subjects and himself. Thus, although there was much of wise and salutary legislation to restrain oppression among his subjects, he himself never meant to be restrained by them, and, no doubt, knew right well that his crown lawyers had established a maxim, that the crown was not bound by a statute unless by express terms mentioned—so that the excellent provisions he enacted for the protection of his subjects from each other, lent them no protection against the crown. Thus, for instance, as to one of the most important provisions of the second statute of Westminster, protecting infants, *femes coverte*, and others from oppression, it was held that the king was not bound by it, so that he might oppress them at pleasure without redress (35 *Hen. VI.*, 62). So, although the legislation of this reign did much to improve the remedies of subjects as between themselves—by action or suit at law—it must be borne in mind that this remedy did not avail as against the king's officers, acting in their official capacity on behalf of the crown. The only remedy allowed in such cases was the petition of right—*i.e.*, a petition to the crown against its own officers—a remedy in that age, it need hardly be said, entirely illusory, so that practically any amount of oppression was practised by the king's officers without any real redress. So as to another enactment in the statute of Westminster (c. xvi.), as to taking of beasts, it is remarkable that though the statute does not in terms except the king or his ministers, yet it was held that, by construction of law, they were excepted, because the king might do it by his prerogative (13 *Edw. IV.*, 2 *Inst.* 191). As in cases of purveyance, as it was called, which led to the most grievous abuses, many of the enactments in the statute of Westminster will be found to have had a direct bearing upon the benefit to be derived to the royal revenue from the administration of justice in the king's courts; as, for example, stat. West. 1., c. 35, which, as Coke says, was pointed to a mischief (in local courts), to the prejudice of the king, in losing his fines in actions, and amerciaments and other profits 2 *Inst.* 229), and the terms of the statute itself are "*en prejudice du roy*: et a damage du people;" but the former being evidently the real grievance. So as to

come now to a series of legislative acts, which, in all periods of the law, have been considered as constituting a necessary, yet difficult branch of study. These furnish an immediate occasion to apply

the pretended limitation set up for the first time in this reign, to the jurisdiction of the county courts, restraining it to cases under 40s., unless the king's writ was obtained (see the comments on the statute of Gloucester), the object of which was to bring business into the king's courts, where the fines, fees, and amerciaments would augment the royal revenue. No doubt the suitors also gained the advantage of better judicature and regular procedure in the supreme courts, but the interest of the subject was not the object, the real object was the necessity for money. The same object was the cause of other obnoxious proceedings of the reign; for example, the oppressive proceeding by *quo warranto*, of which Coke says, "The truth is, that the king wanting money, there were some who persuaded him that none that had franchises by the grants of the king's predecessors had right to them, for that they had no charters to show for the same, for that in truth most of their charters, either by length of time or by casualty, were lost or consumed; whereupon it was openly proclaimed, that every man that held those liberties or other possessions, by grants from any of the king's progenitors, should, before certain selected persons, show, *quo jure* illi retinerent, &c., whereupon many that had long continued in quiet possession were taken into the king's hands. To remedy which, there was a chapter in the statute of Gloucester, passed in the sixth year of the reign" (2 *Inst.* 280). In this and the next reign, writs of *quo warranto* appear to have been very frequent. In *quo warranto*, the party claimed to have a franchise (of toll) in his manor, and said that his father died seised, and this seems to have been held sufficient (*Bro. Abr. Quo Warranto*, fol. 3). In *quo warranto*, the party claimed to hold a court for his tenants in his manor; and it was held sufficient to show that he had the manor (*Ibid.* fol. 4; 17 *Edw. II.*) So numerous were the claims to franchise, as appendant (*Ibid.* fol. 5; 6 *Edw. II.*, fol. 6). Free warren was a franchise sometimes claimed (*Ibid.* fol. 6; 6 *Edw. II.*, 6, 7). So as to fairs, markets, or tolls (*Year-book*, 16 *Edw. IV.*, 10; 15 *Edw. IV.*, 4, 7). Franchises could sometimes be claimed by prescription, that is, by user from before the time of legal memory (*Ibid.* fol. 8; 6 *Edw. II.*, fol. 7). Whenever the subject claimed any power of privilege, whether of holding local courts or markets, or levying tolls, or the like, if he could not support his claim at law, he was liable to be heavily fined for usurping the franchise, and also had to forfeit it to the king, who could then sell it to him or to the highest bidder. Thus the proceedings had a direct effect in augmenting the revenue. This politic prince, in order to give his exactions the colour of legality, and to promote the object he had in view, of enabling himself to derive as large a revenue as possible in accordance with law, and especially from the administration of justice, caused a treatise to be written, and to give it greater weight and authority, to be written in his own name, whereby the law, to the utmost possible extent, should appear to favour the royal prerogative; and, in particular, to base the administration of justice upon the supremacy of the royal authority. As the learned treatise of Bracton was already in existence and quite sufficiently favoured the prerogative of the crown, it is obvious that no new treatise could be really required for the exposition of the law; and, indeed, the new treatise by Britton is, for the most part, based upon that of Bracton; so that it has been supposed to be only a new and popular version of it—Bracton being in Latin, and Britton in the Norman-French of that age. But it differs from that of Bracton in this most important respect, that it is far more favourable to the prerogative, and especially with reference to all possible pecuniary emoluments or exactions to be derived from the subject under the forms of justice or the pretence of law. That it should be so will appear natural enough, when it is borne in mind that it was in effect written under the king's dictation. This appears upon the face of the book, for it begins thus:—"Edward, par la grace de Dieu, Roy D'Engleterre et Seigniour de Irlande, a touts ses feals et ses sujets, pees and grace et Sauvaycon. Desiraunt estre le people que est en nostre protection, par la suffraunces de Dieu (la quels pees ne peut mye bien estre sans ley), avons les leyes que l'en ad uses en nostre royalme avant ses houres fait mettre en escript solonques ceo que ca est ordeine, et volons que soient issent uses et tenues in touts points, save a nous de repealer et de amender, a touts les foits que nous verrons que bon a nous serra par l'assent de nos countes fist un liver deux ans prochein apres le fesance de cet statute, en quel est reherse tout ces statute," which is indeed recited in Britton, fol. 169. Thus, then, it is clear that the book was written

great part of the detail of ancient law that has just been delivered; and as the design and effect of them will be more easily and more naturally comprehended after this preparation, it is trusted the reader will feel himself amply rewarded for the trouble and time

at the direction of the king, and within the first five years of his reign, after the first statute of Westminster, and before the second. It also appears, from the preamble of the book itself, that it was written at the dictation of the king, and with an evident desire to favour the royal prerogative and the jurisdiction of the royal courts et barons, &c. The language of this preamble plainly indicates that the treatise was written under the dictation of the king, and also with the object of effecting some alterations, the nature of which will be apparent from a perusal of it, and a comparison with the tenor of the prior work of Bracton. As to the first point, it was certainly the traditional belief of the age; for in the reign of Henry VI., a chief justice, Prisot, distinctly stated from the bench that the book of Britton was written under the orders of Edward I.; and he fixes the date of its composition. For, speaking of the first statute of Westminster (3 *Edw. I.*), he said :—"C'est statute fuit fait al temps de Roy Edw. I., le quel Roy fuit appurpose d'aver mis tout en certaine, et en esscriture, et commenca de ceo faire livers de et plus sages hommes del ley, s. judges, et auxi il fist en liver deux ans," &c. (*Year-book*, 35 *Henry VI.*, fol 42). It is quite plain that it had a very different object from that suggested, of putting the law into writing, for that had, as to the common law, already been done in the great treatise of Bracton. As regards any alterations considered necessary by the legislature, it was being done by the statutes passed from time to time. The object was to warp and wrest the common law as much as possible in favour of the royal prerogative, and at all events to represent the whole administration of justice as depending on the royal authority, so as to enhance the necessity for its supremacy. Hence, at the outset, in the very first paragraph, all justice is described as resting on the royal authority. "En primes, en droit de nous mesmes, et de nostre court, avous issint ordeine, que pur ces que nous ne suffisons mye en nostre propre persone a oyer et terminer toutes quereles de people, avons party nostre charge en plusurs partres sicome icy est ordeine, nous volons que nostre jurisdiction soit sur toutes jurisdictions en nostre royalme, eyent poer, a rendire, et faire rendre les judgments par la ou nous savons le droite verite come juge." Thus, the supremacy of royal jurisdiction is asserted at the outset in all its plenitude, and that strikes the key-note, so to speak, not only of the treatise of Britton, but of the whole policy of the reign, as to law and justice. Thus the whole system of the administration of justice was deduced from this great fundamental principle. "Et volons que justices errants soient assignes oyer et terminer enchescun counte, &c. En droit des justices que sont assignes de nous suyvre, et tener nostre lieu volons que eux eyent conisaunce de amender faux judgments, et de terminer appels, et trespass faits enconter nostre fees et nostre jurisdiction." That is, the King's Bench—"Et enchescun counte soit un visconte," (the sheriff), "que soit entendaunt au commandements de nous, et de nos justices, que des pleas pledes devaunt eux par nos brefs eyent record." And so of the coroners—"Et enchescun comiti soient corones eslus a la garde de pleas de nostre pees." So much for pleas of the crown; and it is to be observed that the court of king's bench was alone indicated as the highest court of such jurisdiction, and as following the king; whereas, according to Magna Charta, the court of common pleas was fixed, and is so described in the next paragraph, but is with equal care described as deriving its jurisdiction, in each case, only from a special royal authority, conveyed in a writ. "Volons que justices demoergent continuelment a Westminster, ou aillours la ou nous voudrons ordeiner a pleder communes pleas solonque ceo que nous les maundrons par vous brefs, issint que des paroles deduces devaunt eux par nous brefs eyent record." Thus it was established that no one could commence an action without an original writ (as it was called), which, in any case not entirely novel, was utterly useless and unnecessary, and was only required for the sake of imposing a fee, and thus deriving a revenue out of the administration of justice. Next the court of exchequer is mentioned: "Ainsi volons nos que a nous Eschekers a Westminster et aillours eyent nos tresorers et nos barons illeques jurisdiction de choses que touchent leur office a oyer et determiner toutes les causes que touchent nos dettes, et ainsi a nos fees et les incidents choses et que el eyent poer a conutre de dettes que l'on doit a nos dettours, par ou nous puissions plus toft approcher a nostre." It was under this specious pretext that the exchequer claimed

which he has already bestowed on the history of the law. We shall explain these statutes as nearly in the order in which they were passed as the nature of the subject will admit.

The statutes of this reign may be divided into such as relate to

jurisdiction in matters of private debts, if owing to any person indebted to the king, and from the *Mirror* it appears that there were reasons, as may well be imagined, seeing how this court was then composed, for objecting to any extension of its jurisdiction (c. v. s. 1, *Abuses of the Law*). Finally, the opening chapter of Britton closes with an emphatic reservation of supreme and paramount jurisdiction to the king: "Et defendons generalement a touts que nul ne eyt poer de amender nul faux judgement de nous justices, *sauve les justices* que *suivent nous* et *nostre court;* que a ceo sount par nous entitles, en nous mesmes, en nostre conseil. Car ces *reservons nous especialment a nostre jurisdiction*" (*Britton*, fol. 3.) The effect of which in that age was very much to give the king a power practically to determine what the law should be. And it will be manifest that, with servile judges, what the law should be would depend much less on the mere terms of statutes than upon their decisions in interpreting them, especially as the statutes in those days were couched in very general language; while as to the common law it would be perfectly in their power to pronounce it to be what they or the king pleased (especially as there were no legal reports until after this reign), at all events if they were provided with any colourable pretence of authority for so holding. And such authority would be afforded by the very treatise which the astute mind of this wily and sagacious prince had projected and dictated. And it admits of positive proof that, by means of and under cover of this treatise of Britton, the law as laid down by Bracton, and declared or recognised by Parliament, was actually warped and wrested into something entirely different, and indeed opposite, in order to favour the prerogative and increase the revenue of the king. A remarkable instance can be afforded, upon the authority even of as zealous a crown lawyer as Lord Coke, with reference to the privilege of clergy. What the law really was had been lately laid down by Bracton —viz., that a cleric accused of crime could be claimed by the ordinary, and was to be at once delivered to him:—"Cum vero clericus captus fuerit, pro alio crimine ex imprisonatus est, et de eo petatur curia Christianitatis ab ordinario loci. . . . . imprisonatus ille statim ei deliberetur *sine aliquą inquisitione facienda*" (*Bracton*, lib. iii., fol. 123). Then the statute of Westminster 1 recited and recognised the privilege, which enacted that the ordinary should not liberate the accused clerk until he had been put to his canonical purgation. "Que ceux que sont endites, &c., en nul maner ne les deliverent sans due purgation, issint que le Roy vient mestier de mitter auter remedy" (*Statute Westminster* 1, c. 2), upon which it was actually held by the king's judges that they had power to *try the clerk before he was delivered to the ordinary*, contrary to the plain meaning of the act, which implies that he should be put to canonical purgation in lieu of trial at common law. And Britton thus lays down the law: "Si clerk encoupe (*i.e.* indicte) de felony allege clergie, et est tiel trove (*i.e.*, que est un clerk) et l'ordinary demaund donqus serra enquis coment il est mescrue (*i.e.*, culpable), et sil soit nient mescrue, donques il serra aroge touts quits: et sil sort mescrue, *si soient ses chateaux taxes et ses terres prises en nostre maine;* et son corps deliver al ordinary" (*Britton*, c. iv., fol. 11). That is to say that his *goods and chattels should be forfeited and his land seized by the crown*, which betrays the reason for this wresting of the law. It is remarkable that it appears, prior to the reign of Edward I., the subject had a remedy as of right against the king for any wrong or injury by his officers or ministers, but that he ordained that no subject should sue the king, but that he should sue a petition to him, which was deemed a matter rather of grace and favour than of strict legal right, *ex debito justitiæ* (*Bro. Abr. Prerogative le Roy*, fol. 2) (*Year-book*, 24 *Edw. III.* 55). In this reign at all events it was held and firmly established that petition of right was the only remedy against the crown for torts done by the king's officers (case of the Prior of Christchurch, 31 *Edw. I.*, 1 *Rot. Parl.* 59, *Rigby Plac. Parl.* 218, 8 *Edw. II.*, 1 *Rot. Parl.* 319) as to wrongful seizure of goods as distress (John Mowbray's case, 33 *Edw. I.*, 1 *Rot. Parl.* 163, *Rigby*, 218) as for wool wrongfully taken to the king's use (Michael de Harlar's case, 33 *Edw. I.*, 1 *Rot. Parl.* 163, *Rigby* 268). So for wheat seized under pretence of a Royal Commission (14 *Edw. II.*, 1 *Rot. Parl.* 320) as for trespass to land (18 *Edw. II.*, 1 *Rot. Parl.* 416) Robert of Clifton's case, 22 *Edw. III.*, 5, fol. 12). Sometimes permission to sue the king's servants for torts done by them would be granted,

the rights of things, the administration of justice in general, and such as were of a political nature, and concerned objects of very high national importance. We shall speak of these latter first; and shall then be at liberty to consider the others more at leisure.

and it should seem that it was held that without such permission they could not be sued, and that it would not be granted if the king had had the benefit of these torts (De Grey's case, 15 *Edw. II.*, 1 *Rot. Parl.* 391). It will be observed that some of these cases occurred in the reign of this king's son and successor, who only kept up, however, the system his father established. It is manifest that Edward I. only meant, as far as he possibly could, to deprive the subject of remedy. That the opinion of the people was much less favourable to the legislation of this reign than that of the *lawyers*, there is abundant evidence in the *Mirror of Justice*, which bears internal evidence of having been composed or completed about the middle of this reign, since it notices the principal statutes up to the 16 Edward I., and there stops. In the last chapter "Of Abusions of the Common Law," it is said, the first and chief abusion is that the king is above the law, whereas he ought to be subject to it, as it is contained in his oath. It is an abuse that whereas parliaments ought to be twice in the year at London, they are but very seldom, and at the pleasure of the king, for subsidies and collections of treasure. And where the ordinances ought to be made by the assent of the king and of his earls, they are now made by the king and his clerks, and others who dare not contradict him, but desire to please him *and to counsel him for his profit*, though the counsel be not amenable for the common people without calling the counties thereto." So that this gives a very different picture of the legislation of the reign from that presented by the courtly hand of the king's "clerks" who penned the statutes, and the servile lawyers who wrote treatises to extol his laws. The *Mirror* goes on to denounce the abuses in the administration of justice. "It is an abuse that justice is delayed in the king's courts more than elsewhere. It is an abuse that a man who hath done manslaughter of necessity, or not feloniously, is detained in prison until he *hath purchased the king's charter of pardon*. It is an abuse to *hold the goods of fugitives* forfeited before they be attainted of the felony by outlawry or otherwise." Here it appears that there were two heads of royal emolument, which were constantly kept in view—fines and forfeitures; and it will be difficult to find any part of the law or the legislation of the reign which had not some bearing, direct or indirect, upon the enriching of the exchequer. It appears that amercements were grossly abused, notwithstanding the language of the Great Charter. "It is an abuse to assess an amercement without the affierment of freemen sworn to it, or in the absence of those who are to be amerced." The whole tenor of this chapter in the *Mirror* is to show that the impression was that the administration of justice was used, and often abused, for the sake of securing profit and emolument to the crown. The same impression pervades other sections of the chapter, making severe animadversions upon the two principal statutes of the reign—the first and second statutes of Westminster. "Many chapters," says the commentator, "are reprovable in the statute of Westminister I. The chapter of clerks found guilty of felony is reprovable, for they are not to be delivered to the ordinaries, but at the pleasure of the king and his justices. The punishment of officers, disseisors by colour of their office, is reprovable for the smallness of it." So of several chapters in the second statute of Westminster, it is said that they are idle, because not kept or observed. The whole course of justice in this reign was settled in the king's courts, so that the king derived a profit from every step in the suit from first to last, and for every default of either party from the commencement to final judgment. A suit could not be commenced even in the county courts (above a small amount), without a writ of justicies, for which a fee would be paid. Nor could a suit be commenced in the king's court without an "original writ," even although it was a common action, fully established by usage, and for this writ a fee was to be paid; so to enforce appearance there were distresses or attachments of goods, the proceeds of which went not to the suitor but the crown. And so at every stage amercements were levied to the profit of the crown on every default, and on judgment either for plaintiff or defendant—from the defendant for the wrong he had done, or from the plaintiff for his false suit. Thus it was to the end of the suit, on every default of suitors or jurors, and at every step there was some fine, fee, or amercement to the king. These pecuniary impositions on the suitors in the king's courts were regarded with great aversion, and are mentioned with much bitterness in the *Mirror*. It is an abuse that

Of those which are of a political kind, the *Statutum Walliæ*, 12 Edward I., presents itself first; being a sort of constitution for that principality, which was thereby, in a great measure, put on

remedial writs are saleable, and that the king commands the sheriff that he take sureties to his use for the writ. It is an abuse to distrain in personal actions where the profit of the issues come to the king; and no profit accrueth to the plaintiff (c. v., s. 1, art. 68–70). And above all, the practice of imposing arbitrary amercements was complained of: "It is an abuse to assess an amercement without the affeerment of freemen sworn, or to affeer amercements in the absence of those who are amerced (*Ibid.* art. 33–34). It is obvious that the administration of justice had become a source of emolument to the crown, and that this emolument was naturally regarded by the crown as one of its chief objects, and thus justice was made a source of profit to the king, and it became his interest to take care of it, and develop and improve its administration. That this and every other possible source of emolument was diligently made available to the advantage of the royal revenues, the entries with *Memoranda in Scaccario, temp.* Ed. I. (appended to the Year-book of Edward II.) abundantly attest. It appears from thence that there were very few of the affairs or transactions of life at that time which were not, in one way or another, improved to the advantage of the royal revenue, and especially the administration of justice. Undoubtedly, however, there was a vast deal of valuable and useful legislation in this reign, especially with respect to legal procedure and remedies at law; and, although all dictated by an enlightened sense of self-interest, they were not the less valuable on that account. Hence all our lawyers have always spoken in high terms of the advance made by our law at this era, and Lord Coke is quite enthusiastic about it. He says, breaking out upon the initial words of the first great statute of Westminster, "Ceux sont les establishments:" "And justly may not only these chapters challenge that name, but all other the statutes made in the reign of this king, because they are more constant, standing, and durable than any laws which have been made since" (2 *Inst.* 156). It would be as idle to ascribe the improvements in our law to the king's regard for justice, as to attribute the rise of representative institutions in this reign to his love of liberty. The improvements in our political system, as all historians testify, arose simply from the royal necessities and the king's want of money. And the improvements in our legal and judicial systems arose from the same cause. Sir Matthew Hale gives a sketch or summary of the legislation in this reign, (concluding with the passage above cited by our author,) which may usefully be here inserted, as it affords at the outset an admirable and comprehensive view of the whole: "He settled the greater charter and *Charter de Foresta*, not only by a practice consonant to them in the distribution of law and right, but also by that solemn act, 25 *Ed. I.*, styled *Confirmationes Chartarum.* As to which, however, it is to be observed, that the very fact that a confirmation was required, and that it was not conceded until the twenty-fifth year of the reign, tells a very different story, and it is notorious that it was then extorted from the king by absolute necessity, and the imminent dread of a rebellion (*Brady*, iii., app. 34; *West.* 431). "He established and distributed the several jurisdictions of courts within their proper bounds;" as to which, however, the plain truth is (as will seen from Britton) rather the reverse; that he encroached upon, and actually destroyed, the jurisdiction of the ancient county courts, in order to bring all but trivial business into the king's courts, with a view to the profits. At the same time, this no doubt would tend to improve the law and advance justice, and would be for the benefit of the people, although for the profit of the crown, and with the same view the judicature of the superior courts was improved. "He established the limits of the court of common pleas, perfectly performing the direction of *Magna Charta, quod communi a placita non sequantur curia nostra*, in relation to the king's bench, and in express terms extending it to the exchequer by the statute of *articuli super chartas*, c. 4." The first part of this is not quite correct, as appears by Britton and the next paragraph in Hale's own account; for it appears that the jurisdiction of the court of the king was still ambulatory, and obtained to the extent of twelve miles round the king's residence. "He established the extent of the jurisdiction of the steward and marshal," (*i.e.* of the king's court,) vide *articula super chartas*, c. 3; and he also settled the bounds of inferior courts, of counties, hundreds, and courts barons, which he kept within their proper and narrow bounds, for the reasons given before; and so gradually the common justice of the kingdom came to be administered by men knowing in the laws and

the foot of England with respect to its laws and the administration of justice. Of a similar nature, though confined to a few articles of reform, is the *ordinatio pro statu Hiberniæ,* 17 Edward I.,

conversant in the great courts, and before justices itinerant." "He did not only explain, but excellently enforced *Magna Charta,* by the statute, *De tallagio non concedendo,* 34 *Ed. I.;*" as to which, however, it will occur to any one, that the fact that it was only conceded at the close of the reign shows at once how much it had been required, and how reluctantly it was conceded. It is notorious that it was extorted only by political and pecuniary necessity. "He settled the forms and solemnities, and efficacy of fines;" the fees on which were a great source of revenue. "He settled that great and orderly method for the safety and preservation of the peace of the kingdom, and suppressing of robberies, by the statute of Winton or Winchester. He settled the method of tenures, to prevent multiplicity of tenures, which grew to a great inconvenience, and remedied it by the statute, *Quia emptores terrarum,* 8 *Ed. I.,* as to which the object was to prevent subinfeudations, whereby the great lords, and especially the crown, lost the profits incident to the oppressive feudal system. He settled a speedier way for recovery of debts, not only for merchants and tradesmen, by the statutes of *Acton Burnel* and *De Mercatoribus,* but also for all other persons, by granting an exemption for a moiety of the lands by *elegit;*" as to which, under his predecessor Henry III., improvements in procedure similar in object had been made, and with the same purpose, to draw business into the king's courts by improving the remedies of the suitors in those courts. "He made that great alteration in estates by the statute Westminster 2, whereby estates of fee-simple, conditional at common law, were turned into estates tail, not removable from the issue by the ordinary methods of alienation; the object of which was like that of the statute *Quia emptores,* to consolidate and preserve the great estates, so as to enhance the feudal profits of the crown. He introduced quite a new method both in the laws of Wales and in the method of their dispensation, by the statute of Rutland;" with a similar object of extending the jurisdiction of his courts there, and making the subjection of the principality a source of lawful profit. Further, says Hale, "Partly by the learning and experience of his judges, and partly by his own wise interpolation, he silently and without noise abrogated many ill and inconvenient usages both in his courts of justice and in the country. But this course of improvement had been going on silently and surely ever since the Conquest. Trial by jury was introduced as a substitute for the duel in the reign of Henry II., and the ordeal died out in the reign of John. It is only by losing sight of this constant gradual progression that the erroneous idea becomes rooted in the mind of any very sudden or rapid change at any particular era. "He rectified and set in order the method of collecting his revenue in the exchequer, and removed obsolete and illeviable parts thereof." No doubt, to this part of the system of government, the attention, not only of Edward I., but of every sovereign who had any wise regard for the interest of the crown, was carefully afforded. "And by the statutes of Westminister 1 and Westminster 2, and Gloucester 1 and Westminster 3, and of *Articuli super chartas,* he removed almost all that was either grievous or unpractical out of the law and the course of its administration, by such apt and effective remedies and provisions as have stood ever since without any great alteration." But this was only in completing or carrying out changes which had been in course of progress for two centuries, and which were by no means completed even in his time. Trial by jury, for instance, was not yet developed, and was only to be developed by the same course of gradual progress in which it had arisen. And it will be found that the law and the administration of justice owed infinitely more to the quiet, silent development and improvement they received in the courts of law than to any acts of legislation, which, to say the utmost, only removed obstructions out of the way, or afforded facilities for improvements already attempted. The great alteration was in the establishment of a regular and settled judicature, which had been growing up ever since the Conquest, which no doubt was promoted in the present reign, because it was perceived by the monarch that the administration of justice might be made a source of revenue, and that the more it was improved the greater would be the amount of business done, and that there could be no effectual improvements without a settled judicature and a regular procedure. Finally, Lord Hale says: "That the laws did never in any one age receive so great and sudden an advancement—nay, I think I may safely say all the ages since his time have not done so much in reference to the orderly settling and

which gives some directions for better ordering the administration of justice in that country. These two statutes, particularly the former, are monuments of this king's wisdom in planning schemes of juridical improvement for every part of his dominions.

Such of the Britons as had fled from the Saxon invasion into Wales, preserved there, together with their language, and the blood-royal of their kings, their ancient laws and government. (*a*)

establishing of the distributive justice of the kingdom, as he did within the short compass of the thirty-five years of his reign, especially about the first thirteen years thereof. As touching the common administration of justice between party and party, and accommodating the rules and methods and order of proceeding, he did the most at least of any king since William I., and left the same as a fixed and stable rule and order of proceeding very little differing from that which we now hold and practise, especially as to the substance and principal contexture thereof" (*Hist. Common Law,* c. vii.) But both Hale and our author had here somewhat lost sight of the course of gradual progression which had been going on ever since the Conquest, the results of which the present reign realised, and which would amply account for a more rapid development of our legal institutions in this reign. Thus Hale mentions, that in the parliament 18 Edward I., in a petition in the House of Lords touching land, between Hugh Lowther and Adam Edgenthorp, the defendant objected that the plaintiff, if he had any right, had his remedy at common law by action, and therefore demanded judgment that he ought not to answer for his freehold there, and the judgment of the lords in parliament was entered to that effect—viz., "Et quia actio de prædicto tenemento petendo et etiam suum recuperare si quid habere debeat vel posset eidem Adœ per assisam competeire, debet, nec est juri consonum, vel hactenus in curia ista usitatus, quod aliquis sine *lege communi* et brevi de cancellaria de libero tenemento suo respondeat et maxime in casu ubi breve de cancellaria locum habere potest, dictum est præfato Adœ quod sibi perquirat per breve de cancellaria ei sibi viderct expederirc"—that is, that he should sue at law. So (*Rot. Parl.* 13 *Rich. II.*, No. 10) Adam Chaucer preferred his petition to the king and lords in parliament against Sir R. Knolles, to be relieved touching a mortgage which he supposed was satisfied, and to have restitution of his lands, on which a similar judgment was given: "Et apres les raisons et les allegeances de l'un party and de l'autre sembles a seigneurs de parlement, que le dit petition ne estoit petition du parlement deins que le matteer en ciel conprize dovit estre discuss per le commun ley. Et par ces agreed fuit que le dit Adam ne priendroit riens einsque il sueroit per le commun ley"—that is, that he should sue at law. "And," says Hale, "let any man look over the rolls of parliament, and the petitions in parliament of the times of Edward I. to Henry VI., he will find hundreds of answers of petitions in parliament concerning matters determinable at common law endorsed with answers to this or the like effect: 'Suez vous a le commun ley, sequatur ad communem legem, perquirat breve en cancellaria, si sibi videret expedire, ne est petition due parlement, mandetur ista petitio en cancellorium vel justiciariis de Banco, vel thesaurio et baronibus de Scaccario,'" &c. And these, he adds, were *de jure.* So parliament refused to review judgments regularly given in courts of law, except in the regular course by writ of error.

(*a*) Of which some illustrations have already been given in the introduction, as bearing upon the question of the prevalence of Roman laws in this country during the centuries of Roman occupation, and their influence in the formation of our own. These laws were collected by Howell Dha; and as the Britons in Wales were those who had resisted the Saxons to the utmost, and were in hostility to them, these laws must represent their own, and not Saxon laws; added to which, as may be seen from a comparison with the Saxon laws of the same period, the latter were in the last degree rude and barbarous, as compared with the British. On the other hand, as the British were barbarians when the Romans arrived, and had no laws at all, and as these laws correspond remarkably with the Roman laws which for centuries were established here, the inference appears not only natural but unavoidable that these laws of the Romanized Britons were of Roman origin. Hence the interest of the question what the laws of the Welsh were at this period, because, as Hale observes, although he thinks that we have few evidences touching the British laws before their expulsion hence into Wales, yet the usage in Wales seems sufficient evidence of what was ancient British law (*Hist. Com. Law,* c. xi.), which must be taken to mean Roman

The descendants of Cadwallader are said to have governed in that country during all the Saxon times. When William the Conqueror established himself in England, three princes, descended from that ancient British king, reigned over Wales, then divided into three sovereignties; and kept possession of their respective dominions in defiance of the Conqueror and his successors. The way in which our kings carried on war with this people, was to make a grant to certain great lords of such countries in Wales *as they could win from the Welshmen.* Many great lordships were by this policy conquered; and the lords held them to them and their heirs of the kings of England, as lands purchased by conquest. Such was the origin of *Lords Marchers*, who assumed

British law, since, as already observed, before the Roman Conquest the British were mere barbarians, and had no laws at all. And although Hale and our author, because they could not, so to speak, trace the descent of the Roman law from the Romanized Britons through the Saxon period to the present, ignored and disregarded the question of the influence of that law upon the formation of our own, yet when by a more close attention to the course of legal history the traces of that descent are restored, the question becomes one of considerable interest, for so soon as the historic connexion between the Roman law and ours is disclosed, we see in the Roman law the parent of our own, and this at once gives new interest and importance to the study of *that* law, and throws a great deal of light upon the study and the history of ours. Now, on the one hand, it has already been seen that the laws of the Welsh Britons were of Roman origin. And of course, what these laws were when they were forced into Wales, it is only natural to infer the laws of the Britons had been before, or at the time when the Roman occupation ceased—that is, the military occupation of the country by the Romans; for it would be a great mistake (and perhaps this is the greatest of the many mistakes made upon the subject) to suppose that the Roman occupation ever was entirely terminated. For it is not to be supposed that the myriads of Roman colonists and settlers who, during four or five centuries, had established themselves here, and who from the end of the first century had been in a course of amalgamation by marriages and otherwise with the native inhabitants, departed when the Roman legions were withdrawn. They were for the most part, at that time, *born inhabitants of the country*, with all their ties of interest and relationship rooted there. Britain was to them and unto their families home, and Rome was a distant and a foreign land. The Britons had been Romanized (as we read in the pages of Tacitus) as early as the time of Agricola, and the process of Romanizing had been going on for centuries. On the other hand, the descendants of the Roman colonists were Britons, though Roman-Britons, and natives and inhabitants of the country, and those two classes—the Britons who had become Romans, and the Romans who had become Britons—must have formed the great bulk of the civilised inhabitants at the time the Roman empire there had ended. And as during all that period Roman laws and institutions had prevailed, they must have been firmly established. Then when the Saxons came, for the very reason that they were barbarians, they could neither create nor destroy institutions or laws, and it is an entire confusion of ideas to suppose that they ever did so. Barbarians can burn buildings indeed, but they very soon find that it is better to preserve them; and this is more rapidly learned in the case of an invasion intended to be a permanent conquest and settlement, for even barbarians soon cease to destroy what is to be their own. Similar reasons would speedily apply as regarded the inhabitants, for it would be idle to destroy men who could be made useful and profitable by being made tributary, and accordingly we find from the chronicles that so soon as resistance ceased in any part of the country, the Britons were made tributaries, and the whole system of life went on as before. Moreover, as Guizot points out, there was never any sudden, sweeping conquests by the Saxons. There were a succession of invasions and contests, which were local, partial, and successive, and lasted for several centuries, and during the whole of which time, by intermarriages, alliances, and otherwise, there was a consequent course of amalgamation between the two races, insomuch that even in the earliest of the Saxon laws we see them treated on a footing of equality. That being so, the natural theory

every authority and prerogative that was necessary for the due execution of the laws within their respective lordships. These new establishments had a tendency to introduce the English law; which was either mixed with the Welsh, or prevailed in certain places, and with respect to certain persons, in its pure state. In some lordships, in consequence of the singular mixture and mutual toleration of laws last mentioned, the English and Welsh resorted to separate and distinct courts of judicature.

The lords marchers increased in number, till Llewelyn ap Gryffydh, the last prince of Wales, was slain in the eleventh year of this king. Upon this event Edward took the principality into his hands, and gave it to his son, afterwards Edward II. Since

would be that the Saxons, as they appropriated the property of the Britons, should adopt their institutions. And accordingly we find from their history and from their laws that they did so. As to the manorial institutions, this is shown affirmatively from the recognition of them in the laws. As to the municipal institutions, it is shown at first negatively in the absence of any trace of their destruction, and then affirmatively by the strongest recognition of them. All this has been shown in the review of the Saxon period in the former volume. The notion, then, that the Saxons abolished or abrogated the Romanized laws and institutions of the country is an entire fallacy. They simply adopted them and preserved them, endeavouring, no doubt, to engraft on them their own barbarous usages, which, however, were rejected by the nobler stock, and dropped off one by one in course of time, so that in the present reign little of them remained, and even the ordeal had gone. In the meantime, as has been shown in the former volume, there had been, even before the Conquest, and still more so since the Conquest, a gradual course of recurrence to the Roman system of laws and institutions, especially as to the administration of justice, modified no doubt by the Saxon usages and animated by the Saxon spirit; and this process had been aided by large recourse to the same great fountain of the civil law, from which our earliest civilized institutions were originally derived. Thus it happened that by this process of restoration, the laws and legal institutions of this country had become substantially wrought into the same state in which they were in Wales among the remnants of the old Romanized race of Britons. For it is to be observed that in the above statute, the object of which was to assimilate the Welsh laws and institutions to the English, there appears to have been very little to alter, a most remarkable fact. Thus, for instance, in the law of real property there were only one or two points in which the Welsh law varied from the English, and only one in which they were altered. And on one of the points on which they differed, viz., in their land being partible among the heirs male, the law of this country had been so until quite recently, and hence it was agreed not to alter it; and the only point on which it was altered was that bastards inherited, by which probably was meant that the effect of marriage was deemed to legitimate previous issue of the parties, which also was the law in this country in ancient times, and altered in accordance with a later usage in the previous reign. The *Statutum Walliæ*, 12 Edw. I., runs thus—"Aliter usitatem est in Walliæ quam in Anglia quoad successionem hæreditatis: eo quod hæreditas partibilis est inter hæredes masculos: et a tempore cujus non extiterit memoria partibilis extitit. Dominus Rex non vult quod consuetudo illa abrogatur, sed quod hæreditates remaneant partibiles inter consimiles hæredes sicut esse consueverunt: et fiat partitio illius sicut fiere consuevit. Hoc excepto quod bastardi non habeant de catero hæreditates: et etiam quod non habeant purpartes cum legitimis nec sine legitimis." So that there was little difference as to real property. Then as to remedies, especially for real property, it appears from the laws of Howell Dha that the Britons in Wales had a regular system of procedure in real actions, substantially the same as existed in this country at the era we are now considering, after all the learned labours of Glanville and of Bracton. And when it is borne in mind that their works were largely founded on the civil law, and that there was only an amalgamation of it with the Saxon element in our institutions, as in the trial by jury, the inference is obvious that the civilized institutions of Saxons, of Normans, and of Britons had all been derived from the Roman law, and were really of Roman origin.

that time no more lordships marchers were erected; the Welsh, in general, submitting themselves to the kings of England. Edward soon held a parliament at Ruthlan Castle, and there brought forward the following statute, for appointing a juridical establishment in Wales similar to that in England.[1]

Statutum Walliæ.

The *Statutum Walliæ* begins the arrangements it is about to make, by stating what was conceived to be the political condition of that country at that time. It says, that Wales with its inhabitants had hitherto been subject to the king *jure feudali;* but that now, by the divine providence, it had fallen *in proprietatis dominium*, and was annexed and united to the crown of England as a part of the same body. The king therefore, wishing that the people inhabiting *Snaudon, et alios terras nostras in partibus illis* (for to such it was confined, and did not extend to all Wales, as it is now called), who had submitted themselves to the king *de alto et basso*, should be governed by certain laws as the rest of his dominions, had caused the laws and customs of that country to be rehearsed before himself and his nobles. Some of these, by the advice and counsel of his nobles, were abolished; some were permitted to remain; some were altered, and other new ones were ordained: this alteration and modification of the Welsh law was as follows:—

First, respecting the magistrates and officers of justice it was ordained, that the *justitiarius de Snaudon* should have the keeping of the king's peace there and in the parts adjacent, and should administer justice according to the king's writs, hereafter to be mentioned. Further, that there should be sheriffs, coroners, and bailiffs of commotes in Snaudon and the parts adjacent; that there should be a sheriff in Anglesey, one in Carnarvon, one in Merioneth, and one in Flint; the jurisdiction of which last was to extend to the town of Chester; and he was, for the future, to be attendant on the king's *justitiarius* of Chester (which officer of justice of Chester is mentioned as existing in the former reign),[2] and should be answerable for issues at the exchequer of Chester. Coroners were in future to be elected in these counties by the king's writ, inserted in the statute for that purpose; bailiffs of commotes were to be appointed; and they are thereby enjoined to do their duty, as directed by the *justitiarius* and the sheriff. Besides the above sheriffs, who were appointed for Snaudon and the parts adjacent, the statute directs that there should be a sheriff in Carmarthen, and another in Cardigan and Lampader, together with coroners and bailiffs of commotes, as in the former.

The sheriff was to hold his county from month to month; but his tourn only twice a-year, that is, after Michaelmas and Easter. In his county he was to hold plea of the following actions, with or without a writ: Of trespasses against the king's peace; of the caption or detention of cattle, or *de vetito namio;* of debt, and

[1] *Vide* Penn. *Tour in Wales*, vol. ii. appendix. [2] St. de Scac. 51 Hen. III., s. 5.

other breaches of contract. At his county court, he, together with the coroners, was to receive all presentments of felonies and other offences that had happened since the last county; when *Waleschery*,[1] in case of death, was to be presented, the presentment enrolled, and the offenders prosecuted to outlawry, the same as in England: the same in appeals *de plagâ*, mayhem, rape, burning, and robbery.

All persons residing within the commote were to attend at the tourn, except religious men, clerks, and women. The sheriff was then to inquire, by the oath of twelve discreet and lawful men, concerning the *capitula coronæ;* which are inserted in the statute, and are the same, except some local matters, with those delivered to the justices itinerant in England: the jurors were next charged to make presentment of offenders, in the manner as has already been described in the proceedings of the eyre.[2]

As to the coroners, it was ordained that there should be one at least in every commote, who should be chosen *in pleno comitatu* by the usual writ, and be sworn before the sheriff to be faithful to the king, and discharge the office of a coroner with fidelity. Then the manner of holding inquisitions *super visum corporis*, and other parts of his office, in taking appeals, abjurations, and the like, are described in the same way as the office of coroner in England.[3]

After this account of officers, and their duty, there follow forms of the most common original writs for the use of the inhabitants of Wales—namely, a writ of novel disseisin of freehold, of disseisin of pasture, a writ of nuisance, and of mortauncestor; a writ, or commission, appointing a justice and certain associates, whom he should chuse, AD ASSISAS *novæ disseisinæ et mortis antecessoris* CAPIENDAS; and another writ, directing the sheriff to cause all such assizes to come *coram nostro justitiario*, which was the return in the above original writs. It was directed that co-heirs, or any who could not properly have a writ of mortauncestor, should have a writ of that kind *in suo casu*, adapted to their case; by which, probably, was meant a writ *de consanguinitate.* Next follows a form of *præcipe quòd reddat, &c., quòd ei deforceat*, for cases both of right and possession. This writ, like the former, was to be returnable *coram justitiario nostra;* but it might also be had *caram justitiariis in banco.* After this there is a writ of dower *unde nihil*, a writ of debt, and a writ of the same nature in the *detinet*, instead of *debet;* which has since been called a writ of *detinue.* This is remarkable for being the first mention of such a writ. Writs of *debt* were not to be *coram justitiario*, if for a sum under forty shillings; but such small sums were to be sued for in the county court, and in commotes. In case a plaintiff chose to sue in the county, the form of a *justicies* is given by the statute; such suits might be removed, by *pone, coram justitiario.* To these succeed a writ of covenant, with a *justicies* and *pone;* a writ for appointing an attorney; a writ *de coronatore eligendo.*

[1] *Vide ante* 22 of Englescherry. [2] *Vide ante*, 4. [3] *Vide ante*, 12.

When the statute has given all these writs, it goes through the proceedings in each, much in the way in which those actions were conducted in England; only in the allegations of the parties it was recommended that the rigour of practice which declared, *qui cadit à syllabâ, cadit à totâ causâ*, should not be tolerated. Among others, it sets forth the form of proceeding in trespass, but does not give any form of a writ.

Some alterations and regulations were made concerning property (*a*). It had not been the custom in Wales for women to have a title to dower; but now it was declared, that in future they should have dower. Inheritances that had been partible among the heirs, time out of mind, were to continue in the same manner as had been before used; only bastards were no longer to be allowed to inherit. Women, being co-heiresses, were in future to have their equal shares of the inheritance, though contrary to the former custom of Wales. The people of Wales had expressly prayed that the following regulations might be established: *first*, That the truth of a fact might be inquired of by good and lawful men of the vicinage, chosen by the consent of parties; *secondly*, That in all actions for movables, as upon contracts, debts, suretyships, covenants, trespasses, chattels, and the like, they might still retain the Welsh usage; which was, that when a matter could be proved *per audientes et videntes*, and a plaintiff had brought witnesses so qualified, whose testimony could be depended on, to prove his declaration, he should recover his demand against the adverse party; and in cases where there could not be a proof *per audientes et videntes*, that the defendant should be put to purge himself with a greater or less number, according to the quantity and quality of the thing or fact; *thirdly*, That in thefts, if a person was taken with the thing in his hand, he should not be suffered to purge

(*a*) As already shown, though the object was to assimilate the laws of the two countries, there was very little found to alter, the reason being that both had been derived, in the main, from the same source, the Roman. A remarkable illustration of this is afforded in the instance above-mentioned, that of dower. The Roman law did not recognise dower, in our sense of the word—as an endowment of the wife by the husband—but rather in the sense of an endowment of the husband by the wife, as in what our law called *maritagium*. It is thus accounted for why the Welsh had no law of dower—their law being the old Romanized British law. As to inheritance, it has already been adverted to; and it may be observed, that the law of Rome had fluctuated and varied on that head. It will be observed, again, in the above passage, that the Welsh had no barbarous ordeal or brutal battle, but an intelligent system of trial by persons most likely to know the truth, and chosen by the parties: in substance the Roman system, at which the Anglo-Normans had only recently arrived, after centuries of slow progress; whereas these Romanized Britons had retained it ever since the time of the Romans, when they acquired it. Again, there were provided, in cases where the trial by witnesses or jurors was not available as to the facts, a system of purgation, by oath of witnesses to the *credit* of the parties, very different from the absurd miracle of God, which at this very time the English were still so superstitious and so stupid as to desire; for in the *Mirror* it is actually stated as one of the "abuses" of the law that the "miracle of God," *i.e.*, the ordeal, was not allowed, as it had been! This superiority of the Romanized Britons in the principality is a remarkable proof of the vitality of the Roman laws and constitution.

himself, but be judged *pro convicto:* all which were granted, except only in cases of theft, burning, murder, homicide, and manifest and notorious robberies, in which the order of the law of England was to be observed.

This is the whole of the *statutum Walliæ;* which concludes with a reservation to the king of a power to interpret, add to, or diminish it as he pleased, and thought it expedient for the good of the country. After this follows, *in cujus rei testimonium sigillum, &c.* The king affixed his seal, and so executed it rather in the form of a charter than an act of parliament. Thus was the judicial polity of the principality settled in the form in which it continued till the reign of Henry VIII., when some further steps were taken for uniting it more closely with England, by a fuller participation of our laws.

Ordinatio pro statu Hiberniæ.

The *ordinatio pro statu Hiberniæ,* 17 Edward I., contains eight chapters of regulations in matters of a judicial nature. It appears from this act, that the English law prevailed in Ireland, with all its formalities. We find here mention of the king's writs, of assizes of novel disseisin, of the king's justices, the chancery, exchequer, and the like.[1] The first chapter of this statute ordains, that neither the king's justice of Ireland, nor any other officer, should purchase lands or tenements within the limits of his bailiwick, without a license from the king, under pain of forfeiting such purchase to the king. No purveyance was to be made by the king's justice of Ireland, or any other officer, but in cases of necessity; and then it was to be by the advice of the greater part of the council in those parts, and by a writ awarded out of the chancery of Ireland, or out of the chancery of England, by the king's order.[2] They were likewise forbid to arrest ships of the king's subjects who were ready to give security not to trade with enemies; and any officer of the king doing otherwise, was to satisfy the complainant in double damages, and be punished by the king.[3] The fees for the king's seal, and those due to the marshal, were regulated.[4] The justice of Ireland was no longer to have power of pardoning for the death of a man, or other felony, but by the special command of the king.[5] No officer was to receive an original writ without the seal of Ireland; nor was process to be made under any other seal, except only the seal of the exchequer of Ireland, for matters peculiar to that court.[6] Assizes of novel disseisin were not to be adjourned or delayed by the writs or letters of the justice of Ireland, except only in the county where he was present, and during the time he should remain in that county.[7]

Confirmations of the charters.

The other statutes, which we have before mentioned as of a political nature, relate to the observance of *Magna Charta* and the Charter of the Forest. During this reign several acts were passed for confirming and strengthen-

[1] For English statutes binding Ireland, *vide* Harris's *Hibernica*, part ii., pp. 75 to 142, &c. [2] Ch. 1. [3] Ch. 3. [4] Ch. 4, 5. [5] Ch. 6. [6] Ch. 7. [7] Ch. 8.

ing these great pillars of the constitution. In the thirteenth year of this reign, the king was entreated by the parliament to confirm all former charters of the kings, his predecessors: a form of *inspeximus* and confirmation was accordingly agreed upon, not only to be prefixed to the Charter of Liberties, but also to charters of donation to individuals, as is to be seen in a public instrument entitled *Forma Concessionis et Exemplificationis Chartarum,* 13 Edward I., st. 6. Further, respecting charters of donation, it was ordained, that should a doubt arise upon any articles therein, the matter should be argued before the treasurer and barons of the exchequer, together with the justices of both benches.

But, in the twenty-fifth year, there was a more solemn confirmation of the Great Charter in the statute called *Confirmationes Chartarum* (*a*). This contains seven chapters. The first ordains that the Charter of Liberties and of the Forest should be kept in every point, and that they should be sent under the king's seal as well to the justices of the forest as to others; to all sheriffs and other officers, and to all the cities in the realm, accompanied with a writ commanding them to publish the said charters, and declare to the people that the king had confirmed them in every point. All justices, sheriffs, mayors, and other ministers, were directed to allow them when pleaded before them;[1] and any judgment contrary thereto was to be null and void.[2] The charters were like-

(*a*) Not, it will be observed, until near the end of the reign, nor, as history shows, even then, until coerced and extorted by absolute necessity. And it was entirely to the pecuniary necessities of the monarch we owe both the legal and political improvements which were effected in this reign. The mere confirmation of the charters, indeed, would have been of little importance, since they had been confirmed again and again, but in vain. The most important of the demands made upon the crown was that by which it was called upon to relinquish the claim of levying taxes without the consent of the nation, which had been already yielded by John in Magna Charta. But in the great charter of Henry III. it was omitted and reserved, and hitherto had been evaded; and it was now most reluctantly conceded (*Lingard's Hist. Eng.*, ii. c. 7). When the barons took up arms against John, they exercised the right of resistance to oppression; but they took no securities, they made no lasting provision for the time to come. In the second stage of the contest the national leaders obtained, in the Great Charter, a solemn recognition of the rights of the people, and some provisions which, by reserving to a national assembly the power over money taxes, laid the foundation of a permanent and effectual control over the crown. Still the means of redressing grievances lay chiefly in an appeal to arms, a coarse and perilous expedient, always of uncertain issue, and the repetition of which is incompatible with the peace and order of society. Such were the plans of government in the Great Charter, the provisions of the Oxford, and the *mise* or agreement of Lewes. The third epoch is distinguished by the establishment of a permanent assembly, which was on ordinary occasions capable of checking the prerogative by a quiet and constant action, yet strong enough to oppose it more decisively if no other means of preventing tyranny should be left. Hence the unspeakable importance of the new constitution given to parliament by Simon de Montfort; hence, also, arose the *necessity* under which the succeeding king, with all his policy and energy, found himself of adopting this precedent from a hated usurper. It would have been in vain to have legally strengthened parliament against the crown, unless it had been actually strengthened by widening its foundation, by rendering it a bond of union between orders of men jealous of each other, and by multiplying its points of contact with the people, the sole allies from whom succour could be hoped. The introduction of

[1] Ch. 1. [2] Ch. 2. 28

wise to be sent under the king's seal to all cathedral churches, there to be kept and read to the people twice a year.[1] It was ordained, that all archbishops and bishops should pronounce sentence of excommunication against those who, by word, deed, or counsel, did anything contrary thereto; which curses were to be pronounced twice a year; and if any bishop was remiss in doing this, he was to be compelled and distrained to do it by the archbishops of Canterbury and York.[2]

Thus far provision was made not only for the observance but likewise for the preservation of the charters. The remaining three chapters of this statute were to guard the subject against the levying of unlawful aids. The king had, in the present parliament, obtained some aids and subsidies for maintaining a foreign war. Though these grants were with consent of parliament, they created some jealousies, an idea having prevailed that the subject was not bound to contribute towards carrying on the king's wars out of the realm. It is said that on this occasion Bohun, earl of Hereford and Essex, the high constable of England, and Bigot, earl of Norfolk and Suffolk, and marshal of England, being personages who, from their office in the king's armies, seemed called upon to interfere in such a crisis, presented a petition to the king this year in behalf of the commons, in consequence of which it was now ordained that such aids, tasks, and prises should not be drawn into custom or precedent.[3] Further, the king granted for him and his heirs, as well to archbishops, bishops, abbots, priors, and other persons of holy church (who had been taxed likewise in their church-lands), as to earls, barons, and to all the commonalty of the land, that he would on no account take such aids, tasks, nor prises, *but by the common assent of the whole realm*,[4] and for the common benefit thereof, *saving* the ancient aids and prises due and accustomed,[5] which meant, probably, the aids due by reason of tenure. This is the first mention in the statute-book of a renunciation of right to levy money on the subject without consent of parliament. There had been a like declaration in the charter of John; but we have seen that it was omitted in that of Henry III.[6] Further,

knights, citizens, and burgesses into the legislature, by its continuance, showed how exactly it suited the necessities and demands of society at that time. No sooner had events thrown forward the measure, than its fitness to the state of the community became apparent (*Mack. Hist. of Eng.*, v. 1.) It was to this the confirmation of the charters, and, what was far more important, the guarantee of their observance, are to be ascribed. The monarch had convened parliaments, which comprised representatives of the counties, and towns, and cities, who alone had the power of granting him subsidies or supplies; and in consequence of the power they thus acquired, the confirmation of the charters was granted, containing the all-important guarantee that no supplies should be granted but with the common consent of the realm—that is, of the representatives of the realm—in such a parliament assembled. The power of parliament was thus enlarged by this monarch, as by his successors, not only to facilitate grants of money, but to share harsh acts of government, and introduce innovations too daring to be hazarded by the single arm of a wary tyrant (*Mack. Hist. of Eng.*)

[1] Ch. 3. [2] Ch. 4. [3] Ch. 5. [4] *Par commun assent de tut royaûme.*
[5] Ch. 6. [6] *Vide ante*, vol. i., c. viii.

because there had been a particular outcry against a tax of forty *souds* upon every sack of wool, it was declared this should not be again levied without the common assent and goodwill of the commonalty of the realm.[1]

This statute, being in the form of a charter, was sealed with the king's great seal at Ghent, in Flanders, on November 5th, in the twenty-fifth year of his reign, as appears by a memorandum upon the roll. The form of excommunication pronounced by the archbishop of Canterbury against the breakers of it follows in the next public instrument, entitled *Sententia Domini R. archiepiscopi super præmissis*, stat. 25 Ed. I. stat. 2. The next notice of the two charters of liberties is in the preamble to the statute *de finibus levatis*, 27 Ed. I., where the king refers to the former confirmations thereof, and solemnly ratifies them.

In the next year something more was done for confirming the charters. We find there the statute of *articuli super chartas*, 28 Ed. I. stat. 3. This act complains that the charters, notwithstanding the several confirmations of them, were not observed; and this is attributed to there being no certain penalty prescribed for the violators of any points thereof (*a*). They are, therefore, again confirmed by this act; and the following method was appointed for enforcing the observance of them, and for the punishment of offenders. The charters are directed to be delivered to every sheriff in England, under the king's seal, to be read four times a year to the people in full county—that is, at the next county after St Michael, Christmas, Easter, and St John. For the punishing of offenders, the commonalty were to choose in every county court three *able men*,[2] knights, or other lawful, wise, and well-disposed persons, who should be assigned and sworn justices by the king's letters-patent under the great seal, to hear and determine, without any other writ than their commission, such complaints as should be made of those who offended in any point against the charters within the county, as well within franchises as without, and as well of the king's officers out of their places as of others. They were to hear such complaints from day to day, without admitting any of the delays which were allowed by the

(*a*) The want of punishments for infractions of the charters is alluded to by the author of the *Mirror;* but there was, as already observed, a necessity for something beyond the mere enactment of punishments—viz., a power to execute and enforce them. It was in this want of guarantees or securities lay the great difficulty of the age, as Mackintosh and Guizot have pointed out. And these guarantees were but gradually obtained, as the power of law grew up under the protection of the increasing power of parliament. There was thus a close and indeed inseparable connexion between the growth and progress of our political and legal institutions. Law could only be administered and justice guaranteed by a judicature having the will and the power to administer justice according to law; and this will and power could only, as experience had abundantly attested, be obtained under the influence, the control, and the protection of parliament.

[1] Ch. 7.

[2] Such is the term given by the translator to the words *prodes homes;* that is, *prud'homme*, from which there is formed an abstract word, *prud'hommie.*

common law, and to punish all those who were attainted of any trespass against the charters, by imprisonment, ransom, or amercement, according to the trespass. The statute expressly declares that this special proceeding shall only be in cases where there was no remedy before by the common law. It was enacted that if the three commissioners could not all attend, two should be sufficient. The king's sheriffs and bailiffs were to be attendant on these justices. Besides these regulations for the observance of the two charters, several *articles*, as the act calls them, were enacted for amendment of the law, not of less importance than the above provisions. These will be considered in their proper place.

The next public act upon the subject of the charters is the *Ordinatio Forestæ*, 33 Ed. I. stat. 5, containing some regulations about the purlieus of forests (*a*). In the next year is the famous statute *de Tallagio non concedendo*, 34 Ed. I. stat. 4; and another[1] statute concerning the forest, called likewise *Ordinatio Forestæ*.

De Tallagio non concedendo.

The statute *de Tallagio non concedendo*, like the *Confirmationes Chartarum*, was occasioned by the question about levying money for carrying on foreign wars.[2] The king had required that every freeholder of £20 per annum[3] should attend him into Flanders, or pay him a compensation in lieu thereof, to enable him to go to war with the king of France, in behalf of Guy, earl of Flanders. To this the constable and marshal, who distinguished themselves on the former occasion, made an opposition, and being supported by many potent and steady adherents, they at length compelled the king to make a similar declaration with that in the *Confirmationes Chartarum*. There was now more cause for murmuring than before; for the king had, the last year, levied a talliage on all cities, boroughs, and towns, without assent of parliament; to quiet his commons, therefore, as well as to satisfy his nobles, the king consented in the present statute to a parliamentary declaration about levying money. It was declared that no talliage or aid (which included those feudal aids that had been excepted in the statute of *Confirmationes Chartarum*) should be imposed or levied by the king or his heirs, without the will and assent of the archbishops, bishops, earls, barons, knights, burgesses, and other freemen of the commons of the realm.[4] Nothing was to be taken by way of *maletoute* (a tax before mentioned) for sacks of wool.[5] Respecting purveyance, which was in the light of a very severe tax, it was declared, as it had been on other occasions during this reign, that no officer of the king should take any corn, leather, cattle, or other goods, of any one, without the consent of the owner.[6]

After these provisions concerning taxation, the following general

(*a*) Most of the old statutes are repealed, but they are not the less *illustrative of legal history*.

[1] Stat. 5.

[2] Of this statute *vide* Mad. Exch. vol. i. 762.

[3] This is the value of a knight's fee by the statute *de militibus*, in the next reign.

[4] Ch. 1.

[5] Ch. 3.

[6] Ch. 2. *Vide post*, 28 Ed. I., stat. 3, c. ii.

declarations were made in favour of liberties claimed by the subject. That all men, both clergy and lay, should have their laws, liberties, and free customs as freely and fully as they ever were accustomed to enjoy them;[1] and if anything was introduced by this, or any former law or custom contrary thereto, it was declared null and void.[2] There was at the same time a free pardon of the constable and marshal, and all their adherents, who had refused to attend the king into Flanders.[3] For the better observance of the charter, it was directed that all archbishops and bishops for ever should read it in their cathedral churches, and openly pronounce a curse against all those who violated it in any point. The king put his seal to this statute, or rather charter, as did the archbishops and bishops, who all voluntarily swore to observe the tenure of it in all causes and articles, according to the best of their power.[4] Thus was the statute *de Tallagio non concedendo* sanctioned with the solemnities attending the several confirmations of the charters of liberties, as a security of equal importance with those great supports of our free constitution.

Ordinatio Forestæ.

The *Ordinatio Forestæ*, passed in the same year, is ushered in with a preamble expressing very feelingly the king's compunction for the hardships suffered by his subjects from the forest laws. One great cause of these was the abuse of indictments, which, instead of being presentments by the country, were dictated by one or two of the foresters, upon which attachments issued, and the parties were subjected to all the penalties of law, though perhaps clearly innocent of any offence (*a*). These foresters, it seems, were too numerous, and derived their whole subsistence from the plunder of the forest, in taking wood, venison, and the like to their own use. To remedy all these mischiefs it was ordained as follows: First, that all trespasses *de viridi et venatione* should be presented by the foresters within whose bailiwick they were committed at the next swainmote, before the foresters, verderors, regardors, agistors, and other ministers of the forest; that the truth should be there inquired of by the oath as well of knights as other good and lawful men, and the presentment sealed with the seals of the presentors, otherwise to be void;[5] which regulation about the seals of the presentors had been before

(*a*) Thus, even long after this statute, in the reign of Edward III., it appeared that it was a justification for arresting and imprisoning a man that the defendant was forester in fee of a forest, and that at a certain swainmote it was presented by the foresters, verderors, regardors, and agistors, that the plaintiff had hunted the deer in the forest, upon which the defendant came to him and requested him to find pledges to answer for it before the justices of oyer and terminer in the county; but he refused to do so, for which he was arrested and imprisoned until he should do so, according to the statute; and then it was said that the party could not traverse the presentment of the foresters, though as to that the reporter added a query (*Yearbook* of 45 *Ed. III.*, fol. 7). A man could have a "free chase," though not in a royal forest, without a grant (42 *Ed. III.*, fol. 2); and an action would lie for hunting the deer in a free chase (43 *Ed. III.* 8).

[1] *Ita liberè et integrè sicut eas aliquo tempore meliùs et pleniùs habere consueverunt.*
[2] Ch. 4. [3] Ch. 5. [4] Ch. 6. [5] Ch. 1.

made (as will be shown hereafter) in regard to indictments at common law. If any of the aforesaid ministers happened in the meantime to die, the justice of the forest was to put in others, that there might be a sufficient number to make the presentment. Other officers were to be appointed as before; only verderors were to be elected by the king's writ.[1] None of the before-mentioned ministers were to be put on assizes, juries, or inquisitions out of the forest.[2] Any officer who surcharged the forest was to be removed from his place, and imprisoned at the discretion of the justice of the forest; and at every swainmote inquisition was to be made of such surcharges and oppressions committed by the officers of the forest.[3] The justice of the forest was empowered, in the presence of the king's treasurer, to impose fines without waiting for the eyre.[4] These, with some regulations of a temporary kind, were all the alterations made in the system of forest law by this statute.

These are all the acts which may be considered as of a political nature. The other statutes of this king relate to the common justice of the kingdom; the principal of which are, the statute of Westminster 1, statute of Gloucester, Westminster 2, Westminster 3, and *Articuli super Chartas*. It is to these that Sir Matthew Hale chiefly alludes in what he says of the improvements made by this king in the administration of justice. By these, many grievous and impracticable parts of our law were corrected or removed, and others more apt and effectual substituted in their place, which have stood ever since, incorporated into, and, as it were, a part of the common law. We shall now treat of these statutes in the order in which they were made.

The statute of Westminster the first (*a*), (so called to distinguish it from two subsequent statutes, denominated likewise from parliaments holden at Westminster) is the first in this reign, and is stat. 3 Ed. I. It contains fifty-one chapters; and was ordained, says the general preamble, "because the state of holy church had been evil kept, and the prelates and religious persons of the land grieved many ways, and the people otherwise entreated than they ought to be; the peace less kept, and laws less used, and offenders less punished than they ought to be." It provides, therefore, in the course of fifty chapters, for the correction of many irregularities in the exercise of certain privileges and rights, and for the better administration of justice, both civil and criminal. The first chapter ordains[5] generally, that the peace of the holy church and of the land be well kept and maintained in all points; and that common right be done to all, as well poor as rich, without respect of persons. It then provides against an abuse which had lain very heavy upon religious houses and ecclesiastical dignities. Persons who were descended from the founders, and officers in public employments, used to claim the liberty of residing there on their journeys, with

(*a*) A.D. 1273.

[1] Ch. 2. [2] Ch. 3. [3] Ch. 4. [4] Ch. 6. [5] Ch. 1.

board and lodging for themselves, servants, and horses; hunting in their parks, and taking other liberties without the consent, and generally much against the inclinations of the persons encroached upon. All such intrusions are forbid, under pain of fine and imprisonment; though this restraint, says the act, was not to withdraw the grace of hospitality from those who needed it.

Of wreck.

Some points of the common law were recognised, and more firmly established. Concerning wrecks of the sea, it is *agreed*, says the statute,[1] that where a man, a dog, or a cat, escape alive out of the ship, such ship or barge, or any therein shall not be adjudged wreck;[2] but the goods shall be saved and kept by view of the sheriff, coroner, or king's bailiff, and delivered into the hands of such as are of the town where the goods were found; so that if any within a year and a day sued for them, and proved them to be his, or his lord's or master's, and that they were lost while in his care, they should be restored; if not, they were to belong to the king, and to be seized by the sheriff, coroners, and bailiffs, and delivered to the inhabitants of the town, who should be answerable for them, as wreck belonging to the king, before the justices: in like manner, where the wreck belonged to any other person (*a*), a breach of the above regulation was to be punished with imprisonment and fine.

A provision was made to secure the freedom of all elections; a more important object, perhaps, than it is even at this day; for, at that time, sheriffs, coroners, and other officers, who had great sway in the administration of justice, were all elected by the people (*b*).

(*a*) Wreck, *i.e.*, the privilege of taking it, might belong to a private person or public body, by special grant from the crown; and it is mentioned by Britton and Bracton as one of the "liberties," "privileges," or "franchises," which might be granted by the crown to subjects. Thus Bracton mentions "wreckum maris," as one of these franchises (*Lib.* ii., c. xxix., fol. 56). So Britton mentions the franchise "de aver wreck de meer" (fol. x.) Both agree that for the absence of any grant or prescription it would belong to the crown; and see the subsequent chapter of this statute as to franchises held by subjects.

(*b*) Lord Coke, commenting upon this statute, says:—It declared a principle of the common law, for, before the act, the electors had not their free nor due elections, for sometimes by force, sometimes by menaces, the electors were wrought to make election of men unworthy or not eligible, so as their election was neither due nor free. And, he adds, that the statute extends to all elections, and it would seem that it was not confined to popular or public elections, but included cases where parties had a right of option or election to exercise in matters of private right. Thus the statute *de prærogativa regis* said that a woman, married under age, might elect whether she would abide by her first husband—"Et tunc eligat illa utrum maluerit habere virum illum vel alium quem ei rex obtulerit," &c. And upon this it was argued, when the king claimed the value of the marriage, that the female ward had her election, and that it ought to be free; and Huls, "bachelor of law," argued much in Latin about it. And Paston said that the statute which gave an election did not declare the common law, for, at common law, the ward could not be forced to marry; only if she did not marry the person proposed by the guardian, then she must pay the penalty. On the other side it was urged, that if the ward had to pay the value the election could not be without compulsion, and so would not be free. And it was said, "Election est done par le statute et electio est libera" (*Year-book*, 7 *Hen. VI.* fol. 11, c. xii.) Lord Coke quite adopts the view that this was the common law

[1] Ch. 4. [2] *Vide ante*, 9.

It was with a view to these, and not, probably, to any representatives of the people, that this law referred: however, as it is in general words, it may have a construction which will extend it to elections that have been appointed since for any purpose whatever. Because elections ought to be free, says the act,[1] the king commands, that no man by force of arms, nor by malice, or menacing, shall disturb any in making a free election.

A restraint was put on purveyance:[2] constables and chatellains were not to make prises (that is, to purvey) on persons who were not of the town where the castle was: and further,[3] if purveyors did not pay the money they received at the exchequer, as it was a great inconvenience to the creditors of the crown, and a slander of the king, the amount was to be levied of their lands and goods; and if they had none, they were to be imprisoned (*a*). Another hardship on the public consisted of excessive tolls demanded (*b*) in

and that therefore the above act was declaratory; and he says, "This act extends to all elections, in counties, cities, universities, corporations, and other places" (2 *Inst.* 169). And then he refers to c. x., as to elections of coroners; as to which he says—"The office of a coroner was and is eligible in full county by the freeholders, by the king's writ *de coronatore eligendo.*" The reason whereof was, that both the king and the county had a great interest in the due execution of his office, and therefore the common law gave the freeholders to be electors of him. And for the same reason of ancient time, the sheriff who had *custodiam comitatus* was also eligible. This, however, is very questionable. At all events, if popularly elected in Saxon times, the sheriff certainly was not so, after the Conquest, for instances are numerous of persons appointed by the king to be sheriffs of several counties for a course of years or for life; and it was a common thing to make a king's justice sheriff, or a sheriff king's justice (see c. i.) The present king in the 20th year of his reign, in the *articuli super chartas*, restored, says Coke, the ancient election of sheriffs. "Le roy ad grant a son people que ils eient election de lour viscounts en chescun countie, ou viscount n'est de fee, s'ils voullient" (28 *Edw. I.* c. viii. 13). But this, it will be observed, had an important exception, and by subsequent statutes the election was virtually re-vested in the crown (*vide* stat. 9 *Edw. II. de visc.*; 14 *Edw. III.* 7, 12; *Rich. II.*, c. ii.) The coroner, however, continues to be a popular officer.

(*a*) This only appeared when the money had been actually received from the exchequer, so that there had been a species of embezzlement. Ordinarily the remedy for a tortious or wrongful injury, done by the king's officers under pretext of purveyance or otherwise, was by petition of right, as where the king's officers disturbed the taking of tithes (case of the prior of Christ Church, 31 *Edw. I., Rot. Parl.* 59; *Ryley's Plac. Parl.* 208). So of a wrongful distress by the king's officers (John Mowbray's case, 33 *Edw. I.*, 1 *Rot. Parl.* 163). So for wool wrongfully taken for the king's use (Michael de Harla's case, 33 *Edw. I.*, 1 *Rot. Parl.* 163). So for wheat seized under pretence of a royal commission (14 *Edw. II.*, 1 *Rot. Parl.* 320). Purveyance, when really necessary for the support of the royal household, was in that age undoubtedly legal, as a part of the royal prerogative; but then it only amounted to pre-emption and implied payment, and it was grossly abused. Hence it had been the subject of one of the clauses in Magna Charta.

(*b*) Lord Coke's comment upon this is:—"In the troublesome and irregular reign of Henry III. outrageous tolls were taken and usurped in cities, boroughs, and towns where fairs and markets were kept, to the great oppression of the king's subjects, by reason whereof very many did refrain from coming to fairs and markets, to the hindrance of the common weal; for it hath ever been the policy and wisdom of this realm, that fairs and markets, and especially the markets, be well furnished and supplied" (2 *Inst.* 219). As to toll, more is said in the exposition of the second statute of Westminster, *vide post.* It is to be observed, that the present enactment is against outrageous toll, which seems to point to a toll unreasonable in amount, though Coke thought it also included tolls taken when none were due; as to which, however, in

[1] Ch. 5. [2] Ch. 7. [3] Ch. 32.

some towns for the privilege of the market, in others for murage, that is, for inclosing their towns: both these were restricted, under forfeiture to the king of the franchise so abused.[1]

Such were the miscellaneous articles, regulated by this statute, that could not easily be reduced to any of the heads into which the remainder of it will divide itself. These are *tenures* and *property*, the *administration of justice*, and the *criminal law*.

The services and fruits of tenure were an endless subject of jealousy and contest in these times. We have already seen what was done in the last reign to ascertain these claims, and temper the inconveniences resulting therefrom. The heaviest of these were wardship and marriage; and the following attempts were now made still further to regulate them. In the case of heirs being in ward to their lords,[2] it was provided and declared that *Magna Charta* should be observed,[3] that their land should not be wasted (*a*). All spiritual dignities were to be kept

Wards.

the treatise of Bracton, it appears there was a remedy provided already by the common law (*Bracton*, fol. 56). Lord Coke connects the exaction of tolls at markets with the ancient Saxon laws as to witnesses to contracts, for which he cites the *Mirror*, c. i., s. 3. He says—"Toll to the market is a reasonable sum of money due to the owner of the market upon sale of things tollable within the market. And this was at the first invented, that contracts might have good testimony, and be made openly; for of old time, secret contracts were forbidden, and the *Mirror* saith truth, for the ancient law was so." And then he cites the laws of Ina and Athelstan: "Nemo extra oppidum nisi præsents præposito aliusve fide dignis hominibus, quicquam emito. Ne quis extra oppidum quid emat;" in which Coke says—"Oppidum is to be taken for market." He goes on to state that fairs and markets can only be by grant or prescription, and that the grant of a market does not necessarily imply a toll which requires a special grant, and that will require consideration if it be after the establishment of the market. He also points out that no toll can be claimed for things not sold, unless it be by custom, used time out of mind, which custom none can challenge that claim the market by grant within the time of memory, namely since the time of Richard I. (*Ibid.* 221). He further points out, that the king (where he does not prejudice prior grantees) can grant special privilege of exemption from toll, for which he cites two old cases of this and the next reign, one the case of the abbot of St Edward, *Rot. Parl.* an. 18 *Edw. I.* fol. 2; and the other 2 *Edw. II.* the case of the merchants of Brummagham (*qu.* Birmingham) (2 *Inst.* 221). With regard to the proper amount due for the toll, Lord Coke says:—"I can tell what was due of old, and what was ordained in times past to be paid, for the *Mirror* saith:—Que faires et markets se fissent per lieus, et que achators de blee, et beasts donassent toll a les bailifes des seigniours de markets, ou de faires, cest ascavoire maile de dixe soux de biens, et demeynes, meynes, meynes and de pluis, pluis al afferant, essint que nul tol passast un denier de un manere de merchandize, et cest tolle fuit trove par testmoigner les contracts, car chescun privie contract fuit defendue" (*Mirror*, c. i., s. 3). But the value of money fluctuates, so that a penny in Saxon times might be equal to five shillings now; and Lord Coke adds, "But at this day, there is not one certain toll to be taken, but if that which is taken be not reasonable, it is punishable by this statute; and what shall be deemed in law to be reasonable, shall be judged, all circumstances considered, by the judges of the law, if it come judicially to be determined" (fol. 222).

(*a*) Many cases in the Year-books in the following reign illustrate the system of wardships. Thus, in trespass brought by an infant, the defendant pleaded that the plaintiff's father held a house and land of the Prince of Wales by escuage, and died, whereupon the prince seized the wardship, and granted it to the defendant, who thereupon entered (22 *Assize* 44, fol. 12). Here, it will be seen, that the wardships were granted out by the feudal lords—no doubt, to the highest bidder, whose interest

[1] Ch. 31. [2] Ch. 21. [3] Namely, c. 4, 5, 6. *Vide ante*, vol. i. 236.

in like manner, without spoil or waste, during their vacancy. Of such heirs who, being in ward, married without consent of their guardians before they were fourteen years old, it was declared that the statute of Merton should be observed;[1] and it was now further enacted,[2] that those who married without consent of their guardians, after they had passed fourteen years, should forfeit the double value of their marriage, as directed by that act; and moreover, that the ravisher or detainer of such ward should be answerable to the guardian to the full value of the marriage for the trespass, and make amends also to the king, as directed by the same act. Next, as to heirs female, that lords might not prevent their marrying in order to keep possession of their lands, it was ordained, that after they had accomplished the age of fourteen years, the lord should not keep their lands more than two years; and if in that time the lord did not marry them, they were to have an action to recover the inheritance, without giving anything for wardship or marriage. But, on the other hand, if a female ward wilfully refused a marriage provided by her guardian, being such as would not disparage her, he was entitled to hold the inheritance till she was twenty-one years old, and further, till he had taken the value of the marriage.

In protection of wards, it was provided, by another act,[3] that if a guardian or chief lord infeoffed any one of land that was the inheritance of a child who was in ward to the disherison of the heir, the heir should recover by assize of novel disseisin against the guardian and the tenant: and if the land was recovered, the seisin should be delivered by the justices to the next friend of the heir, to whom the inheritance could not descend, who was to improve it for the use of the heir, and answer for the issues when he came of age. If the infant was carried away, or anywise disturbed in pursuing the remedy here given, the assize might be brought by his next friend.

Of Aids.

Another burthen of tenure was the aids demanded by the lord *pur faire fil chevalier*, and *pur file marier*. These had never been ascertained,[4] but had been levied at the discretion of the lord, who sometimes exacted unreasonable supplies in this way, and those much oftener than was necessary. It was therefore declared[5] that, for the future, there should be taken of a knight's fee twenty shillings only, and the same sum for land in socage of ten pounds, and so in proportion. This was not to be levied for making the lord's son a knight till he was fifteen years

it thus became to oppress and impoverish the estate in order to derive the greatest profit. But the worst incident of wardship was, that it applied to the person as well as the estate. Thus, in an action against the prior of a convent for imprisoning the plaintiff twenty-six years before, in the 10 Edward III., the plea was, that the defendant seized the body of the plaintiff as ward, and as heir-apparent to his father, who held his land of the prior by knight-service (22 *Assize*, fol. 109, p. 85).

[1] Namely, c. 6. *Vide ante*, vol. i. 261.
[2] Ch. 22.
[3] Ch. 48.
[4] *Vide ante*, 105.
[5] Ch. 36.

of age, nor for the marriage of his daughter till she was seven. If the father died before he had married his daughter, his executors were to be answerable out of his goods for the sum levied; and should the goods be insufficient, the heir was to be charged therewith. Thus far of the fruits of tenure, and of property in land.

Next as to the administration of justice. Before we consider such provisions as related to the discussion of causes, with the process and proceedings therein, we shall first mention those made for putting the special remedy by distress on a foot of convenience and effect. The provisions made by the statute of Marlbridge were of an important nature, and as they touched the mischief then mostly prevalent, it was above all things to be desired that they should be enforced (*a*). The first statute

Distresses.

(*a*) The statute was explained by a case which arose in the reign of Edward IV. Trespass was brought upon the statute of Marlbridge, c. iv., *quod nullus de cetero duci faciat* distringas, &c., for driving a trespass out of one county into another, and the lord pleaded that the distress was for rent due for land held of a manor in another county, and that therefore the distress was driven thither. The court were divided in opinion as to whether this was an excuse. One judge said the lord could justify, for the intent of the statute was, that before the act the distrainer, even in case of distress *damage feasant*, could always drive the distress into another county, so that the owner could not know where he could sue replevin, and that therefore the words of the act were *si vicinus super vicinum hoc faciat, &c.*, so that the mischief was that, and did not arise where the lord had a reason for removing the distress. A case was cited of the 1 Hen. VI. to that effect, and so the court seemed disposed to hold, but for another fault it would seem the plea was held bad (22 Edw. fol. 12). It has already been observed, in commenting upon the statute of Marlbridge, that wrongful distresses, or rather illegal seizures of cattle under colour or pretence of distresses, were the most common form of oppression suffered by the body of the people in this age, and thus it is that the remedies for this species of wrong were of the greatest and most general importance; and one of the largest chapters in Britton, "De prises des avers," relates thereto. It touches upon the obvious hardship of detention of cattle, and provides a summary remedy, "pur ceo que bestes et autres distresses ne soient mis trop longement detenus emparkes (impounded) que le viscount per simple pleintes, et par plegges, deliverent teles destresses" (fol. 54). That is, that the sheriff, on account of the hardship, might give a summary remedy by replevin; and he might use force for the purpose, and distrain the disturbers, and arrest them (*Ibid.*) Then the bailiffs of the sheriff having got the cattle, and taken pledges for their return should it be accorded, there was a summary procedure provided for the determination of the plaint or suit of replevin, which is carefully described in this chapter x. of Britton (fol. 55). Or the party distraining might avow and justify the taking of the cattle on the ground that they were *damage feasant*, and detained as pledges for reasonable satisfaction; to which the owner might reply, that he offered to make "dues amendes par les taxation de ascun de ses bones veisins (voisins) et il reson refusaunt," &c. (fol. 56), or that he put the matter in arbitration, "en le arbitrement de tiel et tiel, les quêx arbitrement, que il n'y avoit nul damage fait," &c. (fol. 57). This passage is interesting as showing how our ancestors settled the question—which has not been so satisfactorily disposed of in modern times—how the reasonable amends should be adjusted or ascertained. It will be observed that they still made good use of the simple and salutary proceeding by *arbitration of the neighbours*, which, as has been shown in describing the Saxon system, was what the court of the hundred or county virtually came to. Then the chapter goes on to describe the procedure in case the distress is justified on the ground of rent or other service being in arrear. Then it proceeds to declare that these who distrained for more than the value of their demand should be amerced for the outrage, "soient en la mercy pour le outrage;" and those who made a double distress—distraining again, pending the proceeding on a prior distress—were to be imprisoned and fined (fol. 60–62). There is no portion of the law of the age which will be found guarded so carefully, and described so particularly, as that relating to distresses.

of this reign is, in effect, nothing more than an injunction to observe it; for it says,[1] that some persons take and cause to be taken, beasts, and chase them out of the county, which is hereby forbid; and if any offend against this injunction, they shall be fined as directed by the statute of Marlbridge;[2] as shall those who take beasts wrongfully, and distrain out of their fee, who shall, besides, be punished in proportion to the trespass. Thus this act is a confirmation of the statute of Marlbridge, with these differences: that statute speaks only of distresses; this, of all *takings*: that prohibits *all* distresses; this, only distraining of *beasts*: that concerns those *who take*; this extends to those *who cause* to be taken.[3]

The next statute on the subject of distresses goes much further towards removing this peculiar remedy from the hands of individuals, and submitting it to the officers of justice. It is provided,[4] that if any take the beasts of another, and cause them to be driven into a castle or fortress, and there withhold them against gages and pledges, whereupon they are solemnly demanded by the sheriff, or some other bailiff of the king, the sheriff or bailiff, at the suit of the plaintiff, taking with them the power of the county or bailiwick, should endeavour to make plevin of the beasts taken (*a*); and if any obstruct them, or there is no one belonging to the lord or taker to give an answer, or make deliverance, he shall be warned of the matter; and if he does not forthwith deliver the cattle, the king, for the trespass and despite, shall cause the castle or fortress to be beaten down, and no permission shall afterwards be given to rebuild it. The plaintiff shall be recompensed by the lord, or him that took the beast, in double damages for all the loss he sustained after the first demand made by the sheriff or bailiff;

(*a*) The mischief before this act, says Coke, was, that great men, when they took a distress of the beasts of their tenants or neighbours, to prevent the course of justice, or to enforce the owner to yield to their desire, would drive the beasts into a castle or fortress, and then detain and keep them, so as no replevy could be made according to the ordinary course of law, for that, in case of a subject, the sheriff could not break the castle or fortress. This act giveth remedy, that the sheriff, taking with him the power of the county, may make replevin. And note, says Coke, that every man is bound by the common law to assist the sheriff in his office for the execution of the king's writ, or the bailiffs who have the sheriff's warrant. So Bracton, "Et si (vicecomes) aliquem invenerit resistentem assumptis secum (si opus fuerit) militibus et liberis hominibus de comitatu, ad sufficientiam capiat corpora hominum resistentium, et illos imprisona salvo custodiat" (*Bracton*, lib. v. s. 443). And so in the statute Westminster 2, c. xxxix., it was provided that sheriffs should not falsely return that they could not execute the king's writs, but that the sheriff, in any such case, *assumpto secum posse comitatui sui*, should go to make execution (*Stat. West.* 2, c. xxxix.) And statute 2 Ed. III. c. v. provided that the sheriff should be bound to receive writs. And Coke cites a case in the reign of Ed. II., that a sheriff returned that he could not execute the king's writ for resistance of certain persons, and because he did not take the power of the county in aid of the execution, as the statute willed, he was amerced in twenty marks (19 Ed. II. title *Execution*, 24). And it is holden as a maxim of law, that it is not lawful for any man to disturb the ministers of the king in the due execution of the king's writs (2 *Inst.* 194).

[1] Ch. 16.
[2] Viz. ch. 4, 2, and 15. *Vide ante*, 67, 68, 69.
[3] 2 Inst. 191.
[4] Ch. 17.

and if he that took the beasts has not wherewith, the lord shall make the recompense upon the spot, at the time the sheriff or bailiff makes the deliveranse. It was further directed that, in cases where the sheriff ought to deliver the king's writ to the bailiff of the lord of such castle or fortress, if the bailiff will not make deliverance, the sheriff (not waiting for a writ of *non omittas*, as heretofore) shall do his office without further delay; and not only where the writ of replevin is issued, but also upon a plaint, as authorised by the statute of Marlbridge.[1] The statute says, if these violences were committed in the marches of Wales, or anywhere else where the king's writ runneth not, the king, who is sovereign lord over *all*, should do right to those who complained, a clause which at once asserted the king's dominion over that country,[2] and left the measure of its exercise at his discretion.

The first object that draws our attention in considering the administration of justice, is the jurisdiction of courts. Some provision was made towards abolishing inconvenient customs, and regulating the order of hearing and deciding causes (*a*).

A singular custom had prevailed in many cities, boroughs, and towns corporate (*b*), that if any person of one city, society, or merchant-guild was indebted to some one of another city, society, or merchant-guild, and if any other of that city, society, or merchant-guild came into the city, society, or merchant-guild where the creditor was, that the creditor might charge such foreigner with the debt of the other.[3] It was this custom that occasioned the following statute,[4] which enacts, that in no city, borough, town, market, or fair, should any foreigner be distrained for a debt of which he was not the debtor or surety; and such distress was to be

(*a*) It has already been noticed that our municipal institutions are, along with the manorial, the most ancient of our institutions, having undoubtedly been derived from the Romans during their occupation of the country, whether in the form of municipal corporations, or guilds, or colleges, or incorporated companies, which some have supposed to have been of Saxon origin, but which were really of Roman origin. Much of our law was embodied in these institutions, and some of the most ancient of our local customs are the customs of cities which go back to the time of the Romans. Among these ancient customs was that of foreign attachment, as it was called, that is, the custom of attaching the funds of a debtor residing in some other or "foreign" city or town, and so not within the town in which the creditor lived. It is to that the following passage seems to refer.

(*b*) The custom of foreign attachments existed not only in such great cities as those of London and Bristol, in which it still prevails, but in many others in which it is obsolete, as in Exeter, Chester, or Oxford. Thus, in the old reports, there are cases of foreign attachment in Exeter (*Halse* v. *Walker*, 1 *Rolls Abr.* 554). The earliest case in which the custom appears pleaded in the city of London is the case of *Bowser* v. *Collins* (*Year-book*, 22 *Edward IV.* fol. 30), where the custom is set out fully on the certificate of the Records of London. The custom is there stated thus: "That upon a plaint in the court of the mayor, if the defendant had no goods in the city by which he could be distrained to do right, but it appeared that any one in the city was indebted to him, then, unless the party could dispute the debt, it might be

[1] *Vide ante*, 69.

[2] This was seven or eight years before the conquest of Wales, and the making of the *Statutum Walliæ, Vide ante*, 94, 95.

[3] Fleta, lib. ii. c. 56. 2 Inst. 204.

[4] Ch. 23.

immediately delivered by the bailiff of the place, or the king's bailiff, and the offender to be grievously punished.

There was another instance, though not so singular as the former, where these local jurisdictions exercised an authority that required some correction (*a*). Great men, and others who had particular jurisdictions to hold plea of contracts, covenants, and trespasses, when they were made or done within a certain precinct, would attach persons who happened to be within their franchises, by their goods, to answer in their courts of contracts, covenants, and trespasses, which had happened out of their franchise, pretending the same were *transitory*, and, as such, might *be supposed* to be done within the franchise. This was greatly to the prejudice of the king's courts, and of the crown, which lost its fines and amercements; and it brought great inconvenience on the party, who was a stranger, held nothing of the franchise, and was only passing through it. It was enacted, therefore,[1] that any one who should

'attached' in his hands, to answer the claim of the plaintiff." The principle of custom prevailed strongly in our law. Thus, it was enough if the proceedings in the court of a manor were according to the custom of the manor (*Year-book*, 11 *Edward III.* fol. 60). But then the custom must be reasonable, and the custom of foreign attachment was so; but that stated in the text was not so, and therefore was corrected and qualified by the statute *ut supra.* Customary local courts existed in almost all towns and cities for the recovery of debts from persons *residing* there; but, in order to bring a suit in a local court, it was necessary that the debt should have arisen, and that the debtor should reside within the local limit of its jurisdiction. Hence, if the debts arose elsewhere, a difficulty arose; and, in favour of trade, a custom had arisen in our principal cities, that if the debtor had funds or assets in the place where his creditor lived, the latter might attach them; and so, if any one there was indebted to the debtor, the creditor might attach that debt, as payable to himself. This was not unreasonable; but it should seem that in some places it had become misunderstood or perverted, and hence the present enactment.

(*a*) What follows is taken from Coke's comments on the chapter, which give the true reason for its enactment: "The prejudice to the king, in losing his fines in actions, and amercements, and other profits, upon a false supposal, not like to the general jurisdiction and power of the king's courts, through the whole realm; for wherever the contract, &c., were made, the matter being transitory, the plaintiff may allege it in what county he will, and the king can lose nothing" (2 *Institute*, 229). He goes on to say, that, at the common law, one that had a particular jurisdiction within a manor or the like could not hold suit of a matter done *out* of the manor, because it was not within his jurisdiction (*Ibid.* 23). And by statute 6 Rich. II. c. ii., it was enacted that even in the superior courts suits should be brought in the counties where the matters arose. It was of the essence of a local and inferior jurisdiction that it could only be exercised over parties within its local limits, and as to matters which had arisen within those limits, and not over "foreigners"—*i.e.*, parties residing out of those local limits, whence the phrase "foreign attachment," as applied to the peculiar and exceptional custom of attaching funds belonging to "foreigners," or parties residing out of the jurisdiction. The local courts were extremely numerous, being originally, there can be little doubt, the courts of the lords of manors or vills, whence it was that it was sufficient to set up a court according to the custom of the vill (*Year-book*, 11 *Edward III.* fol. 60), and there might be courts of lords of manors by prescription in hundreds (*Longo Quinto*, 349). If there was a castle in the vill, the court might be set up by prescription in the castle, the constable of the castle, like the steward of lord of a manor, being judge; and thus there was such a court in the Tower of London. There can be little doubt that these courts were often set up by *pretended* prescriptions, and that their jurisdiction was used as a cloak to the most atrocious oppressions. The oppressions exercised by constables of castles formed the subject of a clause in Magna Charta, and the evil still continued.

[1] Ch. 35.

cause a foreigner to be so attached should recompense him in double damages. Upon this act have been formed two writs: the one, in nature of a prohibition before the suit began, commanding that the party should not be arrested contrary to the form of this statute; the other, after the commencement of the suit, to recover the penalty of double damages, and the goods distrained.[1]

While measures were taking to secure the king's courts in possession of the proper objects of their cognizance, it was necessary to facilitate the despatch of causes there as much as possible. There was room for regulation in this particular. The method of hearing causes in the superior court had become very preposterous and disorderly. Many times the judges, yielding to the importunity of great men, and others, especially in the late turbulent reign, would put off the business of the day to some future time, and at that time, perhaps, hear some other matter appointed for a subsequent day: so that causes were delayed, parties disappointed, expenses incurred; and after all, when the matter was to be heard, the parties had neither advocate, witnesses, or anything in readiness.[2] To remedy this, it was provided and commanded, as the act says,[3] by the king, that the justices of the king's bench, and of the bench at Westminster, should decide all pleas that stood for determination at one day, before any new matter was arraigned, or new plea commenced the day following.

Another impediment to the administration of justice arose from the canons of holy church, which forbade, under pain of excommunication, that any man should be sworn on the evangelists, or that any secular plea should be held at certain seasons. These are stated by Britton to be as follows: from the Septuagesima to eight days after Easter; from the beginning of Advent to eight days after Epiphany; in the Ember-days; the days of the great litanies; the Rogation-days; the week of Pentecost; in the time of harvest or vintage—that is, from the feast of St Margaret, 13th July, until fifteen days after the feast of St Michael the Archangel, and in the solemn feasts of the acts of the saints. All these times, says our author, were allotted for prayer, to silence debate, to reconcile those that were at strife, or to gather the fruits of the earth, being works either of piety or charity.[4] If these seasons are compared with the scheme of *dies communes in banco*, in the former reign,[5] they will be found nearly to fill up all the remainder of the year that was not occupied by the Terms, and, indeed, to encroach upon some of them. The circuits of the justices, therefore, which, no doubt, were always held in the vacations, and sometimes part of a term, could not, consistently with the canons, be held without a dispensation, for which reason some of those seasons that stood most in the way were now broke in upon. Forasmuch, says the act,[6] as it is great charity to do right to all men, at all time, when need shall

1 Reg. 98. 2 Inst. 230.
2 2 Inst. 256.
3 Ch. 46.
4 Britton, c. 53.
5 *Vide ante*, 48.
6 Ch. 51.

be, it was provided, by the assent of all the prelates, that *assizes of novel disseisin*, *mortauncestor*, and *darrein presentment*, should be taken in *Advent*, *Septuagesima*,[1] and *Lent*, as well as Inquests.[2] This general standing dispensation of the canon in future was obtained of the bishops at the special instance of the king.

Assizes.

The remedy by assize was extended by several statutes to cases where it before had no effect. One was, where escheators, sheriffs, and other bailiffs, under colour of their office (*a*), would seize into the king's hands the freeholds of individuals. The disseisee, in this case, had no remedy but to sue by petition to the king (*b*); but now it was enacted,[3] that he might either pursue the old course, or bring a writ of novel disseisin, in which he should recover double damages, and the offender should be amerced to the king. A provision was made respecting disseisins, which seems to be merely an affirmance of the common law.[4] It is for that reason, probably, that the act says, it was provided and *agreed*, that if any one be attainted of disseisin, with robbery of goods, and it be found by the recognitors in an assize of novel disseisin, the judgment should be to recover his damages, as well of the goods as the freehold; and the disseisor should make fine, and, if present, be ordered to prison: and so was it to be in all cases of disseisin with force and arms, though there was no robbery of goods.[5]

(*a*) That is, not *really* on behalf of the crown, but for their own profit, under colour and *pretence* of acting for the crown. This, it is obvious, would be a mere act of private spoliation, and the parties would, at common law, be liable to the common remedy by action, if not also by indictment; and this perhaps may have been what was meant when it was said that, before the reign of the king, a man could have sued the *king* in the same way as a subject, and that this king ordained that the crown could only be sued by Petition of Right (*Bro. Abr.*, "Prerogative le Roy," fol. 2; 21 *Edward III.* fol. 3). At all events, in this reign it was settled (as already seen) that this was the only remedy for wrongs done by the king's officers for or on behalf of the crown, as where goods were taken for the use and benefit of the crown by virtue of the prerogative of purveyance or otherwise (*vide ante*). But this, it is obvious, would not apply in cases when the officers really seized for their *own* use and benefit, under colour and pretence of seizing for the king's use; and in such cases *they* would clearly be liable at common law, so that this was a mere declaratory enactment; and the practical difficulty would be in applying it, for how could the plundered subject know whether the king's officer seized for his own use or the king's? The author, however, is obviously in error in supposing (as he states in the next sentence) that when the officer seized *under colour* of his office, the only remedy would be by petition of right. That was the remedy when the seizure *really was* on behalf of the king—that is, for the use and benefit of the crown; for if the king should be possessed, whether by right or wrong, the subject should have petition (*Year-book*, 24 *Edward III.* fol. 55).

(*b*) This is not so (*vide supra*).

[1] If *Septuagesima* means here the same period as in the passage just quoted from Britton, it must include *Lent;* which therefore need not have been added, but *ex abundante cautela.* If that is not the sense, it can signify only the Sunday, which seems an absurd provision. In like manner *Quaresme*, which is the next word in the original, either means from Quadragesima, the first Sunday in Lent, to the end of it, or the whole of Lent from Ash-Wednesday.

[2] The expression in the statute seems to convey, that inquests used to be taken before at those seasons. This must have been by a dispensation.

[3] Ch. 24. [4] *Vide ante*, vol. i. 331. [5] Ch. 37.

In cases of disseisin, if it happened either that the disseisee or disseisor died, leaving an heir within age, and a writ of *entry sur disseisin* was brought by the heir of the disseisor being within age, we have seen that the practice was for the parol to demur, until the full age of each respectively.[1] This occasioned great delay, and contributed rather to confirm the injury of the disseisor and wrong-doer. To correct this, it was provided,[2] that for the nonage of the one party or the other, in the above cases, the writ should not be abated, nor the plea delayed; and if it came to a trial, and the verdict was against the heir of the disseisee, he should have a conviction, or attaint (as it was now more commonly called) of the king's special grace, without paying anything. So equitable did they think it to take care that the infant, who was by this act precipitated into a contest at law, to which, by the old practice, he was not liable, should be protected by every legal means. The attaint, as it should seem, not being a writ, that was granted of course.

Of attaints.

Attaints had just before come under the contemplation of the legislature,[3] when the first parliamentary provision was made respecting this peculiar and severe proceeding against jurors. "Forasmuch," says that statute, "as certain persons of this realm doubt very little to make a false oath, whereby many people are disherited, and lose their right; it is provided, that the king, *of his office*, shall from henceforth grant attaints upon inquests, in plea of land, or of freehold, or of anything touching freehold, when it shall seem to him necessary." Many doubts have arisen upon this act. Some are of opinion that, though an attaint did lie upon a false verdict given in a plea of land, yet the king, sometimes, would not grant it without a special suit made to him, which produced great delay, trouble, and expense. The reason of this difficulty in obtaining an attaint in a plea real, more than a plea personal, they say, was, that in the latter the party grieved had no remedy but an attaint, which should therefore be of course, but that in pleas real he might resort to an action of a higher nature, and therefore this extraordinary redress was not absolutely necessary. Others have been of a contrary opinion—namely, that an attaint did not at common law lie in *all* pleas real; and therefore this act provides, that the king shall grant it *ex officio*—that is, *ex merito justitiæ*.[4] Upon the whole, it seems to be the opinion of Lord Coke,[5] that an attaint lay at common law, both in pleas real and personal, and he founds that opinion, as he supposes, upon ancient writers and records.

However, it should seem, from the face of our statute-book, that this writ was not so general as is stated by that learned author.[6]

[1] *Vide ante*, vol. i. c. viii. [2] Ch. 47. [3] Ch. 38.
[4] 2 Inst. 237. [5] *Ibid.* 130.
[6] In confirmation of the statute-book, *vide Rot. Parl.* 18 *Edw. I*, Petit. No. 93. Attaint denied in trespass; and the *Mirror*, where that writer complains of it as an abuse of the common law, that attaints did not lie in pleas personal as well as pleas real. This author, as is supposed, lived towards the close of the reign of Edward II., just before those acts of Edward III. were made. (*Mirror*, ch. 5.)

For, to say nothing of the statute now before us, we find by stat. 1 Edward III. sect. 6 that an attaint was thereby granted in a *writ* of trespass; and it is remarkable, that by stat. 5 Edward III. c. vii. an attaint is granted as well in pleas of trespass *without* writ as by writ, from which it looks extremely likely that each of these was an enlargement of this remedy, which extended no further than the express words of the statutes would carry it. Thus might Lord Coke's opinion be shaken by merely looking into the statute-book; but it is evident, from the former part of this history, that an attaint lay only against jurors in assizes when the assize was taken *in modum assisæ*, and not at all in other cases of freehold, nor in any personal action whatsoever.

It is true that from a passage in Bracton,[1] we must conclude that the writ of attaint was not, even in these cases, obtained in the ordinary course of the chancery, if the party had suffered any time to elapse; but that after a length of time the king was to be specially petitioned to allow it. However, it seems harsh to put any other construction upon this statute than the following: that perjury had grown so common, it was become necessary to declare that an attaint should be had not only in an assize when taken in *modum assisæ*, but in all *inquests* in pleas of land or of freehold, or of anything touching freehold.

If it is necessary to draw any particular inference from the words *de son office,* perhaps the following may be as natural as that above mentioned: not that the king shall grant these writs whenever applied for, *ex merito justitiæ* (a sense which the words *ex officio* surely never bore in any writer of Latin, whether good or bad), but that the king shall *ex officio*, without being sued and applied for, grant writs of attaint to make inquiry of the perjury of jurors. This is the true sense of *ex officio;* and this construction is supported not only by the earnestness with which the statute complains of the crime, but by the words annexed to the grant of this new power to the king, *when it shall seem to him necessary.*

We have seen[2] that the champion in a writ of right was to swear *de visû et auditû proprio*, or that of his father; but things were so altered, that we find a statute made in this parliament[3] to the following effect: "Because it seldom happened, but that the champion of the demandant is forsworn, in that he sweareth that he or his father *saw* the seisin of his lord or his ancestor, and his father commanded him to deraign that right;" it is provided, that henceforth the champion of the demandant shall not be compelled so to swear. But the old oath in other points was to be observed.

Several provisions were enacted to facilitate the course of proceeding and process in actions. In a writ of dower *unde nihil habet*, the old plea of the tenant, whereby it used to be objected that she had received her dower of another man before the writ purchased, was taken away;[4] unless the tenant could show that

[1] *Vide ante*, vol. i. c. viii. [2] *Ibid.* c. viii. [3] Ch. 41. [4] Ch. 49.

she had received part of her dower of himself, and in the same town, before the writ purchased.

Vouching to warranty and casting essoins were put under some wholesome restrictions. These indulgences had been too much abused. In all real actions the tenant was permitted to vouch any person, though he or any of his ancestors never had anything in the land whereof he might infeoff the tenant or any of his ancestors. Again, the person vouched might in like manner vouch another; and when we consider that upon every summons *ad warrantizandum*, there must be a lapse of several months before a return of the writ could be had, the delay was infinite; while every voucher perhaps was false (*a*). To remedy this, it was provided as follows:[1] First, as to writs of possession, as those of *mortauncestor*, *cosinage*, of *aiel* (a writ in nature of a mortauncestor),[2] *nuper obiit* (for so they now called a writ *de proparte*), of intrusion, and other similar writs; if the tenant vouched to warranty, and the demandant counter-pleaded it, and averred by assize or by the country, or otherwise, as the court should award, that the tenant or his ancestor, whose heir he was, was the first that entered after the death of him of whose seisin he demanded the land; then the averment of the demandant should be received,

Vouching to warranty.

(*a*) This is taken from the commentary of Coke (2 *Inst.* 240), who points out that if the vouchee, the party vouched to warrant the title, appeared, he was substituted for the tenant as defendant. "It seemed strange," he says, "that when the original *præcipe* was brought against the tenant of the land that the court should, upon that writ, hold plea between the tenant and vouchee; but it is more strange to make a question of that which hath received an ancient, continual, and constant allowance. The vouchee cometh in *in loco tenentis*, and in judgment of law as a tenant to the demandant" (*Year-Book*, 8 *Edw. III.* 61, *Fitzherbert's Abr.*) The subject has a close connection with the subject of another enactment in the second chapter of Westminster as to the right of those in reversion or remainder to come forward and defend their title in a real action against the *tenant* of the freehold for life; all the old real actions, it is to be observed, being brought against the party seised of some freehold estate. The present enactment relates rather to the right of the tenant to call upon the party from whom he professed to derive title to come forward and defend it; and as the party could not do this unless he had himself been seised, the demandant could counter-plead, as Coke points out, denying his title, so as to show that he had no right to come forward; and the demandant might safely do this if the tenant had himself succeeded to the seisin on the alleged devolution of the title to the demandant, the principle being, that the third party had no right to come forward unless the tenant had really denied title under him as against the demandant. Hence the remedy provided by this chapter, the effect of which was that the demandant might, to avoid delay, insist on the matter being determined between him and the tenant on that simple issue, whether the latter *had* derived title from the third party vouched. This principle has never ceased to pervade the law of procedure in actions for the recovery of real property, and pervades it still. It was always a principle that the party who stood in the relation of remainder-man, or reversioner to the actual tenant sued, could claim to come forward; and the enactment in the second statute of Westminster enforced it as to real actions (*vide post*), and that principle was applied by the practice of the courts to the action of ejectment, in which the *landlord* was allowed to come in and defend (*Salkeld's Reports, title Ejectment*). But then it was only the real and actual landlord who stood in the relation of reversioner to the tenant who could thus claim to come in (*Ibid.*) And thus there has been an entire identity of principle on the subject for six hundred years, from the statutes of Westminster to the present day.

[1] Ch. 40. [2] *Vide ante*, vol. i. c. viii.

if the tenant would abide thereon: and if not, and he had not his vouchee ready to enter immediately into the warranty, he should be compelled to answer over; saving to the demandant such exception against the vouchee, if he would vouch over, as he had against the first tenant.

Moreover it was provided, that in writs of entry which made mention of degrees, none were to vouch out of the line there mentioned. As to writs which made no mention of degrees; as the writ of *entry in the post;* those writs, says the statute, shall not have place, but where the other writs naming the degrees could not be maintained.[1] If the demandant would aver that neither the vouchee nor his ancestor had ever seisin of the land or tenement demanded, nor fee or service by the hands of his tenant or his ancestors, since the time of him on whose seisin the demandant declared, until the time the writ was purchased, whereby he might have infeoffed the tenant or his ancestors; the statute directs this counter-plea should be allowed in the before-mentioned writs of possession, as well as in a writ of right. After all these checks upon vouching, the statute, notwithstanding, has a saving for tenants, who, though ousted of their voucher by the counter-pleas above-mentioned, yet might, perhaps, really have a charter of warranty: as if a person, who neither himself nor any of his ancestors ever had any thing in the land, released to the tenant with warranty; and a writ was brought against the tenant, and he vouched the releasor, and the demandant counter-pleaded the voucher under this statute, namely, that neither he nor his ancestors ever had any seisin; then the tenant was ousted of his voucher; but yet, by the saving here made, he was to have his remedy over by a writ of *warrantia chartæ.*[2]

Essoins were as great a grievance in judicial proceedings as vouching to warranty. To limit these also, it was provided,[3] that because in writs of assize, attaint, and *juris utrùm*, for so the *assisa utrùm* was now called (where the jurors, being returned the first day, suffered most by delays), the jurors had been troubled by reason of the essoins of tenants; therefore after the tenant had once appeared in court, he should be no more essoined, unless he would make his attorney to sue for him; and if not, it was enacted, that the assize or jury[4] should be taken by default.

There was an instance in which the delay of essoins was carried to an infinite length: that was, where there was an essoining *simul et vicissim*, or as it was now called, *a fourcher by essoin;* as when a *præcipe* was brought against two or more tenants, and after each had had one essoin, which was by law due to them, they further delayed the demandant by alternately successive essoins. As for instance, a *præcipe* is brought against *A.* and *B.* *A.* is essoined,

[1] *Vide ante*, c. viii. [2] 2 Inst. 240, 245. [3] Ch. 42.

[4] *L'assise ou la juree*, to comprehend the two characters, the recognitors might by possibility appear in at the trial.

and *B.* appears, and hath *idem dies* given him; at which day *A.* appears, but *B.* casts an essoin: at the *dies datus A.* is essoined again, and *B.* appears; and so alternately: this was called *fourcher*, that is, *to divide;* because they divide themselves, in delay of the demandant by essoins and appearances, interchangeably.[1] The excess to which this practice was now carried, had crept in since the time of Bracton; or at least it was discountenanced by that author; for he lays it down expressly, that an essoin, in such case, should not be allowed at every appearance, on account of the infinite delay it would occasion.[2] The statute made to remedy this abuse[3] recites, that "forasmuch as demandants are often delayed, by reason that many parceners are tenants, of whom none can be compelled to answer without the other; or the tenants may be jointly infeoffed, in which case none may know his several right; and such tenants often *fourch* by essoin, so that every one of them has a several essoin;" it therefore enacts, that for the future such tenants shall not have an essoin, but only at one day, as a sole tenant has; so that they shall no more *fourch*, but have only one essoin.

Of all the various essoins, none put so effectual a stop to justice as that *de ultra mare* (*a*); by which persons would essoin themselves, though they were really within the realm the day of the summons. It was ordained,[4] that this essoin should not always be allowed, if the demandant would challenge it, and be ready to aver that the tenant was in England the day of the summons, and three weeks after; but it should be adjourned in this form: that, if the

(*a*) This is an instance of an important principle embodied in an ancient form. Essoins were excuses for non-appearance. This enactment relates to one species of excuse for non-appearance that the party was *beyond seas,* and this plainly proves that, at common law, a party might be sued although he was beyond seas. The same thing is provable in another way: that is, because summons at the common law was not upon the person, but at the residence (2 *Inst.* 254). Hence the essoin, or excuse for non-appearance, which was allowed for a period of eighty days. Thus Glanville says: "Est aliud genus essoniandi, et necessarrium, cum quis essoniat se de ultra mare, et tunc si recipiatur essonium, dabuntur ipsi essoniato ad minus quadraginta dies" (lib. 1, c. xxv.) Hence Fleta says: "It could be avoided by showing that on the day of the summons the defendant was in England. Sunt tamen quidam, qui, cum, fuerint brevia super ipsos impetrata, extra regnum se divertunt, ne summonitione sint preventi, ut sic jus petentis per essonium de ultra mare deferri possit, et unde provisum est, quod si petens offerat verificare, quod tenens *fuerit in Anglia die summonitionis,* et per tres septimanas sequentes, adjournetur essonium, et si alia die constare possit per inquisitionem, vel alia modo, quod tenens fuit in Anglia die summonitionis, &c., ita quod potuit rationabiliter præmuniri, vertatur essoonium in defaltam" (*Fleta*, lib. 6, c. viii.) Which plainly implies that the summons was not necessarily served personally, or it would be idle to allege that the party was in England on the day of the summons, for summons was always within the realm. If the party sued, when summoned, *i.e.*, at his residence, did not appear, nor cast an essoin, *i.e.*, make an excuse for his non-appearance, and he was within the realm, he could be outlawed, or his property could be taken if he was out of the realm (*Brooke's Abr.*, *title "Utlagary" and "Attachement des biens"*). And a party could be outlawed although out of the realm (*Ebro.* v. *Mathew Carthews Rep.*) although it was an outlawry which could be defeated by a writ of error. Thus, therefore, at common law, parties were suable though beyond seas.

[1] 2 Inst. 250. [2] *Vide ante*, vol. i. c. viii. [3] Ch. 43. [4] Ch. 44.

demandant was ready at a certain day, by averment of the country or otherwise, as the court should award, to prove that the tenant was within the four seas the day he was summoned, and three weeks after, so that he might be reasonably warned by the summons, the essoin should be turned into a default.[1]

Thus far of these obsolete parts of our ancient jurisprudence; which we have ventured to treat so fully, that the history of our law may be better understood, and the causes and effects upon which the changes of our jurisprudence have at different periods turned, may be clearly distinguished.

We have seen what the *solennitas attachiomentorum* was in the last reign.[2] The great delay occasioned by this tediousness of process made it necessary to shorten it very considerably. This design was begun by the statute of Marlbridge, which ordained that the second attachment should be *per meliores plegios*, and then should go the last or great distress.[3] Another step of this process was now taken off; for it was ordained,[4] that should the tenant or defendant, after the first attachment returned, make default, *immediately* the great distress should be awarded; and if the sheriff did not make sufficient return thereof upon a certain day he should be amerced. If he returned, that he had done execution in due manner, and the issues were delivered to the mainpernors, then he was commanded to return issues, at another day, before the justices. If the party came in at the day to save his default, he was to have the issues. If he came not, the king was to have them; that is, the justices of the king were to cause them to be delivered to the wardrobe; the justices of the bench at Westminster were to deliver them to the exchequer; the justices in eyre to the sheriff of the county.

A new time of limitation was fixed in the following manner: (*a*) In conveying a descent in a writ of right, it was enacted,[5] that none should presume to declare of the seisin of his ancestor beyond the time of king Richard; which has since been always con-

(*a*) In the time of Bracton, *temp.* Henry III., the period of limitation was fixed upon the natural aod practical basis of the range of recollection in the jurors or witnesses, who could only testify as to what they had seen or heard from persons who had personal knowledge, and thus, of necessity, there was practically a period of limitation, which was estimated at about forty years, that is, forty years from the time of the matter in question, which probably might be prolonged to sixty years, as society became more settled, and possibly it might be supposed that there was some uncertainty in the duration of the period of limitation upon this principle, which, however, has this advantage, that it was reckoned from the time of the matter in question. In the statute of Merton, A.D. 1236, a certain date was fixed as the commencement of the period of limitation—viz., the coronation of Henry II., which was eighty years back. In 1275, that period having by the lapse of time increased to a hundred and twenty years, the coronation of Richard I., which was sixty-eight years before, was fixed as the date whence the period should be reckoned. The absurdity of such arbitrary modes of reckoning the period of limitation will be manifest; but it was not until 1540, *temp.* Henry VIII., that the rational mode of limitation was restored; that is to say, a limitation reckoned from the occurrence of the matter.

[1] *Vide ante*, vol. i. c. viii. [2] *Ibid.* [3] *Ibid.*
[4] Ch. 45. [5] Ch. 39.

strued to mean the first day of that king's reign. Writs of novel desseisin, and of partition, commonly called *nuper obiit*, were to have limitation from the first voyage of Henry III. into Gascony, which was in the fifth year of his reign (a period that had been fixed for assizes of novel disseisin by the statute of Merton);[1] writs of *mortauncestor*, of *cosinage*, of *aiel*, of entry, and *de nativis*, from the coronation of Henry III. These continued the period of limitation till the reign of Henry VIII., when the policy of measuring the time of limitation, for commencing actions, by a certain number of years, was adopted in the place of these fixed periods. The prohibition about *beaupleader*, made by the statute of Marlbridge,[2] was revived and enforced.[3]

While these improvements were made in the practice of our civil courts, the legislature provided for the due administration of the criminal law, by defining crimes, but more particularly by contriving modes of prevention and punishment.

It should seem that sheriffs, in their tourns, and lords in their leets, had exercised that part of their criminal jurisdiction which related to escapes with too little discretion; for it was enacted,[4] that nothing be demanded, taken, or levied by the sheriff, or by any other, for the escape of a thief or felon, until it be judged an escape by the justices in eyre.

The crime of rape, which, in ancient times, had been felony, and punishable with death, had, in the last reign, been considered in a less heinous light, and punished only by certain mutilations, which were thought peculiarly adapted to the offence.[5] This species of punishment continued till the legislature once more changed it. The king, says the statute,[6] prohibiteth that none do ravish, nor take away by force, any maiden within age, neither with nor without her consent; nor any wife or maiden of full age (that is, twelve years old, being the age of consent), nor any other woman against her will: and if any do, the king shall do common right, at his suit that will sue within forty days; and those who are found guilty shall be punished with two years' imprisonment, and fine at the king's pleasure. If they have not whereof to make fine, the imprisonment shall be increased in proportion to the enormity of the trespass. We shall presently[7] see that this new penalty was changed by parliament to the old one of felony.

Trespasses[8] in parks and ponds (*a*), which were thought not sufficiently punished by a compensation in damages only, were to be

(*a*) Upon this it was held that the statute Westm. 1, c. xx., De malefactoribus imparcis et vivariis, did not extend to forests *ne extendia*, al forest *quod nota* (10 *Edward IV.* 7). This was in accordance with a general principle always recognised in

[1] For the limitations fixed by the statute of Merton, *vide ante*, vol. i. 264. For the limitation of the seisin in a writ of right, *vide ibid.*, 427.

[2] *Vide ante*, c. viii.

[3] Ch. 8.

[4] Ch. 3.

[5] *Vide ante*, c. viii.

[6] Ch. 13.

[7] *Vide post*, Stat. Westminster 2, c. 34.

[8] *Vide ante*, vol. i. c. viii., where the great lords wanted authority to punish such trespassers with a short hand; but the king refused to concur in a statute for that purpose.

punished by imprisonment and fine at the king's suit,[1] and, says the statute, if tame beasts or other thing in the park were taken in the way of robbery, the common law shall be executed upon the offender, as upon one who had committed open theft and robbery.

Several laws were made to guard against the misconduct and extortion of officers of courts, who, from their situation, were enabled to throw obstacles in the way of justice, and so confer favours, or work oppression, to answer their private views. A short mention of these provisions may not be unentertaining, as they tend to show the difficulty under which the administration of justice laboured at that time.

Extortion of officers.

We have before taken notice of a remedy contrived for those who were disseised by escheators, sheriffs, and bailiffs, *colore officii*.[2] It was now ordained, that no officers of the king, either by themselves or any other, should *maintain* suits or matters depending in court, *to have a part* or profit out of the thing in question, according to an agreement made between them, under penalty of being punished at the king's pleasure.[3] No sheriff, or other officer, was to take any reward for doing his office, but was to be content with the king's pay, under the penalty of forfeiting double the sum taken, and being likewise punished at the king's pleasure.[4] One article of expense to the subject in the circuits was, delivering out the *capitula coronæ;* which, it was ordained,[5] should, for the future, be the privilege of the justices' clerks only; and they were not to take more than two shillings of every hundred or town out of which a jury of twelve or six appeared, who were each to have a duplicate of the *capitula*. Prior to this statute, probably, not only the clerks of the justices, but of escheators and other ministers and officers that followed the eyre, used to write out these *capitula;* and, most likely, reduced the value of a perquisite which, it was thought, should belong to the clerks of the justices.[6] If a justice's clerk exceeded the sum here allowed, or any one else took upon him to make out the *capitula*, he was to pay thrice as much as he received, and lose his office for a year. It was also ordained[7] that no clerk of the king, nor of any justice, should accept a presentation to a church concerning which any plea was then depending in the king's court, without special license from the king, under pain of the church being declared void, and of losing his office. At this time many ecclesiastical persons were not only clerks in the chancery, and other of the king's courts, but also stewards of the household to noblemen and other great men, and were therefore in situations to procure favour or discouragement in suits.[8] It was further ordained, that no clerk

the construction of statutes—viz., that penal laws were to be construed strictly (11 *Hen. IV.* 76); whereas beneficial acts were always construed largely and liberally. Statutes which restrained the common law, again, were construed strictly (18 *Edward IV.* 16).

[1] Ch. 20.
[2] *Vide ante*, c. viii.
[3] Ch. 25.
[4] Ch. 26.
[5] Ch. 27.
[6] 2 Inst. 211.
[7] Ch. 28.
[8] 2 Inst. 212.

of any justice or sheriff should take part in matters depending in the king's courts, nor commit any fraud whereby common right might be disturbed or delayed.

There was great complaint that officers, criers, who had an inheritance in their office, and the marshals of justices in eyre, took money of such as recovered seisin of land, or other thing depending in suit; and that fines were levied of jurors, towns, prisoners, and others attached upon pleas of the crown; which abuse was in a great measure owing to the excessive number of those officers. Several penalties were enacted to punish offences and extortions of this kind.[1]

During the late dissolute times, malpractices seem not to have been confined to inferior offices, but to have run through all ranks of persons attendant upon courts. The following provision was occasioned, no doubt, by an experience of this kind. It was ordained,[2] that if any serjeant-pleader,[3] or other, do or consent to any manner of deceit or collusion in the king's court, in order to deceive the court or party, he shall be imprisoned for a year and a day, and shall never after be permitted to plead in that court. If the offender should not be a pleader, besides the imprisonment, he was further to be punished at the king's pleasure, according to the degree of the offence.

We have an instance where corruption and cabal had got upon the bench of justice. It has been seen, that by the statute of Merton,[4] every free suitor of the county and other courts might make his attorney to do suit there for him. Under colour of this license, two mischiefs ensued: first, barrators and maintainers of quarrels[5] were encouraged by the sheriff to become attorneys, to make suit; and accordingly, amongst the other suitors, to give judgment, and sometimes, perhaps, take the lead in pronouncing judgment for, and in the name of, the other suitors: secondly, stewards of great lords, and others, who had no letters of attorney, as required by the statute, would do the like.[6] These were the mischiefs intended to be removed by the following law,[7] which ordained that no sheriff should suffer any barrators, or maintainers of suits in their county courts, nor permit either stewards of great lords, or any other (unless he was attorney for his lord), to make, give, or pronounce judgment, if he was not specially so commanded by all the suitors, and attorneys of suitors, then present in court; and should any one act otherwise, the sheriff, as well as the offender, was to be grievously punished at the pleasure of the king.

Spreaders of false reports.

Thus far of offences against the administration of justice. There remains only one crime, which we shall first mention, before we speak of the regulations made for the improvement of criminal judicature: this is the spreading of false

[1] Ch. 30.
[2] Ch. 29.
[3] In the original *Serjaunt countre.*
[4] Viz. c. 10. *Vide ante*, vol. i. 265.
[5] *Querells* may signify plaints, suits.
[6] 2 Inst. 225.
[7] Ch. 33.

and slanderous reports (a). The cause of this act is stated in the preamble:[1] "Forasmuch as there have been oftentimes found in the country devisers of tales, whereby discord, or occasion of discord, hath many times arisen between the king and his people, or great men of the realm," as had been lately experienced in the unsettled reign of Henry III.; therefore it was commanded, that from henceforth no one be so hardy as to tell or publish any false news or tales, whereby discord, or occasions of discord or slander, may grow between the king and his people, or the great men of the realm; and whoever does so, shall be taken and kept in prison until he has brought into court the first author of the tale. This, from the nature of the thing, became the severest punishment that could well be devised, as it might amount to perpetual imprisonment.

Respecting the office of magistrates, it was provided in the following manner. First, as to coroners. It seems, that of late many mean and unfit persons had been chosen into that office, though the proper qualification for such an officer was that of *probus, legalis, et sapiens.* It was now ordained, that[2] sufficient men should be chosen coroners, of the most wise and discreet knights, who were best skilled and willing to attend their duty; and such should lawfully attach and present pleas of the crown. It was further directed, that sheriffs should have counter-rolls with the coroners, as well of appeals as of inquests, of attachments, or of other things which belonged to that office; and no coroner was to take any fee for doing his office. The particular duties of this important office were more particularly marked out by a subsequent[3] statute, of which we shall take notice in its proper place.

It had been the practice for the common fines and amercements before justices in eyre to be assessed promiscuously by the sheriff, and, as the statute says, by barrators; and upon those who were innocent, as well as upon the guilty; all which was transacted after the justices were gone. These fines were paid to the sheriff and barrators. To remedy this, it was provided,[4] that henceforth such sums should be assessed in the presence of the justices in eyre, before their departure, by the oaths of knights and other honest men, upon those who ought to pay; and the justices were to cause the sums to be put into *estreats*, which were to be delivered into the exchequer.

(a) Lord Coke's comments upon this chapter are quaint and instructive. He says that persons were "the authors of great discord and scandal," sometimes between the king and his commons, and at other times between the king and his nobles, as they wrought secret discontentment that produced public discord and scandal, which did oftentimes break out (in the reign of Henry III.) into fearful and bloody wars. King Edward I., finding by experience the woeful effects of such false reports, therefore did make this law for the redress—"in a temperate manner," adds Coke—"leaving the same to the censure of the common law, by fines and imprisonments" (2 *Inst.* xxii.) He cites both Britton (fol. 33) and Fleta (lib. 2, c. i.) to the like effect.

[1] Ch. 34.
[2] Ch. 10.
[3] Stat. 4 Ed. I., st. 2, *de officio coronatoris.*
[4] Ch. 18.

The chapter of *Magna Charta* concerning the reasonableness of amercements,[1] was re-enacted in more comprehensive terms; for whereas that provision says, LIBER HOMO *non amercietur, &c.*, and so was confined to natural persons, or, at furthest, to *sole* bodies politic; this statute of Edward I.[2] extends it to *cities, boroughs,* and *towns.*

Because the method of pursuing felons by fresh suit had not been so much attended to as formerly, and great obstruction was occasioned thereto by franchises, an act was made to enforce this common law prosecution. It is directed[3] that all persons in general should be ready and apparelled, at the command and summons of the sheriff and cry of the country, to sue and arrest felons, as well within franchises as without. Those who neglected or refused were to be fined at the king's pleasure; and if default was made by the lord of a franchise, he was to forfeit his franchise to the king; if by a bailiff, he was to be imprisoned two years. The sheriff, coroner, or bailiff who showed any favour to a felon, or concealed felonies committed within his district, was to suffer a year's imprisonment, and afterwards pay a grievous fine; or, should he not have wherewith to pay, he was to suffer imprisonment for three years.

Some laws were made for ordering of offenders when taken (*a*). It sometimes happened, that persons committed for murder would sue out the writ *de odio et atiâ*, and, obtaining a favourable inquest before the sheriff, would get themselves replevied till the coming of the justices in eyre. To prevent

Of replevying prisoners.

(*a*) Upon this Lord Coke remarks, "that it applied only to sheriffs and gaolers, and not to the king's justices or judges of any superior court;" for that, being superiors, they are not comprehended in general words; 2. That "the words *queux ont prises ou reteynes prisoners,*" do not include judges; 3. Because in those days prisoners were commonly bailed by the king's writ, *De homine replegiando*, and also by the writ *De odio et atiâ;* both of which were directed to the sheriff (2 *Inst.* 186). And here it is proved, that it is an offence as well to bail a man not bailable, as to deny a man bail that ought to be bailed. And the reason is yielded wherefore the sheriffs and others did so offend, because they would make gain of the one and grieve the other —viz., either for avarice or malice (*Ibid.*) The mischief of the law, Coke says, it was not clear on what charges prisoners were or were not irreplevisable or bailable; and this act says, that those who are taken for homicide did *not* be so: "Forpris ceux queux fuerunt prises pur mort d'homme." According to Glanville: "In omnibus autem placitis de felonia solet accusatus per plegios dimitti, præterquam inplacito de homicidio, ubi aliter statutum est" (*Glanv.*, lib. xiv. c. 1; *Bracton*, lib. iii. fol. 123; *Britton*, fol. 73; *Fleta*, lib. ii. c. 2).

It is very observable that another exception is added—of persons committed by command of the king or his justices: "*Ou per commandment* le roi *ou de les justices;*" upon which, in favour of liberty and law, the judges put a remarkable judicial construction, making it read thus: "By the command of the king—*that is,* of his justices." Coke says, "The opinion of Gascoyne, chief-justice, is notable on this point, that the king hath committed all his power judicial to divers courts; and because some, as the king's bench, are *coram rege*, and others *coram justiciariis*, therefore the act says, "per commandment de le roi, ou de ses justices" (2 *Inst.* 186). But this is sophistical; for it had been held long before, that a matter before the king's justices is before the king, in contemplation of law; and though the argument might be applicable to *judicial* acts, it is not so of acts *not* judicial. There are cases in which

[1] Ch. 14. *Vide ante*, vol. i. c. vii. [2] Ch. 6. [3] Ch. 9.

unfair inquisitions in these cases, it was ordained[1] that such inquests should be taken by lawful men, chosen by oath (of whom two, at least, were to be knights), who had no affinity with the prisoner, nor were for any other reason to be suspected.

But in this article of replevying offenders, suspicion of favour and malice went further than the jurors; for it is stated, in a statute

the king may arrest without judicial warrant, as in cases of treason or sedition; in which, though his ministers might sign the warrant, and be responsible to parliament, the warrant would be legal, and the act be in law the act of the king or the crown. The judges were very jealous of the royal power; but their reasoning was not always good. Thus, Lord Coke quotes Hussey, chief-justice, as reporting (*Yearbook*, 1 Hen. VII. 4), that Sir John Markham said to King Edward I. that the king could not arrest any man for suspicion of treason or felony, as any of his subjects might; because, if the king did wrong, the party could not have his action; which, if meant of a personal arrest by the king's own hands, was a case not often likely to occur; but *qui facit per alium facit per se,* and an arrest by order of the king, would be an arrest by the king; and the judge goes on, according to the report, to say: "If the king command me to arrest a man, and accordingly I do it, he shall have his action of false imprisonment against me"—that is, presuming the king had no good cause of arrest, as he might have; and in such a case the arrest by his order would be an arrest by himself, and would be perfectly legal. And indeed a case occurred in this reign which illustrated this in a remarkable manner, and shows that an arrest by the king's own hand might be legal. There was, it is well known, an attempt to assassinate Edward I. when alone, who, however, overpowered the assassin, and held him until attendants came, when he delivered the man into their custody; an arrest of which no one will doubt the legality. Nor could it be any less clear if the king, observing the weapon, had seized the man upon suspicion, and arrested him, or ordered him to be arrested, for treason. Lord Coke indeed says, that on the statute 1 Rich. II. c. xii., "si non que il soit per briefe, ou auter commandment de le roi," it was resolved by all the judges that the king cannot do it but by writ, or by order or rule of some of his courts of justice where the cause dependeth, according to law; but this evidently is intended of arrests in the ordinary course of justice, which, no doubt, can only be by order of judges or courts of law. There can be no doubt, however, that there always was in the crown a power of arrest for sedition or on suspicion of treason, on the ground of danger to the state; and this power was recognised by the courts after the Revolution. But in ordinary cases the ordinary course must be pursued. Another exception to the statute was of those who were taken in the act. *Ceux queux sont prises sur le manier*, and who were *not* to be bailed; for, says Coke, in such case *non stat indifferenter*, whether he be guilty or not: being taken with the manner—that is, with the thing stolen, as it were, in his hand—which Bracton and Britton call *factum manifestum* (*Bracton*, lib. iii. fol. 12; *Britton*, fol. 22); and so felons, openly known and notorious, were not bailable, *larons apertment escries et notories*, nor those accused of arson or treason. These were not to be bailed or replevied by the *sheriff* by the common writ—*i.e.*, the sheriffs, says Coke, were not to replevy them by the common writ *de homine replegiando*, nor without writ—*i.e.*, *ex officio:* but, he adds, all or any of these may be bailed in the king's bench (2 *Inst.* 189). This statute, as he had already pointed out, only applying to *sheriffs*, not the king's judges, who were presumed to have a sufficient discretion. In other cases the sheriff might release upon sufficient sureties; and if he did not do so, the prisoner might have the writ *De manucaptione;* but this was taken away by the statute 28 Edward III. The statute, it is to be observed, only applied to indictments taken before the sheriff in his tourn; for other prisoners could not be bailed without writ; and the statute 2 Edward IV. c. ii., provided that upon all presentments or indictments taken before the sheriff, he should have no power to arrest or put in prison any person so prescribed or indicted, but should send the indictments to the sessions of the justices of the peace. These justices of the peace practically superseded the criminal jurisdiction of the sheriffs; and the present statute is only valuable for the principles it lays down; and for this reason Coke expounds it fully with reference to the act 1 and 2 Philip & Mary, as to bail. There was a statute of Henry VI. as to bail in civil cases, as to which, *vide post.*

[1] Ch. 11. *Vide ante*, c. viii.

which we are now going to mention, "that sheriffs and others who had the custody and imprisonment of persons[1] charged with felony, used to let out such as were not properly replevisable, and kept in prison such as were, that they might gain of the one party and grieve the other." For this reason, and because it had not been hitherto particularly determined who were replevisable and who not, except in the case of persons taken for the death of a man, or by command of the king, or of his justices, or for the forest, it was therefore expressly enacted[2] what offenders should and what should not be replevisable. First, the following persons were in no wise to be replevisable; neither by the common writ—that is, the writ *de homine replegiando*, nor without writ—that is, *ex officio*, by the general discretion entrusted to sheriffs in this point—namely, persons outlawed, those who had abjured the realm, provors, those taken with the manor, those who had broken the king's prison, thieves openly defamed and known, such as were appealed by provors, so long as the provors were living (if they were not of good name); such as were taken for house-burning, feloniously done, or for false money, or for counterfeiting the king's seal; persons excommunicated, who were taken at the request of the bishop; those taken for manifest offences, or for treason touching the king's person. The following persons might be let out by sufficient surety; but the sheriff was to take nothing for so doing, and was to be answerable for them—namely, those indicted of larceny by inquests before sheriffs and bailiffs by their office; those of light suspicion; those taken for petty larceny that amounted not to more than 12d.,[3] if they were not guilty of some other larceny before; those guilty of receipt of felons, or of commandment, or force, or of aid in felony done; those guilty of some trespass for which a man ought not to lose his life or limb; a man appealed by a provor, after the death of the provor, if he be no common thief, nor defamed.

If the sheriff, or any other person who had the keeping of prisons, let a person to bail who was not replevisable, he was to lose his office for ever, though he held it in fee; and should it be any inferior officer who had done so without the will of his lord, he was to suffer three years' imprisonment, and to be fined at the king's pleasure. Again, if any detained a prisoner who was replevisable, after he had offered sufficient surety, he was to suffer a grievous amercement to the king; but if he took any reward for delivering such a prisoner, he was to pay double the sum to him, and be at the king's mercy.

In this manner was the law of bail in criminal cases settled in the reign of Edward the First. The same statute has been adopted in later times, as[4] the rule by which justices of the peace are to govern themselves.

[1] *Rettez de felonie.* [2] Ch. 15. *Vide ante*, 15.

[3] The distinction between greater and smaller thefts is mentioned only obscurely by Bracton. This is the first passage where the limit of petty larceny is distinctly marked. *Vide ante*, c. viii.

[4] By stat. 1 and 2 Ph. & M. and 2 and 3 Ph. & M.

Having spoken of such laws as were made to bring offenders to justice, it follows that we should treat of such as directed the manner of administering it. It had been the usage (contrary to the general law) in some counties to outlaw persons appealed[1] of command, force, aid, or receipt, before the person who was appealed of the principal fact was outlawed. To render the law uniform in this point, it was ordained[2] that none should be appealed of command, force, aid, or receipt, until the person appealed of the fact was attainted; nevertheless, the appellant was not therefore to delay commencing his appeal at the next county against the accessory any more than against the principal; only the exigent against him was to remain till the principal was attainted of the fact by outlawry, or otherwise. This statute, though it speaks of appeals only, has been construed to extend to indictments.

This account of the alterations made in our criminal law shall be closed with the two following statutes—one relating to the exemption claimed by the clergy, the other concerning a very singular part of our penal code, called *peine forte et dure*.

Of clergy.

We have seen that the clergy had so far established the exemption of their persons from corporal pains (*a*), as for it to be laid down for law in the last reign that a clerk, taken for the death of a man, or any other crime, and imprisoned,

(*a*) This mode of expression seems to represent the clergy as usurping all these privileges or immunities, and as constantly encroaching on the state, whereas it will have been seen from the laws of the Saxons, these privileges and immunities were all established in that age. Thus in the *Mirror* we find that Alfred hanged a judge who had executed a clerk, because as a secular judge he must have known he had no jurisdiction over clerks (*Mirror*, c. v.) And the laws of Canute show that such was the law in the Saxon times. The reason for it is obvious, that the barbarous ordeal was the mode of trial resorted to in that age in criminal cases; and the Church, as Hale says, did all it could to discourage it, and as one mode of doing so, prohibited it as to the clergy, who were supposed to be specially under its charge; and as to the clergy, therefore, the Church adopted the more sensible system of compurgators, who were a species of witnesses or jurors, whose verdict, as Lord Coke says, countervailed or was equal to a verdict of jurors, the only difference being that jurors were sworn *between* the crown and the party, and compurgators were produced by the party, both being equally sworn of their own knowledge or belief, jurors in that age being witnesses. This was, it is obvious, a more rational mode of trial than the ordeal, and was the origin of trial by jury. And by degrees, and by the example of this more rational system of trial for the clergy, it became adopted by the laity. As Lord Hale observes, by the persuasions of the clergy the ordeal became discontinued in favour of the more rational system. It was not likely, therefore, that the bishops (who could hardly have an interest in the immorality of their clergy) should fail to apply the system which the canon law itself enjoined. But then the effect of withdrawing the accused before trial was *that the king lost the benefit of the forfeiture of lands and goods*, which followed upon conviction; and there is too much reason to believe, from the character of the judges in those days, that this often supplied a motive to them for pressing cases to conviction. At all events, it supplied an obvious motive for some legislation, which should afford a pretext to the king's judges for trying the accused clerk before he was delivered to the bishop. This could not be done in any open or direct way, for beyond all doubt it would have been a total alteration of the law. This is clear from Bracton, who had lately laid the law down thus: "Cum vero clericus captus fuerit, pro alio crimine, et imprisonatus est, et de eo petatur curia Christianitatis, ab ordinario . . . imprisonatus ille statim ei deliberetur, *sine aliqua inquisitione facienda*" (Bracton, fol. 123). The statute itself

[1] *Vide ante*, vol. i. 315. [2] Ch. 14.

if demanded by the ordinary to be delivered over to the court Christian, should immediately be delivered, without any inquisition being taken.[1] The pretence of the ecclesiastical court was, that the clerk so delivered should be put to make canonical[2] purgation, and to establish his innocence, or stand convicted of the charge. Whether this was constantly or fairly practised seemed to be a matter of some doubt.

We shall now hear what was ordained by parliament on this point (*a*). It was provided[3] that when a clerk was *taken on a charge of felony*,[4] and was demanded by the ordinary, he should be delivered to him, according to the privilege of holy church, on such peril as usually belonged to it (by which probably purgation is meant), after the custom used in former times; and the king now admonished and enjoined the prelates, upon the faith they owed him, and for the common profit and peace of the realm, that those who had been indicted of such offences by a solemn inquest of good and lawful men in the king's court (*b*), *should in no manner*

indeed recites the law to the like effect, and then proceeds merely to enact that the clerks should not be released by the bishops until they had undergone their canonical purgation. There is not the slightest reason to suppose that they were so; and therefore the real reason for the enactment must be sought in the use made of it by the king's judges, which was upon some strained and monstrous misconstruction of it, to pretend that it gave them power to try the clerk first, before he was delivered, the effect of which would be that if he should be convicted, his lands and goods would be forfeited to the crown. This, it is plain, was the real motive for the statute, and the "pretence" was on the part of the crown lawyers who thus contrived it.

(*a*) It is to be observed that the author here represents it as "provided" by the statute, so as to keep up the impression he had already conveyed that this was a novel claim, or an encroachment on the part of the clergy, whereas, as already shown, it was as old as the Saxon laws, and had been laid down by Bracton in the previous reign as settled law, and was not merely "provided" but recognised and recited by the act. The real reason of the enactment was at the end; and the pretence it afforded to the crown lawyers and the servile judges of the king to warp, wrest, and alter the law.

(*b*) As already seen, the effect of the law was that the clerk was to be delivered to the bishop *before* trial, in order that, *instead* of undergoing trial at common law, he might be put to his "canonical purgation;" and this is recognised by the act, which says that the clerk shall not be liberated until he has undergone such purgation, "Que ceux qui sont endites, &c., en nul maner, ne les deliverent, *sans due purgation*, issint que le roy nilent mestier de mitter auter remedy." Upon this, however, it was actually held by the king's judges that they had power to *try the clerk before he was delivered to the ordinary!* And the king's own law-writer, Britton, accordingly thus laid the law down on the subject, writing soon after the statute, "Si clerk encopie (*i.e.*, indicte) de felony, allege clergie, et est trove (*i.e.*, que est un clerk), et l'ordinary demaund, donque serra enquise comment il est mescrue (*i.e.*, culpable), et s'il soit merit mescrue, donques il serra aroge touts quits (*i.e.*, he shall go quit), et s'il soit mescrue si soient ses chateux, taxes, et ses terres prises en nostre mesne, et son corps deliver al ordinary (*Britton*, c. iv. fol. 11). That is to say, that upon conviction of the clerk his lands and goods should be forfeited to the crown, and then he should be delivered to the ordinary, which supplies the real motive for this piece of legislation.

[1] *Vide ante*, c. viii.

[2] Canonical purgation was that by compurgators, and had been recommended by the canons in lieu of that by ordeal, which, in the canon law, was called vulgar purgation.

[3] Ch. 2.

[4] *Est pris pur ret de felonie.*

be delivered without due purgation, so that the king might have no need to provide any otherwise in this matter.

Peine forte et dure.

We now come to the statute which makes the first mention of anything like what has since been called the *peine forte et dure*; a punishment to be inflicted on such as refused to put themselves on a jury, to be tried for the felony of which they were indicted. The statute ordains,[1] "that notorious felons, and who are openly of evil name, and will not put themselves on inquests of felonies with which they may be charged before the justices at the king's suit, *soient mys en la prisone forte et dure*, shall have strong and hard imprisonment, *come ceux qui refusent etre a la commune ley de la terre*, as those who refuse to stand to the common law of the land. But this is not to be understood of such prisoners as are taken upon light suspicion" (*a*). Great difference of opinion has arisen upon this provision. Some have thought that the punishment of *peine forte et dure* was ordained first by this act, and that at the common law, a felon standing mute should, upon a *nihil dicit*, be hanged, as the law is at this day in case of treason. Others have holden, that at the common law, in favour of life, he should neither have *peine forte et dure*, nor have judgment to be hanged, but be remanded to prison until he would answer. Lord Coke is of opinion that the *peine forte et dure* was a penalty at common law, and not such a one as any judges could have framed upon a general direction of this act, which only says they are to be sent to *prisone forte et dure*; and that the words of this act were designed to refer to a subsisting species of penance, which they sufficiently intimated, though the particular mode of it was not described.[2]

This provision is worthy of serious consideration. The statute says, that *those who will not put themselves on inquest of felonies*,[3] shall be treated *as those who refuse to stand to the common law of the land*.[4] The difference between these two kinds of refusal is a difficulty that stands as much in need of explanation as the manner in which the latter were punished.

Though this statute, from the form of its expression, does not seem to have introduced this penance, but rather speaks of it as a thing already known; yet it does not appear that it is taken notice of in any ancient writer, record, or case, before the reign of this king. On the contrary, some instances are to be found in the preceding reign of persons arraigned for felony standing mute, who

(*a*) The author of the *Mirror* observes upon this that it is reprovable to put persons found guilty of felony, who will not put themselves upon their country, to penance, which may kill them, without regard to their condition, since one may perhaps help and acquit himself otherwise than by his country; and as none is to be put to penance before he is attainted of the offence for which he ought to be pained (c. v. s. 4). This seems to assume that in some way the parties were found guilty of the felony, before being put to the penance. Possibly it may mean the finding of the grand jury. The latter part of the passage appears to confirm the author's view.

[1] Ch. 12. [2] 2 Inst. 178–179. [3] *Ne se voilent mettre en enqueste des felonies.*
[4] *Come ceux qui refusent etre a la commune ley de la terre.*

were, nevertheless, not put to their penance, but had judgment to be hanged. The practice in 5 Hen. III. was, it should seem, of the following kind: If a prisoner stood wilfully mute, a jury of twelve men was impannelled. If they found him guilty, another jury of twenty-four was chosen to examine the verdict of the former; and if they were of the same opinion the sentence was for the prisoner to be hanged.[1] It is true, there is no mention of such proceeding in Bracton; nor does that author at all acquaint us with the method of treating persons who obstinately refused to submit to a fair trial.[2]

It should seem, then, that this method of treating felons who stood mute, was introduced some time between the 5 Hen. III. (or even the time of Bracton) and the 3 Edw. I., and was not established by this act. That it was supported by some other sanction than this act, is plain from the constant practice, which has allowed this penance to hold in cases of appeal, though the act only speaks of the king's suit: and those authors who wrote nearest the time of which we are now speaking, such as Fleta, Britton, and the *Mirror*, mention the penance without referring to this statute.

The manner in which this penance is described by Britton is as follows:—" If they will not put themselves upon the country, let them be put to their penance[3] until they pray to do it; and let their penance be this: that they be barefooted, ungirded, and bareheaded, in their coat only,[4] in prison upon the bare ground, continually, night and day; that they eat only bread made of barley and bran; that they drink not the day they eat, nor eat the day they drink; nor drink anything but water the day they do not eat; and that they be fastened down with irons."[5] In Fleta it is stated in a similar way: *Morti tamen non condemnabitur, sed gaolæ committetur sub diætâ salvo custodiendus, donec iustructus petat inde se legitimè acquietare; consideratio verò erit talis, quòd unico indumento indutus, et discalceatus, in nudâ terrâ, quadrantalem panem hordeaceum tantùm pro duobus diebus habeat ad victum, non tamen quòd quolibet die comedat, sed altero tantùm; nec quòd singulis diebus bibat, sed die quo non comederit, aquam bibat tantùm, et hæc diæta omnibus* LEGEM REFUTANTIBUS *injungatur donec petant quod prius contempserint.*[6]

The penance stated by these two authors is a rigorous method of compelling the criminal to undergo a trial; yet very different from the cruel way in which felons standing mute were treated in aftertimes. The alterations this penance received, and the causes that led to such alterations, will be considered in their proper place.

If a conjecture may be hazarded upon a point that has created much debate, perhaps this statute may be considered as auxiliary towards the establishment of trials by jury, in preference to all others then in use. It may be remembered that *Magna Charta*,[7]

[1] This appears by two curious records in the notes upon Hale's P.C., vol ii. 322.
[2] *Vide ante*, 26–27. [3] *Si soient mys a lour penance.* [4] *En pure lour cote.*
[5] Britt. c. iv., fol. 11. [6] Flet. lib. i. c. xxix. s. 33.
[7] Viz. c. xxix. *Vide* vol. i. c. vii.

in declaring the privilege every man shall have of being fairly tried, mentions two modes; that *per judicium parium suorum,* and that *per legem terræ;* there being methods of trial much more ancient, as we have before seen, than that by jury;[1] and such as therefore might more properly be called the *lex terræ,* than the later invention of trial *per pares.* It is remarkable that Fleta uses the like expression in this sense. After reciting at length the judgment of penance; he adds, this is the course *omnibus* LEGEM *refutantibus,* with all those who refuse to be at the law, or common law; and the particular case he there states as an instance in which that judgment should be passed, is of a criminal, who having said that he would defend himself *per corpus vel per patriam,* as the court should award, would not, as he ought by law to do, make a specific declaration *by which* of those modes he would be tried. This was therefore to be considered as putting himself upon *no trial at all,* which was totally renouncing the decision of the law; and consequently, by the old course recognised in this statute, he was to be sentenced to the penance.

To apply this to the statute before us. The trial by inquest had of late been encouraged, as we have seen in the last reign, and was in more esteem than the barbarous practice of the old jurisprudence; nor was there any object of judicial improvement that more deserved the countenance of a wise legislator than this mode of inquiry. We have seen that Bracton, in his account of the proceeding *per famam patriæ,*[2] says, that a person so indicted might make his purgation, or put himself upon the country. It does not appear from that passage, nor from any other part of that author, whether *the country* there meant was the same which had indicted him, or some other: though it should rather seem, from the whole of his discourse on this subject, that a person indicted was to stand or fall by the verdict of that single jury, unless he made his purgation. However, it should seem, that it was intended by the present statute to make an alteration in this point; and that as a person appealed might put himself upon the country to prove his innocence, so one indicted should no longer make purgation, but should be *compelled* to put himself on an inquest of the country, to try the truth of the charge brought against him by the indictors.

If the statute is read with these sentiments, and a knowledge of these circumstances of the then state of criminal judicature, it will receive a new light, and appear in a point of view in which it never was before seen. It will then very plainly ordain, that persons charged or indicted of crimes who will not put themselves on *inquests* (that is, on the particular mode of trial which it is seen fit to encourage, as the more rational), shall be sent to prison, and treated with the same severity as those who refuse to put themselves on the old method of inquiry, long used by the law of the land. The statute certainly reads as intelligibly in this way as in any

[1] *Vide ante,* vol. i. 376, 248, 198, 195.

[2] *Ibid.* 33.

other, and perhaps more so; and whether this sense of it is not strengthened by the ensuing history of the trial by jury, will be for the reader to judge. One of the most remarkable changes in that proceeding, during this reign, was the invariable resort to a jury to try the indictment, and *deliver* the prisoner of the charge thereby brought against him.

Before we dismiss the statute of Westminster the first, the last chapter but one [1] deserves a slight notice, as it discovers the caution observed in everything that concerned the rights of the crown, both in private instruments and acts of the legislature. "Forasmuch," says that act, "as the king hath ordained all these things to the honour of God and holy church, and for the commonwealth, and for the remedy of such as be grieved," as he had condescended so far for the national benefit, "he would not that, at any other time, it should turn in prejudice to himself or his crown; but that such right as appertained to him should be saved in all points." As the reader goes through the statutes of this reign, he will find many reservations of the king's right even more singular and emphatical than this.

The next statute in this reign is 4 Edw. I. st. 1, and is entitled, *Extenta Manerii;* being a sort of direction for making a survey, or terrier, of a manor and all its appendages. This is followed by the stat. *de Officio Coronatoris*, enumerating the duties of that office more particularly than they had been stated even by Bracton (*a*).[2] It is directed by this statute, that the coroner should go, upon the information of bailiffs, or other honest men of the country, to the places where any were killed, or suddenly dead, or wounded; where houses were broken, or where treasure was found; and should forthwith command four, five, or six assessors of the next towns to appear before him in such a place; and there he was to inquire, upon their oaths, whether they knew where the person was killed, whether in a house, bed, tavern, or in company, and who that company were. He was to inquire who were the principals and accessories; who were present, whether men or women, and of what age. Those that were found guilty by the inquisition in this manner, were to be taken and delivered to the sheriff, and committed to gaol; and those who were discovered, but were not found guilty, were to be attached; that is, were to give pledges to appear at the next coming of the justices, and their names were to be written in rolls. The coroner was to go immediately to the house of the person found guilty of the murder, and inquire what goods he had, and what corn in his granary; and, if he was a freeman, what land he had, and the value of it yearly; and was to cause the land, corn, and goods to be valued, as if for

The office of coroners.

(*a*) In Britton the office of coroner is described very fully. The chapter proceeds very much in the terms of the present statute, and thus affords a curious proof that the treatise of Britton, which was written after the statute of Westminster, was in part composed of the statutes.

[1] Ch. 50. [2] *Vide* vol. i. c. viii.

sale, and to be delivered to the township, which was to be answerable for them before the justices; the land was to remain in the king's hands, till the lords of the fee had made fine for it. After all this ceremony, the dead body was to be buried, and not before. In like manner, inquiry was to be made, when any one was drowned, or suddenly dead, whether any hurt was visible on the body or not; and should it appear they were not killed, yet the coroner was to attach the finders, and all those in the same company.

Besides this inquiry *super visum corporis*, there were other articles which fell under the jurisdiction of the coroner. He was to inquire of *treasure trove;* who was the finder, or suspected thereof; and he was to attach him by four, six, or more pledges. He was to attach persons appealed of rape, and of wounds, especially if the wounds were mortal; and the party offending was to be safely kept till it was perfectly known whether the person wounded could recover. If the person recovered, then he need only attach the offender by four or six pledges, according to the size of the wound; if it was for a maim, by not less than four; for a small wound, two would suffice. All these proceedings were to be enrolled in the roll of the coroner. Accessories were to be taken and kept till the principals were attainted or delivered. *Deodands*[1] were to be valued and delivered to the towns under the direction of the coroners, as was also wreck of the sea, and those that laid hands on it were to be attached: those who did not follow the *hutesium*, or hue and cry, were to be attached. All these objects of police had been, by the old law, intrusted to the coroners, whose office was of great consideration and utility in the preservation of the peace and the prosecution of offenders.

The statute of *bigamy*, called so from a provision made respecting *bigami*,[2] was passed the same year with the former.[3] The general preamble to this short statute (for it contains only six chapters) is very remarkable, and well deserving of notice, as it gives some intimation of the course then pursued in passing laws. It states, that " in the presence of certain reverend fathers bishops of England, and others of the council of the realm of England,[4] the underwritten constitutions were recited;" and afterwards they were heard and published before the king and his council,[5] who all agreed, as well the justices as others, that they should be put into writing for a perpetual memorial, and that they should be strictly observed.[6]

From this recital prefixed to the statute of bigamy, it appears that the statute was digested and framed by a sort of committee of parliament, but that it was the approbation of the king's council, among whom were the justices that determined the king in mak-

[1] Such casualties are called *Bani* in this statute. [2] Ch. 5.
[3] Stat. 4 Ed. I. st. 3. [4] *De concilio regni Angliæ.* [5] *Coram rege, et concilio suo.*
[6] See Pickering's *Statutes from the Cott. M.S.*, where the wording differs from that in some editions of the statutes, as may be seen by comparing it with 2 Inst. 287.

ing it public, and that it was from the concurrence of these two bodies, and not that of the parliament, that it derived its sanction and authority. It was for this reason that Shard, in the time of Edward III.,[1] was of opinion that this was no act of parliament; however, it has always been received as one. It seems to be a declaration of some points of the common law, which was thenceforward to govern the judges in their decisions.

The first chapter is penned expressly with that view. "It was agreed," says the statute,[2] "by the justices and other learned men of our lord the king's council, who heretofore have had the use and practice of judgments," that whereas, in case of a deed and feoffment made by the king, so conceived as that a common person would thereby be bound to warranty, it had been held that the justices could not make an award of recovery over against the king, they had done right in so judging, and the law was so. In the second chapter,[3] a like provision was made respecting *Aid prier*, which was the name now given to the course mentioned by Bracton as a substitute for vouching where the king was warrantor.[4] This was to relieve the king from *aid prier*, where there was no express warranty, or in case of a release or confirmation, where the king granted only as much as in him lay, and the like. Another provision was made about *aid prier* of the king by chapter III. However, as this statute did not get into print till the latter part of the reign of Henry VIII., and, as it should seem, was not commonly known before, *aid prier* had often been granted in opposition to the directions here laid down.

By the fourth chapter,[5] it was agreed that a regulation which, it seems, had been made in the reign of Henry III. about purpestures and encroachments on the king, and which has not come down to us, should be observed (*a*). This ordained that the king should have power to resume into his own hands all such encroachments, whether of franchises or other things.

Then follows the provision which gave the name to this statute[6] concerning men twice married, who were called in the canon law *bigami.* (*b*) These, by a late canonical constitution,[7] had been

(*a*) The subject of "purpresture" is very fully treated of by Britton (as also that of "franchises") under the head of "Droits del Roy," always with a careful view to the interests of the crown, and especially as to the emoluments it derived from fines or forfeitures for purprestures, or any encroachments on the royal rights. Inquiry is to be made, "De toutes maneres de purprestures, faites sur nous, de terres et de franchises," *i. e.*, all kinds of encroachments on our lands and franchises (*Britton*, fol. 28, "Droit del Roy"). And this is more fully expounded under the two subsequent heads of "Franchises" (fol. 30), and "De Plusurs Torts" (fol. 31). It is laid down, that as to purprestures, nusances should be redressed at the cost of the purprestors (fol. 30). Lord Coke derives purpresture from the French *pourpris.*

(*b*) It was a papal constitution which is here alluded to, and was in effect enacted by this chapter. The chapter runs thus, "De Bigamis quos Dominus Papa in Concilio Lugdunensi, omni privilegio clericali privavit, per constitutionem, &c., inde

[1] 2 Inst. 267. [2] Ch. 1. [3] Ch. 2.
[4] *Vide ante*, vol. i. 439. [5] Ch. 4. [6] Ch. 5.
[7] This is the constitution of Gregory X. in the General Council at Lyons; and is to be found in the *Sextus Decret.*, lib. i. tit. 12.

excluded from all the privileges of clerks. However, certain bishops, still grudging that the lay tribunal should gain the advantage which was lost by any individuals of the clergy, had claimed many clerks indicted of felony, notwithstanding they had become *bigami*, alleging that they had married a second time before the Constitution, and therefore, as they said, were not within the meaning of it. As this was an opinion that seemed to have some legal reasoning in its favour, it was necessary to declare by this statute that neither those who were *bigami* before the Constitution, nor those who had become so since, should be delivered to the ordinary, but that justice should be executed upon them as upon lay persons.

The remainder of this act relates to the force and effect of certain words in a deed. It says,[1] that deeds which contained the words *dedi et concessi tale tenementum*, without reserving homage, or without a clause containing warranty, and to be holden of the donors and their heirs by a certain service, should be so construed as that the donors and their heirs should be bound to warranty. This seems to be only a confirmation of the common law, as laid down by Bracton.[2] Where a deed contained the words *dedi et concessi, &c.*, to be holden of the chief lords of the fee, or of any other, and not of the feoffer or his heirs, reserving no service, without homage, or without the above-mentioned clause, it was declared that the heirs should not be bound to warranty, notwithstanding the feoffor, during his life, should be bound by force of his own gift.

The next which presents itself is the statute of Gloucester, 6 Ed. 1., containing fifteen chapters. We shall divide the provisions of this, as we did those of the former statutes, according to their matter; that is, into such as regard tenures and property, and those that relate to the administration of justice, whether civil or criminal.

The remedy a lord had against his tenant for default in service, was by seizing what was on the freehold as a *namium*, and holding it till the arrears were paid: another course was now directed in such situations as were thought likely to produce a defect in

editam," &c., upon which Lord Coke's commentary is, "Bigamus is he that either hath married two or more wives, or that hath married a widow, as it appeareth in the statutes of 18 Edw. III. c. ii., 1 Edw. VI. c. 12." The constitution here mentioned is in these words, "Altercationis antiquæ dubium præsentis declarationis oraculo decidentes Bigamos omni privilegio clericali declaremus esse nudatos, et coercioni fori secularis addictos, consuetudine contraria non obstante, ipsis quoque anathemate prohibemus deferre tonsuram vel habitum clericalem." "This council was holden," says Coke, "Boniface VIII. being pope;" and he cites "Per Decret. Epistol. Gregor. IX. lib. vi. decretal; a Bonifacio VIII. in Lugd. Conc. Edit." The Council of Lyons, no doubt, was in 1274, two or three years after the accession of Edward I., and under the popedom of Gregory X., when twenty "constitutions" were made as to the election of bishops and the ordination of clerks, &c. Pope Boniface VIII. was elected in 1294, twenty years later; but he, no doubt, reaffirmed these constitutions, one of which was here enforced by the legislature.

[1] Ch. 6. [2] *Vide ante*, vol. i. c. viii.

service. It was ordained, that where a man let his land in fee farm, or to find estovers, in meat or in clothing, amounting to the fourth part of the real value of the land, and the tenant suffered the land to lie fresh for the space of two or three years, so that no distress could be found thereon (*a*) whereby to compel a render of the farm or rent, or a performance of what was contained in the deed of lease, then the lessor, after the end of two years, might have an action to demand the land in demesne, by a writ to be had in the chancery. If the tenant came before judgment, and paid the arrears and damages, and found such surety as the court approved for payment of the future demands, he was to retain the land; but if he delayed till after judgment, he was to be barred for ever.[1] The writ framed upon this statute was called a *Cessavit per biennium*, and was considered in the nature of a writ of right. The putting the lord in possession of his tenant's land by this writ seemed to be a recurring back to the ancient remedy of seizing the freehold,[2] under the guard, however, of a formal legal proceeding.

Warranty of tenant *per legem Angliæ*.

Much has been said on the great force of à warranty, one of which was, that as it bound the heir to protect the donee in possession of the land, so it, *à fortiori*, barred him from ever claiming it against the deed of

(*a*) Here again we have an embodiment in an ancient and obsolete enactment of a *principle* which has never been departed from, and has been re-embodied in more modern statutes. That principle is, that if the landlord can find no distress by which to levy his rent, he ought to be allowed to re-enter. At the time of this statute, the tenant meant the tenant of the freehold—at all events, of a life estate; "so as there must be," says Coke, in commenting upon it, "a tenure between the feoffor and feoffee in fee simple, for a *cessavit* lieth not upon such a reservation without such a tenure. At the making of the act, all estates of inheritance were in fee-simple, and therefore the donor on an estate-tail created by a statute made after this act (the statute *De donis, vide post*) shall not have the *cessavit*, for he holdeth not the land as this act speaketh, which *ought to be overt*, and *sufficient to the distress of the lord*" (2 *Inst.* 296). Here is the general principle laid down, which is thus further expounded by Lord Coke: "The land is said in law to be fresh, not only when there is no cattle or other thing distrainable upon the land of the value of the rent, but also yet though there be a sufficient distress to be taken, yet, by construction upon the act, if the land be so immured or inclosed about, as that the lord cannot come to take and carry away the distress, it is said to be fresh, that is, without profit to the lord, for though it be sufficient, yet is not sufficient to his distress; as the land must lie open and sufficient to the distress of the lord, or else it is said in law to be fresh within the statue, which construction is worthy of observation" (2 *Inst.*, 296). As, no doubt, it is, being a very remarkable illustration of that robust construction which was applied by the courts to our old statutes, conceived as they were in terms more general than modern legislation. This, however, was the principle, and it is obvious that it would be equally applicable to landlords in cases of the tenancies more usual in modern times, viz., tenancies for terms of years. But, on the other hand, it was considered necessary to have additional legislation to apply it to such tenancies; and accordingly, it was so applied in the Landlord's Act of 11 Geo. II. c. xix. s. 16, which recited that landlords are often great sufferers by tenants suffering the demised premises to lie uncultivated without any distress thereon, whereby the landlord might be satisfied, and then enacting, that if the tenant should desert the premises, and leave the land uncultivated or unoccupied, so as no sufficient distress could be had, then the landlord might, by a certain summary proceeding, re-enter. Thus, after the lapse of centuries, the principle established in the above ancient act was re-applied.

[1] Ch. 4.

[2] *Vide ante*, vol. i. c. v.

his ancestor. This point of law was not always consonant to reason and equity. Thus, in case of an alienation with warranty, by a person holding *per legem Angliæ*, that warranty, descending upon the heir, barred him from claiming the inheritance of his mother by action; but, considering the inheritance did not belong to the father, this was an apparent injustice to the heir, and therefore the following statute was made to regulate it. It was ordained, that if no inheritance descended to the heir from his father, the father's warranty, though for him and his heirs, should not bind the heir, nor be a bar to his demanding and recovering the land by writ of mortauncestor, of the seisin of his mother: but if any inheritance did descend to him *ex parte patris*, he should be barred as far as the value of the inheritance which descended; and if any descended to him afterwards through his father, then the alienee should recover against him of the seisin of his mother, by a judicial writ, to issue out of the rolls of the justices before whom the plea was, to re-summon the warranty, as was done in other cases where the warrantor came into court, and said that nothing descended to him from the person upon whose deed he was vouched. As the son was to recover by mortauncestor, so his issue might have a writ of *cosinage*, of *aiel*, and *besaiel*. In like manner, the heir of the wife was not to be barred of his action after his father's and mother's death by any deed of his father, if he demanded his mother's inheritance by a writ of entry *sur cui in vitâ*, unless a fine had been levied thereof in the king's court.[1]

This provision seems conceived upon an idea that had long prevailed respecting warranty; for, at common law, the heir was not bound to make recompense, unless *sufficient* to enable him so to do had descended to him from the warrantor; and he was bound *ad excambium* only *pro rata*, as far as the *assets* (as they were afterwards called) would go.[2] In like manner, after this statute, the heir of a tenant *per legem* was not to be barred, unless an equivalent descended to him from his father, who made the warranty. This was going a step further than the common law had gone; for, though an heir was not bound *ad excambium* beyond the assets which descended, it does not appear but that he was bound to warrant, and, of course, barred from claiming the land against the warranty of his ancestor, notwithstanding no assets at all came to him by the same descent.

If the interest of the heir was protected against an unjust alienation of the mother's estate by the father, it deserved no less security against the alienation of the father's inheritance by the mother; not that a gift or feoffment by the tenant in dower could not be avoided by the entry of the reversioner for the forfeiture, but that the mischief was often carried out of the reach of the law in this way. Thus, if the feoffee or any other died seised, the entry of him in reversion was taken away, and he could have

[1] Ch. 3.

[2] *Vide ante*, vol. i. c. viii.

no writ of entry, as the law now stood, until the death of the tenant in dower; at which time the warranty contained in her deed (as most deeds had a clause of warranty, especially when it was with a direct design to bar the heir) would descend upon the reversioner if he was her heir, as he generally was, and so bar him of the inheritance for ever.[1] To remedy this, it was ordained that in such case the heir or other to whom the land ought to revert after the woman's death, should have present recovery; that is, should have right, in her life-time, to demand the land by a writ of entry to be made in the chancery.[2] The writ framed upon this statute was called a writ of entry *in casu proviso*, and the words of it are general, *et quæ post dimissionem factam ad præfatum, &c.*, without expressing any estate, *contra formam statuti de Gloucester de communi concilio regni nostri inde* PROVISI, *reverti debet per formam ejusdem statuti, &c.*[3]

The law of damages underwent some change. Damages used to be awarded in assizes of novel disseisin against the disseisors only[4]; and if they were unable to make amends, the disseisee was without recompense; but it was now ordained, that should the disseisor alien the lands, and not have that whereof damages might be levied, the person into whose hands the tenements came, should be charged with the damages, so that each should answer for the time he held them; likewise that the disseisee should recover damages, in a writ of entry *sur disseisin*, against him who was found tenant after the disseisor (*a*). It was further provided, that whereas damages were not recoverable in a writ of mortauncestor, except against the chief lord, by stat. Marlb.,[5] damages for the future should be recovered in that writ, as in one of novel disseisin; and also in writs of *cosinage, aiel*, and *besaiel.* Further, as damages had been heretofore taxed only to the value of the issues of the land, it was provided that a demandant in future should recover the costs of his writ purchased, together with the damages, not only in the above instances, but generally in all cases where he was entitled to recover damages; which is the first law obliging the unsuccessful party to pay the costs of suit. It was, moreover, enacted, that damages should, in all cases, be rendered where the land was recovered against a man, upon his own intrusion, or his own act.[6]

We have before seen what the common law ordained in cases of

(*a*) "Here," says Lord Coke, "is express mention made but of the costs of the writ, yet it extendeth to all the legal costs of the suit, though not to the costs and expenses of his travel and loss of time; and these costs must appear to the court to be legal costs and expenses" (2 *Inst.* c. 238). And so of the words, "Et tout ces soit tenus en touts cases ou trouve recover damages," he says, "This clause doth extend to give costs where damages are given to any plaintiff in any action by any statute made after this parliament" (*Ibid.* 289). These instances are illustrations of the large and liberal way in which these ancient statutes have been extended by coustruction, rather by their spirit than their terms, when they are enabling and beneficial.

[1] 2 Inst. 309. [2] Ch. 7. [3] 2 Inst. 310. [4] *Vide ante*, vol. i. c. viii.
[5] Viz. c. 16. *Vide* vol. i. c. viii. [6] Ch. 1.

waste,[1] and what provision had been made by stat. 52 Hen. III., cap. 23,[2] and 3 Edw. I., c. 21.[3] It was now provided, that a writ of waste might be had in chancery against one who held *per legem Angliæ;* in which case, it should seem, it did not lie at common law; and, in addition to the former statutes, it was now declared, that it should lie where any one held for term of life, or years, or in dower (*a*). Not that the common law had already provided no redress in all such cases of waste; for we have before shown, upon the authority of Bracton, that a proceeding might be had for waste against a tenant in dower, a tenant for

Waste.

(*a*) Here, again, is an ilustration of the ancient embodiment of a principle which has in later times received an adaptation suited to the alteration of circumstances. As Lord Coke observed in his commentary, the act introduced that which was not at the common law as to persons liable to the action. For the action of waste, like all the old real actions, lay only against the tenants of the freehold; for which reason it appears to have been for permissive waste, as it is called, *i.e.*, allowing a place to go to ruin, as well as for actual commissive acts of waste or devastation, as pulling down buildings or cutting down trees. For it stood to reason that a person who had a freehold estate in the place should keep it from falling into decay, for the sake of the reversioner, who could not, as in the case of a mere tenant, for years enter to do repairs, and prevent the ruin; and, as Lord Coke points out, had not had any opportunity of exacting covenants to do repairs, since in most cases the tenant of the freehold was in by act of law. And thus the allowing a place to fall to ruin was deemed the same thing in effect as doing acts of waste, and indeed seems to have been so called, as the old entries always speaks of waste as being done. Bracton treats of the subject (lib. iv. fol. 315,) and assumes it to be an injury to the inheritance: "Vastum erit injuriosum, nisi vastum ita modicum fuerit propter quod non sit inquisitio facienda," (lib. iv. c. xviii. s. 12, fol. 316.) On account also of the importance of the inheritance, the common law allowed writ of prohibition to prevent waste (which might be irreparable), as well as action to punish it. "Now the remedy at common law," says Coke, "was in two degrees—first, that if he that had the inheritance did fear (for example) that the tenant in dower would do waste, he that had the inheritance might, before any waste done, have a prohibition directed to the sheriff, that he shall not permit her to do waste: "Quod non permittas quod talis mulier faciat vastum," &c. And as Bracton said: "Et hoc faciat tempestive, ne per negligentiam damnum incurrat, quia melius est in tempore occurrere, quam post causam vulneratum remedium quærere" (lib. iv. fol. 315). And the sheriff, having this writ, might, as in the case of a writ of estrepement, take *posse comitatos*, and withstand the doing of any waste" (2 *Inst.* 299). For the same reason, the reversioner, for waste actually done, might recover treble damages, and also the place wasted. But if the law granted away the reversion, the action failed at the common law (for waste done after the assignment), "whereby," says Coke, "it appeareth how necessary it is for the understanding of the act, to know what the common law was, and the reason thereof before the making of the act" (ib. 300). The reason thereof was, that the action was thought requisite for the protection of the inheritance. This statute, however, gave it in tenancies for life, or for years; but it did not alter the description of the character or nature of waste, which remained as before, at all events, as to wilful or actual waste. And it should seem that, in cases of tenancy for life or years, where very small damages were found, the place wasted was not necessarily recovered (*Fitz. Abr.*, "*Waste,*" fol. 111, 8 *Edw. II.*; *ibid.*, fol. 146, 34 *Edw. III.*; *Year-book*, 14 *Hen. IV.* 11; *Bo. Abr.*, "*Waste,*" fol. 70). Waste lay at common law, not only for wilful, but permissive waste; for in the earliest cases in the Yearbooks, we find mention made of extraordinary causes of waste, which would excuse or make an exception to what would otherwise be considered waste, as, for instance, tempests, accidental fires, and the like (*Year-book*, 40 *Edw. III.*, 3, 5, 6, 25; 43 *Edw. III.* 24.) And it was no excuse that a place was feeble when demised, if it fell into ruin through the default of the tenant (42 *Edw. III.*, 21, 22). An infant in ward could, it was held, have the action against his guardian (43 *Ed. III.*, 6). It was con-

[1] *Vide ante*, vol. i. c. viii. [2] *Ibid.* [3] *Ibid.*

life, and a guardian.[1] It ordains, that a person attainted of waste should lose the thing wasted, and should moreover make recompense to treble the sum at which the waste was rated. Whereas it was directed by the Great Charter,[2] that guardians doing waste should lose their custody, it was now declared, that should the remainder of the wardship not be equal to the waste sustained, the guardian should make it up in damages.[3]

The increase of frivolous suits in the king's superior courts occasioned probably the following law (*a*). It was declared that

sidered, in the reign of Edward III., that waste lay in cases of leases for life or for years (34 *Ed. III.*, 5). If a house fell through the default of repairs, as of roofing, it was waste (44 *Ed. III.*, 44). There was, it will be observed, a distinction between the "action for waste," which implied an abuse of a right, and trespass, which implied a bare tort. In the action of waste, the place wasted was recovered with treble damages (41 *Ed. III.*, 23). And waste lay against a tenant for years, or even from year to year; but not against a tenant at will, because the lessor could re-enter at his will, and the tenant would be liable in trespass (48 *Ed. III.*, 25). It was said that no action of waste lay at the common law before the statute of Gloucester, except against tenant in dower and guardians; and by the statute, the action of waste was given against the tenant by the courtesy tenant for term of life, and tenant for term of years, but not against tenant at will; and if he cut trees, trespass would lie (21 *Hen. IV.*, 38). But this was meant, as is manifest, of wilful waste, and there might be a distinction between that and permissive waste. In the reign of Edward III., it was held that a tenant for life was liable for permissive waste; and if a house should be ruinous for want of sufficient roof, and the tenant suffered it to be more ruinous than it was, the action would lie (*Year-book*, 45 *Edw. III.*, f. 3). So waste might be committed in permitting a building to fall into ruins, for the tenant was considered bound to keep it in the same state in which it was when he took it (*Year-book*, 5 *Ed. IV.*, 89). The courts seem, as to the forfeiture, to have entertained an equitable jurisdiction in cases of this kind (*Eldon & Governors of Harrow School* v. *Alderton*, 2 *Bos. & P.* 87). "The doctrine prevailed as early as the time of Bracton, who wrote before the statute of Gloucester" (Heath, J., *ibid.* p. 88). And unless the jury found the place wasted, the plaintiff could not have judgment (*Redfern* v. *Smith*, 2 *Burg.* 262). The courts, in fact, followed the spirit of the action, which was protection to the inheritance. On the same principle, when as the real actions become obsolete, the action on the case was substituted, it was held that it did not lie against tenant for years for mere permissive waste, in not keeping up the premises (*Gibson* v. *Wells*, *B. & P., N. R.*, 290). And when the old action of waste became obsolete, or in cases where it would not lie, as cases of copyholders, equity interfered by injunction (*Dench* v. *Brampton*, 4 *Vesey, Jun.* 706, 3 *Swanston*, 497), or writs of prohibition and assistance were granted out of chancery to prevent a prebendary from committing waste on his prebend (*Ackland* v. *Atwell;* 3 *Swanst.* 499). Thus through the course of six centuries the same principle has pervaded the law on the subject, the general rule of equity being not to interfere except in order to prevent irreparable injury to the inheritance. The writ of estrepement of waste lay to prevent waste being committed *pendente lite* (2 *Inst.* 328), *vide post* on the statute of Gloucester.

(*a*) Lord Coke in his commentary says "The inferior courts, which are not of record, cannot regularly hold plea of debt or damages under 40s." (*i.e.*, as he explains on the next page, without the writ of justices); and then he observes that the ounce of silver was, at the time of the making of this act, but twenty pence, and now it is above thrice so much (2 *Inst.*, 311); but it is manifest that many other considera-

[1] Lord Coke lays down the law of waste in a different manner. He says, that it was punishable at common law in three persons, that is, in tenant in dower, tenant by courtesy, and the guardian; but not in tenant for life, or for years. However, that writer gives no authority for his opinion, unless the following observation is to be considered as such—namely, that the law which created the former of these estates and interests provided a remedy itself against waste, but left the owners of land, who created the others, to provide a remedy in their demise. *Vide ante*, vol. i. 386, and *ante*, 73. 2 Inst. 299. Reg. 72. Bro. Waste, 88.

[2] Ch. 4. *Vide ante*, vol. i. c. viii.

[3] Ch. 5.

sheriffs should continue to hold pleas of trespass in their counties, as before; and further, that none should have writs of trespass before justices, unless they swore by their faith that the goods taken were worth forty shillings at the least (which was the ancient limit to the sheriff's jurisdiction) (*b*); if it was a beating, the plaintiff was to swear that the complaint was true. Wounds and

tions enter into the question of the comparative value of money at two periods, besides the mere price or value of bullion, or the intrinsic value of the coin. There is also the question of prices of commodities, alterations in which may make a penny in one age go further than a shilling or five shillings in another. Added to which, the comparison must be made with the period when the limitation of jurisdiction, if it ever existed, must have arisen—that is, in times anterior to the Conquest. And in Saxon times, when only five pence went to the shilling, and a shilling was the price of a cow, we can hardly have an idea of the value really represented by forty shillings. Even in the reign of Edward IV. (as appears by the old ballad of the king and the tanner) a wealthy yeoman would only give four shillings for a horse, which would now perhaps cost forty pounds. And in the reign of Henry VI. forty shillings per annum was the qualification of the electors of knights of the shire, and even of knights themselves. The difference, therefore, between the real value of such a sum at the time of the Conquest and at the time of Lord Coke, or even of the statute, can hardly be estimated. In a note in the Introduction, cv., some curious illustrations are adduced upon the subject. Elsewhere Lord Coke himself says "a day's work of a ploughman, *i.e.*, including the plough, the horses, and the two ploughmen, was only estimated at the small sum of eightpence," and that no doubt was an exorbitant estimate, as it was *pro servicio regis* (4 *Inst.*, 209). So elsewhere it appears that to take a cart and horses, and a cartload of corn, was not necessarily an excessive distress for four shillings. It is facts like these which help us to understand the real comparative value of money at different periods; and according to the most probable estimate that can be made, the sum of forty shillings at the Conquest would be equivalent to much more than £50 at the present period, so that the compulsory jurisdiction of the county court (subject to removal for good cause) would be fixed at £50. It may, however, be gravely doubted whether it might not safely be fixed at a much higher rate. As to the writ of *pone*, for the removal of plaints into the superior courts, 2 *Inst.*, 339; *Stat. of Westm.*, 2. So in *Brooke's Abr. Jurisdiccion*, fol. 98, *vide Registrum;* that in writ of trespass, where the defendant pleads that it is his soil and freehold, or otherwise the freehold comes in question in the county court; the matter shall proceed there, but not if it comes in issue as a plaint without writ (*i.e.*, writ of *justicies*); that is sufficient to remove the record, *i.e.*, into the superior court. See also cases in *Bro. Ab. Recordare, et vide Year-book*, 30 *Ed. III.*, fol. 22.

(*b*) It has already been seen that this was not so. The *Mirror* states that it was the limit of the jurisdiction of courts-baron and other inferior courts (c. i. s. 15). It was impossible that this or any other amount should have limited the jurisdiction of the county court, seeing that even after the Conquest, and as late as the reign of Henry I., the county court, called "*Curia Regis*," was the *only* court of ordinary jurisdiction. In the reign of Henry I. justices itinerant began to be sent regularly to supersede the county courts in more important cases; and in the reign of Henry II. the court of the king's permanent justices—the justices of the bench, as they were called, in contradistinction from the itinerant justices—had become known as the *curia regis*, and to entertain suits between party and party. And then the county court having virtually to a great extent become superseded in important cases, the notion arose naturally, and was inculcated by the crown lawyers, that the limitation of the jurisdiction of the inferior courts applied to the county court. The consequence was that the king's courts became overburdened with small suits; and the object of the present enactment was to provide a remedy for that grievance. It assumes the limitation of the jurisdiction already alluded to, and the object was to exclude from the superior courts cases within that limitation. In cases of claims or demands for fixed sums or debts there was no difficulty; the difficulty was in cases where the demand was not thus fixed, and was for uncertain damages, the amount of which might be above or below the limitation assumed. And the difficulty was, that as a man could not know beforehand what sum a jury would give for the injury he had sustained, it was impossible to force him to sue in the county court, when per-

mayhems were to be prosecuted as formerly; only the defendants therein were now allowed to make their attorneys if the suit was not by appeal; and if they were absent when attainted, the sheriff was to be commanded to take them, as if they had been present at the judgment. To avoid delays, it was provided that if the plaintiffs in such actions of trespass caused themselves to be essoined after the first appearance, day should be given to the coming of the justices in eyre, and the defendant in the meantime should be in peace. Again, in all actions where there lay the process of attachment and distress, if the defendant essoined himself *de servitio regis*, and did not produce his warrant at the day, he was to give the plaintiff twenty shillings as damages for his journey, unless the justices in their discretion should order more; besides which, he was to be amerced.[1]

The tediousness of the old process was lessened by other regulations. In writs of mortauncestor, *cosinage*, *aiel*, and *besaiel*, after issue joined, the inquest was no longer to be deferred on account of the nonage of the defendant.[2] A former statute,[3] which took from parceners the *fourcher by essoin*, was extended to a man and wife, when co-defendants.[4] In conformity with the common law, it was declared that where there were many heirs, though in different degrees, they might join with him who could bring a mortauncestor.[5]

haps in the superior court he might recover more than the sum limited, though he might recover less. This difficulty still exists, and has caused a distinction to be drawn, in all the county court acts, between claims for debts and for damages; and the endeavour has been to attain the object by means of the deprivation of costs. In the above statute the object was sought to be attained in a more direct way—by means of a preliminary inquiry, *before allowing a party to sue at all in the superior courts;* for though the oath of the party was admitted as sufficient proof of a cause of action of the requisite amount, the *principle* was that of a preliminary inquiry; and it would be quite in accordance with the principle of the enactment to require that a judge should be first *satisfied* that there was a cause of action of an amount sufficient to justify a party in suing in the superior court. Of course the judge could not try the case upon affidavit, and it does not appear that the oath of the party could be controverted. But, on the other hand, it does not appear that the court were obliged to be satisfied with a mere general statement upon oath, and that they could not, in order to carry out the object of the statute, require a more particular statement of the nature of the case, so as to enable them to judge how far it was likely to be sustained. It is to be observed that the principle laid down in this enactment, that the question whether a case was or was not fit to be tried in the superior courts should be determined on the *writ*, upon a summary application, is one of immense practical importance, and appears to be well grounded in the common law. For the law was that a man ought not to sue in the local court in a case above forty shillings, without a writ of *justicies*, nor in the king's court, where the cause of action was under forty shillings; and how could that be determined more properly than when the writ was to be issued? So, when a writ of *pone* was required to remove a cause from the inferior court, as being fit for the superior court, it was applied for upon the plaint being made, which answered to the writ in the superior court. It seems to stand to reason that an objection to the suit being brought in, a particular court should be made when the suit is so brought, and soon as possible.

[1] Ch. 8. [2] Ch. 2. [3] 3 Ed. I. c. 43. *Vide* vol. i. c. viii.

[4] Ch. 10. *Vide ante*, vol. i. c. viii.

[5] Ch. 6. It is laid down by Bracton, that an *assisa* might be joined with a *consanguinitas*, and both be determined upon one writ; as where a sister demanded of the death or

The remaining provisions concerning civil matters are confined principally to the city of London, and other cities and boroughs; and in that light are of less moment than what has just been mentioned. However, two laws in favour of termors, and to prevent waste, though chiefly designed for the city of London, were extended to the whole kingdom. We have before seen that a term for years was of very inferior consideration in the scale of estates, one circumstance that rendered such an interest peculiarly precarious was, that it was subject to the will of the person having the freehold, who, by a collusive recovery of the land, might entirely destroy the term; for the[1] termor would not be allowed to falsify the recovery, it being a rule that none could falsify the recovery of a freehold but one who had a freehold (*a*). To remedy this it was now ordained,[2] that if tenements in the city of London were leased for years, and he to whom the freehold belonged was impleaded by collusion, and made default after default, or came into court and surrendered the freehold, to make the termor lose his term, and the demandant recovered, so that the termor became entitled to a writ of covenant against his lessor; in such case, the statute directs that the mayor and bailiffs

Feigned recoveries.

(*a*) A judgment bound the parties and their privies—that is, in a judgment of land, their privies in estate; and as the title of the termor was derived out of the freehold, he would come within this rule, and be bound by the recovery against his lessor, the freeholder under whom he held, and against whom the recoverer would, if there were no collusion, claim by some title paramount. And as the recovery would lie in a real action, which only lay between freeholders, the termor would have no remedy. If, indeed, he was wrongfully ousted, the law was said to be that he might have an assize of novel disseisin, inasmuch as that remedy rested on unlawful ouster rather than on legal title (*Mirror of Justice*, c. iii. s. 28, title *Disseissin*; and see c. v. s. 1, "Abuses of the Law" art.). And there was also *ejectione formæ*. But if the recovery was rightful, there was no remedy against the recoverer at the suit of the termor. It may, indeed, appear to require explanation how a recovery of the *freehold* could affect the title of the *termor*, which was consistent with the freehold title being in another. The explanation of this is to be found in the nature of real actions, which were grounded on some specific deduction of title; and this would be from a time anterior to the granting of the lease, so as to destroy the title to lease; and then, again, by the judgment in a real action, seisin would be executed, which in those days meant actual seisin, and *prima facie* imported possession. Indeed, this was the real ground of the plea of freehold in an action of *trespass*, that *prima facie* it showed possession in the party pleading it; and although a lease might be replied, and would show possession in the lessee, that was only when a good title to make the lease was deduced from a tenant of the freehold. And in these ancient times "the tenant" meant the tenant of the freehold. In those times fraudulent recoveries were often resorted to; as, for instance, to evade the *condition* on which the land had been taken, and acquire an absolute title. Thus it was held that where a feoffee on condition suffered a man who had right to recover by false title, the feoffer could enter and falsify the recovery (*Year-book*, 44 *Edw. III.*, 8). It was also laid down that even where a man who had cause of action made by covin an entry upon which he recovered, the disseisee could re-enter or have an assize, and the recovery would not aid, by reason of the covin (44 *Edw.* III., 46). But only those who had a freehold title could falsify a recovery, and a real action for it could only be by another seisin of a father, and a son of another sister; in which case the writ would allege. *A. pater B. et avus C. cujus hæredes ipse B. et C. sunt, fuit seisitus in dominico suo ut de fœdo, &c.* (*Bract.* 283 b. *Vide ante*, vol. i. 363.)

[1] We have before noticed an instance where a collusive term was established by statute against the freeholder, by way of penalty for a fraud. *Vide* vol. i. c. viii.

[2] Ch. 11.

might try by an inquest, whether the demandant had right, or sued by collusion to defraud the termor (*a*). If the former was proved, judgment was to be given in the suit; if the latter, it was ordained that the termor should continue to enjoy his term, and execution of the judgment should be suspended till the term was expired. This was the course directed when a suit depended before the mayor of London, in which case the inquiry used to be made by writ in nature of a commission grounded upon this statute. At the close of the act is this clause: "And in like manner shall it be done, in like case, *before justices*, in an equitable way, if the termor challenge it before the judgment." This was a general clause, extending the former part of the act to the whole kingdom; and by virtue of this a termor might before judgment pray to be received to defend the right and interest of his term, on the default, or render, or *nient dedire* of the tenant, but not upon faint pleader. The effect of such interference and receipt of the tenant would be (if he proved the collusion), that execution should be suspended during the term, as in the former case; for the act says, *en mesme le manner*.[1]

This is the first statute that gave receipt in any case; but the principle upon which a person interested was allowed to interpose in a suit that was likely to affect his interest, is to be found in the old practice at common law. Thus, if a tenant for life, or in dower, was impleaded, and neglected to vouch the reversioner in fee, the reversioner might appear unvouched, and enter into the warranty.[2]

A law concerning waste was made for the city of London, and, like the former, was, by a clause at the end, extended to the whole kingdom. This ordains that, *pendente lite* in the city of London, no tenant should have power to commit waste, or estrepement of the land in question; and if he did, that the mayor and bailiffs, at the proper *suit* of the demandant, should cause the land to be safely kept. This was to be observed in other cities and towns, and *everywhere else* in the realm.[3] Upon this act was framed a judicial *writ of estrepement*, which was granted out of the bench where the

real action which required a freehold title. Hence it was held that a termor could not falsify a recovery of the freehold by the common law, for he could not have the estate which was recovered, because it was a recovery of the freehold, and the term was a mere chattel, though the contrary was held by Littleton (9 *Ed. IV.*, fol. 48). And in a case long afterwards, which was not within the terms of the statute, so that it became material to consider what the law was apart from the statute, two judges held that a termor could at common law falsify a recovery (4 *Hen. VII.*, fol. 10), though it was doubted. It would appear, therefore, doubtful whether the view of the law above stated was really correct (43 *Assize*, fol. 41). And probably this statute, like so many others, was declaratory.

(*a*) This was the remedy given by another statute with reference to feigned recoveries in evasion of the law of mortmain. It must always be borne in mind that a recovery, even if really valid, was not binding, except between the parties and their legal privies—that is, privies in estate. Thus the *heirs* would be bound.

[1] 2 Inst. 324. [2] *Vide ante*, vol. i. c. viii. [3] Ch. 13.

principal writ was returned, the old writ of estrepement being, like other original writs, suable only out of the chancery. The judicial writ was in effect a prohibition, upon which there might be an attachment, and the parties would come to pleading.

It seems that in London there was an assize called an assize of *fresh force*. This was not a proceeding by writ, but by bill in the city court; and no damages were recoverable. As it was, on this account, less effectual than an assize of novel disseisin at common law, damages were now given.[1] If in a suit in the city of London, a person was vouched in a foreign country, a difficulty arose, which was now removed by a statute, directing that a *recordari facias* should issue to remove the cause into the bench, and that a *summons ad warrantizandum* should issue out of chancery. After the vouchee had answered in the bench to the warranty, the cause was to be remanded.[2] Some little alteration was made in this proceeding by a sort of writ directed to the justices of the bench, which is now, like some other instruments of the same kind, placed among the statutes as an act of the legislature.[3]

There is only one chapter in this statute that relates to criminal matters. By this it was intended to check the frequent issuing of writs *de odio et atiâ*, and to appoint a course of bringing persons accused to answer for their offences.[4] The king commandeth, says the act, that no writ shall be granted out of chancery for the death of a man, to inquire whether the person killed the deceased by misadventure, or *se defendendo*, or in any other manner feloniously;

Homicide *se defendendo.*

but such person shall be kept in prison till the coming of the justices in eyre, or justices assigned to deliver the gaol, and then shall put himself upon the country, *de bien et de mal:* and if it appears to the country that he did it *se defendendo*, or by misadventure, then the king, upon the record of the justices, may take him to his grace, if he pleases; that is, upon the record being certified into the court of chancery, which court was CORAM REGE *in cancellariâ*, a pardon would issue from the chancellor. It had before been a matter almost of course to grant pardons in homicide *se defendendo*, and by misadventure;[5] which merciful usage, therefore, was only confirmed and secured to the subject by this statute. The act goes on to remedy the obstruc-

[1] Ch. 14. [2] Ch. 12.

[3] This is stat. 9 Edw. I. stat 1. At the close of this statute is a memorandum to the following effect: "That this article was signed under the great seal, and sent to the justices of the bench, after the manner of a writ patent, with a certain writ closed, dated by the king's hand, that they should do and execute all and everything contained in the article aforesaid, albeit that the same did not accord with the statute of Gloucester in all things."—A similar instrument follows also the statute of Gloucester, beginning thus: "After, by the king and his justices, certain expositions were made upon some of the articles above-mentioned." Of a similar nature with these two acts was the statute of bigamy just mentioned. Such facts as these, at a period when law and legislature were more regarded than they had been a century ago, are very remarkable examples to confirm the observation before made respecting the king's authority to frame such legislative acts as were calculated to promote a better administration of justice. *Vide ante*, vol. i. 216, 217.

[4] 2 Inst. 315. [5] *Vide* vol. i. c. viii.

tion occasioned to justices by the frivolous objections, to which the proceeding in appeals was liable. It says, that appeals shall not be abated so easily as they have been ; but if the appellor declare the fact, the year, the day, and hour, the time of the king, the town, and the weapon, the appeal shall be good and valid, and shall not be abated for want of fresh suit, provided the party sue within a year and day after the fact ;[1] so that the old learning about *fresh suit* became henceforward obsolete.[2]

In the next year was passed the famous statute, 7 Ed. I. of mortmain, or *de religiosis*, as it is sometimes called. The object of this law was to aid in enforcing the provision of the Great Charter on the subject of alienation to religious societies, and to carry that restriction somewhat further.[3] Notwithstanding the above law, religious men continued to accept gifts, and to appropriate lands, whereby services that were due for such lands, and that were originally designed for defence of the realm, were withdrawn, and, what was an object of more anxious concern to great lords, the valuable casualties of tenure were gradually diminished(*a*). To prevent this, it was ordained, in the most comprehensive and full expressions that could be contrived, that no person whatsoever, religious or other (*b*), should presume to buy or sell, or under

Statute of mortmain.

(*a*) But it was held that this did not apply to a mere term for years of ordinary duration, *petite terme*—*i.e.*, for twenty or forty years, for that was not deemed to be contrary to the statute *de religiosis*, otherwise if it was of a long term, as of a hundred or two hundred years, so that, by long continuance of possession, the land would be in mortmain ; but of a short term the law would not take regard as within the statute for forfeiture of the land. It was not the intent of the statute, it was said, that there should be an inquiry as to collusion, where all that was recovered was a chattel. The intent of the statute was where the religious house was to recover the fee-simple (*Year-book*, 3 *Edw. IV.*, c. 13). For it was said that, according to Magna Charta and the statute *de religiosis*, the religious houses were not to take lands in fee-simple, and then in this statute it was said that, by *colour* of a term or gift in fee, the land should not be in *mortmain*. Then, as notwithstanding those statutes, religious men would recover by default, by the covin and collusion of the tenants, so that the statutes were eluded ; then for that reason the statute of Westminster 2 was made "*cum viri religiosi*, &c., implacitent aliquem et implacitatus fecerit defaltam," then the collusion shall be tried ;" and that, it was said, was meant of suits in which the lands should be recovered in fee; on the other hand, some of the judges took the opposite view, that the case of a term of years came within the mischief of the statutes, and the arguments form the best possible exposition of them. One of the judges thus stated their scope and effect: "At the common law, before the statutes, every man of religion could purchase (*i.e.*, acquire) lands or tenements as well as any layman or temporal person. And it was mischievous to the country, for many services of the land ordained in defence of the realm were decayed, and for that the statutes of Magna Charta, *de religiosis*, and Westminster 2 were made, restraining the acquisition of land by men of religion and recoveries by them. But this case is out of the statutes." Littleton, however, seems to have been of a contrary opinion, but the actual determination on the point does not distinctly appear. The exposition of the scope and policy of the statutes, however, is equally valuable (3 *Edw. IV.* 15). The action in that case was, it is to be observed, one of *waste*, which lay against the tenant of the freehold, and in which incidentally the land was recovered. But usually a recovery was in a writ of right.

(*b*) Therefore it was held that the statute included and applied to gifts of land to a parson and his successors. It was held, in the reign of Edward III., that if a man give land to a parson and his successors, or to a vicar and his successors, it ought to

[1] Ch. 9. [2] *Vide* vol. i. c. viii. [3] *Ibid.* vol. i. c. vii.

colour of any gift, term, or other title whatsoever, receive from any one, or in any other way, *arte vel ingenio*, appropriate to himself any lands or tenemen ts, so as such lands or tenements should come into mortmain,[1] under pain of forfeiting the same: and if any offended against this act, it was made lawful for the chief lord next immediate, within a year, to enter on the land, and retain it in fee and inheritance. If he neglected during that year, the next superior lord might enter; and if *he* did not enter within half a year, the right of entry was to accrue to the next superior lord; and if all the lords, being of full age, within the four seas, and out of prison, neglected to avail themselves of the forfeiture, the king might take the lands into his hands and infeoff others, saving to the chief lords of the fees their wards, escheats, and other services.

Notwithstanding the solicitude with which this statute seems to have been penned, a method of evasion was soon discovered by ecclesiastics. This was to recover lands by default, in a collusive suit brought against the person who had in contemplation to bestow lands in mortmain (*a*). Although this proceeding was by consent and fraud, yet the justices held that the religious and ecclesiastical persons did not appropriate such lands *per titulum doni, vel alterius alienationis*, as the statute of mortmain expresses it, nor that they were within the words *aut alio quovismodo, arte vel ingenio*. For as recoveries were prosecuted in a course of law, they were by law presumed to be just and lawful; and it was accordingly held by the justices, that they were not within the statute. These fraudulent recoveries were practised very soon after the statute was made, and in a few years grew to such a height as to occasion a parliamentary interference. It was ordained in 13

be by a licence, and this by virtue of mortmain; for the parson and his successors, or the vicar and his successors, are incorporate by the common law (*Year-book*, 40 *Edw. III.*, fol. 27, 28). There appeared to be a question whether a devise of land to raise an income for the support of a chaplain was in mortmain or not. Thus it being found that one R. was seised of land in Wood Street, Cheapside, and devised the rents in fee to pay annually £12 to find two chaplains to chant for his soul *in perpetuum* in the church of St Albans, in Wood Street, it was held not to be mortmain (40 *Assize* 26). But in another case where land was devised in fee to find six marks a year to provide a chaplain in perpetuity, it was adjudged in chancery to be mortmain (43 *Assize*, fol. 33). But Brooke remarks, "*quod mirum*," as there was no *corporation* or incorporate body to receive the rent (*Bro. Abr.*, *Mortmain*, fol. 24), and he refers to other similar cases where it was held that such endowments were *not* within the law of mortmain (*Ibid.* fol. 23, fol. 25; 43 *Assize* 27, 43 *Assize* 34).

(*a*) This proceeding was only effective as between the religious house and the heirs of the virtual donor, the party against whom the recovery was recorded; for it was always a fundamental principle of law that a verdict and judgment only bound parties and privies; that is to say, the original parties to the suit and their legal representatives. The recovery would have no effect as regarded a party claiming by title paramount to the virtual donor, the party against whom the land was recovered, for *he* could "falsify the recovery," not being estopped by it. This, however, did not apply as regarded the lord, whether mesne or paramount, whose title would only accrue in case of forfeiture or escheat, and as the recovery was not a cause of forfeiture, therefore it was effectual for the purpose of a virtual alienation. Hence the present enactment, which declared that the recovery, unless real, and hostile, and grounded on title, should operate as a forfeiture.

[1] *In mortuam manum*.

Ed. I.[1] that when a default was supposed to be made for this purpose, it should be inquired by the country, whether the demandant had any right to the land or not: and that, if it was found he had, judgment should be for him to recover seisin; if not, the forfeiture should accrue in the manner directed by the statute of mortmain (*a*). Every one of the chief lords was to be admitted to challenge the jurors of this inquest, and a challenge might be made for the king. The sheriff was to be charged at the exchequer to answer for the lands in question. After this act it was usual, when land was lost by default, to award a writ, called a *quale jus*, grounded upon this act, in which there was a recital of the recovery; and the sheriff was commanded to summon a jury to try *quale jus idem abbas habuit*, *&c.*[2] Thus were the clergy hunted out of a new device for enriching themselves; but the practice of conveying land by means of a feigned recovery, in a real action, did not cease with this statute: we shall find in a subsequent part of this history that this became a common mode of conveyance, of equal authority with the ancient ones by feoffment and fine.

There are other statutes on the subject of ecclesiastical possessions which, though properly belonging, in point of time, to the latter part of this reign, will, if transposed to this place, more satisfactorily illustrate this important part of the history of landed property.

In stat. West. 2,[3] a regulation was made for preserving to religious societies the property they had already obtained (*b*). If, says

(*a*) It was said, upon this, that where the statute made a judgment by *default* to be mortmain, judgment *per reddition*, by confession or trial, should be taken by the equity of the act, *quod non negatur*. And it was also said that the statute of mortmain extended to rents or commons, *quod non negatur*. But these were mere *dicta*, and it should seem that such extensions of penal acts by construction were not legal (*Year-book*, 3 *Edw. IV.* 14).

(*b*) It is necessary, with reference to what follows in a subsequent portion of this chapter, to draw attention to the nature of the tenure on which ecclesiastical property was held, which the author had omitted to do. "Tenant in frankalmoigne," says Littleton, "is where an abbot, or prior, or another man of religion, or of holy church, holdeth of his lord in free alms." And such tenure began first in old time, when a man was seised of land in his demesne as of fee, and if it enfeoffed an abbot and his convent, to have and to hold to these and their successors, in pure and perpetual alms. In the same manner it is where lands were granted in ancient times to a dean and chapter and their successors, or to any other man of holy church and his successors, &c. And they which hold in frankalmoigne are bound of right before God to make prayers and masses and other divine services for the grantors and their heirs, &c. And therefore they *shall do no fealty to their lord*, because these words, "in frankalmoigne," exclude the lord to have any earthly or temporal service. And if they which so hold fail to do such divine service, the lord may not distrain, but may complain to the ordinary, &c. And note, that where such man of religion holds in frankalmoigne, his lord is bound by the law to acquit him of every manner of service which any lord paramount will have of him for the tenements (*Littleton*, c. vi.) So that if the land were held by the grantor on knight-service, he would have to provide the knight-service due in respect of the land. All this is most important, in order to understand the real merits and the motives of the opposition to ecclesiastical property in this age, and the disposition to restrain it. It is manifest that it arose from the loss of feudal services which were not due in respect of the lands of the church. This is plain from another passage at the end of the section in Littleton on the subject, where he says that where the grantor's estate escheated, then the abbot or spiritual

[1] Westm. 2, ch. 32. [2] 2 Inst. 429. [3] *Vide* ch. 41.

the act, abbots, priors, keepers of hospitals, and other religious houses founded by the king or his progenitors, alien lands given to their houses by him or his progenitors, the land shall be taken into the king's hands to be holden at his will, and the purchaser lose both the lands and the purchase-money; and if the house were founded by any common person, the heir of the donor shall have the following writ, called since a *contra formam collationis* (a). *Præcipe tali abbati, quòd justè, &c., reddat A. B. tale tenementum quod eidem domui collatum fuit in liberam eleemosynam per prædictum B.*[1] (b); *et quod ad prædictum B. reverti debet per alienationem quam prædictus abbas fecit de prædicto tenemento,* CONTRA FORMAM COLLATIONIS *prædictæ, ut dicit.* So also of lands given for

person should hold of the lord paramount in fealty only, "because he cannot hold of him in frankalmoigne," whence it appears that those who held in frankalmoigne did not even hold under the obligation of fealty. It is manifest that this was detrimental to the interest of the feudal lords, and hence this and other enactments directed against church property, in pursuance of the policy of the provision in the great charters against alienations to monasteries for the purpose of avoiding feudal services. It is to be observed that Littleton considered the statute of this reign, *Quia emptores*, to have been framed with the same policy, for he says of it that it prevented any further alienation of property to religious houses or churches. "If a man grant to an abbot or prior lands in frankalmoigne, these words 'in frankalmoigne' are void, for it is ordained by the statute, *Quia emptores terrarum* (which was made *anno* 18 *Edward I.*) that none may alien lands in fee-simple to hold of himself. So that if a man seised of tenements which he holds of his lord by knight-service grants the same by license to an abbot, &c., in frankalmoigne, the abbot shall hold the same by knight-service of the lord of whom his grantor held, and shall not hold of his grantor in frankalmoigne, by reason of the statute. So that none can hold in frankalmoigne unless it be by title of prescription, or by force of grant made before the statute. But the king may grant lands in frankalmoigne"—a case put in quiet irony, for the days had long passed when kings *gave* lands to the church, and now all their study was, as in the present instance, to *take* the lands of the church. For in this statute, which our author with grave humour describes as designed to *secure* the property of the church, the king *takes* it away. The alienation is declared void, the natural result of which would be that the abbey should *retain* it, but instead of that the king takes it, and keeps it, and takes the purchase-money as well. The statute of *Quia emptores* prevented the church from having any more lands, and the present and other statutes were passed to prevent the church from dealing with the lands she had.

(a) Here we see that the principle acknowledged by the statute was that if a religious or charitable endowment failed, from neglect of its duties or its object, the endowments *should revert to the donors*, whence they proceeded. This is in accordance with a general principle pursued by legislation, and recognised both at law and equity. Thus it will be found followed out in other writs in similar cases (*vide post*, c. xv.)

(b) This, it cannot but be observed, was rather an act for securing the property to the king, and it may be remarked that the statute affords the best possible refutation of the notion that ecclesiastical property was inalienable, for it proceeds upon the supposition of an alienation, and then declares the alienation void. Afterwards the supposed inalienability of church property was made an argument *against* such property. It is further to be observed, that this, like all the other statutes as to ecclesiastical property, professed to be based upon the right of patronage arising out of supposed endowment. No trace will be found of any right of interference with church property except upon that principle. The patron and his heirs were supposed to have an interest in the due appropriation of the property of his own dedication, and patronage and endowment were correlative. Hence Littleton laid it down "that none can hold lands in frankalmoigne but of the grantor or his heirs."

[1] Or, *per antecessores prædicti B.*

maintenance of a chantry (*a*), or of a light in a church, or chapel, or other alms, if the land given was aliened. If land given for these latter purposes was not aliened, but the alms were withdrawn for the space of two years, the donor or his heirs were to have an action, to demand the land in demesne, as directed by the statute of Gloucester, by a writ of *cessavit per biennium.*[1]

The following may be noticed as an instance of the claims advanced by the clergy. Persons who were tenants to the orders of Knights Templar and Hospitaller enjoyed at this time great privileges, as well against the king as against other lords; as, to be free from tenths and fifteenths due to the king; to be discharged of purveyance; not to be sued for ecclesiastical causes before the ordinary, *sed coram conservatoribus privilegiorum suorum.* Because the knights of both these orders were *cruce signati*, a cross, as the ensign of their profession, used to be erected on their lands, to notify that they were privileged and exempt; and so sacred were such places held, that, at one time, a felon could enjoy sanctuary

(*a*) The "chantries" were endowments of priests to offer masses for the souls of the donors and their heirs for ever. These endowments are also mentioned all through the subsequent reigns, until suppressed in the reign of Edward VI. There were other endowments to find lights, &c., for churches, for the good of the souls of the donors, &c., but these were generally incident to masses for the dead. The chantries were endowed, in order to have perpetual continuance, but chaplains were often retained by contract for salary to offer masses or perform divine services, and if they failed they were liable to be sued on their contracts (50 *Edward III.* fol. 13). The distinction was between perpetual endowment and temporary contract, but both of these classes of the clergy, the chantry priests and the chaplains, were regarded as distinct from the parochial clergy, who had other spiritual work to occupy them, as visiting the sick, &c., besides the mere performance of the special divine services. The scope of the statute was restricted to *endowments*. The writ of *cessavit* thus given could only be brought by the heirs of the donor, to whom alone the land was to revert (45 *Edward III.* fol. 15). Cessavit against the chaplain of a chantry, supposing by the writ that he held by service of chanting mass every Monday and Saturday throughout the year, and that he and his predecessors, from time whereof memory was not to the contrary, held the lands on that service. It was objected that the statute which gave the action gave it only to the donor and his heirs, and that the plaintiff had not shown that he was donor, or heir of the donor. The statute was read, which ran thus: *Quod competat actio donatori aut ejus hœredes.* And it was held that the writ should abate for the cause alleged, or for that it was so general (*Bellewe's Cases, temp.* Rich. II.) Cessavit against a prior for that the ancestor of the plaintiff had given land to the prior's predecessors to chant mass three times a week in the chapel, and that the prior had ceased (*Bellewe*, fol. 82). It is to be observed that the statute West. 2, c. xxiv. recognised these endowments by providing that a chaplain or chantry priest should have a *juris utrum* to recover the lands of the endowment, as a parson could have to recover the lands of his church (*West.* 2, c. 24). And the present statute was passed, on the other hand, to enforce the continuance of the service. It is to be borne in mind that the continuance could not be kept up without incorporation and perpetual succession, nor could this be without the royal grant, while the royal license also was required to allow of endowment in *land*, as it would be in mortmain. Thus in the reign of Edward III. we find that the king granted to J. N. to found a chantry of twelve priests, and it was laid down that he could do this, and that he could have *quare impedit* (28 *Edward III.* 14). So in the reign of Henry IV. we find a case of disseisin of the chaplain of a chantry (12 *Henry IV.* fol. 19). And in the reign of Edward IV. it was held that where a chantry was founded, and where land was given to the chantry priest and his successors, it was good in law—*i.e.*, as an incorporation, so as to secure its perpetuity (20 *Edward IV.* fol. 2).

[1] *Vide ante*, 145.

by flying to these crosses. To abolish these privileges, it was enacted by st. West. 2, 13 Edw. I. c. xxxiii. that wherever such crosses were erected, the land should be forfeited, as land aliened in mortmain. In the st. *quia emptores,* 18 Edw. I. st. 1, c. iii., it was expressly declared that the license to alien there given should not be construed as giving any power to alien in mortmain.

Another provision was made to check the abuse of clerical possessions, one of which was the waste they suffered by being drained into foreign countries (*a*). This was by a statute passed at the latter end of this reign, *de asportatis religiosorum,* 35 Edw. I. st. 1. It is therein complained, that abbots, priors, and governors of religious houses, and certain aliens, their superiors, used to set talliages and impositions upon monasteries, and houses in subjection to them, so that much of the opulence which was intended for religious service, the support of the poor, sick, and feeble, and maintenance of hospitality, was conveyed out of the kingdom. To prevent these abuses of religious institutions, it was ordained, that no abbot, prior, warden, master, or other religious person whatsoever, should secretly or openly, by any device, carry or send, or cause to be carried or sent, any such tax out of the kingdom, under pain of being grievously punished for such contempt of the king's solemn injunctions to the contrary ;[1] and all alien abbots, priors, masters, wardens, and the like, imposing such tax, were to forfeit for the offence everything they had.[2] The provisions of this statute were in after-times reviewed by the legislature, when it was employed in devising some method to restrain a new contrivance for enriching foreigners with ecclesiastical property, called *provision* (*b*). The persons prac-

(*a*) The effect of which, it will be observed, was that the king could not get at it. No king levied heavier subsidies either upon clergy or laity, but especially on clergy. A few years before this act passed, he levied a *tenth* upon the laity, and demanded from the clergy the *half* of their whole income. He had, some years before this, obtained from the pope the tenth of all ecclesiastical benefices for six years, and, that the grant might be more productive, the assessments were made by a new valuation, taken upon oath (*Dunst.* 593). It was published in 1380, under the title of *Taxatio Ecclesiastico Angliæ,* auctoritate P. Nicholai IV., A.D. 1291). By this were regulated all taxes to pope and king. In 1297 the king demanded a third or a fourth of the income of the clergy, and on their resistance to the illegal imposition, he issued a proclamation of outlawry against them, and took possession of all their property. And the lord chief-justice of the king's bench was not ashamed to give his public sanction to this act of arbitrary spoliation, and pronounce the sentence of outlawry (*Knyghton,* 2491). Before the writs of outlawry issued, the clergy compounded for a fifth (*Brady,* iii. App. xix.) The laity were glad enough to see the clergy plundered, as the more the clergy paid, the less the laity had to pay, and hence king and laity had a common interest in the property of the church; and the object of this act, passed on the eve of the king's expedition into Scotland, when he was more in want of money than ever, was to prevent the pope, or the foreign superiors of the religious houses, from receiving any pecuniary contributions out of their funds. The object of the act was not, as the author's language might lead the reader to suppose, to protect the religious houses, but to preserve their funds for the king, who was desirous that no one but himself should tax them.

(*b*) Here, again, it will be found that the object was to preserve the patronage to the king and other lay patrons (*vide post,* in the reign of Edward III.)

[1] Ch. 2. [2] Ch. 3.

tising this new device were called *provisors*, and were made subject to many penalties and forfeitures.

To return to the order of statutes, from which we have been digressing: the next is the statute of *Acton Burnel de Mercatoribus*, 11 Edw. I. The pressing demands of mercantile concerns made merchants complain of the delays and niceties of the law, and request some speedy course might be appointed for recovering payment of their debts at the appointed days; the want of which, it is said, occasioned many merchants to withdraw from the kingdom. The shortening of the process of attachment in favour of merchants, as was usual in the last reign,[1] was a partial redress, and since the *solennitas attachiamentorum* had been corrected by several statutes, they seem to have enjoyed no distinction in point of process from common plaintiffs. For the support, therefore, of credit, and the welfare of commerce, the following method of securing a ready payment of the debts of merchants was ordained by parliament. A merchant who wished to be sure of his debt was to bring his debtor before the mayor of London, York, or Bristol, as it might be, or before the mayor and a clerk, to be appointed by the king, there to acknowledge the debt and day of payment; and the recognizance was to be entered on a roll by the clerk. Besides this, the clerk was to make a writing obligatory, to which the seal of the debtor, together with the king's seal (which was to be provided for that purpose, and to be kept by the mayor), was to be affixed. If the debtor did not keep his day of payment, the creditor was to apply to the mayor; and upon view of the writing obligatory, and recognizance, the mayor was immediately to cause the chattels and devisable burgages of the debtor to be sold, to the amount of the debt, by the appraisement of honest men; and the money was immediately to be paid to the creditor: if no buyer could be found, the goods themselves were to be delivered to him. As to the sale of the devisable burgages, the king's seal was to be affixed thereto, for a proof of the sale. If the debtor had no movables within the mayor's jurisdiction, the mayor was to send the recognizance to the chancellor, who was to direct a writ to the sheriff of the county where the goods were, to act as the mayor.

Statute of Acton Burnel.

If the appraisers, out of favour to the debtor, set too high a price upon the goods, they were themselves to take them at the price, and be answerable to the creditor for the debt (*a*); but the debtor had no redress if they were sold under their value; it being his own folly, says the statute, that he did not sell them himself, and pay his debt with the produce. If the debtor had no mov-

(*a*) In the reign of Edw. III., this case arose on the statute. Candish (Cavendish ?) came to the bar, and showed how one had made a statute merchant; and he to whom the recognizance was made had sued execution, and that the lands of the recognisor were extended, and the extent returned: and he to whom the recognizance was made, said that they were extended too high, and prayed that the lands might

[1] *Vide ante*, vol. i. 487.

ables, then his body was to be taken, and kept in prison till he or his friends had made agreement with the creditor; and, should he be so poor as not to be able to support himself in gaol, the creditor was to sustain him with bread and water; which expense, as well as the debt, was to be defrayed by the debtor before he could be released. If the creditor was a merchant stranger, the debtor was likewise to pay all expenses attending his extraordinary stay here. If, instead of taking the body, the creditor would accept sureties, or mainpernors, for the payment, they were to bind themselves before the mayor, in like manner as the original debtor, and were to be subject to the same execution; though that was not to be till the goods of the principal were first exhausted.

Complaint, it seems, was made to the king, that this statute had been misinterpreted by sheriffs, and the execution of it delayed, upon various pretences. The king, therefore, in a parliament holden the thirteenth year of his reign, caused the statute of Acton Burnel to be rehearsed, and then several declarations were made by the legislature for enforcing it: these are contained in the *Statute of Merchants*, 13 Edw. I. st. 3. By this act, the recognizance may be taken before the mayor of London, or before some chief warden of a city, or of any other good town where the king shall appoint, or before the mayor and chief warden, or other sufficient men chosen and sworn thereto, when the mayor and chief warden cannot attend; and before one of the clerks to be appointed by the king. The recognizance is to have two parts; one to remain with the mayor or chief warden, the other with the clerks. The seal of the writing obligatory also is to be of two parts; the greater of which is to remain with the mayor or chief warden, the other with the clerk. Instead of the prefatory process against his movables, by this act the body of the debtor, if he is a layman, is to be taken in the first instance, and committed to prison till he has agreed about payment of the debt; and if the keeper of the prison do not receive him, he is to be answerable for the debt: a like power is given to the chancellor, if the debtor is not within the jurisdiction of the mayor. Within a quarter of a year after he is taken, his chattels and land (without confining it to burgages devisable, as the last act did) are to be delivered to him, that he may pay his debts by selling them; and such sale of his lands and tenements during the quarter of a year, for the discharge of his debts was declared good and effectual. If he did not make agreement about payment within the second quarter of a year, all his goods and lands are to be delivered to the creditor by a reasonable extent, *to hold them until such time as the debt is wholly*

be delivered to the extenders, so that he might have execution against them, and thus have the benefit of the statuts of Acton Burnel. And it was awarded by all the justices, that *fieri facias* should issue against the extenders upon the recognizance (*Year-book*, 40 *Edw. III.*, fol. 27; *et vide*, 44 *Edw. III.*, fol. 2; 2 *Hen. IV.*, fol. 17; 2 *Rich. III.*, and 15 *Hen. VII.*, fol. 15). If the conusee once agreed to the extent, he could not disagree afterwards (44 *Edw. III.*, fol. 2).

levied (*a*); and the debtor is still to continue in prison, and be kept on bread and water by the merchant. The merchant is to have such seisin in the lands and tenements delivered to him or his assignee as to be entitled to maintain a writ of novel disseisin, and re-disseisin, as if it was a gift of a freehold to him and his assigns, till the debt is paid. When the debt is paid, the land is to be restored, and the debtor delivered from prison. The statute directs that writs issued by the chancellor for taking the debtor should command the sheriff to certify the justices of one bench or the other what had been done therein, at a certain day; at which day the merchant is to appear, and there sue, if agreement is not made. If the sheriff returned *non inventus*, or that he was a clerk, then they proceeded against the goods and land, as before-mentioned. The creditor is to be allowed all damages, costs, and expenses. If there are sureties, they are to be proceeded against, as the principal debtor is.

It is ordained by the statute, that all lands that were in the hands of the debtor at the time of acknowledging the recognizance, even if given away since by feoffment, are to be delivered to the merchant; and after the debt paid, they are to return to the feoffee. Further, it was added by way of caution, that should the debtor or his sureties die, the merchant shall not take the body of his heir, but shall have his lands, in like manner as if the debtor was living. All persons might enter into recognizances under this act, except only Jews, to whom this statute was not to extend. There was a saving of the old method of acknowledging recognizances, which was to be practised as before. The writ to take the person recited the acknowledgment of the recognizance, and then commanded, *quòd corpus prædicti A. si laicus sit, capias, et in prisonâ nostrâ salvo custodiri facias, quousque de prædicto debito satisfecerit.*

This last statute may be considered as contributing to extend the power of alienating land. In the same sessions, as we shall see presently, any common creditor by judgment was empowered to take half the debtor's land in execution; but we see that, in favour of trade, a merchant who had resorted to this security might have the whole. A recognizance acknowledged with the formalities here prescribed, was in after times called *a statute merchant;* and a person who held lands in execution for payment of his debt, as hereby directed, was called *tenant by statute merchant.*

(*a*) If the land should be "extended" too low (or for too small a sum), the conusor could not have a re-extent, for he could tender the money and have his land again; and if the land was extended at too high a value, the conusee could not have re-extent, for he could pray that the extenders should have it; and they should answer according to the statute of Acton Burnel (the above act); but it ought to be at the first day of the return of the extent, for if he agreed to the extent, he could not refuse it (*Year-book*, 15 *Hen. VII.*, 14). And it was held that the conusee, under statute merchant or staple, should recover his costs, damages, and expenses (*Ibid.*) A statute merchant was extended, and the extent returned, and the conusee came and said that the lands were extended too high, and prayed that the extenders should have it according to the statute of Acton Burnel, and it was awarded (*Year-book*, 40 *Edw. III.*, fol. 21). In another case, the conusee complained that the land was valued too high, that is, at 3s. an acre, whereas it was only worth 1s. an acre (*Year-book*, 21 *Edw. III.*, 21).

CHAPTER X.

EDWARD I.

Origin of Estates-Tail—Regulation of the Eyre—Justices of Nisi Prius—Justices of Gaol-Delivery—Of Replevin—Of Accountants—Waste—Of Execution of Process—Of summoning Jurors—Of Essoins—Writ of Elegit—Bill of Exceptions—Scire Facias—Cui in Vita—Quod ei deforceat—Of Presentations to Churches—Admeasurements of Dower and Pasture—Writs in consimili Casu—Ejectment of Ward—Presentments of Jurors to be sealed—Rape—Statute of Winchester—Statute of Circumspecte Agatis.

THE most distinguished period of this king's reign is the thirteenth year, when great alterations were made in the law by several statutes. In this year we have the statute of Westminster the second, the statute of Winchester, the statute of merchants mentioned in the preceding chapter, and the statute of *circumspecte agatis*. Each of these is an important occurrence in the juridical history of this reign (*a*).

(*a*) The general legislation of the reign, and indeed of any other, may fitly be considered, first, as relating to the titles of transfer of land; and next, and especially, with reference to religion, or the church; and then as regarded the administration of justice. As regards the titles or transfers of land, this reign is remarkable for the attention given by the legislature to the subject of *fines*, which were used as a species of record or registration of a title or a transfer of title. The subject of fines is closely connected with that of recoveries, which only differed therefrom in that both, being founded on suits, or supposed suits for land, a fine was in accord entered into by the parties in cases, and a recovery was a judgment recovered by default. And both had this value that, being records of courts of law, they were preserved under the protection of the king's courts, and were not like private deeds, which might be lost or destroyed, a consideration of no small importance in times of constant turbulence and disturbance. These fines or recoveries were solemn records of titles or transfers of title; and there is abundant evidence in the reports and records of subsequent reigns that they were used as far back as the last reign for purposes of conveyance, or as permanent records of conveyance, the titles or limitations of land. Fines thus used, recording several successive limitations, are mentioned as of the time of Henry III. (*vide Year-books*), and see (*Bellewe's Cases, temp. Rich. II., Fines*). That recoveries were used for the purpose of transfer of land is apparent from one of the earliest statutes of this reign, that of Gloucester (6 *Edw. I.*, c. 11) against feigned recoveries, in which he to whom the freehold belonged caused himself to be impleaded by collusion and made default, or came into court, or gave it up; and the legal effect of a recovery is shown by another statute of the same reign (13 *Edw. I.*, st. 1, c. iv.) "that if a man had lost his land by default, he had none other recovery than by writ of right, which was not maintainable by any that could not claim of mere right as tenants for life or entail" (13 *Edw. I.*, s. 1), and that statute therefore provided that they might recover their estate by another writ than by a writ of right, which lay only for the owner in fee-simple. Thus, then, the effect of a recovery by default was, that those who were not parties or privies could recover in a real action according to their right, but then they were driven to such actions. The effect of a record was always that it bound parties or privies, and this applied to a fine as well as a recovery. And hence the subsequent statute (13 *Edw. I.*, c. 32) against feigned recoveries by religious

In discoursing of these statutes, we shall begin with the statute of Westminster the second. The first chapter of this statute is on the subject of some of those conditional estates of which so much was said in the last reign.[1] It is generally known by the name of the statute *de donis conditionalibus*. This act has occasioned more discussion than, perhaps, any parliamentary provision in the statute-book; and deserves a very particular consideration in this place. The design of it cannot be better understood than from a recital of its contents. It says, that where lands were given upon condition, as to a man and his wife, and the heirs begotten between them; with an express condition that, should the man and his wife die without heirs begotten between them, the land should revert to the donor or his heir: again, where land was given *in liberum maritagium* (which sort of gift, we know, had an implied condition, that, upon the death of the husband and wife without any heir begotten between them, the land should revert to the donor or his heirs): again, where land was given to a man *et*

Origin of estates-tail.

men to avoid the mortmain laws. Thence the statute *de donis* about the same time (13 *Edw. I.*, c. i.) passed against alienations of estates-tail, enacted that fines contrary thereto should be void, so that even the heirs could avoid them. It is observable that there is no prohibition of feigned recoveries to bar estates-tail, although the legislature were well aware that such recoveries were used, having already provided against them in the earlier statute of Gloucester. Then a later statute of the reign (18 *Edw. I.*, s. 4, c. i.) the statute as to the *modus levandi* fines, described the formalities of fines and declared, "And the cause wherefore such solemnity ought to be done in a fine is, because a fine is of so high a bar, of so great a force, and of so strong a nature that it concludeth not only such as be parties and privies thereto, and their heirs, but other people of the world, being of full age, and within the four seas, the day of the fine levied, if they make not their claim of their action within a year and a day." But this certainly was not carried out, for in the subsequent statute (27 *Edward I.*, c. i.) it was provided, that, as fines levied in the courts ought to and do make an end of all matters, and therefore are called fines, but *the parties and their heirs* had been admitted to defeat them by alleging that they or their ancestors were always seised of the land, it was provided that such exceptions should not be allowed in future. The tenor of these statutes strongly shows the extreme importance attached to these permanent records of titles or transfers of land; and their importance in such an age may easily be understood. Nevertheless, as times altered, and as the law became more firmly settled, the courts of law, in spite of the express provisions of these statutes, permitted persons, at first strangers, and then even the heirs, to defeat fines by showing that the parties to the fines had no estate in the land. The Year-books of Edward III. and *Bellewe's Cases, temp.* Richard II., contain numerous cases of fines defeated on that ground. On the other hand, a statute passed in this reign enabled parties to have executions upon fines without being put to a real action. It is remarkable that in the very statute of Westminster 2, in which fines to bar estates-tail were prohibited, the legislature made provision for the summary execution of fines (*St. of Westminster* 2, c. xlv.), reciting that of such things as he recorded before the judges and enrolled in their rolls, process of plea ought not to be made by summons, &c., as in cases of deeds out of court, and it provided that those things which were found enrolled before them of record or continued as fines, that thenceforth they should have such vigour that it shall not need to plead to them; but when the fine was levied within a year, the party should forthwith have execution, and if the fine was levied of a further time passed, there might be *scire facias* to call upon the opposite party to show cause why the fine should not be executed. The practical effect of this was, that although fines to bar estates-tail were prohibited (nothing being said against recoveries, which therefore, there is every reason to

[1] *Vide ante*, vol. i. 294.

hæredibus de corpore suo exeuntibus; it seemed hard, says the statute, to the donor and his heirs, that their will expressed in the gift should not be observed; for, says the act, in all the above cases the feoffees *post prolem suscitatam, et exeuntem ab ipsis*, have hitherto had a power to alien the land so given upon condition, and to disinherit their issue, contrary to the will of the donors, and the express form of the gift. And whereas, if such feoffees had no issue, and even if there had been any issue, which had afterwards died, the land ought, by the express form of the gift, to revert to the donor or his heir; yet the persons to whom such conditional gift had been made, used to infeoff others, and so bar the donors of their reversion; all which was in direct violation of the form of the gift.

These are the mischiefs of which the statute complains; and to remove them it ordains as follows: that thenceforward "*the will of the giver,*[1] *according to the form in the deed of gift manifestly ex-*

believe, continued to be used for that purpose), fines were invaluable as permanent records of the titles to land, and especially of the *limitations* of estates, of estates-tail or otherwise, which were thus placed upon record, and could at any time be executed without putting the party to the delay of a real action, unless defeated by showing that the parties had no estate in the land at the time the fine was levied. And so, in point of fact, fines continued to be used all through this reign and the ensuing reigns (as the reports and records of cases in subsequent reigns show); that is, continued to be used for the double purpose of effecting and of recording transfers of land, and placing upon record the titles to land, and the successive limitations to which it was subject. In point of fact, this was the way in which the titles to land were created, transferred, and recorded, and the country, by this system of fines, had the advantage of a system of registration of titles. With regard to recoveries, they were rather used for alienation, or for the alteration of titles and estates. And the use of fines and recoveries for these purposes formed the great features of the law of this period, so far as it related to landed property. The recovery was in form a recovery in a real action by default, and formed all the proceedings proper for such a cause—one of which was public proclamation. And therefore the statute as to the mode of levying fines required that they be openly read in court. The essence and substance of the proceedings were publicity and notoriety, as a means of notice to persons interested. And therefore all who did not come forward within a year and a day were barred. But as the tenants for the particular estate, as tenants in tail, often failed to protect the rights of the issue, it was thought right to provide that the issue should not be barred; and as in those turbulent times men were often deterred from coming forward, a statute of Edward III. provided that they might come forward at any time. The other head of law relating to the subject is the law of mortmain, which originated in this reign, and was directed against the acquisition of land by the church. The remaining great head of law and legislation in this reign is that which related to the administration of justice. All these matters will be found fully treated of by our author, but it was deemed that it would be of assistance and advantage to the reader to present this general review of the character and tendency of the legislation of the reign, so as to point out or suggest to his mind the connection and mutual illustration of these various heads or subjects of law and legislation.

[1] These words are taken from the translation in our statute-book. In the other parts of the statute, I have strictly adhered to the original; and the language, for that reason, will be found to vary from the common translations. The reader who has passed through the former part of this history, instead of a *deed of gift*, he would expect to hear of a *charter of donation*, and so indeed it ought to be. That it is absolutely necessary to adhere to the language of the time, in pursuing an inquiry like this, every one must know. A curious observation in the next page, upon the construction of this statute, is founded entirely on the expression, and would have been lost, if the common translation had been followed. The reader should be apprised that, from the time of this king, a conflict will inevitably arise between the old and new language of the law, and the victory will in the end be decided in favour of the latter.

pressed, shall be observed;" so that the person to whom such a conditional gift was made should not have power to alien, and prevent the land from *remaining* to his issue, or, upon failure of issue, to the donor or his heir (*a*). It was declared that the second husband of such woman should not claim any thing *per legem Angliæ*, in such conditional gift; nor the issue of such second husband claim anything by descent; but that immediately upon the death of a man and woman to whom land was so given, it should *revert* to their issue, or to the donor or his heir; so that the law, in this particular, as laid down both by Glanville and Bracton, was changed; and the opinion maintained by *Stephanus de Segrave* in the last reign was established.[1] These are the words of this famous law; the great object of which seems to have been to secure the then possessors of land in the power of making dispositions that were to endure to all eternity. The inclination showed by the courts to support the principle of this statute, and the construction they put upon it, soon promised to carry this intention into full effect.

The construction of the judges upon the wording and intention of this statute was, that the donee should no longer have a *fee conditional*, as before, but that the fee should be *entaillé*, cut, or divided, and he should have a *fœdum talliatum*. Indeed, this seems to have been foreseen by the makers of the act; for, in the same parliament, and before the statute could have been agitated in the courts of law, we find the term *fœdum talliatum*[2] as expressing an estate then existing in the law (*b*). It appears, that very early after the statute the judges had gone a great way in pursuing its intention; for they not only cut a fee tail out of a fee simple, but they again divided the fee tail: as for instance, if a person took land by purchase to him and his wife, and to the issue begotten by them in lawful matrimony, nothing would here accrue to the purchasers

(*a*) This plainly alludes to some power of alienation by the tenant in tail to prevent the land from *remaining* to the issue, as *well* as to alienations upon *failure* of issue. And it would appear that this was the alienation by fine or recovery. These modes of alienation being by matter of record, and in actions or suits at law, which were pursued with the same form as if real, and were not to be presumed to be fictitious, would bar the issue in tail as privies in estate; and even as against the donor and his heirs, whose right in reversion would only arise upon failure of the issue in tail, would have a certain effect and operation, putting him to a remote and contingent remedy. The present statute only alludes to *fines*, not recoveries.

(*b*) If land was given in tail, with warranty to donee, and his heirs, and assigns, and the donee aliened in fee and died without issue, the warranty would be a bar to a *formedon* for recovery by the recorder (*Year-book*, 46 *Edw. III.*, 4). It was said that at common law, if land was given to a man and the heirs of his body, or heirs male of his body; if he had issue, then it was a fee simple, for it was a fee simple at common law, though otherwise, since the statute of Westminster 2, c. i., and after issue had, the donee could at common law alien, but if he died without issue and had not aliened, then *formedon a reverter* lay (18 *Assize*, fol. 5). But after the statute, where the donee died without issue, the heir of the donor could recover (35 *Assize*, fol. 14), for it was adjudged an estate tail and not fee simple (*Ibid*). So, since the statute, the donee in tail had not fee simple, *sicut habuit prius*, but the fee simple remained

[1] *Vide ante*, vol. i. c. v. [2] Ch. 46.

but a freehold for their lives, and the *fee* to their issue: if they had no issue, the fee remained in the person of the donor till they had issue; and if the purchaser had no issue, or the issue failed, the land reverted to the donor.[1] In this construction they seemed entirely justified by the terms of the statute; for it speaks of the land not as *descending* to the issue, but as *remaining*[2] or *reverting;* and, notwithstanding the term *descendere* in the writ given by the act, it seems to consider the issue and the donor as in the same light. The numberless consequences which followed from the restriction imposed by this statute, furnish no small part of the discussion to which landed property afterwards became subject; as will be seen in the course of this history.

A remedy was ordained by this act for those who would avail themselves of the new regulation made by it. The following form of a writ was given: *Præcipe A. quod justè, &c. reddat B. manerium de F. cum suis pertinentiis, quòd C. dedit tali viro, et tali mulieri, et hæredibus de ipso viro et muliere exeuntibus, &c.* Or thus: *quòd C. dedit tali viro in liberum maritagium eum tali muliere, et quod post mortem prædictorum viri et mulieris, pædicto B. filio eorundem viri et mulieris descendere debeat per formam donationis prædictæ, ut dicit, &c.* Or thus: *quod C. dedit tali et hæredibus de corpore suo exeuntibus, et quod post mortem illius talis, prædicto B. filio prædicti talis descendere debeat per formam, &c.* The writ here given was for the issue, and was in after-times called a *formedon in discender.* There was no writ of *formedon in reverter*, as it has since been called, given by the statute; the writ whereby the donor might recover when issue fails, (says the act) being common enough in the chancery; though there is no mention of such a writ in Bracton. Lest the efficacy allowed by the law to a fine should prejudice the provisions hereby ordained, it was declared, that if a fine was levied of lands given in the above form, *ipso jure sit nullus,*[3] it should be void; and their heirs, or those to whom the reversion belonged, though they were of full age, within England, and out of prison, should not be under necessity to make their claim.[4] This is the whole of the statute *de*

with donor (*Year-book*, 5 *Hen. VII.*, 14). The effect of this statute may be explained thus by a case in the next reign. Before the statute, if tenant in tail made lease for life and then released, the issue would be bound in a writ of formedon; and so after the statute, where tenant in tail before the statute had made lease for life, and had then released his reversion in tail (*Year-book*, 44 *Edw. III.*, fol. 3). There the issue in tail brought a writ of formedon, and it was pleaded that the ancestor before the statute, leased for life, and then released also before the statute. And it was adjudged that as the lease and release were before the statute, the issue in tail were barred, although it was argued that the fee simple did not pass as the reversion was in tail; it appears to have been held otherwise, but it was implied that it would not be so if the lease and release were after the statute (4 *B.* 44 *Edw. III.*, fol. 3).

1 Britt. fol. 93.

2 An estate *ad remanentiam* in Glanville, signifies an estate in fee. Lib. vii. c. 1.

3 It may be worth remarking, that these very words are used by Bracton to express that a fine was void. *Vide ante*, vol. i. 479.

4 Ch. 1. *Vide ante*, vol. i. c. viii.

donis, to which we shall have frequent occasion to recur in the course of this work.

It has been seen[1] how the administration of intestates' effects came into the hands of the ordinary, who was bound, however, to do such things as the executors would have been liable to had there been a will. It seems, this part of his charge was not sufficiently considered by the bishop (*a*), and therefore the following declaration of the common law was made; namely, that the ordinary should be bound to answer the debts of the intestate, as far as the goods would go, in the same manner as the executors must have done.[2]

Executors could not, by the common law, have an action of account, for an account to be made to the testator, because an account was a matter that was considered as resting in privity between the two parties concerned: for which reason it was ordained that, for the future, they should have a writ *de compoto*, with the same process as the deceased would have been entitled to.[3]

The remainder of this statute consists of improvements in the administration of justice. These were very numerous and important; the change in the order and course of judicature, which was the grand object of Edward's reformation in the law, being principally effected by this statute (*b*). These regulations divide themselves into such as concerned the jurisdiction of courts, and

(*a*) The author, it is conceived, had not rightly apprehended the reason for the enactment, which was, by making it a matter of common law, cognisance to apply the rules of the common law as to debts, the proof of debts, their discharge, and the like; as to which there were various differences between the common law and the civil or canon law. So long as the matter was entirely of ecclesiastical cognisance, the rules of the canon law would be followed; but the effect of the statute was to impose a *statutable* duty on the ordinary; the performance of which would then be enforced by the courts of common law, according to rules of the common law. As regards the duty to pay the just debts of the deceased, there was no difference between the canon law and the common law; but as to what *constituted* debts, or as to the proof of debts, or the discharge of debts, there would often be a difference, and there was no reason why there should be any difference between the liability of the executor and administrator.

(*b*) Not, as has already been seen, from any *regard* for justice (for there never was a more rapacious, unscrupulous, and arbitrary sovereign), but simply (as already explained) because, being a sagacious prince, he was wise enough to perceive that the administration of justice might be made a source of revenue. Hence his legislation was directed to the establishment of royal courts, with a regular judicature and regular procedure; and to the transfer of business as much as possible from the old local popular tribunals to these royal courts; the suits in which, by means of fees and fines, became a fruitful source of profit to the crown. It is a curious and remarkable fact, that although the justices itinerant had been appointed to go circuits so long ago as the reign of Henry II. (or rather Henry I.), yet now we find under this king, justices in eyre, or of oyer and terminer, going only once in seven years. The reason has already elsewhere been mentioned, and is indeed indicated by the chapters in Britton relating to the subject, that these justices in eyre applied themselves far more carefully to fines and forfeitures than the administration of justice, and were regarded more as oppressors than protectors; and hence it was desired that they should come only once in seven years. One great head of their inquiries, and that to which it is believed they applied themselves more closely than any other, was as to franchises; the assumption of which, without proof of legal title, exposed the party

[1] *Vide ante*, vol. i. c. viii. [2] Ch. 19. [3] Ch. 23.

such as made any variation in the course of proceeding. We shall first speak of the former, in the order in which they were made.

The first of these relates to the proceedings at the eyre (*a*). There used to be proclamation made for the delivery of all writs by a certain day, after which no writ was to be received. Suitors trusting to this used to depart, when, by some connivance, writs would be received in their absence, and they lost their land by default. To prevent this, it was ordained that the justices in their eyres should appoint a time of fifteen days, or a month, more or less, according to the size of the county, within which the sheriff was to certify the chief justice of eyre, how many and what writs he had, and none was to be received after that; but all process issuing upon writs received after that was to be null and void. However, to this there were made several exceptions; first, that writs abated might, during the whole eyre, be amended: secondly, that writs of dower of the seisin of men who died within the summons of the eyre,[1] assizes *ultimæ præsentationis*, writs of *quare impedit*, of churches vacant within the aforesaid summons, should be received at any time before the departure of the justices: and lastly, that all writs of novel disseisin, at what time soever the disseisin was done, should be received in the eyre.

Regulation of the eyre.

This chapter makes a provision concerning the appointment of attorneys. At common law, the king might, by letters patent, or by writ under his seal, grant to any demandant or plaintiff, tenant or defendant, to make his attorney in any action, and command the judges to admit such person to be attorney; but now, by this act, for the quiet and good of his subjects, the king *de speciali gratiâ* granted that such as had lands in several shires where the eyre was held, and had a suit there, and were apprehensive that they might be sued in some other county, as before the justices of the benches of Westminster, or the justices *ad capiendas assisas*, or in any county before the sheriff, or in a court baron, might make their *general attorney* to prosecute and defend suits for them in the eyre: which

not only to forfeiture but fine. And every offence against the crown which would involve an amerciament or forfeiture was eagerly inquired into, as appears from several chapters in Britton. Hence it may easily be imagined that every possible excuse for non-attendance was taken advautage of.

(*a*) As to this in Britton's treatise, the king is represented as saying, "Et volons nous que justices errants, soient assignes oyer et terminer en chescun counte de vii. ans en vii. ans." . . . (fol. 1). And then there is a chapter, "De Eyres"—"Quant a nos venues et al eyres de nos justices, volons nous que general crie soit fait solempnement par les cytes et burghes par tout counte, que trestons les franks del counte et touts les mainpris del counte soient, a certein jour que contoigne xl. jours ou meyns devant nous ou ceux justices que serront nosmes en nostre maundement a eyrer en mesme counte, et touts ceux que ascune franchise cleyment en mesme counte soient mesme le jour davant nos ou les justices, et chescun monstre apertement, et des frischement par lettres queles franchises il clayme," &c.

[1] Lord Coke, 2 Inst. 377, construes *infra summonitionem itineris* to signify the space of forty days previous to the coming of the justices in eyre; but I am inclined to think it means, as in Bracton, the district within which the summons of the justices itinerant would run. *Vide ante*, vol. i. 346.

attorneys were to have authority to do all acts, till they were removed, and the plea determined; though they were not on that account to be excused from being put on juries and assizes before the justices.[1] By this parliamentary permission to make attorneys, the king gave up the fees that used to be paid for a special permission to appoint an attorney; and, in proportion, the carrying on a suit became less expensive and troublesome to the subject than it had been.[2]

The next provisions concerning judicature are c. 29 and 30. The former relates to justices *ad audiendum et terminandum*, or [3] of *oyer and terminer*, as they have since been usually called. Of these there is no mention in Bracton, though they are hinted at in a statute of the last reign (*a*). It was now enacted that a *writ* (for so *commissions* were called) *de transgressione ad audiendum et terminandum*, for hearing and determining any outrage or misdemeanour (for

(*a*) These commissions were substituted for the ancient commissions of the eyres or "itinera," and were in substance the same—the result being, when they became regular and settled by prescription and usage, to substitute our modern justices of assize for the old justices itinerant. The commission of oyer and terminer—a commission to "hear and determine," is in fact the most general form of a commission from the crown to administer justice; and it will comprise either civil or criminal matters. It, therefore, is the most comprehensive of the commissions under which judges of assize afterwards sat, and still continue to sit; and it is perhaps the most ancient kind of commission issued by the crown for the administration of justice. There is reason to believe that originally justice was administered under these general commissions very roughly and arbitrarily; but by degrees, as usage settled the general course of procedure all over the kingdom, that general course became established, as the course of the common law (though there were still variances of practice in the different counties), and a commission of oyer and terminer was understood to mean a commission to hear and determine according to the course of the common law. It is to be observed that in these commissions we see the earliest exercise and illustration of the great prerogative of the crown to administer justice; and it is only by usage or prescription that this prerogative is limited, apart from statute. It is not now (as Lord Coke says) competent to the crown to issue commissions, or to establish courts to administer justice in some new mode, except with the authority of parliament; because usage has long settled the terms and the import of these commissions. It has already been seen what, according to Bracton, were the commissions issued to the justices itinerant, which were substituted for those of the justices in eyre. As to these, it appears that their commissions were very general, and in that respect resembled commissions of oyer and terminer" (6 *Edw. II. Bro. Abr., Oyer and Terminer*, 91). Such commissions, before the present statute, could be issued to persons not lawyers or regular judges. Thus we find "a commission issued to Knevit, Thorpe, and Ludlow, knights, to hear and determine all manners of treasons, felonies, conspiracies, confederacies, damages, and grievances, done to the king and the people, whether at the suit of the king or of the party; and also of wards' marriages, escheats, and other things done to the king, in the counties of Essex, Hereford, Cambridge, Suffolk, and Norfolk, and by which they came to the hundred, and had their commissions read, and then called upon the bailiffs of each hundred, &c." (42 *Assize*, fol. 5). This is the course taken at this day, under the commissions of oyer and terminer at the assizes. The commissions issued out of Chancery, and were returned there; and, if required, sent into the king's bench (44 *Edw. III.* c. xliii. & xxxi.) If the commissions expired or were discontinued, the commissions came into the king's bench, as the supreme criminal court of the realm (*Ibid.*); and process would issue out of that high court if necessary (*Ibid.*) It was always held that justices, *i.e.*, judges of assize, could not be made, except by commission (*Mirror of Justice; Year-book*, 5 *Edw. IV.* 3).

[1] Ch. 10. [2] 2 Inst. 378.

[3] It may be remarked that *Oydor*, from *Oyr* to hear, in Spanish, signifies a *judge*.

transgressio is to be understood in a large sense) should not from thenceforth be granted before any justices, except justices of either bench and justices in eyre, *nisi pro enormi transgressione*, unless in cases of particular enormity, where it was necessary to provide speedy remedy, and the king in his special grace should think fit to grant it; nor was a writ *ad audiendum et terminandum*, to hear appeals, to be granted but in special cases, and for certain causes, at the king's command. But, that such appellees might not be detained in prison an unreasonable time, they were to have their writ *de odio et atiâ*, as ordained by *Magna Charta*.[1] It should seem, from the manner in which the writ of *oyer* and *terminer* is here spoken of, that it was usually issued at the suit and prayer of some person, and was not a general commission, like that of gaol-delivery; it used also, one should think, to be directed to private persons, whose names were inserted by the direction of the party suing it out. A writ of *oyer* and *terminer* might be superseded under this statute, *quia non enormis transgressio, &c.*

This is followed by the statute of *nisi prius*, as it has since been called. It will be unnecessary to recapitulate the account formerly given and so frequently recurred to, of the order of judicature, both as it stood at common law, and as it was altered by *Magna Charta*, and subsequent usage[2] (*a*). In further reformation thereof, the following regulation was now made. It was ordained, in the first place, that there should be assigned two justices sworn, before whom, and them only, should be taken all assizes of novel disseisin, mortauncestor, and attaints (*b*). These

Justices of *nisi prius*.

(*a*) Except to observe that ordinarily, and apart from statutable regulation, a cause would be tried in the court in which it was brought, and thus, if an action were brought in the *curia regis*, the parties upon appearance would commence their pleading (which was by parol), and when this came to an issue, that issue would be tried in the same court, and might be tried at once. But as by Magna Charta common pleas, *i.e.*, pleas (or suits) between party and party, could not follow the person of the king, but must be brought in a court fixed in some place, which, by usage, was at Westminster, it followed that, except as to courts of assize, &c. (as to which there was a special clause, that they should be tried in their counties), all causes in the superior courts could be tried at Westminster. The inconvenience of this would be manifest, and led to the practice of sending the records of the cases for trial into the counties where they arose. It seems that, notwithstanding Magna Charta, suits between party and party still continued to be brought in the king's bench. "Assize was taken in *banco regis* in Suffolk, and then the court was removed to Westminster, and yet the court proceeded and awarded the assize, and tried the issue by *nisi prius* in Suffolk (19 *Assize*, fol. 4). So again, if assize was taken in *banco regis* in the county where the court sat, and before it was determined, the court was removed into another county, yet the assize should not cease, but be tried at *nisi prius*; notwithstanding the statute (Magna Charta), which said that assizes should be taken in their proper counties (15 *Assize*, fol. 5). And if an assize was brought in the common bench, of land in Middlesex, and the court was removed, the issue should be tried at *nisi prius*, and it was a case out of the statute (8 *Edw. IV.* 16).

(*b*) Commenting on this, Brooke says, "Note, that by the statute of Westminster 2, c. 30, two justices can take an assize, and try issues of *nisi prius*, of pleas (or suits) in either bench (*i.e.*, in the king's bench or common bench), unless it was a matter of great weight (*nisi magna indigiat examinatio*), and then it should be determined *in banco*, unless both parties prayed that it should be before two justices of the court,

[1] Ch. 29. *Vide ante*, vol. i. c. v. [2] *Ibid.*

justices were to associate to themselves one or two of the discreetest knights of the county into which they came, and to take the before-mentioned assizes and attaints, at most, three times in the year; that is, between the *quindena* of St John the Baptist and the gule of August, that is, the feast of St Peter *ad vincula*, being the first of August; then between the feast of the exaltation of the holy cross, that is, the fourteenth of September, and the octave of St Michael; then between the Epiphany, that is, the sixth of January, and the feast of the Purification of the blessed Mary.[1] These justices were, in every county, before their departure, to appoint the day of their return, that every one might know of their next coming: they were to adjourn assizes from term to term, if the taking of them was deferred by vouching to warranty, by essoin, or by default of recognitors: and if they saw it would be proper for assizes of mortauncestor, when respited by essoin or voucher, to be adjourned into the bench, they were to send the record with the original writ before the justices of the bench; and when the plea had proceeded as far as to the caption of the assize, then the justices of the bench were to remand the record, with the original writ, back to the former justices, before whom the assize should be taken. It was ordained, that the justices of the bench should give four days, at least, in the year in assizes of the above kind, before the said justices assigned, in order to spare expense and trouble.

Thus far the statute provides concerning assizes, which was nothing more than a modification of the institution of justices of assize by *Magna Charta*. It then goes on thus: Besides the above, inquisitions to be taken of trespasses which were in suit before the justices of both benches (unless it was an enormous trespass that required a more[2] solemn inquiry) were to be determined before these justices; as were also inquisitions arising in other pleas depending in both benches, where the issue was of easy examination; as an entry or seisin, or any one single point which was to be tried. But it ordains, that inquests, where great and numerous points were to be tried, which required much examination, should be taken before the justices of the bench, unless both parties joined in praying that the inquest might be taken before *aliquibus de societate*, some associated in the commission, *cùm in partes illas venerint;* which, however, was never to be done in future but by two justices, or one justice, together with a knight of the county, who should be agreed upon by the parties.

or one justice and one knight. And the statute *De finibus* is to the same effect, and so the statute of York, save that it may be before one justice of the place where the plea is, associating to him one prudent man, &c. And by the statute of 2 Edward III. c. 19, a *nisi prius* can be granted in a plea of land, as well at the prayer of the demandant as of the tenant, according to the statute of York. And by the statute 14 Edw. III. c. 15, *nisi prius* can be taken before two, so that one shall be a justice of one of the benches, or the chief baron, or a sergeant-at-law, &c. (*Bro. Abr. Nisi Prius*, 37).

[1] For these feasts and seasons, and the relation they bore to the terms, *vide* vol. i. c. viii., the scheme of *dies communes in banco.*

[2] *Vide ante*, c. ii.

To carry the provision of this act into execution, it was moreover ordained, that no inquest should be taken before any of the justices of the bench, unless a certain day and place was appointed in the county, in presence of the parties, and the day and place inserted in a judicial writ, in these words: *Præcipimus tibi, quòd venire facias coram justitiariis nostris apud Westm. in octabis sancti Michaelis,* NISI *talis et talis tali die et loco ad partes illas venerint, duodecim, &c.* (*a*). Thus the inquest was to be taken at Westminster only upon failure of its being taken in the county; and the trial in the county was in later times, from the clause in the writ, said to be at *nisi prius;* though in the above *venire* given by the statute, the word *prius* is not inserted, as it now is, and indeed usually was at that time; for this clause of *nisi*, or *nisi prius*, was not a new thing. In the reign of Henry III., when it seemed to be arbitrary and promiscuous whether certain writs should be tried at Westminster or in the eyre, we find some of them had this clause, NISI *justitiarii* PRIUS *ad partes illas venerint,*[1] *&c.*

Inquests taken in this manner were to be returned into the bench, where judgment was to be given, and the inquest enrolled; and inquests taken otherwise than in the above way were to be held void, except that assizes of *darrein presentment,* and inquests of *quare impedit,* should be determined in their own county, before one justice of the bench and one knight, at a day and place certain appointed in the bench, whether the defendants consented or not; and there the judgment was to be given immediately. It was further directed, that all justices of the benches in their itinera should have clerks to enrol pleas pleaded before them, as they had been used in time past. It was ordained that justices assigned to take assizes should not compel jurors to say precisely whether it was disseisin or not, so as they showed the truth of the fact, and prayed the assistance of the justices; if they, however, of their

(*a*) Originally, it is to be observed, an action was triable only in the court where it was brought. It was provided by Magna Charta that assizes of novel disseisin and mort d'ancestor, the most common remedies at that time, should, instead of being tried at Westminster, in the superior court, *i.e.*, of common pleas, in which they were brought, (the charter making that court fixed at Westminster, by enacting that common pleas or suits should not follow the king), be taken in their proper counties, and for this purpose justices were to be sent into every county once a year, to take these assizes there. These local trials being found very convenient, it was decreed the system should be applied, not only to assizes, but to other actions; and it is thus provided in the above statute that the juries should be summoned at Westminster only in the event of the trial not previously taking place in the county where the action arose. The venire or court to summon the juries was under the statute framed in this form: "Præcipimus tibi, quòd venire facias coram justitiariis nostris apud Westm., nisi talis et talis tali die et loco ad partes illas venerint, duodecim," &c. This *nisi prius* clause was until lately retained in the proceedings of record; and it is the above enactment expressed by a subsequent one (14 *Edw. II.* c. 16) which authorises at the present day a trial before the justices of assize when of the superior court, and gives it the name of a trial at *nisi prius*; though in reality the enactment as well as the form are obsolete, because the trials now, by reason of the rules as to venire, must take place in the county appointed for the trial, which is (unless changed by order of the court) the county where the matter arose.

[1] *Vide ante,* vol. i. c. viii.

own accord would say generally, that it was or was not disseisin, their verdict was to be taken at their peril (*a*).[1] This caution

(*a*) This reign was the era at which trial by jury became firmly established, and therefore all that related to it became of great importance; and accordingly we find, in this reign, legislation on every part of it, from the summoning of jurors to their final verdict. Further on, will be found a statute as to the qualifications of jurors; and there is the enactment as to bills of exceptions, to which the present is introductory. Britton, who wrote in this reign, enters fully into the whole system of trial by jury. He speaks of challenges, and the impanelling of twelve jurors, who are to be sworn to speak the truth upon the issue, and the justice is to inform them of the nature of the question, and the allegations on each side, though nothing is said of evidence offered to the jurors; for at this time they gave their verdicts on their own knowledge, and thereupon they are to go by themselves and consider the matter; and if they cannot agree, others are to be added. "Et si ils ne purront accorder, soient autres mys en la plus forte partie des jurors, si les parties le vouillent, et si non, *soit juge encontre celuy que ne le voudera* (330). And if the jury could not give any verdict at all, the plaintiff failed. There were many modes of trial; and from various parts of Britton, it appears that the general principle was this, that if the matter, from its nature, *might* be in the knowledge of others, at all events, of neighbours, the proper course was trial by jury. In cases from their nature secret, and between the parties, as in most cases of debt, wager of law was allowed—*i.e.*, trial on the oath of the defendant and compurgators. This was derived from the ancient Saxon system of compurgators—the origin of trial by jurors; for the difference between the compurgators and jurors was only this, at first, that the former swore to their belief, from their knowledge of the defendant, and jurors gave their verdicts on their belief, of their own knowledge, as to the facts of the case. Hence wager of law was allowed in cases where, from their nature, jurors could not have knowledge. Thus, under the head of debt, Britton enters fully into the course of procedure, and describes when it shall be wager of law and when trial by jury: "Et si il tende taille ou suyt et la suyte soit trouve accordaunte, adonques purra il defendre la det par sa ley;" whence it appears, that "the suit," or "secta," meant the compurgators, with whom the defendant waged his law—*i.e.*, denied the debt upon oath. So the defendant might declare the deed not to be his, because he had lost his seal, and had made public outcry about it at the time. "Et sur ceo soit enquys la vente par la visne ou la fait duist estre fait et solone le verdit du pays soit celuy que serra trouve mentour juge a la prison et puny par fyn." Whence it appears, that if the matter pleaded was one which, in its nature, would be within the knowledge of the county or vicinage, it would be tried by the jury *per patriam*. "Et si le fait ne fuit mye fait les nostre poer si que la vente ne purra estre enquys par nous, soit la prouve abounde ou pleyntyfe, essent que si il passe aver par bons tesmoyncs les contractes, soit juge pur le pleyntyfe: et celes *exceptiones eyent* lieu en *nostre court devaunt nos justices* car en countes ne en autres petites courts, ne port nul home foreyn contractes prover sil soit dedit." Whence the advantage of suing in the king's court is pointed out, in that it had a general jurisdiction. If the debtor could not deny his debt, he was to be mulct in debt and damages, and to make satisfaction to the plaintiff and to *the king*, by amercement for his wrongful detention of the debt. The chapter concludes by stating, that other personal actions could be brought before the sheriff by writ of *justicies*, as covenant or account, or detention of deeds, &c., and of nuisances, "que voillent estre pledes par destresse de chateux et par damages, et termines *par jures*." If, on a trial by jury, they could not say one way or the other, the plaintiff failed, as it was for him to prove his case. "Et si les jurours ne sevent veut prouncier la vente ne rien del fait, si remeyne la seisin al tenaint, et le plaintiff en la mercy, pour ceo que il n'ad mye prouve sa entente et sa pleynte (330). It was only in case of wilful and perverse misconduct on the part of the jurors that they were to be coerced by starvation into a verdict. "Et si ils ne voillent le verdict pronouncer en ceo cas pour favour de une des parties ou pur autre enchesun, donques soient, en fermes sauns manger et sauns beyver si la que ils eyent lour verdit pronouncere." Upon their verdict followed judgment, unless there was any reason for doubt. This is treated of under the next head—jugement: "Come ils serront de un accord, tauntost voysent a la barre devaunt les justices, a doner lour verdit, et solone lour verdit soit jugemeut rendu pour un des parties si

[1] Ch. 30.

seems to have been in affirmance of the common law (*a*), and was inserted only to guard jurors from being driven into the danger of an attaint.[1]

This was the manner in which the old appointment of justices was reformed, and that of justices of *nisi prius*, as they were called in after-times, was first made. This latter received afterwards several alterations; some of which were made in this reign. As these contribute to show the history of this important improvement in our judicial polity, it will be proper to mention them now, and bring the whole of this subject into one point of view. It seems, the justices of gaol-delivery, either not returning so frequently into the country as was to be wished, or the persons filling that office not executing it as they ought, it was enacted by stat. 27 Edward I., stat. 1, c. iii., that justices

Justices of gaol delivery.

nul doute ne soit ne nul difficulte par quoy mester soit de examiner par les jurours ou par autres ou de delayer jugement jesque a eu autre jour issent que en le mien temps pussent les justices estre assise, et conseilles quo est soit mieux a faire; si les justices nequedent en verdits soient dotous, et ces jurours ne sout suffisament examines et sorent a les trop avaunt en jugement par les reason de ascune mot ou de ascune reson que puit aver et double entendement en tiels cas tient lieu cele certification par mesure les justices ou par autres. Mes plus sure est as justices d'examiner biens les resons des juraurs essent que ils pussent rendre bon jugement et seyn." And if the verdict was for the plaintiff (in disseisin, for instance), it was to be enforced if he had claimed too much; and if so, he was to be amerced for his excessive claim: "En tiel cas il est amerceable pour sa outrance demaunde" (334). Then follows what is very characteristic of the age. It is to be observed, that the system of trial by jury, in its infancy, viz., that the jurors gave their verdicts of their own knowledge, was a cause of constant difficulty, because, although in very early times, when transactions were few, simple, and open (as feoffments, with livery of seisin, or contracts of sale in markets, and the like), the jurors, coming from the vill, might have knowledge of them, it was otherwise as population increased, and men's affairs grew more numerous, and, from their nature, often secret; as, for instance, private contracts or conveyances. In such cases, the jurors would often be entirely at fault, knowing nothing of the matter; and hence, by degrees, the necessity for hearing *evidence* of sworn witnesses was recognised. But this was only gradually and partially established, and in the meantime much difficulty was often met with, which was dealt with in the way described by Britton: by examination of the jurors, or addition to the jury, until they were agreed. Another mode resorted to was that of returning a special verdict upon the facts *proved*, which relieved the jury of responsibility, both as to the facts and the law. As to the facts, they were liable to attaint for a false verdict; and they were often in this difficulty, that they did not and could not know the truth of a fact from their own knowledge; and yet it was not *given in evidence*, one way or the other; and so, if they did not find it, they might be liable, if it was a fact of an open nature, such as a feoffment; and yet, if they *did* find it, having no evidence of it, their verdict might be false, and they be liable to an attaint. Hence, in such cases, the common law allowed them to give their verdict specially, by setting forth the *facts proved* before them; and thus they escaped the difficulty as to facts of which they could and could not take cognizance without actual evidence, and at the same time also avoided any difficulty as to matters of law, by referring the matter to the court, who gave judgment on the special verdict, and then the verdict became that of the court; for the judgment went on *their view* of the facts, not on the view of the jury (43 *Assize*, 41; 38 *Assize*, fol. 9; 29 *Assize*, fol. 40; 21 *Assize*, fol. 28; 43 *Assize*, fol. 1). Thus, therefore, special verdicts, as Lord Coke says, arose at common law; and the present statute only protected the right of the jurors to give such verdicts.

(*a*) This, in the statute, comes immediately before the chapter as to bills of exception, *vide post*, where it is noticed in that, its proper place.

[1] *Vide ante*, vol. i. c. viii., &c.

assigned to take assizes in every county, after the assizes so taken, should remain together, if they were laymen; and if one of them was a clerk (which was very often the case), then one of the discreeter knights of the county being associated with him who was a layman, they two by the king's writ should deliver the county gaol, as well within liberties as without, as had been done in gaol deliveries formerly, and then proceed to make inquiry of, and punish sheriffs for breaches of the statute 3 Edward I. c. xv., concerning bail and mainprise. Thus were justices of assize and *nisi prius* constituted also justices of gaol delivery.

The times for taking inquests, and the persons who were qualified to be justices of *nisi prius*, were altered by the next chapter of this act, in the following way. Inquests and recognitions determinable before justices of either bench, were by this new law to be taken in time of vacation, before any justice of the same bench where the suit depended, to whom was to be associated one knight in the county where the inquest was taken; though in this, as in the former act, there was an exception of inquests that required great examination. This statute further impowered the justices, in taking inquests, to do that which appeared to them most expedient for the good of the realm, *non obstante* the statute of *nisi prius.*[1]

Further, by the statute *for persons appealed*, 28 Edward I. stat. 2, it was ordained, that where such justices assigned to take assizes and deliver gaols, found any provors in the gaol, the sheriff of the county where the persons appealed were resident should be commanded by the king's writ, upon testimony of such justices, to take the persons appealed, and bring them before the justices, where they should answer. If they would put themselves *super patriam*, the justices were to issue a judicial writ to the sheriff of the county where the felony was committed, *quòd venire faciat* an inquest of the county, to appear before the justices of the place where the provor was then detained.

Thus stood the jurisdiction of these justices at the end of this reign. This institution was found to be a great improvement on the eyre; and, as it received several alterations in the two following reigns to render it still more beneficial and convenient, it soon made that ancient establishment less necessary, and by degrees wholly superseded it. The variety in the taking of inquests, sometimes *in banco*, and sometimes in the county, as was the practice in the last reign, no longer subsisted;[2] but the whole was reduced to one uniform system.

While the superior tribunals were thus ascertained, the excesses committed by inferior courts in extending their jurisdiction, were repressed by an act[3] which gave treble damages against sheriffs, and other bailiffs or lords, who procured suits to be maliciously brought against persons, without any cause of action, in the county

[1] Ch. 4. [2] *Vide ante*, vol. i. c. viii. [3] Ch. 36.

hundred, and other courts. Among other regulations about inferior jurisdictions, a check was imposed upon the judicial authority assumed by certain persons appointed by the Hospitallers and Templars to be their *conservatores privilegiorum:* these were enjoined not to presume to entertain suits of matters belonging to the king's court.[1]

Thus far were provisions made for ascertaining the bounds of judicature, and securing a regular access to courts of different kinds. There were many alterations made in the old remedies, which tended to render the former method of proceeding more easy and effectual. Others, wholly of a new kind, were contrived for ordering a course of redress in cases not already provided for: these consisted chiefly in new writs, upon which real actions were founded, applicable to various purposes. We shall first speak of the improvement made in the remedies at common law, and then of those that were entirely new.

Of replevin.

The next chapter to that, *De donis conditionalibus*, provides a remedy in three cases of suits, *de vetito namio*, which were thought great grievances. When a lord distrained for services, and the tenant replevied either with writ or without, and upon the plaint being made in the county or other inferior court having jurisdiction *de vetito namio*, he avowed the taking to be lawful and just, the tenant might, as we have seen, disclaim any tenure between them; whereupon, as the county could not try the tenure, there was an end of the suit, as far as it could be maintained in that court, and the distrainer would be *in misericordiâ*, and it was not in the power of the court to inflict any penalty on the tenant for disclaiming the tenure.[2] This was one defect, which it was intended to remedy by the following provision. It was ordained that, in future, where lords could not, in the like case, obtain justice against their tenants in the county or other inferior court, they might, as soon as they had been attached, have a writ *ad ponendam loquelam coram justiciariis*, before whom alone justice could be substantially done to such lords; and in the writ of *pone* was to be inserted this clause of removal, *Quia talis distrinixit in fœdo suo pro servitiis, et consuetudinibus sibi debitis, &c.* This allowance of a *pone* to the defendant, says the statute, is no prejudice to the rule of the common law, that forbids[3] any suit *poni coram justitiariis* at the motion and prayer of a defendant; for though, at first sight, the tenant seems to be the plaintiff, and the lord defendant, yet, when it is considered that the lord has distrained, and sues for his services and customs in arrear, he appears rather in the light of a plaintiff. As a rule to the justices to know on what seisin a lord should be permitted to avow a distress upon his tenant, it was agreed and enacted, that a distress should lie of seisin of a man's ancestor or predecessor, *à tempore* that a writ of novel disseisin would run.

[1] Ch. 43. *Vide ante*, c. ix. [2] *Vide* vol. i. c. viii. [3] *Ibid.*

A second inconvenience in cases of distress was, that, after replevying his cattle, the tenant would sell or *eloin* them, as it was called, so as effectually to prevent their being returned to the lord, if the judgment of the court happened to be for a return. To remedy this it was provided, that, in future, the sheriff or his bailiff should, before he made delivery of the cattle, take not only pledges *de prosequendo*, as had been always usual (and indeed the proceeding was thence called *replegiare*), but also pledges *de averiis retornandis*, for the returning the cattle, if a return should be adjudged. If pledges were taken in any other way than this, the person taking them was to answer himself for the value of the cattle; and the lord might have a writ against him, *quòd reddat ei tot averia*, or *tot catalla* (*a*), if the bailiff could not make the amends, his principal was to be liable.

A third inconvenience was, that when a return of the cattle was adjudged to the distrainor, the tenant would again replevy them; but when the lord appeared in court, he would make default, and consequently a return of the cattle would again be adjudged to the lord; and so it might happen several times, to the harrassing of the lord, and the utter contempt of the king's court. To remedy this, it was ordained, that, after judgment for return of the cattle, the sheriff should be commanded by a judicial writ, *quòd returnum habere faciat de averiis*, and therein should be inserted a clause, commanding him not to deliver them again without a writ making mention of the judgment passed by the justices (which could not be but by a writ issuing out of the rolls of the justices before whom the plea was depending); and when the tenant applied to the justices in such case for a new replevin of his cattle, it was to be by a judicial writ commanding the sheriff, *quòd captâ securitate de prosequendo, et etiam de averiis* (or *cattallis*) *retornandis, vel eorum pretio, si returnum adjudicetur, &c.*, since called a writ of *second deliverance*. Upon this the sheriff was to make deliverance of the cattle that were returned; and to attach the distrainer to appear on a certain day before the justices, where the plea was to be heard. If the person replevying should make default, or a return should on any other account be adjudged, in this second replevin, the distress was ever after to remain *irreplevisable;* saving, however, a new distress for any new cause.[1] The writ of *second deliverance* is similar to one of the same kind used in Bracton's time,[2] called a *second caption*, though that was, as it should seem, an original writ. Indeed there is no mention in Bracton of any decisive effect that writ of *second caption* had, more than the writ of replevin; and the making the cattle *irreplevisable* seems entirely a regulation of this statute.

(*a*) Upon this it was held that if the sheriff took *insufficient* pledges he was liable as though he had taken no pledges; a remarkable instance of judicial construction of a statute according to its object and spirit (*Year-book*, 2 *Hen. VI.*, 15).

[1] Ch. 2.

[2] *Vide*, vol. i. c. viii.

Of accountants.

The proceeding against accountants was rendered more strict in all cases of servants, bailiffs, chamberlains, and all manner of receivers who were bound *ad compotum reddendum* (a). It was ordained,[1] that when the lord of servants of that kind assigned them *auditores compoti*, auditors of account, and they were found in arrears, their bodies should be arrested, and they should be sent, on testimony of such auditors, and delivered to the next gaol of the king in those parts, there to be kept by the sheriff or gaoler *in ferries, et sub bonâ custodiâ*, at their own expense, till they satisfied all arrears. If a person so delivered to custody should complain that the auditors had charged him with receipts which never came to his hands, and had not allowed him reasonable disbursements, and could find friends who would become *manucaptors* for him, and undertake to bring him before the barons of the exchequer, he was to be delivered to them. Further, the sheriff, who had custody of him, was to *scire faciat* the lord to appear at a certain day before the barons of the exchequer, with his rolls and tallies by which he made his account; and in the presence of the barons, or auditors whom they should assign, the account was to be rehearsed, and justice done between the parties. If the receiver should be found in arrears, he was to be sent to the Fleet Prison.[2] Upon this clause was framed the writ called *ex parte talis,* for the person imprisoned to bring the inquiry before the court of exchequer.

Thus far of a particular method of proceeding with accountants. It was further ordained generally, in like cases of account, that if the accountant fled, and would not come to account, he was, according to the statute of Marlbridge,[3] to be distrained, if he had anything whereof distress could be made, *ad veniendum corum justiciariis ad compotum suum reddendum ;* and if upon appearing he was found in arrear, and could not pay, he was to be committed to gaol, as before-mentioned. If he fled, and it was certified by the sheriff that he was *non iuventus*, he was to be demanded[4] from county to county, till he was outlawed. It was moreover declared, that persons imprisoned for such matter should not be replevisable, and the sheriff was enjoined not to permit them

(a) By the statutes there was a *capias ad computandum,* an arrest, to compel the party to account, and if he would not account he was condemned in the whole amount of the receipts (*Year-book,* 41 *Edw. III.*, fol. 3). And the auditors could commit the party to prison (45 *Edw. IV.*, fol. 14), that is, to compel payment of the arrears ; but this imprisonment, which was for a specific time, was no satisfaction of the debt, for which the plaintiff could still sue to execution (27 *Hen. VI.*, 8). It was a cumulative or additional remedy which was thus provided by the statute, in favour especially of mercantile debts. After arrest the account was taken, and the certificate of the auditors filed in court (21 *Hen. VI.*, 26). In the *Mirror* this statute is objected to on several grounds, that it gives the remedy only to the master ; and that auditors are assigned without the assent of the servant; that the auditors are not bound to allow anything but at their pleasure without punishment; that recovery is ordained against the servant, and not the surety or the goods; and that there was no check or control on the auditors (*Mirror*, c. v., s. 2).

[1] Ch. 11. [2] Gaola de Fleta (21 Hen. VI. 26). [3] *Vide ante*, c. viii. [4] *Exigatur.*

to go at large, either upon a writ of *replegiare* or otherwise, without the assent of the lord, on pain of answering to him for the damages he had sustained by such servants, according to the amount he could make out *per patriam*, to be recovered in an action of debt. If the gaoler could not make amends himself, his principal was to be liable (*a*). Thus was the process in an action of account become more effectual. We have before noticed that this action was allowed to executors by another chapter of this statute.[1]

A notion it seems had prevailed, that the old writ *de prohibitione vasti*,[2] which issued in cases of waste, required the parties to answer only for waste done subsequent to the writ. To prevent this mistake, this writ of prohibition was wholly taken away by statute;[3] and there was substituted in its place, in all cases of waste, a writ of summons; by which the party complained of was to be summoned to answer for waste done at any time. If he did not appear upon the summons, he was to be attached, and, after the attachment, distrained; and if he did not appear after the distress, the sheriff was to be commanded, *quòd assumptis secum duodecim, &c., in propriâ personâ*, he should go to the place wasted, and make inquiry of the waste, and return the inquisition; and upon that inquisition they were to proceed to judgment, as directed by the first statute of Westminster, ch. 21.[4] It was in another chapter[5] ordained, that when two or more had a wood, a turbary, a fishery, or the like, in common, in which neither knew what was his several right, and one of them committed waste against the will of the others, in such case an action of waste should lie; and the defendant, when judgment was to pass, should have his election to take his share in a certain part to be assigned by the sheriff, and the view of his neighbours chosen and sworn for this purpose; or to take nothing in future from the said common but what his parceners would allow. If he chose to take his share, it was to be allotted him in the place wasted. The writ in this case begun, *Cùm A. et B. teneant boscum pro indiviso, B. fecit vastum, &c.*

Waste.

In favour of infants it was provided, that if they were eloigned, and so prevented from appearing in person, their next friends

(*a*) Upon this a liberal construction was placed which very much enlarged the scope of the enactment. It was held that by the equity of the statute debt should be against the gaoler upon judgment in any other action in case of an escape out of custody (*Year-book*, 15 *Edw. IV.*, 20). This is a remarkable illustration of the principle often laid down in the construction of these ancient statutes—viz., that remedial statutes are to be construed as largely as possible so as to extend them to all cases within "the mischief." Thus it was laid down that a statute made for common remedy for a general mischief shall be taken by equity (*Year-book*, 11 *Hen. IV.*, 76). Thus the statute of 9 *Edw. III.*, c. v., said that the executor who first came by distress should answer, and it was applied to him who first came by *capias*, *quod nota et hoc videtur per un equitie* (24 *Edw. III.*, 48). (So on the statute *West.* 1, c. xxxix.; 40 *Assize*, fol. 2. So 7 *Hen. VI.*, 7, and 3 *Hen. VII.*, 2.)

[1] *Vide ante*, c. ix. [2] *Ibid.* vol. i. c. viii. [3] Ch. 14.
[4] *Vide ante*, c. ix. [5] Ch. 22.

might be admitted to sue for them in all cases where the infants could maintain an action.[1] The eloignment has been considered only as an instance stated for an example, and the statute has always been construed as giving a permission in all cases for infants to appear by their next friend; which, however, is nothing more than a confirmation of the common law.

Several regulations were made respecting process. Sheriffs used to appoint bailiffs to make distresses, who were not known to be regular officers. This was sometimes done in order to tempt persons to make resistance, and incur the penalty of contempt of the law. Thus was it made the means of extortion; but to prevent it in future it was ordained, that distresses should not be made but by bailiffs sworn and known; and that persons convicted of distraining otherwise, should restore damages to the party grieved in an action of trespass, and also be punished as for an offence against the king.[2]

Of execution of process.

The execution of process by sheriffs was regulated by another chapter.[3] The course of justice was much impeded by the neglect of sheriffs in making return of writs, and in making false returns. To avoid such obstacles to justice, if possible, it was directed, that persons who apprehended the negligence of sheriffs, should deliver their writs *in pleno commitatû*, or *in retro commitatû*, as it was called (which it seems was a continuation of the county court, after the hearing of causes, for collecting the king's money and other business), and that a billet should be taken from the sheriff, or under-sheriff, containing the names of the plaintiff and defendant in the writ, with the day on which the writ was delivered, and that at his request the seal of the sheriff or under-sheriff should be affixed in testimony thereof; but if the seal was refused, the testimony of knights and other credible persons present was to be taken, and their seal affixed. After this, if the sheriff did not return the writ, and complaint was made thereof to the justices, a judicial writ was to go to the justices of assize, to make inquiry, by those who were present at the delivery of the writ, what they knew of the delivery; and if it appeared, upon return of such inquisition, that the writ was delivered, damages were to be adjudged to the party grieved, in proportion to the subject of the action, and the inconvenience incurred. The same course was also to be taken when the sheriff returned, that the writ came too late to be executed.

Sheriffs sometimes returned, *mandavi ballivo*, that they had commanded the bailiff of a certain liberty, who had done nothing therein; and then they would name some liberty, which, in truth, had no return of writs. To correct this, it was ordained that the treasurer and barons of the exchequer should deliver to the justices a roll of all the liberties, in every county, that had the return of writs. If a sheriff returned that he commanded the

[1] Ch. 15. [2] Ch. 37. [3] Ch. 39.

bailiff of a liberty not contained in that roll he was punished as a disheritor, says the statute, of the king. But if he returned that he had commanded the bailiff of some liberty inserted therein, he was then commanded, *quòd non omittas propter, prædictam libertatem,* but to execute the writ, *scire faciat* the bailiffs to appear, and say why they did not execute the king's writ. If they came and acquitted themselves, by saying they were not required so to do, the sheriff was to be condemned both to the lord of the liberty and to the party to the suit, who had suffered by the delay. If the bailiffs did not appear at the day, or did not on their appearance acquit themselves in the above way, in every subsequent judicial writ, through the whole action, there was to be the same clause of *non omittas.*

Another instance in which sheriffs frequently failed, was in executing the clause *de exitibus, &c.*, for levying issues; sometimes returning that there were none, or small; and sometimes saying nothing at all of issues. To such return, therefore, it was now ordained, the plaintiff might *offerat verificare* that the sheriff could answer for larger issues; upon which a judicial writ was to go to the justices of assize to make inquiry, in presence of the sheriff, if he pleased to be there, for what issues he could answer, from the date of the writ to the return; and if it was proved that he had not answered for the whole, he was to be estreated into the exchequer for the overplus, and, besides, was to be amerced for the concealment. The sheriff was also enjoined by this statute to consider all rents, corn in the grange, and all movables (except the furniture of horses and household utensils) as *issues.* Sheriffs were to be punished for their first and second offences by the justices of assize; but for the third, only *coram rege.*

It was commanded, that sheriffs should never in future return, that they were prevented from executing a writ by the interference and resistance of some potent lord, as this was a disgrace to the king's authority and crown; and whenever a sheriff was informed by his bailiffs that such resistance was made, he was to proceed immediately with the *posse comitatûs* to support him in executing the king's command. If it was proved to be false, he was immediately to commit the bailiffs to prison; if true, he was to do the same with the offenders, who should not be delivered without the special command of the king. If he was still resisted, he was to certify to the court the names of the resisters, with those who were aiding, consenting, commanding, and favouring them; who were to be attached *per corpora* by a judicial writ to appear *coram rege;* and if they were convicted, they were to be punished at the pleasure of the king.

Of summoning jurors.

Another complaint against sheriffs, hundredors, and bailiffs of liberties was, that they put infirm persons, and those who lived out of the country, upon juries; and summoned a greater number than was necessary, only to get money for dispensing with their attendance; so that, after all, assizes and juries very frequently would not be taken, for want of jurors. It was therefore ordained,[1] that in one assize no more should be summoned than twenty-four; and that old men above seventy, those who were incurably ill, or at the time of the summons were ill, or not resident in the country, should not in future be put on juries, or lesser assizes; nor any one who had not some freehold of the value of twenty shillings per annum within the county where the assize or jury was to be taken, or of forty shillings without it; unless they were witnesses to charters or other writings, whose presence was absolutely necessary (*a*). As to great assizes, where, on account of the small number of knights, it might be inconvenient to affix any such qualification, it would be sufficient if they had freehold of any value in the county. If any officer offended against this act, he was to answer in damages to the party grieved, and be amerced to the king by the justices of assize, who were to hear complaints on this statute. The qualifications of jurors were altered by the statute *de iis qui ponendi in assisis*, 21 Edw. I., st. 1, which requires those who were on juries out of their counties (which was the case in trials at the bar of the courts at Westminster) to have land or tenements of one hundred shillings per annum, and those within the county of forty shillings; those before justices assigned, or other ministers of the king, appointed to take inquests, juries, or other recognitions, forty shillings per annum; but as to those before the justices itinerant, and in cities, boroughs, and other mercantile towns, they were to remain as at common law. Respecting jurors in general, it was enacted by statute *articuli super chartas*, 28 Edw. I., c. 9, that such persons should be put on inquests and juries as were next neighbours; those who were most sufficient, and least suspicious; under pain of paying double damages to the party complaining, and being amerced to the king.

To return to the statute of Westmin. 2. Some further regulations were made for the forwarding of suits; these we shall proceed to mention. As the law now stood, a warrantor, if, upon denying the warranty, it was found against him, suffered no other penalty but an amercement, and being obliged to warrant;[2] but it was now thought proper to make the warrantor, in such case, lose his land, as the tenant would; and further, to prevent collusion

(*a*) The remedy of the party at the trial was challenged; and in Britton there is a chapter on "De chalenge de jurors," in which the various grounds of challenge are enumerated, on conviction of any infamous offence: "Ne ceux que ne ount point descretion ne eux que sont excommenges ne mese ans de commune gents outer, ne prestres ne clers dedens seynt ordres ne femmes ne ceux que sont passes le age de lxx. ans, ne villayns ne ceux que a ascun des partres sent destreynables, ou seigniour, ou conseillers, ou countours" (pleaders). Want of proper qualification has always been deemed a ground for challenge. From this time there was a long series of statutes on the subject, until they were all consolidated in the jury act, 6 Geo. IV., c. 60.

[1] Ch. 38.

[2] *Vide ante*, vol. i. c. viii.

and delay, it was provided, that where the tenant and warrantor were at issue, the demandant might pray a *venire facias,* to try the matter.[1] We have seen what great delay was occasioned by the essoin *de malo lecti.* To prevent the long and tedious course of ascertaining the truth of this essoin by the writ *de faciendo videre,*[2] it was now provided,[3] that the party might, in the iter of justices (which has been extended by construction to the common pleas), take issue whether *languidus* or not; and if it was found against the essoin, that it should be turned to a default. This essoin *de malo lecti* was wholly taken away in a writ of right beween two claiming by the same descent; as between parceners. It had been enacted by statute Marlb. c. 13,[4] that after a person had put himself on an inquest he should have only one essoin; but this is not limiting at what precise stage he should have that essoin, and as defendants would sometimes take it upon the writ of *habeas corpora juratorum,* the consequence was, that the jurors lost their issues, and the inquest was not taken; it was therefore (principally for the ease of jurors) now provided,[5] that the essoin should be taken at the next day; which must be upon the *venire facias,* and not after (*a*). This alteration, like that of the statute of Marlbridge, which it was meant to amend, has been construed to relate only to personal actions. Again, as at common law, no essoin was to be allowed, where a day was given *prece partium,* and the parties agreed to come without an essoin.[6] Again, whereas by the statute Westmin. 1[7] an essoin was taken from the tenant in certain assizes, after appearance, it was now in like cases to be taken from the demandant.[8] Of essoins.

The view, which likewise created much delay in real actions, was dispensed with in some instances. It was ordained,[9] that where land was lost by default, and the loser brought a new action; and where a writ was abated by a dilatory exception, after a view, as by non-tenure, or misnaming of the place; no view should be granted in a second action. In the following cases there was to be no view at all: in a writ of dower, where the land was aliened to the tenant and his ancestor, for he could not but know the land himself; in a writ of entry, after a former writ quashed for assigning the entry wrong, in which there had been a view; and in all writs grounded upon a demise to the tenant himself from the plaintiff or his ancestors, *dum fuit infra œtatem, non compos, in*

(*a*) Upon this it was laid down that a statute must have a reasonable construction, and though the statute said, that after any one had put himself in any inquisition, the next day should be allowed to have an essoin, yet to him who came by the *exigent* or *cape corpus,* and joined issue, there should not be an essoin, for he should remain in custody, or be released on mainprise, and so was present in court (*Yearbook,* 35 *Hen. VI.,* 53).

[1] Ch. 6. [2] *Vide ante,* vol. i. c. viii. [3] Ch. 17.
[4] *Vide* vol. i. c. viii. [5] Ch. 27.
[6] At common law, an essoin was allowed on a day given *prece partium;* but not if expressly given *sine essonio.* Compare *ante,* vol. i. c. viii.
[7] Viz. ch. 42. *Vide ante,* c. viii. [8] Ch. 28. [9] Ch. 48.

prisonâ, and the like. In these provisions, the legislature seems to have acted upon the principles which governed on this subject, in the latter reign.[1]

The other improvements made in the administration of justice were of a more striking nature than those that have just been mentioned, and claim a more particular regard; such as an execution given against land by *elegit;* the introduction of bills of exception; and the proceeding by *scire facias* to revive a judgment of a year's standing. These we shall speak of first, as more worthy the consideration of a modern reader. The remainder of this statute relates to the real remedies so much practised in those days, and which we have reserved to be thrown together at the conclusion of these provisions for the better administration of civil justice.

Both Glanville and Bracton pass over personal actions so slightly as to give us no information concerning the execution that might be had thereon. We have seen that there was a process against the chattels and the land also to compel an appearance,[2] and in cases of outlawry, both might be taken; but it does not appear that the land, like the goods, was ever sold, or delivered to the plaintiff in satisfaction of his debt (*a*). It was only in real actions that the land was taken; except, indeed, in the cases provided for by the late statute *de mercatoribus.*[3] But now it was enacted as follows: that when a debt was recovered or acknowledged, or damages adjudged, in the king's court, the plaintiff should have his election either to have a writ *quòd vicecomis* FIERI FACIAT[4] *de*

(*a*) In the *Mirror* it is stated, that in personal actions on defaults, defendants were distrained to the value of the demand; and for default after default judgment was given for the plaintiff; and that if the defendant had land, he should not be arrested, but the judgment by default was in force, and the plaintiff should have the land to hold until satisfaction was made (c. iv. s. 5), and so in real actions the land was to be adjudged to the plaintiff to hold as a distress (c. vii.) It is plain that it was so, either on default before judgment or after judgment, whether by default or otherwise. The land was looked upon as the real security, and it was only held to enforce appearance, or, after judgment, to enforce payment. So as to mixed actions, which included debt and contract, the defendants were distrainable by all their goods and lands, till they appeared and answered; and the issues (of the lands) came to the profit of the lord of the court (s. 8). Thus the seizure was only as a mode of coercion, there was no power to sell the goods any more than to sell the land. It is manifest it was the same after judgment as before. Nothing is said in the *Mirror* as to execution in the sense of an actual levy of the money. The plaintiff only had power to seize and hold land and goods as a distress, and at common law a distress could not be sold. There was coercion, but not execution, at common law, save in actions for assault or injury to the person, when arrest was allowed on mesne process, and therefore on final process or execution. For the rule seems always to have been that the process allowed on default before judgment, was allowed upon default after judgment; for non-payment of the debt, or non-render of the property in dispute, was in fact a default. Then the present statute gave the plaintiff his option or election, either to have the land to hold, as before, and levy the debt out of the profits, or to levy it on the goods; and it should seem that it was not intended that the creditor should have both, even in succession, so as to enable him to resort to one to remedy the deficiency of the other. That has been by usage. And see *Bracton,* lib. v., fol. 440.

[1] *Vide ante*, vol. i. c. viii. [2] *Ibid.* [3] *Ibid.*

[4] The common language of our law-books has been, that the writs of *levari facias* and *fieri facias* were at the common law. Considering the silence of Glanville and Bracton about execution in personal actions, there is no direct authority either to contradict or

terris et catallis; or one commanding, *quòd vicecomes liberet ei omnia catalla debitoris (exceptis bobus, et affris carucæ),* ET MEDIETATEM TERRÆ SUÆ, *quousq; debitum fuerit levatum, per rationabile pretium, vel extentam.* The statute ordained, that if a person was ejected from a freehold so delivered to him, he should have his writ of novel disseisin, and redisseisin, if necessary.[1] Upon this there was framed a writ of execution, called an *elegit,* from the words of the statute; and if a plaintiff or conusee prayed this writ, the entry on the roll was, *quòd* ELEGIT *sibi executionem fieri de omnibus catallis, et medietate terræ, &c.*, and the writ was, *ac cùm idem H. juxta statutum inde editum* ELEGERIT SIBI LIBERARI *pro prædictis* 20 *libris omnia catalla, et medietatem terræ ipsius R. &c.*[2] Thus was land made directly liable to answer for debts, contrary to the general policy of the feudal institution. We have seen, that in the case of a merchant, lands of a particular kind might be taken in execution; but after this general authority had been given to take lands by writ of *elegit,* the merchant's security was enlarged still further by the second statute on that subject; so that the whole of a man's land was made liable to a statute-merchant, while only half could be taken by *elegit.*

Writ of *elegit.*

The reasons for ordaining[3] a *bill of exceptions* was this: a writ of error might be had, whenever there was error on the record. But it sometimes happened, that the parties might allege matter of exception *ore tenus* in court, as the method was in these days, which the justices would overrule (*a*); and matter that was so

(*a*) The previous clause or chapter throws great light upon the real meaning of the present, as to bills of exception. That clause provided that judges should not force jurors to a general verdict, or one precise to the point, but that jurors might return a special verdict, setting forth the facts for the judgment of the court: "Justiciarii non compellant juratores dicere præcise se sit disseisina vel non, dummodo dicere voluerint veritatem facti et petere auxilium justiciarii." Upon which Lord Coke said: "It hath been resolved that in *all* actions, personal, real, or mixed, and upon all issues joined, general or special, the jury might find the special matter of fact pertinent, and tending only to the issue joined; and thereupon pray the discretion of the court for the law, and this the jurors might do at the common law, not only in cases be-

support that opinion. It seems, however, doubtful whether those writs *eo nomine* are of such ancient date; and it is not improbable that the latter might have obtained both its name and existence from the words of this act. From the mere penning of the statute, the *fieri facias* appears as much a new regulation as the *medietatem terræ.* It is probable that the *distringas per terras et catalla,* which was the mesne process in personal actions, was the process of execution likewise. The legislature seem to have an eye to this process in the terms *de terris et catallis.* But the writ of *fieri facias,* properly so called, never contained anything *de terris.* This defect is supplied by the *levari facias.* Thus these two writs reach all the objects that could be touched by the old process of *distringas;* and were with that view, perhaps, framed after this act, if not upon the authority of it. *Vide ante,* c. ix.

[1] Ch. 18.

[2] 2 Inst. 395.

[3] It appears from the following case, that a *bill* was a mandate of an authority inferior to that of a *writ.* In 8 Ed. II., upon an issue whether ancient demesne or not, a *bill* sealed with the seal of one of the justices of the bench was sent to the treasurer and barons of the exchequer to certify the court of the fact; but they paid no regard to the mandate, as it was only a *bill;* and therefore the same justice sent a writ, returnable in the bench at a general return day. *Mayn.* 277. [The author failed to observe that a bill was not mandatory, as a *writ* is. A bill was rather in the nature of a complaint; hence the process in the king's bench was by bill, in the nature of a petition or original writ. *Bro. Abr.* "*Bill,*" c. xii.]

overruled, as it was never entered upon the record, could not be assigned for error. It was therefore now provided[1] as follows: that

tween party and party, whereof the act putteth an example of the assize, but also in pleas of the crown at the king's suit. And note," he says, "the next clause of the act in affirmance also of the common law." The next clause is as to bills of exception: "Cum aliquis implacitatus proponat exceptionem et petat quod justiciarius eam allocent, quam si allocari noluerint, si ille qui exceptionem proposuerit scribat illam exceptionem, justiciarii apponent sigilla sua," &c. Upon which Lord Coke says: "At the common law, before the enacting of the act, a man might have had a writ of error for an error in law, *in redditione judicii, in redditione executionis*, or *in processu*, and this error in law must be apparent in the record; for the writ of error saith: Quia *in recordo*, &c., error interveniet manifestus. Or for error in fact, by alleging matter out of record, as death of either party before judgment. Now, the mischief was, that when the party did offer to allege any exception, and the justice overruled it, so as it was not entered of record; this the party could not assign for error, because it did not appear upon the record, nor was error in fact but error in law (2 *Inst.* 426). It is, however, to be observed that a party might demur upon the evidence, and on such demurrer bring error; that being in effect an exception allowed, for if the exception or demurrer were disallowed, it would not be entered of record, and then the evidence would not be entered of record; but if it were so, then the other party, the party demurred against, might bring error, if it was ultimately allowed by the bill court (2 *Rolle's Reports*, 117; *Baker's Case, Cro. Eliz.*, 753; *Wright* v. *Pendar, Al.* 18; *Cockridge* v. *Fanshawe, Dougl.* 119; *Rastall's Entries, tit. Demurrer, Scholastica's case, Plowd.*, 405), the evidence being entered on the record, and the demurrer or exception thereto, that is, that it was not sufficient to maintain the issue incumbent on the party offering it. If such demurrer was received, and entered with the evidence, then the exception was so far allowed at *nisi prius* as to be entered of record, and thus to admit of a writ of error. So, again, if the jurors returned a special verdict, setting forth all the facts. But if this was not done, and the judge would not receive and record the "exception," whether in the form of a demurrer to the whole of the evidence, or of objection to the admissibility of any part of it, or otherwise, then there was a necessity for the power given by this statute, enabling the party excepting himself to write down the exception, and making it imperative on the judge to seal it, and return it as part of the record. Such was the scope of the statute which turns on the term "exception." There is nothing in which the influence and effect of usage, in controlling and determining the operation of our more ancient statutes, has been more marked or manifest than in regard to this subject of bills of exception. It is not too much to say, perhaps, that the modern notion of it is just the opposite of its ancient sense and meaning. To begin, what is now understood as the "exception" is always to the ruling of the judge; whereas, in the original meaning of the phrase, it was always applied to an objection to the case of the opposite party. This is the sense in which the term was used in Bracton's *Treatise*, written not long before the statute passed, and in which it was evidently borrowed from the phrase "exceptio," in the Roman law. The last book is entirely occupied with the subject, and is entitled, "De exceptionibus." And it treats of exceptions thus: "In primis videndum quid sit exceptio, et sciendum quod exceptio est actionis elisio, per quam actio perimitur, vel differtur." Then there follows an elaborate disquisition on the nature of exceptions, which comprehends all the objections that could be made to actions. For example, "Exceptio de defectu probationis, per lapsum temporis," &c. (fol. 437). "Excepere etiam poterit tenens *contra petentem* quod licet jus ei descenderit sicut petens dicit, tamen non valet petitio sua nec actio pro defectu probationis" (fol. 438). Thus it was always; the "exception" was against the case on the other side, and usually was against the case for the plaintiff, or it was some answer to it, as, for instance, the party sued might except to the case that it was *res judicata*, "Item competit tenenti exceptio rei judicatæ ut si antecessor petentis rem petitam amiserit per judiciam. . . . . hæc omnia probari possunt per rotulos et recorda justitarii" (fol. 436). So that the "exception" might be one grounded on matter of fact, which required proof; and hence Bracton says that if it failed in proof, the party bringing it forward would lose judgment, "Si quis autem in probatione exceptionis defecerit, amittet per judicium" (fol. 401). And thus, therefore, the exception would always be directed against the case on the other side, and the justices would have to determine upon it; and

[1] Ch. 31.

where any one was impleaded before the justices, and proposed any exception, and prayed it might be allowed, but the justices would

either party—the party excepting, or the party excepted against—might have reason to be dissatisfied with the ruling, either for or against the exception, as the case might be. But as error only lay on matter of record, the result was that whether the exception were regarded or overruled, neither party could appeal against the ruling beyond the court where it was pronounced. The terms of the statute, it will be observed, applied only to the case of an exception disallowed; but according to the usual mode of construing ancient statutes, it was construed largely and liberally, as applying equally to either class of cases—that is, to exceptions allowed or disallowed. Still, it was understood in ancient times that the appeal was on the ruling or decision upon an exception to the case of the opposite party, though it might be to the sufficiency of the proof. The term "bill" used in the statute was the phrase used for a statement of a cause of complaint. Hence it was the form of process in the king's bench; "a man shall have bill *in banco regis*," &c. (*Year-book*, 7 *Henry VI.*, 41); "bill of debt, by which J. S. petit de B.," &c. So the phrase, "bill in chancery" (2 *Richard III.*, 12). In one of the earlier Year-books it is laid down that the order of exceptions was—1. To the jurisdiction; 2. To the person; 3. To the court; 4. To the writ; and, lastly, to the action (17 *Edw. III.*, 74; 19 *Henry VI.*, 10). Britton treats carefully of various kinds of "exceptions," as also does Bracton; and some of these exceptions were such as could be taken at the trial, being to the sufficiency or admissibility of evidence to sustain the issue. The making of an exception, however, did not necessarily raise a question as to the whole of the evidence, and that was the object of a special verdict. It should be observed that the present enactment was confined to cases of *exceptions*; and though this might include cases where the exception was to the whole case on the other side, for insufficiency to maintain the issue, and in such cases the whole of the evidence would be put on the record and brought before the court of error, yet it might be only an exception to part of the case, and it could not apply to cases where there was evidence on both sides, and where the question could not be raised in the form of an exception to the case on one side, the object being to obtain the judgment of the court upon the *whole* of the facts. Thus in such cases the course of the common law presented the procedure by special verdict, already provided for in the previous enactment above-mentioned. That, however, being a rather formal, prolix kind of proceeding, the practice of the courts very soon provided another, less formal and more convenient; and the simple proceeding by special case, in which, on a point reserved at the trial, the counsel stated the case at the bar, and obtained the opinion of the court thereon. The Year-books are full of cases in which it is said that counsel "vient al barre," and stated such and such facts, and prayed the opinion of the court thereon. This was a "special case." In more modern times the "special case" was more frequently stated in writing, especially—and indeed necessarily so—if the question arose on documents; and the reports of Salkeld contain as many special cases as special verdicts. After this statute, as before, the course taken when it was desired to have the judgment of the court upon all the facts, was to have them set forth in a special verdict, or, as they said, "at large" (*Year-book*, 41 *Ed. III.*, fol. 10; 30 *Ed. III.*, fol. 23). And upon the doubt as to the law, the case would be adjourned to Westminster, where the opinion of the court would be taken (43 *Assize*, fol. 1); and then, if necessary, the case could be taken to error, as the special verdict set out the facts at large upon the record. But if the parties were satisfied with the decision of the court in which the action was brought, the case need go no further; so in effect it was a reservation of the case for the judgment of the court. If the jurors were in doubt, they could find the facts at large, and put the matter in the discretion of the court (38 *Assize*, fol. 9; 43 *Assize*, fol. 41; 29 *Assize*, fol. 40). There is reason to believe that the practice upon this ancient statute has hardly been appreciated in modern times, when it has been supposed that the practice of special cases—at all events in error—was entirely of modern origin. On the contrary, it is believed it arose out of the ancient practice *before* the statute. It is manifest that it assumes a power in the justices to enter the facts upon the record, for it provides a remedy for the party if they refuse to do so; and the whole scope of the statute confirms the view of Lord Coke, that it was declaratory of the common law. So, again, the practice of demurrer to evidence, which assumes that the facts are entered on record, implies a power in the court so to enter the facts. And it is believed that, looking at the numerous cases in the Year-books of cases stated at the bar, many of them in

not allow it; then he might write down the exception, and pray the justices to put their seals to it, which they should do; and if one refused, another might do it. If, after this, the king, upon complaint of what the justices had done, caused the record to come before him, and that exception was not found therein, and the complainant showed it written down, with the seal of the justice appendant, then the justice should be commanded to appear at a certain day to acknowledge or deny his seal; and if it was not denied, then they were to proceed and determine whether that exception ought to have been refused or not (*a*). After this statute it should seem that most points of law, whether upon the record or not, might be re-examined in a writ of error.

Scire facias. The nature of the provision about a *scire facias* on a judgment cannot be better understood than from a rehearsal of the statute itself. Because, says the act,[1] where a mat-

courts of error, the practice of entering the facts on record, by way of special case, was even more ancient than the statute, and was confirmed by it. Any exception to the proceedings could be made the subject of a bill of exceptions; for instance, a challenge to a juror, if it were not allowed, the party challenging could have his bill of exceptions upon it, according to the statute, and upon that could have a writ of error (21 *Edw. IV.* fol. 3). Or it might be an exception to any part of the case on the other side; and it should seem that whether the exception was allowed or overruled, it might be the subject of a bill of exceptions; for in one case the exception to a part of the defendant's case being *allowed*, he prayed that it might be entered on the record; and this being refused, he was told to make a "bill" of it, and they would seal it (*Year-book*, 2 *Edw. IV.*, fol. 7). In the reign of Henry VI. an exception was taken in a case of formedon; and the judge (Martin, J.) seems to have treated it roughly. "*Quid ad hoc*," said he. He overruled it, upon which the counsel prayed that it might be entered; but Martin, J., said, "Make your bill of exceptions, and we will seal it; for it shall not be entered on the rolls, to encumber the rolls," &c. "*Quod nota*," says the reporter (4 *Henry VI.* fol. 15). If there be any matter of law that carries with it any difficulty, the jury may, to deliver themselves from the danger of an attaint, find it specially, that so it may be decided in that court where the verdict is returnable; and if the judge overrule the point of law contrary to the law, whereby the jury are persuaded to find a general verdict (which yet they are not bound to do, if they doubt it), then the judge, upon the request of the party desiring it, is bound by law, in convenient time, to seal a bill of exceptions containing the whole matter excepted to, so that the party grieved by such indiscretion or error of the judge, may have relief by the writ of error or the statute of Westminster (*Hale's Hist. Com. Law*, c. xii.)

(*a*) The statute can scarcely be understood without some explanation. The principle of the common law was that a party sued must have notice or warning to defend himself, and as therefore he had the notice by summons in every action, so after judgment he ought to have it whenever there had either been a change of parties, such as might afford ground for some exception, or a lapse of time during which such a change of parties might have taken place; and the common law rule fixed this at a year and a day; after which execution could not be taken out on a judgment without a *scire facias*. Upon this principle also, when it was sought to charge a person upon some obligation or judgment to which he was not a party, but by which he was under a legal liability, as in the case of change of parties, by death, the common law required that he should have notice of the proceeding, and thus be made in some way a party to it, so far as to give him an opportunity of showing cause against his enforced liability to it, and also against the tenants of any lands bound thereby. And on an inquisition or an elegit, strangers, even tenants, would not be bound, as they would be if these made parties by *scire facias*. Thus, if a man be bounden in a recognisance, though the recognisee die, his executors cannot sue forth an elegit to have execution of the recognisance even within the year, without suing forth a *scire facias* against the recognisor. And if the recognisor be dead, then the

[1] Ch. 45.

ter is recorded before the chancellor and the king's justices of record, and enrolled in their rolls, there ought not be thereon the common process of an action, by summons, attachment, essoin, view of land, and other solemnities of proceeding that are usual in cases of contracts and covenants made out of court; therefore, for the future, all things enrolled in a court of record, or contained in fines, (*a*) whether they are contracts, covenants, obligations, services, customs, recognisances, or whatever they may be, if enrolled, and such a

recognisee or his executors must sue a *scire facias* against the heir of the recognisor, and against those who are tenants (*i.e.*, freehold) of the lands which he had (*Fitzherbert's Natura Brevium*, 267; *Year-book*, 38 *Edw. III.* 13; 46 *Edw. III.* c. 29; 2 *Rich. III.* 8). The *scire facias*, so called from the principal words in it, directed the sheriff to make them to know, *i.e.*, to give notice to them, "to show if they have anything to say for themselves why the land which they hold ought not to be delivered, &c." (*Ibid.*) Where, however, the parties, on either side, had not died, *scire facias* was not necessary, except to the tenants of the freehold, for they would be thereby bound. The inquisition *in elegit* would be an *ex parte* inquiry whether the recognisor or judgment debtor was seised of the lands. If this was falsely found, and any one else was seised, he could not be bound by the inquisition, unless he had previously been made party by *scire facias*, in which he could have shown that the recognisor was not seised of the land. Lord Coke and Lord Hale thought *scire facias* lay in all actions at common law, *vide Salkeld.*

(*a*) One important application of this enactment related to the execution of *fines*, which in this age were used as records of titles and limitations of estates. The statute *De donis* shows, by its concluding enactment, prohibiting the use of fines for the purpose of barring estates tail, that they were used for that purpose. After that statute, recoveries were used for the purpose of alienation or alteration of estates; and fines appear to have been used rather for the purpose of creating and transferring and recording titles to land, and especially for recording the successive limitations of estates; and on these estates vesting, the fine could under the enactment be summarily executed without putting the party to the delay of a real action. Before the statute by which *scire facias* was granted to have execution, the party to a fine had no other remedy but the writ *de fine facto*, and that was nothing but a writ of covenant (*Year-book*, 43 *Edw. III.* fol. 13). As before the statute, the writ *de fine facto* lay to have execution by action on the covenant; now the writ of *scire facias* lay to give a more direct and summary remedy by way of execution, without a new action (*Ibid.*); and though it was in the nature of a new action, yet the onus lay on the defendant of showing, by some matter subsequent to the fine, why it should not be carried into execution. The writ or declaration in *scire facias*, which of course set out the fine, could be objected or demurred to on the ground that it did not set forth a fine which would warrant the execution required; but if there was no objection to it in law, then execution was at once awarded (*Ibid.*) The advantage of this system—of a permanent record of titles, and a simple and summary remedy for recovery of land—can be readily understood, and in such an age must have been very great. The reports and records of subsequent reigns contain entries showing that fines were thus used for the purpose of creating and recording titles, at least as early as the time of Henry III., for fines of that reign are to be found mentioned which had evidently been used for that purpose, and the Year-books of the ensuing reigns are full of cases of *scire facias* upon fines. Thus, in the 40 Edw. III. fol. 19, there was *scire facias* brought upon a fine by the Duke of Lancaster and Blanche his wife. If indeed the title did not really depend upon the fine, but on a prior title, the party was left to his real action (41 *Edw. III.* 21). And the writ could be had upon a fine with several limitations; for it was said before the statute, a party could have had the writ *De fine facto*, which was in its nature a writ of covenant, and although different estates were granted by the fine, one writ would have lain upon them, for that they were all in one fine; and so it was with the writ of *scire facias* under the statute (43 *Edw. III.* fol. 23). So *scire facias* lay to execute a remainder on a fine (44 *Edw. III.* fol. 39), or reversion after death of tenant for life (44 *Edw. III.* fol. 39), or it lay for the issue in tail (42 *Edw. III.* fol. 5), for that it was inconvenient that he should be put to the delay of his writ of formedon (*Ibid.*) And upon the *scire facias* there could be no objection taken, unless that

matter to which the king's court might, by the law and custom of the realm, give the authority of a record, shall have such consideration and sanction, as for it not to be needful to make them again the subject of regular action and pleading; that is, by summons, attachment, and so on, as above-mentioned. But when complaint shall be made thereon to the court, and the acknowledgments or *fine* is a recent one, that is, within a year, then a writ of execution shall be had; but if it is of longer date, the sheriff shall be commanded, *quòd scire faciat* the party of whom the complaint is, to appear at a certain day, and show cause why what was contained in the roll or the fine should not be executed. If the party appeared not, or could say nothing why execution should not be had, the sheriff was to be commanded to do execution thereof. It should seem that this statute, from the mention of contracts, covenants, and the like, first gave a *scire facias* in personal actions (that writ being, as we have seen, not uncommonly used in real actions); and that before this act it had been usual to bring a fresh action upon the judgment (*a*).

We come now to the additions which this statute made to the number of real remedies before in use. These we shall speak of nearly in the order in which they were made. The first provision of this kind was in favour of a wife whose husband held land in her right. We have before seen, that where a husband *aliened* a freehold that he had in right of his wife, she, after his death, might have a writ of entry, since called a *cui in vitâ*, to recover it back again.[1] It seemed hard, that when a husband had lost such land by *default*, the wife, after his death, should not have the same remedy, but was to be driven to bring a writ of right. It was

the parties to the fine had no estate of freehold. The statutes as to fines, indeed (18 *Edw. I.*, and 27 *Edw. I.*), declared that fines should bind not only parties and privies, but strangers, and that no allegation against them should be permitted; but, nevertheless, the courts allowed strangers to show that the parties to the fine had no freehold estate (40 *Edw. III.*, fol. 32; 42 *Edw. III.*, fol. 20), and even the heir of the party acknowledging could show that he himself or his ancestor had continued seised (46 *Edw. III.*, fol. 14). A fine was effectual, however, if either of the parties were seised at the time the fine was levied (41 *Edw. III.*, fol. 14). If that were so, *scire facias* would lie to execute it, unless some special matter which had occurred could be shown to avoid it (50 *Edw. III.*, fol. 22). It is manifest that this permanent record of titles, and this speedy and summary remedy for the recovery of land, must have been of great importance in such an age.

(*a*) Upon this an important principle was laid down, that when an act of parliament is made in the affirmative, it does not take away a prior remedy. Thus the common law (it was said), was, that if a man recovered debt or damages, and did not sue execution within the year, he was put to a new action, for no *scire facias* at common law in such case; and the statute Westminster 2, c. xlv., gave *scire facias*, but as it was in the affirmative, that the party might have *scire facias*, it was held not to take away the writ of debt, and the party could have writ of debt after the year, as at common law; and so an action of debt was held to lie on a recognisance, and the party was not driven to a *scire facias* (36 *Hen. VI.* 3). The same principle was laid down—upon the precedent afforded by this statute—in other cases (42 *Assize*, 22). But statutes in the negative were deemed to alter the common law, so that a man could not afterwards resort to the common law, but then it was always also held that statutes which restrained the common law should be strictly construed (10 *Edw. IV.* 7; 18 *Edw. IV.* 16).

[1] *Vide ante*, vol. i. c. vii.

therefore ordained,[1] that in such case the woman should have a writ of entry, *cui ipsa in vitâ suâ contradicere non potuit;* which should be conducted in the following way: If the tenant pleaded against the demand of the wife, that he entered by judgment, and it turned out to have been by default, then he was to answer over to the title under which he claimed upon the first writ brought against the husband and wife; and if he could make out none, it was ordained that the woman should recover, notwithstanding the default (*a*). Again, if a husband refused to defend an action brought for the wife's land, she might, upon her prayer, be received to defend her right.[2]

In like manner, when a tenant in dower, or *per legem Angliæ*, or otherwise for term of life, or by any gift where the reversion was reserved, made default, the heirs, and those entitled to the reversion, were to be received to answer, if they came before judgment (*b*); and if judgment had been passed, either by default or reddition, then, after the death of such tenant, they might have a writ of entry with like process as that above mentioned.

(*a*) Note, by the statute Westminster, c. iii., that where the baron (husband) made default in return, that the wife should be reseised; and the same statute, c. xxv., says that if any one on assize vouched a record and failed, that he should be deemed a disseisor without recognition of assize; and yet in assize against husband and wife, who vouched record and failed, so that at the day the husband made default, the wife should be reseised. And so (it was said) where there are two statutes made together—the one contrary to the other—a reasonable construction shall be made (*Year-book 7 Hen. IV.* 16). A principle extremely useful, and of very general application. It is to be observed that each chapter of the statute is deemed a distinct act—the statute in those ancient times meaning rather a session, or all the statutes passed in a session or parliament.

(*b*) This deserves attention, as affording an illustration of the tenacity of legal principles, and an instance of the existence of a procedure founded on a certain principle substantially the same, during the course of six centuries. At the common law, as already seen when considering the first statute of Westminster (*vide ante*), when a party was sued in a real action, he could "vouch," as the phrase was, the warranty of some one else from whom he had derived title, and who had undertaken to uphold it, and could summon him to come in as a party to the suit. And when the party vouched that the vouchee came forward and appeared, he was made defendant in place of the tenant, and the suit went on. There was an enactment in the first statute of Westminster, as we have seen, directed to this procedure, which was thus explained by Lord Coke: "In ancient times," he says, quoting the *Mirror*, "it seemed strange that, when the original *præcipe* was brought against the tenant of the land, that the court, upon that original, should hold plea between the tenant and the vouchee; but it is more strange to make a question of that which hath received an ancient, continual, and constant allowance. The vouchee cometh in *in loco tenentis*, and in judgment of law, is a tenant to the demandant. And on a similar principle, by the common law, a party in reversion could claim to come forward to defend his title, and the enactment is to carry that act; the former being to enable the tenant to defend himself, the present for the protection of the reversioner. This being the law in real actions, when the action of ejectment superseded, then the same principle was applied to that action, and, by the practice of the courts, the tenant could virtually "vouch" his landlord by letting judgment go by default, unless he appeared, and the landlord was allowed to come in to defend. See Salkeld's *Reports*, title "*Ejectment*" (*Salk.* 257). Then the practice was established by statute 11 Geo. II. c. xix. s. 11-13, and Lord Mansfield, in a case on that statute, said, "In all real actions at common law, before the statute of Westminster, wherever tenant of the freehold made default, the reversioner or remainderman had a right to come in and defend the possession, because, if judgment was had against the tenant

[1] Ch. 3. [2] *Vide ante*, c. ix., as to the first law for receipt.

Where a person aliened any land held in right of his wife, it was ordained[1] that, after the death of the husband, the woman or her heir should not be delayed by the nonage of the heir who ought to warrant; but a purchaser was to stay till the age of his warrantor before he should avail himself of his warranty, for he could not be ignorant that he was purchasing the right of another person, and therefore deserved no favour.

Further provision was made in cases of dower. It was declared,[2] consistently with what the law had uniformly pronounced,[3] that where a husband, being impleaded, had given up the land demanded to his adversary *de plano*, that is, by a regular judicial surrender, the justices, upon a writ of dower, should adjudge the wife her dower. But where the land was lost by default, there was a difference of opinion, some justices holding that the widow was, in such case, entitled to dower, others that she was not[4] (*a*). To remove this doubt, it was now declared, that a woman claiming her dower should be heard in this case, as in the former; and if it was objected to her that her husband lost the land by judgment, so that she ought not to have any dower, and upon inquiry it was found to be a judgment by default, then that the tenant should

in possession, it turned the estate of those behind to a right. This is, however, expressly allowed by the statute Westm. 2, c. iii. It never could be a doubt whether, before the act, a landlord should be admitted to defend when the tenant refused. It is strange that two acts of parliament at five hundred years' distance, viz., Westm. 2 and 11 Geo. II., both upon the same point, should be made, as introductory to a new law which was provided for by the common law long before" (1 *Wm., Blackstone's Rep.* 361). It is true this was said of the provision in the second statute of Westm. as to allowing the owner to come in, but it is obvious that the tenant's power of letting judgment go by default would virtually operate to compel the landlord to come in, unless he was willing to allow the claimant to recover.

(*a*) As already indicated elsewhere (*vide ante*, c. ix.), a recovery was only, even if real and adverse, effective as against the party—the recoveree and his heirs and legal representatives—that is, those "privy" to him in estate. It had no operation as regarded those who were strangers to him in estate, and claimed by title paramount to him. Hence the doubt as to the effect of a collusive recovery as regarded the widow of the recoveree, who, by virtue of her right of dower, might be held to claim rather adversely to than by virtue of the title of the recoveree. There was no doubt, however, that the heir of the recoveree would be bound by the recovery, and hence its efficiency to "bar an estate tail," that is, to bar the issue in tail, who were barred because they were bound by the recovery as being the heirs of the recoveree. The notion that this use of recovery first arose at the time of Taltarum's case is entirely erroneous, and is a remarkable instance of a very common fallacy, that a rule of law, or legal proceeding, first arose at the time when it was first legally disputed and judicially decided. As regards dower, there was a case in the reign of Edward III., that a custom that if a man alien his land and expend the monies between himself and his wife, she should be barred of dower, was a good custom (*Year-book*, 3 *Edw. III.*) The principle on which this custom rested, the principle of equitable compensation, is the foundation of the system of settlement and jointure which, in modern times, has so largely superseded dower.

[1] Ch. 40. [2] Ch. 4. [3] *Vide ante*, vol. i. c. iii.

[4] This losing of land by default was nothing more than another instance where a feigned recovery was made use of to avoid certain restrictions imposed by the law of estates. A recovery having all the forms of a judicial proceeding, without any visible collusion, as in the former case, we find that the judges were startled with its apparent legality, and some held it to convey a clear unencumbered title. We shall see that, in the course of two centuries, the judges in Taltarum's case came to an agreement in favour of a feigned recovery, and adjudged it to convey a title, clear of all possible claims. [But this, it will be seen, was not the effect of that case.—ED.]

further show what he had a right to according to the writ which he had first brought against the husband; and if he proved her husband had no right, nor any one but himself, then that the judgment should be, *quòd tenens recedat quietus*, and *quòd uxor nihil capiat de dote;* but if he could not show that, then that the woman should have judgment, *quòd recuperet dotem suam:* The same where a woman[1] being endowed, or a person tenant *per maritagium, per legem Angliæ,* for term of life, or in fee-tail, lost by default. Moreover, when these tenants claimed their lands so lost by default, and came to such a stage in the pleading as to be obliged to show their right, which they could not do without the aid of their reversioner, they were by this statute permitted to vouch such reversioners to warranty, the same as if they were tenants in the suit; and when the warrantor appeared, the suit was to go on between him and the person in seisin according to the tenor and form of the writ which had been first brought, and upon which the recovery had been by default, and so from several actions, says the statute, they would come to one judgment, namely, either that the demandant recover his demand, or the tenant go quit.

Again, when a woman, having no title to dower, brought a writ of dower, during the infancy of the heir, against the guardian, and he, out of favour to her, made a reddition of the dower, or made default, or defended the suit so collusively that the dower was adjudged to her in prejudice of the heir, it was now provided that the heir, when he came of age, might demand the seisin of his ancestor against her, as against any other *deforceor;* so, however, as she should still have her exception to show her right to dower, and, if she made it out, should go quit and retain her dower, and the heir be amerced at the discretion of the justices; but if not, that the heir should recover his demand.

In like manner, if the heir or any other impleaded a woman for her dower, and she lost it by default, the default was not to preclude her from recovering it back again if she had right, which she might do by the following writ: *Præcipe A. quòd justè, &c., reddat tali quæ fuit uxor tali tantam terram cum pertinentiis in N. quam clamat esse rationabilem dotam suam,*[2] *et quam talis* EI DEFORCEAT, *&c.*, which writ has since been commonly called a *quòd ei deforceat.*[3] To this writ the tenant might plead that she had no right to be endowed, and if he could make it out he was to go quit; if not, she was to recover the land whereof she had been before endowed. Again, a man losing his land by default, had no remedy except a writ of right; but this writ could only be maintained by such as claimed the mere right, which tenants for term of life, *per liberum maritagium*, or in fee-

Quod ei deforceat.

[1] This was not a novelty; for it was the practice in the times both of Glanville and Bracton, that the widow in dower *unde nihil* should not be answered, unless she produced her warrantor, that is, her reversioner. *Vide ante*, vol. i. c. vii.

[2] Or, *de rationabili dote suâ.*

[3] *Vide ante*, vol. i. c. vii.

tail, could not, as there was a reversion in some one else; it was therefore provided, that such defaults should not be wholly prejudicial to the defaulters, and several new writs of *deforceat* were given by this statute instead of the writ of right. The *quòd ei deforceat* for a tenant *in maritagio* was thus: *Præcipe A. quòd justè, &c., reddat B. tale manerium de C. cum pertinentiis quod clamat esse jus et maritagium suum, et* QUOD *prædictus A.* EI DEFORCEAT; that for a tenant for life, *quod clamat tenere ad terminum vitæ; et* QUOD *prædictus A.* EI DEFORCEAT; that for a tenant in fee-tail, *quod clamat tenere sibi et hæredibus suis de corpore suo legitimè procreatis, et* QUOD *prædictus A.* EI DEFORCEAT. Such were the provisions of this statute ordaining the writ of *quòd ei deforceat* for persons possessed of a particular estate.

The writs framed by the last statute were designed as substitutes for the writ of right, either where a recurrence to that hazardous remedy would be inconvenient, or where the persons injured had no title by law to that writ. The statute which follows[1] made some regulations upon the same principle in case of usurpation of churches. This act is very full, and needs no other explanation than what the mere statement of it will give. It begins by saying, that there being three original writs of advowson of churches; one of them *de recto*, the other two *de possessione*, namely, that of *ultimæ præsentationis*, and that of *quare impedit*;[2] it had been the law and custom of the realm, that when a person having right presented to a church a clerk who was admitted, the true patron could recover his advowson by none but a writ of right, which was to be tried by the great assize, or by the duel (*a*); whence it followed, that heirs within age, through the fraud or negligence of their guardians, and heirs, whether of age or not, through the fraud or negligence of tenants *per legem Angliæ*, tenants in dower, for life, for years, or in fee tail, were many times disinherited of their advowsons, or at least put to their writ of right, and perhaps in the event wholly disinherited.

Of presentations to churches.

This was the grievance for which it was now intended to provide,

(*a*) Thus, where a lessee of an advowson presented a vicar to a parsonage which was full, and the presentee continued in possession for seven years, it was said (the case not being within the present statute), that the parson was put to his writ of right by reason of the lay possession (*Year-book*, 44 *Edw. III.* 33). The possessory remedy of *quare impedit* was when the patron was disturbed and resisted on his presentation, upon the vacation of the living (29 *Edw. III.* 26), or upon the avowal of his right to present. Brooke's comment upon this statute makes it very clear: "It appears by the statute Westm. 2, c. v., that each presentment which was admitted put the true patron out of possession, and put him to his writ of right of advowson, and that at once and within the six months, for the six months were given by the statute; and at the common law, if tenant for life, &c., suffered a presentment, that put the reversioner or the heir to his writ of right of advowson, and so if the parson, &c., should suffer usurpation; and this was remedied by the statute by which the reversioner or heir should have *quare impedit* at the next avoidance" (*Brooke's Abr. Presentation al Esglise*, fol. 46).

[1] Ch. 5.

[2] Of the writ *quare impedit*, &c., *vide ante*, vol. i. c. vii.

by preventing such presentations from being prejudicial to the right heirs, or those in reversion after the death of particular tenants. For this purpose it was enacted, that as often as any person, having no right, should present during the wardship of the heir, or during the time of tenants in dower, *per legem Angliæ*, or otherwise for term of life or years, or in fee-tail; at the next avoidance, when the heir was of full age, or when he came into the reversion,[1] after the death of the before-mentioned particular tenants, he should have such possessory writ of advowson as his last ancestor would have had when the last avoidance happened in his time, or before the demise was made for a term, or in fee-tail, as before-mentioned (*a*). The same of presentation to churches of the advowson of married women, during the time they were *sub potestate viri;* the same of religious men, as archbishops, bishops, rectors of churches, and other ecclesiastical persons, who were all aided by this statute, in case of presentations made by persons having no right, during the time such houses, prelacies, parsonages, or dignities were vacant.[2] However, this act was not to be construed as entitling an heir or reversioner to recover, upon suggestion that any of the before-mentioned particular tenants lost by feigned defences, as all judgments were to remain in force till reversed for error, or annulled by attaint or certificate.

Many other particulars upon the same subject were ordained by this act.[3] We have seen the tenant, in a *quare impedit*, might plead that before the writ was brought, the church was full of a parson presented by him, and this was a good plea to bar the action; but it was now ordained that one form of pleading should be observed in writs *ultimæ præsentationis*, and of *quare impedit*, and that the action should not fail by reason of such plenarty, so as the writ was purchased *infra tempus semestre*, within six months, though the party could not recover his presentation within the six months. Sometimes an agreement was made between several persons claiming one advowson, and enrolled before the justices in a roll or fine, to this effect, that one should present on the first avoidance, another on the second, another on the third, and so on. It was now ordained that should any be disturbed in such his pre-

(*a*) It was held that this clause did not bind the king, on the general principle that a statute should not bind the king, if it was not by express words; and that, therefore, if the king usurped upon an infant to a benefice, this should put the infant out of possession; *non obstante*, the statute of Westminster 2, c. v., which aided usurpation upon an infant, *feme coverte*, or those in reversion; for the king is not bound by it. For where a man presents to a benefice of the king, and his clerk was for six months, yet the king shall have *quare impedit* after the six months; for, *nullum tempus occurrit regis*, for a statute does not bind him; otherwise of the case of a common person (*Year-book*, 35 *Henry VI.*, 2).

[1] The words of the statute are, *postquam advocatio post mortem in formâ prædicta tenentium* (one of whom is a tenant *in tail*) *ad hæredem*—REVERTITUR, &c., which corresponds exactly with the passage before quoted from Britton; and is another instance to show that the legislature considered the statute *de donis* as giving only an estate for life to the tenant in tail, and a *reversion* to the issue. *Vide ante*, c. ix.

[2] Sect. 1.

[3] *Vide ante*, vol. i. 145, c. viii.

sentation, he need not bring a *quare impedit*, but should resort to the roll or fine; and the sheriff should be commanded, *quòd scire faciat* the party disturbing, to appear at a short day, as fifteen days or three weeks, according to the distance of the place, to show what he could allege, wherefore the party complaining should not present; and if he did not come, or could not allege anything done since the fine to bar him, the complainant was to recover the presentation.

It was provided, that if, after the death of the person last presenting, the advowson was assigned in dower, or came to a tenant *per legem Angliæ* who presented, and the heir, after their deaths, was disturbed, he might at his election have either a writ *ultimæ præsentationis*, or of *quare impedit*. The like of advowsons demised for term of life or of years, or in fee-tail.[1] In writs of *quare impedit* and *ultimæ præsentationis*, damages were henceforth to be awarded, if the six months elapsed through the disturbance of any one, and the bishop presented; the statute ordains these damages to be to two years' value of the church. If the six months are not past, and the presentation is deraigned within that time, the damages are only to be half a year's value; if, in the former case of presentation by lapse, the disturber has nothing to pay, he is to be imprisoned for two years; and in the latter, where the advowson was deraigned within the six months, he is to be punished by imprisonment for half a year.[2] These writs were thenceforward granted for chapels, prebends, vicarages, hospitals, abbeys, priories, and other houses of the advowson of others, of all which they did not lie at common law.[3]

It was ordained by the same statute, that when a person was prohibited from demanding tithes in another parish by the writ of *indicavit*,[4] the patron of the parson so prohibited should have a writ to demand the advowson of the tithes in question; and that when this plea was deraigned or decided for the demandant, then the plea in the ecclesiastical court might proceed.[5] Upon this clause a writ of right *de advocatione decimarum* was formed.[6] It was declared, that when one parcener presented to an advowson, and usurped upon another, he on whom the usurpation was made should not be wholly barred by his negligence, but should be permitted to present, when his turn came again.[7]

Some statutes were passed concerning admeasurement of dower and pasture,[8] and the condition of tenants in demesne with respect to their mesne and the chief lords. As the law now stood, if an heir within age assigned dower before the guardian in chivalry entered, the guardian could not compel an admeasurement thereof. It was therefore now enacted that a writ of admeasurement of dower should be granted to a guardian; and if he should prosecute the writ collusively, the

Admeasurement of dower and pasture.

[1] Sect. 2. [2] Sect. 3. [3] *Vide ante*, vol. i. c. vii. [4] *Ibid.* vol. i. 141, c. viii. [5] Sect. 4. [6] 2 Inst. 364. [7] Sect. 5. [8] *Vide ante*, vol. i. c. vii.

heir was not to be barred thereby from admeasuring it. A speedier process was directed both in this writ and that for admeasurement of pasture. When it was come to the great distress, a day was to be given, within which [1] two counties might be holden, and open proclamation was to be made for the defendant to come in at the day named in the writ; at which day, if he came not, and the proclamation was testified by the sheriff, admeasurement was to be made by default.[2]

Pasture was admeasured sometimes *coram justitiariis,* [3] sometimes in the county before the sheriff. It might happen that the pasture, after such admeasurement, was surcharged again by the same person with more beasts; it was therefore now ordained that upon the second surcharge the complainant should have the following remedy: If the admeasurement had been *coram justitiariis,* he should have a judicial writ to the sheriff, commanding him, in the presence of the parties summoned, if they chose to appear, to inquire *de secundâ superoneratione.* If the second surcharge was found, it was to be returned before the justices, under the seal of the sheriff and the seals of the jurors; upon which the justices were to award damages, and estreat the value of the beasts put into the pasture after such admeasurement, more than ought to have been; and such estreats were to be delivered to the barons of the exchequer, like others, to be answered for to the king. If the admeasurement had been made in the county, then the plaintiff might have a writ out of chancery for the sheriff to inquire of the surcharge; and the sheriff was to answer to the exchequer for all the beasts put into the pasture above the proper number. That the sheriff might not defraud the king in such cases, a very particular course was directed; that all writs *de secundâ superoneratione* that issued out of chancery should be enrolled, and that at the year's end transcripts of them be sent into the exchequer, under the seal of the chancellor, that the treasurer and barons might see how the sheriffs answered for the produce of them. It was directed that writs of re-disseisin likewise should be enrolled in the same manner, and sent into the exchequer at the end of the year.[4]

The grievances suffered by tenants in demesne, in consequence of any failure in the mesne lord, were very great. The law allowed a chief lord to distrain anywhere within his fee for his services and customs; the distress might therefore fall upon a tenant who had a mesne lord, that was bound to acquit him towards the chief lord; such tenant, however, after he had replevied the distress, could not deny the title of the chief lord to his services and customs; and when he proceeded by writ of mesne against the mesne lord, *he* would perhaps stand out the long process of that writ. All this might happen when the mesne was able enough to make good the de-

[1] To effect this, the scheme of continuances fixed by the statute of *dies communes in banco* must sometimes be disturbed and dispensed with. *Vide* vol. i., c. viii.

[2] Ch. 7. [3] *Vide ante,* vol. i., c. vii. [4] Ch. 8.

mand; but it became much worse when he was not. Again, though the law allowed such tenants in demesne to acquit themselves by paying to the chief lord the demands he had upon the mesne, yet the chief would sometimes refuse it, and persist in receiving them at the hands of his next tenant only; so that tenants in demesne might be ruined through the obstinacy of their chief, and the insufficiency of their mesne lord, though they themselves were able to pay all demands properly due from themselves. All these grievances required some redress, which was provided in the following way.

It was directed, that the tenant in demesne, as soon as he was distrained, should purchase his writ of mesne against the lord that was mesne between him and the chief lord; and if he absented himself till the great distress awarded, and had land in the same county, that the plaintiff should have a day given in the writ of great distress, before the coming of which two counties[1] might be held; and the sheriff should be commanded to distrain the mesne by the great distress, and likewise to cause him to be proclaimed in two full counties, to appear at the day contained in the writ, and answer to the complaint. If he did not appear, he was to lose the services of his tenant, who was no longer to answer to *him* for any of them, but was, for the future, to do such services and customs to the chief lord, as he before did to the mesne; and if the chief exacted more, the tenant was to have all those exceptions which the mesne might have. If the mesne had no property, the tenant was, nevertheless, to prosecute his writ of mesne; and if the sheriff returned that he had nothing whereby he might be *summoned*, then an *attachment* was to go; and if the sheriff returned that he had nothing whereby he could be attached, still the writ of *great distress* was to issue, and the proclamation to be made in the above form, in order to give the tenant the effect of the mesne being forejudged of his fee and services, as before directed. Again, if the mesne had no land in the county where the distress was taken, an original writ of summons was to issue in that county; and upon the sheriff returning that he had nothing in that county, a judicial writ of summons was to issue against him in the county where it was *testified* his land was; and suit was to be made in that county till it came to the great distress, and proclamation, as before-mentioned. Where it happened that the tenant in demesne was infeoffed to hold by less services than the mesne was bound to do to the chief lord, and he was attorned to the chief lord, after the forejudger of the mesne, in the above way, and the mesne excluded, he was nevertheless to answer to the chief lord for all such service as the mesne was bound to.

This was to be the course when the mesne did not appear; but if he did, and confessed he ought to acquit his tenant; or if he was compelled by judgment to acquit him, and after such con-

[1] *Vide ante*, c. ix.

fession, or judgment, complaint was made that he did not acquit him; then a writ judicial was to issue for the sheriff to distrain him to acquit his tenant, and to be at a certain day before the justices, to show why he had not acquitted him. When they had proceeded to the great distress, the plaintiff was to be heard; and if he could prove that he had not, the mesne was to satisfy him in damages, and the tenant to go quit, and be attorned to the chief lord. If he came not at the first distress, another distress was to issue, and proclamation to be made; and upon the return of it, there was to be a judgment, as before-mentioned.

It was not intended by this statute to exclude tenants from any remedy they had against their mesne at common law. This statute was continued to cases where there was *one* mesne only between the chief lord and the tenant, where that mesne was of full age, and where the tenant might attorn to the chief lord, without prejudice to any one but the mesne only. This was to except tenants in dower, tenants *per legem Angliæ,* or for life, or in fee-tail, for whom no remedy was intended by this statute; though, at the latter end of it there is a promise that provision should be made for them.[1]

To go on with the same subject of real remedies; we shall now mention what alteration the parliament made respecting pleading in the writ *de consanguinitate*, and how the writs of *cessavit*, of nuisance, *juris utrùm* (*a*), assize, and redisseisin, were extended to new cases, to which they did not before apply.

It had been a common answer to a writ of mortauncestor, that the demandant was not next heir of the ancestor by whose death he demanded the land; it was now ordained that in writs *de consanguinitate, avo, and proavo* (being of the same nature with a writ of mortauncestor), the same answer should be admitted.[2] We have seen, that by the statute of Gloucester,[3] a writ of *cessavit* was given against tenants in fee-farm who suffered the land to lie fresh; it was now ordained generally, that if any withheld from his lord his due and accustomed services for two years, the lord should have an action to recover his land in demesne by the following writ:—*Præcipe A. quòd justè, &c., reddat B. tale tenementum quod A. de eo tenuit per tale servitum, et quod ad prædictum*

(*a*) The statute of Westminster 2, c. xxiv. made this provision; and by 14 *Edw. III.*, c. xvii., it was provided that any chaplain or chantry priest, &c., could have the writ as well as a parson. In a case in the reign of Edward III., the writ was brought by the vicar of a church to try whether the land belonged to his vicarage or was lay-fee of an abbey to which his church was appropriate, and it was said that the vicar could have the writ to try "utrum sit libera eleemosyna pertinens ad vicariam ad libera eleemosyna pertinens adr ectoriam" (40 *Edw. III.*, fol. 29). It was there also said that in ancient times it had been considered that the vicar could not have an action against the rector, but that this was changed; and as the vicarage was endowed to him and his successors perpetually, and had his possessions for himself, if he was ousted by his parson or by any one else, he could have assize (40 *Edw. III.*, fol. 28).

[1] Ch. 9. [2] Ch. 20. *Vide ante*, vol. i. 363. [3] Viz. ch. 4. *Vide ante*, 145.

B. reverti debet, eò quòd prædictus A. infaciendo prædictum servitium PER BIENNIUM CESSAVIT, *ut dicitur:* and that, not only in this case, but also in cases within the statute of Gloucester, writs of entry should be had for the heir of the demandant against the heir of the tenant, and against those to whom such land should be aliened.[1]

Writs *in consimili casu.*

The 24th chapter of this statute deserves particular notice, as having a very extensive influence on the course of legal remedies in succeeding times (*a*). In the first

(*a*) By reason of the principle it declared and laid down; but that principle was already in the common law, and it was not *only* declared but enforced by this statute, which was therefore, being declaratory, only necessary for the purpose of enforcing and compelling the practical observance of the principle. The principle was that upon which the whole administration of justice depended, and upon which alone any remedial writs were issued—viz., that it was the prerogative or duty of the crown to see that for every legal right, or rather for every injury to a legal right, there was a remedy. It was upon this principle, as it was laid down in the *Mirror* "that every one have a remedial writ from the chancery according to his plaint" (*Mirror*, c. i., s. 3). All the original writs, as they were called, the writs originating actions in the king's courts, were issued; and it was manifest that, on the same principle, any others which were required by law could equally be issued. And that, while the writs already issued would afford established precedents for the same writs in the same cases, they would not preclude different writs in different cases, but on the contrary would embody principles on which other writs could be issued in all cases of injuries to legal rights. The statute therefore could not be legally necessary, and was only (as appears from a note of the author) required, by reason of the ignorance or narrow-mindedness of the clerks in the chancery; and this statute perhaps is the earliest of the numerous acts of legislation which have been required in consequence of this ignorant and narrow-minded adherence to the mere letter of forms, without a due regard to the *principles* they embody, and the objects for which they were established. The principle embodied in this statute was the foundation of that large class of actions commonly called actions "on the case," *i.e.*, on the particular nature and circumstances of the case, as distinguished from the more fixed, formal, and general writs adapted to the more simple cases of earlier occurrence as, for instance, actions of trespass *quare clausim fregit.* The action was a general action, fitted to the common case of entering the land in possession of the plaintiff, but the action by the reversioner for injury to the freehold was an action "on the case." It may be worth while to consider upon what principle a writ was required at all to commence an action in the king's court. For it is to be observed that the original writs were not in the nature of process, for they went not to the *party* sued, but the *sheriff.* This shows that they were rather in the nature of a commission or authority to the court to proceed in the suit. When it is borne in mind that (as already has been amply shown elsewhere) at common law, the original jurisdiction in all suits between party and party was in the *county court,* presided over by the *sheriff,* the necessity for some particular commission or authority to bring the suit in the king's court will perhaps be more apparent, and this also will explain why the writs went to the sheriff. This may be still further illustrated by the distinction between the writ of *justicies,* which directed the sheriff to hear and determine the case, and the original writ returnable in the king's court, which directed him to summon the party to attend there. Thus, therefore, the writ was the warrant to the sheriff to determine the *jurisdiction* of the suit; and if it was to lie in the king's court it was returnable there, and was in the nature of a *particular* commission. Hence it was distinguished from a *bill* of petition to the king in the king's bench or chancery, and therefore it was held that in the common pleas a suit should be commenced by *writ* and not by bill, *i.e.*, by writ from the chancery to the sheriff, not by bill from the party to the court (*Year-book,* 41 *Assize,* fol. 11). And again a writ, which was the warrant to found a particular private suit between party and party, was distinguished from a general commission of *inquiry* (42 *Assize,* fol. 12). For a writ directed the

[1] Ch. 21.

place, it declares,[1] that in cases where complainants were entitled to a writ in the chancery, grounded upon the fact of another,[2] the complainants should not depart from the king's court without remedy, because the land was transferred from one to another; as because there was no writ in the register in the chancery to be found adapted exactly to that special case, but the form of the writ was only to be had against the very person who actually raised the nuisance; so that should the house wall, or the like, which occasioned the nuisance, be aliened to another, a writ was denied.

sheriff to summon a particular party at the suit or complaint of a particular party; and therefore must set forth some legal ground upon which the party to be sued *ought* in law to be so summoned and compelled to answer. For, upon the original writ, process issued in the first instance summons, and then of capias or *distringas* to compel appearance. And for all this the writ, as a kind of warrant in law, must show some legal ground—that is, some good cause of action. But it is manifest that any injury to a legal right would be a good ground of action, whether or not the precise case had ever occurred before. For every case must *once* have occurred for the first time, and the general principle on which any had been issued would warrant any other equally maintainable in law as a ground of action. At the same time, as the nature of the process and procedure varied in different kinds of action, it was thought necessary to distinguish them in the writ, and then when the party sued appeared and orally pleaded, he could object to the writ as not warranted by the real facts, as, for instance, upon a writ of trespass for taking goods, that the goods had been received on a bailment, and that therefore the action should be in *detinue* (*Year-book*, 2 *Edw. IV.*, fol. 25). So an action against an innkeeper ought to be brought against him as such, and not in trespass (*Year-book*, *Hen. IV.*, fol. 45), and the court would set aside the writ. So, on the other hand, if the law had provided a writ as a remedy in a particular case, the party could not frame another for himself, giving a different remedy as on a different ground (*Year-book*, 11 *Hen. IV.*, 64). So in a *quod permittat* for diverting a stream, if it was shown that the stream was turned before the plaintiff had the land, so that the *diversion* was no nuisance to him, the writ could be abated, *i.e.*, set aside (2 *Hen. IV.*, 13), the remedy being an action on the case for continuance of the nuisance if either the defendant did not originally cause it, or if it was not caused in the time of the plaintiff. And that the writs might answer this purpose of practical utility it was required that they should set forth *in brief* (whence the word "brief") the ground and cause of action. It is to be observed that many of the actions "on the case" were deduced from the old real actions, which only lay between *freeholders*, whereas the actions on the case lay by any one possessed of any legal right against any one injuring that right, whether or not a freehold right, or a right pertaining to a *freehold*. The general principle was laid down some centuries after this statute, that when there was any injury to a legal right, "*action on the case lay, if no other remedy was provided*" (*Year-book*, 14 *Hen. VIII.*, 31). That was an action for obstructing a stream, and it was objected that the remedy was an assize, but the court said that the action on the case lay, as it would lie in the case of a partial obstruction of a way (*Ibid.*) So where a man ought to have kept a sea-wall in repair, and had not done so, whereby the plaintiff's land was flooded, it was held that action on the case lay (*Year-book*, 7 *Hen. IV.*, 8); though in such an action the party could do more than recover damages, and could not, as in an assize, have the nuisance abated (*Ibid.*) In general, it may be said, that for nonfeasance or *neglect* of any legal duty the remedy would be action "on the case," trespass being the remedy for any direct act of tort or injury indicated by the words, *vi et armis* (43 *Edw. III.*, 17). So again the ancient action of waste lying against tenant of the freehold, action on the case lay against tenant at will (48 *Edw. III.*, 25). And there were innumerable cases in which there was no remedy *but* action on the case (*Year-book*, 27 *Hen. VIII.*, 24). The statute may be illustrated by one or two cases upon it, which occurred early in the next reign. In one case a writ of entry was brought on this statute *in consimili casu* on an alienation by tenant for life, he being dead, and it was objected that in such a case the statute was not necessary, for that the statute gave the remedy where the tenant for life was still living; because, by the common law, the rever-

[1] Ch. 24.

[2] *De facto alicujus.*

That justice might no longer be delayed for want of legal remedies, it was now enacted, that when a writ was granted in one case, and a thing happened *in consimili casû*, and needing a similar remedy, a writ should be made accordingly. Then the statute gives this instance of a *similar* form: *Questus est nobis A. quòd B. injustè, &c., levavit domum, murum, mercatum, et alia quæ sunt ad nocumentum, &c.* And if the nuisance levied was aliened from one to another, then it was to be thus: *Questus est nobis A. quòd B. et C. levaverunt, &c.*, against both. In like manner, as a parson of a church might recover common of pasture by writ of novel disseisin, it was ordained, that from thenceforth his successor should have a *quòd permittat* against the disseisor or his heir; though a like writ, says the statute,[1] was never before granted out of chancery. Again, as a writ had long been had to try *utrùm aliquod tenementum sit libera eleemosyna alicujus ecclesiæ vel laicum fœdum talis*,[2] in future there was to be a writ to try *utrùm sit libera eleemosyna talis ecclesiæ, vel alterius ecclesiæ*, in instances where it was a contest between two churches to which the freehold belonged.

After the statute had given permission to extend several writs in the above way, there follows this general clause: "And as often as it shall happen in the chancery, *quòd in uno casû reperitur breve, et in consimili casû, cadente sub eodem jure, et simili indigente remedio, non reperitur;* then the *clerici*, or clerks of the chancery, shall agree in making a writ, or adjourn the complainant to the next parliament, and write the case in which they could not agree, and refer it to the parliament, when a writ should be made with the advice of persons learned in the law; lest it might happen that the king's court should for a long time fail in administering justice to complainants" (*a*). The clerks here spoken of are no doubt the same as the persons said by Bracton to be employed in making out *brevia magistralia*. These writs are said by that author to be varied according as cases differed; and, it should seem, they were put in contradistinction to the *brevia formata*, that were not subject to such variation, without permission of the legislature.[3] Thus

sioner was put to wait until the death of the tenant for life. And it was said, per Herle, J., in different cases there are different remedies, and the recovery which is ordained by the statute is during the life of the tenant who has aliened, for, after the death of the tenant, there is a recovery by the common law (*Year-book*, 6 *Edw. II.*, fol. 200). In another case, a writ of entry was wrongly brought on the statute of Gloucester, when it was really founded on the statute Westminster 2, *in casu consimili* (*Year-book*, 3 *Edw. II.*, fol. 75).

(*a*) In the Year-book 7 Edw. II. there is a case in which it was held that the writ of *juris utrum* could be had by an abbot or other ecclesiastical person, to try whether land was or was not held in *frankalmoigne*, or in fine and perpetual alms (7 *Edw. II.* fol. 274). It was, indeed, the only remedy by which an ecclesiastical person could discharge the land he held in right of his church, from services wrongfully claimed by a layman asserting the land to be held of himself.

[1] So says the statute; but this writ was a known and established remedy in such case in the time of Bracton. *Vide ante*, vol. i. c. vii. [This shows, as stated above, that the statute was only declaratory of the common law, and that the necessity for it, as for so many other declaratory acts, arose from the real or affected ignorance of the officials.]

[2] *Vide ante*, vol. i. c. viii.

[3] *Ibid.* c. vii.

it appears, a sort of liberty had always been exercised by the clerks in chancery of adapting the forms of writs to particular cases. It is probable that this discretion might have been exercised under the direction or control of the council, which was resorted to on very particular occasions, where there was a doubt or difficulty which the clerks could not settle among themselves. It was to preclude the necessity of recurring to a higher authority, and to relieve that authority from the burthen of such applications, that this statute confirmed and enlarged the power of the clerks in chancery, though it still leaves the choice of an application to parliament. The use that was afterwards made of this statute, in devising writs *in consimili casû*, will be seen hereafter. Of the many new writs that sprung from this parliamentary permission, one was emphatically called a writ of entry *in consimili casû*. The statute of Gloucester had given a writ of entry to the reversioner, where a tenant in dower aliened in fee, which writ has been usually called *in casû proviso*:[1] the alienation of a tenant by the courtesy was thought to be *in consimili casû* with the former; and upon that idea such a writ was framed for the reversioner. This may serve, for the present, as an example of what were considered at that time as *similar cases* within the meaning of this act.

It should seem, from the next chapter of this statute, that the following were not considered by the legislature as cases of this sort. The writ of novel disseisin being the speediest remedy in the chancery, it was thought proper to extend it further than it had yet gone. It was therefore ordained[2] that it should lie of estovers of woods; profits to be taken in woods by gathering nuts, acorns, and the like fruits; for a corody; for delivery of corn and other victuals and necessaries to be received yearly in a place certain; for toll, tronage, passage, pontage, and the like, to be taken in places certain; for the custody of parks, woods, forests, chases, warrens, gates, and other bailiwicks and offices in fee; and in all the before-mentioned cases the writ was to be expressed *de libero tenemento*, as was the form before. As heretofore[3] it lay in common of pasture, it was now to be granted in common of turbary, piscary, and the like commons (*a*), whether appendant to freeholds, or without a freehold by special deed, at least for term of life. Further, when a tenant for years, or in ward, aliened in fee, and by such aliena-

(*a*) In these early times the right of taking different kinds of profit in the same land was often in different persons. Thus there is a case in *temp.* Edward I., Fitz. *Prescription*, 55: "That a man shall have land, and may plough and sow it, and cut and carry away the corn; and then, after the corn is sown and carried away, another shall have it as his several, and the other shall not meddle in the land, but to plough it and sow it, and to take the corn; and his beasts cannot eat in the land when he comes to sow it, or to plough it, or to carry it, but he shall have no other profit except the corn only; and still the freehold was in him. And this was found by verdict; and it was found that his beasts fed in the land; wherefore the defendant took them damage feasant, and he brought replevin. And all this matter was pleaded, and found by verdict; wherefore it was awarded that the defendant should have return, and also that the plaintiff should be in mercy.

[1] *Vide ante*, c. ix. [2] Ch. 25. [3] *Vide ante*, vol. i. c. v.

tion the freehold passed to the feoffee, it was ordained that there should be a remedy by writ of novel disseisin, and that as well the feoffer as the feoffee should be taken for disseisors; so that during the life of either of them the writ should lie; and if either of the parties died, then there should be a writ of entry. Some of the cases here mentioned are said by the statute, and truly, to be such as could not be redressed by an assize at common law.

A piece of law that seemed to be thoroughly understood in the last reign was now entertained with some scruple.[1] Some had doubted whether, in case of pasturing under a claim of common in the several lands of another, the remedy by assize would lie: to remove this doubt, it was now declared that it should (*a*). Where any false exception was made to defer the taking of the assize; as, that another writ of a higher nature was depending for the same land; and to maintain such exception, rolls or records were vouched to warranty, in order to create delay, while the persons in possession received the rents and other profits; it was now ordained, that though at common law the only penalty in failing to prove such exception was, that the assize passed; yet that the tenant should in future be judged for a disseisor, without taking the assize; and also that he should restore double damages, and suffer a year's imprisonment. If such exception was alleged by a bailiff, neither the taking of the assize, nor judgment for restitution of the freehold and damages, were to be delayed. However, should the master of such bailiff afterwards come before the justices, and allege that a writ of a higher nature was depending, or the like exception, a writ of *venire facias recordum* was to be granted; and if, upon the return, it appeared to the justices that the record would have barred the writ if produced, it was ordained that the other party should be warned to appear to give restitution of his seisin and damages to the defendant, and that he who first recovered should be punished by imprisonment, at the discretion of the justices. Further, if there were any writings, or deeds of release, or the like, which were not (nor could by a bailiff be) shown to the jurors, the justices, on sight thereof, were to cause the party recovering, and also the jurors of the same assize, to be warned to appear; and if it was found by the assize that the writings were true, he who brought the assize, contrary to his own deed, was to be punished, as before mentioned. Further, it was ordained, in all assizes, that the sheriff should no longer take an ox of the disseisee,[2] but of the disseisor only; and if there were many disseisors named in one writ, yet that he should have only one ox. The ox was not to be more than five shillings' price (*b*); nor was he to take more than that price in lieu of it.

(*a*) Upon which, however, it was held that writ of entry in the nature of an assize would not lie (*Year-book* 4 *Edward IV.* fol. 2).

(*b*) The relative value of money at different periods of our history is of great importance, as it not only illustrates statutable enactments, but is necessary to under-

[1] *Vide ante*, vol. i. c. vii. [2] *Ibid.*

The remedy given to the defendant after the assize and judgment had passed, was, as we have seen, called[1] *a certificate* of assize; and now it was allowed by the former branch of this statute upon matters of record; by the latter, upon deeds and quitclaim; and this was to be not only in the assize of novel disseisin, but in those of *darrein presentment*, *juris utrùm*, and mortauncestor.

Several additions were made to some provisions of the statute of Merton. The provisions of the statute of Merton, and likewise of the statute of Marlbridge, about re-disseisins,[2] had three additions made thereto by chapter xxvi. of this act. First, double damages were in future to be given in writs of re-disseisin; secondly, re-disseisors were not to be replevisable by the common writ—that is, by the writ *de homine repligiando;* and, thirdly, whereas in the statute of Merton that writ was provided for such as were disseised after they had recovered *by assize* of novel disseisin, of mortauncestor, or by juries; it was now to lie for those who recovered by default, reddition, or otherwise, without any recognition either of assize or jury.[3]

By chap. 35 of this act several alterations were made in the statute of Merton[4] concerning the taking away of wards, as will be easily seen by comparing the two statutes. The present statute enacts,[5] concerning children, male or female, whose marriage belonged to another, *raptis et abductis*, taken and carried away, that if the person, *qui rapuit*, had no right in the marriage, yet, though he restored the child unmarried, or paid for the marriage, he should nevertheless be punished for the offence by two years' imprisonment; and if he did not restore the child, or married it after the years of consent, and was not able to make satisfaction for the value of the marriage, he should abjure the realm, or suffer perpetual imprisonment. The following writ in such case was given for the plaintiff, called since a writ of *ravishment of ward: Si A. fecerit te securum de clamore suo prosequendo, tunc pone per vadium, &c., quòd sit coram, &c., ostensurus quare talem hæredem infra ætatem existentem, cujus maritagium ad ipsum pertinet, tali loco inventum*

stand them. And to appreciate the real comparative value of money at different periods, it is necessary to notice its relative power at the respective periods with reference to the price of commodities. We see here that an ox was at this period worth only 5s., whereas the price would now be probably £20, whence it appears that the real value of money at that time was not less than eighty times what it is now. The same conclusion may be drawn from an ancient ballad, "King Edward IV. and the Tanner," in which the tanner, who is represented as well off, boasts that his horse had cost him four shillings. A wealthy tradesman would hardly boast now-a-days as to the value of a horse which cost him less than £30 or £40. There are cases in the Year-books which lead to the same result. Thus there is a case in the reign of Edward IV. in which it was held that the taking of a cart laden with corn, and the two horses which were harnessed to it, was not an excessive distress for the sum of *two shillings* (*Year-book* 20 *Edward IV.* fol. 3, pt. 16). These instances may suffice to show the value of a shilling in the age of Edward I. It was near the value of *four or five pounds* at the present time.

[1] *Vide ante*, vol. i. c. vii.
[2] *Ibid.* and *ante*, c. viii.
[3] Ch. 26.
[4] *Vide ante*, vol. i. c. vi.
[5] Ch. 35.

RAPUIT ET ABDUXIT *contra voluntatem ipsius A. et contra pacem nostram, &c.* If the heir was in the same county, then this clause was added: *Et diligenter inquiras ubi ille hæres sit in ballivâ tuâ, et ipsum, ubicunque fuerit inventus, capias et salvò et securè custodias, ita quod eum habeas coram præfatis justic' &c., ad præf. terminum, ad reddendum cui prædictorum A. vel B. reddi debeat, &c.* Upon this there issued process of distress, if he had anything to be distrained by; and if he had nothing, and did not appear, he was to be exacted and outlawed.

If the heir was conveyed into another county, a writ to the same effect issued to the sheriff of that county. If the heir died before he was found, or before he was restored to the plaintiff, the suit was yet to go on, as the ravisher was still to be punished for the offence. Again, if the plaintiff died before the suit was determined, it was to be re-summoned at the suit of the heir; and if the ward belonged to the plaintiff by gift or sale, then at the suit of his executors. If the defendant died, the action was in like manner to go on between the plaintiff and his heirs or executors by re-summons, though the punishment of imprisonment was not to extend to them. In like manner, in the writ *de communi custodiâ*, which began, *Præcipe tali, &c., quòd reddat, &c.* (meaning the writ of right of ward); if either party died, it was to be re-summoned, with distress, and proclamation at three county courts; and if the defendant came not, judgment was to pass, with a saving of his right, if he would afterwards claim it. The same, says the statute, shall be done in the writ *de transgressione*, wherein a person complained that he was *ejected* from wardships of this kind. This is the first mention of the writ *de ejectione custodiæ*, or *ejectment of ward.*

Ejectment of ward.

Notwithstanding what has been said on the case of ward and marriage of an infant heir, when he had two inheritances, one descended[1] *ex parte patris*, which was held of one lord, and another *ex parte matris*, which was held of another, a doubt is expressed in this statute to which of the lords the marriage of the heir should belong. To settle this, it was now declared[2] that the marriage should belong to that lord by whom the child's ancestor was first enfeoffed, not having respect to the sex, nor to the quantity of land, but only to the more ancient feoffment by knight's service, which merely established this point of law upon the foot on which it stood in the times of Glanville and Bracton.

Another provision of the statute of Merton[3] was extended by a subsequent chapter[4] of this statute. The regulation made concerning tenants encroaching on their lords was extended to neighbours, who had as little or less right than a lord's own tenants to encroach on his wastes. This was to hold good in all cases where pasture was claimed as appurtenant to their tenements; but where common was claimed by special grant, or feoffment, for a certain

[1] *Vide ante*, vol. i. c. vi. [2] Ch. 16. [3] *Vide ante*, vol. i. c. vi. [4] Ch. 46.

number of cattle; there, upon the principle that *conventio vincit legem*, the person entitled was to recover conformably with the terms of the grant. It was enacted (*a*), that no person should in future be liable to an assize of common of pasture, on account of any windmill, sheepcote, dairy, or the necessary enlarging of a court or curtelage. Where a person having right to approve had made a hedge or dike, which was thrown down in the night, or at any other time, but the offenders could not be found, nor would the people of the neighbouring towns cause them to be indicted, the neighbouring towns were to be distrained to repair the damage at their own costs (*b*). It was also enacted, that where common was usurped during the infancy of an heir, during the time a woman was *sub potestate viri*, while the pasture was in the hands of a tenant in dower, tenant *per legem Angliæ*, or for term of life or years, or in fee-tail, and the usurper had entered within the time of limitation in a writ of mortauncestor, the parties should not have recovery by an assize of novel disseisin, if they had no common before. This was declared by statute, because some had said that such pastures were to be considered as appertaining to the freehold, and so that a writ of novel disseisin was a proper remedy.

These are the parts of this statute which relate to private rights, excepting only chaps. xxxii., xxxiii., and xli., concerning property in mortmain, which have been mentioned in a former part of this reign.[1]

The regulations made by this statute for the administration of criminal justice were few. It was complained that many procured false appeals of homicide, and other felonies, to be brought by appellors who had no property, either to satisfy the king for the false appeal, or the party appealed in damages; it was therefore

(*a*) These statutes are still in force, and are of great importance with reference to the question of the enclosure of waste lands. It has lately been held that an owner of a common may approve under the statutes 20 Hen. III. c. iv.; and 13 Edw. I., stat. i. c. xlvi.; that the owner of a common may erect thereon a house necessary for the habitation of beast-keepers, for the care of the cattle of himself and the other persons having rights of common there; and that so he may erect a house necessary for the habitation of a wood-ward, to protect the woods and the underwoods on the common (*Patrick* v. *Stubbs*, 9 Mee. & W. 830). In that case, to an action for a continuing disturbance of common, the defendant pleaded an approvement of the *locus in quo*, "leaving sufficient of common pasture for the said plaintiff, and all other persons entitled thereto, together with sufficient ingress and egress to and from the same, according to the form of the statute," &c.—held that the plea sufficiently showed that enough of common was left at the time of the approvement, and in the place where the plaintiff was entitled to enjoy it (*Ibid.*)

(*b*) An approvement could be pleaded in bar to a *quod permittat* for common, as in a case in the 5th Edward II., where the plaintiff craved that the defendant might be summoned on a writ *quod permittat ipsum habere common au pasture;* and the defendant said that he had made an approvement of so much of the land, saving to the plaintiff sufficient common, and he prayed a recognition to be taken whether he had the better right to the land thus enclosed by reason of the approvement; to which the other party could reply that he had not sufficient common (*Year-book, 5 Edw. II.* 160). Here we see the origin of the writ of *ad quod damnum;* and the more modern enclosure acts, based upon the principle of an equitable division of superfluous waste lands, leaving to all parties sufficiency of common.

[1] Ch. 32, 33, 41. *Vide ante*, c. ix.

ordained, that when an appellee was acquitted, either at the suit of an appellor or of the king, the justices before whom the appeal was heard should punish the appellor by a year's imprisonment. The appellor, nevertheless, was to restore to the party appealed, according to the discretion of the justices, the damages he had sustained by the arrest, imprisonment, and disgrace attending it, besides a fine to the king. If the appellor was not able to pay the damages, it was to be inquired (if the appellee desired it) by whose abetment or malice the appeal was commenced; and if it was found by the inquest that any one was the abettor therein, it was enacted that he should be distrained, at the suit of the party appealed, by a judicial writ, to come before the justices, and, if he was convicted, he should be punished as the appellor. It was further ordained, contrary to the ancient practice, that in an appeal *de morte hominis*, no essoin should lie for the appellor, in whatsoever court the appeal might be.[1]

Another grievance was that sheriffs would pretend persons were indicted before them, in the tourn, of felonies and other offences, and upon that would apprehend them and confine them in prison, and so exact money for their discharge, though they were neither indicted by twelve jurors nor guilty of any offence. To put a check upon this abuse of jurisdiction, it was enacted that sheriffs in their tourns, and other places where they had power to inquire of offenders by the king's precept, or *ex officio*, should cause the inquests of such malefactors to be taken by lawful men, and by twelve at the least, who should put their seals to the inquisitions; and persons found guilty by such inquisitions were to be taken and imprisoned as heretofore. If sheriffs imprisoned others than such as were indicted by inquests of this kind, persons so imprisoned might have their writ *de imprisonamento*, as against any other person who imprisoned them without authority; the like of other bailiffs of liberties.[2]

Presentments of jurors to be sealed.

The crime of rape was once more changed into that of felony. It is provided, says the statute,[3] that if a man ravish a woman, whether married, damsel, or other, where she did not consent, either before or after, he shall have judgment of life and member; this was to be at the suit of the party. Likewise, where a man ravishes a woman, whether *dame espouse*, a married lady, damsel, or other, with force, although she consent after, he shall have judgment as before mentioned, if attainted at the suit of the king; and in this case, says the statute, the king shall have the suit. Thus the election given by the old law to the person ravished was wholly taken away.[4]

Rape.

It is said[5] there was a writ at common law, *de uxore abductâ*

[1] Ch. 12. It seems to have been doubtful in Bracton's time, whether an essoin should be allowed to the appellee, in appeals for smaller offences; and, therefore, it is most probable it did not lie in that *de morte hominis*. *Vide ante*, vol. i. s. viii. But in Glanville's time it lay for both parties. *Vide ante*, vol. i. c. v.

[2] Ch. 13.

[3] Ch. 34.

[4] *Vide ante*, vol. i. c. v.; and *vide ante*, c. ix.

[5] F.N.B. 121 K.

cum bonis viri, for the husband, though there is no mention of any such in Bracton; however, this statute provides, *de mulieribus abductis cum bonis viri*, that the king should have his suit for goods so taken, so that such offenders might now be proceeded against criminally, as well as civilly. If a woman willingly left her husband, and went away and continued with her adulterer, she was, upon conviction thereof, for ever to lose her action of dower, unless the husband would willingly, without any coercion of the church, be reconciled to her, and cohabit with her, in which case her right of action was restored. A person who took away a nun, though she consented, was by this act to be punished with three years' imprisonment, to be fined to the king, and make a reasonable satisfaction to the house.[1]

Several statutes were made for regulating the officers of courts, settling their fees, and preventing extortion and imposition upon suitors,[2] similar to some regulations made by the first statute of Westminster.[3] One of these aimed higher than the ministers of courts. The chancellor, says the statute,[4] treasurer, justices, any of the king's counsel, clerks of the chancery, of the exchequer, of any justice, or other officer; any of the king's house, clergy or lay, shall not receive any church, or advowson of a church, land, or tenement in fee, neither by gift or purchase, nor to farm, *ne a champert* (that is, to have a part, or *campi partitio*, since called *champerty*), nor otherwise, so long as the thing is in suit before them, or any other of the king's officers. If any did contrary hereto, both purchaser and seller were to be punished at the king's pleasure. The *dividing* part of the thing in question is a bribe mentioned in the first statute of Westminster;[5] but it is first spoken of here under the name of *champerty*.

After the numerous provisions made by this statute for the amendment of the law, it concludes with a sort of anxiety lest anything should be left not provided for, *super verò statutis in defectum legis, et ad remedia editis ne diutiùs querentes, cùm ad curiam venerint, recedant de remedio desperati, habeant brevia sua* IN SUO CASU PROVISA,[6] referring, as it should seem, to the 24th chapter,[7] which had given the authority to clerks in the chancery to frame writs *in consimili casû.*

Statute of Winchester.

The next act of this parliament is the statute of Winchester; containing some provisions for enforcing the ancient police, and ordaining some new regulations. The act states, that robberies, murders, burnings, and thefts, increased more than ever; and that this was to be attributed to want of a due administration of the subsisting law. It is said to have been very much owing to the negligence or wilfulness of jurors, who, being connected either with felons or receivers, could not be brought to

[1] Ch. 34. [2] Ch. 42, 44. [3] Viz. ch. 26, 27, 28, 30. *Vide ante*, c. ix.
[4] Ch. 49. [5] Viz. ch. 25. *Vide ante*, c. ix. [6] Ch. 50.
[7] *Vide ante.*

indict them: again, jurors were not, as they should be, of the neighbourhood where the offence was committed; nor was there any penalty upon jurors guilty of such concealments and neglects. To remedy this, says the statute, the king hath established a penalty, for such concealment; so that, if they disregarded their oath, they might be in some fear of the penalty. But there being no specific penalty named, it should seem, it must be ascertained by the discretion of the court. It further directed that *cries*, that is, the *hutesium et clamor*, should be solemnly made in all counties, hundreds, markets, fairs, and other places where there was great resort of people, so that none might excuse himself for ignorance: by these means the country would be so well kept, that none could escape for want of fresh suit from town to town, and from country to country[1] (*a*).

Moreover, when it was necessary, inquests were to be made in towns by the lord of the town, and afterwards in the hundred, in franchises, and in the county, and sometimes in two, three, or four counties, in case of felonies committed in the marches of shires, so that the offenders might be attainted. If the country would not answer for the bodies of such offenders, the following penalty was ordained: the people dwelling in the country were to be answerable for the robberies done, and the damages sustained; so that the whole hundred, where the robbery was committed, with the franchises therein, should be answerable for robberies; and if they were done in the division of two hundreds, *both* the hundreds and the franchises within them were to be answerable. The hundred was to have only forty days allowed them to agree for the damages, or answer for the bodies of the robbers.[2] This policy of compelling a certain district to make good secret mischiefs committed therein, had been pursued in the former statute of this year against those who broke down hedges, and committed other acts of mischief in the night.[3] Upon this provision of the statute of Winchester an action has been grounded, by which a person robbed may recover against the hundred the loss he has sustained. This has since been put under certain restrictions by several statutes.[4]

By way of prevention it was enacted, that in great walled towns, the gates should be closed from sun-setting to sun-rising; that no one should lodge in the suburbs, or in any place out of the town, from nine o'clock till day, unless his host would answer for him. Every week, or at least every fifteen days, the bailiffs of towns were

(*a*) This was the earliest of the statutes of "hue and cry," and other statutes, which have been continued to our own time by more modern statutes, all based on the ancient institutions of the hundred and of francpledge, making the hundred responsible for robberies, riots, &c. See a case on the act, *Year-book* Edw. II., fol. 539. The next statute on the subject was that of the 27 Eliz. (*vide post*, vol. iii.); as to which, however, it was held that it merely altered the proceedings, and that the statute which gave the right of action was the above, the statute of Winchester (*Andrew* v. *the Hundred of Lewkner*, *Yelverton's Rep.* 106). The modern statute on the subject was the 8 Geo. II., c. 16.

[1] Ch. 1. [2] Ch. 2. [3] West. 2, ch. xlvi. *Vide ante*, c. ix. [4] Stat. Eliz. &c.

to make inquiry of persons lodged in the suburbs and extremities of the town; and if they found any who had lodged strangers or suspicious persons against the peace (for so it was called), the bailiffs were to do right therein. Watches were to be kept, as has been used in former times, that is, from the day of the Ascension to the day of St Michael; in every city, six men at each gate; in every borough, twelve men; in every town, six or four, according to the number of inhabitants; and these were to watch continually from sun-setting to sun-rising. If any stranger passed by, the watch were to arrest him till morning; and if any suspicion appeared, he was to be delivered to the sheriff, who was to keep him safe till he was delivered in due manner. If any one resisted the arrest, hue and cry was to be raised; and those who kept watch in the town were to follow the hue and cry from town to town till the offender was taken. It was enacted that no one should be punished for arresting such strangers.[1]

It was directed, that highways should be cleared from woods, bushes, and dikes, to prevent any one from lurking there: this was to be for two hundred feet on each side of the road. However, ashes and large trees were not to be felled to make such clearance. If robberies were committed through the owners' refusing or neglecting to clear the roads in the above manner, they were to be answerable for the felonies; and if murder was done, they were to make fine at the king's suit. If the owner could not remove trees and bushes himself, the country were to aid him: the same of the king's demesnes and forests. Moreover, if a park was made by the side of a highway, it was to be at the distance of two hundred feet; or a wall, dike, or hedge, was to be made, that offenders might not come out to commit offences, and then escape back again.[2] It was further directed, that every man should have harness and arms, according to the old assize of arms, with some variations directed by this statute.[3]

Statute of *Circumspectè agatis.*

The next act of this parliament is the *statute of merchants;* which having been mentioned before, we proceed to the statute of *Circumspectè agatis.* This is so called, from the initial words of it; though it is rather in the form of a writ, from the king to his justices, concerning the bishop of Norwich and his clergy, beginning, *Rex talibus judicibus salutem, Circumspectè agatis, &c.,* without any mention of the concurrence of the parliament.[4] However, it has always been considered as a statute; is referred to by a subsequent parliament as such; and, after what has been before observed on the form of our old statutes,[5] the reader may not, perhaps, consider such deficiency of parties or wording as very singular or material.

We have no authentic account of the disputes between the tem-

[1] Ch. 4. [2] Ch. 5. [3] Ch. 6. [4] 2 Inst. 487.
[5] *Vide ante,* vol. i., c. vi.; and *ante,* c. ix.

poral and spiritual courts during this reign[1] (*a*); but it may be collected from the present statute, that some points were thought not to be sufficiently adjusted. This act was designed to ascertain the boundaries of ecclesiastical jurisdiction in some particulars;[2] for which purpose it directs, that the bishop of Norwich and his clergy (a contest with whom might, probably, be the immediate occasion of this act) should not be punished, if they held plea of such things as were *merè spiritualia:* as, for instance, of penance enjoined by prelates *pro mortali peccato*, as fornication, adultery, and the like; in which cases sometimes a corporal, sometimes a pecuniary pain was inflicted, especially if the person offending therein was a freeman: also, if prelates punished any one for having a churchyard uninclosed, a church uncovered, or not decently ornamented; in which cases none but pecuniary penalties could be imposed. So if a rector demanded parochial oblations and tithes due and accustomed, or claimed against another rector tithes, whether large or small, so as they did not amount to the fourth[3] part of the value of the church: again, if a rector demanded a mortuary in places where it was customary; so if a prelate of any church, or a patron, should demand from the rector a pension as due to him; it was ordained that all such demands should be made in the ecclesiastical court. As to the laying of violent hands upon a clerk, and causes of defamation, it was, says the statute, heretofore allowed, that suits of that sort should be heard in the court christian, if money was not demanded, and they went merely *ad correctionem peccati:* the like of suits *de fidei læsione.* In all the above-mentioned cases, says the act, the ecclesiastical judge had jurisdiction, *regiâ prohibitione non obstante.*

(*a*) As already seen, Edward I. was exceedingly arbitrary, and the clergy, and especially the prelacy, felt the pressure of his power and the rapacity of the king. There is an entry of a claim of £20,000 against the Archbishop of York, for a supposed contempt of the crown, in excommunicating civil officers for imprisonment of ecclesiastical officers for execution of ecclesiastical process, although, as both the ecclesiastical process and the power of excommunication were undoubtedly, at that time, recognised by the law, it is hard to see in what the contempt consisted. The prelate, however, was about to be committed to prison for his supposed offence, when he purchased his liberty by paying the enormous sum of £4000—probably equal to £80,000 at the present time (*Year-book Ed. III.* 28). The temporal courts did not allow any interference of the ecclesiastical power with their administration of justice. Thus, for instance, an ecclesiastical inhibition would be no excuse to a bishop in a court of law for neglect or default in the performance of any duty devolved upon him by law in the administration of justice, as by certificate of some matter of ecclesiastical cognisance or the like. Thus, in a case where plenarty was alleged, and reference was made to the bishop in the usual way, to certify as to the fact, and he excused himself from so doing on the ground of an inhibition from the archbishop, it was held to be no excuse, "for the bishop cannot excuse himself against the command of his sovereign in his own land" (*Year-book* 17 *Edw. II.*, fol. 533).

[1] Some statutes and other instruments which are assigned to this reign by Lord Coke, are to be found among the *statuta incerti temporis*, and will be mentioned in the next reign.

[2] For such cases as were allowed to belong to the spiritual jurisdiction, *vide ante*, vol. i. c. viii., &c.; and *ante*, c. ix.

[3] In Bracton's time it was limited to a sixth. *Vide ante*, vol. i. c. viii.

Such is the adjustment made by the statute of *Circumspectè agatis.* In the twenty-fourth year of this king there is a statute upon the same subject of ecclesiastical jurisdiction, which may be more properly mentioned here than in its chronological order: this is called *the statute of the writ of*[1] *consultation.* It seems the writ of prohibition had been resorted to very frequently, in cases where no remedy could be had in the king's court by writ out of chancery; so that persons who could obtain no remedy in the temporal courts were deprived also of such as might be procured in the spiritual. A representation on this subject was made to the king; and it was now ordained, that, in future, when the ecclesiastical judge was stopped by a prohibition, the chancellor, or the king's chief justice for the time being, upon sight of the libel in such case, at the instance of the complainant, if he saw there was no remedy in such case by a writ out of chancery, but that it belonged to the ecclesiastical court to determine it, should write to the judges before whom the cause depended, *quòd in causâ procedant, non obstante prohibitione regia sibi priùs inde directâ, &c.* Thus was it designed to give protection and energy to the ecclesiastical court when it exercised a jurisdiction supplemental, as it were, to the temporal courts, in correcting those excesses for which the poverty of the common law had not yet provided any redress.

A statute for regulating the police of the city of London, entitled *statuta civitatis Londini;* and another, entitled *forma concessionis et exemplificationis Chartarum,* confirming the charters, make the remainder of the statutes enacted in the famous parliament of Westminster, in the thirteenth year of this king.

[1] Stat. 24 Ed I., of the writ of *consultation.* *Vide ante,* vol. i. c. viii.

CHAPTER XI.

EDWARD I.

Statute of Quo Warranto—Statute of Quia Emptores—Modus levandi Fines—Statute de Finibus levatis—Writ of Ad Quod Damnum—Statute of Articuli super Chartas—Court of the Steward and Marshal—Writ of Conspiracy—Of the different Courts—An Action of Debt in the Steward's Court—Common Writ of Debt—Of Detenue—Of Covenant—Of Trespass—The Criminal Law—The King and Government—Statutes and Records—Fleta—Britton—Hengham—Thornton—John de Athona—Miscellaneous Facts.

PASSING over the *Statutum Exonia*, 14 Edw. I., concerning inquisitions taken before coroners (*a*), and some *articuli* upon that statute, as also the *ordinatio pro statu Hiberniæ*, 17 Edw. I., mentioned in the former part of this reign; we come to the eighteenth year of this king, when a parliament was holden, commonly called Westminster the third. This parliament produced four very important statutes. The first is the statute *quia emptores terrarum*; two statutes of *quo warranto*; and one entitled *modus levandi fines*.

To begin with the statute of *quo warranto*, 18 Edw. I. stat. 2.

Statute of *quo warranto*. Before we speak of this statute, it will be necessary to take notice of one on the same subject, and bearing the same title, enacted in the sixth year of the king. This statute was for a long time considered as made in the thirtieth year of this reign; but that is now agreed to have been only a publication of it under the great seal; and indeed it is there recited as having passed in the sixth, to which place we now restore it.

We have before seen the nature of the proceeding by *quo warranto*, or *quo jure*.[1] This writ was brought forward into more notice by the frequent use which the present king caused to be made of it, and by these two statutes for regulating the process, and proceeding therein (*b*). The king, in execution of the plan of

(*a*) It is to these Britton alludes in the chapter De Ministris, *i.e.*, officers of the crown, in the article which states that "soit enquis de prises et de fraudes de coroners et de lour clercs et de lour ministres solonque ce que est contenu en nos statutes de Excestre" (*Britton*, fol. 64).

(*b*) One of the great characteristics of this reign was the unscrupulous recourse to this writ on the part of the crown, and the strict, and indeed strained, enforcement of any prerogatives or rights of the crown which it occasioned. There was probably no species of claim which could possibly be set up by the crown which was not made at this period, and whenever a subject exercised a right which could be shown, or supposed to be a royal franchise, his title to it was challenged. Hence the records of this reign are full of proceedings relating to every possible species of royal franchise or prerogative. Thus, for instance, the crown claimed the sea-shore, and as incident thereto, the right to take wreck, and any one who took wreck was challenged to show his

[1] *Vide ante*, vol. i., c. viii.

reducing the nobles under his sovereign authority, had begun to make strict inquiry into the titles by which franchises and liberties were claimed. Some of these he had resumed by judgment of his courts of law; and many prelates, earls, barons, and others, had days fixed when they were to make out their titles, and the whole would be examined: but to quiet the minds of men till this matter was investigated, it was among other things enacted in the sixth year of the king, that a writ should issue, commanding the sheriff to permit all persons to continue in the enjoyment of such liberties as they had hitherto possessed, till the king's coming (that is, the coming of the king's court) into that county, or the coming of the justices itinerant *ad omnia placita*, or till the king gave some further direction therein. The form of another writ was prescribed, which directed the sheriff to make proclamation for all persons claiming any liberties by royal charter, or otherwise, to come before the justices *ad primam assisam, cùm in partes illas venerint*, to show *quomodo hujusmodi libertates habere clamant, et* QUO WARRANTO, &c.

Thus, instead of a special writ, which called upon a particular person to set forth his title, and which was a sufficiently severe investigation, all persons were by one general proclamation put to defend their rights, and show their titles: war was at once declared with all the liberties and franchises in the kingdom, without stating

title. Thus the Earl of Cornwall had *wreckum maris per comitatum Cornubiæ*, and his title being questioned in *quo warranto*, had judgment (14 *Edw. I. B. R., rot.* 6, *Corn.*) "For the better understanding of this act, says Coke, it shall be necessary out of history to show the cause of the making thereof. The truth is, that the king wanting money, there were some who persuaded him that few or none of the nobility, or clergy or commonalty that had franchises of the grants of the king's predecessors, had right to them, for that they *had no charters to show for them*, for that in truth most of the charters were by length of time or casualty lost or consumed, whereupon it was openly proclaimed that every man that held those liberties or other possessions by grant from any of the king's predecessors should, before certain persons thereunto appointed, show *quo jure illi retinerent*, &c., whereupon many that had long remained in quiet possession were taken into the king's hands." And then this statute was passed to provide a remedy. And for such as lay in point of charter granted before time of recovery, the party grieved had two remedies, either by allowance or confirmation: by allowance before the justices (of king's bench or of eyre), or confirmation by the king under the great seal, and these were sufficient without showing the charter. And if the franchises of either sort were granted within the time of memory, yet if the same had been allowed they might be claimed by force of the allowance without showing the charter." And so, says Coke, the remedy was perfect and plenary (2 *Inst.*, 28), though it was hardly so secure if allowance had not been obtained, and as prescription opposed a non-existing grant, it might have been allowed to prove a grant. "So all men should enjoy their franchises, which they had reasonably used, until the court came into the county. But, says Coke, you will enquire what remedy there was for him that could not produce his charter? To which he answers, That these franchises were of two kinds, the one such as may be claimed by usage and prescription, as wreck of the sea, waif and stray, fairs, markets, and the like, which are gained by usage, and may become due without matter of record; and felon's goods, &c., and the like, which grow not without matter of record, and therefore cannot be claimed by usage *in pais*, but by charter. And yet all these were at first derived from the crown. All these were granted either before or after the time of memory; if before the time of memory, then for the former kind the party might claim by prescription" (*Ibid.*)

any specific ground of complaint. The statute, however, that was made to maintain the proceeding which was hereby set on foot, declares (*a*), that should any object that they were not bound to answer without an original writ; yet, if it appeared they had usurped any liberty upon the king or his ancestors, they should answer immediately without any writ, and abide the judgment of the court: but if they said their ancestor died seised of the liberty, then they were so far distinguished from the foregoing description of persons, that the king was to award an original writ out of chancery, summoning the party to appear *in proximo adventu nostro, vel coram justitiariis, &c., cùm in partes, &c., ostensurus* QUO WARRANTO *tenet visum franciplegii in manerio de N., &c.*, upon which there was to be the same process as in the circuit of the justices. This was, in truth, nothing more than the old common law writ and proceeding.

After this statute, great numbers of writs of *quo warranto* were brought against prelates and others of the clergy, and against temporal lords and others, for their liberties, franchises, and privileges of various kinds. These rigorous proceedings were borne with great impatience. While this unpopular course was taken by the king's officers, complaint was made thereof in the parliament of the eighteenth year of this king; in consequence of which there passed the *statutum de quo warranto* NOVUM, as it is called in respect of that made in the sixth year at Gloucester. Forasmuch, says this act, as writs of *quo warranto*, and judgments to be given thereon, were greatly delayed, because the justices in giving judgment were not certified of the king's pleasure therein (it not being usual, it seems, for judgment to be given till the justices were certified of the king's pleasure by a writ *de libertatibus allocandis*, founded probably upon the statute made at Gloucester); he therefore, of his special grace, and for the affection he bore to his prelates, earls, barons, and others of his realm, granted as follows: That all persons who could make out by an inquest of the country, or otherwise, that they and their ancestors, or predecessors, had enjoyed and used any liberties, whereof they had been impleaded by any of those writs, *ante tempus regis Richardi, consanguinei sui, aut toto tempore suo, et hucùsque*, and had so continued till then, without misusing them, should be adjourned to a future day before the same justices, within which time they might attend the king with the record of the justices, signed with their seal, and also the return; and the king would, by his letters patent, confirm their titles. It was also enacted,

(*a*) It may be convenient here to quote from Britton, in which this statute seems incorporated. In treatises on the articles of inquiry at the eyre, it is said, "Soit enquis quex de counte cleyment return de nos brefs ou franchises, &c., de infangenthefes ou de outfangenthefe (punishment of thieves) et feires ou marches (fairs or markets) ou de aver wreck de meer, ou murage ou pontage, &c.," and then provision is made for the procedure at the eyre, that parties were to be summoned; "*et com eils viendront*," and thus it proceeds as in the present statute, another instance of the incorporation of statute law in Britton.

that those who could not prove the seisin of their ancestors or predecessors in the above way, should be dealt with in the regular course of law:[1] to which the king added this gracious clause, that where judgments had been given against certain persons within a particular time, he would grant them the benefit of the above provision.

To spare the expenses attending such a proceeding as this, where the contest was with the crown, it was ordained, that, in future, pleas of *quo warranto* should be pleaded and determined in the *itinera* of the justices; and that all pleas then depending should be adjourned into the counties, till the coming of the justices.[2] This is followed by another statute of *quo warranto*, making and confirming a restitution to such as had lost their liberties by judgment, and securing others who came within the grace held out by a clause in the former act. Thus was this terrible inquiry by *qua warranto* for a time let loose upon the great men of the nation, till the king at length consented to suspend it, and wholly to abolish the more oppressive parts of that proceeding.

Statute of *Quia emptores*.

The statute *Quia emptores* is entitled in the parliament roll, from the subject of it, *statutum regis de terris vendendis et emendis.* We have before seen the restraint imposed on the alienation of land by *Magna Charta*,[3] with the practice that still subsisted during the last reign,[4] and which gradually led to a violation of that chapter in the Great Charter. As the consequences of this practice were more felt, complaint thereof was made in parliament, and the following statute was passed in order to put this matter upon a new footing. Forasmuch, says the act, as purchasers of lands and tenements of the fees of great men, and other lords, have entered into their fees, to the prejudice of the lords; these purchasers having bought the lands and tenements from the freeholders of such great men to hold of their feoffors, and not of the chief lords of the fees; so that the chief lords have lost their escheats, marriages, and wardships of such lands and tenements, which was a grievance to the great landholders of the kingdom, who thought themselves in a manner disherited by such defalcations in their seigniories: for these reasons it was, at their instance, ordained, that, in future, it should be lawful for every freeman to sell, at his pleasure, his land or tenement, or part thereof, so that the feoffee should hold the land or tenement of the chief lord by the same services and customs by which the feoffer before held it.[5] (*a*) Thus every freeholder, instead of the partial permission he before had under *Magna Charta*, was at liberty to alien *all* his land, pro-

(*a*) It was held by the learned Littleton that at his day a man could not give land to hold in frankalmoigne to an abbey in fee, for by the statute of tenures he should hold of the lord paramount, of whom the donor held, and it was otherwise before the statute called *Quia emptores terrarum*, &c. (12 *Edw. IV*. 3, 4). Hence it is obvious that the statute was partly aimed at the religious houses and the alienation of land to the clergy and other ecclesiastical persons.

[1] Sect. 1. [2] *Ibid.* [3] *Vide* vol. i. c. iv. [4] *Ibid.* [5] Ch. 1.

vided he made a reservation of the services, not to himself, but to the chief lord; so that the practice of creating new seigniories now ceased, and every tenancy in the kingdom was ever after to continue a part of the same fee or manor to which it then belonged; for, if no new reservation of services could be made, no new manor could be created.

This act has two other chapters: one of them is only explanatory of the former, and directs, that where a freeholder sold part only of his lands or tenements, the feoffee should be immediately charged with the services due to the chief lord, in proportion to the quantity of the land or tenement; and the chief lord was to receive it at the hands of the feoffee.[1] It was added [2] by way of caution, that this act should not be construed as authorising the purchase of lands or tenements in mortmain;[3] and that it should relate only to land held *in fœdo simpliciter*; or, as it has since been called, *fee simple*.

Modus levandi fines.

The fourth act passed in this parliament is the *modus levandi fines*; stating the course to be observed in *levying a fine*; for so this transaction was now usually called. The little information to be found, before this statute, on the subject of fines, and the manner of transacting them in court, is derived from Glanville.[4] What is said by Bracton on this ancient security is confined to the nature of claim, and the consequence of *non-claim*.[5]

The passing of fines hereafter rested upon the directions given by this act. It directs, that when the original writ was delivered in presence of the parties, before the justices, a *countor* should say thus: *Sire justice, congê d'accorder* (this was praying the *licentia concordandi*, on which a fine was due to the king); then the justice was to say, *Que donera, sire Robert?* naming one of the parties, When they had agreed upon the sum of money to be given to the king, then the justice was to say, *Criez la peez* (that is, rehearse the concord); upon which the countor was to say, "Inasmuch as peace is licensed thus unto you; William and Alice his wife, who are here present, do acknowledge the manor of *B.*, with its appurtenances contained in the writ, to be the right of Robert, *come cell' que il ad de lour done*, as that which he hath of their gift, to have and to hold to him and his heirs, of William and Alice, and the heirs of Alice, as in demesnes, rents, seigniories, courts, pleas, purchases, wards, marriages, reliefs, escheats, mills, advowsons of churches, and other franchises and free customs belonging to the said manor, paying to Thomas and John, and their heirs, as chief lords of the fee, certain services and customs due for all services."

This was the method of proceeding to be observed in future, and fines were henceforward more uniform in their practice than they had been at the common law. It was declared to be the usage of the

[1] Ch. 2. [2] Ch. 3. [3] *Vide ante*, c. ix.
[4] *Vide* vol. i. c. iv. [5] *Ibid.* c. viii.

common law not to suffer a final accord to be levied in the king's court without a writ original; which was to be returnable before four justices in the bench or eyre, and not elsewhere: it was also to be in presence of the parties named in the writ, who were to be of full age, of good memory, and out of prison; and if a woman *covert de baron* was one of the parties, she was first to be examined by the four justices above mentioned. The reason of such solemnity, says the statute, is, because a fine is so high a bar, of such great force, and of so strong a nature, that it concludes not only parties and privies thereto, and their heirs, but all other people of the world, being of full age, out of prison, of sane memory, and within the four seas at the time of the fine levied, if they make not the claim of their action on the foot[1] of the fine, within a year and a day. In these declarations about *non-claim*, the statute seems to be framed on the principles of the common law.[2]

De finibus levatis.

In the 27th year of this king, there was another statute upon this subject, entitled, *statutum de finibus levatis*, by which it was intended to abolish a practice which had somewhat invalidated fines, and rendered them a less valuable security than they had before been considered. The statute says, that *fines* levied in the king's court ought to make, and did make, an end of all matters; and were so called, because, next to the duel and great assize, *ultimum locum, et* FINALEM *teneant, et perpetuum:* but that, in the late turbulent reign of Henry III. and since, the parties to a fine, and their heirs, contrary to ancient law and practice, had been admitted to annul and defeat such fine, by alleging, that before the fine was levied, and at the levying thereof, and since, the demandants, or plaintiffs, or their ancestors, were always seised of the lands contained in the fine, or of some parcel thereof; which fact used to be tried by a jury, and, if found to be true, was considered as annulling the fine (*a*). Thus where a fine had been

(*a*) A fine could be avoided by the heir of one who was party to it, by saying that he himself was seised at the time of the fine being levied (*Year-book*, 46 *Edw. III.*, fol. 14). And a stranger to the fine could say that the parties to it had nothing in the land (*Year-book*, 40 *Edw. III.*, 32; 42 *Edw. III.*, 20). The fine was effectual if one of the parties was seised of the land at the time of the fine being levied (*Year-book*, 41 *Edw. III.*, 14); but the conusor could not allege that he had nothing in the land, in order to defeat the fine (50 *Edw. III.*, 5). Fines were made use of for the purpose of settlements, and the originals of our modern settlements are to be found in cases upon fines, which were often made with several limitations of estates, as to one for life, their remainder to another in tail, and in default of issue to another for life, and so on (*Year-book*, 43 *Edw. III.*, fol. 13). This statute was incidentally expounded in a case in the reign of Edward III., where it was said, the statute speaks generally that those who are parties to a fine, or their heirs, shall not be received to avoid the fine by saying that their ancestors had nothing in the land, &c. Yet he shall be received to say that his ancestors had nothing at the time of levying the fine, since he himself was seised. To which it was answered, that this was because he showed the right and the possession himself at the time of the fine being levied, and before the fine (*Year-book*, 46 *Edw. III.*, fol. 3). It would appear that the statute was only declaratory of the common law, for the general principle of law always was that records bound those who were parties or legal privies, *i.e.*, privies in estate,

[1] *Sur la pie* are the words in the original; some copies read *pur la pays*.
[2] *Vide* vol. i. c. viii.

levied to a person already in possession, merely to confirm and establish his title, it was rendered entirely ineffective. To put an end to this practice, it was ordained, that such exceptions, answers, or inquisitions of the country should not, in future, be admitted, contrary to such acknowledgments and fines. The statute further directs, that such notes and fines, as were in future levied in the king's court should be read openly and solemnly, and that in the meantime all pleas should cease; and this was to be on certain days of the week, according to the discretion of the justices.[1] Thus was the doctrine of fines settled in the way it continued for many years after.

To return to the 18th year of this king, and go on with the remaining statutes, in the order in which they were passed. In the 20th year there were six statutes. The first is called the statute of vouchers; the next, of waste; the third, *de defensione juris*: these are followed by three upon the subject of the coin. The first three were made for improving some provisions of stat. Westm. 1. Thus the statute of vouchers extends the privilege given to a demandant by the 1st Westm.[2] to counterplead a warranty, if the warrantor was absent, to cases where he was present also. Vouching to warranty had been much abused by litigious men, who would vouch some indigent person; and if such vouchee entered into the warranty, there could be no counterpleading his title before this act, but the duel might be waged, and the demandant obliged to rest the determination of the question upon that decision: all which was prevented in future by this act.

The statute of waste is an authoritative decision in parliament of a point arising in a cause then pending in the bench, upon which occasion the parliament declared how the law should be held in future. The case in the bench was of an action of waste, where the plaintiff died before judgment, and his heir brought a fresh action against the defendant; to which the defendant made answer by saying, he ought not to answer for waste done before the inheritance descended on the plaintiff, and therefore demanded judgment of the action. Upon this some of the justices were of opinion, that the writ of waste, being a writ *de transgressione*, none should obtain redress and recompense thereby, but he to whom, and in

a principle equally applicable to recoveries. The very object of fines or recoveries was to bind the heirs of the conusor or recoveree. In a case in the reign of Edward IV., it was held that a party, heir of the recoveree, might plead that his ancestor was not tenant at the time of the recovery, whereby it was void in law. It was urged that this was not admissible, as the ancestor had appeared and acknowledged his seisin, and that the heir could not deny it, any more than he could allege a continuance of possession in his ancestor in the case of a fine, for it was contrary to the record. But it was answered by several of the judges, and among them Littleton, that the party could show that the recovery was void by reason that there was no tenant of the freehold against whom it had been recovered, and as to the not alleging continuance of possession against a fine, that, it was observed, was by virtue of the statute, *de finibus*, which, however, was denied by another judge, who said the statute only affirmed the common law (12 *Edw. IV.*, fol. 15).

[1] Ch. 1.

[2] Viz. ch. 40. *Vide ante*, 120.

whose time, the trespass was done: others, and many of the king's counsel, were of a contrary opinion. To settle this doubt, it was now ordained by parliament, that an heir (in whose ward soever he might be, and whether within age or not) should have his recovery by a writ of waste in the above cases, and those which were similar, as well of waste in the time of his ancestor, as since the descent upon himself; and should recover the place wasted, and damages as ordained by the stat. Westm. 2.[1] The justices were directed to proceed in that manner in the cause then before them, and in all others. This statute is one instance of the recourse which the courts used to have to the parliament for deciding doubts arising in suits before them.

It was found that abuses followed from the liberty given by stat. Westm. 2,[2] of receiving persons before judgment to defend the inheritance, where actions were brought against tenants *per legem Angliæ*, in tail, in dower, for life or years. To correct these, it was ordained by the statute *de defensione juris*, that the person so received should find such sufficient security as the court should think fit, to satisfy the demandant of the value of the land, from the day he was received till the final judgment. If the demandant recovered, he was to be amerced; and if he had not wherewithal to pay, he was to be committed to prison at the king's pleasure; though he was to go quit, if he could make his title to have been as he stated it when he was received.

Of the three provisions about the coin, the first is entitled *statutum de monetâ;* the second, *statutum de monetâ parvum.* These were against the importation of clipped and counterfeit money. This crime, by the latter act, was punished, for the first offence, with forfeiture of the money, as well in merchants negotiating as importing it; for the second offence, they were, besides, to forfeit all other goods that they had about them; for the third offence, to be at the king's mercy for their bodies and all their goods. The next provision is entitled, *articuli de monetâ*, and is upon the same subject of importing clipped money, which, it seems, was the most common offence against the coin in those days. To bring all the acts upon this article into one view, we shall mention another public instrument in the 27th year of this king, entitled, *statutum de falso monetâ.* It was therein ordained, that persons importing certain coins, called *pollards* and *crokards*, should forfeit their lives and goods, and everything that they could forfeit. It was likewise directed, that officers should be appointed at the seaports to search all persons landing there, to see if they had any unlawful money.

Thus far of the statutes in the 20th year of this king. In the 21st there are two: one entitled, *de iis qui ponendi sunt in assisis* (of which we have before spoken);[3] the other, *de malefactoribus in parcis.* We have before seen with what solicitude the

[1] Viz. ch. 14. *Vide ante*, 180. [2] Viz. ch. 3. *Vide ante*, 191. [3] *Ibid.* 184.

great lords had pressed for laws to punish those who invaded the places allotted for their rural amusement or accommodation.[1] The act last mentioned was for the punishment of persons trespassing in forests, chases, parks, and warrens; and it ordains, that such persons, if they fled, or defended themselves against the warrener, or parker, and were killed, the persons attempting to take them should not lose life or limb, or suffer any other punishment for so doing: but foresters and others were by the same act cautioned that, under pretence of the like trespassing, they did not molest or hurt any one quietly passing, for that in such cases execution should be done as before.

In the 24th year is the statute of the writ of *consultation*, before mentioned;[2] in the 25th, the *confirmationes Chartarum*, and the excommunication of those who offended against the Charters; both which have been considered before.[3] Then comes the statute *de finibus levatis*, 27 Ed. I., the first chapter of which, and that which gives the title to the statute, has been already noticed; as has the third and fourth[4] concerning justices of goal-delivery and of *nisi prius*. Chap. 2 only remains to be mentioned, which puts sheriffs under some check in their accounts of issues, fines, and the like. It ordains, that a baron and a clerk of the exchequer shall go once a-year into the country, to enroll the names of such as had paid, and hear and determine complaints against sheriffs. The other statutes in this year are, one entitled *ordinatio de libertatibus perquirendis*; and another, which has just been mentioned, *de falso monetâ*.

The *ordinatio de libertatibus perquirendis*[5] was so entitled, because it directs some course to be taken for facilitating the transactions of men in several instances where the interest of the crown was concerned. First, it was ordained, that persons who would purchase a new park, and religious men who would amortise lands or tenements, should have writs out of the chancery to inquire upon the points usual in such cases; and it was directed, that all such inquisitions, if of lands or tenements worth more than twenty shillings *per ann.* should be sent to the exchequer, and there (if the inquests had passed in favour of the purchasers) the parties were to pay their fine for the amortisement, or for the emparking; afterwards the inquests were to be sent to the chancellor, or his deputy,[6] who should accept a reasonable fine, according to the quantity of the thing to be conveyed, and then make livery thereof.[7] The same course was to be taken by those who would purchase lands or tenements held of the king in chief.[8] The writ here alluded to was that of *ad quod damnum*, as it has since been called, which has not been mentioned before, notwithstanding it was probably a writ at common law (*a*). It was directed to the

Writ of *ad quod damnum.*

(*a*) The author hardly takes adequate notice of this important writ, which was of far more general application than would be imagined from this vague and incidental

[1] *Vide ante*, vol. i. c. iv.
[2] *Ibid.*
[3] *Ibid.*
[4] *Ibid.*
[5] Stat. 27 Ed. I. st. 2.
[6] *Lieu-tenant.*
[7] Sect. 1.
[8] Sect. 2.

escheator, to inquire whether it would be *to the damage of the king*, or of others, should he permit such a one to alien in mortmain, or otherwise sell his land. After this statute, when a person wanted a license for one or the other, he used to sue to the king to have this writ out of chancery; and upon the return of it, if favourable, the license used to be granted on the terms mentioned in the statute.[1]

As a check upon the abuse of this act, it was ordained by statute 34 Edw. I. st. 3, touching the king's grants to be made upon inquests returned into the chancery concerning lands to be amortised (which plainly means the writ of *ad quod damnum*), that where there were mesne lords, nothing should be done except the religious persons could show to the king the assent of such mesne lords, in letters patent under their seals; and that nothing should pass where the donor did not reserve somewhat to himself,[2] or there was no original writ, or the writ did not make mention of all the circumstances required by the new ordinance of the king, meaning the before-mentioned statute.

It was further ordained,[3] that people living beyond sea, and having lands, tenements, or rents in England, if they would purchase writs of protection, or make general attorneys, should be sent to the exchequer, and there pay their fine for the same; also persons that could not travel, or who lived at a great distance, and were plaintiffs or defendants, were to have a writ out of chan-

mention of it, and was, moreover (as many of our ancient writs and proceedings were) the foundation of some of our most important modern statutes. The writ of *ad quod damnum* was undoubtedly of common law origin (as may be inferred indeed from the incidental way in which it is mentioned in the statute), and it lay as a kind of inquisition to ascertain whether by any proposed proceeding the crown or the public would be damnified (*Fitz. Nat. Brev.*) "*Ad quod-damnum* is a writ which ought to be sued before the king grants certain liberties, as a fair, market, or such like, which may be prejudicial to others. And by it shall be inquired if it should be a prejudice to grant them, or to whom it shall be prejudicial, and what prejudice shall come thereby" (*Termes de la Ley*, p. 15). There is hardly any writ of which there has been a wider or more expansive modern application. Thus one application of its principle was in the statutable provisions to assess compensation to owners of lands taken for highways or other public purposes, of which, perhaps, the earliest instance was the stat. 8 and 9 Wm. III., c. xvi. Another and more direct application of it was to ascertain whether the public or the inhabitants would be injured by the stoppage or diversion of a highway. In this respect it was superseded by the Highway Act, 13 Geo. III., which provided a special proceeding for the purpose, substituting the authority of the justices of the peace for an inquiry before a jury (Davison *v.* Gill, 1 *East's Reports*). The mode of proceeding presented in the Highway Acts was substituted in lieu of the old writ of *ad quod damnum*, which had become inconvenient from the expense and difficulty with which it was attended, and a more compendious and easy method was given; but still the substance of the old proceeding was to be preserved in all essential points (Davison *v.* Gill, *East*, 70). This writ therefore affords an apt and remarkable illustration of the adaptation of ancient and obsolete proceedings to the exigencies of more modern times.

1 F. N. B. 509.

2 This provision seems to take away the power of making any more gifts *in puram et perpetuam eleemosynam*. Indeed, this seems to have been before accomplished by the statute *Quia emptores;* which, by requiring the accustomed services to be reserved to the chief lord, takes away the liberty of making a gift with an exemption from service.

3 St. 27 Ed. I. st. 3.

cery to some sufficient man, who should be received as their attorney when needful.[1]

In the twenty-eighth year we find three statutes: one called the statute *of wards and relief*; the next, *for persons appealed*; the third, the famous statute of *Articuli super Chartas*. The first of these seems to be nothing more than a declaration of the common law in several points relative to ward and relief. In the first place it declares, that where a relief was given, there wardship was incident, and the contrary; that such as held by *serjeanty* to go with the king in his host, were to pay ward and marriage, as incident thereto; that those who held by *petit serjeanty*, as to bear shield or spear in the king's host (which, however, does not agree with Bracton's description of petit serjeanty),[2] should pay neither ward, marriage, nor relief; that a *free sokeman* was not to give ward nor relief, but was to double his rent after his ancestor's death, according to what he had been used to pay to his lord, and was not to be immeasurably burthened. Some declarations were made as to the nature of wards. It declares, that there were two kinds of writs to recover wards—one where the lands were holden by *knight's service*, the other where lands were holden in *socage*; that the ward of the former belonged to the lord till the heir was twenty-one years old, and also the marriage, which was to be, as ordained by the Great Charter, without disparagement; but that the ward of an heir in socage, if the land descended *ex parte matris*, belonged to the next friend on the father's side, and so *vice versa*.[3]

It further declares, that there were three ways in which a writ to recover ward might be brought: one, where the ward both of the land and the heir was demanded; this was where a tenant in knight's service died, and the chief lord demanded the heir and land in ward. Another way, says the statute, is where a man is infeoffed of a piece of land by one, and, after that, of another piece by another man: here the second lord could not have the writ, because the ward belonged to the lord who made the first feoffment.[4] The third way was, when a person possessed the land in ward, but had not the heir, then a writ would lie to demand the heir only.[5] These are the declarations made by this statute. The statute for persons appealed has been mentioned before.[6]

Statute of *Articuli super Chartas*.

The statute of *Articuli super Chartas* was made, as has been before said, to supply certain defects in the Charters; and therefore some of its regulations are upon the same subjects with many of that famous instrument. These we shall divide into such as relate to the king, or were of a miscellaneous nature, and such as related to the administration of justice, civil or criminal.

[1] *Vide ante*, vol. i. c. iv. [2] *Ibid.*

[3] For the nature of *ward* and *marriage* at common law, *vide* vol. i. c. iv.

[4] *Vide* vol. i.; and *ante*, c. x. [5] Of the writ of ward, *vide ante*, c. x.

[6] *Vide ante*, c. ix.

Of the former kind, the first that presents itself is a string of regulations concerning that heavy grievance on the subject, purveyance; the king's household officers taking provisions either without paying anything for them, or paying only what was very much under their value. It was now ordained that none should take such prises (for so they were called) but only the king's takers and purveyors for his house; they were to take nothing but for the use of his house; and all meat, and drink, and the like they were to pay or make agreement for. They were also to have the king's warrant, containing what things they should have authority to take, and this they were to show before they took anything. They were to take only what was sufficient for the king, his household, and children, and for none who were upon wages, or any other; and they were to account in the king's *hostell*, or in the wardrobe, for all things taken. If any took things contrary to the above restrictions, complaint was to be made to the steward and treasurer of the king's *hostell*, and the truth was to be inquired of; and if any was attainted of breaking the above regulations, he was to make agreement with the party, be put out of the king's service, and remain in prison at the king's pleasure. If any one took prises without a warrant, he was to be arrested and put in prison, and if attainted thereof, he was to be treated as a felon, provided the goods required it, that is, if they amounted to more than twelve-pence.

This was the order to be observed in taking meat, drink, and other small things; but as to prises made in fairs, in towns, and in ports, for the king's great wardrobe, the takers were to have the common warrant under the great seal, as before. What they took was to be under a sort of check and control from the mayor, bailiff, or keeper of the fair, and accounted for to the master of the wardrobe.[1]

It was ordained that distresses for the king's debts should not be made upon beasts of the plough, so long as any other could be found, under pain of the penalty inflicted by the statute *de districtione scaccarii*, 51 Hen. III. Too great distresses were not to be made for the king's debts, nor were they to be driven too far, which also had been provided for by the said former act.[2] Further, if a debtor could find able and sufficient sureties until some day before the day limited for the sheriff, within which a man might purchase a remedy to agree for the demand, the distress was to be in the meantime released.[3] Upon this clause a writ was framed, commanding the sheriff to accept sureties, which, if he refused, there would issue process of attachment against him.[4]

Some further provisions were made for regulating the king's revenues. To redress waste done in the king's wards by escheators and sub-escheators, a writ of waste was given, as in other cases of waste.[5] And where land had been seized into the king's hands by

[1] Ch. 2. [2] *Vide ante*, 61. [3] Ch. 12. [4] 2 Inst. 565. [5] Ch. 18.

escheators or sheriffs, and the profits taken, and it was afterwards removed out of the king's hands, because he had no right to seize it; the issues in such case were to be fully restored to the person to whom the land ought to remain, for the damage sustained.[1] Concerning the *removing* the king's hands by a writ called an *amoveas manum*, more will be said in the next year, when a statute was made on that subject.

The principal officers for the preservation of the peace of the county, or for the execution of justice, were, by virtue of the king's writ, chosen by all the freeholders of the county in open county court. It was in confirmation of this ancient usage, which, perhaps, in this instance had been violated, that it was now declared by parliament, that the king had granted to his people that they should, if they pleased, have election of their sheriff in every county where the shrievalty was not of fee.[2] By another chapter[3] of this statute it was ordained, that as the king had granted the election of sheriffs to the people of the county, they should choose such persons as would not overcharge them, or put officers in authority for rewards or bribes, nor lodge too frequently in one place, nor upon poor persons or men of religion. To avoid one great occasion of the oppressions exercised by sheriffs, it was ordained[4] that the bailiwicks and hundreds of the king, or of other great lords, should not be let to farm, as they commonly were, at over-great sums, which gave occasion to burthen the people, that the renters might be enabled to pay their ferms. This was a great evil, and to prevent the extortions to which it led, several acts were made in the subsequent times to correct, and at length to abolish this practice of letting to farm the offices of justice.[5]

The remainder of this statute relates either to the administration of civil justice, or to the criminal law. To begin with the former:

Court of the steward and marshal.

We find a provision made for ascertaining the bounds of jurisdiction in the court of the steward and marshal, a court of which nothing hitherto has been said, and the earliest mention of which is in this statute. This seems, like several others, to have been an emanation from the great court called the *aula regis*, so often mentioned, and to have been designed for the sole purpose of determining questions between persons attending the king in his household. Of the nature of this court, and the manner of conducting suits there, more will be said in the subsequent part of this reign: for the present, we shall proceed to examine the statute now made for ascertaining its jurisdiction. It was ordained,[6] that the stewards and marshals (for the statute speaks in the plural number) should not hold plea of freehold nor of debt or covenant, nor of any contract made between common persons, but only of trespass done within the *hostell*, and other trespasses done within the verge, and of contracts and cove-

[1] Ch. 19. [2] Ch. 8. [3] Ch. 13. [4] Ch. 14.
[5] Stat. 4 Ed. III. c. xv., and 4 Hen. IV. c. v. [6] Ch. 3.

nants that any one of the king's *hostell* should have made with another of the same *hostell*, and in the same *hostell*, and nowhere else. They were to hold no plea of trespass but that which should be attached by them before the king departed from the verge where the trespass was committed; and they were to hold plea thereof speedily, from day to day, so that it might be pleaded and determined before the king departed out of the limits of the same verge where the trespass was done; and if it could not be determined within the limits of the same verge, then the plea before the steward was to cease, and the plaintiffs were to resort to the common law. It was enacted, that the steward should not in future take acknowledgments of debts, or other things, but of persons of the *hostell*, as aforesaid; nor hold any other plea, by obligation *made at the distress* of the stewards and marshals (the nature of which *distresses*, to give jurisdiction to this court, will be considered hereafter); and if the stewards or marshals did anything contrary to this act, it was to be holden for void.

The steward and marshal had a criminal as well as civil judicature, and this, like the former, was confined to the verge; but it happened that many felonies went unpunished, because the coroners of the county had not authority to inquire of felonies done within the verge, but only the coroner of the king's house; and as this never continued long in one place, there sometimes could be no regular trial, no time to put the felon in exigent, and proceed to outlawry. Again, none of the matters cognisable in this court could be presented in the eyre. These failures in the administration of justice tended greatly to obstruct the well-ordering of the police. To correct these in future, it was ordained, that from thenceforth, in cases of the death of a man, it should be commanded to the coroner of the county, that he, together with the coroner of the king's house, should do as belonged to his office, and make enrolment; and those matters which could not be determined before the steward, as where the felon could not be attached, and the like, should be remitted to the common law, so that exigents, outlawries, and presentments should be made thereon at the eyre by the coroner of the county in the same manner as presentments of felonies done out of the verge; however, there was not, on this account, to be any neglect in making fresh attachments against felons by the officers in the verge.

After this provision was made to limit the court of the steward and marshal, it was moreover ordained, that no common plea should thenceforth be held in the exchequer contrary to the form of the Great Charter.[1] From whence it seems, though the words *curia nostra* in the Charter were construed by the legislature to mean the exchequer, as well as the court properly so called, conformably with the account we have before given of this court,[2] yet, that suits between party and party were still entertained there.

[1] Ch. 4. [2] *Vide ante*, vol. i. c. iii.

This had been complained of, and the legislature endeavoured to remedy it in the statute of Rutland, 10 Edward I., where the king says, that whereas certain pleas have been hitherto held in the exchequer, which did not concern us or our ministers of the exchequer; by which means our pleas, and the business of the people, *coram nobis*, are improperly prorogued and impeded, therefore we are willing, and ordain, that no plea be held or pleaded in the exchequer aforesaid, unless it specially concerns *nos vel ministros nostros prædictos;* which statute was thereby directed to be enrolled in the exchequer, for the government of the barons. Thus did the court of exchequer, by these two statutes, seem to be completely deprived of all cognisance, except in the suits of the king, and his ministers and officers; but we shall see hereafter, that this last branch of their jurisdiction was made use of, in subsequent times, to introduce all sorts of causes, under the pretence that they affected the king's ministers or officers.

The following chapter says, that, on the other hand, the king willed, that the chancellor, and the justices *de soen banc*, should follow him; so that he might have at all times near him some sages of the law, who were able duly to order the business that came into the *court*, at all times when need should require.[1] This probably required no more than what was the usage before; as, where the court was, there, of course, were to be the justices. However, when it was thus ordained that the chancellor, who kept the great seal, should always attend the king, it might very easily be declared, as it was in the next chapter, that no writ touching the common law should thenceforth issue under the petit seal,[2] as very likely had before sometimes happened, through the absence of the chancellor.

It was moreover declared by this statnte, in confirmation of the common law,[3] that in pleas of land, the summons and attachments should contain the term of fifteen days at least, according to the common law; unless in attachments of assizes taken in the king's presence,[4] or in pleas before justices itinerant during the eyre.[5] It was directed also,[6] that the stat. Westmin. 2, c. xxxix., about false returns, should be faithfully executed. There was a provision[7] about the qualifications of jurors, which has been noticed in another place.[8] This was the whole of the regulations made as to civil justice, except only a law respecting the jurisdiction of the Constable of Dover Castle; it was thereby declared, that he should not hold plea, within the castle gate, of any foreign matter of the county, except it related to the keeping of the castle; nor was he to distrain the inhabitants of the Cinque Ports to plead

[1] Ch. 5. [2] Ch. 6. [3] *Vide ante*, vol. i. c. viii.

[4] Lord Coke says, that these words should be added, "or before the justices of common bench." It is true, indeed, that the term of fifteen days was not allowed in case of disseisin at common law. 2 Inst. 567. *Vide ante*, vol. i. c. viii.

[5] Ch. 15. [6] Ch. 16. [7] Ch. 9. [8] *Vide ante*, c. ix.

anywhere, or anywise, than according to their charters of ancient franchises confirmed by *Magna Charta.*[1]

The alterations in the criminal law ordained by this statute, consist in two provisions about conspirators and maintainers, and one about the statute of Winchester. It seems a writ had been framed by *Gilbertus de Rouberie, clericus de concilio domini regis,* and allowed by the authority of parliament, in the 21st year of this king,[2] though this statute is usually placed in the 33d year.[3] This writ was against conspirators, inventors, maintainers of false quarrels,[4] and partakers thereof, and brokers of debates, and was as follows:—*Si A. fecerit, &c., tunc pone, &c., quòd sit coram nobis in octabis sancti Johannis Baptistæ, ubicunq; tunc fuerimus in Angliâ, ad respondendum prædicto A. de placito conspirationis et transgressionis,* SECUNDUM ORDINATIONEM NOSTRAM NUPER INDE PROVISAM, *sicut idem A. rationabiliter monstare poterit, quòd ei inde respondere debeat, et habeas ibi nomina plegiorum, et hoc breve, &c.* In allusion to this writ, it is said, in the statute we are now speaking of,[5] that, as to conspirators, false informers, and evil procurers of dozens, inquests, assizes, and juries, the king had provided a remedy for the plaintiffs by a writ out of the chancery. But, notwithstanding this provision, says the statute, the king willed, that his justices of the one bench and the other, and justices assigned to take assizes, when they came into the country to discharge their office, should, upon complaint, award inquests therein without writs, and do right to the plaintiffs without delay.[6]

Writ of conspiracy.

We have before mentioned several statutes against maintenance of suits and champerty, in the parliament of Westm. 1, and Westm. 2;[7] but these were all confined to certain ministers therein named, as the chancellor, treasurer, justices, the king's counsellors, clerks of the chancery, of the exchequer, and of justices, and to those of the king's household, clergy or lay. An act was now made in general terms, which declares, that *nul ministre, ne nul outre,* should take upon him a business in suit, to have part of the thing in question. But this was not to prohibit any one from having the counsel and advice of countors and learned men for his fee, nor of his parents or friends.[8] Some further notice was taken of these offenders in the subsequent part of this reign.

Because crimes and disorders were thought to have increased through a relaxed police, it was ordained, that the statute of Winchester should be sent again into every county, to be read and published four times a-year, and kept as strictly as the two Great Charters, under the pains therein limited. For the observance and maintenance of this statute, it was ordained, that the three knights assigned in the county[9] to redress offences against the

[1] Ch. 7. [2] 2 Inst. 562. [3] St. 3. [4] That is, suits.
[5] Stat. art. sup. cart. [6] Ch. 10. [7] *Vide ante,* c. x.
[8] *Ses parentz e ses procheins.* Ch. 11.
[9] Namely, by ch. 1 of this stat. *Vide ante,* c. ix.

charters, should have charge of this also.[1] This statute concludes with some very minute regulations for assaying vessels of gold and silver. No vessel of silver was to pass out of the hands of the workers till it was assayed by the wardens of the craft, and marked with a leopard's head; and no gold was to be worked worse than that of Paris.[2]

Thus far of the 28th year: in the 29th, there is a statute on the subject of *amoveas manum*, concerning which we before spoke in the statute of *Articuli super Chartas.*[3] It was now ordained, that in all cases where it appeared by an inquest, taken before the king's escheators, that the land did not belong to the king, a writ should be immediately obtained in chancery, commanding the escheators, *quòd manum suam amoveant omnino*, and cause the land, with all issues and fruits of it, to be restored to the right owner (*a*). However, if it should afterwards turn out that the king had any title, the person was to be summoned by writ out of chancery to appear *coram rege*, and show cause why the king should not have the custody of the land; and so, *toties quoties*, an *amoveas manum* and a *scire faciat* might be had by the party and the king. This was with a *non obstante* of the statute made in the preceding year.

In the 31st year there is a statute entitled *tractatus de ponderibus et mensuris:* in the 33d there are several statutes; one called *statutum de protectionibus;* another, containing *a definition of conspirators;* another, called the *statute of champerty;* another, *an ordinance for inquests;* another, *ordinatio forestæ;* another, *an ordinance for measuring of land.*

We[4] often had occasion to mention the obstruction of justice occasioned by the warrant *de servitio regis.* We now find a similar device under the denomination of *protection.* By means of such a writ, a person was protected against all suits in the king's courts, under pretence that he was engaged in the king's service. The statute relating to protections was to prevent some of the evil consequences attending those privileges. It was now ordained, that, in such case, the adverse party might challenge the protection, upon its being shown in court, and aver that the person was within the four seas, or out of the king's service in a certain place, whence he might very easily have come to attend. This challenge was to be entered, and the matter stand without a day, according to the nature of the protection. When it was re-summoned, the party objecting was to demand judgment, and offer to aver his chal-

(*a*) Wherever the court saw that the crown, though not a party to the record, was interested in the matter, it might pronounce judgment for the crown; and if a presumption of title appeared in the crown, the court would suspend execution until the party had interpleaded with the crown (*Adam Pennell's Case*, 29 *Edward I.; Maynard's Memoranda in Scaccario*, 42; 7 *Hen. IV.*, 71; 12 *Hen. VII.*, 12; 16 *Hen. VII.* 12; *E. Stringer's Case*, Lib. Ass., anno 1, fol. 12; *Bro. Abr., de rege inconsulto.*)

[1] Ch. 17. [2] Ch. 20. [3] *Vide ante*, c. x. [4] *Ibid.* vol. i. c. viii.

lenge; and if the country passed against him that cast the protection, and he was tenant in the action, the protection was to be turned into a default: if it was the demandant, he was to lose his writ. This was a very beneficial law, at a time when actions were liable to be totally stopped by such regal interpositions.

The[1] next statute defines conspirators in this way: Conspirators are those who confeder and bind themselves together by oath, covenant, or other alliance, that every of them shall aid and bear the other, falsely and maliciously to indite, or cause others to indite, or falsely to move or maintain pleas; also such as cause children within age to appeal men of felony, whereby they are imprisoned, and sorely grieved; such as retain men in the country with liveries or fees, to maintain their malicious enterprises; and this was to extend as well to the takers as givers. Again, stewards and bailiffs of great lords, who by their seigniory, office, or power, undertake to bear or maintain quarrels, pleas, or debates that concern other people, and not their lords or themselves, were to be considered as conspirators.

Champerty was defined by the same statute. *Champertors,* says the act, are those who move, or cause to be moved, pleas and suits, either by their own procurement or by that of others, and sue them at their own costs, to have part of the land in dispute, or part of the gains (*a*). This definition of champerty is in the English edition of the statutes, but no original text appears to warrant it; and it is probable, that it was added by some reader to explain what followed; for the next statute is entitled, "the statute of champerty," and ordains, after alluding to the former acts on that subject,[2] that all persons attainted of such emprises, suits, or bargains, and such as consented thereto, should be imprisoned for three years, and make fine at the king's pleasure. The ordinance of inquests[3] directs, that when a juror was challenged for the king, the inquisition should not therefore remain; but those who sued for the king should show some cause of challenge, and the truth of such cause should be inquired of according to the custom of the court; after which the inquisition should be proceeded in or not, according as the challenge was established or not. The *ordinatio forestæ* has been noticed in another place.[4] The last of this year is the statute for measuring of land.

In the 34th year there are several acts. The first is the statute

(*a*) This has always been considered a great mischief, tending to encourage litigation, by leading to *speculative* litigation; hence the statute (32 Hen. VIII.) passed in affirmance and furtherance of the old common law on the subject, enacted that no one shall buy or sell, or by any means obtain, any pretenced rights or titles to land, &c., unless he who sells or by whom he claims, shall have been in possession thereof, or have taken the rents and profits by the space of a year; and therefore if any one who has the naked right to lands sells them, it will be within the statute, as if a disseisor, before re-entry, sell his land, *although he has a real right to it.*—*Co. Litt.* 369.

[1] *Vide ante,* c. x.

[2] Viz. 3 Ed. I. c. xxv.; 13 Ed. I., stat. 1, c. xlix.; 28 Ed. I., stat. 3, c. xi. *Vide ante,* c. x.

[3] Stat. 4.

[4] *Vide ante,* c. ix.

de conjunctim feoffatis; the next consists of some articles upon the statute of Winchester; the remaining three have been mentioned in another place,[1] namely, that for amortising lands, that *de tallagio non concedendo*, and the *ordinato forestæ*.

The statute *de conjunctim feoffatis* was to prevent the delay occasioned by tenants in novel disseisin and other writs pleading that some one else was seised jointly with them.[2] It was enacted, that where such a plea was grounded upon a deed, and the plaintiff would offer to aver by the assize that the day of the writ purchased the tenant was sole seised, the justices might retain the deed safely in their keeping till the assize had tried it; and the person named to be joint-tenant by the deed, as well as the tenant, was to be warned to appear at a certain day, and then to answer to the assize, as though the original writ had been brought against both. It was also enacted, if the plea was found to be false, and for delay, that then, notwithstanding the assize passed for the tenants, yet he who alleged the plea should suffer a year's imprisonment and a heavy fine. Further, the plea of joint-tenancy was no longer to be received from a bailiff, who, we have seen, was in some cases allowed to put in pleas for his principal. If it was found that they were joint-tenants, as alleged, the writ was to abate: the same in writs of mortauncestor, *juris utrùm*, and other real actions.

There is the following provision in this statute concerning the writ of *indicavit*, which is a writ of prohibition that has frequently been mentioned.[3] This writ used to be brought at the commencement of the matter in the spiritual court, so that no room was left to judge whether a writ of consultation should go or not. It was therefore now ordained, that it should not in future go till they had proceeded so far in the court christian as the *litis contestatio*, and the chancellor could be certified of the nature of the suit by inspection of the libel.

In the 35th year are two statutes—one, *de asportatis religiosorum*, which has been noticed in another place;[4] the other, which is the last in this reign, is entitled, from the subject of it, *ne rector prosternat arbores in cæmeterio*. Great disputes had happened between rectors and their parishioners, to which of them the trees in the churchyard belonged. It was now declared by this act, that they are sacred property; that they follow the nature of the soil, which is *ecclesiæ dedicatum*, and that the laity had no disposal thereof. However, as they were planted for protecting the church from winds and storms, rectors were prohibited by this act from cutting them, except for reparation of the chancel; nor were they to convert them to any other use, unless the nave of the church needed repair; in which case parsons would do well in bestowing such trees upon the parishioners; though, says the act, we do not command this, but will commend it when done.

[1] *Vide ante*, c. x.
[2] For the practice on this point, at common law, *vide* vol. i. c. viii.
[3] *Vide* vol. i. c. iii. [4] *Ibid.* 157.

We have now travelled through the numerous statutes of this king, and have performed the task, perhaps, with more expedition, and less show of difficulty, than is commonly annexed to the idea of such an undertaking. These statutes have been usually studied with great labour, through the obscurity in which a long lapse of years has involved them; yet the matter of them has been, in all ages of our law, thought so important, as to make that labour be submitted to with patience. These, with the statutes of Henry III., are considered as the foundations of the common law; and indeed, after Glanville and Bracton have been so long neglected, the attention of the student could be directed to nothing more ancient. But with all the importance which is so deservedly attributed to them, and notwithstanding the space which the learning upon them fills, when they are viewed in retrospect by a modern lawyer; yet in the historical account that has been here attempted of our ancient legal polity, they appear comparatively small. It is true, that in the reign of this prince many more statutes were made in a few years, than in many reigns of his predecessors. Those statutes were very important in their object, and many of them very beneficial in their consequences; but antecedent to that period, the slow hand of time and experience had been long moulding our laws and judicature into a form capable of receiving the finishing touches which were made by Edward; and in that respect, perhaps, the turbulent and unprosperous reign of his father Henry was more productive than his. This consideration of the subject will account for the appearance which these statutes, and indeed this whole reign, makes, in point of length, when compared with the former.

Indeed, the changes made in our law by the gradual alteration of opinions during this reign, seem to have been very few. The rules and principles which had been so thoroughly weighed and settled in the reign of Henry III. still operated with all their influence, except in those instances where they were modified by the late statutes. Thus we find the law stated by Fleta and Britton to be the same, almost in every particular, as it was delivered by Bracton, with the addition only of the statutes of Edward I. One exception, however, should not be passed over in silence, which is, that in the law of descent, according to Britton, the half blood was to be excluded,[1] which had not been settled in the time of Bracton.[2]

Very little, therefore, remains to be said on any part of the subject, which was so fully handled in the last reign; and we shall confine ourselves to such heads as were there treated rather cursorily, or not mentioned at all. This will be principally in the jurisdiction of courts, and the nature of personal actions.

Of the different courts.

We have seen what was said by Bracton upon the different courts;[3] they are mentioned by the author of Fleta more fully in the following way: *Habet rex curiam suam in concilio suo, in parliamentis suis, præsentibus prælatis, comitibus,*

[1] Ch. 119. [2] *Vide ante*, vol. i. c. vii. [3] *Ibid.*

baronibus, proceribus, et aliis viris peritis, ubi terminatæ sunt dubitationes judiciorum, et, novis injurii, emersis, nova constituuntur remedia; et unicuiq; justitia, prout meruit, retribuetur ibidem. This is the account of the supreme judicature, in which, it should seem, he includes both the council and parliament (*a*). The next is the court *coram senescallo suo in aulâ suâ.* This officer is described as filling the place of the chief justiciary (an office that was abolished in the last reign), who used to be named in the writs of the earlier periods, determined the king's own causes, and administered justice without writ.[1] In the place of this great officer was now appointed the *senescallus,* or steward of the household. This court has been mentioned before in this reign, and the nature of its jurisdiction was defined by a particular statute.[2] Fleta describes this court as having jurisdiction of all actions against the king's peace within the bounds of the household for twelve miles, *ubicunq ; rex fuerit in Angliâ ;* which circuit of twelve miles was called the *virgata regia,* because it was within the government of the marshal, who carried a *virga* as the badge of his office. According to the same authority, these actions might be brought *recenter*, and without writ, *non obstante privilegio, vel libertate alicujus legem regni expectantis.* This jurisdiction was exercised in the *aula regia,* and the steward might associate with him the *camerarius*, the *hostiarius*, or *marescullus,* being knights ; or any of them, if they could not all be present.

The next court of the king mentioned in Fleta, is that held *in cancellariâ.* After this, he says, there was a court *coram auditoribus specialiter à latere regis destinatis,* whose office was not extended beyond the justices and ministers of the king. The business of these auditors was not to determine, but to report to the king what they had heard, that he might direct what was proper to be done between the parties. After these he mentions *curiam*

(*a*) It appears that cases were brought before the parliament in this and the next reign. Geffrey Scorley and others sued in parliament to have brought up the record of a plea of land, which was before Sir R. de Bellars in the new exchequer, before the king and his council. And it appeared by the record that one E. and others had been cited by writ into the exchequer, to answer to one R. and to the mayor and bailiffs of Southampton, and other men of the commonalty of Southampton, for that whereas they held the port and the vill of the king in fee-farm, rendering £220 to the exchequer, and ought to have all the tolls and customs of the vill and port ; the said E. and others, of Lympton, which is in the precinct of the port, took twenty shillings of a certain person, and would not permit the mayor and commonalty to receive the custom, and assaulted one John, a bailiff of the king, whom they had deputed to receive it. It appeared to be objected that the judgment for the plaintiffs was erroneous, because the suit ought not to have been brought in the exchequer ; on the other hand, it was answered that the plaintiffs were the king's farmers, and that therefore it affected the crown, and the judgment seems to have been upheld (*Year-book, Edw. II.*, fol. 280). It appears also from the *Memoranda in Scaccario, temp.* Edward I. (*Year-book, Edw. II.*) that cases were brought into the exchequer chamber before the king and his barons of the exchequer by way of error, or complaint, or appeal (2 *Edw. I.*, fol. 3). The bounds of jurisdictions were not yet, however, exactly defined.

[1] *Vide ante*, vol. i. 114.

[2] *Ibid.* 235.

suam, et justitiarios suos, tam milites quàm clericos, locum suum tenentes in Angliâ, before whom, and before no others (except before himself, or his council, or special auditors), false judgments and errors of justices were reversed and corrected. Before them also were determined writs of appeal, and other writs in criminal matters; trespasses against the king's peace; and all writs which contained the clause *ubicunq; tunc fuerimus in Angliâ.* Next to these he ranks the *justitiarios residentes ad Scaccarium,* and those *in banco apud Westmonasterium* (*a*); after these, the justices assigned *ad gaolas deliberandas* in different counties; those assigned to take assizes, juries, inquisitions, certificates, and attaints; the justices itinerant *ad primas assisas, ad omnia placita, criminalia et civilia;* and the justices itinerant *ad placita de forestis.* All these were the king's courts; to which might be added, others in the country, as the county, tourn, and hundred courts; those in the king's manors, and those in cities and boroughs.[1]

King's Bench.

Of these courts, that before the steward is the only one which has not been mentioned in the early parts of this history; for which reason it may be proper to add some further account of this court than the short mention made thereof when we were speaking of the statute passed in this reign concerning it. The stewards, says Fleta, had cognizance of all injuries (by which

(*a*) To the Year-book of Edward II. are appended "Memoranda in Scaccario de tempore regis Edwardi Primi," from which much valuable information may be collected as to the legal history of the age. From these it appears that the exchequer, though primarily a court of revenue, yet as the king and his principal barons, sitting there, received complaints as to the administration of justice generally, it had become a court of error. For we find an entry in the second year of a writ of error brought of a judgment given by justices (2 *Edw. I.*, fol. 3). And that it was the *curia regis*, for one of the records commences, "Quia curia regis coram baronibus de scaccario" (5 *Edw. I.*, fol. 6). But that it had no ordinary jurisdiction, save as to debts due to the crown, for in 5 Edward I. a record runs thus: "Cum placita coram baronibus in scaccario secundum legem et consuetudinem regni sui teneri non debeant nisi de debitis regis propriis et ministrorum de scaccario, ac Johannes de Michelden qui non est minister regis implacitet coram Adam de Fraxino coram baronibus de £13, &c., rex, nolens sustinere hujusmodi placita, contra tenorem Magnæ Chartæ, de libertatibus Angliæ alibi quam suis locis propriis et debitis placitari; rex mandavit baronibus quod placitum illud vel aliud placitum commune coram eis non teneant," &c. (fol. 7). And again, in the 12 Edward I. we find this record: "Cum placita de transgressionibus et catallis, et debitis, et alia communia placita coram Justiciariis de banco vel coram Justiciariis Itinerantibus, aut coram viscontibus in suis comitatibus debeant et consueverunt, secundum legem et consuetudinem regni placitari et terminari; et non ad scaccarium nisi tamen placitis de debitis regis, &c., et de debitis ministrorum regis ejusdem scaccarii ac de transgressionibus eisdem ministris," &c. (12 *Edw. I.*, fol. 12). Thus, therefore, it was settled law that common suits ought not to come into the exchequer in the first instance. Numerous entries attest how entirely arbitrary the courts then were in all that regarded the crown, and how eagerly every case was taken advantage of for the purpose of securing some emolument to the royal treasury. Thus, for instance, we find that one Gilbert de Brunholmstead was adjudged to prison for a certain term for some trespass of which he was convicted before the justices itinerant, and he was convicted of felony, and after that demanded his privilege of clergy; but it was not allowed, except on infliction of a fine, "Sed non fuit liver al ordinary postea fecit finem pro imprisonamento;" and then there was a writ to deliver him to the ordinary, if he desired it, but his goods were not to be restored (fol. 28).

[1] Fleta, 66.

are meant trespasses), and all criminal and personal actions, *per inventionem plegiorum de prosequendo*, and were to do ample justice to parties complaining, without allowing any essoin. Thus, when sufficient pledges were found and enrolled by the king's clerk, who had the keeping of the *rotulum placitorum aulæ pro rege*, the marshal was commanded immediately to attach the person complained of, if he was to be found within the limits of the household; otherwise he was not attachable by the marshal. If the complaint was against any *familiaris regis*, he was first to be summoned, and if he did not come at the appointed day, then there was an award, *quòd attachietur* till a further day; and if he did not come then, there was an award, *quòd corpus capiatur* (provided he had received the summons personally within the verge), and brought before the steward; and then, says Fleta, the marshal was to be his pledge; or, in other words, he was to be continued in the marshal's custody, according to the law and custom of the household; and the marshal was to be answerable to the party complainant, if he did not have the body forthcoming. When Fleta has stated this to be the method of proceeding against a *familiaris regis*, he adds, *quòd dictum est de serviente regis, dici poterit de* COMITIBUS, *in tantum quantum paritatem consequuntur*: so that the authority of the steward went beyond the king's servants, properly so called.

As this court followed the king wherever his household removed, and so far suspended all other jurisdictions; the method was, when the king was about to fix his residence at any place, for the steward, in the name of the chief justiciary, whose place he filled, to command the sheriff, *quòd venire facias coram nobis* on such a day, *ubicunq; dominus rex tunc fuerit in ballivâ tuâ*, all assizes of novel disseisin, mortauncestor, *ultimæ præsentationis*, great assizes; all juries, inquests, attaints, pleas of dower *unde nihil*, which were summoned before the justices *ad primas assisas*, all prisoners, and persons manucaptured or bailed; all attachments which belonged to the gaol-delivery; and all the freemen to compose juries. When the steward arrived at the destined place, he began to discharge the business of the county; beginning as the justices itinerant did, with the criminal matters. After he had despatched those,[1] he then proceeded to trespasses committed within the verge against the peace; then to the assizes and fines; and lastly, to debts and contracts, where the debtors had voluntarily bound themselves to the distress of the steward and marshal. Matters that could not be despatched by him while there, were to be adjourned, either into the bench, *ad primas assisas*, into the county, or otherwise, as it seemed most expedient. He might direct proceedings to outlawry, waging of the duel, and everything which belonged to the regular justices itinerant.

The contracting of obligations *ad districtionem senescalli et ma-*

[1] Fleta, 67.

rescalli, or one of them, was the means by which the jurisdiction of these officers might be greatly extended, as the plea of *extra virgatam* would not in such case avail; in these matters, and in all others, except pleas of freehold, the parties were heard without writ.[1] When a person was convicted of a debt before the steward, he was to be committed to the custody of the marshal, till he had satisfied the party for his debt, and the king for his amercement and fine: however, he might be replevied *ex potestate marescalli* for forty days, but no longer.[2]

So necessary and inseparable an appendage to the king's household was this court thought, that when the king was in France, in the fourteenth year of his reign, and a person was charged with a robbery committed in the household, it was allowed by the French king (after the point of jurisdiction had been contested between his court and that of the English king) that the steward should exercise his jurisdiction; and the offender was accordingly put upon his trial, was sentenced and hanged.

It will be seen, in the subsequent part of this history, how the steward occasionally delegated his authority to the justices, *locum suum tenentes in Angliâ*, who thence assumed to themselves the power to hold plea of suits *by bill* against persons in the custody of the marshal.

The chancery is called by Fleta *an office*, though he had before spoken of a *court* held IN *cancellariâ*. This office, says he, was intrusted to some discreet person, as a bishop, or other dignified ecclesiastic, together with the care of the great seal. The department of the chancery was carried on by the assistance of several subordinate officers, who are thus described by Fleta:[3] *cui associentur clerici honesti, et circumspecti, domino regi jurati, qui in legibus et consuetudinibus Anglicanis notitiam habeant pleniorem;* it was the business of these clerks to hear and examine the petitions and complaints of suitors, and give them a remedy by the king's writ, fitted to their case.[4] These *collaterales et socii* of the chancellor, as he calls them, were the superior officers there; and were called *præceptores*, on account of the direction they gave, after hearing a complaint, for making out remedial writs. These *masters* had become of greater consideration since the statute[5] had enlarged their power of making out writs *in consimili casû*. The inferior officers are described as *clericos legaliter expertos*. These likewise were acquainted with the forms of writs, and had a power to allow such as they approved, and reject those that were defective. They were to examine all writs as to the matter and style of them, before they were put to the seal; nor was any to be sealed that did not come through their hands. There were besides six *clerici prænotarii*, who, together with the former, were considered as *familiares* of the king, and were provided with board and clothing out of the profits of the seal, for their trouble of writing out writs.

[1] Fleta, 68. [2] *Ibid.* 69. [3] *Ibid.* 75. [4] *Ibid.* 76. [5] *Vide ante*, c. x.

Besides these, there were other clerks,[1] who are styled *juvenes et pedites*, young persons of inferior condition, who for despatch of business, were, by the favour of the chancellor, permitted to be employed in making out the *brevia cursoria*. These were to be under the superior clerks, who were to be answerable for all their acts; for which purpose it was required, that the writer's name should be noted on every writ.[2]

This is the account given of the chancery, and other courts, by the author of Fleta. The same writer is somewhat minute in relating the proceedings in certain personal actions, particularly that of debt (*a*). We shall give from him, first, the method of commencing such an action of debt in the steward's court, and then add something concerning this action, when brought at common law.

An action of debt in the steward's court.

To commence an action of debt in the steward's court, there needed no writ, as was said before, but only to show the debtor's obligation, and that part of it where he bound himself to the distress of the steward or marshal (*b*); then, after security *de prosequendo* was taken of the creditor, the marshal was commanded to distrain the debtor by his chattels, till he had found pledges (provided he was taken within the bounds of the household) to appear the next law day before the steward to answer the creditor without any essoin, or other delay. If the debtor could be found, he was to be attached *per corpus* till he had obtained his liberty by giving pledges; if he had no pledges, he was to be detained till he answered the creditor, but he was not to be put in chains. Suppose he found pledges, and had a day given him at the end of fifty days, at which he failed to appear, his pledges were amerced, and he was taken,

(*a*) It is to be observed that as the court of chancery was, in its origin, rather an *office* than a *court*, the writs issued out of it were, for the most part, returnable or triable in some *other* court. Thus, the *Mirror* says (c. iv., s. 2, 3): "That writs issued out of the chancery directed, some to judges of other courts, some to officers as sheriffs, &c., and that those writs which were *not* pleadable or returnable before the king were returnable in chancery; implying that those which *were* 'pleadable' were returnable 'before the king,' *i.e.*, in the king's bench." So it would be, for instance, in *scire facias* when a judicial writ. Thus, in *scire facias* on a recognizance in the chancery, brought in the chancery, the defendant pleaded a release, and the plaintiff denied it, and so they were at issue, and the action and process were sent into the queen's bench to be tried; and there the plaintiff was nonsuit, and brought a new *scire facias* there and well, for the record was then there and not in chancery; and so *note, that the chancery shall try nothing by a jury, but the king's bench* (*Year-book*, 24 *Edw. III.*, fol. 45).

(*b*) The court of the "marshal" had jurisdiction over personal injuries within twelve miles of the royal court or residence, wherever he might be, which was the jurisdiction exercised by the court of the king, before the king himself—the supposed origin of the jurisdiction of the court of king's bench in common suits between party and party, although, as that court *had* such jurisdiction before the Great Charter, and was then deprived of it only indirectly and conditionally by the clause enacting that common pleas should not follow the king's court, it would follow that, when the court ceased to follow the king, it recovered this jurisdiction, and the senseless forms and fictions devised under the pretence of *giving* the jurisdiction

[1] Fleta, 77. [2] *Ibid.* 78.

if he could be found within the jurisdiction of the household, and detained, as in the former case; he was not to be again enlarged on pledges till he answered to the suit. If the debtor had been distrained twice, thrice, or oftener, and he at length appeared; yet, before his cattle were delivered, he was to make fine for his contempts, unless he could prove *per legem* that he came as soon as he knew he was called upon to appear; and then, upon giving pledges to stand to the suit, debtors were allowed to have the disposal of their chattels distrained, and were immediately to put in their answer to the creditor.

This was the process against those who bound themselves voluntarily to the distress of the steward or marshal. But the method of proceeding with those who were *comites,* was more gentle. They were first summoned by the marshal; and if they disobeyed, then they were to be distrained; and the third process, if necessary, was an attachment. In the same manner did they proceed against the *familiares servientes* of the king, who were attendant upon him in his house. It was upon this privilege of the king's servants that the saying, then well known, was founded, *quòd servientes regis sunt pares comitibus.*[1]

When the debtor came in to answer, he might allege many things against the creditor by way of exception. He might ask, what he had to show for his debt; and if he had nothing but his own declaration to prove it, the person attached had judgment, *quòd quietus recedat.* But if he produced his *secta,* the debtor was to defend himself *per legem* against the *secta,* the same when the plaintiff produced tallies,[2] unless he was a merchant; for it was permitted *de gratiâ principis,* says Fleta, in favour of merchants, to prove tallies that were denied, by two sworn witnesses at least,

(like the similar forms and fictions resorted to under the like pretence in the exchequer) had their origin really in the desire to multiply forms and accumulate fees. The court of the king, however, retained a species of privileged jurisdiction, copiously explained by Lord Coke in his case of the "Marshalsea" (*Coke's Reports*), and thus described in the *Mirror*: "The king maketh his justices in divers degrees, and appointeth to them jurisdiction, and that in divers manners, sometimes in certain; generally, as it is of commissions of justices in eyre, and of the chief justice of pleas before the king (*i.e.*, the king's bench), and of justices of the bench (*i.e.*, the common pleas), to whom jurisdiction is given to hear and determine fines not determined, the grand assizes, the transaction of pleas (*i.e.*, common pleas), and the barons of the exchequer have jurisdiction over receivers and the king's bailiffs, and of the rights of the crown. Sometimes jurisdiction is given to the justices of the bench by removing of pleas out of inferior courts. To the office of chief justices it belonged to redress and punish the tortuous judgments of other justices, and by writ to cause to come *before the king* (*i.e.*, the king's bench), the proceedings and records, and before such justices are all writs pleadable and returnable, and also it belongeth to their office to hear and determine all plaints of personal wrongs (*i.e.*, as the phrase always means in the *Mirror*, wrongs to the person) *within twelve miles of the king's house*" (*Mirror*, c. iv., 3).

1 Fleta, 131.

2 A tally is thus defined by Spelman:—TALLIUM, *alias* TALEA—*est clavola vel ligni portiuncula, utrinq; complanata, cui summa, debiti insiditur: fissaq; inde in duas partes, una debitori, altera creditori traditur in rationis memoriam.* It seems a tally was a common security for money in those days.

who, upon diligent examination, were found to agree upon the day, place, number, and other circumstances thereof.

If a writing was produced, and any default was found in the name or number, the defendant might say, he was not bound to answer such writing, because it was faulty. He might say, *quòd non est factum suum.* He might say, he had paid it, if he had anything to prove the payment. He might say, he was not bound to the distress of the steward or marshal; and if that was proved, the plaintiff could recover nothing, unless he could reply, that though he was not bound to the distress of the steward or marshal, this could not avail him, for he belonged to the king's household, was always in his service, and in such case he was obliged to answer to the suit; for as he would be entitled to an essoin *de servitio regis* in every other court, there would be an entire stop to justice, if he could not be sued in this. He might say, he ought not to answer, because he was taken without the limits of the household, and not within the jurisdiction of the marshal, but brought there by violence. He might say, that the king did not reside within twelve miles of the place on the day named in the *narratio,* so that the fact could not happen within the limits of the household, and, of consequence, not within the cognizance of the steward. He might say, it concerned his freehold, and so might demand judgment, whether he was to answer concerning his freehold without a writ. He might say, that the plaintiff had complained of the same trespass in another court, where he *quietus recessit, et querens in misericordiâ pro falso clamore.* He might show an acquittance; or say, that another plea was then depending in another court by writ for the same matter. If there was a condition in the obligation, he might say, that he was not bound to pay the debt, because the condition was not satisfied.[1]

If more than one were bound by the obligation, he might demand judgment, whether he was to answer singly for a debt contracted by many in common. Again, if each was bound to pay the whole, he might say, that one of them paid it for all, and he might vouch the record, or an acquittance of the plaintiff; but if he failed of the record or acquittance, at the day fixed for him to produce it, he was, for his delay, to render double damages to the plaintiff, and be grievously amerced in proportion. If he did not appear at all on the day appointed, his pledges were to be further distrained till they satisfied the creditor, or rendered to the marshal the body of the principal and were likewise to be amerced for the failure of the record or acquittance. He might say, that at the time of making the obligation he was *non compos mentis,* or *non sui juris,* because under age, in the custody of such a one, in prison at such place, or oppressed, or coerced by threats: if a wife, she might say, she was not to answer without her husband. Many other exceptions which would defeat the plaintiff's action, might be taken.

[1] Fleta, 132.

It should be observed, that when the obligor died, the obligation died with him, for no one could bind his heir to answer to the distress of the steward or marshal. Again, it must be remembered, that this whole jurisdiction of the steward in matters of debt, which was a *commune placitum*, was against the provision of *Magna Charta* on that point;[1] since which, says Fleta, common pleas were to be confined to the justices of the bench, and justices itinerant *ad omnia placita.* But, adds he, this cognizance of certain special causes was given to the steward by the king, in analogy to the jurisdiction exercised by the exchequer over such common pleas as concerned the king, though equally within the chapter of *Magna Charta:* the latter was permitted in hopes that the king might obtain his own debts, through the debtors of his debtor, with more ease than by levying it on his own debtor's lands and chattels. However, it seems this privilege of suing in the exchequer was rarely extended beyond a person *in debito regis vehementur existentem;* and then it was never done but by special permission from the king.[2]

Actions of debt were also brought in the county, in cities, boroughs, and franchises, in cases of small demands (*a*); and as in the former instance the interest of the king was consulted, in this latter it was for the benefit of the people at large, that they should have justice adminstered near their own homes without much trouble or expense. Debts under forty shillings were recoverable in the hundred, wapentake, trithing, and other inferior courts belonging to the king or to great lords.[3]

The writs of debt were various. One, since called SI RECOGNOSCAT,[4] was thus: *Rex vicecom.· Præcipimus tibi quòd* SI *A.* RECOGNOSCAT *se debere decem libras, tunc distringas præfatum A. ad prædictum debitum præfato B. sine dilatione reddendum, &c.* This gave the sheriff a record of the matter; and if the debtor acknowledged the debt before the sheriff,

Common action of debt.

(*a*) Debts or causes of action to *any* amount were cognisable in the county court *by writ.* The limitation of amount applied only to suits by mere plaint without a writ, which meant a *fee.* "En counties, par devant les viscontes, &c., poient estre pledes *sans nos brefs,* plees de trespass et de dettes, issint que les biens emptes ne les trespass ne les dettes demaundes ne passent mye *xls.* ne de dettes *passant* mesme la summe *sauns nos brefs,* les ques nous volons ascune foits que soient pledes en counties si il ne soient de illonques remues par nos commandements" (*Britton,* "De dette," fol. 62). So the *Mirror,* in its remarks on the clause in the statute of Gloucester as to suits above 40s. in the superior courts, notices that this distinction was lost sight of, and says, "For small trespasses, debts, contracts, and such things, not exceeding 40s., suitors have power to hear and determine *without* writs by ordinary jurisdiction, and by *writs* in other cases, for sheriffs have more jurisdiction in their writs viscontiel," &c. (c. v. s. 3). And at the end of the chapter it is added: "Et sont autres acciones personelles pledables par viscont *par nos brefs de justicies,* de torts faits en contractes, come est de covenants ufreint, ou de accounte, ou de aver commune, ou de chartres detenus, et de nuisances," &c. (fol. 71). Thus, therefore, it is plain that even at this era in the history of our law, the county court had jurisdiction to any amount, provided a writ of justicies was sued out, which only meant that a fee should be paid to the king's exchequer.

[1] *Vide ante,* vol. i. c. v.

[2] See an instance of such permission in Ryley's *Placita Parliamentaria.*

[3] Ryley's *Pla. Parl.*

[4] O. N. B.

he was to be distrained by all his movables till the creditor was satisfied. If the debtor denied the debt, then the plaintiff had the following writ: *Præcipimus tibi, quòd* JUSTICIES *A. quòd justè, &c., reddat B. decem marcas quas ei debet, ut dicit, sicut rationabiliter monstrare poterit quòd ei reddere debeat, ne ampliùs inde clamorem audiamus pro defectu justitiæ, &c.* This was a writ of *justicies*, upon which it had been the practice of the sheriffs not to proceed till pledges *de prosequendo* were found. This, however, is blamed by Fleta, since the writ required no such process, but according to that author, they ought only to *command* the debtor, as they were directed by the writ. If he did not make payment forthwith, it was clear he meant to stand out a suit; and should the plaintiff pray that suit should be made to recover it, then, and not till then, need he offer pledges *de prosequendo.* Upon such security being given, the debtor was to be summoned by two freemen of the vicinage where he resided, to appear at the next county, to answer in the said plea of debt; and it was sufficient if the matter of such summons was related to any of his family. If he did not appear at the day, nor essoin himself, then, on the appearance of the plaintiff, the sheriff was commanded to distrain him till he found pledges to appear, and answer at the next county.[1]

If the debtor appeared, and the debt was proved, the judgment was, *quòd recuperet debitum cum damnis*, which latter were to be taxed by the sheriff and *sectatores* of the county, *if* the defendant prayed it; and the defendant was to be *in misericordiâ:* the bailiff of the hundred where the defendant had most movables was then commanded, *quòd de catallis suis haberc faciat, &c.* Should the bailiff be remiss in this, and not properly execute the writ, or should the debtor, in order to defraud the creditor, have designedly suffered his land to lie unstocked, and no beasts or chattels were to be found thereon; in such case it was advisable for the creditor to remove the plea by *pone* to the superior court, and then execution might be had in any hundred or county; and of the land also, by an *elegit*, grounded on the late statute.[2]

But to save the trouble of such removal by *pone*, it would be better to commence the action originally before the justices of the bench, by the following writ: *Præcipe A. quòd justè, &c., reddat B. decem marcas quas ei debet et injustè detinet, ut dicit: et nisi fecerit, et præfatus B. fecerit te securum de clamore suo prosequendo, tunc summone per bonos summonitores præfatum A. quòd sit coram justitiariis nostris apud Westmonasterium tali die, ostensurus quare non fecerit, &c.* This writ differs very little from the writ of debt in Glanville's time.[3] There was another writ of debt now in use for executors: *Præcipe A. quòd justè, &c., reddat B., &c., executoribus testamenti talis, &c.;* and, on the other hand, one against executors: *Præcipe A. et B. executoribus testamenti C. quòd justè, &c.* Respecting executors, it was held at this time, that

[1] Ryley's *Pla. Parl.* 134. [2] *Vide ante*, c. ix. [3] *Ibid.* vol. i. c. iii.

if they demanded a sight of the instrument by which a debt was claimed against them, they could not afterwards plead, *quòd de bonis defuncti nullam habent administrationem.*[1]

Another writ cognisable in the county was one which has not yet been mentioned, and which was called *de annuo redditû.* This likewise might be pleaded in the county, and was as follows: *Præcipimus tibi, quòd justicies A. quòd justè, &c., reddat B.* DECEM MARCAS, *quæ ei à retrò sunt de annuo redditû tanti per annum, sicut rationabiliter, &c.* An *annuus redditus* might be due in three ways: either where a lord was seised of a certain rent, together with homage and fealty, issuing out of a freehold, or where the lord had assigned over the rent, which remained as a charge upon the freehold into whatsoever hands it passed: the third way was, when the rent was received not out of a freehold, but *de camerâ*, from a chamber, or the like, for the life of somebody. The writ of annuity went for the arrears and damages: to the damages the defendant might answer *per legem;* but to the arrears he could not. This writ would lie upon the mere writing containing the grant, without any seisin having been obtained.[2]

To return to the action of debt. If the sureties were distrained without proceeding against the principal debtor, who yet was able to pay, they might have a writ to the following effect, directed to the sheriff: *Monstraverunt nobis A. et B. quòd cùm ipsi, &c.*, stating that they were sureties only, and were distrained, notwithstanding the principal debtor was sufficient, which ought not to be; therefore, *Tibi præcipimus, quòd distringas præd. C.*, the principal debtor, *pro præd. pecuniâ, et præd. plegiis pacem habere permittas; et averia sua si qua eâ occasione ceperis, sine dilatione deliberari facias, &c.* It has been before seen[3] what provisions had been made in case of sureties for debts due to the king. We now find, that if the sureties had paid the debt of the principal, or had incurred any damage on account of it, they might have the following writ: *Præcipimus tibi, quòd justicies A. quòd justè, &c.*, ACQUIETET *B. de centum solidis unde posuit eum plegium versus C. et nondum eum acquietavit, ut dicit, sicut eum rationabiliter, monstrare poterit, quòd eum acquietare debeat, ne ampliùs, &c.*, which, like other *justicies*, might be removed into the superior court by *pone.* If the action was brought originally in the superior court, the writ was thus: *Præcipe A. quòd justè, &c., acquietet B. de centum solidis, unde, &c.* This writ, nearly in these words, was in use in Glanville's time;[4] but it should seem, it then lay for the creditor only against the surety; now it lay for the surety against the principal; as the surety, by paying the debt, had put himself in the place of the original creditor.

We have seen what was the method of proof in an action of debt in Glanville's time.[5] Nothing is said on this subject by Bracton (*a*);

(*a*) There is a good deal upon the subject in Britton, which our author lost sight of.

[1] Fleta, 135. [2] *Ibid.* 136. [3] *Vide ante*, vol. i. c. iv. [4] *Ibid.* [5] *Ibid.*

but from the practice, which obtained in many actions, of bringing a *secta*, and afterwards a jury, it is most probable the mode of trial in his time was the same as is stated by Fleta in this reign. That writer says, that if the creditor had no writing to show, he was to take some other method of making out what he calls *rationabilem monstrationem* that a debt existed; for, continues he, it had been ordained by *Magna Charta* that no one should be put to answer either *per legem* or *per juramentum* upon the *simple voice* of another.[1] The creditor was therefore to produce a *secta*—that is, the testimony of certain lawful men who were present at the contract; and if these, upon being examined by the judge, were found to agree, then the defendant was to *vadiare legem*, as it was now called, or wage his law against the plaintiff and his *secta*. The mode in which this was done is thus described by Fleta: If the plaintiff produced two witnesses, the defendant was to produce four; if three, he was to produce six; so that the defendant was always to have two *juratos* to the plaintiff's one, till they came to twelve; and they did not ever go further than *duodecimam manum*. In this case, says he, the proof lay upon the person who denied the charge.[2] It was a rule, that where the right was equal, the defendant rather than the plaintiff should be admitted to the proof. The waging of law was considered as making a proof, and always surpassed the presumption raised by the *secta*, according to the rule, that *lex vincit sectam* (*a*). If any of the *jurors* (for so those

The chapter "De dette" is remarkably copious and complete. It first treats of the different kinds of debts: "Obligation doit estre vestere de V. maneres de garniment, de chose, de parole, de escript, de unite de volonte, de bail, de jointure. De chose, quant ascun chose est apprompt de rendre, &c. De parole, corauntо entre le creaunsour et le dettor, per les ques ils donassent per offres et per demandes. L'autre est escript: dont il est simple et sauns condition; et aussi purra l'escript estre conditionel, &c. L'autre est bail, &c. Et adonques les debtors se purrait eyder (aider) en moults des maners par exceptions. Et se il tende taille ou suyte, et la suyte soit trouve accordante, adonques purra il defendre la det par sa ley. Car il purra dedire l'escript, et tendre par pays que ces n'est mye son fait. Et si le pleyntife priè, soit donques enques la verite per les testmoynes nommes en l'escript ou per pays" (*i.e.*, by the attesting witnesses, or a jury); "ou il purra dire que l'escript ne luy doit grever, car quant il le fist il fait dedens l'age de xx. ans, ou que riens ne fuit fait per son seal, et en tiel manere purra et dedire le fait; et sur ce soit enquies la verite par la visne ou le fait duist estre fait, et solonque le verdit du pays soit celuy que serra trouve mentour juge a la prison, et puny per fyn. Et celes exceptions, eyent lien en nostre court devant nos justices" (*Britton*, fol. 66). So of other defences, as acquittance, or condition, &c. Thus, therefore, it appears that the mode of pleading and proving defences was already settled. And it is added: "Et come ascune dette soit recouvere en nostre court, soit le judgment et la execution fait solonque la ordinance de nos statute" (fol. 70), meaning the enactment in the statute of Westminster as to exemption.

(*a*) In Britton the whole matter is very fully described under the title "Dette." The defendant, it is said, might take any exception, and, among others, that he had nothing of the plaintiff for which he was indebted. "Si il eyt rien de luy per quoy il se soit tenu a cet dette rendre;" and upon this he could have wager of law. "Et si il tende taille ou suit, et la suit soit trouve accordante, adonques purra, il defendre la det per sa ley," &c. (*Britton*, fol. 64). Or, again, he might deny a deed, and *that* would go to the country—*i.e.*, a jury. "Car il purra dedire l'escript, et tendre par pays, que ces n'est mye son fait." "Et en tele manere purra il dedire le fait, et sur ces soit enquis la verite par la visne, ou le fait duist estre fait, et solonque

[1] *Vide ante*, vol. i. c. iv.

[2] Fleta, 136.

who swore for the defendant were called) refused to swear, or those produced were not sufficient, the defendant was convicted. If the *secta* varied in their account, the defendant was not put to wage his law against it, but had judgment, *quòd recedat sine die, et querens in misericordiâ.*

What is said of a *secta* to prove the verbal declaration of the plaintiff, held equally where a *secta* was produced to prove a tally; for if a tally was not supported by a *secta*, credit would be given to the single oath of the party *denying* it. But, says Fleta, it is otherwise in cities and fairs, and in causes between merchants, in favour of whom, as was shown before, it was granted *ex gratiâ principis*, that the proof should lie on the party *affirming;* they therefore might prove their tallies, if denied, *per testes et per patriam.* There was this remarkable custom among merchants, that where a tally was produced to support an action, and another was produced to prove that the first was discharged, which tally of discharge was denied, the person whose tally was denied was to prove it in this way: he was to go to nine churches, and upon the nine altars of them he was to swear that the plaintiff gave him the said tally as an acquittance of the debt contained therein, "So help me God and His holy Gospels;" after which the judgment was, *quòd recedat inde quietus in perpetuum*, and the plaintiff *in misericordiâ.*[1] It was because these methods of proof left too much room for debtors to avail themselves of their hardiness in swearing that another method of recovering debts was contrived by the statute-merchant.

This is all that is said by Fleta on personal actions; so that what he has left on this subject is confined wholly to the action of debt, and that *de annuo redditu:* nor is Britton more explicit. For further information therefore on this subject, we must have recourse to other sources. In the *statutum Walliæ* we find mention of other personal writs, with the proceeding upon them, as prescribed for the use of the Principality. There can be no doubt but this detail was copied from the course of proceeding in the English courts, and is particularly worthy of attention on that account. We shall therefore extract from thence what is said on the action of *debt, covenant*, and *trespass.*

le verdit du pays, soit celuy que serra trouve mentour juge a la prison et puny per fyn." The reason for the distinction was, that to a deed there would be witnesses who could be called as jurors, for at this time it must be borne in mind that jurors were still witnesses—that is to say, they gave verdicts of their own knowledge. It followed that in matters to which there were no witnesses there could not be trial by jury. Hence, in cases of private debts, without deeds, the procedure by wager of law or compurgators—that is, the defendant's oath, denying the debt, supported by the oaths of his compurgators. This was the only possible substitute in our age, which had not yet attained to the system of trying cases by the verdict of a jury upon evidence of witnesses. The practice of wager of law was found to lead to abuses; hence a statute afterwards passed in the reign of Henry IV. to check it in cases of account, by means of an examination of the plantiff and his attorney.

[1] Fleta, 138.

The writ of debt hitherto mentioned was for the recovery of money owing; but in this statute we find a writ for the recovery of a chattel belonging to the plaintiff. The following is a writ of this kind: *Præcipe A. quòd justè sine dilatione reddat B. unum saccum lanæ pretii decem marcorum, quam ei injustè* DETINET; *et nisi fecerit, &c.* This writ was in after-times called *detinue;* being in effect nothing else than a writ of debt, which, when brought to recover a chattel, was in the *detinet*, instead of the *debet.*

Of detinue.

The process to be pursued in a writ of debt in Wales was this: Upon pledges *de prosequendo* being found, the debtor was summoned to appear at a certain day, and if he failed, was summoned again. If he failed at the second summons, and did not essoin himself, the debt was adjudged to the plaintiff by default, with damages at the discretion of the justice, or by an inquest of the country, as the justice pleased, and the debtor to be *in misericordiâ.* If the debtor appeared, then the plaintiff was to set forth the ground of his action; and, to prove it, he was to produce his *secta*, or a charter of obligation, or a tally. If the defendant denied the debt, and his obligation was produced against him, the writing was to be verified *per testes nominatos in obligatione*, if they were alive, *simul cum patriâ.* If there were no witnesses, or they were dead, it was to be verified only *per patriam*, and, according to the verdict of the country, judgment was to be given. If the plaintiff had no obligation, but only produced a *secta* or *tally*, the defendant might defend himself either *per legem*, that he owed him nothing (that is, by his own oath and that of eleven swearing with him), or *per patriam*, as he pleased. Again, if the defendant said he had paid the debt, he was to show an acquittance; to which the plaintiff might answer, by denying, either *per legem* or *per patriam,* that he had received anything.

The writ *de conventione*, or *of covenant*, was sometimes for recovery of movables, sometimes of immovables. No forms of this writ are mentioned by Bracton or Fleta; but in the *statutum Walliæ* we find the following: *Præcipe A. quòd justè et sine dilatione* TENEAT *B.* CONVENTIONEM *inter eos factam de uno messuagio, cum decem acris terræ, et quinq; acris bosci, cum pertinentiis in N. Et nisi fecerit, &c. tunc summoneas prædictum A. quòd sit, &c. ostensurus, &c.* These writs varied according to the nature of the covenant, and might be returnable before the justices, or, by a clause of *justicies*, in the county.

Of covenants.

The process in a writ of covenant was as follows: Upon pledges *de prosequendo* being found, the defendant was to be summoned once, and, if needful, a second time. If he did not come at the second summons, nor send on essoin, the *petitio* of the plaintiff was to be heard, and the thing in question, if a tenement, was to be taken into the king's hands; if a chattel, the thing or its value; and another day was given to the parties. If within fifteen days he replieved the thing so taken, and came at the day appointed, he was received to answer and make his defence; but if he did not appear, the claim of the plaintiff was adjudged to him by default, together with damages taxed, as above mentioned in a writ of debt, and he was to be *in misericordiâ*. If the defendant appeared, both parties came to allegations, and at length to an inquest of the country, by which the matter was determined. There is no mention of any *secta* in this action; though it is most probable there was one in this as in other actions.

A freehold was sometimes demanded in a writ of covenant; as when land was demised upon a certain firm or rent, with a condition, that should the firm not be paid, the person demising might enter and hold the land: in such case, should the rent be in arrear, and the demisor not able to make an entry, he might recover the land, together with damages, by a writ of covenant. Again, when an agreement was made between two persons, that one should infeoff the other of a freehold, and give him seisin by such a day; if afterwards he infeoffed a third person of that tenement, then a writ of covenant would lie against him, not to recover the land (which having passed by lawful feoffment could not go back), but money or damages for the breach of covenant. Thus we see, that, in some cases, land could be recovered in a writ of covenant; and in such case it was a real action; in others, only damages; and then it was a personal one. In after-times, the former writ of covenant was that on which fines were generally levied.

Of trespass.

We have seen a provision made in this reign[1] to confine actions of *trespass*, where the damages were not more than forty shillings, to the inferior courts; and another[2] for shortening the process of attachment. Of this action we have been enabled to say very little: neither Bracton, Fleta, nor Britton give any particular account of the nature of the proceeding therein, after the parties were in court; nor do they even exhibit the form of the writ. In the *statutum Walliæ* it is directed, that the justice should command the sheriff, *quòd faciat venire* the person complained of, at an early day. The plaintiff was to set forth his complaint, as in other actions, and the defendant to make his answers thereto. As it could scarcely happen, says the statute, but the defendant would defend himself *per patriam*, the justice was to inquire the truth by a good and sufficient *patria*, by consent of the party: if the defendant was found guilty, he was to punish him by imprisonment, or fine, or *misericordiâ*, and also by damages, which were to be given to the party injured, according to the nature of the trespass (*a*).

(*a*) This was one of those injuries which, being committed with force, was deemed to warrant a fine to the king, and to suggest either indictment or action: a doctrine now confined to actual force and violence, as a forcible entry or assault. The *Mirror* says of such cases—"Si ascun querevit vengeance adonque appuert de attaquer sa action par appele de felonye, et si ils quent denends, des dammages, donque apprest de attainer se action par bref" (c. ii., s. 3). If, indeed, it is really criminal, as a felony,

[1] *Vide ante*, 149. [2] *Ibid.* 124.

This inquisition was to be taken, as we said, by consent of the parties; for if the plaintiff offered to verify the trespass *per patriam*, and the defendant refused the country, he was taken *pro convicto*, and suffered the same penalty as if he had been convicted by the country.

Though the writers of this period say so little upon the action of trespass, it happens that a complete record of the proceedings in trespass, from the writ to the award of a *venire*, is to be seen in Ryley's Collection. As this will furnish a specimen of records in other actions, as well as in trespass, the reader will not think it tedious to read it at length. This record was in the 21st year of the king. It begins with a recital of the execution of the writ of attachment. *A. B. et C. attachiati fuerunt ad respondendum D. personæ ecclesiæ de Cheping-norton de placito, quare, vi et armis, in præfatum D. in suâ domo inventum insultum fecerunt, et ipsum a domo sua extraxerunt, et bona et catalla sua ibidem inventa ad valentiam centum librarum ceperunt, et asportaverunt, consumpserunt, et voluntatem suam inde fecerunt, et alia enormia ei intulerunt, ad grave damnum ipsius D. et contra pacem, &c.* After this, there followed a similar entry of the *narratio* upon the writ, in these words: *Et unde queritur, quòd prædictus A. et alii die sabbati proximâ post festum St Johannis Bapt. hoc anno, vi et armis, venerunt ad domum ipsius D. apud Cheping-norton, et in præfatum D. in eâdem domo inventum insultum fecerunt, et ipsum a domo suâ extraxerunt, et bona et catalla sua ibidem inventa, viz. blada, frumentum, hordeum, avenam, cicerem, et quandam cistam in camerâ suâ ibidem inventam fregerunt, in quâ fuerunt diversa jocalia, ut ciphi aurei et argentei, firmacula et annuli de auro et argento, et alia diversa scripta obligatoria de debitis quaterviginti marcarum et plus, sibi per diversos debitores debitis, et bona illa, et scripta, et alia bona ad valentiam centum librarum ceperunt, et asportaverunt, consumpserunt, et voluntatem suam inde fecerunt, viz. vina biberunt, cicerem, blada sua cum equis, et hominibus suis consumpserunt, et alia enormia ei intulerunt, ad damnum ipsius D. quingentarum marcarum, et contra pacem, &c. Et inde producit sectam, &c.*

Then the plea begun as follows: *Et prædicti A. et alii per attornatum ipsorum B. et C. veniunt, et defendunt vim, et injuriam, et quicquid est contra pacem, &c. Et idem A. pro se et aliis dicit, quòd ipse est persona ecclesiæ de Cheping-norton, et fuit prædictis*

the right of action gives way to the king's suit—"Si autem duo vel plures competunt actiones, contra unum, quarum unum, sit criminales, et altera civiles, criminales prius debet terminari" (*Bracton*, lib. iii., fol. 113). But this only applies when the matter is really criminal, not where it is merely a ground of fine. Thus, in Year-book, 16 Edw. II., fol. 490, is the case of the Prior of Coventry, who brought a writ of trespass against John de Nevill and many others, for a confederacy and riotous assembly, to beat him and his servants; and it was objected that the thing was an offence against the crown, so that the action pertained only to him; but Herle, J., said that the plaintiff only mentioned the riot as matter to aggravate the fine to the king, and that he relied on the trespass to himself, and for that he should recover damages; and though the king could pardon the fine he could not the damages.

die et anno ; et eodem die accessit ipse ad ecclesiam suam prædictam, et ad domos suas eidem ecclesiæ annexas et pertinentes, de quibus domibus omnes prædecessores sui, personæ prædictæ ecclesiæ, fuerunt seisiti tanquam pertinentibus ecclesiæ suæ prædictæ, ut de jure ejusdem ; et sic ipse A. et alii prædictis die et anno ad domos ipsius A. venerunt, de quibus domibus ipsemet jam multo tempore præterito extitit in seisinâ. Sed tam idem A. quàm alii bene defendunt, quòd ad domum prædicti D. prædictis die et anno, vi et armis, non venerunt, nec in ipsum D. insultum fecerunt, nec ipsumæ domo suâ extraxerunt, nec aliqua bona sua ceperunt, asportaverunt, aut consumpserunt, sicut eis imponunt ; et de hoc ponunt se super patriam.

To this the plaintiff replied as follows: *Et prædictus D. bene cognoscit, quòd prædictæ domus sunt pertinentes ecclesiæ prædictæ ; sed dicit, quòd ipse jam undecim annis elapsis extitit persona præfatæ ecclesiæ, et in plenariâ possessione ejusdem, et pacificâ ; et hoc notorium et publicum est per totum comitatum Oxoniæ ; et fuit in pacificâ possessione ejusdem prædictis die et anno quando prædictus A., &c., vie et armis, ut prædictum est, in ipsum D. in domibus suis propriis insultum fecerunt, et ipsum de domo suâ extraxerunt, et alia enormia, &c., ut prædicitur, ei intulerunt, contra pacem, &c. Et quòd ita sit, petit quòd inquiratur per patriam, et prædictus A. et alii similiter.* Then follows the award of a *venire: Ideò præceptum est vicecomiti, quòd venire faciat coram domino rege in octabis St Mich. ubicunque tunc fuerit in Angliâ, &c.,* 24 *tam miletes, &c., per quos, &c. Et qui nec, &c., ad recognoscendum in formâ prædictâ, quia tam, &c.*[1]

It appears from hence that the *narratio* had become of more consideration than in the reign of Henry III. It was now drawn with more form and precision, and was liable to be excepted to if deficient in either. We find in the last reign[2] the order in which a defendant was to state his exceptions was this: first to the jurisdiction of the court; then to the person of the plaintiff; next, to that of the defendant; if they were both proper parties to the suit, then he might except to the writ. The writ, as it contained the ground of the action, and was the only part of the proceedings in writing (the *narratio* and the rest being all alleged *vivâ voce* at the bar of the court), was the most formal part of the proceeding, and that by which principally the defendant was to shape his defence. The only nicety almost in pleading was what arose upon the writ, which was examined, both in its form and substance, with much curious criticism. The *narratio* at that time was subject to no exception ; but we find, in the time of Fleta, that exceptions to the *narratio* were pleas of course, and followed next after those to the writ. As the writ was a brief state of the demand, it was required of the plaintiff to spread out his case more fully in his *narratio*, pursuing still the style and words of the writ, for a

[1] Ryley's *Plac. Parl.*, 1, 2, 5.

[2] *Vide* vol. i. c. viii.

difference between them was a good cause of exception. The next plea after that to the *narratio* was to the action of the writ; and lastly came pleas in bar of the action.[1]

The method in which the pleading in an action was conducted seems to have been this: When the cause came on in court, first the writ was read; next, the advocate for the plaintiff stated his case more fully, which was called *narrare*, or *to count;* from whence such statement was called the *narratio*, or *count;* then the advocate for the defendant put in his *exception*, or plea; and so they went on to reply, rejoin, take issue, or demur, as it seemed advisable. All this was transacted *vivâ voce* by the advocates on both sides; and the prothonotary (or themselves) minuted it down. If the advocates were overruled by the court, or wished to retract or amend, they were at liberty so to do, and it was accordingly done *instanter*. The whole seemed to be managed very much in the way of the scholastic disputations, so fashionable in those days. When pleading was practised in this manner, it had more the appearance of argument than of form.

There was some little variation in the manner of dealing with jurors in civil causes. The method of effecting a unanimity among jurors, by afforcing the assize, as mentioned by Glanville and Bracton,[2] was now in some measure altered. Fleta lays it down for law that, when there was a difference of opinion among the jurors, it was at the election of the judge either to afforce the assize, by adding others till twelve were found who were unanimous, *or* to *compel* the assize to agree among themselves, by directing the sheriff to keep them without meat or drink till they all agreed in their verdict.[3] Another method was to enter the verdict of the major and lesser part of the jurors, and then judgment was given *ex dicto majoris partis juratorum*.[4] Jurors might, in civil cases, give a verdict upon their belief, which two latter modes were also used in the last reign.

The criminal law.

The criminal law continued through this reign much in the state in which we left it in the former. However, the definition of some crimes was a little altered; and there seems to have been a variation in the method of trying persons who had been indicted.

It has been before surmised that the provision about *peine forte et dure* was intended to affect a change in the method of proceeding by presentment, so that offenders, when indicted, should not be permitted to make purgations, but should be obliged to put themselves on an inquest.[5] This seems to be corroborated by Britton in more than one passage, where he treats of presentments. In speaking of those indicted by *presentment*, he says, if they *ne se voillent acquitter*, will not put themselves upon their acquittal, they shall be put to their penance till they pray to do it.[6] As the other

[1] Flet. 116, 117, 118.
[2] *Vide ante*, vol. i.
[3] Fleta, 230.
[4] *Vide* 2 Hal. P.C. 297.
[5] *Vide ante*, c. ix.
[6] Britt. 11.

words of the statute before alluded to are here used, it cannot be doubted but the *acquittal* spoken of must mean the inquest directed by the statute. Afterwards, speaking of a defendant putting himself upon the country, he says, when the jurors came into court they might be challenged; and he states one cause of challenge to a juror, that he was one of those who *indicted* him; and there was a presumption that all who indicted him still bore the same ill-will against him.[1] It is also said by Britton, that a person indicted should have fifteen days for his defence,[2] which adds to the probability that the inquest he was to be put upon for his acquittal was not the same which presented the offence.

The manner in which this second inquest was ordered is thus described by the same author: When the jurors came into court, the challenges were to be made, the principal of which was that above mentioned; and if the prisoner could not or would not challenge them, as there was a sufficient number of jurors unchallenged—that is, to the number of twelve, then they were to go to the book. If there were not sufficient, then the challenges were to be tried; and if they were found true, so that there was not a full *dozen*, another day was to be appointed, and the sheriff was to summon more. When the oath was put, they were to swear, one after another, that they would speak the truth of what should be demanded of them on the part of the king; but there was to be no mention of their *belief* in cases of life and limb, it being required that in matters of so high concern they should speak upon their knowledge only. After this, the justices were to give a charge to the jurors upon the matter concerning which they were to speak the truth. They were then all to go and confer together, and be kept by bailiffs, so that no one should be suffered to go near them; and if any one did, or there was any one of them who was not sworn, he was to be sent to prison, and all the others amerced, as a punishment for merely suffering it. If they should not agree, they were to be separated and interrogated why they could not; and, after all, according to the sense in which Britton is interpreted by a late editor, the opinion of a greater number was to be followed,[3] though no other author speaks of a verdict being taken in a *criminal* case without the concurrence of all the jurors; and such unanimity is expressly required by Fleta.[4] If they all declared upon their oaths that they knew nothing of the fact, others were to be put in their place who did know it; and if he who put himself on the first inquest would not put himself on the new jury, he was, according to our author, to be remanded to penance till he did.

Further, if the prisoner, finding the verdict was likely to pass against him, would say that some of the jurors were about to pro-

[1] Britt. 12.
[2] *Ibid.* 10 b.
[3] See Kelham's translation of that part of Britton which relates to the pleas of the crown, p. 42.
[4] Fleta, 52.

cure his condemnation, at the instigation of the lord of whom he held his land, to obtain an escheat, or from any other motives; then the justices were carefully to question them, and make strict examination and inquiry how they were satisfied of their verdict. They perhaps might say one of their fellow-jurors told it them; and he (proceeds our author) perhaps might say that he heard it asserted for a truth at a tavern, or some other place, by one of the rabble, or such a one as nobody ought to give credit to. If it appeared to the justices that one of the jurors was influenced, or was entreated or procured by the lord, or by the enemies of the indicted, to get him condemned, they were to cause the procurers to be taken and punished by imprisonment and fine. Britton lays it down as a rule, that should the jurors be doubtful of the matter, and nothing certain could be made out, they should in such case always find for the defendant.[1]

It appears very evidently from this account of the inquest upon which a prisoner put himself to establish his innocence, that the jurors were considered as *witnesses*, the same as in other juries, and in assizes; and to call witnesses before them would have been absurd, and not at all consonant with the notion entertained of this proceeding. They were *sworn to speak the truth*, to discharge which duty they must speak from their own knowledge, and not from the testimony of others; and as they came from the vicinage where the fact was committed, none, it was thought, could be better able to perform the office than themselves.

It was many years after this reign, and when the second (since called the *petty*) jury began to be considered rather as judges of the presumption raised by the finding of the presentors than as witnesses of the fact, that a kind of evidence used to be exhibited to them. The first evidence made use of in this way consisted of written papers, such as depositions, informations, and examinations taken out of court: this led by degrees to a sparing use of *vivâ voce* testimony. It was long before they thought it necessary to bring evidence into court in support of the prosecution, and it was still longer before they allowed the prisoner to disprove the indictment by anything else than the oaths of the twelve *jurati*. When a prisoner was permitted to call witnesses to prove such matter as he offered in his defence, it was a high favour, and depended much on the discretion of the court, and the manner in which the charge had been made out by the prosecutors; besides this, the witnesses for the prisoner were never upon oath, which always left a pretence for discrediting their testimony.

The trial by jury at the time of which we are now writing was, to all intents and purposes, a trial by witnesses, and no doubt deserved all the value that was set on it by our ancestors. When the condition of society so changed, that, notwithstanding all the supposition of their personal knowledge of the fact, as coming from

[1] Kelham's Britton, from p. 34 to 45.

the vicinage, they were in reality wholly ignorant of it; and it was necessary the charge should be *proved* to them before they could pronounce on the guilt or innocence of the party; then the old proceeding became a piece of mummery, productive of oppression and tyranny, till at length it was softened by the calling of witnesses to inform the conscience of the twelve jurors. This was the last improvement of the trial by jury in criminal cases, and was not thoroughly effected till the times of Edward VI. and queen Mary.

The inclination in favour of juries had gone so far in this reign that there seemed a backwardness to allow the trial by duel, where a defendant insisted upon it as his right, which could only be in an appeal. Should there be any slip in the proceedings, of which the defendant had omitted to avail himself, the judge was *ex officio* to examine and point it out, in order to stop the duel. Fleta says that this was a trial not to be resorted to rashly,[1] if by any possible means it could be avoided.[2] Another alteration in our criminal proceedings was that the eyre was no longer to be a time of limitation for the prosecution of offenders; but they might be prosecuted at any distance of time.[3]

It has been before shown what was ordained by statute concerning the exemption of the clergy from criminal jurisdiction.[4] The practice, in Britton's time, respecting clerks is thus stated by that author (*a*). If a clerk accused of felony pleaded his clergy, and

(*a*) It appears plainly, by the testimony of contemporary authors, and of Lord Coke himself, that the law was deliberately warped and altered in this matter by the servile judges of the king, with a view to his emolument and advantage. That is, as to privilege of clergy. As to what the law was when the statute passed there could be no doubt, because, as Lord Coke says, it had just been laid down by Bracton, and is admitted and recited in the statute itself—viz., that a clerk arrested or accused of a crime could be claimed by the ordinary, "Cum vero clericus captus fuerit pro morte hominis vel alio crimine, et imprisonatus, et de eo petatur curia Christianitatis ab ordinario loci," &c.; "imprisonatus ille statim ei deliberetur sine aliqua inquisitione facienda" (*Bracton*, lib. iii. fol. 123). Then the statute recited the privilege, and simply admonished the prelates not to deliver or liberate those thus delivered to them, without putting them to their canonical purgation, so that the king should not be put to other remedy, "Que ceux que sont endites, &c., en nul manner ne les delivrent sans due purgation, issinit que le roy neit mestier de mitter auter remedy" (*Stat. Westm.* 1, c. 2). Upon which the king's lawyers actually held that this gave them power to try the clerk *before* he was delivered to the ordinary! the plain meaning of the statute being just the reverse; for if they were to be tried by the common law, why should they be put to their canonical purgation? Yet Britton, writing after this statute, and avowedly writing at the dictation of the king (his treatise indeed beginning in the name of the king, who himself is supposed to be writing), says, "Si clerk encoupe de felony (*i.e.*, endite) allege clergie, et est tiel trouve (*i.e.*, que est un clerk) and l'ordinary demaund donques serra inquise coment il est mescrue (*i.e.*, culpable) et s'il soit nient mescrue, donques il serra aroge touts quits; et s'il soit mescrue, si soient ses chateux taxes, et ses terres prises in nostre maine; et son corps deliver al ordinary" (*Britton*, c. iv. fol. 11). That is, as Coke puts it—"and thereupon an inquisition was taken whether he were guilty of the fact or not; and if he were found guilty, his *goods and chattels were forfeit, and his lands seized into the hands of the king*," which explains the reason of the king's anxiety to have the parties tried, and the readiness of the crown lawyers to warp the law for the purpose. That they did so is manifest; for there is not a word in the statute as to trial by the county, and the tenor of the enactment implies the contrary.

[1] *Cum levitate.* [2] Flet. 51. [3] Wingate's Britt., p. 12. [4] *Vide ante*, c. ix.

was found to be a clerk, and was demanded by the ordinary, it was then to be inquired whether he was guilty; and if he was found not guilty, he was to have judgment of acquittal; if guilty, his chattels were to be appraised, his lands seized into the hands of the king, and his body delivered to the ordinary; and if the ordinary delivered him out of prison before he was acquitted according to the due order of canonical purgation, or if he kept him so negligently as to let him escape, or maliciously kept him in such manner as to prevent his coming to make his purgation; in either of these cases the ordinary, if convicted of such misbehaviour, was to be *in misericordiâ*. Upon the ordinary certifying that a clerk so delivered to him was acquitted by purgation, restitution was to be made of his goods, provided he had not fled. Further, if the ordinary, either in person or by his procurator, demanded one who was a layman or *bigamus*, or not of a condition to be entitled to clergy, he was to be punished by imprisonment, as was also a procurator who in any case presented himself as such without any authority in writing from the ordinary.[1]

There are some variations between the description of offences given by Britton and his contemporary Fleta. Fleta speaks of treason almost in the words of Bracton;[2] but Britton says treason is every mischief which a man knowingly does, or procures to be done, to one to whom he is in duty bound to be a friend. Treasons he divides into *grand* and *petit*, though he does not specify what were to be ranked as the one or the other. Some of these treasons were punished by judgment of death; some by loss of limb, pillory, or imprisonment; and others by a slighter penalty, as the case required. *Grand* or *high treason* was to *compass* the king's death, or to disinherit him of his realm, or to falsify his seal, or to counterfeit or clip his coin. A person might also, says our author, commit high treason against others several ways; as a villein procuring the death of his lord, who was seised of him; and those who drew persons into such perils as to lose life and member, or chattels.[3]

It seems, from this account of it, that the crime of treason was very vague and undefined, so that almost any enormity might, by construction, be brought within the penalty of it. The same author goes on and says that the judgment in high treason was to be drawn, and suffer death for the felony; and, says he, the same judgment ought to be given against those who, in appeals of felony, were attainted of counterfeiting, or otherwise falsifying the seal of their lord of whose dependence or homage they were; or of committing adultery with the wives of their lords; of deflowering the daughters of their lords, or the nurses of their children. A woman attainted of any treason was to be burnt. Those attainted of falsifying the seal, if the fact was of small consequence, were to have judgment of pillory only, or to lose an ear; but if the fact

[1] Wingate's Britt. p. 11.
[2] Flet. 31. *Vide ante*, c. viii.
[3] Wingate's Britt. p. 16.

was of an enormous and heinous nature, as if it produced disherision, or any lasting damage, the offender was to have judgment of death.[1]

Arson was, when any in time of peace feloniously burnt other's corn or houses; such offenders were to be burnt, that they might suffer in the same manner in which they had offended. The same punishment of burning was to be inflicted on sorcerers, sodomites, and heretics.[2]

The crime of *hamsoken* is barely mentioned by Bracton, without any description of it. Offenders of this kind are called by Britton *burgessours*, since called *burglars*, and are described to be such as feloniously, in time of peace, break churches, or the mansion-houses of others, or the walls or gates of cities or boroughs, except they are infants under the age of discretion, and poor people, who through hunger enter the house of another for food, and take under the value of twelve pence; excepting also idiots, madmen, and others, whom the law would not consider as capable of committing felony. *Burgessours* were to be punished with death.[3]

The stat. Westm. 1,[4] seems to consider the stealing of twelve pence as a petty larceny. The statute *articuli super Chartas* seems to require the taking to be more than twelve pence.[5] Fleta says, if a person steals the value of twelve pence, *et ultra*, it shall be death;[6] Britton says, if it is twelve pence *or* more;[7] though in another passage he says that death would follow if the value was under twelve pence. So that it seemed to be not quite settled whether the sum was twelve pence or more that induced the penalty of death. The latter author makes no distinction between robbers and thieves as to this point. If any persons, says he, were indicted by presentment of *robbery* or *larceny*, or of cutting purses, of receiving felons, of enchantment, as pretending to charm people, of cheating, by selling bad things for good, as pewter for silver, of brass for gold, or were guilty of the like small offences, they were to be apprehended; if they could not be found, they were to be outlawed; and if judgment was passed against them, they were to be hanged, or to lose an ear, or to be pilloried, in proportion to their crime and the frequency of committing it,[8] so discretionary and various were punishments at this time.

Again, in petty larcenies, says our author, as for stealing sheaves of corn in August, or pigeons or poultry, if the offender was not suspected of any other crime, and the thing stolen was under the value of twelve pence, he was to be put in the pillory for an hour, and to be disabled from taking the oath of a juror or being a witness. If they were persons of bad character, or offended out of mere malice, and not through want[9] (which was an extenuation, if not even a justification, adopted from the canon law),[10] then they

[1] Fleta, 16 b.
[2] *Ibid.*
[3] *Ibid.* 17.
[4] *Vide ante*, c. ix.
[5] *Vide ante*, c. x.
[6] Fleta, 55.
[7] Britt. 22.
[8] *Ibid.* 23 b.
[9] *Ibid.* 24.
[10] Corv. Jus. Can. lib. iv. tit. 23.

were to lose an ear, and become infamous. For a second offence it was to be in the discretion of the justices either to sentence them to death, or to order their other ear to be cut off; and for the third offence, whether the crime was great or small, they were to suffer death.

Cut-purses were, for the first offence, to be sentenced to the pillory. If they had stolen other things, under the value of twelve pence, then they were to lose their ears; if the value was more than twelve pence, they were to be hanged.[1]

The crime of homicide was at this time extended to persons who seemed to act in authority, and void of all guilt. Felony, says Britton, may be committed under colour of judgment, as through malice of a judge; or under other colour, as by an unskilful physician or bad surgeon; by poison, and sundry other ways. It might likewise be committed by those who, whether for hire or otherwise, had condemned, or caused any one to be condemned, to death, by taking a false oath; so that perjury, if it had the effect of procuring a judgment of death, was punished with death.

Among the additions made to our body of national canon law, we find in this reign the constitutions of the archbishops Peckham and Winchelsey. These were confined to subjects purely of a clerical nature, without touching upon those points of controversy that had so long inflamed the temporal and spiritual jurisdictions against each other.

King and government.

The character of Edward is that of a brave and wise prince, qualities which well fitted him for the undertaking to improve our laws, and maintain the execution of them with vigour (*a*). The king took a personal interest in reforming

(*a*) As already has been seen, the attention paid by this monarch to the administration of justice between subject and subject was the result of his perception of its advantage to himself, by reason of the additions it produced to the revenue; and he was infinitely less attentive to it as between himself and his subjects. Nevertheless, as the power of the commons was very much augmented in this reign, and parliament had begun to acquire a real and potential existence, he was obliged to recognise the claims of subjects for redress against the crown or its officers for extortion or oppression; and in this and the subsequent reigns the remedy by petition of right appears to have become very commonly resorted to, though too often without any results. A petition of right lay against the crown for any tort or wrong done by the king's officers for the king's profit, as for disturbance of a party in the taking of his tithe (the case of the Prior of Christchurch, 31 *Edw. I.*, 1 *Rot. Parl.* 59; *Ryley's Plac. Parl.* 218); or for tithes subtracted by the king's officers (8 *Edw. II.*, 1 *Rot. Parl.* 319); or for wrongful distress (John Mowbray's case, 33 *Edw. I.*, 1 *Rot. Parl.* 163; *Ryley*, 218). So for wool wrongfully taken for the king's use (Michael de Harla's case, 33 *Edw. I.*, 1 *Rot. Parl.* 163; *Ryley*, 248). So for wheat seized under pretence of a royal commission (14 *Edw. II.*, 1 *Rot. Parl.* 320). So for trespass to land (18 *Edw. II.*, 1 *Rot. Parl.* 416); Westmilne's case, for bread and meat supplied to the late king (6 *Edw. I.*, 1 *Rot. Parl.* 1); Everley's case, for an annuity granted by Henry III. (33 *Edw. I.*, 1 *Rot. Parl.* 164; 1 *Ryley*, 25); Ayneshaw's case, for work done as a mason (33 *Edw. I.*, 1 *Rot. Parl.* 165; *Ryley*, 251); Basing's case,

[1] Wingate's Britt., p. 24.

our legal polity, deeming the due and strict administration of justice the best defence against the turbulence of the great barons. By affording protection to his inferior subjects, he at once diminished the power of the great, and reduced the whole nation under the dominion of law.

It was in this spirit that he erected the court of *Trailbaston.*[1] This was a commission of oyer and terminer of an unusual kind, and was issued in the fulness of zeal for the correction of public disorders. The rigour, however, with which this was executed creating some discontents, it was thought expedient, in course of time, to discontinue it.

The heavy penalties inflicted on the judges for malpractices are instances of the concern this king took in the execution of the laws. At one time, all the judges except two were convicted of corruption, and fines were set upon them amounting in the whole to the immense sum of 100,000 marks. It is related, that the offence of one of them, the famous Ralph de Hengham, was altering a record of a fine on a poor man from 13s. 4d. to 6s. 8d. This unseasonable act of humanity was punished with the penalty of 7000 marks—a punishment which struck a terror into all future judges; made every iota of a record be thenceforward most religiously preserved; and perhaps contributed not a little to encourage the scruples which prevailed afterwards with regard to the minutest errors in judicial proceedings.

for wax (35 *Edw. I.*; *Ryley*, 334); Fitzwalter's case, for services in Gascony (33 *Edw. I.*, 1 *Rot. Parl.* 169; *Ryley*, 259); Besney's case, for the price of a horse (33 *Edw. I.*, 1 *Rot. Parl.* 164); Lodelow's case, for money paid for the king (33 *Edw. I.*, 1 *Rot. Parl.* 169); the abbess of Fontevrault's case, for annuity (18 *Edw. I.*; 1 *Ryley*, 82); Bessop's case, for oats (14 *Edw. II.*; *Ryley*, 408), and many others. In the last case, Robert de Clifton brought a petition of right in parliament for injury done to his meadows by the king's keepers of Nottingham Castle, in digging a trench through his land for the supply of water to the king's mill. A commission *ad inquirendum* was issued, upon which the facts were found as stated in the petition; but he found himself as far from a remedy as before, and presented a petition of *grace* (as distinguished from one of *right*), praying some office as a compensation. A similar petition was afterwards presented by his son. Formerly petitions were often presented in cases where the proper remedy was by action. In such cases the course was not to reject the petition, but to endorse it with a direction that the "suppliant" was to pursue his remedy before the ordinary tribunals. Thus a petition was presented by John Offerwest, for lands seized by the king's escheator, without saying "to the king's use," which was answered, "For the land mentioned in the petition, but in the king's hands, let certain persons be assigned to inquire whether the petition is true or not; and the inquisition being returned into chancery, let right be done" (4 *Edw. III.*, 2 *Rot. Parl.*, 376). And see instances of petitions of right for recovery of pecuniary demands for redress for injury done by the officers of Edward II. (22 *Edw. III.* fol. 5). So in the case of torts or injuries by the king's tenants, permission to sue the wrongdoers to judgment and execution was granted upon the petition of right (De Grey's case, 15 *Edw. II.*, 1 *Rot. Parl.* 396). So parties who had been compelled to pay to the crown debts already paid, or from which they were exempt, were to recover the amount by petition (5 *Edw. II.*, 1 *Rot. Parl.* 284). The general result of the cases was, that where the subject was entitled to a right which the crown withheld, or suffered anything which the crown ought to redress, the remedy, either at common law or by Magna Charta, was by petition of right (1 *Rot. Parl.* 421).

[1] Namely, by the statute of Ragman, *de justiciariis assignatis*, among the *statuta incerti temporis.*

The manner in which this inquiry about the judges was made, gives a trait of Edward's character and of that of the times. From the best consideration of the different accounts given of this transaction,[1] it does not appear to have passed in parliament, but to have been a mere exertion of regal power.

Indeed, Edward, through the whole of his reign, however he might exact from others an obedience to the laws, affected to place himself above the restraint of them. The ill grace with which he confirmed *Magna Charta;* his frequent breaches of it; his procuring a dispensation from the oath he had taken to observe it; his levying money without assent of parliament, even after the statute *de tallagio non concedendo;* all these are strong proofs how determined he was to preserve, if possible, the authority which had been once assumed by the crown.

Perhaps one of the strongest acts of power attempted since the granting of the Charters, was executed by Edward. This was when, by an edict signed by some barons then in parliament (but whilst all the prelates were violently excluded from thence), he put the whole body of the clergy out of the protection of law. "No manner of justice," said the ordinance, "shall be done them in any of the king's courts; but justice shall be *had against them* to every one that will complain and require it of us."[2]

It was common to issue letters of protection to stop the ordinary course of justice: this occasioned the statute *de Protectionibus.*[3] This practice, however, continued afterwards, and was the subject of many complaints in the two next reigns.

Statutes and records.

It is unnecessary to observe that in this king's reign there are many more statutes extant than in that of Henry III. It is the opinion of some, that many more were enacted than those which have come down to us; otherwise, it is said, the sudden advance made in the law during this reign, beyond that of any other, could not be accounted for.

The authentic information derived from records is very much increased in this reign. The *Placita Parliamentaria*, collected and published by *Ryley*, contain many records of proceedings before the king in council, and so far give an insight into the nature of that kind of memorials. Besides these, there are extant judicial records of the king's bench, the common bench, and the eyre. It appears from these, that pleadings were very short but perspicuous, without involving the matter in any multiplicity of words. The records are for the most part orderly and clear, relating the several steps made in a suit, with the judgment thereon, and generally expressing the rule and reason upon which the judgment was given.[4]

There are some few broken notes of adjudged cases to be found in Fitzherbert's Abridgment; and there are said to be manu-

[1] *Parl. Hist.* vol. i. 93, 94. [2] *Ibid.* 116. [3] *Vide ante,* c. x.
[4] Hale's *Hist. Com. Law*, 157.

script reports of this period in private hands, but not in any regular series.[1]

Among the steps this king had taken to promote the improvement of the law and the administration of justice, he caused some treatises to be composed,[2] of which Fleta and the treatises of Britton and Thornton are supposed to be some.

Fleta.

Fleta, *seu Commentarius Juris Anglicani* (for so it is entitled), is a treatise upon the whole law as it stood at the time this author wrote (*a*). It is divided into six books, the first whereof treats of the rights of persons, and of pleas of the crown; the second, of courts and officers; the third, of methods of acquiring titles to things; the fourth and fifth, of actions grounded upon a seisin, and of writs of entry; the sixth of a writ of right. The author of this work has followed Bracton in the manner and matter of it, having adopted his plan, and in many instances transcribed whole pages from him. He did not, however, confine himself to Bracton as his sole guide, but had also an eye to Glanville. Many obscure passages in those writers are illustrated by Fleta. It seems as if the author wrote with both these treatises, particularly Bracton's, before him, and that his design was to give a concise account of the law, with the alterations which had been made by parliament since Bracton wrote, supplying such parts as had been left untouched by him, and dilating upon others that had been passed over with too little attention. Thus Fleta serves as an appendix, and often as a commentary to Bracton. But if Fleta contains much which is not to be found in Bracton, it is deficient in much more which abounds in that author, most of the subjects so minutely discussed by Bracton being passed over in a very brief manner; so that, with all its new matter, this volume is not more than one-third of the size of Bracton. The writer of this commentary seems to have followed his master, Bracton, in his acquaintance with the canon and civil law, though he is less frequent in the use of them, and then it is in a manner less likely to mislead the reader. This author was wholly an imitator. As he followed Bracton in the design of his work, he has copied the Prœmium from Glanville, *verbatim;* and, after all, the idea was borrowed from that prefixed to the Institutes of Justinian.

(*a*) Fleta—in this respect resembling Britton—appears to have incorporated the statute law of the time—for instance, the statutes of Westminster—in his text, which is a kind of commentary upon it, and thus he is quoted constantly by Lord Coke as explaining the true meaning. Thus, in commenting on the provision in the first statute of Westminster as to tolls, Lord Coke says, "Fleta collecteth the effect of this part of the act in these words," and then quotes his version of it (*Fleta*, lib. ii. c. xliii.) So he says, "Fleta rendereth the last part of the statute in these words," and then he again quotes him (2 *Inst.*, 222). So all through that book of the Institutes Lord Coke quotes Fleta's version of the older statutes, as affording a valuable commentary thereon.

[1] In Lincoln's Inn and the Middle Temple Libraries. Hale's *Hist. Ibid.*

[2] 35 Hen. VI., 42 a.

This book was written after the thirteenth year of the king, and not much later; at least the statutes towards the latter end of this reign are not mentioned, though that of Westminster 2 is frequently quoted. The occasion of the title to this book is given by the author himself, who says it was written during his confinement in the *Fleet* prison.[1] From that circumstance, it has been conjectured that he might be one of those lawyers who, for malpractices in their office as judges, were punished with imprisonment and pecuniary penalties.[2]

Britton.

The small French tract under the name of *Britton* is thought to have been composed under the direction of Edward (*a*). The singular form of it seems to countenance such a supposition, for the contents of the whole book are

(*a*) This is the proper place in which to offer some account of Britton's treatise. Some notice of it, indeed, has already been taken in the note at the commencement of the reign, but it may be convenient here to offer a more complete analysis of it. It begins, as already mentioned, with a preamble, written in the name of the king, and is avowedly written at his direction. This fact, and the date at which it was written, are also ascertained as a matter of legal history, by the statement, already quoted, of Chief-justice Prisot, in the reign of Henry VI., that it was written at the desire of the king, two years after the first statute of Westminster (3 Edw. I.), which in part it recites. It commences with a preamble in the king's name, which has already been quoted. And the treatise of Britton is, at all events, clear, and each head or title is very distinctly treated of, and it affords very valuable exposition of the common law, and very useful explanation of the statute law of the age, while its study is a highly desirable if not absolutely essential preliminary to the study of the Year-books, which our greatest lawyers have regarded as the richest repositories of the learning of our law. Lord Coke made great use of Britton, as well as Bracton and the *Mirror*, in his notes upon the old statutes (2 *Inst.*) It is to be observed that our author has in some instances had recourse to Britton for the illustrations of the law of this reign, and he might have done so more often with obvious advantage. The editor has ventured to add some references in the notes. The numbers and titles of the chapters in Britton's treatise (which is only divided into chapters, not books) are as follow, after the preamble or preliminary chapter:—Ch. 1. Coroners; 2. De eyres; 3. De chapiters (*i. e.*, the articles of presentments at the eyres, a chapter very much the same as that in Bracton, *De corona*); 4. De faudeours (forgers) de seales et de monoye; 5. De homicides; 6. De murdre; 7. De aventure; 8. De treson; 9. De arsons; 10. De burgessours (burglars); 11. De prisons; 12. De bannys; 13. De inlagerie (reversal of outlawry); 14. De rape; 15. De larcyns; 16. De abjuracions; 17. De troveurs (finders of treasure); 18. De droit de roy; 19. De franchises; 20. De pluseurs; 21. Torts; 22. De ministres (*i. e.*, del roy, as escheators, &c.); 23. De appels (or criminal prosecutions at the suit of the party); 24, 25. De appels de homicide; 26. De appels de robberies et de larcyns; 27. De appels de mahems; 28. De attachments; 29. De prises des avers; 30. De dette; 31. De tournes de viscontes; 32. De mesures; 33. De naifte; 34. De disseissine; 35. De purchas (*i. e.*, acquisition of real property); 36. De douns (donations of land); 37. De commun purchas; 38, 39. De purchas conditionel; 40. De reversions et de escheates; 41. De purchas de villeyns; 42. De chartres; 43. De seisins; 44. De purchas de rent; 45. De disseisene (or assize of novel disseisin); 46. Ou assize ne gist point; 47. De remedie de disseisins; 48. De vues en disseisin; 49. De proces en assises; 50. De title de frank tenement; 51. De exceptions de brefe; 52. De exceptions a la persone le pleyntyffe; 53. De exceptions al action; 54. De assisa turnes en jures; 55. De challenge de jorours; 56. De judgment; 57. De apurtenance; 58. De commune depasture; 59. De remedie de disseisin de commune; 60. De amesurement depasture; 61. De quo jure; 62. De resonable estovers; 63. De nusances; 64. De remedie de nusances; 65. De exceptions de nusances; 66. De termes (*i. e.*, termes or leases); 67. De intrusion; 68. De gards (*i. e.*, wards); 69. De marriages (*i. e.*, of wards); 70. De homages; 71. De reliefs; 72. De mort d'ancester; 73. De action

[1] In Prœm.

[2] Diss. ad. Flet. ch. 10.

put into the king's mouth, and the law so delivered has the appearance of being promulgated by the immediate voice of the sovereign. This work is shorter than the former, and is little more than a compendium. It is attributed by some to John Breton, who was

mixte; 74. De heritage divisible; 75. De resonable partie; 76. De sommonses; 77. De garaunt vocher (voucher to warranty); 78. De exceptions de mesne la descente; 79. De exceptions de la seisine; 80. De exception en son demeyne; 81. De exception de fee; 82. Exception de jour que il morust; 83. De taunt (tenure) des terres ovesque (avec) les apurtenances; 84. Exceptions puis le terme; 85. Exceptions de proeteyne bene; 86. Exceptions qui la terre tient; 87. Exception de felonie al action; 88. De assises tornes en jures; 89. De judgment; 90. De quod permittat; 91. De cosinage; 92. De assise de darreyn presentment; 93. De jour de plee; 94. De exceptions; 95. De exceptions hors de brefe; 96. De quare impedit; 97. Assise de utrum juris utrum (whether the land is of lay or ecclesiastical tenure); 98. De exceptions (*i. e.*, thereto); 99. De atteyntes (attaints of jurors for false verdicts); 100. On atteynte jeste (where attaint lay); 101. De exceptions (*i. e.*, thereto); 102. De proces de judgment; 103. De dowers; 104. De establishments de dower; 105. De assignement de dower; 106. De remedie de dower; 107. De guranties (warranties of title); 108. De exceptions de mort; 109. De exceptions de concubinage; 110. De exceptions de pluralite de femmes; 111. De exceptions par l'ascent le prere; 112. De communes exceptions; 113. De judgment; 114. De plee de droit de dower; 115. De amesurement de dower; 116. De entre; 117. De proces; 118. De exceptions; 119. De droit de la properte; 120. De plus procheynate (*i. e.*, of the heir); 121. De succession; 122. De court de baron; 123. De sommonses; 124. Desaoyns; 125. De essoyne de outre mer; 126. De essoyne de service le roy; 127. De essoyne de mal de venue; 128. De attornes. From this enumeration of the heads of the various chapters, it will be seen that the titles are more numerous and varied than in Bracton; while, on the other hand, they are treated, in general, more summarily, and with far less of scientific method or order, as also with far less learning—in fact, without any citation of authority; whereas Bracton is extremely methodical, regular, and elaborate, and appeals, wherever it is possible, to actual judicial authority. It is, on the whole, manifest that Britton's treatise is far inferior to that of Bracton, although, on the other hand, it is far superior to the *Mirror*, which is extremely loose and rambling, and often obscure and confused, owing to its being built on an older work. It will be observed that the book begins by a definition of jurisdictions and of courts of judicatures, and it is characteristic of the age, and of the reign of Edward I., that so much importance should be attached to matters of that nature, and, above all, to the sovereignty of the king as the source of justice, the origin of jurisdiction, and the guardian of law. And thus the jurisdiction of all courts, and the authority of every judicature, is deduced from the royal power. Thus the book goes on to describe the judicature emanating from the royal authority, "En primes en droit de vous mesmes, et de nostre court avons essint ordyne, que pur ceo que nous ne suffisons mye en nostro propre persone a oyer et terminer toutes quercles de people avons party nostre charge en plusurs partres si come icy est ordine." Then it defines the royal jurisdiction, "Nous volons que nostre jurisdiction soit sur toutes jurisdictions en nostre royalme essint que a toutes maneres de felonies, trespas, contractes, et en toutes maneres de autres accions personelles ou reales eyons poer a rendre et faire les jugements teles come ils afferrount sauns autre proces par la on nous savons la droite verite come juge." Then as to the judicature, first as to the marshal of the royal household and the origin of the king's bench, then as to justices itinerant and of "oyer and terminer." "Et outre ceo, volons nous que justices errauntz soient assignes de mesme le chapitres oyer et terminer en chescun counte de vii. ans and vii. ans." Then, as to the superior courts, great care was shown to preserve to the court of king's bench, which followed the king, the cognizance of all false judgments and appeals, which produced a plentiful harvest of fines, &c.: "De amendes faux jugements et de terminer appels et autres trespas faits encontre nostre fines," &c. Then, great care was shown as to the court of exchequer: "Aussi volons nous que a nous escheators a Westminister, et aillours eyent nos tresours et nos barons illeques jurisdiccion et record de choses que touchent lour office; a oyer et determiner toutes les causes que touchent nos dettes, et aussi a nos fees et les incidents choses, sauns les quex teles choses ne purrount estre tries, et que il eyent poer a conustre de dettes que lou doit a

Bishop of Hereford, and a judge; but as he died in the third year of this king's reign, and this treatise takes notice of statutes made in the 13th, the truth of this account is justly doubted.[1] By others it is considered as nothing more than an abridgment of

nos dettours, par in nos puissons plus toft approcher a nostre." So that the court was to have power to entertain suits against persons indebted to the king's debtors; a wide extension of jurisdiction, which the *Mirror* mentions as a grievance. It is characteristic that, in Britton, far less interest is shown in the office of the sheriff, which had far more to do with the administration of justice, than in that of the coroner, who (as the title indicates) had to do with the pleas of the crown, and in those times had much more to do with profits accrued to the crown than he has now; and the very first sentence in which the duties of coroners are treated of, betrays the secret of this anxiety about their functions: "Et volons que come suite felonieas mes a ventre sont avenue *ou que tresor soit trouve de soult terre*, &c., le coroner *hastivement* mande al visconte," &c. So, great anxiety is shown about escheats, and the first thing to be done of persons indicted is to seize their lands and goods. Then comes a chapter on the justices in eyre, and the articles of eyre; the very first of which is stated to be one in which the crown would feel most interest:—"De fauseours de seals et de monoye;" which latter is copiously treated of, the former being dismissed in a few lines. Then comes chapters on homicide, murder, treason, and arson, all treated very cursorily and briefly. Then comes a long chapter on prisons, in which one of the first things pointed out is, that, if a prisoner escapes through the negligence of the officer, he is to be amerced 100 shillings by the justices in eyre, one of whose principal functions was to look after these amercements. Then comes a chapter on outlawry, of felons fugitives from justice, in which the great feature dwelt upon is forfeiture: "Et volons que chescun home definaunt nostre fees, forface ses chateau a nous," &c. After this, there is a chapter on finders of treasure, as to which careful inquiry is to be made: "Car tresor musce en terre et trouve, volons que soit nostre," &c. Then comes a chapter of some length, entitled "De droit le roi," which commences with the Church: "Et quant de nos fees soit enquis de esglises, cathedrales, parochiales et religious, et de mesones de religion, et de hospitals en cet counte quex sount de nostre avowson; et quex deyvent estre et ne sount mise; et quex demeynes nous tenons en nostre meyns, &c. Et aussi de avowsons de esglises, &c. Et aussi de escheates et de terres et tenements, alienes par felons, &c. Des enfaunts, damoyseles, et wedues que marriages, duissent estre nos maries sauns conge de nous et combien que cest que lour terres vaillent par an." Then there is a chapter, "De fraunchises," under which it is directed that inquiry is to be made as to all persons holding royal franchises, with a special view to discover any defaults which might warrant the crown in seizing them: "Et si ceux persones que sount defaute pour prise de mesme teles fraunchises par nous par lour tort demeyne nos volons que ils soient distreintz, &c. Et come ils viendront en court et ne se purrount desafabler de ceux torts, soit agarde que nous recoverons la franchise; et ils soient desherites de la value, ou en nostre mercy." Then there is a chapter, "De pluseurs torts," under which inquiry is to be made of roads and bridges: "De ponts et de causeys, et de commune cheymyns debruses, ou autrement male altyres, que les duist reperiller ou amender;" and here again special care is to be taken as to forfeitures: "Et si trouve que ceux teigment tenements de nos pur ceux chemyns amend, si soient ceux tenements pris en nostre meyn," and otherwise, "que illes soient en nostre mercy;" which meant that no mercy was to be shown to them: "Et soit comaunde au viscont que il les faux destreindre per lour avers et par lour chateux, et les distresses retenir jusques a taunt que ils eyent les defautis amendis a touts les faits que mester serra." Inquiry is to be made, also, of all nuisances, and of all who have obstructed the execution of the judgments of the king's court, and who are to be punished by imprisonment and fine; also of lands aliened in mortmain, which are to be forfeited: "De terres et de tenements aliens en mortmeyn, et celles terres et ceux tenements soient pris en nostre meyn sauns replevin et les purchasours en nostre mercy." So of ecclesiastics who have held lay pleas: "Soit enquis de clercs que tenent plees de lay gents de autres choses que de testament et de matrimoyne ou de dymes ou que eyent juge ascun lay home en court christeine a ascune compuncion de argent; ou que ount la gent a

[1] Diss. ad. Flet. ca. 2, 3.

Bracton, with the subsequent alterations that had been made in the law, and that it is called *Britton* as one of the names of *Bracton* himself.[1]

This French tract, as it is written in the language which the

fort *excommenge et a tort fait pendre et imprisoner.* Et ausi de ceux que ount autres greves par bulles, par double somonse a un jour en divers lieux per malice, et touts ceux soient punys par prison *et per fyn.*" And finally, inquiry is to be made of all who had committed breaches either of statutes or of the common law: "Et de touts trespassours contre la fourme de nos estatutes," &c. Then follows a very long chapter, "De ministris"—*i.e.*, of the officers of the crown—the first of whom mentioned are the escheators: "De nos escheatours suit enquis queles terres ils eyent seisis en nostre meyn," &c. So as to fines and amercements: "Et aussi de viscontes que eyent par fyns et amerciamentes de gents de lour baillie;" and so of sheriffs or their bailiffs, *who have summoned people vexatiously and wrongfully on juries or inquests;* and so of a great number of other misdeeds, all which are to be punishable by *fine.* So that, whether the inquiry was of fines or forfeitures *already* secured to the crown, or of misdeeds in the king's officers which would warrant the imposition of fines, the inquiry would equally tend to the profit and emolument of the crown. Then, after chapters on appeals on homicide or other felonies, comes a chapter, "De attachements," showing how, when a man had commenced an action and sued out a writ, the first thing to be done was for the plaintiff to find pledges distrainable, and the next was for the sheriff to distrain the trespassers or wrongdoers: "A commencement deliver son brief al viscont, et fines trouve deux pleges destreynables a luy de suer sa pleynte et le viscont face destreyndre ces trespassours per lour avers ou per chateux" (97). And, above all, for every default there was to be an amercement; and the more defaults the more amercements: "Et come ascun que serra destreint viendra en court et ne pusse sa defaute savre tauntost soit ajuge a nostre mercy pur sa defaute; et si plusurs defaute, plusurs soient amerciamentes" (103). Then it is provided, that rolls shall be made up of all fines and amercements, and returned into the exchequer: "Et tauntost soient les amerciaments taxes, et les estretes envoyer a nostre eschcker et ausi de fyns et des chateaux de felons, &c.; soient euroules de deux roules dount l'un remeyne a coroner et al viscont et l'autre *route avesque touts les roules del eyre soient envoyes a nostre escheker,* et savement gardes en nostre tresore" (107). These are the rolls of the exchequer, which are of so much value to our legal antiquaries. Then comes a very long chapter of wrongful distresses: "De prises des avers," (evidently an important subject in those days,)—always carefully providing that the offenders shall be in mercy—and ending by commanding that, if the distress shall have been against the peace—"en contre nostre pease"—the parties are to be made examples of by grievous amercements: "Et par grevous amercements que autres par les ample de cux soient chastises en casu semblables" (119). The next chapter treats of "Dette;" and at the outset it begins by stating that, in the counties, before the sheriffs and the suitors, they have pleas of trespass and debt, so that the goods, or the trespass, or the debt demanded, do not exceed 40s., and not of debts exceeding that sum, *without the king's writs*—"saun nos brefs"—which meant the payment of a fee for an original writ; the pretence for which, that it was necessary to give jurisdiction, was, as has been already pointed out, altogether deceptive, for more reasons than one; for first, after the *first* writ of the kind issued, the jurisdiction of the court over all similar cases would be as well established as after a hundred such cases; and next, if it were not so, the jurisdiction of the courts might have been settled and assured once for all, by the terms of their commissions—and indeed in effect was so—by the definition of their jurisdiction previously laid down on the authority of the king himself. It was not, however, only the first fee on the writ which was involved in the question of suing in the king's superior court, there were all the fees, fines, and amercements imposed in the course of the litigation, which went into the royal treasury; and therefore it was said: "Et ces grauntz (great) trespasses, volons nous que soient plede defauts nous meines." This may suffice as an analysis of the work, and also as illustrations of the state of the law at the time it was written, which was after the statute of Westminster (as it is mentioned), and likewise as specimens of the language in which the Year-books are written. The main importance, indeed, of Britton is, that a study

[1] Diss. ad Flet., ca. 2, 3.

law spoke for many years after, engages the curiosity of a modern reader in a particular manner. In the writings of Bracton and Fleta everything is seen as it were through a cloud, disguised in the terms and phraseology of the Latin tongue; whereas Britton addresses you in the technical, proper style of the law: you here perceive a determinate meaning, conveyed in precise terms, and are enabled to form an opinion from it with more confidence and certainty.

Another treatise composed in this reign, was that of Radulph de Hengham, who had been chief-justice, and was, for misconduct, degraded from his office, with many others of his fellow-justices. This consists of two parts: one called *Summa Magna*, and the other *Summa Parva*. It seems to be a collection of notes relating to proceedings in actions; and must have proved extremely useful to a practiser of those times. The same may be said of the little French tract called *Fet Assavoir*, printed at the end of Fleta.

Hengham.

Chief-Justice Thornton made a *summa*, or abridgment of Bracton, containing most of the titles of the law in a concise form. Though a professed epitomiser, he omits many things in that author, and does not adhere to his method.[1]

Thornton.

The foregoing writers, in addition to Glanville and Bracton, together with the *Mirror* (of which we defer saying anything till the next reign), must have thrown great light on the study of the law in these early ages, and were no doubt for a time of great authority with lawyers. It is true, that we do not find these authors cited in such reports of decisions as have come down to us; but, in later times, Lord Coke, in his inquiries into the grounds of our law, particularly in those works which were chiefly designed for the closet, begins all his investigations, where the subject will allow it, from these old tracts, and thence traces down the confirmations or alterations the law received in succeeding times. The changes which have happened in the law since that author's time, particularly by the abolition of tenures, have made these treatises less read than they were even in his days. Perhaps, of all of them, Fleta is that which is most frequently looked into, owing to its being written after many of king Edward's statutes, and to the comment which it sometimes gives upon them.

The chief of these writers are Glanville, Bracton, Fleta, and Britton. But the comparative merit of these four authors appears very different in the eyes of a modern reader. The copiousness, learning, and profoundness of Bracton place him very high above

of the work is, if not an essential, at all events a highly useful preliminary to the study of the Year-books—those venerable repositories of early law and legal antiquities, without a knowledge of which, Lord Coke says, no one can be well-grounded as a lawyer, and without some acquaintance with which, certainly a man can hardly have much knowledge of our legal history. The Year-books begin with the next reign, so that they follow almost immediately upon Britton.

[1] Dis. ad. Flet. ch. 24.

the rest. It is to him that we owe Fleta and Britton, which would probably never have existed without him. To him we are indebted for a thorough discussion of the principles and grounds of our old law, which had before lain in obscurity. But while we give to Bracton the praise that is due to him, as the father of legal learning, we must not forget what Bracton, as well as posterity, owe to others. Britton delivered some of this writer's matter in the proper language of the law, and Fleta illustrated some of his obscurities; while Glanville, who led the way, is still entitled to the veneration always due to those who first open the paths to science.

Among the monuments of the king's ecclesiastical law, are to be reckoned the provincial constitutions of Archbishop Peckham and Archbishop Winchelsey; but our national canon law acquired in this reign an ornament and support of a new kind. Among the numerous commentators and glossists on the civil and pontifical law, a man of learning stood forth to do equal honour to the English ecclesiastical law. John de Athona, by his copious commentary on the legatine constitutions of Cardinals Otto and Ottoboni, passed in the last reign, set the first example of that kind to our canonists, and laid the foundation of a future body of juridical learning for the guide of our clerical courts.[1]

Miscellaneous facts.

Edward was extremely careful to provide his courts with persons properly qualified to practise there. In the 20th year of his reign,[2] he specially directed John de Mettingham, then chief justice of the bench, and the rest of his fellow-justices of that court, to provide and appoint, according to their discretion, from every county, *attornatus et apprenticios, qui curiam sequantur; et se de negotiis in eâdem curiâ intromittant, et alii non.* It appeared to the king and council that *seven score* would be sufficient; but the justices, if they saw fit, were authorised to exceed that number.[3]

The different orders of practisers are thus stated by Fleta: *servientes, narratores, attornati et apprenticii.*[4] The apprentices, it should seem, were students, who, it is said (and probably by the above ordinance), were first permitted by Edward I. to practise in the king's bench, in order to qualify themselves to become in a course of years *servientes*, or serjeants. Whether *servientes* and *narratores* (or, as they were called in French, *countors*) were two distinct orders, or *narrator* was only an additional description of a serjeant, may be doubted (*a*). It has commonly been taken in

(*a*) From this and from the *Mirror* it appears that, at this time, there were regular pleaders, and, it is to be observed, that the pleading was oral. The authorities, even prior to the reign of Edward I., the treatises of Bracton, and Glanville, and the *Placitorium Abbrevatio,* which contain extracts from the records from the time of Richard I. to that of Edward II., exhibit the gradual growth of a system of pleading. And the very earliest reports in the Year-books, which begin with the reign of Edward II., show the system in a very perfect state. Therefore Mr Serjeant Stephen considers the reign of Edward I. as the period when it was fully estab-

[1] Duck. de Auth. lib. ii.
[2] Plac. Parl. 20 Ed. I. Rot. in dors.
[3] Ryl. Plac. Parl. 104.
[4] Lib. 2, c. xxxvii.

the latter sense, in stat. Westm. 1, c. xxix.,[1] where the same words come together, *si serjeant countor, ou outre;* and that statute ordains imprisonment for a year and a day on a person of that description who was guilty of any collusion in practice. As neither attorneys nor apprentices are mentioned in that statute, we may suppose such persons were not then entrusted with the conduct of business in court; if so, it is probable they had not that authority till the above ordinance; though it may be observed, that Fleta speaks of them as equally subject to this punishment with serjeant countors.

The first mention of *capitalis justitiarius* of the bench is in the first year of Edward I. This style was now conferred, probably for the first time, in conformity with that of *capitalis justitiarius*, assumed in the latter part of Henry III. by the chief justice in the king's bench.[2]

The salaries of the justices were at this time very uncertain, and, upon the whole, they sunk from what they had been in the reign of Henry III. Thomas de Weyland, chief justice of the bench in 7 Edward I. had but £40 per annum, and the other justices there 40 marks. This continued the proportion in both benches till 25 Edward III. then the salary of the chief in the king's bench fell to 50 marks, that is, £33, 6s. 8d., while that of the chief of the bench was augmented to 100 marks; which may be considered as an evidence of the increase of business and attendance there. The chief baron had £40, the salaries of the other justices and barons were reduced to £20.[3]

It seems that it was thought too great a burthen on the justices of the two benches to attend the assizes, according to the late statute of *nisi prius;* the king therefore appointed eight persons to take assizes, juries, and certificates; writs of assize, juries, and recognition, were to be directed to these, and to no other person, except *de speciali gratiâ regis.*[4]

lished, not only as a system, but a science. In the very first year of Edward II., we find pleaders raising matters of law, and putting themselves upon the judgment of the court concerning them: "Nous demurrions en vos discretions si nous etions mest a respond" (*Year-book*, 1 *Edw. II.*, 8. So 10 *Edw. III.*, 23). Thus also pleading in estoppel was understood (*Year-book*, 17 *Edw. II.*, 534). The great practical object of pleading to bring out the question in dispute, and reduce it to a *point*, was as well understood at the end of this reign as at any other time, for, in the first year of the next, we find the court saying to a pleader: "Vous dites chose que veot avoir deux issues, tenez vous al une" (*Year-book*, 1 *Edw. II.*, 14), a principle or rule, which might bear to be inferred in those early times when transactions were few and simple, but would soon become obstructive of justice; and as Mr Serjeant Stephen points out, it did not prevail in the civil or canon law; in both of which the party could resort to as many exceptions as he pleased. "Pluribus defensionibus uti permittatur" (*Dig.*, 60, 44, 61, 111). "Nemo prohibetur pluribus exceptionibus uti quamvis diversæ sunt" (*Ibid.* 8). The judges and pleaders in this reign were, as will be seen in the *Mirror*, laymen, not well acquainted with the civil law, and hence pleading soon became perverted from its primitive simplicity and practical utility. In our times we have altered it.

[1] *Vide ante*, c. iii. [2] Dugd. Or. Jur. 39. [3] *Ibid.* 104. [4] Ryl. Pla. 130.

CHAPTER XII.

EDWARD II.

Statutum de Militibus—Statute de Frangentibus Prisonam—Statute of Articuli Cleri—Sheriffs to be Nominated by the Judges—Statute of Gavelet—Of levying Fines—The Statute Prærogativa Regis—Of Homage and Fealty—Statuta Incerti Temporis—Possessio Fratris, &c.—Gifts in Tail—Of Writs of Formedon—Other real Writs—Writs of Conspiracy and Deceit—Action of Debt—Detinue de Rationabili Parti—Actions of Accompt—Action of Trespass—Of Pleadings and Arguments in Court—The Criminal Law—The King and Government—The Vetera Statuta—The Year-books—The Mirror—Miscellaneous Facts.

THE reign of this king does not make so inconsiderable a figure in our juridical as in our civil history. Notwithstanding the weakness of the executive power, the judicial establishment of our forefathers, and the reformation made therein by Edward I. continued unshaken. In some points this reign has an advantage over all the former, when viewed by a modern lawyer; for the earliest report of cases adjudged in court is the Year-book of this king. This opens in a new source of information, which will enable us to pursue our inquiries concerning the progress of legal knowledge and improvement with more certainty and effect.

We shall divide the matter of this reign into such as is furnished by statutes, and such as may be collected from the decisions of courts; and shall begin with the former.

The first statute in this reign is the *statutum de militibus*, which is said to be not probably a legislative act, but a writ granted by the king in time of parliament, and entered, by his direction, on the record; from which circumstance this, like many other similar instruments, is said to have acquired the name of a statute.[1] In addition to the burthens of tenure, which have been frequently mentioned, there was one, which from the alteration of times and circumstances was becoming very grievous. It was held as a consequence of the military system, that every one possessed of a *fædum militare*, should *suscipere arma militaria*, that is, take upon him the order of knighthood, or what was more desirable to those who exacted this casualty, pay a fine in lieu of it.

We have not yet met with any regulation for ascertaining what should be the parcel of land to constitute a knight's fee; and probably it had been various at different times, depending upon the pleasure of the crown and the compliance of the people. As this was the measure for a particular mode of raising money, it was material that it should be defined with certainty. On the occasion of a new levy, it was now thought convenient that directions

[1] 2 Inst. 593. *Vide ante*, vol. i. c. iii., and *ante*, c. ix.

should be given for the government of the king's officers in collecting this revenue, as was done by this writ; in which the king *granted*, in the first place, a respite to all those who ought, but had omitted, to become knights, and were then destrained *ad arma militari suscipienda*. Further, it directed, that if any complained in the chancery that he was distrained, and had not land to the value of twenty pounds,[1] in fee, or for term of his life, and was ready to verify that by the country, then some discreet and lawful knights of the county should be written to, in order to make inquisition of the matter; and if they found it to be so, he was to have redress, and the distress was to cease. Again, where a person was impleaded for the whole, or for such a part of his land, that the remainder was not of the value of £20, and he would verify the fact, then also the distress should cease till that plea was determined. Again, where a person was bound in certain debts stalled in the exchequer, at a certain sum to be received thereof annually, and the remainder of his land was not worth £20 per annum, the distress was to cease till the debt was paid. None was to be distrained *ad arma militaria suscipienda*, till the age of twenty-one; nor any on account of land which he held in manors of the ancient demesne of the crown, as a sokeman; considering that those lands must pay a tallage, when the king's lands were tallaged.

With respect to those who held land in socage of other manors, and who performed no *servitium forinsecum*,[2] the rolls of chancery in the times of the king's predecessors were to be searched, and it was to be ordered according to the former custom: the same of clerks in holy orders holding any lay fee, who would, if laymen, be liable to become knights. No one was to be distrained for his burgages, though they were of the value of twenty pounds or more. Those who ought to become knights, and who had had their land only a short time; those who were extremely old, or had any infirmity in their limbs; or alleged that they had some incurable disease, or the impediment of children, or law-suits, or other necessary excuses; such persons were to appear before two commissioners appointed, and make fine before them; and these commissioners were to take discretionary fines from such disabled persons, by way of composition. Thus was provision made for the due payment of one of those casualties, which was supported under pretence of defending the realm, while the extreme rigour of these exactions was somewhat abated.

Statute *de frangentibus prisonam.*

There is another act of the same year, called *statutum de frangentibus prisonam*. It appears by our old law,[3] that a prisoner, for whatever cause, breaking out of the king's prison, was esteemed guilty of felony.[4] In the 23d of

[1] *Vide ante*, c. ix. This was the value by which persons were then summoned to attend the king in his foreign war.

[2] *Vide ante*, vol. i. c. iii.

[3] *Ibid.*

[4] A provision was made in the last reign, to restrain the too hasty punishment of gaolers for escapes of felons. *Vide ante*, c. ix.

Edward I. an act was passed in the very words of this we are now going to speak of, making some alteration therein. That act is not in our printed books; and this of 1 Ed. II. probably was nothing more than a recital and affirmation of the former,[1] but has had the success to reach posterity, and render the former unnecessary, and, therefore, forgotten. This act ordained, that none from thenceforth, who broke prison, should have judgment of life and limb for breaking prison only, unless the cause for which he was taken and imprisoned required such a judgment, if he was lawfully convicted thereof.

In the second year of this king there is a public instrument for the purpose of enforcing the statute of *Articuli super Chartas;* and in the following year another, entitled, *Literæ patentes super prisis bonorum cleri,* for observing a statute made in the last reign, in protection of religious societies, and ecclesiastical men, against the taking of their goods without their consent.[2] In the 7th year of the king there are two acts entitled, one, *Ne quis occasionetur pro reditu;* the other, *Pro captione et morte Petri de Gaveston;* after which, in the 9th year, is the famous statute made at Lincoln called *Articuli cleri.*

This act was to adjust some of those ecclesiastical claims of cognizance which have been so often mentioned (*a*). We have seen what had been attempted by the clergy, in the last and the preceding reigns, towards confirming their ancient claims of judicature; and the manner in which the legislature pleased to interpose, in order, if possible, to make some adjustment or compromise in a matter of so much concern, both to the spiritual and temporal polity.[3] Thus did this dispute rest till the present parliament, when Walter Reynolds, archbishop of Canterbury, a person in great esteem with the king, preferred in the name of himself and the clergy, the following sixteen articles, and received by authority of parliament answers *seriatim* to every one of them.

Statute of *Articuli cleri.*

The first four articles were these: That laymen purchased prohibitions generally upon tithes, obventions, oblations, mortuaries(*b*),

(*a*) Some portion of the ecclesiastical law became by use and adoption incorporated with the common law. Thus, the Fourth Council of Lateran enacted this canon—"Quicunque receperit aliquod beneficium curam habens animarum annexam, si prius tale beneficium habebat, eo sit, ipso jure, privatus: et si forte illud retinere contenderit etiam alio spolietur. Is quoque ad quem, prioris spectat donatio, illud post receptionem alterius libere conferat cui merito viderit conferendum." (Note (*a*), to *Gibson's Codex,* tit. xxxvii., ch. 1, p. 904, 2d. ed.) And this canon was recognised by the courts of law, and thus *became incorporated with the common law of the land* (4 *Rep.* 75 *a*). The constitution, it was said, operated as a general sentence of deprivation (Rex *v.* the Bishop of Norwich, *Year-book,* 10 *Edw. III.*, pt. 3, fol. 1). The law, however, was, that the church must be void before a new presentment could be made (Smale's case, *Year-book,* 17 *Edw. III.*, fol. 59).

(*b*) The terms of the statute are, "Item, si rector petat versus parochianos, oblationes, et decimas debitas et consuetas, vel si rector agat contra rectorem, de decimis majoribus vel minoribus, dummodo non petatur quarta pars valoris. Item, si rector petat mortuarium in partibus ubi mortuarium dari consueverit." Similar expressions are used in the statute *Articuli cleri,* 1st., 9 Edw. II., c. i. "Imprimis, Laici impetrant prohibitiones ingenere super decimis, obventionibus, oblationibus, mortu-

[1] 2 Inst. 589. [2] *Vide ante,* c. ix. [3] *Ibid.*

redemption of penance, violent laying of hands on clerks or converts, and in cases of defamation, where spiritual penance was the proper punishment. To these the king answered (conformably with the regulation of the statute of *Circumspectè agatis*), first, that in tithes, oblations, obventions, mortuaries, when they were propounded under those names, the king's prohibitions should hold no place, although for the long withholding thereof they might be estimated at a sum certain; but it was declared, if a clerk or religious man sell his tithes, when gathered in his barn or otherwise, to any one for money, and the money was demanded before a spiritual judge, the king's prohibition should lie; for by the sale, the spiritual goods were made temporal, the tithes being turned into chattels.[1] Secondly, it was answered, if there was a contest about a right to tithes founded upon a right to the patronage, and the quantity of such tithes amounted to the fourth part of the goods of the church, a prohibition was to lie; alluding to the writ of *Indicavit*, that has been so often mentioned.[2] If a prelate enjoined a pecuniary penalty for an offence, and that penalty was demanded, the king's prohibition was to lie; but if the prelates imposed a corporal pain, and the person to be so punished would, of his own accord, redeem such pain by money, a prohibition was not to lie.[3] Thirdly, it was answered, when violent hands were laid upon a clerk, the amends *pro violatâ pace* were to be *coram rege;* those *pro excommunicatione* were to be *coram prælato*, where corporal penance might be enjoined; and if the offender would redeem that by money, paid either to the bishop or the party grieved, it might be demanded before the bishop (as before said), and the prohibition should not lie.[4] Fourthly, the prelates were to have power of correction in causes of defamation, notwithstanding a prohibition.[5] Most of these points had been before considered by the legislature in the statute of *Circumspectè agatis.*[6]

The next may be considered as the fifth article, and was this: That, on the erection of a new mill, if tithe thereof was demanded by the rector, a prohibition of the following kind used to go: *Quia de molendino tali hactenus decimæ non fuerunt solutæ, prohibemus, &c. et sententiam excommunicationis, si quam hâc occasione promulgaveritis, revocetis omninò.* To this it was answered, that such a

ariis" (*Stat. of Realm,* vol. i. p. 116). The terms *oblationes* and *mortuaries* are thus explained (2 *Inst.* 491)—"Oblationes in the canon law are thus defined: 'Oblationes dicuntur quæcunque a piis fidelibusque Christianis offeruntur Deo et ecclesiæ, sive res solidie sive mobiles;'" and in *Gib.'s Cod.* 784, note (*g*); tit. xxx., c. 10, it is said "Oblations are thus described by Lyndwood—'Accedentes ad solemnia nubentium, purificationes mulierum, mortuorium exequias, et alias solennitates divinas et populares solebant aliquid certum offerre.'" From which customary offerings the fees or duties now payable on these occasions did probably spring; and it is added, that "by the common law, as well as by this statute, these profits are recoverable in the spiritual court." Then, as to mortuaries, in 2 *Inst.* 491, it is said, "Mortuarium is a gift left by a man at his death, pro recompensatione subtractionis decimarum ersonalium et oblationum."

[1] Ch. 1. [2] *Vide ante*, vol. i. c. iii.; and *ante*, c. ix. [3] Ch. 2.
[4] Ch. 3. [5] Ch. 4. [6] *Vide ante*, c. ix.

prohibition never issued with the king's consent, and that, in future, it should never go.[1]

The sixth article of complaint was, that when anything of spiritual cognizance had been determined definitively before the spiritual judge, and had passed *in rem judicatam*, and was not suspended by appeal, and afterwards a question was moved before a temporal judge between the same parties, upon the same thing; this was not allowed as an exception in the temporal court. To this it was answered, that because a matter was discussed before ecclesiastical and temporal judges *diversis rationibus* (as in the case of laying violent hands on a clerk), therefore, notwithstanding any judgment in the spiritual court, the king's court might discuss it, if the party should think proper to bring it there.[2] The seventh article complained, that, when persons were excommunicated, the king's letter used to be sent to the ordinaries, commanding them to absolve them by a certain day; or, otherwise, that they should appear and show for what cause they excommunicated them (*a*). To this it was answered, that such a letter should not issue in future, unless where the king's liberty was injured by the excommunication.[3]

The remainder of these articles was as follows: Eighthly, it was complained, that the barons of the exchequer, not content with claiming for themselves the privilege of not answering to any complaint out of that court, extended it to their clerks in office there, who were summoned either *ad ordines* or *ad residentiam;* and that they inhibited diocesans from calling them to judgment, so long as they were in the exchequer, or in the king's service. To this it was answered, that it was the king's pleasure, that such clerks as attended in his service, should, if they offended, be corrected by their ordinary, as other persons; but that, so long as they were occupied about the exchequer, they should not be bound to residence; and it was further added, by the direction of parliament, that it had been used, time out of mind, for the king's clerks who were employed in his service, during the time of their service, not to be compelled to keep residence at their benefices.[4] The ninth complains, that the king's officers, as sheriffs and others, entered into the fees of the church to make distresses, and sometimes took

(*a*) Excommunication at this time was a disability to any legal proceeding by the party, though not to a criminal prosecution. Thus there is this case in the reign of Edward III.: Margaret le Horne brought an appeal of robbery against the chantor of Canterbury, whose counsel pleaded that the appellant was excommunicated, and produced the letters of the bishop. To which the court said that they would adjourn the case until she had got absolution, "tanque el aiet purchase absolucion." The counsel for the prisoner urged that he ought to go quit until she was absolved; but the court said, not so, as he was a prisoner he should not go quit unless acquitted or mainprised; and so he found mainprise until a certain day, *et sic de die in diem quousque mulier absolvator* (*Year-book, Edw. III.*, fol. 63, pt. 33).

[1] Ch. 5.

[2] Ch. 6. This point seems to have been thoroughly established in the famous case of the Duchess of Kingston.

[3] Ch. 7.

[4] Ch. 8. There was a writ entitled *De non residentiâ clerici regis*. Reg. 58 b.

the parson's beasts in the king's highway, where he had no land but such as belonged to the church. To this it was answered, that such distresses should not in future be made, either in the king's highway, or in the ancient possessions of the church, but only in such as were newly acquired to the church.[1] A similar provision, as to distresses in the highway, had been made by the statute of Marlbridge;[2] and as laymen were entitled to an action upon that statute, the parson might have an action on this for distraining in the highway.

The tenth article of complaint was, that when persons fled to a church, and abjured the realm, according to the custom of the realm, laymen, or their enemies, would pursue them, and take them, if they were out of the king's highway; so that they were hanged or beheaded, as persons who has broke the condition of their abjuration. Further, that while they were in sanctuary, in the church, or churchyard, they were kept so closely by persons in arms, that they could not go forth on the calls of nature, or to provide themselves with victuals.[3] To this it was answered, that those who abjured the realm, were, so long as they continued in the common way, in the king's peace, and should not be disturbed by any one; and while they were in the church, their keepers were not to continue in the churchyard, unless some necessity, or the danger of an escape, required it: while they were in the church, they were not to be driven to the necessity of flying from thence, but should be supplied with what they wanted, and be permitted to go out on their occasions. The king was willing, likewise, that thieves or appellors might, when they pleased, confess their offences to priests; but confessors were to take care that they did not erroneously inform such appellors. The eleventh article complains of some instances in which religious men had long been oppressed, and which were provided for by a statute made at the beginning of the last reign.[4] The king now answered, that the said statute should be observed; and the like remedy was to be pursued in cases of corodies and pensions, obtained by compulsion, whereof no mention was made in that statute.[5]

The twelfth article says, that if any one of the king's tenure was called before the ordinary out of the parish where he lived, and was excommunicated for manifest contumacy, and, after forty days, a writ issued to take him, such person would pretend a privilege that he ought not to be cited out of the town or parish where his dwelling was; and for that reason, the king's writ for the taking of him was denied. To this it was answered, that it never was, nor ever should be, denied.[6] The thirteenth article prayed, that spiritual persons presented by the king to church-benefices (if refused admission by the bishop, either for want of learning, or

[1] Ch. 9. [2] *Vide ante*, vol. i. c. viii. [3] *Ibid.*
[4] *Vide ante*, c. ix. And also a writ for the same purpose, *vide ante*, c. x.
[5] Ch. 11. [6] Ch. 12.

other reasonable cause), might not in such cases be under the examination of lay persons, as had been lately attempted, contrary to the canons, but should sue for redress to the spiritual judge. To this it was answered, that the ability of a parson presented to a benefice was to be examined by the spiritual judge; and so the law had always been.[1] The fourteenth article prays, that elections to vacant dignities might be free. To this it was answered, that the statutes made in such case should be observed,[2] alluding to the stat. 3 Ed. I. ch. 5.[3]

The two remaining articles relate to the immunity claimed for the persons of clerks in cases of felony. The fifteenth says, though a clerk ought not to be judged before a temporal judge, nor any thing done against him that concerned life or member, yet temporal judges caused clerks fleeing to a church, and perhaps confessing their offences, to abjure the realm; so that, though they could not properly be their judges, yet by admitting their abjuration, the temporal judges put them in danger of death, if after such abjuration they were found within the realm. To this it was answered, that a clerk fleeing to a church for felony, should not, if he affirmed himself to be a clerk, be compelled to abjure; but, on yielding himself to the law of the land, should enjoy the ecclesiastical privilege, as had long been used.[4] The sixteenth article was on the like cause of complaint; and states, that though a confession of a crime before a person who was *non judex* should not be good, nor sufficient to ground process and sentence upon; yet some secular judges admitted clerks who were not liable to their jurisdiction, and who were charged before them of theft, robbery, and homicide, to confess their offences, and accuse others (that is, become provors), and then would not deliver such provors to the ordinary, when demanded, though the judge acknowledged he had no authority to condemn them. To this the king answered, that the privilege of holy church, when demanded in due form by the ordinary, should not be denied;[5] so that clerks were not to be compelled to abjure, nor were to lose their clergy by becoming provors.

In this manner was the grand question between the ecclesiastical and temporal courts, as it were, compromised by mutual concessions, and settled upon a foot on which it has stood ever since, with very little alteration; the provisions of this act being the rule by which most of these points were afterwards governed, as will be seen in the subsequent part of this history.

In the same year there was a material alteration made in the old judicial constitution, by transferring the appointment of sheriffs from the election of the people[6] (who were confirmed in that privilege by a statute of the

Sheriffs to be nominated by the judges.

[1] Ch. 13. [2] Ch. 14. [3] *Vide ante*, c. ix. [4] Ch. 15. [5] Ch. 16.

[6] We have seen what complaint there was of the extortions and abuses committed by the elected sheriffs; the experience of these mischiefs, probably, justified the measure of taking the nomination from the people, and placing it in the crown. *Vide ante*, c. x.

late king)[1] to a nomination by the judges. It was complained that great damage had been sustained by the king, and great oppressions by the people, owing to the insufficiency of sheriffs and hundredors, by which was meant *bailiffs* of hundreds: in order therefore to avoid the like in future it was enacted, by statute 9 Edw. II. st. 2, that sheriffs should be assigned by the chancellor, treasurer, barons of the exchequer, and justices; and that none should be sheriff, unless he had sufficient land within the county of which he was sheriff, to answer to the king and his people. Further, that nobody who was steward or bailiff to a great lord should be made sheriff, unless he was out of their service, so as to be able to attend the execution of his office as sheriff. It was also enacted, that hundreds, whether they belonged to the king or to others, should be kept by convenient and able persons, who had sufficient land within the same hundred, or within the county in which the hundred was; and they were to be assigned by the chancellor, treasurer, barons, and justices, as above mentioned. Hundreds were to be let to hundredors at a reasonable rent, so that they need not be driven to extortion, in order to pay an exorbitant ferm; but no sheriff or hundredor was to lease his office to another, in ferm or otherwise. The execution of all writs, which came to the sheriffs, was to be made by the hundredors sworn and known in the county, unless there was any default in the hundredors, and then by other persons meet and sworn, in order that people might know to whom to sue such executions. This statute was sent to all the sheriffs in England (according to the ancient mode of publishing statutes, at least such as were of a particular nature), accompanied with a writ, commanding them to cause it to be read *in pleno comitatu*, and to be observed in all points; besides which precaution, it was sealed with the great seal, and sent to the treasurer and barons of the exchequer, and justices of both benches, that they might maintain it in all points.

The *statutum de vicecomitibus, et aliis de viridi cerâ*, 14 Edw. II., contrives a shorter process in the exchequer to compel sheriffs to make acquittances to the king's debtors; and gives some direction for ordering the twenty-four jurors in attaints. This statute also was sent by a writ to the justices *ad placita coram nobis tenenda assignatis*, to those also of the bench, and to the treasurer and barons of the exchequer.

To return to the order of time from which we are digressing.

Statute of *Gavelet.* In the 10th of the king there is the statute of *Gavelet*, as it is called. *Gavelet*, or *Gaveletum*, is explained to be *a leasing, or letting, to pay rent;* and *consuetudo de Gavelet* was when, upon a rent or service being withheld, denied, or detained, a forfeiture of the tenement followed. This was originally the general law of feuds in England;[2] but being elsewhere softened into a distress, remained only the custom in Kent, where lands

[1] *Vide ante*, c. x.

[2] *Ibid.*, and vol. i. c. ii.

were held in *gavelkind;* and there, when no distress could be found on the land, the lord might seize the land itself in the nature of a distress, and keep it a year and a day; within which time, if the tenant came and paid his rent, he was admitted to his tenement; if not, the lord might make a regular entry and enjoy it.[1] The present act was to introduce the like practice into the city of London; for which purpose it ordained, that where a person had rents issuing out of tenements in the city of London, and such rents were in arrear, he might distrain so long as anything was to be found in the fee; and if there was nothing which could be distrained, then the tenant might be impleaded *de gavelet* by a writ *de consuetudinibus et servitiis.* If he denied the services, the plaintiff was immediately to name his *secta*, consisting only of two witnesses, whose names were to be enrolled; and he was to have a day to produce them at the next hustings: if the witnesses then proved, *de pleno visu et auditu*, that the plaintiff had at any time received the rents demanded, the tenant was to lose his fee by the award of the court, and the plaintiff was to recover the tenements in demesne. If the tenant refused to acknowledge the services, and likewise the arrears, the arrears were to be doubled by judgment of the court, and the tenant was to give to the sheriff, for the wrongful withholding, one hundred shillings, if he was worth so much. If the tenant did not come in upon due summons, in the hustings, then the fee was to be delivered to the plaintiff in full hustings, to be held for a year and a day; within which time if the tenant came, and offered to satisfy the plaintiff to the amount of double the arrears, and the sheriff for his amercements, as before mentioned, then he was to have his tenements again; but after the year and day the lands were, by judgment of court, to remain to the lord of the fee in demesne for ever: the same where tenants acknowledged the arrears, and were not able to make satisfaction.

The principal statutes of this king which have not yet been mentioned, are the statute of York, 12 Edw. II., st. 1, the statute of essoins, 12 Edw. II., st. 2, the statute of Carlisle, 15 Edw. II., and the *prærogativa regis*, 17 Edw. II.

It was designed by the statute of York, 12 Edw. II., st. 1, to supply the defect of some former laws relating to the administration of justice. It was found inconvenient that tenants in assizes of novel disseisin could not make attorneys; it was therefore ordained that they should have that power, with a saving, however, of the liberty to plead by bailiffs if they pleased, as had been the practice heretofore.[2] Again, it was *agreed*, says the statute, that when a charter, quit-claim, acquittance, or other writing was denied in the king's court, wherein witnesses were named, process should be awarded to compel such witnesses to appear, as had before been used. But if none of them came at the great distress returned, or if it was returned that they had nothing, or they could not be

[1] Termes de la Ley.

[2] Ch. 1. *Vide ante*, c. x.

found, yet the taking of the inquest was not to be deferred by the absence of such witnesses. If the witnesses came at the great distress, and the inquest, for some cause, remained untaken, the witnesses that came in were to have the same day given them as was assigned for taking the inquest, at which time, if the witnesses did not appear, the issues that were first returned upon them were to be forfeit. The taking of an inquest was not to be delayed on account of the absence of witnesses living within franchises, where the king's original writ did not run.[1]

An alteration was made in the order of taking inquests by *nisi prius*. We have seen what alteration had been made in this establishment by stat. 27 Edw I., st. 1, ch. 4,[2] directing that inquests should be taken before any justice of the place, associating with him some *knight* of the county, if they had no need of great examination. But it was now directed, that inquests and juries in pleas of land that required no great examination, should be taken in the country, before a justice of the court where the plea depended, associating with him a[3] *substantial man* of the country, knight or other; so that a certain day be given in bank, and a certain day and place in the country, in the presence of the parties, if the demandant prayed it. As to inquests and juries in pleas of land that required great examination, they were to be taken in the country, in the above way, before *two justices* of the bench;[4] and the justice or justices were to have power to record nonsuits and defaults in the country, at the day and places assigned, as before mentioned. What they had done in the above places, was to be reported in bank at a day certain, there to be enrolled, and judgment to be given. However, it was not meant that such inquests and juries should not be taken in bank, if the jurors came. It should seem, the practice now had become for the *venire facias* sometimes to be made returnable in bank, preceding the going of the justices; and then, upon the default of the jurors in bank, a *habeas corpora* or *distringas* issued to cause them to come before the justices in the country. It was enacted, this statute should not extend to great assizes.

Further, it was enacted, that a justice of the one bench or the other, associating to himself[5] a *substantial man* of the country, knight or other, at the *request* of the plaintiff, should take inquests upon pleas moved by attachment and distress, and have power to record nonsuits, as above mentioned, and take inquests upon defaults there made. As to assizes of *darrein presentment*, and inquests to be taken on writs of *quare impedit*, they were to be ordered according to the statute of Westm. 2:[6] besides which, the justices were to have power to record nonsuits and defaults in the country, and to give judgment thereupon, as they did in the

[1] Ch. 2. [2] *Vide ante.* c. ix.
[3] So the expression, *prod'home*, rendered by the translator of this statute.
[4] Ch. 3. [5] The expression in the original is the same as in the former chapter.
[6] *Vide ante*, c. ix.

bench, and report what they had done in the bench, where it was to be enrolled. If it happened that the justices did not come into the country at all, or not at the day assigned, yet the parties and the jurors were to keep their day in bank;[1] that is, the day of return of the *venire facias*, or *habeas corpora*, according as the inquest was to have been taken in the country, upon the one or the other.

Complaint had been made, that the returns of writs by bailiffs of franchises were sometimes changed after they had come into the sheriff's hands. To prevent this, it was ordained,[2] that an indenture should be made of such returns, in the names of the bailiff and sheriff: if any sheriff changed a return so delivered, and was convicted thereof at the suit of the lord of the franchise (should he have suffered any damage or scandal thereby), and at the suit of the party who had sustained any loss thereby, he was to be punished by the king, and yield double damages to the lord and the party grieved. It was also ordained, that sheriffs and other bailiffs who received the king's writs returnable in court, should put their own names with the returns, that the court might know of whom they had such returns; and if the name was left out, the person neglecting was to be grievously amerced.

The last chapter[3] of this statute very wisely directs, in order to prevent the abuse of office, that no one who had the office of keeping the assizes of wines and victuals should, while attendant on that office, deal in such articles. This act is deserving of notice, as it directs a method of prosecution which has since been adopted in many similar cases of breaches of a positive statute. It directs, that if any one was convict thereof, the merchandise should be forfeited to the king, and the third part of it given to the person at whose suit the trespassor was attainted. In such cases, a person who would sue for a thing so forfeited, was to be received; and the chancellor, treasurer, barons of the exchequer, justices of one bench and the other, and justices assigned to take assizes, were to receive such plaints, *with writ or without*, and decide upon them.

These are the regulations made by the statute of York, which, like that of Lincoln, was transmitted to the sheriffs and justices for their direction, and also to the chancellor of Ireland, to be enrolled in the chancery there, and to be sent to the different courts and the several counties, to be observed in all points the same as in England.[4]

The statute of essoins, 12 Edward II., st. 2, declares in one or two cases where an essoin should lie, and where not, and more particularly where the essoin *de ultra mare*, and *de servitio regis*, should be allowed; in all which this statute seems to be mostly a declaration of the common law.[5] It declares, in conformity with

[1] Ch. 4. [2] Ch. 5. [3] Ch. 6. [4] *Vide* Pickering's *Statutes*.

[5] N. B. The original and translation of this statute differ; some passages are transposed, and some which are in the latter are not found in the former; these differences are noted in Ruffhead's edition. I have followed the translation.

the common law, that an essoin lay not where the land was taken into the king's hands,[1] nor where the party was distrained by his lands; nor where any judgment was given thereon, if the jurors came; nor where the party was seen in the court.[2] An essoin *de ultra mare* lay not where the party had before been essoined *de malo veniendi;*[3] nor where he had essoined himself another day; nor where the sheriff was commanded *quòd faciat ipsum venire.* An essoin *de servitio regis*[4] would not lie where the party was a woman, unless she was a nurse, a midwife, or commanded by writ *ad ventrem inspiciendum;* neither did it lie in a writ of dower, because it seemed to be in deceit and delay of right; nor did it lie for that the plaintiff had not found pledges *de prosequendo;* nor where the attorney was essoined; nor where the party had an attorney in the suit; nor where the essoiner confessed he was not in the king's service; nor where the summons was not returned, nor the party attached, for that the sheriff had returned *non inventus;* nor where the party had been another time essoined *de servitio regis*, and had not put in his warrant; nor where he was resummoned in an assize of *mortauncestor*, or *darrein presentment*, nor because such a one was not named in the writ; nor where the sheriff was commanded *quòd attachiet eum;* nor where the bishop was commanded to cause a party to appear; nor for that the term was passed. An essoin *de servitio regis* was to be allowed after the *grand cape* and *petty cape*, and after a distress *per terras et catalla*, which latter is an exception from the general rule that was just before laid down concerning essoins.[5]

The statute of Carlisle *de finibus*, 15 Edward II., like other statutes of this reign, is not a legislative act, but a writ directed to the justices of the bench, for their government in taking fines.[6] It ordains, that all parties, whether demandant or plaintiff, tenant or defendant, who would acknowledge or render their rights or tenements to another, in pleas of *warrantia chartæ*, covenant or other, in which fines were levied, should, previous to the passing of the fines, appear personally before the justices, so that their nonage, idiotcy, or any other defect, might be discerned and judged of by them: provided, that should any one, either by age or *impotence decrepit*,[7] or some casual debility, be so oppressed and detained, as not to be able to come to court, then two, or one of the justices, by assent of the residue of the bench, should go to the party so diseased, and receive his acknowledgment in the plea, upon which the fine was to be levied. If there was only one justice, he was to take with him an abbot, a prior, or a knight, a man of good fame and credit; and these by a record were to certify the justices of the bench of the matter. Fines so levied were to have the same effect as was given

Of levying fines.

[1] *Vide ante*, vol. i. c. viii.
[2] This was otherwise at common law. *Vide ante*, vol. i. c. viii.
[3] *Vide ante*, vol. i. c. viii.
[4] For the cases where this essoin would lie at common law, *vide ante*, vol. i. c. viii.
[5] *Vide ante*, c. x. [6] *Ibid.* c. ix. [7] *Œtate decrepitâ.*

to them when levied according to the directions of stat. 18 Edward I., st. 4.

Respecting the appointment of attorneys in general, it was ordained by the same instrument, that none of the barons of the exchequer, or justices, should admit any attorneys, except only in pleas that passed before them and their companions, in bank, and in places where they might be assigned; the power of admitting attorneys was denied to the clerks and officers of the barons and justices; and all admissions in future by such persons were declared void. There was a reservation to the chancellor and the chief justice of their authority to admit attorneys, as formerly.[1]

The *prærogativa regis*, 17 Edward II., st. 1, is a parliamentary declaration of certain prerogatives which by law resided in the king, and which have been occasionally mentioned in the former parts of this History (*a*). To make the king's rights with respect to tenure, and some other royalties more generally and easily known, it was thought proper to bring them into one view in this statute, the contents of which are as follow.

It is in the first place declared, that the king has the custody of all lands belonging to those who hold of him *in capite per servitium militare*, of which the tenants were seised in their demesne as of fee, the day they died (of whomsoever they held else by the like service, so that they held of ancient time any land of the crown), until the heir came of lawful age; except the fees of the Arch-

(*a*) It was sometimes said this statute was only declaratory of the royal prerogative; but it should seem it was an extension of it. There is no doubt that the royal prerogative had advanced greatly in this reign. That, at least, was the impression in those times. Thus, in the reign of Edward III., a case arose as to the construction of a grant of Henry III., whether, by grant of a manor without saying "with its appurtenances," or "advowsons"—an advowson passed; and it was urged, on the part of the crown, that it did not pass, because, by virtue of prerogative, nothing was deemed to be granted by the king without express words. And it was said, in the time of King Henry III., the king was but as a common person; for, at that time a man might have a writ of entry upon a disseisin by the king, and all other manner of actions, as against any other person; and so, at that time, when the king gave a manor, the advowsons annexed to it passed. In a case in the reign of Edward IV., the question was greatly debated, whether or not the statute *De prærogativa regis* was or was not in affirmance of the common law; and the great Littleton strenuously contended that it was, and that indeed it was not in the nature of a statute at all, but rather an exposition of the law (15 *Edward IV.*, fol. 13). "It is not a statute any more than *Des communes in banco*, &c. These are written in our books, and yet are not statutes; but they were made to the intent that what was at the common law should be put in certain. So it was with the statute *De prærogativa regis*, which was only in affirmation." Most of the judges, however, were of a different opinion. To which it was answered, that *prærogativa regis* is no more than a statute *declaring* the prerogatives of the king; for that there could be no doubt that kings had prerogatives before that statute. And Fencot said: "The statute *De prærogativa regis* was, it was said, Quod quando dominus rex det vel concedit aliquod manerium vel terram cum pertinentibus, nisi faciat expressam mentionem de advocationibus ecclesiis, &c., tunc *hiis diebus* Rex reservat sibi eadem, &c.; on which it was urged that those words, 'hiis diebus,' showed that a new prerogative was declared, and that always before the time of the statute it was otherwise; and so in effect the court held, as the grant was *before* the present statute, when by the mere grant of a manor, its advowsons would pass" (*Year-book*, 43 *Edward III.*, fol. 22).

[1] *Vide ante*, c. x.

bishop of Canterbury, the Bishop of Durham between Tine and Tees, fees of earls, and barons in the marches, where the king's writs run not, and whereof the said archbishop, bishop, earls and barons ought to have the ward, though they held of the king in some other place.[1] The king was likewise to have the marriage of an heir within age and in his ward; whether the land of such heir had belonged to the crown of long continuance, or came by reason of some escheat into the hands of the king, or he had the marriage by reason of the wardship of the lords of such heirs, without any respect to the priority of feoffment, although they held of others:[2] all which seems to be only a confirmation of the common law, and of *Magna Charta.*[3]

The king was to have *primer seisin*, after the death of such as held of him *in capite*, of all lands and tenements whereof they were seised *in their demesne as of fee*, of what age soever the heirs were, receiving the issues of the said lands and tenements, until the usual inquisition was taken, and till he had received homage of such heir.[4] The king was to assign dower to widows, after the death of their husbands who held *in capite*, though the heir was of full age, if the widows pleased: and before assignment of dower, such widows were to swear that they would not marry without the king's licence, whether the heirs were of full age or not; and if they married without licence, then the king was to take into his hands, by way of distress, all such lands and tenements which they held of him in dower; though neither the king nor the wife was to take the issues of the lands, but he was to wait till she or her husband satisfied him by paying a fine. In the time of Henry III., this fine, says the statute, was at most one year's value of the dower. Moreover, all women, of whatever age, who held of the king in chief, were to swear not to marry without the king's licence; and if they did, their lands and tenements were in like manner to be taken into the king's hands till they redeemed them by fine.[5] This provision, like the former, was only a confirmation of the law laid down in *Magna Charta.*[6]

If an inheritance held of the king *in capite* descended to several parceners, all the heirs were to do homage to the king; and it was so to be divided, that every parcener should hold his part of the king.[7] If a woman, during the life of her ancestor who held *in capite* of the king, was married before she was marriageable, then the king was to have the ward of the body of the same woman until she was of age to consent; at which time she might have her election whether she would continue with him to whom she was married, or accept a husband that the king would offer. It was declared, in confirmation of *Magna Charta,* that none who held of the king *in capite* by knight's service might alien more of his land

[1] Ch. 1. [2] Ch. 2. [3] *Vide ante*, vol. i. c. iii.; and *ante*, c. x.
[4] Ch. 3. *Vide* st. Marl. c. 16; and vol. i. c. viii. [5] Ch. 4.
[6] *Vide ante*, vol. i. c. iii. [7] Ch. 5. *Vide ante*, vol. i. c. iii.

than that the residue should be sufficient to answer his service, unless he had the king's licence for so doing; but this was not understood of the members and parcels of such land.[1] As to the alienation of serjeanties without the king's licence, it appears that the king had used to rate such serjeanties at a reasonable extent to be made of them, and on that foot it is left by this statute.[2]

It was declared, that where another presented to a church that was of the king's advowson, and a suit arose thereon; if the king recovered by award of the court, though after six months from the time of the avoidance, that should not prejudice him, if he had presented within six months.[3] Of this prerogative there is no mention in any writer before this statute, though it might be understood under the maxim of *nullum tempus occurrit regi*, which had prevailed in the reign of Henry III.[4]

In the two following chapters, the king's right to the custody of idiots and lunatics is declared. These prerogatives are not mentioned by Bracton; but we are informed by Fleta, that certain persons, called *Tutores*, used to have the custody of the lands *idiotarum et stultorum*. It is thought that these tutors, as was natural, were the lords of whom the lands were holden; such unhappy persons being in a sort of perpetual infancy. But this sort of trust, according to Fleta, had been much abused; on which account an act had been made in the last reign, which is now lost, giving to the king the custody of the persons and inheritances *idiotarum et stultorum*, being such *a nativitate;* with a reservation to the lord of all his lawful claims for wards, relief, and the like[5](*a*). In confirmation of this statute it was now declared, that the king should have the custody *fatuorum naturalium*, of *natural fools*, taking the profits of their lands without waste or destruction, and finding them necessaries. This comprehended all persons, of whomsoever they might hold their fees. After the death of such natural fools, he was to restore the land to the right heirs, so that such persous might not alien, nor their heirs be disinherited.[6] Thus far of *natural fools* or *idiotæ et stulti*, mentioned by Fleta. From the

(*a*) This statute is said to have been the ground of the jurisdiction of the crown over the persons and estates of idiots or lunatics (2 *Inst.*, 14). The custody of the persons and estates of idiots and lunatics was a power not originally in the crown, but was given to it by the statute, for the benefit of the subject (Hume *v.* Burton, 1 *Ridgw. P. C.*, 224; *et vide* 2 *Inst.* 14). And now, by the statute *de prerogativâ regis*, 17 Edward 2, c. ix. and x., the king shall have the real estates of idiots to his own use, finding them necessaries; and he shall provide for the safe keeping of the real estates of lunatics, so that they shall have a competent maintenance, and the residue is to be kept for their use (*Ld. Ely's Ca.*, ib. 519, 535). This jurisdiction was administered in chancery, and that court has always adverted to this statute as the basis of its jurisdiction. Thus, in one case, the question whether the court could order timber to be cut upon the estate, was considered upon the terms of this statute (*ex parte* Broomfield, 3 *Bro. P. C.*, 570). It may be doubted, however, whether—especially as the statute was declaratory—the jurisdiction does not rest upon the broader ground of the duty of the sovereign, as *parens patriæ*, to take care of such as are incompetent—a jurisdiction including lunatics as well as infants.

[1] Ch. 6. *Vide ante*, vol. i. c. iii. [2] Ch. 7. [3] Ch. 8.
[4] *Vide ante*, vol. i. c. iv. [5] Fleta, p. 6. [6] Ch.

manner in which that author expresses himself, it should seem, that in his time there was no provision of a similar kind for the protection of the persons and estates of *lunatics*. But now we find it enacted, that when any one, who once had his memory and intellects, should become *non compos mentis*, as those who have lucid intervals; in such case the king was to provide, that their lands and tenements should be kept without waste and destruction; that the person and his family should live and be maintained in a competent manner out of the issues thereof, and the residue be kept for his use, to be delivered to him when he recovered his memory. In the meantime, such lands and tenements were not to be aliened, and the king was to take nothing to his own use. If the party died in such state, the residue was to be distributed *pro animâ* by the advice of the ordinary.[1]

The king's ancient prerogative to have the wreck[2] of the sea was declared, as also to have whales and great sturgeon[3] taken in the sea, or elsewhere within the realm, except in certain places privileged by the king.[4]

In the twelfth chapter there was a provision concerning the escheats of Normans. King John was the last duke of Normandy; for, during his reign, that province was lost. King Henry III., as appears by the latter clause of this chapter, recovered several escheats of land within this realm holden by Normans; who, after they began to adhere to the French king, the king's enemy, and so were considered as traitors, forfeited all their lands to the king, of whomsoever they were held. If the king had given those lands to any other, he could not, according to the system of tenures now prevailing, grant[5] them to hold of himself, but of those of whom they were before holden; and so king Henry III. had made all his grants. It was now declared, that under such terms the escheats of Normans should continue to belong to the king.[6]

It was declared, that where any one holding of the king *in capite* died, and his heir entered into the land, before he had done homage and received seisin, he should gain no freehold by such entry; and therefore, if he died seised during that time, his wife should not be endowed of such land, as had lately been determined in the case of Matilda, daughter to the earl of Hereford, and married to Maunsel, the earl marshal. He, after the death of William, earl marshal of England, took seisin of the castle and manor of Scrogril, and died in the same castle before he had entered *by* the king, and done homage to him; upon which it was adjudged, that the widow should not be endowed, because the husband had not entered *by* the king, but *by intrusion*. But this same doctrine was not applied in socage, and other small tenures.[7]

It was declared, that the king should have escheats of lands belonging to freeholders of archbishops and bishops, if attainted of

[1] Ch. 10. [2] *Vide ante*, c. ix. [3] Bract. 55 b. [4] Ch. 11.
[5] *Vide ante*, vol. i. c. iv. [6] Ch. 12. [7] Ch. 13.

felony during the vacancy of the see, while the temporalities were in the king's hands; and that the king might make gifts of such lands, saving to the prelates the accustomed services.[1] Respecting the king's grants, it was ordained, that when he granted lands, or a manor *cum pertinentiis*, without express mention, in the charter or writing, of knight's fees, advowsons of churches, and dowers when they fell, belonging to such manor or land, it should be considered that the king reserved those things to himself; though it was held otherwise in the case of common persons.[2]

Lastly, it was, consistently with the common law,[3] declared, that the king should have the goods of all condemned felons and fugitives, wheresoever they were found. Their freehold was to be taken into the king's hands, who was to have the profits for a year and a day, with the liberty to waste and destroy its houses, woods, and gardens, and all manner of things belonging to the same land, excepting in case of persons in certain places privileged by the king. After the king had had his year, day, and waste, the land was to be restored to the lord of the fee, who might have had it before, if he had fined to the king for the year, day, and waste. The statute says, that in the county of Gloucester there was a custom for the lands and tenements of felons, after the year, day, and waste, to revert to the next heir, to whom they ought to descend, if the felony had not been committed; the same in Kent; where, says the statute, the maxim was, *the father to the bough, the son to the plough*. The custom of Kent was also recognised as to the descent of lands, namely, that heirs male should divide the inheritance, the same as women: but that women should not divide[4] with men. Another part of their custom was, that a woman after the death of her husband should be endowed of a moiety; and that if she committed fornication in her widowhood, or took another husband, she should lose her dower.[5]

Such are the prerogatives of the crown, which it was thought convenient at that time to ascertain and settle by a solemn declaration in parliament. It is probable there were many other claims, which were either not generally admitted, or too well known to need any declaration of them at present.

There are two other statutes of the same parliament: one entitled, *Modus faciendi homagium et fidelitatem*: the other, *De terris Templariorum*, by which the lands and possessions of the Knights Templar, whose order was then dissolved, were transferred to the knights of St John of Jerusalem.

Of homage and fealty.

The *Modus faciendi homagium et fidelitatem*, 17 Edw. II., st. 2, prescribes the method of doing homage and fealty, much in the way that has been before stated out of Bracton.[6] It directs, that when a freeman did homage to the lord

[1] Ch. 14. [2] Ch. 15. [3] *Vide ante*, vol. i. c. viii.
[4] This agrees with the common-law maxim by Glanville: *Mulier nunquam cum masculo partem capit in hereditate. Vide ante*, vol. i. c. iii.
[5] Ch. 16. [6] *Vide ante*, vol. i. c. iv.

of whom he held his chief messuage, he should hold his hands together between the hands of his lord and say thus: "I become your man from this day forth for life, for member, and for worldly honour, and will owe you faith for the lands that I hold of you, saving the faith that I owe unto our lord the king." If he did homage to any other than his chief lord, he was to add, "and to mine other lords." When he did fealty, he was to hold his right hand upon a book, and say, "Hear you, my lord *R.*, that I, *P.*, shall be to you both faithful and true, and will owe my fidelity unto you for the land that I hold of you, and lawfully shall do such customs and services as my duty is to you, at the terms assigned. So help me God and all the saints!" When a villein did fealty to his lord, he was to hold his right hand over the book and say, "Hear you, my lord *A.*, that I, *B.*, from this day forth unto you shall be true and faithful, and shall owe you fealty for the land that I hold of you in villeinage, and shall be justified by you in body and goods. So help me God and his holy saints!" It is probable, the above regulation was not a parliamentary act, any more than that in the 18th year of the king, called the statute for view of *frankpledge*, which contains those articles of inquiry that were within the cognizance of that jurisdiction, as the *capitula itineris* did those within the cognizance of the eyre. The other statutes of this king relate to the *Despencers* and *Gaveston*. One is for revoking an establishment of the household that had been made in the 11th year of this king; another is the statute of *estreats*, 16 Edw. II., relating to the ordering of those matters in the exchequer.

Thus have we gone through the statutes that are by universal consent ascribed to the reign of Edward II. At the end of these are thrown together in the statute-book some acts, the dates of which are not exactly agreed upon by lawyers, except that they were made either in the reign of Henry III., Edward I., or Edward II., for which reason they are classed under the denomination of *Statuta incerti temporis*. As some of these must have had a very important effect at the time they were made, it will be proper to notice them, that such consequences as after followed from them may be ascribed to their true causes.

Statuta incerti temporis.

Among these statutes is the statute of *Ragman de justitiariis assignatis*, by which particular justices were assigned *to hear and determine* in cases of outrage, trespass, barratry, and the like. This commission was probably the same as was called *Trailbaston*; and if so, this statute properly belongs to the time of Edward I.[1] There is another statute upon the subject of administering justice in the country, entitled, *Statutum de justitiariis assignatis*; which seems, from the recital at the opening of it, to have been passed very soon after the 13 Edw. I., as it was made in aid of the provision for taking inquests in the country by justices of *nisi prius*. This act states, that the justices of both benches, and the justices itinerant,

[1] *Vide ante*, c. xi.

had not time to come into the country at the seasons appointed by that act; and therefore the king, willing that justice should be administered with all despatch, ordained eight justices to take assizes, juries, and certificates, through the whole kingdom; for which purpose it was divided into four circuits. Two of these justices were to go into Yorkshire, Northumberland, Westmoreland, Cumberland, Lancashire, Nottinghamshire, and Derbyshire; two in the counties of Lincoln, Leicester, Warwick, Stafford, Salop, Nottingham, Rutland, Gloucester, Hereford, and Worcester; two into Cornwall, Devon, Somerset, Dorset, Wilts, Southampton, Oxford, Berks, Sussex, and Surrey; two into Kent, Essex, Hertford, Norfolk, Suffolk, Cambridge, Huntingdon, Bedford, and Bucks.[1] Assizes, juries, and recognitions of the county of Middlesex were to be taken before the justices of the court where the issue depended. These eight justices were specially to attend to taking assizes and certificates *assiduè per totum annum*, without any regard to the times prescribed in the before-mentioned statute, in any part of the county that seemed to them most convenient and proper; and no writs of assize, juries, or recognitions were to be granted before any other justices, *nisi de speciali gratiâ regis.*[2] It does not appear how long this establishment of justices continued.

Another statute contains the oaths to be taken in the eyre by the sheriff, his bailiffs, the four hundredors, and the twelve jurors, much in the way in which they had been stated by Bracton.[3] One of these statutes is entitled, *De magnis assisis et duellis*, though it has rather the appearance of a note penned by some lawyer than a legislative act. It says, that battail, or the great assize, should not lie between relations till they had passed the third degree, whenever they claimed by the same descent; but battail might be joined between brothers when one was infeoffed and the other claimed by descent.[4] Battail might be joined, but there could be no great assize, where a man was infeoffed, and he vouched to warranty a charter which he had of his feoffer; for the vouchee might deny the charter *per corpus* of his free man; and in such case no great assize would lie. On the other hand, a great assize would lie, but not battail, where a man sold land to another, and that other sold it to another, and with it gave the charter by which he was infeoffed. After this the heir of the first feoffer came and impleaded him by writ of right; here he could not defend his seisin *per corpus* of his free man, but must put himself, says the statute, *upon God and the great assize.* However, neither the battail nor great assize would lie, where the demandant claimed to hold in frank-marriage, free burgage, or in gavelkind; nor would they lie where he demanded only a small thing, as an acre, or toft;

[1] *Vide ante*, vol. i. c. ii., for the distribution of the counties at the first appointment of circuits.
[2] *Vide ante*, vol. i. c. iii.; and *ante*, c. x.
[3] *Vide ante*, vol. i. c. viii.
[4] *Ibid.* vol. i. c. iii.

but in such cases they might, by award of the justices, put themselves by consent on a jury of twelve free men, in lieu of the great assize.

A similar fragment of old law is entitled, *Statutum de visu terræ, et essonia de servitio domini regis.* This declares, that a view should not be granted in a writ *de custodiâ*, in a writ *de consuetudinibus et servitiis*, or in one *de advocatione ecclesiæ*, unless where there were more churches in one vill of the same saint; nor in a writ *de dote assignandâ* or *nuper obiit.*[1] Again, the essoin *de servitio regis* was not to lie in a writ of novel disseisin, in a writ or dower *unde nihil, ultimæ præsentationis*, nor appeal *de morte hominis.*[2]

The *statutum pro tenentibus per legem Angliæ* bears evident marks of an earlier period than this reign. In stating the law of tenant by the courtesy, it says, that the second husband should inherit, contrary to the express declaration of the statute *de donis*, which altered the common law in this particular; it was therefore written before that act. Again, as it confines the courtesy to estates given *in maritagium*, according to Glanville, without including all inheritances, as Bracton does, it must have been written before the latter author penned his book. But if this was a statute before Bracton's time, that author, where he examines the question of the second husband claiming by the courtesy, and mentions Segrave's opinion against it, could not be supposed to omit noticing any statute that had been made so decisive as this is.[3]

The *statutum de catallis felonum* states the law respecting the land and chattels of felons before conviction, in the same manner as Bracton. Among the statutes *incerti temporis* is one, entitled in English, *Articles against the king's prohibition*, being, in fact, a translation of the latter part of the statute of *Circumspectè agatis*, the substance of which, however, is in the former part of that same statute. Another is entitled, *Prohibitio formata de statuto articulorum*, being a writ of prohibition directed to the Bishop of Norwich, or his official, with a view probably of enforcing the regulations made by the statute of *Circumspectè agatis*, which was made on the occasion of some proceedings in that bishop's court.

The remainder of these statutes are, *an ordinance for bakers; consuetudines et assisa de forestâ, sive articuli de attachiamentis forestæ; statutum armorum ad torniamenta; compositio ulnarum et perticarum; statutum de Judaismo; de divisione denariorum; an ordinance for measures*, none of which are of any great moment. *Statutum de brevi de inquisitionibus concedendo de terris ad manum mortuam ponendis*, has been supposed to belong to the 20 Edw. I. This act directs, that the writ of inquisition (by which was meant the writ of *ad quod damnum*) should not be granted for

[1] View was not allowed in *nuper obiit* at common law. *Vide ante*, vol. i. c. viii.

[2] As to dower and *assisa ultimæ præsentationis*, this was a declaration of the common law. *Vide ante*, vol. i. c. viii. As to the other points, *vide ibid.*

[3] *Vide ante*, vol. i. c. ii., iii.; and *ante*, c. ix.

amortising lands, but that such alienations should be done only by petition in full parliament. We have seen[1] that this writ was afterwards authorised by parliament for this very purpose of aliening in mortmain.

Thus far of the statutes of the king, and of those *incerti temporis*,[2] none of which, except that for the appointment of sheriffs, and that *de frangentibus prisonam*, seem to have made any very material alteration in the common law. They were either collections, and a sort of *summæ*, comprising in one view a number of particulars relating to one object, and necessary to be plainly understood, as the *Prærogativa Regis*, or declarations of the law in certain points that were entertained with some hesitation and doubt.

Having noticed the few regulations made by statute during this reign, we shall now see what was done by our courts. In this branch of our subject we shall circumscribe our inquiries, as we did in the preceding reign, confining our observations principally to such parts of the law as have not been hitherto sufficiently elucidated, and to such modifications of the old law as had arisen from the operation of the numerous statutes made in the last reign; these, from their novelty, being entitled to a more particular attention.

Whatever might have been the doubt, in the time of Bracton,[3] about the succession of the half-blood, we find in this reign the rule of descent was established conformably with what was laid down by Britton in the last reign,[4] that the half-blood should be entirely excluded in the succession to land. In the fifth year of this king,[5] the following question was put to the bench by one of the counsel: What do you say to the imperial law,[6] upon which the law of the land is founded, which ordains, that the heritage shall go to the most worthy; *quòd possessio fratris facit sororem hæredem?* to which the court assented; and in the same place it is stated, in the very terms of the law as held at this day, that if the brother dies and the sister enters, the land shall rather escheat to the lord than descend to another sister of the half blood: "and this (says the book) is the common law, which ought not to be changed." Accordingly, in the case then before the court, they

1 *Vide ante*, c. x.

2 Besides the statutes already mentioned, which are to be found in all the common editions of the statutes, there are about ten more, which have been omitted by later compilers, and are only to be seen in the edition printed by Tottell, which is the book usually quoted by Lord Coke under the title of *Vetus Magna Charta*. These, like many of those we have just been mentioning, contain declarations of the common law, and have the appearance of being the notes of lawyers. They are, except one or two, of little importance, as may be judged from the titles of most of them. The titles are as follow: *Consuetudines Cantiæ—Capitula Itineris—De Homagio capiendo—Contra Vicecomites et Clericos—Capitula Eschætriæ—Juramentum Regis—Juramentum Episcoporum—Juramentum Conciliariorum Regis—Juramentum Eschætorum—Juramentum Vicecomitum—Juramentorum Majorum et Ballivorum—De Divisione Denariorum—De Venditione Farinæ—Abjuratio et Juramentum Latronum.*

3 *Vide ante*, vol. i. c. vii.

4 *Ibid.*

5 5 Ed. II. Mayn. 148, S.P. *Ibid.* 628.

6 *La ley impiel.*

determined that the land in question should go to the uncle, and not to the sister of the half blood. This now became the law, as well in lands descended as those taken by purchase, respecting which we have seen there was a difference in the time of Bracton.[1] After this, the course of descent referred a claimant no further than to the person last seised, and it became the rule, without any exception, that *seisina facit stipitem*—that is, that the seisin of the last possessor was to be taken for presumption of his being of the blood of the first purchaser without investigating a descent, which, in many cases, had become totally obscured by length of time.

It seems to have been very early taken for law, that warranty with assets would bar the issue in tail,[2] but not warranty without assets: thus was a method already proposed of getting loose from the tie of an entail. But notwithstanding this, there appear constructions upon the words, and peculiar limitations of entails, which show a prevailing inclination to extend the statute *de donis* to the utmost. Among others, the two following may be mentioned as strong instances: It was determined that the heirs, as well as the first donee, were restrained from alienation; and that the word *heirs* was left out of the statute by mistake of the clerk.[3] If the *heirs* of the donee were construed to be bound by the statute, there seems no reason to prevent this construction being carried still further to the heirs of those heirs, and so on, *in infinitum*. Thus did the judges completely carry into execution a plan for rendering landed property, for ever after, subject to continue in the families to which it might happen to be disposed by persons living in the 13th year of Edward I., notwithstanding any future possessor might be ever so inclined to part from it.

Gifts in tail.

In order to carry into complete effect the principle of this famous statute, it was found necessary to abrogate and dispense with many of the claims to which a person possessed of such an estate was liable at common law. Such seems to have been the determination in 5 Edw. II.,[4] where the second wife claimed dower out of an estate in special tail to her husband and his heirs by a former wife. In support of this claim it was contended, that the statute only restrained the tenant from alienation, but could not prevent the attachment of a lawful right. To this it was answered, that the tenant never had a fee in him, nor was any more than a joint feoffee; besides, the statute, which requires that the land should descend to the heir specified by the deed of gift, or revert to the donor, virtually took away this claim of dower, as a sort of alienation that would so far prejudice the issue. Such was the manner in which the claim was combated by those who best knew the law of those times. It may be presumption, upon the foundation of

[1] *Vide ante*, vol. i. c. v.
[2] 4 Ed. II. Mayn. 167.
[3] 5 Ed. II. Bro. Tail. 71.
[4] Mayn. 139.

such scanty remnants of old law as we possess, to hazard any other reason than such as is here given; but we cannot help observing, that, as the law of dower stood in the times of Bracton, it seems very doubtful whether the second wife, in this case, would be entitled to dower. And when we consider the estate of a tenant by the courtesy (a claim that seems very analogous to that of dower), the doubts entertained in Bracton's time, and the removal of them by the stat. *de donis*, which declared that the second husband should not be tenant by the courtesy, there seems to arise a certain equitable construction, in this case, in favour of the heir, to relieve him from the second dower.[1]

Probably soon after Fleta wrote the writ of *formedon in remainder* was invented; for we find one in the second year of Edward II.,[2] so that there was now the distinction, wherever an estate was to be limited over to any person but the donor, between a *remainder* and a *reversion;* and a *remainder* was considered as a technical term of limitation, altogether requisite in the wording of the donation. Thus in the eighth year of this king[3] a question arose upon a gift of land in remainder to *J. S.* in tail, and *for default of issue to W. N. habendum* in tail; it was doubted whether this was good without some word importing *a remainder;* and it was held sufficient only by a strained construction, namely, that the former gift in *remainder to J. S.* was to be extended to both.

The most interesting part of that knowledge which is furnished by the reports of this reign consists in the progress made towards bringing into form the remedies lately invented for redressing injuries to land or personal property (*a*). Of these writs we shall now give a short account, beginning with writs of formedon.

(*a*) It was required at that time that the writ should in brief disclose the nature and ground of action. This, which used to be required in every writ (and still is, to some extent, in ejectment), is now true of declaration; and where the plaintiff "counted" or declared that the defendant had broken a covenant, to acquit or indemnify him of all manner of debts and demands in regard to a house, &c., it was objected, that in the writ he ought to have stated, at all events generally, the nature of his claim, and how the plaintiff was damnified, and ought, in his declaration, to show how he had his action. And thus it was said, when a man is summoned into court, the writ ought to be so that the party *may be instructed as to what he ought to answer.* "And perhaps we have an acquittance from you of what you demand, although we have it not here, and you ought not to have judgment against us, because we were not instructed by the writ what we were summoned to answer, and we ought to have time to give a final answer." Westbury agreed, but Herle thought that, as the deed was in its terms general, the writ might be general, and the declaration certain. It was still pressed, however, that if the writ was general the defendant ought to have further information before he pleaded, and this seems agreed to (*Year-book,* 18 *Edw. II.* 600). It is to be observed, that although these real actions had been obsolete even when our author wrote, they embodied the law of *estates,* the principles of which are all to be found laid down in the Year-books. Real actions, it is to be noted, only lay for *freehold* estates. Thus, in an action of waste, the writ must at least state, *tenet ad terminum vitæ* (37 *Hen. VI.* fol. 26). And so any general grant, not limited in extent of duration, and which might last for life, was held to be at least an estate for life (*Burton* v. *Burton,* lib. ass. *anno* 17, fol. 49). And

[1] *Vide ante,* c. ix. [2] Mayn. 40. [3] Bro. don. and rem. 38.

Writs of formedon became in this reign very common, being specific remedies to carry into effect the provisions of the statute *de donis.* These were of three kinds: one was a formedon *in descendre;* another, a formedon *in reverter;* another, *in remainder.* The formedon *in descendre* was ordained, and the form thereof given by the statute, which also speaks of the formedon *in reverter* (not indeed under that name, but by the description of a writ whereby the donor was to recover after failure of heirs) as common enough in the chancery; though, as we observed before, there is no mention of such a writ, nor probably did it exist in Bracton's time. The form of a formedon *in reverter* differed from that *in descendre* only as the two cases differed. It was, *Præcipe, &c. quòd justè, &c. manerium de Bloxham cum pertinentiis, quod Robertus de Grelley dedit Petro de Grelley ad totam vitam suam, et quod Thomas filius, et hæres prædicti B. frater ejusdem Johannæ, cujus hæres ipse est, concessit Isolde de Grelley, habendum, post mortem prædicti Petri, eidem Isolde et hæredibus de corpore suo exeuntibus, et quod, post mortem prædictorum Petri de Isole, præfatæ Johannæ* REVERTI *debet, per formam donationis et concessionis, prædictorum, eò quòd prædicta Isolde obiit sine hærede de corpore suo exeunte, &c.*[1] The formedon *in remainder* was a writ that had originated since the statute, and was founded upon the distinction just mentioned, that had lately been made between a reversion when to a donor and when to a third person, which in the latter case was now called a *remainder.*[2] The writ, therefore, in consequence of this distinction, used in such cases to allege *quæ* REMANERE, instead of *quæ* REVERTI *debet.* So early as the second year of this king, we find this writ to be a settled form of demanding land.[3]

The formedon *in descendre,* as it came in the place of a mort-

so where land was granted generally, without saying for how long, a freehold estate was deemed to arise (*Vavasur's Case,* lib. ass. 11, 29). The remedies by real actions only applying to freehold estates, and, moreover, being carefully adapted to their respective qualities, the law of real property was necessarily involved in that of real actions. Although the "real actions" to which all this learning applies, had become obsolete even when our author wrote, and have long been abolished, they embodied the principles which lay at the basis of the whole law of real property, and formed the foundation for the complicated system of titles and conveyancing which still exists. Thus, for instance, cases in the Year-books as to writs of *formedon,* the remedy for an estate in tail (11 *Hen. VI.* fol. 20; 8 *Edw. III.* fol. 11; 5 *Edw. III.* fol. 17; 21 *Hen. VI.* fol. 36), are cited by Mr Preston in his work on conveyancing, as showing that, in deriving title to an estate tail, it is immaterial whether the party through whom the demandant derives title was seised or not; and it is to be observed, that in tracing titles in an abstract of title required on a sale, very much the same rules prevail as in deducing title in a real action. And all the well established rules and principles of the law of real property or conveyancing are to be retraced to these early times. So the well-known rule in Shelly's case, as it is called—one of the corner-stones of conveyancing—is to be traced back to cases in the very earliest of the Year-books (18 *Edw. II.* fol. 577; 40 *Edw. III.* fol. 9; *The Prior of Beverley's case,* 38 *Edw. III.* fol. 31; 21 *Edw.* fol. 31). That is to say, the rule in the case of land conveyed to a man and his son, and the heirs of his son's body, when the son died without issue in the life of the father (*Ibid.*)

[1] Mayn. 473. [2] *Ibid.* 311. [3] *Ibid.* 40.

auncestor (the only remedy which, before the statute, the heir *per formam doni* had), was in some points considered in the light of that writ. It was looked upon as a writ of possession, and, as such, it was held the demandant must make himself heir to the person last seised.[1] It was argued, that as it would be a good plea for a tenant in mortauncestor to say, that the person last seised died seised of nothing but a fee tail; so, in this writ, it would be good to say he died seised of a fee simple.[2] This writ was held to lie for an infant as well as for a person of full age, not only because it was a writ of possession, of which any one might avail himself, but also because it was expressly ordained by a statute which makes no exception of persons within age.[3] The general plea in this and the other formedons was, *ne dona pas.* It was once pleaded in a formedon *in descendre*, that the donor was not so seised as to be able to make a gift. To this it was objected, that there was no need of inquiring, in this action, about the seisin or title of the donor, and the tenant had nothing else to say but *ne dona pas:* the tenant accordingly amended his plea, and said he could not make a gift *sans ceo*, that he was seised so as to confer a seisin; but it being still insisted that the donor's title was not to be inquired into, one of the justices directed *ne dona pas* to be entered on the roll.[4]

A formedon *in reverter* was also considered as a writ of possession, and therefore where it counted of a seisin so far back as the time of King Richard, as in a writ of right, it was held ill, and it was said that it should be limited to the time of a writ of aiel or motauncestor.[5] However, though a writ of possession, it was held that an infant could not bring it, because it lay at common law, and was not ordained by statute as the formedon *in descendre* was.[6] A formedon *in remainder* was considered in the same light as the former. An objection was made to a writ of formedon *in remainder*, and the clerks of the chancery were sent to, who said it was the usual form of the chancery to make the demandant in such writ heir to the person last seised, and to no other; but they could give no reason for it.[7]

It was not unusual, in a formedon, for the tenant to plead that an ancestor of the demandant aliened with warranty to such a person from whom the land descended to the tenant; and to argue upon this, that it would be absurd for the demandant to claim under the entail as against the tenant, when he was bound by the warranty of his ancestor to defend the tenant in possession of that very land against all the world. To this plea it was common for the demandant to admit the deed of his ancestor, but to say, that assets did not come to him by descent from his ancestor, therefore that he ought not to be bound by it; and if, upon trial of this issue whether he had any value by descent from his ancestor, it

[1] Mayn. 390. [2] *Ibid.* 431. [3] *Ibid.* 16, 150. [4] Mayn. 506.
[5] *Ibid.* 37, 38. *Vide ante*, c. ix. [6] Mayn. 389. *Vide ante*, c. ix. [7] Mayn. 625.

was found that he had, the warranty was held a bar to the action, and otherwise not.[1] That a warranty should bar the heir from claiming against his ancestor's deed, is perfectly conformable with the old law; and as the statute *de donis* had only declared that a fine should not bar, but seems to have left an estate tail open to the effects of a warranty, it was nothing more than a natural conclusion of law, that an estate tail, even after the statute, might be barred by a warranty; but the singularity is, that this warranty was restricted so as to lose its effect, if not accompanied with assets by descent.

We have before seen that the heir of the warrantor at common law was not bound *ad excambium*, but only in proportion to the lands descended to him from the warrantor; he was, nevertheless, bound to warrant, and, of course, was barred from claiming the estate, although he had no lands or assets, as they were now called, by descent.[2] No statute that has come down to us was made expressly to change the law in this point. There seems no other way of accounting for this novelty but by supposing that the judges thought themselves justified by the spirit of the statute *de donis*, to adopt the principle and regulation of the statute of Gloucester concerning alienations of tenants by the courtesy. This statute, proceeding as we have before surmised upon the common-law notion just mentioned,[3] had declared that a warranty of the father should not bar the heir without an inheritance descending *ex parte patris*.

That they had a eye to the statute of Gloucester in their reasoning respecting entails and warranty, seems probable from the following case: A tenant *per la ley* had aliened with warranty, and his heir brought a *formedon*. To this a warranty was pleaded. In reply, the statute was set forth; and it was alleged there was nothing by descent, therefore the warranty was of no force. To this it was objected, that he could not avail himself of that statute, because it was confined to the writs mentioned therein; namely, to writs of mortauncestor, ael, cosinage, and besael. But it was answered, that in like manner as another chapter of that statute, which gives the writ of entry *in casu proviso*, was construed to extend to alienations by tenant for life and *per legem*, though the statute only mentions tenants in dower; so on this chapter might any writ be maintained that was grounded on the alienation of the husband; and it was accordingly adjudged, that the writs named in the statute were only for examples, and that a writ of formedon, or right, would be equally good.[4] Thus, if a formedon *in descendre*, which was specially assigned by statute for the issue in tail, was allowed as a remedy in a case within the statute of Gloucester, there seemed to be an affinity acknowledged between those two parliamentary provisions.

Indeed, when it is considered, that the statute of Gloucester was

[1] Mayn. 45, 564, 641.
[2] *Vide ante*, vol. i. c. viii.
[3] *Vide ante*, c. ix.
[4] Mayn. 324, 325.

made in protection of the heir against the alienation of the ancestor, in case of a gift *in maritagium*, and of a tenant by the courtesy; that gifts *in maritagium* are one of the estates mentioned in the statute *de donis*, which statute was made expressly in favour of heirs; and that there is a special provision therein to protect the heir from being encumbered with the courtesy of a second husband: these two acts must be considered in the light of statutes *in pari materie*; and to be accordingly entitled to such reciprocal assistance as can be mutually communicated from one to the other, by construction. Whatever might be the ground upon which the courts proceeded, we find it decided so early as the second year of this king, that warranty with assets would bar the heir in tail, but not warranty without assets; and it is very explicitly declared in the next reign, as will be shown hereafter, that this piece of law was by equity of the statute of Gloucester.

We are now enabled to see the nature and tendency of some other writs, which have hitherto been mentioned only generally.

Other real writs.

There were at common law two writs for the recovery of the right of wardship—that called *De communi custodiâ*, and that *De transgressione*, for ejectment of ward; neither of which are discoursed of by any author of the preceding ages; but all the knowledge we have of them is derived from two statutes, which make some regulation for their conduct and process.[1] One of those statutes ordained likewise the writ of *ravishment of ward*, which did not lie at common law. All these three writs were in use during this reign; and we are enabled, from some few decisions, to collect their distinct office. It seems the *writ of ward* was, in its nature, a writ of right, and was brought for the mere right, before any seisin of ward had been attained:[2] in this action the defendant might pray in aid, and vouch to warranty, as in other real suits, but the process was that of distress.[3] The writ of *ejectment of ward* lay where a seisin had been obtained, and the plaintiff had been ousted thereof; and, like the former, it lay both for the land and the body of the ward.[4] The writ of *ravishment of ward*, which was given by the 2 Westminster, c. xxxv.[5] was only to recover the body; and this, like the former, only lay where there had been a seisin, and the plaintiff was deprived of his ward: it was held, however, that the defendant should not be permitted to traverse the seisin, but must plead the general issue of *ne ravist point*.[6] This was an action of trespass as well as the former, and therefore it was thought that the writ should be laid *vi et armis;* and though it was said that it was a special writ, which by the form in the statute was only *contra pacem*, and accordingly one laid *vi et armis* had been once held ill, yet, upon reconsideration, it was determined to be good.[7]

The writ of *cessavit per biennium* given by 2 Westm. c. xxi.[8]

[1] *Vide ante*, c. x.
[2] Mayn. 378.
[3] *Ibid.* 213.
[4] *Ibid.* 376.
[5] *Vide ante*, c. x.
[6] Mayn. 378.
[7] *Ibid.* 268, 191.
[8] *Vide ante*, c. x.

was a very common remedy; being usually recurred to where there was a failure of distress. The pleading in this action was ordered in conformity with that for which it was in some cases a substitute.[1] Thus, though a seisin of the services in question was alleged, it was not sufficient for the tenant to say *ne unque seisi* of the service, no more than in an avowry, but he was to answer to the tenure, or it would be taken for granted;[2] so that the general plea was, *nous ne tenons rien de lui.*[3] It was allowed that the defendant might allege, by way of *protestation*, that the services were less than what were demanded; and for answer say, that there was sufficient distress upon the land.[4] A *cessavit* being in the nature of a writ of right would not in general lie against a termor for life; and yet it was allowed, in such case, when the reversioner was plaintiff in the action.[5] Consistent with the principle on which a view used to be denied at common law, it was denied in this action, because the cesser was the defendant's own act;[6] though the aid of a parcener was refused,[7] that of a reversioner was allowed.[8]

There are several writs of *contra formam feoffamenti* grounded upon the statute of Marlbridge, c. ix.[9] The common plea in these was, *ne unque seisi*, before the time of limitation prescribed by that statute.[10] There appears a writ of a similar design with the former, which we have not met with in any of the preceding reigns, called a *monstravit*, but in after-times more frequently termed *monstraverunt*. This writ was at common law, and was contrived for tenants in ancient demesne, who had been burdened with more services than were originally due in that tenure. The litigation of these points generally produced an issue, which was to be determined by Doomsday-book in the exchequer; that being the evidence by which ancient demesne was to be proved.[11] The first process in this writ was a prohibition,[12] and then an attachment.

There appear some few other new actions, grounded either upon the statutes of the two last reigns, or the common law. Of the former kind are the writ *de contributione*, on the statute of Marlbridge, c. ix., to compel coparceners to be aiding to the eldest in performing the services; on the statute of Gloucester, c. vii., the writ *in casu proviso;* a writ of entry, founded on 2 Westm. c. iii., for the heir of the reversioner, after a recovery against his ancestor by default; a writ *contra formam collationis*, on statute 2 West. c. xli.[13] Of the latter kind are the following: the writ of *secta ad molendinum*, for recovering a suit to a mill, where a lord's tenants had been time out of mind bound to grind their corn at his mill, and any had withdrawn or ceased in making such suit; a writ of *quid juris clamat*, for a conusee in a fine levied by a reversioner to procure the attornment of the tenant for life; the writ of office called *diem clausit extremum*, grounded on the statute of Marl-

[1] Mayn. 361. [2] *Ibid.* 195, 560. [3] *Ibid.* 61. [4] *Ibid.* 534.
[5] *Ibid.* 643. [6] *Ibid.* 38, 61, 195. *Vide ante*, vol. i. c. viii. [7] *Ibid.* 38.
[8] *Ibid.* 245. [9] *Vide ante*, c. viii. [10] Mayn. 51, 52. [11] *Ibid.* 280, 455.
[12] *Ibid.* 422. [13] *Ibid.* 101, 67, 91, 515. *Vide ante*, vol. i. c. viii.

bridge, c. xvi. Where a person died seised of land holden *in capite*, this writ issued to seize the land into the king's hands.[1] The proceeding by *scire facias* had become very common, owing to the sanction that had been given to it by a statute in the last reign.[2] The most usual instances in which we find it, were to get execution of recognizances and of fines.

Writs of conspiracy.

The writ of *conspiracy*, which had been framed by the king's direction in the last reign,[3] was put in practice as a mode of redress for parties who were injured by certain combinations and confederacies. One of the objects pointed out by the statute of Edward I. was evil procurers of dozeins. Under that idea this writ was sometimes prosecuted against indictors; and though in support of such writs it was argued, that a procuror of indictments had only to get himself impannelled on the jury, and then he would escape the imputation of *unlawful* confederacy, yet it was more than once held that it would not lie against indictors.[4] It was endeavoured to extend this writ. A writ of conspiracy was brought against several for suing a false statute-merchant, in order to encumber the land of the plaintiff. It was objected to this writ, that it was not within the statute of conspiracy; but there does not appear in the report any opinion of the court upon it.[5] Again, this writ was brought against one person upon the following case: The defendant had brought a writ of entry against the plaintiff, which was adjourned during a certain time, upon agreement between the parties; the demandant in that writ returned to the court, without communicating to the tenant his design of going on with the suit, and, by surprise, recovered by default; upon which the tenant in the writ of entry brought this action of conspiracy against the demandant for redress. But it was held by the court, that this being transacted under the forms of law, could not be called a *false alliance, confederacy*, and *collusion;* therefore that the writ would not lie, but the party must seek redress by demanding the land back again in a writ of right.[6] It was held, that a conspiracy would not lie against women, though no reason is given for so singular an opinion.[7] The count upon the writ used to conclude, *ad grave damnum ipsius W. et contra formam ordinationis, &c., unde dicit quòd deterioratus est, et damnum habet ad valentiam ——, et inde producit sectam, &c.*[8] Where a writ was brought by a baron and feme, and the damages were laid *ad damnum ipsorum*, it was held ill.[9] In such a writ against conspirators for procuring an indictment, it must be alleged that the plaintiff was *acquitted*, otherwise it would be ill:[10] it was held, that all writs of conspiracy should be laid against the statute.

A similar writ to the foregoing was the writ of *deceit*, of which we find no mention till this reign, though it was founded on the

[1] Mayn. 81, 86, 304. [2] 2 Westm. c. xlv. *Vide ante*, c. x. [3] *Vide ante*, c. x.
[4] Mayn. 401, 547. [5] *Ibid.* 81. [6] *Ibid.* 172. [7] Mayn. 509.
[8] *Vide* Mayn. 401, a record in conspiracy down to the award of the *venire*.
[9] Mayn. 347. [10] *Ibid.* 509.

common law. This was to redress a person in damages for any injury he had sustained by reason of collusive, oppressive, or deceitful proceedings in judicial matters. It was brought for levying a fine falsely, and suggesting a false title; for suing a *monstravit*, where the plaintiff was not in ancient demesne; against the demandant in an action, and the sheriff for not summoning the tenant, so that he lost his land by default; against one for suing falsely in a writ of waste, and not properly summoning him, so that he lost his land.[1]

Action of debt.

We shall now view the improvement made in the more common personal actions then in use. We have seen that the action of debt, in the reign of Henry II., was the remedy for recovering money, or a chattel,[2] and that in the reign of Edward I.[3] this action began to split into two; so that a writ of *debet* was appropriated principally to cases where money was to be recovered, and a writ of *detenet* for recovery of chattels. This distinction was still attended to; but the close affinity between these two modes of demanding was such, that they were sometimes included in the same writ. Thus we find an action *quòd reddat* 20*l.* ARGENTI *quas ei* DEBET, *et dimidium* SACCI LANÆ *quod ei injustè* DETINET.[4] However, debt and detinue must be considered as two actions, and the specific differences shall therefore be treated of separately.

It seems that a writ of debt was usually grounded upon a *deed*, or *obligation* to pay money (which was a *writing sealed*); though it was sometimes upon a mere bargain of buying and selling; but so exact were they in their transactions at this time, that a deed was sometimes made for the price of a thing sold. In such a case the plaintiff would state his demand of so much money as the price of the thing sold, and then produce a deed testifying the transaction, and the debt[5](*a*). If the action was grounded wholly upon a deed of obligation, the plaintiff stated that the defendant granted himself to owe so much money, and then he showed the deed testifying it: if it was a transaction without writing, then, after stating the demand, he would offer to produce his *secta*, or suit, to prove it. It was

(*a*) The action of debt was then the common remedy upon contracts, whether for money or for goods, and such contracts appear to have been always by deed, probably because few of the laity could write. In Fitz. *Abr.* several are stated. Thus, for instance, Fitz. *Abr.* title *Variance*, pt. 24, one of the cases is thus stated:—"Tempore Edward I., in debt upon a deed of thirty quarters of barley, at the price of 20s., it was found for the plaintiff, and they (the jury) inquired of the price at the time of (*i.e.*, appointed for) payment; and it was found that at the time of payment a quarter was at 32s., but at the time of making the deed it was only at 3s. The plaintiff recovered £68 for the corn, according to the price at the time of payment. *Et sic nota*, that he recovered the price and not the corn, and yet he demanded the corn." The damages appeared to have been assessed at the difference between the 20s. per quarter, which the plaintiff was to pay for the barley at the market price of the day of delivery—although the figures do not accord; perhaps, however, something was included for costs (*Year-book*, 7 *Edw. IV.*, fol. 49, pt. 6).

[1] Mayn. 104, 214, 245, 587, 681.
[2] *Vide ante*, vol. i. c. iii.
[3] *Vide ante*, c. iv.
[4] 7 Ed. II. Mayn. 241.
[5] Mayn. 375.

not uncommon to have a writ containing two demands; one grounded upon a deed, the other not; in which case the plaintiff, in counting, would produce the deed to prove one, and his *secta* to prove the other.[1]

A deed made at Berwick was offered as evidence in an action of debt, but was objected to as not legal proof, because the place where it was made was out of the jurisdiction and process of the court.[2] This objection was held good, and it was said to be the same of Chester and Durham, and *à fortiori* of Ireland and other places beyond sea.[3] It was held, that a defendant should not be admitted to wage his law against a *specialty*, for so a deed was now sometimes called; and though it was endeavoured to bring a sealed[4] tally within the same reason, it was overruled; yet at the same time it was admitted, that in *accompt* against a bailiff or overseer, he would not be allowed to wage his law against a sealed tally.[5] The reason of the difference is not stated in the report, nor does it seem easy to account for it. The proper general plea against a deed was, *nient le fait*, that it was not the defendant's deed. So strictly was this form adhered to, that where it was pleaded by an abbot, *nest pas lour commune seale*, that it was not the common seal of the convent, he was driven to say, *nient le fait.*[6] A common plea to a deed was *deins age*, not of age, when made.[7] In an action of debt brought upon an obligation to pay so much money, if a book was not returned by such a day, it was pleaded that the book was deposited at such a place, and the plaintiff took it *ante diem;* to which it was replied, he did not take it.[8]

Respecting joint and several actions; a husband brought an action of debt in his own name only, upon an obligation made to his wife while sole, and it was held good; because if she had been joined, *she* would have recovered the money, and so have had a property which she ought not by law to possess, while under coverture.[9] It was laid down as a rule long settled, that executors, when plaintiffs, should all be named in the writ; but when a writ was brought against executors, none need be named but those who had administered.[10] The way of demanding against executors was somewhat different from that against the original debtor; it was, *quæ prædictus Thomas ei* DEBUIT, *et præd. executores injustè* DETINENT.[11] The general plea of executors was *pleinment administre;* to which the replication was, *assez de biens le mort:*[12] that of an heir, when sued on an obligation in which his ancestor had bound his heir, was, *riens per descent;* to which the replication was, *assez jour de brief purchase;* to which it was rejoined, *navoit rien le jour du brief purchase.*[13]

If there was no writing to prove the demand, the plaintiff was to produce his *secta*, according to the old law; though it seems there

1 Mayn. 78, 188. 2 *Ibid.* 24. 3 *Ibid.* 613. 4 *Vide ante*, c. x.
5 Mayn. 178. 6 *Ibid.* 589. 7 *Ibid.* 369. 8 *Ibid.* 379.
9 *Ibid.* 93. 10 *Ibid.* 503. 11 *Ibid.* 490. 12 *Ibid.* 354.
13 *Ibid.* 585.

was not now so much reliance upon the *secta* as formerly. In the 7th of Edward II. it was demanded by the counsel for the defendant, that the *secta* should be examined, as was the method, we have seen, in former reigns;[1] but the counsel for the plaintiff objected to it, that *this court* (meaning the common pleas) never suffered a *secta* to be examined: however, he said he was ready to *aver* the debt, that is, to *prove* it by the verdict of a jury; for such was an averment: and upon one of the justices showing some doubt about examining the *secta*, the averment was received, the defendant pleaded *riens lour* DEUST, *nil debet*, and it went to the country for trial.[2] The suit, however, still continued to be brought, though their examination might be disused. In the 14th Edward II. the plaintiff being asked what he had to show for his debt, said, *a good suit;* upon which the counsel for the defendant prayed they might come to the bar, which they did; and then he tendered his averment *que riens, &c.* that he owed nothing.[3] The wager of law continued as a proof not only upon the issue of *nil debet*, but on some collateral points. An action of debt was brought upon a specialty, and it was pleaded, that the obligation was to be void upon the defendant levying a fine after reasonable request, and no request was made. To this it was replied, that request was made at such a time and place; to which it was rejoined, that he made no such requests, which he was ready to prove *par notre ley*, by wager of law.[4]

We find actions of debt were brought upon three statutes made in the last reign; one upon 2 Westm. c. 11,[5] against a keeper of a gaol for letting an accountant go at large;[6] another on the statute-merchant, for letting a debtor by recognizance go at large;[7] another on 2 Westm. c. 19,[8] which directs that the ordinary should be bound to answer the debts of the deceased, as the executors should have done. There was an action against the executors grounded upon this statute, which after some debate was held good: the plea in such actions was, *non devindrent en mains l'ordinary.*[9]

Thus far of the action of debt; that of *detinue* next claims our notice (*a*). This might be brought, as was before said, for any chattel that was in the hands of the defendant, and belonged to the plaintiff; but as in the former writ it was necessary in counting to show *how* the money was owing, so in this it was required to show in what manner the thing in question came out of the possession of the plaintiff, and into that of the defendant. This

(*a*) A remedy for the recovery of *specific* chattels as distinguished from a mere sum of money. There has always been a broad distinction between actions for the recovery of specific property, real or personal, and actions for recovery of damages, either for the taking or injuring such specific property. In the former case, the chattels or the land, &c., must be described by number and value (*Year-book*, 1 *Edw. V.*, 6), for the execution, which was the effect of the action, would be to deliver up the specific property; but it was otherwise of actions for damages.

[1] *Vide ante*, vol. i. c. vii.
[2] Mayn. 242.
[3] *Ibid.* 420.
[4] *Ibid.* 433, 434.
[5] *Vide ante*, c. ix.
[6] Mayn. 341.
[7] *Ibid.* 138. *Vide ante*, c. ix.
[8] *Vide ante*, c. ix.
[9] Mayn. 490.

was generally stated to be by a delivery by the hands of the plaintiff, or of some other by his authority, or through whom he claimed, or upon some of the terms mentioned at large by Glanville,[1] as a loan, deposit, or the like. As this was the material part of the inquiry, it had become a rule of pleading, that the defendant should not be admitted to deny, or *traverse,* as they called it, the detinue, but should answer to the *delivery,* or *bailment*, that the court might be informed whether the thing came to the defendant's hands by the bailment of the plaintiff himself, or by the hands of some other.[2] There was a particular reason why the plaintiff should state whether the bailment was by his own hands, or by those of another; because in the latter case it was not sufficient to bring a *secta*, but he must ground his action upon a specialty, otherwise the defendant need not answer it.[3] Thus, then, the plea in this action was, *ne bailla pas*, or *navoit pas de son baille.*[4] In this action as well as in others, they went sometimes into a length of pleading which put the inquiry upon another matter; as where it was pleaded that the plaintiff accepted ten acres of land in satisfaction of the goods demanded, and the plaintiff replied, that he was not enfeoffed in satisfaction of the goods now demanded.[5]

Detinue *de rationabili parte.*

There are two instances, where this action, or at least that of debt, was brought, which deserve particular notice. In the first year of this king, a writ, in the *detinet*, was brought by a son against his father's executors for ten marks of the property of the deceased, who died worth thirty; alleging, that, because *pur usage de pais, by the custom of the country,* the third part ought to go to the deceased, a third to his widow, and a third to his children unmarried, therefore he, as son, demanded his third. To this it was pleaded, that he had been advanced by a lease of lands from his father of such value, and therefore the action would not lie. The plaintiff admitted this in his replication, but said the land was worth only so much, and therefore he ought to maintain his action; however, it was decided against him, as this action was grounded wholly upon usage and want of advancement; so that this writ, notwithstanding what was argued, as to the declaration of *Magna Charta,*[6] which was contended to be general and absolute, was held by the court to be founded on the *particular custom* of a certain place.[7] Again, we find, in the 17th year of this king, a writ of detinue of chattels was brought by an infant against his father's executors, reciting that *per consuetudinem regni*, the mother was to have a third, the children a third, and the executors another third, &c. To this the defendant pleaded *pleinment administre.* One of the justices took up the matter, and expressed a doubt whether the action would lie; for, says he, the writ is founded on a custom, but we know no such custom, and the law is otherwise; and when it was urged that the custom was good, as appeared by

[1] *Vide ante*, vol. i. c. iii. [2] Mayn. 545. [3] *Ibid.* 39. [4] *Ibid.* 78.
[5] *Ibid.* 198. [6] Viz., ch. 18. *Vide ante*, vol. i. c. iv. [7] Mayn 9.

Magna Charta in these words, *salvis uxori et pueris suis rationabilibus partibus suis*, he replied, that the Great Charter only saved to the children their *own* goods, which might happen to come into the hands of the father (*a*); but neither the Great Charter nor the common law restrained the father's power over his own effects, to give or devise them as he pleased. It was added by another, that he had often seen such writs, but never knew one of them maintained; so the plaintiff was nonsuit.[1] This was the opinion in the reign of Edward II. respecting the power of bequeathing, where a wife and children were left by the testator. These two cases may be construed as a clear confirmation of the law, as laid down by Glanville. The latter, which applies to the general law of the kingdom, certainly supports that author's declaration, *quòd ultima voluntas esset libera*. The former may be thought to explain the other passage in Glanville, which qualifies, if not contradicts, that general rule; and may, perhaps, serve to show that Glanville should there be understood to speak of certain local customs; which interpretation, however, does not seem warranted by the present state of that author's text.[2]

The most common subjects of actions of detinue were deeds and charters. This was owing to the mode, then in fashion, of assuring land. It was a common practice, when land was let for years, or other estate less than the inheritance, to make a charter of feoffment, and bail it to a third person, as a sort of trustee, who was to return it if the termor enjoyed his term without molestation; and upon any molestation the feoffment was to be absolute. Another way was, to make mutual obligations for performance of covenants, and deposit them in the hands of some third person, with a power, if one of the parties broke his part of the covenant, to deliver his obligation to the other who had suffered by the breach.[3] These deeds, if the purpose of them had been served, or they became forfeited, used to be demanded in actions of detinue, in which the merits of the detainer were discussed.

The actions of *covenant* that occur in this reign are either for land, or some profit or casualty issuing out of, or appertaining to, land. It was laid down, that this action was appropriated for the

(*a*) This, it is obvious, was frivolous, for the reasonable part evidently meant of the father's goods; and there could be no doubt either as to the existence or the meaning of the custom. But then it was a custom which only applied in cases of *intestacy*, and therefore could be *prima facia* answered by an allegation of *administration*, for that meant administration either to creditors in the absence of a will, or to creditors and legatees in the case of a will. This seems the explanation of the decisions, and the real reason on which they proceeded. It was well understood that the reasonable part only applied to the surplus after all debts were paid. What was really held in this case was, that *plene administravit* was a good plea. And it was expressly said at the end, by Herle, J., that the writ and count in the former case were good. And there is another case in the same book where the writ was only abated for a defect in form, and it was plainly implied that it was good in substance (7 *Edw. II.*, fol. 215). The author, therefore, appears to have been in error in supposing the *decisions* were against the *action*.

[1] Mayn. 536. [2] *Vide ante*, vol. i. c. iii. [3] Mayn. 513, 554, b.

recovery of a fee simple or term, and that even a fee-tail had been recovered in an action of covenant;[1] this, however, must have been before the statute. It used to be brought for not doing homage and service, not acquitting the lessor against demands which ought to have been provided for by the lessee, against the lessor for ousting the lessee, and the like. It seems to have been always founded upon some deed containing covenants.

The writ of *annuity* was frequently recurred to. This action was very common between ecclesiastics. The heads of religious houses would grant to clerks annuities, to continue till they presented them to some of those benefices with which they were plentifully endowed. Again, when they performed their promise by presenting, it was not uncommon, if the living was greater than the annuity, or than they meant to bestow, to stipulate with the clerk for a grant of so much money annually, to reduce it to the value they thought proportioned to his merit.[2] In the latter sort of annuities it was no uncommon plea to allege, that the subject-matter was of a spiritual matter, and therefore not proper to be discussed *in foro seculari;* but this plea was always overruled.[3]

The proper way of counting upon a writ of annuity, if there was no deed, was, after stating the title and grant, to allege a seisin by the hands of the defendant; or, if it was so old, by the hands of his predecessor or ancestor, according to the grant, and also by the hands of the plaintiff; *and*, if the case was so, by the hands of his ancestor or predecessor likewise. The plea to this was *nient seisi*,[4] and the replication, *seisi per le mains le donor, &c.*, such a time *avant le jour le brieve purchase*,[5] the title and the seisin coupled together being the ground of action. If an annuity had been granted before time of memory, it was held that a deed was not necessary, but that it was good by prescription.[6] Annuities were sometimes granted with a clause of distress. It had been endeavoured to make such circumstance a plea in bar of an action of annuity, alleging that the plaintiff had another remedy; but this plea was always overruled.[7] When a writ of annuity was brought against a parson, he alleged that, as it was charged upon his benefice, he ought to have the aid of his ordinary, which was granted.[8] A defendant was not allowed to wage his law in an action of annuity,[9] probably because it was upon a deed or a prescription, that was held equivalent, and supposed a deed once to have existed.

Action of accompt.

The writ of *accompt*, as it had been aided with a more effectual process by the statute of Marlbridge and Westm. 2, was rendered a very useful remedy against persons who acted as agents; and so became, either by bailment or receipt, possessed of the goods, or money arising from the goods, of another.

[1] Mayn. 603.
[2] *Ibid.* 224, 416.
[3] *Ibid.* 634.
[4] *Ibid.* 221.
[5] *Ibid.* 205.
[6] *Ibid.* 665.
[7] *Ibid.* 8.
[8] *Ibid.* 416, 524.
[9] *Ibid.* 309.

The object of this writ was to bring the party *to account*, and for that purpose auditors were to be assigned (*a*). The persons who were the objects of this remedy, as they had violated a trust of great confidence, and often of great magnitude, were subjected to a shorter process than any others who had broken a mere civil engagement. They alone, of all other defendants in suits purely civil, were liable to a process against their person;[1] but the legislature had proceeded with tenderness in allowing this process. The statute of Marlbridge[2] gave it only against a man's *bailiff;* which term, though since understood in a very large sense, did at that time probably mean no more than a person who was a hired servant; and then it was to be only where the bailiff had no lands by which he might be distrained. The stat. Westm. 2[3] went further, and extended it to all *servants*, *bailiffs*, *chamberlains*, and all manner of *receivors, who were bound* AD COMPOTUM REDDENDUM; but still it was only to issue in the case of a defendant having no lands, as directed by the former statute. We find the writ of *monstravit de compoto* made use of in this reign, promiscuously with the common *capias*[4] (for so the *habeas corpus* and other writs against the person were now termed, from the word *capias* being introduced in the place of *habeas* in the command to take the body); and it was a good objection in either case to say that the

(*a*) There has always been a close connexion between the subjects of arbitration and of account; for the procedure by action of account was a kind of compulsory arbitration, and the "auditors assigned" were arbitrators appointed by the court. When, after the lapse of centuries, the action of account being obsolete, the legislature gave increased facilities for the procedure by voluntary arbitration, they recited as the reason the fitness of arbitration for matters of account. And when in our own time compulsory arbitration was established, it was in matters of account. The author has altogether omitted to notice the important subject of arbitration, and this may be the convenient place in which to notice it. The Year-books of this and the next reign make such frequent reference to it that it is evident submission to arbitration was very common; and it is mentioned in Britton as arbitration by "neighbours" (Distress). But the great difficulty about voluntary arbitration was, that if the award was against a party who claimed a right of action, and he persisted in suing, there was considerable doubt how far the award or arbitrament was a bar or a defence to the action, as an accounting under the statute would be (*vide post*). One mode adopted to enforce awards—in the absence of statutory power to do so—was by taking bonds to observe awards, with penalties for non-observance. There are cases of such bonds in the Year-books (for instance, 43 *Edw. III.*, fol. 27). In the case it was taken as clear law that if, in an action of trespass, the defendant pleaded an arbitration and an award that he should pay a certain sum, and that he had paid it, that would be a defence, but not unless he had paid it (*Year-book*, 43 *Edw. III.*, fol. 28). It is obvious that in principle it would be the same if the award should be that nothing was due, and that there was no cause of action, and so it was said in that case (*Ibid.*); but it was denied, and seems to have been doubted, and that was the difficulty in arbitration at common law, added to which, indeed, if one party saw it was going against him, and threw up the arbitration, and sued before an award, there was no remedy. In another case, an action of trespass was brought against one party for taking goods, and he pleaded an arbitration and an award that he should deliver some of them to the plaintiff and retain the rest, and that he was ready to deliver to the plaintiff those he was to deliver; the plaintiff having, it

1 Of this subject, and the statutes concerning the process of *capias*, more will be said when we come to speak of stat. 25 Ed. III. st. v., c. 17, which gave this process in debt and detinue.

2 Viz., ch. 23. *Vide ante*, c. viii.

3 Ch. 11. *Vide ante*, c. ix.

4 Mayn. 94, 99, 665.

party had land, and therefore ought not to be taken;[1] though, if he had not lands where the receipt was alleged to be, the writ would still lie. After these statutes, it was usual, in order to have the benefit of them, to charge defendants either as *bailiffs* or *receivors*. It was sometimes objected that the *monstravit* would not lie against a *receivor*, because the statute of Marlbridge speaks only of *bailiffs;* but it was said, and so adjudged, that the writ would be good, at least by Westm. 2, which spoke of *receivors;* for this latter statute was to be considered as having relation to the statute of Marlbridge, and therefore that the two statutes should be construed together as one; so that these writs, which had become very common, were determined to be good under either statute.[2]

If the defendant was charged with being *receivor* of certain money belonging to the plaintiff, the plea might be *ne unque receivour*.[3] If the count charged him as *receivor* of such money, and also with certain goods which were *bailed* to him, to the first he might plead generally *non receptor;* to the second, that he had accounted.[4] The following instance of a special plea and replication is well worthy of notice: The defendant said that he was employed by the plaintiff to buy things at market, of which he every day gave an account, and delivered to him the escrows of the expenses; and in this and no other way was his receivor or bailiff;

is manifest, sued, being dissatisfied with the award, before he had time to do so. It was held a good plea, however; and Belknap said, "last year I pleaded an arbitrament of a quart of wine, and it was held good" (*Year-book*, 45 *Edw. III.*, f. 16). In another case, in an action of trespass, it was pleaded that it was agreed that the defendant should submit to the arbitrament of certain persons, and that in case he "made his law," *i.e.*, swore (with certain others as compurgators) that he was not guilty of the trespass, then he should go quit, and that he had so "made his law." It was insisted that this was no plea, as there was nothing awarded, and so there was no satisfaction; which was absurd enough; for if there was no trespass, why should there be a satisfaction? and the parties had agreed to put themselves upon a certain mode of trying that question. In the result, the court being divided, the defendant withdrew his plea (*Year-book*, 46 *Edw. III.*, fol. 17). In account, however, which was a kind of compulsory arbitration, as it was compulsory on the defendant, the plaintiff was equally bound by an accounting. He who was put to account could swear that he had well and lawfully accounted of his receipts and expenses (*Year-book*, 41 *Edw. III.*, f. 3). So that there was this further resemblance to arbitration, that the party was examinable on oath, in which case it resembled wager of law (41 *Edw. III.*, f. 2). When the party was ready to account, auditors were assigned by the court (41 *Edw. III.*, f. 4); as, for instance, clerks of the court (*Ibid.*); then the defendant accounted before them, that is, set forth what he had received, and how he had dealt with it. Thus in that case it appeared that he had received jewels to sell, and he insisted that it was a matter rather between merchant and merchant; but it was held to be not the less matter of account, and he was adjudged to pay the sum received (*Year-book*, 41 *Edw. III.*, fol. 10). It was enough, however, to show payment (*Year-book*, 42 *Edw. III.*, fol. 22). It was also sufficient to show that he had already fully accounted to the plaintiff (*Year-book*, 45 *Edw. III.* fol. 14). It was urged that it was not a bar to the proceeding in the action, for that it was voluntary, whereas the auditors in the action had compulsory powers; but this was overruled, and it was said it was a good defence before the statute, and was not less so now, and had often been so held (*Year-book*, 45 *Edw. III.*, fol. 15). The writ of *capias ad computandum* issued against the defendant if he absconded, and when taken he was compelled to account (41 *Edw. III.* fols. 3, 13).

[1] Mayn. 99, 186. [2] *Ibid.* 41, 94. [3] *Ibid.* 80. [4] *Ibid.* 151.

and demanded judgment, whether of such receipt and administration, of which he had rendered account, he ought to answer, &c. To this it was replied that he was receivor in the manner above alleged, *sans ceo que*, that he had rendered account.[1] This phrase of *sans ceo que* was merely a denial, as *come ceo que* was an affirmation; and they respectively corresponded with *absque hoc quòd* and *cum hoc quòd*, two phrases that were thoroughly rooted in the law Latin of those days; that of *absque hoc* and *sans ceo* becoming technical expressions to signify a denial or *traverse* in pleading.

It was a general plea to say, *ne unque receivour.*[2] Where part of the action was founded upon a deed, and part upon a *secta*, the plea to that upon the deed was *pleinement account per patriam;* to the latter, *nient son receivour per legem.*[3] To this, as to all other actions, an acquittance might be pleaded.[4] We find an action of account against a guardian in socage, grounded on the statute of Marlbridge, c. xvii.[5] This writ recited the statute, as was usual in writs warranted by statute only.

Action of trespass.

Very little has yet been said on the action of *trespass*, all the writers of the former periods being wholly silent as to the nature and extent of this remedy. We are informed by Bracton that there was a writ *quare vi et armis* any one entered into the land of another; and we have seen the opinion expressed by that writer upon it.[6] There is a record of the reign of Edward I.,[7] which shows that this writ lay also for cases of personal injury, and for taking of goods and chattels, the writ there mentioned containing a complaint of both. In the present reign we find writs of trespass of various kinds, for *battery*, *imprisonment*, *taking and carrying away of goods and chattels*, *breaking and entering lands or houses*, *rescuing a distress*, and the like cases of violent injury. The manner in which the defendant answered to these suits was by pleading not guilty, if he could deny the *fact;* if he admitted the fact, but could say what would justify him in doing it, he then stated such matter specially. Thus, in an action for imprisoning the plaintiff, he might say that he was seised of the plaintiff as his villein, and took him as such; then the plaintiff might traverse that he was seised of him as his villein; or he might plead he took him on suspicion of killing.[8] Though the special matter of justification was usually to be pleaded in a special way, yet where a defendant pleaded not guilty, and the jury found *son assault demesne*, judgment was given for the plaintiff, the same as if he had pleaded it.[9] In trespass for taking and carrying away the goods and chattels of the plaintiff, he might justify as parson, and that he took them for tithes; if for cutting trees, that he had right of estovers; if for rescous, that they were *blada crescentia*, and so not liable to a distress; if for goods, that he took them as

[1] Mayn. 386. [2] *Ibid.* 80. [3] *Ibid.* 590, 651. [4] *Ibid.* 589.
[5] *Ibid.* 487. *Vide ante*, vol. i. c. viii. [6] *Vide ante*, vol. i. c. vii.
[7] *Vide ante*, c. x. [8] Mayn. 412, 344. [9] *Ibid.* 381.

guardian in socage; if for driving away cattle, that he took them for services due; if for entering land, that it was his own soil and freehold; if for beating down a mound, that it was a nuisance, and he beat it down while it was freshly raised.[1]

To such and the like pleas of justification, the plaintiff was to reply by denying the very point upon which the defence was rested. As thus: To a plea of taking for tithes in the fee of *L.*, the replication might be that he did not take in the fee of *L.*, but in the fee of *C.*; to a justification in right of estovers, that they were not appendant to his freehold; to a plea of distress for services, replication *a force et armes, et nient per tiel cause;* to a *nuisance freshement* raised, replication that it stood a year and a day before it was beat down; to the plea of *our soil and freehold*, and title set forth, the replication was, *our soil, and not his*,[2] and so on.

In an action for beating down a dove-house, the defendant pleaded that it was within his soil and freehold, and demanded judgment if he should answer for abating anything in his own demesne. This sort of pleading was objected to on the other side, as *freehold or not freehold* could not come in issue in an action of trespass. The plaintiff contented himself with averring his declaration; but the defendant then set forth his title, after which the plaintiff was driven to reply to the special matter, thus, *that the defendant beat down the plaintiff's dove-house, in the plaintiff's soil, and not in the soil of the defendant*, which issue went to the jury;[3] and so it seems to have been settled that the freehold of the plaintiff or the defendant was a good issue. When this was agreed on, it must be seen that many injuries to land, which used in the reign of Henry III. to be tried in the assize, might be *contested* in an action of trespass.

In the time of Bracton, every injury that entrenched upon the free enjoyment of a man's freehold was considered as a disseisin, and became of course the subject of an assize. The prejudices of the time were greatly in favour of that remedy, leaving it to the nature of the case whether the point in dispute should be finally determined on as a disseisin, or the assize should be turned into a jury, to consider it as a trespass. The action of trespass was rarely brought; and, considering the above application of the assize, was not necessary. It was upon this idea, probably, that Bracton disapproved of the action of trespass, as a writ by which the *mode* of the fact was to be inquired of, instead of the fact itself.[4] In the time of Bracton, most of the cases above mentioned would have been inquired of in an assize, modified in that way; but they had now, by the change in legal opinions and practice, become the objects of an action of trespass. When this change happened, it was thought that the allegation of *freehold*, which was a good

[1] Mayn. 12, 22, 63, 135, 193, 302, 312, 326, 340, 400, 422, 458.
[2] *Ibid.* 63, 302, 400, 422, 458.
[3] 15 Ed. II. Mayn. 458.
[4] *Vide ante*, vol. i. c. vii.

answer in the assize, ought to be a good plea in the writ of trespass that was substituted in its place; and those, on the other hand, who adhered to the prejudices expressed by Bracton, might very consistently contend that *freehold or not freehold* would not be a proper issue in an action which was not for the recovery of a freehold, but merely to inquire of the *mode* and degree of a trespass upon it.

In this multiplication of remedies, assize and trespass were sometimes both brought for the same cause of action; in such an action of trespass, being for entering a house, and taking goods and chattels, and cutting trees, it was pleaded that an assize was depending for the same land; and that because damages would be given in the assize for taking the goods and cutting the trees, the writ of trespass ought not to lie.[1]

As a *capias* and process of outlawry lay in an action of trespass, there was a temptation to recur to this writ in preference to an assize.: but yet the process of *capias* was under some check; for upon a return of *nihil habet* on the *distringas*, the *capias* did not use to issue without a special application to the court to award it.[2] Aid used to be granted in this as in real actions. In an action against a man for cutting trees, on the defendant pleading a right of estovers, and the plaintiff replying *non appendant*, and that issue being to be tried, the plaintiff *prayed aid* of his wife, because he held the land in her right, and it was granted.[3]

We find some actions of trespass of a particular kind. There is mention of a writ of trespass brought by the king on a *cepit et asportavit*, to which it was pleaded that the defendant and his ancestors had had wreck there from time to which the memory of man runs not to the contrary. To this they replied: not seised before time of memory; on which issue was joined.[4] An action of trespass on the statute of Marlbridge, c. xxviii., by a prior for goods taken during the vacancy of the priory. To this it was objected that it should be *detinue*, and not *vi et armis;* but the writ was held good.[5] Another, upon the statute *De districtione scaccarii*[6] (*a*) for distraining beasts of the plough. An action, grounded

(*a*) Thus a plaintiff complained that one William had wrongfully taken her horse. He pleaded that he found it eating his corn, and distrained it, *damage feasant*. She replied that she was lady of the manor, and that the place where the horse was seized she had a right of way, used by her and her ancestors. The defendant objected that she should show how it was her right of way by deed or prescription; but the court held that it would raise a sufficient issue to reply, denying the right of way; and this was done (*Year-book*, 2 *Edw. II.*, 40). Because the substance of the thing was that the claim was a right of way by old user, and thus the great object of pleading was attained (*S. P.*, *Year-book*, 18 *Edw. III.*, 53). It was always a rule in pleading that a man ought to show with sufficient certainty what lay within his own knowledge (*Year-book*, 13 *Edw. II.*, 407). So he must show matter of time, which gives him action (*Ib.*); so in covenant, a matter within the knowledge of both parties equally; otherwise of time, when it relates to a tort done by defendant, and when time is his defence (*Year-book*, 11 *Edw. II.*, 322). Thus in waste, it was objected that as the plaintiff supposed that the defendant held of him by assignment from

[1] Mayn. 272. [2] *Ibid.* 478. [3] *Ibid.* 302. [4] *Ibid.* 435.
[5] *Ibid.* 109. [6] *Ibid.* 583. *Vide ante*, vol. i. c. viii.

upon the statute of Marlbridge, c. xv., for distraining in the highway, seems not to be trespass, but a special action reciting the statute [1] (*a*). Thus far of the action of trespass, of which more will be said in the subsequent reigns. The common form of commencing a plea in trespass, if any title was to be set out, was to deny the force and arms, and then show the special matter of justification; "and says, that as to his coming with force and arms, and whatever is against the peace, he is not guilty, but as to the cutting and carrying away of the trees," &c. &c., and so stating the justification. This is all that appears necessary to be said respecting the progress of opinions and practice during this reign. Before we add some few observations upon the changes in the criminal law, we shall lay before the reader a juridical curiosity of a new sort.

It has been before intimated that the counting and pleading in actions was all transacted *vivâ voce* at the bar; but the method in which this passed we have not been able to observe till this reign, when we meet with the first *report* of proceedings in court. From this we may form some judgment of a legal disputation (for so the pleading in a cause seemed), and the style in which it was *moderated* by the judges (*b*). We shall

Of pleadings and arguments in court.

W. to M., so that of waste done in the time of W. he could not have action, he ought to show in what time the waste was done; but it was answered that the defendant could take advantage of it. Here it will be observed that the defendant would know best *when* he did the waste, as the premises were in his possession.

(*a*) From these disputes also, the general rules and principles of proceeding may be collected. The fundamental principle was that each party should so far propound the nature and ground of his case, as to enable the opposite party to judge what it was. Thus, for instance, there was a writ of entry when the demandant, the plaintiff, alleged that the defendant only had entered under one G., who had wrongfully disseised the plaintiff, and the third party came forward and alleged that he had a reversion in fee, and prayed to be allowed to defend his right; he was compelled by the court to show how he had the reversion (*Year-book*, 3 *Edw. II.*, 64).

(*b*) The method of proceeding to issue had been substantially practised in pleading from the earliest period; from the work of Glanville it appears to have existed in effect in the reign of Henry II. (lib. vi. c. 43). The term "issue" occurs in the very commencement of the Year-books, in the 1st Edward II. (*Year-book*, 1 *Edw. II.*, f. 14). The terms "issue en ley," and "issue en fait" occur almost as early (*Year-book*, 3 *Edw. II.*, 59). In the reign of Edward IV. the Latin term is thus defined, "Exitus idem est quod finis sive determinatio placiti" (*Year-book*, 21 *Edw. IV.*, 35). In the reign of Edward II. pleading was already beginning to be perverted by niceties and formalities which had no practical utility. Thus, for instance, the objection as to negative pregnant, as when a man pleaded that a house was not burnt by his negligence, he was met by the stupid quibble that this might mean that the house was not burnt at all; and so, in the senseless jargon of the age, it was a "negative pregnant with an affirmative," and "ambiguous," and so forth (*Year-book*, 7 *Edw. II.*, 213, 226; 28 *Hen. VI.* 7), an objection which, in after ages, delighted the souls of pedantic lawyers of the Coke school (Slade, *Drake*, *Hob.*, 231), but was as far removed from plain sense as it is possible to conceive. On the principle that the object of pleading was to elicit the real point in dispute, and that with this view, until it was elicited, the pleading was sufficient, if it was, to a common understanding, sufficient to enable the other side to answer—it was held sufficient in an action of trespass to plead that the place at the time was the soil of the defendant, or of one A. B.; in the latter case, adding that the defendant entered at his command—that is, by his authority, to which the plaintiff, if the dispute were as to title, would have to reply it (*Year-book*, 15 *Edw. II.*, 458; 5 *Edw. III.* 49; 3 *Hen. VI.* 14).

[1] Mayn. 624.

now give some specimens of this, with all its formality, strictly adhering to the original report.

The first shall be of an action where several pleas in abatement were overruled, and at length the general issue was pleaded. The prior of Lenton brought a writ of trespass, grounded upon the statute of Marlbridge, c. xxviii.,[1] against the pastor of Bangor, &c., *quare vi et armis bona et catalla domûs et ecclesiæ ipsius prioratus ad valenciam, &c., ad grave damnum, &c., et contra pacem nostram, &c.*, upon which he *counted*, that he took some wool and lambs. Upon this *Herle*, one of the counsel for the defendant, demanded judgment of the writ, for there was no *one* form of account for *live* and *dead* chattels; and if he had wanted to count of lambs taken and carried away, he might have said in his writ *quare* AVERIA *sua cepit et abduxit.* To this *Brab.*,[2] one of the judges, says he has counted of wool and lambs, which can be as well *carried* as *chased*, therefore *respondeas ouster*. Then *Herle* (taking another ground) said, Again we demand judgment, because he says, *bona et catalla domûs et ecclesiæ, &c.*, whereas by right the property of the chattel is not in the church, but in the prior, therefore judgment. To this *Malm.*, for the plaintiff, said, Our writ is given by statute, and we have followed the statute, which was assented to, and so another *respondeas ouster* was awarded.

Then *Pass.* (another counsel for the defendant) said, Again we demand judgment of the form of the writ; for the statute says, that a man should have recovery *ad bono repetenda*, and therefore the prior ought more naturally to have a *præcipe quòd reddat* of *detinue* of chattels, or *replevin*, and not this writ, which goes wholly for damages. What then, says *Malm.*, if the chattels were dead or aliened, should I have no recovery? and there was another *respondeas ouster.*

Again, says *Herle*, This writ is given by statute to successors after the death of their predecessors, against whom every action for recovery of anything ought to be brought; and we say, that the *prior William*, in whose time, &c., is still alive, and therefore we demand judgment of the writ. *Malm.* says, He is dead as to this action, for he is deposed, and so the action as against him is extinct; and if I was to bring an assize *quis advocatus, &c. ultimam personam, &c. quae mortua est, &c.*, though the person in question was alive and at the bar of the court, yet if he was no longer parson, the writ would be good: and (continues he) put a case that a husband aliened land of the right of his wife, and then was outlawed, and his wife brought a *cui in vitâ;* though the husband was actually alive, yet being dead in law, the writ would not abate. Then *Roub.* (one of the justices) said, If an abbot brought a writ

[1] *Vide ante*, vol. i. c. viii.

[2] The name of the judges and counsel in the Year-books are generally abbreviated, if consisting of more than one syllable. I cannot find any name like Brab. or Malm. in the *Chronica Judicialia*. Pass. stands probably for Serjeant Passelegh. *Vide Chron. Jur.* [These matters are explained in Foss's *Lives of the Judges*.]

against an abbot, and the defendant was deposed pending the plea, the writ would not abate; but it is otherwise where such an abbot was plaintiff, for then all cause of action ceased, and therefore he held the writ good in this point: and there was another judgment of *respondeas ouster*.

Again, *Pass.* demanded judgment of the writ, because it was a writ of trespass *vi et armis*, for a wrong done to divers persons; and the statute does not give a recovery of *damages*, but only *ad bona repetenda*. But *Malm.* argued the writ was good as it now stood, for two reasons: first, because the trespass was done in the time of our predecessor, for which trespass we are entitled to our action by the statute: secondly, because of the detinue in our time. *Herle.* Your writ has nothing to do with detinue of chattels, but it is of a fact done with force and arms to another person; so that the king would be entitled to a fine for a trespass done in the time of his predecessor. *Malm.* (repeating what he had before urged), Suppose the chattels were dead or eloigned, I could not recover the things themselves, and then my action must lie in damages, or I should have no recovery at all. *Herle.* Yes, you might recover the value, &c. Then *West*, one of the justices, interposing, said, The force of their *objection* is, that a man shall not recover damages for a trespass done to another; and yet executors may recover damages for a trespass done to another: again, if waste is done in the time of my father, I shall have an action for the waste and trespass, &c. In regard to the first of these cases, it was observed, that the executors recovered not in their own right, but in right of another; and as to the second about waste, that it was by statute, and not by the common law. However, *Rouboury* (another justice), said, they were all agreed that the writ was good, and therefore awarded another *respondeas ouster;* upon which the defendants pleaded *the general issue*, that they did nothing against the peace, *prest, &c. et alii è contra*, and so issue was joined.[1]

In the above case, where there were so many pleas in abatement, as they were all overruled at the instant, they must be considered as successive *amendments;* and none of them were entered on the roll, but only that plea which was finally approved and relied on, namely, the general issue (*a*).

The following is an action where they went on to reply, rejoin, and surrejoin. The case was this: *Aleyne de Newton* brought his writ of annuity against the abbot of Burton-upon-Trent, and demanded £30 arrears of an annual rent of £45 per ann., and he

(*a*) All through the Year-books it will be seen that so soon as a point of law arose, the party was asked if he would stand by it, and if so, it was recorded to be raised and argued on demurrer. Thus Hale says, speaking of an opinion of Lord Coke's, grounded on a decision in the Year-book, "the book of 14 Hen. VIII., fol. 16., upon which he grounded his opinion, was no solemn resolution, but a sudden and extrajudicial opinion, and the defendant had liberty to amend his plea, to the end that it might be judicially settled by demurrer, which was never done; and the constant practice hath prevailed contrary to that opinion."—*Hale, P.C.*, 579.

[1] Mayn. 109.

counted that one John, abbot of Burton, and predecessor of the present, did, by assent of the convent, grant an annuity to *Aleyne*, payable twice in the year, till he was advanced to a convenable benefice, and he exhibited a specialty, containing, that the abbot by assent, &c., did grant an annuity to *Aleyne de Newton Clerk*, in the above manner, as he had counted. Upon this *Willuby* (as counsel for the defendant) prayed judgment of the writ, because of the variance between the writ and the specialty; for in the writ he was named *Aleyne de Newton,* but in the specialty, *Aleyne de Newton Clerk.* *Ward* said, that it was no variance; yet *Willuby* maintained, that as he might have had a writ agreeable to the specialty, if he varied in his own purchase of it, the writ would be ill; but he could in this case have a writ agreeable to his specialty. *Ergo, &c.* And again, as far as appeared by the specialty, it was made to some one else, and not to the person named in the writ. *Stonore,* one of the justices, said, Then you may plead so if you will, but the writ is good; therefore *respondeas ouster.*

Then said *Willuby*, He cannot demand this annuity, because we say, that John our predecessor on such a day, &c., tendered him the vicarage of, &c., which was void, and in his gift, in the presence of such and such persons, which vicarage he refused; wherefore we do not understand that he can any longer demand this annuity. *Shard.* We say this vicarage was not worth 100 shillings; therefore we do not understand it to be a *convenable* benefice, so as to extinguish an annuity of £40. *Willuby.* Then you admit that we tendered you the vicarage, and that you refused it, &c.? *Shard.* As to the tender of a benefice which was not convenable, I have no business to make any answer at all. Then *Mutford*, one of the justices, asked, What sort of benefice they considered as *convenable*, so as to extinguish the annuity? *Shard.* We mean one of ten marks at least. Then *Stonore* said, Do you admit that the vicarage was not worth 100 shillings? *Willuby.* We will aver that the vicarage was worth ten marks, *prest, &c.;* and he has admitted that one of that value should extinguish the annuity. *Shard.* And we will aver that it was not worth ten marks, *prest, &c.*

After this issue, *Willuby* was desirous of recurring back to his first plea, and said, As you declare that the vicarage was not worth 100 shillings, we will aver that it was worth 100 shillings, &c. But *Stonore* interposed, and said, He declares that the vicarage is worth ten marks; and after that there is nothing to be done, but that the issue should be taken on your declaration or his: now it seems that it should rather be taken on yours; for, by your plea, you make that a convenable benefice which is worth ten marks, and such a declaration you ought to maintain, &c. *Willuby.* The mention of the value came first from him, when he said it was not worth 100 shillings; so that it will be sufficient for me to traverse what he had said. But *Stonore* pressing him whether he would maintain his plea, *Willuby* said he would, and accordingly pleaded that the vicarage was worth ten marks, *prest, &c. et alii*, that it was not worth ten marks, *prest, &c.*, and so issue was joined.[1]

The pleadings upon the record in the above case must then have stood thus: The defendant said, a vicarage had been tendered and refused, and so the annuity should cease, judgment of the action. To this the replication was, The vicarage tendered was not worth ten marks, and *so* not a convenable benefice to extinguish the annuity: rejoinder, it was worth ten marks: surrejoinder, it was not.

These instances, without troubling the reader with more, will serve to show the manner of pleading *vivâ voce* at the bar (*a*): everything there advanced was treated as a matter only *in fieri*, which upon discussion and consideration might be amended, or wholly abandoned, and then other matter resorted to, till at length the counsel felt himself on such grounds as he could trust. Where he finally rested his cause, that was the plea which was entered upon the roll, and abided the judgment of an inquest or of the court, according as it was a point of law or of fact.

The criminal law.

The criminal law is exhibited by a writer of this reign in a state somewhat differing from that given by any preceding author. The crime of treason is divided in the following way; into *majesty*, *falsifying*, and *treason*. Majesty, or *læse majesty*, is that treason which is directed immediately against the king's person and dignity: as first, the killing of the king, or compassing so to do; secondly, disinheriting the king of his realm by bringing in an army, or compassing so to do; thirdly, ravishing the king's wife, the king's lawful eldest daughter before she is married, being in the king's custody, or the nurse or aunt of the king, being heir to the king.[2] All these were considered as the crime of læse majesty. But this author has classed many other offences under this head, which have by construction been drawn into it. Of this kind he has collected many, which being what he calls *perjuria*, are, he thinks, properly to be ranked under this offence; because, says he, *every one who commits perjury, lieth against the king*. In pursuance of this notion, he enumerates many misprisions, negligencies, abuses, and extortions of office, whether judicial or other, committed by judges or inferior ministers and officers; all which he considers as offences against

(*a*) This is an instance of the Roman origin of our laws. In the Roman law there was a title extremely peculiar, as to the crimen majestatis; as to which there is the edict: "Etiam ex aliis causis magistatis crimina cessavit meo seculo, nedum etiam admittam te paratum accusare judicem propterea crimine majestatis, quod contra constitutionem meam cum dicis pronunciasse" (*Cod. Just.* lib. ix. tit. 8, sec. 1). Now, in the *Mirror of Justice*, an ancient law treatise, based it is evident upon an earlier one of the age of Alfred, there is this very head of law under the same term of "majesty" or offence against sovereignty, a term so peculiar that it may fairly be presumed to have come from the Roman law. And how was it derived? No trace of such a law, or such a phrase, is to be found in the Saxon laws; and so it was not derived from written law, but by tradition, from the Romans.

[1] Mayn. 634.

[2] *Mirror*, ch. 1, sec. 4.

the majesty of the king, which merited equal punishment with the before-mentioned defined cases of læse majesty.[1]

Falsifying is either of the king's seal or his money.[2] *Treason* he considers as an offence committed by a private person against another to whom he is bound by ties of blood, affinity, or alliance, which causes his death, disherison, or loss of homage; for the quality of treason, says our author, is, *the taking away of life or member, or decrease of earthly honour, or increase of villanous shame*, which he exemplifies in this manner:[3] The strongest alliance is that of service. If one, says he, whom I have rewarded, who does fealty to me, and is seised in demesne of lands held of me; in short, if any one who has a possession, rent, vote, church, meat, drink, or other gift, from me, falsifies my seal, or ravishes my daughter or my wife, or the nurse or the aunt of my heir, or doth anything which is the cause of my death, by a felonious compassing of the same, or to the great dishonour or damage of my body or my goods, or discovereth my counsel, or my confession, which he is charged to conceal; every one of these, says our author, is treason. It seems, after all, that what is here termed *majesty* and *falsifying*, constitute what we have since called *high-treason;* and this which our author calls simply so, is what has since been denominated *petit treason*. The catalogue of treasons, whether defined or constructive, given by this author, makes it unnecessary to look anywhere else for the reasons that induced the parliament in the next reign to fix the limits of this crime by statute.

Arson was described in very comprehensive terms. *Burners* were those who burnt a city, town, house, man, beasts, or other chattel, feloniously in time of peace, for hatred or revenge. If any one put a man into the fire, whereby he was burnt or blemished, although not killed, yet it was the offence of arson, and he was to suffer the penalty of it; as were also those who *threatened* to burn.[4]

It appears by the definition given of *larceny*, that this crime was gradually assuming the appearance which it now bears. Larceny is said to be, *the treacherously taking away from another movables corporeal, against the will of him to whom they belong, by evil getting possession or use of them.* Larceny, says our author, could not be committed of goods not movable or not corporeal, as of land, rent, advowson, or the like; and it is said to be done treacherously, because if the taker conceived the goods to be his own, and thought he might lawfully take them, it was no offence.[5] Many facts were considered as larcenies, which have since been looked upon only as cheats and civil injuries: thus bailiffs, receivors, and administrators, were said to *steal* goods, if they did not give in their accounts: false weights and measures, tricks in trade, and other deceits and impositions, are described in the *Mirror* as instances of larceny.

[1] *Mirror*, ch. 1, sect. 5. [2] *Ibid.* sect. 6. [3] *Ibid.* sect. 7.
[4] *Ibid.* sect. 3. [5] *Ibid.* sect. 10.

The offence of *burglary* was also very large, for it was not only the breaking of a house, but the felonious assault of enemies in time of peace upon those who were in their houses with intent to repose there in peace, whether the assault was with design to kill, to rob, or to beat, was considered as burglary: and although such offenders did not accomplish their purpose, yet if there was a breaking, by the assault of doors, windows, or walls, to enter feloniously, they were guilty of this crime. Those also came within this offence, who feloniously forced their entry into another's house, and did violence against the peace, although the house were not broken; and that, whether by day or by night. This extensive description contains in it those notions which constitute the crime of burglary, as now understood, attended with many additional circumstances, that were gradually pared off in after-times.

Punishments were still various, and in some degree discretionary. Those convicted of *læse majesty* were to be punished according to the ordinance and pleasure of the king.[1] Those convicted of *falsifying*, and of *treason*, were to be drawn and hanged. Those convicted of *burning*,[2] and rape, were to be hanged;[3] and so it was in murder, robbery, larceny above twelve-pence, and burglary, in cases not notorious; but if the offence was notorious, and the party taken in the fact, he was beheaded. Sodomites were to be buried alive;[4] and heretics underwent a fourfold punishment, excommunication, degradation, disinheriting, and burning.

Inferior punishments not capital were these: mending the highways, causeways, and bridges; setting in the pillory and stocks; imprisonment; abjuration of the realm; exile; banishment, either from the kingdom or some particular town, by prohibiting the entering into or going out of such a place; by ransom; and by pecuniary penalties and fine.[5]

Perjury which affected the life of a man was punished, as in the time of Edward I.[6] with a mortal judgment, "to the example," says the book,[7] "of apparent murderers;" but perjury of a less heinous intent was punished with banishment, either for a time, or for ever. The woods, meadows, gardens, and houses of the perjured men were to be razed and destroyed, but his heirs were not to be disinherited.

King and government.

The whole of this unhappy prince's reign was occupied in contests with his barons in defence of his favourites; during which the royal authority and the force of the laws were considerably diminished. The duke of Lancaster, with all his own power, and relation to the person of the king, could not

[1] *Mirror*, ch. 4, sect. 14.
[2] *Ibid.* sect. 15.
[3] *Ibid.* sect. 10.
[4] *Ibid.* ch. 4, sect. 14.
[5] *Ibid.* sect. 17.
[6] *Vide ante*, c. x.
[7] *Mirror*, ch. 1, sect. 9.

obtain a regular and lawful trial, but in time of peace (*a*) was condemned by a court-martial to suffer the punishment of treason.

So entirely was this king subdued, that he was constrained to sign a commission empowering the prelates and barons to elect twelve persons, who should have authority, for a limited time, to make ordinances, with all the force of laws, for the government of the kingdom. These twelve accordingly framed some regulations, which were presented to the parliament for their confirmation. Some of these were, to ascertain the qualifications of sheriffs; to abolish the practice of issuing privy-seals for the suspension of judicial proceedings; to give damages in case of malicious prosecutions; to order the method of making payments in the exchequer; to prevent the adulteration of the coin; and to regulate other matters tending to the preservation of order and good government.[1]

(*a*) The case is thus stated by Sir J. Mackintosh. "The baronial party took arms. In the following year Edward partly obtained a signal victory at Boroughbridge. The earl of Lancaster was made prisoner, and in a few days led to his own castle of Pomfret, where he was shortly after beheaded." From the official account of the battle, published by Mr Palgrave (*Palgrave Chron. Abstract, Edw. II.*, p. 313), it appears that out of two hundred and sixteen knights arrayed against the king, the earl of Lancaster was beheaded, and twenty-eight knights hanged, &c. (*Hist. Eng.*, vol. i.) It hence appears that the earl and the others were taken in arms against the king in open rebellion, though it also appears that the rebellion was over, as a rebellion in this country usually was, when there had been a decisive victory over it in battle, and several days had elapsed. It is remarkable that Hale cites this as a case of martial law, which he admits to be "allowed or indulged in time of war against those of the opposite army," but not in time of peace. "And accordingly was that famous case of Edmond, earl of Kent(?), who being taken at Pomfret, 15 Edw. II., the king and divers lords proceeded to give sentence of death against him as in a kind of military court, by a summary proceeding." There was no case of the earl of Kent in 15 Edward II. The case in that year was that of the earl of Lancaster, above alluded to by our author. The case of Edmond, earl of Kent, occurred in the reign of Edward III., which is thus stated by Sir J. Mackintosh: "The earl of Kent, deceived by a report that his brother, the late king, was alive, wrote a letter to that king, which was betrayed to the earl of March, who without delay assembled a parliament, to which he inveigled the prince, who was convicted of treason, and executed; and in the 3 Edward III., the parliament declared this judgment to have been illegal." To such a judgment such a declaration might be well applied, for it appears to have been a judgment of the peers, though in all probability irregular and iniquitous; and a judgment in parliament might well be reversed in parliament. But that parliament should reverse a summary sentence of court-martial would be an anomaly, if not absurdity; and it appears plainly that Hale had confounded the two cases, and applied to the one what was only applicable to the other, and the language of the record he professes to cite (he does not say from what roll) is applicable only to the judgment in Kent's case, which judgment was afterwards, in 3 Edward III., reversed in parliament. "And the reason of that reversal seeming to the purpose," he proceeds to recite it as entered on the record. "Quod cum quicunque homo ligens Domini Regis pro seditionibus, &c., tempore pacis captus et in quacunque curia Domini Regis ductus fuerit de ejusmodi seditionibus et aliis feloniis sibi impositis per legem et consuetudine Regni arrectari debet et ad responsionem adduci, et inde per communen legem triai, &c. Unde cum notorium sit et manifestum quod totum tempus quo impositum fuit eidem comiti propter malá et facinora fecisse ad tempus in quo captus fuit, et in morti adjudicatus fuit, fuit tempus pacis maximæ cum per totum tempus predictum et cancellario et alia placita curiæ Domini Regis apertæ fuerunt in quibus cuilibet lex fiebatur sicut fieri consuevit: nec idem Dominus Rex unquam tempore illo cum vexillis explicatis equitabat." And accordingly, says Hale, the judgment was reversed, "for martial law, which is rather indulged than enforced in cases of necessity in time of open war, is not permitted in time of peace," &c.

[1] Brady, App. No. 51.

During the weakness of such a reign, the clergy, who had been reduced to some subordination by the late king, made no scruple of insisting on their ancient claims of exemption with firmness, and even with parade. Adam de Orgeton, bishop of Hereford, was arrested, and accused before the king and parliament of high treason. He there pleaded, that he ought not to answer such high matters without the licence and authority of the archbishop of Canterbury, who, next to the pope, was his proper judge. Upon the prayer of the archbishop and his suffragans, he was delivered to the archbishop's custody. When he was afterwards brought to the bar of the king's bench, the bishops came in great form with their crosses, and took him forcibly from the bar, threatening to excommunicate all who should oppose them. The king after this caused an indictment to be found by a jury of Herefordshire against this prelate, upon which his temporalties were seized into the king's hands; yet the bishop, notwithstanding, escaped without any other punishment.[1]

We are now to consider the sources of legal information belonging to this reign. These are the statutes, records, and year-books, together with one law-treatise. The statutes commencing with *Magna Charta*, and ending with Edward II., together with those called *Incerti Temporis* (it being doubtful to which of these three reigns to assign them), compose what have been called the *Vetera Statuta;* and from the accident of their collection and publication in later times, are sometimes spoken of as the *prima* or *secunda pars veterum statutorum*. We have before made some observations upon the form and style of the *assisæ*, or statutes before the reign of Henry III.,[2] great part of which is equally applicable to those made since. The enacting authority is expressed by all these statutes, as subsisting in the king; who *grants*, *directs*, *ordains*, *provides*, sometimes by his council; sometimes by the assent of the archbishops, bishops, abbots, priors, earls, and barons; sometimes the assent of the commonalty is added. In some there is no mention of the concurrence of any part of the legislature. In some very few instances, among which is the statute of Gavelet, 10 Edward II., it is said to be provided by the king and *his justices*, without any mention either of lords or commons. It is evident from the *Mirror*, that laws were often made in this latter way; for the author of that book complains, that ordinances are only made *by the king and his clerks*, and by aliens and others who dare not contradict the king, but study to please him.[3] We must therefore conclude, that the same ideas of legislation prevailed now, which were stated to have governed in the time preceding the reign of Henry III.,[4] and that the calling the commons to parliament, as it gave them certainly no greater place there than the lords had before, could not impart to them a

Vetera Statuta.

[1] *Parl. Hist.*, vol. i. 197.
[2] *Vide ante*, vol. i. c. iii.
[3] *Mirror*, ch. 5.
[4] *Vide ante*, vol. i. c. iii.

greater right to concur in legislative acts, than the lords themselves claimed.

Many of these old statutes do not at all express by what authority they were enacted; so that it seems as if the business of making laws was principally left in the hands of the king, unless in instances where the lords or commons felt an interest in promoting a law, or the king an advantage in procuring their concurrence; and in such cases probably it was that their assent was specially expressed.

There are some circumstances common to all those statutes. All those passed in one session of parliament are strung together, making so many *capitula*, or chapters of one statute; to which is usually prefixed, a memorandum of the time and place of the meeting of parliament, with the occasion for calling it. The chapters are short, and the manner of expression very often too general and undefined; offences are loosely and ambiguously described; rarely any certain penalty is inflicted on offenders; they are to be punished at the king's pleasure, are to make grievous ransom to the king, are to be heavily amerced, and the like; sometimes the acts are merely admonitory or prohibitory, without affixing any penalties, or prescribing any course of process for prosecuting, hearing, and determining the offences. In the time of Henry III. the statutes are mostly in Latin; in the reign of Edward I. they began to be in French also: and the statutes of this reign and of Edward II. are sometimes in Latin, and sometimes in French. Sometimes there occurs a chapter in one language in the midst of a statute in the other; and there is a chapter of Westminster 2, partly in French and partly in Latin.[1] It is difficult to account for such remarkable variations as these. Some have thought that they discovered one rule to prevail through these statutes respecting this change of language; namely, that all such acts as concerned the interests of the church were in Latin; though this is confessed by the person who started it to be subject to so many exceptions as almost to destroy the rule.[2] Perhaps the legislature was governed by no general principle in choosing the languages of their statutes; both the Latin and French were the language of the law, and probably were adopted according to the whim of the clerk or other person who drew up the statute. In the act above alluded to, as it was the revival of the old law, perhaps the scrap of French in which it was worded was taken from some law-book in that language, treating upon the subject, in its original state; or perhaps it was thought more advisable that this article, as it was a repeal of a chapter of Westminster 1[3] should be in the same language as that statute, though the rest of Westminster 2 was in Latin.

The clerical legislature, during this reign, added little to our national canon law. There are no other constitutions than those of archbishop Reynolds.[4]

[1] Namely, ch. 34. *Vide ante*, c. x.

[2] Barr. Obs., p. 65.

[3] Namely, ch. 13. *Vide ante*, c. ix.

[4] *Vide* Johnson's *Canon*, and Spelm. *Counc.*

The materials of legal information grow to a greater size in this reign than in any of the preceding; for besides the statutes and judicial records, which begin now to be more numerous and perfect, at this period begin the *Year-books*, or books of *Years and Terms*, as they were sometimes called (*a*). These contain reports of cases adjudged from the beginning of

Year-books.

(*a*) The origin of all our received law is to be found in the Year-books. Thus, the proposition that the sheriff cannot break the outer door of a dwelling-house to execute a *fi.-fa.* against the possessor (*Year-book*, 18 *Edw. IV.*, fol. 19), is cited and approved in Lee *v.* Gansell, in *Cowper's Reports* 1, and has always been recognised as established law. The point decided in the Six Carpenters' case, 8 *Coke's Reports* 147 (viz., that he who abuses an authority in law is to be deemed a trespasser *ab initio*), was determined one hundred and thirty years before in the Year-book 21 *Edw. IV.*, fol. 19, pt. 22. So as to the law of distress, in Sir John Mantraver's case, in the reign of Edward III., it was held that, if the lord or his bailiff comes to distrain, and before the distress the tenant tenders the arrears upon the land, then the distress taken for it is tortuous, *i.e.*, wrongful. "The same law for distress *damage feasant*, if, before the distress, he tenders sufficient amends" (Mantravers *v.* the Parson of Clare, 30 *Assize*, fol. 38; the Master of St Mark's Hospital case, 7 *Edw. III.*, fol. 8; *Year-book*, 13 *Hen. IV.*, fol. 17). The germ of the whole law as to ratification of authority is to be found in a case in the Year-books of Henry IV., where it was laid down that if the bailiff took a heriot, claiming property in himself, the subsequent agreement or assent of the lord would not amount to a ratification of his authority as bailiff at the time; but if he took it as bailiff of the lord, the subsequent ratification by the lord made him bailiff at the time of the act (*Year-book*, 7 *Hen. IV.*, fol. 35).

The cases in the Year-books during this period related principally to real property, or to rights regarding the realty, as rights of common. Thus, it was held that a commoner could not maintain trespass for damage of the soil or grass, provided his own cattle had pasture enough, for that he had no interest but to take the pasture by the mouths of his cattle (case of the Abbot of St Mary's, York *v.* Hugh de Altoin, 22 *Assize*, fol. 95. So Sir Simon de Harcourt *v.* Spicer, 13 *Hen. VIII.*, fol. 15). So that the commoner's right of action was necessarily rested entirely on the injury to his own right of pasturage, that is, on there not being sufficient for his cattle. So as to the right of *distress, damage feasant*, and the answers thereto, founded on rights of common or of pasturage, the cases are very numerous in the Year-books.

In the Year-books of the next reign are to be found many of the ancient maxims of our laws, thus early established and recognised in our courts: "Res inter alios acta non nocet" (3 *Edw. II.*, 53). "Causa et origo attendenda" (5 *Edw. II.*, 134). "Modus et conventio vincunt legem" (5 *Edw. II.*, 161). "Accessor sequitur suum principale" (12 *Edw. II.*, 384). "Novo casu novum remedium" (18 *Edw. II.*, 570). "Ley est plus favorable a saver que damner" (18 *Edw. II.*, 400). These maxims can, most of them, be found in Bracton, and some of them can be traced back to the *Leges Henrici Primi.*

In the reign of Edward II. an action of replevin was brought against the dean and chapter of St Paul's for taking nets laid upon the banks of the Thames, and they justified the taking of the nets by their bailiffs on the ground that the nets were unlawfully laid upon their soil (*Year-book*, 13 *Edw. II.*, fol. 400; Sir T. Brudnell's case, 1 *Rot. Parl.*, 331). In the reign of Edward III., there was a case in which it was held that an action of account "lay against a goldsmith or taverner who sold by retail as bailiff" (*Year-book*, 46 *Edw. III.*, fol. 3). The plaintiff said he had delivered divers pots and pails (pots et payles) of silver to the defendant to sell, and he sold them at fairs and markets, and thus received a large sum of money. And the court put the case of a man who had a "taverner" to sell his goods (*Year-book*, 46 *Edw. III.*, fol. 3). In another case a man had account of a house with twenty oxen and cows (*Year-book*, 49 *Edw. III.*, fol. 7). In another case there was account against a party who had sold her rings for the plaintiff (*Year-book*, *Edw. III.*, fol. 19). In another case account was made to Sir Nicolas Tamworth of his jewels sold in Brittany (*Year-book*, 4 *Edw. III.*, fol. 10). These cases are, it will be seen, extremely illustrative of the usages of the age.

The cases on contract, especially on special contracts (which in those days were

this reign to the end of Edward III. and from the beginning of Henry IV. down to the end of Henry VIII.

The *Year-books* are said to be so called, because they were published *annually* from the notes of certain persons, who were paid a stipend by the crown for this employment.[1] The establishment of reporters appears to have been first made by this king, or more probably at the latter end of the former reign; for this institution came precisely within the plan of that prince's endeavours to im-

always by deed), are often very illustrative. Thus, in the celebrated case of Pole *v.* Tocher in the reign of Edward III.: "Sir Rauf Pole, knight, brought a writ of debt against Sir Richard Tocher, and demanded of him £72, and as to the sum of 42 marks he set forth an indenture made between them by which the plaintiff was retained by Sir Richard, with three esquires-at-arms in London, for the war with France, for those 42 marks, the moiety of which was to be paid before they went, and as to the rest he set forth a bond for £42, but made in Normandy (*Year-book*, 48 *Edw. III.*, fol. 3).

The actions "on the case" were often exceedingly illustrative of the customs of the age. Thus, it was held, that an action on the case lay against a farrier for laming a horse (*Year-book*, 46 *Edw. III.*, fol. 19). The complaint was that he shoed the plaintiff's horse, and put a nail in the foot of the horse in a certain place, by which the plaintiff lost the use of his horse for a long time. In another case it was held, that an action lay against a surgeon who had undertaken to cure a man of a wound in his hand, and had injured him (*Year-book*, 48 *Edw. III.*, fol. 6). So it was held that an action on the case lay against an innkeeper ("hosteler") upon the customs of the realm (*Year-book*, 42 *Edw. III.*, fol. 11). Some few further illustrations from the Year-books of the next reign may be here inserted, the more so as the author does not appear to do justice to them. They afford the best possible illustrations of the state of the law. Thus a man brought his writ of account against another as receiver of his moneys, and alleged that he had received so much. The defendant denied the receipt; and the plaintiff then objected that he could not be allowed to do so since he had by deed acknowledged the receipt of so much. But it was said that it was too late to set up that as an estoppel, and that the matter must now be brought to proof of the fact (*Year-book*, 18 *Edw. II.*, 598). Miles le Hunt, of Stratford, brought writ of debt against Symond, and demanded of him thirty quarters of wheat of the price of £20, and the defence, failing the inquest, were charged to inquire what was the price of the corn at the time when he ought to have paid it. They said that, at the time of the contract, it was worth only 3s. a quarter, but when it ought to have been delivered, it was worth 12s. a quarter, and they were directed by the court (*fuit avisa la court*) that the damages were taxed too high, and the court abridged the damages, and awarded that he should recover £18 for the corn, and 40s. for the damages, that is, allowing for the corn at the price at the time for the *delivery*. Et sic nota que la ou il demanda bleé, il recovera a le pris de bleé au temps que le bleé duist aver este paye et nemye le bleé (*Year-book*, 12 *Edw. II.*, 375).

If the defendant showed the place was his soil, it was then for the plaintiff to show how he came to have any right to be there. John de S. brought writ of trespass, complaining that the defendant had pulled down his dovecote. The defendant pleaded that the place was his soil and freehold. The plaintiff objected that he ought to show (as he did not deny that the dovecote was his) how he came to have a dovecote on the soil of the defendant, on which he pleaded that he had leased the place to the plaintiff, who had erected the dovecote on the soil and left it there after the lease expired. The plaintiff objected, that the defendant ought to show how the dovecote became his; but the court answered that this would be to call upon him to say what he himself could not, which would be contrary to reason, whereupon the plaintiff took issue on the soil being the soil of the defendant (*Year-book*, 15 *Edw. II.*, 458).

[1] It may be remarked, that *Jaar-Boecken* in the low German signifies *Annals*. *De Jaar-Boeken van* C. Cornelius Tacitus, is the title given to a Dutch translation of that work.

prove our laws, and was the grand means so much wanted, that of *putting them into writing.*[1] However, as we have no fruits of such an appointment till the beginning of this reign, we may suppose it did not take place till then.[2]

As a record is a concise entry of all the real and effective steps made in a judicial proceeding, a report is a short note of the progress towards making those steps; the debate in court concerning some of them; the decision upon their propriety and design; and the grounds and principles upon which the decision was supported (*a*). The reports of this reign, as they were the first essays in this way, fall short of the clearness and fulness with which reports have been made in later times. Being minuted down by the reporter in court at the instant, as the thing really passed, they have in them all the dryness necessarily attending such a formal memorandum, which is much heightened by the starch manner in which these matters were usually then transacted in court. The way is this: The action is first stated; then comes the counsel for the plaintiff, who rehearses the declaration; he is followed by the counsel for the defendant; and so on; till the pleadings on both sides are brought to an issue: and here the report often ceases, concluding with the whole that was done that day, without the least intimation what afterwards became of the cause. The counsel are continually interrupted by occasional observations from the bench on the form and legality of the pleadings; these are argued, altered, or amended; then the counsel proceed till something else arises to draw the notice of the judges. It cannot be denied that this is sometimes managed with sufficient acuteness, and exhibits often a curious piece of judicial disputation. The whole is concise; without any length of deduction, concatenation of argument, or display of learning. The want of these, and the clerical method of the whole, make this first attempt at reporting not a very inviting performance to a modern reader[3] (*b*).

(*a*) Thus in a case in the *Year-book, Edw. II.* fol. 472, Matthew Bellew made his plaint that Luke Morel wrongfully took his cattle. *Schardeburgh* (for defendant)—Luke avows the taking by reason that he found the cattle in his several meadows eating the grass and trampling, and so he took them for damage. *Ingham* (for plaintiff)—We tell you that this Matthew holds a meadow in the town of B., in which meadow was a house and "corve" of land, and that he and his ancestors have had a right to depasture their cattle; and *Schardeburgh* (for the defendant) objected to this; but the court said that, as the plaintiff had said that he and his ancestors were entitled, it was sufficient. Then *Schardeburgh* pleaded for the defendant that, between the ancestors of Luke and Matthew, an agreement was made that the ancestors of Luke should have a road to carry hay over land which belonged to the ancestors of Luke, from the meadow in question to the house of Luke's ancestors, for which easement they granted the right to pasture in the field, and because they were foreclosed of the road they ousted Matthew of the feeding.

(*b*) Thus it was laid down in chancery. Here we adjudge secundum veritatem rei,

[1] The author of the *Mirror*, among the abuses of the law, complains that the law was not sufficiently put into writing. *Mirror*, ch. 5.

[2] There are said to be reports of cases adjudged during the reign of Edward I. in manuscript, in certain public libraries; but these do not appear to be in any series that would justify one in supposing there was a regular appointment like that above mentioned.

[3] An idea of those reports may be conceived from the account before given of the manner of pleading in court. *Vide ante.*

The *Mirror of Justice* is a book whose consideration may properly belong to this reign. This singular work has raised much doubt and difference of opinion concerning its antiquity. Some have pronounced it older than the Conquest;[1] others have ascribed it to the time of Edward II. Both these opinions may be partly right (*a*). There may perhaps have been

The *Mirror*.

and not secundum *allegata*, and if a man alleges by bill that the defendant has done a wrong to him, and the other says nothing, if we can see that he has done no wrong, the plaintiff shall recover nothing. There are (said the chancellor) two powers and kinds of process or procedure: *s. potentia ordinata et absoluta.* Ordinata is a positive law, and has a certain order: *sed lex naturæ non habet certum ordinem*, sed per quem cunquem modum veritas sciri poterit, and therefore it is called absolute procedure; and in the law of nature, it is required (*i.e.*, only) that the parties shall be present (or absent by contumacy), and that there shall be an examination of the truth (*Year-book*, 9 *Edw. IV.*, fol. 15, *Bro. Abr. Jurisdiccion* 50).

(*a*) No doubt can be entertained by any one who has studied the book that this is so, and indeed this already has been amply shown by the extracts from the work presented in the notes to the earlier portions of this work, especially those relating to the Saxon age. Of the legal history of that age, and of the whole intervening period, up to the present reign, it affords the most valuable illustrations. And this, because from its nature and character it is essentially historical, *professing* to have been based upon memorials of the age of Alfred, and to have embodied all the changes of the subsequent period, and *proving* that it was so by many internal evidences of the most certain character. Thus, for instance, that it is founded on memorials of the Saxon age is plain from this, that *all the names appear to be Saxon*, even the names of "justices" or "judges," whereas we know the names of the king's justices or judges since the Conquest, and these are quite different. Moreover, precedents are given expressly assigned to the Saxon age, as, for instance, under the head of "Appeal of Majesty" (or treason), it is said, "according as it was done in this case in the time of King Edward" (c. i. s. 12). Then, again, a long list of punishments, said to have been awarded by Alfred to bad judges, is given, with the names of the judges and of the parties in each case, and with a particularity as to circumstances which afford the strongest marks of verity. All the names are Saxon, especially those of the judges, and it is not likely that, after the Conquest, there would be many Saxon judges. So far as we know, even the sheriffs were all Normans. The character of the contents of the work also leads to the clear conclusion that great parts of it, and parts easily distinguishable by their style and subject-matter, were written soon after the Conquest; and of matters occurring before, or existing at the time of that event, and recorded soon afterwards. It is also most probable, from the tone of the work, that it was written by a Saxon. It betrays throughout a bitter spirit of complaint as to the effects of the Conquest, describing the gradual rise of common freehold tenure out of the better kind of tenure in villenage, tenure by plough-service, and stating that "Saint Edward"—*i.e.*, Edward the Confessor, caused a survey to be made of those who so held of him, and that afterwards, *i.e.*, after the Conquest, many who had thus become freeholders were forced back into villenage again, which could hardly have been written very long after the Conquest. Other parts of the book keep up a chain of legal history from the time of the Saxons to the era of the great charters, and the reign of Edward I. Thus many ordinances of Henry I. are scattered through the work, which of course afford their own date. So of ordinances of Henry II. or Ranulf de Glanville, his great justiciary, and so of a citation of a decision by the celebrated Martin de Pateshall, a great judge in the reign of Henry III., whose decisions are often cited by Bracton. Thus there is an account of the process and proceedings on default, &c., tracing the changes in the law down to the time of Henry III. There is also a chapter on the defects of the great charter, and on subsequent statutes, down to that of Gloucester, in the sixteenth year of Edward I., where the writer stops, which seems to show that the work was finally completed about that time. Thus parts of the book are as clearly of the time of Edward I., and there is an allusion to something occurring in the reign of Edward II., although that may have been added by an editor, and the substance of the work relates to matters prior to the middle of the reign of Edward I. On the whole, there is no book on the

[1] Among these are Lord Coke and Nathaniel Bacon.

a work by this name as early as the date supposed; but whoever judges from the internal evidence of this book will be satisfied that great part of it is of a period much later, and certainly written after Fleta and Britton, for it states many points of law, as it were, in a state of progression somewhat receding from those writers, and approaching nearer to those of later times. It is probable that

law of greater use and value to a legal historian, as illustrative of our legal history, and especially of the transition from the Saxon to the Norman age, and the long period between the age of Alfred and the age of Edward. Lord Coke thought highly of it as an authority, and mentions it in terms of respect in the preface to the tenth part of his Reports, and quotes it repeatedly, as he does Britton, Fleta, and Bracton. And the opinion of Lord Coke and other great authorities is abundantly supported by a study of its contents, of which it may be well to present an abstract. It is in Norman-French, like Britton, and is entitled "La Somme: appelle Mirrori des Justices, vel Speculum Justiciariorum, factum per Andrean Horne," of whom it is said in the preface that he wrote the book before the 17 Edw. II., on account of an allusion he makes in the course of the last chapter to the statute of that year, "De Prerogativa Regis," but, as already mentioned, that may have been added, as it is an isolated allusion, and no other statute subsequent to the 16th Edward I. is quoted. That it was composed, therefore, as a whole, about that time seems quite manifest. The author in his preface describes the work as a summary of the law for the common people, and as written in their language: "Al ecriture et en language plus entendable en aide de vous et de le common people, ceste petit summe de la ley des persons, et des gents, en cinque chapitres:—I. De Peches Contre la Peace; II. D'Actions; III. D'Exceptions; IV. De Jugements; V. D'Abusions." These being the heads of the five chapters into which the book is divided, the contents of the sections of which each is composed are as follow: Section 1. Of the original of the law; 2. Of the coming of the English into this land; 3. Of the first constitutions; 4. Of offences and their divisions; 5. Of the crime of majesty, or offence against the king; 6. Of falsifying (of the king's seal, or money); 7. Of treason; 8. Of burning (arson); 9. Of homicide; 10. Of larceny; 11. Of hamsockne, or burglary; 12. Of rape; 13. Of the office of the coroner; 14. Of the exchequer; 15. Of inferior courts; 16; Of the tourns of the sheriffs; 17. Of the views of frankpledge. Chapter II.: Section 1. Of actions; 2. Of judges; 3. Of plaintiffs or complainants; 4. Of fees or rewards; 5. Of pleaders or countors; 6. Of attachments (*i.e.*, of the person or goods in process in actions); 7. Of appeals (*i.e.*, the ancient proceeding by appeal in criminal cases); 8. Of process in appeals; 9. Of gaols and gaolers; 10. Of bail in appeals; 11. Of appeals of majesty; 12. Of the appeal of falsifying; 13. Of appeals of treason; 14. Of appeals of arson; 15. Of appeals of homicide; 16. Of appeals of robbery and larceny; 17. Of appeals of burglary; 18. Of appeals of imprisonment; 19. Of appeals of mayhem; 20. Of appeals of wounding; 21. Of appeals of rape; 22. Of offences real at the king's suit (a very obscure chapter, alluding to the rolls of ancient kings); 23. Of offences personal at the king's suit; 24. Of venial offences and personal suits; 25. Of assize of novel disseisin; 26. Of distresses; 27. Of contracts; 28. Of villenage and nicfty; 29. Of summons; 30. Of essoins (or excuse for non-appearance); 31. Of attorneys. Chapter III.: Section 1. Of exceptions; 2. The order of exceptions or pleas; 3. Exceptions dilatory; 4. Exceptions of clergy (*i.e.*, privilege of clergy); 5. Replication of bigamy (*i.e.*, twice married); 6. Exception to the power of the judge; 7. Exception to the person of the judge; 8. Exception to the time; 9. To the place; 10. To the person of the plaintiff; 11. As to the person of the defendant (as infancy, &c.); 12. Exception of summons; 13. Exception of vicious writs or counts; 14. Exception to approvers; 15. Exceptions to indictments; 16. Answer or plea to treason; 17. Plea to charge of arson; 18. Plea to appeal of murder; 19. Plea to charge of robbery or larceny; 20. Plea in burglary; 21. Plea in rape; 22. Plea in imprisonment; 23. In mayhem or wounding, and generally of exceptions; 24. Of the juramentum duelli (or trial by battle); 25. Of the order of battle; 26. Of exceptions in personal trespass; 27. Of purprestures; 28. Of treasure-trove; 29. Of wrecks; 30. Of usury; 31. Of defence as to hunting, chasing, or fishing; 32. Of pleas to obligations or covenants; 33. Of attaint (*i.e.*, of jurors); 34. Of the proceeding of attaint; 35. Of oaths; 36. Of homage; 37. Of fealty; 38. Of common oaths; 39. Of final accords. Chapter IV.: Section 1. Of judgment; 2. Of

Andrew Horne, whose name it bears, might take up an ancient book of that name, and work it into the volume we now see, in the reign of this king, or at the end of the former; and if so, we should expect that whatever it propounds was actually law in the reign of Edward II.

This book treats of all branches of the law, whether civil or

authority of judgment; 3. Of jurisdiction; 4. Of defaults; 5. Of defaults in actions; 6. Of defaults in personal actions; 7. Of defaults in real actions; 8. Of defaults in mixed actions; 9. Of pledges and mainpernors; 10. Of defaults in services; 11. Of trial in case of default of services; 12. Of penalties or punishments; 13. Of infamous persons (*i.e.*, those attainted of offences corporally punishable); 14. Of punishment of majesty; 15. Of arson or burning; 16. Of homicide; 17. Of venial punishments; 18. Of false judges; 19. Of perjury; 20. Of the office of justices in eyre; 21. Of the articles in eyre (articles very much resembling Britton); 22. Of franchises; 23. Of satisfaction of judgments; 24. Of verdict and judgment in cases of disseisin; 25. Of amercements; 26. Of taxation of amercements; 27. Of the office of justices in eyre. Chapter V.: Section 1. Of abusions of the common law, in 155 articles, some of which have been already quoted, and the contents of which were written after the time of Henry III., for one of them alludes to the disuse of the ordeal as an abuse, and it went out of use in the course of that reign; 2. Of the defects of the great charter; 3. Of the defects of the Statute of Merton; 4. Of the Statute of Marlbridge; 5. Of the Statute of Westminster 1; 6. Of the Statute of Westminster 2; 7. Of the Statute of Gloucester, 16 Edward I.; 8. Of the Statute of *Circumspecté Agatis*, 13 Edward I. Such are the contents of this curious and ancient work, and, from a mere enumeration of the heads or subjects of which it treats, it will be manifest that it must afford abundant and interesting illustrations of our legal history down to the middle of the reign of Edward I. The author first divides law in general into spiritual and temporal. The canon law, which consisted in spiritual correction of sin: "En amendement des peches espirituelles, per admonitiones, reproofs, excommergements;" and the temporal law, which dealt in temporal penalties: "En correction des peches materielles per sommons, attachements, peines;" "Le spirituel ley guident les prelates, l'autre guidents les lay princes, et se aide l'un per l'autre." Then the common law is defined: "La ley dont ceste somme est fait est escrite de ancient usages, et pur ceo que elle est generallment done a touts est elle appells commun." The next section alone marks the extreme antiquity of the original work, for it treats of the Saxon Conquest evidently in a Saxon spirit: "De la venue des Anglos en c'est terre;" "Apres ceo que Dieu avoit abbatue la nobility des Britons, libera il le royelme al plus humbles, et simples, de gents les pais adjoynants, cest ascavoire, aux Saxons, que le viendront conqueror des parties d'Almayne;" and then it gives a summary of the substance of the Saxon laws, and, without any mention of the Norman Conquest, goes on to say that "Alfred caused the earls to meet twice a year to make ordinances, and that by this estate many ordinances were made by kings until the time of the king that now is" (*i.e.*, Edward I. or II.); and then the whole texture of the work is such as might well be Saxon, with occasional additions, showing how the law had been altered by *later* ordinances. And that the whole body of the work is, with these *express* exceptions, or necessary additions, Saxon, is shown by the remarkable passage already alluded to, and which tallies curiously with the passage just quoted, speaking of the *Saxon* conquest in such a *Saxon* spirit, and *not* mentioning the *Norman* Conquest. That passage is one (c. ii. s. 28) in which allusion is made to the "first conquerors"—*i.e.*, the Saxons—as no mention had been made of any other, "nous primiers conquerors," language which could hardly have been used long after the Conquest. Then, going back to the first chapter, we find it stated that the realm was divided into parts, according to the number of companions (*comites*): "Solonque le number des companions, que remisteront en estate le royaulme," and these were called comities, after the Latin *comites* "Ceux compaignions sont appelles comities apres l'Latin (*comites*), et issint sont a ceo jour ceux pais appelles comities, et in Latin comitatus, et ceo que est dehors ceux comities a les Anglois est de Conquest," a passage which could scarcely have been written after the Norman Conquest. Then it is said (s. 3) that Alfred caused the counts or "comites" to assemble to make ordinances, &c., and that many ordinances had been made from that time to the time of the king that now is (*i.e.*, Edward I. or II.

criminal. Besides this, it gives a cursory retrospect of some changes ordained by former kings; enumerates a list of abuses, as the author terms them, of the common law, proposing, at the same time, what he considers to be desirable corrections. He does the same with *Magna Charta*, the statutes of Merton and Marlbridge, and some principal acts in the reign of Edward I.

And then the rest of the section proceeds to state what these ordinances were, "ordine fuit," &c., expressly intimating that all the subsequent ordinances were included; and the several sections treat of crimes, giving definitions of them extremely ancient, and which even in the reign of Edward I. must have been nearly obsolete, and were evidently of Saxon origin; beginning with the offence of majesty, and defining it, so as to include heresy and sorcery, and perjury against the king, as well as treason, as it was understood in the reign of Edward II., and making treason an offence between subjects. Then there is a head as to "burners de ardours," which evidently belongs to Saxon times, since it speaks of men putting other men into the fire, and burning them alive, for revenge,—a kind of crime of which we read nothing even in Bracton, and which was only committed in the most barbarous times of the Saxons, that race whom the *Mirror* describes as the most humble and peaceful, but who, as their laws show, were most horribly and barbarously savage. Then there is the head of "homicide," which is defined so generally as to include all kinds of cases; and there is no head as to "murder," which, again, is thus characteristic of very ancient age, the distinction between mere homicide and a more secret and deliberate kind of manslaying, called murder, having arisen soon after the laws of the Confessor and the Conqueror as to *murdrum*. Then burglary is described by the old Saxon word, "hamsockne, hamsocked." Mention is made of an ordinance of Glanville as to deodand, and another ordinance of Henry II. as to duels or tournaments, and another ordinance of Henry II. at Clarendon, as to sanctuary. Several decisions of Saxon judges are quoted: "Et Bermond agarda que les chatels aux fugitifs remaissent forfaits au roy: et Isolgrim dit que il n'est my fugitif que soy present en jugement devant ceo que il sort ut lage;" in which it is to be noted that the names of the judges are Saxon, and to be found in no judicial register after the Conquest; and next, they are mentioned as if known, or, at all events, within recollection. This shows that the passage was written in Saxon times,—as also another, which alludes to Canute's ordinances as to murder, or secret killing of a Dane. The next section as to the exchequer, which appears to refer to the time present, when the book was finally compiled, is necessarily of later date. But the next, as to inferior courts, "des mesnes courts," is evidently extremely ancient: for it goes back to the very first origin of county courts in the earliest rude assemblies of the Saxons, probably even before their invasion of this country: "Des assemblies premiers vindrent consistories que l'un *appelle* courts et celles courts sont *appelles* counties, ou le jugements se sont pur les suitors" (s. 15)—a mode of speaking evidently alluding to those first rude assemblies which could not be deemed courts at all. Then it goes on: "L'autre mesnes courts sont les courts de chescun seignior del fief; et ainsi in fayers et markets en soviendra bastrir droit. Sans delay *en les quelles* courts ount conusanse de dets, covenants, &c., et tiels autres petits pechés que ne passent roy 40s. en la valeu." In this there is a remarkable difference from Britton, who makes the limitation of 40s. apply to the county courts, whereas the *Mirror* applies it to the courts-baron and other inferior courts. There can be no doubt the *Mirror* was right, as it was likely to be on a matter of law of Saxon origin; for as the county court was originally the only court of ordinary jurisdiction, it is obvious that there could not have been any limit to its jurisdiction, and that the limitation must have arisen in later times, and subsequently to the Conquest, which is the more clear, because after all it was only a means of imposing a fine on the suitor, since, as Britton states, the suitor could bring any case into the county court, if he could sue out the king's writ of justicies—of no manner of importance, except that it imposed a fee. The course this matter had taken is a curious illustration of the gradual encroachment of the king's courts. Originally, as the *Mirror* states, the remedial writ, which could be obtained from the chancery, was to compel the sheriff to hear the case: "Et ideo tibi precipimus quod causam illam audias et legitime modo decidas" (c. i. s. 3); and now it was insisted by the king's courts that this writ was necessary to enable the sheriff to hear the cause, unless it was above 40s. in value. The contrast is very remarkable all

This book should be read with great caution, and some previous knowledge of the law as it stood about the same period, for the author certainly writes with very little precision. This, with his assertions about Alfred, and the extravagant punishments inflicted by that king on his judges, have brought his treatise under some suspicions. When read with these hints, the *Mirror of Justice* is

through, between the sturdy tone of the Saxon writer in the *Mirror*, who takes the popular view all through, and the subservient spirit of the Norman crown lawyer Britton, who exalts the royal rights and prerogatives to the utmost. Then the court of the sheriffs or tourn is treated of, and the court-leet, the most ancient court in the realm (as it is called in the Year-books), with its jurisdiction as to nuisances, &c. So ends the first chapter. Many passages afford interesting illustrations of the administration of justice. Mention is made of the "chief justices" (*i.e.*, the "chief justiciaries," who were appointed long before there were any regular king's courts, except the justices in eyre): "Et ove les justices commissaires errants" (*i.e.*, de justices itinerant). There is a curious section as to the lawyers, "de loyers," in which it is stated that the officers, or ministers of justice, ought not to take anything of the people; but that they might take 12d. of every plaintiff for the hearing, and not more, and the pleader 6d., "et al countie vi[d]." And for every knight (*i.e.*, gentleman) sworn to testify, 6d.; and any other juror 4d.: "Et chevaler testimoygner jurer vi[d]., et autre juror iv[d]." (in which we see that jurors were still witnesses); "et les deux summoners iv[d].;" every party sued being summoned by his feeholder. Then come two ordinances of Henry I. on the subject, that jurors should take nothing of the suitors, &c. Then comes sect. 5, "des countors" or "pleaders." The countors, who are described as serjeants learned in the law, and as necessary for those suitors who were not so. It is to be observed, that it is provided that the pleader must not be a man of religion—*i.e.*, a monk or friar, nor a man in holy orders, within the orders of sub-deacon, nor a beneficed clerk with the cure of souls; so that the pleaders were mere laymen, and less versed in civil or canon law than they were in the time of William of Malmesbury, who wrote "Nullus clericus, nisi causidicus." The pleaders were sworn to act fairly and honestly for their clients. The section "Des attachments" describes the procedure to enforce the process of the costs. Several actions, it is said, have attachment of the body—*i.e.*, arrest; but it is to be noted, that throughout, in the *Mirror*, personal actions mean actions for injuries to the person; and at common law, it should seem that it was only in actions for such injuries, with force and violence, such as would be an offence against the person, and require a fine to the king for breach of the peace, it was only in these actions there was arrest. In real actions—*i.e.*, actions for recovery of land, the land itself being security, the process was summons; and in mixed actions, first summons, then attachment, that is, first of the goods and then of the body,—mixed actions meaning actions as to personalty, and yet not personal, and so having a mixed process. Personal actions, it is further stated, are for imprisonment, battery, breaking of parks, &c. Real actions are writs of right, or of dower, or of entry. Mixed actions are of customs, distresses, or covenants, and as to which it may be observed, that at common law a special contract was required to be in writing, and as few could write in those days, the contracts were of necessity sealed instead of being signed, and hence all special contracts were what were afterwards called "specialties," *i.e.*, by deed under seal. Then comes various sections as to the procedure in the various kinds of appeals. Then, in the section on criminal offences at the suit of the king, as to which it is mentioned that it was ordained by Henry I., that no one should be arrested on a criminal charge until he was indicted by the oaths of good men. Then comes a passage, evidently of extreme antiquity, giving an indictment for enchantments, whereby the accused took away from another the flavour of his ale, "la flower de sa cervoise," by which he lost the sale thereof. Then comes indictments for murder, larceny, burning, &c. Next is a section of venial offences at the king's suit. Then in the section "De trespasses venial, et personal suites," *i.e.*, of actions for injuries to the person of a man or his chattels. Here it is stated that the action of trespass required surety to sue, and oftentimes, it is added, that the security was by the bodies of plaintiffs who had no other surety to offer than the four walls of a jail. Then it is stated that on account of the hardships that used to be suffered by the offenders in personal suits, it was ordained by Henry I. that they should first be attached by their bodies until they

certainly a curious, interesting, and, in some degree, an authentic tract upon our old law, though, considering the anachronisms in legal knowledge (if they may be so called) with which it abounds, that the antiquated law is promiscuously blended with that of the time in which it was revised, and that the date of such revision is very uncertain, it is to be wondered that some great writers[1] have

found mainpernors (or bail); and if they were not to be found, and could not find mainpernors, then their lands were to be seized. It is added, by way of explanation, that those who are surety for the body of a man, are properly mainpernors, but pledges might be of other things. Then comes a section as to "assize de novel disseisin," as to which it is pointed out, that "assize," in one sense, is simply a session of the justices; in another sense, it was an ordinance by Ranulph de Glanville, that recognitions should be sworn by twelve jurors of the next neighbours, which, it was said, was called assize. There is a section under the head of "attaint," which treats of the mode of trial by jury, the challenges to the jurors, &c. The usage is described to be that the party on whom lay the affirmative, did, in aid of the court, cause the nearest credible neighbours to appear in witness, so that there be twelve at least of the jury, of whom, if by examination they are found of one mind, it is sufficient, and if not, or if they say generally that they know nothing of the matter or are in doubt, it is adjudged against the plaintiff. Then as to the challenges of jurors, it is laid down to be cause of challenge that a juror is an enemy of one party, or a cousin, friend, or relative of the other, which exactly accords with cases in the Year-books, where it was so held. The fifth chapter treats of numerous supposed abuses of the common law, of which not less than 155 are stated, but of which a great many are obviously frivolous or groundless,—as, for instance, that the miracle of God (*i.e.*, the ordeal) was not allowed when other proof failed, and that battle was not allowed in personal actions as well as felonies. These instances show that this last chapter of abuses was by the editor, not the original author, for in the body of the book it is mentioned that battle was allowed in personal actions, and that the ordeal had been disused. The last chapter treats of abuses of the law, and it is obvious that the language of this part of the work, the list of alleged abuses, is that of the editor, and of the reign of Edward II. The opening sentences are quite appropriate to that reign and the previous one. "The first and chief abuse is, that the king is above the law, whereas he ought to be subject to it, as it is contained in his oath. It is an abuse that whereas parliaments ought to be held twice in the year in London, they are there but seldom, and at the pleasure of the king, for subsidies and collections of treasure. And whereas the ordinances ought to be made by the assent of the king and his earls, they were now made by the king and his clerks and aliens, and others who dare not contradict the king, but desire to please him and counsel him for his profit, without calling the counties, and without following the rules of law; whereby it followeth that many ordinances are grounded more upon pleasure than upon law. It is an abuse that the laws and customs of the realm are not put into writing, whereby they may be known to all men. It is an abuse that justice is delayed in the king's courts more than elsewhere. It is an abuse that a man who hath done manslaughter of necessity, or by misadventure, or not feloniously, is kept in prison until he hath purchased the king's charter of pardon. It is an abuse to outlaw a man before it hath been inquired of by the oaths of neighbours. It is an abuse that justices drive a true man to be tried by his country, where he proffereth to defend himself against the accuser by battle (whereby it appears that at that time the judges did drive men to trial by jury in criminal cases; and if it appears singular that what to us seems so invaluable a privilege should in those days have been so little appreciated, it must be borne in mind that the jurors were but witnesses, and if they knew nothing, as they heard no evidence, they could really say nothing, and the trial, under such circumstances, might often be determined by prejudice). It is an abuse that the king's debts lie dormant, and are delayed to be levied by estreats, since the arrears of debts are levied upon sureties. It is an abuse to amerce any man by a presentment made of less than twelve sworn freemen. It is an abuse that a freeman be made the king's officer by any election against his will. It is an abuse to adjudge a man to death by suitors (*i.e.*, by the mere general voice of the freeholders, without twelve sworn triers or jurors), if not in cases so manifest (*i.e.*, cases taken in the

[1] Lord Coke and Nathaniel Bacon.'

relied so much upon this author as to pronounce on the antiquity of many articles of our law merely on his authority.

Miscellaneous facts.

There is nothing but a vague tradition to give us any trace of the places where the practisers and students of the law had their residence before the reign of this king. But in the reign of Edward II. we are informed that such places were called Hostels, or Inns of Court, because the inhabitants of them belonged to the king's courts. There is said to have been one of these at Dowgate, called Johnson's Inn; another in Fewter's (that is, Fetter) Lane; and another in Paternoster Row. An ancient custom is vouched to support a belief that some inn was in the neighbourhood of St Paul's Church. It is said that the serjeants and apprentices, each at *his pillar*, used to *hear his client's case, and take notes thereof upon his knee*, a custom which was remembered by a solemnity observed in the time of Charles I. upon the making of serjeants, for it was then a custom for them to go there in their formalities, and *choose their pillar*.

It is reported that William, earl of Lincoln, about the beginning of this reign, being well affected to the study of the laws, first brought the professors of them to settle in a house of his, since called Lincoln's Inn. The earl was only lessee under the bishops of Chichester, and many succeeding bishops, in after-times, let leases of this house to certain persons, for the use and residence of the practisers and students of the law,[1] till in the 28th year of the reign of Henry VIII. the bishop of Chichester granted the inheritance to Francis Sulyard and his brother Eustace, both students, the survivor of whom, in the 20th year of queen Elizabeth, sold the fee to the benchers for £520. It seems clear that Thavies Inn was inhabited at this time by lawyers. Such are the first inns of which we have any account that can be depended on.[2]

The number of suits so increased in the common bench, that whereas there had usually been only *three* justices there, Edward II., at the beginning of his reign, was constrained to increase them

manner as in the act) that there need no answer." Whence it appears that those men taken in the act could be executed without trial. "It is an abuse to make a man answer to the king's suit where he is not indicted or appealed. It is an abuse that remedial writs are saleable. It is an abuse to distrain in personal actions (*i.e.*, to enforce appearance) when the profit of the issues comes to the king, and no profit cometh to the plaintiff. (Here may be observed the contrast between the tone of the *Mirror* and Britton.) It is an abuse to think that one cannot recover a term for years (a remarkable passage with reference to the theory that the action of ejectment was of later origin, especially coupled with a passage in the chapter on disseisin, in which it is said that the assize of novel disseisin [the *festinium remedium*, as Lord Coke called it] applied to terms for years). It is an abuse that a man be accused of life and member *ex officio* without suit or without indictment. It is an abuse that rape is a mortal offence (which gives the date later than the statute of Westm. 2, making it capital, as it had been before). It is an abuse to compel jurors, witnesses, to say that which they know not, by distress of fine and imprisonment after their verdict, when they could not say anything." Then there is a section on the defects of the charters and other old statutes, which has been already made use of under each statute. Such is the *Mirror*, one of the earliest sources of our legal history.

[1] Dugd. *Or. Jur.* 231.

[2] *Ibid.* 143.

to *six*, who, we are told, used to sit in two places, a circumstance not easy to account for;[1] within three years after, they were increased to *seven*: next year they were reduced to *six*, at which number they continued.

In 17 Edward II. Hervie de Staunton, chancellor of the exchequer, was constituted chief justice of the king's bench, and his former post was to be executed by deputy while he heard causes *in Banco Regis.*[2]

In the sixth year of this king,[3] oyer of a writ being demanded, it was there said by the justices, that as it was purchased a long time ago, it was in the Tower of London, and therefore there must be a writ out of chancery to cause it to be brought at a certain day. While this fact shows where the depository of judicial records then was, it also accounts in some measure for the great destruction and mutilation of them. These occasional removals must bring them into continual hazard of being lost or destroyed.

This reign is, however, marked with the first instance of royal interposition, not only for the better custody and preservation of records, but for the regular sorting and arrangement of them in such manner as would be most conducive to make them answer the end for which they were designed. In the 14th year of his reign, this king, by writ of privy-seal directed to the treasurer, barons, and chamberlains of the exchequer, commanded them forthwith to employ proper persons to superintend, methodize, and digest all the *rolls*, *books*, and *other writings* of the times of his progenitors, kings of England, then remaining in the *treasuries* of *his exchequer*, and in the Tower of London; all which, as he there declares, were not at that time disposed in such manner as they ought to have been, for his and the public service. Again, in his 16th year, the king commanded the treasurer and chamberlains to cause all *papal bulls, charters, and other muniments* touching his state and liberties within England, Ireland, Wales, Scotland, and Ponthieu, then remaining in the *four treasuries of the exchequer*, *the wardrobe*, and sundry other places, to be regularly sorted, and calendars to be made. At the distance of a few months after, he appointed Robert de Hoton, and Thomas de Sibthorp, to examine and methodize all such *charters, writings, and other national muniments* as at that time were deposited in the castles of Pontefract, Tuttebury, and Tunbridge, also such as had been newly brought into the Tower of London, and all those which were then kept in the house of the Black or Friars Preachers within the city of London. The keepers and the constables of those castles, and the prior of the order of Friars Preachers, were strictly enjoined to allow the two persons so appointed to have free access to such records, and to give them all necessary aid and assistance.

There appear in subsequent reigns instances of a similar interposition for the protection of public records. There are now on

[1] Dugd. *Or. Jur.* 38. [2] *Ibid.* 38. [3] Mayn. 190.

record several writs to this effect—*De supervidendo rotulos, &c.—De rotulis et scriptis in recto ordine ponendis, &c.—De scrutinio Chartarum faciendo, &c.*, and the like.

Ever since the separation of the chancery from the *Aula Regis*, the rolls and records of that court had been kept separate, and they had lately multiplied to a great number. To relieve the chancellor from this concern of keeping the records, a particular officer was appointed for that purpose in this reign. William de Armyn was, with the consent of the chancellor, John de Sandale, appointed *master*, or *keeper of the rolls*, and had the custody of them committed to him in the 20th year of this reign.[1]

[1] See Ayl. Chart. Introd. 25.

CHAPTER XIII.

EDWARD III.

Of Judicature in Ireland—Lancaster made a County Palatine—The Charters —Of Purveyance—Tenures—Of the Clergy—Scire Facias for Tithes—Of Provisors—Of Præmunire—Probate of Wills and Intestacy—The Statutes of Labourers—Trade and Commerce—The Statute of the Staple—Forestalling—Children born out of the Realm—Of Sheriffs.

THE reign of this king fills a great and distinguished space in the history of our law, whether we regard the statutes that were passed or the decisions made by the courts (*a*). The order of proceedings,

(*a*) At the opening of this long reign, which lasted half a century, and was one of the most important in our legal history, it is natural, and it will be useful, to present a general review of it, in order to convey an idea of its general character, of the general course and progress of our laws, and to mark distinctly in the mind the more important features of the law and legislation by which it is distinguished. Every age has some distinct character—some great distinguishing feature. And as the great general character of the age of Edward I. and his son, was that of alteration and improvement of the law, especially as to procedure, so that of Edward III. is the quiet practical development of the system of law thus altered and settled. There were indeed several important alterations of the law, but with two great exceptions, they were rather in the nature of development or supplement of previous legislation. These exceptions were the laws as to the church and the statutes of labourers. With these exceptions, the legal history of this long reign might be stated shortly thus—that the country, under the royal authority, so firmly established by Edward I., and so firmly resumed by his illustrious descendant, reaped the benefit of the wise legislation of the former reign, and quietly carried out and applied the law as it was then settled, especially under those two great heads, the administration of justice and the nature and transfer of titles to landed property. And as one of the great objects of legal history is to trace its course and progress, and keep up its continuity, and another is to show the principles embodied in, and the objects of practical utility answered and attained by, ancient institutions, long since obsolete, so as to give them more of interest, perhaps even utility, in our own times—it may be proper, before noticing the new legislation of the reign, to take a general view of the law as it existed and continued upon the two important subjects above mentioned—the administration of justice, and the transfer of titles to real property. As regards the first, it remained as in the reign of Edward I., except that it gradually progressed, improved, and developed; and also with the exception that on account of the growing importance of trial by jury, a statute (as is noticed in the next chapter, c. xiv.) was passed to settle the qualifications of jurors, so as to secure that they should at least be respectable and substantial men; and another to provide a remedy, by the penal proceeding of attaint, in cases of false verdict. The procedure in real actions, however, *i.e.*, actions for the recovery of real property, remained as before (*vide* c. xv.), and were extremely slow and dilatory. This was because the titles to real property, in an age when everything turned upon the property in land, and there was very little property besides, was of such immense importance: on which account also there was the system of entail established, as already described under the statute De donis. The times, too, were turbulent, and it was most important to have the titles to real property put as much as possible beyond dispute, especially in cases where it was or might be limited by settlement or other-

both civil and criminal, were amended in many instances by statute; and in the course of half a century, there was hardly a title or ques-

wise, for times to come. In an age of violence and turbulence, titles, so long as they rested upon mere parchment, were not felt to be secure; men might be robbed of their deeds, and hence the tendency of the age was still, as it had been, in favour of *public* transfer or records of the titles of real property. One mode of public transfer was feoffment with livery of seisin, *i.e.*, open delivery of possession in the presence of neighbours; the other was the system of fines or records in a court of law, of solemn deliberate settlements. And here it may be of some interest, and may also be of some use, to direct attention to the mode in which titles and conveyances of real estate were recorded or registered under the operation of the system of fines, too hastily perhaps abolished in our own age without any substitutes; and by the abolition of which, the country lost the immense advantage of a system of a record or registration of titles. Fines were neither more nor less than *recorded conveyances*, *i.e.*, conveyances recorded in courts of law. The effect of the fine, as matter of record, was to place the *limitations* of the estate beyond a doubt, supposing the fine to be valid, and that would be the only point that could be raised; and as it would be valid if either of the parties to it were seised, the only question that could be raised was that they were *neither* of them seised, as that he who levied the fine had only an estate for years, and that the freehold was in some one else, not party to the fine (*Year-book*, 42 *Edw. III.*, f. 20). But if he who levied the fine had a freehold, although it was only an estate for life, the *fine* would be good, unless it had been avoided by entry, although it transferred the reversion wrongfully to another, for that would operate as a transfer of the title, although a wrongful transfer; for if the man who levied the fine had any possession of freehold estate, the fine was good; and on *scire facias* to prove execution of it, it could only be got rid of by showing that the parties to it had *no* freehold estate at all (*Ibid.*) There can be no doubt that all the conveyancing of this age was by means of *fines*, on account of their nature as records in courts of justice, and on their efficacy as fixed and permanent and conclusive evidence—a matter of vast practical importance in times of turbulence and disturbance, not merely as settling the right and nature of the estate, but also ascertaining *what the lands were* which were so held. The common form of the fine suffices to show this; for in most cases the fine simply put on record a gift in tail, so that the object could not have been to alter but to ascertain the nature of the estate and also the lands settled. Thus the fine would run thus:—"Between R. Cardolfe and one T., by which fine Cardolfe confessed the lands to be the right of T., as those which he had by force of his (T.'s) gift, by which confession T. granted the lands to Cardolfe and his wife, and the heirs of their body, and in default of issue, the remainder to one W. and his heirs, &c., and for default of issue, to one G. and his heirs, and in default of issue, to one H. and his heirs," &c. (*Year-book*, 42 *Edw. III.*, fol. 20). Now here it will be seen there were not less than four limitations, one of an estate tail, and three successive remainders in default of issue, and by means of the fine, all these limitations were placed upon record, and remained, generation after generation, thus recorded, so as to put the title beyond a doubt, so long as the muniments and records of the king's courts of justice were preserved. And the importance of these "fines" or records of conveyances was all the greater on this account, that by the statute of Westminster, *execution* upon the fine could at any time be had (by means of *scire facias*) without the slow and tedious process of a real action. That is to say, execution on the fine, as a record of a judgment in a court of justice, as distinguished from a mere right of suit upon a *deed*, which could be protracted by the forms of real actions almost to any time, to the evident injury of the party entitled to the land; the title to which would all that time be in uncertainty. Now, as real actions were designed to try the title when it was really in dispute, it was clearly contrary to their object and design to allow them thus to be perverted to purposes of delay and injury in cases where the title was *not* in dispute. And if it was placed on record by means of a fine it *could* not be in dispute, at all events as between the parties to the fine and their representatives, or, in the language of the law, their privies. This was by virtue of the principle of estoppel—one of the most important heads of our law—whereby a man, or those privy to him in blood or estate, were precluded from disputing what was declared by a judgment or a record, to which he was a party. Hence the immense practical importance of fines, and of the procedure by way of summary *execution* upon fines, as a means of precluding litigation. The practical effect was that there

tion that did not, at one time or other, undergo some discussion in court. The judicature of parliament and of the council, as well as

was a system of registration of titles to landed property, with a summary power of enforcing them without any suit. Thus, therefore, it was always of very great importance to have execution upon a fine, without being put to a real action; and if the title of the party really depended on the fine he was allowed such execution. The party claiming, however, to have a fine thus summarily executed was only entitled to it when the title appeared to depend upon the fine, which it would not if it depended on some prior title, in which case he was put to his real action. Thus, for instance, where the fine itself recited, and showed that the title rested on a precedent settlement, the court said—In this case, the thing which ought to take effect is proved by the fine, and you who are privy to it (*i.e.*, in blood), cannot say the contrary to that which the fine supposes; and the fine supposes that your ancestor was seised by force of the gift, *i.e.*, the gift in tail. And the court held that the demandant could not have *scire facias* for execution on the fine, but was driven to sue in formedon on the gift, *i.e.*, according to the form of the gift (*Year-book*, 41 *Edw. III.*, fol. 14). The court there thought that a fine, merely in pursuance of a gift in tail, was of no effect to give any new right, so that the only use or object of a fine, in such case, could have been to place the entail on record, so as to have conclusive evidence of it, and also of the lands which were entailed, by virtue of the principle of estoppel, by which the parties to any record, or their privies in blood or estate, were precluded from questioning it. In an age of constant turbulence and disturbance, this must have been of no slight importance. When, however, the title depended upon the fine, supposing it to be valid, even upon *scire facias* to have execution upon it, a party could only "falsify" or defeat it, by showing that the parties to it were not seised of any freehold estate (*Year-book*, 40 *Edw. III.*, fol. 30). It was only, it is to be observed, the parties to fines—or the privies or legal representatives of those parties—who were estopped by it, so as to be precluded from disputing it (*Ibid.*, fol. 30); but even those who were not estopped from disputing it could only dispute it by denying that either of the parties to it had any freehold in the land. And so the law was that the issue in tail could have execution by *scire facias* upon a fine, settling and recording the limitations of the settlement in order to avoid the delay and litigation of a real action (42 *Edw. III.*, fol. 6). Thus, therefore, there was in effect a system of record or registration of titles, and a summary remedy upon the title thus recorded. The efficacy and utility of this system of fines, as records of title and conveyancing, would be all the greater by reason of the number of local courts in which fines could be levied and recorded. Thus we read in the Year-books of the reign of fines levied in the court at Exeter (44 *Edw. III.*, fol. 37). So we find claims of cognizance allowed in pleas of land—or to levy fines—in various local courts (44 *Edw. III.*, 28), as in the court at Coventry (44 *Edw. III.*, 17), in the court of the abbot of Reading (44 *Edw. III.*, 28), so there was a court at Bristow (Bristol), and that court still remains (46 *Edw. III.*, 4). Thus these local courts were one of the great features of the age, and they are frequently mentioned, whether in claims of conusance, writs of error, or of false judgment, or in other ways (45 *Edw. III.*, fol. 1). There were these local courts not only in the great cities but in almost all towns, and these not mere courts-barons, but regular courts of record, in which fines could be levied and recorded. This must of course have added immensely to the advantage and utility of the use of fines as records of titles and conveyances. It appears that a practice of enrolling deeds, as the next best thing to the levying of a fine, had come into use; and thus we find that the lord of Typloft came into court to enrol a charter of feoffment (44 *Edw. III.*, fol. 7). By the custom of London and other places, wills of land were enrolled (49 *Edw. III.*, fol. 17), and so were deeds (12 *Hen. IV.*, fol. 12). And by the custom of London, deeds enrolled bound parties and privies as fines did at the common law (24 *Edw. III.*, fol. 14), that is, as *quasi matter* of record. This shows what was the great use and advantage of fines, and that our ancestors fully understood the benefits derived from a record or registry of titles. It has been seen that statutes of Edward I., as to the mode of levying fines, required that they should be openly read in court. This was as a means of obtaining publicity and notoriety by way of notice to those interested. But after a year they were barred. But as in those turbulent times that was not sufficient, therefore in this reign the statute of non-claim, as it was called, passed, which provided that non-claims should be no bar

that of inferior courts, was adjusted; the claims of the clergy were qualified and settled; the crime of treason was defined; justices of

to the parties who desired to defeat a fine, *i.e.*, if they could do so. So much as to the law of real property in the age of Edward III. It remains to mention some of the alterations in the law. Mention may here be made of the law on some other subjects connected with procedure on property. It has already been observed that the legislation of the reign, with the exceptions above mentioned, was in the way of supplement or development of the legislation of the previous reigns, especially of Edward I. Thus, for example, the statute of Westminster 2, c. xxiv., had a provision as to *juris utrum*—the procedure to try the right as to the nature of the tenure of property, whether it was lay or ecclesiastical; and the 14 Edw. III., c. xvii., carried that out, and a man could have *juris utrum* to try the question, utrum sit libera eleemosina talis ecclesiæ vel alterius ecclesiæ, vel sit libera eleemosina talis ecclesia vel laicum feodum talis, vel utrum sit libera eleemosina pertinens ad vicarium an libera eleemosina pertinens ad rectoriam (*Year-book*, 40 *Edw. III.*, fol. 30). That is to say, not merely to try whether or not land was held as ecclesiastical and not lay tenure, but whether it belonged to one church or another, or to the vicar or the rector. The statute 25 Edw. III. c. xvii. gave process of capias in debt, which had before been given in actions of trespass and account (40 *Edward III.* fol. 1). The statute 9 Edw. III. c. xiii. gave a remedy in debt against one of several executors, and judgment against all of them (40 *Edward III.*, fol. 1). The statute 14 *Edward III.*, c. vi. made provision for amendment of process in case of verbal and clerical mistakes (40 *Edw. III.*, fol. 4). The statutes 28 Edw. III. fol. 8, and 34 Edw. III. fol. 7, extended the remedy (such as it was) by the penal process of attaint, in cases of false verdict (40 *Edw. III.*, fol. 31). The stat. 14 Edw. III., fol. 17, gave the writ *de juris utrum* by one person against another (40 *Edw. III.*, fol. 27). These are some of the minor statutes of the reign, and it will be seen that they were of far less importance, with the two great exceptions already mentioned, than the practical operation and application of the laws already in existence. So much may suffice, at all events, for a general review of the legal history of the reign, with those two exceptions, which deserve a more particular consideration. The two principal heads or subjects of *new legislation* which require consideration in the legal history of this reign, are those which relate to the church, and those which relate to the condition of the villeins and labourers. With respect to the church, this reign is marked by the celebrated statutes of *præmunire*, and of provisors of benefices, which, especially the former, laid the ground for that ascendancy of the temporal power over the spiritual or ecclesiastical, which, soon after the close of the next century, resulted in the separation of the English church and nation from the see of Rome. When it is remembered that the primary and principal weapon then made use of to effect that object was the statute of *præmunire*, its importance will be recognised, and the reign in which it was enacted would, for that reason alone, be strongly marked in our legal history. It has already been remarked on various occasions in the course of these notes, that it is all important, in the study of legal history, to attend to the gradual course and progress of our laws and institutions, and to observe that, for the most part, the changes in them have been the result of causes of slow and progressive growth. And the legislation in this reign with reference to the church, and its result in the course of a century or so in separation from Rome, afford a striking illustration of this remark. It is a fallacy to imagine, as most persons do, that the separation was the result of any novel cause which suddenly arose. No doubt, such cause there was, which tended greatly to accelerate, perhaps one should say precipitate, the change; but the law, and the mind of the nation as indicated by its law and its legislation, had been long slowly but surely working in that direction, and tending to that result. It has been seen that, in the reign of Henry III., it had been laid down by Bracton that, not only wherever the matter was temporal, but even where spiritualty was mixed with temporalty, which was held to be the case wherever there were endowments annexed to spiritual offices, the king's courts had jurisdiction, and, moreover, that it was entirely for the king's courts to determine whether the matter was in its nature spiritual or temporal; and we have seen that, in the reigns of Edward I. and Edward II. these principles were asserted by the legislature and the courts of law. The king's courts could issue prohibitions to the spiritual courts whenever the king's courts deemed that any temporal interest was involved, and as, according to the law, the right of presentation to a benefice was of temporal value, the king's courts took cognizance of it. The see of Rome

the peace were established; the inferior ministers of justice were regulated. The learning of the law received considerable accessions.

recognised the right of patronage, and the courts of law claimed to determine upon it. By a natural analogy, they held that bishoprics were benefices in the royal patronage, as part of the royal prerogative, and that, indeed, the constant tendency was to render it absolute, so as to make bishoprics donative instead of merely presentative; in other words, to compel the pontiff to accept the royal nominees. The king always had it in his power to do this, and there were numerous instances in which bishops appointed by the see of Rome were refused (*Angl. Sac.*) The crown lawyers, in fact, did not hesitate, as the royal pretensions advanced, to insist that bishoprics were donatives of the crown; in short, that the king could absolutely appoint the bishops. A little reflection upon this will satisfy any one that it really involved, as a practical result, the royal supremacy; for of course, if the crown could appoint the bishops, the crown could insure the subserviency of the episcopate. And such, in fact, was the ultimate result, so that, a little while after the close of the ensuing century, the episcopate, with hardly a single exception, recognised the royal supremacy. There were, however, still, at the commencement of this great era of the reign of Edward III., two great obstacles to this consummation; the one was the right of appeal to Rome, and the other was the papal right of presentation to bishoprics or other benefices. That there was such a right in certain cases can easily be shown. It has been seen that the king's courts claimed jurisdiction to determine on the right of presentation to benefices, and if the papal donation, by way of provision, as it was called, which was claimed in certain cases, was not recognised by the law of the land, the courts would simply disregard it, and give the benefice to the patron's presentee. But it is believed that no case can be found in which a papal provision was ever contested in a court of law. And when the Roman Catholic church was established by law, and the see of Rome recognised as its head, it would have been difficult to ignore the right of presentation recognised by that church. Hence the necessity for some new law to prevent these papal provisions, and hence the statute of provisors of benefices, passed, be it observed, with the assent of the lords spiritual as well as temporal—for the bishops' right of donation was often interfered with by the papal provisions, and they quite concurred in the measure. The papal power of presentation being thus destroyed as to ordinary benefices, the most obvious analogy would point to the application by the crown of the same principle to *bishoprics*, and when once the crown could appoint to the episcopate, its power over the church would only be restrained by the right of appeal to Rome. The law recognised such right of appeal in cases in which the spiritual courts of the bishops would be allowed to exercise jurisdiction; but in others, the king's courts would restrain the spiritual courts by prohibition, and it was an obvious analogy to restrain, by legislation, appeals to Rome in such cases as the law would not allow to be the subjects of episcopal jurisdiction. Hence the statutes of *præmunire*, which were passed, no doubt, primarily to prevent matters being drawn in question out of the realm, *i. e.*, in Rome, which the king's courts did not consider matters of spiritual jurisdiction. What was this but asserting for the crown a superiority over the see of Rome? For it was asserting a power in the crown to restrain the recourse to Rome by way of appeal, and thus indirectly to restrain the exercise by the see of Rome of its supremacy. The crown asserted the power, with the sanction of the legislature, to say when the supremacy should be exercised, and when it should not be. This was entirely in accordance with the assertion, by the king's courts, of the right to restrain the exercise, by the bishops, of their spiritual jurisdiction, for indeed that was in itself indirectly an assertion of a right to control the exercise of the papal supremacy. For it was asserting a right to determine the fundamental question, what was spiritual and what was not—what was or was not a proper subject for the exercise of episcopal jurisdiction. There was thus a close connexion between the subjects of prohibition and of præmunire, as the object of both was to restrain the exercise of ecclesiastical jurisdiction, though the former lay rather in cases where the matter, in its own nature, was within the ecclesiastical jurisdiction, and the ecclesiastical court had only gone beyond it (46 *Edw. III.*, fol. 32), and præmunire lay rather where the matter was considered in its nature out of ecclesiastical jurisdiction. There can be no doubt, however, that the main object of the statute of præmunire was to restrain appeals to Rome. And enough has now been said to show the immense importance of these

Entails and remainders, discontinuances and remitter, actions upon the case; all these were new subjects of argument. While these

statutes of provisors and of præmunire, which, it will be observed, had a conjoint operation, the latter working in aid of the former. The effect and scope, and the views taken in this age of the papal supremacy, at least as regarded its practical exercise, may be illustrated by one or two cases after the passing of these statutes. In a case in the 41st of this reign, it was admitted in a court of law, that when a bishop was elected he required to be confirmed by the pope, and that the pope might refuse him, and that the pope could, upon the vacation of a see, "reserve" to himself the benefices held by the late bishop, and that the royal patent conveying the temporalities to the bishop recited the gift of the episcopate by the pope. But then it was also laid down as law, that the bishop elect was not bishop until consecration, which followed the conferring of the temporalities by the king, and that it was the union of the spiritualty with the temporalty of the see which constituted the episcopate (*Year-book*, 41 *Edw. III.*, fol. 6). It is manifest that the statute was directed against papal bulls—in other words, against the papal supremacy. The statute of provision of benefices was passed in the earlier part of the reign, and enacted that no one should accept a benefice by collation, reservation, or provision from Rome, or procure bulls from Rome in support of any such provision, or in disturbance of the right of patronage (21 *Edw. I.*, c. xl.). And upon this statute a prohibition and attachment were sued by the king and the incumbent, for that the king had presented the incumbent to a benefice, and that the defendant had brought bulls from Rome in disturbance of him, against the statute, and he was adjudged to perpetual imprisonment (21 *Edw. III.* fol. 40). It is obvious that this was actually making penal the recourse to the see of Rome, and that see would of course be driven either to abandon its supremacy, or to assert it by its spiritual weapon of excommunication. Hence the subsequent statute of præmunire. The statute of præmunire, 27 Edward III. c. i., enacted that any one who sued in a foreign court, "curia Romana," or elsewhere, in any matter which might be brought within the courts of the realm, or sought to impeach in such court any judgment given in the king's court, should be liable to be put out of the king's protection, to forfeit all lands and goods, and be imprisoned at the king's pleasure. It was manifest that this was aimed at any recourse to Rome against the exercise by the crown or the king's courts of their power to restrain the ecclesiastical courts, or to control the appointments to the episcopate, and that the scope and spirit of the statute would extend to the obtaining of papal bulls in any way opposed to these assertions of royal supremacy. And accordingly, in the next reign, a supplemental statute declared that persons procuring bulls from Rome should incur the penalties of præmunire (16 *Richard II.*, c. v.). And judicial construction soon extended and applied it to every case in which there could be recourse to Rome, whether as to papal provisions (2 *Hen. IV.*, fol. 37) or papal sentences of any kind; and so at last it was laid down that if a clerk sued a man in the *curia Romana, even in a spiritual matter*, where he could have a remedy within the realm, in the court of the ordinary, it was a case for the penalties of præmunire, for it was drawing a matter in suit out of the realm (*Year-book*, 9 *Edw. IV.*, fol. 3). Enough has been said to show the immense importance of these celebrated statutes, as tending to that separation from Rome in which they ultimately resulted; and it need hardly be said that, considering the effects of that separation, the passing of such measures must be deemed to have made this reign a memorable one in our legal history. The other great head or subject of law and legislation in this reign was that of the condition of the labouring part of the population. This important subject has reference to villenage and the statute of labourers, which had a close connexion. The obnoxious system of villenage was in this reign still in full operation. Emancipation had, indeed, as has been pointed out in the notes in the former volume, been long going on, but so slowly and gradually that it was almost insensibly; and as yet the odious system was little affected. Not only could the lord seize any goods acquired by the fruits of the villein's labour, but the villein could not marry without the lord's will (43 *Edw. III.*, fol. 5); and if a man married a "nief," or female villein, and took her away, he was liable to action (46 *Edw. III.*, fol. 6). A man could seize his villein as he could seize his beast, only it was laid down that he could not seize him in the presence of the king (27 *Assize*, fol. 49). The issue of the villein were villeins. Nay, it was laid down that if the villein married, even in the blood of his lord, the issue should be villeins; and it was even said, "If

novelties were introduced, the old law was modified, real writs were better understood, and personal actions more considered. Such are

my villein marry with my mother, and they have issue, they shall be my villeins; and so one brother shall be villein to the other, when they are of the half blood" (3 *Edw. III., Bro. Abr., Villenage*, fol. 72). So odious and oppressive a system must have been infinitely obnoxious; and there can be no doubt that it led to many insurrections in the Middle Ages. It was serfdom, though not slavery; the villeins went with the estates, and could be granted or sold like cattle along with the estates, and in some instances even separate from any estate. There were, indeed, many modes of emancipation, but for the most part indirect or incidental, and therefore gradual. One of the most important, and probably frequent, was by the villein's departure to and residence for a year, unclaimed, in a borough. Such residence could hardly take place without his entering into some service, or exercising some trade or art; and there would be the strongest possible motives for the practice of such industry by the villeins—seeing that, on the one hand, they thus obtained the fruits of their labour; and, on the other hand, every week of such labour in a borough led them nearer to their emancipation. Added to this, other villeins, merely from idleness, would run away and become vagrants. There can be little doubt that this led to the statute of labourers (23 *Edw. III.*, c. i.), which, on the one hand, provided that idle vagrants should be made to work; and, on the other hand, recognised the right of the lords to the services of their villeins. The statute expressly provided that lords should be preferred in a claim to the services of their villeins; and it is manifest from the statute itself, and the cases upon it, that numbers of persons who were villeins, and had gone away from their lords, were in service as free labourers or artificers in other places, where they were often reclaimed by their lords, or sometimes were induced by other employers to leave their masters. The statute applied, it is to be observed, both to labourers and artificers, *i.e.*, to husbandmen or rural labourers, and to artisans working in towns. And as the statute recognised the right of the lord to the services of his villein, it was allowable to the lord to take away his villein, although he was in service to another person (47 *Edw. III.*, fol. 16; 50 *Edw. III.*, fol. 22). On the other hand, any one could seize a vagrant, without visible means of subsistence, and compel him to work; and there is a curious case in the Year-books of the reign, in which a man sued for false imprisonment, and the defendant justified seizing him as a vagrant and putting him to work; and the other said he had a cottage and two acres of land, and ten cows, and goods and chattels (47 *Edw. III.*, fol. 18). The cases on the statute were so numerous throughout this and the ensuing reigns, that it is manifest they mark an important era in our legal history, as the age in which villenage was beginning to merge in free labour, and in which the value of labour began to be appreciated. For it is obvious that the great object of the statute was to enable those who had the right in labour, either by villenage or contract, to enforce it (50 *Edw. III.*, fol. 22; 47 *Edw. III.* 16). One of the cases on the statute shows that apprenticeship was coming into vogue, for it was held that an apprentice was not within the act (39 *Edw. III.*, fol. 22). The terms of the statute were "servants and labourers," but this was held to comprise persons employed as artificers, as, for example, embroiderers (47 *Edw. III.*, fol. 22); and so of servants in the ordinary sense, as cooks, butlers, horsekeepers, &c. (21 *Hen. VI.*, fol. 9). But the statute was held not to apply to persons not employed as servants or labourers; for instance, collectors of rent (19 *Hen. VI.*, fol. 53). It is curious that it should have been attempted to enforce the statute against priests retained to chant divine service (46 *Edw. III.*, fol. 14); or a chaplain (50 *Edw. III.*, fol. 15). Of course it was held that such persons were not within the statute, as they were not common servants, but servants of God (*Ibid.*); but it is strange the attempt should have been made. In the latter case there was a distinction drawn between the parochial clergy and the chanting priests, as they were called, greatly to the disadvantage of the latter; for it was said satirically that a parochial chaplain might with more truth be called a labourer than another chaplain who owed service only for a single person; for a parochial parson had many things to do besides chanting his masses and other divine services, for it behoved him to visit the sick, &c. There were many endowments in those times for such divine services, for the benefit of the souls of deceased persons, and the performance by the priests of the duties of such services were deemed primarily matters for ecclesiastical cognizance, unless express contract existed, as where a priest covenanted to chant masses (42 *Edw. III.*, fol. 3), in which case action lay at law. In

the principal heads of inquiry in this king's reign. We shall begin with the statutes.

The great length of this reign, and the frequent sitting of parliament, contributed to give birth to more acts of legislation than are to be found in any of the preceding reigns. The statutes being very numerous, and at the same time multifarious and short, it seems advisable, in discoursing upon them, to deviate from the method that has hitherto been observed; and, instead of treating this part of our subject chronologically, it will be, perhaps, more conducive to a thorough understanding of what was done by the legislature towards meliorating our jurisprudence, to digest the statutes, according to the object of them, into heads, and then speak upon them in that order which the history of each head may seem to require; so that, notwithstanding the course of time may be disregarded as to the whole, the several parts will be considered as nearly as can be in a historical way. The same method will be followed for the same reason, in all the subsequent reigns.

A very large portion of the statutes of this reign may be ranked under the title of regulations for the better administration of justice, both civil and criminal. The remainder, which cannot properly be classed under that head, are of so important a nature, as to deserve a separate consideration. Of this kind are the statutes that relate to the political condition of the king's dominions, or the executive authority of the crown; those relating to tenures, or to the clergy; the statutes of labourers, and the laws made for the protection of trade and commerce. We shall first take a view of the regulations made by these particular statutes, and then proceed to those relating to the administration of justice.

Of judicature in Ireland.

The principal act of a political kind is the *Ordinatio pro statu Hiberniæ*, 31 Ed. III. st. 4. This, like a statute of the same title enacted in the reign of Edward I.[1] was made for the correction of certain irregularities in the administration of justice in Ireland. It appears by this act, that Ireland was then furnished with courts of record corresponding, and bearing the same names with ours. The two superior tribunals of this kingdom, those of the *parliament* and of the *council*, seem to be imparted to that kingdom, or confirmed by the present statute. Matters of a

cases even of endowments, however, an ancient statute had provided a remedy for the founder or donor, or his heirs, in cases of cessation of the services. This was by writ, called a writ of *cessavit*, by which he could recover the lands, after a cessation of the services for two years; and in this reign there were cases of the writ being brought to recover lands held on condition of such services (45 *Edw. III.* 15). It is manifest that the foundations were now being laid of that vast system of private endowments for the perpetuation of religious exercises for the benefit of the souls of the donors, which was destroyed so suddenly in a subsequent age, but the destruction of which may have been more or less the result of causes of slow and gradual growth. It remains only to be mentioned that the statutes of labourers formed the basis of others in the reign of Elizabeth, which were the foundation of more modern legislation. This may suffice for a general review of the legal history of the reign.

[1] *Vide ante*, vol. i. c. viii.

more important and arduous kind, says the act, shall be agitated and determined, either in council *per peritos consiliarios nostros, ac prœlatos et magnates, et quosdum de discretioribus et probioribus hominibus* of the neighbourhood where the council happened to be held; or in parliament, *per ipsos consiliarios nostros, ac prœlatos et proceres, aliosque de terrâ prœdictâ*, according to the custom and law of the country.[1] It seems, at least from this mention of the council and parliament in regard to judicial matters, that the constituent members of each were not ascertained with any great exactness.

The remaining provisions of this act were of a very general nature, being chiefly to enforce such laws as had been made in the time of Edward I., and had been, or were now intended to be, engrafted on the Irish constitution; such as the statute of Winchester, those against maintenance, champerty, and other extortions and mal-practices of ministers belonging to courts;[2] and also some made in this reign, as those against purveyors, particularly stat. 4 Edw. III. c. iv.[3] In the same spirit which dictated some laws to restrain the too easy granting of pardons in England, it was directed, that the justiciary of Ireland should not grant pardons of offences but in, and with the assent of, the council and parliament; pardons were not to be general, but specifying the crime pardoned.[4] It was ordained, that the mayors and constables of staples should not hold any pleas but according to the statute of the staple (meaning the English statute);[5] nor should any pleas be held in the exchequer against the statute, that is, the stat. *Artic. super Chartas.*[6]

It seems the justiciary of Ireland used to go circuits twice a year, together with others who were associated with him on the occasion; these were held in every county. It was now directed, that he should once a year associate with himself a prelate and earl, the chancellor and treasurer, and some of the discreeter justices of the two benches, and barons of the exchequer; and make inquiry into the conduct of other judges, by the oaths of good and lawful men, as well clerks as knights, and certify to the king the result of such inquiry.[7]

These were the principal matters contained in this statute. Although this act refers to several English statutes with the same familiarity as if they were the law of Ireland, without enacting them, or taking notice how or when they were adopted there, yet it intimates that that country had customs peculiar to itself; for it directs that certain things should be ordered *secundum legem et consuetudinem terrœ nostrœ Hiberniœ.* Perhaps the usual way of introducing English statutes into Ireland, was to transmit them thither under the great seal, as they were sent into English counties to the sheriffs. Thus when the ordinance, of which we are now speaking, directs that felonies shall not be pardoned generally, but

[1] Ch. 2. [2] Ch. 3, 5, 10, 18. *Vide ante*, c. ix., x. [3] Ch. 4. [4] Ch. 6.
[5] Ch. 9. [6] Ch. 11. *Vide ante*, c. ix. [7] Ch. 17.

that the fact shall be specified, it goes on, *juxta tenorem cujusdam statuti per nos et consilium nostrum Angliæ editi, et missi ad Hiberniam observandi*,[1] alluding to a statute of this king, which will hereafter be mentioned.[2] We have before seen that the statute of Lincoln, 12 Edw. II. st. 1, was transmitted to Ireland to be enrolled in the chancery there, and to be sent to the different courts, and also into the several counties, to be observed the same as in England.[3] The whole business of legislation was, in these days, extremely arbitrary and irregular, as well in the manner of executing and enforcing statutes, as in that of making of them.

To return to English affairs. As Edward had assumed the title of France, some persons apprehended that should the two crowns hereafter unite upon one head, this, being the smaller, might be treated as the subject kingdom. To quiet these jealousies, the king caused it to be declared in parliament, by stat. 14 Edw. III. st. 5, that this kingdom should never be in subjection to him or his heirs, *as* kings of France; but this is one of those laws to which it has pleased Providence there should be no occasion to resort.

Some years after, towards the close of his reign, the king dealt less scrupulously with the crown and its prerogatives, by investing one of his subjects with a part of its royalties. We have seen that William the Conqueror, soon after he was settled, had given to the earl of Chester the royalty and prerogatives of a county palatine in Chester; the same princely franchise had for many years been enjoyed by the bishops of Durham in their bishopric.[4] In imitation of these, the king, in the twenty-fifth year of his reign, having promoted his favourite son John, who had married a daughter of the late Henry duke of Lancaster, to the title of duke of Lancaster, did in reward of his great services in the French war, confer on him the county of Lancaster, with the power of having a chancery, and writs issuing therefrom; the appointment of justices for all pleas, civil or criminal, with officers for the due execution of justice; *et quæcunq; alia, libertates et jura regalia ad comitatum palatinum pertinentia, adeo liberè et integrè, sicut Comes Cestriæ dignoscitur obtinere.* So distinguished an honour as this was conferred in open parliament.[5]

[1] Ch. 6.

[2] It may be remarked, that at this period, while laws were thus imposed on the Irish nation by the legislature of this country, and at the pleasure of the crown, that country had a parliament of its own.

[3] *Vide ante*, c. x.

[4] *Ibid.* vol. i. c. i.

[5] Tyrr. vol. iii., 567. We are told that "in the 36 Edw. III. the king in full parliament did gird his son John with a sword, and set on his head a cap of fur, and upon the same a circle of gold and pearls, and named him duke of Lancaster, and thereof gave to him and to his heirs-male of his body, and delivered him a charter. This was the third duke England ever saw. Again, in full parliament, anno 50 Edw. III., the king erected the county of Lancaster into a county Palatine, and honoured the duke of Lancsster therewith for term of his life." So says Lord Coke, 4 Inst. 204. The grant was thus: *Concessimus pro nobis et hæredibus nostris præfato filio nostro quod ipse ad totam vitam suam habeat infra comitatum Lancastriæ cancellariam suam, ac brevia sua sub sigillo suo pro officio cancellarii, deputando et constituendo justitiarios suos tam ad placita coronæ quàm ad quæcunq; alia placita communem legem tangentia, tenenda, ac cognitiones eorundem et quascunq; executiones per brevia sua, et ministros suos faciendas; et quæcunq; alia, libertates et jura regalia ad comitatum palatinum pertinentia, adeo liberè et integrè sicut Comes Cestriæ dignoscitur obtinere.*

The lords marchers on the confines of the principality of Wales exercised franchises somewhat similar to those of counts palatine.[1] To keep these barons under the sovereignty of the king, it was enacted by stat. 28 Edw. III. c. ii., that such lords and lordships should be attending and annexed to the crown of England, as they had been in all times past, and not to the principality of Wales, into whatsoever hands the principality might come. The dependence of these lords on the crown of England was extremely necessary towards the peace and quiet of the neighbouring counties.

In no time was there greater show of solicitude to secure the subject in the enjoyment of his rights and privileges than all through this reign. It was in this spirit that the stat. 4 Edw. III. c. xiv. was made, ordaining that a parliament should be held every year once, and more often if need be; which was renewed by stat. 36 Edw. III., st. 1, c. x. It was intended by the frequent and regular meeting of that assembly that resort might always be had thither for the correction of disorders, and the amendment of the law. The Great Charter and the Charter of the Forest being considered as the corner-stones of the English law and constitution, were confirmed over and over again. It seemed to be a matter of course all through this reign to prefix a confirmation of the Charters to every statute of any length or consequence. To these two Charters were sometimes added a confirmation of all franchises and privileges enjoyed by cities, boroughs, or individuals; and sometimes, though less frequently than in former times, a confirmation of the liberties of the church.[2] Not content with these general confirmations, particular parts of *Magna Charta*, which were esteemed more calculated for protecting the rights of the people, were specially re-enacted. It was declared by stat. 5 Edw. III. c. ix. (in conformity[3] with the express words almost of *Magna Charta*, c. xxix.), that no man should from thenceforth be attached on any accusation, nor forejudged of life or limb, nor his lands, tenements, goods, nor chattels, seized into the king's hands against the form of the Great Charter and the law of the land; and again, by stat. 28 Edw. III. c. iii., that no man, of what estate or condition soever, should be put out of his land or tenement, nor taken, nor imprisoned, nor disinherited, nor put to death, without being brought in to answer by due process of law.

The Charters.

Among other grievances provided against by the Great Charter, and also by statutes in this reign, was that of *purveyance*. Very early in this king's time some laws were made to regulate purveyors; and these were followed by several others, made in different parts of the reign. It was enacted that there should be no purveyance but for the house of the king and

Of purveyance.

[1] *Vide ante*, c. viii.

[2] Stat. 1 Ed. III., st. 2, c. 1, 9. Stat. 2 Ed. III., c. 1. Stat. 5 Ed. III., c. 1. Stat. 14 Ed. III., st. 1, c. 1. Stat. 31 Ed. III., st. 1, c. 1. Stat. 37 Ed. III., c. 1. Stat. 38 Ed. III., st. 1, c. 1. Stat. 42 Ed. III., c. 1. Stat. 50 Ed. III., c. 1, 2.

[3] *Vide ante*, vol. i. c. iv.

queen, and their children, which too was to be at a fair appraisement;[1] and it was made felony to take anything, by way of purveyance, without a lawful warrant.[2] Many other checks were imposed on purveyance. The commission of purveyors was to be under the great or privy seal, and none other;[3] they were not to take timber,[4] and the king's butler was not to take more wine than should be appointed.[5] Purveyances under twenty shillings were to be paid immediately, and those above that sum within a quarter of a year;[6] afterwards, it was directed that poultry and other small articles should be paid for with ready money, and all other things within a month or six weeks.[7] At length it was enacted that the *heinous name* of *purveyor* should be changed, and he should be named *buyer*; and accordingly, that statute all through speaks of it as of *buying and selling,* and calls them *buyers and sellers.* This statute confines such prerogative-*buying* to the house of the king and queen only; nor was it to be made but where there was plenty. The commissioners were to be people of sufficient estate, their commissions to be renewed half-yearly. All takings and buyings were to be for ready money only; and to take any otherwise than ordained by this act was made felony,[8] as we have seen it had been upon the former method of purveyance. There were likewise penalties inflicted on buyers, if they favoured some and charged others.[9] Commissions were to be awarded to inquire what things buyers had taken, and what they had delivered, and punishments inflicted for defaults either in taking or delivering.[10] Thus was the great oppression of purveyance gradually fined down to a more gentle form, till it amounted to little more than a pre-emption, or preference in favour of the king and queen's household.

Having considered such statutes as related to the political condition of the king's dominions, and the executive authority of the crown, we come now to the statutes that made any alteration in the law of tenure. We have seen how the law stood as to the alienation of the king's tenants *in capite*, by the statute *De prœrogativâ regis.*[11] Notwithstanding the sort of liberty there admitted to be in tenants *in capite*, these landholders could never safely alien without the king's licence; and if they did, the land used to be seized into the king's hand as forfeit, according to the rigour of the old law between lord and vassal. This was, however, now thought a severe penalty; and it was ordained by stat. 1 Ed. III., stat. 2, c. xii., that the king should not in such case hold the land as forfeit, but that in all cases of such alienation, he should have a reasonable fine in the chancery to be levied by due process. Thus forfeiture for alienation was wholly

Tenures.

[1] Stat. 4 Ed. III., c. 3. Stat. 34 Ed. III., c. 2.
[2] Ch. 4. St. 5 Ed. III., c. 2. St. 14 Ed. III., st. 1, c. 19.
[3] St. 25 Ed. III., st. 5, c. 1.
[4] Ch. 6.
[5] Ch. 21.
[6] Stat. 28 Ed. III., c. 12.
[7] Stat. 34 Ed. III., c. 3.
[8] Stat. 36 Ed. III., st. 1, c. 2.
[9] Ch. 3.
[10] Ch. 4, 5, 6.
[11] Viz., ch. 6. *Vide ante*, c. xi.

taken away, and in lieu thereof a fine was paid by the king's tenants as a matter of course, either before or after alienation. Some years after, in order to quiet property, a statute was made[1] to confirm all alienations of tenants *in capite*, made in the reign of Henry III. or before; saving to the king his prerogative, as to all that had been made in the time of Edward I., Edward II., and in the present reign. Because some lands holden of the king, as of an honour, had been seized for alienation, under pretence of their being tenancies *in capite*, contrary to *Magna Charta*, which had explained this matter,[2] it was declared by the same statute,[3] that no man should be aggrieved by reason of such purchases.

To qualify some of the king's feudal claims, it was declared, by stat. 25 Edw. III., st. 5, c. xi., that a reasonable aid, *pur faire fil chevalier*, and *pur file marier*, should be levied according to the statute,[4] and in no other way; that is, of every knight's fee held immediately of the king, twenty shillings, and of every twenty pounds of land holden immediately of the king in socage, twenty shillings and no more. The services of tenure were made a pretence for exacting more attendance than tenants were by law bound to perform. Such excesses made it necessary to declare, by stat. 25 Edw. III., st. 5, c. viii., that no man should be constrained to find men of arms, hoblers, nor archers, except they held by those services, and then by common assent and grant of parliament; so that even the common dues of tenure were no longer to be demanded, than when they were called forth by an act of parliament. These regulations strongly show that the feudal constitution had now ceased to answer the purposes of its first institution, and was hastening to the decay and neglect into which it soon after fell. In the time of Edward II. the ministers of that prince had compelled many to enter into obligations to be attendant on the king with arms and accoutrements; all which were declared void in the first year of this reign,[5] and ordered to be cancelled. To such expedients had they recourse, as substitutes for the ancient military policy, which was now found inadequate and useless.

Tenures were principally considered as a source of revenue to the crown; in that light they were as strictly kept up as ever, and became very often the occasion of great oppression. The ascertaining of the king's right, in these instances, depended on the escheators; and many statutes were made in this reign for the better ordering of that office, as well to secure the king in a due receipt of all his lawful casualties, as to protect the people against the malpractice of officers entrusted with so much power. It seems the number of escheators had been reduced to two; one to act on this side Trent, the other beyond it. But a statute was made to

[1] Stat. 34 Ed. III., c. 15.
[2] Viz., ch. 31. *Vide ante*, vol. i. c. iv.
[3] Stat. 1 Ed. III., st. 2, c. 12.
[4] Viz., Westm. 1, ch. 36. *Vide ante*, c. ix.
[5] Stat. 1 Ed. III., st. 2, c. 15.

increase the number to what they had been when the king first came to the throne; which number, however, is not mentioned by the act. It was further ordained, that those escheators should be chosen by the chancellor, treasurer, and chief baron of the exchequer, taking to them the chief justices of the two benches, if they were present, the same as in choosing sheriffs, which will be mentioned hereafter. No escheator was to continue in his office above a year.[1] Escheators were not to do waste in lands belonging to the king's heirs, but were to return the writ of *diem clausit extremum*, with a true extent, into the chancery forthwith; and if the next friends of the heir pleased, they might have the lands in farm till the heir's age, yielding the value to the king, by agreement with the chancellor and treasurer. The heirs, when they came of age, were to have an action of waste against such guardians and farmers.[2] Escheators were to be anwerable to the king for the value of the forms of the mills and other profits belonging to the king's heirs, in proportion to the time they were in the king's hands:[3] they were to take the inquests by good people and lawful, of sufficient inheritance and good fame, and of the same county where the inquiry should be; and the inquests so taken were to be indented between the escheators and the jurors; if not, they were to be void: the inquests were also to be taken in good towns, openly, and not privately[4] (*a*). Wherever lands were

(*a*) Thus, if an escheator took goods of a man supposing him to be an outlaw, and they were the goods of a stranger, the stranger could bring trespass, and proving his property before a jury, recover damages; but if the escheator took an office (*i.e.*, an inquisition *virtute officii*), and the goods were found to be those of the outlaw, then the owner could not have an action of trespass against the escheator, though he might *traverse* the inquisition, and they would not be without remedy, for, on proving his property, he would recover the goods, though he could not recover damages against the escheator for taking them, as he took them under due course of law (*Year-book*, 34 *Hen. VI.*, 12). The mere conviction for felony, although it involved a forfeiture, did not determine what lands were actually forfeited. And on the principle that there could be no estoppel against one who was not a party even where the king had been duly entitled by an inquisition of office after an attaint for felony, although the conviction for felony was conclusive against all the world; yet, as there had been no binding determination of the *status* or title to the *land*, before the king could take it there must be a writ of *scire facias* against the person *in possession* of it, to give him notice of the claim, and opportunity of showing cause against it, and he might set up title paramount to that of the felon, though he could not dispute the forfeiture by the felony. Where the king is entitled by office, providing H. S. was seised in fee and leased for life to J. H., and was afterwards attainted of felony, and J. H. was dead, but some one else was in possession, and thereon *scire facias* issued against that party, he could come forward and show that the felon had *not* the estate in fee, but another through whom he derived title (40 *Assize*, 24). He could not, however, controvert the felony or forfeiture, and must show what the felon's title really was, and could not put the crown to prove it, *scire facias* being the remedy against strangers to a record, not legal privies (*Year-book*, 21 *Hen. VII.*, 18). The principle, it will be seen, was the same as between subject and subject. So *scire facias* on forfeiture by felony might issue against the lords, mediate or immediate (9 *Edw. IV.*, 24). So, on a false presentment before forest justices allowing a false claim, the party interested might traverse it in the court of king's bench, and have a *scire facias* against the party who had made the false claim, to come in and support it if

[1] Stat. 14 Ed. III., st. 1, c. 8.
[2] Ch. 13.
[3] Stat. 28 Ed. III., c. 4.
[4] Stat. 34 Ed. III., c. 13.

seized into the king's hands by office of the escheator, on account of alienation without licence, or the tenant *in capite* dying and leaving his heir within age, it was returned into chancery; and if the tenant would *traverse the office* so taken by the king's command, and say that the lands were not seizable, he was to be received so to do, and process was to be sent into the king's bench to try it according to law [1] (*a*).

he could (*Year-book*, 21 *Edw. III.*, fol. 48). So if on statute-merchant the conusor was dead, the conusee had *scire facias* against the heir and the parties in possession of the land (*Year-book*, 2 *Rich. III.*, 8). On this principle the writ of *scire facias* went to strangers to the record, and provides to record recoveries, &c., for *scire facias* lies on matter of record, &c. (27 *Hen. VI.*, 7; 3 *Hen. VI.*, 35). The inquisition itself might sometimes suffice to vest the title in the crown, but sometimes *scire facias* would be necessary. The principle was, that where a common person could lawfully have entered without bringing suit to recover the land, then the king, after inquisition, might do so without a *scire facias*. But where a common person by his title could not enter without suit or action, then, though the matter of fact had been found for the king by inquisition, he had not thereby in law possession, but must have *scire facias* against the party in possession of the land, to give him the opportunity of defence. The principle was the same, whether between the crown and a subject, or between subjects in this respect. "Office found," as it was called,—that is, the finding upon an inquisition taken as to any claim or right of the crown of the character of forfeiture,—was, it may be readily conceived, a matter of great and constant importance in those times, and there were numerous cases upon it. The courts went strongly in favour of the crown. Office being found for the king, and afterwards, as was suggested, by "false surmise" being found in favour of the party, it was nevertheless held that this did not *discharge* the office found for the king, for it *is only* an inquest of office. And inquest of office found for a subject does not bind any one (*ne lœra ascun party*), for it is no more than *evidence*; but an inquest of office found for the king shall bind until it is traversed (*Year-book*, 21 *Edw. III.*, 1). So a false presentment taken before forest justices, finding a title in a party, might be traversed by any one interested, and *scire facias* went to the party to come in and support it if he could (*Year-book*, 21 *Edw. III.*, 48). Inquests found, it was held, was only matter of fact, not of record (*Year-book*, 3 *Hen. VII.*, 1). It was thus a general principle that, although an inquisition found for the king should bind all the world until reversed by a fresh finding, it might be traversed and reversed by any one who had an interest; and that an inquisition found for the *subject* should *bind no one*, for, as it was not *between party and party*, it was merely evidence; and thus, on the other hand, to reverse an office so found, there must be notice to the party to come in and support it (*Year-book*, 21 *Edw.*, *III.*, 48).

(*a*) By 8 Hen. VI., c. xvi., it is provided that escheators shall take no inquest but by such persons as be returned by the sheriff, and that no land seised on any inquest be let by the king until the inquests are returned, and that, within a month, the party grieved may traverse the inquest (36 *Edw. III.*, st. 1); and that escheators shall return the inquests within a month. Then the 18 Hen. VI., c. iv., enacts that no lands shall be granted until the king's title be found by inquisition; and 23 Hen. VI., c. xvi., provides that inquests of office should be taken openly and publicly, and that inquests of office taken should be traversed. In the reign of Henry VI. the abuses of escheators gained a great height, and a statute of 1 Henry VIII. passed to afford a further remedy. Where the king is entitled by double matter of record, as by attainder for felony and by office (*i.e.*, inquisition by virtue of office), the party grieved shall not traverse, but petition; but where the king is *entitled* (only) by the office, then the party may traverse (*Year-book*, 4 *Edw. IV.*, 21). That is, where the king is in legal possession by the inquisition, without further suit the party must traverse in chancery (as in case of commons), but otherwise in the suit which the king has to bring upon the inquisition (*Year-book*, 14 *Hen. VII.*, 22; 15 *Hen. VII.*, 6). Thus, on a traverse of the office in chancery it was at common law sent to the king's bench to be tried; but office, *virtute officii*, always went to the exchequer, and thence to chancery, and thence to king's bench (4 *Edw. IV.*, 21; 14 *Edw. IV.*,

[1] Stat. 34 Ed. III. c. 14.

At length it was ordained more fully by stat. 36 Ed. III., st 1, c. xiii., that land seized into the king's hands because of ward should be kept without waste; that the escheator should have no fee of wood, fish, venison, or other thing; but should answer yearly to the king for the issues and profits; and if he did otherwise, and was attainted thereof, he was to be ransomed at the king's will, and yield to the heir treble damages: the same was to be in all cases of lands seized into the king's hands by office taken before escheators. The escheator was to send the inquest, within a month, into the chancery, and a writ was to be delivered to him to certify the cause of seisin; and then any party might be heard to traverse the office, and show his right, as directed by the above act; only there is added by the present statute the pain of two years' imprisonment in case the escheator acted otherwise. By stat. 42 Edw. III., c. v., no person was to be escheator unless he had £20 at least of lands in fee, and discharged his office in person. There was great complaint that escheators, sheriffs, and other officers of the king, seized the lands, goods, and chattels of many, surmising that they were outlawed; which was often grounded upon a person having the same name with the person meant in the writ, who was not sufficiently distinguished by an addition, or particular description. To prevent the oppression consequent upon such mistakes, it was ordained, by stat. 38 Edw. III., c. ii., that persons so injured should have a writ of *idemptitate nominis*, a writ that was in use before this act, but of which we have not yet had occasion to say anything. Besides that, the following course of redress was now directed. The party whose land or goods were seized was to find surety before the officer who had the warrant of seizure, to answer for the value to the king; and this was to be done without any fee, on pain of double damages to the party grieved, and being heavily punished at the king's suit. Thus, in one instance, was a very summary method devised for those who were injured by these officers.

Several statutes were made in this reign to settle such claims of the clergy as still remained exposed to the jealousy of the temporal power, and were not secured by any parliamentary provision. The great subject of discussion between the

Of the clergy.

1, 7). There could be no traverse after a conviction for felony, for it could not be reversed (7 *Edw. IV.*, 1, 2). But if there had not been a conviction for felony, the finding on the inquisition gave the king no title though it found the felony, for that could not be determined save on indictment to which the accused should be party (8 *Hen. IV.*, 21). It was always a fundamental principle that no one was concluded by a proceeding to which he was not a party. Hence, in inquisitions by officers of the crown, either by writ out of chancery, or merely by virtue of their office, as in many inquisitions by the sheriff, they not being *inter-partes*, but only to inquire, and no one but the officers being a party to the inquiry, it follows that no one is concluded by the verdict, and any one interested may "traverse" or dispute it, and where the title rests on the inquisition, and inquisition is traversable, the title of course is traversable; but where the title is already on record, and is irreversible, as in the case of a conviction for felony, then the verdict is not traversable.

spiritual and temporal authority had hitherto been upon the jurisdiction of causes, and the personal exemption of clerks from the secular courts. This dispute had been so adjusted by the statutes of *Circumspectè agatis*, and of *Articuli cleri*, in the two last reigns,[1] that no further clamour was kept up on that head. Some points, however, respecting the property of the church, called for regulation; others that had been lately occasioned through the ambition and avarice of the pope, created new apprehensions, and became fresh subjects of discontent in this and the next reign. It was endeavoured to restrain these new usurpations by the statutes of *provisors*. These, and the other statutes relating to the clergy, exhibit the clerical state in a new point of view, and are well deserving attention. We shall, therefore, take a view of them in the order in which they were made.

The first statute on the subject of ecclesiastics and ecclesiastical property, is stat. 1 Edw. III. st. 1, c. x., by which the king binds himself not to demand of bishops and religious houses any pensions, prebends, churches, and corodies for persons, but in cases where he in conscience might do it. The next are stat. 4 Edw. III. c. vi. and stat. 5 Edw. III. c. iii., both confirming the statute of Carlisle, 35 Edw. I. st. 1:[2] then follows stat. 14 Edw. III. st. 4, which was occasioned, as the act says, by many oppressions and grievances done in divers manners by the king's servants to people of holy church. To prevent these in future, it was enacted, in the first place, that the king's purveyors should take nothing within the fees of holy church against the will of the owners.[3] The other provisions of this act relate to the temporalities of bishops. As the law now stood, the exception of plenarty, in a writ for recovery of a presentation, was never allowed against the king, because he was not within the stat. Westm. 2, c. v.,[4] and was, besides, protected by the old maxim, *nullum tempus occurrit regi*. It often followed from this, that persons were turned out of their benefices after long possession, by reason of the temporalities of bishops and advowsons of infants coming into the king's hands. To remedy this in future, it was ordained that the king, in such cases, should not make collation or presentment after three years from the avoidance; nor should any one, after such time, be bound to answer to the king in a *quare impedit*:[5] and further, the king declared that he would not seize into his hands the temporalities of bishops, abbots, priors, or other people of holy church, without just cause, according to and by judgment of law.[6]

Because the king's escheators and other keepers of temporalities had been used to commit great waste, it was ordained, that such persons should do no waste or destruction; they should sell no underwood, nor hunt or fish thereon, nor rack the tenants: and in order to put the custody of temporalities into safer hands than those

[1] *Vide ante*, c. x.
[2] *Ibid.* c. ix.
[3] Ch. 1.
[4] *Vide ante*, c. ix.
[5] Ch. 2.
[6] Ch. 3.

of the king's officers, they were to be offered to the dean and chapter, to whom they were to be demised by the chancellor and treasurer at a reasonable rate, according to the remembrances in the exchequer; so that escheators should have no right to intermeddle therein; saving, however; to the king all knight's fees, advowsons of churches, escheats, wards, marriages, reliefs, and services of the fees.[1] The letting such lands to the dean and chapter was founded upon the same policy as that before mentioned, of letting the lands[2] to the next friends of the heir; these persons having a sort of interest in the lands, at least such a relation to them as was likely to restrain them from committing destruction or waste thereon.

Another statute was made for the better ordering of clerical property, entitled, *A statute for the clergy*, stat. 18 Edw. st. 3. One provision of this was to secure the execution of the statutes of mortmain passed in the time of Edward I.[3] If prelates, says the act, clerks beneficed, or religious people, who have purchased lands in mortmain, were impeached thereof before justices, and they showed the king's charter of licence and process thereupon made by an inquest of *ad quod damnum*,[4] or the king's grace, or by fine, they should be left in peace, without any further disturbance: and if it should not appear that they entered by licence, they should be received to make a convenient fine for the same, and so the matter should cease.[5]

The following provisions relate to matters of jurisdiction. Besides the grant, that an archbishop should not be impeached criminally before the king's justices, and what related to the trial of bastardy[6] (both which will be mentioned in another place), it was declared, that no prohibition should be awarded out of the chancery but where the king had cognizance.[7] And because commissions had of late been given to justices to inquire into the conduct of ecclesiastical judges, whether they made just or excessive process in causes testamentary, and others that notoriously belonged to the church, upon which commissions many spiritual judges had been indicted; it was now enacted, that such commissions should be repealed, and no others should be granted, except only of such articles as used to be in the eyre.

Scire facias for tithes.

It was a common process to institute an inquiry about tithes by a *scire facias* against some ecclesiastical person, warning him to answer in the chancery concerning his tithes, and there show cause wherefore the tithes in question should not be restored to the demandant; which *scire facias* was as well for the king as the party. It was enacted, that such writs should no longer be brought.[8]

In the 25th year of the king there was another statute for the clergy, better known by the title of *Statutum de clero*, 25 Edw. III. st. 3. By the first chapter of this act, the king gave up all right

[1] Ch. 4, 5. [2] *Vide ante*, c. xi. [3] *Ibid.* c. ix. [4] *Ibid.* c. x. [5] Ch. 3. [6] Ch. 1, 2. [7] Ch. 5. [8] Ch. 7.

to presentations that belonged to his ancestors in right of any other person. But having made this renunciation of right to enforce old claims, it was, in return, thought proper that the limitation which had been set by stat. 14 Edw. III. st. 4, c. ii., to his presentations,[1] should be repealed; and so it was by chap. ii. of this act. Because the king sometimes made presentations upon untrue suggestions of clerks, where he had no right, it was ordained, that if at any time before judgment, it should appear upon examination that he had no right, the presentation should be instantly repealed, and the other party have all proper writs out of chancery to reinstate him in his rights.[2] Again, after a lapse to the bishop, a judgment would sometimes be obtained by the king, through the collusion of the patron, in order to defraud the bishop of his right of presentation by lapse; and it was not the usage to admit the bishop or his clerk to defend the right, and counterplead the king's title. To remedy this, it was enacted, that where bishops so presented, and then the king presented and brought his action against the patron, who suffered the king to recover without trying the right; in such case, the bishop should be received to counterplead the king's title, although he claimed nothing in the patronage.[3] Because the ecclesiastical cognizance of avoidance of livings had been lately encroached upon by the secular justices, it was declared, that the said justices should receive challenges in favour of the clerical jurisdiction, when made by any bishop.[4]

That bishops might not be brought into the danger of having their temporalties seized into the king's hands, so often as they had been, for contempts, in not obeying writs of *quare non admisit*,[5] it was ordained, that the justices might receive a reasonable fine, according to the degree of the contempt, in lieu of such forfeiture.[6] The remaining provisions of the statute *de clero*, concerning privilege of clergy and indictments, belong to another part of this work.

We have seen the jealousy entertained in the reign of Edward I. of foreign ecclesiastics, who were trying all means of draining church-property out of the kingdom: this was checked in some degree by the statute *De asportatis religiosorum*, made at Carlisle.[7] At the time of that act, another method than that aimed at by the act, of conveying the riches of the church into the hands of foreigners, had grown into practice. The persons acting in this new device were called *provisors*: but though the parliament were then apprised of this new encroachment, no special regulation was made to restrain it, and it was left merely with the judgment of the legislature against it[8] (*a*). Since that time this

Of provisors.

(*a*) There had arisen the most entire opposition between the views taken of presentation to the cure of souls—by the church, and by the secular law. The view of

[1] *Vide ante*, c. xi. [2] Ch. 3. [3] Ch. 7. [4] Ch. 8.
[5] *Vide ante*, vol. i. c. viii. [6] Ch. 6. [7] *Vide ante*, 157, 376.
[8] For the description of provisors, *vide* post, the preamble to the stat. of provisors.

evil had grown to such a height, and so exasperated were the nation, that in the first year of this king's reign there was a petition from the commons, praying that no alien *provisor*, nor any procurator for him, should come into the land, or go out of the realm or

the church was, that although it was endowed it was not the less spiritual; the view of the secular law was, that because it was endowed it was temporal. There was at the Council of Lyons a papal constitution declaring *quod collatio beneficii est res spiritualis*, and it was so, as we have seen, by the Saxon laws (*vide ante*, c. i.); but the temporal law had held otherwise since the time of Henry II., and so it is laid down in the books of our common law since that era (*Britton*, fol. 225; *Fleta*, lib. ii. c. xxxii.; *Bracton*, lib. iv. fol. 247). That being so, remedies were provided in the courts of law to recover or protect their rights of presentation. Under the head "De Droit de Roy," in Britton, there is this:—"Et quant a nos fees soit enquis de esglises, cathedrales, parochiales et religious, et de mesons de religion, et de hospitals en cel counte quex sount de nostre avowson, et quex deyvent estre et ne sount mie; et par quex ils ount este sustretz et coment, et quex demeynes nous tenons en nostre meyn en cel counte, &c. Et ausi des fees, et de avowsons de esglises," &c. (fol. 28). The assize of De dareyn presentment was the remedy to try the right of possession of the advowson of a church, which would lie in him who had last presented to it (fol. 222); or, in other cases, there was the writ of *quare impedit*, in which the right would be decided in the king's court, and the writ of prohibition would go to the bishop to prevent him from interfering to obstruct its judgment (fol. 234). And thus the king's courts had the determination of such questions entirely in their own power. And so Bracton had laid it down that prohibition would issue even against a a papal delegate, to prevent him from interfering in the right to an advowson or presentation (lib. v. fol. 400–410). Thus, after treating of prohibition to the bishop in such cases, he proceeds:—"Si autem delegatam ut si delegati fuerunt a Domino Papa, tunc sic prohibemus vobis, ne teneatis placitum in curia Christianitatis auctoritate literarum Domini Papæ, de advocatio ecclesiæ," &c. (fol. 402, lib. v. c. iii.) And, of course, *à multo fortiori*, such prohibition lay in cases where the king's right of presentation was concerned. "Est et aliud genus prohibitionis cum ipse Rex presentaverit clericum et episcopus vel prior substitutus, veniat contra presentationem Regis" (fol. 414). This followed necessarily from the doctrine of the common law, that an advowson or right of presentation to a benefice being a thing of temporal value, was therefore of secular cognizance. But by the law or custom of the church the pope had power of presentation by way of provision, in certain cases, and this often interfered with the right of presentation, either of the king or of a private patron, and excited great discontent, especially when the papal presentees were foreigners, as frequently happened. The contemporary chronicles showed that this had caused a vast degree of excitement in the previous reigns on the part of private patrons, whose patronage was thus interfered with; and there were constant struggles between the crown and the see of Rome as regards the appointments to the episcopate. Now, it might naturally occur to any one that if, indeed, these "provisions" by the see of Rome were really contrary to law, they would be entirely ineffective, and the patrons would have an easy remedy by assize of last presentment, or by *quare impedit*, and the courts could summarily interpose by writ of prohibition. And therefore these papal provisions would practically be no interference with the right of presentation, and would simply be disregarded as idle and illegal pretensions. And certainly there could not possibly be any necessity for any new legislation against them. The difficulty, however, in that view in theory would be, that the Roman Catholic church was not only recognised, but established by the law of the land, and that those papal provisions were in accordance with the law or custom of that church. And, practically, it is plain that the law of the land did not regard these provisions as illegal and invalid, or the courts would simply disregard them and set them at naught, and there would have been no necessity for legislation on the subject at all. And it is remarkable that although Bracton is very copious upon the subject of prohibitions in ecclesiastical cases, there is no instance given of a prohibition in the case of a papal provision. The conclusion is, that the papal provisions were legal; and that for that reason there was a necessity for legislation to protect the rights of patrons. The very name and terms of the proceedings under the statutes showed that the papal provisions could be no offence against the temporal law. Thus an attachment upon a prohibition was brought by the king and incumbent, for that the king had presented

the king's power, in order to prosecute any *provision*, under pain of life and member; but the further consideration of this matter was adjourned till the king should come of age[1] (*a*). We find nothing done on this subject by the legislature till the 25th year of

him to a benefice, and that the defendant brought bulls of Rome in disturbance of it (en disturbance de ceo); but if the only "disturbance" was in bringing a bull which had no legal effect, it is difficult to see how it could be in a legal sense a "disturbance." If, indeed, it was endeavoured to enforce the papal bull by excommunication and citation into the ecclesiastical court, it might be otherwise; but then, assuming the papal provisions to have been illegal, this "disturbance" would have been equally illegal at common law; but no cases of prosecutions for them can be found before the statutes. Even after all the statutes of provisors there were not wanting authorities to show that papal provisions, apart from the terms of the statutes, were legal. Thus in a case in the reign of Henry IV., it was held that the presentee of the king should not oust the other without suit, and that he had a provision of the pope, and pardon and licence of the king to put it in use, and had possession until it was ousted by the defendant, and he said that he had possession by the presentment of the king before the plaintiff had possession by the provision, and that was held to be a good issue, for (says Brooke, in abridging the case) "to this day, if a benefice is void, and the pope shall make provision before the patron has presented, the provisee shall have it," although the king was patron (*Year-Book*, 8 *Henry IV.* 21); and though he adds that "it was permitted for a long time by usurpation, until the time of Henry VIII.," there was no usurpation allowed to the papacy in that age.

(*a*) To enable the reader to understand this subject, it may be well to cite some cases from the Year-books in the reign *previous* to the statutes of provisors, in order to see the grounds on which they were supposed to rest. These cases show that the crown or the lay patrons could claim nothing but patronage, and in virtue of endowment. In the seventh year of the reign, *in quare impedit* it was pleaded that William the Conqueror had granted the church to be annexed to a prebend, and so "appropriate." Herle, J., said, "How show you the appropriation?" Parnell (counsel) said, "At that time the law was, that the king could give a church to hold to the granter's own use." Herle, J., "If the law was so then, I know it is not so now." Parnell urged, "The charter gives the church, and does not say advowson." But Herle, J., answered, "That when a man would grant the advowson he would use the word 'church;'" and added, "The king has granted—as far as in him lay—that you should have the church to your own use; but it does not follow that you do so hold." And another of the judges said, "The king by his grant could not appropriate the church." Parnell urged, "In ancient times, before a new constitution of the pope, the patron of a church could grant tithes in his parish to another parish;" but the court did not alter its view (*Year-book*, 7 *Edw. III.*, 3–8). And the case appears to show that the king and other lay patrons had only right of presentation, and by virtue of endowment, and had not an absolute right even over the endowment; and further, that the papal authority was recognised by the law, and in the king's courts, upon this very subject, and even as to the temporalities, to prevent their alienation. Other cases lead to the same conclusion, and the general principle, it will be observed, applied equally, as regarded the crown, to bishoprics as to other benefices of which the crown might be patron. In the tenth year of this reign there was a case of the bishop of Norwich—relating to the right of patronage belonging to a bishopric; it was said that the bishopric was a thing spiritual, which could not come to the king, though the temporalities of the see might, and that the king could not as pope give the bishopric, including the spiritualities; and one of the judges said, "The spirituality without the temporality can be a bishopric; but if the temporality be joined to the spirituality, the pope cannot give the temporalities, except at the will of the king. The temporalities, however, may remain in the hands of the king, and yet a bishop can be created" (*Year-book*, 10 *Edw. III.*). And Lord Coke cites this case to show that though the possessions of a see are taken away, it may remain a bishopric. The distinction drawn is clearly defined between the spirituality over which the pope had power, and the temporality over which, and over which alone, the king or lay patron had power, and only power of presentation. So in the seven-

[1] Parl. Rot. 1 Edw. III., 26.

the king, when complaint was again made of those "who purchase in the court of Rome *provisions* to have abbeys and priories in England, in destruction of the realm and of holy religion." To remedy this it was then enacted, by a chapter at the latter end of the statute of purveyors, stat. 25 Edw. III. st. 5, c. xxii., that whoever purchased such provisions of abbeys or priories, both himself, his executors, and procurators, who sued and put in execution such provisions, should be out of the king's protection, and be treated as the king's enemies; and all persons who did any wrong to the persons or property of such provisors, were to be liable to no action for the same.

In this manner did the parliament begin with these ecclesiastical offenders: but it did not stop here; for in the same year a special act was made, entitled, *A statute of provisors of benefices*, 25 Edward III., st. 6, and again, in the very next parliament, there was another statute of *provisors* (*a*), 27 Edward III., st. 1.

teenth year of the reign, in a case relating to the deanery of York, claimed by the king against the archbishop, it was said by one of the judges that the king was sovereign patron of the bishopric, and in ancient times the king gave the bishopric; and though now he gives leave to the chapter to elect, yet the patronage remains in him, and as he finds the thing vacant the presentment is for him, and that the archbishop had the right of examination, &c. (*Year-book*, 17 *Edw. III.*). These cases, and several similar, were before the statute now in question, and their result appears to be this, that the law recognised the right of the pope to confer the spirituality, that is, the spiritual office; but of the king or the lay patron to confer the temporalities. And the precedents were according to this view of the law, and the popes had been in the habit of appointing to bishoprics, with a request to the crown to confer the temporalities, and to present to other benefices, by provision, as it was called; and instances as to bishoprics will be found in Wharton's *Anglia Sacra*, and as to other benefices, the king himself had recognised the practice, and had obtained papal presentations for their own chaplains (*Rym. Fœd.* ii. 551, fol. 82). At the same time there was a disposition to press the claim of the crown, by virtue of the temporalities, to confer the bishoprics; and of the lay patrons in like manner to confer the benefice. And it was now sought to uphold this claim of the crown and lay patrons by means of legislation, which, however, it will be seen, clearly implied that it was an alteration of the law. In 1343, however, attempts were made to prevent the exercise of this right, which, it was plainly implied, was legal, as otherwise it could have been resisted in the king's courts. An act was passed forbidding, under the pain of forfeiture, any person to bring into the realm, or receive, or execute any provisions or reservations which should be contrary to the rights of the king or his subjects (*i.e.*, their rights of patronage or presentation), and ordering that such documents might be seized, and that provisors or others who, in consequence of them, should institute actions against the patrons of benefices or their presentees, should be brought before the king to receive judgment (*Rot. Parl.* ii. 144). This act, it will be observed, implies most plainly that these papal provisions were legal, or otherwise they would have been held null and void in the king's courts upon writs of *quare impedit*, and hence the necessity for these enactments.

(*a*) These statutes were of great importance with reference to the control of the crown over the elections of bishops and deans. The charter of king John granted to the church freedom of election, not *de novo*, or as a concession of a new right, but as a confirmation of an ancient right. The precise terms are as follow: "Ut de cætero in universis et singulis ecclesiis et monasteriis, cathedralibus, et conventualibus, totius regni nostri Angliæ, liberæ sint imperpetuum electiones quorumcunque prælatorum majorum et minorum salvâ nobis et hæredibus nostris custodia ecclesiarum, et monasteriorum vacantum, quæ ad nos pertinent. Promittimus etiam quod non impediemus nec impediri permittemus vel faciemus per nostros, nec procurabimus, quin in singulis, et universis ecclesiis, et monasteriis memoratis, postquam vocaverunt prælaturæ, quemcunque voluerint libere sibi præficiant electores

These two are the statutes of provisors mostly referred to on this subject, and prescribe the whole method of proceeding against such offenders, and others of the like sort.

The first of these statutes opens with a long preamble setting forth the grounds upon which such restrictions were to be justified, and the present necessity there was for making them. This preamble, together with the enacting part of the statute, gives a perfect idea what *provision* and *provisors* were; for which reason we shall state the substance of it, preferring this to any other account of these two words that might be extracted from writers of a later date, however learned or accurate; this being the method that has been adhered to through the whole of this History, to pursue the language of our statutes and law-books as the best guides in matters wholly of a legal nature, without recurring to the aid of modern writers, except on some very few and very particular occasions.

The preamble recites, that it had been shown to the parliament

pastorem petita tamen *prius* a nobis et hæredibus nostris licentia eligendi, quam non negabimus nec differemus; et si forte (quod obsit) denegaremus vel differemus, procedant nihilominus electores ad electionem, canonicam faciendam, et similiter post celebratam electionem noster requiratur *assensus*, quam non denegabimus, nisi aliquid rationabile proposuerimus, et legitime probaverimus, propter, quod non debeamus consentire." It was afterwards said that, prior to the charter, the bishoprics were mere donatives of the crown, which, however, is directly opposed to the language of the previous charters. No doubt the statutes of provisors of benefices and the statutes of *præmunire*, went a long way towards establishing the pretensions set up by the crown in the time of Henry II., and contained the whole principle of the royal supremacy. With regard to the deaneries, they were all (except the last, that of Exeter) founded prior to the Great Charter, which granted to chapters that they should have the election. "Quorumcunque prælatorum majorum et minorum;" and the charter to Exeter, in accordance with the Great Charter, granted "Ut in Exoniensi ecclesia temporibus nostris et in perpetuum canonice a capitulo et de capitulo unus de canonicis eligatur decanus et solempniter instituatur;" and this was stated to have been, "ad imitationem aliarum cathedralium, ecclesiarum ordinatarum." The statutes of provisors (25 Edward III. s. 3) and of *præmunire* (Edward III. & Rich. II.) went a long way towards establishing the claims set up by the crown to the absolute appointment of bishops and of deans, although the statute 25 Edward III. st. 6, in theory and in terms, directed that the election of archbishops, bishops, and all other dignities, &c. shall hold from henceforth, in the same manner as they were granted by the king's progenitors and the ancestors of other lords, founders of the said dignities; but the *subsequent* statutes of *præmunire* still secured to the sovereign all the real practical power of excluding the interposition of the see of Rome in protection of freedom of election. In the reign of Edward III. a case occurred as to the right of the crown to control the elections of deans. It was a case of *quare impedit* by the crown with regard to the deanery of York; and the dean pleaded the right of the chapter to elect to the deanery, freely and without the leave or licence of the crown (17 *Edward III.*, c. xl. fol. 17). The case is cited, with others in the abridgments, as proving that *quare impedit* lies of a deanery by the king, although it be elective by others; and cases are collected, whence it appears that the remedy was given to the person who had the nomination, although he had not the presentment (18 *Edward III.*, f. 15; *Bro. Abr.*, *Quare impedit*; Fitz. *Nat. Brev.*, *Quare impedit*, 32). On the whole, the practical effect of these statutes was to give the crown the control over the elections of bishops and deans whenever it chose to assert the power. Lord Coke professed to consider that the right of the crown with respect to the ancient deaneries, was the same as with respect to the bishoprics; and he stated that in the old deaneries the election was by the chapter, under a *congè d'èlire* from the crown; and Mr Hargreaves follows that view in his note to the passage (*Co. Litt.*, 95). He appears to have supposed that the right of free election of prelates was conferred or created, for the first time, by the charter of John, and that the passage in

of Carlisle, 35 Edw. I., that the Church of England was founded by the kings and nobles of the realm, for their instruction and that of the people, and also for keeping up hospitality, and alms, and other works of charity in places where churches were founded; for which purposes, sees and rents to a great amount had been appropriated by the said founders to the prelates and other beneficed persons, from which resulted that right of collation and presentation claimed by the king and his nobles; and that the higher orders of such clergy constituted a considerable part of the king's great council, to advise him in national affairs. This being the nature and condition of the national church establishment, it was considered as a great grievance that the bishop of Rome, *accroaching* to himself the seigniories of such possessions and benefices, did grant the same benefices to aliens, who never dwelt in England; to cardinals, who, by the rule of their order, never could dwell here; and to others, as well aliens as denizens, as if he was patron, and had the advowson of such dignities and benefices, contrary to the known law of the kingdom; so that, in a short time, if the bishop of Rome went on in that manner, there would scarcely be a benefice in the realm that would not be in the hands of aliens or denizens by virtue of such *provisions*, without the concurrence, and against the will, of the founders and patrons of the advowsons, to the entire destruotion of all the purposes for which such ecclesiastical establishments were made. It was therefore at that time adjudged, in full parliament, that such oppressions should not be suffered. The preamble of the statute goes on

the charter, "*prælatorum minorum*," referred to the deans; but in both these views he appears to have been in error, for beyond a doubt, as is shown by the *Leges Henrici Primi* and the earlier charters, wherein it plainly appears, that free election was the ancient right of the church, which had been infringed upon by the Norman sovereigns, and was restored and confirmed to it by the Great Charter; and moreover, the term "*minor prelates*," would appear to have referred rather to abbots than deans—*i.e.*, to abbots not mitred. At all events, there can be no doubt that, throughout this and the following reigns, elections to bishoprics and deaneries went on as ordinarily, in canonical form, and that questions which arose thereon were referred to Rome, by way of appeal. On election of a bishop by the archbishop, confirmation was required; and if it was refused for any cause, the validity of that cause was referred to the pope, just as, on rejection of a priest presented to a bishop, the matter went to the archbishop and the pope by appeal. In such cases, it is obvious, the matter was purely spiritual in its nature; and before these statutes and afterwards, they equally went to Rome by appeal. Numerous instances will be found in Wharton's *Anglia Sacra*. As the statutes were directed only against matters *not* spiritual, not properly referrable to Rome by appeal, there was nothing in them to interfere with such appeals as related to matters purely spiritual. That appeal lay to Rome on matters spiritual is shown by these very statutes themselves, which purported to restrain appeals upon matters not purely spiritual, but rather ecclesiastical, and relating to matters mixed with temporalities, or on which the canon law contravened statute or common law—as, for instance, with reference to marriage and legitimacy; as to which, under the canon law, marriage legitimated the issue already born, whereas, by the statute of Merton, the contrary was declared to be law; and hence, in the reign of Henry III., the king prohibited an appeal to Rome in a case where the archbishop had been required to certify the legitimacy of the plaintiff in an assize of mort d'ancestor (*Rot. Chan.*, p. 629; 8 *Henry III.*). The reason was, that the legitimacy might depend on the effect of marriage; and on that ground the canon law and the common law were at variance; and the title to

and recites, that in the present parliament, 25 Edw. III., a further complaint was made on the subject, namely, that the above-mentioned mischiefs daily increased more than ever, and that now of late the bishop of Rome (*a*), by procurement of clerks and otherwise, had *reserved*, and did daily reserve, to his collation, generally and specially, as well archbishoprics, bishoprics, abbeys, and priories, as all other dignities and other benefices of England, which were of the advowson of people of holy church, and give the same as well to aliens as to denizens, and took of all such benefices the *first-fruits*, and many other profits, so that great part of the wealth of the country was expended in the purchase of such livings; and many clerks who had been presented by their lawful patrons, and had holden their benefices for a long time peaceably, were put out. To remedy all these mischiefs, and in pursuance of the opinion of the parliament in the 35th year of Edward I., it was now enacted as follows:

In the first place, it was enacted, that all elections to church preferments that were elective should be free, as in times past, and that all persons collated and presented should enjoy the same freely, in the manner in which they were *infeoffed* by their donors; secondly, in case any *reservation*, collation, or provision was made by the see of Rome, of any church benefice, in disturbance of such free election, collation, or presentation, then, for that time, the king was to have the collation to such archbishoprics and other dignities as were elective, and of his advowson, in the same manner

land depended upon legal legitimacy. So the scope of the statutes was to prohibit and prevent appeals to Rome upon matters which involved temporal rights, as presentations to benefices, or the like—the law regarding advowsons as temporal property; but when the matter was in its nature purely spiritual, and was not mixed, as the law said, with temporality, there can be no doubt that appeals to Rome were recognised and allowed. The statutes to restrain them showed this; for, if such appeals were not allowed by law, then the courts would simply ignore them, and they would be idle nullities. It was because they were legal, and therefore the courts would recognise them, unless prevented by statute, that statutes were passed to prevent them. Prior to this reign, however, there were no statutes to prevent appeals upon matters purely spiritual. And as the ecclesiastical courts in this country were restrained whenever their jurisdiction would clash with that of the courts of law, it followed that appeals to Rome might, as a general rule, be safely allowed in cases from the ecclesiastical courts of this country (*Year-book*, 20 *Henry VI.*, 25). Thus the law stood after these statutes. Thus, where a *significavit* issued out of chancery to enforce the sentence of an inferior ecclesiastical court, an appeal to Rome, duly certified by the king in chancery, entitled the party to a *supersedeas* (*Year-book*, 20 *Henry VI.*, 25). So stood the law long after these statutes, only that appeals to Rome as to episcopal elections, or from the ecclesiastical courts, were allowed. But the effect of these statutes was practically to give the courts of law power to determine what should be deemed spiritual and what should not; and there was a growing tendency to restrict the right of appeal; and thus, in a subsequent reign it was laid down that the scope of the statutes of præmunire was to prevent appeals to Rome, even in matters spiritual (*Year-book*, 9 *Edward IV.*, 3); and it will be seen that, in a still later reign, such a construction was placed upon these statutes as made them the engines for effecting an entire separation from Rome.

(*a*) The words are, "nostre sanct pere le Pape," which Coke, whom our author follows, translates, "the bishop of Rome." The language of the courts of law, however, at the time was that of the statute, "our holy father the Pope" (*Year-book*, 10 *Edw. III.*) And no doubt he was the head of the English church.

as his progenitors enjoyed it before free elections were granted (*a*), under certain forms and conditions; such as, to demand of the king a *congè d'èlire*, and after the election to have the king's assent, which, says the act, ought to be the form observed now; and if it was deviated from, and the conditions not kept, it was but reasonable, continues the act, that the thing should return to its first nature. In like manner, if it was of any house of religion of the king's advowson, the king was to have the collation for that time; and so also of any church, prebend, or benefice, of the advowson of any person of holy church. But if such houses of religion or church benefices belonged to the advowson of any lord, or other person, then the collation, in the above cases, was to fall to him; and if such patrons did not present within half a year after the avoidance, nor the bishop by lapse within a month after such half-year, then the presentation was to belong to the king.

It was enacted, if the persons presented by the king or any of the before-mentioned patrons were disturbed by such *provisors*, that such provisors, their procurators, executors, and notaries should be attached by their bodies, and brought in to answer; and if convicted, should abide in prison without bail or mainprise, till they

(*a*) It will be observed that this act is founded upon the assumption which, it has been seen, had been set up in the courts of law on the part of the crown, that originally the crown had the absolute right of appointment by virtue of the right of patronage arising from endowment, and not the mere right of presentation, and that it was a concession to allow of canonical election, a supposition opposed to all the charters, which uniformly admitted that to be the ancient right of the church. However, upon that assumption the statute is framed, and, by analogy, the same assumption appears to be applied in the case of all other benefices; and, indeed, the papal provisions were mostly complained of in the inferior benefices, which, of course, were far more numerous, and in which they far more frequently interfered with rights of lay patronage. To prevent them was the object of this statute, the enactments of which, it will be observed, plainly imply that they were legal, and that the statute made an alteration in the law—for otherwise, the papal provisions would be simply set at nought in the king's courts as null and void, whereas, on the contrary, they were still treated as valid after the statute as before. And upon carefully inspecting the terms of the statute, it will be seen that they plainly imply the legality of the provisions, for they merely provide that, if they are made, the king shall have the collation, and the provisors be punished; the first of which merely gives the crown a power, at its option, by virtue of the statutory enactment, of disregarding the provisor; and the other, merely by virtue of a statutory enactment, renders the provisors liable to penalties, both enactments implying that, but for the statute, the provisions would take effect, and the subsequent cases in the courts show this clearly. Many years afterwards, and after further statutes against provisors, *quare impedit* was brought by the king against the bishop of Salisbury for a prebend, and the bishop actually pleaded a papal provision or reservation. "'We say that, after the death of our predecessor, our holy father the pope reserved to himself the bishopric, and gave it to us; and afterwards, before we were consecrated, the king, reciting by his patent that the pope had presented us to the bishopric, granted to us the temporalities.' And the counsel for the crown do not dispute, but adopt this, and say, 'You confess that the pope had presented you to the bishopric, by which your other benefices were avoided.' Upon which one of the judges said, 'If one be elected bishop, his benefices are not void until he is consecrated, and if the king grant him the temporalities afterwards, the king shall not have the presentment.' The counsel for the crown reply, 'True; but then, after he is elected, he has to be confirmed by the pope, and the pope might refuse him.' To which the judge answers, 'When the pope has given the benefice to a bishop, he has time to accept or not; when he is consecrated, he cannot refuse.' And another judge says, 'When

had made fine and ransom to the king, at his will, and gree to the party grieved; and before they were released, they were to make renunciation, and find sufficient surety not to do the like in time to come, nor to sue any process by themselves, or by any other, at the court of Rome or elsewhere, on account of such imprisonment or renunciation, or other matter relating thereto. In case such provisors, procurators, executors, or notaries were not found, the *exigent* was to run against them by due process, and writs were to issue to take their bodies, as well at the king's suit as at that of the party. In the meantime, the king was to have the profits of such benefices so occupied by provisors, except abbeys, priories, and other houses that had colleges or convents; and in such houses the colleges or convents were to have the profits. In order to suppress these practices as soon as possible, this statute was to relate as well to such collations in times past as in time to come.

We have seen that these provisors were to find security not to sue process in the court of Rome with design to invalidate any of the regulations of the last act against provision. The suing in the court of Rome was another mischief that was heavily felt at this

he is confirmed by the pope, and his temporalities are delivered to him by the king, he has all that a bishop should have, for he has both spiritualities and temporalities, and then his benefices are avoided'" (*Year-book,* 41 *Edw. III.*) Now, here the remarkable thing is, that the court and the king's counsel assumed the papal reservation to have been legal and valid. So in another case soon after, *in quare impedit,* it was pleaded, before the bishop was consecrated, the king granted to him the temporalities, &c. To which it was replied, that he was bishop of the pope's provision (*pur la purveyance del pape*) long before, &c. (*Year-book,* 44 *Edw. III.*) So, again, it seemed to be admitted that the statute only applied to benefices in lay patronage. For in a case upon the statute of provisors, the case was, that the dean and chapter of St Paul's had leased a manor with a vicarage (*i.e.,* the advowson), so that it was said the vicarage became severed from the cathedral church and of lay patronage, and that the defendant had sued in the court of Rome a provision. The defendant's counsel set up, that it was a thing spiritual; and the counsel for the crown argued that the vicarage was made lay patronage by reason of the lease and the severance of the spirituality, &c. (*Year-book,* 44 *Edw. III.*) So, in a subsequent reign, even after several other statutes on the same subject, it was admitted in the courts of law, that at common law the papal authority was supreme, as that of sovereign patron of the church. Thus, in a case where the king claimed a prebend on the ground of its vacation by the appointment of its occupant to a see, the bishop pleaded "that our holy father the pope (*l'apostle*), in his bull declaring that he should be bishop, recited also that he should hold his other benefices." To this the counsel for the crown demurred, not on the ground that the bull could not be pleaded, but to its effect. It was urged, that it could not have the effect of interfering with the king's right; to which it was answered, that the king's right only accrued upon the vacation of the benefice, and that this did not, by reason of the papal bull, take place. The suit was abandoned, it being admitted that it could not be sustained at common law; and then a suit was brought upon this statute, and again the papal bull was pleaded, and no question was raised as to its lawfulness, but only as to its legal operation and effect, and the legality of papal provisions was recognised, for Thermug, J., said, "When the pope (*l'apostle*) makes provision, he does it as sovereign patron of holy church" (*Year-book,* 11 *Hen. IV.* fol. 2). Judgment was given against the crown, and the case is thus stated in *Brooke's Abridgment:* "The pope had granted to one that he should be bishop, and that he might retain his other benefices, and held not within the statute of provisors, for the statute refers to him who accepts a benefice by collation, reservation, or provision of Rome, and it is not either of these, for they are by bulls executory, and it is here matter executed," and the case, it was added, cannot be taken as within the equity of the act, for it is a penal statute.

time, and loudly complained of, not only as a personal vexation to suitors, but as an infringement upon the law of the country and the independence of the nation. To restrain these applications to a foreign tribunal, the following regulations were made by the stat. 27 Edw. III. st. 1, c. i., which also is called in the statute-book *A Statute of Provisors.* It was ordained, that all people of the king's ligeance, who should draw any one out of the realm in plea, the cognizance whereof belonged to the king's court, or concerning things whereof judgment had been given in the king's court; or who sued (*a*) in another court to defeat or impeach the judgments given in the king's court, should have a day, containing the space of two months, *by warning* to be made to them, in the place where the possessions in question lay, or where they had lands or other possessions, by the sheriffs, or other the king's ministers, to appear before the king and his council, or in his chancery, or before the king's justices in the one or other bench, or before other justices deputed for that purpose, to answer in person to the king for the contempt; and if they came not at the day, then that they, their procurators, attorneys, executors, notaries, and maintainers, should from that day be put out of the king's protection, their lands, goods, and chattels forfeited to the king, and their bodies taken and imprisoned, and ransomed at the king's pleasure. Thereupon a writ was to be made to take their bodies, and to seize their lands, goods, and possessions, into the king's hands; and if this writ was returned *non inventus*, they were to be put in exigent and outlawed. The appearance of the offender any time before the outlawry was to entitle him to be received, to abide the judgment of the court, but such appearance was not to save the forfeiture.

Of Præmunire.

The subject of *provisions*, and *citations* out of the court of

(*a*) One of the principal heads of offence under this celebrated statute was the attempting to enforce papal "provisions or presentations contrary to the statutes of provisors of benefices" (*vide ante*). Thus, an attachment upon a prohibition was brought by the king and an incumbent, for that the king had presented the incumbent to a benefice, and that the defendant had brought bulls from Rome in disturbance of it (*contra formam statuti*), and the defendent confessed it, and the court awarded that he should suffer perpetual imprisonment! (*Year-book*, 21 *Edw. III.* fol. 40). It was held on this statute, that if a clerk sued another man in *Curia Romana*, even of a spiritual matter, when he could have a remedy in the realm, in the court of the ordinary, it was within the statute (*Year-book*, 9 *Edw. IV.* 3), a view according to which appeals to Rome were abolished, and the separation from Rome virtually accomplished by the operation of these acts. On the other hand, it was said that, as the terms of the statute were "in curia Romana vel alibi," which was to be understood of the court of the bishop, therefore, if a man was excommunicated for a thing which appertained to the common law, the case was within the statute, and the penalties of præmunire incurred (*Year-book*, 5 *Edw. IV.* 6). There can be no doubt that the effect of these statutes, if carried out, would have left little, if anything, to be achieved at the Reformation. There can be as little doubt that they were departures from the common law. This has been shown already as to the statute of provisors, and as to the present statute, it was said that the præmunire lay not at common law (*Year-book*, 14 *Hen. IV.* 14; 9 *Edw. IV.* 2). It was doubted, as already mentioned, whether even a spiritual matter could be carried to Rome after these statutes (*Ibid.*)

Rome was taken up again, some few years after, and a new course was delineated for restraining practices so detrimental to individuals, and to the country at large: this was by stat. 38 Edw. III. st. 2. In the first place, the statutes 25 & 27 Edw. III. were thereby confirmed, except only that prelates and lords were not to be subject to the arrest or imprisonment which had been ordained by those acts. Further, in addition to those two acts, it was ordained, that persons who had purchased or obtained, at the court of Rome, citations against the king or any of his subjects, or had procured deaneries, archdeaconries, provisties, and other dignities, offices, chapels, or benefices of holy church, belonging to the collation or gift of the king, or other lay patron of the realm; and also persons who obtained churches, chapels, offices, benefices, pensions, or rents, amortised, and appropriated to churches cathedral or collegiate, abbeys, priories, chauntries, hospitals, or other poor houses; and also all maintainers and abettors of such persons, and those suspected of such pursuits, should be arrested and taken by the sheriff of the place, and justices in their sessions, deputies, bailiffs, and other the king's ministers, by good and sufficient mainprise, replevin, bail, or other surety (the shortest that might be), and be presented to the king, *or* his council, there to remain and stand to right, to receive what the law would give them; and if they were attainted of any of the above matters, they were to suffer the penalties ordained by stat. 25 Edw. III. before mentioned.[1]

If a person suspected of any of the above offences was not within the realm, or could not be attached, he was to be proceeded against according to stat. 27 Edw. III.[2] If any person attempted anything against this statute, he was to be brought to answer in the above manner, and if found guilty, was to be out of the king's protection, and punished according to the stat. 27 Edw. III. On the other hand, all persons suing maliciously upon this statute were to be punished at the discretion of the king or his council. All the lords and commons bound themselves to see this act fully executed. Upon the stat. 27 Edw. III. was formed a writ to *garnish*, or *warn* such offenders to appear; which writ was in after times, from the initial word of it, called a *præmuneri*, or rather *præmunire, facias*, a piece of law Latin for *præmoneri facias, &c.*

The stat. 38 Edw. III. st. 1, c. iv. may be reckoned among the laws for restraining the clergy from drawing money out of the kingdom to the court of Rome. It says, that whereas many people were bound in *another court* out of the realm (namely, that of Rome) by instruments, and in other manner, *such* penal bonds in the third person (which form was peculiar to them) should be void.

To return to the 31st year of the king. The parliament had been

[1] Ch. 1. [2] Ch. 2.

frequently solicited to make some regulation about the probate of wills, a matter which had been managed by bishops' officers at their pleasure, without much regard to the duties of their trust, or the accommodation of the public;[1] but nothing could be obtained further than recommendations to the bishops to amend and correct abuses (*a*). In the 31st year, it was complained that the ministers of bishops and other ordinaries took grievous and outrageous fines for the probate of testaments, and for making acquittances thereof. Upon this a statute was made, stat. 31 Edw. III. st. 1, c. iv., ordaining, that as the king had charged the archbishop of Canterbury and other bishops to have this amended, if they neglected so to do, the king should cause his justices to inquire of such oppressions and extortions, and determine upon them, as well at his own suit as at that of the party (*b*).

Probate of wills and intestacy.

If a man died intestate, we have seen that the chattels went to the ordinary, who disposed of them as he pleased for the good of the deceased person's soul; but it was presumed the ordinary would answer all debts and demands upon such effects, to which he was also bound by the statute of Westm. 2.[2] However, as the law now stood, the relations, as it should seem, were entitled to nothing, at least in the *dead man's* part, whatever claim they might be thought to have in the other two-thirds (*c*). But this was put

(*a*) By this statute, 4 Edw. III. c. vii., executors are enabled to bring actions for trespasses to the estate of the testator during his lifetime; and administrators have always been held to be within the equity of the statute. Hence, it was held that an administrator may maintain an action for taking away the goods of an intestate after his death, and before the grant of letters of administration (*Year-book*, 18 *Hen. VI.* fol. 22; 30 *Hen. VI.* fol. 8), just as an administrator or executor may sue for trespasses in the lifetime of the deceased, and just as an executor may sue for trespasses to the goods after the death and before the probate of the will, although it was endeavoured to contest the doctrine on the ground of the distinction, that the executors derive their title from the will, and the administrators from the letters of administration. In the 18 Hen. VI., fol. 22, Ascough, C. J., said, that administrators were but deputies of the ordinary, and derived their title from him, and had the occupancy of the goods in his right. But in 36 Hen. VI., fol. 8, Prisot, C. J., said, the administrator shall have action of goods carried away before administration, because it is an administration from the time of the death.

(*b*) "Cum post mortem alicujus decedentis intestati et obligati aliquibus in debito, bona deveniant ad ordinarium disponendum, obligetur, de cætero ordinarius ad respondendum de debitis eodem modo quo executores respondere teneantur." Coke says this was an affirmance of the common law, by which he means, the obligation to pay the debts; but the action was given by the statute, as the 31 Edw. III. c. xi. gave the action against the administrator. The notion that the common law gave the ordinary the goods of the deceased to apply in pious uses, without any obligation to pay the debts, is quite unfounded; and Coke, on the contrary, says that the law gave the ordinary the goods to be well administered, *i.e.*, as he himself says, according to the canon law, to pay the debts of the deceased in the first instance, whatever might be done with the residue (2 *Inst.* 397). And from Bracton, who wrote long before the stat. Westm. 1, it is clear that the jurisdiction as to debts of deceased persons was in the king's courts, however it might be as to legacies or bequests, which would be by the testament, and so in testamentary course, whereas debts are precedent to the death or testament.

(*c*) This was an error of the author's, and it has been already shown that he completely misunderstood this subject, through not observing that, according either to canon law or common law, the distribution of assets could not commence until the

[1] Parl. Roll. 21 Ed. III., 51.

[2] *Vide ante*, c. ix.

upon another footing by stat. 31 Edw. III., st. 2, c. xi., which ordains and declares, that where a person dies intestate, the ordinary shall depute *the next and most lawful friends* [1] of the intestate to administer his goods. In order to give the full effect to this trust, the statute ordains, that such *deputies* shall have an action to demand and recover as executors the debts due to the intestate, in the king's court, to administer and dispend them for the soul of the dead; the pretence under which they had in former times been claimed by the ordinary.[2] These deputies were to answer also in the king's court to persons to whom the said dead person was *holden and bound* (that is, in obligations) in the same manner as executors should; and further, they were, like executors, to be accountable to the ordinaries. From this it seems, that the next friends of the deceased were to act merely as *deputies* to the ordinary, who was finally, as before, to have a sort of resulting trust in the overplus, besides the election and patronage of delegating the administration to such of the next friends as he pleased.

The next parliamentary regulation relating to the clergy was stat. 36 Edw. III., st. 1, c. viii., which was occasioned by the late plague, which had depopulated the church, as well as the laity. The priests having from thence taken occasion to make high demands for their service, certain limits were fixed by statute on the attendance of parish and other priests. The next was in matter of tithes. The clergy had claimed tithe of wood of the age of twenty years or more, when felled for ship-building or other uses, under the name of *sylva cædua*. Complaint of this had often been made to the parliament.[3] It was declared, by stat. 45 Edw. III. c. iii., that a

claims of creditors were satisfied, so that the church could have no interest until then. The scope of this statute was altogether different from what the author supposed. It was to enable the church and the relatives to get at the assets. The jurisdiction to recover the debts and assets of the deceased was, and always has been, in the king's courts, and as there was an inconvenience in, and indeed at canon law an incapacity for, suits by or against the ordinary, it was provided that executors, where they were appointed, and when not appointed, that administrators should be appointed to sue and be sued; to sue the debtors, and be sued for the debts of the deceased. That is to say, the object was to enable the next of kin to recover the debts due to the deceased, and realise the assets. This is the true scope of the statute 31 Edward III. 11, which is utterly misrepresented by Blackstone (2 *Comm.* c. vii.), and most legal writers on this subject. Coke points out that though the ordinary was bound to pay the debts, he could not recover the assets (2 *Inst.*, 398), from which of course it followed that when, by the statute Westm. 2, an action was given against the ordinary, some provision should be made for actions by or under the direction of the ordinary. Hence the statute 31 Edw. III. 11, which ran thus:—"In case a man dieth intestate, the ordinary shall depute the next of kin, &c., to administer the goods, which deputies shall have an action to recover, as executors, debts due to the intestate, for to administer for the soul of the deceased (*i.e.*, first paying his debts, which above all things was deemed for the good of his soul), and shall answer also in the king's court to others to whom the said person was bound, in the same manner as executors shall answer; and they shall be accountable to the ordinaries as executors be in the case of testament, omitting this last clause, and taking no notice of the clause as to administration for the good of the soul." Blackstone represents that the ordinary at canon law did not pay the debts, and that this statute was passed to supersede him, whereas it is plain it was rather to aid and assist him.

[1] *De plus procheins, et plus loialx amis.*

[2] *Vide ante*, vol. i. c. viii.

[3] Cott. Abri. 21 Ed. III., 48.

prohibition and attachment should lie in such case. Respecting prohibitions in general, it was ordained by stat. 50 Edw. III. c. iv., that where a *consultation* was once duly granted upon a prohibition made to a judge of holy church, the judge might proceed in the cause by virtue of that consultation, notwithstanding any other prohibition, provided the matter of the libel of the said cause was not engrossed, enlarged, or otherwise changed.

In the same parliament a new sanction was given to the privilege of person claimed by clerks. It was complained, that divers priests, *bearing the sweet body of our Lord Jesus Christ to sick people*, with their clerks, and other people of holy church, while they attended divine service in churches and churchyards, and other places dedicated to God, were often arrested; which, says the statute, was an offence to God, and a disturbance of divine service: it was therefore enacted, by ch. v. of this statute, that the same should not be done in future. This is the last provision concerning the clergy in this reign.

The statutes of labourers.

The great plague, which was just mentioned, gave origin to the first statute of labourers, which is the next subject that comes under consideration. This public calamity having thinned the lower class of people, servants and labourers took thence occasion to demand very extravagant wages; and rather than submit to work upon reasonable terms, they became vagabonds and idle beggars (*a*). It was found necessary to take some compulsory method, in order to reduce this rank of people to subordination; an ordinance was therefore made by the king and council, to whom it was thought properly to belong, as an article of police and internal regulation, especially as the parliament were prevented from sitting by the violence of the plague. This ordinance was afterwards by stat. 3 Rich. II. st. 1, c. viii., made an act of parliament, and constitutes stat. 23 Edw. III. The contents of this act are well worthy of notice, as they are the first provisions of the sort, and they laid the foundation of that system of government to which this part of the community were subjected for many years after.

In the first place, it was ordained, that every man and woman, of whatsoever condition, free or bond, being of able body and within the age of threescore years, not being engaged in merchandise, and not exercising any craft; neither having of his own whereof he

(*a*) And no doubt their number was largely augmented by the gradual emancipation of the villeins, which, as already observed in an earlier chapter, had been proceeding ever since the Conquest. In this reign villenage still existed and was recognised. Thus, in an action for false imprisonment, the defendant might plead that the plaintiff was his villein, *regardant* to his manor; and such a plea was pleaded, but it failed in proof, and the defendant had to pay 100 merks as damages, an enormous sum in those days, a merk being 13s. 4d., and every shilling being worth at least £4 at our day, so that the sum was equivalent to £5000 in our time. It may be easily imagined that it would be a perilous thing to set up a claim of villenage; and yet many vagabond persons would be known to be villeins, who probably had ran away from their lords, and who could not be followed and recovered.

might live, nor land of his own where he might employ himself in tillage, nor being in the service to any one; every person of such description, if required to serve in a station that suited his condition, was to be bound to serve, when so required, for the wages and upon the terms that were usual in the five or six years preceding the 20th year of the king; and any person so refusing, upon his refusal being proved by two true men before the sheriff or the king's bailiffs, or the constables of the town, was to be taken to the next gaol, there to be detained till he found surety for so serving.[1] Any workman or servant departing from his service before the time agreed for, was to be imprisoned, and also those who received or retained such servant.[2] All persons paying or receiving, or demanding more than the above wages, were to forfeit double the sum;[3] and lords of manors so doing, to forfeit treble.[4] Moreover, any artificer or workman refusing to work for the prices usual at the above-mentioned periods, were to be committed to the next gaol.[5]

In aid of this process for the regulation of the poor, it was also enacted, that provisions should be sold at a reasonable price, having respect to the price they bore in the places next adjoining; and any person selling for more, was to forfeit to the party damnified double the price taken. Mayors and bailiffs of cities and boroughs were to have authority to inquire of such offences; and if they neglected to act, and were convicted thereof before the king's justices, they were to forfeit treble the price to the party damnified, and to be fined to the king.[6] Again, to prevent the poor from being encouraged to take to an idle life, in preference to working at some trade, it was ordained, that none, under pain of imprisonment, should give to such as could labour anything in the way of alms or charity, nor in any manner favour them.[7] Because it was found that people would not sue for the forfeiture against servants and workmen taking more than the above-mentioned wages, it was afterwards ordained, that such forfeiture should be assessed by the king's officers, to go in alleviation of so much of the dismes or quinzimes to be levied on the township.[8]

In the 25th year of the king, the commons complained in parliament that the above ordinance was not observed; wherefore a statute was made, ordaining further regulations on the subject (*a*).

(*a*) In a case in Year-book, 47 Edw. III., fol. 4, p. 13, which was on the statute of labourers, against a servant for departing within the term for which he was retained, the plea was, "We were never in your service." Finchden said this, which was agreed to by the whole court: "At common law, before the statute, if a man took my servant out of my service, I should have writ of trespass; now the statute was made for this mischief, that if he never comes into my service after he has made covenant to serve me, but eloynes himself away from me, I shall have such writ, and suggest that he was retained in my service and departed, wherefore it is necessary to traverse the retainer, which was accordingly done, and so issue *ad patriam.*" So in a case in the Year-book, 11 Hen. IV., Mich. fol. 33, p. 46, it was held that

[1] Ch. 1. [2] Ch. 2. [3] Ch. 3. [4] Ch. 4.
[5] Ch. 5. [6] Ch. 6. [7] Ch. 7. [8] Ch. 8.

It was enacted [1] that carters, ploughmen, and other servants should be allowed to serve by the year, or by some other usual term, and *not* by the day. All workmen were to bring their implements openly into towns, and there be hired in a common place and by no means in a secret one.[2] Certain prices were fixed for a day's work of mowers, reapers, and others. Servants were to be sworn twice a year before the lords, stewards, bailiffs, and constables of every town, to observe these ordinances; and those who refused to

at common law an action lay where the defendant had caused and procured the servant's departure from his service. The statute was always held to apply only to those who worked with their hands. In Year-book, 50 Edw. III., fol. 13, p. 340, case in which the parson of B. sued F., a chaplain, on the statute, and counted of a covenant made with him to serve in the office of seneschal, and to be his parochial chaplain for a certain term, and complained of a departure within the term. As to the office of seneschal, the defendant denied the covenant, and as to the residue, contended that the statute was only made for labourers and artificers, and that he was neither the one nor the other, but the servant of God, and so was not bound by the statute. Clopton, for the plaintiff, took a distinction between a parochial and a private chaplain, contending that the former, from the variety and daily pressure of his duties, was in many respects to be regarded as a labourer, and within the statute, as any other person of the people. The case was adjourned, and the judges of the king's bench were consulted, and the decision was that a chaplain was not bound by the statute. The same law is to be found in a case in the Year-book, 4 Hen. IV., Mich., fol. 4, p. 7, where the count on the statute was, that he was retained by the plaintiff to be his chaplain, and also his proctor and collector of tithes, and to serve him "*as pees et as maines*" for a certain time. The retainer to be proctor and collector was specially traversed, and it was pleaded that his retainer as chaplain was only to do divine service. The decision is not clearly stated, but Fitzherbert appears to have understood that it was against the defendant, for he abstracts the case shortly, and adds, "*quod mirum*, for he shall not be compelled again to serve, but the statute is in *servitio congruo*" (*Fitz. Abr.*, *tit. Labourers*, fol. 51). Immediately afterwards he abstracts a case in 12 Hen. VI., "action on the statute of labourers is not maintainable against an esquire." In Year-book, 19 Hen. VI., fol. 53, is a case where the defendant pleaded that he was retained to collect rents, and so was not a labourer, which was held to be a good plea. The case in Year-book, 11 Hen. IV., fol. 23, p. 462, T. F. brings writ of trespass at the common law against the defendant for his close broken, and one J., his servant, taken out of his service (*pris hors de son service*), and certain sheep driven away. As to the servant, Tremaine pleaded, "We found him wandering on a certain place in another county, and then he came and offered his services to us, and made covenant with us to serve us, and so he demands judgment." Skrene, for the plaintiff, replies, "He has admitted that the servant was in our service, and that he has received him into his service, and so he has admitted our action." Hankford says, however, "when the servant was wandering, if the defendant had not conusance that he was in your service, then this first receiver cannot be adjudged a wrong done by the defendant, but by the servant." Upon this Skrene amends his pleading, and says "that the servant made a covenant with the plaintiff to serve him in the office of trencher for a whole year, within which the defendant procured our servant to go out of our service, by force of which procurement he went out of our service." On which Hill avers, "this writ of trespass does not lie upon the matter shown; for the plaintiff says that the defendant did nothing but procure the servant to go out of his service, by which procurement he went out of the service, and was retained by the defendant, in which case action on the statute was given." Skrene argues, "If a man procures my servant to go out of my service, and retains him upon that, he does me wrong." Hankford and Hill both say, "True it is that he does you wrong; but you shall not have a remedy on this manner of writ as it is here." Culpeper, "This action is taken upon an action at common law, and the actions which were at common law before the statute were not taken away by the statute, and if a man procures and abets my servant to go with him in his service, action at common law lies well." Hill, "No, certes, action of trespass at common law does not lie in such a case of trespass, for such a pro-

[1] 25 Ed. III., stat. 1.

[2] Ch. 1.

take such oath, or to perform the work they engaged for, were to be put in the *stocks* by the above officers, for three days or more, or to be sent to the next gaol, there to remain till they would justify themselves.[1] As the wages of servants in husbandry were settled by the above chapter, that of certain artificers, as masons, carpenters, and the like, were likewise ascertained; and power was given to the justices thereto assigned to lower the rate of such wages at their discretion.[2] It was further enacted, generally, that *all other*

curement cannot in any way be said to be 'against the peace.'" Thermug, "If my servant, before the statute, went out of my service, I suppose well that no action is given to the master, but if a man took my servant out of my service, then action of trespass lay at the common law, and still lies; and if I am beaten by the abetment and command of a man, the commander is guilty of trespass. So in the case here, when he shall procure this servant to depart, and retains him with him, he seems guilty of trespass." But Hill answers him, "Sir, in your case there is no marvel, because the principal actor in your case is guilty of trespass; but the case at bar is different, for the procurement only is not a trespass against the peace, nor is the departure of the servant a trespass against the peace. I well agree that the defendant in this case is guilty as of a thing done against the provisions of the statute, and the matter is as clearly within the statute as it could be, both as to the servant who has departed from his service, and as to the defendant who has presumed to retain him in his service." Hankford, "I am of the same opinion as my master has expressed, that if my servant depart out of my service, at common law I can have no action, and the cause was for that between me and my servant it is a contract, upon which no action lay at the common law without a specialty, and for this mischief the statute was made, and action given on it." Culpeper says, "If a man procure my ward to go from me, and he goes by my procurement, I shall have (a writ of) ravishment of ward against him." Hankford admits this, and says, "The reason is, *because the ward is a chattel*, and vests in him who has the right." After some more discussion, Skrene says, "He came to our house, and procured our servant, and took him as we have supposed in our writ." And Tremaine being ordered to answer, pleads, "He was wandering and offered his service to us, and we received him, without taking him in the manner alleged by the plaintiff." And upon this in the end the issue seems to have gone to the county (*Year-book*, 11 *Hen. IV.*, fol. 23). In Year-book, 10 Hen. VI., fol. 8, p. 30, the prior of W. brought writ on the statute against a chaplain, and counted that he was retained in his service with him for a year to do divine service, and that he departed within the year. Defendant demanded judgment on the writ. "For you see well how he brings the action against a chaplain, and the statute is only to be understood against labourers in husbandry." Strange, "The writ is not maintainable by the statute, for you cannot compel a chaplain to sing at mass, for at one time he is disposed to sing and at another not; wherefore you cannot compel him by the statute." An argument which would be better understood then than now, because the rules of the Roman Catholic Church might often preclude a priest from celebrating mass. Cottesmore to the same intent, "For it was not made but for labourers in husbandry; as in the case of a knight, or esquire, or a gentleman, you cannot compel him to be in your service by the statute, for that the statute is not to be understood of labourers who are in grant, and have nothing whereby to live; but a chaplain hath whereof he may live, in common understanding, as a gentleman." And judgment was for the defendant. "It will be observed," says Mr Justice Coleridge, "that many of these cases were with respect to chaplains. At this distance of time it may be difficult, without more inquiry into history, to assign a reason why there should be such a majority of cases relating to chaplains. It must be referrible, of course, to some circumstance in the state of society at those periods. It may be collected from a royal mandate to the archbishops and bishops, that the services of stipendiary chaplains were, at the date of the statute, much in request. The bishops are required to enforce their services for their accustomed salary, under pain of suspension and interdict. This mandate is printed in the statutes at large at the end of the statutes." The truth is, the chantry-priests were not much respected.

[1] Ch. 2. [2] Ch. 3.

servants not expressly named in the act, should be sworn before the justices to exercise their crafts as before the 20th year of the king; and any servant, workman, labourer, or artificer, acting contrary to such oath, was to be punished with imprisonment and fine at the discretion of the aforesaid justices.[1] The above officers were to be sworn before the justices to execute this statute; and the justices at their sessions were to make inquiry therein and award process of *exigent* after the first *capias* against offenders.[2] The justices for the execution of this act were to hold their sessions four times a year at least; that is, at the Annunciation, on St Margaret, St Michael, and St Nicholas's day; and also as often as they in their discretions should think needful.[3] The commission to execute the statute of labourers was usually directed to the same persons who were in the commission of the peace; the due ordering of such persons as were the objects of this statute being one of the most important articles in the police of the country.

Again, by stat. 34 Edw. III., c. x., it was ordained, that labourers and artificers who absented themselves from their services, should be branded with a hot iron on the forehead with the mark of the letter F, to denote the *falsity* they had been guilty of in breaking the oath by which they had bound themselves, according to the former statute, to serve; though this stigma might be dispensed with by the justices. Further, a servant, labourer, or artificer, who had absented himself, might be demanded of the mayor or bailiffs of the place; if they refused to deliver him up, they might be sued before the *justices of labourers*, and if convicted were to forfeit £10 to the king, and 100 shillings to the party grieved. This was to prevent such fugitives from being harboured, and to interest all persons in enforcing this statute. To promote the executions of these provisions, it was ordained, by stat. 36 Edw. III. c. xiv., that the fines arising from the penalties inflicted under statutes of labourers, instead of going into the exchequer in part of the king's taxes, as directed by a former act, should be distributed among the inhabitants by the collectors, under the control and account of the justices of the peace. Thus far of the statutes of labourers.

Trade and commerce.

Trade and commerce had been patronised by our kings, and encouraged by our legislature, in the earliest times of our history; of which, without looking further back, the indemnity and protection held forth to foreign merchants by *Magna Charta*,[4] is a manifest instance. The great productions of this country, and which were objects of commerce with foreign nations, were wool and lead. Many regulations had been devised by our kings to make the advantage of this traffic centre in the kingdom. Some of these consisted in markets, or *staples*, as they were called, where the buying and selling of these articles was put under certain terms. Of these staples, some were in England, and some beyond sea. All these were experiments on the com-

[1] Ch. 4. [2] Ch. 5. [3] Ch. 7. [4] *Vide ante*, vol. i. c. iv.

merce of the kingdom, a subject not then well understood; and as the experience of times varied, the policy of national trade took a different turn. In the early part of this reign it was enacted, by stat. 2 Edw. III. c. ix., that the staples, whether beyond sea or in the kingdom, should cease; and that all merchants, as well aliens as natives, should go and come with their merchandise in England according to the Great Charter.

In the 27th year of the king, other notions prevailed concerning the vent of the national produce. It was thought expedient to confine the mart or *staple* to certain great towns in England, where foreigners might resort to purchase, and that no Englishman should, under great penalties, export these commodities himself. It was thought the trade conducted in this manner would bring more wealth into the country, than if transacted by the English on the Continent. Upon this idea was made *the statute of the staple*, 27 Edw. III., st. 2, a constitution containing a set of regulations for the establishment and government of the staple. As many of these are wholly of a mercantile import, and are now become obsolete, they are not objects of curiosity to a historical lawyer; but others, that are of a judicial nature, are not, because out of use, less within the compass of this work, as they show the turn and modifications which have, on particular occasions, and for particular purposes, been given to our laws, to accommodate them to the ends of justice in all cases. As the staple was intended, in its very institution, for the resort of foreign merchants, it was wise and expedient that some mode of administering justice between parties should be devised, which would be more consonant with the ideas of foreigners, and more adapted to the nature of mercantile transactions, for ease and despatch, than the common process of the law.[1] To these we shall principally confine ourselves in considering the statute of the staple, noticing little more of the remainder of the act than will be necessary to make them intelligible.

The statute of the staple.

The statute begins by enacting, that the staple of wools, leather, woolfels, and lead, produced in England, should be held at the following places:—For England, at Newcastle-upon-Tyne, York, Lincoln, Norwich, Westminster, Canterbury, Chichester, Winchester, Exeter, and Bristol; for Wales, at Kaermerdyn; and for Ireland, at Dublin, Waterford, Cork, and Drogheda, and nowhere else. All the above articles were to be brought to these places, and there sold.[2] In order that this whole business might be transacted at the staple, it was ordained, that no merchant, English, Welsh, or Irish, should carry out of the realm any of the above articles, on pain of life and limb, of forfeiture of the merchandise, and of other their goods and chattels to the king, and their lands and tenements to the chief lord. There were proper guards in the act to prevent any collusion or fraud, by the interference of foreign

[1] *Vide ante*, vol. i. c. viii.

[2] Ch. 1.

merchants, to give colour to exports really made by English,[1] the great object being to bring foreigners into the country.

In order that disputes might be decided among merchants in the staple conformably with their own ideas, it was enacted, that the justices of either bench, of eyre, of assize, or the marshalsea, or any other justices, if they came to the places where the staples were, should not interfere or have cognizance of such things as were within the jurisdiction of the mayor and ministers of the staple.[2] The jurisdiction of the mayors and constables of the staple was declared in this way: they were to have cognizance within the town where the staples were, of people, and of all manner of things touching the staple. All merchants coming to the staple, and their servants, were to be governed by the *law-merchant* in all thing touching the staple, and not by the common law of the land, nor by the usage of cities, boroughs, or other towns; nor were they to implead, or be impleaded before the justices of such places, in pleas of *debt*, *covenant*, and *trespass*, of things touching the staple; but were to implead all persons, as well those who were not of the staple as those who were, being found therein; and were to be impleaded only before the mayor and justices of the staple, of all manner of pleas and actions whereof the cognizance belonged to the staple. Again, in all contracts whatsoever between merchant and merchant, or other, if one party was a merchant, whether the contract was made within the staple or without; and also of trespass done within the staple to merchants or ministers of the staple by any stranger, or by any of them against a stranger, the plaintiff might either sue in the staple, or at common law.

In pleas relating to the king's house, the steward and marshal of the household were to sit with the mayor, to see right done. All pleas of land were to be at the common law. If any merchant committed felony, or was slain, robbed, or maimed, the mayor of the staple and other proper persons were to be assigned justices, to hear and determine the matter within the staple according to the common law; and if an indictment was taken without the staple of a fact committed within, it was to be transmitted to the mayor and the justices assigned within the staple. If a matter was to be tried by an inquest within the staple, and the parties were both strangers, it was to be tried by strangers; if denizens, by denizens: if one was an alien, and the other a denizen, then the inquest was to consist of half denizens and half aliens.[3]

In order that contracts made within the staple might be better observed, and payments readily obtained, a course similar to a statute-merchant was directed. The mayor of the staple was empowered to take recognizances of debts which any one would enter into before him, in the presence of the constables of the staple, or one of them. There was to be in every staple a seal, to be kept by the mayor, and all obligations made upon such recognizances

[1] Ch. 3. [2] Ch. 5. [3] Ch. 8.

were to be sealed with that seal; by virtue of such sealed obligation, the mayor might hold in prison the body of the debtor, after the time of payment had arrived, if he was found within the bounds of the staple; and there he was to be detained till he had made agreement with the creditor for the debt and damage: he might also take his goods found within the staple, and deliver them, by true estimation, to the creditor, or sell them to the best advantage, and pay the debt. In case the debtor, or his goods to the amount of the debt, were not found within the staple, a certificate was to made to the chancery, under the mayor's seal; upon which a writ would be issued to arrest the debtor's body, without mainprise, and to seize his lands and tenements, goods and chattels. This writ being returned into chancery, with a certificate of the value of the lands and goods, due execution was thereupon to be made in the same manner as was prescribed by the statute-merchant; so that the creditor should have an estate of freehold in the lands and tenements delivered to him by virtue of the process, and recovery by writ of novel disseisin, if ousted; but the debtor was to have no advantage of the quarter of a year allowed by the statute-merchant.[1]

A piece of old law which had been abolished in the reign of Edward I.[2] had been revived in this reign in the case of the Lombard merchants. It was found that Lombard merchants, with which the kingdom at this time abounded, would sometimes escape out of the country without satisfying their creditors. In order to interest all the community in preventing such frauds, it had been enacted by stat. 25 Edw. III. stat. 5, c. xxiii., that if any merchant of the company of Lombards acknowledged himself bound in a debt, the company should answer for it, provided, however, that a merchant *not* of the company should not be liable. The spirit of this proviso was carried into full execution by the present statute, for it was ordained that no merchant-stranger should be impeached for another's trespass or debt, wherein he was neither debtor, pledge, nor mainpernor.[3] It was enacted that justice should be administered in the staple from day to day, and from hour to hour, whenever complaint was made, that merchants, whose occupations required them to be passing and repassing the sea, might not be delayed unnecessarily.[4] In every staple town the mayor was to be chosen yearly, and he was to be well acquainted with the law-merchant, to qualify him for the government of such a concern. There were to be at least two constables. All complaints against the mayor and constables were to be redressed upon complaint to the chancellor and council.[5]

These are the judicial parts of the statute of the staple. Some small alteration was afterwards made in the jurisdiction of the mayor and constables, for whereas it had been ordained, generally, that they should have cognizance within the towns where the staple

[1] Ch. 9. [2] *Vide ante*, c. ix. [3] Ch. 17. [4] Ch. 19. [5] Ch. 21.

was, of the people, and of all manner of things touching the staple, and of felonies, mayhems, and trespass done within the staple, it was thus altered by stat. 36 Edw. III. stat. 1, c. vii., namely, that they should have cognizance only of debts, covenants, and contracts, and all other pleas touching merchandise, and surety of merchandise between merchants; but process of felony, and all other pleas, as well within the staple as without, were to be at the common law, as they were before the statute of the staple, with this exception, that merchants *alien*, whether plaintiffs or defendants, might sue plaints, as well of trespass as of any other matter, before the mayor of the staple, by the law of the staple, *or* at the common law. Some other statutes were made respecting the trade of the staple, which are not much worthy of notice, as stat. 28 Edw. III. c. xiv., xv., and stat. 31 Edw. III. stat. 1, c. vii.

Other laws were enacted for the encouragement of trade and manufactures, particularly that of woollen. It had hitherto been the course of trade to suffer our wool to be exported into the Low Countries to be manufactured; but it being thought more conducive to the welfare of the nation to manufacture it at home, some laws were made first to give protection to such cloth-makers as would come to reside here from foreign parts;[1] secondly, to restrain the wearing of any cloths but such as were made in England, Ireland, or Wales. This measure was first commenced in the 11th year of the king. When manufactures were thus set on foot, the next step was to attend to the quality of their productions, which occasioned the *statute of cloths*, 25 Edw. III. stat. 4, prescribing the size, texture, and properties of cloths: this act was followed by others.[2]

It was not to the natural productions of the king's dominions that the parliament confined their attention. They endeavoured, in various ways, so to regulate other articles of commerce, both import and export, as to keep up the orderly and regular course which must be preserved in commerce if intended to be permanently beneficial. Among other circumstauces of trade, *forestalling* was restrained, as prejudicial to the fair trader. Forestallers of wine, victual, wares, and merchandises, if attainted at the king's suit, or that of any other, by indictment or otherwise, were to forfeit to the king the thing forestalled; and if that was sold, and the party had not whereof to make fine, he was to suffer two years' imprisonment.[3] *Ingrossing* likewise was restrained: merchants ingrossing were to forfeit the thing ingrossed, and also pay a fine.[4] Besides those above mentioned, to compel labourers and artificers to work, many laws were made to direct persons who were industrious to their proper object. Artificers and handicraftsmen were to confine themselves to one trade only, in order that they might excel the better therein.[5] The sumptuary regulations that were

[1] Stat. 11 Ed. III., c. 5.
[2] Stat. 27 Ed. III.
[3] Stat. 25 Ed. III., st. 4, c. 3.
[4] Stat. 37 Ed. III., c. 5.
[5] Stat. 37 Ed. III., st. 6.

made by stat. 37 Edw. III. may be considered as a branch of the laws concerning trade and manufacture. By that act, the apparel of almost all ranks of persons in the state, from knights and esquires down to workmen and servants, was prescribed, so that no whim or extravagance of dress might be indulged to the ruin of the wearer.[1] This scheme of *economy* went so far as to the diet of the inferior sort.

While so much solicitude was expressed for the interest and welfare of trade, no less regard was shown to that great medium of it, *money*. No *sterling*, nor silver in plate, nor vessel of gold, was to be carried out of England, under pain of forfeiting the same, unless the king's special licence was obtained.[2] No sterling halfpenny or farthing was to be melted, and any goldsmith or other so doing was to be committed to prison till he paid to the king the value of that which he had melted.[3] The importing of false money was by stat. 9 Edw. III. punished by forfeiture thereof,[4] but we shall hereafter see that in the 25th year of the king it was made high-treason. Proper authority was given to search for false money suspected to be imported.[5] Many other laws were made on the subject of the coin, all now of very little importance.[6]

Before we come to those statutes that relate to the administration of justice, it will be proper to mention some few which do not strictly belong to that head, nor to any of the foregoing: one of these was for the denization of children born beyond sea, one relating to *non-claim* upon fines, and another concerning fraudulent assurances.

Children born out of the realm.

The stat. 25 Edw. III. stat. 2 was made to remove some doubts which were entertained about the denization of children born of English parents out of the kingdom; for which purpose the statute explicitly declares the law of England always to have been, that the children of the kings of England, whether born in the kingdom or without, ought to have the inheritance after the death of their ancestors: and respecting others, it declares, generally, that all children inheritors who should thenceforth be born out of the king's ligeance, if their fathers and mothers, at the time of their birth, were of the faith and allegiance of the king of England, should enjoy the same benefits and advantages, to have and bear their inheritances within the king's allegiance, as well as those born within the allegiance of England, provided their mothers passed the seas with the licence and wills of their husbands. And because there was some doubt about children born at Calais, that place not being *out* of the king's ligeance, it was declared by stat. 42 Edw. III. c. x. that they should be held within the benefit of the above law.

It was the old law of the land that a fine, properly levied in court, should bind all parties who did not make their claim within

[1] Ch. 8–15. [2] Stat. 9 Ed. III., st. 1, c. 1. [3] Ch. 3. [4] Ch. 2.
[5] Ch. 9, 10, 11. [6] Stat. 25 Ed. III., st. 5, c. 12, 13, 20. Stat. 15 Ed. III., c. 6.

a year and a day; and this was recognised and confirmed by the statute of *Modus levandi fines*, 18 Edw. I.[1] (*a*) The great principle upon which *fines* were to be defended was the peace and quiet thereby given to the possession of property, though a solicitude not to preclude any one from obtaining justice, if he had a lawful *claim*, dictated the indulgence of a year to make it in. In this reign the desire of being always at liberty to do justice seems to have got the ascendant over that to preserve quiet; for it was at the distance of twelve years from the petition for that purpose,[2] ordained by stat. 34 Edw. III. c. xvi., that the plea of *non-claim* of fines should not be taken nor holden for a bar in time to come. The endless litigation to which property was subjected after this law produced an alteration in the reign of Richard III. and of Henry VII., when the doctrine of *non-claim* was revived with respect to fines levied in a particular manner.

Statute of non-claim.

The last act but two in this long reign is upon a subject which will be more fully discussed in the subsequent parts of our History —namely, *the possession of land by one man to the use of another*.

(*a*) In order to understand this statute, and the whole system of conveyances formed by means of fines and recoveries, it is necessary to have regard to their nature, their reason, and their history; and also, to consider this statute in connexion with several others, which the author either does not notice, or notices separately in other places. Originally, as Mr Hargreave says, fines were concords of real suits, and hence the term fine, derived from *finalis*, as making a final end. So Glanville says: "Contingit autem aliquando loquelas motas in curia per amicabilem compositionem et *finalem concordiam* terminare" (*Glanv.* lib. viii. c. i.). And thus he gives the reason for the name, "Dicitur talis concordia finalis eo quod finem imponit negotio adeo ut neutra pars litigantium ab eo de cætero poterit recedere" (*Ibid.*). So Bracton: "Finis est extremitas uniuscujusque rei hoc est, idem in quo unaquaque res terminatur, et ideo dicitur finalis concordia quia imponit finem litibus." This was the nature of fines, however, only so long as they were concords of real and adverse existing suits. But they had ceased to be so long before the statute of fines, where it was declared: "Quia fines finem litibus debeat imponere et imponunt, et ideo fines vocantur maxime cum post duellum et magnam assizam in suo casu, ultimum locum finalem teneant imperpetuum;" it was intended rather of *future* litigation, and it was considered that, in order to conclude future claimants, there should be something which might operate as notice to all parties interested to come in and make their claims. (See the *De finibus*, 18 *Edw. I.*, *vide ante* c. ix.) Therefore, in order to provide the best possible substitute, the statute of fines provided that fines should be openly and publicly read, which it was supposed was grounded upon the usage of making proclamations in cases of recoveries by default. Upon such recovery, it was held that all the parties and their heirs were barred for ever, unless they put in claim within a year (*Year-book*, 5 *Edw. III.*, fol. 50), though properly the recovery ought to be executed by delivery of the land, in order to operate as a bar (7 *Edw. III.*, fol. 76). These conditions, however, either not being observed, or from the nature of the times, men being prevented from putting in their claims, the statute 34 Edward III., c. xvi., ousted non-claim, as it was called—that is, provided that, in order to avoid a fine, it should not be necessary for the heir or the reversioner to put in their claim within the year and day, as at common law. There was no substantial distinction between a fine and a recovery by default, unless there was any difference in the degree of notoriety or publicity which the statute of fines regard as the substance. And it should seem that there was some such difference. After recovery in a court of right, where the trial had taken place, either of battle or the grand assize, non-claim for a year and a day barred future claimants, on account of the notoriety of such a recovery. And, in cases of recoveries by default, it was said that proclamations used to be made before judgment, in order that people might have notice of it, and in those days, when all transactions were public, espe-

[1] *Vide ante*, c. x.

[2] Cott. Abr. 22 Ed. III., 21.

In what degree this practice of modifying property had obtained at the time of which we are now speaking, may perhaps be collected from a recital of the statute itself. The stat. 50 Edw. III. c. vi. complains that many people inheriting divers tenements borrow goods in money or merchandise, and then give their tenements and chattels to their friends, *by collusion, thereof to have the profits at their will*, and afterwards flee to the franchise of Westminster, of St Martin-le-Grand in Londen, or other privileged place, and there live a great time *with high countenance, of another man's goods, and profits of the said tenements and chattels*, till their creditors are glad to take a small part of the debt, and release the remainder. This was the grievance meant to be remedied, for which end the statute ordains, that should such gifts be found to be made by collusion, the creditors should have execution of the tenements and chattels, as if no such gift had been made. One would have thought a stroke like this, as it wholly destroyed the end of such confidential gifts, needed not to have been repeated; but such was the ingenuity and perseverance of mankind, that these collusive gifts rather increased after this act, and were carried to such

cially as to land, and the only other usual mode of conveyance by feoffment was accompanied with open delivery of seisin, such proclamations were really effective means of public notice. Therefore, it was thought that a fine or recovery ought to have been executed by delivery of possession in pursuance thereof, for the sake of public notoriety, though this did not always take place. Before the statute of Edward III., which ousted non-claim, a stranger who had right might come in within the year, and put in his claim upon the record of the fine: "Talis venit et apponet clamcum suum ad terras infra scriptas." There were four claims at the common law to avoid fines—two by record, and two *in pais*. By record—that is, by a declaration brought within the year, or by entry of claim in the record of the fine. *In pais*—that is, a lawful entry into the land by him that had right, and an expulsion of the tenant, or by continual claim. The mischief was, that by the *laches* of the tenant of the particular estate, those in reversion or remainder were bound; this occasioned the making of the 34 Edward III., c. xvi., the statute which "ousted non-claim,"—*i.e.*, ousted parties of the right to set up non-claim within the year as a bar. All that was enacted, however, by that statute was that persons, notwithstanding non-claim, might come forward and make their claims. Whether their claims would succeed depended upon the common law and the previous statutes as to the effect of fines. This matter has been much misunderstood; and it has been supposed that the statute of Edward, by doing away with the effect of non-claim, quite destroyed the finality of fines. That is an error; all that the statute did was to remove a bar to a claim. But at common law a fine, as matter of record, bound the parties and their heirs or privies; and it should seem that even a stranger could only avoid the fine by showing that the parties who levied it had no freehold estate in the land at the time it was levied, by showing some title paramount to the fine. This seems the effect of these cases on the subject, though no doubt it is obscure; and it is difficult to get at their precise effect. What, however, was the effect of a fine at common law as a record binding parties and privies,—that is, the parties and their heirs, with the exception that by the statute *De donis* a fine did not bar the issue in tail (*i.e.*, of their real actions), such effects they continued to have, and they were in fact feoffments of record, and had some of the advantages of public registers of title, not indeed after this act indefeasible, but still, coupled with the statute 27 Edward I., of considerable validity and value. And the records and reports of this and subsequent reigns show numerous instances of fines, containing limitations of estates, in fact, amounting to settlements,—all placed on record among the muniments of the courts of law, a matter of no small importance in those turbulent times. For the same reason, however, men might be deterred from making their claims, and hence the present statute, which, as Bacon says, "was fitted for times of war."

lengths as to baffle the operation of many statutes framed more specially, and upon better experience than the present.

To the account that is to be given of the alterations made in the administration of justice, it may be convenient to prefix a short view of the laws enacted for the better regulations of some offices immediately connected with, and assistant to, courts of justice, such as those of the sheriffs, coroners, bailiffs, and the like.

Of sheriffs.

First, of sheriffs. The statute of Lincoln, 9 Edw. II. st. 2, directing that sheriffs, hundredors, and bailiffs should be chosen from such persons as had lands in the same shires or bailiwicks, and that sheriffs and bailiffs of fee should cause their counties and bailiwicks to be kept by such as had lands therein, was a provision so well calculated to promote the dignity of the office, that it was required by stat. 2 Edw. III. c. iv., and in the next parliament by stat. 4 Edw. III. c. ix., to be strictly observed; the same was more explicitly re-enacted by stat. 5 Edw. III. c. iv., which requires the lands to be sufficient to answer to the king and his people, if grieved.

The farming of counties and hundreds led to much oppression and disorder. It seems that in former times all the counties in England were assessed to a certain ferm; and all the hundreds and wapentakes in the sheriff's hands were rated to this ferm. Afterwards, says the act, approvors were sent into some counties, who increased the ferms of some hundreds and wapentakes, notwithstanding the crown had, at divers times, granted out parts of the same hundreds and wapentakes for the old ferms only; but now of late the sheriffs had been charged with the whole increase, amounting to a great sum, which was a sort of disherison to sheriffs, and tending to the oppression of the people. It was thought this would be remedied by annexing to the counties such hundreds and wapentakes as had been let by the present king; and this was done by stat. 2 Edw. III. c. xii., which also directs that they should never again be severed. Again, because sheriffs had left hundreds and wapentakes at so high a ferm, that the bailiffs could not pay the ferm without extortion and malpractices, it was enacted by stat. 4 Edw. III. c. xv., that sheriffs should let them at the old ferm, and not above; and if they did, they were to be punished by the justices.

To prevent one instance of extortion, it was enacted by stat. 4 Edw. III. c. x., that sheriffs and gaolers should receive and safely keep all thieves and felons delivered to them by constables and townships, without taking anything for so doing; and they were to be punished by the justices of gaol-delivery if they acted otherwise.

In the 14th year of the king, the office of sheriff underwent a fuller consideration, and some provisions of a more general nature were devised for the reformation of it. It had been the practice for sheriffs sometimes to have grants of their bailiwick from the king for term of years; this was found to render them more secure in their misconduct, and all the evils complained of became thereby more inveterate. It was now ordained that in future no sheriff should continue in office more than a year, and then a new one should be appointed in his place by the chancellor, treasurer, and chief baron of the exchequer, taking to them the two chief justices, if they were present; this was to be done on the morrow of *All Souls*, at the exchequer.[1] Besides re-enacting the before-mentioned provisions about letting hundreds to ferm, it was ordained that sheriffs should put in bailiffs and hundredors, having lands within the bailiwick, for whom they would answer. The sheriff's business was to be done by such bailiffs and hundredors, and their under-bailiffs, without any *out-riders*, as they were called, and others who had lately been employed by sheriffs, and had committed great excesses; the same of *bailiffs-errant,* as they were termed, who were no longer to be in counties, but where they were used in the time of Edward I., and no more than one in a county. These *bailiffs-errant* and *out-riders* were deputies to the above officers; and as they were on that account less responsible, so were they more iniquitous in their employments. All others who had bailiwicks or hundreds in fee were to put in such bailiffs as they would answer for; and if they let them, it was to be on the old ferm. If sheriffs, or their fermors, offended against this act, the hundreds and wapentakes where the default was, were to be seized into the king's hand, and themselves committed to prison till they had made fine to the king; the same of those who had bailiwicks in fee, upon default of their bailiffs;[2] sheriffs were also to put in such gaolers as they would answer for.[3]

Notwithstanding *Magna Charta* had directed that sheriffs should hold their tourn after *Easter*, and after *Michaelmas;* yet it seems some sheriffs, not attending to that act, held their tourn sometimes in *Lent*, and sometimes after the *Yule of August*, seasons heretofore set apart for devotion and harvest. It was therefore enacted by stat. 31 Edw. III., st. i. c. xv., that the tourn should be held twice a year—once within a month after *Easter*, and once within a month after *Michaelmas;* and if a sheriff held it any otherwise, he was to lose his tourn for the time. The last act about sheriffs in this reign was stat. 42 Edw. III. c. ix., which, besides some directions about transmitting their estreats into the exchequer, ordains, not only that no sheriff, but that no under-sheriff, nor sheriff's-clerk, should abide in his office more than a year.

As to coroners, it was enacted by stat. 14 Edw. III., st. i. c. viii., that no coroner should be chosen unless he had lands in fee in the same county, sufficient to enable him to answer the people. Again, all coroners were to be chosen in full county by the commons of the county, of the most meet and lawful people that were to be found in the county, to execute the office, except in cases where the king or any lord, by his franchise, had a right to appoint.[4]

1 Ch. 7, confirmed by Stat. 28 Edw. III., c. 7.
2 Ch. 9.
3 Ch. 10.
4 Stat. 28 Edw. III., c. 6.

CHAPTER XIV.

EDWARD III.

Judicature in Parliament—In Council—The Court of the Steward and Marshal—The King's Bench—Error in the Exchequer—Justices of Assize and Nisi Prius, &c.—Attaints—Process of Outlawry—Execution of Writs—Qualifications of Jurors—Law Wager—Statute of Jeofail—Pleadings to be in English—Statute of Treasons—Riots—Of Indictments—A Jury de Medietate Linguæ—The Benefit of Clergy—Of Pardons—Process of Capias and Exigent—Origin of Justices of the Peace.

Several regulations were made by the parliament in this reign for the better and more regular administration of justice (*a*). These consisted partly in a new disposition or arrangement of the courts, and partly in providing new remedies. We shall first speak of the former.

(*a*) These might be divided, as the author appears to have intended, into alterations as to *judicature* and as to *procedure*. As to the former, it is not necessary to add anything here to his copious statements. As to procedure, it is proper to observe that they arose chiefly out of the growth of trial by jury, and that this mode of trial still remained in its nature what it had always hitherto been—viz., a trial by jurors, not as judges, but rather as *witnesses*. It is necessary to bear this in mind, because in it will be found the key to the connexion, and the explanation of various measures passed at this time, and mentioned in this chapter. At first sight, the connexion between statutes as to attaints, as to qualifications of jurors, and as to wager of law, might not appear to have any connexion; but upon a consideration of the *true nature of trial by jury*, as it still existed, it will be seen that the connexion between these different subjects was extremely close, and that they all arose out of *that* cause. Thus, for instance, as the jurors found their verdicts of their own knowledge, it was very material that they should come from the immediate neighbourhood of the parties, and as near as possible to the scene of the cause of action; and hence, in the statute as to qualifications of jurors, it was recited as a reason for it that the jurors often were brought from a distance *who had no knowledge* of the cause of action (*vide post*). For the same reason, if they gave a false verdict, it would most probably be wilfully false; and hence the penal proceeding by attaint in cases of a false verdict. And further, as the jurors only found their verdicts of their own knowledge, there was, as has already been pointed out in the notes to the early part of the first volume, when treating of the Saxon system of compurgators, no very wide difference between the present system of trial by jury and the system of wager of law, which was derived from the old Saxon system, and was simply the oath of eleven men, with the defendant, which thus, as Lord Coke long afterwards explained it, "countervailed a jury." The jurors swore on their knowledge of the parties and the matter; the compurgators swore on their knowledge of and belief in the defendant; and the two proceedings had so near a resemblance that it is not, when this is borne in mind, matter of surprise that the system of wager of law still continued to exist as a mode of trial, along with trial by jury. The fundamental principle upon which the distinction between them rested was, that if the matter was in its nature such as that the country, *i.e.*, the neighbours, might be presumed to have knowledge of it, then the trial must be by them, *i.e.*, *per pais;* if otherwise, and in its nature privy or secret between the parties, as in most cases of simple contract, debt, or of private contract, then wager of law would be allowed; or, in the language of the old law-books, "ley gager." Thus, in a case upon an alleged retainer of a surgeon to cure a man of a wound, he denying the retainer, offered to wage his law, which was objected

The most striking change made in any of the courts was that which regarded the high court of parliament. The judicature exercised by this supreme tribunal has been explained in the former part of this History.[1] What was then said was founded upon the testimony of very scanty materials, confirmed by the analogy observed in contemporary judicatures, and the experience of later times. To these later times we are now arrived. In the reigns of Edward I., II., and III. we find records of proceedings in parliament, which incontestably verify what was before delivered on the judicial character of this assembly, and furnish materials for forming an accurate judgment of its judicature, whether civil or criminal. From them also may be collected some intimation of the judicature of the council, and the way in which that court, and the courts of exchequer, king's bench, chancery, and common pleas were connected with, and dependent upon, the court of parliament. If we had adhered in this instance to the method we have rigorously pursued in all other parts of our historical deduction—that is, to take notice of juridical facts as early as the remains of antiquity afford any notice of them, we should have introduced the present observations in the reign of Edward

Judicature in parliament.

to, as the matter, it was said, would be in the knowledge of the neighbours; but the court thought otherwise, and that the defendant was entitled to wage his law. He, however, waived the right, and took an issue to the country, when it was objected against the plaintiff that he had not stated in what place the retainer was, so that the court could not know from what "vill" to make the jurors come, and for this the plaintiff failed (*Year-book,* 48 *Edw. III.* fol. 6). Here it will be observed that the connexion between the two systems was so close that probably some of the very same men who might have been called as compurgators would have been summoned as jurors; and in either case they would probably have acted very much on the same ground—their knowledge of and belief in the defendant. One practical result of the system of trial by jury thus still prevailing was that it was not applicable to matters which had happened beyond seas, as in the curious case of Sir Nicholas Tamworth, who brought a writ of account against one John, of certain jewels worth £400, which, as he said, he had delivered to John in Brittany. John set up some matter of defence occurring there. Thorpe, C. J., said, "How is it to be tried? we are here at common law, and it is not triable here" (41 *Edw. III.* fol. 4, 9). So there were various matters not deemed in law fit for trial by jury, as matter of record (50 *Edw. III.* fol. 20). So the lawfulness of espousals was, as a general rule, for the bishop, but a marriage in fact for the country; and so of a question whether a man was or was not born in matrimony (42 *Edw. III,* fol. 8). So wills of personalty were proved before the ordinary, though sometimes an issue could be raised for the country as to intestacy (44 *Edw. III.* fol. 16; *vide post,* c. xvi. as to trial *per pais* and trial by proofs, &c.) The close connexion with, and indeed part of this head of trial, or at all events of procedure, is a subject which had altogether escaped the author's attention, that of arbitration, which appears to have been often resorted to at this period, and probably had originally arisen in the old Saxon system of referring disputes to the neighbours, which had never entirely died out, and indeed was in more ways than one adhered to and retained in our system of procedure. The courts of the county in the hundred came virtually, as has been shown in the first volume, to a rude kind of arbitrament by neighbours; and this system had been so far retained, even in trial by jury, that it was necessary that jurors should come from the "vill" or the hundred, for the very reason that they would be likely to have knowledge of the parties, and therefore probably of the truth of the matter in dispute. It was therefore a fundamental principle of the law derived from our Saxon ancestors, and still tenaciously adhered to, that disputes should, as far as possible, be referred to arbitrators. And be it

[1] *Vide ante,* vol. i. c. i.

I.; but they were deferred to avoid repetition, and to accommodate the narrative to the reader's attention, which, as it was necessarily to be much engaged, in this reign, on the alterations made in the court of parliament, it was thought would be better prepared for such alterations by a statement of the whole subject at the time, than by scattering it in different places. It must therefore be understood, that what is now said of the jurisdiction of the court of parliament is equally applicable to the reigns of Edward. I. and

observed, that in an age when the jurors gave their verdicts, not on evidence, but on their knowledge or belief of the truth of the matter, there was a near resemblance between trial by jurors and arbitrators. The main distinction was that arbitrators chosen by the parties would either know about the matter, or would be able to hear evidence about it, which jurors did not. The difficulty was, that arbitration was voluntary; so that the party, finding it likely to go against him, might revoke his submission and insist on suing; or that, even after an award against him, he might decline to perform it or adhere to it, and either resort to law, or put the other party to do so. It was attempted to obviate these difficulties by getting both the parties to execute a bond to submit to arbitration, and stand by the award, with a penalty in case of breach. Thus, in this reign, it was said that in case of an arbitrament, that one party should have bond out of the possession of the other; if the latter should refuse it, the other would have no remedy, unless he had a bond to stand by the award (*Year-book*, 21 *Edw. III.* fol. 26). So, in another case, in an action on a bond, it appeared that the condition was that the parties should put themselves on the arbitrament of four persons named, and that they commenced their arbitrament, and continued it until they awarded, that the parties would stand to the award of two persons, who awarded that one should pay eight marks to the other, &c. (*Year-book*, 27 *Edw. III.* fol. 21). There were difficulties often raised as to whether an arbitrament was a bar to an action, unless performed; for otherwise, it was said, there was no satisfaction (*Year-book*, 45 *Edw. III.* fol. 16; 46 *Edw. III.* fol. 17; 43 *Edw. III.* fol. 27; 45 *Edw. III.* fol. 16). There was a close connexion between arbitrament and wager of law, when the defendant pledged his oath; and indeed there were cases in which the arbitrators awarded that the defendant should wage his law, and that if he did so, the plaintiff should release him (46 *Edw. III.* fol. 17). It was doubtful, however, whether an arbitration pending was a bar to an action (11 *Hen. IV.* fol. 12, 44). The principle was that the force of an arbitration depended on the submission (8 *Hen. VI.* 18); and that while it lasted the parties made the arbitrators their judges (16 *Edw. IV.* fol. 8). In this and in the subsequent reigns arbitration continued to be much resorted to, and it has ever since formed, and still continues to form, one of the most important and salutary means of settling disputes without the delay and vexation of litigation. There can be little doubt that the resort to arbitration was largely the result of dissatisfaction with trial by jury, which, it must be borne in mind, was not a trial by judges of the fact upon evidence, but only a trial by the jurors upon their own knowledge. It was no doubt constantly observed that this, in a great variety of cases, was an extremely imperfect and unsatisfactory mode of determining disputes; and hence a natural disposition would arise to resort to arbitration, a proceeding in which the arbitrators either knew about the matter, or heard evidence and examined into the truth and justice of the case. Indeed, in one important class of cases, those which involved matters of account, the law had provided a kind of compulsory process of arbitration; for the parties were compelled to come to an account before "auditors," or arbitrators appointed by the court. In this action of account the process was summary; and, by a statute already mentioned in a former chapter, a *capias* issued to arrest the party, and compel him to account in a *capias ad computandum*, as it was called; and upon his being brought into court, auditors were at once assigned by the court (generally the masters or officers of the court), and then he was compelled to account before them; and their award was final, and had the force of a judgment (Sir N. Tamworth's case, 41 *Edw. IV.* fol. 3). There were therefore several classes of cases in which trial by jury, such as it was, gave way to other modes of proceeding; wager of law, in which the defendant pledged his oath; account, in which he was compelled to show his accounts before auditors; and arbitration, in which both parties were examined, and the case was decided upon evidence.

II., and indeed, as we conjecture, to all the reigns preceding, from the origin of the Norman constitution.

The great extent of the jurisdiction of parliament in judicial matters, seems owing to the idea of superintendence and supremacy attributed to that assembly by the people. It was thought, that the parliament was to redress all wrongs, to remedy all abuses, and remove all difficulties, with which a man was pressed either in his person or property. In consequence of this notion it happened, at every meeting of parliament, that *petitions* poured in from all quarters, not only upon subjects of public and national concern, but for relief in private affairs. These petitions were exhibited by all sorts of persons, upon all sorts of matters, and to obtain every species of relief which the petitioners thought most desirable in their situations. When petitions were so numerous, and the objects of them so multifarious, it could not but happen that many were frivolous, and many were such as evidently belonged to another jurisdiction. To distinguish between those that were properly within the cognizance of parliament, and those that were not; and also in order that those which belonged to other courts, might be duly remitted thither; certain prelates, earls, barons, and others, were appointed in every parliament to be *receivors and tryors of petitions.* These were to examine all petitions, and upon full consideration thereof, were to indorse upon them what course was to be pursued by the petitioner to obtain redress; referring him, according to the nature of the case, either to the full parliament, to the council, to the chancery, or to some of the other courts. It was for this reason that *the receivors and tryors of petitions* are ranked by Fleta among the king's courts; though, as he says, their business was not to determine, but only to hear and examine, and make their report.[1] This is the outline of the court of parliament, the features of which deserve further consideration.

There was one circumstance common to all these petitions, that they were addressed either *a nostre seignour le roi, et a son conseil, &c.*, or to the king singly, without naming the council at all; though the former was the more common form. As to the matter of these petitions, it will be difficult and unnecessary to speak of them particularly: the curious reader, by casting his eye over the parliament rolls of this and the two preceding reigns, will judge whether what was above said of the extent of this judicature is well founded. Petitions were infinite as to the particular objects of them; but they may be divided into two general heads, namely, such as were the original commencement of a suit, and such as complained of error or delay in any suit depending in the courts below.

The manner in which petitions were treated, is best seen by the answers they received. Petitions that were originally for redress very commonly contained matter which was properly cognizable only at common law; in such case *the receivors and tryors*, upon

[1] *Vide ante*, c. xi.

examination of the matter, would indorse the following answers: *Sue a la comein ley, sue brief de trespass, et aixi de manace s'il vou;* [1] and the like. If it was in some matter of the revenue, the answer would be, *Soit mande as tresorer, et barons de l'exchequer, que viewes et serches les roules et remembrances de l'exchequer, et aissi appellé aucuns de justices, s'il besoigne, facent outre en discharge le dit——et que ley et reson demandent.*[2] If the petition related to any of the king's charters or grants, the reference was usually to the chancery, which seemed to have a nearer connexion with the council than the other courts. An answer to one petition is thus: *Soit ceste petition mande en chancellerie, et illoeq; soient bons genz assignez d'enquere, en la presence des auscuns de la chambre, s'ils y veuillent estre, si les choses contenue en la petition soit veritables: et l'enqueste issint prise, et retourne en chauncellerie, le chaunceller vene le fait, &c.,*[3] *et, appellez le seneschal de la chambre, ou son lieutenants, et les serjeantz le roi, et auscuns des justices, solonc ce qu'il verra que soit a faire, et oiez les resons pur le roi et pur la partie, face outre droit et reson.* To another: *Soit ceste petition maunde en chancellerie, et illoeq; appelle le counsail la roigne, et oiez les resons d'une part et d'autre, soit ent outre fait droit.*[4] If it was a matter proper for the cognizance of the council, an answer to this effect used to be given: *Veigne devant la counsaile et declare la matere contenue en la petition.*

These are some instances, out of many others, of the manner in which the parliament dismissed certain applications for redress. The petitions themselves are rather examples of what the people expected from the parliament, than of the jurisdiction really exercised by it. Among the petitions to parliament we find some indorsed with these answers: *Corum rege et magno concilio;* and sometimes an answer concluded with these words, *et issint fuit respondu en plein parlement.* These and the like answers, it should seem, signified that the parliament had heard and decided upon the petition judicially, by a solemn judgment and an award made upon it. Matters that were determined in this manner by the parliament were those for which the common law had no remedy, or which were of too great importance to be referred to the council, the other tribunal, next the parliament, for supplying the defects of the common law. In this way were *original* petitions in parliament exhibited and disposed of.

The manner in which petitions for direction in suits depending in the courts were entertained by parliament, will appear from a few instances where such interposition was made. In the 21st year of this reign there is a petition to the king and council, stating that the parties were impleaded by writ of *scire facias* before the justices of the common bench; which plea had been six years depending, and the judges could not yet agree upon the judgment, though they had been frequently commanded by the

[1] 21 Ed. III., Pet. Parl. 24 No. [2] *Ibid.* [3] *Ibid.* 69. [4] *Ibid.* 70.

king so to do; the petitioners, therefore, stating themselves to be greatly aggrieved by such delay, prayed the king that he would command the chancellor, or the clerk of the privy seal, to send a writ to the justices to cause the record in the said plea to come into full parliament, that the matter upon which they doubted might be debated before the peers of the land, and so might be finally determined by their advice and that of other learned men:[1] the answer to which was, that the record and process should be brought before the council, and upon view thereof, due discussion should be had. Many instances of such applications to parliament might be produced.[2]

It was not only by petition of the parties that suits depending in the courts below were brought into parliament, but also on the motion of the judges themselves, who, in cases of doubt and difficulty, would rather take the advice of parliament, than hazard their own judgment. In the 40th year of this king,[3] Thorpe says, that he and Sir Hugh Green went together to the parliament, where there were present at least twenty-four bishops and earls, and asked the opinion of those who had been the makers of the late statute of jeofail, concerning the alteration of a record. "At another time," the same judge says,[4] "we were commanded by the council, that when any case of doubt should happen, we should not go to judgment without good advice: therefore," adds he, in the case then before the court, "go to the parliament,[5] and as they will have us do, we will, and otherwise not." Instances of this kind of reference were frequent in this reign, when the constant sitting of that assembly afforded more opportunity for this intercourse, than in any of the former periods. It was in the spirit, and in pursuance of the practice then in use, that the famous statute of treason, 25 Edward III. ordains, that when any new case of supposed treason should arise, not precisely within the terms of that act, the judges should not proceed upon their own conceptions, but should take the opinion of the next parliament.

What we have been saying of petitions in parliament related chiefly to civil affairs. It was not less common to petition parliament in criminal matters: upon which the parties would be directed to sue a writ of oyer and terminer, or take such other steps according to their case, as the common law prescribed. But criminal prosecutions were instituted in parliament in another way than by petition. The lords constituted a great inquest, which was to present and try each other. There are numberless instances of such a jurisdiction all through this reign. In the fourth year we find a string of articles charging Roger Mortimer with certain treasons, felonies, and misdemeanours. At the end of the record it is said, that the king charged the earls, barons, and peers of the realm, with the same; upon which the said earls, barons, and

1 21 Ed. III., Pet. Parl. 82.
2 See Cotton Abri., p. 30, a long case reported.
3 40 Ed. III., 34.
4 39 Ed. III., Mich. 35.
5 *Counsel.*

peers, having examined all the articles, returned back to the king in the same parliament, and all pronounced by the mouth of one of them, that the matter contained in those articles was notorious to them and to all the people; wherefore they, the said earls, barons, and peers, as judges of parliament, by assent of the king in the same parliament, awarded and adjudged, that the said Roger should be drawn and hanged as a traitor; and order was accordingly given to the earl marshal to execute the sentence.[1] It appears very clearly from this case *who* were the judges in such parliamentary trials; namely, that the lords were to sit in judgment on each other, as peers. But the enormity of the offence which was to be punished in this parliament, and which was nothing else than the murder of the late king, excited a sort of resentment in the parliament, and carried them further than the lawful bounds of their jurisdiction; for they passed sentence of death upon several commoners. To prevent, however, this being drawn into precedent in future, the parliament caused the following memorandum to be entered on the roll: That it was assented and agreed by the king, *et toutz les grantz*, in full parliament, that though the peers had taken upon them to give judgment, with the king's assent, upon certain persons who were not peers, yet no peers in future should be held or charged to give judgment on any other than their peers.[2]

In conformity with this resolution, it appears in the same parliament, among the *placita coronæ*, when Sir Thomas Berkeley was to be tried for the same offence of murdering the king, and he alleged he was out of Berkeley Castle at the time, and therefore not consenting to the murder, that the record runs thus: *de hoc, de bono et malo ponit se* SUPER PATRIAM. *Ideo venerunt inde* JURATORES *coram domino rege in parliamento suo, &c.*[3]

All these prosecutions in parliament were brought forward by articles exhibited; but who were the persons appointed to exhibit such articles, and to stand forth as prosecutors, does not appear. Towards the latter end of this reign the commons took this burthen upon themselves; and among their other petitions, began to exhibit *accusations* for crimes and misdemeanours against offenders who were thought to be out of the reach of the ordinary course of the law. In these prosecutions the king and lords were considered as judges. The first of these is in the 42d year of the king, when Sir John Lee was impeached by the commons for malpractices while steward of the household, and for fraud in some private transactions; concerning all which he was heard before the *great council.*[4] In the 50th year the commons preferred impeachments against many delinquents, and these were tried by the lords. Thus was this formidable mode of prosecution by impeachment of the commons first set on foot.

[1] 4 Ed. III., 1 Roll. Parl.
[2] *Ibid.* 6.
[3] *Ibid.* 16.
[4] 42 Ed. III., Rot. Parl. 20.

The tribunal next in authority to the parliament was *the council.* As the parliament was often called by this name, and there was besides more than one assembly of persons called *the council*, much difficulty has arisen in endeavouring to distinguish between them. We have seen that petitions to parliament in private matters were addressed *a nostre seignour le roi, et a son conseil.* The king had a council which consisted of all the lords and peers of the realm, who, it should seem, were called together by him at times when the parliament was not sitting: this was called the *grand council*, as well as the parliament (being probably the original *commune concilium regni*, before the commons were summoned thither), and was so termed to distinguish it from the other *council*, which the king used to have most commonly about him for advice in matters of law. This last council (which in effect approached very near to what has since been called the *privy council*) consisted of the treasurer, chancellor, justices, barons, the keeper of the rolls, the masters in chancery, the chamberlains of the exchequer, justices in eyre, justices assigned, justices in Wales, the king's serjeants, the secretaries of state, clerk of the privy-seal, clerk of the wardrobe, and such other persons as the king was pleased to advise with.[1] In both these councils the king sat as judge, and causes heard there were said to be *coram rege in concilio.*

Judicature in council.

The nature and constitution of the former of these two councils is less known to us than that of the latter; but it may be discerned, that both of them kept up a very close correspondence with the parliament; so that causes were adjourned from thence into either of the councils, and were there heard and finally determined. Instances of such adjournments into the inferior of these councils were very common, on account of its being almost always in readiness to be called together, the king being seldom without some of the persons constituting this council about him: such references are to be found almost in every page of the parliamentary rolls. But adjournments into the *great council* were not so common, as it was seldom called; and when it did sit, it was generally after the dismission of the commons, to make ordinances, or determine matters that were agitated and remained unfinished in the last parliament. The impeachment before mentioned which the commons preferred against Sir John Lee in the 42d year of the king, was finally determined by the *great council*:[2] and probably many other matters which appear by the rolls to have been determined by *the council*, might have been heard by the *great council*; but owing to the appellation being equivocal, it is not now easy to distinguish the one from the other. The method of address to the two councils was, like that to the parliament, by petition; and the objects of jurisdiction there were such questions, whether civil or criminal, for which the law had not sufficiently, or not at all, provided. The king's council used to sit in different *chambers* that

[1] *Vide* Stat. 14 Ed. III., st. 1, c. 5.

[2] Parl. Rot., 27.

were about the palace; sometimes *en la chambre de peincte;* sometimes *en la chambre blanche*, or *en la chambre de marcolf;* and, as some say,[1] *en la chambre des etoiles;* to which place of their sitting the general return of certain writs in this reign, *coram nobis in camerâ*, referred:[2] it very often sat in the *chauncery*.

Having premised these observations upon the state of the judicature in parliament and the council, the alterations made in both by some statutes passed in this reign will be better understood. There was only one statute that at all affected the judicature of the parliament. This was stat. 14 Edw. III. st. 1. c. v., which was intended, partly, to relieve that assembly from the burthen of answering all applications from the courts below, and partly, by establishing a sort of perpetual committee of parliament for that purpose, to render the course of obtaining advice and direction in judicial matters more regular and easy. The statute complains, that many mischiefs happened through delays of judgment, as well in the chancery as in the king's bench, common bench, exchequer, before justices assigned, and other justices appointed to hear and determine; which delays were occasioned by the difference of opinions among the judges, and by other causes. To remedy this in future, it was ordained, that henceforth there should, at every parliament, be chosen a prelate, two earls, and two barons, who should have commission and power from the king to hear, by petition delivered to them, all complaints of delays or grievances done to them. Such lords were to have power to cause to come before them at Westminster, or elsewhere, the tenor of records and processes of such judgments so delayed, and to cause the justices who were then present to come before them to hear the cause and reasons of such delays: which cause and reasons being so heard, they, by advice of themselves, and that of the chancellor, treasurer, the justices of the one bench and of the other, and others of the king's council, as many and such as they should think convenient, were to proceed *to take a good accord, and make a good judgment;* and according to such accord so taken, the tenor of the record, together with the judgment so accorded, were to be remanded before the justices where the plea depended, for them to give judgment immediately according to the record. However, if the difficulty seemed so great that it could not well be determined without assent of parliament, it was enacted, that the said tenors should be brought by the said chosen lords to the next parliament, and there a final accord and judgment should be given, according to which the judges should be commanded to proceed to give judgment. To put this act into immediate execution, a commission of this sort was immediately issued to the archbishop of Canterbury and four lords.

Thus was a subsisting council of resort provided during the intervals of parliament; but the supreme court of parliament, which had distrusted the judges, would not confide their whole authority

[1] 4 Inst. ch. 5.

[2] *Vide* Parl. Rot. passim.

even to this delegation out of their own body, but by the express provision of this statute reserved to themselves the final decision in all points of difficulty and doubt. It appears, even after this act was passed, that the judges did not cease to recur to the parliament for advice immediately;[1] and as there are through all the rolls many instances of such petitions to the parliament, it may be doubted whether this statute and the establishment thereby appointed were much attended to.

While the intercourse between the courts of ordinary justice and the house of lords was endeavoured to be checked by the former statute, the supreme judicature exercised by the council, in matters both civil and criminal, was put under some restraint by several statutes. These restraints were at that time considered as in support of the Great Charter of liberties, which had forbid all imprisonment or disseisin of freehold but by the judgment of a man's peers, or the law of the land: the process and proceeding before the council were looked upon as derogatory to this great standard of common justice, and therefore not to be tolerated.

The jealousy entertained of the power of the council was justified by the present state of our judicial polity, compared with what it had been in times less settled and polished. The judicature of the king in council had been admitted for wise reasons originally, though as wise ones might now be urged for its abrogation. It was principally calculated for times of disorder, when the common course of justice was circumscribed to very narrow bounds, and ordinary judges were unable to enforce the execution of the law against powerful subjects. When the state of society was altered, and things grew more settled, such supreme powers seemed no longer necessary. Again, the common law during this and the preceding reigns had arrived to such a degree of perfection, that arguments from the incompetency or defect of ordinary provisions were now of no avail: the remedies of the law were so increased in number, and their execution so effectually secured, that it was no longer requisite to recur to the judicial character of the king, to supply by his prerogative the insufficiency of law. All injuries now found redress in the courts below, and to recur to any other jurisdiction was thought unnecessary, dangerous, and burthensome to the subject.

Such arguments of convenience and propriety co-operating with the dread impressed by an authority that was as much, or more, perhaps, of a political than judicial nature, contributed to raise a clamour against the council, and occasioned several acts of parliament, which had the effect of discountenancing any unnecessary application to the king in council, and allowed it only on such terms as, it was thought, might prevent an abuse of it. We shall consider these parliamentary regulations in the order in which they were passed.

[1] *Vide ante*, c. xiii.

The first statute on this subject was made in the 25th of Edw. III.,[1] which enacts, that, according to the Great Charter, none should thenceforth be taken by *petition* or *suggestion* made to the king or his council, unless it was by indictment or presentment of good and lawful people of the same neighbourhood where the fact was done, in due manner, or by process of writ original at the common law. Thus far of criminal inquiries. Further, as to civil matters, it enacts, that none should be ousted of his franchise or his freehold, unless he were duly brought in to answer, and was forejudged of the same *by the course of the law;* and if anything was done otherwise, that it should be redressed, and held void. It was thought not sufficient to declare such proceedings to be void; but, suggestions to the king being often false or malicious, it was enacted, by stat. 37 Edw. III. c. xviii., that, to prevent such for the future, all persons making suggestions should be sent with them before the chancellor, treasurer, and the council, there to find surety for prosecuting their suggestions; and if the suggestions were *found evil*, that the party should incur the same penalty as the adversary would if convicted, and then the matter should be left to the process of the law. This latter clause was repealed in the next year, and instead thereof it was ordained,[2] that a person failing in proof of his suggestion, according to the former statute, should be commanded to prison, till he had agreed with the defendant for the damage and slander he had sustained, and besides, made ransom and fine to the king.

Either the evil was not abated by these statutes, or the uneasiness of the people required further declarations of the parliament on this subject. We find, about four years after this, an act which seems to give a finishing blow to all extraordinary judicature whatsoever, whether civil or criminal. The commons having again complained that persons were brought before the king's council by writ, *and otherwise upon grievous pain,*[3] against the law, it was enacted, by stat. 42 Edw. III. c. iii., that no man be put to answer before justices without presentment or matter of record, or by due process and writ original, according to the old law of the land, and that anything done to the contrary should be void. Some plausible exceptions, no doubt, were devised to prevent the full operation of this statute, as the council still continued in the exercise of its judicial authority, both civil and criminal.

Thus much has been said of the supreme courts held *coram rege* in parliament and in council. We now proceed to the inferior courts. If these were taken in the order to which they seem entitled by the dignity of their style, we should first speak of the two courts *coram rege*, that *ubicunque fuerit in Angliâ*, and that *in cancellariâ*. But we shall first speak of the court of the steward and marshal, a tribunal, as we have seen, once of great eminence, but now sinking both in jurisdiction and importance, owing to the in-

[1] Stat. 5, c. 4. [2] Stat. 38 Edw. III., st. 1, c. 9. [3] *Sur greve peine.*

creasing authority of the king's bench, which derived perhaps some of its cognizance from this court.

The court of the steward and marshal.

It was enacted, by stat. 5 Edw. III. c. ii., that inquests before the steward and marshal of the king's house should be taken by men of the country thereabouts, and not by men of the king's house, except in cases of contracts, covenants, or trespasses made by men of the king's house of the one part and of the other, and within the household, according to the statute made in the time of Edward I.[1] It was ordained, that if any one would complain of error in this court, he should have a writ to remove the record and process before the king in his place —that is, in the king's bench: so that the king's bench was confirmed in that appellate jurisdiction which the court of the steward and marshal possessed once over the other courts. This act was confirmed, or rather re-enacted, in ch. ii. and iii. of stat. 10 Edw. III.

The re-enacting the provisions of this act, and the petitions of the commons against this court during this reign, show that its jurisdiction created great jealousy and discontent. In the 25th year of the king, the commons prayed, that none of the king's servants implead any one in the marshalsea, which was refused, as indeed it would have been confining this court wholly to those of the household.[2] In the 50th year, it was prayed, that the steward and marshal should hold plea of nothing but what was contained in the statute of *Articuli super chartas*, and that the limit of twelve miles might be reckoned either from the king's presence, or the place of the household, and not from both, and that the steward should keep his session within three miles of the king's presence. To this it was answered, that the twelve miles should be reckoned either from the king's presence or from the household, and not from both.[3] In the same year it was stated to the parliament by the commons that there was great complaint of the marshal's court throughout the realm, in answer to which the parliament desired that the grievances might be specified.[4] In the following year it was prayed that the marshal might not intermeddle in that part of Southwark which was called guildable;[5] and again, that it might be declared by statute what pleas the marshal should hold, and that prescription might be allowed before him, as well as before other justices of the king.[6] But after all these complaints, this court was left to continue upon the ground of the above statutes and the old common law.

The king's bench.

There appears nothing new respecting the court *coram rege ubicunque, &c.*, commonly called the king's bench, unless the frequent mention of the *marshal*, as the officer and gaoler, may be considered as such. We find the marshals of the king's bench spoken of very familiarly at the beginning of this

[1] *Vide ante*, c. xi. [2] Cott. Abri., 25 Edw. III., 34. [3] *Ibid.* 50 Edw. III., 82.
[4] *Ibid.* 153. [5] *Ibid.* 31. [6] *Ibid.* 38.

reign, especially in stat. 5 Edw. III. c. viii., relating to the bailing of felons. As this act states some things very particular, it may be well to give it at length. It begins with complaining that persons indicted of felonies, robberies, and thefts, used to remove the indictment before the king, and there surrender themselves; upon which they would be let to bail by the marshal of the king's bench, as were also persons appealed, against whom an exigent had been awarded. As this was letting dangerous offenders loose upon the country, it was necessary some restraint should be put on the marshal's power of bailing: it was therefore enacted, that such persons should be kept in prison; and if any marshal was complained of within term for doing otherwise, that the justices should do what was right. At the end of every term the marshals were to choose before the justices, previous to their departure from the place (supposing, as was sometimes the fact, that the king's bench sat in many different parts of the kingdom in different terms) in what town they would keep their prisoners; and there they were to hire houses at their own costs for keeping of such prisoners, and were not to suffer them to wander abroad, neither with bail nor without; and if any were found wandering, the marshal was to be imprisoned for half a year, and ransomed at the king's will. After the statute had made this provision for the marshals of the king's bench, who, it should seem, were deputies entrusted on occasion of removals of that court, it enacts, respecting *the marshal*, that it should be done within the *verge*, as reason should require. A distinction, and at the same time a sort of connexion is here marked between the marshal of the verge and the marshals of the king's bench, which seems to justify a conjecture that this officer was adopted from the court of the steward and the marshal. In the 22d year of the king, the commons wanted to carry this law against the marshals still further; for they prayed, that if they let anybody at large who was committed for the peace, they might answer in damages; but this was refused.[1]

When *Magna Charta* declared that common pleas should be held in a certain place, it seems to have been understood as of a certain *court* for such pleas, and not of a *certainty* of *place* where that court should be held; for we find the common bench had been removed like the king's bench, though perhaps not so frequently, as it did not in its style import to be attendant on the person of the king. To prevent the expense and mischief which happened to suitors by such removals, it was ordained by stat. 2 Edw. III. c. xi., that before such removal the justices should be warned thereof, in order that they might duly adjourn the parties, and so prevent the losing of their process.

The court of exchequer underwent some parliamentary regulations. The exchequer was a depository of records, and therefore by stat. 9 Edw. III. stat. 1, c. v. it was ordained, that justices of assize,

[1] Cott. Abri., 22 Edw. III., 20.

gaol-delivery, and of *oyer and terminer*, should send all their records and processes determined and put in execution to the exchequer at Michaelmas every year; and that the treasurer and chamberlains should receive them under the seals of the justices, and keep them in the treasury, as had been usual heretofore: the justices, before making out the estreats, were to send to the exchequer as formerly.

The course of appeal from judgments in the exchequer was, after several petitions to parliament, at length settled by statute (*a*). In the 21st year of the king, the commons petitioned that judgments given in that court might be redressed and reversed, if erroneous, in the king's bench, the same as error in the common pleas, and not before themselves, who gave the judgment, as it should seem the course then was. To this it was answered, that such error should be amended by the chancellor, treasurer, and two justices.[1] But it was afterwards, somewhat differently, declared by stat. 31 Edw. III. stat. 1, c. xii., that where a man complained of error made in process in the exchequer, the chancellor and treasurer should cause to come before them in any chamber of council[2] near the exchequer, the record of the process out of the exchequer, taking to them the justices, and such other sage persons as should seem proper, and should cause to be called before them the barons of the exchequer, to hear their informations and the causes of their judgment, and thereupon duly examine the business; and if any error was found, should correct and amend the roll, and afterwards send them into the exchequer for execution to be done thereof.

Error in the exchequer.

These are all the provisions made by parliament for the better ordering of business in the court of exchequer. But the commons had frequently petitioned for other alterations in the practice of this court, which, though they were unsuccessful in obtaining, may be worthy of notice, as they exhibit something of the usage of the court, and the opinion then entertained upon that subject. In the 22d year the commons prayed that an accomptant in the exchequer might not be run to issues before he had been warned to appear. To this it was answered, that the process should be first a *venire*

(*a*) The statute, it is to be observed, applies generally to error in the exchequer, whether in actions or informations; and, beyond all doubt, revenue cases upon such informations were decided in the court of error under this act, as well as cases between party and party. Thus there is the following case in the reign of Edward IV.: In the exchequer chamber, before the justices of the one bench and the other (*i.e.*, the king's bench and common bench), a great matter was rehearsed: how an information was made in the exchequer that a merchant had shipped certain goods, &c. (then the case is stated, as it appeared on the information, and the return of the party to a writ issued out of the exchequer), "and upon that there was a demurrer by the attorney-general, and the matter was argued. And it was said that the crown could either demur or answer" (4 *Edw. IV.* fol. 4). That appears to have been upon the record, but there are other cases in which the facts appear to have been somehow stated in the exchequer chamber before the court of error, perhaps on special verdict.

[1] Cott. Abri. 21 Edw. III., 26.

[2] *En auscune chambre du conseile.*

facias, and then a *distringas*.[1] Towards the close of this reign they prayed that a man might have the privilege of waging his law in the exchequer as in other courts; but this, being excluded in that court by the king's prerogative, who was either plaintiff or interested in all suits there, was not granted.[2] In like manner, when it was prayed that attaints might be had of verdicts in the exchequer, as in other courts, it was refused.[3]

We find it had become a practice to sue in the exchequer upon *suggestions*, in the way which had been so often complained of before, respecting the council. The whole proceeding by suggestion being a prerogative course, might, upon that idea, have obtained in the exchequer, which was a court for ordering and governing the king's revenue, and therefore, of all others, best entitled to the same extraordinary and summary way that was affected by the council. In the 40th year of this king we find a case which somewhat explains what this course was. It was said by Lud, a baron in the exchequer, that though no process was made against the king's debtor, yet if he was found present in the exchequer, he should be bound to answer to the king. To this another, named Fitz-John, said, that so it would be, provided it appeared of record that he really was a debtor; but not, if it only appeared by *surmise or suggestion made*, for *then* he ought to be brought in by process, &c.[4] This was putting it upon the footing of the other courts; and accordingly, in the 47th year, the commons prayed that some remedy should be had where persons were called into the exchequer upon suggestion *without* process, contrary to the statute made in the 42d year of the king[5] before mentioned. The answer to this was, that if any special complaint was made, remedy might be had;[6] so that these suggestions in the exchequer (which were in fact no other than petitions, or *bills*, as since called) were left upon the ground of stat. 42 Edw. III.

Justices of assize, and *nisi prius*, &c.

Equal pains were taken to improve other parts of our judicial establishment. The commissions of assize and *nisi prius*, of *oyer and terminer*, and of gaol-delivery, received several modifications. It was complained that felonies had been very much encouraged, not only by too easy pardons, but also through an inattention to a statute made in the time of Edward I.,[7] which directed that the justices assigned to take assizes, if laymen, should make deliverance of the gaol; and if the one was a clerk, and the other a layman, then that the lay-judge, together with another of the country associated with him, should deliver the gaol. It was therefore enacted by stat. 2 Edw. III. c. ii., that justices should be appointed, as directed by that act; and that assizes, attaints, and certificates, should be taken before the justices commonly assigned, being good men and lawful, and

1 Cott. Abri., 22 Edw. III., 17.
2 *Ibid.* 50 Edw. III., 83.
3 *Ibid.* 29 Edw. III., 27.
4 40 Ass. 35 pl.
5 *Vide ante*, c. xiii.
6 Cott. Abri., 47 Edw. III., 34.
7 Viz. Stat. 27 Edw. I., st. 1, c. 3. *Vide ante*, c. ix.

having knowledge of the law, as directed by another statute of Edward I. In addition to this it was now further provided, that writs of *oyer and terminer* should not be granted but before justices of the one bench or the other, or the justices errant; and that only *for great hurt and horrible trespass*, and of the king's special grace, as ordained almost in the same words by the statute of Westminster 2.[1]

The next provision relates to the commission of *nisi prius*. The last alteration made in this commission was by the statute of *York*, in the preceding reign,[2] which confined it to cases, "*if the* DEMANDANT *pray the same.*" It was now enacted,[3] that all such inquests to be taken in a plea of land should be taken as well at the suit of the tenant as of the demandant, with a saving of all other process, as appointed by the said statute of York. By stat. 4 Edw. III. c. ii., it was ordained, respecting three of these commissions, that good and discreet persons, other than of the places, if they could be found sufficient, should be assigned in all the counties in England to take assizes, juries, and certifications, and to deliver gaols; and that was to be three times a year, and more often, if need were.

The commission of *nisi prius* was further materially altered by two statutes, which at length put it into the form into which it has continued ever since: these are stat. 14 Edw. III. c. xvi., and stat. 20 Edw. III. c. vi. We have seen that by the original establishment of these justices,[4] inquests and juries upon issues arising in the court of king's bench or common pleas, were to be taken before one or more justices of the same place; but it often happened that in many counties no justice of that description came, which brought great inconvenience on suitors and on the jurors impannelled. To remedy this it was ordained by stat. 14 Edw. III. c. xvi., that in the king's bench, a *nisi prius* should be granted before any justice of the court, if any of them went into that part; if not, then before any justice of the common pleas, at a certain day to be agreed; and a tenor of the record was to be delivered or sent to him, under the seal of the chief justice of the place; at which day he was to take the inquest, and return the verdict under his seal, with the writ, the tenor, and the pannel. These were to be received in the king's bench and enrolled, and thereupon judgment given according to the verdict. Such justice of the common pleas was to have power to record defaults and nonsuits, the same as if the *nisi prius* had been granted before some justice of the king's bench; after which defaults so recorded and returned, the justices were to give judgment upon the record. Thus far respecting issues depending in the king's bench: the like course was to be pursued in regard to issues in the common pleas. Further, it was provided that should no justices of either bench come into the country where inquests or juries were to be taken, then the *nisi prius* should be granted before

[1] Viz., ch. 29. *Vide ante*, c. ix. [2] *Vide ante*, c. xi. [3] Stat. 2 Edw. III., ch. 16.
[4] 13 Edw. I. Westm. 2, c. 30; 12 Edw. II., st. 1, c. 3, 4. *Vide ante*, c. ix. and c. xii.

the chief baron of the exchequer, *if he be a man of the law* (which it seems at this time he sometimes was not), with the same powers as were given to the justices of the one bench or the other. If neither any justice nor the chief baron came into the country, then the *nisi prius* was to be granted before the justices assigned to take assizes in those parts, so that one of the justices assigned was a justice of the one bench or the other, or the king's sergeant sworn, with the same authority as was above given to the justices of the one bench or the other. It was also directed, that should one party demand the tenor of the record, to deliver to the justices before whom the *nisi prius* was granted, in order to prevent any fraud or damage being done to the other party or the inquest, another tenor of the record should be given to the other party if he required it. As the justices of *nisi prius* were authorised by the statute of York to give judgment in the country upon verdicts of assize and of inquests, and upon nonsuits and defaults, it was ordained that the justices appointed by this act should have the same authority.

In the 20th year of this[1] king, it was ordained that justices of assize should have commissions authorising them to inquire in their sessions of sheriffs, escheators, bailiffs of franchises, and their under-ministers; and also of maintainers, common embraceors, and jurors in the country, if the said officers took anything for the execution of their office, as for making pannels or putting in jurors suspected and of evil fame; and if the said maintainers, embraceors, or jurors took reward of the parties to prevent the course of justice. This proceeding was to be as well at the suit of the king as that of the parties; and therefore, says the statute, the king has commanded the chancellor and treasurer to hear the complaints of all persons so aggrieved, and to ordain speedy remedy.

The other material alteration in the proceeding at *nisi prius* was effected by stat. 42 Edw. III. c. xi. It was complained that the pannels of inquests were not returned before the sessions of the justices at *nisi prius*, and otherwise; so that the parties could not have knowledge of the names of the persons to pass on the inquest, whereby, says the statute, divers of the people have been disinherited and oppressed. To remedy this it was now enacted, that no inquests, but assizes and deliverances of gaols, should be taken by writ of *nisi prius*, nor in other manner, at the suit of any one, before the names of all those who were to pass in the inquest were returned into court. Thus far of *nisi prius*. As to assizes, it was directed that sheriffs should array the pannels in assizes, four days at least before the sessions of the justices (*a*), under the penalty of £20, so that the parties might have a view of the pannel if they

(*a*) Upon this took place one of the most important decisions ever pronounced, and one which may well be studied as a leading case upon the construction of statutes as to procedure. It was held that notwithstanding the peremptory words of the statute, yet—though there were only two days before the assize—it sufficed; for that a statute was in the affirmative, as this was, did not "toll," *i.e.* take away, the common law (43

[1] Ch. 6.

required it. It was further directed, in order to facilitate the above regulation, that bailiffs of franchises should, under the like pain, make their return to the sheriff six days before the sessions.

These two acts of the 14 and 42 Edw. III. deserve a particular notice. It is probable, that before the 14 Edw. III. there used to be no record made out for the trial at *nisi prius;* which being before a justice of the court where the issue was joined, there was less need of any copy of it to inform the judge; and the authority to try the issue rested wholly on the judge's commission of *nisi prius.* Whether before this act there might not be sometimes such a copy made, can only be collected from probable conjecture; but after this act, it became both expedient and requisite that a tenor of the record should be made, which has since been called the *Nisi Prius* Record: upon which the judge "returned the verdict," as the act says, making what has been since called the *Postea,* from the initial word in the form of the return.

The alteration effected by stat. 42 Edw. III. was this. We have seen that heretofore certain writs used to be made returnable before the justices itinerant, sometimes with a clause of *nisi prius,* sometime without.[1] It is probable this practice was not yet wholly out of use, and that this statute alludes to it when it speaks of "writs returned at the sessions of the justices at *nisi prius and otherwise."* We have also seen [2] that this clause of *nisi prius* was inserted not only in the writ of *venire facias,* as directed by the statute of *nisi prius,* but also in the writs of *habeas corpora juratorum* and *distringas,* when the jurors were brought in by either of those writs, after their default on the *venire facias.* The practice had continued, as formerly, irregular and unsettled; but when this act directed that no inquest should be taken by "*nisi prius,* or other manner," before the names of the jurors were returned into court, it is probable that, in order to attain this object, the jury-process began then first to be arranged in this way: The *venire facias,* instead of containing the clause of *nisi prius,* was made returnable on some day in term, with the pannel annexed; then, after the parties had had the opportunity of making their challenges, as designed by this statute, the process of *distringas* or *habeas corpora* would issue, with a clause of *nisi prius* in it, returnable the following term; and upon this writ the trial was had. Thus, ever after, it was necessary in all causes that went to trial, to have both a *venire* and a process of contempt, either a *distringas* or a *habeas corpora* against the jurors.

Some few regulations were made respecting justices of *oyer and terminer,* independent of the other commissions, and which, for

Assize, fol. 22). That is to say, in more modern language, the act was directory; it merely said that there should be so many days' notice of the proceeding; it did not say that if there were not the proceeding should not be valid. It would be difficult to find a more important decision, or one establishing a principle more beneficial (*vide* 3 *Hen. VII.,* fol. 2). And it would be well if it had been followed in later times.

[1] *Vide ante,* vol. i. c. vii.

[2] *Ibid.* c. viii.

this reason, we have reserved to be mentioned last. In the statute of Northampton, stat. 2 Edw. III. c. vi., which contains many provisions for the better keeping of the peace, and punishment of offenders, it was ordained by chap. vi., that whereas by the statute of Winchester the justices assigned had power to inquire of defaults in the execution of that statute, and make a report thereof to the king in parliament, to be remedied by the king, which course did not seem effectual; it was now enacted that the said justices should have power to punish all disobedient persons. This was in the early part of the reign, before the *keepers*, or, as they were afterwards called, *justices of the peace*, were commissioned with such high powers as they afterwards received.

By another chapter[1] of the same statute there is a special authority given to the justices of *oyer and terminer*, which seems to be a confirmation of the court of *trailbaston* instituted by Edward I. For the punishment of felonies, robberies, manslaughters, trespasses, and oppressions of the people, it was enacted that the king should assign justices in divers places, within the king's bench and elsewhere, as was done in the time of Edward I. of great men of the land, being of great power with some justices of one bench or the other, with other learned men in the law, to inquire, as well at the suit of the party as at the king's suit, and *to hear and determine* all manner of felonies, robberies, manslaughters, thefts, oppressions, conspiracies, and grievances done to the people against the law, statutes, and customs of the realm, as well within franchise as without; and also to inquire of the sheriffs, coroners, under-sheriffs, hundredors, bailiffs, constables, and all other ministers within liberties and without. We shall see afterwards that the authority of justices of the peace was thought more conducive to such end than this commission of *trailbaston*, and that the latter was gradually superseded thereby. In the 34th year of this king[2] it was ordained that the justices assigned in writs of *oyer and terminer* should be named by the court, and not by the party, as we have seen might be, and was usually the course.[3]

Thus stood the commissions of assize and *nisi prius*, of *oyer and terminer*, and gaol-delivery at the close of this reign. Though attempts had been made to expedite causes when they had come to that stage in which a *nisi prius* should issue, it was prayed by the commons, in the 50th year of the king, that the process of such as were at issue, and did not within one year after sue out their *nisi prius*, should be discontinued and held void: again, if the plaintiff or defendant did not, upon the return of the *habeas corpora*, sue out his *nisi prius*, that the whole process might be discontinued: and further, that every man might have his *nisi prius* granted as well against the king as others, without sueing to the privy seal: but neither of these applications succeeded;[4] any more than a

[1] Ch. 7. [2] Ch. 1. [3] *Vide ante*, c. ix.
[4] Cott. Abri., Edw. III., 146, 174.

petition that such as sued forth assizes should not be obliged to pay for the justices' patent, as had always been the usage.[1]

A statute was made in the 20th year of the king, which had a reference to all the courts we have been mentioning, and was founded in a zeal for the due administration of justice to all the king's subjects. This statute opens by stating that the king *had* commanded his justices to do equal law and execution of right to all his subjects, whether rich or poor, without any regard to persons, and without delaying to do right on account of any letters or commandment from the king or any other; and it enacts, that should any letters, writs, or commandments come to the justices, or to others deputed to do law and right, according to the usage of the realm, in disturbance of the law, or execution thereof, the justices and others deputed should proceed to hold their courts and processes as if no such interference had been made. It recites that the king had caused all his justices to be sworn, to take no fee nor robe (that being the denomination under which part of their salary was paid) of any one, but the king only, during their office; and to take no gift nor reward, by themselves or by others to their use, of any one who had any matter depending before them, except meat and drink, and that of small value; and further, to give no counsel to any where the king was party, or was interested, under pain of their body, lands, and goods. At the same time an increase was made in the judges' fees.[2] The same was ordained respecting the barons of the exchequer; and they were expressly commanded, in the king's presence, to do right and reason to all the king's subjects, without the delays that had been so much complained of in that court.[3] It was also ordained, that justices assigned to hear and determine, and those who were associated to them, justices of assize to be taken in the country, and of gaol-delivery, and those associated to them, should take such an oath as should be enjoined them by the council in the chancery, before their commissions were delivered to them.[4]

The impediment thrown in the way of judicial proceedings by protections, was a great grievance to the nation; and, notwithstanding the fair appearance of the king's intention, as expressed in the above statute, these protections were granted all through this and the subsequent reigns, and the commons frequently, though in vain, petitioned against them. From a perusal of stat. 25 Edw. III. st. 5, c. xix., we find the king had granted protections to several persons, being his debtors, discharging them from any other actions of debt till they had satisfied the king. It was provided nevertheless, by that act, that such persons should answer suits against them, but that execution of the judgment should be suspended till the king was paid; though such plaintiffs, if they would undertake for the king's debt, might have immediate execution against the

[1] Cott. Abri., 45 Edw. III., 35.
[2] Ch. 1.
[3] Ch. 2.
[4] Ch. 3.

defendant. Very early in this reign it was enacted,[1] that no command either under the great or little seal should issue to disturb or delay common right; and if any such command was to come, the justices were to disregard it. As there was still complaint of fines being exacted for *beaupleader*, the statute of Marlbridge was again[2] directed to be observed.[3]

After the several courts, the remedies of the law constitute the next objects of consideration. Nothing more was done by the parliament on this head than enlarging and modifying those already in use, making no addition to the old stock.

The writ of attaint, of which so much has already been said,[4] was the only redress to which those could resort who had suffered by an unjust verdict; this was now rendered more general and more expeditious by some few regulations. It was ordained by stat. 1 Edw. III. st. 1, c. vi., that a writ of attaint should be granted, as well upon the *principal* as the damages in a writ of trespass, and that the chancellor should have power to grant such writs without speaking thereof to the king. Further it was enacted, that the justices should not omit taking the attaint, because the damages for which it went were not yet paid; which it seems was before held a good objection upon the trial, as the party plaintiff could not say he had been damnified till he had paid the damages given by the wrongful verdict. To avoid the great delays to which attaints as well as other suits were liable, but which were particularly grievous in an action that was made necessary by the misconduct of jurors, who had failed of doing their duty, it was enacted, by stat. 5 Edw. III. c. vi., that no essoin of the king's service nor protection should be allowed in such juries, any more than in assizes of novel disseisin;[5] that five days[6] in the year at least should be given before the justices of the common bench in such juries; and that there should be a *nisi prius* in this, as in other writs. Again, by the next chapter of the same act the provision of stat. 1 Edw. III. concerning attaints in trespass, was enlarged; for it was enacted, that attaints should be allowed as well in pleas of trespass moved *without* writ as by writ, before justices of record, if the damages adjudged were more than forty shillings. This was carried still further by stat. 28 Edw. III. c. viii., which gives this writ as well upon *a bill* (which had lately become a common way of instituting suits) as a writ of trespass, without any regard to the quantity of damages.

In the meantime, the parliament had been solicited to make this remedy more general. In the 21st year there was a petition praying that attaints should be granted in writs of debt, and in all other writs and bills where the demands or damages did not amount to forty shillings; and further, in actions where a person sued *tam pro*

[1] Stat. 2 Edw. III., c. 8. [2] *Vide ante*, c. viii. [3] Stat. 1 Edw. III., st. 2, c. 8.
[4] *Vide ante*, c. ix. [5] *Ibid.* 315.
[6] This must considerably shorten the returns prescribed by the stat. *Dies communes in banco. Vide ante*, c. viii.

domino rege, quàm pro seipso, as the king's ministers and others frequently did, where, as the whole principal and damages recovered went to themselves and not to the king, it was thought hard that neither a writ of error nor attaint should be had. But though it was granted that writs of error should lie, this, as well as the former application about attaints, did not receive a favourable answer.[1] The parliament, however, at length complied with the wishes of the people, and it was ordained by stat. 34 Edw. III. c. vii., that an attaint should be had by the person against whom a verdict passed, as well in pleas *real* as pleas *personal;* and that it should be granted to the poor, would *affie* that they had nothing whereof to make fine, saving their countenance, without paying any, and to all others upon an easy, fine. After this, the proceeding by attaint grew more common, being open to all persons who were aggrieved by a false verdict.

It was complained, that executors could not by the old law have an action for a trespass done to their testator, as of goods and chattels carried away; to remedy which it was enacted by stat. 4 Edw. III. c. vii., that they should have actions in such cases, and recover damages, as their testators might. And further by stat. 25 Edw. III. st. 5, c. v., it was ordained, that executors of executors should have actions of debt, accompt, and of goods carried away, of the first testator; and further, should have execution of statutes-merchant, and recognizances made in courts of record of the first testator as he would have had if alive. Such executors of executors were to answer to others for so much of the goods of the first testator as came to their hands, in the same manner as the first executors should have done if alive.

We have before seen, that an *assisa utrùm,* or, as it had now long been called, a *juris utrùm,* would not lie for any other than a parson;[2] but it was now ordained by stat. 14 Edw. III. st. 1, c. xvii., that parsons, *vicars*, wardens of chapels, and provosts, wardens and priests of perpetual chauntries, should have writs of *juris utrùm* of lands and tenements, rents and possessions annexed to vicarages, chapels, and chauntries, and recover by other writs in their case, as parsons of churches or prebends (*a*). The writ of *deceit* was extended by stat. 2 Edw. III. c. xvii., which enacted, that it should be maintainable as well in case of garnishment touching pleas of land,

(*a*) In the reign of Edward II. it was held that an abbot or other ecclesiastical person could have a writ of *ne injuste vexes,* in respect of land held in *frankalmoigne* (The abbot of Baring's case, *Year-book*, 7 *Edward II.*, 234). The abbot there complained of one Ralf for taking his cattle, and Ralf set up that the abbot held of him by rent-service, of three shillings, for which he seized the beasts. To which the abbot replied, that he held the land in pure and perpetual alms (*en pure et perpetuel almoigne*), discharged of all manner of service; on which it was said, that if the rent-service was wrongfully claimed, the abbot could be discharged by the writ of *ne injuste vexes. Et nota,* per Inge, C.J., in isto placeto, quod abbas potest habere le ne vexes ubi tenet in pura et perpetua eleemosina (fol. 235).

[1] Cott. Abri., 21 Edw. III., 23, 24.

[2] *Vide ante*, vol. i. c. vii.

where such garnishment was given, as in case of summons in a plea of land.

Such were the alterations made in some old writs by parliament. The commons endeavoured to obtain a change of the law in two real writs, but were not successful. They complained, that where land was given to a man and his wife, and the heirs of their body begotten, though they had no issue between them, yet if one died, the other, as the law then stood, might commit waste, not being within any of the laws of Edward I. made against waste.[1] This was thought a great hardship on the reversioner, as the estate of the first takers (though the survivor of them was called *tenant in tail, after possibility of issue extinct*) could be considered as in effect only an estate for term of life; it was therefore prayed, that a writ of waste might lie in such case. Again, as a writ of possession would not, by the old law, lie of land devisable,[2] although not actually devised, and this was felt to be a considerable impediment to justice, it was prayed that writs might be granted of such lands, saving to the tenants their plea in case of an actual devise. The answer to both these petitions seems to intimate that they should be ordained by statute,[3] but no such statute appears to have been made.

The first statute of this king that relates to process and proceeding, is stat. 2 Edw. III., c. xiii., which is principally worthy of observation, because it shows the opinion to have then been that the death of the king somewhat affected, if not destroyed, an action that was grounded on a fact against the king's peace; for this act declares, that like process should be made of trespass done in the time of Edward II., as of trespass done in the time of this king.

Process of outlawry.

We have seen in Bracton's time, when the process of distress had taken the defendant's goods and chattels, in what manner he was satisfied out of them for his damages.[4] Several rules were laid down by stat. 5 Edw. III., c. xii. and xiii., for a similar redress in cases of outlawry in civil actions; that where the plaintiff recovered damages, and the defendant was outlawed at the king's suit, no charter of pardon of his outlawry should be granted, except the chancellor was certified that the plaintiff was satisfied for his damages. Where a man was outlawed by process before his appearance, no such charter was to be granted, except the chancellor was certified that the person outlawed had yielded himself to prison before the justices of the place from whence the writ of exigent issued; as before the king's bench, common pleas, or justices of oyer and terminer; but if the last were not sitting, then before the justices of the king's bench; and in such case the record also with the process was to be removed before that court (*a*).

(*a*) A statute, 8 Henry VI., passed to prevent abuses of outlawry through want of proper proclamations, and statutes passed in the reign of Henry VIII. and Elizabeth, to afford further remedy.

[1] *Vide ante*, c. viii.

[2] *Ibid.* vol. i. c. vii.

[3] Parl. Rot. 21 Edw. III., 46, 47.

[4] *Vide ante*, vol. i. c. viii.

Upon the party surrendering, the justices were to warn the plaintiff to appear at a certain day; at which day, if the warning was duly witnessed, and the plaintiff appeared, then they were to plead upon the first original writ, as though no outlawry had been pronounced. If the plaintiff did not appear, the defendant was to be delivered according to his charter.[1]

Again, because persons duly outlawed had avoided their outlawry by reason of imprisonment, which had been supported by the false testimony of sheriffs and others, it was enacted, that if any would defeat an outlawry by such testimony, he should surrender himself to prison, and then the justices of the king's bench should cause the party at whose suit the outlawry was pronounced, to be warned to appear before them at a certain day; at which day, if he would verify that the testimony was untrue, such verification should be received. In like manner the king's serjeant, or his attorney, or any other that would sue for the king, was to be received to have the same averment against such testimony, where the outlawry was pronounced at the king's suit.[2]

It may be just mentioned here, though it more properly belongs to that division where we treat of the criminal law, that a declaration was made by stat. 18 Edw. III., st. 1, in what cases an exigent should issue; some small alteration in which was made by stat. 2 of the same year, c. v., both which will be spoken of more particularly in their proper place. We next come to stat. 25 Edw. III., st. 5, c. xvii., which gave a greater scope to the process of outlawry in civil actions; for it enacts, that such process should be made in a writ of *debt*, and *detinue* of chattels, and in taking of beasts by writ of *capias* and process of exigent, as was used in a writ of accompt.

This statute, and those relating to the writ of accompt, and here alluded to, have been long considered as introducing a novelty into the process of personal actions. It is laid down by Lord Coke, and has been repeated by others without examination, that no writ of *capias* lay at common law for debt, or damages, but only in actions *vi et armis*. But this opinion is contradicted by the history we have before given of process. We find in the reign of Henry III. that the process in all personal actions was as follows: If the party did not appear upon the summons, then he was attached by pledges; and afterwards by better pledges: if he still did not appear, the sheriff was commanded *quòd habeat corpus*, to take the body: if the sheriff returned *non inventus*, there issued a *distringas per terras et catalla;* after that, another *distringas*, commanding him also take the body; after that, another *distringas*, *ne manum apponat;* and lastly, a writ to take the land and chattels into the king's hands.

Thus there might be one summons, two attachments, a *capias* (as it was afterwards called), and four distresses. To this it is added

[1] Ch. 12. [2] Ch. 13.

by Bracton, that should the defendant not be found, nor have any lands or goods, whether the action was for money or for a trespass, he was to be demanded from county to county, and outlawed;[1] and persons so outlawed were condemned to perpetual imprisonment or to abjure the realm.

Such was the process to compel appearance in court. It happens that no ancient author has furnished us with any information concerning the process of execution in personal actions; but whether we consider the analogy of the two cases, or the rule that was afterwards laid down respecting the process before appearance and after judgment, we cannot avoid concluding, that there was, at least, as effectual a process upon the judgment, as upon the original writ.

This being the state of process at common law, we shall now consider the alterations that had been made by some late statutes. In the first place, it was enacted by the stat. Marlb. c. xii., that in all cases of attachment, after the second attachment should immediately follow the last distress.[2] By this provision, a very material alteration seems to have been made in all personal actions; for not only the three former *distringas's* were now superseded, but also the writ of *habeas corpus*, which, at common law, followed immediately after the second attachment; and of course, as it should seem, the process of outlawry no longer could follow; for, according to Bracton, it was only where the defendant had no lands, *and could not be found*, that he was to be demanded and outlawed; and the return of *non inventus* could not be made but upon the *habeas corpus*, and the second *distingas*, both which were now taken away.

If this was the construction, at that time, put on this provision, the consequence seems to have been very early discovered; for in the same parliament, a provision was made respecting accountants, which restored the process against them very nearly to the same state in which it had been before the late act. It was ordained by stat. Marl. c. xxiii., that if bailiffs, who ought to account with their lords, withdrew themselves (that is, were *non inventi*), and had no lands or tenements by which they might be distrained, they should be attached by their bodies, so as the sheriff might cause them to come to render an account.[3] The process, framed upon this act, differed from the common law process in this respect only; instead of a writ to take the body before the *distringas*, it was not to issue till it appeared that the party had no lands or tenements; and accordingly a special writ, called a *monstravit de compoto*, was framed for that purpose.

The next regulation about personal process was by stat. Westm. 1, c. xlv., which directed that the last distress should issue immediately after the first attachment.[4] After this, we meet with the stat. Westm. 2. c xi., which enacted, that when accountants were

[1] *Vide ante*, vol. i. c. viii. [2] *Ibid.* [3] *Ibid.* [4] *Ibid.* c. ix.

found in arrears by auditors, their bodies should be arrested, and sent to gaol till they satisfied all arrears; and further, that if they fled and would not come to accompt, and had nothing whereby they could be distrained, and were returned *non inventi*, they should be demanded from county to county, and outlawed.[1]

Putting together all these statutes, the process seems to have been reduced to this form. In accompt it was summons, one attachment, one (being the last) distress, *capias*, and outlawry; and in all other personal actions, a summons, one attachment, and one (being the last) distress, and there it ended. The statute, therefore, of this king now in question had the effect, it is true, of giving to the action of debt a process against the person, which it then had not; but this appears to be only bringing it back to the condition it was in at common law, with the improvement of such changes as had been made by the before-mentioned statutes, to lessen the number of writs of attachment and of distress.

What has just been said of the process of *capias* and outlawry in personal action, must not be construed to extend to trespass, which was in the nature of a criminal proceeding, and on that account entitled to the writ of *capias* and process of outlawry.[2]

For the due execution of these and all writs in general some alteration was made in the stat. Westm. 2, c. xxxix. For whereas that directs writs to be delivered to the sheriff in the *full* or *rear county*, and that in such case the sheriff should thereupon make a bill; it was now enacted by stat. 2 Edw. III., c. v., that at whatsoever time or place in the county a man delivered a writ to the sheriff, or under-sheriff, they should receive the same, and make a bill according to the above statute, without taking anything for so doing; and if they refused, others who were present might set their seals to it; and the sheriff or under-sheriff should be liable to the penalties of the above statute, if they failed in returning the writ. Power was given to the justices of assize to hear all com-

[1] *Vide ante*, c. ix.

[2] The validity of these acts, and of the two relating to the process of *capias* in accompt, has been questioned in a very particular manner by Mr Burgess, in his *Considerations on the Law of Insolvency*. He contends that, according to *Magna Charta*, no man should be imprisoned but by the verdict of his equals, or by the law of the land; that by the law of the land no man could be imprisoned for debt; that the statutes of Marlbridge and of Westminster 1, which authorised imprisonment of accountants, were repealed by such statutes as were made to confirm *Magna Charta;* so that the present statute of Edward III. referred to a nullity; that this statute also was repealed by subsequent confirmations of *Magna Charta*, and more especially by stat. 42 Edward III., which expressly repealed all acts contrary to *Magna Charta;* that the statute Henry VII., which gave the same process in trespass on the case as was allowed in debt and accompt, referred to statutes that were not in existence, and was therefore void; so that, upon the whole, this writer concludes, that there is no parliamentary provision whatever authorising imprisonment for debt. This hypothesis depends wholly on the force he attributes to the words *lex terræ* in *Magna Charta*. It seems a very singular construction to confine their sense to what was the law of the land at the time of passing the charter, as if the Parliament was to be for ever tied up from making any future alteration. Besides, as it appears from Bracton, that process against the person was, in his time, the usual procedure in personal actions, it is very probable that such was the *lex terræ* at the time of passing *Magna Charta*.

The obvious sense of *lex terræ* in this passage is probably the true one: namely, every lawful process and proceeding. That an arrest by writ was no violation of *Magna*

plaints on this subject, and award damages to the aggrieved party. It had been enacted by stat. 1 Edw. III., st. 1, c. v., that a man might aver against the false returns of bailiffs of franchises, who had full returns of writs, and recover as well against them as against the sheriff, where too small issues were returned, and in other cases, so that it was not to the prejudice of the lords and their franchise, or that of holy church, and that the punishment fell wholly on the bailiffs. So many expedients were tried to secure the regular execution of process.

Some of the rigorous consequences of the ancient process were removed. We have seen, that a tenant whose land was taken by the *magnum cape*, lost it if he did not replevy in a certain space of time.[1] By stat. 9 Edw. III., st. 1, c. ii., this old law of *non plevin* was taken away; for it was enacted, that none should lose his land by reason of *non plevin*. By chap. iii. of the same act, the *fourcher* by essoin was taken from executors, as it had been from other co-defendants by some statutes of Edward I.[2] It was ordained, that in a writ of debt brought against divers executors, neither they, nor any of them, should have more than one essoin before appearance, that is, at the summons or attachment; and after appearance but one, as the testator should have had; so that the executors were to be considered only as one man representing the testator. Further, by the same act, a course of process against executors was thus directed, namely, that though the sheriff answered at the summons that some of them had nothing whereby he might be summoned, yet an attachment should still be awarded against them. And if the sheriff answered, that he had nothing whereby he might be attached, the great distress should be awarded; so that at the return thereof, he or they who first appeared in court should answer to the plaintiff: and though some of them had appeared in court, and made default at the day on which the great distress was returned upon the other, yet still he

Charta is confirmed by a statute of the present king, which was made for explaining and enforcing this very provision. The statute 25 Edw. III., st. 5, c. iv., runs in these words: *Whereas, it is contained in the Great Charter of the Franchises of England, that none shall be imprisoned, nor put out of his freehold, nor of his franchises, nor free customs, unless it be* BY THE LAW OF THE LAND, it is accorded, assented, and established, that from henceforth none shall be taken by petition or suggestion made to our lord the king, or to his council, unless it be by indictment or presentment of good and lawful people of the same neighbourhood where such deeds be done, in due manner, or by process made by *writ original* at the common law. [The extraordinary notion embodied in the work above alluded to, and so justly condemned by our author—that statutes subsequent to *Magna Charta* are void if contrary to it—is clearly contrary to constitutional principle, and offends against a well-established legal maxim, that later laws abrogate former ones not consistent therewith, *leges posteriores leges priores abrogant*. *Magna Charta*, putting it at the highest, was but an Act of Parliament, and, as Lord Coke says, declaratory of the common law. And it would be a strange doctrine that the legislature could not alter the common law. The notion that it is in the power of the parliament to restrict or preclude the exercise of legislative power on any subject for the future, is surely idle, and was long ago refuted by Lord Bacon, who observed, in allusion to such an idea: "The force and obligation of this law was in itself illusory, by a precedent Act of Parliament to bind or frustrate a future; for a supreme and absolute power cannot conclude itself, neither can that which is in its nature revocable be made fixed" (*Hist. Hen. VII.*, fol. 83). Yet this strange notion has been revived in our own time.]

[1] *Vide ante*, vol. i. c. viii.

[2] *Ibid.* c. ix.

or they who first appeared at the great distress should be put to answer. In case the judgment passed for the plaintiff, he should have his judgment and execution of the goods of the testator, against those who pleaded, *and* against all others named in the writ, as well as if they had all pleaded. The statute, however, contains a saving for those who chose to proceed after the old course at common law.

As the law now stood, a demandant in a plea of land was often delayed by the tenant vouching to warranty a dead man, against which voucher the demandant was not received to aver that he was dead; but it was now enacted, by stat. 14 Edw. III., st. 1, c. xviii., that such averments should be received. Again, as by the old law,[1] a question upon a *false judgment* from an inferior court was to have been tried by duel, it was enacted by stat. 1 Edw. III., st. 1, c. iv., to correct so barbarous a proceeding, that when a record came into the king's court by writ of false judgment, if the party suggested that the record was otherwise than the court alleged it to be, the averment should be received *of the good country*,[2] *and of those who were present at the court when the record was made*, if they were returned by the sheriff with the others of the country; and if they came not, the inquest was to be taken by the good country.

Two other laws were made respecting trials; the one for the trial of deeds, the other of bastardy. It was complained that great delay happened in actions by the parties pleading in bar a release, quit-claim, or other special deed made within a franchise where the king's writ did not run. To remedy this obstruction to justice, it was enacted, by stat. 9 Edw. III., st. 1, c. iv., that when such deeds were exhibited in bar of an action, bearing date in a place within a franchise, although there were witnesses of the same franchise named in the deed, yet if the deed was denied, process should be awarded into the county where the plea was moved, to have the inquest of the country *and* the witnesses to appear; and if the witnesses came not at the great distress, the justices were not on that account to omit proceeding to take the inquest, but were to go on in like manner as if the deed had been made in the county; a course similar to one directed in a similar case in this reign, and which must gradually lead to the practice of no longer summoning the witnesses to be joined with the jurors. In stat. 25 Edw. III., st. 2, which communicated to children born of English subjects in foreign parts the privileges of natural-born subjects, it was ordained, that in questions of bastardy arising upon that act, the matter should be certified by the bishop of the place where the demand was, the same as where bastardy was alleged against persons born in England.

Some matters of pleading were altered by stat. 25 Edw. III., st. 5, c. xi. The exception of non-tenure of parcel was not to abate any

[1] *Vide ante*, vol. i. c. iii.

[2] *Soit receu averrement de bone pais.*

writ, but only for that quantity concerning which the non-tenure was alleged.[1] Again by c. xviii. of the same statute, it was ordained, that notwithstanding adjournment made in the eyre by writ *de libertate probandâ,* purchased by villeins, to delay their lords of their actions against such villeins, the same lords should be received to allege the exception of villenage against their villeins in all writs, whether such writs *de libertate probandâ* were purchased by deceit, or in other manner; and that the lords might seize the bodies of their villeins, as they might before the writ *de libertate probandâ* was purchased. But a more effectual check was given to pleas of villenage (which were very common at this time) by stat. 37 Edw. III., c. xvii., ordaining, that no writ should be abated by the exception of villenage, if the demandant or plaintiff would aver that he who alleged the exception was free the day of the writ purchased.

Qualifications of jurors.

Nothing could be of more importance than that trials by jury should be conducted with impartiality, and free from all external influence; but, considering the persons who constituted this tribunal, it was found very difficult to keep it clear of imputation. Of what sort the imperfections of this mode of trial were, will best appear by the statutes made in this reign to correct them. By stat. 5 Edw. III., c. x., it was ordained, that if any jurors in assizes, juries, or inquests, took of the one party or the other, and was thereof duly attainted, he should not in future be put on assizes, juries, or inquests, and besides, should be imprisoned and ransomed at the king's will; which offence was to be inquired of by the justices before whom such assizes, juries, or inquests, were had. Again, in the 34th year (because sheriffs arrayed their pannels of people procured, to effect which they would take persons living at any distance from the county, who had no knowledge of the fact upon which the inquest was to pass), it was enacted, by c. iv. of that statute, that pannels should be made of of *the next people,*[2] who were not suspected or procured; and if the sheriff acted otherwise, he was to be punished by the justice in proportion to the offence against the king, and the damage sustained by the party. Again, by c. viii. of the same statute, either of the parties (or any stranger for the king) might have his plaint by bill against a juror who had taken anything of him, or the other party, for the verdict; which bill was to be before the justices before whom the jury were sworn, and the juror was to be put to answer immediately; and if he pleaded to the country, the inquest was to be taken immediately. If the juror was fined at the suit of any but one of the parties, the person was to have half the fine, and the parties to the suit to recover their damages by assessment of the inquest; the juror was besides to suffer a year's imprisonment, which the statute declares should be redeemed by no fine: the party was also to be at liberty to sue by writ before other jus-

[1] *Vide ante,* vol. i. c. viii.

[2] *De plus prochiens genta.*

tices. In addition to the provisions of this act, it was further ordained by stat. 38 Edw. III., st. 1, c. xii., that such corrupt juror should forfeit ten times as much as he had taken, one half to him that would sue, the other to the king. All embraceors procuring such inquests were to be punished in the same manner; and if such embraceor or juror had not sufficient to pay the above penalty, he was to be imprisoned for a year. No justice or other minister was to inquire *ex officio* of such offences, but only at the suit of the party, or of some other. Such guards was it thought necessary to put upon this trial, though a favourite with the nation.

Besides these statutes, that are more properly confined to civil actions, there were some that made similar provisions respecting jurors in criminal matters, and in inquests before escheators, and others; all which will be considered in their proper places.

Law wager.

The right of waging his law was secured to a defendant in an instance where, in the time of Edward I., he was by law entitled to it[1](*a*). It said in stat. 38 Edw. III., st. 1, c. v., that many people were grieved and attached by their bodies in the city of London, at the suit of citizens, surmising that they were debtors, and could be proved so by their papers, though they had no deed or tally to produce: it was therefore enacted, that every man should be received *to his law* by people sufficient of his condition against such papers, and the creditor should not put the party to plead to the inquest unless he chose; but if he would wish to do so in future, he must take care to have some other security than mere papers. Thus the wager of law against mere papers (and *à fortiori* against verbal testimony) was secured to the citizens of London, as firmly as it was before practised in the common law courts.

As to the end and object of suits, whether civil or criminal, it was ordained, by stat. 38 Edw. III., st. 1, c. iii., that all fines taken before justices should be in the presence of the pledges, and the pledges were to know the sum of the fine before they departed.

Statute of jeofail.

We have before seen [2] how scrupulous and nice the old pleaders were in every point of the process and proceeding in an action, so as to cavil at mistakes in syllables and letters. As many of these mistakes were owing to the negligence of clerks, and they were never in themselves of such importance as to deserve all the attention that had been paid to them, it was thought prudent to remove some of those frivolous objections by a parliamentary declaration. It was accordingly enacted, by stat. 14 Edw. III.,

(*a*) But, on the other hand, provision was not made by the practice of the courts to prevent its being abused or resorted to in cases to which it did not justly pertain. That is, by the procedure called examination, *i.e.*, examination of the plaintiff or his attorney, in order to ascertain what was the real nature of the case, and whether it was one in which the defendant was entitled to wage his law. This procedure by way of examination was afterwards required by statute in the case of action of account. By that statute the defendant could be examined on oath; and by custom of London the plaintiff could be examined at the defendant's instance (*Year-book*, 21 *Edw. VI.*, 44).

[1] *Vide ante*, c. iv.

[2] *Ibid.* vol. i. c. vii., and c. viii.

st. 1, c. vi., that by the misprision of a clerk, in any *place* (that is, *court*) whatsoever, by mistaking in writing one syllable or one letter, too much or too little, no process should be annulled or discontinued; but as soon as the thing was perceived, by challenge of the party or in other manner, it should be hastily amended in due form, without giving advantage to the party that challenged the same, on account of such misprision. This is the first of those provisions, which in latter times have been called *Statutes* of JEOFAIL *and Amendment.*

Some further regulation on this subject was made by stat. 36 Edw. III. st. 1, c. xv., which act is better known by the alteration it made in the language of courts, directing that all matters should be there debated in English, and not in French as heretofore. The statute sets forth as a reason why the laws were so ill obeyed, because "they were pleaded, showed, and judged in the *French* tongue, which was much *unknown in the realm;* so that the people (says the act) which do implead, or be impleaded in the king's court, and in the courts of other, have no knowledge nor understanding of that which is said for them, or against them, by their serjeants or other pleaders:" for the better observance, therefore, of the law, it was enacted that pleas pleaded in any courts whatsoever, whether in the king's or other courts, before the king's justices or others, should be pleaded, showed, defended, answered, debated, and judged in the *English* tongue, and should be entered and enrolled in *Latin;* which latter was no more than confirming the ancient practice; records of courts always having been in Latin.

Pleadings to be in English.

Thus the language which the Conqueror had imposed upon our courts (the strongest badge of servitude, perhaps, that could be devised) was suffered no longer to maintain its ground. The victories of Edward having given the English a declared superiority over the descendants of their former masters, seemed to mark this as a proper time for such a revolution. Though the language of our courts, in all argument and decision, was henceforward to be English, the French still continued the *written* language of the law, being that in which it had used to lisp in its infancy, and to which in its maturer years it was still attached as a sort of mother-tongue. Thus, many apt and significant terms and phrases were still retained in debate and conversation upon topics of law; and the reports of what passed in court were still taken and published in French, and so continued for hundreds of years after. It was foreseen and intended by the makers of this act, that much of the old language should still remain; for after the above change is ordained, there are added the following reservations—namely, "that the laws and customs of the realm, *terms* and *processes* be holden and kept as before had been; and that by the ancient *terms and forms of counting* [1] no man should be prejudiced, so that the

[1] *Les aunciens termes formes de counter.*

matter of the action be fully showed in the declaration and in the writ;" which only meant that though such established and known forms of expression were not in English, yet it should be no breach of this statute.

Our criminal law received some improvement from statutes passed in his reign. The reducing the crime of treason to a certainty by a parliamentary definition, as it freed the subject from the entanglement of ambiguous and unknown law, and, consequently, from the arbitrary decisions of judges, very eminently distinguishes this period in the history of our penal law. The offence of treason in its original notion, as a crime against the state, lay open to a great latitude of construction; not only direct breaches of allegiance to the supreme power, but violating the persons who were nearly related to, or attendant on, the person of the supreme magistrate; disorders of a public nature tending to confusion and civil commotion; bold and riotous breaches of the peace; affectations of extraordinary influence and authority, with speeches of an ambitious import, had at divers times been brought within the bounds of this offence, as conducing in their consequences to subvert the established order of allegiance and subordination in government. This had been remarkable in the early times of our law; when it was left, in a great measure, to the breasts of judges to fix and determine by their judgment, in particular cases, what was treason and what was not. Killing the king's father or brother, or even killing his messenger, had received the punishment of treason.[1] In the present reign they had gone still further. In the 21st year of the king, a knight of Hertfordshire forcibly detained a man till he paid him £90: this was held treason, *because* he was in so doing guilty of *accroaching* (as they called it), or attempting to exercise royal power.

Perhaps one great motive to raising these constructive treasons, was the forfeiture which in such case belonged to the king. On the other hand, the loss thereby sustained by lords, who would be entitled to an escheat in case of felony, and who at any rate incurred a diminution of the casualties of tenure by such forfeiture, might be a spur to them to obtain some parliamentary definition of this crime. The whole kingdom was interested in a question that touched the lives of all. The determination above mentioned created such an alarm, that a petition was presented by the commons, in the same year, stating that certain justices had lately adjudged some matters before them to be treason and accroachment of royal power; they therefore prayed, that it might be declared in parliament *what is the accroachment of royal power* which should occasion to lords a loss of forfeiture, and to delinquents a loss of clergy. To this petition there was given this evasive answer, that wherever such judgment was given, the points of such treason and accroachment were declared therein.[2]

[1] Britt. ch. 22.

[2] Pet. Parl. 21 Edw. III., 15.

Though the commons were disappointed at this time they did not fail of their object; for, in the 25th year of the king, there was a solemn declaration by statute,[1] defining very particularly what should be considered as treason, and what not. The treasons declared are under the following heads:—To compass or imagine the death of the king, queen, or that of their eldest son and heir; to violate the king's companion, or the king's eldest daughter unmarried, or the wife of the king's eldest son and heir; to levy war against the king in his realm, or be adherent to the king's enemies in his realm, giving to them aid and comfort in the realm or elsewhere; of which a man must be *provably attainted of open deed* by people of his own condition. Again, to counterfeit the king's great or privy seal, or his money; to bring into the realm false money counterfeit to the money of England, as the money called *Lushburgh*, or other, like to the money of England, knowing it to be false, to merchandise, or make payment in deceit of the king and his people; to slay the chancellor, treasurer, or the king's justices of the one bench or of the other, justices in eyre or of assize, or any other justices assigned to hear and determine, being in their places doing their offices: all the above cases, says the statute, shall be judged treason that extends to our lord the king and his royal majesty; and of such treasons the forfeiture of the escheats belongs to the king, as well of lands and tenements holden of another, as of himself.

Statute of treason.

After defining what should be considered as treason against the king's person and dignity, in which case the forfeiture belonged to the king, the statute goes on, and says, there is another manner of treason; that is, when a servant slays his master, a wife her husband, or when a man secular or religious slays his prelate, to whom he owes faith and obedience: and in these treasons, says the statute, the forfeiture of the escheat is to go to the lord of the fee.

Thus far did this act specify cases of treason, whether *high* or *petit;* the distinction by which they have since been known. "And because," says the act, "many other like cases of treason may happen in time to come, which cannot be imagined or declared at the present time, it was accorded," that should any other case, not above specified and supposed to be treason, happen before any justices, they should tarry, without going to judgment, till the cause was showed and declared before the king and his parliament, whether it ought to be adjudged treason or other felony: a method which we have seen it was usual for the judges to take in other cases of doubt and difficulty. This is followed by a clause that was intended, probably, as a satisfaction to the commons, and an answer to their petition above mentioned. "If," says the statute, "any man of this realm ride armed, covertly or secretly, with men of arms against any other to slay him, or rob him, or take him, or retain him, till he has made fine or ransom for his deliverance, it is not

[1] Stat. 25 Edw. III., c. 2.

the mind of the king, nor his council, that in such case it shall be judged treason; but shall be judged felony or trespass, according to the laws of the land of old time used, and as the case required."

It was also enacted, that should any lands or tenements before that time have come into the king's hands, by judgment of treason, for any of the above offences, and have been granted to any others, the parties injured might have writs of *scire facias* against the *terres tenants*, in which no protection was to be allowed. If such lands remained in the hands of the king, writs were to be granted to the sheriffs to deliver them out of the king's hands without delay. By this provision some partial redress was also given to those who had already suffered by the oppression of the old law.

Thus did Edward, by abolishing the many constructive treasons that had before been conjured up at the pleasure of the crown and its judges, make his subjects easy on a point the most important in our whole legal polity. This statute may be regarded in the light of a new *Magna Charta*, and a new pillar in our free constitution; the crime of treason, if indeterminate and vague, being of itself, according to the opinion of a fashionable writer,[1] alone sufficient to make any government degenerate into arbitrary power.

The law of treason was further reformed by stat. 34 Edw. III. c. xii. Complaint was made to parliament that escheators had seized, by colour of their office, divers lands and tenements as forfeit to the king, for the treason of persons then dead who had not been attainted during their lives. It is declared by the above statute that the king and his progenitors had been seized of *the forfeitures of wars of all times*, of which right he did not mean to divest himself, but would continue such forfeitures as had fallen in his time or that of his father (which is a declaration that the king was entitled to certain forfeitures, without attainder, if the person fell in war); yet the king of his special grace granted, that respecting all forfeitures which fell in the time of his grandfather and other progenitors, as soon as an inquest was returned by the escheator, or other commissioner into the chancery, the tenant should not be put out of possession, but should be summoned by *scire facias* to state what answer he had to make. In all other cases of dead persons not attainted of treason it was ordained that they should not be subject to any other forfeiture than the forfeitures of old time adjudged after the death of persons, by presentment in the eyre or in the king's bench, as of felons *de seipso*, or of others.

It may be doubted how strictly this statute was observed; for, in the latter end of this reign, the commons petitioned that none of the king's officers might seize lands or tenements of persons not attainted of treason or felony in their lifetime.[2]

When it was declared that riding armed should no longer be construed treason (unless, indeed, when accompanied with such circumstances as made it a levying war) disorders of Riots.

[1] Esp. des Loix, liv. 6, c. 7.

[2] Pet. Parl. 50 Edw. III., 73.

that sort fell back into the consideration they lay under at common law. Provision had been made by the statute of *Northampton*, 2 Edw. III. c. iii., against such offenders, who, it seems, in these times were very common, and created very great alarm; the course of justice, as well as the peace of society, being liable to disturbance from such armed force. The nature of these tumults may be imagined from the words of this statute, which provided for their suppression. It was enacted that no man great or small, of what condition soever, except the king's servants in his presence, and his ministers in executing his precepts or the precepts of their office, and those in their company assisting, and also upon a cry made for arms to keep the peace,[1] and that in the places where the occasion happened, be so hardy as to come before the king's justices, or other of the king's ministers doing their office, with force and arms; that none bring force in affray of the peace, nor go or ride armed by night or by day, in fairs or markets, or in the presence of the justices or other ministers, or elsewhere, upon pain of forfeiting their armour to the king, and their bodies to prison at the king's pleasure. It was further enacted that the king's justices in their presence, sheriffs and other ministers in their bailiwicks, lords of franchises and their bailiffs in the same, mayors and bailiffs of cities and boroughs within such cities and boroughs, and borough-holders, constables, and keepers of the peace within their wards, should have power to execute this act. The justices assigned were, at their coming into the country, to inquire how such officers had executed this act and to punish all defaults. These were the methods prescribed by the statute of Northampton, and they were often recurred to, in subsequent times, to suppress riotous and tumultuary meetings.

To go on with the laws made for the punishing of offenders. Hawks, as they were instrumental to the diversions of the great, were put under the protection of the law, and guarded with more solicitude than other animals. A person finding a stray hawk was[2] to bring it to the sheriff to be owned, who, after four months and proclamation made, was to keep it, making the finder (if he was a *simple man*, says the statute) some compensation; if he was a *gentleman*,[3] and *of estate to have the hawk*, the sheriff was to re-deliver it to him, taking reasonable costs for the time he had it in his custody. If any one took such a hawk and concealed it from the lord or his falconers, or took it from the lord, he was, upon conviction, to suffer two years' imprisonment, and yield to the lord the price of the hawk; and by stat. 37 Edw. III. c. xix., if any stole a hawk and carried it away, not observing the aforesaid ordinance, he was to be dealt with as a thief who stole a horse, or any other thing. Thus was a severe example set by the legislature, to be followed in certain regulations that were afterwards made for the protection of the game.

[1] *De fait darmes de pees.* [2] Stat. 24 Edw. III., c. 22. [3] *Gentils homme.*

Two felonies were created as sanctions to some commercial regulations, which, however, were soon repealed. By stat. 27 Edw. III. st. 1, c. v., it was made felony to forestall or ingross Gascony wine; but this act was repealed by stat. 37 Edw. III. c. xvi. By the statute of the staple, 27 Edw. III. st. 2, c. iii., it was made felony for any man, English, Welsh, or Irish, to export wools, leathers, wool-fells, or lead, out of the kingdom: but by stat. 38 Edw. III. st. 1, c. vi., the penalty of life and member was repealed, and that of forfeiture of lands and tenements, goods and chattels, still remains.

In the early part of this reign, two new felonies had been created: one, by stat. 5 Edw. III. c. ii., before mentioned (which was confirmed by several [1] others), ordaining that purveyors should be subject to the same punishment as thieves and robbers, if they exceeded the limits of their authority:[2] another is, stat. 14 Edw. III. st. 1, c. x., which enacted that a keeper of a gaol who should by too great duress compel a prisoner to become an approver, should have judgment of felony.

Several laws were made to remove the great impediments thrown in the way of justice by conspirators, champertors, and maintainers of quarrels and suits, against whom the legislature in the reign of Edward I. had made so many provisions.[3] In stat. 1 Edw. III. st. 2, c. xiv., the king commanded that none of his counsellors, nor of his house, nor of his ministers, nor any man of the realm, great or small, should by himself, or by others, in sending letters, or by other means, take upon him to maintain quarrels and parties in the country, to the disturbance of the common law. To forward the prosecution of such offenders, it was ordained by stat. 4 Edw. III. c. xi., that the justices of one bench or the other, and the justices of assize, when they came to hold their sessions, or to take inquests by *nisi prius*, should, either at the suit of the king or the party, inquire of and determine respecting maintainers, bearers, and conspirators, and those who committed champerty, the same as justices in eyre before might; with a power to adjourn such matters as could not be determined, through the shortness of time, into the court to which they belonged. A similar injunction about maintenance was made in stat. 20 Edw. III. c. iv., and by chap. v. of the same act, great men were enjoined to dismiss from their service all maintainers, and others who took upon them to interfere in suits, and impede the course of the law. The writ of champerty was still considered only as a criminal proceeding; for in the 50th year of the king the commons prayed that the chancellor might in such cases grant a writ at the suit of the party, to recover damages in his suit; which, however, was denied by the king.[4]

The other statutes upon the subject of criminal law may be considered as making some alteration in the course of bringing offenders

[1] Stat. 25 Edw. III., stat. 5, c. 15; stat. 36 Edw. III., c. 2.
[2] *Vide ante*, c. xiii.
[3] *Vide ante*, c. ix.
[4] Pet. Parl., 50 Edw. III., 80.

to justice, the manner of proceeding there, and the execution of the law upon them.

The statute of Winchester, passed in the reign of Edward I., and all laws for the ordering of the police, may be treated as ordinances calculated for the better discovery and bringing to justice of suspected persons, that being one of their great objects. It had been ordained by the statute of Winchester,[1] that any stranger passing the country in the night, might upon suspicion be arrested, and delivered to the sheriff. It was now ordained, that because many felonies had lately been committed by persons called *roberdesmen, waisters, and draw-latches*, any person suspected of being such might be arrested, *by day or by night*, by the constables of the town (if within a franchise, by the bailiff), and delivered to the sheriff, to be kept in prison till the coming of the justices of gaol delivery. In the meantime the sheriff and bailiffs of the franchise were to make inquiry about the arrest, and return the inquest, with the finding, to the justices when they came; and if they did not make such inquiry, they were to be amerced, and the justices were to do it before they proceeded to the deliverance. In the 10th year of the king certain *articles of the peace* were transmitted into different counties; but it was specially resolved by the parliament that they should not be considered as a statute. By stat. 28 Edw. III. c. xi., strong injunction is given for the execution of the 2d chapter of the statute of Winchester (concerning hue and cry, and recovery against the hundred), which is specially there re-enacted.

Thus far of bringing offenders into court; next, as to the proceeding there. It seems, that at this time suits for defamation were generally brought in the ecclesiastical court, being avowed subjects of spiritual cognizance only. But this proceeding was carried to great lengths, when persons indicted in sheriffs' tourns, and afterwards acquitted before the justices by a procured inquest, would bring a suit in the ecclesiastical court against the indictors for defamation. This being complained of by the commons, it was enacted by stat. 1 Edw. III. st. 2, c. xiii., that every person so grieved should have a prohibition in the chancery, formed upon his case.

Of indictments.

To insure the due prosecution of indictments when found, it was enacted by chap. xvii. of the same statute, that sheriffs and bailiffs of franchises, and all others that took indictments in their tourns or elsewhere, should take them by roll indented;[2] one part of which was to remain with the indictors, the other with him who took the inquest. This was done in order to prevent the embezzlement of indictments, which, it seems, too frequently happened.

Some abuses arose out of the new practice of introducing a second jury to try an indictment.[3] Thus, it was a common course for

[1] *Vide ante*, c. x.
[2] A similar provision had been made in the time of Edward I. *Vide ante*, c. xii.
[3] *Vide ante*, c. xi., pp. 164, 165.

indictments to be taken before sheriffs and other inferior magistrates; but the trial of them, or, as they called it, *the prisoner's deliverance*, used to be deferred till the justices came into the country for that purpose. It is not to be wondered that, in such an interval, many unfair practices were attempted. This interval also gave room for the indictors to get themselves put on the inquest of deliverance; and therefore it had become one of the commonest challenges taken to a juror, that he was one of the indictors. But, notwithstanding the old law allowed this challenge, it is doubtful how far it was observed; for we find a petition of the commons in the 14 Edw. III.[1] for a law to confirm it. This was at length done by stat. 25 Edw. III. st. 5, c. iii., which enacts that no indictor should be put on inquests upon deliverance of the indictees of felonies or trespass, if he was challenged for such cause by the person indicted.

It seems that sheriffs extremely abused this authority to take indictments. It is recited by stat. 28 Edw. III. c. ix., that these officers used to procure commissions and general writs empowering them to take indictments; and having, under such authority, caused many to be indicted, would take fine and ransom, and then deliver them, instead of keeping them in custody till the coming of the justices, as the regular course was. It was declared that all such commissions and writs should be void, and that in future none such should issue.

Another oppression was practised, not only by sheriffs, but gaolers and keepers of prisons, as well within franchises as without, who by duress and severities would compel their prisoners to become approvers, and appeal innocent people, in order to obtain fines for dispensing with their imprisonment. By stat. 1 Edw. III. st. 2, c. vii., the justices of the one bench and the other, and justices of assize and gaol delivery, were empowered to hear all complaints of this sort by bill, as well at the suit of the party as of the king. We have before seen that this offence in keepers of prisons (for sheriffs are not named) was made felony by stat. 14 Edw. III. st. 1, c. x.

As the law now stood, a felon who was appealed, indicted, or outlawed, in one county, and dwelt in another, being out of the sheriff's jurisdiction, could not be attached. It was therefore enacted by stat. 5 Edw. III. c. xi., that the justices assigned to hear and determine such felonies should direct their writs to all counties in England, to take persons so indicted; a remedy which effectually removed all difficulties.

Jury *de medietate linguæ.*

We have seen the privilege granted by the statute of the staple[2] in favour of foreign merchants, to have an inquest mixed of natives and foreigners, where one of the parties was of this country, and one of another. This was confined to matters of contract; but by stat. 28 Edw. III. c. xiii. it was extended to criminal cases in the following explicit manner: It was enacted,

[1] Pet. Parl., 14 Edw. III., 30.

[2] *Vide ante*, 277.

that in all inquests and proofs to be taken or made amongst aliens and denizens, whether merchants or others, as well before the mayor of the staple as any other justices or ministers, *although the king be party* (as in all criminal cases he is), the one half of the inquest or proof should be denizens and the other aliens, if so many aliens and foreigners were in the place: if not, then as many as could be found, and the remainder to be denizens. This liberal spirit towards foreigners had been distinguishing itself through the whole of this reign, particularly in matters that concerned the interests of commerce. Some years before, the invidious distinction that had been kept up between English and French by presentments of *Englishery*, was removed, by the entire abolition of that proceeding.[1] However, the reason stated by the stat. 14 Edw. III. st. 1, c. iv., for this alteration is of a different kind, namely, that counties were amerced without any knowledge of presentments of Englishery, which was a surprise and oppression to the people; and for this reason they were no more to be received by the justices errant.

The benefit of clergy.

The exemption from all secular animadversion claimed by the clergy for the persons of clerks, made a considerable head of inquiry in the criminal law of these times. Notwithstanding the firmness with which it was demanded on one side, and the indulgence which the laity in general gave to the claim; though it was confirmed by solemn declarations and aided by long prescription, it was always viewed with jealousy, and considered rather as a usurpation, which for particular reasons was endured, than an established and unquestionable part of the old common law. Under such a title, this privilege must depend on the circumstances of times for its support: we accordingly find it one while respected, and at another disregarded, by the government. In the 18th year of the king it was enacted,[2] that an archbishop should not be impeached criminally before the king's justices. This might perhaps be rather a law in protection of the peerage than of the clergy, and was occasioned by the late disputes the king had with the archbishop. In the 25th year of this king the clergy complained in parliament that a certain knight, being one of the clergy, had judgment of treason given against him, to be hanged and quartered: they complained also of a like judgment against a priest for killing his master. These encroachments, as they termed them, or at least these symptoms of the precariousness of the privilege claimed by clerks in criminal questions, required an act of parliament to adjust and define it with more certainty. Accordingly, in the famous statute *de clero*, 25 Edw. III. st. 3, which was made to ascertain some other of their claims, two chapters were inserted for this very purpose. By chap. ii. it was enacted, that all manner of clerks, as well secular as religious, who should be convicted before any secular justices for treason or felony touching other persons

[1] *Vide ante*, c. viii.

[2] Stat. 18 Edw. III., st. 3, c. 1.

than the king himself or his royal majesty, should from thenceforth freely have and enjoy the privilege of holy church, and should, without any impeachment or delay, be delivered to the ordinaries demanding them. In consideration of this grant, and that it might not be productive of an entire failure of justice, the statute says, the archbishop promised the king that he would procure an ordinance to be made for the punishment and safe custody of clerks so delivered to the ordinaries, in order that no clerk might be encouraged to offend through want of correction.[1]

Another complaint of the clergy was, that when clerks were demanded by their ordinary, they were often remanded to gaol by the justices, under surmise that there were other charges against them; though the common law, as they said, required that a clerk should not, in such case, be remanded to gaol, but ought to be presently arraigned of *all* his offences, or otherwise delivered to the ordinary: accordingly, it was ordained in chap. iii. of this statute, that all justices and secular judges throughout the realm should observe this point.

The consequences that followed from this last chapter of the statute will be seen hereafter. The former, though nothing more than a declaration of the common law with respect to the persons entitled to clergy, yet, from the general way in which it is worded, had the effect of extending this privilege to some felonies which did not before enjoy it; and took it from some treasons where before it was allowed. Thus, among other felonies, it was hereby extended to the felonious burning of houses; an offence which at common law was not allowed clergy. On the other hand, by the common law recognised by this statute, all treasons except those against the king's person and dignity were entitled to clergy: accordingly, the offence of coining and some others were entitled to this benefit. But the crime of coining being by the statute of treasons expressly raised from the order of common treasons to the rank of one against the king's person and dignity, it became *eo nomine* excluded from clergy by the exception of treasons against the king's person in the statute *de clero*, chap. ii. Thus, when these two statutes are put together, we find the old distinction between treasons clergyable and not clergyable still remained; and was grounded upon the same principle as at common law, namely, as they were, or were not, against the king's person. Treasons not against the king's person, namely, those which have since been called petit treason, were still entitled to their clergy; and treasons against the king's person (which have since been denominated high treason) were *eo nomine* deprived of clergy.

Of pardons.

There was through all this reign much complaint of the too easy granting of pardons, which contributed greatly to encourage manslaughters, robberies, and other trespasses. To put some check upon this, it was ordained by the statute of

[1] *Vide ante*, 47.

Northampton, stat. 2 Edw. III. c. ii., that charters of pardon should not be granted except where the king could do it consistently with his oath; which the statute explains by saying, where a man slayeth another in his own defence, or by misfortune.[1] That statute was confirmed by stat. 10 Edw. III. st. 1, c. ii., and as a further security, it was ordained by chap. iii. of the same statute, that all those who already had charters of pardon should, by a certain time, come before the sheriffs and coroners of the counties, and find six good and sufficient mainpernors to bear themselves well and lawfully; and the charters of such as did not find such mainprise, or, having done so, broke the peace, were to be void. In case of future pardons, the parties, within three months after the granting, were to find the like mainpernors, and the pardons to be void as in the former case. This was doing something more than had been effected by the general declaration of the statute of Northampton; and stat. 14 Edw. III. st. 1, c. xv. went still further, by declaring all pardons granted contrary to that statute to be void. In the 21st year of the king there was a petition of the commons on this subject; when the king answered, that he would advise with his council, so that no such charter should be granted, unless it was for the honour of himself and his people.[2] At length the evil of improper pardons was attributed to the feigned and untrue suggestions upon which they had been obtained. It was therefore enacted by stat. 27 Edw. III. st. 1, c. ii., that in every charter of pardon granted on the suggestion of any one, the suggestion, and the name of him that made it, should be comprised in the charter; and should the suggestion be afterwards found untrue, the charter was to be void. The justices before whom they were alleged were to inquire of such suggestions, and if they appeared untrue, they were to disallow the pardon: this was to extend as well to pardons already granted, as to those in future. This seemed the most effectual of all the remedies hitherto devised, as it, after all, left the party to the judgment of the common law.

Process of *capias* and *exigent*.

There was an act made for the government of process before justices of *oyer* and *terminer*, that deserves notice, as it settled that point very particularly. It was enacted by stat. 25 Edw. III. st. 5, c. xiv., that after a person was indicted of felony before the justices in their sessions of *oyer* and *terminer*, it should be commanded to the sheriff to attach his body by writ or precept, called a *capias;* and if the sheriff returned in the writ that the body was not found, another writ of *capias* should incontinently be made returnable at three weeks; and in the same writ or precept it was to be comprised, that the sheriff should cause his chattels to be seized and safely kept till the return-day of the writ. If the sheriff returned that the body was not found; and the indictee came not, the *exigent* was to be awarded, and the chattels forfeit, as the law of the crown ordained; but if he came and

[1] *Vide ante*, p. 64. [2] Pet. Parl., 21 Edw. III., 53, 62.

yielded himself, or was taken by the sheriff or other officer before the return of the second *capias*, then the goods and chattels were to be saved.

In the 18th year of the king two acts were made to settle the process of *exigent* and *outlawry* in particular cases. It was enacted and declared by stat. 18 Edw. III. st. 1, that an *exigent* should lie in the following cases, and in no other: against those who receive the king's money or wools, taking them of the people, and then carrying them away, in fraud of the king; against those who bring wools to the parts beyond the seas, without being cocketed, or paying custom or subsidy, according to the assessment; against customers and finders [1] who connive at the same; against lay ministers who receive the king's money and retain it; against conspirators, confederators, and maintainers of false quarrels; against those who bring routs in the presence of the justices or other the king's ministers, or elsewhere in the counties, in affray of the people, to obstruct the course of law; against those who bring, or procure false money to be brought. If none of the above offenders could be brought in by attachment and distress (for that was always to be the first process), then an *exigent* was to go.[2] It is clear this parliamentary declaration was only to settle the course in the particular cases there mentioned; and it was not intended (notwithstanding the general way in which it is worded, *and not against any other*) that an *exigent* should lie in no other case; for if so, it would not have lain in robbery, murder, and many other felonies, contrary to the plainest reason of the thing. It appears that it was only intended to remove some doubts which were entertained at this time concerning process of outlawry in certain cases of *trespass*, of which sort were most of the instances recited in the above statute; for it was in the same year enacted by stat. 18 Edw. III. stat. 2, c. v., in a more general way, that no *exigent* should thenceforth issue, in a case where a man was indicted of *trespass, unless it was against the peace, or* of things contained in the before-mentioned act. We see that there had already grown a distinction between trespasses; some being considered as against the peace, and others not. When this had once prevailed in cases that were treated criminally, the way was opened for improving on the idea in civil writs of trespass, which we shall hereafter see were, upon this principle, branched out into such as were *vi et armis*, and such as were not.

It was endeavoured to make an alteration in the law of forfeiture in cases of felony, but the attempt did not succeed. In the 21st of Edward III., the commons complained that a man indicted or appealed of felony, who did not surrender himself at the *exigent*, forfeited his chattels, although he was acquitted of the felony, without inquiry [3] whether he fled or withdrew himself. Now, as a man might be indicted in a foreign county, and be ignorant of any proceeding against him, they prayed that no man should lose his

[1] *Quære*, if not searchers. [2] *Vide ante*, vol. i. c. viii. [3] *Ibid.*

chattels but where it was found by verdict that he fled. To this it was answered, that the ancient law should be kept till the king by advice of his council should otherwise ordain.[1]

It was also attempted to change the law as far as regarded the forfeiture of the wife's dower by the felony of the husband.[2] The commons presented a petition to this effect in the 1st of Edward III.,[3] but it was not assented to.

The law had always required allegations in writs to be particular and precise; the same in appeals: but nothing has yet appeared of the forms of indictments. As it was not till the time of Edward I. that these were put into writing, there had not been sufficient leisure to discuss the circumstances and property thereof. But we find that certain indictments against ordinaries and their ministers, for extortions and oppressions, had occasioned clamour, because they did not sufficiently *put in certain* the offence charged. To remedy this, it was enacted, by stat. 25 Edward III., st. 3, *de clero*, c. ix., that justices should not put ordinaries or their ministers to answer upon indictments for *general* extortions or oppressions, unless they put in certain in what manner such extortions or oppressions had been committed.

Origin of justices of the peace.

In this reign several regulations were provided for the keeping and maintenance of the *peace;* which, besides increasing the powers of ancient magistrates, new-modelled some of them, and created new ones which were thought to be better calculated for such an employment. The statute of Winchester was the great system of police in these days, and on the full execution of that was thought to depend the domestic peace of the whole kingdom. For punishing breaches of that statute, and restraining other offences more immediately concerning the police, was the commission of *oyer* and *terminer*, called *trailbaston*, instituted by Edward I.[4]

The *peace*, in the most extensive sense of the word, took in, perhaps, the whole of the criminal law; and as most offences were said to be against the peace, all those magistrates who had authority to take cognizance of such offences, might be considered as a sort of guardians of the peace *ex officio:* such were the king's justices, inferior judges, and ministers of justice, as sheriffs, constables, tythingmen, headboroughs, and the like; all these were *ex officio* guardians and conservators of the peace. Others were conservators of the peace by tenure or prescription; others were elected in full county court, in pursuance of the writ directed to the sheriff for that purpose. Besides these, extraordinary ones were appointed occasionally by commission from the king.[5] The manner in which these officers might exercise their authority was, by committing to custody those whom they saw actually breaking

[1] Parl. Pet., 21 Edw. III., 35.
[2] *Vide ante*, vol. i. c. viii.
[3] Parl. Pet., 21 Edw. III., 13.
[4] *Vide ante*, 314.
[5] Lamb. Iren. book i., c. 3.

the peace; or, as is said, they might admit them to bail, or oblige them to give sureties for keeping the peace. This might be done by them all, even down to the constable.[1]

The violent conclusion of the last reign by the imprisonment, deposal, and murder of the old king, succeeded by the elevation of a minor to the throne, occasioned the appointment of certain new officers, in whom the court could have more trust than in the common conservators. Apprehending that some might be alarmed at the proceedings of the court, and that others might take advantage of the unsettled state of the executive power to raise disturbance, special orders were issued, in the name of the new king, to every sheriff to preserve the peace of the county; and, in a few weeks after, it was ordained by stat. 1 Edward III. c. xvi., "for the better keeping and maintenance of the peace, that in every county, good men and lawful, that were no maintainers of evil, or barrators in the county, should be assigned to keep the peace." This short and general act gave a very confined authority to these new officers; the persons appointed by this act being nothing more than *conservators of the peace* nominated by the crown, as auxiliary to those who were such by the titles above mentioned. Indeed, they seem very little more than such officers as were appointed in the reign of Edward I. for the particular purpose only of attending to the due execution of the statute of Winchester;[2] from which ordinance probably it was that the present hint was taken.

Three years after this, these officers were intrusted with greater powers, having the additional authority to take indictments. It was enacted by stat. 4 Edward III. c. ii. (after some regulations for the appointment of justices of assize and gaol-delivery), that there should be *assigned* good and lawful men in every county to keep the peace; and that at the time of the *assignment,* mention should be made, that such as should be indicted or taken by the said keepers of the peace, should not be let to mainprise by the sheriffs, or their ministers, if they were not by law mainpernable; and that such as were indicted should not be delivered but at the common law. The justices of gaol-delivery were to have power to deliver the gaols of such as were indicted before the keepers of the peace; and such keepers were directed for that purpose to send their indictments before the justices. It was further enacted, that such keepers should have power to inquire of sheriffs, gaolers, and others, in whose ward such indicted persons should be, if they made deliverance, or let to mainprise any so indicted and not mainpernable; and they were to punish such officers, if they did anything against this act.

After this, there was no alteration in their authority till the 18th of this reign, when they were empowered to *hear and determine.* It was enacted by stat. 18 Edward III. st. 2, c. ii., that two or

[1] Lamb. Iren., pp. 14, 15.

[2] *Vide ante*, 121.

three of the best reputation in the counties should be assigned keepers of the peace by the king's commission; and when need should be, they, with others wise and learned in the law, should be assigned by the king's commission to *hear and determine* felonies and trespasses done against the peace in the same counties, and to inflict punishment according to law and reason, and the circumstances of the fact. When, in the twentieth year, it was prayed by the commons, that they might have a power to hear and determine felonies, it was answered, that the king would appoint learned persons for that office.[1]

So beneficial was this establishment of keepers of the peace considered by the people, that it became a favourite in the country, and was exalted in preference to some institutions that were more ancient. In the twenty-first year of the king, the commons being charged to advise the king what was the best way of keeping the peace of the kingdom, they recommended that six persons in every county, of whom two were to be *de plus grantz*, two knights, and two men of the law, and so more or less as need should require, should have power and commission out of chancery to hear and determine the keeping of the peace; and that all courts of *trail-baston* should cease, they being oppressive to the people, and contributing nothing towards preserving the peace, nor the punishment of felons or trespassors.[2]

In conformity with these several statutes and petitions, commissions had been at various times framed, *assigning* certain persons to execute the powers which the statutes authorised the king to confer. In these commissions were inserted, besides the general powers for keeping the peace, a special charge to enforce the observance of certain statutes. Thus, in the second year of this king, they had the statute of Winchester in charge; in the twentieth year the statute of Northampton, and stat. 5 Edward III. c. xiv., against roberdsmen, draw-latches, &c.[3] In the twenty-fifth of this king, by the statute called the statute of labourers, we find that *justices* were to be assigned for the execution of that act;[4] and they were to hold a session in all the counties of England four times in the year; that is, at the feast of the Annunciation of Our Lady, of St Margaret, of Saint Michael, and of Saint Nicholas.[5] It is most probable the persons assigned *justices* to execute this statute were the keepers of the peace, who, having already by stat. 18 Edward III. an authority to hear and determine, might with propriety enough be called *justices;* though there is no trace of their being actually so called till seventeen years after. Indeed, the authority given by that statute is to them, not singly, but jointly with others, as occasion should require; their own commission going no further than the bare keeping of the peace.[6] As the

[1] Parl. Pet., 20 Edw. III., 29.
[2] *Ibid.* 21 Edw. III., 70.
[3] Lamb. Iren., b. 1, c. 9.
[4] Ch. 3.
[5] Ch. 7.
[6] Lamb. Iren., 20–23.

general standing authority to hear and determine was not given till stat. 34 Edward III., it was not probably till then that they were commonly reputed and called *justices*, as we find they are by stat. 36 Edward III.

The stat. 34 Edward III. c. i. is more full than any of the former in setting forth the qualifications of these new officers, and the extent of their power. It enacts, that in *every* county there should be assigned for the keeping of the peace, one lord, and with him three or four of the most worthy[1] in the county, with some learned in the law. These were to have power to restrain offenders, rioters, and all other barrators, and to pursue, arrest, take, and chastise them according to their trespass or offence; and cause them to be imprisoned and duly punished, according to their discretion and judgment. The act further directs them "also to inform themselves, and to inquire of all those who had been pillors and robbers in the parts beyond the sea, and were now returned, and went wandering about, not labouring as they were wont in times past, and to take and arrest all they found, by indictment or by suspicion, and to put them in prison; and to take of such as were not of good fame, wherever they were found, sufficient security and mainprise of their *good behaviour* towards the king and his people, and to duly punish others, to the intent that people, merchants, and other travellers might not be endangered by such riotors and rebels; and also to hear and determine, at the king's suit, all manner of felonies and trespasses done in the same county, according to the laws and customs of the realm." This was the first authority they had to take *sureties for good behaviour*, and, indeed, the first mention of it in any statute or law book (*a*). By ch. v. of the same act, those who were assigned to keep the peace

(*a*) This power to arrest suspicious characters upon a general suspicion, and keep them in custody until they find surety for their good behaviour, embodies one of the most important principles in our law, and one which, having been in modern times greatly neglected, has given rise to serious mischief. The present enactment must be coupled with the provisions in the statute of Winchester on the same subject (*vide ante*, c. x.) The object of both statutes was *prevention*, and the present was evidently passed in aid of the former, which merely provided for the arrest of suspicious characters, and did not prescribe, as the present statute does, what was to be done with them: that is to say, they are to be made to find surety. This statutable power of arrest upon a mere general suspicion, and to hold to surety for future good behaviour and for the prevention of felony, must be distinguished from the common law power of arrest on suspicion of a felony actually committed. They have, however, this close connexion, that in the latter, as in the former, ill-fame, vagrancy, and bad company have always been held good grounds of suspicion (*vide Year-books*, 7 *Edward IV.* 20; 9 *Edward IV.* 26; 10 *Edward IV.* 17; 11 *Edward IV.* 6; 2 *Henry VII.* 5; 4 *Henry VII.* 2–18; 5 *Henry VII.* fol. 5; 26 *Henry VIII.* 41; *Brooks' Abridgment*, "*Faux Imprisonment*" and "*Trespass*"). Hence it was long ago laid down that "every man may take night-walkers who go by the way, for it is for the common profit" (*Hussey, C.J.; 4 Henry VII.*, fol. 2). The same law is laid down in effect by Lord Coke, who says "that this species of surety, *de bono gestu*, consists chiefly in this, that a man behave himself well in his port and company" (4 *Institute*, fol. 180); and so Hawkins lays the law down (*Pleas of the Crown*, book 11, c. xii. s. 20, fol. 77; c. xiii. s. 12, fol. 83). The law has been disused, *sed vide post*, p. 333, note (*a*); *vide ante*, p. 322.

[1] *Des multz vauez.*

were empowered to inquire of measures and weights, according to stat. 25 Edward III. st. 5, c. ix. (*a*).

The last statute concerning the keepers of the peace is stat. 36 Edward III. st. 1, c. xii., which enacts, that in the commissions of *justices* of the peace (for so they were now called) and of labourers, express mention should be made, that they hold their sessions four times in the year; by one session *in octabis* of the Epiphany, the second within the second week in Lent, the third betwixt the feast of Pentecost and St John the Baptist, the fourth *in octabis* of St Michael.

Thus stood the commission of the peace at the close of this reign. The keepers of the peace were become justices, presiding over a court, where many matters of considerable importance to the order and quiet of society were cognizable, besides the important jurisdiction over felonies and trespasses. The consideration of these magistrates was greatly heightened by the accession of business that was thrown upon them by later acts of parliament, which have gradually entrusted them with matters of very material concern to the property and liberty of the subject.

(*a*) In the reign of Edward IV. a case arose upon these statutes. Error was brought upon an indictment of felony, "coram A. B., &c., *justices of the peace* for the county;" and the error assigned was, that it did not appear that they had any commission of *oyer* and *terminer*. And it was argued that the powers of the justices of the peace were different by divers statutes; and that under some of these there would be no authority to take indictments. On the other side, it was urged that it was to be presumed they had the requisite authority, the contrary not appearing (22 *Edward IV.*, fol. 13; *et vide* 13 *Henry VI.*, fol. 52). In the reign of Edward IV. a statute passed to take away the jurisdiction of the sheriff in the tourn to take indictments or presentments for felony, and to transfer the jurisdiction to the justices of the peace (*vide post*). There is an important subject of which our author appears to have lost sight, and which may be mentioned here. Magna Charta renders illegal all kiddles or weirs in navigable rivers. The words of the statute are—"Omnes kidelli deponantur per totam Angliam nisi per costeram maris,"—that is, that all weirs shall be put down throughout all England except only by the sea-coast. Then the Act 25 Edward III. cap 4 (1350), recited that the common passage of boats and ships on the great rivers of England was often annoyed by the enhancing of weirs, mills, stanks, stakes, and kiddles, and enacted that all such weirs, mills, stanks, stakes, and kiddles set up in the time of the king's grandfather, whereby the ships and boats be disturbed so that they cannot pass as they were wont, shall be utterly pulled over. This was followed and confirmed by various statutes to the like effect: 42 *Edward III.*, c. ii.; 1 *Henry IV.*, c. xi.; and 12 *Edward IV.*, c. xvii. The scope of these statutes seems to have been the *navigation;* but subsequent statutes provide for the protection of fisheries.

CHAPTER XV.

EDWARD III.

Of Descent—Limitations in Tail and Remainder—Tenant in Tail after Possibility, &c.—Wills of Land—Of Warranty with Assets—Of barring Entails—Of Chattels—Of Entry congeable—Discontinuance—Remitter—Of Assizes—Of Colour—De Ejectione Firmæ—Writs of Entry—Entry ad Terminum qui præteriit—Entry in le quibus—Difference of Writs in the per, per et cui, and post—Entry sur cui in vitâ—Entry ad communem Legem—Entry in consimili Casu—Writs of Formedon—Writs of Right—Other real Writs—Writ of quòd permittat.

THAT system of law which was discoursed upon so fully in the reign of Henry III. continued still to prevail, with such small alterations in the form and circumstances as had been suggested by the courts, or imposed by parliament in the two intermediate reigns. Other seeming changes had also crept in, which, upon examination, appear nothing more than new words and terms to express old ideas. These, however, cannot be passed over in a work whose design is to throw new light upon the law by considering it historically (*a*), a novelty in expression being alone sufficient to obscure a subject otherwise ever so well understood.

(*a*) The author here hints at the true use and object of legal history, which cannot reject what is old or even obsolete, because it deals professedly with the past, and its use is to help to understand the past. As Hale pointed out, in his preface to *Rolle's Abridgment*, even in his time a great part of the law of this age had become obsolete, though he says that the mutations which have taken place, have not been so much in the law as in the subject-matter of it. He points out that the titles of tenures and villenage were obsolete; that the title of dower had grown much out of use by reason of jointures; that the title of descents had been much abridged; that the title of attornments, once so great and difficult, had, with all its incidents, *quid juris clamat*, &c., grown out of use by reason of new modes of conveyance; that the titles of discontinuance and remitter, which were great titles at common law, and full of curious learning, had been much narrowed. So he says, "The remedy by assizes, and the forms of proceedings relating thereto, were great titles in the Year-books; but use and practice had in a great degree antiquated the use of them in recovering possessions, and the action of *ejectione firmæ* was substituted. And real actions, as writs of right, writs of entry, &c., with their numerous incidents, grand *cape*, aid-prayer, voucher to warranty, &c., were great titles in the Year-books, but now much out of use. So wager of law was a great title in the Year-books, but had gone quite out of use by reason of the resort to actions on the case. *Quod permittat* and assizes for commons, *secta ad molendinum*, assizes of nuisance, &c., were much turned into trespass and actions on the case. So garnishment and interpleader were large titles at common law, but now much out of use, for actions of detinue had been turned into actions on the case. And so in many other instances." But then the history of the law shows why they went out of use, and, in showing that, often shows that the *principles* upon which they were based were sound, and that it was only by reason of the forms of proceeding becoming obsolete that the remedies became so. And even where this is not so, the history of these old proceedings is necessary in order to render the law-books of the time intelligible, and to throw light on the history of the age.

We shall therefore take a view of the changes made in the law by the determination of courts during this reign, pursuing the following order: first, of the rights of persons and of things; then of the administration of civil justice; afterwards we shall consider the alterations that took place in the nature of crimes, and the administration of criminal justice.

Notwithstanding the canonists had failed in the reign of Henry III. in their attempt to introduce their law of legitimacy,[1] by which a child born before marriage, if marriage followed, was considered as legitimate; yet the law of England had suffered such issue to obtain a degree of right and preference before other children born out of wedlock. A child so born was called a *bastard eignè*, to distinguish it from the child born after marriage, of the same mother, which was called *mulier puisnè*, *mulieratus* being the appellation applied to a legitimate son by Glanville and our other old writers.[2] It had become the law of descent, that if a person died seised in fee, leaving issue a *bastard eignè*, and *mulier puisnè*, and the bastard entered and died seised, such regard should be paid to this undisturbed possession, sanctioned afterwards by a descent in a lawful way on his issue, that the mulier should be precluded from entering on the issue. Such was the law in the early part of this reign, and, no doubt, long before.[3]

Of descent.

Many points arose upon this new piece of law, and many were settled in this king's time. It was said that the right in the issue accrued by the dying seised of the ancestor; therefore, if anything happened that in other cases would take off the effect of a dying seised, the mulier was not barred. Thus it was held, that should the descent happen while the mulier was within age, he should not be barred.[4] Again, where the bastard entered and continued seised for eight years, and then infeoffed another, who died seised without any interruption, it was thought that such a dying seised would not bar the mulier; but that case happened to be decided upon the nonage of the mulier.[5] This privilege of the bastard only availed his issue as against the mulier and his issue, and not against a stranger; nor would it avail against the issue of the mulier, if they claimed under an entail. Thus where land was given in tail, with a remainder over in tail, and the first tenant in tail had issue a bastard and mulier, and died seised; the bastard entèred, continued in possession, had issue, and died seised; the issue entered, the mulier died without issue; it was held, the second remainder-man should have a formedon, not being bound by the descent on the issue of the bastard.[6]

The maxim of *possessio fratris de fœdo simplici facit sororem esse hæredem*,[7] or, in a more general sense, the rule of excluding the half-blood, was held to as strict a construction as that about

[1] *Vide ante*, vol. i. 265. [2] *Ibid.* 104. [3] 21 Edw. III., 34.
[4] 31 Ass. 18, 22, and Bro. descent, 49. [5] 36 Ass. 2. [6] 39 Edw. III., 38.
[7] *Vide ante*, vol. ii. 317.

mulier puisnè. If a person was seised in tail, and died leaving two sons by different venters, the youngest would inherit to the eldest, *per formam doni*, being heir of the body in tail, though not in fee-simple. Thus this maxim[1] and the exclusion of the half-blood was confined to estates in fee-simple wholly, and to such as were strictly in *possession.* Upon the point of possession, many doubtful cases arose. A man, having a son and daughter by one venter, and a son by another, gave his land to his eldest son in tail, and then died, so that the fee descended on the eldest son, who, being now seised in tail with a reversion in fee, died without heirs of his body; in which case it was held, the youngest son should have the land, and not the daughter.[2] Again, land was given to a baron and feme, and the heirs of their body, remainder to the right heirs of the baron; they had issue a son, and the feme died; the baron married, and had issue another son and died; the eldest son entered, and died seised without issue: here it was held, that the land belonged to the younger son of the half-blood; for the elder, as in the former case, was only seised of the entail, and was not in possession of the reversion.[3]

In order for this rule to take effect, the reversion should come into *actual possession.* A man seised in fee leased his land for life, and then had a son by one venter, and a daughter by another, and died, after the time at which the rent was payable, but without receiving it; then the son died before the next day of payment; so that he had only a seisin in law of the rent, and not in fact; after this, the tenant for life died; and it was held that the reversion went to the daughter, and not to the heir of the son, because the father was the person last seised; the reversion never having fallen into actual possession during the life of the eldest son.[4] Yet, on the other hand, where a guardian entered during the infancy of an elder son, and assigned dower to the widow, it was held that the possession of the guardian was sufficient seisin of the heir, to exclude the half-blood; but the part held in dower prevented that seisin, and that the land so holden descended to the half-blood.[5]

Limitations in tail and remainder.

The interpretation of the statute *de donis*, and the whole doctrine of entails and remainders, were debated in every point of view. Limitations of a new impression were devised for the purpose of ordering property conformably with the wishes of its owners; and doubts were sometimes raised upon these, whether they were within the meaning of that famous act.[6] Although no more than three species of entails are mentioned in that act, the courts had been disposed to bring almost every sort of conditional fee within the equity of it. We find in this reign the following gifts in tail and remainder: First, to a baron and feme, and the heirs that the baron shall beget on the feme. Secondly, to a man and his heirs, if he has

[1] 37 Ass. 14, 24 Edw. III., 30.
[2] 24 Edw. III., 13.
[3] 37 Ass. 4.
[4] 35 Edw. III., Bro. discent, 28.
[5] 8 Ass. 6.
[6] 21 Edw. III., 43.

issue of his body; and if he dies without heirs of his body, remainder over. Thirdly, to a man and his heirs, if he has any *de carne suâ;* if not, the reversion to the donor. Fourthly, to a baron and feme, *et uni hæredi de corpore suo legitimè procreato, et uni hæredi ipsius hæredis.* Fifthly, to a man and his sister, and the heirs of their two bodies begotten. Sixthly, to two men, and the heirs of their two bodies begotten. Seventhly, to a man, and the heirs male of his body. We find remainders of the following kind: to a father for life, with remainder to the eldest son, and his wife in tail, remainder to the right heirs of the father; a lease for life, remainder over in fee; a gift in tail, remainder to the donor for life, remainder over in fee; and the like limitations, which may be easily imagined after these instances.

The first of the above-mentioned limitations was considered as a special tail, as well in the feme as in the baron.[1] In the second and third entails, it was argued, that the gift was in fee-simple on the condition and terms of the tenant having heirs of his body, which event taking place, the estate descended to his right heirs; but this construction was overruled, and they were held to be limitations in tail.[2] The entails to *two men*, and those to *a man and his sister*, and the heirs of their bodies, were allowed sufficient and lawful upon this reason—that they might each respectively have such *heirs* of their bodies as would satisfy the description of the entail.[3] The gift to a man *and the heirs male of his body*, called upon the court to explain at large the force of the statute as to descents in tail. The donee in that case had issue a daughter, who had issue a son, and then died; and it became a question, whether the grandson should succeed. It was argued, he should be heir in tail, because in such a gift at common law the issue would inherit in fee, on account of the word *heirs*, and the power the ancestor, after issue, had of aliening; and as the statute only restrains from alienation, when that was complied with, and the land was left to descend, it was contended that the grandson should take as before the statute, that is, in fee-simple. But it was resolved, this was a gift in tail, which did not give an inheritance so largely as a gift to a man and the heirs of his body; upon which the other side seemed to argue, that there indeed the grandson would inherit by regular descent in fee-tail *general;* but here the entail was to a *special* heir, and the grandson did not convey the descent to himself in the special manner required, as he claimed through his mother, who could not be heir under a limitation to *heirs male.*[4] On another occasion, a gift to a man and his heirs male, without saying of his body, was adjudged in parliament a fee-simple.

Where land was given to a man and his wife in special tail, and

[1] 21 Edw. III., 43.
[2] 35 Ass., 14; 37 Ass., 15.
[3] Edw. III., 78 b.
[4] 18 Edw. III., 46 a.

either of them died without issue, the survivor was by law to hold it for life, and was termed *tenant in tail after possibility of issue extinct.* It was held, that as such tenants once had an estate of inheritance, the survivor was, though in effect only, tenant for life,[1] not to be impeached of waste.

Tenant in tail after possibility, &c.

One of the rules which had been established respecting remainders was, that they should take effect immediately upon the failure of the preceding estate, or otherwise they should be void. Thus, where there were a brother and sister, and land was given to A. for life, remainder to the right heirs of the brother, and he died; after which the tenant for life died, and the sister entered; there, though the wife of the brother was afterwards delivered of a posthumous son, it was held, that the sister should retain the land; and it was said, that wheresoever a remainder or purchase vested, there it should continue; but it would be otherwise of a descent in the like case. Again, where there was a tenant for life, remainder to the right heirs of I. and N., I. had issue, and died; then the tenant for life died, and the heir of I. entered; after which N. died: here it was, conformably with the above case, determined, that the heir of N. took nothing; for he was not heir to N. at the time the remainder fell, for *nemo est hœres viventis:* and it was said, that where there was a tenant for life, remainder to the right heirs of I., the remainder was in abeyance during the life of I.; and if he survived the tenant for life, the remainder became void, because there was no person *in esse* to take it when it fell.[2]

Another rule of remainders was, that they took effect at the same time when the first estate was created, and their continuance depended upon the continuance of that, all standing or falling together. Thus, where lands were given for life, with condition to perform certain duties, remainder over, with the same condition; if the heir entered on the tenant for life for breach of the condition, the remainder was likewise defeated.[3]

Many of the remainders litigated in this reign are to be explained upon one or other of these rules. Thus, where there was tenant for life, remainder over, if the tenant for life died, and he in remainder agreed to the limitation, he stood in the place of the tenant for life; the particular tenant and remainder-man making but one degree in a writ of entry. If a termor or guardian leased for life, remainder over, and he in remainder agreed, he was equally a disseisor with the tenant for life, it being, in law, all one estate.[4]

The giving an estate to a man for life, with remainder to his right heirs, was a species of limitation invented since the time of Bracton, and probably since the statute *de donis* gave an example and an authority for making strict settlements. The object of this new mode of conveyancing, no doubt, was to give the heir a title

[1] Old tenures.
[2] 30 Ass. 47 Bro. Don. & Rem. 21.
[3] 29 Ass. 17.
[4] 50 Edw. III., 21.

by purchase, instead of one by descent, which was clogged with the heavy appendages of wardship, relief, marriage, and the like. But the courts put a construction on such gifts that wholly defeated the design of the makers. Where a gift was made to a man for life, remainder to another for life, remainder in fee to the right heirs of the first taker; it was held, that the first tenant for life might, by virtue of the limitation to his heirs, either give or forfeit the fee-simple, although it did not properly rest in him during the mesne remainder.[1] And where an estate was given for life to a father, remainder to the first son and his wife in tail, remainder to the right heirs of the father; the father died, and then the eldest son and his wife died without issue; the lord was permitted to avow upon the younger son for the relief, as heir of his elder brother to the remainder in fee; though the younger son contended he came in as purchaser, under the words *right heirs of his father*, and that the tail and the fee could not be *simul et semel* in his elder brother.[2]

Wills of land.

We have supposed the above settlements to have been made by some common-law conveyance in the donor's lifetime; that is, by fine, by feoffment, or some other grant with livery of seisin; or such a conveyance as countervailed a feoffment, as a lease for life, or for years, with a release.[3] These were the only methods for a voluntary transfer of freehold, by the general law of the kingdom. But there prevailed in certain places a custom, by which the inhabitants enjoyed the privilege of devising their lands by *testament*. The existence of such customs has been testified by Glanville and Bracton; but the particular influence of them, and the form of such wills, are wholly unnoticed by those writers; so that till the reign of this king there is little or nothing to be met with in any law-book upon the subject of devises of land. What hints are to be found in Bracton and Glanville relate rather to the nature of wills in general; which too, being an object of clerical judicature, were hardly thought a part of their subject.[4] We now find many adjudged cases upon wills of lands; and some of those rules were now laid down, which governed afterwards when devises became the general law of the kingdom.

If lands were devisable, it was mostly in boroughs; and the course by which the devisee was put in possession was different. In some, it was the duty of the bailiff of the place to give him seisin; in others (and that was the most common practice) there lay a writ called *ex gravi querelâ*, which was to be executed by the officer of the town.[5] It was held for settled law, that a husband might give land to his wife by last will,[6] though he could not by deed; but a wife was not allowed to make a will of lands to her husband, as it would be construed to be the act of the husband, or at least to be done by his coercion; though it was allowed that

[1] 24 Edw. III., 70.
[2] 40 Edw. III., 9.
[3] 44 Edw. III., 3; 31 Ass., 25.
[4] *Vide ante*, vol. i. c. iii., v.
[5] 39 Ass., 6.
[6] 44 Edw. III., 33.

she might, by the assent of her husband, devise the moiety of her husband's *goods*, and make executors, who should prove the will by the husband's assent: which nearly corresponds with what was laid down for law in the times of Bracton and Glanville.[1] If the husband, after her death, would prohibit the proving of the will, he might, and the will would be void.[2] So stood the law as to the wills of *femes covert*. It was not uncommon to devise land to executors to make distribution for the good of the testator's soul; in which case, should the executors refuse or neglect to do it, and take the profits to their own use, the heir might enter, and have an assize.[3] It was held, that should one executor die, the rest might lawfully sell.[4] There seems to have been a difference between a devise of land *to* executors to sell, and a devise of land to be sold *by* executors: in the latter case, they were considered as having no possession,[5] but merely an authority.

There are some instances of an inclination to keep a gift of land by will within some of the strictness with which gifts by deed were construed. Where a man gave his land by will, and it was alleged that he afterwards sold it, and took it back in fee to defeat his will, it seems to have been construed as a revocation; upon the idea, we may suppose, that the fee he died seised of was considered as a new purchase since the will was made, and therefore such as could not be conveyed by an instrument made before.[6] Again, it was held, that where land was devised without any express mention of the estate, the devisee could properly have it only for life; so that, in this respect, a devise and a livery agreed: however, it was at the same time admitted, that a devise to a man *in perpetuum*, or to a man *and his assigns*, would convey a fee-simple.[7]

The courts, indeed, began to make allowance in the construction of wills, which were never indulged to deeds; and it became a rule, that the intention of the devisor was to be sought out by all possible investigation, and observed with strictness, however untechnically it might be expressed. Thus, where a remainder was limited by will *propinquioribus hæredibus de sanguine puerorum* of the devisor, it was held, that, upon the devisor dying, leaving two sons who died without issue, and a daughter who had issue Isabel, and then died, that Isabel should take, and was sufficiently described by the will.[8]

Of warranty with assets.

We have seen,[9] in the last reign, that the warranty of tenant in tail, with assets in fee-simple descending upon the issue, was held a bar to his claiming anything under the entail. We now find the courts expressly declaring that this was admitted to be a bar, upon the equity of the statute of Gloucester, which ordained that the issue should not be barred by the act of the father to demand the seisin of the mother, unless he had value

[1] *Vide ante*, vol. i. c. v.
[2] Bro. Devise, 34.
[3] 38 Ass., p. 3.
[4] 39 Ass., 17; 49 Edw. III., 36.
[5] Bro. Devise, 46.
[6] 44 Edw. III., 33.
[7] 22 Edw. III., 16.
[8] 30 Ass., 47.
[9] *Vide ante*, c. xii.

in recompense by descent from the father. But the courts were more strict in requiring a *bonâ fide* recompense to the issue of tenant in tail than to the issue of tenant by the curtesy. For if the former had assets by descent, and aliened those assets in fee, and died; then, though himself having received assets, was barred, yet his issue, or, if he had none, his youngest brother, would not be barred; every heir in tail being considered as privy to the recovery of the land in tail, unless he had had recompense by descent in fee-simple. On the other hand, if a tenant by the curtesy aliened, and value in fee-simple descended to his issue, it was a good bar, though the issue should afterwards alien the fee-simple, and die leaving issue; it being a rule, that, as the issue was once lawfully barred, the issue of that issue should have no title to demand anything of the mother's seisin.[1] As warranty implied that it was accompanied by a recompense, the law took care that such recompense should really continue; and such great force was allowed to a warranty so circumstanced, that it was held sufficient not only to bar the issue, but the reversion, even if in the king.[2] But assets without a warranty were of no more effect than a warranty without assets.[3]

When assets were considered so necessary a requisite to give effect to the warranty of the person aliening an estate in prejudice of his issue, it was merely in compliance with the rule which had been adopted from the statute of Gloucester; the warranty being of itself sufficient, at common law, to bar the issue from making any claim against it:[4] and the statute *de donis*, which had forbid the alienation of the tenant, had not taken away the force of his warranty.

Of barring entails.

And so it was held in another instance of warranty; for if the uncle, or other ancestor, or cousin *collateral*, who was not privy to the entail, aliened with warranty, or made a release with warranty, and died without heirs of his body, so that the *next issue in tail* was become his right heir, such issue would be barred by his ancestor's deed with warranty.[5] As for instance, where there was a tenant in tail, the remainder to E. in tail, the remainder to C. in tail, and the first tenant in tail died without issue; E. in the first remainder made a feoffment with warranty, and had issue, and died, and then the issue died without issue; so that C. in the second remainder became heir to E.; here, though the issue of E. would not be barred, because there were no assets by descent, yet C. was held to be barred by the warranty.[6] The same if an uncle of tenant in tail released with warranty to an alienee of the tenant, this would bar the issue from claiming, though the uncle never had possession or right in the land.

Thus an estate tail might be barred by the warranty of an ancestor under whom the estate *was* claimed, if accompanied with assets; and by the warranty of an ancestor under whom the estate

[1] O. N. B., 145 b., 144 a.
[2] 46 Edw. III., 28. 46 Ass., 6.
[3] 38 Edw. III., 23.
[4] *Vide ante*, vol. i. c. viii.
[5] O. N. B., 143 b., 144.
[6] Bro. Gar., 8.

was *not* claimed, without any assets; which first warranty has since been called *lineal*, and the latter *collateral*, because collateral to the title by which the estate was claimed. These were treated as bars to which an estate tail was subject in its very creation, and which were unaffected by the prohibition of the statute *de donis*. When all this efficacy was attributed to a warranty, it was convenient that it should not be misapplied so as to protect wrong-doers, and to defeat the injured from pursuing their rights. If therefore a guardian or tenant at will aliened the land of the heir, or of the lessor, with warranty, as this conveyance amounted to a disseisin, the warranty was void as against the heir or lessor.[1] This was afterwards called *warranty commencing by disseisin*.

The alienation of tenant in tail being somewhat opened by the above means, and the remaining restraint being perhaps still more felt than ever, application was made to parliament more than once during this reign, for the assistance of a statute to adjust the difficulties complained of. In the 17th year of the king, the commons petitioned that the statute of Westminster might be declared as to the cases in which the issue in tail might lawfully alien;[2] but this was refused, and the petitioners were referred to the law as it then stood. In the 50th year, there is a petition of the commons upon the subject of collateral warranty, which, however, makes no mention of its effect on an estate tail, but merely notices the common case of a warranty, as it regarded estates in fee-simple. The petition states the law long to have been, *and with good sense and reason*, that where any one was disseised of his freehold, and a collateral ancestor of the disseisee released to the disseisor, then being in possession, with a clause of warranty; that the disseisee, should the warranty descend on him, would be for ever barred of his right. But, continues the petition, in many other cases *not here named*, the warranty of a collateral ancestor is considered as a bar, though nothing descend from the ancestor, which is a great damage and disherision of many. It was therefore prayed, that no such warranty thenceforward to be made should be a bar in any action, unless tenements to the value had descended on the demandant from such ancestor, according as it had been ordained by the statute of Gloucester.[3] But this application not succeeding, collateral warranty continued as effectual as before.

The idea of an *excambium*, or, as it was now more usually termed, a recompense in value to the issue, was the prevailing principle by which entails were governed and modified. In the 46th of this king, where a man had given land and rents in tail, with permission that the donee might alien for the benefit of the issue, it was said in support of it, that the donor might as well give an estate tail under conditions, as make a simple gift in tail.[4] An alienation after a gift circumstanced like this, so far from a violation of the

[1] 43 Edw. III., 7.
[2] Rot. Parl., 17 Edw. III., 47.
[3] *Ibid.* 50 Edw., 77. Note, this is No. 68 in Cotton.
[4] 46 Edw. III., 4 b.

statute, seemed to be in the very spirit of it; for the will of the giver expressed in the deed of gift, would, by such alienation, be strictly adhered to. In the following case, where the alienation had no authority but the tenant's own act, and the reasons he could give in justification of it, the decision depended wholly on the efficacy then attributed to a recompense, or, at least, an apparent benefit and advantage to the issue. This is the case of Octavian Lumbard. A younger brother, in the absence of the elder abroad, entered on the lands entailed, enjoyed them for some years, and then died seised, leaving issue; at some distance of time the elder brother returned, and, raising a question about his title, he and the tenant in possession came to a compromise; the elder brother released his title, in consideration of which the issue of the younger granted him a rent out of the land, with a power of distress. It was held, that this rent-charge should be levied against the issue, notwithstanding the entail, and should continue, into whatever hands the land should come[1] (*a*). Thus was the quieting of the title considered as a sufficient consideration and value to the issue for the defalcation they suffered by the rent-charge, though it was plainly a breach of the donor's will, at least of the interpretation which had been put on that part of the statute which forbids alienation.

Of chattels real.

These were the observations that occurred concerning the novelties that had lately been introduced into the doctrines of real property. The learning of real property fills the reports of this reign, and leaves very little space for information respecting chattels and personalty. It may be sufficient from that little just to remark, that *chattels* were now divided into *real* and *personal*. Thus a term for years was called a chattel real;

(*a*) The author somewhat misunderstood and mis-stated this case, and appears to deduce from it a doctrine for which it affords no authority. It does not appear that it was a case of entail at all. Octavian complained that John took her cattle, and he set up that his father died seised (*i.e.*, in fee-simple), having issue himself and a sister, and, that he being abroad, she entered and had issue, and died seised (*i.e.*, in fee-simple), and left issue Nicholas, who entered; and then John returned and claimed the land, and upon that Nicholas granted him the rent-charge. So that neither of them considered it as a case of entail. In answer, however, to this charge, Octavian, the plaintiff, set up that the sister had the estate granted to her and her husband in tail, and that she herself, the plaintiff, was their issue. To which John replied, denying the entail, on which issue was taken. And then it is said that the opinion of the court was, that, inasmuch as Nicholas, who charged the land, had nothing, unless in the tail, and upon him John, who was right heir when he returned, could have entered; and, by accord between them to make a release, he (N.) granted him the rent, that the rent-charge should be levied upon the issue in tail, and against any one else (44 *Edw. III.*, fol. 22). That is, the contest between the parties was, whether or not it *was* an estate tail, and it was insisted that if it *were not* so, there would be no power to charge the issue in favour of a stranger (since John was a stranger to an entail in favour of his sister), and the court held that even although, in point of fact, it *was* an entail, nevertheless, as it was *disputed*, the release by the right heir was a good consideration for the rent-charge. It will be seen that the case has nothing to do with the doctrine as to barring estates tail, but merely illustrates the law of accord.

[1] 44 Edw. III., 21 b.

other movables were called chattels personal.[1] Certain limited interests in real property, besides terms for years, were called chattels, as the next avoidance of a living. A security by statute-merchant belonging to a woman, as it went to the husband if she married, was therefore said to be only a chattel.[2]

So much has been said in the former chapter on the jurisdiction of courts, that nothing need be added; passing over them, therefore, we shall proceed to speak of such actions as were now in use, beginning with assizes and real actions.

Before anything is said of the alterations which the assize and other actions had undergone, it will be proper to premise some observations upon those ousters of freehold that were the ground of such remedies. The old law by which assizes and writs of entry were governed, was founded on principles that naturally and necessarily led to the conclusions that began now to be founded thereon, and which had grown to considerable magnitude as well as curiosity in this reign.

If a man was deprived of his freehold in a way that was termed a *disseisin*, we have seen that he might make an *entry* thereon; and if that failed of recovering the possession, or he chose rather to resort to legal remedies, he might have an assize of novel disseisin.[3] This *entry* was *congeable*, as they now called it, during the life of the disseisee, unless the land descended from the disseisor to his heir, and then the *descent* was said to *toll the entry*, and the disseisee was driven to a writ of entry. This right of entry must be kept alive by an entry within a year and a day before the death of the disseisor; or, if the disseisee was prevented by danger or menace from actual entry by a *claim;* and in such case he might have his assize even against the heir, notwithstanding the descent.

Another way in which a man might be deprived of his freehold was by what was called a *discontinuance.* In such case the party injured could not by law make an entry, and of course could not have a remedy by assize; but he was obliged to resort to his writ of entry. Thus, in order to decide whether an assize or a writ of entry was the proper remedy, it was often necessary to discuss some or all of these questions, whether the *entry* was *congeable;* whether it was *tolled by descent;* whether it had been kept on foot by *claim,* or, as it was in after times called, *continual claim;* or whether it was not such an ouster as amounted to a *discontinuance.* All these composed, as it were, new titles in the law, though deducible from principles before laid down in the time of Bracton.[4] As these points now entered more or less into most questions that arose upon the doctrine of estates, it will be necessary to consider them somewhat particularly. After some few observations upon a *disseisin,* which is the foundation of the rest, we shall go on to treat of these articles more minutely.

[1] Old tenures.

[2] 39 Edw. III., 37; 37 Ass., 11.

[3] *Vide ante,* vol. i. c. vii.

[4] *Vide ante,* vol. i. c. vii.

The very large sense in which the term *disseisin* was understood in the time of Bracton might preclude the necessity of saying much to show the great extent in which it was now received; the decisions of this reign seemed to be only confirmations or explanations of that author's doctrine; but as such they are worthy of notice.

It appears from Bracton, that any encroachment upon or disturbance to the free use of a man's freehold was a disseisin.[1] In the same spirit of the old law, it was now held and decided that to dig in a man's ground, to fish in his water, to cut a tree,[2] to enclose so as to prevent a man enjoying his common,[3] a rescous, or even replevin, or enclosure to prevent a distress for rent *service;* and a detainer, rescous, replevin, and enclosure, accompanied with a denial of a *rent-charge*, or a menace to prevent making a distress in either case, were all disseisins of the freehold.[4] A command not to enter was held a disseisin of the lawful owner.[5] Again, conformably with the same cases stated by Bracton,[6] it was held that if a termor for years made a lease for life, he and his lessee were disseisors; a guardian making a feoffment in fee, or devising, was a disseisor, and the feoffee was now held to be equally a disseisor.[7] Since Bracton's time the limitation of remainders had become more common; and it was now held, that where a guardian leased for life, the remainder in tail, the remainder-man was equally a disseisor with the guardian; the same where a tenant for years aliened in tail, with a remainder over. If the tenant in tail died without issue, and the remainder-man entered, he was a disseisor.[8] In short, wherever a man was seised wrongfully (if the entry was not tolled), he was a disseisor; as, for instance, dower was assigned to a woman, with all the usual forms of law; but it turning out that she was not really married, she was therefore considered as a disseisor.[9] If an attorney made livery of seisin not exactly in the way in which he was authorised by his warrant, it was a disseisin to the feoffer, even where the warrant was to give a simple livery, and he made it upon condition.[10] Entry under a void grant was held a disseisin.[11] A devisee entering under a devise of an infant's land made by a guardian was considered as a disseisor.[12] All commanders and counsellors, and those who agreed afterwards to a disseisin, were disseisors.[13] Such of these cases as were not deemed disseisins at common law were warranted by the principles delivered in Bracton, or at least by the statute made since his time, for extending the writ of assize.[14]

When a man was disseised of his freehold, it was a provision of our law that he might repossess himself of it by an actual entry thereon; by doing which he again became in legal seisin, and the

[1] *Vide ante*, vol. i. c. vii. [2] 11 Ass., 25. [3] 8 Ass., 18.
[4] 21 Edw. III., 34; 49 Ass., 5; 3 Ass., 8. [5] 26 Ass., 17.
[6] *Vide ante*, vol. i. c. vii. [7] 50 Edw. III., 22. [8] 50 Edw. III., 22; Bro. Diss., 85.
[9] 21 Edw. III., 45. [10] 12 Ass., 24. [11] 24 Edw. III., 32.
[12] 28 Ass., 11. [13] 27 Ass., 31; 37 Ass., 8; Bro. Diss., 104.
[14] Westm. 2, ch. 25. *Vide ante*, c. xii.

continuance of the wrong-doer amounted to a disseisin, for which an assize would lie. This entry was sufficiently performed by putting the foot upon the land.[1] The time of making this entry, and of pursuing it with force, so as to regain the possession, was limited, in the time of Bracton, to the space of a few days, unless the party was then out of the way upon a journey, or the like; but all through this reign it seems to have been a rule that an entry should not be made on a person who was in by title, unless in very special cases; and where the tenant was party to the fact, it seems to have been limited to a seisin for a year and a day[2] (*a*). However, after such entry, the right of bringing the assize still continued during the life of the person making the entry, which right is sometimes meant when the right of entry is spoken of.

Of entry congeable.

The following were cases where such a right of entry was permitted: If a tenant for life infeoffed the first remainder-man, who died without issue, then the second remainder-man might enter.[3] If a tenant for life, or tenant after possibility of issue extinct aliened, the person in reversion might enter.[4] If a tenant for life aliened in fee, and the remainder-man in tail died without entering, the next remainder-man in fee might enter.[5] This right of entry would be taken away, if the land in question passed by descent to the present possessor, the law in favour of descent allowing a presumptive title to him, which was not to be defeated by an entry; but if the person who had the right of entry was an infant, he would not be foreclosed of his right of entry: the same, if he was in prison, or under any of those disabilities which the law in many cases allowed as a sufficient excuse for neglect in pursuing legal remedies. Such claim so established the right of entry, as to convey it to the heir.

Every advantage which a man secured to himself by entry might be acquired by *claim*, if he was deterred from making his entry by a fear of death, or of maiming: a claim made under such circumstances would give the same seisin as an actual entry.[6] In the 38th year of this king, an assize was maintained by a person who had right by descent, at the death of the person last seised; it appeared

(*a*) Hale says, speaking of this age, "In those times the learning of the common law consisted principally in assizes and real actions; and rarely was any title determined in any personal action, unless in cases of titles to rents, by replevin; and the reasons thereof were principally these—because those terms were great favourers of the possessor; and therefore, if a disseisor had been in possession by a year and a day, he was not to be put out without a recovery by assize. Again, if a disseisor had made a feoffment, they did not countenance an entry upon the feoffee, because thereby he might lose his warrantry, which he might save if he were impleaded in an assize or writ of entry. They were willing to quiet men's possessions; and therefore, after a recovery or bar in an assize or real action, the party was driven to an action of a higher nature." Afterwards, he observes that in cases of descents and discontinuance, which necessarily drove the demandant to his *formedons* or *cui in vitâ*, &c. But, he adds, the descents which tolled (*i.e.*, took away) entries, were rare, because men preserved their rights of entry by continual claim (*Hist. Com. Law*, c. viii.).

1 22 Edw. III., 15.
2 Bro. Ent. Cong., 85.
3 41 Edw. III., 21.
4 45 Edw. III., 21, 25.
5 43 Ass., 45.
6 49 Edw. III., 34.

ıat his ancestor was residing in the town where the land was, and y parol claimed the tenements among his neighbours, but durst ot approach the land for fear of death, or some bodily hurt:[1] many ases of the same kind appeared in this reign. The case just men-ioned was adjudged to have the effect of continuing to the heir the ight to bring an assize, instead of being driven to his writ of entry; that this new idea of perpetuating a right of entry by claim had ltered the law in this point since Bracton's time; for then the ssize could not be prosecuted by the heir of disseisee, unless it had een actually commenced by the disseisee, and he had gone so far s a view, or the swearing of the jurors;[2] but he was driven to a rit of entry. A *claim* would likewise prevent the consequence of descent from the disseisor to his heir; for it was decided, where here had been a claim, and debate raised against the seisin of the erson in possession, and he died, and then the disseisee died, and he heir of the disseisee entered on the heir of the disseisor, the ntry was congeable, and the assize was the proper remedy.[3] This, ike the former, was an alteration of the law since the time of Ienry III.

A discontinuance was a disseisin, and something more: it was where a person aliened lands to which another had a right, but was prevented by such alienation from making n entry; and so was driven to some of those writs of entry that ave been so often mentioned. Thus where an abbot aliened the ands belonging to his abbey, and died, his successor could not nter, though he had a right, but was obliged to bring his writ of ntry *sine assensu capituli.* Again, where a men aliened lands which he had *jure uxoris*, and died, the wife could not enter, but nust bring her writ of entry *cui in vitâ.* So, if tenant in tail in-eoffed another, and died leaving issue, the issue could not enter, ut must bring a *formedon.* All these were now called *discon-inuances.* Though this efficacy was allowed to a feoffment when nade by a tenant in tail, on account of his being in possession, and he force attributed by the law to a livery of seisin, which carried fee simple; yet a release of a tenant in tail in possession was held ıot to be a discontinuance, unless accompanied with a warranty;[4] ınd a grant of a reversion even with a warranty was adjudged to e no discontinuance.[5]

Discontinuance.

We cannot dismiss the subject of disseisin and discontinuance, without saying something upon another head of law, which was a very frequent consequence of the two ormer. This is a *remitter;* the meaning of which was this, that where a man was in possession of land by an elder and a latter title, he law construed him to be in possession under the first, and not ınder the last; so that he was said to be *remitted* to his first estate, r, as it was sometimes expressed, *en son primer estate, en son*

Remitter.

[1] 38 Ass., 23. [2] *Vide ante*, vol. i. c. vii. [3] 25 Ass., 12.
[4] 24 Ass., 28. [5] 36 Ass., 8.

meliour droit, en son melior estate, and the like.[1] This construction of law was with a design of maintaining the original settlement of estates, whenever broke in upon by the present possessor; and as this was mostly attempted by tenants in tail, the law of remitter seemed to operate in aid and in the spirit of the statute *de donis.* Thus, where baron and feme tenants in tail had issue a son, and discontinued their estate by fine, and took back an estate to themselves and the heirs of the body of the baron *only,* they were adjudged to be remitted to their former estate.[2] Again, where tenant in tail made a feoffment, and died, and the feoffee infeoffed the issue within age, it was held a remitter to the elder estate.[3] Where there were remainders over, a remitter of the first taker was a remitter of all the following remainders, so as to take the estate out of those on whom it had been entailed by the new settlement.[4] If a disseisor infeoffed the disseisee and two others, the whole accrued to the disseisee only, and that by remitter.[5]

Thus have we given a sketch of these new terms, though not wholly new doctrines, of *congeable entry, descent that tolls entry, discontinuance,* and *remitter;* all which were intimately connected with and dependent upon each other, and were afterwards worked up into a very complicated system of learning; there being, perhaps, no question in any branch of artificial knowledge more problematical than such as arose upon entries, and upon discontinuances of estates.

Having considered the nature of disseisin, and the circumstances attending it, we come to treat of the assize of novel disseisin. Whatever difference there may appear between this proceeding in the present reign, and in the time of Henry III., when so much was said upon it, it is more in *terms* than in reality, the substance and form being nearly the same as they were originally. The most striking difference seems to be in the silence about *turning assizes into juries;*[6] a piece of practice that was so much discussed in the early ages of this proceeding. But as this distinction was occasioned by the penalty of attaint, to which recognitors of assize were subject, but not jurors, it no longer was necessary to keep up this distinction, since the legislature had granted attaints against jurors in all pleas of land. Though we hear, therefore, no more of the modification thereby expressed, the thing was practised as often as the assize was put to inquire of any matter besides the mere seisin and disseisin.

Of assizes.

An assize, in the present language of the law, was considered as capable of being taken four ways, that is, first, in point of assize; secondly, out of the point of assize; thirdly, for damages; fourthly, at large. An assize *taken in the point of assize* was, when the recognitors tried the general issue, *nul tort, nul disseisin.* An assize *out of the point of assize* was, where the tenant pleaded some

[1] Edw. III., *passim.* [2] 44 Edw. III., 26. [3] 40 Edw. III., 43.
[4] 41 Edw. III., 17. [5] 29 Ass., 26. [6] *Vide ante,* vol. i. c. vii.

special matter in bar, showing why the assize should not be tal as a release, or some foreign fact to be tried in another county. assize *taken for damages* was, when such special matter was fo against the tenant, or he confessed the ouster, and the assize charged to inquire only of the damages. An assize *taken at la* was, when, notwithstanding some deed or special matter plea the title and all the circumstances were sent to be tried by recognitors; all which seems very reconcilable with the accoun taking assizes given by Bracton.[1]

The taking an assize *at large* was considered as the most lib mode of doing justice between the parties; it was breaking thro the plea which was designed to stop the assize being taken, an was throwing the merits of the question, whether it depended u a fact or a title, fairly before the recognitors. Whenever ei the plaintiff or tenant were infants, and a deed or a fine or other matter was pleaded in bar that in a common case would l stopped the assize passing, it was the practice for the judge to di the assize to be taken at large.[2] Instances of this are nume all through the book of assizes. An assize would be taken at l upon a defect in the pleadings; for as the direct point in this ceeding ought to go to the assize, if what was pleaded in orde prevent the assize, by throwing the question upon another failed in so doing, the result was that the assize should Thus, it was laid down as a rule, that where a bar was plea and the plaintiff in reply made out his own title without traver the bar, and the tenant omitted to rejoin to the title, the a should not be taken upon the title but *at large;* and if the a found the plaintiff seised by any other title than that he had st he would recover. Again, where a tenant pleaded a release, the plaintiff in his reply made title since the release, wit traversing the bar, there the assize was taken at large, nan upon the seisin and disseisin, under any title whatsoever[3] (*a*). seems from these instances that the taking an assize at large the same as taking it in the very point of assize, only the l

(*a*) The great object of pleading, as Sir J. Mackintosh observes (*Hist. Eng.* was to separate the law from the fact, and prevent the jury, who were the la from determing any question of law. To allow them to do so would be to l the advantages of the substitution of the king's courts for the county courts, a regular judicature for a popular tribunal. The suitors in the county court the judges, determined both law and fact; and as their notion of law wo custom, there was no certainty or uniformity. The object of a regular judi and the jury was, that the lay part of the tribunal should only decide questi fact. Hence in Bracton, the jurors are called *judices facti*. All through the books, therefore, the utmost care is shown to prevent the jurors—the laymen-having anything to do with the law; and for this purpose any mode of ple which should set forth the facts and take the judgment of the court upon the in substance sufficient. Thus, in an action for procuring the plaintiff to be in for robbery, the defendant could plead the grounds of suspicion to take the jud of the court upon their sufficiency, because of the doubt of the laymen, *per do lay gents* (*Year-book*, 8 *Hen. IV.*, 6; 22 *Hen. VIII.*, 2; 22 *Assize*, 27).

[1] *Vide ante*, vol. i. c. vii.

[2] 8 Ass., 28; 10 Ass., 1; 28 Ass., 6; 11

[3] 28 Ass., 17.

was upon a plea of the general issue, the former upon a defect in the pleading to issue after a bar. Another instance in which an assize would be taken at large was where, after pleading in bar, the tenant made default.[1]

The grand object of the tenant in an assize being delay, his business was to plead such matter in bar, as would prevent the assize from being taken. To effect this, he was often under a necessity of suggesting some pretended title, which, being unfit for the judgment of the *lay gents* (*a*), must be determined upon by the court; and however it might turn out in the event, if it deferred the assize, it had answered the purpose for which alone it was designed. One way of effecting this was by admitting in the plaintiff some *colour* of a title, but such a one as could not be supported against the real one that resided in the tenant; and then praying the judgment of the court, if the assize ought to inquire of a disseisin, where no disseisin could possibly be committed by the tenant who had the better title. This was said to be *giving colour* to the plaintiff. This sort of pleading will be better explained by an instance. A case happened where a prioress had granted a lease to a man and his wife for years; the wife died and the husband married again, when the prioress entered, with consent of the husband, and gave livery of seisin to him and his wife for their two lives; then the husband died, and the prioress entered, upon which an assize was brought by the woman. The prioress, in order to prevent the assize being taken, pleaded in bar the above matter, only stating, instead of the livery of seisin to the husband and wife for their lives, that they came to her and prayed her to enlarge their estate; upon which she granted them a *confirmation* for their two lives, and upon the death of the husband she ousted the wife, as she by law might. It was argued upon this, that the plea was no bar, because it *admitted* no *colour* of title in the plaintiff, but a mere confirmation, at a time when the plaintiff had no estate upon which it could enure, besides which she was a feme covert at the time, and so upon the whole the confirmation was utterly void. It was therefore, they said, only a plea to the assize, and they prayed the assize might be taken; meaning that it contained no matter of law, but was a mere denial of the disseisin. But it was answered, that this was a *colour* in the plaintiff; for it had been adjudged a good bar to say, that a woman entered after the death of her hus-

Of colour.

(*a*) Thus where prescription of villenage was alleged in the plaintiff and in his blood, it was held that the plaintiff might properly say he was a bastard, "because the matter" (*i.e.*, prescription of villenage) "is doubtful to the jury," and bastards destroyed it (*Year-book, 5 Hen. VII.*, 11). So it was held that a party ought not to say that he held in "socage," nor in chivalry, for the jurors do not know what is socage or what is service in chivalry; but he ought to say that he holds by so much rent—which was socage—and so make a direct, simple, intelligible issue of fact for the jury (*Year-book, 5 Hen. VII.*, 11). So dying sole seised of land, was held matter of fact fit for a jury; so of forcible dispossession (*Year-book*, 1 *Edw. IV.*, 9).

[1] 22 Edw. III., 4.

band, and claimed dower: for though it was necessary that dower should be formally assigned, yet as she had *colour* to claim it, it was reckoned a bar. It was for the like reason so adjudged in the present case, and the plaintiff was put to reply, and then he stated the truth of the case as above related.[1]

The point to be considered in these pleas was, whether they were a good bar—that is, whether they contained such matter as should not be trusted to the determination of unlettered jurors. Too scrupulous an attention to men's rights, and a jealousy of the interference of juries in matters of law, induced the courts to entertain all such pleas, as upon the face of them purported to be pregnant with good matter in law: the truth of such suggestion remaining to be sifted by the replies and rejoinders that were to follow.

The action of trespass, which in many other respects bore an affinity with, and of late had become in many cases a substitute for, the assize, did in this particular also resemble it; and *colourable pleading* was as common and as expedient in trespass as in assize. The following is a case in trespass, where this sort of pleading was resorted to. In trespass for taking and carrying away the plaintiff's corn, the defendant pleaded, that he let the land where the trespass was supposed to be committed, to one *John* for life; which John died, and the defendant entered; after which came the plaintiff and sowed the ground, and then the defendant cut the corn; he therefore prayed the judgment of the court, if he ought to answer for this as a trespasser. It was contended by the other side, that this amounted to saying that he did not carry away the plaintiff's corn, and it was accordingly offered to join issue thereon: but the defendant's counsel said, they had *admitted* (that is, given colour) that the plaintiff sowed in the defendant's land, and that the defendant cut it, as he well might, and that if the plaintiff pleased he might have had an assize. The plaintiff's counsel, maintaining the first objection, said, if it was not growing on our land, then it was not our corn, and therefore it amounted only to a denial of carrying away the plaintiff's corn. But one of the justices said, that it was a good plea in bar to say, that it was the defendant's freehold, without more; and he has said more, namely, that the plaintiff sowed the land; therefore, if he has any special matter, it would be more reasonable to show it in a reply, than to send it upon the general issue to the *lay gents*, who have no knowledge of law; so that the plaintiff was obliged to reply.[2] These are some examples of pleading with *colour*, which began now to be practised, but was not yet so thoroughly explained upon principle as in after times, when it was wrought into a very curious piece of learning.

Assizes were to be taken in the county where the land lay, as ordained by *Magna Charta*.[3] If at the assizes a foreign matter was pleaded, triable in another county, the way was to remove or adjourn the assize into the common pleas; from thence a *venire*

[1] 40 Edw. III., 23, 24. [2] 38 Edw. III., 28. [3] *Vide ante*, vol. i. c. vi.

was issued into the proper county; and then a *nisi prius;* upon the return of which, with the issue tried, if it was found for the plaintiff, it would perhaps be remanded into the first county, for the assize to find the damages, and for judgment to be there given. If there was nothing in the case but the foreign matter, then it was usual for the justices of the common pleas to give final judgment. It was not uncommon, after the plea in bar was tried, whether in the proper or in a foreign county, for the assize to be put to inquire of the circumstances. If the lands lay in Middlesex, then, as there were no justices of assize in that county, the assize might be brought in the king's bench. Together with the writ of assize, it was usual for the plaintiff to sue out a *patent* of assize; this being necessary to entitle him to have a trial before the justices of assize; and if he had it not, the tenant might have judgment.[1]

Next to the assize of freehold, those of common of pasture and of nuisance present themselves; but neither of them seem to differ from those in the time of Bracton. The assize of nuisance, if brought in the county, was called *de parvo nocumento.* The proper objects of such viscontial writs were expressed in two quaint Latin verses.[2]

The doctrines of nuisance and desseisin stood now in the same relation to each other, and were governed by the same principle as in Bracton's time,[3] and the distinction by which the injured person was to be governed in resorting to one or the other was still the same; only the conclusion from that distinction was now different; for instead of having his choice of the two, he was *confined* by the nature of his case to one only. It was laid down, that where a person turned a course of water, so that his neighbour's mill could not work, an assize of disseisin would lie, if the turning of the water and the mill were in the same vill; but if in different vills, then the remedy must be, an assize of nuisance in the vill where the *turning* happened.[4] If the place where the nuisance was raised, appeared upon evidence to be the freehold of the plaintiff, he would be non-suited, as having chosen a wrong remedy; this being a case where he should have had an assize of disseisin, or writ of trespass.[5] The judgment in assize of nuisance was to compel the party to remove it.

We find in this reign a more particular mention of the *assize of fresh force;* a writ which has been glanced at in the reign of Edward I.[6] This lay where a man was disseised of tenements *devisable,* as they were by custom in the city of London, and in some other boroughs and towns. The disseisee was to lodge his plaint in the court of the franchise; when, upon showing he was

[1] 29 Ass., 21.

rica ca gultum ges es
[2] *Fab fur porta, domus, vir gur mol murus, ovillo.*
Et *pons,* tradantur, hæc vicecomitibus.

[3] *Vide ante,* vol. i. c. vii. [4] 9 Ass., 19. [5] 32 Ass., 2.

[6] *Vide ante,* c. x.

disseised, twelve men were appointed to try it, as in an assize of novel disseisin. This was called *fresh force*, because the entry of the plaint, and the recovery thereon, were to be within sixty days, or the plaintiff would be barred of this remedy, and driven to an assize at common law. To quicken the execution of a judgment herein, the plaintiff might have a writ out of chancery to the bailiffs of the franchise.[1]

The writ of *quare ejecit infra terminum* was[2] now always followed by the process of summons, attachment, and distress; and an outlawry might be had thereon; the real process used in Bracton's time being now obsolete; and of course, instead of *Præcipe*, it now always began with *Si te fecerit securum, &c.* (*a*). But a writ of trespass had lately been contrived for redress of termors who had been ejected from their term: this was called *De ejectione firmæ*. The words of this writ were: *Si A. te fecerit securum, &c., ostensurus quare vi et armis in manerium de I. quod C. præfato A. dimisit ad terminum decem annorum, qui nondum præteriit, intravit, et bona et catalla ejusdem A. ad valentiam, &c., in eodem manerio inventa cepit et asportavit, et ipsum A. a firmâ suâ prædictâ ejecit, et alia enormia ei intulit, ad grave damnum ipsius A. et contra pacem nostram, &c.*[3] This was a common writ of trespass for entering land, and taking away goods, with the addition of certain words adopted from the *quare ejecit infra terminum*, namely, *quod dimisit ad terminum decem annorum, qui nondum præteriit, &c., de firmâ ejecit, &c.*, and the appellation of *ejectione firmæ* might be copied from the *ejectione custodiæ*, which was likewise a writ of trespass. This action lay not only against strangers, but against the lessor, notwithstanding the

De ejectione firmæ.

(*a*) The action having been framed from the obvious analogy to real actions, as it related to realty, while, as it regarded only a term for years, it was in that aspect a personal suit. In the reign of Edward I. it was held that in *quare ejecit*, the plaintiff should recover his term, and damages (*Stat. Abr.*, *quare ejecit; ibid.*, *et vide* 6 *Edw. II.*, fol. 177). At common law there lay a writ of covenant by lessee against lessor for ejectment, by reason of a failure of his title, and it was held that the giving of the writ *quare ejecit terminum* against a feoffee who ousted the tenant, did not deprive the latter of his common law remedy by writ of covenant against his lessor; and indeed it was doubtful whether he could not recover both against the lessor and his feoffee (*Year-book*, 46 *Edw. III.*, 4). If a man leased for years, and then sold the freehold to a party who ousted the lessee, the latter could have *quare ejecit terminum* against the third party, and recover his term and damages, *et sic vide*, that in this action a man could recover the possession of the land (19 *Hen. VI.*, fol. 56). This writ of *quare ejecit terminum* lay when against him who was in by title, and the writ of *ejectione firmæ* lay against him who was in by wrong; it lay against a wrong-doer, and not one who was in by title. This latter remedy lay against a third party who ejected the lessee; and the action included trespass, so that damages could be recovered, even if the term was at an end; but it was also an action for recovery of the term (33 *Hen. VI.*, fol. 42). It is an error, therefore, to imagine that in these actions the plaintiff did not recover the term; in both actions it was recovered. Such was the course of the common law, and that implies that it was so from time immemorial. But these actions were only remedies for *actual termors;* and in after ages, the remedy was adapted by practice to those who were supposed to be so.

[1] O. N. B., 96. [2] *Vide ante*, vol. i. c. vii. [3] O. N. B., 122.

old argument, that a man could not enter *vi et armis* into his own freehold;[1] the possession of a termor for years being now considered as equally sacred with the seisin of a freeholder, and to be protected even against the freeholder himself. This writ went only for damages (*a*), the term being to be recovered in the old writ of *quare ejecit infra terminum*, or the still older of covenant[2] (*b*).

Little need be said of the writ of *mortauncestor*. This remedy was less recurred to than in the time of Bracton, it being in many

(*a*) This, it is conceived, was an error of the author's. It is believed that, in both the writs of *ejectione firmæ* and *quare ejecit infra terminum*, the term was recovered, if it was still in existence; otherwise, it is true, damages could only be recovered; and it is believed that some *dicta*, which had reference to that distinction, misled most of our legal writers into the notion which is above adopted by our author. The truth is, that the whole spirit of our ancient procedure was in favour of *specific* remedies, and it is far more likely that they were lost by disuse, than that they did not exist in ancient times. The writ of covenant is a remarkable instance of this, for its form was, that the defendant do *keep* his covenant (*Fitz. N. B.*); so in replevin and detinue, the goods were recovered. This being so, it is not likely that it would not be so as to land. So long ago as the reign of Edward I. it was said to be an abuse that a term was not recoverable by an assize of novel disseisin, as it originally was; and there can be no doubt that when the assize was disused for that purpose, *ejectione firmæ* was substituted, or that of *quare ejecit*, and the term was recovered. It is admitted that it was so afterwards; and that of itself shows that it was so always, for the judgments in our actions were carefully settled upon precedent.

(*b*) The author is in error here, having been misled by an error of Lord Hale. In both actions of *quare ejecit* and *ejectione firmæ*, the term could be recovered, if it was not expired; but if it were, then the proper remedy was *ejectione firmæ*, because it was more in the nature of a writ of trespass, and damages could be recovered for the ejectment, though the term was ended; whereas the writ of *quare ejecit* lay chiefly for the recovery of the term; moreover, it was not grounded on a bare tort, but rather upon title. In the previous reign, one John brought *quare ejecit infra terminum* against one Richard, and said that he had wrongfully deposed him of land which one Agnes had leased to him for a term of years; since which she had sold the land to Richard, who had ejected the lessee. The defendant denied that she had sold it to him, and it was said that he ought to answer to the ejectment, which was the principal matter; but it was answered, that in this action the sale was material (to show that defendant was not a bare wrong-doer), so both matters were denied (*Year-book*, 18 *Edw. II.*, s. 99). In 3 Edw. I. it is said, in *quare ejecit* the plaintiff shall recover his term and damages, by reason of the sale (*Stat. Abr.* 227). In the 46 Edw. III., fol. 4, it was said that if a lessee is ousted of his term by reason of a feoffment by the defendant, the lessee is put to his writ of *quare ejecit*, implying that otherwise he could have the writ of *ejectione*. In 26 Edw. IV., fol. 14, it was said that *quare ejecit* was where a man was in by title; *ejectione firmæ* where he was in by wrong; but in both equally the term could be recovered, if it was not expired; but if it were, then in *ejectione* the damages could be recovered. As already seen, Bracton mentions the writ, and there can be no doubt that the writ of *ejectione firmæ* was instituted after the statute of *consimili casu*, to obviate the inconvenience, incident to *quare ejecit*, that it required a lawful alienation to the defendant to be alleged, and that it was doubtful whether, if the term had expired, damages could be recovered. It has been said, that the first recorded instance of *ejectione firmæ* is 44 Edw. III., fol. 22; but that is a mistake. The case was one of trespass, for that the defendants had entered with force and arms, and would have ejected the plaintiff from a manor he held for term of years; the defendants set up title to the land as tenants in tail, and the court said, they can oust the plaintiff of his term, for that he has not done a trespass; and the party having the freehold could enter, saving the estate to the plaintiff, for that it was only a term (*Year-book*, 44 *Edw. III.*, fol. 22). This, it will be seen, had only a remote bearing on the subject. It is plain, however, that the two actions were the same, except as already mentioned, and that in both the term could be recovered, if it had not expired.

[1] 44 Edw. III., 22.

[2] *Vide ante*, vol. c. vii.

cases supplied by the *formedon in discendre*, and several wri entry. The same may be said of writs of *cosinage*, of *ael et be* which, being of similar import with the mortauncestor, foll its fate in the revolution of legal remedies.

Writs of entry.

Next to the assize of novel disseisin, the most common ren in ousters of freehold was the writ of entry. Wri entry were various even in the time of Bracton;[1] still being of a special form, and confined to certain circumsta of freehold and estate, it had been found necessary in the reig Henry III.,[2] and again in that of Edward I.,[3] to accommodate t writs to new cases of injury to freeholds. Owing to these pa mentary enlargements, writs of entry had become very nume and common. To bring into one point what has already been in different parts of the foregoing History, and give the read just idea of the variety and comprehensiveness of *real* remedie may be proper to recapitulate shortly these writs, with some sory observations upon them, as they now stood.

Entry *ad terminum qui præteriit.*

The writ of entry which first presents itself, and which fron simplicity deserves our consideration first, is that *terminum qui præteriit.* The form of the writ *Præcipe A. quòd justè, &c., reddat B. unum mes gium, &c., quod eidem A. dimisit ad terminum qui præterii dicitur. Et nisi, &c., et prædictus B. fecerit te securum, &c., summone, &c.*, corresponding precisely with the form in the of Bracton.[4] This was the remedy resorted to by a lessor, w lands or tenements were let for a term of years, and the te held over his term. Instead of bringing this writ, the lessor m enter, and, if he was ousted, he might have an assize of novel seisin. This writ of entry lay also where there was a lease for life of another, and the lessee held over; or if the tenant for aliened and died. If the land was recovered against the tenant life, and he died, the reversioner might have this writ in the *pc* for this, like all other writs of entry, might be had in the *per, et cui*, and *post.* But if the reversion was granted over, and tenant for term of life aliened and died, the grantee of the revers being a stranger, could not have this writ, which lay only for lessor, or his heir. For a similar reason, it did not lie for the versioner after the death of a tenant in dower, or by the court who took an estate by the common law, and not by lease. It pears by stat. Westm. 2, c. xxv.,[6] that if a tenant for years guardian in chivalry aliened in fee, the lessor or infant might l an assize of novel disseisin, and the feoffer and feoffee should l be named disseisors: the assize might be brought during the li any of them, but if they were all dead, recourse must be had t writ of entry.

If this or any other writ of entry was in the *post*, the follov

[1] *Vide ante*, vol. i. c. vii. [2] *Vide ante*, vol. i. c. viii. [3] *Vide ante*, c. i
[4] *Vide ante*, vol. i. c. vii. [5] *Vide ante*, vol. i. c. vii. [6] *Vide ante*, c. :

clause, which subsisted even in Bracton's time,[1] was always inserted, *et unde quæritur quòd prædictus A. ei deforceat, &c.*, but never in those in the *per*, and *per et cui.* Again, wherever a person demanded of the possession of an ancestor, it should always be by title, as *quod clamat esse jus et hæreditatem suam, &c.;* but when he went upon his own possession, he was never to make title. There was an exception to this, where a woman demanded her inheritance or *maritagium*, that had been aliened by her husband, or her dower aliened by another husband; for in such cases, in a *cui in vitâ* to recover, she was to make title in the above manner.[2]

We have seen that in Bracton's time, where a gift was alleged to be made by a person *non compos mentis*, an inquisition used to be made, whether the donor was of sane mind. But now there was a remedy, by a writ of entry *dum non fuit compos mentis;* which was in this form: *Præcipe A. quòd justè et sine dilatione reddat B. unum messuagium, &c., quod clamat esse jus et hæreditatem suam, et in quod idem A. non habet ingressum nisi per C. patrem prædicti B. cujus hæres ipse est, qui illud ei dimisit dum non fuit compos mentis, ut dicit, &c.*[3] This writ lay for the heir of the person who was *non compos mentis*, and who was dead; and the general opinion was, that it would not lay for the person himself who had made the alienation; because no one was to be received to disable or *stultify* himself, as it was afterwards expressed: however, it was laid down in the register of writs, that he might maintain this writ, and in such case the heir would be received.

Another writ to recover land that had been conveyed by a person disabled in law to make a gift, was the writ of entry *dum fuit infra ætatem.* This writ originated since the time of Bracton, and was in this form: *Præcipe A. quòd justè, &c., B. qui plenæ ætatis est, ut dicit, duas acras terræ, &c., quas idem B. ei dimisit, dum fuit infra ætatem, ut dicit, &c.*[4] Where an infant aliened land that had descended to him during his infancy; or that he had purchased to himself for life, or in fee; he might, when of full age, have recovery thereof by this writ. But if an infant leased his land for a term of years, and afterwards made a confirmation, or release, before he came of age, he could not when of age have this writ, because this was no alienation; for an infant could not make a *demise* of the freehold, till livery of the land was made to him: but, in such case, he might have an assize of novel disseisin.

If an infant aliened in fee, and died leaving issue; his issue, when of age, might have this writ for the lands so aliened by his father. It was expressly held, that neither this nor any other writ of entry would lay for the issue till he was of full age, excepting the case of the issue of a disseisee, as directed by stat. Westm. 1, c. xlvii.[5] Where the father aliened land descended to him in tail, and died

[1] *Vide ante.* vol. i. c. vii.
[2] O. N. B., 123 b.
[3] *Vide ante,* vol. i. c. vi.
[4] O. N. B., 125.
[5] *Vide ante,* c. xii.

leaving issue, the issue were to have a *formedon in descendre*, and not a writ of entry *dum fuit infra ætatem.*

If an infant aliened his land, he might enter, and if ousted, might, when of age, have an assize of novel disseisin; but if he had not made such entry, he could, when of age, only have this writ of entry. And yet in the third year of this king, where an heir did not enter till he was of full age, and an assize was brought against him, the judges held it could not be maintained, because the tenant was not seised of the freehold after the heir was of age; that is, the space of a year and a day had not elapsed, and therefore that the freehold could not accrue.[1]

Entry *in le quibus.*

The writ of entry *super disseisinam in le quibus*, was that which approached the nearest to the assize of novel disseisin, and is the first writ of entry mentioned by Bracton as a remedy, where the assize failed by the death of one of the parties.[2] The form of it was this: *Præcipe A. quòd, &c., reddat B. unum messuagium, &c., quod clamat esse jus et hæreditatem suam,* DE QUO *idem A. injustè et sine judicio disseisivit C. patrem prædicti B. cujus hæres ipse est, post primam transfretationem domini regis, &c., in Vasconiam.* This writ was always to contain the words DE QUO, or DE QUIBUS *A. disseisivit B. patrem, &c.*, and from thence was named *disseisinam in le quo*, or *in le quibus.*

Where a person was disseised and died, this writ lay for his heir against the disseisor; and it lay for none but the heir of the disseisee; so that in this writ, the demandant was always to make title as heir to his father (*a*). It lay notwithstanding the nonage of the heir, as appears from stat. Westm. 1, c. xlvii.[3] (*b*). This was on account of the fresh suit; for if it was brought against the issue of the alienee of the disseissor, the parol would demur for his nonage, this not being within the statute.[4]

Difference of writs in the *per*, *per et cui*, and *post.*

Before we proceed any further to inquire into the nature of different writs of entry, it may be proper to consider more particularly those changes to which they were all equally liable; namely, under what circumstances it was that they were to be drawn in their simple form, or were to be in the *per*, the *per et cui*, or in the *post.*[5]

(*a*) On writ of entry against heir of heir of disseisor—where fresh suit was made—it was held upon this, that the parol could not demur, and so he was ousted of his nonage (24 *Edw. III.* 25, 46), although he was not immediate heir, yet he was heir.

(*b*) In a writ of entry *in le quibus* by the heir of C., the disseisee, the tenant, pleaded that J., whose heir the demandant was, being seised in fee, gave to T. in tail, who had issue C., and that C. dying without issue of his body, J. entered as reversioner, and enfeoffed the tenant, and afterwards released to him all his right with warranty. It was held that the release would be a good title (*Year-book*, 24 *Edw. III.* fol. 75, pl. 98). That is to say, that the donor of an estate tail, failing issue in tail, could enter and oust the heir of the tenant in tail, and could alienate the land and create a good title; in a case in which the entail had not been barred by fine or recovery.

[1] O. N. B., 126.
[2] *Vide ante*, vol. i. c. vii.
[3] *Vide ante*, c. ix.
[4] O. N B., 128 b.
[5] *Vide ante*, vol. i. c. viii.; *et vide ante*, c. ix.

The above form of the writ of entry *super disseisinam*, is the simple one: the same, if in the *per*, was thus: *Præcipe A., &c., quòd justè, et sine dilatione reddat B. unum messuagium, &c., quod clamat esse jus et hæreditatem suam, et in quo idem A. non habet ingressum nisi* PER *E. qui illud ei dimisit qui inde injustè et sine judicio disseisivit C. patrem prædicti B. cujus hæres ipse est, post primam transfretationem, &c., et unde queritur, &c.* It was the characteristic of this writ always to allege, *et in quod idem A. non habet ingressum nisi per E. qui illud ei dimisit, qui injustè, &c.* This writ was the proper remedy when the disseisor aliened to another, or died and his heir entered; for then the disseisee or his heir might have this writ against the alienee, or the heir of the disseisor; and he could have it against no other person. During the life of the disseisor no writ of entry lay for the disseisin, but only an assize of novel disseisin. The assize in such case might be brought against him and the alienee both; and if the disseisor would not pay all the damages, the alienee must, according to the stat. Gloc. c. i.[1] But if the disseisor aliened and died, and the alienee aliened to another person; or if the disseisor died, and the heir entered and died, and *his* heir entered; then the disseisee or his heir was to have a writ of entry *sur disseisin* in the *per et cui*; and the writ was to allege, *et in quod non habet ingressum nisi* PER *talem,* CUI *talis illud ei dimisit, qui inde, &c.* These writs in the *per*, and *per et cui*, could be maintained against none but the real tenant, who was in by purchase or descent of the inheritance, as appears by the wording of the two writs, one stating a descent, the other a demise.

If the alienation or descent was without the degrees, so as the writ could not be in the *per*, nor in the *per et cui*, it was then to be in the *post;* and it was a rule, that when an alienation or descent was without the degrees, and in the *post*, no writ should ever after be had on such alienation or descent in the *per*, or *per et cui*. There were five events that put a writ out of the degrees—namely, intrusion, election, judgment, *disseisin sur disseisin*, and escheat.

Thus, as to *intrusion:* if the disseisor died seised, and a stranger abated, the disseisee or his heir could have no writ in the *per*, but must bring it in the *post;* for the abator was in neither by descent nor purchase, but by a wrong of his own. As to *election:* if the disseisor was a man of religion, and died, and his successor entered, the disseisee or his heir could have no recovery against the successor by any writ but one in the *post;* because the entry of the successor could never be supposed congeable by the predecessor, so as that he should be adjudged in by his predecessor, the same as a son is in by his father. As to *judgment:* if a man recovered against the disseisor, and the disseisor died, the disseisee or his heir could have no other writ of entry *sur disseisin* but one in the *post*, because the tenant entered neither by descent nor purchase, but by

[1] *Vide ante*, c. ix.

judgment. There were, however, some cases where a judgment did not put a writ out of the degrees. Thus, where an abator had issue and died, and the issue was ousted by a stranger, against whom the issue recovered by assize of novel disseisin; if a writ of entry *sur disseisin* was brought against the issue, it should be within the degrees, because this recovery put the issue in his first estate—namely, in the same descent in which he was after the death of his father. As to *disseisin sur disseisin:* if the disseisor was disseised and died, the first disseisee or his heir could have no recovery but by a writ in the *post;* for the tenant entered neither by descent nor by feoffment, but only by disseisin. As to *escheat:* if the disseisor died without heirs, or committed felony, and was attainted, and then died, and the lord entered, as into his escheat, the disseisee or his heir could have no writ of entry but in the *post;* for the lord was in neither by descent nor by feoffment, but by escheat.[1]

The writ of entry *sine assensu capituli*, was in use in the time of Bracton.[2] The writ was as follows: *Præcipe A. quòd justè, &c., reddat B. abbati sancti Augustine de N. unum messuagium, &c., quod clamat esse jus monasterii sua prædicti, et in quod idem A. non habet ingressum nisi per C. quondam abbatem monasterii prædicti, qui illud ei dimisit* SINE ASSENSU *et voluntate* CAPITULI *monasterii prædicti, ut dicit, &c.* Where an abbot, prior, or any one who had a convent or common seal, aliened lands or tenements belonging to his church without the assent of the convent or chapter, and then died, his successor might have this writ.[3]

The writ of entry *sur cui in vitâ*, like the former, was in use in Bracton's time, and has been frequently mentioned since.[4] The form of the writ was thus: *Præcipe A. quòd justè, &c., reddat B. quæ fuit uxor D. unum messuagium, &c., quod clamat esse jus et hæreditatem suam, et in quod idem A. non habet ingressum nisi per prædictum D. quondam virum ipsius B. qui illud ei dimisit,* CUI *ipsa* IN VITA *suâ contradicere non potuit, ut dicit, &c.* Where the wife was seised for term of life, or in tail, or in fee, and took a husband, and the husband aliened and died, this writ might be brought to recover the land (*a*). Notwithstanding this writ was grounded upon the widow's own seisin, yet she was to make title by purchase or descent; and if it was a fee-simple, the writ was always required to allege, *quod clamat esse jus et hæreditatem suam;* if it was only an estate for life, *quod clamat tenere ad terminum vitæ suæ;* and so *mutatis mutandis,* if in fee-tail.

Entry *sur cui in vitâ*.

We have before seen, that by stat. Westm. 2, c. iii.,[5] the widow should recover her land after her husband's death, if it was lost by default during the coverture, in an action brought against the hus-

(*a*) And by the equity of the statuts of Westm. 2, where she was divorced, she could have a writ *cui ante divorcium* (14 *Hen. VII.* 17).

[1] O. N. B., 129 b. [2] *Vide ante,* vol. i. c. viii. [3] O. N. B., 131 b.
[4] *Vide ante,* vol. i. c. viii.; and *ante,* c. ix. [5] *Vide ante,* c. ix.

band and wife; but if the recovery was against the husband solely, whether it was by default or by action tried, the widow might have an assize of novel disseisin, and not *cui in vitâ;* because she was no party to the judgment, and was ousted by the recovery of her freehold.

By stat. Westm. 2, c. xl.,[1] it was ordained, that where a widow brought her *cui in vitâ* against the alienee of the husband, and the alienee vouched the heir of the husband, being an infant, the parol should not demur. But it was otherwise where the widow brought her *cui in vitâ* in the *per et cui*, and the tenant vouched him by whom the entry was supposed, and he vouched over the heir of the husband, being within age, and prayed the parol might demur till the full age of the heir, for in this latter case the parol would demur; because the statute is only to be understood of the alienee of the baron vouching the heir of the baron.

If the widow died, her heir would have the same remedy by writ of entry *sur cui in vitâ.* But if the woman was tenant in tail, and the husband aliened, or the husband and wife lost by default, the heir must resort to a *formedon in descendre*, and could not bring a *cui in vitâ.* If the issue brought a *cui in vitâ* on an alienation by the father, he was not to be barred by the warranty of his father, as appears by the stat. of Gloc. c. iii.,[2] unless he had land to that amount in fee-simple to descend on him from his father; for if it was from any other ancestor, or in fee-tail, it was not a bar. If a husband leased land held in right of his wife for term of years, and afterwards made a confirmation for life, or in fee, and died; it was held that the widow could not have a *cui in vitâ*, but must bring an assize of novel disseisin, and the heir a writ of entry *sur disseisin;* for the writ was not to suppose such alienation to be made by confirmation or release.[3]

A new writ of entry had lately made its appearance, adapted to cases where a divorce happened between the man and woman after the alienation; for then the woman, instead of *cui in vitâ*, might have a writ called *cui ante divortium* to recover the land (*a*). This agreed entirely with the former; only instead of *cui in vitâ*, it alleged *cui ipsa` ante divortium inter eos celebratum, &c.*, and the writ, in its nature and practice, was precisely the same with the foregoing, to which it was a sort of appendage.[4]

We find another new writ of entry of the following tenor: *Præcipe A. quòd justè, &c., reddat B. unum messuagium, &c., quod idem B. ei dimisit*, CAUSA MATRIMONII INTER EOS PRÆLOCUTI, *qui eam duxisse debuit in uxorem, et nondum duxit, ut dicit, &c.* This was from the words of it, called a writ of entry *causâ matrimonii prælocuti.* It was no uncommon practice, and seems to have originated from gifts *in maritagium*,[5] for a woman to give lands or tenements,

(*a*) 14 Hen. VII. fol. 17.

[1] *Vide ante*, c. ix.
[2] *Ibid.*
[3] O. N. B., 131 b.
[4] *Ibid.* 134.
[5] *Vide ante*, vol. i. c. vii.

or a rent to a man, on condition that he should marry her within a given period. If after this the man would not marry her within the time, or if he disabled himself by marrying another, or entering into religion, or by being ordained presbyter, the woman or her heirs might recover the land by this writ; and might follow it by a writ in the *per*, *per et cui*, or the *post*, into whatsoever hands it went. This condition to marry was to be by deed indented, or the writ could not be supported.[1]

In the time of Bracton there were two writs of intrusion: one was *pone per vadium, &c.*, which was to be brought recently after the intrusion;[2] the other was a writ of entry, and was the remedy when the claimant had chosen to lay by for a space of time.[3] The former of these seems now to have gone out of use, and the latter alone continued, which was in this form: *Præcipe A. quòd justè, &c., reddat B. unum messuagium, &c., quod clamat esse jus et hæreditatem suam, et in quod idem A. non habet ingressum nisi* PER INTRUSIONEM, *quam in illud fecit post mortem C. quæ fuit uxor G. quæ illud tenuit in dotem de dono prædicti G. quondam viri sui, patris prædicti B. cujus hæres ipse est, ut dicit, &c.* Where a tenant for term of life in dower, or tenant by the courtesy, died seised of lands or tenements, and a stranger entered, the person in reversion might have this writ against the abator, or whoever entered after the decease. If an intrusion was made *tempore vacationis*, the successor might have this writ against an abator into any lands or tenements belonging to his church; and this was by the stat. Marl. c. xxviii.[4]

Entry *ad communem legem.*

We find a writ called a writ of entry *ad communem legem*, which was in this form: *Præcipe A. quòd justè, &c., reddat B. unum messuagium, &c., quod clamat esse jus et hæreditatem suam, et in quod A. non habet ingressum nisi per C. quæ fuit uxor D. quæ illud ei dimisit, et quod illa in dotem tenuit de dono prædicti D. quondam viri sui, patris prædicti B. cujus hæres ipse est, ut dicit, &c.* Where a tenant for term of life, by the courtesy, or in dower, aliened in fee and died, the reversioner might have this writ to recover the land, into whatsoever hands it passed; and this was by stat. Westm. 2. c. iii.[5] In the case of a tenant for life losing by default and dying, the reversioner might, at his option, have a writ of entry *ad terminum qui præteriit*, or a writ of entry *ad communem legem;* but a tenant by the courtesy, or in dower, could not properly be called a *termor;* so that the former writ of *ad terminum qui præteriit* could not lie against *them*, but only the writ of *ad communem legem*, as provided by the above statute. Further, should a tenant by the courtesy alien, or lose by default and die, the person in reversion might have recovery by assize of mortauncestor, *ael*, or, *cosinage*, and the like writs, notwithstanding the seisin of the tenant by the courtesy, as appears

[1] O. N. B., 155.
[2] *Vide ante*, vol. i. c. vii.
[3] *Ibid.*
[4] *Vide ante*, c. ix.; O. N. B., 135 b.
[5] *Vide ante*, c. ix.

by the stat. Gloc. c. iii.,[1] or he might have this writ of entry *ad communem legem.*[2]

The writ of entry *in câsu proviso* was given by the stat. Gloc. c. vii.[3] The form was as follows: *Præcipe A. quòd justè, &c., reddat B. unum messuagium, &c., quod clamat esse jus et hæreditatem suam, in quod idem A. non habet ingressum nisi per C. quæ fuit uxor D. quæ illud ei dimisit, quæ illud tenuit in dotem de dono prædicti D. quondam viri sui, patris prædicti B. cujus hæres ipse est, et quod post dimissionem per ipsam C. præfato A. contra formam statuti Glocestriæ de communi consilio regni Angliæ, inde* PROVISI FACTAM *in fœdo ad præfatum B. reverti debeat per formam ejusdem statuti, ut dicet, &c.* Where a tenant in dower aliened in fee, or for term of another's life, the reversioner, by the statute of Gloucester, might bring this writ against the person in possession. It was always to be brought in the life of the tenant in dower.[4]

Entry *in consimili casû.*

The writ of entry *in consimili casû* was of kin to the former, and owed its origin to the stat. Westm. 2, c. xxix.,[5] which permitted writs to be made in *consimili casû.* Accordingly, as the former was a remedy where a tenant in dower aliened, this was a remedy for the reversioner, where a tenant for term of life, or by the courtesy, aliened in fee. This, like the former, must be brought during the life of the tenant by the courtesy, or for life. The form was this: *Præcipe A. quòd justè, &c., reddat B. unum messuagium, &c., quod clamat esse jus et hæreditatem suam, et in quod idem A. non habet ingressum nisi per C. qui illud tenuit per legem Angliæ post mortem D. quondam uxoris suæ, matris prædicti B. cujus hæres ipse est, et quod post dimissionem per ipsum C. præfato A. inde factam in fœdo ad præfatum B. reverti debeat per formam statuti in consimili casû provisi, &c.*[6]

Thus far of writs of entry; the fashionable remedies in those days in most cases of ouster of freehold. To these may be subjoined, as nearly allied both to the writ of entry and writ of right, a writ in use for recovery of a freehold, called *quòd ei deforceat,* which was given by stat. Westm. 2, c. ii.,[7] to tenants in tail, in frank-marriage, dower, courtesy, or for term of life, when they had lost by default. This writ came in lieu, and may be considered in the nature of a writ of right. It could be brought only by the very person who lost the land.[8]

Writs of formedon.

The grand remedies for persons claiming under entails, were the writs of *formedon in descendre, remainder,* and *reverter.* The forms of these writs have been already shown;[9] and nothing remains to add, but some few observations on their distinct natures, as laid down by the lawyers of this reign.

[1] *Vide ante,* c. ix.
[2] O. N. B., 136.
[3] *Vide ante,* c. ix.
[4] O. N. B., 137.
[5] *Vide ante,* c. x.
[6] O. N. B., 137 b.
[7] *Vide ante,* c. ix.
[8] O. N. B., 140 b.
[9] *Vide ante,* c. ix., x., xi.

In all cases of a gift of lands, tenements, or a rent in fra marriage, or to a man and woman and the heirs of their bo engendered, or to a man and the heirs of his body; if, after death of such man or woman, leaving issue, a stranger abated if an alienation was made, with fine or without; or if there wa disseisin, or recovery by default, after default; then after the de of the donee, the issue might have his writ of formedon *descendre* to recover the land.

The issue could recover on the possession of his ancestor by writ but this. But of his own possession he might, if ousted, h an assize of novel disseisin, or writ of entry, as the case might so that this was now considered as a writ[1] of right for the hei tail. It was now taken for settled law, as has been before observ that in this writ it was a good bar to plead the feoffment of ancestor with warranty, with an averment that the issue had as by descent in fee-simple. If a tenant in tail in possession ente into religion, his issue might have this writ, alleging, *quòd p suus habitum religionis assumpsit, &c.* But if the father mac feoffment before he took the habit of religion, the issue could have this writ till his father was dead. In this writ, the takin the profits was to be laid only in the person of the first donee, the demandant was to make himself heir in tail to the person seised. In this writ, and that *in reverter*, the demandant n not show a deed; but in that *in remainder*, he must show a de

The writ of *formedon in remainder* lay for the remainder-n whether the remainder was in fee, in tail, or only for life, aga any one who entered after the death of the person seised of preceding estate, if he was seised only for life, or if he was se in fee-tail, and died without issue. If the tenant in tail remainder was once seised and died, his issue could have no but a *formedon in descendre;* but if he had never been seised could have no writ but a *formedon in remainder.* This writ was before said, could not be maintained without a specialt prove the limitation *in remainder.* If there was a tenant for with remainder over, and the tenant for life was impleaded, vouched the lessor, and recovered in value; the remainder-n after the death of the tenant for life, might demand such l recovered in value in a *formedon in remainder*, the same as might the original lands; because the tenant for life recoverec virtue of the same entail on which the remainder was limi But it was otherwise of a reversion that was granted over, bec the recovery was founded on another deed than that by which reversion was granted; and therefore such recovery in value w go to the lessor: yet if the tenant for life had vouched the gra of the reversion, and he had vouched over the lessor, the rec pense would go to the grantee, and not to the lessor. If a te in tail with remainder over aliened with warranty, and died w

[1] *Vide ante*, c. x. [2] *Vide ante*, vol. i. c. viii. [3] O. N. B., 14

out issue, so as that the remainder-man was his heir, this warranty would be a bar without assets; because it was out of the provision of the statute, and at common law every warranty was a bar. The remainder-man, in like manner, might be barred by the deed of an ancestor who was no party to the entail.

Notwithstanding the demandant could not require an answer of the tenant, unless he had a deed, yet the tenant could take no issue on the remainder, but he was to answer to the gift. Where this writ was brought after the death of tenant for life, for a fee-simple, or fee-tail, the demandant was to allege esplees in the person of the donor, as in case of a fee-simple, and in the person of the tenant for life, as in a freehold. But if he claimed as tenant for life, he was to lay esplees only in the person who made the deed.[1]

The writ of *formedon in reverter* lay for the reversioner, or his heir, after the death of a tenant in tail, and never after the death of a tenant for life, or any other term. In this writ, the esplees were to be laid both in the person of the donor and donee.[2]

The writ of dower *unde nihil habet*, the writ of right of dower, and admeasurement of dower, seem to be in their form, process, and learning, the same as has been already shown.[3] The writ of right of dower was to be directed to the heir, or, if he was in ward, to his guardian; but if the heir had no court, then to the chief lord; and it was removable the same as a writ of right patent, as will be more fully shown hereafter. The writ of right of advowson and the assize of *darrein presentment* were much in the same condition as in Bracton's time.[4] But the old writ of *quare non permittit* was now called *quare impedit;* and the *quare impedit*, as it was used in Bracton's time, together with the appellation of *quare non permittit*, as a distinct writ, had long become obsolete.[5] The other auxiliary writs in these clerical remedies, as used in the time of Bracton, were still in force.[6] A writ had been framed since his time, called *quare incumbravit;* and lay against the bishop for filling the church, while a suit was depending for the presentation. This writ was formed upon the model of the prohibitory writ mentioned by Bracton under the name of *ne incumbraret.* The process in this new writ was summons, attachment, and distress.[7] Another auxiliary writ had been contrived, and called, *de vi laicâ removendâ:* this was recurred to, when a suit was depending between two persons for a church, and one of them came with force, as was sometimes done, and took possession. This writ directed the sheriff to remove such force, and, if he was resisted, to take the *posse comitatûs*, and attach the offenders, so as to have their bodies *coram nobis* to answer for their offence. This writ was never granted without a certificate from the bishop, testifying such resistance.[8]

[1] O. N. B., 147 b.
[2] *Ibid.* 149 b.
[3] *Vide ante*, vol. i. c. vii. and viii.
[4] *Ibid.*
[5] *Ibid.*; and *vide ante*, c. ix.
[6] *Vide ante*, vol. i. c. vii.
[7] O. N. B., 33.
[8] *Ibid.* 37.

The writ of *juris utrùm*, which had been gradually opened several statutes, was still further enlarged by the constructior those statutes (*a*). The statute 14th of this king, st. 1, ch. xv which allowed this writ, amongst other persons, to guardians *wardens of chapels*, was held to extend to wardens of *hospit* such a variation being justified (it was said) by the statute Westminster,[2] as being *in consimili casû*. Those who had a c vent, or foundation with a common seal, could not maintain writ, but such persons were obliged to resort to the writ of e1 *sine assensu capituli, &c.*[3] The process in this writ was summ and re-summons, as in a writ of mortauncestor.

Writs of right.

We now come to consider the nature of writs of right, as plained in the writings of this period. A writ of ri was said to be either *patent* or *close*. A wri right *close* was directed to the sheriff; a writ of right *patent* directed to the lord of whom the land in question was hold commanding him to do right and justice between the part This writ might be removed out of the lord's court into the cou by *tolt*, and out of the county to the common bench by *pone*, if demandant so pleased; for which reason the writ contained clause of *et nisi feceris, vicecomes, &c., faciat, &c.*: for the being all along in the custody of the demandant, he might rem the plea without stating the cause in the *pone*; though, if the was at the suit of the tenant, it must contain the cause of moval. The plea might also be removed *per saltum* out of lord's court to the common pleas, by *recordari* with cause, at suit of the tenant.[4] How far this corresponds with the acc before given of writs of right in the lord's court in the tim Glanville and Bracton, may be seen on comparing them.[5] ' wording of the writ now in use agreed exactly with that Glanville.

We find a writ of right, entitled, *Quia dominus remisit cur suam domino regi*, which has not been before mentioned by

(*a*) In the reign of Edward II., there was this case. The abbot of Tewkesl parson of the church of Cranborne, brought a writ of *jure de utrum* against on and prayed that it might be inquired by the jury whether a verge of land was in) frankalmoigne of the church of Cranborne, or the fee (*i.e.*, property) of it. A. came and said that the abbot ought to demand nothing, for it was lay fee. the jury found that the land was appendant to the chapel of Woburn: that he the church to his own use; and that in the reign of king John, one Abbot predecessor of the present abbot, gave the tenement to one William, his servan his services, rendering to him and his successors six shillings a year; and that liam enfeoffed the ancestor of the present tenant to hold to him and his heirs o chief lord, which facts the jury submitted to the court for their judgment: in a special verdict. It was argued for the abbot that the tenement was held in f almoigne, and that the alienation, without the assent of the ordinary, coul change the tenure, to which it was answered that the ordinary *had* assented. It not appear what the judgment was, but it is apparent that the *juris utrum* wou for lands held in frankalmoigne, and that alienation might take place with the a of the ordinary (*Year-book*, 7 *Edward II.*, fol. 234).

[1] *Vide ante*, c. xi.
[2] Viz., ch. 24; *vide ante*, c. x.
[3] O. N. B., 39 b.
[4] *Ibid.* 2.
[5] *Vide ante*, vol. i. c. v., vii., '

name, though it was the kind of writ which might have been resorted to in Glanville's time, when a court was proved *de recto defecisse.*[1] This writ of right, *quia dominus remisit curiam,* lay where lands or tenements, holden of some inferior lord, were demanded in a writ of right, and the lord held no court: in such case he, at the request of either of the parties to the writ, would transmit the writ to the king's court, *remitting his court,* for that time, *to the king's court,*[2] with a saving of his seignory on any future occasion; upon which there issued this writ, *Quia dominus, &c.,* returnable before the justices of the common pleas: this writ was always *close.* This writ agreed with the common form of a writ of right, only there was added after *teste meipso, &c.,* a clause signifying the reason of issuing the writ, *quia capitatis dominus fœdi illius inde remisit nobis curiam suam, &c.* The process in this was summons, *grand cape* and *petit cape,* the same as in other writs of right.[3]

There was a writ of right in London, directed to the mayor and sheriff of the city, which was *patent,* and not *close;* for though the cause of the distinction was, that the latter writs were directed to the sheriff, and the former not, yet this, being directed to the mayor as well as the sheriff, was *patent.* This writ also did not contain the clause *nisi feceritis, vicecomes faciat, &c.,* and therefore it could not be removed like the others. It was, however, removable in some particular cases. Thus, where a foreigner happened to be vouched, the mayor and sheriffs were to adjourn to a certain day before the justices of the bench, and send the record, which, when the warranty was determined, was to be returned by a judicial writ, commanding the mayor and sheriffs to proceed, the justices having no further authority.[4] This course corresponded with that which was directed in the like case of foreign voucher in Bracton's time.[5]

The writ of right *de rationabili parte* is only hinted at by Bracton,[6] and not mentioned by Glanville. This writ lay between privies in blood, as between brothers and sisters, between nephews and nieces, and never between strangers. It lay even though the ancestor had made a lease for the life of the lessee, and so died not seised of the freehold, leaving co-heirs; in which case, should any of the co-heirs intrude after the death of the lessee, the others might have this writ. This writ did not lie between relations past the third degree; it lay between brothers and sisters, where one claimed by charter, and the others by descent; for it was principally contrived for trying the privity of blood. It was a writ of right patent, directed to the lord of whom the land was holden, with process of summons, and *grand* and *petit cape;* but it did not admit the duel, or grand assize. The words of this writ were:

[1] *Vide ante,* vol. i. c. vi.

[2] Where a lord adjourned a difficult matter into the superior court, it was termed by Glanville, *curiam suam ponere in curiam domini regis. Vide ante,* vol. i. c. vi.

[3] O. N. B., 18.

[4] *Ibid.* 4.

[5] *Vide ante,* vol. i. c. viii.

[6] *Ibid.*

Plenum rectum teneas, &c., de uno messuagio, &c., quod clamat RATIONABILEM PARTEM *suam, quæ tum contingit de libero teneme quod fuit N. patris sui, &c., quod ei deforceat, &c.*[1]

The writ of right *secundum consuetudinem manerii*, was a v close. This was confined to the court of ancient demesne. are told that every writ sued upon the custom of a manor called a writ of right close,[2] which seems an exception to the ab distinction between writs patent and close. In the form of it agreed exactly with the writ of right patent, having the additio words above mentioned, *Præcipimus, &c., quòd sine dilatione, secundum consuetudinem manerii nostri, &c., plenum rectum,* but this writ could not be removed by the demandant into county, and common pleas, like the other. Yet, if he complai that right was not done, he might have a writ out of the chanc to the sheriff, commanding him to go in person with four knig of the county, to see that right be done.[3] The writ of right *præcipe in capite*, which was for the king's own tenants, wa writ close, and agreed in its practice with the proceedings so fu related before.[4]

Besides the above, there were several others which were c
Other real writs. sidered as writs of right, merely because they were tal by reason of a seignory. In some of these the gra assize and duel lay; in some they did not, but the issue was to tried by a common jury; according as the demandant counted his own seisin, or of that an ancestor.

These we shall now enumerate, as they occur among seve other writs for the recovery of land and other heritable rigl without attempting to arrange them in any particular order.

The writ *de rationabilibus divisis*, mentioned by Glanville,[5] settling boundaries was still in use: the process in it was su mons, *grand* and *petite cape*.[6] There was another writ that applicable to the same occasion, and existed in Bracton's tin called *de perambulatione faciendâ*, in which there was no proce but the sheriff was to go to the place where the encroachment l been made; and there, in the presence of the parties and chief n dwelling in the neighbourhood, he was to make perambulati and mark the boundaries of seignories, as they had been in forn times. This was an amicable proceeding, and the writ was alw obtained by agreement of the parties; which agreement was to entered into in the chancery, and there enrolled, before the v would be granted.[8]

There was a writ contrived for persons living in towns where custom lands were devisable: this was the writ *ex gravi quer* of which there is no mention before this reign. If such la were devised, and the heir or any other entered thereon, the dev

[1] O. N. B., 10. [2] *Vide ante*, vol. i. c. vii. [3] O. N. B., 1
[4] O. N. B., 12 b.; *vide ante*, vol. i. c. viii. [5] *Ibid.* c. v.
[6] O. N. B., 85 b. [7] *Vide ante*, vol. i. [8] O. N. B.,

or his heir might have this writ against the intruder, who was summoned before the mayor, or other principal officer of the town, to show cause, at a certain day, wherefore execution should not be done pursuant to the will; and if no cause was shown, the devisee was put into possession.[1] The writ of *nuper obiit* is only glanced at by Bracton,[2] without any discourse put upon it. This was nearly allied to the writ *de rationabili parte;* it lay between privies in blood, as that did, and the wording of both is the same: the difference between them consisted in this; that the writ *de rationabili parte* was a writ of *right*, and lay though the ancestor did not die seised; the present was a *possessory* remedy, and could not be supported unless the ancestor had died seised of the land in question. A *nuper obiit* was to be brought by all those that were deforced, and not by one only: though some might not choose to sue, yet all were to be named; and he who sued might have a *summoneas ad sequendum simul.* If they did not comply after this, the person suing might have judgment and execution for his own portion singly. The process in this writ was summons, *grand* and *petite cape.* As the writs of *mortauncestor*, *ael* and *cosinage*, were always to be brought against strangers, they differed in that respect from these two *family* writs (if they may be so called); for a *nuper obiit* and *de rationabili parte* always lay between privies in blood.

The writs of *cessavit per biennium*, and of *cessavit per biennium de fœdi firmâ*, given by statute in the reign of Edward I.[3] were still in use. The former of these was the more general and more common. There now appeared another writ of this kind, called *cessavit de cantariâ per biennium.* This was, when lands were given to a church, for some religious service; as to pray for the donor's soul, to give alms, to perform divine service, or the like. If this was intermitted for two years, and there was no distress on the ground, the donor's heir might have this writ against the *terre tenant.* This, like the two former writs, made general mention of the statute; *quæ ad præfatum R. reverti debet per formam statuti de communi concilio regni provisi;* and like the writs of entry before mentioned, they might be in the *per*, *per et cui*, and *post.*[4] Similar to the last of these writs,* but grounded upon another statute,[5] was that *contra forma collationis;* which was, where an alienation was made by an abbot, or other religious person, of lands left in pure alms, for divine purposes: this writ lay against the sovereign of the religious society, and not against the tenant of the land.

The remedies for the recovery of common deserve a particular attention. The principal of these was the *Quòd permittat* (*a*). The

(*a*) An approvement of common could be pleaded, showing sufficient common left.

[1] O. N. B., 27.
[2] *Vide ante*, vol. i. c. viii.
[3] *Vide ante*, c. ix.
[4] O. N. B., 140.
[5] *Vide ante*, c. ix.

form of this writ was: *Præcipe, &c., quòd justè, &c., permittat B. habere communiam pasturæ in N. de quâ C. pater prædicti B. cujus hæres ipse est, fuit seisitus ut de fœdo tanquam pertinente ad liberum tenementum suum in eâdem villâ die quo obiit, ut dicit, &c.* This was the remedy where a man was disseised of common of pasture, and the disseisor aliened and died, or died and his heir entered; and it lay either for the disseisee or his heir. If neither of those events had happened, the remedy was by assize of common.

It may be remarked here that there was in the time of Glanville and Bracton [1] (*a*) a writ, *quòd permittat habere rationabile estoverium*, either *in bosco* or *in turbariâ;* but in the place of that writ, the resort after stat. Westm. 2, chap. xxv., was to the assize of novel disseisin.[2] That act ordains that if any one was disseised of his turbary, piscary, or the like, appertaining to a freehold, he should have an assize of novel disseisin. The writ of *quod permittat* had been extended by stat. Westm. 2, ch. xxiv.,[3] which enacted, that where a parson was disseised of common of pasture, he should, during the life of the disseisor, have an assize, and his successor should have a *quòd permittat*, either against the disseisor or his heir. Where several persons had common by special deed or covenant, and the lord built a mill, or otherwise injured the common, the commoners could not have an assize, but could only proceed on their covenant, or specialty, as appears by stat. Westm. 2, ch. xlvi.[4]

The writ of *quod permittat* might be in the *debet* and *solet*, or in the *debet* without the *solet*, according to the nature of the demandant's claim. Thus, if the disseisor died and his heir entered, the writ should mention the disseisin; if, after the death of the disseisor and his heir, a stranger entered, the writ would make mention of the *debet et solet*, to try the right. If the demand was in right of the demandant's ancestor, who was seised in fee the day he died, the writ was not to make mention of the disseisin of the ancestor, but was in the nature of a mortauncestor; if the ancestor was disseised, then the writ was to mention his disseisin. When the writ was in the *debet,* without the *solet*, the demandant was invariably to count of the seisin of his ancestor, and in this the battel and great assize would lie. This writ, like that of trespass, had the process of attachment and distress, and not *grand* and *petit cape.*

(*a*) The writ of *quod permittat* was also a remedy for any permanent nuisance to real property. These real actions, it will be observed, as they were called, as they lay only by parties possessed of freehold estates, were the originals of the modern actions in the case; as, for instance, for nuisance. Thus, in a *quod permittat* for nuisance, the plaintiff showed the manner of the nuisance; to wit, that the smoke entered into the house, so that no man could live there (*Year-book, 4 Edw. III.*, fol. 36, Dalby's case). So a case in which the plaintiff complained of a nuisance occasioned by a lime kiln (*toraile par arder chaux;* Danbey *v.* Berch, 4 *Edw. III.* fol. 36; *Liber. Ass. anno* 4, fol. 6; 5 *Edw. III.* fol. 43).

[1] *Vide ante*, vol. i. c. vii.

[2] *Vide ante*, c. x.

[3] *Ibid.*

[4] *Ibid.*

If a person having a freehold was ousted of his common of pasture by his lord, or if the lord approved contrary to the stat. Mert. ch. iv., and stat. Westm. 2, ch. xlvi., so that the tenant had not sufficient pasture, he might have an assize of novel disseisin; and if the pasture was surcharged by a freeholder, his remedy was by writ of admeasurement of pasture. But if the tenant surcharged the pasture, the lord's remedy was not by admeasurement, but by assize of freehold. He had no other remedy, and some doubted even of this remedy. A writ of *quòd permittat*, in the nature of a mortauncestor, could never be pleaded in the county; that *ad certum numerum averiorum* might be pleaded either in the bench, in the county, or in the iter.[1]

Where a person had common of pasture time out of mind in the several land of another, the person who had the several land might bring a writ of *quo jure*[2] (a writ mentioned by Bracton as applicable to this purpose), and force the commoner to show by what title he claimed his common. It was in this form: *Si A. fecerit te securum, &c., tunc summone, &c., B. quòd sit, &c., ostensurus* QUO JURE *exigit communiam pasturæ in terrâ ipsius A., &c., sicut idem B. nullam habet communiam in terrâ ipsius A. nec idem B. servitia ei fecit, quare communiam in terrâ A. habere debet, ut dicit, &c.* A lord who meant to question his tenant's claim of common could not oust him at once, because he would then be liable to an assize of novel disseisin; his remedy, therefore, was by this writ, which was given in order to try the right. The process was summons, attachment, and distress; and if the party had pleaded and then made default, there issued the grand distress, and not a *petit cape*.[3] This writ was to be determined by the battel, or great assize, or other writs of right.[4]

The writ of *admeasurement of pasture* might be brought by a commoner who had common appendant to his freehold, and complained that another commoner had surcharged the common; the consequence of this writ was, that as all the commoners were admeasured, the process was that which had been ordained by stat. Westm. 2, ch. vii.,[5] summons, attachment, and distress peremptory, with proclamation made in two counties; and if the party did not appear to the proclamation, the admeasurement was made by default.[6]

When admeasurement had been made under a writ directed to the sheriff, as just mentioned, and the person who surcharged was again guilty of surcharge, then the party grieved might have a writ, called *de secundâ superoneratione pasturæ*. This writ was sometimes original, and sometimes judicial. The practice on this writ seemed to rest wholly on the stat. Westm. 2, ch. viii.[7]

After the regulations that had been made in the time of Edward I.

[1] O. N. B., 68.
[2] *Vide ante*, vol. i. c. viii.
[3] *Vide* stat. Westm. ii., ch. xlvi.; *vide ante*, c. xi.
[4] O. N. B., 70 b.
[5] *Vide ante*, c. xi.
[6] O. N. B., 71 b.
[7] *Vide ante*, c. xi.; O. N. B., 72 b.

about waste, the remedies in such cases stood thus: there was a writ of waste, grounded on Westm. 2, c. xiv.[1] This writ was for the reversioner, against tenants for life, in dower, by the courtesy, guardians in chivalry, or tenants for years;[2] it had the process of summons, attachment, and distress, and on default, the proceeding directed by that act.[3] Next to this was the writ of *estrepement*, given by the statute of Gloucester, ch. xiii.,[4] which was a sort of prohibition to stop waste, while a *præcipe quòd reddat, &c.*, was depending for the lands. This writ, in term-time, was judicial, issuing out of the roll of the principal cause; if it was not term-time, it issued out of chancery. The process was attachment and distress; and, for default of distress, process of outlawry.[5]

The writ in use for recovery of services, where the person or his ancestor had not been seised within the limitation of an assize, was that *de consuetudinibus et servitiis*, being a writ of right, in which might be had the duel and the great assize.[6] Where a person was distrained for more services than he was bound to by his original infeoffment, he might have the writ *contra formam feoffamenti*, given by the stat. of Marlb. ch. ix.[7] The other writ in cases of services was the writ of *mesne*, with the proceedings so fully stated in the reign of Edward I.[8] Next follow the *quid juris clamat*, the *per quæ servitia*, and *quem redditum reddit*; each of these writs was to obtain an attornment of the tenant,[9] after a grant of the reversion by fine. These were judicial, and issued out of the record of the fine. The process was summons and distringas. The writ of right *sur disclaimer* was known in Bracton's time, but not by that or any particular name to distinguish it from others.[10] This writ lay, when the lord had avowed, and the tenant *disclaimed* to hold of him; upon which, there being an end of the suit in replevin, the lord was driven to this writ, and, if he made out his title, recovered the land. This was where the suit had been in the common pleas; for if it was in the county or court-baron, where the proceeding was not of record, the lord would be in mercy, as in Bracton's time.[11] There were other actions besides replevin for recovery of services, where the tenant might *disclaim*, one of which was a *cessavit;* in all such actions the lord must resort to this special writ of right.

The old writs of ward were still the usual remedies in such cases—namely, the writ *de communi custodiâ*, *ravishment of ward*, and *ejectment of ward*. All these have been sufficiently discoursed of already.[12] But there now appeared a new writ, called *entrusion de garde*, which lay where the infant within age entered into the lands, and held the lord out.[13] The writs *for the value of a marriage*, and *for forfeiture of marriage*, made up the remainder of the

[1] *Vide ante*, c. xi.
[2] *Ibid.*
[3] O. N. B., 41.
[4] *Vide ante*, c. xi.
[5] O. N. B., 43.
[6] *Ibid.*, 86.
[7] *Vide ante*, c. x.
[8] *Ibid.*, c. xi.
[9] O. N. B., 168, 172.
[10] *Vide ante*, c. x.
[11] O. N. B., 162.
[12] *Vide ante*, c. xii.
[13] O. N. B., 100.

remedies contrived for guardians. The writ of *escheat* was still the remedy for lords claiming under that title.[1]

Other writs in use, but less frequently resorted to than the former, were these: First, the writ of *monstraverunt*, which was for tenants in ancient demesne, when they were distrained for other services and customs than they performed in the time of William the Conqueror.[2] The writ of *ne injustè vexes*, which was for common tenants when they were distrained by their lords to do more services and customs than they were wont to do. We find this writ in the time of Glanville:[3] it was considered as a writ of right patent and ancestral, and might be determined by the battel or grand assize: the process in this and the *monstraverunt* was one prohibition, one attachment, and then a distress.[4] We find also the writ of *secta ad molendinum*,[5] the writ *de contributione faciendâ*,[6] and that *de partitione faciendâ*, for parceners who claimed land;[7] that *de warrantiâ chartæ*,[8] and the writ of *diem clausit extremum*, which had no process, but was a writ of office.[9] When a person had been found heir to the deceased by the last of these writs, he might, when he came of age, have the writ *de ætate probandâ* to prove that fact: this, like the former, being a writ of office, had no process.[10] The writ of *quo minus* was for a person who had a grant to take estovers every year out of another's wood; it was considered as in the nature of a writ of waste, and seems to have come into the place of an old writ, called *quod permittat habere rationabile estoverium*, and just alluded to;[11] the process was attachment and distress.[12] The writ of *ad quod damnum*, of which so much was said in the time of Edward I.,[13] was still in use, as were likewise the writ of *quo warranto*;[14] the writ *de idemptitate nominis*,[15] which has been mentioned before this reign;[16] that *de libertate probandâ*, and that *de nativo habendo*.[17]

Among others was the old writ *de moderatâ misericordiâ* for a person who had been amerced in a county court, or court baron, with great rigour, without due regard to the nature of the offence.[18] The writ of *decies tantùm* was given by stat. 34 Edw. c. viii.,[19] and lay where a jury had taken money of one of the parties for their verdict: they were by this writ to pay ten times as much as they had received, and if they had nothing to pay, they were to be imprisoned for a year. This writ lay also against embraceors and procurors of such inquests.[20] The writs in ecclesiastical matters were *prohibition*, *indicavit*, and *consultation;* and when a person was excommunicated, there lay a temporal process against him by writ of *excommunicato capiendo:* when he was to be delivered, he

1 *Vide ante*, vol. i. c. vii.
2 O. N. B., 16 b.
3 *Vide ante*, vol. i. c. iv.
4 O. N. B., 14 b.
5 *Ibid.*, 67.
6 *Ibid.*, 114.
7 *Ibid.* 157 b.; *vide ante*, vol. i. c. vii.
8 *Ibid.* 161 b.; *vide ante*, vol. i. c. viii.
9 *Ibid.*, 162 b.
10 *Ibid.*, 163 b.
11 *Vide ante*, vol. i. c. v. and vii.
12 O. N. B., 159 b.
13 *Vide ante*, c. xi.
14 O. N. B., 160.
15 *Ibid.*, 166.
16 *Vide ante*, c. xii.
17 O. N. B., 47; *vide ante*, c. xiv.
18 *Ibid.*, 53; *vide ante*, vol. i. c. vi.
19 *Vide ante*, c. xiv.
20 O. N. B., 131 b.

might have the writ *de excommunicato deliberando.*[1] The two writs of *disceit* and *conspiracy* were still in use.[2]

We have hitherto been speaking of original writs for the commencement of judicial proceedings; the following were the writs relating to judgments, and execution thereof. The writ *de executione judicii* lay where the sheriff or bailiff prolonged the execution of the judgment in favour of the tenant. The writ *de falso judicio* was, where false judgment was given in the county, hundred, or court baron. This writ was to bring the record before the justices in bank, or in eyre, which corresponds with the very account given of this writ in Glanville's time.[3] The writ *of error* was for the similar purpose of correcting false judgments. Where false judgment was given in the common pleas, this writ was returnable in the king's bench: if false judgment was given in the king's bench, such judgment was to be reversed in parliament, or by the king's great council upon petition.[4] The writ *de errore corregendo* was a writ of error directed to the justices before whom the judgment was passed, commanding them to correct the error therein, and is what has been since called *error coram vobis, &c.*[5] The writ of *auditâ querelâ*, like the former, was to take off the effect of a judgment; but this was to be upon the allegation of some fact that had taken place since, and entitled the party to avoid the judgment. It was commonly used, where, after a statute-merchant, a compromise or release of the debt had been made; then if execution was sued, this writ might be had returnable in the common pleas.[6] The writs of *dedimus potestatem*, for making an attorney and for levying a fine, have been mentioned before.[7] The writ of *quale jus* was devised after the stat. Westm. 2, c. xxxii., to enforce the provisions of that act. It was a judicial writ, which an abbot or other religious person, after recovery of land by default, was, before execution, to sue to the escheator, to inquire whether he really had a title to the land, or it was lost by collusion.[8]

Perhaps the reader will be better satisfied with this concise enumeration of real writs, than if they had been treated fully and at length; but those which remain deserve a more particular attention, and will therefore be reserved for more deliberate consideration in the following chapter.

[1] O. N. B., 33, 35, 36, 37, 39. [2] *Ibid.* 56, 63. [3] *Vide ante*, vol. i. c. vi.
[4] O. N. B., 18–20. [5] *Ibid.*, 61. [6] *Ibid.*, 74.
[7] *Ibid.*, 23, 114; *vide ante*, c. xiii. [8] *Ibid.*, 177; *vide ante*, c. xiii.

CHAPTER XVI.

EDWARD III.

Action of Debt—Of Detinue—Of Accompt—Of Trespass—Of Actions on the Case—Proceedings by Bill, &c.—Of Pleading—The Secta, and Law-Wager—Trial by Proofs, and other Trials—Trial per Pais—Of the Venue—Of Process—The Crime of Treason—Homicide—Larceny—Burglary—Appeals—Indictments—Of Penance—Trial by Battle and Jury—Sanctuary and Clergy—Of Forfeiture—The King and Government—The Nova Statuta—Reports—Old Tenures—Natura Brevium—Novæ Narrationes—Miscellaneous Facts.

HAVING dismissed the numerous real actions that were now in use, we come to personal actions: these constitute a subject of inquiry that has survived the changes to which the former have long yielded; and a considerable portion of what we shall say upon them makes a part of the law of the present time (*a*). The per-

(*a*) Attention has already been directed (in the note at the commencement of c. xiv.) to the close connexion between trial by jury, wager of law, and arbitration, whether voluntary or compulsory, as in the action of account; and it has been seen that trial by jury was merely trial by the knowledge of the jurors, such as it was, of the matter in dispute; and that the unsatisfactory nature of such a mode of trial had led the law to allow of the awkward procedure by compurgators, and to provide a special procedure in matters of account, and had also allowed the parties to resort to the convenient procedure by arbitration. These other modes of proceeding were chiefly resorted to in personal actions, and it was probably in these that the imperfection of the system of trial by jury, as a trial of their own knowledge, first and most frequently was made manifest. So long as the matter which arose related only to the possession of land, which was open and notorious, the defects of the system were less apparent, and so even as to personal property and personal contracts, so long as men's transactions were few, and simple, and public. But as wealth increased, and as trade advanced, and men's transactions became more numerous and complicated, the necessity for a more efficient and intelligent mode of trial must have been more and more manifest, and hence, in this reign, the great recourse to arbitration and the action of account. Of these different modes of trial or adjudication, it is to be observed, that, although arbitration, being voluntary and by consent, was at the election of the parties, provided they could both agree to it, it was not left to them, or either of them, to elect between the other forms of compulsory procedure. Thus, it was not in the power of the defendant, at his pleasure, to wage his law in every species of action, but only in such as were deemed not fit for trial by *pais*,—*i.e.*, by the "country," or the jury, which virtually meant the neighbours, giving their verdict of their own knowledge. This mode of trial, it was obvious, was only applicable to matters which were, from their nature, likely to be within their knowledge, and for such as were not so, and were, from their nature, likely to be secret between the parties, as most private contracts, wager of law was allowed (40 *Edw. III.* fol. 40). On the other hand, the plaintiff was not allowed to resort to the procedure by account, except in cases in which the procedure was properly applicable, the matter really being one of account. The law left him in other cases to an ordinary action of debt, in which, in most cases, the defendant could wage his law. The defendant, again, in action of account, could not avoid the obligation to account by wager of law, although, in an action of debt for arrears of account, he could wage his law (44 *Edw. III.* fol. 2). It was there objected by the plaintiff, that the matter was one which lay within the knowledge of the "country" (*i. e.*, the neighbours), but it

sonal actions now in practice were the action of debt, of detinu annuity, accompt, replevin, trespass, and trespass upon the cas Of these we shall speak in their order, beginning with the actio of debt.

Action of debt. The action of debt was the common remedy in most contrac for the recovery of money; and since its process ha been strengthened by a statute of this king, it becan more efficacious and useful. The process now was summon attachment, and distress; and on default of distress, three *capias* and an *exigent* proclaimed in five counties, and then to outlawry.

The writ of debt was the same in form as in the reign of Edwa I.[1] We have now an opportunity of seeing the forms of son *declarations* in this action, which are furnished by a book of pr cedents collected in this reign: some specimens of these may n be unacceptable to the curious. The formal beginning of such declaration was the same as the beginning of a petition to parli ment, *Ceo vouz monstre I. R., &c.* Being of a date previous to sta 36 Edw. III., these declarations are in French: a literal translati may serve as well for specimens as the original. *Ceo vouz monstr &c. This showeth unto you, A., who is here, that B., who is ther unjustly*[2] *detains from him, and will not render him* £10 *of mon which he owes him; and therefore unjustly, because, at such a da*

was said by the court that possibly he might have paid the money since the accou ing (*Ibid.*) In debt, upon a contract, also, the defendant could plead payment to all or part, and wage his law as to that part (46 *Edw. III.*, fol. 6), as well as in denial of the debt (42 *Edw. III.* fol. 10). It has been seen how summary and eff tive the procedure in the action of account was (41 *Edw. III.*, fol. 31 ; 21 *Edw. II* fol. 9), and it was therefore a matter of considerable importance whether or not t procedure was allowable, and there are therefore numerous cases on the subject the Year-books of this and subsequent reigns. And here arises an importa matter of procedure. Supposing the form of action objected to, it is obvious that would be desirable that it should be objected to at the earliest possible stage, and the writ in those days was special, and disclosed what the form of action was, it obvious that the exception to it could conveniently be taken upon the writ, and, soon as the party sued, came into court, and so in effect it was. For it is to borne in mind, that, as the records and the Year-books show, the pleading in th days was oral, and began so soon as the parties came into court—that is, upon t appearance of the party sued (38 *Edw. III.*, fol. 28)—when the plaintiff "declare or "counted," that is, simply recited the effect of his writ, perhaps a little m fully—the office of the writ or "brief" being to state it shortly—and thereupon t defendant could plead in abatement of the writ (46 *Edw. III.*, fol. 26), *i.e.*, all some matter of fact against it, or could demur to it, or take some legal objection it: as, that the form of action was not applicable for instance, that it was in acco when it ought to be in debt, or in debt when it ought to be in covenant, and forth; and as the procedure in different kinds of action varied, as we have se according to the nature of the action, and a mode of trial would be proper in which would not be allowed in another, it is manifest that the sooner this determined the better for both parties. And it is evident that in an age wl pleading was oral at the bar, and began so soon as the defendant appeared, t matter could be and was settled very soon at the outset of the case, and so the Y books show. In the course of this and the ensuing reign, however, it was found t it would be convenient summarily to examine the plaintiff or his attorney, in acti of account, on oath, as to whether or not the matter was or was not matter account, and accordingly such examination was allowed by statute in the reign Henry IV. *Vide post.*

[1] *Vide ante*, c. x.

[2] *A tort.*

year, and place, the said B. granted himself to be bound to the aforesaid A. in £10, *to be paid at such a day, year, and place; at which day the said A. went to the aforesaid B., and requested him to pay him the aforesaid* £10, *and he would not pay it, nor yet will,* à tort et à ses damages of 100 *shillings; and if he denies it, he can bring* GOOD SUIT, &c.

The declaration, or counting upon the writ of debt, was various, according to the special nature of the demand: the following are the substance of different declarations. Upon a *lending*, it might be thus: *Therefore unjustly, because on such a day, year, and place, the said A.* LENT *to the said B.* £10, *to be paid on such a day, at which day he did not pay it, &c.* Upon a *selling*, thus: *Was obligated to the said A. in* £10, *for a horse*, or *for corn*, namely, *&c.*, or *for a bag of corn, &c.*, or *for ten quarters of corn, which he* SOLD *to him, to be paid on such a day, at which day, &c.*, and then go on as before. Again: *And therefore wrongfully, for that whereas the said A. was bound to one Robert Fox in* £10, *which the said A.* BAILED *to the aforesaid B. to pay to the aforesaid Robert, the said* £10 *to the aforesaid Robert he paid not; by reason of which the said Robert the aforesaid* £10 *against the said A. on such a day, and year, and place, before such justices, did recover; by reason of which the said A. hath often come to the aforesaid B. and requested him to* REBAIL *the aforesaid* £10, *but he has never been willing so to do, nor yet will,* A TORT, ET A DAMAGES, *&c.* Upon a *bailment* of money, thus: *And therefore wrongfully, for that whereas the said A. by a writing obligatory was bound to one Robert in* £10, *which the said A.* BAILED *to the aforesaid B. to pay the aforesaid Robert, so that he might be acquit of the aforesaid* £10, *the said B. the said* £10 *to the aforesaid Robert did not pay; by reason of which the said Robert the aforesaid* £10 *such a day, year, and place, before such justices, against the said A. demanded; pending which plea, the said A. came to the said B. and requested him to acquit him of the said* £10, *and he would not acquit him; by reason of which the said Robert the aforesaid* £10 *against the said A. for default of acquittance of the said B. did recover; by reason of which the said A. requested that he would rebail to him the aforesaid* £10, *&c.*, as above. Again, on a bailment of money: *And therefore wrongfully, for that whereas the said A. such a day* BAILED *to the said Abbot, and one Robert a monk there,* £10 *to keep till he demanded it of them; by reason of which the said A. at such a day, year, and place, demanded the aforesaid* £10, *and they would not pay it, &c.* For rent on a lease: *And therefore wrongfully, for that whereas the said A. on such a day, &c.,* LEASED *to the aforesaid B. one carve of land in C. for the term of ten years, the term commencing such a day, &c., to pay* £10 *per annum during such term; and the payment of the two first years amounting to* £20 *is arrear; by reason of which the said A. has frequently come to the aforesaid B. and requested him to pay the aforesaid*

£20, *which he has never been willing to do, nor yet will,* ‹ Against a pledge, or collateral security, thus: *And therefore wro fully, for that whereas the said A. sold to one Robert Fox quarters of corn for* £10, *to be paid on such a day, &c., for wh the said B. became his pledge; at which day the said Robert* ‹ *not pay anything; for which reason the said A. often came to said B., and requested him that he would pay him the said* £10, *he would not so do, &c.* Upon a conditional promise to pay: *A therefore wrongfully, for that whereas the aforesaid B. granted make a feoffment to the said A. of one carve of land, &c., in C. such a day, &c., and if he did not, that he was bound to the afo said A. in* £10, *at which day he did not infeoff him; for wh reason he requested him to pay him the aforesaid* £10, *yet he* ‹ *not been willing, &c.* Upon the stat. Westm. 2, c. xi., agains keeper of a prison:[1] *And therefore wrongfully, for that whereas* ‹ *Robert Fox on such a day, &c., tendered accompt to the said before X. Y. Z., auditors assigned by the said A. to hear accompt of the said Robert, of the time that he was bailiff of manor of R., &c.,* or thus: *receivor of his money arising from tunnels of wine of the said A., sold by the said Robert, for the pr of the said A. at Oxford, and remained* £10 *in arrear before aforesaid auditors; by reason of which, by the testimony of auditors aforesaid, the aforesaid Robert was committed to prison of B., according to the form of the statute of our lord king in this matter provided; and there such a day, year,* ‹ *place, &c., and by the aforesaid B., then keeper of the prison afo said, was received, and in the said prison detained from the afo said day to such a day, when the aforesaid B., without the ass of the said A., and without gree being made to the said A., let said Robert go out of the aforesaid prison; by reason of whi according to the form of the aforesaid statute, an action hath accr to the said A. to demand the aforesaid* £10 *of the aforesaid B.,* ‹ *the said A. hath often come to the said B. and requested him to* ‹ *the aforesaid* £10, *and he was not willing so to do, &c.*[2] Th may be sufficient specimens of the form in which narrations u the writ (as they were then called) were conceived.

It next follows, that we should take notice of such decisions tended to reduce this action nearer towards the form in whic appeared in later times. We have seen, in the last reign, tha deed made in a place not within the process of the court could be the subject of an action, as deeds made in Chester, Durh Ireland, and other places beyond sea.[3] As to Chester and Durh the difficulty was probably now removed by stat. 9 Ed. III. st c. iv., and in other cases they seem to have hit upon an expedi to avoid this objection. But places out of the realm caused same difficulties as heretofore, and drove lawyers to the necessit resorting to expedients to remove them. Thus, where an obli

[1] *Vide ante*, c. x. [2] Novæ Narr., fol. 37 b. to 39 b. [3] *Vide ante*, c. xiii

tion was made at Harfleet in Normandy, the plaintiff counted upon it as made at Harfleet in Kent; and though it was objected that there was no such place in Kent, the objection seems not to have been attended to. This bond concerned a retainer of men to serve in France in the wars. It was argued, that this being for duties to be performed out of the kingdom in foreign parts, it ought to be tried before the *constable and marshall* (a new jurisdiction, of which nothing was heard till this reign); but it was held that the action would well lie in a court of common law. It was at the same time held, that where a demand was grounded on an obligation, the plaintiff could not go for less than the whole sum, unless satisfaction was confessed for the remainder.[1]

It was held, that an action of debt would lie for damages recovered in a real action; so that, should the ancestor die before execution, the heir might have execution of the land, and the executor of the damages.[2] Where money was given to a man to make a profit of it for the plaintiff (as in one of the declarations above stated), he might, at his option, have either an action of debt, or accompt.[3] Where a person came to a creditor and engaged to him, that, should his debtor not pay him, *he* would become his principal debtor, and pay him at such a time, it was held that an action of debt would not lie without a specialty, for this was no discharge of the first debtor; though it would have been otherwise if the promise had been by deed.[4] If a man committed a felony, it was held he did not forfeit his debts without specialty, though he did those upon specialty: for if the king brought an action for the former, the defendant would be deprived of his law-wager by the prerogative, which the law would not suffer.[5] Such differences were made between specialties and common debts. Where two were bound severally in an obligation, two several *præcipes* were brought, and they were held good. Where a bond was accompanied with a condition, the defendant might aver the payment *at the day* without a specialty; for though he could, upon a single bond, compel the obligee to give an acquittance, he could not in case of a bond upon condition. But a plea of payment *after* the day, though the acceptance of the obligee was alleged, would not prevent the plaintiff from recovering.[6]

In debt for rent, if the lessor's estate was determined by the entry of any one upon him, as of the disseisee upon the disseisor, the person who infeoffed upon condition or the like, all this would be a good plea in bar of the action. If a man holding for years leased his whole term, he could not distrain, because he had no reversion; but he might have an action of debt for the rent.[7] If a lessor entered it would be a good plea to discharge the rent accruing since.[8] If a man leased for his own life, debt lay for his executors

[1] 48 Edw. III., 2. [2] 43 Edw. III., 2. [3] 42 Edw. III., 9.
[4] 44 Edw. III., 21. [5] 49 Edw. III., 5; *vide ante*, c. xi.
[6] 46 Edw. III., 29. [7] 45 Edw. III., 8. [8] 45 Edw. III., 4.

without a specialty: in like manner if the lease was for the life of t lessee, it lay against the executors of the lessee without specialt; A lease was made to two by indenture, which one sealed but t other did not; yet the other was held bound to pay the rent by t *occupation*, though he was not bound to the conditions of the leas It was held an action of debt would lie for rent, notwithstanding right of re-entry was reserved;[3] but if the plaintiff entered tl might be pleaded in bar of the action.[4] Where rent was reserv in kind, the writ was brought in the *detinet* only, and not in t *debet;* and though it was urged that this, being a rent, should demanded as a debt, it was answered that the chancery would ne make a writ in the *debet*, except it was for money; the writ w accordingly adjudged to be good.[5]

Where an action was brought against a baron and feme damages recovered against her *dum sola*, the writ was *debent et c tinent:* when it was strongly contended that it should be only the *detinent*, it was decided to be good. Again, where an acti was brought by an abbot or prior on an obligation to his pre cessor, it was laid in the *debet et detinet*, though it would be diff ent in the case of executors:[6] yet where one executor sold goods the testator, he might have his writ alone, and as for a debt of l own.[7] If a feme died the baron was discharged from all her del and deprived also of all her credits *dum sola*.[8] Where money w paid for instructing a child in a certain trade within so many yea and the child died before the time expired, it was held debt wo not lie to recover the money; and if the money had not been pa the instructor would not have been entitled to an action.[9] It w held, that where a man promised to give so much money to *I.* if he would take his daughter to wife, debt would lie; but if t money had been promised *in marriage*, it would not lie on acco of the word *marriage*, it being then become an object of spirit cognizance.[10] If an heir pleaded falsely he was to be charged his own land, which he took by purchase, as well as in that he t by descent.[11]

A defendant pleaded to an obligation that he had performed t conditions upon which it had been made, that accordingly plaintiff restored it to him, and afterwards took it with force a arms; this was held a good plea.[12] Again, in another action pending in the exchequer, the same was allowed as a good plea debt, though it was not in trespass, where nothing but dama recovered could be a bar.[13]

It may be proper here to mention the writ *de plegiis acquietan* which was a common remedy for a surety against the princi debtor after having paid the debt for which he was bound. T writ was in use in Glanville's time;[14] and, though word for w

[1] 44 Edw. III., 42. [2] 38 Edw. III., 8. [3] 38 Edw. III., 22. [4] 45 Edw. III. [5] 50 Edw. III., 16. [6] 47 Edw. III., 23. [7] 38 Edw. III., 9. [8] 49 Edw. III. [9] 21 Edw. III., 12. [10] 22 Ass., 70. [11] 21 Edw. III., 9. [12] 43 Edw. III. [13] 43 Edw. III., 27. [14] *Vide ante*, c. iv.

the same, it then lay for the creditor against the surety. The present notion of suretyship was, as has just been observed, that such a collateral engagement to pay, on default of the real debtor, was not good without writing; and therefore the writ *de plegiis acquietandis* could not be maintained against the original debtor without writing.[1] The writ of *si recognoscat* was still in use.[2]

The action of *detinue* still preserved very strongly its original affinity with the former: the wording of this writ was the same as in the reign of Edward I.[3] Respecting these two writs, when they were to be in the *debet* and when in the *detinet*, we find the following rule: In a writ for chattels it was never to be alleged *quæ ei debet;* nor in a writ of debt, if brought by an executor, or by any other against an executor, whether it was a debt or a chattel, and in whatsoever court the writ was brought; for it was always required to be *injustè detinet.* In other respects there was a difference between the practice in the common-pleas and before the justices itinerant; for in the former it might be *debet et detinet,* if they were not chattels, nor against or for executors or administrators, for then it should be *detinet* only: in the latter, if for debt it was to be *debet* only, and for chattels *detinet.*[4]

Of detinue.

The following are some specimens of declarations upon a writ in the *detinet.* First, upon a *bailment: Ceo vous monstre, &c. This showeth you A. that B. wrongfully* DETAINS *from him chattels to the value of £20, and therefore wrongfully, for that whereas the said A. on a certain day, year, and place,* BAILED *to the aforesaid B. linen and woollen cloth, to keep till he demanded it, the said A. on such a day, year, and place, requested the said B. to return the aforesaid chattels, yet he was not willing to return them, nor yet will, &c.* For restoring, after a divorce, certain goods given in frank-marriage: *Ceo vous monstre, &c. This showeth you Ellen, who was the daughter of A. who is here, that N. Fox, who is there, wrongfully detains and will not return to her chattels to the value of £10, and therefore wrongfully, for that whereas the said A. on such a day, year, and place, gave the aforesaid N. chattels to the value of £10—namely,*[5] *corn and grain, in frank-marriage with the said Ellen, the said N. after espousals solemnly had between them, came and procured one Alice to demand him as her husband, by precontract made between them; so that at the suit of the said Alice, and by the procurement of the said N. a divorce was had between the aforesaid N. and Ellen on such a day, year, and place, before the ordinary, &c., by reason of which divorce an action hath accrued to her to demand the aforesaid chattels given with her in frank-marriage in the form aforesaid; by reason of which the said Ellen hath often come to the said N. and requested*

Detinet.

[1] 43 Edw. III., 11; 44 Edw. III., 21.
[2] *Vide ante,* c. xiii.
[3] *Ibid.*
[4] O. N. B., 63.
[5] *Scilicet.*

him to return the aforesaid chattels, yet he has never been will to return them, &c.[1]

Very little need be said on this action, as distinguished from t of debt; they may perhaps be considered as identically the same all their properties, process, circumstances, and form, with difference that one was for the recovery of a chattel, the other money. Any one who had a right to a chattel, though he l never been in possession thereof, might have this writ to reco it; as where a deed was bailed to *A.* to deliver to *B.*, *B.* was titled to detinue.[2] So an heir might have detinue for an *heir-lo* though he never had had possession thereof.[3] There was anot writ of *detinue*, which had been held maintainable without possession, but which, after some discussion in the former reig upon another point, was at last held not to be warranted by law (This was an action by a widow against the executor, for her reas able part of her husband's goods. These actions, notwithstand that decision, continued to be brought, and were variously trea by the courts.

The point upon which this question rested seems to have other authority in the law books than a chapter in *Magna Char* and a passage in Glanville.[6] That chapter of the Great Cha is directly upon the subject of distributing the effects of decea persons; but having ordained a surer method of levying the ki debt, it adds, as a security to the subject, that all the rest shall long to the dead person, *saving* their reasonable parts to the v and children: a saving which seems sufficiently necessary, i were only on account of the particular customs in some coun and other places, which required a man always to leave someth to his wife and children, and which would otherwise have b abrogated by the general scope of the former provision. It not, therefore, seem a necessary conclusion from thence, that s a distribution of the effects was the general law of the kingd As to the passage in Glanville, there seems in it an ambiguit not a contradiction. That author might be quoted as well in fa of as against the proposition, *that it was the general law of kingdom for a man's wife and children to be entitled to a pro tion of his effects, notwithstanding a will.* Upon these authori together with the determinations mentioned in the last reign, s this question, when it underwent the following discussion.

In the third year of the king we find an action of detinue bro by a husband and wife against the executors of the wife's fat for a child's portion: it was laid upon *the custom of the count Northampton*, and she alleged she was not advanced by her fat The cause went off upon the issue, whether married and adva

(*a*) *Sed quære.* This seems to have been a mistake of the author. He took which showed the action answered, as showing that no such action lay. It on in cases of intestacy, and was answered by a plea of *plene administravit.* *Vide*

[1] O. N. B., 40 b., 41 a. [2] 39 Edw. III., 17. [3] 39 Edw. III.
[4] *Vide ante*, c. xiii. [5] *Vide ante*, c. xi. [6] *Ibid.*, 111, 1

by her father, without any question arising about the point of law.[1] In 17 Edw. III. such a writ of detinue was brought by a baron and feme, for her *reasonable part* of her former husband's goods, against his executors; which writ made mention of the custom of the realm;[2] but this went off upon another point. In the 30th year there was another writ of detinue, stating, *Cùm, per consuetudinem totius regni Angliæ hactenus usitatam et approbatam, uxores debent et solent a tempore, &c., habere suam rationabilem partem bonorum maritorum suorum, ita videlicet, quòd si nullos habuerint libros, tunc medietatem, et si habuerint tunc tertiam partem, &c.* It was objected to this writ, that it made mention of common usage through the whole realm, which could mean nothing but the common law; and if it was the common law, he might have a simple writ of detinue: for if a man brought a writ of ael or assize of mortauncestor, reciting that heirs ought by the common custom of the realm to inherit to their ancestors who had died seised, the writ should abate. The same here: for should a traverse be taken to this part, it could not be tried by an inquest, because the issue would be what was the common law of the land; which could not be tried by a *pais* of a particular county, but could only be tried by the court. They admitted that a man might have a writ of the custom of a particular place, for it might be tried by the country. With respect to the present writ it was added, that such a one had been abated before Sir Wm. Herle; meaning, no doubt, that before mentioned in the 17th year of Edward II.[3] It was argued that in that case the writ was abated, because it purported to be founded on the Great Charter.

In like manner, should a woman bring a writ of dower and demand a moiety, if the custom was comprised in the writ, it would be bad; and therefore she should make her demand in the writ generally, and upon that should show special matter to maintain her demand: so it might be here, and the plaintiff might count according to his case. Then Stamford, one of the clerks, showed a writ that was brought by an infant not advanced, containing all the matter of this writ, which, he said, was held maintainable. Here the debate upon the form of the writ rested; and when the executors began to resort to other points—namely, that they were to account before the ordinary, and that this question of distribution belonged rather to the spiritual than the temporal court, they were told they were not to plead to the jurisdiction after they had objected to the writ; so that, upon the whole, it should seem as if the writ was there approved of.[4]

The next action that appears in the books was grounded upon the custom of the county of Sussex, which was stated as allowing a

[1] Bro. de Rati. Parte 8, 3 Edw. III.

[2] 17 Edw. III., 9.

[3] *Vide ante*, vol. ii., 334. [But this seems to have been a mistake. It was held that the writ was good, and that the action lay, but that it was answered by plea of administration, as it only lay in cases of intestacy, and as regarded the surplus after payment of all debts.]

[4] 30 Edw. III., 25, 26.

reasonable part of the *intestate* father's goods to go to the son; l this being upon an intestacy, led to no debate upon the befo mentioned point; though it was said, this custom precluded t father from making a will in prejudice of his wife and childre On that occasion, it was said, that this writ, in case of intestacy, h always been admitted by the ordinary. The next is in the 40th y of the king. This is grounded upon the custom of a vill, by wh the children were to have a reasonable part of their father's goo but it does not appear whether it was brought against executors upon an intestacy: however, the defendant set up an advancem as a plea in bar (a); to which the plaintiffs replied, the gift m tioned was only a reversion, and therefore no lawful advancem to bar their reasonable portion. The defendant said it was, a demanded judgment, which drew from the bench the followi observations. Thorpe, one of the justices, said, *How can we g judgment when you have accepted an action which is contrary the law*, and have pleaded matter in affirmance of it? and Mo bray, another justice, said, *The lords in parliament would ne grant that this action should be maintainable by any comm custom or law of this realm.* But as the plaintiff had not plea to the writ, the justices took time to advise what should be dor The writ in question being grounded on a *particular* custom, a it not appearing whether it was brought in the case of a will, or an intestacy, we are left quite at a loss for the grounds on wh the judges pronounced the above-mentioned opinion; for thou there might be arguments against such a *general* custom, or agai alleging it in the writ, it is difficult to say that such a particu custom might not be good; though Thorpe doubted of it in former case from Sussex, saying, it was hard to restrain a m from making a will of his own effects.

Thus, the law stood at the latter end of this reign, as it did at

(a) That is to say, admitting the custom as alleged, which, there is little do was general, and was so pleaded, it will be observed, in several of the cases; but courts were so strongly adverse to it that it was attempted to set it up as a l custom, rather than as general law. It seems strange that it should have been al assumed that it was a claim notwithstanding a will; and so a claim to restrain power of making testamentary dispositions. And if it were considered only to applied in cases of intestacy, it ought to have been so stated; but it was not so st And this seems to have been the cause of the objection the courts entertained to claim, as a claim to restrain the power of testamentary disposition. And as, on other hand, it was admitted that an advancement did away with the applicatio the custom, it would seem that a testamentary provision in favour of the party w have like effect; at all events, if the bequests were to an amount equal to the sl And it is not likely, of course, that a party who had a share by will would sue f on the custom. Practically, therefore, the customary claim was a claim to a sha the goods, either in case of an intestacy, or of a will, not including the claiman that virtually, in cases of wills, it did interfere with the power of testamentary dis tion, and hence the aversion with which it was regarded. And the reader wil serve that the aversion is actually avowed and assigned as a reason for holding law to be otherwise. The legislature, in the statute of distributions, afterw adopted the principle in cases of intestacy; but all attempts to control wills ceased; and the remedy to enforce administration was in chancery.

[1] 39 Edw. III., 9, 10. [2] 40 Edw. III., 38 b.

close of the former(*a*); and conformably with this opinion against the writ, it is not inserted in the old *Natura Brevium*, which has only the writ of right *de rationabili parte*. It is remarkable, that this writ of right is omitted in Fitzherbert, and the writ of detinue now in question adopted, under the denomination of *de rationabili parte bonorum*. There is in the *Novæ Narrationes*, a book certainly long prior to the above determination, a declaration in detinue by a widow against an executor for a moiety; and it is added in a note, that the same would lie *pro hærede de tertiâ parte*, if the wife was alive; and if dead, for a moiety.[1] What deference was paid to the last decision will be seen in the sequel. It seems strange that a question of so extensive importance, and so frequent recurrence, as the disposition of a deceased person's effects, whether by will or administration, should remain a doubtful case at this time. Perhaps the jurisdiction that the spiritual court had exercised over testamentary matters, tended to keep this point of law in obscurity, and undecided. After all, it is difficult at this time to account for so singular a difference of opinion.

To return to the common writ of *detinue*. In a declaration upon a bailment of sheep, the defendant pleaded, that they were bailed to him to feed his ground, and that he gave notice to the plaintiff to take them back, which he neglected; so that the defendant distrained them damage feasant. This was held a good plea in discharge of the bailment, without any other possession in the plaintiff afterwards; and therefore he was put to traverse the notice.[2] If a bailment was made to a baron and feme, detinue was held to lie against the baron alone, and the writ would abate if brought against them both; but if a chattel came to a woman's custody as executrix, and she took a husband, the action might be against the husband and wife jointly.[3] It was once held, that should a chattel come to the hands of one executor, detinue would lie against him alone, upon the idea that he was charged upon the possession only, and not upon the bailment;[4] but this was afterwards overruled, and upon a plea that there were other executors.[5]

It was observed in the former reign,[6] that the writ of detinue was frequently brought to recover charters that had been deposited for assuring land, and other purposes. This was a very common action, but was considered as of a particular nature, and differing from the common action of detinue. Thus, after the statute of

(*a*) There are numerous cases of actions of account in this and the ensuing reigns. Thus, in this reign there were many, which will be found reported in the Year-books, especially Sir N. Tamworth's case, 50 Edward III.; and there were a great many in the reign of Richard II., some of which will be found in *Bellewe's Cases, temp. Rich. II.* In one of these cases it appears that, when the auditors were assigned, if the defendant before them claimed an allowance which was objected to, or if in any other way a question of law arose, it was referred to the court.—(*Bellewe's Cases, temp. Rich II.*, fol. 13).

1 Nov. Narr., 40. 2 43 Edw. III., 21. 3 O. N. B., 64.
4 39 Edw. III., 5. 5 41 Edw. III., 30. 6 *Vide ante*, c. xiii.

this king which gave process of outlawry in debt, and detinu chattels, it was held that *charters*, as they appertained to the fi hold, should in an action for them be privileged as the freeh was, concerning which no process of outlawry lay. A *detinue charters* therefore was not a *detinue of chattels*, and the pro was only summons, attachment, and distress.[1] The writ *de ch tis reddendis* did not, however, in other respects, differ from common action of detinue, except in the description of the subj It was, *Præcipe, &c., quòd reddat quandam cistam cum cha scriptis et aliis munimentis, ac diversis chartis et bonis in eâd cistâ contentis serurâ ipsius B. clausam, quam, &c.;* or, *quand chartam*, or *duas chartas*, or *quoddam scriptum obligatorium, quoddam scriptum conventionale, &c.*, and so on, as in the comm writ.[2] A declaration upon a writ *de chartis reddendis* might thus, &c.: *Two charters, two writings obligatory, and one q claim, which he wrongfully detains; and therefore wrongfully, that the said A. such a day, year, &c., bailed to the said N. charters—that is to say, one charter by which one Robert Map feoffed him of a mese in C., one charter by which one John P. feoffed one Jordan at C., of the manor of L.; and two writi obligatory—that is to say, one writing by which one G. H. bound to the said A. in* 100 *shillings, and another by which one R. was bound to the said A. in* 20 *shillings; and one quit-cla in which it was contained, that one S. T. to him released and q claimed all the right which he had in the manor of W., to k till he demanded them; by reason of which the said A. often ca to the said N. and requested him to return him the aforesaid ch ters and writings, yet he was not willing so to do, &c.*, A TORT A DAMAGES, *&c.*[3]

There arose much debate whether a writ was to be considered a common writ of detinue, or of the latter kind; and the disti tion depended on the action being generally for a box of chart or specially for certain charters by name and description. It laid down as a rule, that if the plaintiff did not count of a box t closed, or sealed, he should count of the charters specially, for such case he might easily inform himself of them.[4] In detinue a bag of charters it was held, that if the defendant was retur *nihil*, the plaintiff might have a *capias*, because the *bag* was onl *chattel;*[5] but if the writ was for charters in special, *capias* wo not lie.[6] Sometimes, when the writ was general for *a box charters*, the count should be special, naming the charters; wh way of declaring was not at first looked upon as consistent,[7] was at length allowed.[8] The advantage gained by this new was, that the tenant was thereby excluded of his law-wager, which he was entitled upon a general declaration in detinue. So

[1] *Vide ante*, c. xiv.
[2] O. N. B., 65.
[3] Nov. Narr., 41
[4] 39 Edw. III., 7, 8.
[5] 40 Edw. III., 25.
[6] 42 Edw. III.,]
[7] 41 Edw. III., 2.
[8] 44 Edw. III., 41.

difficulty was raised in these actions by the property of the box and that of the charters being in different persons: the former belonging, as a chattel, to the executor; the latter, as a muniment of his estate, to the heir. Yet charters did not, of course, go with the title to the land. It did not follow that the feoffee upon his feoffment became entitled to the charters of the estate; for it might be necessary for the feoffer to keep them, to enable him to make his claims of warranty and the like against his lord paramount.[1] It was laid down, that where charters were burnt, the plaintiff should recover damages to the value of the land to which they related, if the action was *de chartis reddendis;* but if in trespass, he was to have only damages for the taking against the peace: in the former case, therefore, it was proper to allege the value of the land in the declaration.[2]

The writ of *annuity* was nearly allied to the writ of debt, being a demand for arrears of annuity which were detained. This writ agrees with that in the time of Edward I.[3] The following is a specimen of a declaration: *Ceo vous monstre, &c. N. wrongfully detains, and will not render to him four marks of silver, which are in arrear of an annual rent which he owes him; and therefore wrongfully, for that whereas the said N. on such a day, year, and place, obligated himself by this deed here present, to the aforesaid E. in two marks to be paid to the aforesaid E. on the day of Easter from year to year, during all the life of the said E., of which the said E. was seised by the hands of the said N. till two years before the writ purchased, which he has withdrawn to his damage, &c.*[4] The process in this writ was summons, attachment, and distress. It was held, this writ would not lie for executors, who, in lieu of this action *de annuo redditu*, were to have a writ of debt in the *detinet.*[5] If the annuitant assigned his annuity, the assignee could not recover arrears by the writ of annuity, for that would be granting a right of action which the law did not allow.[6] It was held, that an heir should not be charged with an annuity by prescription, by the mere payment of his ancestor.[7] And whether an annuity was demanded on a prescription or grant by deed, the plea of *rien arrere* could not be supported without an acquittance.[8] If an annuity was granted to a physician, or a lawyer (as was very common), *pro concilio impenso et impendendo*, or *pro auxilio, et concilio habendo*, it *became discharged on a refusal* in *the former to attend the grantor*, or in *the latter to give advice;* for it was *said, a lawyer was not to be expected to come to his client.* If such a grant was with the general reservation *pro concilio habendo*, and the like, it would be interpreted to mean that which the grantee was best qualified by his profession to give.[9] Annuities were frequently charged upon land, which gave the grantee a power of distress, and, if interrupted in such distraining, an assize of novel disseisin.

[1] 44 Edw. III., 1. [2] 17 Edw. III., 45; 21 Edw. III., 20. [3] *Vide ante*, c. x. [4] Nov. Nar., 37. [5] O. N. B., 75. [6] 41 Edw. III., 27. [7] 49 Edw. III., 5. [8] 44 Edw. III., 18. [9] 22 Edw. III., 7; 41 Edw. III., 6, 19.

There were two ways of proceeding with a person who was liable to *accompt.* One was, for the party to bring him to account before himself, or before auditors assigned by himself; the other was, by an original writ of *account* summoning him into court to make his account there. If a person took himself the account of his receivor or bailiff, who was found in arrears, he had no further remedy but an action of debt for these arrears: if the account was passed before auditors assigned, he might have his action of debt for the arrears, or proceed in a more summary way, by imprisonment under the stat. Westm. 2 c. xi.;[1] and the accountant, if falsely charged, might have his writ of *ex parte talis* to re-examine the account in the exchequer, as directed by that act.[2]

Of accompt.

If the plaintiff chose neither of these courses, or the party could not be brought to account, he might resort to the writ of account. The writ was thus: *Præcipe, &c., quòd justè, &c., reddat B. rationabile compotum suum de tempore quo fuit ballivus suus in C.*, or, *receptor denariorum ipsius B., &c.*[3] The following are specimens of declarations in account: *Ceo vous monstre, &c., A. that N. &c., wrongfully will not render him a reasonable accompt of the time that he was his bailiff in C.; and therefore wrongfully, for that whereas he was his bailiff of the manor of C., which was worth* £100 *per annum, having the administration of its stock—namely, oxen, cows, hogs, and sheep, and other chattels—from such a day and year to such a day and year, by reason of which the aforesaid A. often came to the aforesaid N. and requested him to render him an account of the issues arising from the said manor, which he refused, and still does,* A TORT ET A DAMAGES *of* £100. As receivor, *&c., Adam Pye, &c., that R. Fox, merchant, wrongfully will not render his reasonable account of the time he was receivor of the moneys of the said Adam; and therefore wrongfully, for that whereas the said R. on such a day, &c., received of the said Adam* £10 *to merchandise and improve for the use of the said Adam, he has merchandised with the said* £10, *and received the profits from the aforesaid day till such a day, without rendering any account thereof;*[4] *by reason of which the said Adam has frequently come to the said R. and prayed him to render an account of the same, &c.* Again, *And therefore wrongfully, for that whereas the aforesaid N. was the bailiff of the said A. from such day continually for a whole year to such a day, of the goods and chattels of the said A.—namely, of corn, grain, &c., to the value of ten marks, by reason of which the said A. often, &c.*[5]

This action was the common remedy in mercantile transactions, and in almost all cases where there were dealings and an unliquidated demand (*a*). The common way of charging the defendant

(*a*) This perhaps may be a convenient and proper place in which to mention a matter of considerable importance, which our author appears to have overlooked—viz., arbitration. The action of account, it will be observed, was a compulsory pro-

1 *Vide ante*, c. x. 2 O. N. B., 60. 3 *Ibid.*, 57 b. 4 SANS CEO QUE.
5 Nov. Narr.

was either as *bailee* or *resciever;* and some significant reasons were given why he should be charged in one or the other character. Where silver wares were bailed by the plaintiff to the defendant, to be sold, and he sold them, and received the money for them, it was said he should be charged as bailee, and not as receivor: the same where one employed a person to sell his wines.[1] Again, where herrings were intrusted to a man to sell, it was held the action should be against him as bailee, not as receivor; and the reason given was, that a receivor was allowed no costs, but a bailee was: therefore the defendant, who might have been obliged to go from one place to another to sell these articles, suffered an injustice, if he was declared against as a receivor of money where he would not be allowed his expenses.[2] But this action would lie against others than receivors and bailees. Where a lord had entered into lands as guardian in chivalry, and it was meant to try whether they were not socage, an action of account was brought against him *as occupier* for the profits he had received;[3] though perhaps, in this case, the proper idea was that of a *receivor*, which was an universal character that suited every one who had received money or profit to the use of another, for which he ought to account. Upon this principle it was that the following actions were supported. Two being possessed of an ox in common, and one having sold it, the other might have account against him: so where trees were cut by one who held *pro indiviso* with another.[4] If tenant by *elegit* committed waste, the remedy was a writ of accompt, and not waste.[5] Money was bailed to have a security of land given for it; if not, to be rebailed; upon no security being given, an action of accompt lay.[6] One joint lessee for years might have accompt against another, if he took the issues and profits to his own use; for he would otherwise be without remedy, as he could not have an assize. But one executor could not have account against the other, because they took nothing to their own use, and they were bound to account before the ordinary. If two guardians were in common, and one took the entire profits to his own use, accompt lay, and the count was to be against him as receivor to

cedure for the appointment of arbitrators or auditors, who were, in effect, arbitrators of matters of account; and it is a curious and instructive instance of the unchanging character of the exigencies arising out of the common affairs of life, and the good sense of our ancient institutions, that one of our latest improvements in civil procedure was the restitution of this old jurisdiction in account, by establishing a compulsory reference of matters of account to auditors or arbitrators; but from the earliest period voluntary references of matters in litigation to arbitrators was to the utmost encouraged, and if there was a reference in an action by order of the court, by consent it was enforced; though, in after times, great difficulties were raised, arising out of the interest the officers of courts had in fees, as to an award being a bar to an action on the same matter; and this, of course, greatly diminished the benefit of arbitration when the award was in favour of a defendant. On the other hand, when it was in favour of a plaintiff, difficulties were often raised from the same motive by arbitrary rules of law. For instance, in the reign of Henry IV., it was held that arbitrators could not make an award of *freehold*, so as to adjudge the land of one to another; although the arbitrament might perhaps be pleadable in bar of an action (*Year-book*, 14 *Henry IV.* 19.)

[1] 46 Edw. III., 3.
[2] *Ibid.* 9.
[3] 49 Edw. III., 10.
[4] 42 Edw. III., 22.
[5] Bro. Accompt, 36.
[6] 41 Edw. III., 7.

their common use: so of coparceners; but not so of tenants in common, for they might have an assize.[1] If a defendant was counted against as receivor, the plaintiff must allege by whose hands he received; but if he could not put this in certain, he might charge him as bailee, and then it would not be necessary.[2]

In this action there were two judgments: the first was *quòd computet*, upon which auditors were assigned; and after the account made, then came the final judgment for the arrears. As the writ was grounded upon a complaint that he refused to account, it was reasonable that *plenè computavit* should be a good plea to the action, and an account before the plaintiff would be sufficient.[3] He might plead *ne unque receivor*, or *ne unque receivor per main I. N.*, the person through whose hands the declaration alleged him to have received monies; that he was not bailiff to the plaintiff of such a manor, but lessee. He might plead a release of all receipts; he might plead nonage;[4] and if any of the above pleas were found against him, there would be a judgment *quòd computet.* He might plead *prist d'accompter;* and then there was of course the same judgment, and auditors would be assigned. Before the auditors he would be allowed to allege such matters as would go in discharge of himself. He might plead payment to the plaintiff without showing an acquittance.[5] Upon the judgment to account, there lay the process of *capias* and outlawry against the defendant, according to the stat. of Westm. 2.[6] It was held, that the first judgment was not such as could be revived by *scire facias* upon the death of the plaintiff before the account taken; nor could a writ of error be brought thereon; yet the plaintiff could not be nonsuited after it.[7] It was on the final judgment only that execution could be had. It was held, that where there were two defendants, and one was sued to outlawry and then taken, and the other not, the proceeding might be against him alone that was taken.[8]

An action of *covenant* was the common remedy where an indenture of agreement was sealed and properly executed by two parties, and one of them did not perform his part. This writ was always founded upon such a specialty; and the process was summons, attachment, and distress. The following is a specimen of a declaration upon a writ of covenant: *A tort, &c., wrongfully keeps not the covenant made between them, to maintain honourably the aforesaid Edward in living and clothing, as long as the one and the other lived; and therefore wrongfully, for that whereas on such a day, year, and place, a covenant was made between the aforesaid Matthew and Edward, by which the aforesaid Matthew granted by his deed here shown, to maintain honourably the said Edward in living and clothing, as long as the one and the other lived; and therefore wrongfully, for that whereas on such a day, year, and place, a covenant was made between the aforesaid Matthew and Edward,*

[1] 49 Edw. III., 27. [2] 43 Edw. III., 21. [3] 41 Edw. III., 3, 9; 45 Edw. III., 14.
[4] 49 Edw. III., 10; 21 Edw. III., 8; 24 Edw. III., 32, 67; 10 Edw. III., 7.
[5] 41 Edw. III., 25. [6] *Vide ante*, c. x. [7] 21 Edw. III., 9, 32. 42 Ass., 11.
[8] 41 Edw. III., 9.

by which the aforesaid Matthew granted by his deed here shewn, to maintain honourably the said Edward in living and clothing as long as the one and the other lived; yet the said Matthew the aforesaid Edward according to the form of the aforesaid covenant maintains not; by reason of which he has often come to him, and prayed him to keep this covenant according to the form of the writing aforesaid, but he would not, nor yet will, a TORT, *&c.*[1]

A writ of covenant was that upon which fines were most commonly levied. In such case, the declaration was, A TORT, *and wrongfully keeps not his* FINE *made in the court of, &c. &c.*, unless the covenant to convey had been made out of court, and then it was termed a mere covenant. Indeed, in most cases, there was not actually a previous fine or covenant, but the writ of covenant was brought upon such *supposed* transaction; and, being an amicable proceeding, it passed of course without inquiry, and was afterwards maintained for the assurance of estates, and the quiet of property. These were called covenants *real;* the writ of covenant in this instance having the effect of actually transferring the land, and so producing a *specific* effect. Other writs of covenant were said to be *personal*, because damages only were recovered for the breach of them. There was one instance in which a doubt seems to have arisen, whether this writ was real or personal. We have seen, that a writ of covenant[2] was the remedy which a termor for years had against his lessor when ejected, and that the *quare ejecit infra terminum* was contrived in aid of this writ. However, it was still held, that where a lessor ousted his lessee, the latter might in covenant recover both his term and damages; and if the term was expired, he would recover the whole in damages.[3] In the 38th year, when it was said that a term should be recovered in covenant, it was denied by Thorpe and Skip, who said the plaintiff should recover only damages;[4] though by a case in the 47th year it should seem, the general opinion was, that in covenant by the lessee against the lessor, he should recover his term.[5]

Another point of debate in covenant was, whether the obligation and benefit of such agreements descended on the representatives of the covenanters and covenantees respectively. It was clearly held, that an executor was not bound to perform a covenant, if the covenantor had not bound his executors expressly; for covenants only bind those who make them, and not their heirs or executors, unless named[6] (*a*). But where land was let to one *habendum* to him and his

(*a*) The law upon the subject has long since been settled by the statute of distributions (*Charles II.*), which substantially legalises and establishes the ancient customs in cases of intestacy; and there can be no doubt that, but for the narrow rule of law, that an action will not lie for what is matter of trust, however clear and plain, an action might be maintained against an administrator for the reasonable share after payment of debts. As it is, the remedy is in equity by an administration suit, in which accounts are taken of debts and assets, and the residue, if any, is divided among the next of kin according to the statute, and upon the general principle established by ancient custom.

[1] Nov. Narr., 44 b. [2] *Vide ante*, vol. i. c. vii. [3] 26 Edw. III. Fitz. Cov. 3.
[4] 38 Edw. III., 24. [5] 47 Edw. III., 24. [6] 48 Edw. III., 1.

assigns for years, it was said that the assigns might have an action of covenant against the lessor, even though they were not named in the deed.[1] And where one brought an action of covenant as heir against an abbot for not performing service in the manor-chapel, and it was objected he had an elder brother, and so was not heir; it was agreed by the court, that if he was *terre-tenant* it was sufficient, and he might have the action without the privity of heir, because it was a covenant that went along with the land. Again, where, upon a partition between parceners, one covenanted to discharge the other from all suits, it was held, an alienee should have covenant if he was not discharged.[2] And this seems to have been the principle upon which representatives might claim the benefit of, or be liable to, covenants, namely, if such covenants were attached to, and dependent upon, the land which they enjoyed.

The action of *replevin* might be prosecuted either before the sheriff or *in banco*. If in the latter, this action might be in two ways; either by original writ at common law, or by *pone*, according to stat. 1 Westm. 2, c. ii.[3] The following is a specimen of a declaration *in banco: Ceo vous monstre, &c., that D., &c., wrongfully took the cattle, &c., namely, &c., such a day, year, and place, and chased them to his house, and there impounded them, and them so impounded detained from such a day to such a day then next ensuing, when deliverance was made by John, &c., a bailiff of our lord the king, sworn and known, &c., à tort et à damages, &c.*[4] The process in this action was summons, attachment, and distress. If the sheriff could not find the cattle to make replevin, we have seen that, in Bracton's time, he was to take some of the defendant's cattle; and if the defendant had no land or chattels, then he was to be personally attached. The same course still obtained, only some new terms had been adopted: the cattle so removed were said to be *eloigned;* and upon the sheriff returning the *averia elongata*, there issued a process to take the defendants, called *capias in withernam;* and if that failed, there went a *capias* against the person.[5] With these immaterial alterations in expression, the proceeding in replevin stood upon the foot of the practice in Bracton's time, and the statutes of Edward I. The requisites to this action are said to be six; 1st, very tenant; 2d, very lord; 3d, services; 4th, arrear at the day of taking; 5th, seisin of the service; 6th, within his fee.[6] As the defendant in his avowry was to set forth his title to make the distress, the obliging him to allege *seisin* kept the inquiry within bounds, and prevented a debate upon the *right*, which was not to be decided by any trial but the duel of great assize, neither of which could be had in this action. The seisin had been limited by the stat. Westm. 2,[7] to the time allowed for bringing an assize. Thus every question of title that might be agitated in a writ of novel disseisin, might be brought forward by

[1] Bro. Cov., 45. [2] 42 Edw. III., 3. [3] *Vide ante*, cc. ix. x.
[4] Nov. Narr., 62 b. [5] 43 Edw. III., 26. [6] O. N. B., 41 b.
[7] *Vide ante*, c. x.

a writ of replevin, but with a different effect; as the former only gave the seisin of the distress, the latter the seisin of the land. However, it naturally followed, that many titles to real property were tried in replevin. The process upon the writ of *recaption* was the same as that upon the *pone* and replevin. There was a writ *de catallis nomine districtionis captis reddendis,* which could only be maintained within a borough, where it was the custom to take the doors, windows, or grates, in the way of distress.[1]

Before we take our leave of this action, we should notice a replevin of a particular sort, the writ *de homine replegiando*. This lay where a man was imprisoned, but was by law replevisable; a writ, therefore, for his being replevied issued to the sheriff to the following effect: *Præcipimus tibi, quòd justè et sine dilatione replegiari facias A. quem B. cepit, et captum tenuit* (or, *quem B. cepit, et tu captum tenes*, as the case might be) *nisi captus sit per speciale præceptum nostrum, vel capitalis justitiarii nostri, vel pro morte hominis, vel pro aliquo alio facto, quare secundum consilium regni nostri Angliæ non sit replegiabilis, &c.* This writ was a justicies, and not returnable. If the sheriff did not obey this writ, there issued a *sicut alias*, or *causom nobis significes*, and then a *pluries;* and if the sheriff still disobeyed, then an attachment followed against the sheriff, directed to the coroners, who were also to see the first writ executed.[2]

The action of *trespass* became in this reign still more general than in the former; and though simple in its first origin, it was by construction and legal intendment rendered applicable to an infinitude of cases where an injury was done, either to the person or property. The manner of declaring upon this writ was rather general, without stating much particularity of circumstances. The following are some examples of declarations, &c. *Wrongfully came, such a day, &c., and vi et armis, namely, &c., the aforesaid N. took and imprisoned, and in prison him detained from such a day to such a day, on which he was delivered by the king's writ; and other harms, &c., namely, &c.,* A TORT, *and against the peace of our lord the king, &c.* For various trespasses: *Ceo vous monstre, A. &c., that C., &c., such a day, year, and place, came with force and arms, namely, &c., in the part of the aforesaid A., at J., in the said county, and there entered, and therein being without his license and will, six deer chased and took, and his trees there growing, namely, &c., of the value of* 10 *marks, cut; and in his several fishery fished, and his fish, namely, &c., of the value, &c., took and carried away, and other injuries to him did,* à tort et à damages, *&c., and against the king's peace.*[3]

When this writ was brought for a trespass on land, it led to a justification upon a title, like the avowry in replevin: but this happened very rarely, it not being so usual to bring on questions

[1] O. N. B., 73. [2] *Vide* stat. Westm. 1, ch. xv.; *vide ante*, c. x.; O. N. B., 40.
[3] Nov. Narr., 74 b., 66 b.

upon titles in this as in the writ of replevin. When a title was set out in this action by the defendant, it was not necessary for the plaintiff to do the same, but merely to deny or traverse the defendant's supposed title; the plaintiff, as he was in possession, was presumed to have a right to that possession, and therefore the law would not put him to state it specially.[1] Thus, where right of common was pleaded, the plaintiff only replied, *de son tort demesne, sans ceo qui il ad common, prist, &c.*[2] Where a defendant justified as taking possession under the escheator, the reply was, *a votre oeps demesne sans tiel cause.*[3] The same idea prevailed in other writs of trespass that did not relate to land; and the defendant, as a wrong-doer, was expected to make out a justification, when called upon by the plaintiff who had sustained the injury.

The principal and most common actions of trespass now in use were three; namely, those for an injury to the person, as for battery or assault; those for taking goods, that is, a *cepit et asportavit*; and those for entering land or a house, or, as it has been since called, a *clausum fregit.* In order to understand the notions now entertained concerning these actions, we shall consider some cases applicable to each of these heads, beginning first with *battery.*

Actions for a battery were usually laid with an assault also; *insultum fecit, et ipsum verberavit, vulneravit, et malè tractavit, &c.* In the twenty-second year, a jury found that the defendant struck at the plaintiff with a hatchet, but did not hit him; and they prayed the discretion of the court as to the law upon the point, when the damages were ordered to be taxed for the assault only, and the judgment against the defendant was *capiatur.*[4] Again, where a defendant was found guilty of the assault, but not guilty of the battery, the plaintiff recovered damages for the former, and was amerced for the latter.[5] Thus an assault began to be considered as a distinct and independent cause of action. The day on which the battery and assault were laid began to be considered as of no consequence; for where a battery was found to be on the day, and on a day after, and even where they found it on another day, it was held sufficient to support the declaration.[6] It was esteemed a good justification in assault and battery to say that the plaintiff was in a rage, and the defendant only restrained him from doing mischief.[7] If a person had recovered damages in an appeal of mayhem, this was looked upon as a recompence only for the wounding, and he might afterwards have an action for the battery.[8] However, in an action of battery, the plaintiff might give in evidence a mayhem,[9] as he was not to be deprived of redress for the mayhem, though he chose to resort to an inferior remedy. If a wife was beat, an action of battery lay for the husband and wife; and though the husband only would have the damages recovered,

[1] 40 Edw. III., 5. [2] 22 Ass., 42. [3] *Ibid.* 57. [4] *Ibid.* 60.
[5] 40 Edw. III., 40. [6] 39 Edw. III., 1; 45 Edw. III., 24. [7] 22 Ass., 57.
[8] *Ibid.*, 82; 43 Ass., 39. [9] 39 Edw. III., 20.

yet, being originally a redress to which the wife was entitled, it might be laid *ad damnum ipsorum.*[1] An action of battery would lie for the master against any one who beat his servant.[2] An action of *vie et armis* would lie also for the taking away of his servant,[3] and *à fortiori* for taking away his villein; but if any one married a female villein, and afterwards took her away, the lord had no remedy *vi et armis* against the husband.[4] A man might have trespass for taking away his eldest son.[5] These were properly trespasses on a *cepit et asportavit;* as was that *de uxore abductâ cum bonis viri,* in which it was held to be no plea to say that the plaintiff was divorced from his wife; for the action was for damages, which should equally be recovered if they were married at the time.[6] However, it was agreed that where two were married before years of consent, the husband could not have this action till he had arrived at such age, and they had assented or dissented from the marriage.[7]

When trespass was brought for goods, it sometimes became a question what should be construed a *taking*, and what a taking *vi et armis.* A defendant pleaded that the goods were thrown into the sea in a storm, and he took them, and when he came to land he gave them the plaintiff's servant to his use; and this was held a bar of the taking and trespass.[8] One tenant in common might have trespass of another of things severed from the land, as corn, hay, and the like; but not of things fixed to the freehold, for then they might have waste *pro indiviso.*[9] Yet, where goods were left to an executor, and another to distribute, it was held that trespass could not lie for the one against the other.[10] Again, though an heir might have a detinue of charters against an executor, he could not have trespass.[11] The *primâ facie* right was held to privilege such persons from the imputation of trespassors. Where a person, acting under authority of law, any ways abused that authority, he became a trespassor. As in trespass for taking and killing the plaintiff's horse *contra pacem,* the defendant justified as taking it *damage feasant*, and impounding; and because it had leaped several times over the pound, he tied it, and *so* the horse strangled itself; which plea was held ill upon demurrer.[12]

When the writ was for breaking a house, or entering land, the plaintiff was not to allege a *continuance* of the trespass, because it was a single act: but where it was for depasturing grass, and the like, it might be laid with a *continuando.*[13] There was long time a doubt how far this action would lie for a lessee against his lessor, and the contrary. This being for a trespass *vi et armis,* was thought not to lie against the lessor, though he had been guilty of violating his lessee's possession, in direct opposition to his own

1 46 Edw. III., 3. 2 39 Edw. III., 1. 3 39 Edw. III., 37. 4 46 Edw. III., 6.
5 29 Ass., 35. 6 23 Edw. III., 23; *vide ante*, c. xi. 7 Bro. Tresp., 420.
8 46 Edw. III., 15. 9 21 Edw. III., 9, 20. 10 27 Ass., 64.
11 43 Edw. III., 24. 12 27 Ass., 64. 13 46 Ass., 9.

lease. This was upon the idea of the lessor's freehold,[1] and the right he had of entering upon any part of it; while the lessee was construed to have a precarious possession, that made him little more than bailiff to his lessor. But the opinion of a farmer's interest was now altered, and the plea of freehold had long been disregarded; therefore, where a lessor distrained, or did any other act upon the land which in the case of a common person would be trespass, the lessee for years might have trespass *vi et armis*.[2] On the other hand, where in a lease to one for life there was a reservation of certain trees; which trees the tenant cut: there it was held, that trespass *vi et armis* would lie by the lessor against the lessee for cutting the trees.[3] Trespass was a remedy grounded upon the actual possession of the plaintiff; therefore it was a rule, wherever a person was any way put out of possession, he could not maintain trespass till he had made a re-entry.[4]

Respecting trespass in general; it had long been held, that there were no accessaries in trespass, but all were principals; and therefore, that a person, by assenting afterwards to a trespass committed, was liable to an action.[5] A writ of trespass, as it was for a wrong done, was to be brought against the wrong-doers individually, and therefore it would not lie against a corporation, against which no *capias* could issue:[6] and it was agreed, that more trespasses than one might be joined in one writ. It was a common plea in trespass for hunting, to say, that the defendant had licence.[7] In all actions of trespass, any matter stated as a recompense to the plaintiff might be pleaded in discharge; as, recovery in another action; amercement in an inferior court;[8] that he had *agreed* with the plaintiff for the trespass;[9] or even such as was only in a course of giving the plaintiff satisfaction, namely, that an action of replevin was depending for the same taking.[10] An officer might justify in trespass under the process of a court, however erroneous; but not so, if the cause of action arose without the limits of the court's jurisdiction.[11]

Of actions on the case.

But not content with the writ of trespass in its old form, they endeavoured to make it more universal, by enlarging its scope, and modifying its terms, so as to adapt it to every man's *own case;* in doing which they availed themselves of the statute of Westm. 2, authorising writs to be framed *in consimili casû*.[12] This novelty did not show itself till towards the middle of this reign; and when it appeared in court, it underwent a discussion and debate that indicated great doubt about the propriety and nature of the innovation.

The first case of this sort, to be found in the reports, is in the 22d year (*a*); when an action was brought against a man, for that

(*a*) This is a mistake. There are cases of the "action sur le case" in the Year-

1 *Vide ante*, c. xii., &c. 2 48 Edw. III., 5, 6, 7; *vide ante*, c. ix.
3 46 Edw. III., 22. 4 44 Edw. III., 18. 5 38 Edw. III., 18. 30 Ass., 6.
6 22 Ass., 67. 7 42 Edw. III., 1, 2. 8 47 Edw. III., 19. 9 22 Ass., 51.
10 38 Edw. III., 35. 11 22 Ass., 64. 12 *Vide ante*, c. xii.

he had undertaken to carry the plaintiff's horse in his boat over the Humber, safe and well; but that he overloaded his boat with other horses, by which overloading the plaintiff's horse perished, *à tort et à damages, &c.* It was objected to this writ, that it supposed no *tort* in the defendant, but on the other hand proved the plaintiff should rather have a writ of covenant. But it was said by one of the judges, that the defendant committed, as it should seem, a trespass in overloading the boat, by which his horse perished, and that the action would lie.[1] Thus the notion of a trespass, or a *malfeasance*, was the principle upon which the application of this new remedy was explained, and justified, even in this instance, which seems to approach nearer to the nature of a contract.

It was taking the idea of trespass in a very large sense, to consider this and some writs which follow to be at all allied to it. From this time to the 42d year, we find mention of several actions, and *dicta* concerning remedies, which could be no other than actions formed upon the special *case* of the party, without including any trespass, except of the vague kind above supposed. It was said that should a contract be made between two men, that one should give the other £10 in case he would marry his daughter, an action would lie for the money.[2] This action could not be such an one as we have hitherto in the course of this History met with; for covenant, which seems the only writ applicable to such a case, would not lie but upon a deed: it must therefore have been a special writ upon the case. We find several of the same kind: an action against a sheriff for quashing the plaintiff's essoin in a plea of replevin before him, without the assent of the suitors:[3] an action against a sheriff for a false return of summons;[4] for directing a wrong officer to summon a panel, which was therefore quashed:[5] an action of slander for calling the plaintiff traitor, felon, and robber;[6] an action against a man because he took certain cattle from another, and offered them to sale to the plaintiff as his own, who, confiding in his word, bought them, and they were afterwards taken from him by the true owner:[7] all these were actions of a new form; those against the sheriff being writs of *deceit upon the case* (mentioned under that name in the old *Natura Brevium*) introduced in the room of the writ of deceit which has been mentioned before, and were merely for the purpose of recovering damages against the sheriff. Two of them were such for which the old law provided no remedy, matters of scandal being wholly of spiritual cognizance; and the last being within the scope of none of the common-law writs which we have met with in former reigns.

book Edward II., and one or two earlier than that here mentioned in that of Edward I. There can be no doubt that this class of actions had originated in the statute of *consimili casu* of Edward I., and had been gradually gaining ground ever since.

[1] 22 Ass., 41. [2] *Ibid.*, 70. [3] 26 Ass., 45. [4] *Ibid.*, 48.
[5] 38 Ass., 13. [6] 30 Ass., 29. [7] 42 Ass., 8.

The same may be said of the following: *Trespass* (says the Report) was brought against an innkeeper and his servant; upon which the plaintiff counted, that whereas it was a custom and usage through all the realm of England, that in all common inns the innkeeper and his servants should take good care of what things their guests had in their chamber in the inn, the plaintiff came to the defendant's inn, and left certain things in his chamber there; and while he was gone out, some persons came and took them away, through the neglect of the defendant and his servants, *per tort, et enconter les peas*, and to the damage of the plaintiff, &c., and he had (says the Report) a writ upon the whole matter *according to his case;* and the action was held good.[1]

In the foregoing cases there was no debate upon the form of the action; in the following some few objections were started, which serve to give a better idea of the notion they then entertained of these special writs. An action of trespass was brought against a farrier, for that being employed to shoe the plaintiff's horse, *quare clavum fixit in pede equi sui in certo loco per quod proficuum equi sui per longum tempus amissit, &c.* To this writ it was objected, that it was in trespass, and yet was not laid *vi et armis.* It was answered, that the plaintiff's writ was according *to his case*, and therefore good; and though it was still urged that the writ should say *vi et armis*, or *malitiosè fixit*, and if any trespass was done, it ought to be *against the peace*, yet the writ was held good.[2]

This seemed to be giving up the idea of trespass entirely. But notwithstanding this reasoning, we find the name was still preserved; for, two years afterwards, there is a report of a writ of *trespass sur son case* brought by a man against a surgeon, much upon the same ground as that just mentioned. The writ stated, that the plaintiff's right hand had been hurt, and the defendant undertook to cure it; but by the negligence of the defendant, and his want of care, his hand was made so much worse, as to become a mayhem, *à tort et à ses damages*, and the writ was neither *vi et armis*, nor *contra pacem.* However, this was held good, and treated as an action of trespass: and yet, because it did not allege force and arms, and *contra pacem*, it was considered, so far, as differing from trespass, properly so called; and for that reason it was the opinion of one of the justices, that the defendant should be admitted to wage his law.[3]

The following is termed by the Reporter trespass *upon the case*, and yet is laid *vi et armis*, and *contra pacem.* It was brought against a miller, and the writ charged, *quòd cùm prædictus Johannes, &c., et antecessores sui à tempore cujus memoria non existit, molere debuerunt sine multurâ, &c., prædictus defendens, &c., prædictum querentem sine multurâ molere vi et armis impedivit, &c.* Upon this the plaintiff declared, that when he came

[1] 42 Edw. III., 13. [2] 46 Edw. III., 19 pl. [3] 48 Edw. III., 15.

to have his corn ground, the defendant took two bushels, &c., with force and arms. It was objected to this, that as the plaintiff, in his declaration, stated that the defendant *took toll*, he might have had a general writ of *cepit et asportavit* his corn with force and arms, and not this special writ. To this it was answered, that surely the plaintiff, if he had sustained an injury, was entitled to a remedy applicable to his case. But the court decided, that as he must have brought a general writ if all his corn had been taken, so he must if part was; and therefore it was held that this writ was not good.[1] However, about three years afterwards the same writ was held good.[2] Again, we find an action of trespass against a woman for burning the plaintiff's house with force and arms. There was no debate upon the form of the writ, though the jury found that the house was burnt by negligence, and not with force and arms, or malice, and that the house in question was rented by the woman from the plaintiff, from year to year.[3]

From the foregoing instances it appears not to have been well agreed when the proper remedy was a general common law writ of trespass, and when a special writ; nor again, when a special writ should be laid *vi et armis*, and when not. These were difficulties in this new remedy, which were left to be settled by the refined notions that obtained in after-times upon this subject. The great motive to inserting *vi et armis* was, that the plaintiff became thereby entitled to process of *capias*, and the defendant could not wage his law; whereas in a writ not containing that suggestion, there lay only *distringas*, and the defendant might wage his law.

Proceedings by bill, &c.

Thus far of particular actions: we shall next speak of the proceeding and process, which were more or less applicable to all the foregoing writs. Whatever conjectures may be formed concerning the origin of proceedings *by bill*, it is beyond all question that actions were brought in this way during all this reign, and the books are full of them. But we are not enabled to pronounce upon the nature and properties of this new method, as no debate arose upon it. We can only say, that they proceeded by bill on all the three courts, of king's bench, common pleas, and exchequer; that the bill begun *A. queritur de B., &c.*, and went on as a common writ; nor does it appear, from any of the cases reported, that in bills in the king's bench there was any mention of the custody of the marshal. If that was the ground of jurisdiction, it was so understood, and not thought necessary to be alleged. The bills in the exchequer are in general against sheriffs, who may be considered as privileged persons, in the light of king's officers. The bills in the common pleas were sometimes for and against attorneys. There is one brought *qui tam pro domino rege quâm pro seipso;* and was for an assault by a person, who, being plaintiff in an action in that court, was, while bringing a writing thither to prove his case, attached by the defendant.[4] This being a

[1] 44 Edw. III., 20. [2] 44 Edw. III., 20. [3] 48 Edw. III., 25. [4] 30 Ass., 14.

contempt of the king's peace and justice, might for that reason be considered as the subject of an action in that form. It was laid down, that a person might have an appeal by bill in the king's bench of any matter that touched the king, whether mediately or immediately.[1] For further information on this subject, we must wait till we arrive at later times, when they began to speak more plainly about the commencing of actions by bill, and the extent of this privilege was explained upon certain and settled rules.

There was another course by which matters used to be commenced or forwarded in court, which was by *surmise* or *suggestion.* In one sense of these terms, (and the original one,) in all probability, nothing more was meant than a verbal application, praying that process might issue for carrying on a suit already commenced; and in that sense we frequently meet, in the Reports of this reign, with a *suggestion to the court.*[2] But there certainly was in the exchequer an original commencement of a suit, as has been mentioned in another place, by a mere verbal surmise or suggestion;[3] and though this was sometimes disputed in the case of common persons, yet it was still held to be the course of that court, and, in the case of the king, was not attempted to be withstood.[4] This was the shape in which that proceeding first showed itself, which afterwards grew into an *information.*

Of pleading.

Pleading in causes was carried on through great part of this reign much in the way in which it was described in the former period (*a*); but it is said,[5] that about the middle of this reign it became the practice to draw up the declaration and pleas out of court, and deliver them in writing to the prothonotary, from whom the adverse party received a copy, to enable him to give in his plea in answer. The book entitled *Novæ Narrationes* is

(*a*) It is most important to bear in mind that, during this age, as the pleading was only oral, upon any objection taken at the bar by reason of demurrer, the other party could at once discuss it, and, if he saw any ground for it, demand his pleading; and it was only if both parties insisted upon the point—one on his pleading, and the other on his objection—that they remained in judgment, as it was called, and even then, before judgment, either party could withdraw his pleading (*Bellewe's Cases, temp. Rich. II.*, fol. 131). It was only when the parties remained in judgment that the demurrer was entered (*Keilway*, 81). It is evident therefore that the rules of pleading might well, under such a system, be safely enforced, for the judgment could never be given upon the pleading unless it was really material. The author, following Gilbert, supposes that the ancient practice was changed in this reign, but it appears by the case cited from *Bellewe's Reports* that it was not so; and all through the Year-books of this and ensuing reigns there is no trace of any alteration of the practice, but pleading went on orally at the bar, either party amending upon any objection made, if he elected so to do at the time; and if ever pleadings were put into writing, it could only have been when the parties either "remained in judgment" on demurrer, or, on the other hand, when they had "pleaded to issue;" and of course the record was made up for *nisi prius.* It would indeed have been idle to reduce the pleadings to writing until they were finally settled, either on a demurrer or an issue of fact, the pleading being undoubtedly oral, in the first instance, all through the Year-books, up to the reign of Henry VIII. But no doubt when the parties had agreed as to their pleading, the prothonotaries entered then of record, and to that end required each party to present his pleading in writing.

[1] 17 Ass., 5. [2] *Passim.* [3] *Vide ante*, c. xiv.
[4] 40 Ass., 35. [5] Gilbert's *Orig. of King's Bench.*

adduced as a confirmation of such conjecture. But this seems to give little credit to a conjecture otherwise without foundation. There appears nothing in the Reports of this reign to assure us of any such alterations; for they state the pleading on both sides in the same manner as the Reports of the time of Edward II., as though they were debated *vivâ voce* in court. Yet it cannot be denied, that, towards the latter part of this king's time, pleading was brought to more certainty and system than it had before exhibited; such as it was natural should follow from the deliberation with which proceedings might be penned when drawn out of court. It is therefore truly said by Sir Matthew Hale, that pleadings were now somewhat more polished than in the former reign, without running into uncertainty, prolixity, or obscurity.[1] The putting of pleadings into writing was the first step towards the refinement and subtlety affected by pleaders in after-times; though at present they went no further than was necessary to bring the matter in question before the court with due clearness and precision.

Sufficient has been said, in speaking of different actions, to give some idea of the state of pleading at this period: what remains to be added will be very short and general. It seems that in the beginning of this reign the order of pleading to the count before the writ began to obtain in practice; for it is said in the 4th year that after *oyer* of the writ, (which was necessary previous to its being pleaded to,) the defendant should not plead to the count;[2] and though afterwards[3] the contrary was permitted, yet a few years after, namely, in the 30th year, it seems to have been settled in the following way: that a defendant should plead first to the jurisdiction, then to the person of the plaintiff or defendant, then to the count, then to the writ, and lastly to the action.[4] There might be reasons of convenience and propriety which contributed to establish this course. When pleadings were put into writing, it was natural that the count should become more strict and formal; and, as it contained the substance of the writ, it was sufficiently full and explicit to become the first object of criticism to the defendant, as the writ had been in earlier times;[5] the defendant therefore in his defence was expected first to take notice of that, or entirely to waive all objections to it.

The fashion of these times was to state special matter of justification or title in almost all actions, and to avoid as much as possible the general issue: this led to much vying and revying on both sides. Perhaps this arose from the nature of assizes and real actions, which, being special in their form and for the trial of some title, necessarily called upon the parties to be particular in their pleadings: the personal actions in use naturally partook of the prevailing taste; not to mention that in trespass and replevin some question of title was very often litigated.

[1] *Hist. Com. Law*, 173.
[2] 4 Edw. III., 133, 134.
[3] 24 Edw. III., 35, 47.
[4] *Thel. Dig.*, lib. 10, c. i., 21.
[5] *Vide ante*, vol. ii. c. xii.

The *secta* and law-wager.

We have seen in the preceding reign,[1] that the practice of examining the *secta* of the plaintiff had ceased, though they still continued to be produced; but since they had thus become almost useless, it may be doubted whether now they continued even to be produced; at least, there is no mention of the *secta* all through this reign; though the formal conclusion of declarations by *inde producit sectam*, as it was still used, preserved a remembrance of the old practice. The *secta*, however, were still produced by a defendant, who waged his law, though it may be presumed they were never examined, as the only object of such examination had formerly been to confront them, and weigh their evidence against that of the plaintiff's *secta*.

The law-wager did not seem to be settled upon such fixed principles as to leave no doubt about the instances where it should and where it should not be allowed. We find some difference of opinion upon this point. The state in which this piece of old law stood in this reign will be better understood from a short view of some adjudged cases.

We have before seen that a defendant was not permitted to wage his law against an obligation. However, though he could not deny the obligation, and the debt grounded thereon, in this way, he was allowed, in an action upon a deed, the privilege of waging his law of non-summons, and the like, in the same manner as had long been used.[2] The following are some instances of law-wager. In accompt, the defendant said that he gave the plaintiff a statute for the debt, and a tunnel of wine for the damages; to which the plaintiff replied that he never received them, and tendered his law, which was received;[3] the issue being considered as in the nature of the general issue in detinue, where the law-wager was the common trial. In an action of accompt, where the receipt was alleged to be by the hands of another, the law-wager was allowed;[4] the same also in debt upon the arrear of an account.[5]

In detinue of charters law-wager was allowed,[6] notwithstanding it was urged that charters being things relating to the freehold, ought to take the action out of the common course, like an obligation upon which an action of debt was founded. In another action, some years after, for detaining charters, this matter was argued again, and a difference seems to have been taken between a *general* declaration of charters and one that specified the charters detained, upon which the plaintiff had leave to amend; and, after specifying the charters, the defendant was forced to plead to the country.[7] This, however, was of a bailment to the predecessor of the defendant, who was dean of a church, which was an additional reason for putting it to the country.

It was held that law-wager should not lie in debt for recovery of

[1] *Vide ante*, c. xii.
[2] 28 Edw. III., 100 a; 29 Edw. III., 44 b.
[3] 30 Edw. III., 4 b.
[4] 47 Edw. III., 18.
[5] 49 Edw. III., 3; 43 Edw. III., 1 a.
[6] 38 Edw. III., 7 a.
[7] 44 Edw. III., 41 b.

rent, because it was connected with the realty.[1] The rent in this case consisted not in money, but in corn and other things; and the action was laid, not in debt, but as for a *detinet* of those articles, upon which ground it was that the defendant offered his law-wager, and upon the above reason it was refused.

In an attachment upon a prohibition, the defendant was not suffered to wage his law; for it was said that suing in the spiritual court was a trespass and contempt of the king's writ and authority, and in such case no wager at law could be allowed.[2] Notwithstanding this determination it was allowed in a subsequent case, though in another they returned back to the first resolution, and so settled the law.[3] Indeed it was held generally that no defendant could wage his law against the king,[4] for which reason it was never allowed in the court of exchequer. It was held, that where a testator might wage his law his executors might also.[5]

Trial by proofs, and other trials.

The trial by *proofs*, which is so often mentioned in Glanville and Bracton,[6] continued still in use, though its application was extremely circumscribed (*a*). It seems to have been resorted to only in such cases where the matter could not, by construction of law, be supposed to be within the knowledge of the *pais* or country. The most common instances we meet with of this trial were, where the husband was alleged to be alive in another county. Thus, in an assize brought by a woman, *quæ fuit uxor B.*, the tenant said that B. was alive in another county, and he was ready to *prove* it, that is, to put it on the trial by proofs. To this it was answered by the other side, that this amounted to the issue of *covert baron*, which was triable by the assize; therefore they prayed the assize might pass. But it was the opinion of the court, that this point had formerly been always tried by *proof*, and so it must continue; yet, they said, had the assize been brought without the plaintiff alleging *quæ fuit uxor B.* it would have been otherwise. If the deed of an ancestor was pleaded, and it was contended on the other side that such ancestor was alive in another county, or beyond sea, it was the opinion of some that this should be tried by the assize, and not by *proofs*.[7] In an assize against baron and feme the baron did not appear, but the wife did, and pleaded the death of the baron in a foreign county; upon which the plaintiff prayed the assize, without alleging the baron to be alive in the first county; but this creating a difficulty the justices

(*a*) Trial by witnesses was applicable, anciently, to an issue arising on the death of the husband in an action of dower; and in some other cases (*Abbot of Strata-Marcella's case*, 9 *Rep.* 30 b.; *Grace Faux* v. *Barnes*, *Lord Raym*, 174). In dower, if tenant pleads that the husband is still living, the trial shall not be by jury, but witnesses (1 *Bulst.*, 131). In case of trial by witnesses, the court upon issue of writ orders that both parties produce in court, at a given day, their respective witnesses. The judges examine and decide, and the judgment is pronounced accordingly. On this trial the affirmative must be proved by two witnesses at least (3 *Blo. Com.* 336).

1 50 Edw. III., 16 b. 2 18 Edw. III., 4 a. 3 24 Edw. III., 39 a; 44 Edw. III., 32.
4 50 Edw. III., 1. 5 29 Edw. III., 36 b., 37 a.
6 *Vide*, vol. i. c. iv. v. vi.; and *ante*, c. x. xi. 7 36 Ass., 5.

adjourned it to Westminster, where it was adjudged that it should be tried by *proofs*.[1] Again, in an appeal in the king's bench, by a woman for the death of her husband, in the county of B., the defendant said that he was alive in the county of N., and they had a day given them to bring their *proofs* on both sides; one to prove the death, the other the life of the party.[2] This trial in appeal was considered as peremptory; and therefore, if there was a doubt of succeeding, they would withdraw that plea, and plead the general issue, not guilty.[3]

The foregoing trials were all upon one point. The following was of another sort. In an assize there arose the issue, whether the priory of D. was donative and removable, or perpetual; and the Reporter says, it should seem this ought to be tried by the assize, and not by *proofs*, because it lay in the knowledge of the *pais* whether the priors had enjoyed the land all their lives, and acted as lawful owners all that time; but it was said by Percy that as the prior was a prior alien, and the chief priory was beyond sea, it should be tried by *proofs*.[4] It may be observed, that the formal words by which a party signified that he meant to make out what he asserted *per pais*—namely, that he was ready to *verify* it—seemed to import a higher confidence in this decision than in any other; and again, while the evidence of proofs could no more than *prove* the matter on one side and the other, the determination of the jury was called *veredictum*, that is, as it should seem, a verity not to be controverted.

There were other methods of inquiry, which might be called trials *per proves*, and were the remains of the old jurisprudence. A recovery by default in dower on a *petit cape* was pleaded in an assize, and the plaintiff said the land in question was not comprised in that recovery. This was to be tried by the summoners and viewers in the first action; and if it had been upon a *grande cape*, then by the summoners, viewers, and pernors.[5] In other cases, where land was to be identified, there was a mixed trial, consisting partly of the *pais* and partly of proofs; as where, in an assize, there arose an issue whether the land in question was extended, and put in execution under a statute merchant, there process was awarded against the extendors to be joined with the assize to try the issue.[6] Where a recovery was pleaded in a former assize before the same justices, and the plaintiff said they were not the same tenements, he put himself to prove it *per primos juratores et per alios,* and it was tried in that manner.[7] This trial by the former jurors and by others was very common where a former recovery was in question.[8] The practice of joining the witnesses in a deed to the pannel of jurors was very ancient, and continued still in use, as will be seen presently.

Another mode of trial was by the certificate of the bishop, who

[1] 39 Ass., 9. [2] 41 Ass., 5. [3] 43 Ass., 26. [4] *Ibid.* 4.
[5] 48 Edw. III., 11. [6] 31 Ass., 6. [7] 22 Ass., 16. [8] 40 Ass., 4

had cognizance in certain questions of a supposed spiritual nature. Much debate had been occasioned by the contests about spiritual jurisdiction between the lay and ecclesiastical courts. When the grand bounds of these two tribunals were settled by parliament, and by long usage, there apparently still remained disputes about terms, which led into many subtle explanations and artificial distinctions. Though it was beyond all question, that, in cases of general bastardy, matrimony, profession, divorce, and the like, the court christian was to determine; yet it was held that even those points might be brought into debate in such a way as to draw the cognizance of them from the spiritual to the lay tribunal. It depended therefore upon the pleading and the form of the issue[1] (*a*) whether they were to be tried by certificate or *per pais*. So minutely were these pretended distinctions refined upon, that they did not always escape the charge of contradiction.

In an assize by baron and feme, it was alleged by the tenant, that there had been a divorce between the plaintiffs, and one of them had since been married to the tenant, therefore she was the wife of the tenant, and not of the plaintiff. After much debate and argument, it was held, this should be tried by the *pias*, and not by

(*a*) Glanville, "inde de quis versus aliquem hæreditatem aliquam tanquam hæres petat et alias ei objiciat, quod hæres inde esse non potest, eo quod ex legitimo matrimonio non fit natus, tunc quidem illud in curia Domine Regis remanebit, et mandabitur episcopo loci, quod de matrimonio ipso cognoscat et quod inde judicaverit, id Domino Regi vel ejus justiciis scire faciat" (lib. vii. c. xiii.) So Bracton lays it down: "Cum autem talis proponatur exceptio quod dotem habere non debeat, eo quod fuit tale non (per quem petit) matrimonialiter dispensata vel legitimo matrimonio copulata: hujusmodi inquisitio fieri non potest nec debet in fori seculari cum sit spirituale: et ideo demandetur inquisitio facienda ordinario loci sicut episcopo, &c., quoniam hujusmodi causæ cognitio ad forum spectat ecclesiasticum" (fol. 302). So Britton, s. 107, p. 252, "Exceptionis de concubinage, tolle non effert." So Fleta, "Super contentionem autem despensationis et divortii celebrationem non poterit justiciarius procedere in fori seculari, ideoque demanditur inquisitio facienda episcopi loci, quia hujusmodi causarum cognitio spectat ad forum ecclesiasticum; quod convocatis convocandis veritatem diligenter inquirant et inde certificant justiciariis per literas suas patentes (lib. v. c. xxviii.) Thus in the Year-books of Edward II., Katerine de Ravensdon brought trespass against Philip de Hardwick, who pleaded that she was his wife: "dit que fuit sa feme:" which she denied, and demanded where he married her? He said at Ravensdon, within the jurisdiction of the bishop of N.; upon which the court sent a writ to the bishop, who gave proof to the parties which showed that she was not his wife. "L'evesque dona prove a les parties que prova quel ne fuit mys sa feme." It was set up that the place was in the jurisdiction of another bishop, but this the court would not regard (*Year-book*, 7 *Edw. II.* 22). Thus in an assize of novel dissessin of lands in the diocese of Winchester, when the plea of bastardy was set up, and a marriage alleged to have been had in London, the writ to certify was sent to the bishop of Winchester, and not to the bishop of London (38 *Assize*, fol. 30, p. 231). So in a writ *sui cui in vitâ*, where bastardy was pleaded, and a marriage replied in the county of S., the writ was awarded to the bishop of E., where the lands were (*Year-book*, 7 *Hen. V.* 7). So in an assize of mort d'ancestor the tenant pleaded bastardy in the demandant, who said he was born in another diocese, and prayed a writ to the bishop of that diocese to certify the writ was sent to the bishop of the diocese where the lands lay (35 *Assize*; 7 *Bro. Abr.*, *Certificate d'Evesque*, fol. 14). In 11 Hen. IV. fol. 78, it is said that a trial of matrimony by certificate was only in *dower*. It was not allowed in personal actions (*Mackell* v. *Garett*, 3 *Salk.* 64).

[1] *Vide ante*, vol. i., c. viii.

certificate of the ordinary; and this was on account of the conclusion of the plea, *et essent nient son feme*[1] (*a*): for if he had rested upon the divorce only, that being wholly a spiritual matter, must have gone to that tribunal; but the conclusion being a matter *in pais*, brought the whole before the country.[2] This distinction may help to reconcile many of the cases. Thus, where the issue in *quare impedit* was *void*, or *not void*, it was to be tried by the country; but otherwise if it had been *full*, or *not full*; for plenarty was to be tried by the court christian,[3] which alone could judge of it. Where the issue was, whether the maker of a deed was professed the day he made it, it was tried by the country; because, though the profession was properly to be tried by the certificate of the ordinary, yet here the profession was admitted, and the doubt was only upon the time when the deed was made.[4] On the other hand, where imprisonment was alleged in the ordinary's prison, at the time of the outlawry, it was tried by certificate.[5] It seems that it had become the practice to try by the country even the direct questions of profession, general bastardy, and the like, if alleged in a person who was dead, or a stranger to the action. This had been done in some possessory actions, particularly in assizes, where dispatch might be thought some apology for the innovation; but this was not universally approved, and they seem to have recurred sometimes to one tribunal, and sometimes to another, according to the opinion of different judges.[6]

Upon the whole, the law seemed to stand thus: That the issues of *feme* or *not feme covert*, of *sole parson* or *not parson*, born before espousals or after, and the like points, which were mere temporal facts, were to be tried by the *pais*; but the direct points of general bastardy, *ne unque accouple in loyal matrimony*, profession, bigamy, divorce, ability in a parson, and the like matters of spiritual cognizance, were to be tried by the bishop's certificate. Yet, owing to the forms of some actions, as well as to the way of pleading above stated, these direct issues on spiritual matters were mostly avoided. Thus, where a woman demanded land of her own possession, or of a possession with her husband, as in an assize, in a *cui in vita*, and other possessory writs, the issue of *ne unque accouple, &c.*, could not arise; but it was otherwise in dower, and an appeal *de morte viri*, for there she claimed *through* her husband.[7] The nature of pos-

(*a*) The rightfulness of espousals, whether they made lawful matrimony or not, was always triable by the bishop; and so of bastardy, where it was of party to the writ, and then of right it was tried by the certificate. But whether a woman was *feme sole* or *coverte* was always inquirable by the country (*per pais*, *i.e.*, the jury); as where a *feme sole* brought assize with another as *covert*, and the tenant said she was *covert* of another man. But whether a woman was *accouple en loyal matrimonie* or not, was triable by the bishop. The lawfulness of matrimony was always tried by the bishop and not by the country (*Year-book*, 49 *Edw. III.* fol. 18; 40 *Edw. III.* fol. 40; 44 *Edw. III.* 12; 42 *Edw. III.* 8). If the bishop was out of the realm, the vicar-general sent the certificate (41 *Edw. III.* 10).

[1] 39 Edw. III., 31. [2] 39 Ass., 8. [3] 40 Edw. III., 20. [4] 44 Ass., 10.
[5] Bro. Trial, 140. [6] 38 Ass., 30.; 41 Edw. III., 37; 42 Edw. III., 8.
[7] 40 Ass., 17; 40 Edw. III., 25; 49 Edw. III., 18; 50 Edw. III., 19.

sessory actions was such, that the above issues seldom arose between the parties, but connected with such circumstances as made them very proper objects to be inquired of by the country; which consideration was assisted by a general propensity rather to commit the trial to a jury, than to the ecclesiastical judge.

In proportion as any of the foregoing trials gave way, the trial by the country succeeded in its place; this mode of trial became every day more common (*a*). As it grew more frequent, its nature and properties were more discussed and better understood, and the rules by which it was to be governed became settled upon principle. The learning upon this mode of trial consisted in the qualifications of the jurors, the manner of giving their verdict, and the subject matter that was within their cognizance.

Trial *per pais.*

The idea of jurors being of the vicinage where the fact to be tried had happened, was in some measure given up; for they were now to inquire for the body of the county, and it was sufficient if there

(*a*) There was a close and intimate connexion between the county court system and the trial by jury, which was trial *per pais*, *i.e.*, trial by the country, which meant the county, in the ancient language of the law. Hence a party was said to put himself upon the country, that is, the men of the county; and thus trial by jury was trial by men of the county—the only difference being, though a *vital* difference, that the jury were selected and sworn. In the county court, the suitors, *i.e.*, the general body of the freeholders, were the judges (*Year-book*, 7 *Edw. II.*, fol. 249). A jury was only a sworn and selected number from the same general body. And as the men of the county, and among them the men of the hundred or vill, were the judges in the county court, because they were of the vicinage, so a jury was composed of men of the vicinage. If there were not enough of the vicinage in the local court, the case would go to the king's court. As where an issue joined in a writ of right in a local court, only six suitors could be obtained to try the case, and so it was removed into the king's court, and a jury awarded *de vicineto* (*Year-book*, 7 *Edw. II.*, 238.) Thus the same men who would try the case in the county court might try it as a jury in the king's court, for which reason, if it was desired to avoid this, the jury were summoned from a different hundred or vill (*Year-book*, 7 *Edw. II.*, fol. 231). This applied not only to the local courts, but to the king's courts of oyer and terminer, which are essentially courts of the county, though not county courts. The courts of assize, and oyer and terminer, sitting under commissions, limited to particular counties, were in reality courts of the county, though not county courts, and could only try cases arising, or supposed to arise, within these counties, and by juries from those counties respectively. Hence it was often necessary to remove cases into the king's superior courts, in order to get witnesses from other counties. Thus in an assize of novel disseisin, where the tenant set up a claim, the witnesses to which were in divers counties, the case was adjourned to the king's court at Westminster, which had jurisdiction over the whole country (*Year-book*, 7 *Edw. II.*, 231). The courts of oyer and terminer had, as to parties, and indeed still have, as to jurors and witnesses, process of their own; but extending only to the county in which the commission is opened. The jurors being as much men of the counties as the suitors in the old county courts, were equally exposed to influences which might affect their impartiality. This was so well understood in ancient times, when trial by jury was established, and the courts of the hundred and county, and other local courts, had still an actual practical existence, that where the venue came from a hundred or manor in which the suitors or freeholders were tenants of one or other of the parties, and was removed, for that reason, in order to secure a fair trial, it was removed to the next hundred, not to the country at large; "for then it would be tried by the tenants of the same manor or hundred," *i.e.*, by the very same set of men, or some of them, along with others, whom it was desired should not try the case (*Year-book*, 3 *Hen. VI.*, 39). And trial by jury has always been trial by men of the county.

were two of the hundred to inform the rest; however, it was a good cause of challenge if there were no hundredors[1] (a). If the venue was awarded out of two counties (as it was in some cases) each sheriff was to return twenty-four jurors, and there ought regularly to be six of each upon the inquest; though should it appear upon examination of the jurors that there were not six in town, the inquest might be supplied from others.[2] In all cases where there were not sufficient of the jury returned, after defaults or challenges, the plaintiff might pray a *tales*, as it was called, to the amount of ten, but not further;[3] for though *decem tales* was common, says the book, we never heard of *undecim tales;* notwithstanding, in an attaint eighteen *tales* were allowed to make up the jury of twenty-four.[4] Where an assault happened in Westminster Hall, and it was prosecuted by a bill in the king's bench, a jury was awarded of those persons who kept shops in the hall.[5] In order that the jury might be above all exception, the causes of *challenge* were very numerous; these were either to the *array*, or to the *polls.* If a juror was nominated by either party, if the sheriff was *des robes*, as they called it, to either party, these were challenges to the array; the sheriff not being supposed sufficiently impartial to return an indifferent jury[6] (b). If a juror was a relation, even in the remote degrees, as in the eleventh degree, or if he held lands in lease of either party, it was a good challenge to the *poll.*[7] When such distant apprehensions of favour in jurors were regarded as legal

(a) It was very early recognised that so much was knowledge of the matter on the part of the jurors of the essence of trial by jury, and so little did the law dread it, or desire to avoid it, that unless a juror was challenged as favourable to one side or the other, it was no good ground for such challenge that he had merely declared himself disposed or resolved to find for one side, supposing that he said this, not merely from private feeling, but from knowledge of the matter, and his impression of the merits of the case. Thus when a juror was challenged for favour, the judge thus charged and directed the "triers," who were to try the cause of challenge: "Observe what is understood by favour. It is favour if he resolved that, whether the matter be true or false, he will pass with the one side or the other; in that case, he is favourable to that side, but though a man has said twenty times that he will pass with one side or the other, yet you must inquire whether the cause is the affection he has for the party, or for the knowledge he has of the matter in issue; and if for affection, then it is favour; but otherwise not so. And so, though he has more affection to one side than to the other, yet if he has full knowledge of the thing in issue, and if he were sworn he would say the truth, notwithstanding the affection he has for one party, yet he is not favourable, *i.e.*, in a sense to sustain the challenge" (*Year-book*, 7 *Hen. VI.*, fol. 25). So two centuries afterwards, a verdict was set aside, because the foreman had said that the plaintiff should never have a verdict *whatever witnesses he produced* (*Dent* v. *Hundred of Hertford*, 2 *Salk.* 645).

(b) Thus a juror was challenged because he held land of the party (*Year-book*, 7 *Edw. IV.*, 4, 5; 3 *Hen. VI.*, 39). So of a gossip or godfather (*Ibid.*, 10 *Hen. VI.*, 24). So 49 Assize 1. So of any direct relationship to one of the parties (21 *Edw. IV.*, 63; *Mir.* 220). So if the juror was in any way favourable to the opposite party (*Year-book*, 10 *Hen. IV.*, 18; 7 *Hen. IV.*, 25; 20 *Hen. VI.*, 40). But as to challenges to the favour, founded upon knowledge of the parties, or of the matter, it is to be observed that as the original theory of trial by jury was that the jurors found on their own knowledge, mere acquaintance with the parties of the matter would not be a cause of challenge.

[1] Ass. 12. [2] 48 Edw. III., 29. [3] 47 Ass., 11. [4] 21 Edw. III., 43. [5] 42 Ass., 18. [6] 38 Edw. III., 25; 49 Edw. III., 1. [7] 41 Ed. III., 9; 21 Edw. III., 41.

objections, it is easy to imagine how much argument might be raised on the subject of challenges.[1]

A challenge of the array used to be tried by the coroners; and if it was found against the sheriff, the *venire* would be directed to the coroners (*a*). A challenge of the *polls* would be tried by two of the jurors already sworn, if so many were sworn, otherwise by some persons *de circumstantibus*.[2]

We have seen the method which had got into practice in the time[3] of Edward I. of compelling a jury to agree in their verdict. This authority over jurors seems to have been exercised by judges with very little scruple. Some instances of the treatment experienced by jurors in this reign will show the notions entertained by our ancestors concerning this proceeding. In the eighth year of the king, in a writ of mortauncestor, a juror who had delayed his companions a day and a night, because he would not agree with them, and this (as the book says) without any good reason, was committed to the Fleet, and was afterwards let to mainprize, till the court were advised what step to take with him. In the third year, where, in an action of trespass, one of the jury would not agree, the judge took the verdict of the eleven, and committed the twelfth to prison.[4] The same was done in the twenty-third year.[5] But the taking a verdict *ex dicto majoris partis juratorum*, though conformable with the old practice,[6] began to go out of use towards the latter end of this reign; for in the fortieth year, when eleven gave their verdict without assent of the twelfth, they were fined by the justices.[7]

In the next year this point was debated, and finally settled. In an assize, all the jurors were agreed except one, who could not be brought to concur with them; they were therefore remanded, and remained all that day and the next without eating or drinking; and then, being asked by the justices if they were agreed, the dissentient answered No, and that he would first die in prison; upon

(*a*) A cause of challenge to the array went to impeach the partiality of the sheriff as summoner of the jurors. Thus it was a challenge to the array that the sheriff was plaintiff,* and returned the pannel of the jurors, though not that he had in his official capacity returned the pannel in a suit in which he sat as judge.† And it was a cause of challenge against an array or the polls, that the sheriff‡ or the juror§ had been appointed as the arbitrator by either side in a previous arbitrament of the matter, though not so if both chose him as indifferent.

* *Year-book*, 14 *Hen. VI.* 1.

† Thus it was said, a man may be his own judge. As, "suppose a redisseisin is directed to the sheriff, there he shall be judge and also minister, for the writ will be that he inquire of those who were of the assize and others, and he also shall make process against them; and he is judge, and executes his own judgment; and it is not challenge to that array to say that he is favourable, for he is judge, and it shall be presumed that he is indifferent" (*Year-book*, 8 *Hen. VI.* fol. 21).

‡ *Year-book*, 20 *Hen. VI.* 39. So it was a cause of challenge that the sheriff had empannelled a jury at the approval of the one side or the other (*Year-book*, 19 *Hen. VI.* 9).

§ *Year-book*, 7 *Hen. VI.* 24. Thus it was said, "If the plaintiff and the defendant should both refer themselves to the arbitrament of certain persons to act for both, it would be no challenge; but where one side chose one, and the other another, then, although they are to be indifferent as arbitrators, yet as each is unknown to the other, it is good cause of challenge; and as it appeared that the juror was chosen only by one side, the challenge was allowed."

[1] *Vide ante*, vol. i. c. i.
[2] 21 Ass., 26; 20 Ass., 10.
[3] *Vide ante*, vol. ii. c. x.
[4] Fitz. Verd., c. i.
[5] Bro. Jurors, 53.
[6] *Vide ante*, c. v.
[7] 40 Ass., 10.

which the justices took the verdict of the eleven, and committed the single juror to prison. But when judgment was prayed in the common bench upon this verdict, the justices were unanimously of opinion, *that a verdict from eleven jurors was no verdict at all:* and when it was urged that former judges had taken verdicts of eleven, both in an assize and trespass, and particularly mentioned one taken in the twentieth year of the king; Thorpe, one of the justices, said, that it was not an example for them to follow, for that judge had been greatly censured for it;[1] and it was said by the bench, that the justices ought to have carried the jurors about with them in carts till they were agreed. Thus it was settled at the close of this reign, that the jurors must be unanimous in the verdict, and the justices were to put them under restraint, if necessary, to produce such unanimity. If the jurors, when committed to the care of the sheriff, ate or drank, or went at large, the verdict was void, and the party might have a new *venire.*[2] It happened, when a jury were put together to consider of their verdict, one of them secretly withdrew himself: for this contempt he was fined and imprisoned, and another sworn in his place.[3] This compulsory power over jurors extended even to the pannel; for where a false return of jurors was made by the bailiff of a franchise, the justices reformed the pannel.[4]

To relieve themselves from the difficulty of deciding, the jurors might find their verdict *at large*,[5] as it was called; that is, they might state the special circumstances, and leave it to the discretion of the court to make the conclusion thereon: and they might do this as well on a special as a general issue.[6] In such verdicts, it was not uncommon for the jury to find *fines*, and other matters of record; for though they could not be compelled to find matters of record, they might, if they so pleased.[7]

There was great doubt, how far the jurors might take cognizance of matters that happened out of the county; nor does there seem to have been any principle yet agreed upon, which enables us to pronounce with confidence as to the general law upon this point. Perhaps, the distinct jurisdiction between counties depended much on the same sort of reasoning as that between the spiritual and temporal courts; so that though the jury of one county could not find a fact which was *necessarily* of a *local* nature, and had happened in another county, yet they might judge of matters that were only *accidentally* so, or dependent upon such local fact. Thus it was held, that the jurors in assize could not find a *dying seised* in another county, but they might find the *dying* simply.[8] It may be observed, that the general propensity of courts was, to confine jurors to the cognizance only of such things as happened within their own county.

[1] 41 Ass., II. [2] 4 Edw. III., 24. [3] Bro. Jur., 46. [4] 41 Edw. III., 26.
[5] *Vide ante*, c. xiii. [6] 22 Ass., 60; 38 Ass., 9; 18 Ass., 3; 30 Ed. III., 23, and *passim*.
[7] Bro. Jur., 39; 26 Ass., 50. [8] 1 Ass., 16.

If there was any doubt concerning the competency of the jurors of one county to take notice of facts happening in another, there was not less difficulty in deciding from what county the jurors should be chosen to try an issue when joined. It was usual in pleading, for the parties to allege the locality of facts conformably with the real truth; so that in the course of pleading, two or more different counties might be mentioned as the places where several scenes of the transaction in question had passed (*a*). When a fact was said by one party to have happened in the county of A. and by the other in the county of B., and the writ perhaps had been brought in the county of C., it required some technical distinctions to ascertain whence the jurors should be brought to try the fact in dispute. One sort of reasoning prevailed at one time, a different one at another; and there seem to have been very few cases where any fixed rule was laid down, to govern the court in awarding the *venire facias* to one county or another.

Of the venue.

It was repeatedly debated, whence the vicinage should come to try the issue of villenage. It seemed natural to try this by the vicinage where the villenage was alleged to be, and so it was in the old law.[1] We find in the 39th of the king, that practice still continued; for being at issue, whether the demandant was a villein regardant to the manor of T., in the county of N., or a bastard; and the manor was in one county, and the birth alleged in another; the venue was awarded in the county where the manor was.[2] But in the next year, when an issue arose like the former, the venue was not awarded where the manor lay, but where the writ was

(*a*) It is to be observed that as the pleading was oral, and originally the case was tried in the court where the action was brought, and, to avoid delay, would be tried at once when the pleading was at an end, it was the practice for each party in pleading anything he had to prove to produce at once his "suit" (*secta*) of witnesses to prove it, and to offer at once to do so. So Bracton says: "Non sufficit quod petens intentionem suam sic proponat et fundet, nisi sic fundatam probaverit ut dicatur in fine intentionis fundatæ, et quod tale sit jus suam offert" (373 b.). And so of plea on the other side; so throughout the *Placitorum Abbreviatio*, the pleadings are always held insufficient without offer of instant proof. "Isabella de B. petit versus R. dimidium, &c., et jus suam et hereditatem et ipse venit et defendet jus suam, et ipsa nullam sectam adduxit. Eat sine die (*Plac. Abr.* fol. 2; *Staff. rot.* 7, *temp.* 10 *Johan*) Gilbertus de Beville petit duas virgatas terræ quæ eum contingunt de socagio quod fuit patris eorum in eadem villa Wilhelmus defendit quod socagium illud nunquam partitum fuit nec debet partem. Et hoc offert defendere, quia Gilbertus nullam probationem produxit, consideratum est quod W. eat inde sine die (*Plac. Abr., temp. Johan*). So in an assize of novel disseisin, the tenant pleading that he had recovered the land in an assize of mort d'ancestor. "Et inde producit milites de comitatu qui eodem assisæ capiendæ interfuerunt et hi idem testantur." And then the plaintiff says in reply, that after this he gave it to them "et inde posuerit se super visnetum," as that would be a fact in the knowledge of the vicinage (*Plac. Abr.* 81, *Bed. rot.* 4.) So in an assize of mort d'ancestor it is recorded that the tenant, "nihil quam defensionem illam dixit vel obtulit nec sectam quod ipse J. (the plaintiff) primogenitum fratrem habuit quoduxit, nec curiam aliquam in qua placitum eis et inter eos," &c.; wherefore judgment was given for the plaintiff (*Plac. Abr.* 20, *Hertf. temp. Rich. I.*).

[1] *Vide ante*, vol. i., 143.

[2] 39 Edw. III., 36.

brought.[1] Again, in the 43d year, an issue of villenage arising, the venue was awarded where the manor lay, and not where the birth was alleged.[2] Yet the next year they seemed to have returned back to the practice of the year 41; and that seemed to be relied upon as the better opinion.[3] But in the 47th year, the court were still in doubt; and in order to settle the practice, they suspended the issue of the *venire* till they had consulted parliament, whether the *venue* should be of the county where the villenage was alleged, or where the writ was brought.[4] What was the result of this application of the judges, we do not know; but in the 50th year there was a petition to parliament, praying, that wherever a question arose concerning a man's birth, in pleas of freehold or inheritance, the inquest might be of the county where the birth was laid, and not where the writ was brought; this petition, however, was rejected.[5]

The two guides for settling the venue seemed to be the *land*, and the *fact* alleged; and when the balance was thought to stand equally between them, there was sometimes a venue from both. Where it was indifferent, the jury naturally came from the county where the writ had supposed the transaction. All this will be better understood by some examples. In the first place, of land. It was settled, that in debt for rent on a lease for years, if any fact, as payment, an agreement, or the like, was alleged in another county, it should, notwithstanding, be tried where the land lay,[6] although there was an issue upon the very deed granting the lease.[7] In a writ of *per quæ servitia*, non-tenure was pleaded; and though the manor was in N., and the writ brought there, yet, the land being in S., the venue came from thence.[8]

Secondly, as to the *fact*. In a writ of annuity, where the seisin was alleged in a different county from that where the land lay, and that where the writ was brought, the venue came from the county where the seisin was alleged.[9] In debt by an administrator, the defendant pleaded, that the deceased made executors, and died in a foreign county; the plaintiff replied, that he died intestate: here the venue was in the foreign county.[10] A release was pleaded; the venue was, where the deed bore date, and not where the land lay.[11] In a plea of covenants performed in a foreign county, the venue was from thence; and this was laid down as a general rule;[12] but not so where conditions were pleaded, and alleged at another place.[13] If imprisonment was pleaded, the jury was to come from the place where the imprisonment was alleged.[14] In an action of debt, there was a plea of a bailment in pledge at L., and the venue was awarded from L. In dower, where the tenant pleaded elopement of the

1 40 Edw. III., 36.
2 43 Edw. III., 4.
3 44 Edw. III., 6.
4 47 Edw. III., 26, 27.
5 Cott. Abrid., 50 Edw. III., 152.
6 44 Edw. III., 42; 45 Edw. III., 3.
7 45 Edw. III., 8.
8 21 Edw. III., 18.
9 49 Edw. III., 5; 48 Edw. III., 26.
10 44 Edw. III., 16.
11 *Ibid.*, 34.
12 *Ibid.*, 42.
13 45 Edw. III., 15.
14 45 Edw. III., 15.

demandant from her husband at D., in the county of S., and residing with the adulterer in London, the venue came from London.[1] In accompt, the defendant pleaded infancy at the time of the receipt, and said, that he was born at B., in another county; but the jury came from the county where the receipt was alleged.[2] Again, in *quare impedit*, upon disability pleaded, the plaintiff said he was examined at D., in the county of C., and the writ was brought in D., but the jury came from C.[3] When the venue was governed by the fact, it always followed the plea of the defendant, and not the replication; as where the defendant said, that the plaintiff and others took away his wife in the county of K., and there detain her; the plaintiff replied, that she was at large in C.; here the venue came from K.[4] So when the tenant pleaded a warranty in the county of S., and the plaintiff replied that the warrantor was still alive in D., the venue was from S;[5] these being cases where the fact alleged by the defendant would in subsequent times have been traversed, and so brought directly in issue.

A replevin was brought in Middlesex, the defendant avowed for homage; the plaintiff pleaded tender of homage in the county of Sussex, and the venue was awarded in that county.[6] Where there was eloignment in one county, and receipt in another, and issue was joined on the receipt, the venue was in the county where the receipt was alleged.[7] In an assize of rent, upon the issue of *ne charga pas*, the venue came from the county where the deed was made; which was said to be a constant rule where *non est factum* was pleaded.[8] Yet, in a *quare impedit*, it was doubted whether the deed of grant of the advowson should be tried where it was made, or where the church was.[9]

The following were instances where a venue of two counties was agitated or awarded. In an assize they were at issue on a special bastardy, and the espousals and birth were alleged in a foreign county. There seemed an inclination to try it by a venue of both counties;[10] but in the next year a bastardy alleged in a foreign county was tried by the assize.[11] Yet, in the same year, where a bastardy was alleged in an assize, it was tried by a venue of both counties, though not without long argument.[12] And thus stood the law as to bastardy at the close of this reign. In trespass in the county of E. the defendant justified for common appendant to land in the county of W., and the venue was awarded of both counties.[13] Where trespass was laid in B. against two, and one defendant pleaded not guilty, and the other a release at A., there was a venue of both counties.[14] Again, where a release was pleaded, and the party replied that he was within age when he executed it, the venue was awarded both of the county where the deed was made and

[1] 46 Edw. III., 30; 47 Edw. III., 25. [2] 21 Edw. III., 7, 8. [3] 39 Edw. III., 2.
[4] 11 Ass., 7. [5] 11 Ass., 18. [6] 21 Edw. III., 11. [7] 21 Edw. III., 48.
[8] 26 Ass., 3. [9] 43 Edw. III., 1. [10] 45 Ass., 12. [11] 46 Ass., 3.
[12] 46 Edw. III., 6. [13] 49 Edw. III., 19. [14] 50 Edw. III., 1.

where he was born.[1] As a venue might be had out of two counties, so might it out of two districts, or smaller jurisdictions. In an assize of common in one franchise, appendant to land in another franchise, the jurors were to come from both the franchises; and it was said, the assize could not be taken by the men of one franchise alone, any more than in an assize in *confinio comitatûs,* which could not be taken by the men of one county only.[2] Again, in an appeal of mayhem in the ward of Cheap, the defendant pleaded *son assault demesne,* and in his own defence, in the ward of Cornhill; and the jury came from both wards.[3]

If no venue was laid in the plea (which sometimes, though not often, did happen), the fact was taken to be in the county alleged by the plaintiff.[4] The option of the plaintiff to choose the county in which he would bring his action seemed of little value; for if he laid it in a foreign county, he might be brought back, by the pleading of the defendant, to try it in the true one: or if he brought it in the true county, some justification or discharge might be set up which would carry the trial to another; the consequence of which was, that there was little debate about the venue which the plaintiff chose for his declaration. There are, however, some determinations upon that point. It was held that an action of accompt against the bailiff of a manor should be brought in the county where the manor was. Detinue might be brought either where the detinue or where the bailment was alleged. *Warrantia chartæ* might be brought in another county than where the land lay.[5] An action on the statute of labourers might be brought either where the retainer was, or where the departure of the servant was alleged.[6] An attachment on a prohibition was to be brought where the summons to appear had been served.[7] Where a person was taken in one county, and carried into another, it was said there might be separate actions of false imprisonment: the same where a distress was taken in one county and carried into another.[8] A *quare impedit* was to be brought where the preferment lay that was in question; but we find the king brought a writ in a foreign county, and it was held well.[9] Forfeiture of marriage was to be brought where the tender was;[10] a writ of ward in the county where the land lay.[11]

Whenever the witnesses to a deed were joined with the jurors, they so far differed from the pannel that they could not be challenged, nor was their concurrence necessary to complete the verdict.[12] It was a rule that the jurors should be exempt from attaint, if the witnesses agreed with them; but if they dissented, the jurors were liable as in other cases. Process might be had against witnesses, even where a deed was not denied directly, but the issue was upon the effect and consequence of it; as, *il ne charga pas per le fait, ne releasa pas,* and the like.[13]

[1] 38 Edw. III., 17. [2] 30 Ass., 42. [3] 41 Ass., 21. [4] 21 Edw. III., 10.
[5] 40 Edw. III., 4. [6] 41 Edw. III., 1. [7] 42 Edw. III., 14. [8] 38 Edw. III., 34.
[9] 21 Edw. III., 5; 4 Edw. III., 9. [10] Fitz. Visne, 4. [11] 31 Edw. III., 42.
[12] 12 Ass., 12; 23 Ass., 11. [13] 23 Ass., 11; 43 Edw. III., 2; 41 Ass., 23.

Very little has yet been said on the process of *capias*, and writs of execution: the latter are passed over in silence by Bracton, and it was of late that the former had become of much use. We have seen that the writ of *capias*, being a process of contempt,[1] did not issue without special award of the court; and in granting it, whether in cases where it lay at common law, or where it had been ordained by the late statutes, the court exercised a discretion according to the circumstances of the case. In an action for a bag of charters, it was said that this was a matter of too little importance to award a *capias*, and therefore it was denied.[2] The bag, and not the charters, being the only pretence for the writ, they thought themselves justified if they were governed by the value of that, without any regard to the importance of the charters; for these, being considered as chattels *real*, were not, they said, such chattels whose detinue could entitle the plaintiff to a *capias*, under the statute of this king. Again, in an action of trespass against an innkeeper for goods which a guest lost while in his inn, the court would not award a *capias* upon the judgment, though the writ was *contra pacem;* saying that it was found by the jury to be only negligence; and a man was not to be sent to prison for negligence only, where he had committed no *tort*.[3] It seemed to be held, that where the defendant appeared upon the *distringas* in the mesne process, he was not liable to a *capias ad satisfaciendum* upon the judgment, but only to a *distringas ad satisfaciendum*:[4] and a *capias* in no case was allowed against an archbishop, bishop, abbot, or prior, nor against an earl, baron, or knight, because it was presumed that such persons must have sufficient whereby they might be distrained.[5]

Of process.

The common writs of execution were *elegit*, *fieri facias*, and *capias;* besides that above mentioned of *distringas ad satisfaciendum*, where the defendant was to be compelled to make specific redress as in detinue. It was settled that a *capias* might be issued after a *fieri facias*, and a *nihil* returned.[6] But after taking the body, no *fieri facias* nor *elegit* could be had, the person of the defendant being considered as a full execution;[7] nor could the body be taken after an *elegit*.[8] An *elegit* might be sued into as many counties as the plaintiff pleased.[9] As the land was bound from the time of the judgment only, an application had been made to parliament that it might be bound from the date of the original writ; but no alteration was made.[10] Upon an *elegit*, all chattels were to be levied, under which were included, as we have seen, a lease for years, lands in ward, or in execution under a statute.[11] A gift of goods after judgment was void, and the officer might levy them under an *elegit* or *fieri facias*, notwithstanding any sale or gift, they being bound by the judgment.[12] A

[1] *Vide ante*, c. xii. [2] 42 Edw. III., 13. [3] 42 Edw. III., 11.
[4] 49 Edw. III., 2; *vide ante*, c. ix. in the note. [5] O. N. B., 61.
[6] 45 Edw. III., 19. [7] 22 Ass., 43. [8] 50 Edw. III., 4.
[9] 47 Edw. III., 26. [10] Cott. Abr. [11] 31 Ass., 6. [12] 22 Ass., 72.

person taken upon a *capias ad satisfaciendum* was not to be suffered to go at large, though he had found mainpernors: the same if he was charged on a *capias pro fine.*[1] And if he escaped, another *capias* might be had, as well as an action against the gaoler.[2] The established practice was, upon the return of the first *capias ad satisfaciendum*, to issue an *exigent*, and so to proceed to outlawry.

Several statutes were made in the reign of Edward I. to enforce the execution of process, and to punish the neglects of sheriffs or bailiffs in serving it.[3] In the time of Henry III. it had been usual to amerce sheriffs for omissions and defaults of that sort; but the method of levying such amercements does not appear. A practice had now obtained to deal with these officers in a more summary way; for the courts used to issue process to the coroners to *attach* the sheriff, and, according to the nature of the case, he used afterwards to be amerced.[4] Where an under-sheriff, having the charge of jurors, had suffered them to eat and drink, and to go at large, a *capias ad respondendum* was awarded against him out of the king's bench.[5]

Though we have met with several statutes[6] to qualify the abuses following from writs of protection, there has not yet occurred any particular mention of them, so as to enable us to state what the tenor of them was. The two principal writs of protection were distinguished by the clause of *nolumus* and *volumus.* The latter was the most general and most ample. It was usually obtained by persons going, or pretending to go, out of the kingdom in the suite of some great man on the king's service; and it was under the great seal. The writ, or letters patent, was directed to all bailiffs and others, signifying that the king had taken the bearer and all his lands and goods into his protection *quià profecturus, &c.*, because he was going out of the kingdom on the king's affairs: and they were commanded accordingly to see that his person and property were protected from all harm or injury; which protection was to last to a certain time therein mentioned. Then there followed this clause, *Volumus etiam, &c.*, signifying the king's pleasure, that he should be free from all pleas and plaints, except pleas of dower *unde nihil, quare impedit*, assize of novel disseisin, darrein presentment, and attaint, and certain other pleas summoned before the justices in eyre. The protection *cum clausulâ nolumus*, was of a more confined nature: it was only had in cases where a person was in apprehension that the king or some common person might take his corn, hay, horses, charters, or the like; and it might be granted by any master in chancery without a privy seal, which was necessary to obtain the former. The clause from which the writ was named, was *Nolumus, &c.*, signifying the king's pleasure, that no one should presume to take the property of the person so protected.[7]

[1] 22 Ass., 74.
[2] 26 Ass., 51; 41 Ass., 15.
[3] *Vide ante*, c. xi.
[4] 43 Edw. III., 26; 47 Edw. III., 28.
[5] 24 Edw. III., 24.
[6] *Vide ante*, c. xii.
[7] O. N. B., 21.

We shall now consider such alterations as were made in the criminal law during this reign. The crime of treason was brought to somewhat more certainty by the famous statute made in the 25th year of this king.[1] All the treasons enumerated in that act were considered as treasons before; and many that are not there mentioned were, however, still continued by the courts to be construed treasons, notwithstanding the strict injunction of that act. In order to set this subject in a true light, we shall first mention such cases of treason in this reign as are recorded to have happened before, and then such as happened after that act.

The crime of treason.

In the 12th year of the king, a girl of 13 years old killed her mistress, and was burnt; which shows that it was considered as a treason;[2] so that killing a mistress was held equally criminal with killing a master. The punishment of such an offender was to be drawn and hanged without any benefit of sanctuary.[3] How conformable the statute of treason was with the common law as it then stood, may be judged by the following passage of a report in the 22d of the king, which was the year when the petition was first presented to the parliament for the declaration of treason. Treasons that touch the person of the king are there instanced as follows: Imagining his death, according with his enemies, falsifying his seal, counterfeiting his money, and the like: so that coining was considered among the higher order of treasons, as stated by the *Mirror*, though it had been otherwise in the earlier times of our law. In all these treasons, on account of their heinous nature, and their near connexion with the royalty, the law allowed no person but the king to derive any emolument from them; and therefore he had the forfeiture of lands and goods. But where a master was killed by his servant, and in other inferior treasons, the escheat belonged to the lord of whom the offender held his land; all which corresponds with the language of the statute of treasons. The case in which the law was so laid down was, where a person was indicted for killing a king's messenger; which, on that occasion, was held to be of the higher order of treasons.[4]

After the passing of the statute of treason we find the following cases:—A servant departed out of his service, and a year afterwards killed his former master, upon a malice that he had conceived against him while in his service; and for this he was drawn and hanged.[5] Shard, who was the judge on that occasion, forbade, under pain of imprisonment, that any one should furnish the prisoner with a hurdle or other thing to be drawn upon; but directed that he should be dragged by horses out of the hall where judgment was passed to the gallows. Thus *drawing* was a serious part of the sentence. In the 38th year it was held, that adhering to the king's enemies in Scotland was only felony, and not treason;[6] for

[1] *Vide ante*, c. xiii. [2] 12 Ass., 30. [3] 21 Edw. III., 17.
[4] 22 Ass., 49. [5] 33 Ass., 7. [6] Bro. Cor., 36.

what reason, it is difficult to say. However, where a Norman was captain of an English ship containing several Englishmen, and they committed many robberies on the sea; it was held by Shard that, inasmuch as the former *did this in the Norman tongue*, it was only felony in him; but in the others, *who did it in English*, as the Report expresses it, the fact was treason. This case is very remarkable: first, as it was neither expressly within the statute of treasons, nor declared by the advice of parliament; secondly, as it was upon the high seas; from which it should seem that the admiralty as yet did not exist, or at least affected no jurisdiction of that sort.[1] The above case was held for law by the court; and it was at the same time agreed, in the case of a servant who had procured another to kill his master, that as this, if committed, was only felony in the principal, it could not be treason in the accessary.

Homicide.

The ideas of homicide which prevailed in the time of Bracton seemed still to govern.[2] This was particularly observable in what was called homicide *se defendendo*, where the defendant was required to make out the absolute necessity he was under to act in his own defence. Where one pursued another with a stick, and struck him, and the person stricken again struck the pursuer, of which blow he died; here, because it was proved that the person killing might have fled, but would not, rather choosing to assault the pursuer, it was held to be felony.[3] Where the deceased had thrown the defendant to the ground, and drew his knife to kill him, and the defendant, while upon the ground, also drew a knife, upon which knife the deceased, in a hurry to do the act, fell, and was killed; this was held not homicide *se defendendo*, but not felony at all, the death having followed from the motion of the deceased himself. This distinction was material to the defendant; for notwithstanding *se defendendo* was a killing under an absolute necessity in defence of one's self or property, it was still homicide, and the goods were forfeited upon conviction. So was it held at common law; and as the statute of Gloucester[4] had only ordained that the convict should have a charter of pardon, the forfeiture remained as before.[5]

In respect of homicide when committed in defence of a man's property, it was held, that where a thief assaulted a man, and pursued him, if he killed the thief, the killer should go quit.[6] Again, where it was proved that the deceased and another came to the house of the defendant with a design to burn it, and the defendant, being then at home, shot an arrow, and killed the deceased; this was adjudged not to be felony. It was at the same time said, that where a thief had robbed and killed a merchant, and the merchant's servant came suddenly upon the thief, and killed him, it was not felony.[7] It will be seen presently, that such killing was sometimes esteemed *justifiable*.

[1] 40 Ass., 25. [2] *Vide ante*, c. ix. [3] 43 Ass., 31. [4] *Vide ante*, c. x.
[5] 44 Edw. III., 44; 21 Edw. III., 17. [6] 26 Ass., 32. [7] *Ibid.*, 23.

Most of the foregoing were cases of homicide, which Bracton calls *ex necessitate*. We shall now consider such as he denominates *ex justitiâ*. This was, when the killing happened in the execution of lawful process. And here the defendant, instead of pleading not guilty, might state the special matter in the way of a justification; and if it was proved true, he went quit, without a charter of pardon. In such case of justification, the jury were charged to find if the thief, against whom the process was directed, could have been otherwise taken; so strictly did they require, even in *justifiable* homicide, that a plain *necessity* should be made out to warrant the killing. It was at the same time said, that a man might in many cases *justify* a killing; as where thieves came to rob, or burglariously to break a house, they might safely be killed, if they could not be otherwise taken: the same of a jailer, if he had a weapon in his hand, and was attacked by his prisoners:[1] so that it should seem, the killing a thief or a burglar, if he could not otherwise be taken, was not homicide *se defendendo*, but *justifiable*. In reading our old writers on criminal law, it should be remembered, that they made a distinction between homicide *se defendendo* from necessity, and *se defendendo* justifiable; the former being felony, the latter none at all.

There was no allowance in our old criminal law for the infirmities and passions of men's minds. A killing, if in a quarrel or sudden affray, was equally felonious with any deliberate act of killing: it was so in Bracton's time,[2] and so it still continued; therefore, where two men were fighting, and another interposing to part them was killed by one of them; to adjudge this felony, was perfectly consonant to the notions of law that had long prevailed.[3] In Bracton's time it was held, that to procure an abortion, after the fœtus was formed and animated, was homicide: the courts now began to think otherwise. A man beat a woman big with two children, of which one then died; the other was born alive, and baptized, but died two days after of the injury it had received; and all this was stated in an indictment: but it was held by the court not to be felony.[4] It was the governing opinion all through this reign, that to kill a child *in ventre sa mere* was not felony; the reason given for it being, that a child, as it never was *in rerum naturâ*,[5] could not properly be said to be *occisus*; though the same reason would not apply to one that was born, and died of the injury it had received *in ventre*, as in the foregoing instance.

The practice was, if a jury acquitted a man of homicide, to direct them to find *who* was guilty of the killing,[6] in order that so heinous a crime might not go unpunished. We find where a jury had acquitted a man who was indicted for the death of another, and they were directed to say *who* killed the deceased, they said that he was in a passion, and fell upon his knife, and so killed himself.[7]

[1] 22 Ass., 55. [2] *Vide ante*, vol. i. c. viii. [3] 22 Ass., 71. [4] 3 Ass., 2.
[5] 22 Ass., 94. [6] 21 Edw. III., 17. [7] 37 Ass., 13.

It was common to indict a person *de morte ignoti*, which was held sufficient; but in an appeal, the name of the deceased was always to be mentioned; the latter being a suit that belonged only to the relations, who must of necessity know him; the former being a presentment by the jurors for the king, without any knowledge of the deceased.[1] There is an opinion, that persons outlawed for felony, as they were *capita lupina*, might be killed by anybody; though Bracton lays it down otherwise;[2] and says, that even where a sentence of law was not executed in due order, it was an offence. Very early in this reign we find a person arraigned for killing an outlaw for felony.[3] In the 27th year, in an appeal of death by a woman, the husband's outlawry for felony was pleaded, and, though overruled, a case was mentioned where it had been allowed.[4] It is probable, that the slayers of such unhappy objects went without punishment, rather from some peculiarity in the circumstances of the prosecutions then in use, than from any principle of law authorising such barbarity. The heir of a person so outlawed could not have an appeal, because of the corruption of blood; and therefore, till the time of Henry III., when the proceeding *per famam patriâ* became more common, there was no regular method of bringing such offenders to justice. But now, when indictments were preferred almost as frequently as appeals, it is no wonder that those who committed violence on such persons were brought to punishment.

Larceny.

The crime of *furtum*, or *larceny*, as it was now commonly called, began to be more minutely explained. The new learning upon this head related either to the things taken, or the mode and circumstances under which they were taken. A forester was indicted *quòd felonicè succidit et asportavit arbores*, &c., upon which indictment the justices refused to arraign him, because the trees were annexed to the soil, and so not *movables corporeal*, as they were required to be by the *Mirror*;[5] and therefore felony could not be committed of them even by a stranger, much less by the forester, who had the custody of them. As to the trees being annexed to the freehold, it was suggested, that it would be different, if they had been cut by the lord, and *afterwards* taken away by some one.[6] It was held, that doves, fish, and other animals, being *feræ naturæ*, were not such things as a man should suffer death for taking them; *nisi* (says the book) *fuerunt felonicè furata extra domum vel mansionem*.[7] A person who lived a servant in a house got up in the night, took some things out of a chamber into the hall, with intent to take them away; and in going to the stable for his horse, was stopped by the ostler: this was adjudged a sufficient *taking* to make it a larceny.[8] Taking away a woman with the goods of her husband upon her, was held

[1] 1 Ass., 7; 22 Ass., 94.
[2] *Vide ante*, vol. i. c. viii.
[3] 2 Ass., 3.
[4] 27 Ass., 41.
[5] *Vide ante*, vol. i. c. v.
[6] 12 Ass., 32.
[7] 22 Ass., 95.
[8] 27 Ass., 39.

a felony of the goods, if it was against the woman's will; though it should seem to be otherwise if she consented to the going away.[1] There appears to have been a difference of opinion about the offence of receiving stolen goods. A man was appealed by a provor, *quòd receptavit latrocinium sciens de feloniâ illâ*, &c., and the justices would not put him to answer; though Shard said, that Scrope used to punish such offenders.[2] It was laid down, that *theftbote* was not when a man took his own goods from a thief, but only when he accepted the thief's goods, in order to favour and screen him.[3]

We have seen in the reign of Edward I.[4] there was a difference of opinion as to the sum which constituted grand or petty larceny. It was said by Thorpe, in the twenty-second year of the king, that a man should be hanged if he stole twelve pence; to which the reporter adds: *Dixit tamen, quòd laici dicunt* QUE NON *nisi summa excedat* 12d.[5] That the vulgar opinion differed from that of lawyers, appeared plainly from the verdicts of juries, who, when they found a man guilty of the fact, and yet wished to make it petty larceny, in order to make sure of being right, would find the goods to be worth only *ten pence.*[6] The better opinion seemed not to be that of Thorpe, but that which he attributed to the lay gents.[7] A conviction of petit larceny produced a forfeiture of goods;[8] and the punishment was to be sent to prison *d'aver penance*,[9] which probably meant no more than custody and confinement.

Burglary.

Burgessours, as they were called by Britton,[10] or *burglars*, as they were now called, are in this reign described somewhat differently than they had been by that author. He seems to include the circumstance of stealing as a requisite to constitute the crime; but in the twenty-second year of this king they are described as those "who feloniously in time of peace break houses, churches, walls, or doors; for which burglary" (says the book) "a man would be hanged, even though he took nothing."[11] Thus the offence consisted in the violence done to a man's house, and not to his other property, for it carried in it no idea of stealing. Again, *robbery* consisted principally in the violence done to a man's person; for if only a penny was taken, yet the robber would nevertheless be hanged.[12]

Respecting all these offences, it must be observed that the intent was considered as equally criminal with the fact; and persons were often executed as offenders who, in the language of the present time, would be thought to have actually committed no offence. It was said by Shard, in the twenty-seventh year of the king, that a person taken *deprædando vel burgulando* should be hanged, though he did not put in execution his design; the same of a man who

1 13 Ass., 6.
2 27 Ass., 69.
3 42 Ass., 5.
4 *Vide ante*, vol. i. c. iv.
5 22 Ass., 39.
6 18 Ass., 1.
7 *Vide ante*, vol. i. c. iv.
8 Bro. Cor., 219.
9 18 Ass., 1.
10 *Vide ante*, vol. i. c. iv.
11 22 Ass., 95.
12 *Ibid.*, 39.

assaulted with intent to rob, though he took nothing.[1] This noti was of very ancient date, and prevailed all through this reig When common offenders were pursued with such violent presum tions, the severity with which state crimes were prosecuted cann be wondered at. The statute of treasons seems only to have p treasons upon the same foot with felonies; for by that statute su delinquents were not to be convicted, unless they had signifi their intent by some manifest *overt* act, like that of *deprædando burgulando* in a felon.

If the law punished those who only attempted to commit offence, it is not to be wondered that those who were accomplic to the commission of the fact were subject to the animadversion the law. Little is said on the subject of *principal and accessa* by Bracton. Some decisions in this reign give an insight into t distinct marks of these two degrees of offenders. If a man receiv a felon, so as to aid or favour him in his felony, he became accessary; but if he aided him *per bon parol, ou suist*, or se letters for his deliverance, this did not make him an accessar The idea of accessary was carried very far; for if an accessary w received by any one, such receiver became accessary to the acce sary, and might be appealed as such.[3] A man might be tried accessary after he had been acquitted as principal; for where person on a plea of not guilty was acquitted, he was afterwar indicted for receiving the man who had committed that sar felony, after he had been outlawed for it; and he was arraign and obliged to plead to it;[4] for it was said his acquittal could ha no effect to discharge him of an offence which he had committ since. It was a general rule that an accessary should not be p to answer in any case of felony till the principal was attainted; a this was the practice all through this reign.[5] Every precauti was used to prevent the accessary being tried for an offence befc it was proved that the principal had really committed it, to avc the absurdity of making a man accessary to a crime which did n exist, or at least had not been proved on the person who committ it. For the same reason, where a man claimed his clergy, and w found guilty by an inquest of office, yet the accessary was n arraigned, because there was a possibility that the principal mig make his purgation before the ordinary;[6] and should the accessa have been found guilty and hanged, this incongruity would bri a scandal on the justice of the kingdom.

If the principal was found guilty of justifiable homicide *se* (*fendendo*, and had his charter of pardon, as there was no felo proved upon the principal, the accessary went quit.[7] Again, wh the principal and accessary were both indicted, it was held a gc plea for the accessary to say that the principal was dead; and the principal was hanged for any other felony, the accessary was

[1] 27 Ass., 38. [2] 26 Ass., 47. [3] *Ibid.*, 52. [4] 27 Ass.,
[5] 44 Edw. III., 7. [6] 5 Ass., 5; 18 Ass., 13; 26 Ass., 27. [7] 15 Ass.,

be discharged.[1] Thus it became usual in all cases, not excepting homicide itself, where the principal was not yet attainted, to let the accessary to mainprise.[2]

By the old law, judgment of felony did not use to be passed against an infant within age; but we have before mentioned the case of a girl of thirteen years who was burnt for killing her mistress; this was in the twelfth of this king; they seemed, however, to think that the propriety of executing judgment of death on a child was to depend on the appearance of capacity and understanding, which would be different in different persons. If a child did anything which showed he was sensible of having acted wrong, they pronounced that *malitia supplet ætatem*, and proceeded as with an adult.[3] Married women were in Bracton's time considered as *in potestate viri*, and so privileged in cases of felony; but that was with a distinction which has not been observed so much as the good sense of it deserved.[4] A married woman in this reign would have confessed the felony, and that she did it by the command of her husband; but the judge would not take the confession; however, he directed the jury to find that she did it by coercion of her husband, and upon that she went quit.[5] A woman might plead her pregnancy to respite her execution; but this would not be allowed a second time.

The offence of conspiracy, the legal consideration of which had become a great object since the reign of Edward I.,[6] might be prosecuted either at the suit of the king or of the party; and the judgment in those two cases was different. In the latter it was for a recovery of the damage sustained by the plaintiff, and for imprisonment of the defendant; in the former, the offender underwent a similar pain with attainted jurors—namely, that he was to lose his *liberam legem*, to be no more put on juries or assizes, nor to be a witness; and, if he had any business in the king's court, he was always to make an attorney to sue for him; he was not to come within twelve miles of the king's residence; his lands and chattels were to be seised into the king's hands, his houses to be destroyed, his wife and children turned out, his trees cut down, and his body imprisoned.[7] By what authority the *villainous judgment* (for so this was called) was made the punishment in cases of conspiracy, does not appear; it was not prescribed by the statutes of Edward I., which gave the writ of conspiracy. The affinity which this offence bore to the false swearing of jurors (being often the cause and motive of it) might naturally dictate a like mode of punishing those who were guilty of it.

Appeal.

We have seen that the statute of Gloucester[8] had taken away the necessity of making fresh suits in prosecuting an appeal, provided the party commenced it within a year

[1] 22 Ass., 40.
[2] 40 Ass., 8.
[3] 12 Ass., 30.
[4] *Vide ante*, vol. i. c. viii.
[5] 27 Ass., 40.
[6] *Vide ante*, vol. i. c. iv.
[7] 46 Ass., 11.
[8] *Vide ante*, c. ix.

after the fact. The method of prosecuting an appeal in this reign was as follows: The prosecutor was to come in full county within a year and day after the fact, and find two sufficient pledges of prosecution; the coroner was then to enter his appeal on the roll, and forthwith command the bailiff of the place to have the body of the appellee at the next county; and if the bailiff testified at two counties that he was not to be found, then he was to be demanded from county to county till he was outlawed. Should the plaintiff make any default, the *exigent* was to cease, as in Bracton's time, till the coming of the justices in eyre, and the plaintiff lost his suit.[1] It was held, very early in this reign, that appeals would lie before justices of gaol delivery. It was agreed that an appeal would lie in the king's bench at Westminster of a robbery in Yorkshire, on the idea that the justices there were the sovereign coroners of the land, and therefore they might do such acts as the sheriffs and coroners did with relation to appeals in their respective counties.[2] Appeals, like other records, might be removed from before the coroners into the king's bench.

The stat. Westm. 2, which gave imprisonment and damages in case of false appeals, occasioned some discussion.[3] It was held, that though the defendant was acquitted, yet there should be no inquiry of the damages, or abettors, if an indictment had been preferred; as thereby a fair presumption of guilt was raised, sufficient to take away all charge of malice in the plaintiff. But the appeal and indictment must appear to be precisely for the same offence; for if they did not agree, as where one was against the party as principal, the other as accessary, there the defendant might have his damages; the same if the indictment was brought after the appeal.[4] If the jury found it homicide *se defendendo*, there would be no inquiry of damages or of the abettors, because the jury had thereby pronounced there was no malice.[5]

The object in an appeal of robbery, or larceny, was the restitution of the thing stolen, which could not be obtained by conviction upon an indictment. In order to do justice to the person who had been spoiled, it was held, that though the defendant had his clergy, yet the plaintiff should be entitled to a restitution.[6] A difficulty arose where a man was appealed by three different persons, and being convicted at the suit of one, was hanged: it was said, the others should have no restitution, but that the goods should be all forfeit. Yet one of the justices directed an inquest to try whether the thief was taken by the other persons, and whether the goods were theirs; and both these issues being found in the affirmative, they had restitution, as being no ways in default.[7] The same method was taken if the defendant stood mute upon an indictment, and an appeal was then depending:[8] in like manner where the defendant, after pleading not guilty, fled to sanctuary[9] and abjured.

[1] 22 Ass., 97. [2] 17 Ass., 5. [3] *Vide ante*, vol. i. c. iv.
[4] 40 Ass., 18; 22 Ass., 39; 40 Edw. III., 42. [5] 22 Ass., 77. [6] 44 Edw. III., 44.
[7] *Ibid.* [8] 22 Ass., 16. [9] 26 Ass., 32.

There was commonly both an indictment and an appeal depending for the same fact; and the appeal would sometimes, on default of the appellor, be arraigned at the suit of the king. A woman appealed a man, and he was acquitted, the offender and several others were afterwards indicted of the same fact; upon which she brought a fresh appeal: but it was held, that when she had brought one appeal, and the defendant was acquitted by nonsuit after appearance, or in any other way, she could not have a second appeal against any others: so they were arraigned at the king's suit.[1] If an appeal was null or defective in form, and so the plaintiff could not prosecute it, neither could it be arraigned at the suit of the king.[2] An acquittal upon an indictment within a year after the fact, was thought to be no bar to an appeal;[3] the plaintiff being entitled, it should seem, to bring his appeal at any time within the year. The higher suit was the appeal, which was therefore more favoured than the indictment. An heir brought an appeal after an indictment, and the declaration agreed neither in year, day, nor weapon, with the indictment; afterwards the parties compromised the matter, and the plaintiff was nonsuit after declaration: but notwithstanding this, the defendant was arraigned upon the declaration, and not upon the indictment, and a *cesset processus* was entered on the indictment.[4] In an appeal by an infant, the parol used to demur; and if the party was arraigned on the indictment and pleaded not guilty, he would be let to mainprise till the infant was of age to prosecute the appeal.[5] It has been before remarked, that the attainder of the ancestor was held a good plea to bar the heir of an appeal, though it would not bar the widow; the former being an action which accrued by reason of blood, the latter not.[6]

It had long been agreed, that, should a person be struck in one county and die in another, an appeal might be brought in the county where he died: and if the defendant was arraigned at the suit of the king, a jury should be summoned out of both counties.[7] But where an appeal was brought against two, one for killing in one county, and the other for receiving the offender in another, it was agreed that an appeal could not be laid against a principal in one county, and an accessary in another, unless where it was in one vill that extended into two counties; the former cases, however, were admitted to be law.[8]

Appeals by provors were still a common mode of prosecution, and many decisions happened which show the nature of this proceeding. It was agreed that none but such as were in prison for felony could become provors.[9] If a provor received the king's pardon after the appeal, the appellees went quit; but should a provor disavow his appeal, or die, between the joining battel, or issue, and the trial, the appellee was to be arraigned at the suit of the

[1] 47 Edw. III., 16.
[2] 27 Ass., 25; 13 Ass., 11.
[3] 17 Ass., 1.
[4] 4 Edw. III., 10.
[5] 32 Ass., 8.
[6] 2 Ass., 3; *vide ante*, c. ix.
[7] Bro. App., 149; 41 Edw. III., 6, 19.
[8] 45 Ass., 9.
[9] 21 Edw. III., 18; *vide ante*, vol. i. c. viii.

king; so that in this respect it was like a common appeal or an indictment.[1] The following cases may give some idea of the effect and consequences of this mode of prosecution. A provor was hanged, and the appellee was not arraigned at the suit of the king.[2] A provor was nonsuited, and then offered to plead that he was taken out of sanctuary; but this plea was not allowed after he had confessed the felony by becoming a provor, and he was adjudged to be hanged.[3] A man after pleading not guilty was not permitted to become a provor.[4] A provor was hanged for appealing persons out of the kingdom, who being out of the reach of the law could not be attainted:[5] so strictly were these persons held to the performance of the terms on which they were to have their lives. A provor disavowed his appeal, on pretence that he made it by duress; the coroner denied this; and the record of the coroner was judged sufficient evidence of his being voluntary in the appeal, and he was accordingly hanged.[6] Where a defendant in an appeal of robbery wanted to approve the appellor, and demanded a coroner for that purpose, it was held that he could not make an appeal of any other than the goods in question.[7] It was a good plea against a provor to say he had abjured the realm, and so was out of the common law; and if it was found to be so by the rolls of the coroners, he would be hanged, and the appellee go quit:[8] outlawry was likewise a good plea against a provor.[9]

Indictments.

The proceeding by presentment and indictment became more common in cases of felony, than it had been in any former period. As indictments were, by a statute of Edward I., directed to be in writing and indented,[10] they after that, were framed with deliberation and in form. Wherever an indictment was presented for a matter which by the old law might have been prosecuted by appeal, it was natural to adopt the words and phrase of such appeals; so that an indictment differed very little from an appeal of the same offence, except in the introductory part: *Juratores pro domino rege super sacramentum suum presentant quòd, &c.*

The commissions of *oyer et terminer*, besides enumerating specific offences, authorised the commissioners to hear all "damages, grievances, extortions, and deceits," done to the king and his people. Owing to this, an idea had prevailed, of the great extent of the inquisitorial authority with which the presentors before such commissioners were invested; and many misprisons and irregularities were attempted to be prosecuted in this way, which were perhaps not before considered as criminal, but were thought to be fitter objects of a civil action.

The following are experiments in this liberal sort of penal jurisprudence. An indictment against a person for taking 20s. of such

[1] 47 Edw. III., 5. [2] 21 Edw. III., 17. [3] *Ibid.* [4] 21 Edw. III., 18.
[5] 1 Ass., 2. [6] 12 Ass., 29. [7] 40 Ass., 39. [8] 11 Ass., 27.
[9] 21 Edw. III., 17. [10] *Vide ante*, vol. i. c. iv. c. viii.

a one when he was collector of the taxes, was held good as for extortion; but an indictment against a man as "a common misfeasor" was held ill for the uncertainty: the same of a "common thief;" as a man should be brought (it was said) to answer not for every act of his life, but for some particular fact.[1] An indictment for concealing the custom, in order thereby to get advantage of the market, and to enhance the price of merchandise, was held good.[2] But where some justices of *oyer et terminer* were indicted for changing some presentments, by entering on the roll as felonies what were only trespasses, they demurred to the indictment.[3] An indictment, *quòd cepit et asportavit* certain charters concerning land was held ill, as not being of a criminal nature.[4] An indictment for voluntarily suffering a felon to escape,[5] and against an indictor *felonicè* for discovering the king's counsel, were held good: the latter, which seems to be a singular case of felony, was said by Shard to be treason.[6]

In the time of Bracton the presentment of offences was, by a jury of twelve, returned for every hundred in the county.[7] But that practice had now received some small alteration; for towards the close of this reign we find, at a commission of oyer and terminer, that besides the return of an inquest for every hundred by the bailiff, the sheriff likewise returned a pannel of knights, which, says the book, were *le graunde inquest.* The inquests for the hundreds still made their presentments, as in Bracton's time;[8] and if they presented, they likewise, no doubt, found indictments; but these were confined to their different hundreds. The grand inquest probably was to inquire at large for every hundred in the county (*a*); and the hundredors became jurors in inquests *de bono et malo*, or *ex officio*, when called upon; and if a commission of assize and *nisi prius* were sitting, they filled the place of jurors occasionally in assizes and juries in civil causes. When the practice began of returning a grand inquest to inquire for the whole body of the county, the business of the hundred-inquest must naturally decline, till at length the whole burthen of presenting and finding indictments

(*a*) Many local courts had criminal jurisdiction, but their jurisdiction could seldom be exercised, because it could only be executed against persons residing within the local limits of their jurisdiction. Thus, in the Year-book, 50 Edward III., it was said by Belknap, J., if a stranger come into the Cinque Ports, and commits a transitory trespass, and afterwards goes out of their jurisdiction, he to whom the trespass is done may have an action at the common law; for it is more for his benefit to have the suit at the common law than within the Cinque Ports; for they have no power to summon any man that is out of their jurisdiction, viz., in the county of Kent or elsewhere, into the limits of their jurisdiction. And thus an appeal of felony was held to lie in Kent for a murder within their jurisdiction, "because, although the Cinque Ports have several liberties (*i.e.*, local courts), yet the reason of the grant of these liberties was for the ease and benefit of the inhabitants, and not for their prejudice" (*Crispe* v. *Virol*, Yelverton's Rep. 13); and it would be for their prejudice if they could not follow murderers or debtors out of their own limited local jurisdiction.

[1] 22 Ass., 73. [2] 43 Ass., 38. [3] 27 Ass., 18. [4] 30 Ass., 27. [5] 27 Ass., 62. [6] *Ibid.*, 63. [7] *Vide ante*, vol. i. c. i. [8] 42 Ass., 5.

devolved upon the grand inquest, and the hundredors continued to be summoned merely for trying issues.

Of penance.

If there remains any doubt whether prisoners were subject to a sort of penance before the stat. Westm. 1, it seems to be wholly removed by some cases reported in this reign; where this penance was inflicted without the least authority from that statute.[1] In the 21st year a man was appealed of robbery, and was taken at the plaintiff's suit with the manor: he then stood mute, and an inquest *ex officio*, as was usual, being empannelled to try whether he could speak, and they finding that he was mute of malice, it was adjudged that he should be hanged; and it was at the same time said, that had it been at the suit of the king, he would have been put to his *penance*, there being this difference between an appeal and an indictment.[2] But this distinction did not hold universally, at least as to the appeal; for in the 43d year, when a woman appealed a man of the death of her husband, and he stood mute, and it was found by an inquest *ex officio*, that he had spoken that same day, he was ordered to the *penance*.[3] It is probable that the latter was the most usual course, and that the robber in the former case was hanged, merely because he was found with the manor. Conformably with this idea, we find that in the 26th year a man after he had adjured the realm, was arraigned, and standing mute, was put to his penance; but it was at the same time said, that a prover standing mute should be hanged.[4] The confession of the prover, and the being taken with the manor, were considered as convictions in themselves, upon which it might be safe to execute an obstinate offender; though it would be rigorous indeed to presume guilt in every one who stood maliciously mute.

Trial by battel and jury.

It was endeavoured by all means to avoid the trial by *battel*, and to encourage that by *jury*.[5] Thus, in an appeal for breaking the king's prison the battel was not allowed. If the defendant was taken at the suit of the appellor, and had escaped, he was ousted of his battel, that being a sort of prison-breaking;[6] the same where a defendant was taken with the manor.[7] The trial by jury, or *per pais*, in civil causes, and the manner in which it was now ordered, has been already mentioned: this trial, in criminal cases, preserved an analogy with it, being distinguished by very few peculiarities. It was no longer the custom, as in Bracton's time,[8] for the defendant to put himself upon a particular *pais* or hundred, or for the judge to direct the fact to be tried by one *pais* in preference to another. The prisoner put himself *upon* the country generally, which implied a jury of the county where the fact arose; but so much of the old practice continued that the *pais* were to consist of some hundredors belonging to the hundred

[1] *Vide ante*, vol. i. c. viii.
[2] 27 Edw. III., 18.
[3] 43 Ass., 30.
[4] 26 Ass., 13.
[5] *Vide ante*, c. ix.
[6] 1 Ass., 3, 6.
[7] *Vide ante*, c. ix.
[8] 4 Ass., 1.

where the vill in which the fact was said to be done was situated. Thus, though the idea of the jury coming from the vicinage, and being therefore acquainted with the fact they were to testify, was, in some measure, given up, this legal privity was, however, still preserved in construction of law; for though the people of one hundred were permitted to try a fact committed in another, the people of one county were not supposed to know, nor were suffered to try a fact arising in another. Therefore, where a man was taken in the county of S. with goods that he had stolen in the county of N., it was said that the justices in the county of S. might put him to answer; and if he pleaded not guilty they might send him for a *pais* in the county of N., no jurors in the county of S. being competent to the trial of a foreign fact.[1]

We have seen a statute made in this reign, ordaining that no indictor should be put on the deliverance of the prisoner whom he had joined in indicting;[2] such therefore was a good challenge to a juror. In order to enable the defendant to make such challenge it was usual to put the indictors' names to the indictment; and it was a good exception to an indictment if it was without them.[3] A doubt might be raised who were meant by the indictors; and it seems that it signified not only the jurors who presented, but those also who were sworn to inform them, or who, in the modern language of the law, preferred the indictment; and in that sense was the word *indictor* taken at this time.[4] If so, the practice now was to challenge *them*, as well as the presentors; and it was probably their names, as well as those of the presentors, that were required to be on the bill of indictment.[5]

The courts seem to have carried the construction of the above statute further than the bare letter of it warranted; for where one of the indictors in trespass got himself to be made foreman of the jury to try the issue in an action brought for the same trespass, he was committed to the Marshalsea and paid a heavy fine; for (they said) he ought to have challenged himself.[6] What other causes of challenge were allowed by the court have been shown before in speaking of jurors in civil actions; but to prevent defendants in criminal cases creating delay, and avoiding a trial by repeated challenges, it was laid down as a rule that where a defendant challenged generally three inquests without cause, he was not to be considered as refusing the law; but if he showed sufficient cause of his challenge, he might challenge even more.[7] If a defendant did not appear to take his trial, process of *capias* issued against him; and nothing else could be done, for it was a rule that an inquest should never be taken by default in criminal cases.

[1] 26 Ass., 32. [2] *Vide ante*, c. ix.

[3] 44 Edw. III., 43. The *seals* of the indictors were, by statute, required to be annexed to indictments. *Vide ante*, c. xiii. [4] 27 Ass., 12.

[5] Though the practice of annexing the presentors' name is out of use, the names of the prosecutor and witnesses are still endorsed; but the point of law which made either of them necessary has been long obsolete.

[6] 40 Ass., 10. [7] 17 Ass., 6.

Sanctuary and clergy.

Sanctuary, abjuration, and clergy, had undergone very little alteration. The law upon these heads stood at present as follows: If a person had been drawn violently from the place where he had taken sanctuary, he might plead this to an appeal or indictment. Where a provor was nonsuit in his appeal, and then pleaded that he was forcibly taken from such a church, where he had fled for sanctuary, and prayed to be restored; it was adjudged that as he had omitted to plead that at first, he should be hanged upon the nonsuit.[1] A person delivered to the sheriff to be executed, if he escaped to a church, was not allowed the privilege of sanctuary.[2] Of all these places of sanctuary (and they were very numerous), the principal was one at Westminster, which belonged to the abbot of that religious house. This was enjoyed under a grant from one of our kings. It was endeavoured in this reign to extend the privilege of this place to debtors and accomptants, and to other cases besides felony; but upon exhibiting the charter granting the privilege of sanctuary to the abbots, they appeared to claim under the following words: *Quòd quisquis fugitivus de quolibet loco pro quâcunq; causâ cujuscunq; conditionis fuerit, si ipse* SANCTUM LOCUM *Westmonasterii fugiens intravit, membrorum et vitæ impunitatem consequatur;* and it was decided by all the justices, notwithstanding the seemingly general exemption given by some of those words, that the sanctuary was confined to felons.[3] The resort of felons to this place, being in the metropolis of the kingdom, must have been very great, and productive of great disorders. The abbot of Westminster was, besides, the ordinary of the king's bench, and had a prison (which in later times was the Gate-house), where he kept those clerks that were delivered to him from the Marshalsea.[4]

The manner of delivering clerks to the ordinary, if clergy was claimed upon the arraignment, was the same as in Britton's time.[5] A jury used to be empannelled *ex officio* to try the fact of clergy; and this was the practice in the last reign. Clergy was allowed to a defendant in appeal as well as on an indictment, and a provor might have his clergy.[6] It seems that a clerk had not his privilege if he was not demanded, or was disowned, by the ordinary. A clerk was found guilty of felony, and showed his clerkship by reading, but nobody challenged him; however, he was not hanged but sent to prison: and this was the usual course, as it should seem, where the party was found guilty by the inquest *ex officio* only. For where the same clerk, choosing to risk a trial rather than suffer indefinite imprisonment, renounced his clergy, pleaded the country *de bono et malo*, and was found guilty, but again claimed his clergy, and no ordinary appeared to challenge him, he was hanged.[7] Again, where a man was found guilty, and upon his claiming his clergy, was refused by the ordinary, because he had broke the archbishop's

[1] 21 Edw. III., 17. [2] 27 Ass., 54. [3] 29 Ass., 34. [4] 21 Ass., 12.
[5] *Vide ante*, c. ix. [6] 43 Edw. III., 42; Bro. Clerg., 26. [7] 12 Ass., 15.

prison, he was hanged by the advice of all the justices.[1] A clerk was attainted of breaking the bishop's prison and claimed his clergy; but it was answered by the judge, *frustra legis auxilium invocat, qui in legem committit.* He said, if the bishop would claim him he might have his privilege; but the ordinary disclaimed him and he was hanged.[2] As there was this distinction between a conviction by the jury *ex officio*, and that *de bono et malo*, it was advisable for a clerk to claim his clergy on the arraignment, lest he should not be demanded by the ordinary after conviction.[3]

When the privilege of clergy thus depended upon the will and pleasure of the ordinary, it was reasonable enough to allow it in the offence of sacrilege, the church being at liberty to pardon offences against itself. It was therefore held that stealing a chalice did not preclude a man from his clergy, if he was claimed by the ordinary[4] (*a*). If a clerk had acknowledged that he was not a

(*a*) This was shown remarkably in the determined endeavour to recover all franchises exercised by subjects. There were many cases of *quo warranto* in the course of the reign, and are to be met with not only in the Year-books of the reign, but in the cases in the time of Edward III., cited in Keilway. There is one case there reported at great length, and which was one of some historical interest, and is extremely illustrative. The abbot of St Peter's was summoned to answer to the king by what warrant he claimed a market and view of frankpledge, and privilege of exemption from the sheriff, and of various franchises he claimed in divers vills and manors. The counsel for the abbot set up a prescription confirmed by Richard I., and showed a charter of confirmation. Then the counsel for the crown demanded by what right the abbot claimed eight hundreds, and the abbot still relied on the prescription and the charter of confirmation, and he also set up an allowance of the charter in the last eyre. The abbot was challenged to show some other title than prescription, and he produced a charter of king Edgar. The counsel for the crown said that king Edgar was before the Conquest, and that by the Conquest all franchises devolved into the hands of the king. It was answered that the Conqueror had not come for the ouster of those who had rightful possession, but of those who occupied wrongfully in disherison of the crown; and, it was added, that many religious houses were founded before the Conquest, whose foundations still continued. The counsel for the crown appears to have been ashamed of the objection and withdrew it, but a number of others were taken and urged with extreme tenacity, and it is manifest that all claims of franchises were in this reign obstinately contested (*Keilway*, 144). The cases of *quo warranto* form the great majority of the cases in that book, entire pages are filled with them, and it is clear that the crown was engaged in a resolute attempt, in pursuance of the policy of Edward I., to seize all franchises upon every possible pretext. It was hardly possible to maintain a franchise in the face of the captious objections taken by the counsel for the crown. If the party claimed by prescription, he was told that the subject could not claim a royal franchise by prescription, but must show some special grant; if he showed a grant he was told that he must show some allowance of it, and if he showed such a charter of confirmation, whether it was before or after the time of legal memory, some exception was certain to be taken. Most of the grants shown were by Henry III., and they were generally, on some ground or other, got rid of (*Keilway*, 152). In another case of *quo warranto* against the master of the Hospital of St Bartholomew's in London, he set up a charter of king Henry III., confirmed by king Edward II. (*Keilway*, 147), and in another case a charter of Henry III. was shown (148), and in another the defendant set up a charter of confirmation by Henry III. to have the franchise in the same way as king John had granted to one C. It was objected by the counsel for the crown that this showed a

[1] 12 Ass., 39. [2] 27 Ass., 42.

[3] Brooke, not observing the difference between a conviction by these two juries, concludes that, as some such disclaimed clerks were hanged, and some not, it rested wholly on the discretion of the justices. Bro. Clerg., 9. [4] 26 Ass., 27.

clerk, yet he would afterwards be permitted to read and show that he was one. Reading seems to have been the grand evidence of clergy: however, we find Shard adopting the saying *quòd literatura non facit clericum nisi habet sacram tonsuram;* and that an ordinary challenging one who was not a clerk should lose his temporalities.[1] A priest who had abjured returned without the king's licence; and being arraigned for this offence and pleading his clergy, he was sent to prison, and it was said he would have been hanged had he been a layman.[2]

Another plea which prevented the going on to trial, was that of *autre foit acquit* of the same felony; upon which the defendant was expected to produce the record of acquittal.[3] It seems not to have been settled whether *autre foit convict* or *attaint* (for no distinction was yet made between[4] them), should be a plea to avoid a second trial. Where a man was appealed by three appeals of robbery, and was convicted on one, the justices had great doubt whether he should be put to answer to the rest or hanged upon that conviction. This doubt was entertained through tenderness to the other appellors, who could not have restitution without a conviction; but, upon consideration, the man was hanged without being arraigned upon the other appeals, and the parties had restitution of their goods *without* a conviction.[5] When this mode was struck out it probably soon became settled that *autre foit attaint* should be a good plea to an indictment or appeal.

Of forfeiture.

The law of forfeiture was strictly enforced in these times, and the occasions of exercising it seem to have been as eagerly caught at. It was held that where a defendant claimed his clergy after verdict of conviction, the judgment was *suspendatur per collum*, and by virtue of this he forfeited his goods. This was another reason for praying clergy before verdict; for then there being no pretence for such a judgment, there was not properly a forfeiture;[6] though there are not wanting instances where the forfeiture was enforced even in such cases.[7] It should seem that no interval was left between the verdict and judgment, but that it was usual to enter it immediately; and therefore, in all the old books, the *conviction* and *attainder* are spoken of without any distinction, as if they were the same thing. The forfeiture in the time of Bracton seems to have been more general than it was now held to be; they then forfeited *all* rights of action.[8] The law now was, that though debts by obligation were forfeit, yet simple contract debts were not: the reason for which was, as has been before observed, that the defendant, who might wage his law in

title by prescription, commencing in the time of king John, long before the time of legal memory; but it was answered, although every king since the time of memory had confirmed, yet it would be still a title by prescription. It was replied that it was a grant by king John, &c. (*Keil.*, 149).

[1] 26 Ass., 19.
[2] 1 Ass., 4.
[3] 26 Ass., 15.
[4] *Vide ante*, c. xii.
[5] 44 Edw. III., 44 b.
[6] 40 Edw. III., 42.
[7] Fitz. Ass., 116.
[8] *Vide ante*, vol. i. c. viii.

such case, would be deprived of that privilege when sued by the king.[1] The goods were forfeited by the issue of the *exigent*, though the party might be afterwards acquitted of the felony.[2] One who fled to a church for felony forfeited his goods, as in other cases of flight, with the profits of his lands; and if he abjured he forfeited his lands also.[3] It was said that land purchased after a felony committed, was forfeited equally with that enjoyed before.[4] In case of a feoffment to baron and feme in fee, if the baron committed felony, the land was not forfeited, but survived entire to the feme, on the idea that the feme could take no moiety with her husband.[5]

Where a person, being issue entail, was outlawed for felony during the life of the tenant, and had his pardon, he might enter, after his ancestor's death, as heir in tail, though it would be otherwise with the heir in fee-simple; but it was thought, that should the ancestor die before the pardon, the heir in tail could not enter, because the king would be entitled to the profits during the life of the outlaw.[6] The striking of a juror for giving a verdict against a man in the hall of Westminster, was an offence that was punished with loss of lands and goods, besides amputation of the right hand.[7] Not to bring this calamity of forfeiture on a man before he was proved guilty, the law still preserved the humanity it professed in Bracton's time.[8] The sheriff was not to seize and carry away the goods of a felon immediately upon his being indicted, but to take surety of the party that they should not be withdrawn; and if he would not give surety they were to be put into the hands of the neighbours to be kept till the event of the prosecution was known.[9]

The king and government.

The dominion of laws and of a settled government seems fully to have established itself under the great power and popularity of this prince (*a*). The law was a protec-

(*a*) This may well be doubted, at all events if it be understood as of something established in this reign; for nothing could be more arbitrary than the system of government pursued by this monarch, although, no doubt, the spirit of resistance to arbitrary power was gradually growing, and, perhaps, the principles of law were slowly gaining ground, so that at the end of this long reign they had acquired a strength which proved itself in the struggles of the next reign. The spirit of resistance, however, asserted itself rather in the reign of the king's weaker successor, just as, after the severe and oppressive reign of the first Edward, it asserted itself under Edward II.; and thus the weaker princes bore the brunt of a reaction caused by the oppressions of the more powerful. Certainly, nothing could be more arbitrary or oppressive than the government of that great monarch, Edward III. Innumerable illustrations might be adduced of this from the legal records of the reign. John, bishop of Winchester was arraigned in the king's bench for that he came to a parliament by summons, and departed without the king's leave. And it was urged by the counsel for the bishop that the matter was one only cognizable in parliament; and it was answered slavishly by the counsel for the crown, that it was the will of the king to prosecute the prelate in this court, no doubt because the judges were likely to be more servile to his will. The court, however, seemed ashamed of the case, and shrunk from determining it, so it ended with an adjournment. "Sir," said the

[1] 50 Ass., 1. [2] 22 Ass., 21, and *passim*. [3] Bro. Forf., 121.
[4] 48 Edw. III., 2. [5] 4 Ass., 4. [6] 29 Ass., 61.
[7] 41 Ass., 25. [8] *Vide ante*, vol. i. c. viii. [9] 43 Edw. III., 24.

tion to the property and lives of the people: and there generally appeared in the reigning power an anxiety to preserve it unviolated. However, it cannot be denied that this king, as well as his predecessors, discovered a strong attachment to the old prerogatives; and there are not wanting instances wherein he acted illegally, and infringed the undoubted rights of the people.

The many confirmations of *Magna Charta*, and the statutes made to prohibit protections, are strong proofs of the practices which called for such parliamentary interposition. All the ancient prerogatives of the crown were, at one time or other, exercised by this king. The levying of money without assent of parliament; the dispensing power; an oblique confirmation of that power by statute 1 Edw. III. c.; monopolies, loans, imprisoning members of the house of commons for freedom of speech, extensions of the forests, renewal of the commission of Trailbaston,[1] pressing men and ships, levying arbitrary fines, the council obliging people to find recruits;[2] all these extraordinary exertions of power were kept on foot by Edward III.

The regard paid by this prince to the sanction of the legislature is shown in one strong instance: Having found it necessary to consent to an act of parliament by which the control over his great officers had been taken from him, and conferred on the parliament; he issued an edict, in which he affirms, that he *only dissembled*

bishop's counsel, "parliament est assemblie des peeres de la terre, pur profit del Roy et de people, doncques quant un des peeres ne vient pas, ou vient et depart sans conge, cel default est auxy bien fait as gents comme al Roy: ou des choses touchants parliament, les peeres serront judges, et ceo chiet en lour record sil depart sans conge de Roy: per que n' entend my que de celuy chose que fuit fait en le place pluis haut, voles cieins conustre que est place pluis base." Scroop (counsel for the crown) said, "Ceux que sout judges de parliament, sont judges de lour peers nes le Roy n'ad my peere en sa terre demesne, per que il nedoit pas per eux estre judge, doncques alors que cy ne port il estre judge, *et la volunt le Roy, est de faire sa suit* vers celuy que luy trespass, ou que luy plerra per que avises vous, and *adjornatur*" (*Year-book*, 3 *Edw. III.*, fol. 63, pl. 32). It does not appear what became of the case. No doubt the object was to terrify the prelate and extort a fine, and probably he compounded with the crown lawyers to obtain peace and protection from further litigation. But that such a prosecution should have been attempted is most significant. In the 20th year of the king (1347), a case occurred, strongly illustrative of the difficulty of obtaining legal redress for injuries done by the ministers or servants of the king. A complaint was made to the king in council by one Geways, that some wool belonging to him had been seized by the king's taxers, in a house in London in which it had been deposited, for the sum of which the owner of the house had been assessed, and a fifteenth granted to the crown. That he had sued to the sheriff and to the court of mayor and aldermen in vain, as the taxers had taken away the wool. That he had sued in the exchequer, but "that through menaces there were none of the country so bold as to come at the summonses," and that he was threatened to be put to death by the taxers unless he abandoned his suit; wherefore he prayed the king in council for remedy, seeing that by no suit at law could he come at a remedy. The answer of the council was simply to send him back to the city, for it was, "Let the mayor of London be commanded to execute the process, and it is not proper that the king should give him any other remedy" (2 *Rot. Parl.*, 186). What this "remedy" was practically worth the unhappy applicant had already proved, and no doubt was fated to prove again; the truth being that the mayor and sheriffs durst not execute their process against the king's collectors, who simply set them at nought. What became of Geway or his suit does not appear. Very likely he realised his own prediction, and was "put to death," to get rid of a troublesome suitor.

[1] 2 Edw. III., 41.

[2] Hum., vol. ii., 490.

when he seemed to ratify that act, but that he had never in his own breast given his assent to it. To prevent, therefore, the inconveniences which he thought he foresaw would follow from that law, he, with the advice of his council, and *some* earls and barons, *thereby abrogated* and annulled it. The next parliament, so far from taking any notice of this extraordinary proclamation, consented to a regular repeal of the statute.[1]

When the parliament was thus contemned in its legislative capacity, the king could have no trouble in managing its judicial decisions according to the exigency of his own occasions.

The earl of Kent was attainted by parliament, without any formality of inquiry (*a*). Roger Mortimer, who had procured that attainder, was himself accused before parliament, and condemned by the lords upon the mere exhibition of the articles, "without any further inquiry, because everything therein contained was notorious, and known to themselves."[2] About twenty years afterwards this attainder was reversed in favour of his son; and the reason there given was the illegality of the proceedings. It is observed that the principles of law and justice in these times were established, not in such a degree as to prevent an iniquitous sentence against a devoted person, but sufficient to serve as a reason for its reversal on a change of things in favour of himself or his party.[3]

The next objects of inquiry are those monuments of legal antiquity which contribute to furnish information through the reign of this king. These are the Statutes, Parliament-rolls, Year-books, and some small law tracts.

The Nova *Statuta.*

The statutes from the beginning of this reign are called *Nova Statuta*, as contra-distinguished from those which preceded. It seems that the commons began now to take some partial share in the legislature, for most of the principal acts made in this reign were made upon petitions of the commons.

(*a*) It was well recognised that the common law only applied in time of peace. Thus, where one Ralph Bassett claimed a manor against John of Derby, on the ground that Ralph, his grandfather, was seised in time of peace, in the time of Edward I., and died seised, he was met by a denial of the averment that it was in time of peace; and said that the allegation was "de substantia rei, car il n'avera pas action de nul seisine en autre temps qu'en temps de pees;" and then it was alleged that Ralph Bassett, the elder, was with Robert, count of Ferrers, in the first war of Lewes, and in the battle took the defendant, John of Derby, prisoner, and held him in prison at Kenilworth or elsewhere while he occupied the manor, until the battle of Evesham, and there died; and so he was not seised except in time of war, and that was held a good issue (*Year-book, 7 Edw. II.*, 226). The principle involved in this case was that the common law was the law of peace, and that rebellion is war; and this principle was implied in many other cases. Thus it was held that it was a good issue that a presentment was or was not in time of war (*Year-book, 7 Edw. II.*, 245, 605); and it was held that a presentment in time of Henry III., in time of war (*i.e.* rebellion), would not make a title (18 *Edw. II.*, fol. 605). The principle lies at the basis of the law of treason, for it is treason to levy war against the crown, and rebellion is held to be war, and, indeed, there can be no other war by subjects against the crown. On the same principle, as already shown in the notes to *Magna Charta*, the celebrated clause, "nullus liber homo," &c., was never supposed to apply to a state of war or rebellion.

[1] Hum., vol. ii., 414; *Parl. Hist.*, vol. i., 264. [2] *Ibid.*, 223. [3] Hum., vol. ii., 379.

However, even in these instances where the motion for a law originated with the commons, and after the answer of the king was favourable, it still remained with the king and his council to digest the whole into the form of a statute, as in former times: the answer to the commons very often intimated that the king would consult with others before he granted the petition; and this was never thought derogatory to their rights.

This will appear plainly from several petitions and answers on the parliament-rolls. In the 21st year of the king, to a petition requesting the king to increase the fees of the judges, he answered, that he would call to him the great persons, and mention the matter to them, and upon their advice would ordain such remedy as should be proper.[1] Again, upon another petition in the same parliament, he answered, he would advise with his council. When petitions were delivered in, they were sometimes not attended to with so much despatch as the commons expected. In the 22d year the commons prayed they might be answered presently; to which it was answered, that they should be answered after Easter.[2] Notwithstanding these remonstrances, it continually happened that the making of laws was delayed; for though the petition might be answered at the session in which it was presented (and this was not always the case), yet sometimes several years elapsed before it was framed into a law. Most of the acts which in the statute-book appear in the 25th year of the king, were answered in the 21st year; some were delayed longer. The petition about error in the court of exchequer was presented first in the 21st year, and answered; but the petition and answer were both forgotten, and the commons petitioned again the next year, when the former answer was referred to by the king;[3] and after all, it was not put into a statute till the 31st year.[4] Many instances are to be found of the like delay.

When statutes were framed so long after the petition and answer, it is not to be wondered that they did not always correspond with the wishes of the petitioners, but were modified according to some after-thought of the king's officers who had the care of penning statutes. The commons often complained of this. In the 22d year they prayed that the petitions answered in the last parliament might not, under pretence of any fresh bill or petition, be altered or changed. But, notwithstanding this remonstrance, the petition and answer were not always adhered to, as the exact model for the statute. In the 25th year, a petition was exhibited against suing before the council, when part of it was granted; as to the rest, the king said he would be advised;[5] and yet stat. 25 Edw. III. stat. 5, c. iv., enacts the whole. Again, in the famous stat. 36 Edw. III., stat. 1, c. xv., about law proceedings, after the words of the petition

[1] Cott. Abri., 21 Edw. III., 6.

[2] *Ibid.*, 22 Edw. III., 7.

[3] *Ibid.*, 21 Edw. III., 26; and 22 Edw. III., 25.

[4] Stat. 31 Edw. III., st. 1, c. xii.

[5] Stat. 25 Edw. III., 16.

are added, "*that they be entered and enrolled in Latin*," of which there is no notice at all in the petition.[1]

The variations above mentioned do not appear to be very material; they did no more than explain in a fuller manner what perhaps was the sense and aim of the petition. It was more important, when a petition was granted, and afterwards never heard of, an instance of which is to be found in 21st year, when a petition, praying that writs of error might be allowed in actions, *qui tam*, was granted by the king, though there appears no subsequent statute to carry it into execution.[2] There are many intimations in the parliament-rolls of acts being to be made, of which, however, we find no other trace whatever.[3]

It is not probable that these petitions and answers were wholly disappointed of their effect, though they were not thrown into the form of a statute. It seems the parliament, upon the petitions of the commons, exercised two branches of authority, by one of which it legislated or made new laws; by the other, it interpreted the then existing law. When, therefore, a declaration of some point was prayed by petition, it was the business of the receivers and tryers of petitions to consider whether the matter prayed could be complied with, conformably with the then existing law, or whether it would be new and inconsistent with it; for in the former case, an answer, accompanied with some instrument to testify it, would of itself be sufficient to warrant it; in the latter, there must be an express statute. It is in this way that the following words of stat. 15 Edw. III., c. vii. are to be understood: "That the petitions showed by the great men and the commons be *affirmed* according as they were granted by the king; that is to say, some by *statute*, and the others by *charter* or *patent*, and delivered to the knights of the shire, without paying anything."

Many examples of a like distinction may be produced out of the parliament-rolls. In the 21st year of the king, it was prayed by the commons that a plaintiff in debt or trespass might have execution of the land which the defendant had the day of the writ purchased. To this it was answered that it could not be done *without a statute*, upon which the king would advise with his council.[4] Again, where the king granted lands forfeited for treason, the commons prayed it might be *declared* whether in such case the donees held of the king, or of the lord of whom the traitor held. To this it was answered that for the present it should remain as it had formerly been; but if *declaration* thereof was to be made, it should be by good advice, among other articles whereof *new law* was required.[5] A similar answer was given to several other petitions in that parliament.[6]

These passages very clearly intimate that there was another par-

[1] Cott. Abri., 36 Edw. III., 39.
[2] *Ibid.*, 21 Edw. III., 24.
[3] Among others, *vide* Cott. Abri., 8 Edw. III., 20–22, and *passim* through that Abridgment.
[4] Cott. Abri., 21 Edw. III., 13.
[5] *Ibid.*, 43.
[6] *Ibid.*, 46, 47, 52.

liamentary way of settling the law than by *statutes*, and that way must have been the *charters* and *patents* mentioned in the above act. Laws of this sort had no other sanction than the parliament-roll, where the answer was written; and these were probably what were called *ordinances*, being of equal force and validity with *statutes*, but less solemn and public, because they were only a declaration, and not an alteration, of the law. A statute was drawn up with the advice and deliberation of the judges and other learned men, and was entered on a roll called the *statute-roll;* afterwards the tenor of it was annexed to a proclamation-writ, directed to several sheriffs to proclaim it in their county.[1] Ordinances were never proclaimed by the sheriff, but it was sometimes recommended by the king to the commons (probably by a *charter* or *patent*) to publish them in their county.

Though these were the peculiar and distinct offices of statutes and ordinances, it is still clear that many things which were mere *declarations* of the old law, were done by statute, as appears by the formal words, and by the contents of several: and as everything might be done by statute that could be done by ordinance, it depended perhaps on the nature of the subject, and the wish of the managers of it, whether the old law should be declared by one or the other. A statute was an ordinance, and something more; and therefore, though statutes may sometimes be called ordinances, yet no inattention to language would excuse the converse of the proposition. Though an ordinance could be altered by a statute, yet a statute could not be altered by an ordinance. After all, perhaps, the principal mark of a statute was its being entered on the statute-roll.

The rolls of parliament during this reign begin to be very complete, and form a very valuable accession to the documents of legal information. They give us an account of proceedings whether judicial or legislative; and in the former are more particularly full and satisfactory.[2]

Reports.

The reports of this reign fill four volumes. Three of these are distinguished as *Year-books*, and are called the *first*, *second*, and *third parts* of Edward III. The other volume is called *Liber Assisarum*, being a collection of cases that arose on assizes, and other trials in the country. The first part contains the first *ten* years of this king, very completely reported: the second part is incomplete, containing the 17th, 18th, 21st, 22d, one term of the 23d, the 24th, and so on to the 30th inclusive; then there is a chasm till the 38th and 39th, which closes the book. The third part begins with the 40th year (and thence it is commonly called the *Quadragesms*), and goes on regularly to the end of the reign. The *Liber Assisarum* contains every year regularly all through the reign.

[1] For the statute rolls, parliament rolls, and bundles of petitions, see *Hale's Conjectures, Jurist*, p. 64.

[2] Manuscript copies of the parliament-rolls are to be found in many public libraries; and they have lately been printed by the authority of parliament.

These books of reports have not maintained an equal reputation with posterity; the book of assizes and the *Quadragesms* having been generally preferred to the rest. But this comparative value is owing perhaps more to the accidents of time and circumstances, than to any intrinsic merit of their own. It happened that many points of learning discussed in the first and second parts became more obscure and less known than those in the third part, in consequence of which, very few cases are abridged from the second part by Fitzherbert and Brooke, and hardly any from the first; and as these two abridgments became in after-times the principal clue to the Year-books, not to say the substitutes for them, the first part of these reports sunk into oblivion, and the second was little regarded; while the *Quadragesms* and the *Liber Assisarum* were alone consulted as depositories of the law in this reign. It should seem this neglect of the older Year-books had, unhappily, an effect upon the still older writings of Fleta and Bracton. A still wider chasm was made between those authors and the latter end of this reign; and as the chain of legal history by which their fidelity as lawyers would be best demonstrated was broken, their credit and authority were considerably diminished.

However, viewing these volumes with the prepossession of a modern lawyer, we must certainly concur with the opinion long entertained in favour of the *Quadragesms* and book of assizes; for, besides that questions are there discussed with more precision and clearness, they contain more of those points of law that have survived to the present times. In regard to precision and clearness, all the reports of this reign excel those of the preceding; but the merit of these volumes is of a peculiar kind, and has a very different appearance from what has in later times been considered as excellent in this way. We find here no learned argument, no quotation of cases, compared, distinguished, and applied to the point in debate. The bench rarely deliver a solemn judgment, setting forth the principles and grounds upon which they proceeded, or alleging any former determination by which they were swayed: a report is little more than a state of the facts, with *dicta* of law on both sides, unsupported by any authority. That the allegations and arguments of counsel should be unsupported by adduced authorities, is not at all remarkable at a time when there was such a scarcity of published reports. This want of written memorials of the law was repeatedly lamented in the reign of Edward I.; and one of the wisest means used by that king towards improving the law, was the ordering of law-books to be written; but the effect of such an undertaking must be slow. We find, in the reign of Edward II., the author of the *Mirror* complains that the law in his time was not sufficiently reduced into writing.

During such a state of things, the knowledge of the law must be confined to the practisers, and subsist rather in the experience of old professors than in volumes of reports; of which there must, in the nature of things, be few in this reign, and those kept, no doubt, with sufficient jealousy, for the use of their owners: the consequence of which would naturally be, that, with the use, the authority of them in a great degree would be confined to their possessors. There were certainly no reports of established and general credit; otherwise it is not easy to imagine why no adjudications are vouched for what is laid down as law in the Year-books of this reign. According to the form of these reports, everything is to be taken on the bare authority of the person pronouncing it.

However unsupported they may seem, the reports of this reign have always had great weight with posterity, though received upon their own authority alone: nor is this without great show of reason. These volumes seemed to claim a higher regard than any which had been produced in the preceding reigns. The law here spoke out in its own written annals, and was delivered by the oracles of it, the judges sitting on the seats of justice. The whole method of legal proceeding was exhibited to the reader. This was a lively way of transmitting the knowledge of our laws; it commanded a more serious regard, and seemed to carry in itself an incontrovertible authority; unlike the treatises written by private men, who, however learned or experienced, could not aim at an equal degree of authenticity. This consideration placed reports in the highest rank of law-books, and made them a sort of authorities in themselves; while the treatises of Bracton and Fleta grew to be less considered, and at length became obsolete.

The reports of this reign engage the attention of a modern lawyer more readily than those of the former, and have always been held in great esteem. The learning, however, of these volumes is of a peculiar kind. Through all the reports of this reign there is perpetual debate on matters of form, which were so repeatedly discussed, and so fully examined, that numberless points of the utmost importance in the practice of those times were settled. The greater part of the reports of this reign seem to be on this subject. To say nothing of the first forty years of this king, upon turning over the celebrated *Quadragesms*, it will appear that nine parts in ten relate to the forms of writs, of pleadings, and of practice; and of these nine, six parts concern real actions.

While the same state of things remained, and the same learning was in vogue, the reports of this reign must have been of great use, and accordingly deserved every encomium which the grateful student could bestow on them; they were accordingly held in great estimation during most of the succeeding reigns, till the time of Henry VII. and Henry VIII. But when another order of things took place, when real actions went out of use, and the learning concerning them was forgotten, the legal annals of this reign must be viewed with a very different eye. Amid heaps of endless curiosity about proceedings in real actions, we find a very small space occupied by decisions on great and leading principles of law. This anxious minuteness in the form and conduct of actions had so loaded and entangled the practice of the courts, that it was found necessary, in after-times, to get rid of them altogether by a revolution in the course of legal remedies. The law-learning in the reign of Edward III., and the scholastic learning of those times, exhibit alike an unhappy misapplication of sagacity and diligence (*a*); and it is only by a partial redemption that the volumes which contain the one have escaped that oblivion which has long overwhelmed the other.

The reign of this king has furnished three small tracts on law subjects: the *Old Tenures*, *Old Natura Brevium*, and *Novæ Narrationes.*

Old Tenures.

The *Old Tenures* (so called to distinguish it from Littleton's book on the same subject) gives an account of the various tenures by which land was holden, the nature of estates, and some other incidents to landed property. It is a very scanty tract, but has the merit of having led the way to Littleton's famous work. The *Natura Brevium* contains those writs which were then most in use, annexing to each a short comment concerning their nature, and the application of them, with their various properties, effects, and consequences. This work became a model to Fitzherbert, in writing his valuable treatise on the same subject. The collection called *Novæ Narrationes* contains pleadings in the actions then in practice. It consists principally of declarations, as the title imports; but there were sometimes pleas, and the subsequent pleadings. The *Articuli ad Novas Narrationes* is usually subjoined to this little book, and is a small treatise on the method of pleading. It first treats of actions and courts, then goes through each particular writ, and the declaration upon it, accompanied with directions, and illustrated by precedents. The book on *The Diversity Courts* is said[1] to have been written in this reign.

Natura Brevium.

Novæ Narrationes.

Miscellaneous facts.

It is beyond dispute that the Temple was inhabited by a law society in the reign of Edward III. Upon the dissolution of the order of Knights Templar in the last reign, their possessions came to the crown. The *New Temple,* as it was then called, to which they had removed from their house in Holborn, about the beginning of Edward II.'s reign, was granted by the late king successively to the earl of Lancaster, the earl of

(*a*) It is curious to observe how early the lawyer's legal technicalities were employed to neutralise the beneficial, amicable jurisdiction of arbitration. Thus it was said that in trespass, an arbitration would be no defence, unless the arbitrator had awarded that something—be it little or much—be given to the plaintiff (*Year-book*, 43 *Edward III.*, 28); and yet it is obvious the trespass might be so trivial that the arbitrator might well award that nothing be given for it. So, again, it was said to be no defence in an action of trespass for taking goods, that there had been an award that the defendant should deliver part, and retain the rest; nor, in an action of debt, that he did pay a part of the sum claimed (*Year-book*, 45 *Edward III.*, 16), although it might be that no more was really due.

[1] 2 Inst., 552.

Pembroke, and Hugh Despencer the son, upon whose severa attainders this property again devolved to the crown. In pursu ance of a decree made by the great council at Vienna, A.D. 1324 respecting the possessions of the Templars, king Edward III granted this building to the Knights Hospitaller of St John o Jerusalem; and they soon afterwards, as the tradition is, demise it at the rent of £10 per annum to divers professors of the law who came from Thavies Inn in Holborn.[1] At the general disso lution of religious houses, when the inheritance of this house agai fell to the crown, king Henry VIII. granted them a lease, an they continued tenants to the crown till the sixth year of kin James I., when that king granted *hospitia et capitalia messuagi cognita per nomen de le* INNER *et le* MIDDLE TEMPLE *sive Nov Templi*, to Sir Julius Cæsar and others, to them and their heir for the use and reception of the professors and students of the law.

It is said that some professors of the law resided in Gray's In during this reign, under a lease from the Lord Grey of Wilto who was seised of the inheritance, and had a mansion there. Th inheritance was, in 20 Edw. IV., purchased by the prior and monk of the monastery of Sheene in Surrey, to whom the students con tinued tenants, at the rent of £6, 13s. 4d. per annum. At the dis solution of religious houses, Henry VIII. granted the inheritanc to the society at the above rent in fee-farm.[3]

The most authentic memorial of any settling of the law-societie in this reign is a demise in 18th of Edw. III. from Lady Cli ford, *apprenticiis de banco*,[4] of that house near Fleet Street, calle Clifford's Inn.

The chancery, as well as the king's bench, followed the cour and the chancellor and his officers were entitled to part of the pu veyance made for the king, till the 4th of Edward III., when h fixed his seat at Westminster. The place where the chancell held his court was at the upper end of Westminster Hall, at great marble table (which is said to be covered by the courts sin erected there), to which there was an ascent by five or six steps.[5]

The salaries of the judges, though they had continued the sam from the time of Edward I. to the 25th of this reign, were agai become very uncertain. In 28th of Edward III. it appears that o of the justices of the king's bench had 80 marks per annum. In 3 Edw. III. the judges had in that court £40. The chief and oth barons in 36 Edw. III. had £40. In 39 Edw. III. the justices the bench had £40, and the chief of the king's bench 100 marks.[6]

A house had been founded by Henry III. for the reception convert Jews. The presidency of this house had been usual granted to some of the clerks in chancery—namely, those *de prim formâ*, who were always ecclesiastics, and lived as a part of t chancery in the king's palace till the 4th of Edw. III. In the 15

[1] Dugd. *Or. Jur.*, 145.
[2] *Ibid.*
[3] *Ibid.*, 272.
[4] *Ibid.*, 141.
[5] *Ibid.*, 37.
[6] *Ibid.*, 105.

Edw. III. the headship of this house was annexed by charter to the keepership of the rolls, which was confirmed by act of parliament in the 51st year of this king. The keepership of the rolls was thereby rendered more considerable; being endowed with this house of the gift and patronage of the king, the nomination of clerks of the rolls was by degrees assumed by the crown, in exclusion of the chancellor. This officer for keeping the rolls was anciently called, *Gardein de Rolls; Clericus et Custos Rotulorum;* then *Clericus Parvæ Bagæ, et Custos Rotulorum et Domûs Conversorum.* In no statute is he called *Master*, till the 11th of Henry VII. cap. xviii.; and again, in 25th chap. of the same statute, he is called *Clerk.* This office was considered as a preferment for ecclesiastics (*a*).[1]

(*a*) The most ample and interesting information upon all these subjects may be found in the "Lives of the Judges," by Mr Foss, one of the most valuable and interesting works of the present age.

[1] *Hist. Chanc.*, 21.

CHAPTER XVII.

RICHARD II.

Copyholds—Statutes of Liveries—Of the Clergy—Heretics—Vicarages—Mo main—Statutes of Labourers—Of Pernors of Profits and Uses—Judicat of the Council—Of the Parliament—Origin of the Court of Equity Chancery—Court of the Constable and Marshal—Of the Admiral—Cour Exchequer—Statutes of forcible Entries—Of Treasons—Scandalum M natum—Game Laws—Justices of the Peace—The King and Gove ment.

In the reign of Edward the Third we took a short view of the la in general, comparing it, in many instances, with its ancient sta as delivered by Bracton and the older writers. It seemed that great object would be attained if a connexion and dependence cou be shown between the learning of these two periods in our ancie law. After this, perhaps, the reader will be content that the r mainder of the subject should be drawn into a smaller compa and treated less in detail.

However, this wish to set bounds to our inquiry must be govern by the nature of the materials. The progress made in the alter tion or improvement of the law by decisions of courts, is by mar and those very short steps; and to pursue these with minutene if at all possible, would, when on questions not wholly new, be u entertaining and tiresome: but it is very different with statutes they make a long stride at once, and the advance thereby effect is too discernible to be passed over in silence. It appears, therefo incumbent upon a juridical historian, whatever liberty he may ta with one part of his materials, at least to state the substance statutes with fulness and fidelity. Conformably with this idea shall, in the remainder of this work, continue to give the statut at length, as in the former reigns; but in what relates to the d cisions of courts, we shall be more sparing; sometimes confini ourselves to such adjudged cases as relate to the new points whi were now arising in many branches of our jurisprudence.

In the present reign we shall omit all notice of the decisions courts; partly because the reader, who has just left the precedi reign, will perhaps, for the reason above mentioned, not wish partly because no Year-book of this reign is existing, and the rem nants and abstracts of adjudged cases, which are to be found different compilations, are not of much importance, and wou hardly add a link to the chain of our historical deduction. In t meantime, the parliamentary alterations of the law are of gre moment, and will amply make up for the deficiency in the oth head of inquiry. We shall therefore take a view only of the statute-law of this reign; and we shall divide it into such as is of a miscellaneous kind, and such as relates to the rights of property, and the administration of justice.

To begin with the former. A statute was made in the 21st year of the king, to annex to the county of Chester certain forfeit lands which had belonged to the earl of Arundel; it was, at the same time, enacted that the county of Chester should thenceforward be called *The Principality of Chester*, and should always go to the king's eldest son, with the rights and franchises thereto belonging.[1]

In order to secure the regular attendance of persons in parliament, it was thought fit to make a statute, in the 5th of the king,[2] ordaining that all persons and commonalties which from thenceforth should have summons to come to parliament, should attend, as they were bound to do, and had formerly done: and it was enacted, that if any so summoned, whether archbishop, bishop, abbot, prior, duke, earl, baron, banneret, knight of the shire, citizen of city, burgess of borough, or other singular person or commonalty, absented himself (unless he could reasonably and honestly excuse himself to the king), he should be amerced, and otherwise punished, as formerly; the same of sheriffs who were negligent in making returns of parliamentary writs, or who left out of the returns any cities or boroughs which were bound, and formerly were wont to come to parliament. The election and return of members to serve in parliament were further considered in the two subsequent reigns.

In the 12th year of the king, an act was made to remove some doubts which were entertained about the levying of the expenses of knights of the shire upon lands held by lords. To settle this, it was enacted that they should be levied as formerly, with this consideration, that if any lord, or any other man, spiritual or temporal, had purchased lands or tenements, or other possessions, which were contributory to such expenses before the time of the purchase, they should continue contributory as before.

The feudal bond between lord and vassal had been of late years growing weak; and we find now, that villeins and land tenants had begun to break out into violent demands for an exemption from the servitude in which they were held by their tenures. In the first year of this king's reign a statute[3] was made, appointing commissioners to inquire into these differences. It seems that many of these claims were pretended to be founded on the evidence of Domesday book; which was nothing more than demanding, in other language, to be put in the condition of landholders in the time of Edward the Confessor; the cry that had been kept up in the early times of the Norman constitution. These matters, as far

[1] Stat. 21 Rich. II., c. ix. *Vide ante*, vol. i. c. i.
[2] Stat. 2, c. iv.
[3] Stat. 1 Rich. II., c. vi.

as the claim of right went, were referred to the examination of th parliament, while the justices of the peace were commissioned t suppress the tumults and outrages committed by the claimant The impatience expressed by these inferior landholders might b encouraged by the ancient title which they now seemed to posses in their lands. Instead of the precarious holding at the absolut

Copyholds.

will of the lord, as originally, we find in the latter en of the last reign, mention of *tenants by copie of court rol* which indicates that villenage was, in some places at least, becom of a more stable nature; and villein-tenants were enabled to set u a species of *title* against their lord. However, this tenure *by cop* is not mentioned in the Old Book of Tenures, nor does any discu sion upon it appear in the reports of Edward III. We must ther fore wait till a later period, when it was more generally acknov ledged, for a better account of this new species of tenure.

Statutes of liveries.

The condition of the times, and the turn of manners which no prevailed, made it desirable and necessary for gre lords to supply this defection in their tenants by oth expedients.[1] It accordingly had become the custom to *retain* pe sons in their service, to be at call when their lords' affairs neede their support: and in order to distinguish different partisans, well as to give a splendour to such retinue, they used to dress the in *liveries*, and *hats* of a particular make or colour. This distin tion of dress gave origin and strength to a spirit of party, whi became very general. Besides those who were retained by gre men, fraternities used to be formed of persons concurring in t same sentiments and views, who bound themselves to support ea other on all occasions, and denoted their union by similarity dress. Thus, the country everywhere abounded either with t adherents of great men, or societies which were ready to becor such; and persons of weight and influence could never want a s of determined followers to maintain and abet them in any pub violence or dangerous scheme of ambition. (*a*)

These confederacies became a terror to the government, a were the occasion of the *statutes of liveries* passed in this and t

(*a*) Some immaterial alterations were made in this statute under Henry VI. (*v post*, c. xx.); but in substance the statute remained as now enacted, although it very little enforced in this reign, or that of Henry VI., and it was reserved for stricter and sterner rule of Henry VII. really to carry them out. In an informat in that reign, on the statute of liveries, it was objected that there were several s statutes as that of Edward III. and Henry IV., which apparently was a mistake Richard II. and Henry VI. (*Year-book*, 5 *Hen. VII.* fol. 17). In that reign the statu were rigidly enforced; in this reign not at all. Had they been so enforced in reign, it would not have had such a tragical issue, and the country would have b spared the civil wars which ravaged the country for so many years. The mischief wh the statutes were intended to prevent was well described in one of the cases in reign of Henry VII.: "If (it was said) a man gave liveries, he should have a g company of men at his disposal, so that men would fear to execute the laws aga him" (6 *Hen. VII.* fol. 13). It would be impossible to describe the evil more tru and the history of this and the ensuing reigns amply illustrates it. The country no peace or security until these statutes were rigidly put in force.

[1] *Vide ante*, c. xiii.

following reigns. The first of these is stat. 1 Ric. II. c. vii., which ordains that no livery be given by any man for maintenance of quarrels and other confederacies, upon pain of imprisonment and grievous pain to the king. This statute speaks of *esquires*, as well as others, being the sort of people who used to be retained in this way. By stat. 16 Ric. II. c. iv., it was provided that no yeoman, nor other of lower estate than an *esquire*, should use or bear livery, called *livery of company*, of any lord, unless he was menial and familiar, and continually dwelling in the lord's house. There is no earlier mention of an esquire than in these acts; it seems to have been not a very high rank in the orders of society, being only next above a yeoman.[1] As the giving of liveries was a matter in which *the peace* was principally interested, we find in stat. 20 Ric. II. c. i., for enforcing the statute of Northampton, and declaring *lancegaies* and armour to be unlawful, a clause ordaining that no lord, knight, nor other should go or ride armed by night or by day, nor bear pallet nor skull of iron, nor of other armour, except the king's officers and ministers; and moreover, that the above statutes of liveries and hats should be observed. The cognizance of these statutes was first submitted to the jurisdiction of the justices of assize, and afterwards to that of the justices of the peace.

Of the clergy.

Notwithstanding the precarious authority which Richard held among his contending nobles, he maintained with firmness the opposition begun by Edward III. to clerical usurpations.[2] New statutes of provisors were enacted; and while the independence of the national church was vindicated, some steps were taken towards preventing the bad effects of *appropriations;* some regulations were also made for the security of tithes, and the personal privilege of clerks. We shall mention these provisions in the order in which they were made.

The first act relating to the clergy was stat. 1 Ric. II. c. iii., which gives prelates and clerks an action of trespass against purveyors to recover damages for a breach of any of the statutes made in the last reign against those oppressors of the people.[3] This was because they could not by any of those acts proceed criminally against purveyors. Complaint was made that indictments used to be preferred against prelates and clerks suing for their right in the spiritual court, and even against spiritual judges for entertaining the suit; and under colour of such indictments they used to be imprisoned, and otherwise vexed, till they entered into obligations and promises to desist from their suits. It was enacted by the same statute, c. xiii., that such obligations should be void; that the procurers of such indictments, if the party was acquitted, should be prosecuted as directed by stat. Westm. 2, c. xii.,[4] and that the justices before whom the acquittal was, should have power to inquire

[1] The *Franklein*, as described in a contemporary work, I mean Chaucer's *Canterbury Tales*, seems to have been a higher order of yeomen; such as a *wealthy farmer*, or *gentleman farmer*. *Vide Canterb. Tales*, the *Franklein's Tale*.

[2] *Vide ante*, c. xiii. [3] *Ibid.* [4] *Ibid.*

of such procurers, and punish them as they deserved. Again, it was provided by the following chapter of the same act, that where an action for goods taken and carried away was brought for tithes against a parson, and he pleaded that it was a matter of tithes belonging to his church, the general averment should not be taken without showing specially how they were his lay chattel.

Complaint was made in the last reign of priests being arrested in church, and a general provision had been framed to prevent it;[1] but now it was more specially ordained, that any of the king's ministers so doing should be imprisoned, and pay a fine to the king, and compensation to the party; only this was not to extend to clerks who held themselves within churches or sanctuaries by fraud or collusion. The persons entitled to this privilege are thus described by the preamble of the statute: Clerks in cathedral or other churches, or churchyards, and those bearing the body of our Lord to sick persons.

Notwithstanding the statutes made in the last reign [2] to restrain the gifts of church-benefices to aliens, that practice still continued; and, many livings being held by foreigners, all the ill consequences following from non-residence were miserably felt. A new act was now made to prevent, if possible, this irregular and destructive practice. It was enacted by stat. 3 Ric. II. c. iii., in the most explicit terms, that no one without the licence of the king should receive procuracy, letter of attorney, ferm, or other administration of any benefice within the realm, from any person except the king's liege subjects. As foreign incumbents could not manage the revenues of their benefices but by some of the above means, it was intended hereby to make them ever after unproductive to the possessor. It was, moreover, ordained that every one who had accepted such procuracy or administration from aliens, should abandon it within forty days after publication of this act. None were to convey money or other things out of the realm for the use of such alien incumbents. If any was guilty of a breach of this act, he was to incur the penalties of the statute of *provisors*, 27 Edw. III., by the process ordained in that act; in addition to which process it was now ordained, that should the offenders be out of the realm, and not beneficed, nor have any possessions within the realm, where they might be warned, then a writ should be made in the chancery grounded upon this ordinance, directed to the sheriff of the county where they were born, returnable in one bench or the other; which writ was to issue at the king's suit. This writ was to command that proclamation be made for them to appear at a certain day in the bench where the writ was returnable, at the distance of half a year, to answer the matters contained in the writ; and upon the return thereof, the justices were to proceed in the above form. It was also ordained that no bishop should meddle with the benefice of such alien by sequestration, or in any other manner.

[1] *Vide ante*, c. xiii. [2] *Ibid.*

It is said[1] that the lords spiritual did not assent to this statute; which, it may be observed, is all through termed an *ordinance.* Indeed, the higher clergy were not much interested to suppress this practice; as they still enjoyed their bishoprics, and might have views at the court of Rome, which they would be very ready to promote by a connivance at practices so advantageous to the pope and his adherents. But though these pious prelates did not contribute their sanction to a national provision for the maintenance of alms and piety, they were not ashamed to palm upon the country an ordinance of their own fabrication as a legislative act, though the consent of the commons was never taken. But this was a case in which their influence and dignity were concerned, and where they did not think it wise to be over-scrupulous. The act alluded to is stat. 5 Ric. II. st. 2, c. v., which was levelled at the followers of Wickliffe, who by their lives and doctrines, as well as by their numbers, had become a terror and reproach to the higher orders of the church. These people are described as persons who went from town to town under pretence of great holiness, and without the licence of the ordinary, or other authority, preaching daily in churches, churchyards, markets, fairs, and other open places, uttering in their sermons heresies and notorious errors. To give better colour to violent measures, it is added that they preached divers matters of slander to engender discord and dissension between divers estates of the realm.

Heretics.

These preachers had been frequently brought before the bishops, but without their admonitions producing any effect. To make quick work, it was now ordained that the king's commissions should be directed to the sheriffs and other officers, or other learned persons, in pursuance of certificates from the bishops, to be made in the chancery from time to time, to arrest all such preachers, with their maintainers and abettors, and hold them in prison till they would justify themselves according to the law and reason of holy church (*a*). Thus was the secular power to be let loose upon the

(*a*) It is to be observed that the king's commissions were required to allow of these proceedings, and that the authority of parliament was given to the issuing of these commissions; and further, it is to be remarked that, as the statutes of provisors and of præmunire, passed in the same reign, show, the influence of the church would not have procured this law to be passed, had it not, for some reason, obtained the support of the commons and the lay lords. And there is abundant evidence in contemporary history, that, rightly or wrongly, these "Lollards" were regarded—as our author appears to hint—rather as political fanatics than merely as religious heretics, and that at all events they were looked upon as sectaries whose notions were dangerous to property. In short, the "Lollards" were looked upon as levellers; and therefore it would be unfair to attribute this law entirely to the influence of the church, or to the spirit of religious bigotry. It had its rise really in the hostility felt by persons of property to a new sect, apparently regarded as inimical to the established order of things. In an age like that, in which the nation was as yet immersed in ignorance, and the criminal code was still in the last degree barbarous, and marked by horrid penalties, it would be natural, however lamentable, that to this new offence, which was regarded as savouring not only of heresy but rebellion and revolution, some cruel punishment should be inflicted; but a fair view of the law can

[1] *Vide* Cott. Abri., *ad locum.*

followers of Wickliffe, whenever it seemed good or expedient to the bishops. This provision was highly resented by the commons, who, in the next year, declared they meant not to bind themselves and their heirs to the prelates any more than their ancestors had done; and that they therefore never consented to the law: it was accordingly revoked by the king.[1]

In the seventh year of the king, the subject of *alien-incumbents* was again taken up; the statute made in the third year was confirmed: and it was, moreover, enacted by stat. 7 Ric. II. c. xii., that the provisions of it should extend to all aliens purchasing, or who had purchased benefices; and they were likewise to incur the penalties of stat. 25 Edw. III. st. 5, c. xxii., made against those who purchased provisions of abbeys or priories. The king likewise commanded all persons to abstain from praying of him licences for such purchases. To facilitate the execution of this and the former statutes, it was the same year ordained,[2] that persons against whom writs of *præmunire facias* were sued,[3] and who were then out of the realm, or should go out of the realm by the king's licence, if they were of good fame, might appear by attorney.

These practices of the churchmen were pursued still further by the legislature. In stat. 12 Ric. II. c. xv., it was ordained that no liegeman should go or send out of the realm by licence or without (unless he had the special leave of the king himself), to provide or purchase for him a benefice; and that any such person should be considered as out of the king's protection, and the presentation be void. Again, by stat. 13 Ric. II. st. 2, c. ii., the stat. 25 Edw. III. st. 6, was confirmed;[4] and it was, moreover, enacted that if any one accepted a benefice contrary to that act, and was beyond sea, he should remain exiled and banished out of the realm for ever; and his lands and tenements, good and chattels, forfeited to the king: if within the realm, he was to leave it within six weeks next after his acceptance, and remain banished for ever; and any one receiving such banished person was to be punished in the same manner. It was, moreover, provided, if any one sent or sued to the court of Rome, whereby anything was done contrary to this act; such offender, if a prelate, should forfeit one year's value of his temporalities; if a temporal lord, the value of his lands and possessions not movable for a year; if any inferior person, he was

only be had by comparing it not with our own humane code, but with the general character of the laws of the age. Neither would it be fair to regard this as a law passed against mere heresy, seeing that, rightly or wrongly, the professors of the new doctrines were regarded as holding political views hostile to society as then established. Still the fatal precedent appeared to be set—of a penal law against the profession of religious opinion; and the fatal principle of prosecution appeared to be established, which, in subsequent reigns, was so cruelly carried out on both sides; and therefore this statute, taking the fairest and most dispassionate view of it, forms an era in our legal history of sad and sinister significance. Nevertheless, to form a fair judgment upon it, the general character of the laws of the age must be regarded.

[1] Cott. Abri., p. 285, s. 52.
[2] Ch. 14.
[3] *Vide ante*, c. xiii.
[4] *Ibid.*

to pay the value of the benefice for which suit was made, and be imprisoned for a year. But if any man brought or sent within the realm, or within the king's power, any summons, sentences, or excommunications against any one *for the cause of making motion*, assent, or execution of the said statute of *provisors;* he was to be taken, arrested, and put in prison; he was to forfeit his lands and tenements, goods and chattels for ever, and, moreover, incur the pain of life and member. If any prelate made execution of such summons, his temporalities were to be taken into the king's hands till due redress and correction was made therein; and a person of less estate was to be imprisoned, and make fine and ransom according to the discretion of the king's council[1] (*a*).

The two last acts struck deep into the papal authority, and were viewed not without jealousy by the bishops, who were thus gradually withdrawn from the protection of the papal see, and left to the common course of the laws. To show their apprehensions on this subject in a way that would carry an appearance the least offensive, they preserved a silence respecting themselves, but ventured to discover great concern for the interest of the pope. Towards the close of this parliament, we find that the archbishops of Canterbury and York, for themselves and the whole clergy of their provinces, made their solemn protestation in open parliament, that they in no wise meant, nor would assent to any statute or law made in restraint of the pope's authority, but would utterly withstand the same; which protestation was at their desire enrolled.[2]

However, on another occasion, the clergy acted in conformity with the wishes of the commons, though with a reservation of their opinion. This was at the passing of the stat. 16 Rich. II. c. v., which subjected those who purchased bulls from Rome to a *præmunire.* The statute is introduced by a long preamble, which states that all the lords, both spiritual and temporal, had been singly asked in parliament, whether they would support the king in maintaining his authority against the pope's bulls, which were purchased to prevent the execution of judgments passed in the secular courts about advowsons (*b*).

(*a*) A case came before the court in this reign, which tends strongly to show that the papal presentations or "provisions" were legal, and that this was the very reason why the procuring them was made penal. The parson of a church brought an action of account of moneys received for him, and the defendant pleaded that he himself had been parson of the church; and the plaintiff sued a provision in the court of Rome until he had recovered the church against him, and said that these moneys, which were claimed, were oblations and offerings at the church during the time he was parson. This was not denied, and therefore the plaintiff was non-suited (*Bellewe's Cases, temp. Rich. II.* fol. 13). This case seems to show that the papal presentee had actually, notwithstanding the statutes, recovered the benefice upon the papal provision.

(*b*) The principle involved in these statutes, and their practical operation and results, appear to have been of such immense importance that it is proper to draw attention to their terms. The statute of the sixteenth of Richard II. recites, "That our lord the king, and all his liege people ought, and of old time were wont, to recover

[1] Ch. 3.

[2] Cott. Abri., p. 332, s. 24.

The temporal lords declared such interference to be a violation of the old established law of the land; and the lords spiritual having made protestation that it was not their mind to deny nor affirm that the bishop of Rome may not excommunicate bishops,

their presentments to churches, and other benefices to which they had right to present, cognizance of plea of which presentment belongeth only to the king's courts; and when judgment was given therein in such cases, archbishops, bishops, &c., have made execution of such judgments. But of late, divers processes be made to our holy father the Pope, and censures of excommunication against certain bishops of England, because they have made execution of such commandments; and it is said that our holy father the Pope hath ordained and purposed to translate certain prelates of the realm (some out of the realm), without the king's assent and knowledge, and without the assent of the said prelates which shall be so translated, by which the statutes of the realm would be defeated, and the said subjects of the realm carried away, and also the substance of the realm," &c. Thus, therefore, the mischief complained of was the exercise of the papal supremacy *as to temporalty;* and it is to be noted that the prelates concurred in resisting such exercise of it. For they, "protesting that it is not in their mind to affirm or deny that our holy father the Pope may excommunicate bishops, &c., said, that if any executions of processes made in the king's courts, as before" (*i.e.*, according to the old law), "be made, and censures of excommunication be made against any bishops, &c., for that they have made execution of such judgments, and if any translations be made, &c., so that the substance of the realm may be consumed" (as the commons then alleged), "that the same is against the king and his crown, and that the said lords spiritual will, and ought to be, with the king in these cases, in lawfully maintaining his crown, and in all other cases touching his crown and his regalty, as they be bound by their legiance." Whereupon it was ordained, with the assent of the lords spiritual as well as the lords temporal: "That if any purchase or pursue in the court of Rome, or elsewhere, any such processes and sentences of excommunication, bulls, or any other things which touch the king, against him, his crown, and his regality, or his realm, as aforesaid, then they shall be put out of the king's protection." That is to say, that spiritual sentences or censures by the see of Rome, upon any matters which affected the rights of the crown, or interfered with the decisions of its courts, were to be regarded not only as null and void, but as unlawful, criminal, and punishable in all who attempted to put them in force. Now, practically of course, this would include anything which the crown claimed, or which its courts held to belong to it; but the principle affirmed was, that it was not for the pope to interfere in temporal matters. This, therefore, was not a claim on the part of the crown to limit, control, or restrain the exercise of the papal supremacy; nor was it in any way asserting the royal supremacy in spiritualty. The courts of law well knew how to draw the distinction; and so in the next reign we find it laid down that the scope of the statutes was lay patronage and temporal rights, and that in that sense "the Pope (called 'the Apostle') could not alter the law of the land;" but that he had supreme spiritual power to decline or dispense with the law of the Church; but that the scope of the statutes was to prevent spiritual censures being used to interfere with the enforcement of legal and temporal rights (*Year-book*, 11 *Hen. IV.* fol. 76; 10 *Hen. IV.* fol. 2). And it was afterwards said, "Nota, that this statute of præmunire runs, 'in the Roman court or elsewhere,' which means the court of the bishop; so that if a man be excommunicated in the court of the bishop for a thing which pertains to the royal majesty—*i.e.*, a thing at common law, he shall have præmunire, and so it was adjudged" (5 *Edw. IV.*). It is true that the crown lawyers were bent upon following out the principle thus affirmed by parliament with the assent of the prelates; and they did not cease from doing so until they had pushed it to what they considered its logical result—separation from Rome: by reason of the substitution of the royal for the papal supremacy. When that was done, however, in the reign of Henry VIII., it will be found that it was by confusing the principle thus laid down, and by means of perverting the statutes now passed. For it was by coercion of a prosecution under the statutes of præmunire the clergy were forced to acknowledge the royal supremacy—that is, to acknowledge it in spiritualty, under the idea that virtually it was involved in these statutes, which established the right of the crown to limit, control, and restrain the exercise of the papal supremacy as to temporalty.

or make translations of prelates, after the law of holy church (the doing this without the king's consent being one of the grievances now complained of, and upon which they had been questioned in the same manner as upon the other); they said, that censures of excommunication against any one for executing the process of the king's courts were *against the king and his crown.* It was therefore enacted, that if any purchase or pursue, or cause to be purchased or pursued, in the court of Rome or elsewhere, any such translations, processes, sentences of excommunication, bulls, instruments, or any other thing against the king's crown and dignity; or receive, or make notification, or any other execution within the realm, or without; they, their notaries, procurators, maintainers, abettors, and counsellors, should be put out of the king's protection; and their lands and tenements, goods and chattels, be forfeit to the king. Such offenders were to be attached, if they could be found, and brought before the king and his council; or process of *præmunire* was to be awarded, as in other cases of provisors, and of those who sued in any court in derogation of the king's royal authority.

When the encroachments of a foreign ecclesiastical power were repressed, it remained to provide for the eternal welfare of our own church, which could not be better effected than by securing a competent maintenance to the parochial clergy. The manner in which the clerical office was discharged, and the state of dependence and poverty in which the labouring part of the priesthood were kept, through the practice of appropriations, particularly those of the monasteries, called aloud for the interposition of the legislature. Pensions, which had been put under the sole cognizance of the bishops by stat. *Articuli Clerici*[1] (*a*), had thereby

Vicarages.

(*a*) The 14 Edw. III. c. xvii. provided that parsons, vicars, wardens of chapels, and wardens and priests of perpetual chantries, shall have their writs of *juris utrum*, of lands and tenements, rents and possessions annexed, or given perpetually in alms to vicarages, chapels, or chantries, and recover by other writs in their cases, as parsons of churches or prebends: "Come parsones des eglises ou provendres." And in the reign of Edward III. there was a case upon the statute in which it was held that a vicar could have the writ against the rector or impropriator, to try whether the land in question pertained to the vicarage or not (*Year-book*, 40 *Edw. III.* fol. 27). It was there said by the court that in ancient times it was held that a vicar could not have an action against the parson, but that this was changed for the better (*Finchden, C.-J.*). It was said also that a parson could not alien all the lands of his church without license, but that he could give to the vicar without license, with the assent of the patron and ordinary. If a vicar, it was said, purchased (or acquired) land from a layman with the license of the king (*i.e.*, to hold lands in mortmain), and a question arose about it between the parson and the vicar, the suit should be in the king's courts; and if the parson disseised the vicar, he should have an assize. Again, it was said by the court, that it had been held that the vicar could not have an action for his possessions against the parson, but that this was changed, and that, therefore, for this reason, when he was endowed to him and his successors in perpetuity, and was ousted by the parson, or by any one else, he should have his action. And, further, that if a layman granted land to the vicar and his successors, the parson or the ordinary could not oust him. And it was said that the vicar could have a writ of *juris utrum*, to try utrum sit libera elymosyna vicariæ vel libera eleymosina de rectoriæ (40 *Edw. III.*

[1] *Vide ante*, c. x.

suffered some restraint; and having been lately condemned as uncanonical by a decree of Pope Clement III., the patrons of church benefices were set upon practising more frequently the stratagem of appropriations.

Instead, therefore, of exacting arbitrary rents and pensions from the poor clergy whom they had presented to benefices, they got into the habit of taking the whole profits of such livings into their own hands, by a license *to appropriate*; and after that, they provided for the cure of the parish (being only a secondary concern) in some other way (*a*). The monks who enjoyed such appropriations sometimes resided on the cure, and officiated by turns: this they performed by some settled rotation among themselves; and as it was a burthen, the service was not unfrequently imposed as a penance.

fol. 29). It was held in the same reign that if a canon professed was made vicar, he was discharged of obedience, but not of profession (44 *Edw. III.* fol. 4). It is to be observed that vicars and their successors, like parsons and their successors, being known to the law, had perpetual succession, as "corporations sole," and thus were capable of receiving perpetual endowments, which, according to the statute, were to be secured to them. It was not so of the chantry priests, who were not known to the common law, and therefore required special incorporation, which could only be granted by the crown; and so of the licenses to hold lands in mortmain, which, so soon as they were thus incorporated, would be required to enable them to take the endowments to them and their successors. Hence there was always in the case of a chantry a grant from the crown, both of incorporation and license, to hold lands in mortmain. These endowments had been long recognised, for, as we have seen in the reign of Edward I., the statute of Westminster 2 contained an enactment as to a writ of *cessavit*, to enable the donor or his heirs to recover the land upon cessation of the divine services (*vide ante, et vide* 45 *Edw. III.* fol. 15). Thus it will be observed that this related to the remedy of the parties entitled to the services against the spiritual person endowed. As regards the converse case of the remedy of the spiritual person to recover his endowment, if, as in the case of a parson or vicar, the lands themselves were vested in him, he could have his action at law, but if otherwise, the remedy would be either in the spiritual court or in a court of equity, upon the doctrine of uses or trusts. In the earlier age the former and more simple course would be taken; in a later age, when uses were established, and the jurisdiction of equity to enforce them, they would be resorted to in cases of private endowments. The present statute, however, related to cases of parochial clergymen whose spiritual duties were rather of a public nature—at all events, related to the parishioners generally, not to individuals, or the performance of particular services; and the distinction between the two classes of the clergy will be found very strongly marked in the cases on the subject. The parochial clergy, it was said, had other duties to perform than the mere performance of the divine services; they had to visit the sick, &c. Their endowments, therefore, were assured by the common law; those of others required special incorporations to secure their perpetuity.

(*a*) The author appears not to have been aware that appropriations could not and did not take place without the license of the crown, as well as of the bishop; and indeed the crown lawyers at this time set up the right of the crown to make appropriations at its own pleasure. Thus, in one of the earliest cases on the subject in the previous reign, it was set up that William the Conqueror had granted a church to two prebendaries and their successors, to have to their own use, and so an appropriation; and when the court asked how this showed an appropriation, the counsel urged that the king in ancient time could give a church to hold to the grantee's own use; but the court said that the law was not so; and that when the church was granted, it would mean the advowson or right of presentation. It was then pleaded that the king's grandfather, Edward I., had granted the advowson to the defendants and their predecessors, to their own use and the use of their successors. But the judges said that the king by his charter could not appropriate a church (*Year-book*, 7 *Edw. III.*, fol. 8). It was then said that before a new constitution of the pope, the patron of a church could grant tithes of his parish to another church, but the

A duty discharged in this way was, on many pretences, shifted from one to another: these changes produced intermissions and neglect in the pastoral care, and occasioned great scandal. As a remedy for this, the monks would depute some person to do the duty regularly, upon a scanty salary: and this was the constant practice with lay-patrons, as the only method by which they could serve the cure. The miserable subsistence of these *curates* could not fail of bringing their persons and office into a degree of contempt. The bishops had often interposed in order to correct these abuses; by degrees they restrained the monks from taking upon themselves the cure of souls, and obliged them to retain fit and able deputies, with competent salaries annexed to their appointment. These were called *curates, vicars*, or *capellans*, according to the notions prevailing in different places.

license of the bishop and of the king was required. In the same reign the appropriation of an advowson was pleaded as of the time of king Henry III., by license of the king and of the bishop, and the dean, chapter, and of the apostle (*i.e.*, of the pope, so described in the Year-books of the age, as the successor of St Peter), and the person who appropriated was patron, *ut oportet semper sur appropracion* (46 *Assize*, fol. 4; 19 *Edw. III., Fitz. Abr.* 124). So in another case, in the last reign, it was laid down as law that an appropriation must be by the patron, with both the license of the bishop and the crown (2 *Edw. III.*, fol. 5). So in another case in that reign, it was said that an appropriation could be made by the king with the patron and the bishop (50 *Edw. III.*, fol. 26). The author, however, not having made himself acquainted with the law on the subject, as laid down in the courts at the time, had imagined that it rested entirely with the parties promoting or profiting by the appropriation; and he seems to have supposed that all appropriations were to religious houses, and that all monks were priests—a very common error, which Guizot points out. The monks, on the contrary, were mostly laymen, and could not themselves perform the divine services of the church appropriated, and hence the necessity for vicars. And the assent of the bishop was required to an appropriation, for the very purpose that he might insist upon a proper provision for the support of the vicar and the performance of divine service. Thus in the next reign a case occurred of an apppropriation to the college of Windsor; and upon the appropriation the vicar was endowed (10 *Henry IV.*). If there was not in every case an adequate endowment, it was the fault of the crown, the patron, and the bishop, the concurrence and consent of whom was required for the very purpose of securing it. The author goes on to confound curates, vicars, and chaplains, who were all perfectly distinct. Vicars pertained properly to appropriations; for vicars were endowed in the place of rectors in cases of appropriations, when there were no rectors; and the vicars were in place of the rectors, and had endowments out of the benefices; so that vicars could only be of benefices, and must be endowed. Curates,—if the phrase was used at all in those times—meant originally those who had cure of souls; and then afterwards the phrase was applied to those who officiated for or assisted the incumbents, and were paid by them, so that they were the opposite of vicars. Chaplains, again, were priests retained or paid, whether by means of endowments or otherwise, and often by contract, to perform divine service for special purposes, and in particular places, where there were no benefices, as, for instance, chantries, colleges, or chapels. Thus there were the chantry priests, who said masses for the souls of the founders and their heirs; and there were the domestic chaplains of lords of manors or others, employed to perform special services, or services in special places, as private chapels and the like. These, it is manifest, were as distinct from vicars or curates as they were from rectors or incumbents of benefices; and mention is made in the Reports of the time of all these classes of clergy. But the present subject of appropriations has only to do with *vicars;* for vicars were only upon appropriations, and appropriations properly required vicars, and endowments of vicars, and sufficient endowments; so that this statute was only in affirmance of what was already recognised as law, though probably it was not in all cases practically observed (*vide* 10 *Henry IV.*, fol. 2).

The injunctions of the bishops were at length seconded by the legislature. An act was made in this reign, with a design of putting this institution of vicars and curates upon a more permanent establishment, and also to provide for a due application of such portion of the profits of benefices as was designed for alms and hospitality; for it was enacted by stat. 15 Rich. II. c. vi., that in every license to be made in the chancery for the appropriation of a parish church, it should be expressly contained therein, that the diocesan of the place, upon the appropriation of such church, should ordain, according to the value of the church, a convenient sum of money, to be distributed yearly, of the fruits and profits thereof, to the poor parishioners, in aid of their living and sustenance; *and also, that the* VICAR *be well and sufficiently endowed.* The parliament went no further at present than to make this general injunction, which was more particularly explained and enforced in the next reign.

Mortmain.

Before we dismiss the subject of the clergy and of clerical possessions, it will be proper to take notice of a new statute of mortmain enacted in this reign. The ingenuity of the ecclesiastics was still employed in devising methods to evade the restraints of the mortmain act.[1] One of their contrivances was to consecrate land, as for a burying-ground; and under that pretence they purchased considerable property in mortmain. This used to be done without the license of the king or chief lords, merely by authority of *bulls* from Rome. As this was a sort of device which seemed to be within the terms *arte vel ingenio* of the statute of mortmain, the parliament, by stat. 15 Rich. II. c. v. declared it so to be, as likewise the purchase of lands *to the use* of religious persons. This act also declared, that the statute of mortmain should be extended to lands, tenements, fees, advowsons, and other possessions, purchased to the use of *guilds* and *fraternities.* Moreover, because mayors, bailiffs, and the commonalty of cities, boroughs, and other towns, which have a perpetual commonalty, and others that have offices perpetual, were *as perpetual* as religious institutions; it was declared, that any purchases by them, or *to their use,* should be within the statute of mortmain. Thus was the jealousy originally excited by the wealth of the clergy felt in respect to lay corporations, which were, therefore, now subjected to the same restraints in making purchases of lands and tenements.

Another device practised by ecclesiastics was to get their villeins to marry free women who had inheritances, so that the lands might come to their hands by the right which the lord had over the property of his villein. The commons, in the 17th year, petitioned against this contrivance: the answer given was, that sufficient remedy was provided by the statute;[2] meaning, probably, the words *arte vel ingenio* in the statute of mortmain; which, how-

[1] *Vide ante,* c. x.

[2] Cott. Abri., p. 355, s. 32.

ever, had been already found ineffectual in other instances that appeared entitled to the same construction.

The statutes of labourers, made in the last reign, were confirmed, and further regulations were made on this subject. The lower orders of people were, in consideration of law, divided into *servants*, *labourers*, *artificers*, and *beggars;* and different regulations were provided for them, as they came under one or other of these descriptions. One great point in the policy of managing *servants* and *labourers* was to prevent their wandering from place to place. It was enacted by stat. 12 Rich. II. c. iii. that no servant (either man or woman) should depart at the end of his service out of the hundred, rape, or wapentake where he dwelt, to serve or dwell elsewhere, unless he brought a letter patent, containing the cause of his going, and the time of his return, if he was to return, under the king's seal; for which purpose a seal was to be in the keeping of some good man of the hundred, city, or borough, at the discretion of the justices; and a servant or labourer found wandering without such letter was to be put in the stocks, and there kept till he had found surety to return to his service, or to serve or labour in the town from whence he came. Persons receiving such wanderer not having a letter, were to be fined by the justices, if they harboured him more than one night.

Statutes of labourers.

Artificers, and persons of mysteries that were not very needful, were to be compelled to work at harvest-time. The wages of labourers[1] in agriculture were fixed by statute; and those giving or taking more were subjected to the penalty of paying the value of what they gave or took beyond the stated wages: for the third offence, the taker, if he had not wherewith to pay, was to be imprisoned for forty days. In order that there might always be hands to do country work, it was ordained,[2] that all men and women who had been used to labour at the plough and cart, or other service or labour in husbandry, till they were twelve years of age, should abide at the same time without being put to any mystery or handicraft; and all covenants of apprenticeship to the contrary were declared void.

To prevent disorders, it was ordained,[3] that no servant, labourer, nor artificer, should carry a sword, buckler, or dagger, under pain of forfeiting the same, except in time of war, or when travelling with their masters; but they might have bows and arrows, *and use them on Sundays and holidays.* They were required to leave all playing at tennis or football, and other games called quoits, dice, casting of the stone kails, and other such *importune games.* All offenders against this statute might be arrested by sheriffs, mayors, bailiffs, and constables, and their arms taken away. This is the first statute that prohibited any sort of games and diversions.

Thus far of servants, labourers, and artificers, being the industrious part of the lower class of people. Next, as to *beggars.* It

[1] Ch 4. [2] Ch. 5. [3] Ch. 6.

was enacted,[1] that persons who went begging, and were able to serve or labour, should be treated as those that departed out of the hundred without letters testimonial; and beggars *impotent to serve*, were to abide in the cities and towns where they were dwelling at the time of the proclamation of this statute. If such towns were not able to provide for them, they were then to withdraw themselves to other towns within the hundred, *or* to towns where they were born, and there continue during their lives.

Thus we find no other provision for the poor than begging within a certain district. The idea of provision might be encouraged by the plan on which church benefices and religious houses were bound to dispose of part of their incomes. A certain portion of every living was for the maintenance of alms and hospitality, the proper disposal of which, we have seen, was secured by a statute in this reign;[2] and the gates of religious houses were daily attended by troops of beggars, who received a regular donation of food, and sometimes of money. These institutions, no doubt, contributed to increase the number of idle beggars, and made it necessary for the legislature to observe a distinction between those who were able to serve and labour, and those who were impotent.

The conclusion of this act makes mention of two very remarkable sort of beggars, which are worthy of observation, as they mark, in a particular way, the manners of the times. It enacts, that all those who go *in pilgrimages* as beggars, and are able to travel, shall be treated in the same manner as servants and labourers, if they have no testimonial of their pilgrimage under the great seal; and that *scholars* of the university who went begging in that manner, should have letters testimonial of their chancellor, under the penalty of being treated in the same manner. The going on pilgrimages is mentioned, more than once, in the statutes of this time, as a dissolute custom in all sorts of persons, and was particularly so when made a pretence for beggars wandering about the country.

Another set of wandering beggars were persons returning or pretending to be returning to their own houses from abroad. It was required[3] that all such persons should have letters testimonial of their captains, or of the mayors or bailiffs where they arrived; and the mayors and bailiffs were to inquire of them where and with whom they had lived, and where they had dwelt in England; and then make them letters patent under the seal of their office, testifying the day of their arrival, and where they had been, according to their own account. The mayors and bailiffs were to cause them to swear, that they would hold their right way towards their country, except they had letters patent under the great seal to do otherwise. If any such person was found travelling without his testimonial, he was to be treated in the manner in which servants and labourers were. Thus were vagabonds to be *passed* to their own home. In

[1] Ch. 7. [2] *Vide ante*, c. xv. [3] Ch. 8.

the above regulations we see the first outline of our present system of poor-laws: the course here traced out was amended and corrected by subsequent statutes as occasion required, or later experience pointed out defects, till the whole was reconsidered in the reign of Queen Elizabeth, and after some alteration and improvement was thrown into one principal statute.[1]

There was an alteration made in one of the above acts, by stat. 13 Richard II. c. viii. Upon consideration it was thought advisable not to let the rate of wages continue as fixed by that statute, which, by the alteration in the prices of provisions, might become very hard and inadequate; and therefore by this new act, the justices in their sessions between Easter and St Michael were to make proclamation, according to the dearth of victuals, how much every mason, carpenter, tiler, and other craftsman, workman, and other labourer, should take by the day, as well in harvest as in other parts of the year.

Having disposed of the statutes of a miscellaneous nature, we come now to those on private rights, and the administration of justice. The statute made in the last year of Edward III.[2] against fraudulent gifts of lands and goods to avoid the executions of creditors, was followed up by two others of a similar nature, enacted in the first two years of this king. The stat. 1 Richard II. st. 2, c. ix. went further, and aimed at these collusive transactions, when practised for other purposes than defrauding creditors. It was complained, that many people having right and title to lands, tenements, and rents, and also to personal actions, were delayed of their rights and their actions, because the occupiers and defendants commonly made gifts and feoffments of their lands and tenements in question, and of their goods and chattels, to lords and other great men of the realm, against whom the claimants dared not make suit. Again, many disseisins were committed; and immediately the disseisors made alienations and feoffments, sometimes to lords and great men of the realm, to have maintenance; and sometimes to persons whose names were wholly unknown to the disseisees, in order to delay them from their recovery. To remove these mischiefs, it was ordained, in the first case, that such feoffments and gifts of lands and goods should be void; and, in the second case, that the disseisees should have their recovery against the first disseisors, as well of the lands and tenements as of their double damages, without having regard to such alienations, so that the disseisees commenced their suits within a year next after the disseisin. This was to hold in every plea of land where feoffments were made by fraud and collusion, so as recovery might be had against the first feoffer; though this was to be understood where such feoffers *took the profits.*

Of pernors of profits and uses.

When persons making such feigned gifts withdrew into privileged

[1] That is, 5 Eliz., to which may be added the statute of the same reign about vagabonds.

[2] *Vide ante*, c. xii.

places, and there continued taking the profits of their lands and goods, it was enacted, by stat. 2 Richard II. st. 2, c. iii., in all cases of *debt*, that after the *capais* was awarded, and the sheriff returned that he had not taken the defendant, because he had fled to a privileged place, another writ should issue, commanding proclamation to be openly made at the gate of the place, by five weeks continually, once a week, admonishing the party to appear at a certain day before the justices, to answer to the plaintiff; and if the party came not in person, or by attorney, judgment was to be had against him for the sum in demand, and, after the collusion and fraud proved, execution levied of such lands and goods as he had out of the privileged place.

These gifts of lands, which are termed collusive and fraudulent, were a modification of real property that was now growing very common, and was better known afterwards under the title of *gifts to a use*. The legal possession of land by one man while another enjoyed the profits, seems to have been not unknown before this reign; though it was not till lately that it had become common, and begun to undergo some discussion. The idea upon which they made this division between the land and the profit, was that of raising a *trust;* namely, when a man would confide in the conscience of another with more security than in his own possession. This was likely enough to happen at all times, and in all places, and must be recognised more or less by all systems of law. There is mention of such uses very early in our juridical history. When an ancestor infeoffed his[1] eldest son, in order to avoid the claim of guardianship, he, no doubt, retained to himself a right to the profits during his life: but when the effect of such feoffments was taken away by the statute of Marlbridge, such uses were no longer resorted to, or thought of. It became an opinion in later times than those of which we are writing,[2] that, after the statute of *Quia emptores*, if a feoffment was made without consideration, the use resulted to the feoffor; and therefore, that the origin of uses is to be ascribed to that period.

But, without straining the fancy after conjectures, there are some authentic notices of an early period clearly evincing that land might be in the seisin of one person, while a right to the emoluments was in another. To say nothing of the statute of Kilkenny[3] made in the reign of Edward II., in which act there is mention of such secret feoffments in Ireland, we find, in the eighth year of Edward III., a case in our books, where, a fine being levied by consent, the entry of the conusee was said to be *en auter droit.*[4] Towards the close of that reign, we find another where the feoffees were sued by a petition to the king.[5] In the second year of Richard II. there is a case in parliament, which fully shows the manner and circumstances of these gifts. It there appears that Edward III. had infeoffed the

[1] *Vide ante*, c. ix. [2] *Tempore*, Hen. VIII. [3] *Vide*, the Irish Statutes.
[4] 8 Ass. [5] Bro. Feof. al. Use, 9.

duke of Lancaster and others in fee by deed, and caused livery of seisin to be made without any condition whatsoever. Long after, the king, by verbal declaration, prayed the feoffees, that they would, out of the lands, provide for the friars of Langley, and certain other religious persons. It was now demanded, in full parliament, of all the judges and king's serjeants, whether such subsequent charge to the feoffees should be adjudged by law a *condition*, and so make the feoffment *conditional;* and they were of opinion, that as nothing was said before, nor at the time of the gift, nor yet upon the livery, the king's request afterwards could not make a *condition.*[1] Other examples there are of such gifts, and a declaration to apply the produce of them to other purposes than the interest of feoffees, and they are invariably considered as *conditions*, and in that light and no other were pronounced to be good or bad.[2]

Among these instances, to contest for the origin of uses is disputing for words. Whether they were called *conditional enfeoffments, entries en auter droit*, or the like, the thing was certainly understood before the time of Richard II. But the stat. 50 Edward III., which says that lands so collusively given should be liable to the execution of creditors, *if they took the profits*, by that phrase seems to come nearer to the proper idea of a *use*, as since understood, than anything before in the annals of the law. The earliest mention of this kind of property, under the *name* of *a use*, is in the reign of Richard II., when there is the first evidence that the words *ad opus et usum* got into deeds and assurances of land.[3] We also find in the statute of provisors, 7 Richard II. c. xii., the term *use;* and in the statute of mortmain, 15 Richard II. c. v., the possession of land *to the use of another*, is spoken of in the same language that was ever after held on this subject.

A use, as now understood, was when a man infeoffed another to the use of himself, or of a third person; in this case, while the feoffee was seised of the land, the feoffor, or third person, was seised of the use. The motives for throwing property into this shape were many and powerful. A person, conscious that his land was liable to forfeiture for any crime, or to the burthen of some legal charge, might rid himself of both by disposing of his land to another who was in a better condition than himself. In the meantime, by reserving to himself only the use of it, he had property that was not liable to the like hazard and encumbrance. This invention is by some attributed to the ecclesiastics, who practised it to evade the statute of mortmain. It might be argued that the prohibition to take *land* was no prohibition to take *the use* of it; when, therefore, an alienation in mortmain was designed, it was advised to infeoff some person *to the use* of the religious persons intended to be benefited, who thereby became seised of the use. Whether the churchmen were the first who suggested the idea of

[1] Cott. Abri., p. 169, s. 26.
[2] *Ibid.*, p. 185, s. 25, &c.
[3] Bacon's Reading on the Statutes of Uses.

dividing the profits from the land, it is certain that the term *use* (as far as we can judge from the statute book) was first applied to their transactions, as appears by the statutes before mentioned, concerning provisors and mortmain.[1] If this was the origin of uses, many reasons concurred for adopting the device—reasons of more common and frequent application than alienations in mortmain. Besides those of forfeitures and legal liens, the power of devising a use by will, at a time when the owner had not the same power over his land, contributed perhaps more than any other consideration to make this sort of property desirable.

This disposition of property, though a novelty in the law, was not incompatible with any known rule. If a person seised of land might give it in one way, there was no reason why he might not give it in another. Conformably with such general principles of equity, these gifts, though not capable of being enforced by any common law process, seemed, equally with many other questions, to deserve the cognizance of the supreme tribunal of the kingdom; and they were accordingly entertained by parliament on petition exhibited to the king. While uses were created merely as a mode of ordering property more suitable to the views of the owner than a conveyance at common law, they were entitled to the equitable consideration they received from the parliament. But we have just shown that they were resorted to for other purposes; a debtor, in the agony of some pressing occasion, would transfer his property in this manner, in order to avoid the process of the law. In such instances, *a use* became a fraudulent and collusive transaction; and the legislature provided a remedy against the effect of it by the statute 50 Edw. III., and the two statutes of this reign before mentioned.[2] When *a use* was resorted to as a medium by which land could be conveyed to a religious house, it was transacted with more deliberation, as well as more secrecy, than in the former case; and the injury, if any, was more remote than that of withdrawing property from the immediate execution of creditors.

It was not, therefore, till the fifteenth year of this reign that the legislature imposed any restraint upon such gifts; and then a statute of mortmain was made, adapted to this new modification of property. It was enacted[3] that all those who were possessed by feoffment or other manner, *to the use* of religious people, or other spiritual persons, of lands and tenements, fees, advowsons, or any other manner of possession, to amortise them, and whereof the said religious and spiritual persons *took the profits*, should cause them to be amortised within a certain time by the license of the king and lords, or else alien them to some other use; and all future purchases in that way were to be considered as within the statute of mortmain. Such was the progress of this new species of property, and this was all the notice that had hitherto been taken of it by the legislature.

[1] *Vide ante*, c. x. [2] *Vide ante*, c. xii. [3] Chap. 5.

The title to dower was considerably affected by a statute made in this reign concerning *ravishment* (which meant no more than what has since been called stealing) of women. The stat. 6 Rich. II., st. 1, c. vi., says that the ravishment of ladies and the daughters of noblemen and other women, in every part of the realm, was now more violent and more frequent than had formerly been. To take away part of the temptation to these outrages, it was enacted, that whenever such ladies, daughters, and other women were ravished, and, after such rape, consented to the ravisher, both the ravisher and ravished should be *ipso facto* disabled from claiming any inheritance, dower, or joint-feoffment after the death of the husband or ancestor ; and that the next of blood to the ravisher or ravished should have title immediately after the rape to enter upon the ravisher or ravished, and hold the land. The husbands or fathers of such women might sue the ravishers, and have judgment of life and member, notwithstanding the women afterwards consented to such ravishers, and the defendant was not to be permitted to wage battel, but the truth was to be tried by the country.

Judicature of the council.

We come now to such statutes as relate to the administration of justice. The judicature of the parliament, and even of the council, was exercised in all its amplitude, notwithstanding the attempts made in the last reign to draw all causes and questions from both, and particularly from the latter, to the decision of the common law.[1] The statutes then made respecting the council seem not to have been observed with much strictness ; for through the whole of this reign similar complaints were repeatedly preferred to parliament. In the first year of Richard II., it was prayed that no suits between parties should be *ended* before any lords or others of the council, but before the justices only.[2] In the following year it was prayed that no man should answer before the council, by writ or otherwise, concerning his freehold, but only at the common law ; to which it was answered that no man should be *forced to answer finally* there on such matters, though all persons should be obliged to answer before the council concerning *oppressions*.[3] Thus a limit seemed to be fixed to the jurisdiction of the council, by allowing it to entertain all sorts of suits commenced originally there by complaint or otherwise ; but instead of determining *finally*, to refer them, as it should seem proper, according to the subject of debate, to the different courts of common law. This had been the practice in the last reign,[4] and we find instances of it continually in this, in all sorts of questions that could arise upon property.[5] Besides the business that would perpetually engage the council, when it acted in this manner, as ancillary to the judicial determinations of the courts of law, it was laid down by parliament that *oppressions*

[1] *Vide ante*, c. xii.
[2] Cott. Abri., p. 162, s. 87.
[3] *Ibid.*, p. 178, s. 49.
[4] *Vide ante*, c. xii.
[5] Cott. Abri., p. 176, s. 34, 35, *et passim*.

might be determined there *finally* ; and in all times, particularly those of disorder and change, numberless are the causes which the council might draw to itself under the idea of *oppressions*, many matters of dispute between man and man being liable to that construction.

For the despatch of all this business, we have seen that a regular standing council was established towards the close of the last reign, as a substitute for the council which the king had about him by the old constitution. The confirmation of this appointment was more than once prayed by the commons in this reign ; they petitioned the king that he would discharge the great council of lords, and appoint about him a standing council, consisting of the great officers, as the chancellor, treasurer, keeper of the privy seal, the chief chamberlain, the steward of the household, and the like.[1] It should seem that this was at length complied with, and that the summoning of the great council became less frequent; while the standing council gradually assumed judicial powers of a very extensive nature, equal to those exercised by the great council of lords. Questions, both of a civil and criminal import, were brought before the council, as a regular part of the judicial establishment of the kingdom. Besides the original commencement of suits, the judges used to adjourn causes before the council, if any doubt or difficulty occurred, as they used in former reigns to adjourn them into parliament.[2] Probably the appointment directed to be made by stat. 14 Edw. III. of certain lords and bishops to decide such adjourned causes was not kept up ; and such inquiries being therefore excluded from the parliament, the council was the only superior court that remained for judicial information of that sort.[3] It was not this part of the jurisdiction of the council, but the former, that continued to raise jealousies. These at length occasioned the following stat., 17 Rich. II. c. vi., for the suppression at least of all *false* suggestions ; the chancellor was thereby authorised, upon any suggestion being found and proved untrue, to award damages according to his discretion to the person injured.

Of the parliament.

The parliament still continued to determine causes brought before them upon petition, as in the former reign, while their criminal judicature maintained all the authority it ever possessed. Indeed, there is no period of our history in which the criminal judicature of parliament was called forth into action so frequently ; nor was this confined to the persons of peers, but commoners were equally subject to this supreme court, notwithstanding the protestation of the lords at the beginning of the former reign.[4] The modes of proceeding being various, and none of them quite consonant to our present ideas upon this subject, it may be acceptable to the reader to give a sort of report of some trials of this kind.

[1] Cott. Abri., p. 183, s. 12 ; 3 Rich. III.
[2] *Vide ante*, c. xii.
[3] Cott. Abri., 282, s. 17.
[4] *Vide ante*, c. xii.

To begin with the inquiry instituted against Alice Piers: This lady was brought before the lords, where Sir Richard Le Scrope, steward of the household, at the command of the prelates and lords, recited in her presence an ordinance, which it seems had been made in the 50th Edw. III., declaring that no woman, especially Alice Piers, should prosecute anything in the king's court by way of maintenance, under penalty of forfeiture, and banishment out of the kingdom. The steward informed the lords that she had incurred this penalty; and, to support the charge, mentioned two instances where she had used her intercession with the late king respecting some appointment in the state. The facts adduced seem hardly within the meaning of the ordinance; however, they were held breaches of it; and accordingly, without calling any witness to prove what had been alleged, he demanded of her what she could say to clear herself. She said she was not guilty, and offered to produce witnesses who would disprove the charge. A day was assigned for the examination of these witnesses; when, after they had deposed upon oath what they knew of the transaction, twelve other persons were called in, who were most of them witnesses, says Tyrrell; and they, in the nature of a jury or inquest, being sworn, and charged to speak the truth, whether the said Alice was guilty or not, found her guilty.[1] This was a mixed and very singular proceeding. It was the trial of a commoner before the lords, by the verdict of a jury. This, though warranted by a similar proceeding in the former reign,[2] appears more singular than the putting her upon her defence, without calling a witness to prove the charge.

The method of prosecuting by impeachment, which had been first exercised against the Lord Latimer in the last reign, was pursued in the reign of Richard II. In the tenth year of this king, an impeachment was preferred against the chancellor, Michael de la Pole, at the instigation of the duke of Gloucester, who at that time had the house of commons at his devotion. In the 20th of the same reign, the commons impeached the archbishop of Canterbury.

There was a fierceness discoverable in all the proceedings of Gloucester, and the confederate lords, against the king's favourites; yet as some of these purport to be judicial inquiries, they must be specimens of proceeding in criminal prosecutions, and as such deserve our notice. When the five lords appealed the archbishop of York, the duke of Ireland, Michael de la Pole, earl of Suffolk, Robert Tresilian, and Sir Nicholas Bramber, of high treason, they offered to prove their accusation in the old way; they threw down their gloves, protesting on their oaths to prosecute the charge by battel; but the king referred it to the next parliament, and there it was resolved that battel lay not in that case. Afterwards, articles were exhibited in writing to the number of thirty-nine, in many of which those persons were charged with accroach-

[1] Tyrr. Hist., vol. iii., 834.

[2] *Vide ante*, c. xii.

ing royal power: the accused were summoned, but not appearing, their default was recorded: the judgment, however, was deferred till the king and lords had advised upon the articles.[1]

In the meantime, the judges, serjeants, and others, learned in the common and the civil law, were directed to advise the lords how to proceed in this appeal.[2] Their answer to the lords was, that the appeal was not made, nor brought, *as the one law or the other required.* Upon this answer the lords entered into deliberation, and then declared, that in so high a crime as that laid in this appeal, which touched the person of the king and the estates of the realm, and was perpetrated by persons who were peers, as well as by others, the cause could not be tried anywhere but in parliament, nor by any law but that of parliament; and that it should be done in this case by the assent of the king, by the award of parliament; since the process of inferior courts was only as they were entrusted with the execution of the ancient laws and customs of the realm, and the ordinances and establishments of parliament: and they declared that this appeal was well brought.

Accordingly, upon the default of the first four defendants, they were adjudged guilty of the treasons and other crimes in the accusation charged. Sir Nicholas Bramber, being the only one of them in custody, was brought before the lords; he there waged his battel, which was refused him: and though the lords said they would take due care by all ways to inform their consciences of the matter of the accusation, there seems to have been nothing stated by way of proof. It is indeed said, that divers companies came from London to *aggravate* the charge; but this sounds more like a popular clamour than an examination of legal evidence. However, upon this, the knight, not having an answer to make, was adjudged guilty, as were all the others.

As this prosecution was called an appeal, and under that name assumed the pretence of a legal proceeding, we are more struck with any irregularity in it, particularly with the decisive manner in which the lords overruled all attempts to reduce it to the order of the common law. The impeachment exhibited by the commons against the judges, being a prosecution *entirely* parliamentary, was more unquestionably, according to the opinion just given by the lords, exempt from the rules of the common law, and to be judged of only by the law of parliament; a distinction which, we find, in those days made some difference as to the probability of the party being acquitted or convicted.

The proceedings against the judges must therefore be explained by the parliamentary law of those times. They were all, except Skipwith and Tresilian,[3] arrested upon their seats in Westminster Hall, on a charge of high-treason, in giving answers to questions propounded to them by the king; which questions tended to calumniate and destroy the supreme authority that had been conferred

[1] Stat. Tri., vol. i., 11. [2] *Ibid.*, 11. [3] *Ibid.*, 5.

on certain lords by commission from the king, and confirmed in parliament. They were all adjudged guilty of treason, and, though their lives were spared, they were obliged to submit to banishment.[1]

Thus much of these famous proceedings against Richard's favourites and ministers. During the same reign, there were other prosecutions of great men, which serve to illustrate the criminal proceedings of parliament in those times.

The appeal brought against Richard's old enemies, Gloucester, Arundel, and Warwick, is related in this manner: In the great hall of Nottingham Castle, the king then sitting with the crown on his head, seven lords appeared, who exhibited a bill of appeal of treason: this was read, and then, by the advice of the lords, and those of the council about the king, the lords accused had a day given them to appear in the next parliament. The principal charge against these lords was *the accroaching of royal power*, in the transaction which happened in the 10th of Richard II., and is to be found in all the histories of those times. Of these offenders, Gloucester was murdered abroad, and the other two pleaded the king's pardon; which plea was overruled, because the pardons had been avoided by a late statute; sentence, therefore, was passed upon them at the prayer of the appellants without proving the charge: the sentence was pronounced by the duke of Lancaster, lord steward, by the command of the king, the lords temporal, and the *procurators* for the prelates and clergy; an appointment which had been devised just about this time.

Appeal against the duke of Norfolk.

The appeal between the dukes of Hereford and Norfolk is the most singular judicial proceeding (if it can be called one) within this period. In the 21st of Richard II., the day before the parliament ended, the duke of Hereford came before the king, and presented him with a schedule, containing the substance of an accusation, of which he had before given the king some intimation, against the duke of Norfolk: it related to some disrespectful words spoken by that nobleman against the king's person and government.[2] This being read before the king and lords, the next day (being the last of the parliament) it was ordained by the king, with the assent of the estates, that this matter should be determined by the advice and discretion of the king, and the committee, which had already been appointed by the parliament to represent the legislature, with all its authority, and to continue to despatch such matters as were left unfinished by the parliament.

Afterwards the king and the committee agreed, that the matter should be determined by the law of chivalry, if other sufficient evidence or proof could not be found for ending it by the ordinary course of law. Accordingly, as the one persisted in maintaining his assertion, and the other in denying the charge, and no proofs

[1] Stat. Tri., vol. i., 14.

[2] Tyrr., vol. iii., 984.

were brought, it was remitted by the above authority to be decided by single combat at Coventry. There the two lords met, with all necessary formality, the king and the committee attending. Everything was arranged, the ceremonial was adjusted by the constable and marshal, and the combatants were spurring on to the attack, when the king put a stop to the engagement, ordered them to be disarmed, and retiring for two hours to the committee to consider of some expedient to prevent the effusion of blood, the following sentence was at length pronounced: "That the king, by the advice of his council, to avoid the shedding of blood, had decreed, that, instead of fighting, the defendant should be banished for life, and the appellant for ten years."[1]

This unexpected sentence, to get rid of a mode of proceeding not now much favoured, was considered as the judgment of the whole parliament; the committee, who represented the lords, being assisting to the king at the trial. However, that this singular sentence might not be questioned hereafter, it was solemnly ordained by the committee, that whoever attempted to reverse any of those acts of the king, so done with the assent of the committee, should be deemed a traitor: and to make everything sure, an oath was exacted of every lord for the observance of them. From the foregoing relations may be formed an idea of the criminal law of this period, when administered by the supreme judicature of the kingdom.

Origin of the court of equity in chancery.

The court of chancery has hitherto been spoken of in no other light than as a common law court; except when causes were referred thither, either by the parliament or council, and were there finally determined; which determination was not usually made by the chancellor alone, but by a sort of committee of the council, who frequently adjourned thither for that purpose. It has been a received opinion, that the chancellor began, in this reign, to enlarge his judicial authority, by entertaining suits not cognizable at common law; and that he thus gave rise to the *court of equity*, which has since become the principal object of the chancellor's attention, so as to eclipse the jurisdiction belonging to his ancient court of common law.

We have seen in the reign of Edward III.,[2] what steps the legislature had taken to preclude suitors from making application to the king in council. By these means, while questions of common law went to the courts of common law, equitable obligations, which made another branch of the jurisdiction of the council, were, in some degree, left only to the conscience of men to fulfil, without a tribunal to give them effect. A state of judicial polity like this, was extremely defective; and it became expedient, from considerations highly concerning the justice of the kingdom, that an authority should reside somewhere, to mitigate the rigour and supply the inefficacy of proceedings at common law.

[1] Tyrr., vol. iii., 986 to 988.

[2] *Vide ante*, c. xiv.

In the distribution of judicature, tribunals were established for the administration of right, which were guided in their procedure and judgment by a settled form of things calculated for the ordinary course of redress, and conceived to meet the common instances of wrong and injury. To preserve regularity and ease in business, such forms were adhered to, and proceedings upon them became precedents for future cases. But this system, founded on the known custom and written laws of the kingdom, was inadequate to the purposes of universal justice. There still remained many injuries to property against which the common law did not relieve, and many wrongs which an adherence to the letter of the law would only confirm and aggravate. To do complete and substantial justice, it was seen that something besides *law* must be administered; something that would supply its defects, and yet not contravene its rules; by which justice might be upheld without intrenching on the established order of judicature.

Innumerable are the instances in which such an authority was wanting. It will be sufficient to consider only the following: When a person was to found a claim by virtue of a deed which was detained in the hands of another, so that he was prevented from making a regular profert of it, he was thereby utterly deprived of the means of obtaining justice according to the forms of law: If a deed of grant of rent, common, or annuity were lost, as these claims could only be substantiated by the evidence of a deed, they vanished together with it: If a person had neglected to take, or had lost an acquittance for money paid, in an action of debt on a specialty, the defendant could not discharge himself on the plea of *nil debet*, because it was a rule of law that a deed could only be dissolved by some instrument of as high authority. All these cases were rendered harder by another rule of law, that a party to a suit should not be obliged to answer questions relating to the matter in dispute; in consequence of which, that light which could be derived only from an examination of the persons concerned, was quite shut out.

It was highly reasonable that some remedy should be applied in these and the like defects of law, or the judicature of the kingdom would have been incomplete. The resort in such cases had been to the king in council, in whom resided everything respecting law and justice that was not declared by any known rule, or not distributed among some of the judicial departments. But it will now be seen, that the consideration of such matters passed from that supreme tribunal to the chancellor.

This great officer, standing in an immediate and confidential relation to the king's person and service, was the principal of those counsellors who assisted by their advice in deliberating on such matters as were brought before the council by petition. From an adviser, it was natural, that in length of time his high rank and knowledge might constitute him almost the sole judge; and filling already a department that made him the first spring in the administration of justice, as he framed original writs, by which alone justice was to be obtained; and being already in the exercise of a considerable judicial office, in determining on the expediency of the king's grants and patents; it was obvious, when petitions of this kind increased, to delegate the consideration of them to the chancellor, who, in quality of a learned and pious ecclesiastic, might safely be trusted for a conscientious discharge of this important duty.

It was not unlikely, that the frequent reference to the chancellor in these cases might lead to a shorter course of redress; and that the chancellor might be petitioned, in the first instance, to grant that relief which, it was foreseen, he would have to direct upon a reference for that purpose being made to him by the council, had the petition been originally there. It is probable, that after the jurisdiction of the council was restricted by the statutes made in the last reign, it became the practice, if it had not been so before, to address petitions and bills of complaint to the chancellor himself.[1]

Even the ordinary common-law business of the chancellor carried in it some appearance of a court of equity. The holding of pleas concerning the king's grants, and determining on their validity from considerations of policy and fitness; the exercising a kind of guardianship over the estates and persons of such of the king's subjects who were not able to protect themselves, as idiots and lunatics; this was a scope of judicature not like that of any other court of common law. Less clamour was likely to be raised by those who were jealous for the common law, when they observed the equitable judicature of the council exercised by a judge like this, who was already of high rank and authority in an ancient judicial department, and whose jurisdiction was already of a nature somewhat similar.

There was another part of the chancellor's office which afforded an opening to an innovation like this. The permission given to the chancellor by stat. Westm. 2, to frame writs *in consimili casu* had enlarged to so great an extent his remedial authority, that every sort of relief seemed within his jurisdiction. When he had gone as far as the analogy of the common law would allow in forming writs of a liberal conception, he might think it inconsistent with his office to dismiss any one from the chancery without relief of some kind; and he might venture, in his own court, to entertain and decide such matters of an equitable nature, as he foresaw it would be in vain to send to the courts of common law. Whatever were the grounds the chancellor rested his jurisdiction upon, it is evident that he had begun, about this time, to exercise certain judicial powers of a new and equit-

[1] The statute of Henry VII. for new-modelling the star-chamber, directs that bills or informations should be put to the chancellor *for the king*. Stat. 2 Hen. VII., c. i.

able kind, unknown to the ancient courts of the realm. The fixing the chancery at Westminster about the 4th of Edward III., might contribute to establish the chancellor in these new powers, as he became, by his residence there, more accessible at all seasons.

It is said that John Waltham,[1] bishop of Salisbury, who was keeper of the rolls about the 5th of Richard II., considerably enlarged this new jurisdiction; that, to give efficacy to it, he invented, or, more properly, was the first who adopted in that court, the writ of *subpœna*, a process which had before been used by the council, and is very plainly alluded to in the statutes of the last reign, though not under that name.[2] This writ summoned the party to appear under a penalty, and answer such things as should be objected against him; upon this a petition was lodged, containing the articles of complaint to which he was then compelled to answer. These articles used to contain suggestions of injuries suffered, for which no remedy was to be had in the courts of common law, and therefore the complainant prayed advice and relief of the chancellor.

Some have attributed the origin of this court of equity to Cardinal Beaufort, the son of John of Gaunt, who was bishop of Winchester in the reign of Henry V. It is an opinion also,[3] that the chancellor assumed his extraordinary judicature in order to be in a situation to favour the avarice of the churchmen. Uses, contrived first by the clergy, it is said, with a view to enrich them in defiance of the statute of mortmain, were of a new impression, and entirely out of the rules of the common law. A person *seised* of a use had no means of obtaining the execution of it but the conscience and honour of the feoffee. To give effect to these dispositions, the chancellor, who was himself an ecclesiastic, applied, it is said, this new writ of *subpœna*, to compel a feoffee to answer before him respecting such trust; and upon the truth of the matter appearing, he would decree such execution of the use as the feoffee was bound in conscience to make. This is suggested by some writers as the occasion on which the court of chancery first exercised its *equitable* jurisdiction.

After what has been before observed, it will not be easily credited that this was the origin of the court of equity. Yet it is not at all improbable that such motives might have induced clerical chancellors to entertain suits of that kind with great readiness; and that the frequency of them might have brought the court into such a sudden repute, as would have very much the appearance of an entire new creation. The consequence was, that later times have dated the birth of the equitable jurisdiction in chancery, from the period when it grew into more notice by the accession of this new subject of litigation.

[1] So it appears from *Rot. Parl.*, 3 Henry V.

[2] *Vide ante*, c. xiv.

[3] Gilb. *For. Rom.*, 17.

The chancellor was not suffered to continue increasing this new authority unnoticed or unmolested. He was watched by the legislature, and such checks were occasionally applied as were thought necessary to keep it within just bounds. In the 13th Richard II.[1] the commons petitioned the king that the chancellor might make no order against the common law, and that no judgment should be given without due process of law. In another petition they prayed that no one should appear before the chancellor where recovery was given by the common law; to both which the king's answers were to the like effect, that it should continue as the usage had been heretofore. These applications to the king carry in them an admission that such a power of judicature did reside in the chancellor so long as he did not determine against the common law, nor interpose where it furnished a remedy; and the answer as clearly demonstrates that such an authority residing somewhere was recognised by the usage and constitution of the realm.

But the stat. 17 Richard II. c. vi. (before mentioned) recognises this new judicature in the most explicit terms, and, by coupling it with the council, seems to intimate its origin to have been as we have just supposed. This statute recites, that people were compelled to come before the king's council, or in the chancery, by writs grounded on untrue suggestions; and on that account it enacts, that the chancellor, presently after such suggestions were duly proved untrue, should have power to award damages, according to his discretion, to the person so grieved. This statute seems to give the first testimony to the legitimate authority of this court, and may be considered as a legislative sanction to its establishment, for after this it enlarged its judicature with great freedom.

Court of the constable and marshal.

Besides the court of equity in chancery, two other new jurisdictions had lately grown into notice—that of the *constable* and *marshal*, and that of the *admiral*. Of these, there is very little notice before this king's reign. The former is mentioned in a report-book of the last reign as a court[2] which was to decide upon contracts made in martial affairs. We hear no more of this court till the 2d of Richard II., when the commons petitioned that the constable and marshal might surcease from holding plea of treason or felony, which should be determined only before the king's justices. It seems, the heirs to whom these two offices had descended being then within age, they and the offices were in the custody of the king, and for this reason the parliament refrained from making any alteration in this new tribunal.[3] The objection to this court was, that it was governed by *the law of arms*, and not by the general custom of the kingdom; and at a second meeting of this same parliament, it was stated by the bishop of St David's, who happened to make the usual speech at the opening of the parliament, as a grievance, that

[1] *Rot. Parl.*, 13 Rich. II. [2] *Vide ante*, c. xvi. [3] Cott. Abri., p. 171, s. 47.

the law of arms and the law of the land did not concur.[1] To quiet the minds of the people upon this subject, a statute was at length made; but this was so general, that it left things in the same state they were in before. It was noticed by stat. 8 Rich. II. c. v., that divers pleas concerning the common law, and which ought to be examined and discussed by that law, were now of late[2] drawn before the constable and marshal of England, to the great damage and disquiet of the people; and it was therefore declared and ordained that such pleas and suits should not be brought in that court, but this matter should stand as it did in the time of Edward III. This seems to be calculated for satisfying the present discontent of the people, without disturbing things, till the office was out of the wardship of the king; but in the 13th year of this reign (when probably that event had taken place) an act of a more special nature was made, which seems to define the authority of that court very exactly. Considering the daily encroachments made by the court of the constable and marshal, in holding plea of contracts, covenants, trespasses, debts, detinues, and other matters cognizable at common law, it was intended by stat. 13 Rich. II. st. 1, c. ii. to make a declaration of the jurisdiction of the constable (for the act does not in this place name the marshal) in the following way: "To the constable," says the act, "belongs the cognizance of contracts touching deeds of arms, and of war out of the realm, and also of things which touch war within the realm, which cannot be determined nor discussed by the common law, with other usages and customs to the same matters appertaining, which other constables before that time had duly and reasonably used." It was also ordained, that every plaintiff should declare plainly his matter in his petition, before any one should be sent to answer thereto; and if any would complain that a plea was commenced before the constable and marshal which might be tried by the common law, he might have a privy seal of the king without difficulty, directed to the constable and marshal, to surcease in the plea, till it was discussed before the king's council, whether the matter belonged to the common law or to that court.

The marshal, who was joined with the constable in the presidency of this court, filled a different office from him, who was associated with the steward; though it was not uncommon for them both to be held by the same person, as well as other offices which likewise conferred the title of marshal. This appears from a transaction in the 20th year of this reign, for the king granted to the earl of Nottingham, and to the heirs male of his body, the office, name, and title of earl marshal of England, the office of marshal of the king's bench and exchequer, the office of proclaimer marshal, and of the steward and marshal of the king's household.[3]

While the crown was in possession of territories on the continent, as during the latter part of Edward III. and the reigns of Richard

[1] Cott. Abri., p. 173, s. 8. [2] *Jam de novo.* [3] Cott. Abri., p. 363, s. 32.

II. and the two Henrys, there must have been great employment for this court, notwithstanding the fiction[1] that had been devised in the time of Edward III. to make matters arising beyond sea cognizable by a jury from an English county. We shall also find there was conferred on these two officers a criminal jurisdiction, by which they tried crimes committed beyond sea; and this they exercised so low down as the reign of Queen Elizabeth, though it was in part rendered less necessary by the statute of Henry VIII. for trying treason committed beyond sea.

Of the admiralty court.

The office of admiral is considered by the French as a piece of state invented by them; nor does it appear that any officer of this kind was constituted in England till about the time of Edward I., and from thence the place of high admiral had been conferred on some of the first nobility. We have yet met with nothing concerning the judicial authority of this officer; but in this reign there had arisen a like jealousy of his authority, as of that of the constable and marshal. It was the port-towns, which had franchises of their own, that raised most of the complaints against the admiral.[2] To satisfy them, an act was at last made, in the 13th year of the king. The preamble of this act[3] states the complaints as arising, because admirals and their deputies held their sessions within divers places of the realm, as well within franchises as without, *accroaching* to them greater authority than belonged to their office, to the prejudice of the king, and of persons possessed of franchises: to remedy which it was declared, that the admiral or his deputies should not meddle with anything done within the realm, but only with things done upon the sea, as had been used in the time of Edward III.

This, like the first act about the jurisdiction of the constable and marshal, was too general to have any effect in working a reformation. It was therefore soon followed by stat. 15 Rich. II., c. iii., where the admiral's jurisdiction was more particularly marked out. First, it was declared that of all manner of contracts, pleas, and quarrels, and all other things arising within the bodies of counties, as well by land as by water, and also of wreck of the sea, the admiral's court should have no manner of cognizance or power, but these were to be determined by the common law. Nevertheless, the admiral was to have cognizance of the death of a man, and of a mayhem done in great ships, being and hovering in the main stream of great rivers, only below the *bridges*[4] of the same river near the sea, and in no other places of the same rivers. It was further ordained, that he should have power to arrest ships in the great fleets for the great voyages of the king, and of the realm, saving to the king all manner of forfeitures and profits thence arising: he was also to have jurisdiction on such fleets during such voyages,

[1] *Vide ante*, c. xvi. [2] Cott. Abri., p. 339, s. 33. [3] Ch. 5.

[4] *Paraval les pountz.* In the Old Abridgment it is *portes*; in Pickering it is *bridges*; in the *Nova Statuta*, it is *pointz*.

saving also to lords, cities, and boroughs, their liberties and franchises.

It may be asked by what law was the court of the constable and marshal, and that of the admiral, governed? It has been said by later writers, that the proceeding in the former was a course directed by the civil law;[1] but *the law of arms* was surely not to be found in the volumes of imperial jurisprudence. The laws of Oleron, as they were called, might constitute a national code of maritime law, for the direction of the admiral; and whatever was defective therein was supplied from that great fountain of jurisprudence, the civil law, which was generally adopted to fill up the chasms that appeared in any of the municipal customs of modern European nations.

It should seem that the old laws[2] respecting the bounds of the steward and marshal's court were not observed; for in the beginning of this reign, the commons petitioned that the jurisdiction of the marshal might be limited, and that all persons within the verge might have their liberties:[3] and it was enacted by stat. 13 Rich. II. c. iii., that the jurisdiction of the court of the steward and marshal of the king's house should not pass the space of twelve miles, to be reckoned from the king's lodging: which was conformable with some petitions in the former reign.[4] After this there were no further parliamentary declarations on the subject of this court, except a short act in the reign of Henry VI.

Court of exchequer.

Having said thus much upon these courts of a particular and special nature, we come now to the ordinary courts of law, respecting which some regulations, well deserving of notice, were made by parliament. Great complaint was made of the dilatory and oppressive course of the court of exchequer; where, in addition to the rigour which was experienced from the natural order of things, the clerks practised many unfair devices upon accountants. Among other hardships, the heirs and executors of persons who had accounted at the exchequer, were not allowed to plead the discharge of their ancestor or testator, without a writ or privy seal authorizing them so to do. By this act the necessity of such writs was removed, all persons were admitted to plead as in other courts, heavy penalties and imprisonments were inflicted on clerks who issued process to recover debts already paid. Besides this, the business of the exchequer, as far as concerned the king's revenue, was better regulated by several acts of parliament.[5] It seems, as the court of exchequer was not within the act of *nisi prius*, whenever an issue in a foreign county was to be tried, a special commission used to be made out: it was now enacted, that no more than two shillings should be given for such commission as the clerk's fee for making it out, and the same for the record of *nisi prius* with the writ.[6] The people were not satisfied with the

[1] Duck de Auth. Jur. Civil, 336, 340.
[2] *Vide ante*, c. xiii.
[3] Cott. Abri., p. 160, s. 65.
[4] *Vide ante*, c. xvi.
[5] Stat. 1 Rich. II., c. 5; Stat. 5 Rich. II., c. 9, 11, 12, 13, 14, 15.
[6] Stat. 5 Rich. II., c. 16.

course of appeal established from this court by the statute of the last reign;[1] but it was again prayed (though without effect) by the commons, that errors in the exchequer might be redressed in the king's bench or parliament.[2]

The substance of the oath which had been ordained by stat. 18 Edw. III. s. 4, to be taken by the judges and barons, was put into a statute in the 8th year of this king.[3] This act ordains, that they should not take any robe, fee, pension, gift, or reward of any but of the king, except reward of meat or drink, which should be of no great value: they were to give no counsel to any in matters where the king was party, or where the king was any ways concerned; nor were they to be counsel with any man in any cause or matter depending before them, upon pain of losing their office, and making fine to the king. It was one of the charges against the archbishop of York, Robert de Vere, and Michael de la Pole, that they on many occasions tampered with the judges, and those suspicions might have produced the above act. But, whatever was the motive for making it, we find it was repealed the next year by stat. 9 Rich. II. c. i., *because* IT WAS VERY HARD *and needed declaration.* It was by another chapter[4] of the former statute enacted, that if any judge or clerk was convicted before the king and council of false entering of pleas, razing of rolls, and changing of verdicts, to the disherison of either of the parties to the suit, he should be punished at the discretion of the council. To prevent the possibility of partiality or favour in magistrates, it was ordained by the same act,[5] that no *man of law* should be justice of assize, or of the common deliverance of gaols, in his own county. This prohibition was confined to such persons in the commission as were men of the law, because the persons associated with them were, by some former statutes, expressly required to be persons of the county.

Further regulations were made concerning these provincial judicatures. By the last mentioned act it was ordained, that the chief justice of the common bench should be assigned among others to take assizes and deliver gaols; but that, as to the chief justice of the king's bench, it should be as had been for the most part the last hundred years. What the practice had been for the preceding hundred years does not appear by any statute, report, or book, but it should at least seem from this act, that the chief justice of the common bench did not use to go circuits. By stat. 20 Rich. II. c. iii., it was enacted, that no lord, nor other of the country, little or great, should sit upon the bench with the justices to take assizes in their sessions, upon pain of great forfeiture to the king; and the statute says, the king had charged the justices not to suffer this order to be broken. This, like some of the former laws, must have been occasioned by late discoveries of the interference and sway of great men in judicial matters. It was ordained by stat. 6 Rich. II.

[1] *Vide ante*, c. xvi.
[2] Cott. Abri., p. 164, s. 105.
[3] Ch. 3.
[4] Ch. 4.
[5] Ch. 2.

st. 1, c. v., that justices of assize and gaol delivery should hold their sessions in the principal and chief towns of every county where the shire-courts were held; but in stat. 11 Rich. II. c. xi., this was said to be found in part prejudicial and grievous to the people in many counties; and on that account the chancellor was thereby empowered to remedy it by the advice of the justices when occasion required.

The delays in suing writs of *nisi prius* still continued.[1] Complaint was made, that persons were impannelled on juries, and after that, the parties would not sue their writ of *nisi prius*, but delayed it from year to year; by which it was said jurors suffered great loss, sometimes to more than the yearly value of their land. To remedy this, it was enacted by stat. 7 Rich. II. c. vii., that in all pleas where a *nisi prius* might be had of course, after the grand distress thrice returned, and served before the justices against the jurors, and thereupon the parties demanded, if none of such parties would sue the writ of *nisi prius*, then it might be made at the suit of any of the jurors present; and this might be in the exchequer as well as the other courts.

Very little was done towards adding to or improving the remedies formerly in use. By stat. 7 Rich. II. c. x. it was ordained, that an assize of novel disseisin for rent due out of tenements in divers counties should be had *in confinio comitatûs* within which the tenements lay, in the same manner as had before been used where a common of pasture in one county was appendant to land in another.[2]

The statutes of *forcible entries* had a more extensive effect, by abrogating the old method of redress in cases of disseisin. We have seen, that in the time of Bracton,[3] a person disseised might recover seisin by force, with a multitude of friends to assist him, provided he made this attempt *flagrante disseisinâ*. But the state of things was so altered, and the ideas of men were so different, that these forcible vindications of a man's property were thought incompatible with a well-ordered government. It was accordingly enacted by stat. 5 Rich. II. c. vii., that none should enter lands and tenements but where an entry was given by the law; and in such case, not with strong hand, nor with multitude of people, but only in a peaceable and easy manner; and if any one did the contrary, and was thereof convicted, he was to be imprisoned and ransomed at the king's pleasure. Thus, a disseisee, if he entered with force, became punishable in the same manner as a disseisor with force had been before.

A more summary method was pointed out by stat. 15 Rich. II. c. ii., which directs, that upon complaint made to any justice of peace of such forcible entry, such justice should take sufficient power of the county, and go to the place where the force was; and if he found any persons holding the place forcibly after such entry

[1] *Vide ante*, c. xvi. [2] *Vide ante*, c. xvi. [3] *Vide ante*, vol. i. c. vii.

made, they were to be taken and committed to the next gaol, there to remain convict by the record of the justice, until they had made fine and ransom to the king. The sheriff and all the people of the county were thereby required to attend the justices. The same of forcible entries into benefices, or offices of holy church.

In order that those in reversion might not be losers by the collusion of the particular tenants, the following statue was made. It was enacted by stat. 9 Rich. II. c. iii., that if a tenant for term of life, tenant in dower, tenant by the courtesy, or tenant in tail after possibility of issue extinct, was impleaded, and pleaded to an inquest, and lost by verdict, or by default, or in any other manner, he to whom the reversion of such tenements belonged, his heirs and successors, should have an action by writ of attaint, or by writ of error, as well in the life of such tenants as after their deaths; and if he succeeded in such writ, the tenant who lost should be restored to his possession, with the issues arising in the meantime, and the party suing, to the arrears of the rent, if any were due; and if the tenant were dead, then to the land in question. Moreover, although the particular tenant was alive, yet if the reversioner so suing alleged that he was of covin and consent with the demandant who recovered against him, the tenements were to be restored to the reversioner. The tenant, however, might afterwards have a *scire facias* out of the judgment so reversed, if he would traverse the covin alleged. This was a redress similar to that which had been allowed to termors for years, by a statute of Edward I.[1]

Another way in which the particular tenant could injure the reversioner, was by making *default*, if impleaded for the freehold; in such case the reversioner was entitled by a statute of Edward I.[2] to be received to defend the right; but there was no remedy where he *pleaded in chief* such pleas by which he knew the inheritance must be lost. To remedy this, it was now enacted, by stat. 13 Rich. II. st. 1, c. xvii., that where any of the before-mentioned tenants were impleaded, and he in reversion came into court and prayed to be received to defend his right, at the day the tenant pleaded to the action, or before; he should be received to plead in chief to the action, without making any delay by voucher, aid-prayer, nonage, or other delay, by essoin or protection.

The laying the venue in personal actions, which before had been almost optional[3] (*a*), was somewhat restricted by stat. 6 Rich. II.

(*a*) The whole of the proceedings in an action were grounded upon the original writ, and among others the venue or place of trial—*vide* the judgment of Blackstone, J., in Santler *v.* Heard, 2 W. Blackstone, 1031, deducing the history of the law as to venue. So long ago as 6 Rich. II. c. ii. a statute was passed in furtherance of the common law, to compel plaintiffs to bring their actions in the counties where the cause of action arose; and the stat. 4 Hen. VI. c. xviii. was also passed in furtherance of the same policy. The notion that a plaintiff had a right in transitory actions to lay his venue where he pleased is of much later origin, and indeed is quite modern, and has not only no foundation in the ancient law, but is utterly opposed to it. If the wrong venue was laid in a transitory action, no doubt it was not error, as in a

[1] *Vide ante*, vol. i. c. vi. [2] *Ibid.* [3] *Vide ante*, c. xvi.

st. 1, c. ii. It is thereby provided, that in actions of debt, accompt, and *all other such actions*, if the declaration stated the contract to be in any other county than that contained in the original writ, the writ should be immediately abated (*a*). It was ordained by ch. iii. of the same statute, that the writs of nuisance, commonly called *viconteil*,[1] might be brought, either in the old way, or else in the nature of assizes determinable before the justices of the one bench or the other, or of assize to be taken in the country; so that the distinction between these writs, so much attended to in the last reign, began to be of less moment. It was a doubt in the last reign, whether the question of a priory being donative or not, should be tried *per proves*, or *per pais*.[2] But it was now ordained, by stat. 9 Rich. II. c. iv., that such an issue should be tried by the certificate of the ordinary of the place; and this was to be, as well where the ordinary was not a party, as where he was. Notwithstanding the precaution taken by the legislature in making stat. 25 Edw. III. st. 3, c. iii.,[3] yet the king's presentees, either by the favour of ordinaries, the partiality of inquests, or perhaps by the parties not being duly warned, would get themselves forced into benefices, and the incumbents put out. To remedy this, it was now provided, in addition to the course there directed, that where a benefice was full of an incumbent, the king's presentee should not be received till the king had recovered by process of law; and if any was received otherwise, and the incumbent put out, he was to commence his suit within a year after the induction of the king's presentee.

It was held in the time of Edward III. that[4] a prisoner in custody upon a judgment should not be suffered to go at large without the consent of the plaintiff; but it was now complained, that such persons were frequently let at large by the warden of the Fleet-prison, sometimes by mainprise or by bail, and sometimes

local action, but the jury could only come from the venue laid (*Lee* v. *Lacon*, *Yelv.* 69; *King* v. *Andrews*, *ibid*, 57); and if this came from a larger or different venue, it was error (*Wilcocks* v. *Lovelace*, *Yelv.*) The object of these statutes was to force the plaintiff to lay the proper venue.

(*a*) Upon this a practice arose of examining the plaintiff as to where the contract was made or the cause of action really arose, a practice which seems to have originated with reference to wager at law, and to have been applied in various other cases. Thus in debt on a deed said to have been made in one county, the defendant alleging that it was made in another, the defendant prayed that the plaintiff might be examined; and he was so (*Year-book*, 5 *Hen. V.* fol. 1). But if the defendant said the deed was made beyond seas, the plaintiff was not examined upon the date; he left it at large, not saying where it was made, and although in fact it was made at Rome, for it could be alleged to have been made here (21 *Edward IV.* fol. 74; 3 *Hen. VI.* fol. 29). This it was said was by the equity of the statute (*Ibid.*), so the plaintiff in an action of detinue was examined as to where the bailment was (3 *Hen. VI.*, 38). The effect of the statute was said to be that, if a man brought a writ in one county and declared upon a contract in another, the writ should abate (3 *Hen. VI.*, 15). And by the practice of the courts, examination of the plaintiff was allowed to discover where the contract was made. This was by mere force of practice, and is a precedent of great importance.

[1] *Vide ante*, 27. [2] *Ibid.*, 100. [3] *Ibid.*, vol. ii., 378. [4] *Vide ante*, 115.

without any mainprise, with a *baston*[1] of the Fleet: that such persons went into the country about their private affairs, continuing out many nights and days without the consent of, or any satisfaction made to, their plaintiffs. To prevent this, it was enacted by stat. 1 Richard II. c. xii. that no warden of the Fleet, upon pain of losing his office, should suffer a prisoner by judgment to go out in any of the above ways, without making gree to the parties at whose suit he was there, unless it was by writ or other commandment of the king; and if he was attainted of such neglect by due process, the plaintiff might have recovery against him by writ of debt. It was usual, when an action was commenced in another court against a prisoner, for him to be removed into the prison of that court: this had been abused in a way that caused the following provision, declaring, that if any prisoner in execution in another prison, would confess himself voluntarily, and by a feigned cause, debtor to the king, and by such means to be judged to the Fleet, there to have *greater sweet of prison* than elsewhere, and so delayed the party of his recovery, the recognizance so confessed should be taken as a true one; so that the party being remanded to his first prison till he had satisfied his first plaintiff, should then be brought back to the Fleet, and there detained till he had satisfied the recognizance.

Two laws were made to correct the abuse of *protections;* a species of privilege which created great obstacles to the course of justice. We have seen[2] that some protections had the clause of *volumus*, and some that of *nolumus:* we now find, that as the clause of *volumus* was usually accompanied with the clause of *quia profecturus*, simply alleging that the party was going abroad; so other protections had in them a clause *quia moraturus*, signifying that he was to reside abroad. By stat. 1. Richard II. c. viii. it was enacted, that no protection with a clause of *volumus* should be allowed before any judge, for victuals taken or bought upon the voyage or service of which the protection made mention, nor in pleas of trespass, or of other contracts, since the date of the protection. It was not uncommon to purchase these protections, both with a clause of *volumus* and of *quia profecturus*, after a plea was actually commenced, merely to delay the proceedings, without any regard to the king's service, in which the parties pretended to be employed; for they in the meantime continued to stay at home. This misapplication of protections occasioned the following act, 13 Richard II. st. 1, c. xvi., ordaining, that no protection with a clause of *profecturus* be allowed in any plea commenced before the date of the protection, if it was not in a voyage where the king went in person, or in some voyage royal, or on the king's messages for business of the realm; but such persons were to make their attorneys to answer for them, or were to stay themselves. Not-

[1] That is, an under-keeper of the jail having a *baston*, or wand, and walking with the prisoner.

[2] *Vide ante*, c. xv.

withstanding this restraint on the above protections, the protection *quia moraturus* was to be allowed in all cases, as before. It was likewise provided, that if any person remained in the country, without going on the service for which he was retained, the chancellor might repeal the protection. Thus far of the statutes which had any influence on the administration of civil justice.

The commotions which happened in this reign, and the vicissitudes experienced by the several contending parties, had an effect upon our criminal law. When that could be made an instrument in the hands of either to destroy their opponents, they never failed of availing themselves of it; and at every revolution they endeavoured to give a new edge to the sword of justice. In no period of our history was the crime of treason imputed so promiscuously to all sorts of resistance and opposition. Of treasons. This extravagance was not confined to the lords in parliament, who might be hurried into violent measures by the heat of contest and the flush of success; but we shall find the sages of the law giving deliberate opinions of the same import, upon questions stated in writing: so that the subject seemed to derive little benefit from the statute of treasons.

The first alteration made in the law of treason, was by act of parliament. It was enacted by stat. 5 Rich. II., st. 1, c. vi., that if any made or begun any manner of riot and *rumour*, *or the like*, and the same was duly proved, it should be done of him as of a traitor to the king and realm. A declaration of treason like this, might perhaps be excused by the late riots, which had been carried to a length sufficient to endanger the safety of the government. Two years before that statute, it happened that one John Imperial, an ambassador from the state of Genoa, was killed in London: this had been deemed treason by the judges, and that sentence was confirmed by parliament; the reason alleged being, that it affected the king's majesty.[1] In the 17th year of the king, we find the duke of Lancaster, steward of England, and the duke of Gloucester, constable of England, complained in parliament that Sir Thomas Talbot, with other adherents, conspired the deaths of the said dukes. This was adjudged by the king and lords in parliament to be open and high treason.[2] The parliament made the above declarations by virtue of that power which was acknowledged to reside in it, by the statute of treasons; and which it could not be denied to possess, as necessarily belonging to its legislative authority.

The famous opinions given by the judges had not that sanction, and therefore should have been founded on principles of known and established law. The following was the occasion on which these opinions were taken: The king being compelled to sign a commission and call a parliament, at the instance of a great part of his nobles, wished to get rid of the act he had done under such

[1] 3 Rich. II.; Cott. Abri., p. 183, s. 18.

[2] Cott. Abri., p. 353, s. 20.

compulsion; and, thinking the law on his side, caused certain of his judges and others to be consulted on different questions, calculated to stigmatise and declare void the late proceedings. In the 11th year of this reign, in the presence of the king and some lords at Nottingham Castle, were summoned Tresilian, the chief-justice of the king's bench, and Belknap, chief-justice of the common bench; Holt, Fulthorpe, and Burghe, judges of the common bench; and Lokton, one of the king's serjeants-at-law. To these persons were propounded among other questions, the following, which received the annexed answers. Being asked, How those ought to be punished who procured the above-mentioned statute, ordinance, and commission? they answered, By capital pain; as ought those likewise *who excited the king to consent* to the said statute. Those who *compelled* the king to consent, they said, should be punished as *traitors;* as should those also who interrupted the king in the exercise of those things that belonged to his royalty and prerogative. The following question, namely, Whether, if the king *limited* to the lords and commons certain articles to be debated, and they proceeded upon others, and would not go upon the king's articles till he had answered theirs, the king should be obeyed? they answered, That such as disobeyed this rule of the king, should be punished as *traitors.* If the king dissolved the parliament, and any proceeded therein afterwards, they said, he was to be considered as a traitor. They said, it would be treason to impeach in parliament any of the king's officers, or justices; and that the person who moved that the statute whereby Edward II. was indicted should be sent for, and he who, by force of such motion, brought it into the parliament, were guilty of *treason.*

The judges who concurred in these opinions, were afterwards prosecuted as offenders; but things taking another turn, in the 21st year of the king, these opinions were read in full parliament, and there received the sanction of the legislature; and at the same time they were pronounced by Sir Thomas Skelton, and Hankford, and Brenchley, the king's serjeants, to be *good and lawful.* But it is recorded in the same statute of 21 Rich. II. that Thirning, and Clopton, successively chief justices of the common bench, and Richehill, a judge in that court, gave a more discreet opinion upon the act of these judges; they said, that the declaration of treason not declared belonged to the parliament; and *if the offender were a lord*, or peer of parliament, and those questions had been put to *him, he* would have given the like answers: which was intimating that they were not consonant to the law, as established and known, but were fit enough to be declared treason by parliament.

In the same stat. 21 Rich. II., c. iii., some points of treason which had been settled by the statute of treasons, were re-enacted, together with some others that were not within that act. Thus, it was ordained, that every one who compassed or purposed the death of the king, or to depose him, or to render up his homage or liege-ance; and he that raised people, and rode against the king to make war within the realm, and was judged and attainted thereof *in parliament,* should be considered as guilty of high treason, and should forfeit his lands, as well those in fee-tail as those in fee-simple. The difference between this act and the statute of treason is, that this did not require an overt act to be proved; but then it was to be judged of only in parliament; and lands in fee-tail were forfeit thereby. It was made treason to procure, or counsel to repeal or annul, any judgments given against statutes made in the parliament 11th Rich. II., which the king now procured to be declared void;[1] and it was also declared treason for any one to attempt to repeal the stat. 21 Rich. II.[2]

Besides the above provision about riots, other statutes were made for the suppression of those disorders, which had lately grown to a height that threatened the existence of government. In stat. 2 Rich. II. st. 1, c. vi., there is a lively picture drawn of the riots which then very commonly happened. People used to come in great bodies, sometimes under pretence of taking possession of lands to which persons pretended they had a right; they would pillage a whole neighbourhood, carry off women and children, and commit all such acts of violence as might be expected from an invading enemy. To maintain the peace against such extraordinary attacks required more than the ordinary means. Among other methods it was ordained, that the statute of Northampton should be kept in all points; and moreover, that certain sufficient and *valiant persons,* lords, or others, should be assigned by the king's commission, with authority to take such rioters, without waiting for an indictment, and commit them to custody till the coming of the justices. But this new authority was repealed by stat. 2 Rich. II. st. 2, c. ii., the statute of Northampton being thought quite adequate to the purpose. This repeal was procured by some great lords, who were too much interested in the outrages committed by these people (many of whom were their retainers and partisans)[3] to suffer any greater restraint to be put on their meetings. When the *villeins,* about a year or two after this, had risen in different parts of the country, and compelled manumissions and privileges to be granted them, it was enacted, as we have seen, by stat. 5 Rich. II. st. 1, c. vi., that rioters should be punished as traitors. The discontents of the villeins continued all through this reign. Upon the occasion of new disturbances made by this order of the people, particularly in Cheshire and Lancashire, it was enacted by stat. 17 Rich. II. c. viii., that sheriffs, and other the king's ministers, should take such offenders; and that all lords, and others of the realm, should be assisting therein. We shall see what course was pursued in the next reigns, for the suppression and punishment of such disorderly persons.

The two statutes against *the spreaders of false rumours* are said

[1] Ch. 4. [2] Ch. 20. [3] *Vide ante.*

to have been procured by the Duke of Lancaster, who was extremely unpopular, and, at the time of the insurrections among the villeins, had been singled out as a principal object of their fury. The first of these is stat. 2 Rich. II. st. 1, c. v. (*a*). The design of this act will be best understood from the preamble. "Of the devisors" (says the act) "of false news, and of horrible and false lies of prelates, dukes, earls, barons, and other nobles and great men of the realm; and also of the chancellor, treasurer, clerk of the privy seal, steward of the king's house, justices of the one bench or of the other, and of other great officers of the realm, of things which by the said persons were never spoken, done, or thought; in great slander of them, and whereby debates and discords might arise betwixt them, or between them and the commons, and great mischief to the realm:" these were the objects meant to be aimed at by this statute; and it was enacted, that none, under grievous pain, be so hardy as to devise, speak, or tell any false news, lies, or other such false things, of the above-mentioned persons, whereof discord or slander might arise within the realm; and those who offended therein were to be liable to the statute of Westm. 1,[1] which directs such offender to be taken and imprisoned till he had found the person by whom the speech was moved: but this not being likely to produce the effect intended, it was enacted that by stat. 12 Rich. II. c. xi., that, should he not be able to find such person, he should be punished by the advice of the council, notwithstanding the said statutes.

Scandalum magnatum.

We have hitherto met with nothing on the subject of *public* nuisances: we find now a statute,[2] ordaining proclamation to be made for removal of public nuisances; such as offal thrown in the streets and ditches near towns; with a penalty of forty shillings on offenders; who were to be called before the chancellor by writ, if they refused to remove the annoyance. By another act, the laws against maintenance were directed to be enforced.[3]

Notwithstanding the act passed in the last reign[4] to prevent the frequent granting of pardons, great clamour was still made on this subject. We find the commons had petitioned that the king might grant no more pardons. To this the king refused to consent, but agreed to the following act,[5] ordaining that no charter should be allowed before any justice for murder, or for the death

(*a*) In the reign of Richard II. a case occurred in which it was held that this statute did not apply to slanderous matter put forth in an action or prosecution. Lord Beauchamp brought an action on the statute against Sir Richard Croft and another, for that they had slandered him as a forger of false deeds; and they pleaded that he had brought a writ of forger of false deeds against Lord Beauchamp, and that this was the slander of which the action was conceived, and the plea was held good, for that the statute was not intended to oust men of their lawful actions (*Lord Beauchamp* v. *Croft*, *Keilway's Rep.* 28). The statute was intended, it was said, to punish men who, without any cause, slandered great men, not such as merely pursued their lawful actions or prosecutions, whether truly or falsely.

[1] *Vide ante*, c. ix.
[2] Stat. 12 Rich. II., c. 13.
[3] Stat. 1 Rich. II., c. 4.
[4] *Vide ante*, c. xvi.
[5] Stat. 13 Rich. II., st. 2, c. i.

of a man slain by await, assault, or malice prepense, for treason, or rape of a woman, *unless* the fact was specified in the charter. Where the pardon of the death of a man was exhibited without specifying the fact, the justices were to inquire, by an inquest of the vicinage where the fact was committed, whether the murder was by await, assault, or malice prepense; and if it was found to be either, the pardon was to be disallowed. If any one sued for a pardon for the death of a man slain in either of the above ways, the chamberlain was to indorse on the bill the name of the person suing, upon pain of a thousand marks, and the under-chamberlain upon pain of five hundred. These bills were always to be directed to the keeper of the privy seal; nor was any warrant of the privy seal to be made out without a bill so signed and indorsed. No charter of pardon of treason, or felony, was to pass the chancery without a warrant of the privy seal, but where the chancellor might[1] grant it *ex officio,* without speaking to the king; and great penalties were to be paid by those who sued pardons in any of the above crimes; that is, an archbishop or duke was to forfeit a thousand pounds, and so in proportion of lesser dignities; a clerk, bachelor, or other of less estate, two hundred marks. But the whole of this statute, except that relating to a specification of the fact, and an inquiry of the truth of it by an inquest, was repealed by stat. 16 Rich. II. c. vi.

The statute 2 Richard II. c. iv., may be ranked among the penal laws of this reign. This ordained, that mariners, who had been *arrested* and retained for the king's service, and then fled, should, besides forfeiting double what they had taken for wages, suffer a year's imprisonment: this offence was to be inquired of before the admiral, or his lieutenant.[2] It appears by this act, that mariners used then to be *compelled* into the service in a way which the legislature did not scruple to call an *arrest;* signifying as compulsory a method as the law made use of on any occasion. The carrying of gold or silver out of the kingdom was forbidden by statute 5 Richard II. st. 1, c. ii., under the penalty of forfeiting all that the offenders could forfeit: prelates were not to export their payments, even by exchange, without license. All persons were by the same act restrained from going beyond sea, without the king's license, and then it was to be only at certain ports: those who offended therein were to forfeit all their goods, and the persons carrying them to forfeit their vessel. This law continued in force till the time of James I.[3]

Some grievances in the manner of executing the forest laws were removed by stat. 7 Rich. II. c. iii. and iv.[4] It was provided, that no jury should be compelled by any officer of the forest, or other, to travel from place to place, out of the place where their charge was given, unless they so pleased; *nor were they,* says the act, *to be con-*

[1] *Vide ante,* c. x.

[2] *Ibid.,* 197.

[3] Stat. 4 James I., c. i. s. 22.]

[4] *Vide ante,* c. ix.

strained to give a verdict otherwise than according to their conscience. Again, no one was to be taken or imprisoned by any officer of the forest without indictment, or being taken with the manner, or trespassing in the forest; nor was any one to be compelled to make an obligation or ransom to an officer of the forest; and any one offending against this act, was to pay the party damnified double damages, and be fined to the king.

While these restrictions were imposed on the old forest law, a sort of new forest law began to show itself; which, since the enlargement it has received in later times, is endured with as little acquiescence as the old; being calculated, like that, to promote the pleasures of the great by restricting those of the lower orders of society. This new system is, perhaps, attended with particular circumstances of aggravation; for whereas the old law was for the protection of the king's diversions, and was local, this is in favour of all lords and great landholders, and extends to every spot of ground in the kingdom: so that, coming more nearly home to the observation of men, it is more generally felt, though indeed less severely, than the forest law.

Game Laws.

The design of the legislature in the first act on this subject will appear from the preamble, which informs us, that "divers artificers, labourers, servants, and grooms, keep greyhounds and other dogs, and on the holidays, when good Christian people be at church, hearing divine service, they go hunting in parks, warrens, and connigries of lords and others, to the very great destruction of the same; and sometimes under such colour they make their assemblies, conferences, and conspiracies to rise, and disobey their allegiance." Thus was the safety of the state, as on other occasions, made a reason for imposing the following restrictions; for it was ordained by stat. 13 Rich. II. st. 1, c. xiii., that no artificer, labourer, nor any other layman, not having lands or tenements of forty shillings per annum, nor priest, or other clerk (if not advanced to the value of ten pounds per annum) should keep any greyhound, hound, or other dog to hunt; nor use ferrets, keys, nets, harepipes, nor cords, or other engine, to take or destroy deer, hares, conies, or other *gentlemen's*[1] game, on pain of a year's imprisonment; to be inquired of by the justices of the peace. This was the first stone in the present fabric of *game laws;* and seems merely a regulation of police, to confine the lower class of people from misspending their time in a way that was neither useful to themselves nor the community.

Justices of the peace.

The authority of justices of the peace was considerably enlarged in this reign, and several regulations were made for the due holding of their sessions, the proper choice of persons to fill this office, and other matters concerning their jurisdiction. By stat. 7 Rich. II. c. v., they had power to inquire of vagabonds, and to compel them to find sureties for their good

[1] *Des gentils.*

behaviour, otherwise to commit them to prison till the coming of the justices of gaol delivery. The next statute respecting justices of the peace is stat. 12 Rich. II. c. x., which enacts, that in every commission of the peace there should be assigned but six justices, besides the justices of assizes (who were always put into the commission); and these six justices were to hold their sessions every quarter of a year at least, and by three days, if need were, on pain of being punished at the discretion of the king and council, at the suit of any one who would complain. They were to inquire if mayors, bailiffs, and others properly executed what was required of them in the ordering of beggars and vagabonds, servants and labourers; and were to punish defaults. The justices were each to have four shillings a day during the sessions, and two shillings for their clerk; this to be paid by the sheriff out of the fines and amercements arising at the sessions. By stat. 13 Rich. II. st. 1, c. vii., it was ordained, that justices should consist of the most sufficient knights, esquires, and gentlemen of the law, of the county, without any exemption for the stewards of lords, as was granted by the former act; and they were to be sworn to put in execution all the statutes relating to their office. By stat. 14 Rich. II. c. xi., there were to be eight justices in every county. As some lords had been put into the commission at that parliament, it was ordained that no duke, earl, baron, or banneret should take any wages: and the wages were to be paid by indenture between the justices and the sheriff. The next statute relating to these justices was stat. 15 Rich. II. c. ii., before mentioned, which gives them authority to proceed in a summary way in cases of forcible entry. By stat. 17 Rich. II. c. ix., they were made conservators of some old statutes for preservation of salmon, and the fry of fish. The last act on this head is chap. x. of the same statute, which ordains, that in every commission of the peace there should be, if need was, two men of the law of that county, who should make deliverance of thieves and felons as often as they might think it convenient.

Such is the progress that was made by parliament in altering our law during this reign. The decisions of courts, for the reasons before given,[1] we shall pass over in silence.

The king and government.

The law is not much indebted to this king. It is said to have been the inclination of Richard and some of his favourites to countenance the encroachments of the civil law; though this, probably, went no further than a partiality for such parts of it as favoured high sovereign authority (*a*).

(*a*) There is no foundation for this suggestion, and the author has passed over the great events of the reign in a constitutional point of view—the audacious attempt made by the principal nobles to supersede the royal authority by a permanent com-

[1] *Vide ante.*

In the reign of this prince, when the sovereign authority often changed hands, when the nation was governed at one time by the king, at another by an authority delegated to certain lords, who, in the struggle for power, pursued each other with the most unrelenting animosities, it is not to be wondered that the law was occasionally made subservient to the successful party, and taught to speak that language which would confirm their interests, and destroy all those who opposed them. Most of the extravagancies which arose from this state of things, consisted in judgments of treason, and attainders of obnoxious persons, without due examination or trial.

It was in this spirit, that conspiring the death of the dukes of Lancaster and Gloucester, the king's uncles, was, as before mentioned, declared by the king and lords to be high treason;[1] that Sir Thomas Haxey was condemned to die the death of a traitor, for having moved in the house of commons, that economy might

mission of regency. This had been attempted in previous reigns, with more pretence of excuse; the authority of parliament not being then so firmly established as to afford adequate guarantees for the due observance of the laws by the crown. But that was not so now; for, as Sir J. Mackintosh observes, after the accession of Richard II., there are no examples of any pretension to lay new and general taxes on the people otherwise than by the estates of parliament. The parliamentary power of the purse was then as much an acknowledged principle of the constitution as it is now. The right of the commons to appropriate supplies to specific services was first regularly introduced in the minority of Richard II. (*Hist. Eng.*, vol. i.) When, therefore, after an abortive attempt at a prosecution of the chancellor (for which there was not a pretence), the powerful party headed by Gloucester forced the king, by actual threats to his life, to sign a commission delegating to them, in effect, the royal authority, it was clearly only a struggle by them for supreme power, and it was simply an act of treason. The commission appointed them a permanent council, authorised them to inquire into all alleged grievances of the people, to hear and determine all complaints which could not be redressed by common course of law, and to provide such remedies for all abuses as should to them appear proper. This, it is evident, transferred to them the authority, not only of king, but of parliament, and vested in an absolute oligarchy the supreme power of the state. The king afterwards consulted the judges, who, as advisers of the crown, gave it most rightly as their opinion that the commission was subversive of the constitution, and that its having been extorted from him by threats of violence was an act of treason. The subsequent conduct of Gloucester and his party, in pretending to accuse the judges and the king's advisers of treason, was simply a continuance of their own treasonable rebellion. When they appealed or accused the five lords, including the chief justice, who had been the king's chief adviser, they arbitrarily and illegally arrested all the judges who were the constitutional advisers of the lords on an impeachment; and it was then that the king called upon the sages of the common and civil law to give to the lords their opinion on the bill of impeachment. They all declared it to be illegal. The oligarchical party, however, proceeded in their illegal course; and it was on that occasion they said they were bound by no other law than the law and custom of parliament (which meant in this instance their own will); that the kingdom of England had never been governed by the civil law, nor would they be guided by the opinion of the other courts of the realm. In other words, that they would not be governed either by civil law or common law, or by any law at all except their own will, which was to murder their political opponents, as they accordingly did. This is another illustration afforded in our annals that there might be as much tyranny exercised by an oligarchy as by a monarchy, and that it is necessary that the powers of the aristocracy, not less than of the crown, should be under the constitutional control of parliament, and in subjection to the law.

[1] Cotton's Abrid., 354.

be promoted at court, and that to attain such end, the court should not be so much frequented by *bishops* and *ladies*.[1] Of the like kind was the prosecution before the committee of parliament, against Henry Bowet, attorney to the duke of Hereford, who having solicited for the duke concerning the possession of his father's estate, was adjudged a traitor; but in this case the punishment of death was changed to banishment.[2] These and the like abuses of law and justice must be ascribed to the violence of the times.

There is no Year-book of the reign of Richard II. in print; but Sir Matthew Hale says, he had seen the entire years and terms of this king in manuscript.[3] There are some cases of this reign to be found in Jenkins's *Centuries*, some in Keilway, some in Benloe, and some in Fitzherbert's *Abridgment*. All these scattered notes have been collected by Bellewe, and digested under heads; making a sort of substitute for a Year-book of this king.

[1] Cotton's Abrid., 362. [2] Tyrr., vol. iii., 991. [3] *Hist. Com. Law*, 175.

CHAPTER XVIII.

HENRY IV.

Election of Members—Of the Clergy—Vicars instituted and inducted—Statutes of Labourers—The Parliament and Council—Attorneys—Repeal of Treasons—Heretics—Multiplication—Pardons of Provors—Insidiatores Viarum, &c.—Riots—Actions upon the Case—Of Assumpsit—The criminal Law—Peine forte et dure—The King and Government—The Statutes—Reports.

THE judicial history of Henry IV. has an advantage over that of his predecessor; for the decisions of courts as well as the provisions made by parliament during this reign have come down to our times (*a*). Our attention, however, will be principally engaged by the latter. The laws of this king are upon many of the subjects which were canvassed by parliament in the former reign. One article of regulation was wholly new, and distinguishes this king's reign as the period when the first provisions were made for securing to the people a due and faithful choice and return of their representatives.

(*a*) Upon the accession of this the first sovereign of the House of Lancaster, afterwards continued by that of Tudor, a question of some interest suggests itself as to the view which was taken by the kings of this race, as to their position with reference to the laws and liberties of the realm. The question suggests itself in consequence of the repeated confirmations by this king, and his successor, of the Great Charters, which one would have thought had by this time, after centuries of acquiescence and confirmation, become sufficiently established. No doubt this king was, in strict law, a usurper; and against such a sovereign the parliament might naturally be disposed to take guarantees. But it is conceived that this is hardly of itself an adequate explanation of the matter, and that its real causes would refer, and have much bearing upon subsequent events. There is strong ground for supposing that all the sovereigns, since the Conquest, had cherished the notion that the Conqueror had acquired the realm by conquest, in the strict legal sense; the result of which would have been an entire abrogation of all the laws and liberties of the nation, and hence a necessity for grants or confirmations of them from the crown. At all events, it is a fact, that even at this period of our history, centuries after the Great Charters, they were not once, but again and again confirmed, a fact which shows some latent distrust: and there is the further fact, that Henry VIII., on his accession, appears to have styled himself ostentatiously the eighth from the Conquest. Not only in that age, but in an age long subsequent, much importance was attached to the theory of a conquest; for Lord Hale wrote his *History of the Law* in a great degree to refute it, and argues against it elaborately. The age of the accession of the House of Lancaster would be a natural occasion for the assertion of such a theory, especially as Henry IV. was the first sovereign, since the Conquest, who had really attained to the crown by force of arms, as no doubt he had. Hence, on the other hand, parliament would be anxious to restrain the supposed right of conquest, by repeated confirmations of the Great Charters; and scarcely a parliament was summoned during the present reign, in which there was not such a confirmation. Thus, in the very first act of the first session of parliament, we find a confirmation of the liberties of the church, and of all statutes not repealed, and of all laws and usages of the realm (*Hen. IV.*, c. i), that holy church have and enjoy all her rights, liberties, and franchises, and that the Great Charters and other good ordinances and statutes made in the time of the king's progenitors, and not repealed, be firmly holden and kept;

In the fifth year of the present king a special act was passed for the punishment of a person who had assaulted, beat, and wounded a menial servant to one of the knights representing the county of Somerset, during the time of parliament. It was enacted,[1] that proclamation should be made where the fact was done, commanding the offender to appear in the king's bench within a quarter of a year; if not, to be attainted of the fact, and pay the injured party double damages, to be taxed by the judges, or, if need were, by an inquest; and further pay a fine to the king; *and so* (says the act) *shall it be in all similar cases.* It was in the same parliament prayed, that all persons who arrested a knight, or burgess, or any of their servants, knowing them to be such, should be fined at the king's pleasure, and render treble damages to the party grieved. To this it was answered, that there was a sufficient remedy already.[2] What this remedy was does not appear, unless it is to be collected, that the privilege was so notorious and established, as to entitle the party injured to an action.

It was complained in parliament, that the election of knights of counties was sometimes made according to the pleasure of the sheriffs, and generally against the form of the

Election of members.

and that the peace be kept, so that all his liege subjects may safely dwell, according to the laws and usages of the realm; and that good justice and equal right be done to every person. This was in terms confirmed by 2 Hen. IV., c. i; 4 Hen. IV., i; and 7 Hen. IV., c. i. These repeated confirmations of themselves suggest a sense of suspicion, distrust, and insecurity, arising, no doubt, from the notions of a conquest, long latent in the breasts of the Plantagents, and now perilously revived by the accession of a usurper, who attained the crown by force of arms. And it is very observable that in the later of those confirmations, there are added those remarkable words, "saving to the king his regality and prerogative" (7 *Hen. IV.*, c. i.) This prerogative was upheld, even as against the church. There was, it will be observed, a confirmation of the statutes of previous reigns (a confirmation needless except with reference to the notion of conquest), and among those were the statutes of liveries, passed in the reigns of Richard II., for the suppression of combinations, &c. So in this reign statutes were passed against disseisors with force; that is, great persons, who make forcible entries, with force and arms and numbers of men, into other men's lands (4 *Hen. IV.*, c. viii.); and against riots or routs (3 *Hen. IV.*, c. vii.); and the policy of these statutes was carried out in the subsequent reigns. So with reference to the church, there was no relaxation of the statutes passed in previous reigns against the exercise of papal supremacy, so as to interfere with the temporal rights; but, on the contrary, they were not only, in general terms, re-enacted, but were reaffirmed and aided by several other statutes. Thus there was a statute that if any do accept a provision granted by our holy father the pope (*nostre sanct pere le pape*), to any person in religion, to be exempt from obedience, he should be within the danger of the statute of provisors (2 *Hen. IV.*, c. iii.); and another statute enacted penalties for procuring bulls to be discharged of tithes (2 *Hen. IV.*, c. iv.) And there was a subsequent statute, that no provision, license, or pardon, should be granted of a benefice full of an incumbent (7 *Hen. IV.*, c. viii.) This statute enacted that many mischiefs arose because of many provisions made by the pope, and licenses granted upon the same by the king, from which it appears that the crown assumed the power of granting licenses to dispense with the statute of provisors; and then got from parliament power to invalidate its own licenses. Parliament, however, was always ready to aid the crown against the church, and this sovereign sought to rule with the support of parliament. And this was the spirit and policy of all the sovereigns of this dynasty, and of the House of Tudor, which succeeded them.

[1] Ch. 6.

[2] Cott. Abri., p. 433, s. 74.

writ directed to the sheriff. To prevent this in future, it was enacted by stat. 7 Hen. IV. c. xv., that the election of knights should be in the following way; namely, at the next county to be held after the delivery of the parliament writ, proclamation was to be made in the full county of the day and place of the parliament; and that all those then present, as well suitors duly summoned for that cause, as others, should enter upon the election of knights; and then, in full county, they were to proceed freely and indifferently, notwithstanding any request or command to the contrary. After they were chosen, their names were to be written in an indenture, under the seals of all those who chose them, and tacked to the same writ of parliament; which indenture, so sealed and tacked, was to be held for the sheriff's return of the said writ, as far as concerned the knights of the shire. It was also enacted, that in the writs of the parliament, in future, this clause should be put; *et electionem tuam in pleno comitatu tuo factam distinctè et apertè sub sigillo tuo, et sigillis eorum qui electioni illi interfuerint, nobis in cancellariâ nostrâ ad diem et locum in brevi contentos certifices indilatè.* But because no penalty was inflicted by this statute on sheriffs who did not conform thereto, it was ordained by stat. 11 Hen. IV. c. ii., that the justices of assize should inquire of such returns in their sessions; and if it was found by inquest, and due examination before them, that a sheriff had made a return contrary to this act, he was to be fined one hundred pounds; and knights so unduly returned were to lose their wages. Before these two acts there was no statute relating to this matter, unless the statutes of Edward I.,[1] for free elections could be considered as such.

Of the clergy.

The two grand objects of reformation in church matters, the restraining the interference of papal authority, and providing for the regular maintenance of vicars, were pursued in this reign. The weapon now used against the pope and his adherents was the statute of provisors, 13 Richard II. st. 2, c. iii., which had put the proceeding by *præmunire facias* into a stricter course.[2] Many new cases were now brought within the penalty of this law. It was enacted by stat. 2 Hen. IV. c. iii., that if provision was made by the bishop of Rome to any person, religious or secular, to be exempt from obedience regular, or to have any office perpetual within houses of religion, or as much as one regular person of religion, or two, or more, had in the same, and such privisors accepted the same, they should incur the pains of stat. 13 Richard II. st. 2, c. iii. Again, because complaint was made that the *Cistertians* had purchased bulls to be discharged of tithes, and that this exemption used to be extended to their tenants, it was enacted,[3] that they should continue in the condition they were in before the purchase of such bulls; and they and all other orders which purchased bulls, or by colour of any bulls pretended to avail themselves of a discharge from tithes, were to be warned to appear

[1] *Vide ante*, c. ix. [2] *Vide ante*, c. xiii. [3] Ch. 4.

in two months by writ of *præmunire facias;* and if they made default, or were attainted, they were to incur the penalties of the before-mentioned act of Richard II.

Such were the securities provided for the due payment of tithes, when an act was passed in aid of the statute of Richard II.[1] concerning vicars (*a*). It was by stat. 4 Hen. IV. c. xii., enacted, that the former statute should be duly observed; that licenses of appropriation made since should be reformed according to the effect of that act; and if such reformation was not made within a certain time, the appropriation and license were to be void. All appropriations of vicarages since the first year of Richard II. were declared void. And further it was enacted, that in every church so appropriated, or to be appropriated, a secular person should be ordained vicar *perpetual*, canonically *instituted and inducted*, and *convenably endowed* by the discretion of the ordinary, to do divine service, to inform the people, and to keep hospitality; and no religious person was to be made vicar in any church so appropriated. Thus was it at length ordained, that vicars should have institution and induction, which gave them the same tenure as parsons; and to avoid the abuses which had been so long complained of, religious houses were no longer suffered to appoint any of their own body to such appropriated vicarages as belonged to them.

Vicars instituted and inducted.

The religious orders were no longer in such consideration as they had been. A statute was made in this parliament restraining the four orders of friars, that is, the *friars minors*, *Augustines*, *Preachers*, and *Carmelites*, from taking any person into their order, under fourteen years of age, without the assent of the parents of

(*a*) As already has been seen, it has been held, even before the statute of Richard II., as to endowment of vicarages, that vicarages could be endowed; and that if so endowed, the vicars could recover their endowments by legal process, either against the parsons or strangers (40 *Edw. III.*, f. 12). After the above act of 4 Henry IV., that is in the 10th of Henry IV., a case arose in the courts of law, in which an appropriation was involved, and which is worth quoting, as showing the strong tendency of the courts to make all things relating to the church establishment matter of secular cognizance:—"The abbey of Saltash was appropriate to the college of Windsor, and upon the appropriation the vicar was endowed, &c., and was bound in a great sum before the collector of the pope (*del Pape*) in England (with the assent of the ordinary), to pay to the chamber of the pope, upon condition that he should do certain things, which he had failed in; wherefore the dean of the college came to the chancery, and showed that he had sued him in a plea before the collector of the pope, and that the vicar had, on the suggestion that the plea of covenant or of debt on contract made within the realm, pertained to the courts of the king, obtained a prohibition to the collector of the pope, directing him to disseise his plea. The collector prayed a writ to proceed: Thirning, J., at first said the 'writ' should go. Hankford said: The king is well informed by all the archbishops, and bishops, and others, who have spiritual jurisdiction. And when the collector of the pope came to England, he brought two bulls, of which the king has one, and he himself the other. But I do not think he can intervene, and sue in this matter. And afterwards by counsel of the archbishop of Canterbury, a consultation was refused" (10 *Hen. IV.*)

[1] *Vide ante*, c. xiii.

the child; and the chancellor was authorised, upon complaint duly made before him, to inquire into breaches of this statute, and to punish the heads of the society according to his discretion.[1]

Further provision was made for the regular payment of tithes. It was enacted by stat. 5 Hen. IV. c. x., that farmers and occupiers of the possessions of aliens should be bound to pay all tithes due to parsons and vicars, notwithstanding they were seized into the king's hands, or any prohibition to the contrary. Again, it was ordained by stat. 7 Hen. IV. c. vi., that no person should be discharged of tithes by colour of any bulls; and if any were molested by pretence of such bulls, the offenders were to be liable to the penalty inflicted on the *Cistertians* by stat. 2 Henry IV. c. iv. Because it had sometimes happened, that provisions from the pope had been licensed by the king, it was enacted,[2] that no license or pardon so granted should be available, if the benefice was full of an incumbent at the time it was granted. These *licenses* showed that the statutes against provisions were not executed with rigour. However, in the ninth year of this king, a statute[3] was made, confirming all the statutes against provisions and translations of bishops, and[4] declaring that the election to spiritual preferments should be free. The other laws relating to church matters were such as were made against heresies; but these, unhappily for the first promoters of reformation in our church, were of a sort which obliges us to rank them amongst those that make a part of our penal law.

Statutes of labourers.

Nothing remarkable was ordained respecting the lower class of people, except a regulation about apprentices made by stat. 7 Hen. IV. c. xvii. It was complained, that, notwithstanding the statute of Canterbury,[5] ordaining that no person who had worked in husbandry till twelve years of age should be permitted to be put to any mystery or handicraft, yet the children of many persons having no land or rent, were bound apprentice to crafts in cities and boroughs, "*for the pride of clothing, and other evil customs that servants do use in the same;*" which produced a scarcity of labourers and servants. To prevent this, it was enacted by the above act, that no one should put his son or daughter apprentice to any craft or labour within a city or borough, except he had land or rent to the value of twenty shillings per annum at least; but he should put them to other labour as his estate required, on pain of one year's imprisonment. Any person willing to make his child apprentice, was to bring to the mayor or bailiff of the place a bill sealed by two justices of the peace, testifying the value of the parent's lands. Any person taking an apprentice contrary to this act, was to forfeit a hundred shillings, to be recovered by complaint to the justices of the peace. All labourers and artificers were annually to be sworn at the leet, to observe the statutes relating to their wages and service; and if they refused, they were to be put in the stocks for three days. To facilitate this, it was provided,

[1] Stat. 4 Hen. IV., c. 17. [2] Ch. 8. [3] *Ibid.* [4] *Ibid.*, 9. [5] *Vide ante*, c. xiv.

that every town or seignory not having stocks should be fined a hundred shillings.

The laws passed in this reign respecting the rights of property were few; being only those which concerned the king's grants. It should seem that Henry, as well as Richard, had been too easy in making grants to his favourites: to prevent this in future, it was endeavoured to avoid the misrepresentations and deceits which used to be imposed on the king to obtain such grants. Thus it was provided, by stat. 1 Hen. IV. c. vi., that all those who demanded lands, tenements, rents, offices, annuities, or any other profits, should make express mention in their petitions of the value of the thing, and also of such things as they before had of the gift of the crown; and in failure of this, the grant was to be void. Again, it was ordained,[1] that where lands were granted to the king without title found by inquest, or the king being otherwise entitled to enter, those who were disseised by the king's patentees should have a *special assize*, without the chancellor speaking to the king; and if they recovered, should have treble damages. The statute requiring the value of the thing petitioned for, to be specially mentioned, was explained by stat. 2 Hen. IV. c. ii., which, among other matters, excepts all confirmations and licenses to be made by the king: these were not to be void, though the petition did not mention the value. Stat. 4 Hen. IV. c. iv., went still further than the first; for, after declaring that the king would make grants to none but those who deserved it, and as it should seem best to himself and his council, it ordained, that all those who made any demand contrary thereto should be punished by the advice of the king and council, and never have their demand. After this, a further explanation was made of stat. 1 Henry IV. by excepting the queen and the king's son.[2]

An attempt was made by the commons to effect an alteration in the judicature of parliament. The commons, who had been called to parliament in the reign of Edward I. merely to consent to taxes upon themselves and their constituents, when they had discharged that office, were not any further considered, nor looked upon as a necessary part of the *legislature*. The attention which had been occasionally shown to their petitions for redress of grievances, by making statutes in pursuance of them, was a matter of grace in the king and lords, and was usually conferred either to reward them for, or to purchase, a supply of money. In proportion as the king stood in need of this resource, those who held the purse of the nation grew into importance.

The parliament and council.

The annual sitting of parliament during the long reign of Edward III. had familiarised the commons so much to the condition of parliament men, that they began to consider themselves as part of the *legislature;* and their claim was so far favoured, that their assent is mentioned not only to the

[1] Ch. 11.

[2] Stat. 6 Hen. IV., c. 2.

taxing of their constituents, but sometimes to general laws for the government of the kingdom. Notwithstanding this, matters purely of a judicial nature were still considered as within the exclusive province of the king and lords.[1] It was a part of their original constitution to be the supreme court of the nation; and (it was thought) the admission of the commons to assent to general laws could make no precedent that would entitle them to interfere with the judicature of parliament.

But the consequence of allowing the commons to assent to laws in the time of Edward III. was, that during the reign of Richard II. this was settled by long usage into a matter of right; and in the reign of Heny IV. they advanced their pretensions so far as to claim a participation in that judicial capacity which the lords had deemed to be solely their own. In this attempt they might reason upon very just ground. The awards, they might say, made by the king and lords in matters of private property were agreed to be the highest judgments that could be given; they are upon subjects which are not within the cognizance of inferior courts; and the relief afforded is of a kind which dispenses with and overrules the general course of the law; but the law cannot be dispensed with, nor altered otherwise than by an act of the legislature; therefore the assent of the commons, as a part of the legislature, is necessary in all these judgments on private petitions. In this manner might the commons have argued; and probably such reasoning as this encouraged them in the following instance to advance their claim to this supposed right.

In the reign of Henry IV. there was a petition to the king in parliament on behalf of the restored archbishop, praying that he might have recovery for sundry wastes and spoils against Roger Walden, who had been appointed to the see during his exile. The king instantly granted it, and it became an award in the usual way. But the commons hearing of this, prayed the king, that since *they* were not made privy to the judgment, no record might be made to charge or make them parties therein, a language which was artfully enough contrived to conceal any consciousness that their interference might be thought new or ill-founded. But the king was more explicit in his answer: the archbishop, by his command, told them, *that the commons in parliament were only petitioners; and that all judgments belonged to the king and lords, unless in statutes and the like;* which ordinance the king willed should be from that time observed.[2] The commons acquiesced in this command of the king, and no further attempt was made in this and the two next reigns to participate in the judicature of the king and lords.

The jurisdiction of the parliament and council was still viewed with a jealous eye.[3] It was complained, that after judgment given in the king's courts, the parties were made to come, *upon*

[1] *Vide ante*, c. xiv. [2] *Parl. Hist.*, vol. ii., 50. [3] *Vide ante*, c. xiv.

grievous pain, sometimes before the king himself, sometimes before the king's council, and sometimes to the parliament, to answer there anew; which was considered as subversive of the common law, as well as a great grievance to the people (*a*). To prevent this in some degree, it was enacted, by stat. 4 Hen. IV. c. xxiii., that after judgment given in the king's courts, the parties and their heirs should continue in peace until the judgment was undone by attaint or error, according to the old laws.

Though the preamble of this statute is only aimed at *subpœnas* summoning persons before the king himself, the council, and the parliament, yet the enacting clause is so general, that it might be, and afterwards was, construed as applicable to the equity jurisdiction in chancery. It was an easy construction to say, that all equitable considerations arising on such judgments should be silenced; and that no court, upon any ground whatsoever, should presume to discuss their propriety, or suspend their effect.

The commons had two years before gone further than the provisions of this act respecting the two new courts of equity, for they prayed that no *subpœna* might issue out of the chancery or *exchequer*.[1] It was also prayed in the same parliament, that there might issue out of the *exchequer* no more writs of *datum est nobis intelligi*. But to this it was answered, that the old usage should continue.[2]

It seems, that while the chancellor was trying all means to establish his judicature, there began silently to obtain in the court of exchequer a practice to entertain suits in the like manner by *subpœna*, and suggestions by bill, which proceedings are here complained of as equally new and illegal with those in chancery. It was not at all unnatural, that an equitable jurisdiction should be exercised by the court of exchequer; for the cognizance of the king's debts being confined to that court, it would have been hard indeed that suitors there should be deprived of those equitable remedies which all common suitors might have in chancery; and as this court had a chancellor of its own, there seemed nothing

(*a*) The statute is in these terms, as it is in the original statutes in c. xxii.: "Item, come sibren en ple roial come personel, apres judgments rendez en les courts notre seignieur le roy les parties sont faitz vener sur greveuse peine a le faits devants le roy mesmes et a le faitz devant le conseil du roy, et a le faitz en parliament dent rendre de novel a grand amentissement des parties suis dets et en la subversion del commune ley del terre ordeines est et establies que apres judgments rendus en les courts le roy les parties et lour heires ent soient en pees tanque al judgment soit anientes per atteint ou per errour si errour y ad come il ad estes uses per la ley en temps des progenitours notre dit seignieur le roy." This statute is mentioned in no other law-book but *Doctor and Student*, and in Coke's *Institutes*. In the former work, it is said that its effect was, that judgments given in the king's court should not be examined in chancery or elsewhere (which certainly is not according to the terms of the statute, in which there is no mention of the chancery nor "elsewhere"), but he adds that it did not prohibit equity, but only undue interference with judgments at law, and he admits equity (*Doctor and Student*, lib. i. c. xvii., xviii.). In the *Institutes* it is cited against the jurisdiction of chancery, but it is conceived it was aimed at the council.

[1] Cott. Abri., p. 410, s. xcix.

[2] *Ibid.*, p. 413, s. xcix.

wanting to complete the form and circumstance of a court of equity. Thus, as common persons sued in chancery, it became the custom for the king's debtors to file their bill in the exchequer. So ill founded is the opinion, that the court of equity in the exchequer was not heard of till the time of Henry VIII., and that it was founded on stat. 33 Hen. VIII. c. xxxix.[1] At length, the connexion between a chancellor and a court of equity became so inseparable, that it will be hardly too general to pronounce, wherever that officer was, there was also that jurisdiction.

At another time, we find it was prayed by the commons, that the statutes about *suggestions* made in the reigns of Edward III. and Richard II. should be observed.[2] With all this solicitude to keep the jurisdiction of the council within bounds, there is more frequent mention of it, and more instances of its judicial powers, than in any former period.[3] Many applications were made to parliament concerning the bounds of jurisdiction in the constable and marshal, and the steward and marshal;[4] but no statute was enacted on either of those points.

The jurisdiction of the court of admiralty still continued to excite jealousies, and many applications were made to parliament on the subject. These produced a statute in the second year of the king, by which it was enacted that the statute of Richard II. should be observed; and, moreover, that whosoever felt himself grieved contrary thereto, should have his action by writ grounded upon the case against him who so sued in the admiral's court, and recover double damages. The party was also to forfeit ten pounds to the king.

Next, as to the course of proceeding, and other matters relating to the ordinary administration of justice. The grievous injury done by those who made forcible entries, and otherwise got violent possession of land, occasioned some statutes that rendered the proceeding by assize rather more expeditious: this was by granting of course a *special assize*, to inquire of the fact immediately, without waiting for the general commission, which issued only twice a year. The first instance in which the parliament resorted to this method, was where persons had obtained grants of the king, and by virtue of such patents had turned out the true owners. It was enacted by stat. 1 Hen. IV. c. viii., that where lands were granted by the king's patent, without title found by inquest or otherwise, and the king had no entry by law, the person so disseised should have a *special assize* of the chancellor's grant, *without any suit to the king;* and if he recovered, he was to have treble damages. The next instance in which special assizes were to be granted without suit to the king, was where[5] any one made forcible entry to the use of himself or of another, by way of maintenance, or took and

[1] 4 Inst., 118.
[2] Cott. Abri., p. 422, s. xxviii.
[3] Cott. Abri., Hen. IV., *passim.*
[4] Cott. Abri., p. 411, s. lxxix; p. 432, s. lxiv.
[5] Stat. 4 Hen. IV., c. 8.

carried away any goods from the possessor of the freehold after such forcible entry; in such cases the party attainted was to suffer a year's imprisonment, and yield double damages. In such special assizes was to be named a justice of one of the benches, or the chief baron, if he was a man of the law.

We have seen,[1] that by the statute of Richard II. a disseisee was enabled to bring his assize against the disseisor if he took the profits, and the assize was brought within a year; this limitation was now thought too short, and therefore, by stat. 4 Hen. IV. c. vii. the disseisee is allowed to bring his assize against the first disseisor at any time during the disseisor's life, if he took the profits. As to other real writs, the demandant was to commence his suit within a year against the person who was tenant of the freehold at the time the action accrued to him, if such tenant *took the profits* at the time the suit was commenced. This provision was followed by several others of the same nature in subsequent reigns, and they were usually called *statutes of pernors of profits.*

Because in assizes of novel disseisin, and other real writs, it had been common, where lands lay in ancient demesne and within franchises, to charge the bailiff, lord, mayor, or other chief officer, as a wrong-doer, in order to deprive him of the benefit of his franchise in that instance, it was enacted by stat. 9 Hen. IV. c. v. that in such cases the justices of assize should (if the persons required it) first inquire by the assize in the country whether they were really disseisors or tenants; and if it was found that they were named by collusion and fraud, the writ was to be abated, and the plaintiffs to be in grievous mercy. The other statute relating to real writs is stat. 4 Henry IV. c. xxii., concerning the remedy incumbents were to have if ejected by the king's presentee; these persons were hereby permitted to sue at any time without being confined to the term of a year, as they had been by some late acts.[2]

Some few regulations were made respecting personal actions, and actions in general. It was enacted by stat. 2 Hen. IV., c. vii., where a matter was adjourned on account of some difficulty, after a verdict, that if the verdict had passed against the plaintiff, he should not be nonsuited; meaning that he should be barred by the verdict. This expedient of plaintiffs resorting to a nonsuit was used on other occasions. The commons prayed, that when the defendant had waged his law, the plaintiff might not be nonsuited; but no statute was made to prevent it.[3] It had lately become the practice, that a defendant should not be admitted to wage his law against an account settled before auditors, though this was contrary to the usage in the time of Edward III.[4] It was complained, that this new point of law had been much abused;

[1] *Vide ante,* c. xvii.

[2] *Ibid.*, c. xiv.

[3] Cott. Abri., p. 466, s. xxxiii.

[4] *Vide ante,* c. xiii.

for plaintiffs would, in an action of debt upon arrears of account, surmise that the defendant had accounted before auditors; which auditors might, perhaps, be only apprentices or servants to the plaintiff; and in truth no account had been taken, nor was anything really due; but the plaintiff would get a favourable inquest, and so obtain a recovery. To prevent this, it was enacted, that the justices in the king's courts, and other judges before whom such actions in cities and towns were brought, should have power to examine the attorneys and others (*a*), and thereupon receive the defendant to his law, or try the point by inquest, according to their discretion.

Some statutes were made for the government of process. It was enacted by stat. 5 Hen. IV., c. xii., that when a statute-merchant was certified into chancery, and a writ awarded, and returned into the common-pleas, and the statute there *once* shown, the justices might recontinue the process till full execution was had, without a second view of the statute. Because many people were outlawed by erroneous process, and by reason of sickness could not appear in person, as the law required, to reverse such outlawries, it was enacted by stat. 7 Hen. IV., c. xiii., that the justices and chief-baron should examine such persons, and thereupon admit their attorneys: however, the writ of *capias ad satisfaciendum* was to continue as at common law. That the execution of process might not be defeated by those who had the custody of persons imprisoned, it was enacted by stat. 7 Hen. IV., c. iv., that, in an action against a gaoler for an escape, no protection should avail.

(*a*) Here the practice of examination, which had arisen in wager of law, and had been applied by the courts to the subject of venue (*vide ante*), was expressly applied by the statute to the ascertainment of real and proper cases of account. The precedent thus set, and the principle thus established, are of great practical importance. In debt upon arrears of an account, the defendant prayed that the attorney of the plaintiff might be examined if the matter lay in account or not, *et sic fuit*, non obstante, that no issue was tendered. And upon the examination of the arrears, it appeared that it was for stuff bought by the defendant of the plaintiff, upon which he tendered his law, and it was admitted (*Year-book*, 14 *Hen. IV.*, fol. 19). In another case it was found, upon the examination, that the plaintiff had let a manor to the defendant for a term and certain stuff, and they accounted at the end of the term, and found that much stuff was wasted, and for the real debt on the lease would lie, and for the goods wasted, an action of detinue, upon which the defendant waged his law (*Year-book*, 20 *Hen. VI.*, fol. 16). In other cases, the plaintiff or his attorney asserted on oath that the matter was as stated in the declaration (19 *Hen. VI.*, fol. 43, 35). If an executor sued, he might be examined as to the matter, not precisely, but as to any matter within his knowledge which might show whether the case was one fit for an account (21 *Hen. VI.*, fol. 55). It is obvious that the principle of this practice would equally apply to ascertain the truth on the issue of the writ. In debt for arrears of an account, the defendant could "tender his law" (*i.e.*, offer to "wage" it, by the oaths of himself and twelve "compurgators") *quod nihil debet*, and could pray that the plaintiff should be examined if the matter lay in account or not, and if it appeared by the examination that it did not lie in account, he should have his law, and otherwise not so; and the party or his attorney should be sworn to speak the truth, and such examination was upon oath (35 *Hen. VI.*, 5; 33 *Hen. VI.*, 24). The procedure by "wager of law" was not, it will be observed, admissible if the matter was one of account, in which case it was to be referred to auditors.

For the safe keeping of records, and also to preserve them entire and unaltered, it was ordained by stat. 11 Hen. IV., c. iii. (as had been before provided),[1] that the justices of assize should cause to be delivered into the king's treasury all records of assizes of novel disseisin, of mortauncestor, and of certifications (with all appurtenances and appendages), before them determined. And further it was provided, that the records and process of pleas, real and personal, and of assizes of novel disseisin and mortauncestor, certifications and others, whereof judgment was given and enrolled, or things touching such pleas, should in no wise be amended or impaired by new entering of the clerks, or by the record or thing certified, in witness, or commandment of any justice, in any term after judgment given and enrolled.

The extortion of sheriffs, and the ferms of their bailiwicks, occasioned some few regulations of the same sort with those that have been frequently before mentioned.[2] At length it was enacted by stat. 4 Hen. IV., c. v., that sheriffs should abide in their bailiwick during their office, and should not let it to ferm to any one: and these two points were to be inserted in the sheriff's oath.

Attorneys.

The parliament began to make some provision for ordering *attorneys*, who had now become a very considerable body of men.[3] Complaint had been made of the mischiefs arising from their ignorance and want of knowledge in the law; and therefore, to make sure of their qualifications, it was ordained by stat. 4 Hen. IV., c. xviii., that all attorneys should be examined by the justices, and by their discretions their names should be put in a roll: they were to be *good and virtuous* and *of good fame;* and if they appeared to be such, they were to be received and sworn well and truly to serve in their offices, and especially that they make no suit in a foreign county: all other attorneys were to be put out, and such as were passed in the above manner were to be put in their places by their *masters*, that is, by their clients. It was enacted, that when qualified attorneys died, or ceased to act, the justices might appoint others in their room, being virtuous and learned, and sworn as above mentioned. It was enacted, that if any attorney was found notoriously in default, of record, or otherwise, he should forswear the court, and never be received to make suit in any of the king's courts: this ordinance was also to be observed in the exchequer, at the discretion of the treasurer and barons. It was again ordained, by chap. xix. of the same act, that no steward, bailiff, nor minister of lords of franchises, having return of writs, should be attorney in a plea within the franchise.

It seems as if some act was made on this subject in the 11th year of this king, though it does not now appear; for in the 13th year the clerks and attorneys of both the benches prayed a revocation of it. The answer of the parliament to that petition was,

[1] *Vide ante*, c. xiv.

[2] *Ibid.;* and *vide* stat. 1 Henry IV., c. 11.

[3] *Vide ante*, c. xiii.

that the justices of both the benches should consult about it, and also concerning other mischiefs in the said courts.[1] In this reign some acts were made for settling the fees of courts; as those of the marshal, of the chirographer, the clerk of the crown, and the like.[2] Some regulations were also made to prevent the embezzling of writs on which fines were levied, and substituting other fees, and notes of fines, in the place of the true ones.[3]

We now come to the consideration of such statutes as relate to the criminal law. The vindication of Henry and his adherents required that the articles of treason enacted in the 21st year of the last reign, should not be suffered to continue in force (*a*). In the 1st year of Henry IV., it was enacted, that whereas in the 21st year of Richard II. divers pains of treason were enacted by statute, *insomuch that no one knew how he ought to behave himself, to do, speak, or say, for doubt of such pains;* therefore, in no time to come any treason should be adjudged otherwise than as was ordained by statute in the preceding reign; meaning the statute of treasons 25 Edw. III. This measure of repealing new enacted treasons, by declaring all void but those contained in the statute of Edward III., was resorted to in later times,

Repeal of treasons.

(*a*) The author omits to notice the remarkable act against appeals in parliament passed in this same year, no doubt with reference to the various sanguinary proceedings which had taken place in the last reign. The petition of the commons, the answer, and the statute thereupon passed, afford admirable illustrations of the language of the legal history of the age. The petition is: "Supplyont les communs que desore en avant nul appele de traison ne de autre felony quelcunque, soit accept ou recieve en le parlement ains en vous autres courts dedans vostre realme dementiers que en vous dits courts purra estre terminer come ad ote fuit et use anciennement. Et qne chescun person qui en temps, a venu serra accuse ou empeach en vostre parlement ou en ascuns des vos dits courts per les seigneors et communs de vostre realme ou per ascun personel defence ou response a son accusement ou empeachment, et sur son response reasonable record jugment et tryal come de anciennemcnt temps ad estre fait et use per les bones leges de vostre realme nient obstant que les dits empeachments ou accusements soient faits per les seigneors ou communs de vostre realme come que de novel en temps de Rich., nadgarius Roy ad estre fait et use a coutier, a tres grand mischief et tres grand maleveys exemple de vostre realme." The king would readily assent to this, for he, when earl of Derby, had interceded in vain with Gloucester for the life of the gallant Burley, one of the finest knights of the age, who was murdered by that minister, and the royal answer was in these terms: "Le Roy voet que de cy en avant toutes les appeles de choses faits dans le realme soient tryez et terminer per les bones leys faits en temps de tres noble progenitors *de nostre dit seigneor le Roy*. Et que toutes les appelles de choses faits hors du realme soient triez et terminez devant le constable, &c. Then the statute was in these terms: "Pur plusieurs grands inconvenences et mischiefs que plusieurs fait ont advenus per colour des plusieurs appeles faits dans le realme avant ces heurs ordain est et establiez, que desore en avant touts appeles de choses faits dans le realme soient trier et determiner per les bones leys de le realme faits et vires en temps de tres nobles progenitors de dit nostre seigneor le Roy." This was evidently enacted with a view to overrule the monstrous contention of Gloucester's party, that upon impeachments they were not bound by any law, civil or common, but only by what they chose to call the custom of parliament, by which they deprived their victims of all power of fair defence. The above statute established that, even upon parliamentary impeachments, the general principles of law must be observed, though not of course ordinary forms.

[1] Cott. Abri., p. 483, s. xlix.

[2] Stat. 2 Hen. IV., c. 8, 10, 23.

[3] Stat. 5 Hen. IV., c. 14.

when the law had been occasionally overstrained to answer particular purposes.

The same motives of favour to his partisans which induced Henry to concur in the above act, led him to consent to some laws of an opposite nature; for in the next year after this humane statute was passed (*a*), the king, at the instigation of the clergy, by whom he had been materially served at the time of his claiming the crown, consented that some rigorous measure should be devised against the *heretics* or *Lollards*, as they were then called. The punishment of *heretics* by burning is mentioned in Bracton: and this was in England, as in all other Christian countries, the pain which religious zealots had agreed in inflicting upon all those who oppugned the established superstitions. Notwithstanding this, it has been a doubt whether the writ *de hæretico comburendo* was a common-law process, or was given by this statute: though it should seem, from the scope and wording of this act, that nothing more was meant than that the bishop should be enabled to direct execution without the intervention of this writ; for it enacts, that *credence should de given to the diocesan* by the sheriff, who was to receive the offender, and cause him to be burnt. So far, therefore, from appointing or even confirming this writ, the present act seems in some degree to supersede it.

At present there was no temporal law in force against heresy; for the statute of Richard II., which was the first made on the subject, and had been obtained surreptitiously, was repealed the next year, as has been before shown[1] (*b*). The stat. 2 Heretics.

(*a*) Thus, it will be observed, that this is a mere suggestion of the author's, without any authority, and it is opposed to all contemporary testimony and the opinion of the most important historians, who refer these statutes rather to the general spirit of the age. Added to this, indeed, the purview of these and similar acts was not mere heresy, as our author supposes, for, rightly or wrongly, the "Lollards" were regarded as *levellers*, and the history of the time, and the recitals of the statutes, show that the legislature were apprehensive of political revolution from the communistic and destructive tendencies of the new sect. The practice of punishing for heresy as a crime against the state had been, as Sir J. Mackintosh observes, introduced by the Roman emperors, and he and Dr Lingard concur in representing it as taught by Roman law, which, as they two say, was the common law of Europe. And under monarchs most hostile to the church (as Henry II.) this policy had been pursued. But the very fact that, though the new doctrines in religion had been introduced in the reign of Edward III., there had been no attempt until now to put this policy in execution, shows that there was some particular cause in operation at the time, and that cause is to be found in the records of contemporary history, which show that the sectaries had proceeded to press their views to conclusions fatal to property.

(*b*) Upon this statute a case arose in the reign of Henry VII., which is reported in the Year-books of that reign. In an action of false imprisonment, the defendants pleaded that in the act of 4 Henry IV. it was enacted that if any one should be accused of heresy, or should hold any opinion contrary to the laws of holy church, the bishop of the diocese should arrest him and safely keep him until he could make his purgation or abjuration within three months next after the arrest. And it was alleged that the law of holy church is that each parishioner ought to pay his tithes to his curate, and that the plaintiff was residing in the parish of St Dunstan, and that notice came to the bishop of London, the diocesan, that he had said that he was not

[1] *Vide ante*, vol. ii. 163.

Hen. IV., c. xv., was now made, containing, like other acts upon clerical matters, a minuteness and length not usual in the other statutes of this period. The meetings of heretics in their conventicles and schools are stigmatised in this act with the name of confederacies to stir up sedition and insurrection; the very pretence that had been made use of by the Romans against the primitive Christians, and which had been adopted by the Romish church ever since, to suppress all opposition or inquiry into its errors (*a*). To prevent persons of this description from escaping out of the bishop's diocese, it was now ordained, that none should presume to preach openly or privily without the licence of the diocesan of the place first had and obtained, except curates in their churches. None were to hold, teach or instruct, openly or privily, or write any book contrary to the Catholic faith or determination of holy church, nor make conventicles, or hold schools; nor were any to maintain those who did. All persons having such books or writings, were to deliver them to the diocesan within forty days from the proclamation of this statute; and those who did not so deliver them, or who otherwise offended against this act, and all those defamed and evidently suspected thereof, were to be arrested by the direction of the ordinary, and committed to prison till they canonically purged themselves, or abjured their opinions. The ordinary was to proceed according to the canonical decrees, and determine the matter within three months from the arrest. If the party was canonically convict, he was to be confined in prison at the discre-

bound to pay his tithes to his curate, upon which he was accused, by reason of which the bishop ordered the defendants to arrest him, which they did, and committed him to the care of the bishop, but he escaped within the three months. The plea was objected to on several grounds, the most serious of which seemed to be that it was so vague, and that no authority appeared for the accusation in presentment, nor process, nor summons to the party, nor opportunity of defence, nor any authority for the arrest beyond mere word of mouth, and no writ or writing. It was urged that the intention of the statute was, that if a man was detected in or accused of any heresy, or of anything contrary to the faith, the bishop could arrest him; and, before the statute, they had no other power than to make process against the party by citation, and that the intention of the statute was, not that the bishop should arrest any one who held any opinion contrary to their constitution, and in this case it might be that what the man said was right, for the pope might have granted him a dispensation from payment of tithes. It was argued on the other hand that the statute was, not only as to heresy, but as to holding any opinion contrary to the laws or constitutions of the church, and that as there was a constitution of the Council of Lateran that tithes should be paid by every one to his curate; the opinion of the plaintiff that he was not bound to do so was against that constitution, and so came within the statute (*Year-book*, 10 *Hen. VII.*, fol. 18). It does not appear how the case ended, but the bare fact that a man could be summarily arrested and imprisoned on mere *ex parte* accusation, and on a mere verbal authority from one who never saw or examined him, and that it should be contended in a court of law, and apparently with some colour of ground that it was lawful, speaks volumes as to the vexatious and oppressive character of this ecclesiastical jurisdiction, and it will be found that, under the Tudor dynasty, in little more than a century, the pressure of it had helped greatly to estrange the nation from the ancient faith and the ancient church.

(*a*) But the difference was that, in the former instance, the plea was a false one; in the present instance, according to contemporary testimony, it was true. Knighton, who had actually attended the meetings of these sectaries, states that they held

tion of the ordinary, and moreover *to be put* to the secular court, (except in cases where, according to the canonical decrees, he was entitled to exemption,) to pay a fine to the king; which fine was to be assessed by the diocesan, and certified to the exchequer, to be levied by process from thence.

Thus far of those canonically convicted; but farther if persons sententially convict refused to abjure their opinions, or after abjuration relapsed, a more rigorous course was directed. Such persons were by the canons to be left to the secular arm; and it was now enacted, that in such cases *credence should be given to the diocesan,* or his commissary, and the sheriff, and mayor or bailiff of the place, should be present when the sentence was given, if required by the diocesan or commissary; and, after sentence promulgated, should receive, *and them before the people in a high place caused to be burnt,* to the example and terror of others. It is observed respecting this first statute against the preachers of new opinions, that the print differs materially from the record, so as to give a sharper edge to this proceeding.[1]

We find it recorded in this same parliament, that a writ was sent to the sheriffs of London for the burning of William Sawtree, clerk, convicted by the clergy.[2] This was according to the ancient course, by issuing the writ *de hæretico comburendo;* for the new method directed by this act put the whole authority into the bishop's hands; and as he might direct his sentence to be executed without the writ, the persecution against the followers of Wickliffe was likely to be more warm than before. In the 8th year of the

language of the most extreme character. They described an established church as unlawful, and told the people not to pay their tithes. The only reliable evidence is contemporary testimony, and the best is the recital of the statute itself, passed at the request of the commons, not less than the clergy. The petition was presented in these terms: "Prælati et clerus ac etiam *communitates* in eodem parlemento existentes domino regi supplicarent," and it was granted "a les prier de communes" (*Stat. of Realm* 2, 126; Wilk. *Conc.* 3, 328). It recited that divers unauthorised teachers went about misinforming the people, and daily committing enormities, &c. And the lords and commons five years afterwards presented a petition to the king, stating that the sectaries excited the people to take away the possessions of the church, of which the clergy were as assuredly endowed as the temporal lords were of their inheritance, and that unless these evil purposes were resisted, they would perhaps move the people to take away the possessions of the latter, and have all things in common, to the open commotion of the people and the subversion of the realm (*Rot. Parl.* iii., fol. 583). The purview of these statutes, therefore, was not merely polemical but political. Rightly or wrongly, the parliament were apprehensive, not of heresy only, but of spoliation, revolution, and communism. And events soon showed that these apprehensions were well grounded; for, in the next reign, these sectaries actually rose in open revolt; and the commons, in their address to the king, stated that the insurgents sought to destroy the faith, the king, the spiritual and temporal estates, and all manner of policy and law; to which the king replied, that they meant to destroy him and the lords, to confiscate the possessions of the church, to secularise the religious orders, to divide the realm into confederate districts, and to appoint a president of the commonwealth, all which is borne out by the contemporary records and chronicles (*Wols.* 385; *Rot. Parl.* iv. 24; *Rym.* ix. 89, 193). It is manifest that, at all events, it was the belief of the age, and that these statutes were not the acts merely of the clergy, but of the nobility and commonalty of the realm.

[1] Cott. Abri., p. 409, s xlviii.

[2] *Ibid.*, p. 407, s. xxix.

king the prelates procured a long and sanguinary bill to be exhibited in parliament against the spreaders of new opinions, under the name of Lollards. This bill was to empower every officer or minister whatsoever to apprehend and inquire of such Lollards, and that no sanctuary should be allowed them. But the churchmen were not gratified in this instance.[1] In the 11th year it was prayed by the commons, that persons arrested under stat. 2 Hen. IV. might be bailed and freely make their purgation, and that they might be arrested by none but sheriffs, or the like officers, nor any havoc be made of their goods; but this intended relaxation of the new course against heretics was not passed into a law.[2]

Multiplication.

The notion of producing gold out of other metals, by a chemical process, and the infatuation with which these vain hopes were pursued, occasioned a law to be made in this reign against these experiments. This process was sometimes called *multiplication*, and to *multiply*, because it was with a view to increase the quantity of metals, though in reality it seldom had any other effect than diminishing that which the credulous adventurer possessed before the operation began. The pretence of possessing this secret of changing metals had been practised by cheats, to draw supplies out of the pockets of the weak and ignorant; and had been ridiculed, before this time, in one of Chaucer's Tales.[3] Besides the mischiefs here mentioned, which, perhaps, might be better left to experience to correct, without making them the object of legislative notice, it is most probable that this imposture was many times held forth as a cover to the real operation of coining base money, in which light it became a matter of serious and national concern. It was for this reason, and perhaps under some small apprehension lest the process of changing metals might by possibility succeed, that it was enacted by stat. 5 Hen. IV. c. iv., that any one who multiplied gold or silver, or used the craft of multiplication, and was attainted thereof, should incur the pain of felony.

Because many persons had lately been beat and maimed, and afterwards had their tongues cut out or their eyes put out, it was by the same statute[4] made felony for any one *so* to cut tongues or put out the eyes of any one, if it was proved to be done with malice prepense. This shows that mayhem was not now considered as a felony of life and limb; for though cutting out tongues did not come under that construction, yet putting out eyes was a mayhem at common law.[5] These were all the felonies enacted in this reign. The misdemeanours, besides what may have been mentioned in different parts of this reign, were few. The statute 12 Rich. II. c. vi.,[6] against unlawful games, was confirmed by stat. 11

[1] Cott. Abrid., p. 456, s. lxii. [2] *Ibid.*, 472, s. xxix.

[3] A person who had been tricked of his money in this way, after a minute account of the process and the deception, is there made to say, "*Lo, which advantage is to* MULTIPLIE!" *Cant. Tales*, vol. iii., p. 95. Edit. Tyrwh.

[4] Ch. 5. [5] *Vide ante*, vol. i., c. viii. [6] *Ibid.*

Hen. IV. c. iv., and it was moreover ordained, that labourers and servants offending against it should be imprisoned for six days. All mayors, bailiffs, and constables of towns were to put this statute in force.

Several laws were made to regulate criminal proceedings. The *appeals* in the reign of Richard II. brought against lords and others, were of a singular nature, and probably occasioned the stat. 1 Hen. IV. c. xiv., which states that many and great inconveniences had arisen heretofore from appeals. To prevent the like in future it provides that all appeals of things done within the realm should be tried and determined by the good laws of the realm; and of things done out of the realm, before the constable and marshal of England. No more appeals were to be in parliament.

Pardons to provors.

The too easy granting of pardons to provors was restrained by stat. 5 Hen. IV. c. ii. This act states, that divers common and notorious felons would, upon their arraignment, in order to save their lives, become provors; so that in the meantime by brockage, grants, and gifts to be made to several persons, they might obtain their charters, and after their deliverance become more notorious felons than they were before. To prevent this the act provides, that if any person sued for a pardon in such case, his name should be inserted in the charter, with mention that it was granted at his instance; and if the provor became afterwards a felon, the person suing the pardon was to forfeit £100.[1]

Insidiatores viarium, &c.

Some circumstances relating to the personal benefit of clergy were settled and explained. It was stated by stat. 4 Hen. IV. c. ii., that the king was willing to be gracious to the clergy in their affairs, in return for the part they had taken in his favour when he came to the crown; and therefore he confirmed in the fullest manner the statute *de clero*, 25 Edw. III., and further, considering that the words *insidiatores viarum, et depopulatores agrorum* (which had been mentioned in a petition of the clergy to parliament) were not commonly used in indictments in the time of Edward III. and his progenitors; and being willing, for the quiet of the people, to avoid such novelties, he caused it to be enacted that such words should not be used in indictments, arraignments, appeals, or any other impeachments; and though indictments to that effect might be taken, neither those words nor words to that effect should prevent any one from having the privilege of holy church, but they should be delivered to their ordinaries without any impeachment.[2] As the Lollards were stigmatised with the suspicion of being disorderly vagabonds, who wandered about the country doing great mischief, the above general charge was contrived to be inserted in indictments against *them;* and it had been the opinion of the judges that persons so convicted should be deprived of their clergy. In the next chapter of the same statute

[1] *Vide ante*, c. xiii.

[2] Ch. 2.

it is recorded that the archbishop of Canterbury, for himself and the other bishops, had promised the king that whenever a clerk, religious or secular, convicted of treason not touching the king, nor his royal majesty, nor a common thief, and so notoriously holden, should be delivered to the ordinary as such, that the ordinary should keep him safely and surely, and according to a constitution provincial *to be* made by the archbishop and bishops, in pursuance of letters of the late archbishop, dated 12th March 1351,[1] in which constitution were to be ordained certain pains for the observance of it; and it was enacted that no such convict should make his purgation contrary to the form of that constitution. The constitution here mentioned was to be shown to the king in this parliament, but there is no evidence that it was even made.

All the acts that have hitherto been mentioned requiring jurors to be of a particular description and qualification, related only to those jurors who tried issues; but some presentments having lately been made at Westminster by outlaws, and sanctuary-persons, not properly returned by the sheriff, it was provided by stat. 11 Hen. IV. c. ix., that no indictment should be made but by inquests of the king's lawful liege people, returned by the sheriffs or bailiffs of franchises, without any nomination to the sheriffs or bailiffs of franchises of the persons that should be returned, except by the officers sworn and known; and all indictments contrary to this act are declared void. Notwithstanding the many alterations made in the qualifications of jurors in subsequent times, and the solicitude shown to choose them from among those that were thought, from their rank and character, to be temptations to corruption, nothing further was provided respecting those jurors who found indictments.

Because the people of the county of Chester committed felonies in the neighbouring counties, and then escaped into that principality, it was ordained that process of exigent should be issued against such persons in the county where the fact was done: if they escaped into the county of Chester, the outlawry or exigent was to be certified to the officers and ministers of that county, who should take the party and seize his lands and goods as forfeit to the prince or lord of the principality, the king still having his year-day and waste; but the lands out of the principality were to go as those of persons living in other counties. The same method was to be observed in case of trespasses committed out of the county of Chester.

Riots.

The last statute in this reign[2] made some alteration in the summary method which had lately been devised[3] to suppress and punish rioters. It was thereby ordained, whenever any riot, assembly, or rout of people was made against the law, that the justices of the peace, three, or two of them at the least, and the sheriff and under-sheriff, should come with the power

[1] *Vide ante*, c. xvi. [2] Stat. 13 Hen. IV., c. 7. [3] *Vide ante*, c. xvii.

of the county (if need were) to arrest them, and should have authority to record what they found done in their presence against the law; by which record the parties were to stand convicted, in the same manner as had been before provided by the statute of forcible entries.[1] If the offenders were gone before the justices and the sheriff came, then they were to inquire within a month after the fact, and hear and determine it according to law. If the truth of the matter could not be found in the above way, they were to certify the king and his council of the matter; which certificate was to have the force of a presentment by twelve men; the offenders were to be put to answer thereon, and, if found guilty, were to be punished at the discretion of the king and council. If the parties traversed the matter so certified, the certificate and traverse were to be sent in to the king's bench, and there tried and determined. If the offenders did not appear before the council, or in the king's bench, at the first precept, then a second was to issue; and if they were not found, then the sheriff or under-sheriff, was to make proclamation in the full county next ensuing the delivery of the second precept, that they should appear in the council or king's bench; or, if in time of vacation, in the chancery, within three weeks then next following; and if they did not appear they were to stand convicted. The justices dwelling nearest the place, with the sheriffs and justices of assize, were to execute this statute, under the penalty of £100 for every default.

The above act tended to increase the authority of justices of the peace, who were daily growing in consequence, many matters relating to the police being submitted to their cognizance by different acts of parliament. This authority was sometimes abused. We find that constables of castles would get themselves to be assigned justices of the peace, and under colour of that commission would imprison in their castle those whom they wished to oppress, till they made fine for their deliverance. It was for this reason ordained by stat. 5 Hen. IV. c. x., that none should be imprisoned by justices of the peace but only in the common gaol, with a saving to such lords as had franchises. Thus far of the alterations made by statute in this reign.

Out of the decisions of courts during this reign, we shall select for consideration the single head of actions upon the case, and some few alterations in our criminal law. To return to any of the topics that have been so recently and so fully canvassed, seems entirely unnecessary at present. When we have made some further advance in our history, they will be of course reconsidered, and many of them placed in a new point of view.

Actions upon the case.

During the reign of this king, actions upon the case had grown very common. We find this action brought—for disturbing a way—against an ostler for horses lost—for negligently keeping fire and burning the plaintiff's house—for not infeoffing after promise—for

[1] *Vide ante*, c. xvii.

not doing suit—for selling bad wine—for not repairing banks—for enticing away a servant—for keeping a school near an ancient one.[1]

These writs of trespass were not only applied to a variety of new cases, but they were likewise more nicely considered, and their peculiarities better understood. In the reign of Henry IV., we find the term of *trespass sur le case* in familiar use: before, they were more usually called actions of trespass simply; but the marks of discrimination between *trespass* and *trespass upon the case,* began now to be distinctly ascertained. It was held that the former must always be *vi et armis,* the latter never. The nature, however, of injuries is often so complex, and their consequences so various, that the truth of a matter sounding in case could not be properly set forth without sometimes alleging circumstances which carried evident *force* in them: therefore, in 12 Henry IV., where an action on the case was brought for stopping a sewer, so as several acres of ground were flooded, it was held good that the stopping the sewer was laid *vi et armis,* that being a malfeasance, and the remote cause of the injury sustained by the plaintiff, though the consequential damage, which was the immediate cause, and the gist of the action, was in case,[2] a distinction which was many years after adopted as a just one. It was then laid down that the *causa causans* (as they called it) might be forcible, as in this instance of stopping the sewer, and be laid *vi et armis* even in an action upon the case, though that action is properly grounded upon the *consequence* of such stoppage: this consequence they distinguished by the appellation of *causa causata.*

This was the manner in which they refined on this new action. It was in its conception so near of kin to the action of trespass, that it required no small degree of sagacity to perceive the instances in which the old form failed, and it was necessary to make a special writ. The cases in the reign of Edward III., and those in this period, which we have hitherto considered, are founded upon *malfeasances,* or such instances of *neglect* as were in the nature of a malfeasance, both which were so much *in the like case* (according to the requisition of the statute of Westminster) with the old writ of trespass, that the admitting of them to be objects of this special writ of trespass was obvious and easy.

Of *assumpsit.*

But the action upon the case was found so convenient a remedy, that it was wished to extend it still further. They wanted to apply it to cases of *non-performance of promises;* but these did not so kindly fall within the analogy of former instances. It was thought somewhat harsh to give the name of trespass to a thing which was never *done;* it took, therefore, some time, and needed the concurrent force of some strong motives to induce the courts to admit these new writs. The present state of the remedies in use, where contracts were not performed, operated, very probably, towards gaining a support for

[1] The Year-book of Hen. IV., *passim.*

[2] 12 Hen. IV., 3.

these new actions upon the case. If a man performed not his covenant, an action of covenant lay; but it had been long held that an action of covenant must be grounded on a specialty; so that where the parties had not so bound themselves, that remedy failed. If a man did not pay money which he owed, the remedy was by action of debt; in which the defendant might discharge himself by wager of law, unless the demand was founded upon a specialty: the same in detinue, which indeed was only another form of the action of debt. To obviate these and the like defects, and to legitimate an action of a more effectual nature in matters of contract, was worth the attempt. Several actions of this kind were brought into court before they were allowed and authenticated by a judicial decision in their favour.

The first case of this kind upon record was in 2 Henry IV. It was an action against a carpenter; *Quare cùm, &c., assumpsisset, &c.*, to build a house within a certain time, he had not done it. It was objected that this was in covenant; and as no writing was shewn, the action must fail. This was supported also by Brian, who at the same time conceded that perhaps if the writ had said that *the work had been begun,* and had afterwards *through negligence* been stopped, it might be otherwise; thereby adhering to former determinations respecting *malfeasances* and cases of *negligence.* He pronounced, however, this remedy inadequate where the contract was *executory,* and where the only complaint against the defendant would be for his *non-feasance* or *non-performance.* The cause was dismissed on the above objection.[1] In the 11th of the same king there was exactly the same case before the court: the same objections were raised, the same concession was made, but in plainer terms; and the cause was dismissed on the same grounds as the former.[2] Thus the court seemed to have determined against the very conception of this kind of action. It is remarked upon this case by an author of later times,[3] that in these cases there was no consideration alleged; that it was *nudum pactum,* and therefore the action could not lie, which, it cannot be denied, may be an additional objection, but it was not taken at the time, and the cause appears by the report to have been dismissed both times upon the same defects, namely, the want of a written covenant; and the prevailing opinion which confined these actions to instances of malfeasance and negligence, where the defendant had really *done* something.

It must be observed of these determinations, that they left all persons who had made agreements without deed (for, if a mere writing, it could not be declared on in covenant), and where nothing had been done to execute the contract, entirely without redress. It is not improbable that the repeated decision of this point might have driven parties so circumstanced into chancery, where they could have these agreements decreed to be specifically performed.

[1] 2 Hen. IV., 3 b. [2] 11 Hen. IV., 33. [3] Bro. Act. sur Case, 40.

This, perhaps, as well as other considerations, might incline the courts to review this grand point, and try if they could accommodate the notions of law, as then understood, to the exigency of the occasion; and thereby not only draw back into its proper channel the current of decision from the chancery to the courts of common law; but, by rendering this action more general, put the nation in possession of what was then much wanted, a more effectual common-law redress in matters of contract. This was not accomplished till some years after.

The criminal law, as practised in this reign, was in general governed by the same principles and rules as in the reign of Edward III.

The criminal law.

Some few points are now to be met with in the books which did not before occur, and others that somewhat deviate from the more ancient practice: of the former sort is the account given in the first year of Henry IV. of the trial of a peer. In all cases of life and limb, the lords possessed a judicature, by which every peer had, according to *Magna Charta*, a right to be tried. In this capacity the lords acted as judges, and sat as in a court, being bound to hear and determine according to the rules of the common law. This judicial character, it should seem, was supported with more scruple, and with a closer attention to legal formalities, than their parliamentary one, where they often decided on the lives of men without any evidence of guilt, or even the pretence of a trial.[1] The proceedings on the trial of a peer are thus related in a case that happened in the beginning of the reign of Henry IV. An indictment of treason had been found against a peer, under a commission directed to the lord mayor and others for that purpose: after this the king granted a commission to an earl, reciting the above facts, and that the place of steward of England was vacant, and thereby appointing him to that office, to do right to the lord indicted, commanding all lords to attend, and the constable of the tower to bring his prisoner before him. The trial was held in Westminster Hall, where the steward sat under a cloth of state, the lords sitting down the hall on each side, and the judges round a table in the middle. The justices then delivered in the indictment, which on that occasion was confessed by the defendant, and judgment accordingly given: but, says the book, if it had been denied, the steward was to begin with the lowest lord, and ask all their opinions *upon their conscience*, without administering an oath.[2]

Some points on the law of principal and accessary are also to be found in the books of this period. We have seen the prevailing doctrine in the reign of Edward III. was, that an acquittal or pardon of the principal should operate in favour of the accessary.[3] Thus it was now held by Thirning, justice, that where a man was indicted, and cleared, either by pardon, clergy, or abjuration, the

[1] *Vide ante*, c. xvi. [2] 1 Hen. IV., 1. [3] *Vide ante*, c. xiv.

accessary should not be arraigned; for it was a settled rule, that wherever the principal was saved by law, the accessary should go quit;[1] and so the law continued to be understood in after-times. So strictly were persons held to the observance of the legal dependence between the character of the principal and accessary, that where a principal was attainted at the king's suit upon an indictment, the accessary could not be put to answer in an appeal at the suit of the party,[2] for both must be attainted at the suit of the same person. If a principal was found guilty of homicide *se defendendo*, it was held that the accessary should not be arraigned.[3] The general tenor of cases in the reign of Edward III., seems to indicate that a person being present, aiding and assisting, was considered only as accessary; but the opinion of lawyers seemed now to have altered, and a person who was present, aiding and assisting, at a murder, was held to be a principal.[4] If a person taken by process died in prison, the coroner was always to view the body.[5]

We have seen that the petty jury, when they gave a verdict of acquittal on an indictment of homicide, used to be required to say *who* was the person that really committed the fact.[6] It had now grown into practice not to require this, unless the indictment had been found before the coroner.[7] That officer being in duty bound to find who had committed the murder, it seems, as if the law expected the jury who tried the traverse, and had defeated his inquisition, to supply it by finding another. It was decided that justices of the peace could not assign a coroner, if a person indicted before them was desirous of becoming a provor;[8] such an appeal being adjudged void by the court of king's bench. A person was appealed by three different provors, and having vanquished one, he was, very properly, declared to be acquitted as against all.[9]

There was great care taken that a person once acquitted should not be again arraigned for the same offence. But where the first arraignment was either without an original or with a bad one, he might be newly arraigned at the suit of the king. However, if the original was good, whether it was an appeal or indictment, he could not afterward be arraigned, though the mesne process, or return, was ever so bad.[10] In like manner, if the plaintiff was nonsuit in his appeal, the defendant might be arraigned at the king's suit.[11] It was held that where a felon was within the benefit of a statute-pardon, the court were *ex officio* to decline arraigning him, though he made no claim[12] of it. A man was convicted of robbery, in an appeal at the suit of the person robbed, who released the *execution;* and afterwards the king also, reciting the release, pardoned the *execution;* this was held to be no pardon of the *felony*, which must be expressly named.[13] We find it laid down

[1] 7 Hen. IV., Bro. Cor., 18.
[2] 7 Hen. IV., 27 and 35.
[3] 11 Hen. IV., 93.
[4] 7 Hen. IV., 27, 35.
[5] 3 Hen. V., Bro. Cor., 168.
[6] *Vide ante*, c. xiii.
[7] 11 Hen. IV., 93.
[8] 9 Hen. IV., 1.
[9] 11 Hen. IV., 93.
[10] 9 Hen. V., 2.
[11] 11 Hen. IV., 41.
[12] *Ibid.*
[13] 8 Hen. IV., 22.

for clear law that an appeal of murder could not be brought beyond a year and day from the fact; which seems to imply that all other appeals might be commenced at a more distant period.[1]

Peine forte et dure.

The severe penance to which prisoners were subjected, *if* they refused to plead, was now inflicted in a different manner from that which is described in Fleta and Britton.[2] They were now to be put *en diverses measons bases et estoppes, que ils gisent par la terre touts nuds forsque leur braces, que il mettroit sur chacun deux tant de fer et poids quils puissent porter, et plus, issint quils ne puissent lever, et quils naver ascun manger, ne boire, si non le plus pier pain quil puissent trouver, et de leau plus pres al gaole (excepte eau courant) et que le jour quils ont pain quil nayent de leau, et e contra, et quils* GISSENT ISSINT, TANTQUILS FURENT MORTS.[3] Thus they were to lie under a *peine* (for so it was now called instead of *prisone,* which is the word in the statute) *till they were dead,* an event that was likely soon to follow from the account here given of the weights to be placed upon them. By what authority this proceeding was altered between the time of Fleta and the reign of Henry IV. can only be determined by conjecture. It is probable so material a change in judicial proceedings as one which affected life would not have been hazarded without the sanction of the executive power at least, if not of parliament; but no mention is to be found of any such order or direction. In later times we find[4] a further alteration in the mode of compelling prisoners to stand a trial; and if an authority had been given by parliament or the council for this second change, it is less likely that no trace of it should be left, as it must have been given since the reign of Henry IV., when public memorials have been kept with more security than in earlier times. Whatever was the authority for the first change, the motive to it has been thus accounted for: It has been thought to arise from the justices in eyre and justices of gaol delivery not staying above two or three days in a county town, who therefore could not wait for the tedious method, before used, of forcing the criminal to plead, as it lasted sometimes forty days,[5] the probability and justness of which conjecture must be determined by the reader.

If a person charged with felony stood mute, it was usual to impannel a jury *ex officio,* to try whether this silence was a device of the prisoner, or an infirmity that had actually fallen upon him, in order that so grievous a punishment might be inflicted on none who were disabled by the visitation of heaven.[6] It had now become a settled practice to inflict the *peine forte et dure* as well in appeals as upon indictments,[7] a point concerning which there seems to have been[8] some difference of practice in the reign of Edward III.

[1] 12 Hen. IV., 3.
[2] *Vide ante,* c. xiv.
[3] 8 Hen. IV., 1.
[4] At Cambridge, 1471.
[5] Barr. Stat., p. 86.
[6] 8 Hen. IV., 3.
[7] 8 Hen. IV., 1, 2.
[8] *Vide ante,* c. xiv.

There appears nothing remarkable in the reports of this reign relating to the description of offences; these stood generally upon the foot of determinations in the reign of Edward III. However, we find the following point of treason. A man had taken the seal of an old patent, and put it to a new commission, by authority of which he collected much money, and otherwise imposed upon the world; this was held to be forging the king's seal, and the offender was accordingly drawn and hanged.[1] It seems to have been long agreed that lands entailed were not to be forfeited for treason,[2] and of course not for felony. Where a man had a felon in his house, and permitted him to depart, this was held to be no escape of a felon, because he had not arrested him for felony;[3] and again, where a man was struck, and afterwards died of the plague, the offender who escaped out of the custody of the constable was adjudged not to be guilty of felony.[4]

It does not appear that our jurisprudence was under any particular obligation to this king (*a*). After the reign of Richard II., it was an advantage that the reigning prince had no prejudices against the ancient common law. The law in general was suffered to take its course. If it was ever turned aside from its proper direction, it was in the instance of certain obnoxious persons who were to be destroyed by this instrument, as one more effectual and safe than open violence. The king and government.

In the 6th of Henry IV. that monarch did not scruple to proceed against the archbishop of York for rebellion and treason. Sir William Gascoigne, the chief-justice, having some doubt about acting in so hazardous an enterprise, the king appointed Sir William Fulthorp for judge, who pronounced sentence of death, which was followed by immediate execution. This seems to have been with very little formality of trial, and is the first instance in this country of a capital punishment inflicted on an archbishop. The Earl of Nottingham was condemned in a like summary manner. In the following reign, the Earl of Cambridge, some other lords, and Sir Thomas Grey, were indicted by a jury of commoners of

(*a*) But in this reign the most decisive and rapid progress was made in constitutional government. Lord Hale had observed, that owing to the defect in the king's title, he was deferential to the people. "Under Henry IV. I find no complaint of any imposition set on merchandise. It concerned him to be pert (*i.e.*, polite) to the people" (*Sir M. Hale on "Customs,"* c. xi.) At a subsequent chapter, indeed, the same remark is applied to the king's successors (c. xii.–xiv.) Sir J. Mackintosh observes, "The right of the commons to appropriate supplies to specific services was exercised without resistance under these parliamentary kings. In this reign, as well as in that of his son, parliaments were almost annually holden; and Henry IV. only delayed the success of the commons in their first attempt to make the redress of grievances a condition preliminary to the grant of supply (*Rot. Parl.* iii. 458). The memorable reformation of 1406, which required the king to govern the realm by the advice of a permanent council, who, being present, took an oath in parliament to observe and defend the reformed institutions, has been justly characterised by the highest authority as a noble fabric of constitutional liberty, hardly inferior to the petition of right" (Mackintosh, *Hist. Eng.*, vol. i., quoting Hallam's *Middle Ages*, i. 302).

[1] 2 Hen. IV., 25. [2] 7 Hen. IV., 32. [3] 9 Hen. IV., 1. [4] 11 Hen, IV., 12.

high treason. The evidence upon the indictment was, that the constable of Southampton Castle had sworn that they had separately confessed their guilt to him. Upon this evidence Sir Thomas Grey was executed. But the lords pleading their privilege, the king thought proper to summon eighteen barons, with the Duke of Clarence as their president, to try them. The evidence given to the jury had been put into writing, and was now read to the lords; it does not appear that the prisoners were even produced in court, but they were in this manner convicted and accordingly executed.[1]

The statutes.

Several statutes were made in the reign of Richard II., without the assent of the commons; but they had acquired during that reign an ascendancy which gave them importance; and in the first of Henry IV., though foiled in their attempt to share in the judicial department of the lords, they drew from that house, as we have seen, an express resolution that they had a legislative authority in all statutes, grants, and subsidies.[2] This was a declaration expressly in favour of their right. It was, nevertheless, so little regarded in practice, that in the very next year it was invaded; for the famous statute 2 Henry IV. c. xv., against Lollards, was passed without the assent of the commons, who are said to have expressly protested against it[3] (*a*); notwithstanding which, this act has always been held to be an act of parliament, and was occasionally enforced as such, till repealed in the reign of Henry VIII. It was afterwards revived, and carried into severe execution, in the reign of Philip and Mary, but was finally repealed in the reign of Queen Elizabeth.

Instances like this produced the petition in the 8th of Henry IV., in consequence of which it was enacted, at the request of the commons, that certain of the commons' house should be present at the engrossing of the parliament-roll. The grievance complained of was not remedied entirely by this precaution. It had got into practice, upon entering the bill on the statute-roll, to make additions, diminutions, and alterations, whereby the act was made to vary, and that sometimes materially, from the substance of the commons' petition; and the roll was not unfrequently drawn up

(*a*) This is a very gross mistake, the only pretext for which is that the statute does not say it was passed with the assent of the commons, the reason for which is manifest, that it was passed on their petition, "Prælati, et clerus ac etiam communitates domino regi supplicarunt;" and it was in the usual manner granted by the king, with the assent of the lords, "Qui quidem dominus rex ex assensu magnatum concessit ordinavit et statuit" (*Stat. of Realm*, ii. 126; Wilkin's *Conc.* iii. 328). It was taken for law in that and succeeding reigns; and the idea of the commons, then rising rapidly into power, having allowed a statute of that kind to be fraudulently foisted into the statute-roll, and put in execution, without remonstrating and protesting, must appear idle to any one who has paid any attention to the constitutional history of the reign. For it happens that in this reign, by reason of the defect in the king's title, he was particularly deferential to the commons, and specially engaged at the outset of his reign to pass no measure without their concurrence, a pledge to which they rigidly kept him. In the 25th Henry VIII. the statute is referred to as valid.

[1] Hum., vol. iii., 97. [2] *Vide ante*, c. 17. [3] 4 Inst., 51.

directly contrary to their sense and intention.[1] A practice like this required redress. The commons remonstrated in 2 Henry V., and contended that, considering they were as well *assertórs* as petitioners, statutes should be made according to the tenor of the writing of their petition, and not altered. We do not find that this representation of the commons produced any answer or immediate correction of the cause of complaint.

Reports.

The Year-book of this king's reign is complete; and many cases are likewise to be found in Jenkins and Benloe. The reports of Henry IV., as they contain matter that bears a nearer affinity to the state of our laws at this day than the books of Edward III., are more likely to engage the attention of a modern reader. Their form is less irksome, and the subject more intelligible; they have less the style of an entry than the old reports, and give a state of the case, and what was said upon it, more in the way of a narrative (*a*). Notwithstanding these advantages in their favour, it is the opinion of a learned writer[2] that the reports of this reign, as well as those of Henry V., do not arrive, either in

(*a*) The Year-books are extremely illustrative of the ideas and usages of the age. The cases as to claims of villenage in this reign are curious, and from the reluctance shown by the claimants to take direct issues on the question of villenage (which would go to a jury), it may be surmised that juries were hostile, and that it was not safe to refer such an issue to them, as they were very likely to find the villein free (*vide Year-book*, 2 *Henry IV.*, fol. 24; 11 *Henry IV.*, fol. 48). The cases on the statute of labourers in this reign shew that the villeins were beginning to wander away from their lords, and to become vagrants, a state of things, indeed, the beginning of which had probably given rise to the statute itself, and which, in ensuing reigns, led to statutes of still greater severity against vagrants. In one case in this reign, it appears that it was a moot-point whether, if a villein wandered away, and was found vagrant, and was put to work under the statute of labourers, he could be reclaimed by his lord, which Gascoigne, C.J., denied (*Year-book*, 3 *Henry IV.*, fol. 13). In this reign there occurred a case under the statute of labourers, in which it was held that it did not apply to *un petit damosel* under the age of ten years, nor, it would seem, under the age of twelve, the age of marriage, for the scope of the statutes, it was said, was ability to labour (*Year-book*, 2 *Henry IV.*, fol. 19; 7 *Henry IV.*, fol. 5). It was held that the statutes did not apply to jurists, or persons in the position of gentlemen. So a distinction was drawn between a common labourer and an artificer; as a carpenter, who was to be retained and employed in his particular art, and could not be put to other work (11 *Henry IV.*, fol. 34). There was a curious case in which Thomas Chepesyde brought an action against the Guardian of the Friars Minors and his brethren, for that they wrongfully took his servant out of his service, and they pleaded that the servant came to them and asked them to receive him into their order to do divine service, and that they received him: that the man was professed, and was their spiritual son. What the result was is not stated (*Year-book*, 3 *Henry IV.*, fol. 13); but it should seem that it was a legal bar to the action. The most important, however, of the cases of this reign were those which related to the boundaries of the spiritual and temporal jurisdiction, and especially of the royal and papal supremacy. The questions which arose in this reign upon the subject were of some nicety and difficulty. Thus, a vicar, in an appropriation, having been bound in a sum payable to the papal chamber, if he should seek to alter the endowment made upon the appropriation, and he having forfeited the obligation, was sued in the spiritual court of the papal collector, and the vicar thereupon appealed to the king's court for a prohibition, upon the ground that a matter of debt was of temporal cognizance. The point was much

[1] *Vide* Cotton's Abrid. Table, Statutes, &c.; and *vide ante*, c. 17.
[2] Hal. *Hist.*, 175.

the nature of the learning contained in them, or in the judiciousness and knowledge of the judges and pleaders, or in any other respect, to the perfection of those in the last twelve years of Edward III.

debated, and it was said the king is apprised of all his judges, as well spiritual as temporal, as the archbishops, &c., who have spiritual jurisdiction; and when the collector of the pope came into England, he brought two bulls, of which the king had one and he himself the other, but he had no power to hold pleas within the realm. And in the result, by the advice of the Archbishop of Canterbury in the council, it was ordered that the prohibition should stand (*Year-book*, 2 *Henry IV.*, fol. 10.) Several cases on the statutes of provisors and præmunire occurred in this reign, whence it should seem they were enforced; but it also appears that there was great doubt as to the extent of their operation, and that they were not deemed to interfere with the ecclesiastical jurisdiction in matters spiritual, of which there was no jurisdiction in the king's courts, as there was in mattere of patronage. Thus, for instance, a suit upon the statute of *præmunire*, for suing in the court-Christian for a mortuary appears to have failed (*Year-book*, 10 *Henry IV.*, fol. 2). There it appears that the defendant had sued in the court of Rome, and yet there was no judgment against him. The scope of the statutes, it is plain, was the temporal rights of the king or his subjects, as the legal right of patronage, or the jurisdiction of the king's courts to determine thereon. The most important case, however, and one which may well be called a leading case on the subject, is one which occurred in the 11th year of the reign. It was a case of *quare impedit* by the king against the Bishop of Salisbury, who had been created bishop at the court of Rome, and in order to avoid the king's title to the presentation, alleged to have arisen from the incumbent's being created bishop, pleaded that before he was created bishop, he had a papal bill of dispensation to hold the living. The chief-justice said, "The pope's grant cannot change the law of the land, for if the king had title by reason of the voidance of the benefice, the 'apostle'" (so the pope was called in the courts of law) "could not deprive him of his right." Another of the judges answered with what seems, in these days, to have been a legal maxim, "*Papa omnia potest*," and he went on to argue that the papal power was sufficient to dispense in such cases, so that there had been in truth no voidance. The chief-justice replied, "It was so in ancient times, and I do not dispute the power of the apostle; but I do not know that he, by his bulls, can change the law of England" (11 *Hen. IV.*, fol. 37). And he said that though the case was not within the terms of the statute of provisors, it appeared within its spirit and scope, as it interfered with the king's right to patronage by means of a papal presentation (fol. 76.) In a subsequent year the court held that they could not allow the papal excommunication to disable a party from suing on the statute of præmunire in the court of Rome, for this would be to enable the court of Rome to get rid of these statutes or of any other laws it did not approve of, and so would be unreasonable (*Year-book*, 14 *Hen. IV.*, fol. 14). If a bishop, it was said, excommunicated a party contrary to law, there could be a writ issued out of chancery to compel the bishop to release the party, or he should be deprived of his temporalities, but no such writ could be issued to the pope; and therefore an excommunication could not be allowed as a legal disability in such a case (*Ibid.*) It will be seen that the law was already carried almost to the utmost extent possible short of an interference with the papal supremacy in matters purely spiritual. In all matters at all mixed with temporality the crown was absolute. And there was a remarkable incident in this reign which our author failed to notice—viz., that in this reign the king so little regarded the privileges of the clergy that he actually had an archbishop not only tried by a secular court, but by a mere summary tribunal, so utterly illegal, that Gascoigne, the chief-justice, refused to sit upon it, and there is reason to believe lost his office in consequence, for his name is not afterwards to be found in the Year-books. In this reign, also, the commons suggested the confiscation of church property, which was only spared by the king. It is manifest that so far from encroaching, the church was losing ground, and had no longer any real power in the State.

CHAPTER XIX.

HENRY V.

Qualification of Electors—The Clergy—The Statute of Additions—Statute of Amendments—Laws against Heretics—Forging of Deeds—Riots—Of Truce and Safe-Conduct—The King and Government.

The few changes made in the law by parliament during this military reign, consist principally in such provisions as were framed to promote the design of several statutes passed in the time of the two preceding princes (*a*). The election of knights and burgesses,

(*a*) In the third year of the reign there was a confirmation of the liberties of the church (3 *Hen. V.*, c. i.) "That holy church have all her liberties and franchises, and that the lords spiritual and temporal, having liberties and franchises, have and enjoy all the liberties and franchises which they have had of the grants of the king's progenitors, and of the confirmation of the same by our lord the king or his grant, except always those franchises and liberties which he repealed in this present parliament, and those that he repealed by the common law." And in the same reign there was another statute (c. iv.), "That all provisions, licenses, and pardons of a benefice full of an incumbent shall be void," reciting a stat. of Henry IV. (7 *Hen. IV.*, c. viii.) against papal provisions, and enacted that, notwithstanding several persons having provisions of the pope of divers benefices, and licenses royal to execute the provisions, had, by colour of the provisions and licenses, excluded divers persons of their benefices, in which they had been incumbents for a long time, of the collation of the patrons spiritual; and then enacted that "the king had ordained and established that all the incumbents of the collation patronage, or presentation of spiritual persons, may peaceably and quietly enjoy their benefices, without being in any wise grieved or molested by colour of such provisions or licenses; and that all licenses and pardons made upon such provisions shall be void" (3 *Hen. V.*, c. iv.) And that if any felt grieved or molested by colour of such provisions, &c., the parties molesting them shall incur the pains and penalties contained in the statutes of provisors (25 *Edw. III.*, st. 4) and the statutes of præmunire (10 *Rich. II.*, c. v.); and this was enacted with the assent of the lords *spiritual*. In the same reign there passed an act that ordinaries should inquire of and reform the estates of hospitals, reciting that many hospitals which had been founded for poor men and women, &c., have for the most part decayed, and their revenues withdrawn and spent in other uses by divers persons, as well spiritual as temporal, enacted that, as to hospitals of royal foundation, the ordinaries should inquire by the *king's commission*, and if other hospitals, they should inquire by the law of the church (2 *Hen. V.*, st. 1). There was a more important statute or ordinance enacted or ordained in this reign, which does not appear on the statute-book, and which our author has omitted to mention, but the importance of which it is impossible to overrate. This (as Mr Justice Coleridge observed, in one of his elaborate and learned judgments, by which he added the reputation of a jurist to his high character as a judge), "This was the period of the great papal schism. There were three anti-popes; Henry V., preserving a neutrality between the rival candidates, treated the see of Rome as vacant, and by consequence, those bulls and briefs which had become established as necessary to the completion of episcopal election, could not be procured from any one. An act therefore passed, reciting that for this reason confirmations could not be made, and great inconveniences followed; and enacting that, during the avoidance of the holy see, bishops elect should be confirmed by the metropolitans, without excuse or delay on that account; and that the king's writs should issue to the metropolitans, straitly charging them to perform the confirmations, and all that to their office pertains; and also to the elected, that they should effectually pursue their confirmations

the punishment of provisors and heretics, and the suppression of riots, were favourite objects in this, as they had been in the two former reigns. The statutes upon those, and some few other articles of reformation, constitute the whole of the juridical history of this reign, the decisions of courts during nine years furnishing nothing of any great importance.

Qualification of electors.

The statutes hitherto mentioned concerning the representatives of the people, relate to the mode of election.[1] The first act in this king's reign is to ascertain the *qualifications* of the *electors* and person to be *elected* (*a*). Knights of the shire, says the act, shall not be chosen unless they are resident within the shire the day of the date of the writ of summons; and knights, esquires, and others who are to be choosers of the knights of shires, are to be resident within the shire in the manner and form aforesaid. Again, citizens and burgesses of cities and boroughs are to be citizens and burgesses resident, dwelling, and free in the same, and no other person, nor in any other manner whatever.

The clergy.

We have seen that in the last reign vicars were established in possession of their benefices;[2] we now find an act for limiting the salaries of curates and chaplains; the former were to have eight, and the latter but seven marks per annum.[3] The subject of provisors, and the possession of ecclesiastical benefices by aliens, occasioned several acts in this reign. The stat. 13 Rich. II. c. iii., prohibiting Frenchmen from holding church benefices, was enforced by stat. 1 Hen. V. c. 7, with an exception of priors alien conventual, and other priors having institution and induction, so as they were catholic, and found surety not to disclose the secrets of the realm. The penalties of a præmunire were inflicted by stat. 3 Hen. V. c. iv. on persons obtaining provisions, licenses, or pardons against the stat. 7 Hen. IV. c. viii.[4] The same jealousy which had been long entertained of foreign churchmen in this kingdom was shown by the Irish parliament in the last reign, when they passed an act prohibiting the Irish people from accepting any church benefice whatever; by the *Irish* were meant those original inhabitants of the country who had almost always been in a state of resistance to the English settlers. This act of the Irish parliament was now confirmed by the stat. 4 Hen. V. c. vi.; and further, if any archbishop, bishop, abbot, or prior of the Irish nation made any collation or presentment contrary to

before the archbishop" (3 *Hen. V.*, *Rot. Parl.*, vol. iv. pp. 2, 71). In the fourth vol. of *Rymer's Fœdera*, part ii. p. 156, will be found the writs accordingly issued to the bishop elect and the metropolitan for confirmations." (See the judgment of Sir John Coleridge in the case of the Archbishop of Canterbury, 11 *Queen's Bench Reps.*, 593). It is rather strange that this most remarkable statute should have escaped attention in the history of the reign, seeing that it was the earliest direct and avowed assumption by the crown of the spiritual supremacy of the holy see.

(*a*) This was provided for as to pecuniary qualification by the stat. Henry VI.

[1] *Vide ante*, c. 17. [2] *Ibid.*, 222. [3] Stat. 2 Hen. V., st. 2, c. 2. [4] *Vide ante*, c. 17.

that act, or brought with them, as servants, any Irish rebels to parliament, to learn and discover the secrets and state of the English, it was ordained that their temporalities should be seized into the king's hands till they had made fine to the king.

Fees for the probate of testaments were settled by stat. 4 Hen. V. c. viii. By another act, the ordinary was empowered to inquire into the government of hospitals (*a*); and if they were of the king's foundation, he was to certify the state of them to the chancery; if of another's foundation and patronage, then he was to make correction and reformation according to the laws of holy church.[1]

One statute was occasioned by the old dispute about ecclesiastical jurisdiction. Complaint had been made to parliament, that persons were sued in the ecclesiastical court, as well for matters touching freehold, debt, trespasses, covenants, and other things (the cognizance of which belonged to the king's court), as on questions matrimonial and testamentary; and when a person appeared upon citation and demanded a libel, in order to be informed what he was to answer, or purchased a writ of prohibition, the libel used to be denied. That persons might not in this manner be deprived of their remedies at common law, it was enacted by stat. 2 Hen. V. st. 1, c. iii., that the libel should be delivered to the party, without difficulty, at the time when by law it was grantable (*b*).

Some amendments were made in the course of process and proceeding. We have seen what remedy was given by statute in the time of Edward III. for persons whose goods were seized as the goods of an outlaw by mistake of the sheriff.[2] The great use of the writ *de idemptitate nominis* was to ascertain whether the person so injured was the party really meant by the exigent. To make this process more accurate and certain, it was prayed in the last reign, that no man might be outlawed without his surname, and

(*a*) It is to be observed that the author has omitted to mention the remarkable statute passed in this reign as to hospitals, &c. This was the statute 2 Hen. V., c. 1, reciting, "That, forasmuch many hospitals within the nation, founded as well by the kings of this realm, as by lords and ladies, spiritual and temporal, and by divers other estates, to the honour of God, and of his glorious mother, in aid of the souls of the founders; to which hospitals the founders gave goods and lands wherewith to sustain poor men and women, &c., and the same be now for the most part decayed, and the goods of the same withdrawn; and then enacting that as to hospitals of the royal foundation, the king's commissioners should inquire, and, of others, the ordinaries; making reformation thereof according to the laws of Holy Church (2 *Hen. V.*, c. i.)

(*b*) In a subsequent chapter (c. xxiv.), a full account is given by the author of the canon law and the jurisdiction of the ecclesiastical courts; and there can be no doubt that its vexatious exercise had a painful influence in estranging the nation from the ancient church. As the officers of the courts had an interest—being paid by fees—in extending their jurisdiction, they were always trying to do so, and even within its legal limits it was capable of being very vexatiously exercised. Indications are not wanting of the irritation and dissatisfaction this excited among the people, even apart from the former serious question of the interference of the law as to heresy with freedom of thought and of discussion. And the present statute is one of the earliest and most significant indications of the growth of that feeling of discontent and impatience of ecclesiastical jurisdiction which had a powerful influence in promoting separation from Rome.

[1] Stat. 2 Hen. V., st. 1., c. 1.

[2] *Vide ante*, c. 13.

the name of his town and county.[1] At length a statute was passed to ascertain this matter, and it was enacted by stat. 1 Hen. V. c. v., that in every original writ of actions personal, appeals, and indictments, in which the exigent shall be awarded, to the names of the defendants *additions* should be made of their estate or degree, or mystery, and of the towns, or hamlets, or places and counties of which they *were*, or *be*, or in which they be or were conversant (*a*), otherwise the outlawry to be void; and before the outlawry pronounced, the writ and indictment may be abated by exception of the party. It was also provided that, though the writs of additions personal were not according to the records and deeds, if such addition was surplusage, the writ should not be abated on that account. The clerks of the chancery, if they left out such additions, were to be punished, by fine, at the discretion of the chancellor. This *statute of additions*, as it was afterwards called, removed those inconveniences that used to be occasioned by the want of naming particularly the parties in a writ.

The statute of additions.

(*a*) This statute must be considered with reference to the statute of Richard II. (589), as to the law of *venue*, from which the necessity for it arose. According to that law, the action must be brought, *i.e.*, the original writ issued, in the county where the contract was made or the cause of action arose. That, however, might not be the county in which the party sued resided at the time of action, still the original writ was the ground of subsequent process, and hence it might be that the proclamations preliminary to outlawry might be made in a county in which the defendant did not reside. And as the outlawry was founded upon a supposed contempt in not appearing, according to the exigency of the writ, it was right that there should be reasonable notice of it. Hence the necessity for the present statute, which required that the original writ should state the county where the defendant resided or lately resided, which, in the absence of any knowledge of his removal, might be presumed to be in the county where the contract was made or the cause of action arose; since there, at all events, he had, it must be supposed, resided. But this was not necessarily so, since he might have made a contract in one county, residing in another, or he might have removed. And the object was, that his true place of residence at the time of action, or his last known place of residence, should be specified in the writ, in order to indicate where the proclamation of the process, with a view to outlawry, in case of non-appearance, should be made. Under this statute it was held that the residence meant place of household, but that if a man had household in two places, the residence might be said to be in either (*Year-book*, 33 *Hen. VI.*, fol. 9), and so a place where a man was residing for business (*Ibid.*) The plea in abatement to the writ (which, as pleading was oral, came in effect to an application to set it aside) would state, that the party at the time of action was "conversant and resident" (or commorant) at another place, and not that stated in the writ; and if this was admitted or proved, it was set aside (21 *Hen. VI.*, fol. 54). It was admissible to describe the defendant as lately of such a place (22 *Edw. IV.*, fol. 13). The exception of account of proper addition of the residence was only to be received either in abatement of the writ or for reversal of an outlawry founded on the defective process, as it did not go to the courts (33 *Hen. VI.*, fol. 53; 21 *Hen. VI.*, fol. 54). Upon this statute, if there was no proper addition of the residence, the outlawry would be set aside summarily or reversed on error (8 *Hen. VI.*, fol. 37). And so it was if the defendant alleged that he was residing at a place different from that stated in the writ (19 *Hen. VI.*, fol. 80; 21 *Hen. VI.*, fol. 21). The plaintiff, on the other hand, could maintain the proceeding by showing that the defendant was, in point of fact, residing where he was stated in the writ to have been residing (28 *Hen. VI.*, fol. 1; 21 *Hen. VII.*, fol. 13). The object of the writ was carried out by subsequent statutes (6 *Hen. VIII.*, and 31 *Eliz.* c. 4), and the principle thus embodied was preserved in the uniformity of process act, 2 and 3 W. IV., c. 39, which used the very same words, "supposed residence."

[1] Cott. Abri., p. 422, s. 82.

A statute of *jeofail and amendment* was made, in order to remove some doubts which had arisen upon stat. 14 Edw. III. st. 1, c. vi.[1] It was ordained by stat. 9 Hen. V. c. iv., that the justices before whom such plea or record was made or was depending, should have power and authority, as well by adjournment as by way of error or otherwise, to amend such record and process, according to the permission of the former statute, as well *after* judgment as *before*, so long as the record was before them. Thus this act did no more than extend the powers of the statute of Edward III. by allowing such amendments to be made *after* judgment. In the second year of the king, a statute had been passed to secure plaintiffs in the full fruits of a judgment obtained. It had been common for defendants in custody on execution, to sue out a *certiorari* or *corpus cum causâ,* and when brought before the chancellor, they would be discharged upon bail or mainprise, and sometimes without either, against the will of the plaintiffs, whom they thus defeated of their judgments: to prevent this, it was enacted by stat. 2 Hen. V. st. 1, c. ii. that if upon such writs it was returned, that the person was a prisoner on a judgment, he should be remanded immediately, and there remain without bail or mainprise till he had agreed with his plaintiff.

The statute of amendments.

Another regulation was made by stat. 2 Hen. V. st. 2, c. ii. concerning the qualifications of jurors. The statute complains that many were disinherited, because the persons who passed on inquests were "common jurors, and others that have but little to live on but by such inquests, and nothing to lose on account of their false oaths, whereby they offend their consciences the more largely:" it was therefore now provided, that none should be admitted to pass on inquests upon the trial of the death of a man, nor between party and party in pleas real, nor in a plea personal, where the debt or damage declared for amounted to forty marks, unless he had lands or tenements of the yearly value of forty shillings above all charges; and if he had it not, it was a cause for which either party might challenge him. Because the under-officers of sheriffs continued in their offices from year to year, it was found no easy matter for an injured person to obtain redress against them: it was therefore enacted by stat. 1 Hen. V. c. iv., that those who were bailiffs of sheriffs in one year, should not be in office for the three years next following, except bailiffs or sheriffs inheritable in their sheriffwicks; nor was any under-sheriff, sheriff's clerk, receiver, or sheriff's bailiff, to be attorney in the king's courts during the time he was in office with such sheriff. By stat. 9 Hen. V. c. v., the stat. 14 Edw. III. st. 1, c. vii., concerning the appointment of sheriffs was dispensed with for a time; and the reason given was, that the late pestilences and wars had not left in the country sufficient persons of substance to answer the requisites of that act; the king therefore was authorised, during four years, to appoint sheriffs and escheators at his pleasure.

[1] *Vide ante*, vol. ii. 448.

Laws against heretics.

The whole secular power seems, at the beginning of this reign, to have been made subservient to the ends of the prelates in suppressing the Lollards. (*a*) It was enacted by stat. 2 Hen. V. st. 1, c. vii., that the chancellor, treasurer, justices of both benches and of the peace, sheriffs, mayors, and bailiffs of cities and towns, and all other chief officers of places, should, upon entering into their office, take an oath, to use their whole power and diligence to destroy all heresies and errors, commonly called *Lollardies*, and assist the ordinaries and their commissaries as often as required by them, so as they paid their expenses of travelling. Nevertheless they were enjoined by the act not to postpone the king's service to that of the church. Besides the penalties to which Lollards were before liable, they were now to suffer forfeiture of goods and lands, as in case of felony; only the lands such convicts held of the ordinary or his commissary before whom he was convict, were to be forfeit to the king; but no heretics thus left to the secular arm were to forfeit their goods till they were dead; in which particulars this new provision did not conform to the law of forfeiture for felony. The justices of the king's bench, of the peace, and of assize, were empowered to *enquire* (that is, take indictments) of Lollards and their maintainers, and award process; but because heresy was a spiritual offence, they were to deliver the party, when taken, to the ordinary by indenture, within ten days after the arrest, to be tried by the laws of holy church. The indictment was not to be used as evidence, but only for information before the spiritual judge, who was to commence his process, as if no indictment had been found. This was the famous act against the Lollards, upon which many of those people suffered. In the preamble they are loaded with the imputation of state crimes, as a pretence to delude the people into a concurrence with the churchmen in their persecution; they are said to be united in confederacies to destroy the king, and all other estates of the realm, both lay and spiritual, *and all manner of policy, and finally the laws of the land:* so sensible were they that the charge alone of difference in religious opinions could not justify to the people such sanguinary proceedings.

Some statutes were passed relating to the coin. It was made felony by stat. 3 Hen. V. st. 1, c. i., to make, buy, or import certain coin then prohibited by proclamation, called *gally halfpence, suskins,* and *dodkins;* and the payments in these coins subjected the party to certain penalties. Much doubt had arisen whether clipping, washing, and filing, was an offence within the statute of treasons; and it was accordingly so declared to be by stat. 3 Hen. V. st. 2, c. vi., and cognisance thereof, and of every other falsity of money, was given to the justices of assize: the justices of the peace, likewise, might still enquire thereof; that is, take indictments and issue process of *capias,* but no farther. The suspicions entertained of the treasonable practices of the Welsh still contiuued; and it

(*a*) Prelates had little power in these times. *Vide ante.*

was enacted by stat. 3 Hen. V. st. 2, c. iii., that all such Britons dwelling in the queen's house, and others abiding near the house, and elsewhere, not made denizens, should be voided out of the realm by a certain day, under pain of felony. And because many Welch made inroads into Shropshire, Hereford, and Gloucestershire, and took away people by force, the justices of the peace were authorised by stat. 2 Hen. V. st. 2, c. v., to enquire, hear, and determine such offences, award process of outlawry, and certify this to the lords of seignories where such plunderers harboured, who were to order execution to be done thereon. By another statute it was ordained,[1] that all Irishmen and Irish clerks-beggars, called *chamber-deacons*, should be voided out of the realm by a certain time, on pain of losing their goods, and being imprisoned at the king's pleasure; excepting graduates in the schools, serjeants and apprentices of the law, those who were inheritors in England, religious persons professed, merchants of good fame and their apprentices, and those with whom the king would dispense. All Irishmen having estates and benefices were to dwell on them. This act is stated to be made for the quiet and peace of England, and the increase and restoring of Ireland.

The law respecting forgery, as stated by our old writers,[2] seems to have become obsolete, as a statute was now made, imposing a less penalty than the old law, and yet adding something to the then existing law. It is said by stat. 1 Hen. V. c. iii., that people possessed of lands or tenements suffered losses, because persons *subtily imagined and forged new divers false deeds and muniments to trouble and charge their lands:* it was enacted, that a person so injured should have recovery of his damages against the party making and publishing, who was also to make fine at the king's pleasure. This was substituting a civil in the place of a criminal proceeding.

Forging of deeds.

Several laws were passed to facilitate the execution of process against offenders living in places where the king's writ did not run. Because felons living in Tyndal and Hexham escaped the process of the law, which could not be executed in those franchises, it was provided,[3] that process should be made at common law, till they were outlawed; and when that was pronounced and returned before the justices, they were to certify it to the ministers of those franchises, who were immediately to seize the lands, goods, and persons of the offenders. This statute was afterwards extended to persons living in Ridesdale, another franchise.[4] It was likewise provided,[5] that persons outlawed in the county of Lancaster should not forfeit their lands or goods in other counties.

Respecting offenders in general, who absconded to avoid the process of the law, it was enacted by stat. 2 Hen. V. st. 1, c. ix., that

[1] Stat. 1 Hen. V., c. 8.
[2] *Vide ante*, c. 9.
[3] St. 2 Hen. V., st. 1, c. 5.
[4] Stat. 9 Hen. V., c. 7.
[5] *Ibid.*, c, 2.

where murder, manslaughter, robbery, battery, assemblies of people in great numbers, riots, and insurrections happened, and the offenders fled, and any one came to the chancery to complain thereof, a bill should be thereupon made; and the chancellor, after the bill to him delivered, if he was informed of the truth thereof, should have power to make a writ of *capias* at the king's suit, into the county where the offence was committed, returnable in chancery at a certain day. If the party was taken or surrendered, he was to be put in ward, or mainprise, as the chancellor pleased; if not, and the sheriff returned that he could not be taken, then the chancellor was to make a writ of proclamation directed to the sheriff, returnable in the king's bench at a certain day, to make proclamation in two counties, for him to appear at the day, or stand convicted of the offence charged in the bill, the substance of which was to be contained in the proclamation; and if he came not by the return of the proclamation, he was to stand attainted. If the offence was a riot, the suggestion thereof was to be testified to the chancellor by letters under the seal of two justices of the peace and the sheriff, before the *capias* was to issue. If the fact happened in the county of Lancaster, or other franchise, where there was a chancellor and a seal, the chancellor was to write to the chancellor thereof all the suggestions in the aforesaid bill, commanding him to make execution in the above way.

In the preceding chapter of the same statute a very special course was directed in case of *riots*. It was found, that the persons intrusted with the execution of stat. 13 Hen. IV. c. vii.,[1] concerning riots, were dilatory and negligent therein: it was now enacted, that should default be found in the two justices of peace, or justices of assize, and the sheriff and under-sheriff, then there should issue, at the instance of the party grieved, under the great seal, a commission, to inquire as well of the truth of the case and the original matter, as of the default of the justices and sheriff, to be directed to sufficient and indifferent persons at the nomination of the chancellor; which commissioners were to return presently into the chancery the inquests and matters found before them. The panel was to be returned by the coroner, and the juors to have lands of £10 per ann. with severe issues and penalties on default. The chancellor, moreover, when he had knowledge of any riot, was to send a writ to the justices and sheriff, enjoining them to put the above statute of Hen. IV. in execution; and the justices were to be paid by the sheriff the costs of suppressing such riots. Persons attainted of heinous riots were to be imprisoned for a year at least, without bail or mainprise; those attainted of petty riots to be imprisoned as it should seem best to the king. All persons were to be assisting to the justices and commissioners, on pain of imprisonment and fine.

Riots.

Because indictments in the county of Lancaster sometimes charged offences to be committed in places that did not exist, under pretence

[1] *Vide ante*, c. 16.

of some fabricated name to assume jurisdiction of the crime, it was provided by stat. 7 Hen. V. that the justices should, before the exigent on such indictment was awarded, inquire *ex officio* whether there was such a place; and if there was found to be no such place, the indictment was to be void, and the indictors punished by imprisonment and fine.[1] It was at the same time declared, that process of *capias* and exigent, as in trespass, should lie against the forgers of false deeds.

The authority of justices of the peace was further established by several acts. Justices were empowered by stat. 2 Hen. V. st. 1, c. iv., to send their writs to take fugitive labourers in any county. All the statutes of labourers were to be exemplified under the great seal; an exemplification was to be sent to every sheriff, to make proclamation in full county, and deliver it to the justices of the peace named of the *quorum*, to remain with them for the better execution thereof. It was further directed, that justices of the *quorum* should be resident with the county, except lords, justices of the two benches, the chief baron, serjeants-at-law, and the king's attorney, and that they should hold their sessions four times a-year; namely, in the first week after St. Michael, the Epiphany, the close of Easter, and the translation of St. Thomas the Apostle; and the justices were to hold their sessions throughout the realm in the same week every year. Justices were authorised by this act to examine labourers, servants, and artificers, with their masters, upon their oaths. Again, by stat. 2 Hen. V. st. 2, c. i., justices of the peace were to be of the most sufficient persons dwelling in the county, except lords and justices of assize, and were to be named by the advice of the chancellor and king's council.

Of truce and safe-conduct.

We must rank among the penal acts of this reign a statute made in aid of the law of nations, to punish the breach of *truce and safe-conduct*. This was stat. 2 Hen. V. st. 1, c. vi. It complains, that during the continuance of a truce, many people having the king's safe-conduct had been slain, robbed, and spoiled by the king's subjects, as well upon the main sea as within the ports and coasts of England, Ireland, and Wales; and such spoilers were abetted and received, to the breach of truces and safe-conducts, and the dishonour of the kingdom. It was now declared that such manslaughter, robbery, spoiling, breaking of truce and safe-conduct, and voluntary receipt, abetment, procurement, concealing, hiring and sustaining of them, as well by land as by sea, should be adjudged high-treason. The king was to assign by letters patent, in every port, a person to be called *a conservator of the truce and the king's safe-conduct*, who was to have power by such patent, and also by commission of the admiral, to inquire of all such treasons and offences upon the main sea out of the body of the counties, and out of the franchises of the *cinque* ports, and to

[1] Because this statute was supposed not to be in force, it was re-enacted by statute 18 Hen. VI., c. 12.

punish all those indicted before him, at the king's suit, or that of the party, by such process, examination, proof, determination, judgment and execution, as the admiral might have done; saving the determination upon the death of a man, which was to be reserved to the admiral. Upon land, within the body of a county, he was to inquire of all the above offences, as well within liberties as without, and to make process by *capias* and *exigent.* Two persons learned in the law were to be associate in every commission made to such conservator, and they together were to make deliverances of gaols, according to the law of the land. The act contains some other particulars of less importance. Thus far of the statute-law in the reign of Henry V.

The king and government.

A prince like Henry, engaged during almost the whole of a short reign in the pursuit of conquest in a foreign country, could not be supposed to have any turn for the arts of legislation. The youthful sallies of this prince have furnished juridical history with an anecdote that shows him to have once been a contemner both of justice and those who administered it. (*a*)

The legal annals of this reign have come down to us imperfect; for of the Year-book of this king, the third, fourth, and sixth years are wanting.

(*a*) This is hardly just to the character of this king, for, according to the version of the story commonly given in history, the offence, that of striking a judge, was committed by the *prince*, and nobly atoned for by the *king*, seeing that upon his accession he received with marked respect the judge—Chief-Justice Gascoigne—whom he is said to have struck. But as to how far the story is correct, and as to numerous interesting details relating to the more personal portion of the legal history of the reign, the reader is referred to the *Lives of the Judges*, by Mr Foss. It seems that Gascoigne was displaced in the former reign for refusing to take part in the murder of Archbishop Scrope. There is a remarkable entry in the Year-book of the first year of this reign: "Note, that if any minister of the king arrests a man by command of the king, and rescue is made of him by any baron, earl, or duke, or any abbot; if the sheriff or other officer return that the rescue is made, the judges shall award a writ of *capias* against him who made the rescue, notwithstanding the law that they are not liable to *capias*—(*i.e.*, in civil suits)—because of their disobedience to the law (*Year-book,* 1 *Hen. V.*, fol. 14).

CHAPTER XX.

HENRY VI. (*a*).

Statutes of Henry VI.—Members of Parliament—Of the Council and Chancery—Statutes of Pernors of Profits—Attaints—Writs of Proclamation—Statutes of Jeofail—Juries—Sheriffs, and Execution of Process—Attorneys—Treason to Burn Houses—Process in Criminal Causes—Forcible Entries.

THE history of such alterations as were made in the law by the decisions of courts, during these two reigns, is so intimately connected, that it will be extremely convenient to unite them into one period, and so consider them together (*b*). In the meantime, the alterations made by parliament are not so interesting or important as to give a distinguished juridical character to either of these reigns, and to make it absolutely necessary that they should be treated separately. In the present chapters, therefore, we shall consider the statutes of both these kings (*c*), beginning with those of Henry VI.

(*a*) The author had in this and the following chapter blended together the statutes and the law of the reigns of Henry VI. and Edward IV., occupying a period of about sixty years in our history; and then, after these chapters, in which the law of real property, the system of pleading, and the ecclesiastical law and the ecclesiastical courts are described, he had devoted a *separate* chapter of two or three pages to the nominal reign of Edward V. and the brief reign of Richard III. It appeared to the editor (for reasons more fully explained in the ensuing note) to separate the two reigns of Henry VI. and Edward IV., devoting these two chapters entirely to the former, and throwing into a later chapter of the volume the reign of Edward IV., which, for reasons explained in the note to that chapter, is considered to have commenced a new era in our legal history, and therefore properly commences the *next* volume.

(*b*) The present editor ventures to differ from the author in this view, as he differed from him as to the propriety of blending together the reigns of the sovereigns from the Conquest to John. The reign of Henry VI. lasted forty years before his title was disputed, and, on the other hand, he soon *after* that ceased virtually to be sovereign, and the reign of his successor, Edward IV., lasted above twenty years. To mix up together two such long periods of our history seems calculated to confuse the reader's ideas, and there were statutes and some events and incidents of Henry's reign which require to be noted, and deserve to be distinctly remembered; for instance, the act as to bail on arrest, and the act as to electoral qualifications. Without altering the *text* of the work, (which it is desired to adhere to), it is difficult to amend this defect in its place; but as the present chapter is altogether occupied with matters which belong to the reign of Henry VI., it is entitled by the editor of that reign; the next, which equally belongs to that reign (being mainly made up of the treatise of Littleton, written at that time), is entitled Henry VI. to Edward IV., and the following chapter as to pleading is entitled as the author entitled all three, Henry VI. and Edward IV.

(*c*) The editor has ventured to differ with the author upon this point, and to think that these two reigns, on account of their respective duration, and the importance and distinctive character of the legislation and the law laid down in each, require that they should be kept separate and distinct. The reign of Henry VI. lasted from 1422 to 1460, nearly forty years, and that of Edward IV. from 1460 to 1483, nearly a quarter of a century, periods far too long to be mixed up together and thrown into

Statutes of Henry VI.

The legislature in the reign of Henry VI., as in the times of his two predecessors, was rather employed in furthering and improving the policy of some statutes made in the preceding period, than in introducing any novelties.

one in the consideration of legal history. Such a course is surely calculated to leave the mind in great confusion and obscurity. The long reign of Henry VI. had in it much that was important and distinctive, both in a legal, as well as in a political, or constitutional point of view. Hume observes that during the reigns of the Lancastrian princes the authority of parliament seems to have been more confirmed, and the privileges of the people more regarded, than during any former period; and, in particular, the long minority of Henry VI. encouraged the lords and commons to extend their influence, and they assumed the power of giving a new arrangement to the whole administration (*Hist. Eng.*, vol. iii. c. xxi.) He adds, that the people were now become of some importance, and the laws were beginning to be respected by them (*Ibid.* c. xxi.) In the time of those kings the distinction between their reigns was sufficiently marked most strongly. In the reign of Edward IV. the three previous kings were denounced as usurpers in parliament, and their grants were held void in the courts of law. Thus, in the seventh year of the reign of Edward IV., there was a great case of assize continued till the ninth year. One Bagot complained that he had been disseised of the office of one of the clerks of the crown, and he set up a grant from Edward IV. The defendant pleaded that Bagot was an alien, and he, in reply, set up letters of naturalisation granted by Henry VI. in the thirty-sixth year of his reign. Upon which the defendant set forth that, in the first parliament of Edward IV., it was declared (reciting it at great length) to the effect that Henry, late Earl of Derby, "by force and arms against his faith and ligeance, reared war against King Richard II., and intruded upon the royal power, estate, and dignity, taking upon him usurpously the crown and name of king and lord of the realm, &c., and that, after the decease of the said King Richard, the right and title of crown did descend and belong to Edmund, Earl of Mortimer, and of right belongeth at this time unto our sovereign lord, King Edward IV., as cousin and heir to Richard II.; and he, after the decease of his father, Richard, Duke of York, took upon him to use his right and title to the realm, and entered into the exercise of the royal estate and power of the crown, and the reign and governance of the realm, and removed Henry VI., son to Henry V., son to the said Henry, Earl of Derby, from the occupation, usurpation, intrusion, reign, and governance of the realm; and that he was *in right, from the death of the prince, his father,* very just king of the realm of England, and in full possession of the realm, with the royal power belonging to the crown." And the date of this accession was fixed in the act—*i.e.*, the 4th March then last, the date of the death of Richard, Duke of York. So that it is manifest that, in the view of parliament, the reign of Edward IV. did not commence until then; that is, the right did not descend to him until then; and he did not pretend to have been in *possession* until then. On the other hand, it is equally manifest that from that time he claimed to have been king *de jure* and *de facto,* having removed Henry VI. from the throne, and assumed the actual power and title of king. And it is to be observed that the letters of naturalisation of Henry VI. were pleaded as of Henry, lately *de facto, et non de jure,* Rex, &c. They were pleaded, however, necessarily as of a *de facto* king, or they would not have had any colour of legality; and it should seem that they were two or three years anterior to the date fixed by parliament as that of Edward's accession. But the act declared that Henry IV., V., and VI. had only usurped and intruded, and the court said it seemed that, "as the patent was that of an usurper and intruder, it was void;" but they first gave another ground for their judgment against the plaintiff, and from the act itself it is clear that the reign of Edward IV. was not deemed to commence until the death of the Duke of York, which was in December 1460. That, therefore, makes it clear that in the view of parliament and of the courts of law, the year 1461 was the first of King Edward IV. The case in the Year-books just quoted speaks, in the ninth year of King Edward IV., of his accession to the throne as having taken place in the first of those years—that is, the ninth, reckoning backwards from the year of the book, which makes that year to be 1470. In the March of 1461 Edward was proclaimed king, and received the homage of the peers. In 1471, which would be the 10th of Edward IV., the power of Warwick gained for Henry VI., who still lived, a temporary ascendancy,

The parliament made another law to restrain the immigration of the Irish into this kingdom. It was ordained by stat. 1 Hen. VI. c. iii. that those who did not leave the kingdom within a month after proclamation of that statute, should forfeit their goods, and

and accordingly, just after the 10th Edward IV., the Year-book has a few cases entitled, "Of Michaelmas Term," "Of the 49th of Henry VI.;" or, rather, it is headed thus: "De Termino Michaelis anno ab inchoatione Regni Henrici Sexti, xlix., et recaptionis Regiæ potestatis primo;" but that was only, at the utmost, a momentary interruption of Edward's sovereignty, whose reign had really lasted since 1461, and recommenced almost immediately afterwards; and the next book is "Te Termino Trinitatis, anno xi., Regni Regis Edwardi Quarti;" so that it is plain the year was reckoned on continuously as one of Edward IV., and from thence the Year-books go on continuously to the 23d year of Edward IV. There can be no doubt, therefore, as to the dividing point of the two reigns, and each of them, the one lasting nearly forty years, and the other above twenty, was long enough to constitute a distinct period in legal history. The great dynastic struggle which marked the latter part of the reign, and in which the adherents of both parties had to appeal to parliament and the people for support, and urge all possible arguments in order to obtain it, "sharpened the minds of men" (to use the expression of the historian), and made them, on the one hand, familiar with topics of vast constitutional importance, and, on the other hand, rendered them more and more aware of the influence of parliamentary sanction, and the importance of legal and constitutional title, while the terrible civil war which ensued impressed upon them more deeply the inestimable value of law and order. In such a reign it was natural that measures of political legislation should take precedence and have prominence. The most remarkable law which passed in this reign was that for the due election of members of parliament in counties. After the fall of the feudal system the distinction of tenures was in some measure lost, and every freeholder, as well those who held of mesne lords as the immediate tenants of the crown, were by degrees admitted to give their votes at elections. This innovation was indirectly confirmed by a law of Henry IV. (7 *Hen. IV.* c. xv.), which gave a right to such a multitude of electors as was the occasion of great disorder. In the eighth and tenth of this reign, therefore, laws were enacted limiting the electors to such as possessed forty shillings a year in land (free from all burdens) within the county (8 *Hen. VI.* c. vii.; 10 *Hen. VI.* c. ii.) The sum was equivalent to nearly twenty pounds a year in our money, and it were to be wished that the spirit, as well as the letter, of the law had been maintained (Hume's *Hist. Eng.*, vol. iii. c. xxi.) The preamble of the statute is remarkable: "Whereas the elections of knights have of late in many counties of England been made by outrages and excessive numbers of people, many of them of small substance and value, yet pretending to a right equal to the best knights and esquires, whereby manslaughters, riots, batteries, and divisions among the gentlemen and other people of the counties shall very likely arise and be, unless due remedy be provided." We may learn from these expressions what an important matter the election of a member of parliament was now become in England. That assembly was beginning in this period to assume great authority. The commons had it much in their power to enforce the execution of the laws, and if they failed of success in this particular, it proceeded less from any exorbitant power of the crown than from the licentious spirit of the aristocracy, and perhaps from the rude education of the age, and their own ignorance of the advantages arising from a due administration of justice (*Ibid.*) Upon this subject the statute of "forcible entry" and the contemporary evidence, such as the *Paston Letters*, or the records of the courts of law, disclose a state of the country in which the rising spirit of law was struggling with the spirit of a somewhat turbulent independence, in which men were very wont to take the law into their own hands. Contemporary history, and the cases in the courts, disclose the mischief, and the remarkable statute referred to was passed to provide a remedy. In the *Paston Letters* we find bodies of armed men laying siege to places instead of resorting to the regular process of law, and the statute, which Lord Coke regarded as only declaratory of the common law, while Hallam is disposed to regard it as a new law, prohibited such assertion of right by means of force and violence, and so upheld the supremacy of law. At the same time, there can be no doubt that in this reign the supremacy of regular law made great progress, and showed the breadth and strength of the popular basis upon which our

be imprisoned at the king's pleasure. It is remarkable that the Irish who principally created suspicion were persons beneficed there, and scholars resorting to the university of Oxford. It was now ordained, that no scholar should enter England without a testimonial under the seal of the lieutenant or justices of Ireland, testifying that he was of the king's obedience; and if he did, he was to be deemed a rebel.[1]

The article of *safe-conducts*, which had received some parliamentary sanction in the last reign,[2] was again considered by the legislature; and several regulations were made for the better ordering of those public protections.[3] After this, it was thought so severe a penalty as that of high-treason imposed by stat. 2 Hen. V. stat. i. c. vi. on the violators of safe-conducts might be repealed.[4]

The election and privilege of members of parliament engaged some of the attention of the legislature in this reign. The importance which the lower house was daily assuming, made it necessary to enlarge and adjust the rights they claimed individually as members.

Members of parliament.

The first act concerning members of the lower house is stat. 6

institutions were founded. Nothing more proved this than the development of trial by jury, which in this reign appears to have reached its modern form of a trial upon evidence. In the Year-books of the reign is a case in which it was held that a man might enter the park of another to show him his evidences in a law-suit, and numerous cases show that juries heard evidence and gave their verdicts upon it, and not merely upon their own knowledge. Sir John Fortescue, in his celebrated treatise, *De Laudibus Legum Angliæ,* thus describes the system of trial by jury, and dwells upon it as one of the most distinctive and important of our institutions, especially pointing out that it required an independent body of freemen from which juries could be chosen (*De Laudibus Legum*, c. xxxvi.) In that remarkable treatise, which in itself would be enough to characterise the reign, all the main principles of constitutional law, of civil procedure, and of an intelligent administration of justice, are clearly laid down. He lays it down that a king is appointed to protect his subjects, in their lives, properties, and laws; for this end he has the delegation of power from his subjects, and he has no just claim to any other. The king cannot, in England, levy taxes; he cannot alter the laws or make new laws without the consent of the whole kingdom in parliament assembled. The laws of England in all cases declare in favour of liberty (*Ibid.* c. xii.) No doubt all this was merely laid down in theory. There was a sad contrast in ensuing reigns between the theory and the reality, and it took more than one century, and more than one revolution, to carry out and to realise these great principles. But they were, at all events, laid down for future ages to appeal to; and a reign in which such principles were laid down by one who was a chief-justice and a chancellor may well deserve a separate study and a distinct consideration and regard. The parliaments in this reign showed the progress of a growing jealousy of the exercise of the papal supremacy, which, under the next dynasty, produced a tremendous religious revolution, which, for want of attending to its progress during this reign and the next, is usually regarded as sudden, whereas it was the result of a steady and progressive growth. No new laws were passed against the papal see, but that was only because no further legislation was possible short of absolute separation from Rome. But the laws which had been made were enforced, as the records of parliament and the courts show, with great rigour. The commons petitioned in this reign that no foreigner should be capable of preferment, which betrayed the real motive of the statutes against "provisors" of benefices—*i.e.*, papal presentees. The tone used towards the see of Rome in the courts of law, or in

[1] *Vide* stat. 2 Hen. VI., c. 8.

[2] *Vide ante*, c. xix.

[3] Stat. 15 Hen. VI. c. 3; stat. 18 Hen. VI., c. 8; stat. 20 Hen. VI., c. 1; stat. 29 Hen. VI., c. 2; stat. 31 Hen. VI., c. 4.

[4] Stat. 20 Hen. VI., c. 11.

Hen. VI. c. iv., and relates to their election. By stat. 11 Hen. IV. c. i.[1] the justices of assize had been empowered to inquire by inquests of office of the return of members: it was now ordained, that such members and sheriffs as had inquests of office found against them should be allowed to traverse them, and should not be damaged by such inquest till they were duly convict. In stat. 8 Hen. VI. c. i. it was complained, that as well the clergy who came to convocation, as their servants and familiars coming with them, were commonly arrested and molested; to prevent which it was now ordained, that they and their servants should in future use and enjoy such liberty or defence, in coming, tarrying, and returning, as the great men and commonalty called to parliament enjoyed. What was the privilege they enjoyed may be partly inferred from the following case, mentioned in the rolls of the same year. It is there said, that a servant to William Lake, a burgess for London, being committed to the Fleet in execution for debt, was delivered by the privilege of the commons' house; but authority was given by the chancellor to appoint by commission certain persons to apprehend him after the end of the parliament.[2]

the councils of the realm, was very contemptuous, and this is an infallible indicator of the tendency of public opinion in that direction. In one case in a subsequent reign it was said by the Bishop of London that when the pope wrote letters to Henry VI. in derogation of the royalty, Humphrey, Duke of Gloucester, *put the letters in the fire* (*Year-book*, 1 *Hen. VII.*) An age in which such things were said by prelates was an age in which the papal power had already lost its ascendancy; and it is an important fact that during this period, when anti-papal laws were enforced with the utmost rigour, and the papal supremacy was reduced to a mere name, the chancellor and chief ministers were ecclesiastics, and one of the most powerful and influential persons of this reign was Beaufort, the Cardinal Bishop of Winchester. Both as regards the law and the legislation of this long reign, it had a marked and distinctive character, and in it many statutes of importance were passed which are known by its name, such as the statute as to bail in actions at law, (the basis of our whole system of bail in civil suits,) the statute of forcible entries, one of the most remarkable in our annals, and to this day still in force; the statute of pernors of profits, the first of a series of statutes directed to remedy the inconvenience caused by the separation of the beneficial from the legal interest, by the operation of uses, the laws as to jurors, electors, attorneys; these and other similar statutes certainly are sufficient to give a distinctive character to the legislation of the reign. With regard to the law of this reign, as apart from its legislation, the Year-books of the time have a distinctive character. Lord Hale says that the times of Henry VI. and Edward IV. were times that abounded with learned and excellent men. "There is little difference," he observes, "in the usefulness or learning of these books, only the first part of Henry VI. is more barren, spending itself much in learning of little moment, and now out of use; but the second part is full of excellent learning" (*Hist. Com. Law*, c. viii.) He observes also that "real actions and assizes were not so frequent as formerly, but many titles of land were determined in personal actions, partly because the statute 8 Henry VI. (of forcible entries) helped men to an action to recover their possessions by a writ of forcible entry;" he adds, "even while the method of recovery of possession by actions of ejectment was not known or used." But this statement of Lord Hale's is one in which he was not followed by our author, probably from his not referring to the Year-books themselves, in which it would be seen that though the action of ejectment was used, yet, as most estates in those times were still freehold, and most ejections were actual and forcible, the statute of forcible entries (which only applied, be it observed, to freehold estates) afforded a more frequent remedy (*vide post*, p. 549).

[1] *Vide ante*, c. xix.

[2] Cott. Abri., p. 596, s. 57. *Vide ante*, c. xix.

In the same year we find the famous act for fixing the qualifications of the electors and elected in county elections.[1] The reason for this regulation is stated in the preamble of the act in the following words: "Because elections of knights of shires have now of late been made by very great, outrageous, and excessive numbers of people dwelling within the same counties; of the which most part was of people of small substance, and of no value, whereof every of them pretended a voice equivalent, as to such elections to be made, with the most worthy knights and esquires dwelling within the same counties, whereby manslaughters, riots, batteries, and divisions among the gentlemen and other people of the county shall very likely arise, unless due remedy was provided." The remedy prescribed by the statute[2] is this: that the knights of the shire should be chosen by people dwelling and resident in the county, having free land or tenement to the value of forty shillings by the year at the least above all charges (*a*). The persons

(*a*) The sum of forty shillings, as already has been noticed, was the sum fixed in the reign of Edward I. as the limit of the jurisdiction of the county courts and other inferior courts, and observations have already been made, in commenting upon that regulation, to show that it must have been a very considerable sum in those times. Of this the present enactment affords a remarkable confirmation for a sum fixed as the qualification of the electors or members for parliament, and must have been something considerable. The value of money indeed depends upon so many considerations and comparisons, that it is difficult to get at an accurate idea of its comparative value at different periods in our history. It depends, it is manifest, not merely on the price or value of the precious metals, but upon the price or value of commodities and the purchasing power of money at the time; that is, as the "price or value" of coin and commodities must be correlative terms—the one being the measure of the other, and representing how much of one can be got for a certain quantity of the other, they must needs be closely connected; and really represent rather the relative degrees of plenty or scarcity at different periods than any precise calculation of equivalents. The only way to get at an idea of the real practical amount or effect of a pecuniary qualification or limitation is therefore to see *what so much money would buy or procure of necessary commodities* at the time when it existed. And as prices have constantly *risen* since the reign of Edward I., and now are enormously, almost incalculably, higher than they were then, the difference in the relative value of money will be found to be immense. The matter is one which, from its nature, defies calculation, and can only be understood by these comparisons and actual illustrations. Nor are there wanting numerous data for the purpose, many of them to be gathered from the law books. The first, the fundamental *datum*, is the price of *corn*. Now in the reign of Edward I., as we find from Britton, corn was often, indeed ordinarily, at twelvepence per quarter; for in that reign such was the price fixed as the rate at which the assize of bread was to be calculated: "De quant le quarter de frument est vendu a xiid.," &c. (fol. 74). And in the Year-books of Edward IV., is a case in which it was held, that a cart loaded with corn, with the two horses attached to it, could not be an excessive distress for the sum of four shillings; while, in the same reign, there was a ballad, the well-known ballad of the *Tanner of Tamworth*, in which the tanner is represented as boasting of a horse for which he had, he said, given four shillings. The rate of wages settled by a statute of 1491, the statute of labourers, fixed the yearly wages of a farm-bailiff at the sum of forty shillings, including his clothing. And a man's diet was estimated, in the same statute, to cost 2d. a day; a sum amply sufficient, seeing that long afterwards, in the reign of Henry VIII., an act was made (24 and 25 Hen. VIII.) settling the price of beef at *a halfpenny per pound*. And in the household of a great nobleman 2½d. was estimated as the whole daily expense of a servant, including meat, drink, and firing (Wade's *Hist. of Eng.*, p. 108). These data may suffice to show that 40s. in the time of Henry VI. represented at least £40 or £50 now.

[1] *Vide ante*, c. xix.

[2] Ch. 7.

chosen were also to be dwelling and resident within the county The statute further provides, that he who had the greatest number of those who might expend forty shillings a year as aforesaid should be returned by the sheriff, by indenture sealed between the sheriff and the choosers; and the sheriff had authority given him to examine upon the Evangelists every such chooser how much he expended by the year. If the sheriff returned any one contrary to this act, the justices of assize might inquire of it; and if the sheriff was attainted thereof by inquest, he was to forfeit one hundred pounds to the king, and to be imprisoned for a year without bail or mainprise. Moreover, the knights were to lose their wages. In addition to the above affirmative designation of qualified voters there was annexed, in abundant caution, this negative clause, that those who could not expend forty shillings per annum as aforesaid should not be choosers. It was further enacted, that in all writs to sheriffs to elect knights mention should be made of this act.

It appears by the wording of this statute that the qualification of electors was narrowed, and thereby numbers of the inferior people excluded; but what was the particular description of those people, and what was the qualification of electors before this act, is a question much agitated by writers on the constitution of parliament. To such writers we refer the reader, this being a point not within the compass of a work principally confined to subjects of a juridical nature. In the 10th year of the king,[1] this new regulation received an amendment; for, as it was not specified whether the freehold should be in the county where the elector dwelt, it was now declared that it should. To prevent any personal insult to members of either house it was enacted by stat. 11 Hen. VI. c. 11, that if any assault or affray was made upon a lord spiritual or temporal, knight of the shire or burgess, come either to parliament or to any other council of the king, and there attending, proclamation should be made for the offender to appear in the king's bench within a quarter of a year, otherwise he should stand attainted of the fact, and pay the party grieved his double damages, (to be taxed by the justices or inquest,) and should likewise be fined to the king. The method of levying the wages of knights of the shire was prescribed by stat. 23 Hen. VI. c. 11. They were to be assessed in the county court, after proclamation for the attendance of the coroners and chief constables; and severe penalties were inflicted on sheriffs who failed in the levy or payment thereof to knights.

The order of electing members to serve for counties, cities, and boroughs was reconsidered in the 23d year of the king,[2] when reference being made to stat. 1 Hen. V. c. 1,[3] and stat. 8 Hen. VI. c. 7, it was ordained that those acts should be fully observed. But because a sufficient penalty had not been provided as a security for their observance, it was now enacted as follows: That every sheriff, after delivery of the writ to him, should make and deliver

[1] Ch. 2. [2] Ch. 15. [3] *Vide ante*, c. xix.

a sufficient precept under his seal to every mayor and bailiff within the county, reciting the writ, and commanding him by such precept to elect citizens and burgesses to come to parliament; which precept was to be returned to the sheriff by indenture between them, declaring the election and the persons chosen, and the sheriff was to make a return thereof, together with the writ. Every person acting contrary to this or other acts for election of members was to incur the penalty ordained by stat. 8 Hen. VI., and moreover pay to every person chosen, but not returned, (or any other who would sue in his default,) £100 with costs, to be demanded in an action of debt, wherein no wager of law or essoin should be allowed. Mayors and bailiffs were in the like case to incur the penalty of £40, and pay in like manner £40 to the party injured, or those who sued. A sheriff not making due election in convenient time, (that is, in full county, between the hours of eight and eleven in the forenoon,) and not making a good and true return of such election of knights, was to forfeit £100 to the king, and £100 to the party suing; but these actions against the sheriff by the party grieved were to be instituted within three months after the parliament commenced; if not, the cause of action would lapse to another. At the end of this act, there is a clause requiring that the knights of shires should be notable knights of the county for which they were chosen, or otherwise such notable esquires, gentlemen[1] of the same county as were able to become knights, and no man of the degree of a yeoman[2] or under. Thus stood the election and qualification of members of parliament at the close of this reign.

Next to those that relate to the parliament are to be considered such acts as were made for regulating certain classes of individuals, such as servants, labourers, persons exercising various trades, and other matters of a miscellaneous kind.

The policy which had been marked out by the statutes of labourers, passed in the reign of Edw. III.,[3] was still pursued; while many changes were made therein, as occasion required, the general course and order of it continued the same[4] (*a*). Some immaterial alteration was also made in the statutes of livery and maintenance.[5] While these provisions were framing for the government of the inferior orders of the people, the interest of trade was considered, and many statutes passed to prescribe rules and bounds to be observed by merchants and traders in their dealings.[6] The numerous provisions made by parliament for the protection of the coin and bullion, were other instances of the great solicitude now felt for the advancement of commerce.[7] The staple of Calais was kept

(*a*) They were rapidly, however, becoming inapplicable by reason of the growth of trade; and in the reign of Elizabeth were virtually superseded by another statute, which in its turn was superseded by the act of Geo. IV., the master and servants act.

[1] *Gentils hommes del nativite.* [2] *Vadlet.* [3] *Vide ante*, c. xiii.
[4] Stat. 6 Hen. VI., c. 3; Stat. 23 Hen. IV., c. 13. [5] Stat. 8 Hen. VI., c. 4.
[6] Stat. 2 Hen. VI., c. 7.
[7] Stat. 1 Hen. VI., c. 1, 4, 6; stat. 2 Hen. VI., c. 6, 9, 12, 13, 14; stat. 8 Hen. VI., c. 24; stat. 27 Hen. VI., c. 3.

up with great strictness.[1] Instead of any new statutes against purveyors, those already made were directed to be proclaimed in every county four times a year.[2] Some acts relating to escheats and other points arising in the management of the revenue accruing from tenures, are little worthy of notice.[3]

There are two statutes relating to the jurisdiction of the council and chancery.

Of the council and chancery.

In the thirty-first year[4] of the king a statute was passed to give effect to the process by which persons were brought before the council (*a*). This act is very particular in the terms of it; and as it throws some light upon the nature of that jurisdiction, it may be proper to state it minutely, leaving the reader to make that application of it which the former part of this history will naturally dictate. It says, that upon suggestions and complaints made as well to the king as to the lords of his council against persons for *riots*, *oppressions*, and *grievous offence* by them done against the peace and laws, he used to give commandment by writs under his great seal, and by his letters of privy seal, to appear before him and his chancery, or before him and his council, to answer for the above offences. Because these writs had not met with regular obedience, it was now ordained that where such writ or letter issued, commanding any one to appear before the king or *his council*, and the person refused to receive it, or withdrew himself, or did not appear, and such disobedience was duly certified to the council, then the chancellor should have power to direct writs of proclamation into the county where the party dwelt, or the next adjoining county, *and also* into London, commanding the sheriff, under the penalty of £200, to make open proclamation in the shire-town and in the city three several days immediately after delivery of the writ, for the party to appear before the council or the chancellor within a month after the last day

(*a*) There can be no doubt that this was what afterwards, under the Tudor dynasty, was called the "Star Chamber." From the earliest times, before the superior courts of law had become established, the king's council exercised a kind of controlling or appellate jurisdiction over the old common law courts of the country—the county courts—supplying defects and failures of justice, and hearing complaints of miscarriages either in civil or criminal tribunals. By degrees, as the superior courts became established, the *ordinary* administration of justice came under their jurisdiction; but the king's council still retained and exercised its ancient and extraordinary jurisdiction, which, although liable to be abused, was, as Hume observes, useful in that turbulent age, for the purpose of repressing outrages, disturbances of justice, or audacious violations of law. In Hudson's learned and elaborate "*Treatise of the Court of the Star Chamber*," which was approved of by Finch, who was chief-justice and lord-keeper, and cited by Lord Mansfield (4 *Burrows*, 2554), a great number of instances are adduced of the exercise of this jurisdiction by the king's council, to which he traces the origin of the court which, under the Tudors, was distinguished by its well-known name. And it is very observable that this author describes the power and jurisdiction of the council as having vastly grown and augmented during the reign of Henry VI., especially during his long minority, when the council practically administered the whole royal power. Further on, in the next chapter, the author mentions a case debated in the Star Chamber (*vide post*).

[1] Stat. 2 Hen. VI., c. 4, 5.

[2] Stat. 1 Hen. VI., c. 2.

[3] Stat. 8 Hen. VI., c. 10; stat. 18 Hen. VI., c. 7; stat. 23 Hen. VI., c. 17; stat. 39 Hen. VI., c. 2.

[4] Ch. 2.

of proclamation; the writ to be returned into the chancery within seven days after the proclamation, under the same penalty.

If the party did not appear within the month, then he was to forfeit, if a lord, all offices, fees, annuities, and other possessions that he, or any one to his use, had of the grant of the crown; and if upon the issuing of a second writ and proclamation he still made default, he was to forfeit his estate and name of lord, and place in parliament. If he had no grant from the crown, then he was to forfeit his name and estate of lord, and place in parliament, and also all his lands and tenements; but all the above forfeitures were only for life. If the party was a commoner, he was to be punished for disobedience to the first writ by fine, at the discretion of the two chief-justices; but if he had no livelihood whereof to pay a fine, he was to be put out of the king's protection. There was the usual proviso in favour of persons under the disabilities of sickness, imprisonment, being out of the realm, and the like.

While the legislature by this statute gave new vigour and energy to the authority of the council, they did not forget the regard which should be paid to the courts of common law; for in the conclusion of it the statute declares, that no matter determinable by the law of the realm should be determined otherwise than by the course of the law in the king's courts.

The same jealousy as formerly[1] was entertained of the new jurisdiction exercised by the chancery. In the second year of the king, we find a petition to parliament praying that no man be bound to answer in the chancery for a matter determinable at common law, under the penalty of £20, to be paid by the plaintiff suing there,[2] the answer to which was, that the stat. 17 Ric. II. should be executed.[3] It was upon the idea suggested by this petition that stat. 15 Hen. VI. c. 4 was passed, by which it is enacted that no writ of *subpœna* should be granted till surety was found to satisfy the party grieved and vexed for his damage and expense, if the matter of the bill should not be made good.

The authority of other courts was affected by the interference of parliament. It was complained, that the steward and marshal held pleas of debt, detinue, and other personal actions between parties who were not of the king's household;[4] and that when they were mentioned in the record to be of the household, they were not permitted to take their exception to such allegation. It was enacted by stat. 15 Hen. VI. c. 1, that in every surety thenceforward to be taken for a defendant, he should not be estopped by the record, to say that himself or the plaintiff was not of the king's house, as supposed by the record. By stat. 24 Hen. VI. c. i., justices of *nisi prius* were empowered to give judgment in all cases of felony and treason, as well upon acquittal as conviction, and to award execution. By chap. iii. of the same act, the assizes for Cumberland are directed to be held at Carlisle.

[1] *Vide ante*, c. xix.
[2] Cott. Abri., p. 566, s. 41.
[3] *Vide ante*, c. xix.
[4] *Ibid.*, c. xiv.

The following are the few alterations made in the course of proceeding in different actions. Some statutes were made in this reign to correct some of the inconveniences that followed from the late device of separating the legal from the equitable estate; the object of which was to make[1] the *pernor of the profits*, as he was called, liable to such demands and burthens as he would be subject to, if he was legally seised of the freehold (*a*). The first act of this kind is stat. 11 Hen. VI. c. iii. It had been held, that the stat. 4 Hen. VI. c. vii.[2] was confined to an assize of novel disseisin; but by this act it was declared, that the same remedy might be had in all manner of writs grounded upon novel disseisin. Again, because tenants for life, and for years, would let their estate to persons unknown to their lessors, but still continued to occupy and take the profits to their own use, and commit waste, it was enacted by chap. v. of the same act, that the reversioner might maintain a writ of waste against such pernors of the profits, as well after as before the grant.

Statutes of pernors of profits.

An act was made to prevent plaintiffs in assize charging the sheriff as a disseisor, in order that the writ might be directed to the coroners: it was provided by stat. 11 Hen. VI. c. ii. that the tenant might aver that the sheriff was not a disseisor, nor tenant, but was named disseisor by collusion; and if it was so found, the writ was to be quashed, and the plaintiff amerced.

Some helps were contrived for rendering the proceeding by attaint more expeditious and effectual. The delay of attaints was heavily complained of. It was said, that when the grand jury appeared in court, and were ready to pass, one of the tenants or defendants, or one of the petty jurors named in the writ, would plead false and feigned pleas not triable by the grand jury, so that the taking of the grand jury was delayed till such pleas were tried; and after such pleas had been tried for the plaintiffs, another of the jurors, tenants, or defendants, would plead another feigned plea, *puis darrein continuance;* the rest might do the same; and though all were found against them, they were subject, says the act, to *no pain*. In order, therefore, to prevent such studied delays, it was provided by stat. 11 Hen. VI. c. iv. that the plaintiffs in such attaints should recover their damages and costs against all such tenants, jurors, and defendants. When it is considered that there

Attaints.

(*a*) "Pernor of the profits" was he who took the profits of the land as real *owner*, not as mere landlord; and thus, where a plaintiff charged the defendant as pernor of the profits, and he said that he took nothing but as rent incident to the reversion, it was held a good answer (*Year-book*, 22 *Hen. VI.*, fol. 16). Where two disseisors made a feoffment, and one took the profits to the use of the other, they were both charged as "pernors" generally (*Year-book*, 39 *Hen. VI.*, fol. 65). The statutes of pernors of profits prove that uses were at common law, for the pernancy of the profits is a use (27 *Hen. VIII.*, 8). And uses were at common law, though before the statute of *Quia emptores* (*Edw. I.*) they were not common (*Bro. Abr.*, fol. 331, pl. 40); for the statute of Marlbridge (*temp. Hen. III.*) was directed against feoffments to uses, to deprive lords of the benefits of feudal tenure (27 *Hen. VIII.*, 8).

[1] *Vide ante*, c. xix. [2] *Ibid.*

could not be less than thirteen defendants in an attaint, and that each of these might have a several plea, it is easy to conjecture to what a number of obstacles it was liable. The last mentioned act being thought too general, it was ordained by stat. 15 Hen. VI. c. v. (*a*), that should any foreign plea he found against the defendant, there should be the same judgment against him as if the grand jury had passed against him, without any prejudice to the co-defendants. The same statute provided likewise for the qualifications of jurors in attaints, as did also stat. 18 Hen. VI. c. ii.

In some cases of a particular kind, a special mode of redress was prescribed by several statutes. It had often happened that women were stolen away, and till they had signed some obligation or engagement for payment of money, sometimes married by force, or kept under restraint. As a more expeditious remedy than the law hitherto had provided, it was ordained by stat. 31 Hen. VI. c. ix. that in all such cases the party bound might have a writ out of chancery, containing the matter of complaint, and commanding the sheriff to make *proclamation* in the next full county after receipt of the writ, for the person offending to appear at a certain day before the chancellor or the justices of assize for the county, or some other *notable person* to be assigned by the chancellor, who was to examine the parties; and if the obligations were found to be so made, they were to be declared void, as well as all process and execution thereon, whether the offender appeared at the day or not. There was a penalty of three hundred pounds upon sheriffs not executing the writ, half to the king, and half to the party suing the writ, to be recovered in an action of debt, in which action no protection, wager of law, or foreign plea, was to be allowed.

The writ of proclamation was applied in another instance by stat. 33 Hen. VI. c. 1, where servants availing themselves of the consternation prevailing in the family upon the death of their master, would violently and riotously take away the goods of the deceased: it was by that statute provided, that in such cases the chancellor, by the advice of the chief-justices and the chief-baron, or two of them, should, upon the application of two executors at least, direct such writs as they thought proper to sheriffs, to make proclamation in cities, boroughs, towns, or other places, two market-days, within the space of twelve days next after delivery of the same writs, to appear in the king's bench at a certain day, so as the last proclamation should be made within fifteen days before the day of appearance. If the writ was returned, and the party did not appear at the day, he was to be attainted of felony: if he appeared, he was to be committed to prison, till he answered to such actions as should be brought against him by the executors, either by bill or by writ, for the aforesaid riot, taking and spoiling, provided the action was brought without delay, and not in order to keep the offender mali-,

(*a*) This subject was dealt with by the statutes of Henry VII. and Henry VIII. where it will be found fully treated of in the next volume (*et vide post*, p. 540).

ciously in prison. This act, like the former, contains penalties for the neglect of those who were intrusted with the execution of it. Executors had before been provided with a new remedy for keeping together the effects of the deceased, by stat. 9 Hen. VI. c. iv., which gave them the writ of *idemptitate nominis*[1] in the same manner as the testator might before have had it.

The remaining statutes concerning the administration of justice relate either to process and proceeding in general, or to the methods of trial, and the duty incumbent on officers of courts. Some statutes of *jeofail* and amendment were passed. The first act of this sort, which was made in the time of Edward III., had been extended by an act of the last king,[2] to amendments as well after judgment as before; but this statute, being temporary, had expired with that king's reign: it was therefore now afresh enacted by stat. 4 Hen. VI. c. iii. that the act of Edward III. should be in force in every record and process, as well after judgment given upon a verdict passed, as upon a matter in law pleaded; and moreover, that it should be perpetual; but it was not to extend to records and processes in Wales, nor to proceedings where process of outlawry lay. After reviving the statutes of Henry V. and that of Edward III., the legislature made further provision on the subject of amendments. It was enacted by stat. 8 Hen. VI. c. xii. that for error assigned in any record, process, or warrant of attorney, original or judicial writ, panel, or return in any places of the same rased or interlined, or in any addition, subtraction, or diminution of words, letters, titles, or parcel of letters found therein, no judgment should be reversed, or record annulled; but that the judges of the court should have power, with their clerks, to examine the same, and reform and amend (in affirmance of the judgment of such records and processes) all that which to them, in their discretion, seemed to be misprision of the clerks, so that no judgment should be reversed, or record annulled, by reason of such misprision. Out of this act are excepted all appeals and indictments of treason and felony, and outlawries for the same; nor was it to extend to cases where the substance of the proper names, surnames, or additions were left out in original writs or writs of exigent, according to stat. 1 Hen. V. c. 5, or in other writs containing proclamations.

Statutes of jeofail.

Some further regulations were made by this act respecting records. If any record, process, writ, warrant of attorney, return, or pannel, was certified defectively, it might now, upon the challenge of the party, be reformed, and amended according to the original; and if such original, being in any of the four courts at Westminster, or in the treasury of such courts, was stolen by any clerk or other person, by reason whereof any judgment should be reversed, he and his aiders were to be considered as felons. This fact was to be tried by the judges of the two benches, and a jury, half of which was to

[1] *Vide ante*, c. xix.

[2] *Ibid.*

consist of men belonging to the courts. Again, it was provided by ch. xv. of the same statute, that the king's justices should amend all misprisions or defaults in records or processes, or in the returns of the same, made by sheriffs, coroners, bailiffs of franchises, or others, by misprisions of clerks of the court, the sheriffs, or their clerks and other ministers, in writing one syllable too much or too little. Thus did the statute follow almost the words of the statute of Edward III., with the same exception of records and process in Wales, and those of outlawry in felony and treason.

Some laws were made for the better ordering of juries. Because, in *special* assizes, the parties were not furnished with pannels of the jurors before[1] (*a*) the day of the sessions, and therefore had not time to see that they were all duly qualified, it

Juries.

(*a*) At this time, trial by jury appears to have advanced very near to what it became in modern times—a trial by the jury, not on their own knowledge, but on the evidence of witnesses. For in the Year-books of this reign there is a case in which it was held that one might enter the park of another to show him his evidence in a law-suit (*Year-book*, 17 *Hen. VI.*, fol. 1). It had taken some centuries, however, to bring trial by jury to this; for originally the jurors were witnesses, and determined on their own knowledge. This might suit the usages of a primitive age. It had been found, however, as the transactions of life grew more numerous, and less open and public, that cases must be decided on the evidence of witnesses examined before the jurors. This is well put by Fortescue, c. 26: "Twelve good and lawful men being sworn, &c., then either party, by himself or his counsel, shall open to them all matters and evidences whereby he thinketh he may best inform them of the truth; and then may either party bring before them all such witnesses on his behalf as he will produce . . . not unknown witnesses, but neighbours," &c. And then in c. 28: "The witnesses make their depositions in the presence of twelve creditable men, neighbours to the deed that is in question, and to the circumstances of the same, and who also know the manners and conditions of the witnesses, and know whether they be men worthy to be credited or not." At that time, it will be observed, the jury had ceased to determine merely upon their own knowledge, and had evidence given before them, on which they gave their verdict. This rendered it still important that they should come from the locality whence the witnesses came. From and after the time of Edward III. we find frequent mention of "evidence" in the cases in the Year-books, though the jury were still required to find upon, and take cognisance of, any facts within their own knowledge, whether or not formally proved, or given in evidence. This often put them in great difficulty, as there were facts of which it was presumed they had knowledge, of which they in truth had not knowledge, and hence they took refuge in special verdicts. It has already been mentioned in the reign of Edward I., under the head of "special verdict," and "bill of exceptions," that the jury were allowed, on account of any doubt on their minds as to the legal effect of the facts proved, to set them forth at large in a special verdict, which protected them from any liability under an "attaint," for a verdict contrary to facts, not indeed proved, but presumed to be within their knowledge. Thus, if the disseisee re-entered and enfeoffed the disseisor, and then brought assize against him, and recovered, the feoffment not being pleaded or given in evidence, the jury would be liable on an attaint; for that they ought to have taken notice of the brief of seisin, which was presumed to be a fact open and notorious in the "vill;" though otherwise of a release, as that was a particular fact of a private nature, which would require to be given in evidence. But if the jury found the facts specially, and set them forth in the verdict as proved, referring it to the court, then they would not be liable (assuming the verdict true according to the evidence), for then the judgment would be that of the court (43 *Assize*, fol. 41; 29 *Assize*, fol. 40). Hence the special verdict was a resource for the jury in cases of doubt as to the facts, and also in cases of doubt as to the law; as they set forth the facts, and referred the matter to the discretion of the court (38 *Assize*, fol. 9; 43 *Assize*, fol. 1). There was often doubt as to what matters a jury could take cognisance of as occurring in

[1] *Vide ante*, c. xiv.

was enacted by stat. 6 Hen. VI. c. 2, that the panels should be arrayed, and an indented copy thereof delivered by the sheriff to the parties (if they demanded it) six days at least before the sessions of the justices. The jury *de medietate*, which had been granted by stat. 28 Edw. III. c. xiii.,[1] was thought to be repealed by stat. 2 Hen. V. st. 2, c. iii., which requires jurors to be freeholders, a qualification that could not possibly be enjoyed by aliens. To repel this inconvenient construction, it was enacted by stat. 8 Hen. VI. c. xxix., that those qualifications should extend only to inquests to be taken between denizen and denizen. Because the sheriff or his officers were often bribed to return favourable juries, an action was given by stat. 18 Hen. VI. c. xiv., to recover ten times the money given for such purposes; and what is remarkable, the statute authorises the justices to inquire of the truth, *as well by examination of the defendant* in such suit for the penalty, as by an inquest. But this was only a temporary act, and expired with the then parliament. Another temporary act directed,[2] that all foreign pleas, pleaded after the return of the *venire*, should be tried where the writ was brought (*a*). Some other statutes upon the

a "foreign" county, *i.e.*, a county different from that in which the action was brought, and the case tried (*Year-book, 7 Edw. IV.*, fol. 15), and this difficulty led necessarily to the trial of cases more upon evidence of witnesses than on personal knowledge by the jurors. The truth is, that the nature of trial necessarily, but gradually, altered as the nature of the transactions and affairs of life altered. When these were few and simple, open and public, and matter of general notoriety in the neighbourhood, the jurors who came from the neighbourhood could certify of their own knowledge; but as the affairs of life became more numerous and complicated, and also more private, the jurors of necessity had to listen to *evidence* upon them, and give their verdicts more and more upon facts proved. The change was very gradual; and through even this reign we find distinctions drawn between feoffments with livery of seisin (*i.e.*, open transfer of possession) and private writings, such as deeds or written contracts, of which, from their nature, juries could only know by their being put in evidence before them; and it was said that they could only take cognisance (*i.e.*, of their own knowledge) of facts done upon the land, such as seisin or disseisin, and the like, but of private contracts or conveyances they would require express proof (*Year-book, 7 Hen. VI.*)

(*a*) The law had attached great importance to the trial of cases by jurors who came from the localities where the matter arose. For originally they gave their verdicts of their own knowledge, and even now, when they had tried cases on the evidence of witnesses of which they were to judge, it was important that they should come from the place where the witnesses lived, which would usually be where the matter arose. This advantage, however, was counterbalanced in that turbulent age by the violence which was often exercised by parties interested, to overawe juries and influence their verdicts. Many cases could be cited to illustrate this. An assize was arrayed before Sir William Babington and Strange, in the county of Cumberland, and it was adjourned before them at Westminster, and Fulthorpe asked of the justices the cause of the adjournment, and Babington said, that it was because it was a great matter, and the parties in their own counties came with great routs of armed men, more as though they were going to battle than to an assize ("les parties en leur propre counties, viendront ove graund routs des gents armes, pluis semble pur vener a battaile que al assize"), and so for danger of the peace being disturbed, and also that counsel were in London, and the parties could be better seised in their right, the case was adjourned (*Year-book, 7 Hen. VI.*) See Year-book 32 Hen. VI., 9, where a trial in the county was denied in a cause between the Duke of Exeter and Lord Cromwell, because there had been a great rout, and a greater would ensue if

[1] *Vide ante*, c. xiv.

[2] Stat. 23 Hen. VI., c. 12.

same subject were made at different times in this reign, but, being of short continuance, were soon forgotten.[1]

It seems, that the officers of the court would sometimes make the entry of *obtulit se in propriâ personâ*, when in truth the plaintiff had never appeared; but it was ordained by stat. 10 Henry VI. c. iv. that no filazer, exigenter, or other officer, should make such entry, unless the plaintiff appeared in proper person before some of the justices where the plea was depending, and was there sworn upon a book, that he was the same person. The act permits that his counsel, or some other person, might make the oath for him. Again, because in many outlawries the entry was, that the parties appeared by their attorney, where, in truth, the attornies had no warrant of record, on which account the outlawries used to be reversed, it was enacted, that every attorney, who had not his warrant entered of record in all suits wherein process of *capias* and *exigent* were awardable, the same term in which the *capias* was awarded, or before, should be fined forty shillings by the justices.

It was endeavoured to put the office of sheriff, and other minis-

the trial should take place there, for my Lord of Exeter is a great and potent prince in that county ("un graund et prepotent prince"). The *Paston Letters* afford many instances of similar proceedings at assizes about the same period. In modern times the courts have always recognised that it is good cause for removing a case into another county for trial, that there is a popular excitement and doubt of the possibility of fair trial. Nor was it only from violence that the integrity of trial by jury was interfered with or endangered; it was also in danger from acts of seduction or corruption of a very coarse and vulgar character. For it seems that our ancestors, by reason of their robust appetites, suffered severely from their seclusion in the jury-box, the rule being, that after they had gone from the bar to consider their verdict, they could not be allowed to eat or drink (2 *Hen. IV.*, 21). Hence they were peculiarly open to the temptation presented for eating and drinking, and hence "manger et boyer" is a common head in the Year-books for cases of verdicts alleged to be vitiated from this cause, *i.e.*, from irregular eating and drinking by the jurors. The courts had often to consider these cases, and found them so frequent, that if they had held the mere irregularity enough to avoid or vitiate a verdict, probably few verdicts would have stood; and hence they laid it down, that the mere eating and drinking would not have this effect, unless it was at the cost of one or other of the parties, and the *verdict went for that party*, in which case, they held the verdict vitiated by the corruption; otherwise, though the jurors would be punishable for the irregularity, their verdict would stand (*Year-book*, 14 *Hen. VII.*, 29; 20 *Hen. VII.*, 3). And if they separated and went at large, and ate and drank, it was thought so suspicious that their verdict was not taken (*Year-book*, 24 *Edw. III.*, fol. 24). One of the cases on the subject is so curious an illustration of the usages of the age, that it may well be quoted here. In a case tried in Essex, between a bishop and the county of Kent, the jury were sworn at the bar, and when the evidence was about to be given to them, there came a great storm of wind and rain, and the jury went away, "*as they were standing in the street unsheltered!*" and one juror went into a house, where they said to him that he should take care what he did, for the case was better for the county than the bishop, and they prayed him to eat and drink, and he did so; and afterwards the storm ceased, and the jury returned and were put into an inn, and they found for the bishop. And the matter being shown to the court, they thought that the juror was punishable, but that the verdict was not vitiated, as it was *against* the county; though it seems it would have been otherwise if it had been for the county (*Year-book*, 14 *Hen. VII.*, 29). Such were the perils of trial by jury in those days.

[1] Stat. 4 Hen. VI., c. 1, 2; stat. 8 Hen. VI., c. 13; stat. 11 Hen. VI., c. 7; stat. 20 Hen. VI., c. 2; stat. 33 Hen. VI., c. 7.

ters of justice, upon a footing which would render the execution of them more regular, effectual, and incorrupt (*a*). Two acts had been made in the reign of Edward III.,[1] ordaining that no sheriff should stay in office more than a year: again, by stat. 1 Richard II. c. xi. no one who had served was to be chosen again within three years. Notwithstanding these acts, it seems that sheriffs used to be continued ten or twelve years in their office, which led to great abuses in the administration of it. To prevent these, it was now again enacted by stat. 23 Henry VI. c. viii. that the former statute should, in future, be duly observed; with an exception of the under-sheriffs, and all other officers in the city of London; of such counties where several persons were inheritable to the office, and had a freehold therein; as also with an exception of letters-patent made of the office, and the under-sheriffs and clerks of such patentees. And it was further ordained, that if any sheriff, under-sheriff, or sheriff's clerk, occupied his office in violation of the above acts (with the above exception), he should forfeit £200 yearly, half to the king and half to the person suing, as long as he continued therein. All pardons of this offence, and all patents granting the office for years, for life, or in fee, contrary to this act, are declared void, notwithstanding any clause of *non obstante;* and the persons accepting such patents are declared for ever disabled to hold the office.

Sheriffs and execution of process.

This act was succeeded by another in the same year,[2] containing several regulations for their government in discharging their office, and that of others in the like employment, as under-sheriffs and their clerks, coroners, stewards of franchises, bailiffs, and keepers of prisons. It was enacted, in order to avoid *perjury*, *extortion*, *and oppression*, that no sheriff should in any manner let to ferm his county, or any of his bailiwicks, hundreds, or wapentakes, as had been[3] before forbid by several acts; nor should any sheriff, under-sheriff, bailiff of franchises, or other bailiff, return upon an inquest any bailiffs, officers, or servants of any of the before-mentioned officers; and that none of them should, by occasion or colour of his office, take anything by himself or by others to his use, profit, or avail, from any person by them to be arrested or attached, for omitting an arrest or attachment, or for showing ease

(*a*) Upon this subject our author had forgotten one or two statutes of considerable importance at the time when they were passed, as to abuses of escheators or other similar officers in taking what are called "inquests of office," by which the Crown became entitled to property. By 8 Henry VI. c. xvi., lands seized by the escheator are not to be let to farm before the office was fully returned, which was to be done in a month. By 18 Henry VI. c. vi., no lands were to be granted before the king's title was found by inquisition. The recitals to these statutes show that enormous abuses prevailed in this matter, and they were the subject of numerous cases in the Year-book of this and the ensuing reigns. If a man aliened land in mortmain without licence, the title to it would not be vested in the king without "office found" (*Year-book,* 9 *Henry VI.* 22); so as to the lands of a party in outlawry (9 *Henry VI.* 20); so in the case of a tenant of the king dying (3 *Henry VI.* 5). The cases in which an office was necessary in that age were innumerable.

[1] *Vide ante*, c. xiv. [2] Ch. 10. [3] *Vide ante*, c. xiv.

or favour, except only the fee of twenty pence to the sheriff, and four pence each to the bailiff and the gaoler, if he was committed to ward. Nor were they to take for the making of any return, or pannel, and the copy of a pannel, more than four pence.

After these restrictions as to fees, there follows the famous clause concerning letting to bail upon arrests, which is worded in the following way (*a*): That sheriffs, and all other officers and ministers above mentioned, should let out of prison all manner of persons arrested by them, or being in their custody by force of any writ, bill, or warrant in any action personal, or by cause of indictment of trespass, upon *reasonable sureties of sufficient perons, having sufficient within the counties* where such persons were let to bail or

(*a*) It appears plainly from this statute, and from the cases both before and after it, that the object of arrest and "mainprise" was to enforce appearance (47 *Edward III.* 21), which long before this statute might be by attorney (1 *Henry VI.* 4). Thus in the reign of Henry IV., after *capias* had issued, and the sheriff had returned *non est inventus*, the defendant appeared by attorney, and it was objected that he could not do so, but must appear in person, as a *capias* had been awarded against him; but it was held otherwise (*Year-book*, 3 *Henry IV.* 2). There was, it is to be observed, a distinction between mainprise and bail—mainpernors being sureties for the person (42 *Edward III.* 7); bail being for appearance (7 *Henry VI.* 4)—and it appears that before the act mainprise was allowed (47 *Edward III.* 21; 11 *Henry IV.* 57). But mainpernors however forfeited nothing on non-appearance (39 *Henry VI.* 21); but it was otherwise of bail, and hence the statute requires sufficient sureties. The statute, it is to be observed, speaks of the party "keeping their days," *i.e.*, appearing at the return of the process. Just before the act it was held that a party could not be allowed to appear when the process was not returned served, except in cases where a *capias* could be issued (22 *Henry VI.* 20); but in such cases, to avoid arrest, he might do so; and after the act it was held, that in an action personal, the defendant not appearing at the return of the original, the plaintiff could have an award of a *capias* (27 *Henry VI.* 23). If a man had mainprise, and "kept not his day," *capias* should issue against him and his mainpernor (2 *Henry IV.* 14). After appearance, the process in personal actions was distress (*distringas*), and so *ad infinitum*, not outlawry, which only lay before appearance (21 *Henry VI.* 50). The statute required the sheriff to take reasonable, *i.e.*, sufficient sureties, that is, sufficient to satisfy the debt (11 *Henry VI.* 31), whereas mainpernors were only sureties for appearance, and were merely finable, not liable for the debt (11 *Henry VI. fol.* 31). Upon this construction a practice was established, upon which security was required not merely for the appearance, but for the satisfaction of debt and costs at any termination of the suit in favour of the plaintiff,—that is to say, after "common bail," as it was called, had been taken by the sheriff for appearance, "special bail," or security for the claim, was taken for the benefit of the suitor; and this was by force of judicial construction upon the general terms of the statute, "reasonable surety" for "keeping their days," *i.e.*, not merely appearance at the return of the writ, but appearance at any time afterwards when required. There might be default after as well as before appearance, and, as already seen, after appearance there was only *distringas*, until final judgment, on which a *capias* could issue, and so to secure the plaintiff, bail to the action was taken to the full amount of debt and costs. That the object of the arrest was only to enforce appearance is manifest from an exposition of the statute almost contemporaneous; for, in the reign of Edward IV., it was held that the bail-bond must be given to the sheriff by the defendant, and to "keep his day" (*i.e.*, the day for appearance), and therefore that if the bond was given to the plaintiff it was void (7 *Edward IV. fol.* 6). Thus it appeared that the form of bond to be taken by the sheriff was that the obligor, the defendant, would keep his day in the court out of which the *capias* issued (7 *Edward IV.*, *fol.* 6). The bond therefore, was not for security of the plaintiff, but of the sheriff, who was bound to have the defendant in court on the day for appearance, and was only bound to that and nothing more, and so took the bond for that and nothing more. The practice of taking special bail had no warrant in the express terms of any statute.

mainprise, to keep their days in such places, as the said writs, bills, or warrants required; with an exception of the following persons, namely, those in ward by condemnation, execution, *capias utlagatum*, or *excommunicatum*, surety of the peace, those committed by special commandment of any justice, and vagabonds refusing to serve according to the statute of labourers. Nor was the sheriff, or officers before mentioned, to take an obligation for the above causes, or by colour of their office, but only to themselves, and by the name of their office, and upon condition written, that the prisoner should appear at the day and place contained in the writ, bill, or warrant; and all other obligations taken by colour of their office were declared void; fourpence was the utmost he was to take for making such obligation, warrant, or precept. It was further ordained, that all sheriffs should yearly appoint a deputy in the court of chancery, king's bench, common pleas, and exchequer, to receive all writs and warrants to be delivered to them; and this was to be done before they returned any writs. Any of the above officers breaking this act, were to forfeit to the party grieved treble damages; and, moreover, £40, half to the king and half to the party grieved. Charge of this act was given not only to the justices of assize, and of the two benches, but also to justices of the peace, who were empowered to hear and determine *ex officio*, without special commission, all breaches thereof. As a caution in favour of the old course, which otherwise might be thought to be waived by the above clause about bailing, it was added, that sheriffs who made a return of *cepi corpus*, or *reddidit se*, should still be chargeable to have the body at the day of return, as before the making of the act. The warden of the Fleet and of the king's palace at Westminster were excepted out of this act.

An act was made in the early part of this reign,[1] requiring, that all officers appointed by the king's letters patent, within his courts, and who had power to nominate clerks and ministers, should be sworn to appoint such persons as they would answer for, and who would regularly attend their duty there. These were the measures now pursued for securing the chaste administration of justice, instead of increasing the number of statutes passed in the reign of Edward I. against maintenance and champerty, and extortion, so much practised at that time by the officers of courts.[2]

There is an act relating to attorneys, which deserves some notice for the singularity of the facts it contains. This is stat. 33 Henry VI. c. vii., which says, that not long since in the city of Norwich, and in the counties of Norfolk and Suffolk, there were only *six* or *eight* attorneys at most, coming to the king's courts, in which time great tranquillity reigned in those places, and little vexation was occasioned by untrue and foreign suits. But now, says the act, there are in those places *fourscore* attorneys, or more, the generality of whom have nothing to live upon but their practice, and besides

[1] Stat. 2 Hen. VI., c. 10.

[2] *Vide ante*, vol. ii., 240.

are very ignorant. It complains, that they came to markets and fairs, and other places, where there were assemblies of people, exhorting, procuring, and moving persons to attempt untrue and foreign suits for small trespasses, little offences, and small sums of money, which might be determined in courts-baron; so that more suits were now raised for malice than for the ends of justice, and courts-baron became less frequented. These are the motives the act states for making a reformation; which was, that in future there should be but *six* common attorneys in the county of Norfolk, the same number in Suffolk, and in the city of Norwich only *two*: these were to be admitted by the two chief-justices, of the most sufficient and best instructed; and persons acting as attorneys in those parts without such admission were subjected to heavy penalties.

The first statute that anywise affected the criminal law in this reign is stat. 2 Henry VI. c. xvii., which made it treason for any to escape out of prison if he was indicted, appealed, or taken on suspicion of high treason. The penalty of treason was inflicted on other offenders of different kinds. Because letters had been sent to persons demanding money to be put in certain places, with threats to burn their houses if they did not comply, it was enacted by stat. 9 Henry VI. c. vi. that all such burnings should be judged high-treason. However, that the landholders might not be prejudiced by such an extension of the stat. 25 Edward III., it was declared that the forfeitures should be saved to lords, as in cases of felony: the like exception was inserted in stat. 20 Henry VI. c. iii., which made it high-treason for any inhabitant of Wales or the Marches to carry away cattle out of the English counties. This plundering had occasioned an act in the reign of Henry IV.,[1] among other regulations for restraining the outrages of the Welsh. Again, by stat. 23 Henry VI. c. iii., the sheriff of Herefordshire was enjoined under penalties to take all offenders coming out of Wales to market, and to levy hue and cry after them. The above stat. 20 Henry VI. being left to expire after it had been continued by an act in the last parliament,[2] the like provision was again enacted by 28 Henry VI. c. iv., which likewise extended it to the people of Lancashire and other parts; for if any one took any goods, chattel, or *person* out of the counties and seignories royal in Wales and the duchy of Lancaster, and carried them to any other places, it was adjudged felony.

Treason to burn houses.

Other felonies were enacted by statute. It appears, that masons used to hold confederacies and meetings, to concert schemes for opposing the statutes of labourers. To prevent the effects of these, it was enacted by stat. 3 Henry VI. c. i., that any one causing such *chapiters or congregations* to be assembled, should be adjudged guilty of felony. Among other penal laws for the regulation of trade, it was by stat. 11 Henry VI. c. xiv. made felony to carry

[1] *Vide ante*, 241.

[2] Stat. 27 Hen. VI., c. 4.

any goods and merchandise of the staple into creeks, as was often done to avoid the customs: this was a temporary act, which expired in three years. Again, it was by stat. 18 Henry VI. c. xv. made felony to carry wools or woolfels to other places than the staple at Calais. Trade and commerce had now become very important objects in the contemplation of the legislature, and many other acts of a penal nature were made for the protection of them.

Process in criminal causes.

*The alterations made in criminal proceedings are of more consequence to the historical lawyer: these relate principally to process, to indictments, and to jurors. A law was made for the government of process in the king's bench, where, as it is represented by the statute, it was common to get a person indicted "by suspect jurors, hired and procured to the same by confederacy and covin of the said conspirators;" upon which a *capias* used to be awarded to the sheriff of the county where the bench was, returnable within two or four days; when, if the party came not, an *exigent* would be awarded, and so the goods of the party became forfeit. It was now enacted by stat. 6 Henry VI. c. i., that before any *exigent* was awarded in such case, a writ of *capias* should be directed as well to the sheriff of the county where the party was indicted, as of the county whereof he was named in the indictment; and this *capias* was to have the space of six weeks or longer, at the discretion of the justices, before the return; and any exigent awarded or outlawry pronounced before such return, was declared to be null and void. This act was confined to cases where the defendant lived in the same county in which the king's bench then was. The commons had petitioned in the preceding reign, that where a defendant indicted in the king's bench lived out of the county, there might be three *capiases*, with fifteen days between each, before the exigent was awarded.[1]

The preferring of indictments and appeals in foreign counties, and within liberties and franchises, was practised as a mode of oppression against defendants, who might in this way be put in *exigent* by surprise, before they knew of any indictment against them. To remedy this, it was provided by stat. 8 Hen. VI., c. x., that before any *exigent* should be awarded, a second *capias* should issue presently after the first, into the county whereof the defendant was named in the indictment, returnable on a certain day, containing the space of three months from the date of the last writ to the return, where the counties were held from month to month; and where they were held from six weeks to six weeks, containing the space of four months. The second *capias* was to command the sheriff to take the party, if he was to be found, and if not, then to make proclamation in two counties before the return, for him to appear at the day contained in the writ; and if he came not, then the exigent was to be awarded; and all exigents issued or outlaw-

[1] Cott. Abri., 547, s. 37.

ries pronounced in any other manner were to be void. This act relates to all cases, whether treason, felony, or trespass. It was further provided that wherever a person was indicted, or appealed in the manner aforesaid, and was duly acquitted by verdict, he should have a writ and *action upon his case* against every procurer of such indictment or appeal, and like process as in a writ of trespass *vi et armis;* and if the procurer was attainted, he should recover treble damages. The process against persons living in the same county, in cases of treason or felony, was to continue as formerly.

Because the above statute was thought to have no force but where the *capias* was returnable before the justices or commissioners who had taken the indictment, it used to be evaded by removing the indictment into the king's bench or elsewhere by *certiorari,* and then issuing the common-law process; to prevent which, and in explanation of that act, it was declared by stat. 10 Hen. VI., c. vi., that in such case the same process should be had as in the former case, otherwise the exigent and outlawry should be void.

The stat. 2 Hen. V., st. 1, c. ix.,[1] was revived by stat. 8 Hen. VI., c. xiv., with this alteration, that before the *capias* was awarded, it should be testified by two justices of the peace that a common fame and rumour ran of such riots; and when the fact was in the county palatine of Lancaster, or other franchise where there was a chancellor and a seal, after complaint so testified by a justice or sheriff, the chancellor was to award a proclamation and writ, as the chancellor of England might by the former act.

It had been ordained by stat. 20 Hen. VI., c. ii., that persons attainted in the county of Lancaster should forfeit only such goods as they had within the county; but it being observed that offences were more common within that county than elsewhere, which was attributed to this circumstance concerning forfeiture, that act was repealed by stat. 33 Hen. VI., c. ii.: however, to check the abuse of hasty indictments in a local jurisdiction, it was by the same act required that the jurors who found indictments should have certain qualifications in land, or the indictment should be void.

A passage in the famous 29th chapter of *Magna Charta* was explained by stat. 20 Hen. VI., c. ix. It was there said that no mention was made in that chapter how ladies of great estate, such as duchesses, countesses, or baronesses, were to be put to answer, or before what judges they should be judged on indictments of treason or felony: it was now ordained that they should, in such cases, whether married or sole, be tried as *peers* of the realm.

The summary proceeding in case of *forcible entries,* which had been appointed by stat. 15 Rich. II., c. ii.,[2] was enlarged and rendered

[1] *Vide ante,* c. 19.

[2] *Vide ante,* c. 17.

more effectual by stat. 8 Hen. VI., c. ix. (a) The defects of the former act were that it did not include a detainer with force, after a peaceable entry, nor cases where the persons entering forcibly were removed before the coming of the justices: again, there was no penalty on the sheriff, if he neglected to obey the precept of the justices. Owing to these defects, many wrongful and forcible entries were daily made, followed with gifts, feoffments, and discontinuances, sometimes to lords and great persons for maintenance, and sometimes to persons unknown.[1] To comprehend all these mischiefs, it was provided generally that where any one made forcible entry into lands, tenements, or other possessions, and held them forcibly, after complaint to the justices, they

Forcible entries.

(a) This statute requires attention not only as an illustration of the history of the age, but on account of the close connexion between the history of this action and that of *ejectione firmæ*, the original of our modern action of ejectment. Nothing is more illustrative of history than these alterations in the law which betray the *necessity* for such alterations on account of some changes in the circumstances of the times. And nothing is more important to legal history than to observe the manner in which successive changes in the law have thus arisen. This is particularly the case with the history of these actions. As regards the action for forcible entry itself, it was an alteration of the law arising out of the altered circumstances of the times. The assize of novel disseisin was the ancient remedy for a dispossession of the freehold, and the action of forcible entry was an attempt to provide a still more effective and summary remedy. The first statute was restricted to the case of forcible dispossession of property, but it was found that as time went on, a more common case was that of property wrongfully and forcibly withheld. The party who had the possessory right, or right of entry, could make such an entry if he could do so peaceably or without terror or peril of personal violence; but this he could not do if the property was held with force and violence: and hence the necessity for the second statute, under which, in such cases, the sheriff or justice could take a sufficient force, and give possession to the party manifestly entitled to possession (21 *Hen. VI.*, 5; 22 *Hen. VI.*, 19, 37). But a man who had held peaceable possession for three years could defend his possession with force (22 *Hen. VI.*, 18). A party disseised with force could re-enter peaceably, or if not, he could have his action of forcible entry (22 *Hen. VI.*, 37). The cases of force in those times were numerous (37 *Hen. VI.*, 20). In an action of trespass and false imprisonment the defendant pleaded that K. and others were seised of a manor in Cornwall until ousted with a strong hand by the plaintiff, and that they came to a justice of the peace to remove the power out of the manor, and that he came to the manor and found the plaintiff keeping it with force and arms, and arrested him, and sent him to the king's gaol at Launceston, of which the defendant is constable, who, by force of his warrant, detained him (*Oliver* v. *Michel*, *Year-book*, 26 *Hen. VI.*, fol. 5). See also the case of *Paston* v. *Ledlaw*, 37 *Hen. VI.*, fol 20, and the collateral illustration of the subject afforded in the *Paston Letters* written in this reign. Lord Hale says that the statute of 8 Hen. VI. helped men to an action to recover their possessions by a writ of forcible entry, even while the method of recovery of possessions by an action of ejectment was not known or used; and that in consequence of this, real actions began to go out of use (*Hist. Com. Law*, c. viii.) The most numerous cases of dispossession in that age were by force; and hence the remedies by force were applied. But the remedy by *ejectione firmæ* was, it is believed, always in existence, although it applied only to termors. It was held that executors could have a writ *ejectione firmæ* for ouster of their testator from a term which still continued; and the ground upon which the court gave judgment was, that by the stat. 4 Edw. III. c. 6, executors could have actions of goods fallen out of the possession of their testators, and that a term was only a chattel, which plainly implied that the action was for recovery of the term (*Year-book*, 7 *Henry IV.*, fol. 7), and refutes a notion which our author elsewhere appears to have adopted, that the action only took that form in the reign of Edward IV. The application of it to recovery of freeholds was of a later date, and will be explained in the next volume.

[1] *Vide ante*, c. 17.

should cause the said statute to be executed; and whether such offenders were present or departed before their coming, yet the justices, or justice, in some good town next to the tenements, or in some other convenient place, should inquire of the matter by the people of the county, and upon their verdict put the party in possession. If the party making the entry had made a feoffment or discontinuance to any lord, or other person, to disappoint the possessor of his recovery, and such conveyances were found in an assize or other action to be made for maintenance, they were declared void. In order to make the above inquiry, the justices were to issue precepts to the sheriff, to cause to come before them sufficient and indifferent persons dwelling next about the places, having lands of the yearly value of forty shillings above reprises, under pain of £20 penalty. It was enacted that the party disseised might, in all the above cases, have an assize or writ of trespass, and recover treble damages, and a fine should be paid to the king. This act was not to extend to persons who kept forcible possession if they, or their ancestors, or they whose estate they enjoyed, had been in possession for three years.

Justices of the peace.

The authority of justices of the peace was still increasing by the number of articles of small concern which were submitted to their direction and superintendence. Many of these have been already mentioned. The following acts were made to govern them in the exercise of their jurisdiction. We have seen that by stat. 2 Hen. V., c. iv. the justices were to hold their sessions four times a year: it was now stated in stat. 14 Hen. VI., c. iv. that, considering the high courts of justice were held in the county of Middlesex in the four terms, at which time the commons were to attend to inquire of such articles as were inquirable there; and that the justices held their sessions immediately after the term, more to avoid the penalty of the statute than for any business they had to transact; and that bringing the people together again on that occasion was harassing them both in term and out; under all these considerations, it was enacted that the justices of Middlesex should be discharged of the penalty while the court of king's bench sat in that county, provided they sat twice a year at least, and oftener if need were.

It is complained in stat. 18 Hen. VI., c. xi., that notwithstanding the laws made for ascertaining the qualifications of justices, yet many were of small fortunes, and necessitous, so as to become contemptible, as well as guilty of great extortions: wherefore it was now provided that none should be assigned who had not lands or tenements to the value of £20 by the year. A person assigned who had less than that was to give notice thereof to the chancellor within a month; and if he did not do so, or made any warrant or precept, he incurred the penalty of £20, and was to be put out of the commission. However, if there were no sufficient persons having lands and tenements of the above value, who were learned in the law and of good governance, the chancellor had a discretion to put in others. Again, all cities and places were excepted out of the act if they had justices of the peace living therein, by commission or warrant from the king.

Thus far of the statutes made in the long but turbulent and unfortunate reign of Henry VI. (*a*)

(*a*) The author omitted to notice a very important matter which marked this reign—viz., the rise of the statutes of sewers. In the reign of Henry IV., cases had occurred which showed the necessity for some more prompt and effective remedy for the inundations which constantly arose through non-repair of sea-walls, or neglect of the internal drainage of the country. Several cases occurred, showing that the mischiefs as to want of sufficient repairs of the sea-works or internal drainage of the country were beginning to be experienced, which, in the reign of Henry VI., led to the issuing of commissions of sewers (7 *Henry IV.*, fol. 8). That was an action against the Abbot of Stratford for not repairing the banks of the Thames, which, it was alleged, that by reason of prescriptive tenure he ought to repair. It was the necessity for a more speedy and summary remedy which led to the issuing of commissions of sewers, for while the legal obligation was being litigated, the land was being overrun. Hence, in 1427, there was an act to authorise commissions of sewers, reciting the great damage and losses which had of late happened by the great inundation of waters in divers parts of the realm, and that much greater damage was very likely to ensue, if remedy were not speedily provided. The commissioners were to inquire of annoyances, and by whose default they happened, and also who had lands common or fishing there, and who might have loss by the annoyances, or benefit by the repair of them, and all were to be assessed for the necessary reparations. The effect was, that all who would be benefited should contribute (6 *Hen. VI.*, c. v.) The subject was settled by statute (23 *Hen. VIII.*, c. v.)

CHAPTER XXI.

HENRY VI. AND EDWARD IV.

Tenures—Knight's Service—Escuage—Socage—Serjeanty—Homage—Fealty—Villenage—Of Copyholds—Of Rents—Estates Tail—Perpetuities declared Void—Of Dower—Tenant at Will—Estates upon Condition—Mortgages—Of Parceners—Joint-tenants—Tenants in Common—Attornment—Feigned Recoveries—Of Uses—Their Nature and Properties—An Executory Devise—Of Chattels—Of Contracts.

THE decisions of courts during these reigns present many interesting points of historical investigation (*a*). Among other subjects of improvement, we see the birth of that system of equity which is administered by the court of chancery; we find the doctrine of uses, and the application of a common recovery to the barring of estates tail, fully established. These were topics unknown to our old law (*b*). In the meantime, the learning of real actions gradually gave way (*c*), personal writs became more frequent (*d*), and

(*a*) Their interest, however, depended in a great degree on their order in point of time, because this exhibits the course of progression in the gradual development of our law, and its adaptation to the exigencies of the age. But this the author had to a large extent lost, in mingling together in the same chapters the incidents in the legal history of the two reigns of Henry VI. and Edward IV., occupying a period of nearly seventy years. For this reason, as already explained, the statutes, and the legal decisions, and other distinctive incidents of the two reigns, have been separated, and for other reasons, explained in a note to the reign of Edward IV., that reign has been removed to the next volume. The present chapter is mainly occupied with the law of tenures, drawn from the celebrated treatise of Littleton, which, though written in the reign of Edward IV., when he was a judge, describes the law as it was in the reign of Henry VI., when he was at the bar, and so is not unfitly placed here.

(*b*) This was a great error of our author. As there are instances of fines in the Year-books as old as the reign of Henry III., so it was more than once stated from the bench that uses were older than the statute of *quia emptores*, though not *common* until after that act, which implies that they *were* common after that act, which was *temp.* Edward I. (27 *Hen. VIII.* 8; *Bro. Ab.*, *Feoffments al uses*, fol. and pl.) And it was said that uses were at common law; for that the statute of Marlbridge (*temp.* Hen. III.) was directed against their application to deprive lords of the profits of feudal tenure (*Ibid.*) And as to the use of recoveries to bar estates tail, the statute *de donis* itself, *temp.* Edward I., shows that means were then used for that purpose, which could only have been fines and recoveries, and it only prohibited *fines* (the reason for the distinction being founded on the difference of the two modes of procedure as regarded the degree of publicity and notoriety); and as the statute of Gloucester, *temp.* Edward I., shows that recoveries were used to evade the law of mortmain, there can be no doubt they were used after the statute *de donis* to bar estates tail. The author himself, in a subsequent chapter, in effect says so; though he so far yields to one of the false traditions of legal history as to give countenance to the notion, which had somehow become current, that this use of recoveries arose, or became established, in the reign of Edward IV.

(*c*) This, Lord Hale says, was owing to the use of the action of forcible entry, which gave men a speedy and easy remedy, either for land forcibly withheld or forcibly seised; but then these statutes only applied originally to the freeholder, and to cases of actual force. Out of this action, however (or rather the use allowed to be made of it), and the action of *ejectione firmæ*, arose the action of ejectment, which really superseded the old real actions.

(*d*) This was not only in such real actions as were for the recovery of real property,

pleading grew into a science of much nicety and refinement (*a*): in short, the whole face of the law seems to be assuming that character which it has retained to this present day (*b*). So large a field is here opened, that should we only go into such passages of this period as seem properly to belong to the juridical historian, we might, perhaps, engage further than every reader would be disposed to follow: we shall therefore content ourselves with selecting certain heads of inquiry that stand more eminently distinguished from the many others which are furnished by the valuable reports of these times.

Tenures.

In the times of Glanville and Bracton, when tenures were in all their vigour, we gave an account of their different kinds from the works of those two writers (*c*.) Since those days, great revolutions had happened in this sort of property, which, however, did not so much alter the law as obscure the evidence by which distinct tenures were to be known. Thus, *knight's service* and *socage* were still the principal species of tenure; but as the *servitium militare* was performed by very few, and that rarely (this service having given way to the employment of hired troops), and as the *servitium sokæ* was now nowhere known, but was universally commuted for certain rents and other compensations, it was necessary to recur to other evidences of these two tenures, in order to pronounce which was *knight-service*, and which was *socage;* or, in other words, which was and which was not to be burdened with ward, marriage, relief, and other casualties; those being the grand points which interested both lord and tenant.

In order therefore to ascertain this, many circumstances were to be considered; such as whether the tenant did homage or fealty; whether he rendered services that were certain or uncertain, and the like: and from a comparison of these properties and incidents, the conclusion was to be drawn, whether the land in question was held by *knight's service* or in *socage;* for under one of those it must be ranked, whether it was *escuage*, *grand* or *petit serjeanty*, *burgage*, or any other special denomination, which was merely descriptive of certain modifications of those two principal holdings. Our curiosity is naturally led to inquire into the alterations that had taken place in so important a part of the law of real property as tenures, since those early periods when this subject was can-

but such as were remedies for injuries to real property—deprivation of incorporal rights relating thereto, and the like. The real actions, it is to be borne in mind, were only remedies for the freeholder, and therefore lay by the freeholder against the freeholder, always presupposing something permanent and annexed to the freehold; as a nuisance arising out of stoppage of a way, or of a stream, or the like (39 *Hen. VI.* 32; 22 *Hen. VI.* 14; 11 *Hen. IV.* 26).

(*a*) The next chapter treats fully of the subject of pleading.

(*b*) There can be no doubt that the law, during the long period covered by these two reigns, was in a state of progress and transition; and therefore it is of the more importance to *observe the order of time* which displays that course and progress.

(*c*) The former and greater part of the chapter, however, is occupied with the tenures from Littleton.

vassed so much at length. Some statutes had been made at different times to correct the inconveniences arising from tenures, and some small variation had been effected by the resolutions of courts; but upon the whole, the leading ideas still maintained their ground.

Knight's service.

For example, in *knight's service*, it was still the law, that when the tenant died, leaving an heir-male under twenty-one years, the lord should have the land till he arrived at such age; and if he was not married, the lord was also to have the marriage. But if it was an heir-female, and she was of the age of fourteen or more, the lord had neither the land nor body in ward; because she might marry one who was sufficient to do the service. If she was under fourteen years, and unmarried, then he might have the wardship of the land till she was sixteen years old; concerning which point some provisions had been made by the stat. Westm. 1, and the stat. Merton, and which are mentioned in their proper places.[1] By these parliamentary provisions was the law of ward and marriage governed at the time of which we are now writing. As to relief, the law was, that where the tenant held by a whole knight's fee, the relief should be 100 shillings, and so in proportion.[2]

Escuage.

The *servitium militare* had become so generally commuted for the *servitium scuti*, or *scutagium*, as mentioned by Bracton,[3] that *escuage* was in these days considered almost as a substitute and convertible term for *knight's service;* so that Littleton, in order to clear the subject, felt himself under the necessity of declaring expressly, "that many tenants held by *knight service*, who yet did not hold by *escuage*."[4] It is for this reason that the same writer, in his Book of Tenures, begins with *escuage* as the chief and most general holding in the kingdom, and then goes on to *knight's service*, *socage*, *serjeanty*, and the others. We have seen, in the time of Bracton, that this *servitium scuti*, or *scutagium*, was called sometimes *servitium regale*, because it was to be performed to the king, and *servitium forinsicum*, because it was not performed to the lord, but was done *foris*, and without the lord's jurisdiction. The account of the tenure by *escuage*, as given by Littleton, corresponds with all these terms. The instance he gives is, when the king made a voyage royal into Scotland; and then those who held by *escuage*, were to be assessed according to the number of their knight's fees.[5]

Though *escuage* was due by tenure, yet because it concerned almost the whole kingdom, it could not be assessed but by authority of parliament; and it is said that *escuage* had not been assessed since the eighth year of Edward II. When Richard II. made a voyage royal into Scotland, the payment of *escuage* was remitted at the petition of the commons.[6] When *escuage* was so

1 *Vide ante*, vol. i., c. 7; and *vide* Litt., 103.

2 Litt., 112; *vide ante*, vol. i., c. 7.

3 *Vide ante*, vol. i., c. 7.

4 Litt., 111.

5 *Ibid.*, 97.

6 1 Inst., 72 b.

assessed by parliament, every lord used to receive the sum assessed on his tenants,[1] and those who held of the crown paid their *escuage* to the king. After such parliamentary assessment, a lord might have a writ to the sheriff of the county, to levy the sum due,[2] or he might distrain; but to such distress the tenant might plead, that he was with the king for forty days in his voyage royal; and the issue would be tried by the certificate of the marshal of the king's host, in writing under seal. So obsolete had this personal service become in the reign of Edward IV., that the author before quoted speaks of this method of proof as depending on a traditionary opinion, which had not been confirmed by any recent experience.[3] Such was the form in which tenure by *knight-service* now mostly showed itself.

Socage.

The idea of socage-tenure was now confined to this definition; namely, where a tenant held by *certain* service for all manner of services, provided such service was not *knight-service;* as where a man held his land by fealty and certain rent, for all manner of services; or held by homage, fealty, and certain rent, for all manner of services;[4] or if a person held by fealty only: in short, every tenure which was not a tenure in chivalry, was tenure in socage.[5] And the principal difference between these two tenures was, whether the service was *certain* or *uncertain;* the latter being the grand criterion that distinguished knight's service, and the former socage-tenure: for even escuage, if it was a certain sum, was considered as a socage-tenure. Thus, if a man was to pay half a mark for escuage, whenever that assessment was made by parliament, whether at a greater or less sum, this was socage, on account of the sum being certain and unalterable; but where the escuage was *uncertain*, notwithstanding it might have been lowered by agreement to one half or one quarter of the parliamentary taxation, yet such a holding was still by an *uncertain* escuage, and so was deemed knight-service.[6] Again, if a certain rent was to be paid for castle-guard, it was socage-tenure; but if the tenant ought to do castle-guard in person, or by another, it was knight-service.[7]

We have seen how the law stood in the time of Glanville and Bracton, concerning the wardship of socage-tenants.[8] What had been delivered by those authors is, for the most part, now confirmed by our great oracle on the law of tenures in later times. If a tenant in socage, says Littleton, died, leaving issue within the age of fourteen years, then the *prochein amy*, or next friend to the heir, who could not inherit the land, was to have the wardship of the land and the heir, till his age of fourteen years, under the title of *guardian in socage*. Thus, if the inheritance came *ex parte maternâ*, the guardian was to be the next cousin on the part of the father, and so *vice versâ*, according as it had been laid down by

[1] Litt., 100. [2] *Ibid.*, 101. [3] *Ibid.*, 102. [4] *Ibid.*, 117. [5] *Ibid.*, 118.
[6] *Ibid.*, 120. [7] *Ibid.*, 121. [8] *Vide ante*, vol. i., c. 7.

Glanville and Bracton. When such heir arrived to the age of fourteen years complete, he might enter and oust the guardian, and occupy the land himself. The guardian was not to take the profits of the inheritance to his own use, but was to render an account thereof to the heir, with an allowance of all reasonable costs and charges; and if such guardian married the heir within the age of fourteen years, he was to account for the value of the marriage, although he took nothing for the value; for the law expected he should, and *it was his own folly,* says Littleton, if he did not; but he would be excused, if he had procured him a match of as much value as the marriage of the heir.[1] A stranger who occupied the inheritance as guardian, would be equally liable to account; for he would not be permitted to plead he was not next friend, but must answer, whether he had occupied the land or not. If the guardian continued to occupy till the heir was twenty-one years of age, it was a doubt whether the heir should have account against him as guardian or as bailiff.[2]

There was this difference between a guardian in chivalry and in socage, that if the former died during the minority of the heir, his executor had the wardship; but it was not so of a guardian in socage who died before the heir had attaiued his fourteenth year; for then it went to another *prochein amy*, to whom the inheritance could not descend: this difference was owing to the former guardian's taking the profits to his own use, and the latter not. It was held, that no writ of account lay against the executors of a guardian in socage, unless it was for the king.[3] The relief in socage-tenure was a year's rent;[4] and because the lord had no wardship in this tenure, he had relief in all cases, whatsoever might be the age of the heir; and he might distrain for it forthwith upon the death of the tenant.[5] Indeed, if the rent happened to consist in paying a rose, or some other production of the earth, he must wait till the season would furnish it.[6]

The title to ward, like most other considerations arising upon landed property, was perplexed with the modifications that estates had been made subject to in the present mode of conveyance. However plain the law might be when the lord and tenant held in fee-simple, it was a matter of some nicety to decide what tenant should be in ward, where there were reversions and remainders. The courts had long laid down some rules upon this head, and many points of this sort were agitated during the present period.

It had long been held, that where land was leased for life, with a remainder over in fee, and the remainder-man died during the life of the particular tenant, leaving a son under age, the lord should not have the son in ward; but whenever the tenant for life died, and the son entered, he was to be in ward, because he was in as heir to his father. But where a lease was made for life, reserving

[1] Litt., 123. [2] *Ibid.*, 124. [3] *Ibid.*, 125.
[4] *Ibid.*, 126. [5] *Ibid.*, 127. [6] *Ibid.*, 129.

the reversion to the lessor, the lord would in such case have the ward and marriage.[1] The same if a gift was made in tail with a reversion; for the donee was considered as holding of the reversioner, and the issue was to be in ward to him; the reversioner continuing to hold of the lord paramount:[2] whereas in case of a remainder, the tenant for life, or in tail in possession, was the very tenant to the lord paramount. The title to wardship was frequently involved in difficulties from the following considerations: from the king's prerogative, where a tenant held one fee of the king, and others of common persons; from a feoffment made by collusion to avoid the wardship of the heir; from claims depending on priority and posteriority; and either of these, when mixed with questions of estates, with discontinuances, disseisins, and remitter, tended very much to perplex the law respecting rights of wardship.[3]

Having considered the nature of socage in general, we shall make some few observations upon the several species of it. Successive determinations had contributed to make some alteration in the notion of tenure by *serjeanty*, which is now described as differing somewhat from the same tenure in the time of Bracton.[4] It was now laid down, that *grand serjeanty* must be a holding of the king, and of him only, by such services as ought to be done in proper person to the king; as to carry the king's banner or lance; to lead his army, to be his marshal, carry his sword before him at the coronation; to be his carver, his butler, one of his chamberlains of the receipt of the exchequer, or other service:[5] to find a man for the war[6] was also a grand serjeanty. The same service made the tenure different, accordingly as the land was held of a private person, or of the king. Thus land held by the service of cornage, to wind a horn when the Scots came into the country, was grand serjeanty, if held of the king; yet if held of a private person, it was not grand serjeanty, but knight-service, and drew to it ward and marriage; for none could hold by grand serjeanty but of the king only.[7] Grand serjeanty again differed from escuage, inasmuch as those who held by escuage ought to do their service out of the realm; but those who held by grand serjeanty were to peform their service within the realm, as appears by most of the above instances.[8] One who held by grand serjeanty, was considered as a tenant by knight-service; for he was liable to ward, marriage, and relief; but no escuage could be demanded of him, unless it was also a tenure in escuage.[9]

Serjeanty.

Tenure by *petit serjeanty* was now, like the former, always a holding of the king, and him only; to yield to him a bow, a sword, dagger, knife, lance, a pair of gloves, an arrow, or other small things belonging to war. This service was considered in effect but as socage; for the tenant was not obliged to go, or do anything in

1 O. N. B., 96.
2 2 Edw. IV., 5.
3 33 Hen. VI., 55; 33 Hen. VI., 14; 15 Edw. IV., 10.
4 *Vide ante*, vol. i., c. 1.
5 Litt., 153.
6 *Ibid.*, 157.
7 *Ibid.*, 156.
8 *Ibid.*, 155.
9 *Ibid.*, 158.

person touching the war, but merely to pay yearly certain things to the king.[1] Such were the natures of grand and petit serjeanty at the period of which we are now writing: there are several marks of difference between this description and that given by Bracton; the principal of which is, that both were now required to be held of the king.[2]

There was a species of socage called *tenure in burgage;* which was, where there was an ancient borough, and those who had lands therein held them of the king, or of some lord, by a yearly rent.[3] This was so called, says Littleton, "because they were holden of the lord of the borough."[4] It was besides reasonable, that this species of socage should be distinguished from others, as lands under this description were governed, very often, by a peculiar custom differing from the common law. Thus, in some boroughs it was the custom for the youngest son to inherit such burgage-tenures; which usage was called *Burough English:*[5] in others, the wife used to have all her husband's lands in dower: in others, a man might devise his lands in fee-simple by his last will, and the devisee might enter without livery of seisin.[6]

There were two ancient tenures that had received a great blow from the statute of *quia emptores, &c.*, 18 Edward I. These were tenures in *frankalmoigne*, and by *homage ancestrall.* Tenure in *frankalmoigne* was, when land was granted to an abbot, dean and chapter, a parson, or other religious person, and his successors, *in puram et perpetuam eleemosynam.* Such persons were bound before God to make orisons, prayers, masses, and other divine services for the soul of the grantor and those that were his heirs, and the prosperity and long life of those who were not. Such tenants, says Littleton, did no fealty, or other earthly service, all which they supplied by the above spiritual acknowledgment and remembrance; and there was no remedy, in case of remissness in such service, but complaint to the ordinary or visitor.[7] However, if the service so reserved was specifically and certainly named, as to sing a mass every Friday, or every year at such a day to sing a *placebo et dirige, &c.*, and the like; or to find a chaplain, or to distribute alms of one hundred pence to a hundred poor men at such a day; in such cases, the lord might distrain for failure of service, and he should have fealty: but this was not properly a tenure in *frankalmoigne*, but was called tenure *by divine service;* and seems, in some measure, to correspond with what Bracton calls *in liberam et perpetuam eleemosynam*, which was subject to service, because the epithet *puram* was not added in the deed of gift.[8] But Littleton seems to consider these two expressions as equally signifying frankalmoigne, and he makes the distinction to consist in the specification of service; for none, says he, can hold in frankalmoigne, if there be expressed any manner of service.[9]

[1] Litt., 159, 160.
[2] *Vide ante*, c. 12.
[3] Litt., 162, 163.
[4] *Ibid.*, 164.
[5] *Ibid.*, 165.
[6] *Ibid.*, 166, 167.
[7] *Ibid.*, 133-136.
[8] *Vide ante*, vol. i., c. 7.
[9] Litt., 137.

Since the statute of *quia emptorés*[1] no gifts could be made *in pure alms*, or in frankalmoigne; for that statute ordains, that none should alien, or grant lands or tenements in fee-simple to hold of himself: if, therefore, any held lands by knight's service, and granted by license in frankalmoigne, the religious grantee would immediately hold by knight's service of the same lord of whom the grantor held, and not of the grantor. The king, however, not being within that statute, might still grant lands in frankalmoigne.[2] Again, if a tenant in frankalmoigne aliened the land to a secular person in fee-simple, the grantee would be required to do fealty to the lord, because he was not able to hold in frankalmoigne, and the law would not allow the lord to be deprived of all service.[3] It was for a similar reason that lands in frankalmoigne could only be held of the grantor; for if there was lord, mesne, and tenant, and the tenant held in frankalmoigne, and the mesnalty escheated to the lord paramount, then the tenant would cease to hold frankalmoigne, and would hold of the lord paramount by fealty.[4] Such mesne grantor, before escheat, was by the nature of this tenure bound to acquit his tenant in frankalmoigne against the lord paramount.[5]

The tenure by *homage ancestrall* is another holding that received a check by the statute *quia emptores;* which provision, as it enlarged the power to alien, gave tenants an occasion of breaking the mutual connexion on which this tenure depended. For this tenure subsisted only where there was a double prescription, both in the blood of the lord and of the tenant; that is, where the tenant and his ancestors had held the same land of the lord and his ancestors time out of memory of man, and had done homage. This tenure is spoken of by Bracton as a very common holding in his days: most of that which he says on the dependence between the lord and his homager, and upon the warranty that followed from the doing of homage, seems to refer to this pure and original tenure by homage.[6] As alienation became more frequent and easy, the number of these holdings diminished, and probably very few were in being in the reigns of Henry VI. and Edward IV. However, the legal consideration of homage ancestrall was treated in the same way as in the early period of our law. Thus it was held, that the service of homage ancestrall drew to it an implied warranty, and an acquittal against the lord paramount, when homage had been once done by the tenant to the lord.[7] So strictly was a privity and prescription required by law, that should such a tenant alien and take back an estate in fee from the alienee, though he held the land by homage, yet it would not be homage ancestrall, nor could he have the warranty and acquittal incident to such tenure.[8] It is plain, from the nature of the thing, that a tenant by homage ancestrall might hold either by knight-service or socage.[9]

[1] *Vide ante*, c. 10.
[2] Litt., 140.
[3] *Ibid.*, 139.
[4] *Ibid.*, 141.
[5] *Ibid.*, 142.
[6] *Vide ante*, vol. i., . 7.
[7] Litt., 143, 144.
[8] *Ibid.*, 147.
[9] *Ibid.*, 152.

This brings us to speak of *homage* in general, which, as well as *fealty*, is treated by Littleton in the way in which it had been delivered by our ancient writers. Homage and fealty were the great bonds between lord and tenant, and, when once established, were too sacred to be altered in substance. Notwithstanding they have been frequently mentioned before,[1] yet the nature of our inquiry calls upon us to lay before the reader such new lights as are furnished in the more advanced stages of the history of our tenures.

Homage. Homage is stated by Littleton to be the most honourable and most humble service of reverence that a frank tenant could do to his lord; for he was to be ungirt and his head uncovered; the lord was to sit; the tenant was to kneel, and hold his hands jointly together between the hands of his lord, and say thus:—"I become your man from this day forward, of life and limb, and of earthly worship; and unto you shall be true and faithful, and bear you faith for the tenements that I claim to hold of you, saving the faith I owe to our sovereign lord the king;" and then the lord, still sitting, was to kiss him. But if the tenant was a man of religion, or a woman sole, it was thought not decorous for such a person to say, "I become your man, or your woman;" therefore they used to say, "I do to you homage, and to you shall be faithful and true; and faith to you shall bear for the tenements I hold of you, saving the faith I owe to our sovereign lord the king."[2] If the tenant held also other lands of other lords, he added likewise this exception, "And saving the faith I owe to my other lords:"[3] which ceremony corresponds with the precedents of former times.

It was still held, as in Bracton's time, that none were to do homage but those who had an estate in fee, or in tail, in their own right, or in the right of another; for it was a maxim of law, "that a tenant for life should neither do nor receive homage." Thus, if a man became tenant by the courtesy, he was to do homage; but if the wife died before homage done by the husband, then he was not to do homage, because he had but an estate for life.[4] Homage was to be done only once in the tenant's life; therefore, though he was obliged to do fealty to the heir of his lord, he was excused from homage.[5] The same if the lord granted the services, and the tenant attorned, he should not be compelled to do homage, but should do fealty, notwithstanding he had done it before; for fealty was incident to every attornment of the tenant, when the seignory was granted. But it was not the same upon a recovery as upon a grant; for if a stranger recovered against the lord upon a *præcipe*, the tenant was obliged to do homage again to the recoveror.[6] Many cases are stated by Bracton, where the lord might transfer

[1] *Vide*, vol. i., c. 7; and *ante*, c. 12.
[2] Litt., 85-87.
[3] *Ibid.*, 89.
[4] *Ibid.*, 90.
[5] *Ibid.*, 148.
[6] *Ibid.*, 149.

the homage, and the tenant, of course, be compelled to do homage a second time, all which seem now not to be law.[1]

Fealty.

When the tenant did *fealty*, he was to hold his right hand upon the book, and say thus: "Know you this, my lord, that I shall be faithful and true to you, and faith to you shall bear for the lands which I claim to hold of you; and that I shall lawfully do to you the customs and services which I ought to do at the terms assigned, so help me God, and his saints;" and then he was to kiss the book. He was not to kneel when he did his fealty, nor make such humble reverence as in homage. Again, homage could only be done to the lord himself; but the steward of the lord's court, or bailiff, might take the fealty.[2]

Fealty was incident to all manner of tenure except tenure in frankalmoigne; and it was no uncommon tenure to hold by fealty only.[3] Thus, if lands were let for term of life, without reserving any rent, the tenant was still to do fealty to the lessor, because he *held* of him. For the same reason it was said, that a termor for years should do fealty to the lessor, such a lessee being said, in the writ of waste, to *hold* of the lessor; but a tenant at will, as he had no sure estate, was not to do fealty. Those who held by copy of court-roll, by the custom of a manor (which new description of tenants will be considered presently) were bound to do fealty.[4]

We have hitherto confined our discourse to free tenures; it remains to add something upon the subject of tenure in villenage, and the new tenures that had lately been growing out of it.

Villenage.

Since the time of Henry III. little has been said of *villenage*, considered either as a condition in society, or as a *tenure*.[5] The proper and primary notion of villenage was, when a person, being villain to a lord, held also of that lord certain lands or tenements at the will of the lord, to do villain-services, as to carry the lord's dung out of the city, or off the manor, to put it upon the land, and similar predial labours. But such had been the revolutions in society, and the changes of property, it now very commonly happened that some persons who were free had become possessed of lands burthened with such services, and such tenure was still called villenage, though the persons themselves were no villains. Others, on the contrary, who were villains, had yet no land at all to hold in lieu of such services, which they were, nevertheless, still bound to perform. Another change that had taken place was, that the villain services were no longer indeterminate, and wholly at the will of the lord, as in the time of Bracton, but were universally limited (as even in his time they were in the case of one sort of villains, called villain-sockmen) by the custom that had immemorially prevailed in the manor.[6] Thus the universal character of tenure in villenage was a *holding according to the custom of a manor, or otherwise at the*

[1] *Vide ante*, vol. i., c. 7. [2] Litt., 91, 92. [3] *Ibid.*, 130, 131.
[4] *Ibid.*, 132. [5] *Vide ante*, vol. i., c. 7. [6] Litt., .172

will oj the lord.[1] With this qualification, the law of villena stood mostly on the footing it was on in the age of Bracton.

As to the persons of villains, they were either such by prescri tion, so that a villain and his ancestors had been villains time c of mind of man, or by acknowledgment and confession in a coı of record.[2] Again, villains were said to be *regardant*, or *in grc* The former were in the nature of the original and proper villains namely, such as had belonged, they and their ancestors, to a mar time out of the memory of man. The latter were such as h been granted by deed from one to another, in consequence of whi they became villains in gross, and not regardant: a man and l ancestors might perhaps have been seised of a villain and l ancestors, who were such in gross, beyond the memory of ma A man who confessed himself a villain in a court of record, was villain in gross.[4] A female villain was called a *niefe.*[5]

These were the divisions and species of villains. Some poiı of law, as now understood, concerning this sort of persons were follow. If a villain took a free woman to wife, and had issue, t children were considered by the law as villains; on the other hand a niefe married a freeman, the issue were free. In this, an analo seems to have been preserved towards our law of descents, whi gave a preference to the male line, in direct contradiction to t civil law, which in a similar case pronounced that *partus sequit ventrum.*[6] The sentence of the law against a bastard, that he w *quasi nullius filius*, was permitted, in this instance, to operate favour of such persons, for no bastard could be a villain by desceı nor, of course, any otherwise than by confession in a court record.[7]

It was an old rule, that *quicquid per servum acquiritur, domino acquiritur*, and this still prevailed with all its influen Thus, though a freeman, by purchasing land held in villena; did not lose his freedom, yet a villain might make free land becoı villain to his lord; as where a villain purchased land in fee-simp or fee-tail, the lord of the villain might enter thereon, and oust t villain and his heirs for ever, and, if he pleased, might afterwaı grant the same land to the villain, to hold in villenage.[8] But the villain aliened before the lord entered, then the lord was p cluded from entering at all, having nothing to blame but his o neglect: the same of goods, if the villain sold or gave them befı they were seized by the lord. In case of goods, it was sufficient the lord claimed the goods openly among the neighbours, a seized part in name of the whole, for this gave him a compl possession of the whole;[9] but in both cases of lands and goods, t king might follow them into whatsoever hands they passed, *nullum tempus occurrit regi.*[10] Where a reversion or an advows

[1] Litt., 172. [2] *Ibid.*, 175. [3] *Ibid.*, 181, 182. [4] *Ibid.*, :
[5] *Ibid.*, 186. [6] *Ibid.*, 187. Fortescue, c. 42. [7] Litt., :
[8] *Ibid.*, 172. [9] *Ibid.*, 177. [10] *Ibid.*, 178.

was purchased by a villain, it was enough for the lord to claim it in the above way during the life of the particular tenant or incumbent.[1] A villain was held competent to sue all manner of actions against any person but his lord; and even against him he might have an appeal of his ancestor's death. A niefe might have an appeal of rape; a villain might have an action as executor against his lord, because it was to the use of the testator. But in all these cases it was expedient for the lord to make protestation that the plaintiff was his villain, otherwise he would be enfranchised, even though the matter was finally determined for the lord, and against the villain. It was the opinion of Littleton that a villain could not have an appeal of mayhem against his lord, because he would recover only damages, which the lord might by law retake, as soon as they were taken in execution; but he might unquestionably have an indictment,[2] for the lord was not allowed by law to maim his villain.

If a villain was made a secular priest, his lord might seize him, though he was not permitted to recover him, if he had entered into religion, because he was then considered as dead in law; nor could he retake his niefe if a freeman married her: but in both these cases he might have an action; in the latter against the husband, and in the former against the sovereign of the house, for damages in taking his villain without his license.[3]

Manumissions were generally performed by deed, but many acts were considered as implied manumissions. Thus, if the lord made an obligation to his villain for a certain sum of money, or granted him an annuity, or let him lands for a term of years by deed, or by a feoffment without a deed with livery of seisin, these were implied enfranchisements; but not so if he made him a lease at will, whether with deed or without, because it carried no certainty with it.[4] If the lord sued a *præcipe quòd reddat* against his villain, and recovered, or was nonsuit after appearance, this was construed to be a manumission, because he might by law have made an entry without suit: in like manner, if he brought an action of debt, accompt, covenant, trespass, or the like; for such suit was wholly unnecessary, as he had, by law, a power to imprison the villain, and take his goods; but the same conclusion would not be drawn from an appeal, because, says Littleton, the lord could not hang him without such a suit. However, if the appeal was found against the lord, and no indictment was pending to save the damages, the villain, it was thought, would be enfranchised on account of the judgment for damages against his lord.[5]

Thus stood the law respecting such persons as still continued in a state of villenage. These were greatly diminished in number; but it appears, from what has just been said, that their condition was not alleviated from what it had been in the earlier times of

[1] Litt., 179, 180. [2] *Ibid.*, 189, 190, 191, 192, 194. [3] *Ibid.*, 202.
[4] *Ibid.*, 204-207. [5] *Ibid.*, 208.

our law. While the *persons* of villains were left to labour unc all the rigours of the ancient villenage, the *tenure* of villenage h been long in the habit of increasing its franchises, and had n obtained some degree of emancipation. The tenure in *pure vill age* (as was before observed) was nowhere now to be found; b all tenants of that description had obtained those privileges whi Bracton gives to such as, in his time, held in what was call *villain socage.*[1] These privileges were silently obtained by cust and usage, confirmed by lapse of time, and defended by the leg security of prescription. As the land so holden ceased to be p sessed in a precarious way, it began gradually to lose its ancie denomination. In the 4 Edw. I. we find mention *custumarii tenentes*, which probably meant the ve persons in question.[2] Towards the latter end of the reign Edward III. we meet with a new appellation; and as the form new term expressed the foundation and *title* to their estate, t latter denoted the *evidence* of such title: they are called *tenants p roll solonque le volunt le seigniour.*[3] In the reign of Henry I they are called *tenants per le verge*, which was expressive of th peculiar mode of conveyance;[4] and in the next reign[5] they a called *copyholders*,[6] meaning the *copy* of the *roll* of the lor court.

Of copyholds.

At the period of which we are now writing, this new holding h become an acknowledged branch of the law of tenures, and is treat by Littleton with his usual precision and fulness. He says th "*tenant by copie of court-roll*, is where a man is seised of a man within which there is a custom that has been used time out mind of man, that certain tenants within the same manour ha used to have lands and tenements to hold to them and their hei in fee-simple, in fee-tail, or for term of life, &c., at the will of t lord, according to the custom of the same manour."[7] This is t description of copyholds given by Littleton. These tenants, as h been before observed, could not alien their lands by deed, for in su case the lord might enter as for a forfeiture; but the course was surrender the land in court, according to the custom, into the han of the lord, to the use of him who was to have the estate; up which occasion an entry used to be made on the roll to the followi effect:—*Ad hanc curiam venit A. de B. et sursum reddidit eâdem curiâ unum messuagium, &c., in manus domini, ad usum de D. et hæredum suorum. Et super hoc venit prædictus C. de et cepit de domino in eâdem curiâ messuagium præd., &c., habe dum et tenendum sibi et hæredibus suis, ad voluntatem domi secundum consuetudinem manerii, faciendo et reddendo inde re ditus servitia et consuetudines inde priùs debita et consueta, &c., dat domino pro fine, &c., et fecit domino fidelitatem, &c.* A co

[1] *Vide ante*, vol. i., c. 7. [2] Stat. Extenta Manerii, 4 Edw. I. [3] 42 Edw. III.,
[4] 14 Hen. IV., 34. [5] 1 Hen. V., 11. [6] 1 Inst, 58.
[7] Litt., 73.

of this court-roll was all the evidence or muniment of such an estate.[1]

If these copyholders did not purchase and convey their estates by the same solemnity as was used in the transfer of common-law estates, so neither could they implead or be impleaded for their lands by the king's writ; but the course was to enter a plaint in the lord's court, to this effect: *A. de B. queritur versus C. de D. de placito terræ, videlicet, de, &c., cum pertinentiis, et facit protestationem sequi querelam istam in naturâ brevis domini regis mortis antecessoris, &c., ad communem legem, &c., &c. Plegii de prosequendo, &c., &c.*[2]

Although copyholders had an inheritance, yet it was only an inheritance by the custom of the manor; as such an estate was still, in its very nature, and by the common law of the land, at the will of the lord. This mark of their original baseness hung about copyhold estates so heavily, that it continued to be the opinion of some, even so low down as the reign of Edward IV., that if the lord should oust such a tenant, he had no other remedy but to sue to the lord by *petition;* for if he had any remedy that was at all compulsory, it was asked, how could he be said to hold *at the will* of the lord? Notwithstanding this argument, from that part of the description of these tenants by which they were made to depend on the will of the lord, yet it might be answered, that this will was not to violate the established and immemorial custom of the manor, which was always too reasonable to permit a lord to do injustice to his tenants.[3] And it was the opinion of Sir Robert Danby, chief-justice of the court of common-pleas in the 7 Edward IV., and afterwards of Sir Thomas Brian, his successor, in the 21st year of that king, that the copyholder doing his customs and services should, if put out by his lord, have an action of trespass against him:[4] and this seems to be the inclination of Littleton's opinion on the same point.

Copyholders, in some parts of the country, were frequently denominated from the symbol and ceremony of surrender and grant, and were called *tenants by the verge;* because when land was to be surrendered, the tenant used to have a little verge or rod in his hand, which he delivered to the steward or bailiff, who delivered to the person taking the land the same verge, or another, in name of seisin.[5] There was another method of surrender and grant, which does not seem, however, to have acquired any particular name; as a surrender to the bailiff or reeve, or to two *probi homines* of the same lordship, who used to present such surrender at the next court; and in both these cases, the *copy of the court-roll* was still the evidence of the title.[6] Besides these, there were many other different customs in different manors, too numerous to recount; all which the law in this as well as other cases would recognise, so long as they were reasonable.[7]

[1] Litt., 73–75. [2] *Ibid.*, 76. [3] *Ibid.*, 77. [4] 1 Inst., 61.
[5] Litt., 78. [6] *Ibid.*, 79. [7] *Ibid.*, 80.

As to the length of time that was necessary to give validity to customs and usages, it was laid down that no custom was to be allowed, but such as had been used by title of prescription, that is, *from time out of mind.* But there was a difference of opinion as to what should be deemed time out of mind; some reckoning it from the limitation in a writ of right, which, by the stat. Westm. 1, was fixed at the beginning of the reign of Richard I. Others, again, admitted such to be a good prescription; but, they said, there was another title of prescription at the common law, long before that statute, and that was, where a custom had been used for time, *whereof the memory of man runneth not to the contrary.* They founded their notion upon the form of pleading a custom, which was by suggesting it in the above phrase; and this was the same as saying, that no man then alive had any proof or knowledge to the contrary.[1] This seems to be the opinion of Littleton, and that which is consonant to reason and practice; for otherwise no custom could have gained birth after that distant period, though great part of the common law, which is custom, had confessedly originated since.

Of rents.

We cannot dismiss the subject of tenures and services without taking notice of a title in the law which was connected with them, and had now grown to a considerable size: this is, the title of *rents.* A rent, in its original form, was a compensation reserved to a grantor, in acknowledgment of a grant of lands or tenements; and in this light it may strictly be ranked among the other services we have just been mentioning: but a rent issuing out of land carried with it such a permanency, as put it on the footing of real property; and for that reason a charge of this sort was created on many other occasions than where a proper service could be reserved. Rents were purchased and transferred with less ceremony than land; and on that account recommended themselves, like uses, as a commodious species of property. All through the reigns of Edward III. and his successors, rents in different shapes had been a common object of conveyance, and the law relating thereto underwent various discussion. Very little regard has yet been paid to this branch of the law in the present historical inquiry; but now it had become of too much importance to be passed over.

Rents were of three kinds: that is, *rent-service*, *rent-charge*, and *rent-seck.* The former of these was (as was before mentioned) where a tenant held his land by fealty, and certain rent; or by homage, fealty, and certain rent; or by any other service, and certain rent; and if such rent was not paid at the day, the lord was authorised by the common law to distrain for it,[2] even though the gift was made without deed: this was also the case where lands were given in tail, or a lease was made for life, or for years, rendering rent.[3] But, in order to make this a rent-service, the rever-

[1] Litt., 170. [2] *Ibid.*, 213. [3] *Ibid.*, 214.

sion must remain in the donor or lessor; for if a feoffment was made in fee, or a gift in tail, with a remainder over in fee, without deed, reserving a rent, this reservation would be void, because no reversion remained in the donor, and the tenant held his land immediately of the lord, of whom his donor before held.[1]

It was the alteration in tenures, made by the statute *quia emptores*, that occasioned this difference in the nature of such rents. Before that act, if a man made a feoffment in fee, yielding a certain rent to him and his heirs, this was a rent-service, because there was a tenure subsisting between such feoffor and feoffee:[2] but since that statute, such a feoffment in fee, or a feoffment in tail, or for life, with a remainder over in fee, would not make a tenure between the feoffor and feoffee, for the feoffee would hold of the chief lord paramount. If a rent therefore was reserved by deed, on such a feoffment, with a clause enabling the feoffor and his heirs to distrain, this would be a rent-charge, and not a rent-service, because it arose by force of the writing only, and not by operation of law; and if there was no clause of distress, it would be a rent-*seck*.[3] Again, if a man granted a yearly rent to be issuing out of land to another in fee, or in tail, or for life, and the like with a clause of distress, this would be a rent-charge; and if it was without a clause of distress, it would be a rent-seck. Rent-seck, says Littleton, was, as it were, *redditus siccus*, because no distress was incident to it.[4]

There were many ways in which a rent-service might become a rent-seck. Thus, if a tenant held by fealty and certain rent, and the lord granted the rent by deed, reserving the fealty, and the tenant attorned; here, because the tenements were not holden of the grantee, but of the lord who reserved the fealty, the rent would be a rent-seck.[5] If the lord granted the homage of his tenant, reserving to himself the remnant of his services, and the tenant attorned, the tenure would be of the grantee, and the rent was seck.[6] The same if land was let for life, and the lessor granted the rent to another, reserving the reversion, this rent would be seck, because the grantee had nothing in the reversion.[7] Under the name of "reversion," the rent and services would all pass, as incident thereto.[8]

If a person who had a rent-charge, or rent-seck, was once seised thereof, and the tenant did not keep up his payments, his remedy was to go to the land, and demand it; and if it was denied, or the tenant was not there ready to pay it, which amounted to a denial, in either case this was a disseisin of the rent, for which he might have an assize; and if after recovery and execution it was again denied, this was a re-disseisin.[9] But if the grantee was denied the rent at the first day of payment, then he had no seisin, and so no remedy whatsoever to recover it; and therefore it was usual for the tenant, when he attorned to the grantee, to give a penny, or some-

1 Litt., 215. 2 *Ibid.*, 216. 3 *Ibid.*, 217. 4 *Ibid.*, 218. 5 *Ibid.*, 225. 6 *Ibid.*, 226. 7 *Ibid.*, 228. 8 *Ibid.*, 229. 9 *Ibid.*, 233.

thing, in the name of seisin of the rent, which entitled him to a assize after a denial; for the delivery of the deed of grant gave no such a seisin of the rent as to maintain an assize.

The remedy for recovery of rents was sometimes twofold. Thus in case of a rent-charge, the grantee might choose whether he would sue a writ of annuity or make a distress: but he could not d both; for an avowal of a taking would charge the land and dis charge the person.[1] If a grantor chose not to be liable personally he might add a clause, providing, that the grant should not exten to charge the person by writ of annuity, but only to charge th lands and tenements, &c.[2] Again, should the deed of grant ru thus, "that if A. of B. be not yearly paid at the feast of Christmas for the term of his life, twenty shillings, then it shall be lawful fo the said A. of B. to distrain for it in the manor of G., &c.," here because no annuity was expressly granted, but only that the grante might *distrain* for such an annuity, the person was considered a not charged, but only the land.[3]

There was some curious points of law on the extinction and ap portionment of rents. If a man had a rent-charge to him and hi heirs, and purchased in fee any part of the land out of which i issued, the whole rent was extinct, and could neither be recovere by distress nor by writ of annuity. Yet, if it was a rent-service, i would not be an extinguishment of the whole, but the rent woul be apportioned according to the value of the land. In some in stances, however, a service would be extinguished; as where lan was held by the service of rendering to the lord yearly, at such feast, a horse, a golden spear, or a clove-gilliflower, and the lik If the lord purchased part of the land, the service, as it could nc be severed or apportioned, would be taken away.[4] But where man held by homage, fealty, and escuage, and certain rent, there in the above case, the rent and escuage would be apportioned, an the homage and fealty abide entire to the lord for the rest of th land.[5] It being required by law that the land should be held b some service, and as these were not expensive, they could not com under the same reason as a horse, golden spear, or other entir service, which the tenant, after the land was divided, might not b able to provide.

There was likewise a difference, where the grantee of a rent charge came to part of the land by his own act, and where b course of law. For if a man had a rent-charge, and his fathe purchased part of the land, and this part descended to the son, the the rent-charge would be apportioned according to the value of th land.[6]

There were other circumstances which amounted to a disseisi of rent; and such as were a disseisin in the case of one sort of ren were not so in the case of another. This has been touched before

[1] Litt., 219. [2] *Ibid.*, 220. [3] *Ibid.*, 221. [4] *Ibid.*, 222.
[5] *Ibid.*, 223. [6] *Ibid.*, 224. [7] *Vide ante*, 17.

and the law seems now to be laid down nearly in the same manner; that is, there were three causes of disseisin of a *rent-service*, namely, rescous, replevin, and enclosure.[1] There were four causes of disseisin of a rent-charge, namely, rescous, replevin, enclosure, and denial, and only two causes of disseisin of a rent-seck, namely, denial and enclosure: a menace to prevent a distress was a disseisin of the three kinds of rents.[2]

Such was the shape in which the law of tenures appeared in the reigns of these two kings. From thence we shall proceed to consider the nature of estates.

After what has been said in the reign of Edward III. on the law of entails and limitations in remainder, very little need be added to this part of our subject. The curiosities that arose on these topics constitute no small part of the learning of real property during this period. To enter into a detail of such inquiries would lead us too far; and the great outline of estates-tail, as delivered by Littleton, corresponds so exactly with what has already been mentioned,[3] that it would be an unnecessary recapitulation to adopt much from this great authority. Estates-tail.

The manner in which this author divides estates-tail is this: If lands were given to a man and the heirs of his body begotten, this he calls a *general tail;* because, whatsoever woman he married, every one of his issue by possibility might inherit as issue of his body. A *special tail* was where lands were given to a man and his wife, and the heirs of their two bodies begotten; because none could inherit but the issue of those two persons: all these, as well as gifts in frank-marriage, were specified in the statute *de donis.* Other estates-tail, says our author, were, by the equity of the statute, as lands to a man and the heirs-male of his body-begotten, or heirs-female of his body begotten.[4]

Among other instances of agreement with the old law of entails, it is expressly laid down by Littleton that in case of a limitation in tail-male, and the donee having issue a daughter who had issue a son, such son could not inherit *per formam doni;* because he ought to convey his descent wholly by the heirs-male.[5] Opinions, though of no great authority, had gone so far as to say it would be otherwise in a devise.[6] Where a limitation was made in tail-female, the daughter would take by descent in exclusion of the son; and this was by force of the statute: but it was not so in case of a purchase. For where land was given for life, with remainder to the heirs-female of the body of T. S., who died and left issue a son and a daughter, after which the tenant for life died, here it was held that the daughter could take nothing, because she was not heir; for she must be both *heir* and *heir-female* to answer the limitation of the deed, which she could not be during the life of her brother.[7]

[1] Litt., 237. [2] *Ibid.*, 238–240. [3] *Vide ante*, c. 13.
[4] From Sect. 14 to 21. [5] Litt., 24. *Vide ante.* [6] 1 Inst., 25.
[7] 9 Hen. VI., 23.

If lands were given to a man and his wife, and the heirs of the body of the man, there the husband was construed to have an estate in general tail, and the wife but an estate for term of life: if to the husband and wife, and *the heirs of the husband* which he should beget on the body of his wife, there the husband had an estate in special tail, and the wife an estate for life;[1] but if to the husband and wife, and to the *heirs* which the husband should beget on the body of the wife, there both of them had an estate-tail, because the word *heirs* was not limited to one more than the other.[2] If it was to a man and his heirs which he should beget on the body of his wife, there the husband had an estate in special tail, and the wife nothing.[3] A gift to a man and his heirs-male, or to a man and his heirs-female, was held to be a fee-simple, because it was not limited of what *body* the heirs should be;[4] for these estates were not only *fees* but *fees-tail;* and therefore, as it was necessary to have the word *heirs* to convey a fee, it was likewise necessary to have the word *body* to create a fee-tail.[5]

The title of *tenant in tail after possibility of issue extinct* is described by Littleton with more latitude than in the *Old Tenures.*[6] It is there instanced in a special tail to a man *and* his wife; but now we find if lands were given to a man and his heir which he shall beget on the body of his wife, where the wife had nothing, and the husband was donee in special tail, the husband might be tenant after possibility.[7] No one could be tenant in tail after possibility of issue extinct, but one of the donees being donee in special tail for a donee in general tail was always within the possibility o having issue; and for the same reason the issue to such donee ir special tail could never be tenant in tail after possibility of issu extinct.[8]

There is one species of estates in special tail called estates ir *frank-marriage,* which were very ancient gifts at common law, an are mentioned in the statute *de donis;*[9] since which it was hel that land given with a wife in frank-marriage was, without an other limitation, an estate to the husband and wife, and to th heirs between them begotten; and therefore, that the issue of th second wife could not inherit it.[10] Since the times of Glanville an Bracton, who speak very particularly of these gifts, the law ha altered as to the exemption allowed to such donees and their heir from doing service. It is clearly laid down by both those writer that the third heir, or, as Bracton[11] more particularly calculates i the issue in the fourth degree (reckoning the donee as in the fir degree) should commence doing the services; whereas it is said b Littleton that the fourth degree should pass, and the issue in the fift degree should do the first service.[12] The reason given for requirin them then to do the accustomed services is, that the issue past th

1 Litt., 26, 27. *Vide ante,* 6. 2 *Ibid.,* 28. 3 *Ibid.,* 29. 4 *Ibid.,* 3
5 Bro. Tail, 3. 6 *Vide ante,* 6. 7 Litt., 33. 8 *Ibid.,* 3
9 *Vide ante,* vol. i., c. 7. 10 Litt., 17.
11 *Vide ante,* vol. i., c. 7. 12 Litt., 19.

fourth degree might marry by the canon law: no reason is given for the different limitation made by our older writers. This exemption from service did not, however, include fealty, which must be performed by the donee and the immediate issue;[1] and after the fourth degree, homage and the other services were to be performed. In the early times of our law, all gifts to a woman in order to her marriage, were called *maritagia;* and were distinguished into those that were *free* and those that were not; but now the term was used only as coupled with the former epithet, and we no longer hear of any but gifts in FRANK-*marriage*.

The title of tenant *per legem Angliæ*, or *by the courtesy of England*, was, in our old law, derived from gifts *in maritagia*.[2] When land was given in such a way to a woman, and a child was born, the husband, after her death, enjoyed it for life as tenant *per legem Angliæ*. Thus the law stood in the time of Glanville. In the time of Bracton, this *jus mariti* was extended to *all* inheritances. So the law continued; and conformably thereto it is laid down by Littleton that when a man took a wife seised in fee-simple, or in fee-tail general, or, as Littleton adds, seised as heir in special tail, he should be tenant by the courtesy if any issue were born.[3] Thus a much larger field was opened for this claim of the husband than was warranted by the opinions of our older lawyers.

Thus stood the law respecting estates that were founded on the statute *de donis*.

Perpetuities declared void.

The ill success of some attempts that were made to refine on the restrictions of the statute *de donis*, and the manner in which such attempts were treated by the courts, show that some doubts began to be entertained concerning the wisdom and policy of long entails. We are told[4] that in the reign of Richard II., Richel, a judge of the common pleas, having issue many sons, made a settlement on them in tail, one after another, with a condition that if any one of the sons aliened in fee, or in tail, then his estate should cease and be void, and the land should immediately remain to the next in the entail—a condition which became now necessary for those to make who apprehended the consequences of the judgment in Octavian Lumbard's case, determined in the reign of Edward III.[5] The framer of this deed, probably, did not doubt but such a condition would still be thought deserving the support once given to entails. But that inclination was gone off, and this new device of the judge was declared void by the court of common-pleas in the 2d year of Henry IV. A like settlement made by Justice Thirning,[6] in the reign of Henry IV., was also solemnly adjudged bad in the 21st year of Henry VI. It is not enough to say that entails were no longer favourites in our courts, for Littleton gives three learned reasons why the limitations above-mentioned were substantially void in law in their original creation. First,

[1] Litt., 19.
[2] *Vide ante*, vol. i., c. 3, 4.
[3] Litt., 35.
[4] *Ibid.*, s. 720.
[5] *Vide ante.*
[6] 1 Inst., 377 b.

because a remainder that commences by deed ought to vest in him to whom it is limited, when livery of seisin is made to him who has the particular estate. Secondly, because if the son alien in fee, the fee-simple and freehold is in the alienee, and in none other; and, therefore, that such remainder could not possibly commence immediately after the alienation to a stranger. Thirdly, because upon the breach of the condition the donor ought to enter, and not the person in the remainder, who was no party to the condition; for all which reasons this newly-invented perpetuity, says he, was void in law.[1]

But it was not sufficient to repress these extravagant refinements on entailments. The statute *de donis* still operated with great force on landed property; and it was thought expedient to contrive some method of a general nature, which, to a certain degree, should have the effect of a repeal. In the course of the long contention for power between the houses of York and Lancaster, some temporary motives might contribute to promote such an attempt. An impoverished gentry, and a nobility exhausted by the expenses of the field, were eager to obtain a power of exchanging the slow produce of their inheritances for the common medium, which was current everywhere; and which could now be procured from a commons daily increasing in riches by the cultivation of foreign and domestic trade. Nor was this the only motive for making alienations of land. To persons of unembarrassed circumstances, to whom money afforded no temptation, a full dominion over their own property, if not a desire to alien, was extremely grateful. These were as much inclined as the former to avail themselves of any legal means of enlarging that dominion. To such, the possession of a clear fee-simple was far preferable to land, when under the tie and encumbrance of an entail; the owner might then satisfy his caprice in the full management and disposal of it, regardless how it lay open to the forfeitures and penalties which the law might enforce on property not entailed. The wishes of all these were at length gratified in the reign of Edward IV. and we shall now consider the steps which led to this important event.

We have seen,[2] in the reign of Edward I., that the clergy had invented a method of conveying in mortmain, by means of a *feigned recovery*, upon a *præcipe quòd reddat, &c.* *Feigned recoveries* continued still to be used as a mode of conveyance; and when they were not to the prejudice of any of the persons protected from them by the statutes of Edward I. (*a*), they were accounted a

(*a*) There was nothing in the statute *de donis* against recoveries; the statute was restricted to fines. One reason for the distinction, which goes to the root of the whole subject, was, that recoveries purported to be adverse. Another was, that they were public. The essence and substance of a proceeding to bind the rights of others than the parties to it, would be publicity, as a means of notice to all the world. It was upon the principle of the presumed reality and publicity of the proceed

[1] Litt., s. 721–723.

[2] *Vide ante*, vol. ii., 155.

good assurance to a purchaser, and recognised as such by the courts of law. During all the reign of Edward III., and his successors, there is repeated mention of recoveries, which can be understood in no other light than as modes of conveyance. But these, like other conveyances, if defective in any of their properties and requisites, were liable to be questioned by the parties or their heirs; which was usually done by *falsfying the recovery*, in some action, either by assize or by *præcipe*. If the person suffering a recovery was tenant in fee, he was such a complete owner of the estate, that, provided all due forms were observed, none but termors could falsify such recovery. But if he was tenant in tail, an idea had prevailed, that the issue possessed a title paramount the tenant, which would enable him to falsify the recovery. This notion seems to have governed for some time; till at length, in the reigns of Henry IV. and V., some doubts began to be entertained whether a recovery suffered by tenant in tail was not good against the issue; and it had accordingly become the practice for tenants in tail, who wanted to get rid of the entail and sell their land, to convey under the sanction of a pretended recovery against them on a *præcipe quòd reddat, &c.;* for this (said they) being a solemn judgment, and supposed to be upon a right tried, the issue, who could have no better title than their ancestor, must acquiesce

ings and records of courts of justice, that the great rule of law became established on which the force and efficacy of fines and recoveries entirely depended, viz., that judgments or records bound the parties and their privies, as, for instance, their heirs; so that if a man acknowledged a fine, or suffered a recovery, it would bind his heirs. And on this principle it would bar the issue in tail, for, although it was continually sought to evade the force of this principle in their behalf by pretending that they took under the deed, and not by descent, this, now obviously a fallacy, was never judicially affirmed, and was, wherever it was distinctly brought forward, negatived. In order, however, to protect the issue in tail, the statute *de donis* adopted that principle, and declared that fines should not prejudice the issue. There was no such enactment as to recoveries; and, no doubt, one reason was this: that a recovery in a real action, even by default, could not be without public proclamation, and which would be notice to all the world, and therefore to those interested in ascertaining the rights of the issue, born or unborn, to come forward and disclose the gift in tail, and thus lay a ground to defeat a fraudulent recovery without injury to an honest recoveror. So at least the law was stated by the judges in a case in a subsequent reign to have been, and so it will be seen it was (*Zouch* v. *Stowell, Plowden's Reports*). And that this was so will seem more probable when it is borne in mind that the statutes of Edward I., as to fines, were directed as to secure publicity; and there never was any such statute as to recoveries. Moreover, fraud would vitiate a judgment, and a fraudulent and collusive recovery would be avoided. And if a party recovered on a false and pretended title, the party really interested could recover the land (*Year-book*, 44 *Edw. III.*, 8; 44 *Edw. III.*, 46). It was doubtful whether even a termor could not falsify a recovery (9 *Edw. IV.*, 48; 4 *Hen. VII.*, 10). This was the remedy given by another statute with reference to feigned recoveries in evasion of the law of mortmain. It must always be borne in mind that a recovery, even if really valid, was not binding except between the parties and their legal privies, that is, privies in estate, as the heirs of the recoveree. And, though the ground for the notion that the issue in tail were not barred by a recovery was, that the issue derived title from the deed and not by descent, and so were not privies in estates, a notion which, as the author shows, was judicially negatived, and, although often put forward at the bar, was never judicially established. It would be quite a different thing for the issue to falsify the recovery by showing that it was collusive and feigned, and was not *really* a recovery.

in the same judgment which barred him. Of this opinion was the court in the 3d of Henry VI. A writ of right was there brought against the tenant in tail; and upon his making default, the court showed great reluctance in passing judgment, because, said they, it will bar the issue.[1]

An opinion so explicit as this was sufficient to encourage this application of a recovery upon a *præcipe.* It seems delivered by the court as a common point of learning; it was probably nothing more than was generally admitted, and the very object, perhaps, the parties to that suit had in view. However, this continued, like many other prevailing notions which have not received the sanction of a judicial determination, without any very general effect; and the consequence of a feigned recovery barring an estate tail, was not a settled and established point of law; for in 7 Hen. VI.,[2] it was said, if a tenant in tail lose by *false plea*, his issue may have a formedon against the demandant. But notwithstanding what was held respecting a *false plea,* it was contended as a thing of course, in 37 Hen. VI., that a recovery *by default* in a writ of right might be pleaded in bar of the issue in a formedon.[3] This was not allowed by the counsel on the other side, who seem, notwithstanding, to agree that such a recovery might bar all mesne charges, but not the issue, for they claimed paramount. It does not appear what judgment was given; for the cause was adjourned. This proves, that whatever the practice might be, there was at least a difference of opinion concerning this point in the reign of Henry VI. (*a*).

But this difference of opinion seems to have been confined principally to cases where the tenant suffered the recovery to be had against him by a plain and palpable collusion of *his own,* without maintaining his title, as he ought, by going to a fair and real trial. Of that complexion are all the cases that have hitherto been mentioned; and another which might be added from Littleton.[4] But there was another method of suffering a recovery, than by the tenant's default; and that was by the tenant making his defence, and vouching over a warrantor, *whom* he might procure to make default; and then, the recovery not being by the covin or collusion of the tenant, who had done all he could in vouching his warrantor, the judgment of recovery was complete by all the rules of law. Such recoveries are mentioned by Glanville, Bracton, and all the old writers, and were as fair a proceeding as any other adjudged cause could be.

The grounds upon which a recovery might be falsified were various. The plea of no tenant to *præcipe* (*b*) was the most com-

(*a*) Not at all. It was mere argument, and the author had forgotten the judicial decision he had just cited on the previous page (3 *Hen. VI.*, 55).

(*b*) That is in effect that there was no recovery against the real owner of the freehold estate in possession. The recoveree could not set up this, but the real owner of the freehold could; *i.e.*, he could show that it was not a recovery against him.

[1] 3 Hen. VI., 55 b. [2] 7 Hen. VI., 39. [3] 37 Hen. VI., 31 b. [4] Litt., s. 688.

mon. Another ground was covin; as if the entry of one who had right to the land was taken away, and he got another to enter covinously, and then recovered against the person so entering; this might be falsified, though the party recovering had good title. Thus, where a woman had title of dower and got another to enter, and then she recovered against him that entered, this might be falsified for the covin.[1]

It seems to have been laid down as a general rule, that no party or privy to a recovery should falsify in the point tried by verdict. Thus, on an issue of *non dedit*, if a verdict was found against a tenant in tail, this being a decision of the title, neither he nor his issue would be permitted to falsify, but they must resort to an attaint, otherwise, if the issue had been upon a collateral point, and not upon the title; or if the recovery had been by default.[2] Yet, notwithstanding this rule, where the party could not have an attaint, he might in some cases falsify in the point tried: for it was laid down, that where a man seised in borough-English lost by false oath, as the attaint belonged only to the heir at common law, the younger should be permitted to falsify in the point tried.[3] Though this restriction was laid on parties and privies on account of their being in most cases entitled to another remedy, either by writ of error or attaint, yet a stranger, who had not such remedy, was allowed to falsify in the point tried, or allege any matter which would prove the recovery, or the title of the demandant, to be void.[4] Thus a recovery, with all the sanction of a judicial proceeding, and of a record, was subject, like other conveyances of estates, to be canvassed and made void, if irregular, or if suffered by persons who had no title, or not such an estate of inheritance as was by law completely in their disposal.

Of uses.

The most novel mode of conveyance was a feoffment to a use. We have already taken notice of the origin of uses, in speaking of the several statutes that were passed for correcting the inconveniences suffered from this new species of property. Notwithstanding the distance of time since those statutes were made, there appears nothing in our books relating to *uses*, till the reign of Henry VI. (*a*). Though it is probable that a

(*a*) The inference here suggested, that therefore uses were not unknown from times much more ancient, is an instance of a fallacy into which the author often appears to have fallen, and against which it is necessary to guard in the study of legal history, viz., the fallacy of assuming that, because proceedings are not mentioned as judicially decided upon, they did not exist. It is forgotten that law, especially in matters of conveyancing, would be in a great degree a matter of traditional use and practice, and that nothing could be judicially decided until it had been disputed, and that, therefore, if a practice had become well established, it would not be disputed, and would therefore not become the subject of judicial decision until some extreme or exceptional case had arisen, which happened to come into court perhaps in an incidental and collateral way. And so it might be that a practice had existed for ages before it was mentioned in the books. Thus it was as to the use of fines and recoveries, and thus it was as to uses. It was mentioned in a subsequent reign as a matter

[1] 9 Hen. VI., 41.
[2] 34 Hen. VI., 2; 19 Hen. VI., 39.
[3] 22 Hen. VI., 28; 26 Hen. VI., 18.
[4] 36 Hen. VI., 32.

proper use was meant even by the stat. 50 Edw. III., and it i certain this property was well known in the reign of Richard II and Henry IV., yet it is pretty clear that *uses* were not carried t any great extent till the foreign wars of Henry V. and the civi dissensions between the houses of York and Lancaster made i necessary to find out some method of conveying and concealin real property from the reach of debts and forfeitures. The ex penses and attainders which then threatened the nobility, mad them resort to uses, as the most convenient method of shelterin their lands from the consequences of both.

We have now sufficient light to enable us to trace the steps b which *uses* gradually arose, and took the form in which they after wards appeared. As low down as the 7th of Henry VI., this kin of property was so little regarded, that we find it stated by one o the judges as a thing not allowed by law, and entirely void, if a man made a feoffment with a proviso that he himself should tak the profits[1] (*a*). It was not till the 33d year of the same reign that judicial opinions seem to have altered in favour of these feoff ments; and then, upon a question of collusive feoffment to th heir to avoid guardianship; where it was agreed by the bench tha a feoffment to the heir and a stranger, and to the heirs of the heir was lawful, and no collusion, on account of the interest of a stranger. Again, where a feoffment was to the son to enable hin to marry his daughter or to pay debts.[2] In both these cases, i was agreed that a subpœna lay against the feoffees to compel then to perform the trusts; but it was held that if the feoffees in eithe of these cases infeoffed another person, there was no remedy agains the second feoffee. In the 37th year of this king there is a cas

of legal tradition and legal history, that uses were before the statute of *qui emptores* (*temp. Edw. I.*), though they were not common before that statute, whicl plainly implies that they were common after that statute (*Bro. Abr., Feoffment al uses* fol. 40, 24 *Hen. III.*) And again in another case, it was said that the better opinio was that uses were at common law, for that it appeared that, by the statute of Marl bridge (*temp. Hen. III.*), it was usual for men to make feoffments with intent tha the refeoffments should be made to their heirs at full age, in order to evade the in cidents of feudal tenure to which the lords would otherwise be entitled (*Bro. Abr. Feoffment al uses*, fol. 4, 27 *Hen. VIII.* 8). Thus uses were in existence from the ear liest periods of our legal history. So of fines and recoveries as modes of assuranc or conveyance. In the reign of Henry VII., there was an instance of a fine so use in the reign of Henry III. And the statute of Gloucester, *temp.* Edward I., men tions that feigned recoveries were used to evade the mortmain law, and no doubt ha been also to evade the burdens of feudal tenure.

(*a*) It is strange that the author should have failed to notice the distinction between a feoffment to the use of another, and a feoffment with condition that the feoffor shoul take the profits—that is, should himself be seised, which would be in manifest repug nancy to the feoffment and the apparent livery of seisin to the feoffee. The distinction ha always been drawn between such a feoffment, or a feoffment to a man to his own use, an a feoffment to one for the use of another—that is, with intent that the feoffee should b seised and take the profits, but for the benefit of another; and although in practic the *cestui qui trust* would be allowed to be in possession, yet it would be necessary t avoid the appearance on the face of the conveyance of the legal repugnancy of on man being seised, and another taking the profits. Perhaps it may have been partl for this reason that fines were so generally used as conveyances to uses.

[1] 7 Hen. VI., 43 b. [2] 33 Hen. VI., 14.

which sets forth the state and application of uses, and the course they were then in of being enforced in chancery. A man had signified his desire that his feoffees should make a feoffment to a person to whom he had to go to law, and it was agreed that the intention of the feoffor should be declared by some writing, and not by a verbal message; and that where one devised by his will that his feoffees should make an estate for life to one, remainder to another, the remainder-man should have a subpœna to establish his estate even in the life of the tenant for life.[1]

Of dower.

Since the period when we had occasion to consider the subject of dower a very material change had taken place in the judgment of the law on the subject. Glanville reckons three sorts of dowers thus: *ad ostium ecclesiæ*, the *ex assensu patris*, and the *rationabile dos*, assigned by the common law. The two former were appointments made at the time of the marriage, and if these were not made the widow had a title to claim the third of her husband's freehold, but this was to be a third of such freehold as the husband was *seised of on the day of the marriage.* In the same manner is the *rationabile dos*, spoken of by Bracton and Fleta.[2] But in the reign of Edward III., we find the widow's dower is said to be a third of all that was her husband's *in his life* in fee-simple or fee-tail, as if acquisitions made after the marriage were to be liable to dower. Whatever might be the origin of this doctrine, it was so thoroughly established in the time of Henry VI., that it was then laid down, that where a man was seised of lands "or tenements in fee-simple, fee-tail general, or as heir in special tail, his wife should be endowed of the third part of such lands and tenements as were her husband's *at any time during the coverture;*" so that not only what had been acquired since the marriage, but also such as had been conveyed away were now subject to the claim of dower.[3]

Again, dower *ad ostium ecclesiæ* was not permitted in the time of Glanville to amount to more than a third; and if it was more, it would be admeasured down to a fair third. But it was laid down by Littleton, that such endowment might be of the whole of a man's land. To make such a dower, the man must be of full age and seised in fee; it was to be done after affiance and troth plighted; and after the husband's death the widow might enter without any further assignment, the quantity and certainty of the parcels having been openly declared at the time of the endowment.[4] Dower *ex assensu patris* could likewise only be where the father was seised in fee; the person endowing was to be son and heir-apparent; and the parcels were to be assigned with certainty, so that the widow might enter without any further assignment. It was thought that a deed should be made testifying the father's assent.[5] There was this difference between these two dowers, that a widow might waive that *ad ostium ecclesiæ*, and resort to her dower

[1] 37 Hen. VI. [2] Fleta, v., 341. [3] Litt., 36. [4] *Ibid.*, 96. [5] *Ibid.*, 40.

at common law, contrary to the usage in Glanville's time; but if she had once entered she would be precluded from such option.[1]

If a woman was not above nine years of age at the death of her husband, the law pronounced that she should not be endowed.[2] A woman could not be endowed of lands or tenements which her husband held jointly with another, but otherwise of land he held in common.[3] Neither a tenant in tail of full age, nor a tenant in fee within age, could endow *ad ostium ecclesiæ;* yet an infant could endow *ex assensu patris*, this not being construed to be an act of his own,[4] but of his father.

Thus far of the three species of dower mentioned by the oldest writers upon our law. To these there is added by Littleton another, which he calls *de la pluis beale.* This was where a man seised, for instance, of forty acres of land, held twenty acres of one by knight's service, and the other twenty acres of another in socage, and took a wife, and died leaving a son within age, so that the lord entered into one part as guardian in chivalry, and the widow into the other as guardian in socage. If the widow brought a writ of dower against the guardian, he might pray the oourt that she should endow herself *of the most fair* of the tenements she held as guardian in socage, according to the value of the third she claimed in the tenements held by knight's service; upon which judgment would be given for the guardian in chivalry to hold his lands quit of the dower.[5] After this judgment the widow might call together her neighbours, and in their presence endow herself by metes and bounds of the fairest part of the tenements held in socage.[6] Such regard was paid to the interest of the guardian in chivalry. Another species of dower mentioned by our author is *dower by the custom.* Thus, in some counties, the widow might have the half of the tenements; and by the custom of some town or borough the whole.[7] Thus he reckons in all five species of dower; namely dower by the common law, dower by the custom, dower *ad ostium ecclesiæ*, dower *ex assensu patris*, and dower *de la pluis beale.*[8]

The two estates of *tenant by the courtesy* and *tenant by dower* seem to have borne some relation to each other, as if the claim of the wife in one case and of the husband in the other were founded on equal considerations in law and in policy. Thus a seisin in fee, in fee-tail general, or as heir in special tail, was laid down by Littleton as the proper estate in the husband to give a title of dower and in the wife to make her husband tenant by the courtesy. And afterwards he states it still more specially, that where one of the parties was seised of such an estate, as by possibility, the issue that might be had between them would inherit to its ancestor, there the other party should be entitled, as the case might be, to dower or the courtesy, and otherwise not. For where tenements were given to a man and the heirs that he should beget on the body of his

[1] Litt., 41. [2] *Ibid.*, 36. [3] *Ibid.*, 45. [4] *Ibid.*, 46, 47.
[5] *Ibid.*, 48. [6] *Ibid.*, 49, 50. [7] *Ibid.*, 37. [8] *Ibid.*, 51.

wife, which made the husband donee in special tail (not being one of the above-mentioned estates), if he died without issue, yet the wife should be endowed; because the issue which she by possibility might have had by such husband would have inherited the land. But if she had died, and he had taken another wife, this second wife would not be endowed, for the reason above-mentioned;[1] which latter case confirms likewise the above rule respecting the husband, he being neither seised in fee, nor in fee-tail general, nor heir in special tail. There was this great difference between the donee and the heir in special tail, that the latter was emancipated from all the peculiarities of the entail, and became a tenant in tail general.

The law concerning tenants for years had undergone no great alteration since the time of Bracton.[2] It seems to have been governed by the same principles, and subject to the same rules. Such leases might be made by deed or without; and if there was a remainder over for life, in tail or in fee, the lessor was obliged to make livery of seisin to the lessee for years, or nothing would pass to those in remainder by the entry of the lessee. If the termor entered before livery made, then the freehold and reversion were construed to remain in the lessor.[3] When land was so let for years, the lessee might enter after the death of the lessor, because he derived his title from the lease, which differed from a feoffment; for if livery was not made during the life of the feoffor the feoffment was void, and the land descended to the heir of the feoffor.[4] It was not uncommon to let tenements for the term of half a year, or quarter of a year; and if such tenants committed waste, the writ would nevertheless say, *Quod tenet ad terminum annorum*, for no other form of writ could be had.[5]

The precarious possession described by Bracton[6] seems still to have continued under the title *of tenant at will*. Littleton describes this as "a letting to have and to hold at the will of the lessor;" but it was understood to be at the will of the lessee, as well as of the lessor;[7] and therefore if a lease was made at the will of the lessor, the law inferred that it was also at the will of the lessee, for it must be at the will of both parties. When Littleton therefore says, that such a tenant had no certain nor sure estate, but might be put out whenever the lessor pleased, it should be added that the lessee also might leave the land whenever he pleased. Nevertheless, the will of the lessor was not to be exercised in defiance of all justice and equity; for if the lessee sowed the land, and the lessor put him out before the corn was ripe, the lessee was to have free entry, egress and regress, to cut and carry the corn. But a lessee for years, who knew the end of his term, had not the like indulgence; for if he was so inconsiderate as to sow the land, when he knew his term would end before it was

Tenant at will.

[1] Litt., 52, 53. [2] *Vide ante*, vol. i., c. 8. [3] Litt., 60. [4] *Ibid.*, 66.
[5] *Ibid.*, 67. [6] *Vide ante*, vol. i., c. 8. [7] 18 Hen. VI., 1.

ripe, the lessor or reversioner would have it by law.[1] A tenant at will was not bound to sustain and repair as a termor for years was; but if he committed voluntary waste, in pulling down a house, felling trees, and the like, the lessor might have an action of trespass.[2] The lessor might distrain or have an action of debt for rent reserved on a lease at will.[3] A feoffee to whom no livery of seisin had been made was construed to be a tenant at will; for the words of the deed indicated the feoffor's will that he should have the land;[4] but there being no livery, or specification of estate, he could not have it but at the will of the feoffor.

Estates upon condition.

Conditional estates had always made an important title in our law. They are treated of at large by Bracton;[5] and the useful purpose such modifications of property answered in providing for the contingencies of men's circumstances made them very common, and they were brought into frequent discussion in our courts in every period from the reign of Henry III. to that of which we are now writing.

The principal *conditional estates*, in the earlier times of our law were such as had been converted into estates tail by the statute *de donis*. These had long since fallen under a different head, the supposed condition being no longer a subject of consideration. The chief estates upon condition that now appear in our books, are such as were made to secure a loan of money, and were termed *mortgages*. The others cannot easily be ranked under any particular denomination.

Estates upon condition, in a legal view of them, were of two sorts; that is, upon condition in deed, and upon condition in law. An instance of a condition in deed is where a man infeoffed another in fee, reserving to him and his heirs a certain rent payable at a certain day yearly, with a condition that if the rent was behind, it should be lawful to the feoffor and his heirs to enter; in such case the feoffor might enter, and entirely oust the feoffee.[6] Sometimes the condition was for the feoffor to hold the land only till he was satisfied, in which case he would enter and take the profits as a distress; but when he was satisfied, the feoffee might re-enter.[7] The words constituting such conditions were various, as *sub condition quòd, &c.; proviso quòd, &c.; si contingat quòd, &c.; tunc, &c.;* and in all these instances the feoffee had an estate upon condition.

Mortgages.

The principal of these estates upon condition by deed was mortgage, or *mortuum vadium*, a security well known in the time of Glanville, who states it, however, as hard bargain, and such as subjected the lender to the imputation and punishment of usury.[9] The common way of making this security was for the borrower to infeoff the lender in fee, upon condition that if the feoffor paid to the feoffee at a certain day such

[1] Litt., 168.
[2] *Ibid.*, 71.
[3] *Ibid.*, 72.
[4] *Ibid.*, 70.
[5] *Vide ante*, vol. i., c. 7.
[6] Litt., 325.
[7] *Ibid.*, 327.
[8] *Ibid*, 328–330.
[9] *Vide ante*, vol. i., c. 4.

sum the feoffor might enter.[1] Sometimes a gift in tail, or a lease for life or years, was made in mortgage.[2] It was held, that should such feoffor die before the day of payment, his heirs or executors[3] might tender the money and enter, though there was no provision to that effect in the deed; for the heir was considered as having an interest in the condition, and the grand object was that the money should be paid at the day, which might be as well done by the heir as the feoffor; but a stranger who had no interest could not make such tender.[4] If the feoffee refused the money so tendered, and the feoffor entered, the feoffee had no remedy by law to recover the money which he lost by his own default and obstinacy.[5] If the condition was for the feoffor to pay, not at *a certain day*, but *generally*, and the feoffor died before payment, this was held differently, for, in such case, the heir could not make the tender, because a condition for the feoffor to pay was the same as saying he should pay during his life; and when he died the time of the tender was past.[6] Many similar questions upon the performance of conditions by heirs are to be found in Bracton.[7] If the feoffee in mortgage died before the day of payment, the feoffor ought to pay the money to the executors, and not to the heir, the estate being given in lieu of money, which would otherwise have come to the executors. But sometimes the deed expressly stipulated that the money should be paid to the feoffee or his heirs.[8]

Some doubts had arisen about the place where the feoffor in mortgage was to tender the money. Some said upon the land, because the condition, it was said, depended upon the land. But Littleton was of opinion that he was bound to seek the feoffee whersoever he was in England, the same as if money was to be paid on a common condition in a bond; in which case the obligor was bound to seek the obligee, if in England, otherwise the obligation would be forfeited. He likewise thought that the estate might more properly be said to depend upon the condition, than the condition to depend on the land.[9] There was this difference between a sum in gross, and a rent issuing out of land, that the latter need only be tendered on the land.[10] It was therefore advisable and safe for the feoffor in mortgage to appoint by the deed a special place for the payment; and such was commonly the practice, as, "in the cathedral of St Paul's Church in London, within the four hours next before the hour of noon, at such a pillar within the church," and the like specifications, which ascertained to a certainty both the time and place.[11] Though the feoffee was not bound to receive the money in any other than the place limited, yet, if he so pleased, it would equally avail the feoffor; and so it would, if the feoffee accepted any other thing in satisfaction of the money, though not a twentieth part of the value.[12] Thus stood the law respecting mortgages in the reign of Edward IV.

[1] Litt., 382. [2] *Ibid.*, 333. [3] *Ibid.*, 337. [4] *Ibid*, 334.
[5] *Ibid.*, 335. [6] *Ibid.*, 337. [7] *Vide ante*, vol. i., c. 4. [8] Litt., 339.
[9] *Ibid.*, 340. [10] *Ibid.*, 341. [11] *Ibid.*, 342. [12] *Ibid.*, 344.

Where estates were to be raised or defeated by performance of a condition, it appears from the above cases that any person who had an interest in the condition, or in the land, might make offer to perform that condition. Again, where a feoffment was upon condition, that if the feoffee paid to the feoffor at a certain day so much money, the feoffee should have the land to him and his heirs, and if he failed, the feoffee might enter; if the feoffee, before the day of payment, made a feoffment to another, and the second feoffee tendered the money, he would have the estate without the condition being so expressed; and this was because he had an interest in the condition for the safeguard of his estate. The same if the first feoffee tendered it, because he was privy to the condition.[1]

Concerning these conditions for *entry*, it should be observed that they, as well as rents, could be reserved or given to no person, but only to the feoffor or donor and his heirs. For if a man let lands for life, rendering rent, with a clause of re-entry for non-payment, and then granted the reversion with attornment, the grantee of the reversion might distrain for the rent as incident to the reversion, but could not enter, the right of entry being gone for ever.[2] In like manner, if a reversion came to a lord by escheat, the lord might distrain, but could not avail himself of a condition of re-entry.[3]

It was laid down as a rule, that wherever land was granted for a term, with condition to hold in fee on paying a certain sum, it was always necessary that livery of seisin should be made upon the grant when the lessee first entered; for the fee and the freehold could not pass without livery, this being one of the most established rules of the ancient law.[4] A question of law arose upon such a livery made to a termor for years, which has been debated since with great difference of opinion. Where land was granted to a man for term of five years, on condition that if he paid to the grantor within the first two years forty marks, he should have the fee-simple, or otherwise should hold it only for the five years, and livery of seisin was made upon the grant, Littleton says that the grantee in such case had a *fee-simple conditional;* but if he did not pay the forty marks within the two years, then the fee and freehold would be immediately adjudged in the grantor. For notwithstanding the common rule, that in feoffments upon condition the feoffor had not the freehold before his entry, yet, says he, that was confined to cases where he could lawfully enter, which he could not here; for the grantee had still a title to occupy for three years and during that occupation, if he committed waste, the grantor might have a writ of waste, which Littleton considers as another proof that the reversion was in him.[5] The doubt, however, with later writers has not been whether the reversion was in the grantor at the end of the two years, but rather how it passed out of him

[1] Litt., 346. [2] *Ibid.*, 346, 347. [3] *Ibid.*, 348. [4] *Ibid.*, 349. [5] *Ibid.*, 350, 351

during the two years—that is, how the grantee could have a fee conditional.

Those who differ from Littleton say that, as the fee-simple was to commence on a condition precedent, it could not pass till that condition was performed; and in support of this opinion, they vouch authorities in the reigns of the three Edwards and of Richard II. But the cases relied upon seem, many of them, to differ from this in the grand circumstance which constitutes the foundation of Littleton's opinion, for it is not expressly said in any of them that livery of seisin was made; and Littleton has himself said, in the preceding section, that without livery nothing of the freehold and inheritance passed. It is therefore argued on the other side, with some show of reason, that when the lessor made livery, as in the present case, it would not be consistent that against his own livery a freehold should remain in him; and, secondly, it being a rule of law that livery must pass a present freehold to some person, and cannot give a freehold *in futuro*, therefore the freehold and inheritance must pass immediately, and not expect till the condition was performed. These were principles well known in the time of Littleton; and his commentator declares that there is both reason and authority on his side.[1] Upon the shifting of the freehold and inheritance on conditions and contingencies, Bracton had been very explicit, as we have shown in the former part of this work.[2]

If, by the act of God, a condition was rendered impossible to be performed, the law permitted the party to acquit himself by acting as nearly as could be according to the spirit and design of it. Thus, if a feoffment was made on condition that the feoffee should give the land back to the feoffor and his wife, and the heirs of their two bodies, with remainder to the right heirs of the feoffor; there, if the husband died in the lifetime of the wife, before any estate in tail was made, he might fulfil the condition by making an estate as much like the other as possible, which Littleton thinks he would do by giving the wife an estate for life, without impeachment of waste, with remainder, after her decease, to the heirs of the body of the husband, remainder to the right heirs of the husband; for as she could not have an estate in tail, it was reasonable she should at least have an estate without impeachment of waste, which was one advantageous property of an entail.[3] If the husband and wife both died, leaving issue before the gift was made, then our author thought an estate should be made to the issue, and to the heirs of the body of his father and mother, remainder to the right heirs of the father.[4] Again, if there was a condition to infeoff several persons to them and their heirs, and they have all died before the estate was made, then an estate should be made to the heir of him that survived of them, *habendum* to him and the heirs of the survivor;[5] for this would keep the land in the line for which it was

[1] 1 Inst., 217. [2] *Vide ante*, vol., i., c. 4. [3] Litt., 352.
[4] *Ibid.*, 353. [5] *Ibid.*, 354.

intended; whereas, if the limitation had been to the heirs of th son, then it might, upon failure of heirs on the part of his father go to those *ex parte maternâ.*[1]

If the feoffee did anything that affected the land, and disable himself from making as good and complete an estate as when h was infeoffed, the feoffor might enter. As if a feoffee, before th performance of the condition, infeoffed another, or made an estat for life or years to another;[2] if he married before the conditio performed (for his wife became entitled to dower out of the lan whether he made the estate or not);[3] if he charged the land wit a rent, or bound himself in a statute, the feoffor might enter nevertheless, when the feoffor entered, all incumbrances an charges made by the feoffee were defeated and void.[4]

The last order of estates upon condition and deed, now in use was where a restraint was imposed on the feoffee with regard t alienation, or any other circumstance. In the early ages of ou law a feoffor considered a grant so much in the light of a gratuit that he subjected it to almost any sort of restraint and conditio which did not tend to the evident breach of some law. Wit respect to alienation, it was very common, in the clause of per mission to alien, to add *exceptis viris religiosis et Judœis;* an when a clause was necessary to enable the feoffee to alien, it wa not remarkable that it should be given with certain restrictions. It was not uncommon to add a prohibition from aliening at all, an very frequent to impose a fine for alienation. These and man other checks were thought to be lawful and reasonable for feoffo to affix to their grants, in consideration of the possibility of reverte which the law supposed to remain in them after their feoffment but the statute *quia emptores* took away the force of this reason, a since that act nothing remained in the feoffor after the feoffmen in fee. We find it accordingly laid down by Littleton that feoffment in fee, upon condition that the feoffee should not alie was void in law; for the law annexing to the tenant in fee th power of alienation, it would never endure a condition that was t take away all the power it gave.[6] But it was still held that partial restraint might still be imposed, as that the feoffee in fe should not alien to a particular person.[7]

Such conditions were good, when calculated not to defeat, bu rather to favour, the great designs of the law. Thus restraints o alienation carried a more plausible colour when connected wit estates tail, the law having pronounced that those should be mai tained in the form which was given to them by the donor. I therefore, land was given in tail, on condition that none of th tenants in tail should alien in fee, in tail, or for the life of anothe but only for their own lives; this was adjudged a good conditio because such alienation and discontinuance would be contrary t

[1] Inst., 220 b. [2] Litt., 355, 356. [3] *Ibid.*, 357. [4] *Ibid.*, 35
[5] *Vide ante*, vol. i., c. 4. [6] Litt., 360. [7] *Ibid.*, 36

the will of the donor.[1] Again, a gift in tail might be made upon condition that if the tenant in tail or his heirs aliened in fee, in tail, or for term of another man's life; and also, if all the issue of the tenant failed, then it should be lawful for the donor and his heirs to enter. Such conditions were held to be good, so as not to defeat, but to save the entail to the reversioner, that being the course in which the law would otherwise dispose of the land.[2] We have before seen that such conditions for preserving entails were sometimes carried further than the judges thought proper to support them.[3]

Thus far of estates upon condition by deed: estates held upon condition in law might, in the full extent of the term, include most estates in the law, as there was hardly a holding that did not bind the tenant to certain terms, which might be said to be the conditions on which he held his estate. Thus, if a parkership was granted for life, there was a condition in law annexed to such office, that the parker should do his duty, or otherwise the grantor might oust him.[4] There were many instances of that kind, which can very easily be supplied by the imagination of the reader.

All the different estates beforementioned might belong to more persons than one; and when an estate was so possessed, the owners were either *parceners*, *joint-tenants*, or *tenants in common.* The nature of such tenancies has not hitherto been sufficiently discussed; but they were now become too important an article to be passed over. We shall begin with *parceners.*

Of parceners.

These were, when daughters or other female heirs took an estate in fee or in tail by descent; and in such case they were all reckoned but as one heir. As some might feel an inconvenience in possessing land in this way, the law had furnished a writ *de partitione faciendâ,* which we find mentioned so early as the time of Bracton as a judicial proceeding, by which one or more parceners might compel the others to come into a partition of the estate amongst them.[5] A partition was sometimes made by deed or by parole,[6] with the general consent of all the parties. Thus, either some friends would divide the land as nearly in equality as could be, and the eldest made the first choice; or it would be agreed between them, that each should have certain particular tenements.[7] In these cases, the part the eldest sister had used to be called, by way of distinction, the *enitia pars.* If the eldest sister made the partition, it was thought a reasonable piece of equity that she should choose last, *cujus est divisio alterius est electio.* Another voluntary partition was by lot: they used to write upon separate scrolls different parts of the land, and these being rolled up in wax, and mixed together, the eldest sister drew the first ball, and then the others.[8] If they could come to no agreement about either of these amicable methods, they

[1] Litt., 362. [2] *Ibid.*, 364. [3] *Vide ante.* [4] Litt., 387.
[5] *Vide ante*, vol. i., c. 5. [6] Litt., 250. [7] *Ibid.*, 243, 244. [8] *Ibid.*, 246.

then had recourse to the compulsory one, by writ *de partitione faciendâ*.[1]

The judgment upon this writ was, that partition should be made between the parties, and that the sheriff should go in person to the land, and, by the oaths of twelve men of his bailiwick, make partition, assigning a part to each parcener: no mention was to be made in this judgment of any preference to the eldest sister beyond the others;[2] but it was left wholly to the sheriff to assign as he pleased; and he was to certify the partition to the justices.[3]

A partition need not be made between all the parceners; for if there were three parceners, and the youngest would have partition, and the other two would rather hold in parcenary, then one part might be allotted in severalty to the one who wished it. But this was in case of partition by agreement only; for on a writ, there must be a partition of the whole.[4]

Whether partition was made by the sheriff under the sanction of law, or by the parties upon an agreement, the great object of both was to obtain an equality; and therefore, when property was circumstanced in a particular way, there was some difficulty so to marshal it that every claimant might have a lawful equality. For instance, if two houses descended to two parceners, the one producing twenty shillings, the other ten shillings rent *per ann.*, partition might be made in this manner: each parcener might have a house, and she who had that worth twenty shillings *per annum* would be required to pay a yearly rent of five shillings issuing out of her house to the other parcener and her heirs.[5] This, though without deed, being a rent-charge, might be distrained for, into whatsoever hands the land went.[6]

If a partition was made between tenants in fee, and it was found afterwards to be unequal, it was, nevertheless, binding on all parties; but not so between tenants in tail; for though they were bound during their lives, yet the issue of either might disagree to the partition, and enter upon the land, and occupy the whole in common, as if no partition had been made.[7] In like manner, if a partition was made by a parcener's husband, she might enter after his death.[8] The same of a parcener within age, who might enter either before or after she came of age; but if, when of full age she took all the profits of her allotment, this would be construed such an agreement as would confirm the partition.[9]

The statute *de donis* created some difficulties in the way of partitions. Thus, if lands descended to two daughters in fee and in tail, and, upon a partition, one took the lands in tail, and the other those in fee; if she who took the land in fee aliened it, and then died leaving issue, the issue might enter into the lands in tail, and hold them in purparty with the aunt.[10]

[1] Litt., 247. [2] *Ibid.*, 248. [3] *Ibid.*, 249. [4] *Ibid.*, 276. [5] *Ibid.*, 251. [6] *Ibid.*, 252, 253. [7] *Ibid.*, 255. [8] *Ibid.*, 256. [9] *Ibid.*, 258. [10] *Ibid.*, 260, 261.

There was a species of estates-tail that created still greater difficulties in making partitions, and these were estates in *frank-marriage*. If a man was seised in fee, and had two daughters, and on the marriage of the eldest he gave lands in frank-marriage, and afterwards died seised of lands of greater value than those given in frank-marriage; it was a rule, in such case, that neither the husband nor wife should have any purparty in such remnant of the estate, unless they would put their lands held in frank-marriage into what was called *hotchpot* with the remnant, and so make an equal division of both together: if she would not agree to this, then the youngest might hold the remnant to her separate use.[1] A gift in frank-marriage being an advancement to a child, it was collected from such refusal to put into hotchpot, that she was conscious she was sufficiently advanced; and therefore it was but reasonable, that she should have no claim on what remained for the other child.[2] This law of hotchpot held only where the lands descended from the donor; and it did not take place if they came from any ancestor of his;[3] nor where the lands in frank-marriage and the others were of equal value;[4] nor in any case where lands did not descend in fee-simple:[5] all donees but those in frank-marriage might have their purparty in such descended land without coming into hotchpot.[6]

It was a rule, that should one of the parceners be evicted of her part by one who had lawful title, she might have a claim upon the other allotments, as if no partition had been made.[7] Thus, if land, part of which was possessed by just title, and part acquired by disseisin, descended on two parceners; and the disseisee being an infant, and so not barred of his entry by the descent, entered on the parcener to whom the land of which he had been disseised was assigned, then she might enter upon her sister, and hold her share in parcenary with her. But if she had aliened the land in fee, and the infant had entered on the alienee, it was held, the parcener could not then enter on her co-parcener; but she might, if she aliened only a particular estate, and continued seised of the reversion.[8] If one parcener aliened, the others might have a writ of partition against the alienee.[9]

Thus stood the law concerning parceners. Parceners were usually females; none but females being able to take an estate together, by the general law of the kingdom. But by the custom of gavelkind, males might hold lands in parcenary; the descent there being to all the males equally.[10]

Joint-tenants.

The condition of *joint-tenants* bore some apparent affinity to that of parceners, but there was a material difference between them. The first difference was, that joint-tenants took their estate by purchase, and not by descent.[11] Again, the

[1] Litt., 266–268. [2] *Ibid.*, 269. [3] *Ibid.*, 272. [4] *Ibid.*, 273. [5] *Ibid.*, 274. [6] *Ibid.*, 275. [7] *Ibid.*, 263. [8] *Ibid.*, 262. [9] *Ibid.*, 264. [10] *Ibid.*, 265. [11] *Ibid.*, 277.

nature of joint-tenancy was, that the surviving tenant should have the entire estate to himself. Thus, if three were enfeoffed in fee, and two had issue and died, yet the third would take the whole. But it was different with parceners; for if there were three parceners, and one died leaving issue, that issue took the part belonging to the parcener; and if she died without issue, her co-heirs would take her part as parceners, and not as joint-tenants.[1] It was not only among joint-tenants of estates of freehold that survivorship prevailed, but it held also between those who had a joint estate or possession of a chattel, real or personal; as of a lease for years, or of a horse:[2] the same of a debt or duty; for if an obligation was made to many, the survivor would have the whole debt: the same of other covenants and contracts.[3] But this did not extend to merchants; for it was laid down by our law, that *jus accrescendi inter mercatores pro beneficio commercii locum non habet.*[4]

An estate was sometimes so limited, that the feoffees were joint-tenants for their lives, and tenants in common of the inheritance. As where lands were given to two men and to the heirs of their two bodies begotten; in this case, the donees had a joint estate for their lives, and yet they had several inheritances; for if one of the donees had issue and died, the other would have the whole by survivorship for his life; and if the survivor had likewise issue and died, then the issue of one would have the one moiety, and the issue of the other the other moiety, and they would hold them in common. For the former words gave a complete estate to the donees for their joint lives; and as they could not by possibility have an heir between them, the law gave them such an inheritance as they could take; namely, to the heirs which each should respectively beget in marriage: the inheritances, therefore, must of necessity be several, without any survivorship between the issue. Again, if lands were given to two and to the heirs of one, they were joint-tenants for life, and one of them had the fee-simple; and if he who had the fee-simple died, the other tenant had the entirety by survivorship.[6]

The title of survivorship superseded all charges and encumbrances made by the joint-tenant: thus, a rent-charge granted by a joint-tenant would be good during his life, but void as against the other joint-tenant. It was otherwise in case of a parcener; because the surviving parcener took by descent from the parcener who died, which the joint-tenant did not.[7] If a joint-tenant could not encumber the estate, so neither could he devise it; but a parcener could devise her moiety.[8] The survivorship was a title paramount to everything that the joint-tenant could do; the whole estate was considered as belonging to each, and therefore it would be disposing of the property of others for one to have prevented its coming to the longest liver in as perfect a state as when the gift was orig

[1] Litt., 280. [2] *Ibid.*, 281. [3] *Ibid.*, 282. [4] 1 Inst., 182.
[5] Litt., 283. [6] *Ibid.*, 285. [7] *Ibid.*, 286. [8] *Ibid.*, 287.

ually made to them. It is upon this idea that joint-tenants were said to be seised *per my et per tout;* or, as Littleton more fully expresses it, " In every parcel, and by every parcel, and by all the lands and tenements in one tenant jointly seised with his companion."[1] So great a favourite was this joint estate in the law, that though it might be parted by the agreement of the joint-tenants, yet there was no writ to compel a partition as between parceners.[2] Notwithstanding the above piece of law, upon a rent-charge granted by a joint-tenant, if a lease was made by a joint-tenant who died before the lessee entered, the lessee might, notwithstanding, enter; and the reason of this difference is stated by Littleton to be, because the tenant had a right in the land by force of the lease, and therefore the state of the land was altered in the life of the tenant, which was not the case in the rent-charge.[3] If land was given to a husband and wife and another person, the husband and wife took only half, because they are reckoned but one person in law.[4]

The title of parceners, as was before seen, accrued only by descent; that of joint-tenants, by purchase; but tenants in common might be by both titles; and tenants of both the above descriptions might become tenants in common. Tenants in common were such as came to lands by several titles, but held them in common *pro indiviso*, so that neither knew the part that belonged to him. Thus a joint-tenancy might become a tenancy in common; as if one joint-tenant aliened in fee to another, such feoffee would hold in common with the other joint-tenants, because he took his estate by a different title from that of the joint-tenant with whom he held;[5] but if the joint-tenants were more than two, those who had not aliened held their part jointly with the usual survivorship.[6] If an estate was given to two persons, without more saying, the construction of law upon it was, that they were joint-tenants; but if it was to two abbots, or to an abbot and a secular man, and the like, this was held to be a tenancy in common.[7] If land was given to two to hold, the one moiety to one and his heirs, the other moiety to the other and his heirs, it was a tenancy in common.[8] The same if a man infeoffed another of the moiety of his land, the feoffee and feoffor held in common.[9]

Tenants in common.

If there were two joint-tenants in fee, and one let the part that belonged to him for the term of his life, it was held, that in such case the reversion was severed, and the lessor held in common with the other joint-tenant,[10] according to the opinion of Littleton, though some thought otherwise. Again, if there were three joint-tenants, and one released all his right to another of them; the person to whom the release was made, would hold such third part with his companions in common.[11] If one parcener aliened to a

1 Litt., 288.
2 *Ibid.*, 290.
3 *Ibid.*, 289.
4 *Ibid.*, 291.
5 *Ibid.*, 292.
6 *Ibid.*, 294.
7 *Ibid.*, 296, 297.
8 *Ibid.*, 298.
9 *Ibid.*, 299.
10 *Ibid.*, 302.
11 *Ibid.*, 334.

stranger,[1] the alienee would hold in common with the other parceners.

The different condition of joint-tenants and tenants in common occasioned a difference in the actions they brought; they were sometimes to be joint, and sometimes several. In like manner, tenants in common in some cases might join, and in some were driven to bring several actions. For example, if two tenants in common were disseised, they must have two assizes, because they were seised by several titles; but it was otherwise of joint-tenants, who, on account of their joint-title, must join in one assize.[2] The heirs of two parceners, though they came in by several titles, would, notwithstanding, be entitled to one assize, as long as the land remained undivided.[3] Where two tenants in common let their land, reserving a certain rent, and a pound of pepper, and a hawk, or a horse; if they distrained for this, and the tenant made a rescous, in such case, as to the rent and pound of pepper, they might have two several assizes, but as to the hawk or horse, they could have only one. The reason of this difference, as given by Littleton, is, that the rent and pound of pepper might be apportioned to each according to his moieties; but as no moiety of a hawk or horse could be had, therefore, notwithstanding their several titles, they could have but one assize of such things.[4]

Though tenants in common were properly to have several actions of such things as concerned the realty, on account of their title to the realty being several, yet in personal actions they might join; as of trespass, for breaking their houses, breaking their closes, feeding and spoiling their grass, cutting their woods, fishing in their piscary, and the like.[5] In like manner, they might bring a joint action of debt for rent, because it was in the personalty; but if they avowed for the rent, they ought to sever, because it was in the realty.[6] Tenants in common might make partition by agreement; but they could not be compelled by law to do it.[7]

As persons might be tenants in common of a freehold, so might they of a chattel, whether real or personal; and in a similar way might one joint-tenant of a chattel make the person to whom he aliened his moiety tenant in common with the other joint-tenant.[8] One tenant in common of a term for years might have an *ejectione firmæ* against the other; so might a guardian have an ejectment of ward for lands held in common; these being things that might be apportioned and severed. But one tenant in common could not have trespass *quasi clausum fregit* against the other, because by the nature of their estate, each might enter and occupy *per my et per tout.* And in chattels personal, if one tenant in common took the whole, there was no remedy in law for the other; but he must retake it, if he could. The same of chattels real, that could not be severed; as the wardship of the body (though we have seen

1 Litt., 309. 2 *Ibid.*, 311. 3 *Ibid.*, 313. 4 *Ibid.*, 314.
5 *Ibid.*, 315. 6 *Ibid.*, 316, 317. 7 *Ibid.*, 318. 8 *Ibid.*, 319–321

was otherwise of the land), where the one guardian could only ıke the body out of the possession of the other, when he saw a fit ime.[1]

Next to the nature of estates, we are led to consider the modes y which they were created and conveyed. The most ancient ways f conveyance were by feoffment and by fine, both which have been requently mentioned. Deeds of release and of confirmation had ately become more common; and the discussion of their design nd effect filled some space in the learning of real property.

A person might convey all the right he had in lands or tenements y a *release*, the form of which was, *Noverint universi, &c., me emisisse, relaxâsse, et omninò de me et hæredibus meis quietum lamâsse totum jus, titulum, et clameum, quæ habui et habeo.*[2] We re told by Littleton, that some releases went further, and added, *uæ quovismodo in futurum habere potero;* but these words, says hat author, were null and void, for no right passed by a release, ut that which the releasor had at the time. Thus, where there vere father and son, and the father was disseised, and the son, luring the father's life, released by deed to the disseisor all the ight he had or might have without clause of warranty, and then he father died, the son might enter, notwithstanding the release; because he had nothing in the land during his father's life, but the ight descended to him after the release.[3]

In cases of release of all a man's right in lands, the relessee should have a freehold in deed or in law, to make the release good.[4] Thus the son of the disseisor had a freehold in law by the descent without an entry, and a release so made to him would be good.[5] In some cases, where there was no freehold either in deed or in law, as where the disseisor let the lands for life, with reversion to himself, a release to the disseisor would be good, by reason of the reversion.[6] So if there were remainders over, a release to any of the remainder-men was good.[7] But if the tenant for life was disseised, a release to a remainder-man would be void, because he had not a remainder in deed, but only a right to a remainder.[8] Every release that was good to a reversioner, or remainder-man, was good to the freeholder;[9] and so *vice versâ* of a release to the freeholder.[10]

The form of a deed of confirmation was this: *Ratificâsse, approbâsse, et confirmâsse, &c.* A release and a confirmation differed in many respects. As for instance: If a man let lands for life, and the tenant for life let them for forty years, and the first lessor confirmed the estate of the tenant for years, and afterwards the tenant for life died during the term for years, the first lessor could not enter.[11] But a release by the first lessor to the tenant for years would in this case be void, because there was no privity between him and the tenant for years; for it was a rule, that a release to a

[1] Litt., 323. [2] *Ibid.*, 445. [3] *Ibid.*, 446. *Vide ante*, vol. i., c. 5. [4] *Ibid.*, 447. [5] *Ibid.*, 448. [6] *Ibid.*, 449. [7] *Ibid.*, 450. [8] *Ibid.*, 451. [9] *Ibid.*, 452. [10] *Ibid.*, 453. [11] *Ibid.*, 516.

tenant for years was not good, unless there was a privity between him and the relessor.[1] Thus if the disseisor made a lease for years, and the disseisee released to the termor, it would be void, but a confirmation would be good.[2] If the disseisor confirmed the estate of the disseisee, he had a clear fee-simple, although the confirmation was expressed to be in tail, for life, or for only an hour.[3] A confirmation to a tenant for life would not, like a release, avail the remainder-man or reversioner; but a confirmation to the remainder-man would bar the confirmor from entering on the tenant for life; because such entry, by defeating the estate for life, would also defeat the remainder, against his own confirmation.[4]

If there were two disseisors, and a release was made to one of them, such relessee might hold his companion out. But according to some opinions, a confirmation would not have the same effect: for nothing was confirmed but *his estate,* and that was a joint one.[5] The same if one joint-tenant confirmed the estate of the other; but if in such case the following words were added, "to have and to hold to him and to his heirs all the tenements," &c., it would become a sole estate in fee-simple. It is therefore recommended by Littleton, that instead of confirming *the estate*, the words should be, "to have the said land to him and his heirs," or for life, as the case might be; applying the words of confirmation not to the estate, but to the land.[6]

Sometimes the words *dedi* or *concessi* had the same force as *confirmavi;* as if the disseisee made a deed to the disseisor, saying *dedi et concessi* the land in question, this would operate without livery, as a confirmation.[7] So if a man was in possession under a lease for years, and a deed was made to him by the words *dedi* or *concessi* for life, in tail, or in fee, it would enure by force of the confirmation to enlarge his estate.[8] Where the words *dedi et concessi* would not enure as a confirmation, they might as a new grant; as where the person to whom the deed was made had nothing in the thing on which the confirmation would enure.[9] Sometimes such grant operated in extinguishment of the thing given or granted; as where a tenant held of his lord by certain rent, and the lord by deed granted to the tenant and his heirs the rent, the rent thereby became extinct.[10]

In like manner a release was sometimes construed to enure to enlarge an estate, and sometimes *de mitter*, and vest a right according to the fact and circumstances of the case. Thus if a reversioner released to his tenant for a term, he must specify the estate he meant to give, whether for life, in tail, or in fee; and if there was no mention of heirs, the estate was enlarged only for life.[11] But if a disseisee released all his right to the disseisor, as this was nothing more than *remitting* the right of the disseisee, there needed n

[1] Litt., 517. [2] *Ibid.*, 518. [3] *Ibid.*, 519, 520. [4] *Ibid.*, 521.
[5] *Ibid.*, 523. [6] *Ibid.*, 524. [7] *Ibid.*, 531. [8] *Ibid.*, 532, 53
[9] *Ibid.*, 541, 542. [10] *Ibid.*, 543. [11] *Ibid.*, 465.

mention of heirs; for the relessee had a fee-simple at the time of the release made, and that which was before wrongful was thus made lawful; and if the release was to him only for an hour, it would enure in fee; for a right being once gone, was gone for ever.[1] A release was said also to enure by way of extinguishment, where he to whom the release was made could not take the thing released; as where a lord released to a tenant all the right he had in the seignory, or the land: the same of a release to the tenant of the land of a rent-charge, or common of pasture.[2]

A confirmation, as the name implies, was designed to substantiate a defeasible estate, which had been obtained either by right or by wrong; and therefore it was rarely, if ever, made in concurrence with the party who gave rise to the imperfect interest which it was meant to confirm. But a *release,* though applicable to divers cases, where it was certainly a subsequent transaction, and made upon an after-thought, as to divest a right, or enlarge some pre-existent estate; yet was not unusually adopted as an original conveyance for the transfer of the freehold and inheritance. The way was this: A deed of *lease* was made to the party intended to be the purchaser for three or four years; and when he had entered on the possession immediately, or very soon after, a *release* of the inheritance was given to him; and thus he became seised as completely as if by fine, or feoffment with livery of seisin.[3] Thus *a lease and release* were practised as a full transfer of the freehold and inheritance. This, as well as a feoffment to a use, which will be considered presently, was a deviation from the common law conveyances, which, we shall soon find, began to give place to these and other new modes of transfer, grounded upon the doctrine of uses.

Attornment.

In considering the nature of conveyances at this time, we must not forget to speak of *attornment*, which was a necessary requisite for the completion of some grants that were particularly circumstanced. Attornment was the agreement of the tenant to a grant of a seignory, or of a rent; or the agreement of a donee in tail, or termor for life, or for years, to a grant of the reversion or remainder. In the time of Henry III.[4] we had occasion to mention this, among other topics arising upon the subject of tenures, but since that time great alterations had taken place in it. What was there said, is confined to attornment of the former kind—namely, upon a grant of the lord—which doctrine, however, appears in a very different point of view, as exhibited by Littleton. As this subject leads us to consider very particularly the relation between lord and tenant, it is well worthy of attention. We shall therefore take a short view of it, and shall begin with grants made by lords, and then proceed to grants made of reversions and remainders.

If a lord granted by deed the services of his tenant, the tenant

[1] Litt., 466, 467.
[2] *Ibid.*, 479, 480.
[3] 32 Hen. VI., 8.
[4] *Vide ante*, vol. i. c. vi.

must attorn during the life of the grantor, or the grant would be void. The form of attornment was either by saying, "I agree to the grant made to you," or, "I am content with the grant made to you;" or, as were the most common forms, "I attorn to you by force of the said grant," or, "I become your tenant;" or by delivering to the grantee a penny, or anything by way of attornment.[1] So much did the validity of such a grant depend on the attornment that if the lord made a second grant, and the tenant first attorned to the second grantee, he would have the services, and any attornment afterwards to the first grantee would be void.[2] If a manor was sold, it was necessary all the tenants should attorn, except those at will, for they need not.[3] If any tenant had made a lease for life or in tail, saving the reversion, the reversioner was to attorn, and not the tenant for life, or in tail, for they were not immediately privy to the grantor.[4] So in case of lord, mesne, and tenant, the mesne should attorn to a grant of the services by the lord, and not the tenant peravaile.[5] But it was otherwise when the grantee of a rent-charge, or rent-seck, granted it over, for then the tenant of the freehold, on which the rent was charged, was to attorn; for the avowry was not to be made on any person, but as in lands charged with the distress.[6] So where lands were let for life, with remainder over in fee, and the lord granted the services, it was sufficient if the tenant for life attorned; for he in remainder could not be said to be tenant to the lord to this purpose, till after the death of the tenant for life. Yet if such remainder-man died without heir, the lord would have the remainder by escheat.[7]

Thus far of attornment, where it was necessary to complete a grant of services or of rent. We have before said that it was also necessary where land was let for years, for life, or in tail, and the reversion was granted either for life, in tail, or in fee; for in such cases it was requisite that the tenant for years should attorn to the grantee in the life of the grantor; and by such attornment the freehold would pass without any livery of seisin.[8] In like manner if land was let in tail, or for life, with remainder over in fee, the remainder over could not be granted without the attornment of the tenant of the land.[9] Where land was let for years, remainder to another for life, reserving a rent to the lessor, and livery of seisin was made to the tenant for years; if the reversion was granted, and the tenant for life attorned, the grantee by force of such attornment might distrain the tenant for years for rent due after such attornment; for where a reversion depended upon an estate of freehold the attornment of the freeholder was sufficient.[10]

We have hitherto been speaking of a grant by deed: there was some difference where the grant was made by fine. For if the lord granted his services by fine, they were immediately in the grantee by force of the fine, but yet the lord could not distrain for them

[1] Litt., 551. [2] *Ibid.*, 552. [3] *Ibid.*, 553. [4] *Ibid.*, 554.
[5] *Ibid.*, 555. [6] *Ibid.*, 556. [7] *Ibid.*, 557. [8] *Ibid.*, 567, 568.
[9] *Ibid.*, 569. [10] *Ibid.*, 571.

without attornment. However, if the tenant died, leaving an heir within age, the grantee would have the wardship, the seignory being in him by the fine without attornment: the same of an escheat.[1] So if a reversion dependent on an estate for life was granted by fine, the reversion was immediately in the grantee by force of the fine, but he could have no action of waste without attornment; yet, if the tenant for life aliened in fee, the grantee might enter, such alienation being to his disherison, as he had the reversion.[2] The lord in the above case could not have relief without attornment, because this was a matter that lay in distress, and he could not avow the taking to be good and lawful, as was before observed, without attornment. To establish wardship or escheat, there needed no distress but an entry, which he had by force of the fine.[3] So, if there were lord, mesne, and tenant, and the mesne made a grant of the services of his tenant, and then the grantee died without heir, the services of the mesnalty would escheat to the lord paramount, and he might distrain for them, notwithstanding there had been no attornment; and this for two reasons, given by Littleton: First, because the mesnalty was in the grantee by force of the fine, and so, being very tenant to the lord paramount, he might avow upon him, though he was not compelled so to do; and if the grantor had died without heir, during the life of the grantee, he could have been compelled to avow upon the grantee. Secondly, because the lord paramount claimed the mesnalty, not by force of the grant by fine, but by virtue of the seignory paramount.[4]

In like manner, for a similar reason, if a reversion dependent on an estate for life was granted by force, and the grantee died without heir, the lord would have the reversion by escheat, and also a writ of waste, notwithstanding that there was no attornment; but where a person claimed by force of a grant by fine, as heir, or assignee, he could not distrain, nor avow, nor have waste without attornment.[5]

This doctrine of attornment did not reach to devisees, for if a rent-tenure or rent-charge was devised by will, the devisee might distrain without attornment,[6] and the devisee of a reversion might have waste without attornment. The reason stated by Littleton is, that the will of the testator should be performed, whereas it might be defeated if made dependent on the attornment.

Thus far of attornment to complete conveyances that were lawful, but if a grant and fine stood in need of this assent of the tenant to perfect the transfer of the land, much more should an unlawful act, as a disseisin, intrusion, or abatement. Thus it is laid down by Littleton, that if the tenants of a manor did not attorn to the disseisor, then, though he died seised, and his heir was in by descent, yet might the disseisee distrain for the services, because all the manor did not descend to the heir.[7]

[1] Litt., 579. [2] *Ibid.*, 580, 581. [3] *Ibid.*, 582. [4] *Ibid.*, 583.
[5] *Ibid.*, 584. [6] *Ibid.*, 585. [7] *Ibid.*, 587.

The last species of conveyance, if it can be so termed, and that which was nearly connected with gifts to a use, was that by will. The distinction between gifts of land by deed and by will became more strongly marked; and although in a gift by deed, if the tenant of the particular estate refused to accept the livery, the remainder was void, yet, if the first devisee refused, the remainder was still good, and he took in possession immediately.[1] Another distinction was this: if land was given to a man and the heirs-male of his body, and he had issue a son and a daughter, and died, the son entered, and the daughter had issue a son, and died, and then the donee died without issue-male, here the son of the daughter was not to have the land, though he was heir-male, but if it had been by devisee he would.[2]

A notion had begun to prevail respecting the devise of a chattel which was entirely novel. A gift of a chattel without any specification, or if for life, was heretofore considered as a gift for ever; a chatte not being respected by the law in the light of such permanent property as might be limited over from one to another, after the deatl of the possessor. But, at length, the following method was hi upon, by which a chattel might be bequeathed over, in like manne with real property. It was held that a man might give, by will, a book to one of his executors, *to have and use* for the term of hi life; remainder to his other executor, to have and use for the tern of his life; and then to the parishioners of such a parish. Th reason of this opinion was, because only *the use* was given for life and therefore a sort of remainder over night might be reasonabl and consistent therewith. Such was the origin of tha sort of gifts which in later times have been calle *executory devises*.[3]

An executory devise.

In following the history of revolutions in the laws relating t property, the reader's attention has been principally taken up wit that artificial and refined system upon which a title to land an inheritances was governed; the magnitude as well as the difficult of the subject requiring a very close and serious examination. Th law of *chattels* is of a less complicated nature, an being regulated upon principles of plain sense, inde pendent of the influence of any peculiar system of things, is mor easily comprehended. The few opportunities that have hithert presented themselves of speaking on this part of our inquiry, wer when we considered the several actions in which chattels migh become the objects of judicial discussion; and such idea of th kind of property as could be collected from thence, must be ver imperfect. As personal property had of late years been growin into greater consideration, owing to the increase of trade an manufactures, it became more agitated in our courts; and lawye bestowed upon it some share of that attention, which seems befo

Of chattels.

[1] 3 Hen. VI., 4; 37 Hen. VI., 37.
[2] 27 Hen. VI.; 11 Hen. VI., 12.
[3] 37 Hen. VI., 30; Bro. *ibid.*, 13.

to have been wholly engrossed by the learning of real property. The reports of this period furnish several cases upon the qualities and incidents of this sort of property, with the nature of contracts and agreements and other methods of transferring it from one to another. These are almost new subjects; and as they constitute the foundation of what has since been raised in modern times to such a height as nearly to overshadow and obscure the law of estates, they become extremely deserving the curiosity of a juridical historian.

The first point to be considered on this subject is what things were deemed of sufficient importance to come under the denomination of property. Animals that were properly *feræ naturæ* were not considered as being the property of any one. However, there was a sort of incomplete property that accrued *ratione soli*, and gave the owner a title to an action for an injury done to them. Thus it was laid down, that a person who had a park or a warren, had not therefore such a property in the game thereof as in an action of trespass for taking them to call them *lepores suos* or *damas suas;* but yet he might declare for *mille lepores*, or *damas viginti;* and so it was adjudged over and over again.[1] The same of doves and hawks.[2] The idea was carried so far as for it to be laid down for law, that no gift could be made of a deer in a park; and this seems to have been a general opinion; but Chief-Justice Brian endeavoured to make this exception to it, that a white deer, or any that seemed to be identified by some peculiarity, might be given away as a thing in which a man had a clear property:[3] and this distinction seems to conform with what had been laid down in a former period, that a man might have property in a tame deer.[4] The scruple concerning the meaning of *meum* and *tuum* was once carried to a very extravagant length; for in an action *de malè ignem custodieno*, the writ was *ignem suum*, which was excepted to because no one could have *property* in fire; but the objection was overruled as frivolous.[5] If a man came into the freehold of another and cut trees and made timber of them, the property was considered as remaining in the owner of the soil till it was carried away.[6] If a sow was taken by way of distress, and then pigged, the owner might have replevin of the pigs as well as the sow, and recover damages for both.[7]

It was a very old rule of law, that a man's property in any thing should not be transferred by the wrongful taking of it; a thing therefore so taken remained the property of the owner, whatsoever hands it might pass through, or by whatsoever means, except only by a sale in market overt; to which the law, for the security and confidence necessary in the dealings of men, allowed such credit for fairness, as to convey a clear title to a purchaser. But if goods

[1] 3 Hen. VI., 55; 7 Hen. VI., 38; 22 Hen. VI., 59.
[2] 16 Edw. IV., 7.
[3] 18 Edw. IV., 14.
[4] 43 Edw. III., 24.
[5] 2 Hen. IV., 18.
[6] 35 Hen. VI., 2.
[7] 12 Edw. IV., 5.

were sold in this public manner by a collusion between the buyer and seller, or if the buyer knew that the vendor had taken them wrongfully, then the property would not be changed;[1] and some went so far as to hold, that if the toll of the market was not paid, the property would not be changed.[2] In such cases, and where the sale was not in market overt, the law was, that the owner might take his goods wheresoever he found them; but the seller would nevertheless be entitled to all the price agreed for between him and the buyer, who had no recompense but the admonition of *caveat emptor* to make him more circumspect on other occasions.[3] If a man took the goods of another, and offered them to an image, the superstition of the age had allowed this to be as complete a change of property as a sale in a market or fair; but if they came back to the hands of the first trespasser, the owner might take them.[4]

The construction of the common law upon the law of nations was, that any one might seize the goods of the king's enemies imported into the kingdom; and also the goods of Englishmen taken by such enemies, to the exclusion of the king, the admiral, and the owner, unless he came the same day they were taken, and claimed them *ante occasum solis*.[5]

Of contracts.

The most usual mode by which chattels were transferred from one person to another, was by bargain and contracts of several kinds, the law of which began now to be tolerably well understood. The foundation of every contract required that there should be a mutual benefit to both parties, that is, a *quid pro quo;* otherwise it was a *nudum pactum,* and such to which the law would not give effect. Thus where a man brought an action upon the case against another for not building a mill by a certain day, according to his engagement, the declaration was held ill, because it did not state that the defendant was to have been paid anything for his labour, in which case the bargain would have been void.[6] A promise to give a person a sum of money if he married his daughter, was a contract whose validity was much questioned, on the idea of there not being a *quid pro quo.* An action of debt upon such a promise was debated with some difference of opinion. In support of it many instances of bargains were quoted by Prisot, which he thought bore some similarity to the present, and were esteemed good in law. Thus if A. sold a horse for £10, and had no horse at the time, yet he might have an action of debt for the money, though there was in fact no *quid pro quo;* but because if A. had a horse the buyer might take it, the bargain was to be supported in law. Again, if one sold his land for £100, debt would lie for the money immediately, though the purchaser could not have the land without the ceremony of livery. Again, if a person was retained to be counsel for a certain sum, he might have an action for the money.[7] It seemed to be thought that though a pur-

[1] 33 Hen. VI., 5. [2] 35 Hen. VI., 29. [3] 9 Edw. IV., 1.
[4] 34 Hen. VI., 10. [5] 7 Edw. IV., 14. [6] 3 Hen. VI., 36.
[7] 37 Hen. VI., 8.

chase of things for the use of a society, if agreed to by them, would charge them with the price; yet if the purchase was for them, it would not bind them without an apparent agreement: it might, however, be questioned whether the law would not interpret their use of the things purchased as an agreement, and so it was afterwards determined.[1]

[1] 20 Hen. VI., 22.

CHAPTER XXII.

HENRY VI.

The Court of Equity in Chancery—Cases determined before the Chancellor—Of Proceedings by Bill in the King's Bench—Ejectione Firmæ—Action: upon the Case—Action of Forcible Entry—Of Forger of Deeds—Damage: and Costs—Of Protections—The Criminal Law—Larceny—Of Appeal: —Of Provors—Of Battel—Of Clergy—Judicature in Parliament—Origin of Private Acts—Of the King and Government.

THE administration of justice during these two reigns affords ai object of inquiry equally interesting and important with the law o private rights. The novelties in this part of our juridical systen consist principally in the perfection to which the science of plead ing had arrived, the introduction of such new actions as had beer given by some late statutes, and some slight variation in the forn of judicial proceedings.

The court of equity in chancery.

The court of chancery grew into great consideration in the reign of Henry VI. and Edward IV. Indeed the statute 1: Hen. VI. may be considered as adding a new suppor to this court; which, by restraining a wanton and in considerate application of its authority, confirmed it in a due an regular administration of justice. That the legislature should a different times express a jealousy of this new judicature by *subpœnc* and impose checks upon the exercise of it, is not to be wondere at: the idea upon which this court had taken upon itself to decid according to principles of equity and general justice, was novel an adventurous. It was to afford relief to suitors, upon circumstance of hardship, fraud, or trust, where the king's courts allowed non This was, in effect, an appeal from the ancient customs and statut of the realm to the conscience and discretion of a single persoi It appeared like changing the rules of right; like renouncing th government of law, and preferring that of arbitrary will. Adde to this, when it is considered that the chancellor presided thei alone, without the influence of common-law judges (except whe he choose to call in their advice) to control the force of his ow particular notions; that he was a person unlearned, for the mo part, in the common law, and an ecclesiastic bred up, as was the usual, in the study of the civil and canon law; from these conside ations it was extremely probable, that, in the course of time, a s of rules and maxims of justice would gain ground in that cou differing from and derogatory to the common law. These we natural apprehensions, and in the event proved not to be whol unfounded.

Not only the education of the judge who there presided, but t very intent and design of his jurisdiction naturally led to what w foreseen.* The canon and civil law furnished a system of rules and a course of proceeding extremely well adapted to the objects of inquiry in a court of equity. The large principles of universal justice taught by the imperial law, were calculated for any set of people and any state of things. These furnished grounds of reasoning to model, correct, and qualify the untoward consequences of our partial municipal customs; while the ecclesiastical jurisprudence supplied a method of proceeding, in the examination of witnesses and of the party, peculiarly contrived to sift the conscience of a designing and fraudulent defendant. The chancery being, like other courts, at liberty to form its own method of proceeding, adopted that which best answered its design; and accordingly, a proceeding formed from the civil and canon law together, gradually became the practice of the court of chancery, without any interference or control of the legislature. But the chancellor was not left at liberty entirely to establish the rules of justice dictated by the civil law. This was a matter of much more importance in its consequences than the other. In this instance he was narrowly watched by the judges, who, in many cases where their advice was called in, put some check on the liberal conclusions derived from those plausible topics, the fitness, and convenience, and the substantial justice of a cause, which were the principal grounds on which the chancellor used to rest his equitable decisions.

It is beyond a doubt that this court had begun to exercise its judicial authority in the reigns of Richard II., Henry IV. and V., as appears from what has been before mentioned.[1] But we do not find in our books any report of cases there determined till 37 Henry VI., except only on the subject of uses; which, as has been before remarked, might give rise to the opinion, that the first equitable judicature was concerned in the support of uses. Leaving uses to be considered hereafter, we shall now take a view of such points as were resolved in this court during the reign of Henry VI. and the subsequent one; being the earliest notices we have, in the annals of our law, of the nature and progress of this new court of equity.

Cases determined before the chancellor.

The following case was before the chancellor in 37 Hen. VI. A person bought up some debts owing to another, and gave him a bond to the amount. He now preferred a bill in chancery to be relieved from the obligation, alleging that as *choses* in action were the subject-matter of the contract, and these were not transferable, he had in reality received no consideration, and should therefore in conscience be discharged from the obligation. The chancellor, having doubts, adjourned it into the exchequer-chamber, where it was agreed, with the concurrence of all the judges of the king's bench and common-pleas, that the obligation should be cancelled, and if the defendant refused, that he should be committed to the Fleet till he complied.[2] But when this matter was afterwards pleaded to the obligation

[1] *Vide ante*, 188.

[2] 37 Hen. VI., 13; Bro. Consci., 4.

sued in the common-pleas, the plea was overruled, and the deed was considered as still in force; it being conceived that the only power the chancellor had of enforcing his decrees, was by inflicting imprisonment on the contumacious party, who might still prosecute his legal rights in a court of law, notwithstanding they had been determined in chancery to be unconscionable.

A grant was made, by letters-patent, of goods forfeited by a person attainted; the grantee brought his bill in chancery against the person who had then the possession of them, for this reason, that as the king could not have an action at law for the goods of an outlaw or one attainted, before they had been seized for the king's use or found by matter of record, much less could the grantee maintain a common-law action without having had the possession. Accordingly it was held, that the *subpœna* was his only remedy; and the defendant was ordered to exhibit an inventory of the things the next day, on pain of being committed to the Fleet.[1]

Of proceeding by bill in the king's bench.

The new jurisdiction in the court of king's bench had assumed a novel appearance. We have seen that in the reign of Edward III., a practice had obtained of commencing actions, by bill, in either of the three courts in Westminster Hall: but nothing has yet been said on the nature of that proceeding: the books preserved a silence thereon, until the reign of Henry VI.,(*a*) when there happened some cases, which show that such bills in the king's bench were used to charge the defendant as *in custodiâ mareschalli*, intimating that circumstance to be the foundation for the proceeding. It seems, that the persons in the custody of the marshal of that court might be declared against by bill for any cause of personal action, notwithstanding the prohibition of Magna Charta, which was construed not to extend to this privilege claimed against prisoners. The court, however, guarded this custom, which it had suffered to obtain, by a strict adherence to the notion of law on which it originated; they required that the person should be an actual prisoner of the court. Thus in 7th of Henry VI., where a man was out on bail, it was held,[2] that a bill could not be filed against him as in custody. It was moreover required that there should be some proof on record of the defendant being in custody;[3] for otherwise it was said, it lay at his option whether he would plead to the bill.

Many devices were contrived to effectuate this requisite of custody; one of which seems to have been the exhibiting of articles of the peace;[4] so strenuously did they endeavour to preserve the proper character of this tribunal as a criminal court. However, in

(*a*) Here we see another reason for preserving the distinction between the legal history of these two reigns. The beginning of the long reign of Henry VI. marks pretty clearly the commencement of what may be called the modern jurisdiction of the court of king's bench, as a court of ordinary jurisdiction, in suits between party and party: and this is an important era. Between that time and the middle of the reign of Edward IV., there was a period of about half a century.

[1] 39 Hen. VI., 26 b. [2] 7 Hen. VI., 42. [3] *Ibid.*, 41. [4] *Ibid.*

31 Henry VI. they seem to have relaxed a little on this point. It was then held, that if it appeared that a person was out on bail, this of itself was sufficient ground to the court to proceed against him as in custody, whether the cause of his commitment appeared or not. Thus the ground of the court's jurisdiction became a fiction, and the king's bench began to entertain suits against persons who were only *supposed* to be in custody, provided there were some slight grounds to warrant the supposition. It was sufficient therefore to file a bill with pledges to prosecute, and then by a copy of that bill or by *latitat*[1] to arrest the defendant, who gave bail to appear; and then, though out of custody on bail, he still was deemed liable to plead to a declaration filed against him in any action, and this became the settled practice towards the latter end of the period of which we are now writing.

When the proceeding in this court by bill was rendered so easy, it may be supposed that suits of every kind were brought here in that way very frequently, and that the civil business of the court began considerably to increase. The number of actions upon the case (which too could be brought by original here) increased the subjects of judicial cognizance in this court to a nearer proportion with those of the common-pleas than it had ever before exhibited.

The declaring against persons *in custodiâ mareschalli* is a singular phenomenon in the history of practice in the court of king's bench; and it became more extraordinary when extended, as we see here, to all persons, without any regard to the actual custody of the marshal. It has been intimated in a former part of this work, that the jurisdiction of the steward and marshal was communicated to the court of king's bench, and particularly discovered itself in this proceeding by bill.[2] The reader may be better able to judge after he has weighed the following considerations, whether this is a probable conjecture to account for the novel proceeding of which we have just been speaking.

It has been before related, on the authority of Fleta, that the steward determined the king's own causes without suit: that he had cognizance of all actions against the king's peace within the verge, *ubicunq; tunc rex fuerit in Angliâ;* that such actions were to be brought *recenter.* In another place he tells us, that the steward had cognizance of all trespasses and personal actions, *per inventionem plegiorum de prosequendo,* without allowing any essoin; that upon pledges being found and enrolled, the marshal was commanded to attach the party, if he was within the verge; that this court removed with the king, and by its presence suspended all commissions of eyre, assize, gaol-delivery, and others within the same county, the business of which courts was summoned before the steward; that he despatched them first, then proceeded to the trespasses within the verge, and to debts and contracts where persons

1 It may be remarked that the absconding from process is expressed in Bracton by the verb *latitare.* *Vide ante,* vol. i. c. viii.

2 *Vide ante,* c. xiv.

had bound themselves to the distress of the steward and marshal.[1] Such are the principal features of the steward's court, according to the practice in the reign of Edward I. To this may be added what is mentioned by Britton, that the steward was allowed that singular privilege, which none but himself and the justices of Ireland and Chester had, of delegating his judicial authority without a special permission from the king.[2]

It is not unlikely that the steward used to avail himself of this power to delegate, and it is natural that the judges of the king's bench should be the persons whom he delegated, they being, like him, obliged to attend *ubicunq ; rex tunc fuerit in Angliâ.* This is rendered more probable by the similarity of jurisdiction which we see in after times exercised by the judges of the king's bench. We see the king's bench by its presence suspend all courts within the same county; we find that it had marshals who travelled with it through the several counties; and that in a statute of Edward III. these marshals are coupled in a remarkable manner with the marshal within the verge.[3] When, therefore, we find also a proceeding in this court *per inventionem plegiorum;* when a person, merely because he was supposed to be *in custodiâ mareschalli*, might be proceeded against for debts and contracts; where can we look for the origin of such innovations, but to the model preserved in the ancient history of the steward's court?

The judges of the king's bench, when once in the habit of exercising this jurisdiction within the verge, may easily be supposed, in the usual course of judicial aggrandisement, *ampliare jurisdictionem*, to extend this new proceeding to all persons, whether within the verge or not. While the king's bench was moulding this borrowed piece of judicature so as to aggrandise its authority, the ancient court of the steward and marshal, under the presidency o less active managers, sunk into discredit. It was, at various times expressly restricted by parliamentary regulations[4] to its origina boundary of the verge; and the steward never reviving thos branches of his supreme jurisdiction which had been so often dele gated, the court became of no more consideration than others tha are confined to a small local jurisdiction.[5]

Ejectione firmæ.

Next to the jurisdiction of courts, the objects which presen themselves are the various actions now in use. Bu these being the same as were so fully examined in th reign of Edward III. it will be unnecessary to add anything to th account there given, except by an observation on the action (*ejectione firmæ*, and a short view of the decisions that were mad

[1] *Vide ante*, c. x.

[2] Britt., 10 edit., Kelh.

[3] *Vide ante*, c. xiv.

[4] *Ibid.*

[5] However, the marshalsea court, situated near the prison of the marshal of t king's bench, may be regarded as retaining so far some mark of the ancient stock fro whence the latter flourishing branch of judicature has sprung. It was not without very substantial reason that the king's bench originally sent their prisoners into anoth county for confinement; and the neighbourhood of the ancient court of the stewa and marshal seems to point out that reason with some show of probability.

respecting the nature and properties of actions on the case. Some opinions began to prevail respecting the effect of the writ of *ejectione firmæ*, which led the way to an important change in real remedies. In the reign of Edward III., and again in that of Richard II., (*a*) the action of *ejectione firmæ* became more frequently used, as a substitute to the many real writs for recovering possession and trying titles to lands.

Actions upon the case.

The action most favoured was that of *trespass upon the case*, which, during these two reigns, expended itself in a manner that made it applicable to numberless cases for which the common law had not before provided any remedy. In addition to those we have already seen, we now find it brought against an escheator for a false return of an office:[1] against a man whose dog bit the plaintiff's sheep, the defendant knowing the dog was used so to do:[2] against a clerk for not entering a *nisi prius* record as he assumed to do:[3] for suing a writ against the plaintiff without consent of the principal:[4] for arresting the plaintiff while he was coming to answer in a cause depending against him: against an under-sheriff for embezzling a writ:[5] for beating the plaintiff's servant:[6] for erecting a mill near an ancient one, at which the tenants were used to grind their corn:[7] against an abbot who ought to find a chaplain to do divine service at a manor chapel, but neglected so to do:[8] for disturbing the plaintiff's steward in holding a leet:[9] against an innkeeper for not lodging the plaintiff:[10] against a victualler for not providing victuals for the plaintiff:[11] for not performing a promise or undertaking.[12]

(*a*) The author refers this change to the reign of Edward IV., where, therefore, the passage on the subject is transferred, and where it is noticed. At present it is enough to say, that the action was resorted to in this reign, and was fully established in law, only from the nature of the times the action of forcible entry was most frequent, being the remedy for recovery of the freehold. Thus, in a case in this reign it was said, if a man lease for term of years, and sell to one who ousts the termor, he shall have a *quare ejecit* to recover his term and damages (19 *Hen. VI.* 56). For in the same case it was said, that if the lessor ousted the tenant before the conveyance, the remedy would lie against him in *ejectione firmæ*: but if after the conveyance, the feoffee ousted the tenant, the remedy would lie against the feoffee, and would be *quare ejecit infra terminam* (*Ibid.*) It is manifest that the judgment in both actions was the same; both actions being grounded on a term and on an ouster: the difference being that one was favoured rather on the right as against the lessor, the other rather on the wrong against a stranger; for it lay against any one who ousted the termor. It is said by Choke, J., in 33 Hen. VI. fol. 42, that if after a lease for years, the lessor aliened and gave livery of seisin, that is upon, the land, the lessee could have a *general* writ of trespass, although he was not actually ousted, and as the feoffment was good; and so he could have a *general* writ of trespass, as well as one of *quare ejecit*; but in the writ of trespass, he could only recover damages; whereas in *quare ejecit* he could recover the term if it was not expired, or, if it was ended, he could recover all in damages, to which the reporter adds *quære*, in writ of covenant and *ejectione firmæ*; as much as to say, that they were the proper remedies, if the term was ended, to recover damages. This is actually referred to by some writers as showing that in *ejectione firmæ* the term could not be recovered.

1 9 Hen. VI., 60. 2 28 Hen. VI., 7. 3 34 Hen. VI., 4. 4 7 Hen. VI., 43.
5 19 Hen. VI., 29. 6 21 Hen. VI., 8. 7 22 Hen. VI., 14. 8 22 Hen. VI., 46.
9 28 Hen. VI., 16. 10 39 Hen. VI., 18. 11 39 Hen. VI., 18. 12 *Passim.*

The discussion which arose on these new actions upon the case, as well as on others which have been before mentioned, is well worthy the attention of the reader, as we therein see the principles which led to the establishment of this liberal and comprehensive action.

The action against the escheator was founded on the same principle as the many we have already mentioned against sheriffs for false returns. Sheriffs and escheators, though *officers* of record, were not justices of record, even when in the employment of taking inquisitions; for if so, it was held no action could lie[1] (*a*). It seems not to have been a settled point that an action would lie against an innkeeper or a victualler. It is laid down by Moile that it would, but by Prisot that it would not, in which Danby seems to concur;[2] and Prisot referred it to the constables of the place to give directions.

The old questions upon the distinct properties of trespass, trespass upon the case, and nuisance, still continued unsettled.[3] Some distinctions were made, which seem to furnish a principle by which the separate office of these actions might be known. If a road was straitened or embanked, an action upon the case lay; if it was entirely stopped, an assize of nuisance, says Moile, to which Prisot assented, provided it was stopped by the tenant of the soil; for if it was by a stranger, he held it should be an action on the case.[4]

One of the old remedies trenched upon by the new action upon the case was *deceit;* and, in like manner, it often became a question when the old writ of deceit was the proper remedy, and when an action upon the case. Where a person made a promise to do anything, and broke that promise, there trespass on the case lay; but if he performed it in words, and by some false dealing rendered the performance of no effect, there deceit lay; as if a man who had undertaken to infeoff another, first charged the land and then made the feoffment, or first infeoffed a stranger, and then entered and made the feoffment he had promised to make, this was a proper subject for the old writ of deceit.[5]

This brings us to actions upon the case for non-performance of promises, which had been so repeatedly canvassed in the reign of Henry IV.[6] All the topics then agitated were again brought forward during the period of which we are now writing; but the courts showed great inclination to overrule the scrupulous objections which were thrown in the way of this action. In the 3 Hen. VI. the distinction that had been made between a non-performance and a negligence or malfeasance, was denied. An action on the case was brought against a mill-maker for not making a mill by a certain day, as he had undertaken. It was objected, upon the principle of the determinations in the time of Henry IV. that i

(*a*) See mention made of the statutes on the subject in a previous chapter—c. xx

1 9 Hen. VI., 60. 2 39 Hen. VI., 18. 3 *Vide ante*, 27.
4 33 Hen. VI., 26. 5 20 Hen. VI., 34. 6 *Vide ante*, 244.

the mill had been made ill, the covenant would have been turned into a tort, and trespass on the case would lie for the mis-feasance; but here was a *non*-feasance, which sounded merely in covenant. To this Babington answered, that if one made a covenant to cover a house by a certain day, and he neglecting to do it, the rain came in and damaged the house, the owner might have an action of trespass on the case for the damage: the same, said Cockain, if a man neglected to make a ditch, according to his covenant, and my corn was thereby damaged: the same, said Strainge, if my covenant-servant neglected to do what I ordered him. After this manner of arguing, it was observed by one who was inclined against the action, that if this was allowed, every covenant that was broken might be made the subject of an action upon the case.[1]

Notwithstanding these decided opinions, we find, a few years after, similar topics were urged against these actions upon promises. It was said, that where a man was retained to purchase a manor for me, and he did not do it, I could have no action against him, unless it was by deed, and then I might have covenant; but if he assisted another in making the purchase, this was a deceit upon me, and I might have an action on the case; and this distinction was recognised by most of the court.[2]

An action was brought against a man who had undertaken to procure certain persons to give releases, which undertaking he did not perform: it was on the case, and the same arguments were used against it as against the former. This being, they said, merely a *non-feasance*, the remedy must be in covenant. But this was explicitly denied by Iuyn, the chief justice, and Paston; and they stated the common cases of a carpenter, a surgeon, and the like, who, if they undertook, and did nothing towards the performance of that undertaking, should be liable in an action on the case, and the party should not be driven to an action of covenant.[3] When an action on the case was brought against a man for not delivering wine according to his undertaking, the same arguments were again urged against the form of the action, and the same answers given: [4] as the parties in that case came to an agreement, there was no judicial determination of the point.

However, it sufficiently appears from what had been thrown out, that the opinions upon this question were now somewhat changed; and the best lawyers began to think, that an action upon the case was a proper remedy to recover damages for *non-performance* of an agreement, as well as for any *mis-feasance* in the performance of it. Accordingly we find it laid down by Newton in 22 Hen. VI.[5] that if land was sold, the vendor might have debt for the money, and the vendee might have an action upon the case, if he was not infeoffed of the land, which passed without any contradiction. We have every reason to suppose that the *promise* meant in the reports

[1] 3 Hen. VI., 36. [2] 11 Hen. VI., 18. [3] 14 Hen. VI., 18.
[4] 21 Hen. VI., 55. [5] 22 Hen. VI., 44.

of this period was an *actual* undertaking which could be proved and not such an *implied* promise as was in after times pronounced to arise in point of law in cases where a duty was previously due It was also generally agreed, that a consideration for such promise should be stated in the declaration, as it would otherwise be a *nudum pactum*, to which the law would never give effect.

The action upon the case sometimes applied, amongst others, to instances where the old remedy was by detinue. The wager of law, which was allowed in that old writ, made it very desirable to substitute the action upon the case in its room.

Thus was the action upon the case by degrees adapted almost to all purposes; sometimes as a remedy where the common law had furnished none, and sometimes in the place of the old established actions, which were found less adequate than this to obtain the ends of justice. It was the usual mode of redress in most instances of *malfeasance* or *negligence*, whether of private persons or of those in office; and the party thereby received a recompense in damages for the wrong sustained. Numerous are the instances in which this action had already been applied, the reports of which have come down to us. These afforded a groundwork to extend it by a reasonable analogy to all the consequences which have since been built upon it: so that the specific writs before in use, as the writ of deceit, of conspiracy, of detinue, and others, began gradually to go out of practice; and actions upon the case, of a liberal conception, were framed in the nature of those remedies. It only remained to give efficacy to the actions of *assumpsit*, as a substitute for the action of debt; and then the method of legal redress in regard to personal injuries will have suffered a complete revolution. During this period, the steps above recounted were made towards effecting this change.

It will be proper to take notice of two actions which had lately made their appearance, and were founded upon statutes passed in the preceding reigns: these are the actions of forcible entry, and of forger of false deeds.

Action of forcible entry.

The[1] statute of Henry VI. had given an assize or writ of trespass to recover treble damages for a violent possession of lands or tenements; but the action most in vogue being trespass, an assize was not so frequently brought. It was therefore in an action of trespass for a forcible entry that these statutes were enforced, if it was meant to proceed civilly; if criminally, there might be a presentment, or one justice might proceed in a summary way, as directed by one of those statutes.

These statutes, being for the suppression of force and violence, seemed to require a more rigorous construction than the judges had put on them (*a*). Thus it was held by them, that the issue in this

(*a*) The decisions on this subject formed one of the steps or stages in the course of progress by which, out of the use or practice of this action, there arose a use or prac-

[1] *Vide ante.*

ıction should be on the title, and never on the force; and if the ;itle was found against the defendant, he would, it is true, be *o facto* convict of the force; but if the title was found for him, ;he force would not be at all considered.[1] The force, however, night be punished in an indictment afterwards, notwithstanding ;he title was with the defendant. On the other hand, if possession was restored to a disseisor by virtue of the statute, because he had)een three years in peaceable possession, yet the disseisee might 'e-enter peaceably, or have an assize.[2] It was held, that forcible ıntry would lie of a rent as well as of land; for a man might be lisseised of a rent, and might have a writ of entry sur disseisin.[3] Process of outlawry lay for a forcible entry, as was natural in an ıction of trespass.[4] The statute only gave treble damages; but it was the opinion of the judges that treble costs should likewise be 'ecovered.[5]

Of forger of deeds.

The action of forger of false deeds was a civil remedy for re-:overy of damages for the injury sustained by the party interested n the effect of such fictitious deeds. This remedy was founded on ɜtat. 1 Hen. V. c. iii.,[6] and the construction put on it was as 'ollows.

It was a good plea to this action to say, that the plaintiff had ıothing in the tenements at the time the deed was forged and pub-lished.[7] The degree of interest was, therefore, an object to be con-ɜidered in this action. It was doubted at one time, whether a remainder-man had a sufficient estate to entitle him, under the ɜtatute, to bring an action for forging a deed that affected his inter-ɜst. On one hand it was contended, that he had possession of the remainder, though not of the demesne; and it was said, that where ın estate was made for life, the remainder over, the deed belonged to the tenant for life during his life; and yet if a stranger got pos-ɜession of it, the remainder-man might have an action for it, and ;he tenant for life might have another action.[8] An heir ıad been allowed to maintain this action against a)erson who had forged a release during his father's life.[9] But this atter opinion (at least where the publication was not till after the 'ather's death) was afterwards denied, for the heir had no right luring the father's life. The deed, to be a subject of this action,

ıce of the action of *ejectione firmæ*, which rendered it a remedy for recovery of the 'reehold. The action of forcible entry, it is to be observed, was primarily a remedy 'or the party entitled to an estate of freehold in possession; while the action of *ejectione irmæ*, on the other hand, was the remedy for a termor. Both were grounded on a right ıf entry and on ouster or dispossession of the land; but, as in the latter, so, according o these decisions, in the former, the question of title could be raised, for if the)laintiff had no right of entry, then his action failed. This was the common ele-nent which connected them, and in the subsequent reigns it will be seen how, out of he use and practice of these actions (*i.e.*, the use of one by the termor, and of the ıther by the freeholder), the action of ejectment arose for the trial of title in all cases ıf freehold or leasehold.

[1] 21 Hen. VI., 39. [2] 22 Hen. VI., 17. [3] 22 Hen. VI., 23; 20 Hen. VI., 11.
[4] 37 Hen. VI., 23. [5] 22 Hen. VI., 37. [6] *Vide ante.*
[7] 21 Hen. VI., 51. [8] 33 Hen. VI., 22. [9] 7 Hen. VI., 34.

must be both published and forged; but if the action was brought against two, it was sufficient if the forgery was proved upon one, and the publication on the other, for the plaintiff would then be entitled to recover.[1]

From actions, the transition is natural to proceedings therein, and the nature of pleading. The latter is a branch of the law which was cultivated with great attention during this period, and deserves a very particular consideration: we shall therefore reserve what we have to say on that subject to a chapter by itself, and at present go on to speak of some other points which relate to proceedings in actions. The first of these will be the adjudication of damages and costs, the nature of which has not yet been at all noticed.

Damages and costs.

Damages and *costs* might either be assessed by the jury in a gross sum,[2] or separated, so much for damages and so much for costs. It should seem, the court exercised a discretionary power to abridge or increase damages and costs; but this was with some distinction. Thus, after a writ of inquiry, they might either increase or abridge both the damages and costs as they pleased, because this was only an inquest of office to inform the court, who might have assessed the damages without an inquest. But where an inquest passed on an issue joined between the parties, there, though the court might increase the costs, they could neither increase nor diminish the damages; because there the party might have an attaint if he was dissatisfied, which could not be in case of a writ of inquiry. However, even in such case, if the damages were excessive, the court would sometimes suspend the judgment till the plaintiff released so much of the damages as would reduce them to a reasonable sum.[3]

It had, indeed, on a former occasion been held, that where the principal demand was certain, the court might, after a verdict upon an issue, increase the damages as well as the costs (*a*). This was in an action of debt, and the jury having found a gross sum for the damages and costs, the plaintiff prayed that the damages might be severed from the costs, in order that the latter might be increased; which the court declined, upon the idea that they, in this case, had an authority over both (*b*).[4] Again, in trespass, where the jury had found greater damages than were laid in the declaration, the court took upon them to abridge the damages down to the sum in the declaration (*c*).[5] Whatever doubt there might be

(*a*) Thus, it was very early laid down, that where the demand was certain, as in debt, the court could increase the amount adjudged (*Year-book*, 10 *Hen. VI.*, 25).

(*b*) Thus, in trespass for taking goods, the damages would be far more than the value, according to the circumstances, in the opinion of the jury (*Year-book*, *Edw. II.* The jury were always asked to assess the damages (*Year-book*, 19 *Edw. II.*, 625).

(*c*) There was this distinction between trial by jury and mere inquisition or inquiry

[1] 20 Hen. VI., 11; 14 Edw. IV., 2.
[2] 18 Edw. IV., 23.
[3] 19 Hen. VI., 10
[4] 10 Hen. VI., 24.
[5] 2 Hen. VI., 7.

respecting damages or costs after a verdict, there seems none concerning either after a writ of inquiry, or upon confession, and the like. We find upon a plea of *tout tems prist*, and judgment of *sit inde quietus, &c.*, that the plaintiff used to be admitted to make an averment *pro damnis suis occasione detentionis*, and to pray that such damages might be allowed him.[1] What is still more striking, there are instances of such averments against the sheriff for not returning greater issues upon jurors; and on these averments it is to be supposed the court used to award damages according to their discretion.[2]

Much confusion seems to have arisen from the mixing of damages and costs together, which was done not only in the verdicts of jurors, but also in the award of the court. When they were confounded in the verdict, it was not uncommon for the plaintiff to pray they might be severed;[3] it being his object to see that the costs were not taken into the amount of the damages, as that might create difficulty should an attaint be afterwards brought. The entry of costs, when increased by the court, was always stated to be at the prayer of the plaintiff: *Ideo consideratum est, quòd recuperet versus A. prædictum debitum suum prædictum, et damna sua prædicta ad 40 shill. per juratores prædict. in formâ prædictâ assessos, nec non 40 shill. eidem B.* AD REQUISITIONEM *suam pro misis et custagiis prædictis per curiam hic* DE INCREMENTO *adjudicatis, quæ quidem* DAMNA *in toto se attingunt ad, &c.*[4] The court had awarded increased costs to a plaintiff for the delay he had suffered by being hung up by injunction;[5] but in the following year the like costs were refused.[6]

The mode of trial by law-wager was still open to much discussion. The principal actions in which law-wager was used were debt and detinue; it was also allowed in accompt in some instances. A statute had been made in the time of Henry IV. to prevent defendants being precluded from waging their law, by the suggestions of plaintiffs that the debt arose upon the settlement of an account.[7] That statute gave the judges an authority to examine the plaintiff's attorney and other persons, and to allow or refuse, according to their discretions, the wager of law to the defendant (*a*). The rule by which the judges chose to

Wager of law.

by a jury to assess damages—that, in the latter case, the inquisition was only to inform the mind of the court, and it was at their discretion whether they would award judgment for the amount found by the jury; whereas, upon a trial, they had no jurisdiction to interfere as to the amount of damages in cases of tort, except as to costs. And upon courts of inquiry to assess damages in cases of tort, the court always assumed a power to reduce the amount if excessive; and though they had no direct jurisdiction to do so in trials of actions for torts, they have evidently done so by refusing to enter up judgment unless, in outrageous cases, the plaintiff will either consent to reduce the amount, or to a new trial (*Year-book*, 19 *Hen. VI.*, 10).

(*a*) This is an instance of those illustrations which ancient and obsolete proceedings often afford of an enduring and invaluable principle. The principle here illustrated, as described by the author a little further on, was this: that as the law pro-

[1] Rast., 158. [2] 8 Hen. VI., 12. [3] 18 Edw. IV., 23. [4] Rast., 172. [5] 21 Edw. IV., 78. [6] 22 Edw. IV., 37. [7] *Vide ante.*

govern their discretion was the preamble of the act, which seems to admit, that against an accompt settled before persons not properly and legally auditors, a defendant might wage his law.[1] We find in the reports of this period many instances of the plaintiff being examined, according to the direction of this act, and several cases where the judges went further than the object of the preamble of the statute.

An action of debt was brought on arrearages of an accompt, upon which the defendant tendered his law, and prayed the plaintiff might be examined: this was done, and it appeared by such examination that it was a debt upon a contract, and so was no matter of accompt.[2] Again, it appeared upon examination of a plaintiff, that he had let to the defendant a house and furniture, and at the end of the term they came to accompt before auditors, upon which part of the rent was found to be in arrear, and part of the furniture destroyed; and because he might have debt for the rent, and detinue for the furniture, the defendant was allowed to wage his law.[3] In debt on accompt before auditors, upon examination, it appeared to arise on an award by arbitrators; but these were held not to be auditors, and therefore the defendant was admitted to his law (*a*).[4] These cases were not within the preamble of the statute; but the judges availed themselves of the discretion given them by the enacting clause, and took this summary method of discovering whether the plaintiff had chosen his proper remedy: if not, they permitted the defendant to discharge himself by making his law.

vided appropriate remedies for different cases, there should be a discretionary power of discovering, by summary examination, whether the plaintiff had chosen the proper remedy—whether, by arbitration, by trial, or otherwise. If, as is self-evident, that was a course useful and salutary, then it would be equally so now—in fact, infinitely more so, since cases are infinitely more numerous, and the mass of litigations far greater and more burdensome. The procedure in the action of account was by compulsory reference to auditors or arbitrators appointed by the court, with greater and more coercive powers than could be conferred on mere arbitrators. The effect of the statute was, that if the plaintiff proposed to take that course, and the defendant objected, the court should summarily inquire whether it was proper and admissible, and if so, enforce it upon the defendant, and if otherwise, then to leave him to the proper remedy. The same principle would justify a statute enabling the defendant to apply to the court to fine the plaintiff to the action of account in cases where it was the proper course. And as the action of account was only a compulsory mode of arbitration by official arbitrators, the same principle would justify a statutable enactment enabling either party to apply to the court to enforce upon the other, if the case was proper for it, the procedure by arbitration.

(*a*) This is a proper place in which again to notice the important subject of arbitration, which the author has unaccountably neglected. Throughout this and the ensuing reigns, arbitrament was constantly resorted to voluntarily. This appears from the cases reported in the Year-books generally, upon the question how far the arbitrament was a bar to an action by the defeated party. Thus, it was held in this reign that an award, that one of the parties should "go quit" of the other, was good (10 *Hen. VI.*, 14). The difficulty as to voluntary arbitration was, that before an award, either party could revoke his submission (21 *Hen. VI.*, 30); for arbitrament depended upon the submission (8 *Hen. VI.*, 18). Hence the distinction between arbitrament and account before auditors whose power was coercive and whose award was matter of record, (3 *Hen. IV.*, 5).

[1] *Vide ante.* [2] 8 Hen. VI., 15. [3] 20 Hen. VI., 16. [4] 20 Hen. VI., 41.

The only case precisely within the act was the following, where, upon examination, it turned out that the accompt was not before *auditors*, but in the presence of *one* only, and the defendant was for that reason admitted to his law.[1]

If auditors were assigned, and it appeared that there was a surplus due from the lord to his bailee, and the bailee brought debt on arrearages of this accompt, yet the lord might wage his law; for the auditors were by the statute, and, according to the common law, were considered as judges of the bailee only, and not of the lord; and it was upon the idea of the matter having been discussed before competent judges that a defendant in such case was restrained from making his law.[2]

A notion had prevailed, that in debt against a person for board and eating, the defendant should not be permitted to wage his law; and, after it had been repeatedly decided, generally, that where the party was at liberty to provide or not, the defendant might have this privilege,[3] this point was denied by Prisot and Needham in the latter end of Henry VI.'s reign.[4] However, in a very particular instance, namely, where victuals had been provided by the warden of the Tower for a person imprisoned for treason, the obligation of common humanity was esteemed of such force as to leave the plaintiff without an option, and therefore the defendant was not permitted to wage his law against this meritorious creditor.[5] Again, where the boarding was connected with a sort of realty, as where the plaintiff had let a room to a man, and then took him and his wife to his table at so much a week, the defendant was not allowed his law. In the same manner, if land was let with a stock upon it in debt for the rent, law-wager would not be allowed, on account of the stock being coupled with the land, though it would lie in debt founded on a lease of the stock only.[6]

The above doubt might have arisen from the difference between the common law, as collected from the analogy of other cases, and the custom of London; for it was positively held, that by the custom a defendant could not wage his law, in debt for board: by the same custom a defendant was excluded from this law, if an alderman of London testified the truth of the contract.[7]

It was agreed, that where persons were *compelled to serve* by the statutes of labourers, as were ploughmen, shepherds, and all servants in husbandry, and they brought an action for their wages, the defendant should not have his law, because there was no option in the plaintiff whether he would serve or no; and yet it was held, that though a tailor, carpenter, or other artificers, if they departed from their service, were liable to an action under the second chapter of the statute, yet because they were not compellable to serve, they might be deprived of their debt by law-wager.[8] No

[1] 20 Hen. VI., 16.
[2] 14 Hen. VI., 24.
[3] 22 Hen. VI., 13; 15 Edw. IV., 16.
[4] 39 Hen. VI., 18.
[5] 28 Hen. VI., 4.
[6] 9 Edw. IV., 1.
[7] 1 Edw. IV., 5.
[8] 38 Hen. VI., 14, 22.

retainer of a servant, but under the compulsory part of the statute of labourers, was to exclude a defendant from law-wager. Upon a similar idea it was, that in an action brought by an attorney of the common-pleas for his fees, Fortescue, chief justice, held that the defendant should not wage his law, saying, that the justices could compel him to act as attorney for a suitor, though it was otherwise in inferior courts. But where an action was brought by a serjeant who had been retained for two years, law-wager was allowed; because, said they, notwithstanding he was compellable to be of counsel, yet he was not compellable to be retained so long as for two years.[1]

It was now settled, conformably with some opinions in the time of Edward III.,[2] that in a general declaration for a box of charters, the defendant might wage his law, because they partook of the nature of the box; but where one of them was specially noticed, the defendant, as to that, was obliged to plead to the country, and this had become the established practice.[3]

In detinue, if the bailment was in one county, and the declaration alleged it to be in another, the defendant might wage his law.[4] There was this difference between detinue and accompt, that in the former, if the bailment was alleged to be by the hands of another, law-wager was allowed the same as if it had been by the hands of the plaintiff himself,[5] but in accompt it was not allowed; though where it was by the hands of the wife of the plaintiff, they being considered as one person, the law-wager was allowed; the like as between an abbot and one of the same society.[6]

It was held by many, that, according to the custom of London, if a defendant waged his law, the plaintiff might produce a bill testifying the contract, and that would oust the defendant of his privilege.[7] But this opinion is directly against a statute made in the reign of Edward III., which expressly declares that a man might wage his law against a Londoner's papers.[8] Law-wager was allowed in debt upon an arbitrament,[9] but was denied in debt on a recovery in court of ancient demesne,[10] and for an amercement in a leet.[11] An infant was not permitted to wage his law.[12] Executors, when charged as such, could not wage their law, because no man could wage his law but upon a contract of his own: they could not therefore be charged on a bailment to their testator, but might yet be liable to an action on their *possession* of goods that had been bailed to their testator, and in such case they might wage their law.[13] It had been held, contrary to an opinion in the time of Henry V., that a defendant might wage his law against a *quo minus* in the exchequer:[14] this violated the rule laid down in an earlier period,[15]

[1] 21 Hen. VI., 4.
[2] *Vide ante.*
[3] 19 Hen. VI., 9; 22 Edw. IV., 7.
[4] 21 Hen. VI., 35.
[5] 8 Hen. VI., 10.
[6] 15 Edw. IV., 16; 10 Edw. IV., 5.
[7] 39 Hen. VI., 34.
[8] *Vide ante.*
[9] 33 Hen. VI., 4.
[10] 34 Hen. VI., 64.
[11] 10 Hen. VI., 7.
[12] 11 Hen. VI., 40.
[13] 3 Hen. VI., 38.
[14] 32 Hen. VI., 24.
[15] *Vide ante.*

that no man should wage his law against the king; and it was on that account overruled by the practice of later times.

Protections were a greater source of delay to justice than even essoins; for a protection might be cast where an essoin could not, and, besides, had the sanction of the great seal to back it; while an essoin, being only the surmise of the party, was open to cavil and rejection. Thus a protection might be cast by a person who was in prison, or let to mainprise, but such a one could not cast an essoin.[1] It might be cast at *nisi prius*, which an essoin could not.[2] Protections stood upon the ground of decisions before mentioned to be made in the reign of Edward III., and the alterations introduced by the late statutes.[3] They were of two kinds, namely, *quia profecturus*, and *quia moraturus:* they were for a year only, and were disallowed in *quare impedit*, assize, attaint, dower *unde nihil*, darrein presentment, and certain other pleas before justices in eyre; and a protection that was offered in any of such cases would not be allowed.[4]

Of protection.

The effect of a protection was to put the plea *sine die* for a year, and the common manœuvre was to cast it at *nisi prius*. In such a case the entry would be thus: *Postea continuato inde processu, &c.*, mentioning the respite of the jury, and the appearance of the parties *in banco*, after which it might go on, *Et super hoc loquela prædicta remanet sine die, eò quòd idem A. in obsequio domini regis in guerris domini regis in partibus transmarinis profecturus est* (or as the case might be) *moraturus est. Et habet literas domini regis de protectione patentes, quarum datum, &c. per unum annum tunc proximè sequendum duraturas, &c.*[5] The justices of *nisi prius* had no power to allow or disallow the protection, but were merely to discharge the jury, and make a return of the protection, which was allowed or disallowed at the day in bank. If the inquest was taken after the protection cast, it was void. It often happened at the day in bank, that the plaintiff would present to the justices an *innotescimus* to repeal the protection; upon which there would issue a re-summons, or re-attachment against the defendant, and a new *venire*, or new *distringas* (for after much variety, either practice was held good)[6] to try the issue. The discharge, however, of the jury at *nisi prius* was still right, as the protection was good till repealed: so, if it expired before the day in bank;[7] but if it was disallowed on the day in bank, it was otherwise, for then it was the same as none.[8] Sometimes the defendant would make default at *nisi prius*, and not cast his protection till the day in bank, when it might be allowed; and if the inquest had been taken by default, the default would be saved.[9] Where a defendant appeared and challenged some jurors, and cast a protection, it was disallowed; because, as he

[1] 9 Hen. VI., 58; 38 Hen. VI., 23.
[2] 9 Hen. VI., 55.
[3] *Vide ante.*
[4] 39 Hen. VI., 39.
[5] Rast., 453.
[6] 5 Edw. IV., 2; Bro. Prot., 69.
[7] 35 Hen. VI., 58.
[8] 21 Hen. VI., 20.
[9] 21 Hen. VI.; 10 Bro. Prot., 50.

had appeared, he could not be demanded, and a protection was to excuse a default.[1]

It was a rule where there was more than one defendant that a protection cast by one, whether before appearance or after, should put the parol *sine die* for all.[2] But if the plaintiff had the precaution to sue several *venires*, then a protection cast by one defendant at *nisi prius*, or in bank, would stand only for that one.[3] A protection could only serve a defendant; and even a defendant in replevin, if he avowed and so made himself an actor, could not have a protection.[4] It was argued at one time that a *garnishee*, after plea pleaded, when he made title to a deed, was an actor, and therefore should not have a protection.[5] There is a case of a garnishee, even after plea pleaded, casting a protection;[6] but the former seems the better opinion.[7] It was held, he might cast a protection to the *scire facias*, because then at least he was not an actor.[8] A vouchee and prayee in aid were held entitled to cast a protection to the writ of summons, upon the ground that they might have an essoin, and were liable to judgment by default.[9] But where resceit was counterpleaded, the prayee was not allowed to cast a protection, because he was no party to the suit till he was received.[10]

Besides the substantial requisites to constitute a legal protection before mentioned, it was likewise not to vary[11] from the original writ by containing more or less;[12] it was not to be dated since the time of the default to be saved;[13] in either of which cases it would be disallowed. A corporation could not have a protection, because they could not be supposed to be all in *servitio regis*.[14]

The criminal law received some impression from the decisions of courts during these two reigns. What is laid down by Newton in the 19 Hen. VI.[15] as the law of treason, militates so plainly with the statute of treasons, that it can hardly be taken to be the better opinion of lawyers in his time. He says that if a man imagined the death of the king or his consort, he should be put to death for such an imagination, without having done anything, *i.e.*, without an overt act. Perhaps the slight circumstances that were then construed overt acts of treason might, in some degree, justify the opinion.

The criminal law.

By statute of Edw. II.,[16] no one was to be construed guilty of felony for breaking prison, unless the crime for which he was committed was felony. This act does not seem to have been violated by a determination in the beginning of the reign of Henry VI., where a person outlawed for felony was imprisoned in the king's bench; and being afterwards indicted for breaking prison, knowing certain traitors to be there confined, and letting them go at

[1] 4 Hen. VI., 22. [2] 21 Hen. VI., 41. [3] 22 Hen. VI., 3. [4] 22 Hen. VI., 28. [5] 3 Hen. VI., 18. [6] 4 Hen. VI., 9. [7] 9 Hen. VI., 36. [8] 3 Hen. VI., 18. [9] 3 Hen. VI., 30. [10] 37 Hen. VI., 2. [11] 7 Hen. VI., 22. [12] 28 Hen. VI., 1; 4 Hen. VI., 22. [13] 21 Hen. VI., 10. [14] 21 Edw. IV., 79. [15] Litt., 47. [16] *Vide ante*, c. xii.

large, he was adjudged guilty of treason, and accordingly drawn and hanged.[1]

Where a man had killed the wife of his master, it was agreed that it was treason.[2]

It was agreeable with the old law to denounce the pains of felony against any one who took away the life of an attainted man, otherwise than by the forms of law.[3] It was held a good justification in an appeal of homicide to say, that the deceased appealed the prisoner of treason in the court of the constable and marshal, and they waged battel thereon, and so he killed him.

With regard to larceny, it was only such things in which a man had a *property* could be feloniously taken and carried away.[4] The old maxim of criminal law that *voluntas refutalitur pro facto* continued to prevail in the reign of Henry IV.[5]

Of appeal.

Some points arose on the mode of proceeding by appeal. The appeal of death was the action of the heir to the deceased. A case of a peculiar kind was stated by Thirning, in the reign of Henry IV., when the heir was within age and died, and was succeeded by several heirs within age. It was said by that judge that the last of these heirs should have the appeal; but Gascoigne was clearly of another opinion.[6] A case happened in the reign of Henry VI. which brought forward this point again; for there a man was outlawed, and having a pardon, he sued out a *scire facias* against the plaintiff, who was returned dead by the sheriff, and, after much argument, it was determined by the court that no *scire facias* should go against the heir;[7] which seems like a decision that the heir was not entitled to the appeal. We find a curious point in the law of descent as to appeals much argued at this time: whether a person who derived his descent through a female could entitle himself to an appeal as heir? A case of this kind was brought into the exchequer chamber in the 20 Hen. VI., when Fortescue, chief justice, declared that he and his brethren were agreed upon the matter, but were willing to hear what could be said upon it. The objection against such an appeal was founded on the express words of Magna Charta, that no one should be taken on the appeal of a woman except for the death of her husband. The woman not being enabled to maintain an appeal, it was argued that an ancestral action like this having never descended on the woman could not descend through her to the appellant. Upon this reasoning the court determined that the appeal would not lie.[8]

Of provors.

Very little alteration happened in the ideas upon which provors were admitted to appeal. The statute 7 Henry IV. had discountenanced this mode of proceeding, and gave a warrant to the courts to go on in discouraging such suspicious accusers. In the 14 Henry VI., a man, being convicted of robbery, confessed the felony, and appealed two men of the same fact. Pro-

[1] 1 Hen. VI., 5. [2] 35 Hen. VI., 50 [3] 37 Hen. VI., 20. [4] 22 Hen. VI., 59.
[5] 13 Hen. VI., 85. [6] 11 Hen. IV., 11. [7] 38 Hen. VI., 13. [8] 20 Hen. VI., 63.

cess was issued against one of them; the other came to the bar and joined battel with the provor. A day was given them at Tothill, where they fought, and the appellee was worsted and severely wounded in the head. Upon this the justices demanded of him if he would have any more of the battel, to which he answered that he neither could nor would; adding upon the oath which he had taken that he was not guilty of the crime wherewith he was charged. Upon this he was adjudged to be hanged. After this the other appellee came in, and pleaded not guilty. Then judgment was given against the provor also to be hanged; for whether he who had pleaded guilty was acquitted or attainted, the provor, says the book, ought to be hanged on his own confession of the felony, and accordingly execution was instantly done upon him.[1] It was laid down that the appeal of a provor was for the benefit of the king, and not of himself, and that it was in the election of the justices to admit the appeal and avoid process against the appellees, or to direct the provor to be hanged on his own confession.[2] This was putting it nearly upon the footing of that courtesy which, in modern times, has been indulged towards offenders who will consent to give evidence for the crown against their accomplices.

It had been the common law for prisoners to claim the benefit of the clergy upon their arraignment; this was thought prejudicial to the party, for he had no challenge to the inquest *ex officiis, ut sciatur qualis* or *de nono liberari debeat*, by which connexion, nevertheless, he forfeited his goods and chattels, together with the profits of his lands, until he had made purgation. To remedy this, Sir John Prisot, chief justice of the common pleas, in concert with the other judges, in the reign of Henry VI., made an alteration, which was thought more advantageous to prisoners than the old practice. This was not to allow the benefit of clergy upon the arraignment, but to recommend to the prisoner to plead to the felony, and put himself on the jury *de bono et male*. Thus he had the advantage of his challenger and the chance of an acquittal on the events, and after all, if convicted, he might still claim his clergy. This was a variation in the practice of our criminal law, which was greatly commended, and was followed by most of his successors.[3]

[1] 19 Hen. VI., 35. [2] 24 Hen. VI., 28. [3] 2 Inst., 164.

CHAPTER XXIII.

HENRY VI. AND EDWARD IV.

Of Pleading—The Declaration—The Defence—Of Argumentative Pleading—A Traverse—A Negative Pregnant—Of Double Pleading—A Protestation—Departure in Pleading—Colour in Pleading—Aid Prayer—Of Garnishment—Of Interpleader—Plea of hors de son Fee—Of Non-tenure—Of Joint-tenancy—De son Tort Demesne—Summons and Severance—Forms of Pleading—Of Demurrer—Of Jeofaille and Amendment—Of Repleader (a) *The King and Government—The Statutes—Fortescue—Lyndwood—Treatises and Law Books—Miscellaneous Facts.*

Of pleading.

THE science of pleading makes a distinguished feature in the learning of this period, particularly of the last twenty years of Henry VI. and the reign of Edward IV. Whatever industry and whatever ingenuity had been exercised in the reign of Edward III., in adjusting the constitution and conduct of real actions, seems to have been transferred to pleading; which succeeded, as it were, to that ancient branch of learning like a descendant of the same family. Everything which concerned the frame and proceedings of actions was now agitated and refined upon with the greatest dexterity and skill. The writ, the declaration, the consequent pleadings, the process, the judgment, all these were debated under every possible consideration, and the forms and course of them were settled upon solemn deliberation.

Pleading had become so much the fashionable study, and it constituted such an essential part of the qualifications of a lawyer, that Littleton, in the reign of Edward IV., declares it to be "one of the most honourable, laudable, and profitable things in the law, to have the science of well pleading in actions real and personal;" and therefore he advises his son "especially to employ his courage and care to learn it."[1] The reports of the time of Henry VI. and Edward IV. are full of points of pleading, which are started, in one shape or other, in almost every question debated in court. Pleading was cultivated with so much industry and skill, that it was raised to a sudden perfection in the course of a few years.

In the former parts of this history, frequent occasion has been given to speak upon the nature of pleading in different actions, and the reader is not unapprised of the progress made in this branch of our law. But this retrospect will hardly satisfy the curiosity of

(a) As this chapter is occupied entirely with pleading, and there is no material difference in the law of the two reigns on that subject, they need not be separated.

[1] Litt., s. 534.

the historical inquirer, when he is arrived at a period in which pleading was brought to a state of consistency and accuracy that has entitled it, in the language of lawyers, to the name of a science. Almost everything substantial in pleading, which was practised from this time down to the present, was settled by judicial determinations in the reigns of these kings. The precedents of this period became ever after the standards of good pleading, and the rules and maxims of pleading now settled have governed ever since in our courts. It seems, therefore, proper to inquire what these precedents and what these rules and maxims were; in order to which we shall take a view of pleading in general, confining our observations to such formal parts as apply to most actions, whether real, personal, or mixed.

The whole of pleading was so much a matter of form that it may appear strange to distinguish any by calling them formal parts; but the forms of pleadings seem to be of two kinds. Thus, there are the forms of commencing and concluding a declaration or plea; the form of a traverse, of a protestation, of giving colour, and the like. These are the same, whatever is the substance and matter of the declaration, plea, traverse, protestation, or colour, and are properly and emphatically matters of form. But there is also a form in stating the substance of a declaration or plea; thus, a bond, a fine, a lease, a record, all have due forms, in which, and in no other, they ought to be pleaded. Such formal parts, therefore, whether of the former or latter kind, as were now settled, and had grown into common use, are the objects of our present consideration, without entering into such matters as might, by possibility, be made the substance of a declaration or plea, those being as infinite as the causes of action and grounds of defence that might arise upon the various modifications of rights, whether of property or persons, in the law of England.

The declaration.

The first part of pleading that naturally presents itself is the count or declaration. The declarations which were laid before the reader in the reign of Edward III.[1] seem to differ in form from those that had grown now to be in use. The first difference which strikes us is, that they were now no longer in French, but seem, in the first instance, to have been put into such Latin form and style as the entry on the roll was finally to be; the consequence of which was likewise this, that instead of being in the first person, the counting part, like the writ, was now in the third. Another alteration was, that the writ was invariably recited in the count, and made a necessary part of it. The count or declaration, was, therefore, the same as the roll or record of the court, down to the production of the *secta*, suit. In like manner the plea began with a recital of the defendant's appearance, and then stated his defence and plea in the third person; and this plea constituted, in like manner, the following part of the roll o

[1] *Vide ante*, c. xiii., c. xiv.

record of the court: the same of the replication and subsequent pleadings.

The following is a specimen of a declaration in an action of debt, according to the practice now established: *B. &c. summonitus fuit ad respondendum A. de placito quòd reddat eidem A. £20 quas ei debet, et injustè detinet. Et unde idem A. per C. attornatum dicit, quòd cùm prædictus B. tali die et anno, &c., apud S. comput âsset cum eodem A. de diversis denariorum summis ipsius A. per præfatum B. ad compotum inde eidem A. cùm inde requisitus fuisset, reddendum, ante id tempus receptis, et super compoto illo prædictus B. inventus fuisset in arreragiis erga ipsum A. in £20 per quod actio accrevit eidem A. ad exigendum et habendum de præfato B. prædictus £20: idem tamen B. licèt sæpiùs requisitus, prædictus £20 eidem A. nondum reddidit, sed illas ei hucusq; reddere contradixit, et adhuc contradicit; unde dicit quòd deterioratus est, et damnum habet ad valentiam 40s. &c. et inde producit sectam.*[1]

Such was the form of the delaration; but whether it was drawn out in this form on paper or parchment by the party's counsel, and delivered over to the adversary's counsel, or, what is more probable, was entered, in the first instance, upon the roll of the court, it is not easy to determine with precision: in point of effect, it would be the same; for the roll might be amended by the leave of the justices, during the term in which the declaration or plea was entered, and it must, at any rate, be entered on the roll as of that term; in both which cases the roll became afterwards, in construction of law, a record: so that the power the justices exercised over the roll during the term is, on one hand, sufficient to show the possibility of making the amendment of pleas without resorting to the supposition of there being paper pleadings; and the different construction the judges put upon the same roll of parchment, after and during the term, satisfies us that to constitute a record, there was not required a transcript from any less solemn paper or parchment, to one that was more so. If we were to judge from the reports of this period, in which there is frequent mention of the roll, with the above distinction of the same parchment being a roll in the term, and a record afterwards, without any allusion that could induce one to suspect the pleadings were, in any stage, to be sought for elsewhere, we cannot help adopting the above opinion; which likewise seems to be rendered more probable when it is considered that neither paper nor parchment was then an article to be consumed so profusely as now-a-days, in multiplying copies of the transitory nature these must have been.

It seems, therefore, a reasonable conjecture that whenever pleading *ore tenus* went out of use, it became the practice for the counsel to enter the declaration or plea upon the roll, in the office of the

[1] Rast., 147. Whenever it is necessary to illustrate what is here said on the doctrine of pleading, we shall make use of Rastell's Entries; most of the records in that collection being of the period of which we are now speaking.

prothonotary; that the counsel of the other party had access to it, in order to concert his plea, or take his exceptions to it; and that when these were to be argued, the roll was brought into court, as the only evidence of the pleading to be referred to. This course was certainly attended with some difficulties, and led to the expedient of putting the pleadings into paper, and handing this paper from one party to the other, the entry on the roll being deferred till the end of the term, an improvement which greatly facilitated the perusal and correction of pleadings, both of the party and his adversary, and made the affair of amendments more easy and decorous than in the old method, which must deface the roll. But this could not be indulged till a period arrived in which so useful a commodity as paper was become cheaper and more common; (*a*) and after all it must be confessed, whatever advantage might be attained by the convenience of paper-pleadings, the old method had simplicity to recommend it; for the declaration or plea, when once entered on the roll, answered all the purposes of paper-pleading during the term, and of a record afterwards.

To return to the delaration, and its form. As the declaration was to set out with a recital of the original writ, it is plain that where the writ was to attach the defendant, it should begin *B. attachiatus fuit ad respondendum, &c.* The general rule for framing a declaration was, that after setting forth the nature of the action, as was done by the recital of the writ, it should state the time and place, and the cause of action, in which should be comprehended how, and in what manner, the action accrued; and lastly, the conclusion, in which the plaintiff averred his damage, and offered to prove his suit. Respecting the degree of accuracy with which all this should be stated, it was a rule, founded on stat. 36 Edw. III. c. xv.,[1] that a declaration should not abate for want of form, so as it had matter of substance, nor should it abate for surplusage.[2] In mixed and real actions the plaintiff was not to count of the day, year, and place, as in personal actions.[3] If there was any defect in the declaration, the writ likewise, as well as the declaration, was abated.[4]

Defence.

The plea of the tenant or defendant begun with the *defence*, which varied according to the nature of the action or the plea; that is, whether it was first to the jurisdiction, next to the person, then to the count, and then to the writ, all which were called pleas in abatement, or, lastly, to the action, which was called a plea in bar.

Thus in some actions, as in assize, dower, *darrein presentment*, mortauncestor, *per quæ servitia*, attaint, and *scire facias*, the de-

(*a*) It did not, it is believed, take place until near the reign of Elizabeth, and led to this mischief, that it greatly increased the expense of pleading, and intervened obstacles in the way of that easy and speedy amendment of the pleading which, under the old system, at once disposed of all objections purely formal.

[1] *Vide ante*, c. xiv.

[2] 9 Hen. VI., 25.

[3] 9 Hen. VI., 115, 116.

[4] 35 Hen. VI., 40.

fence was *venit et dicit.* In others, as in every writ of *præcipe quòd reddat,* of intrusion, ayel, escheat, and the like, the defence was *venit et defendit jus suum quando, &c.* In others it was *venit et defendit vim et injuriam quando, &c.*, as in debt, accompt, detinue, covenant trespass, trespass upon the case, ejectment, *ne injustè vexes,* partition, *quare impedit, quo jure,* replevin, rescous, *recaptione averiorum, parco fracto, recto rationabili parte bonorum, rationabilibus estoveriis,* actions of debt or trespass given by statute, actions of waste, and other personal or mixed actions. In other actions the defence was more special; thus, in a writ of right, *quando dominus remisit curiam,* the defence was *venit et defendit jus prædicti petentis et seisinam suam quando, &c.* Again, in the writ *de nativo habendo,* the defence was *venit et defendit jus suum et omnem nativitatem quando, &c.* In others it was still more special, as in a prohibition upon the statutes of Richard II. and Henry IV., it was *venit et defendit vim et injuriam quando, &c., et omnem contemptum, et quicquid, &c.;* the same in actions upon the statutes of maintenance and labourers.[1] Those defences, however, that were most special were much contracted from the form of defences in the reign of Henry III., when it was usual to set forth *verbatim* the remaining part of the defence, which now was signified by the *et cætera.*

The foregoing were called *full defences,* to distinguish them from a *half defence,* which consisted in closing the defence without adding the words *quando, &c.* Thus, in pleas to the jurisdiction or to the person, the defendant could only make a half defence; for if he added the words *quando, &c.*, the jurisdiction and ability of the person would be thereby admitted.[2] Again, a misnomer was to be pleaded before any defence at all.[3]

After the substance of the plea was stated, the next point was to conclude it in proper form. Thus it was to conclude either to the jurisdiction, to the writ, to the count, or to the action. If the defendant pleaded to the writ, and concluded to the action, it would be repugnant and bad, because by the conclusion he admitted the writ; the same if he pleaded to the jurisdiction, and concluded to the writ.[4] Yet, on the contrary, if the plea was to the action, and the conclusion to the writ, the plea would be taken for a good one in bar.[5]

The commencement, therefore, and the conclusion of a plea might be in some or other of the following ways:—If to the action *Et prædictus B. per attornatum suum venit et defendit vim et injuriam quando, &c. Et dicit quòd ipse de debito prædicto, &c., onerari non debet, quia dicit, &c. Et hoc paratus est verificare, unde petit judiciam si prædictus A. actionem suam prædictam versus eum habere debeat, &c.* If to the writ, *Et prædictus B. venit et defendit vim et injuriam, et petit judiciam de brevi originali*

[1] *Vide* Bro., Defence.
[2] 2 Edw. IV., 15; 40 Edw. III., 36.
[3] Bro., Defence.
[4] 37 Hen. VI., 48.
[5] 37 Hen. VI., 24

loquelæ prædictæ, quia dicit, &c. Et hoc paratus est verificare, unde petit judiciam de brevi illo, et quòd breve cassetur, &c. If to the declaration, the alteration was *mutatis mutandis, judicium de narratione*, and *quòd narratio cassetur.*[1] A very material part of the conclusion of a plea was the general averment, or *paratus est verificare;* and this was required in all pleas, replications, or other pleadings containing matter of affirmation. But a plea that was the general issue, or in the negative, ought not to be averred. The nature of replications, rejoinders, and the other pleadings, wherever they differed from a plea in the form, will be better seen in what will hereafter be said upon the different parts of pleading.

Of argumentative pleading.

The great object of pleading being to bring the question between the parties to a certain point, it was expedient to hold the plaintiff and defendant to a strict way of stating his allegations, so that the adversary's plea might be answered directly and plainly, without leaving the sense to be collected by argument or inference. Thus it was held that in trespass for depasturing the plaintiff's grass, it was not sufficient for the the defendant to say *non depacit herbas*, for this they would call an *argumentative plea*, which the law would not allow; but as it meant that the defendant was not guilty of the charge, he should be compelled to say so in the formal and established plea of *non culpabilis.*[2] Again, in trespass for entering a garden, and where the defendant pleaded that there was no such garden, this was held to be argumentative; and as it amounted to the general issue, the defendant was driven to plead *non culpabilis.*[3] These might seem to be prejudices in favour of an established form of words, rather than instances where great precision was effected by rejecting such argumentative answers. The most common instance in which argumentative pleading seemed to mislead and confound was where some special matter or circumstance was stated; and the other party, instead of a direct denial of it, set up some contrary circumstance, as apparently incompatible with it, and therefore in effect amounting to a denial; as where it was pleaded that a person was resident at B., and it was replied that he was resident at F.;[4] or where it was pleaded that one of the defendants was dead before the writ purchased, to which it was replied that he was alive;[5] or where a defendant was declared against as executor, and he pleaded that the party died intestate.[6] All these were pronounced such pleadings as the law would not allow, though they had been very common in the reign of Edward III.,[7] and were then the occasion of much difficulty. For, without considering the want of precision in such allegations, it was a great difficulty, when an issue depended upon two affirmatives, to decide from which place the venue should come, whether from the place alleged by the plaintiff, or that alleged by the defendant. This, and other consequences from

[1] Rast., *passim.* [2] 22 Hen. VI., 37. [3] 10 Hen. VI., 16. [4] 19 Hen. VI., 1.
[5] 19 Hen. VI., 4. [6] 20 Hen. VI., 1. [7] *Vide ante.*

this old way of pleading, had induced the courts of late to lay it down as a rule *that every affirmative in pleading should be answered by an express negative.*[1] Conformably with this rule, the above pleas ought to have gone on, and concluded with a denial of the adversary's affirmative allegation, which was usually done by an *absq; hoc*, or *sans ce*, or, as they more commonly called it, a *traverse*. The effect of this was, that whatever new matter was started, the pleadings could not go on without an issue being soon raised, to be decided either by the court or by a jury.

A traverse.

Thus, where the declaration was for rent for the occupation of twenty acres of land, and the defendant pleaded a lease for twenty acres and twelve more, he was bound to traverse the lease for twenty acres.[2] When the plaintiff claimed an annuity by prescription, and the defendant pleaded an annuity by grant, he was to traverse the annuity by prescription.[3] Where a plaintiff claimed title to an advowson in gross, and the defendant set up a next presentation, he ought to traverse the advowson in gross.[4] Notwithstanding it was now considered as a general rule that two affirmatives could not make an issue, there still remained some vestige of the old forms, which were now taken as exceptions to that rule. Thus, if it was averred that the defendant was of full age, there needed no traverse that he was not within age.[5] If no negative went before, an affirmative would be sufficient without a traverse: thus the plaintiff might say that I. S., who appears, is I. S., of D., and the party sued is intended to be I. S. of C., without a traverse;[6] and some other cases still existed where the issue was held sufficient without a traverse.

This was the general idea upon which a traverse was introduced; and when the matter pleaded consisted of one fact only, the application of it was obvious and easy; but where a plea alleged several facts and circumstances, it was a consideration of no small difficulty to decide which of them should be picked out by the traverse as the main point to be denied, and of course to rest the issue upon. Much argument arose upon a doubt of this sort, where a *formedon in discendre* was brought on a gift to the father and mother of the demandant in tail. The tenant pleaded that he, long before the donors had anything in the land, was seised thereof in his demesne as of fee; and being so seised, and being within the age of twenty-one years, he infeoffed the donors, to have and to hold to them and their heirs; and the donors being so seised made a gift to the donees in tail, who had issue the demandant, and died; and that the tenant, being within age, entered, by force of which entry he was seised in his remitter, and so he demanded judgment of the action. To this the demandant replied, that the donors made the gift to the donees, as had been stated in the declaration, *sans ce* that the tenant infeoffed

[1] 18 Hen. VI., 8–10. [2] 32 Hen. VI., 3 b. [3] 32 Hen. VI., 4, 5.
[4] 35 Hen. VI., 33, 34. [5] 19 Hen. VI., 54. [6] 33 Hen. VI., 10.

the donors in the manner they had pleaded. It was objected to this replication that the feoffment was only the conveyance to the bar, and that it was not the conveyance, but the matter and substance of the bar which should be traversed, confessed, or avoided; and there was great debate whether the *seisin* or the feoffment should in this case be traversed; but the court held the feoffment to be the substance of the bar, and therefore that it was properly traversed.[1]

This was a question, whether a *seisin* or a *feoffment* was the proper point to be traversed; in the same year we find a case where the like doubt arose between a *disseisin* and a *feoffment*. In trespass *quare clausum fregit*, the defendant pleaded that one Richard Rawlins was seised of the same close in fee, and long before the trespass infeoffed the defendant in fee; and he gave colour to the plaintiff by the said Richard, and said the plaintiff entered, on whom the defendant re-entered and committed the trespass. To this the plaintiff replied, that true it is that Richard was seised in his demesne as of fee; but being so seised, he infeoffed one Peter Bennett in fee, by force of which he was seised, and upon him the said Richard entered against his own feoffment, and *disseised* the said Peter; and the said Richard being so seised, made the feoffment to the defendant, as he supposed, upon whom the said Peter entered and was seised in fee, and being so seised, infeoffed the plaintiff. To all this the defendant made no other rejoinder than that the said Richard did not disseise the said Peter. It was objected by the plaintiff that this traverse was not properly taken, because the disseisin was not the force of the title, but the feoffment made to the person whose estate the plaintiff had before the feoffment to the defendant. This feoffment, they said, was the force of the title, and the disseisin only the conveyance to it. It was alleged in the argument on one side, that the common practice had been to traverse the feoffment; it was as strongly contended on the other side that it had never been so adjudged; but that, on the contrary, it had been determined that the traverse of the disseisin was the proper pleading. To this effect, indeed, we find a rule laid down so far back as 9 Hen. VI., which says, that wherever a disseisin was alleged in a bar or replication, it should always be traversed.[2] Afterwards, indeed, it was laid down by Needham that the traverse might be *either* to the feoffment or the disseisin;[3] and in the present case they held the traverse to the feoffment to be good,[4] without any regard to or indeed mention of the above rule, and left it for after times to reconcile these differences, by holding, according to the opinion of Needham, that in such case either traverse was good.

When pleadings were long and special, they of course drove one of the parties to a traverse, and occasions were continually furnished

[1] Long. 5 Edw. IV., 9-12.
[2] Scien. de Plead., 355.
[3] Long. 5 Edw. IV., 136, 137.
[4] *Ibid.*, 138.

to inquire what matters were traversable and what not, whether in pleas or in declarations. This made one of the nicest and most curious parts of the science of pleading. To enter minutely into it would carry us too far: from what has been already said, it appears that a traverse should be directed to that which is the substance and matter of the title; but such was the subtilty with which points of law were treated, that this general rule stood in need of many auxiliary ones to assist the mind in judging of the particulars that should or should not be traversed.

The same love of precision which induced the courts to discountenance *argumentative pleading*, led them to pass a like judgment, and with the same justice, on what was called a *negative pregnant*. An instance of this may be seen, where in an action on the case against an innkeeper, for goods lost by his default, the defendant pleaded that they were not taken by his default, which answer was construed to be a denial *pregnant* with an admission that they might be taken, though not by his default; and therefore the court, in that case, compelled the defendant to plead the special matter.[1] Again, where an action was brought against a man for burning the plaintiff's house by negligently keeping his fire, the defendant pleaded that the house was not burnt by his default in keeping his fire: this was held a negative pregnant, for the same reason as the before-mentioned plea.[2] There seems, therefore, to be this sort of affinity between an argumentative plea and a negative pregnant; that as the latter is a negative pregnant with an affirmative, so is the former an affirmative pregnant with a negative; and the cure for both is, in most cases, to add, or at least to substitute, a direct denial of the substance and git of the plea or declaration which is to be answered.

A negative pregnant.

If the courts would not admit a plea that did not directly answer the adversary's allegation, neither would they allow one that contained a multiplicity of matter, to each of which a distinct answer ought to be made: such was called a *double plea*. Thus where bastardy was pleaded as to one acre, and joint-tenancy as to another, this plea was held double, because bastardy went to both.[3] Again, where a defendant, in avoidance of a bond, pleaded imprisonment at one place, and detainer till he made an obligation at another, this was held double.[4] In debt for four marks of rent, the defendant pleaded first that one only was due; and further he pleaded, as to part a tender, and as to the remainder an entry before the day: this was held double.[5] The remedy in this and other cases, where the party thought he had more points than one to object, and he would not willingly preclude himself of one by stating only the other, was to set forth that one in a *protestation*.

Of double pleading.

There were cases where multiplicity of matter might be stated

[1] 22 Hen. VI., 38, 39.
[2] 28 Hen. VI., 7.
[3] 32 Hen.
[4] 37 Hen. VI., 15.
[5] 3 Hen. VI., 16, 19.

without the charge of duplicity. Thus where the plea concluded with a *non est factum*, all the special reasons for the deed being void might precede.[1] Again, a plea with a traverse was not double, because the traverse was held to waive the plea;[2] the conveyance to the traverse being no more considered than what was taken by protestation. In some cases, however, double pleading was allowed: thus in justification for false imprisonment, twenty causes might be alleged without the charge of being double.[3] Again, in favour of life, it was allowed in an appeal to plead some special matter, and then to plead over to the felony.[4]

A protestation.

A protestation was likewise necessary where the party would otherwise be concluded by force of the plea; as if a lord pleaded *nil debet* to debt brought by his villein, this would operate as an enfranchisement, because it admitted him capable of having property: he might therefore protest that the plaintiff was his villein, and for plea say, that he owed him nothing. For these reasons a protestation in after-times was very significantly termed "exclusion of a conclusion." The rule in making a protestation was, that it should not be repugnant to the matter stated by way of plea. Thus where a defendant in replevin protested that he did not take the cattle, and for plea said there was no such vill, and then avowed to have a return;[5] this was held to be such a repugnancy between the protestation and the avowing for a return, that they could not stand together. If the plea was found for the party pleading the protestation, the protestation would serve; but if against him, it would not serve the purpose it was designed for. Thus where a defendant in replevin avowed for rent, alleging that the plaintiff held by homage, fealty, and rent; and the plaintiff said that he held by the rent, and nothing of the rent was arrear, and pleaded on, protesting that he did not hold by homage; there, if the plaintiff barred the defendant of his avowry, he should be excluded from demanding homage afterwards. Again, where in forger of false deeds the defendant took the forging by protestation, and traversed the publication, and that was found against him, the protestation would not aid him.[6]

Departure in pleading.

It was not sufficient that every single plea was drawn with the precision and accuracy above required, unless the successive pleas alleged by the same party were pursuant to and fortified what went before. It was therefore required that the matter first alleged should not be *departed* from, but that whatever was added in the subsequent plea should be in support and aid of it, otherwise the plea was bad: if therefore a defendant in his bar should allege a title to the whole estate, and in his rejoinder he should make title only to a moiety, this was held a departure, and as such the rejoinder was bad.[7] The construction of pleas in

[1] 38 Hen. VI., 26, 27.
[2] 9 Hen. VI., 26.
[3] 7 Edw. IV., 20.
[4] 22 Edw. IV., 39.
[5] 20 Hen. VI., 28.
[6] 9 Hen. VI., 26 and 59; 33 Hen. VI., 45.
[7] 22 Hen. VI., 51.

these cases was very strict, as may be seen in the following instance. A tenant pleaded a devise to him: the plaintiff replied that the devisor was an infant; to which the defendant rejoined, that infants might devise by custom: this rejoinder was held a departure from the bar, which alleged a devise generally.[1]

Colour in pleading.

We come now to consider the nature of *colourable pleading*, a device of which we found some instances in the reign of Edward III.,[2] but which was now grown into a settled form of pleading, and was explained upon grounds and principles that appeared satisfactory to the minds of lawyers. This pleading was used in assizes, in writs of entry in nature of an assize, and in trespass. The matter suggested in this way was always a fiction, and owed its origin to two circumstances: first, a jealousy in defendants of trusting certain special points of defence to the verdict of jurors; and secondly, a rule of law, that if such special points amounted in fact to nothing more than the general issue, they should not have the effect of taking the cause from the verdict of the jury to the judgment of the court, but the defendant must plead the general issue in the usual form; as, *nul tort, nul disseisin*, in assize; *ne disseisa pas*, in a writ of entry; and *not guilty*, in trespass.

Thus suppose *A.* had infeoffed *B.* of certain land, and an assize was brought by a stranger against *B.*; in such case the tenant would be led by the inclination of his own mind not to plead the general issue, because then the validity of the title and feoffment would be decided on by the jury; but he would endeavour to state a sufficient bar to the assize, and bring the question to the opinion of the judges, by saying, that *A.* was seised, and infeoffed by him, by force whereof he entered, and then he would pray judgment if the assize would lie. But here the law would pronounce that this plea was not good, for it amounted to the general issue, which he must be compelled to plead in terms, or the assize would be awarded. The tenant therefore, in order to attain the object of having the matter decided by the court, used to give the plaintiff *colour*, that is, *a colour of action*, by which it would appear dangerous for the tenant to trust the matter, he had pleaded, to the judgment of unlettered men. Thus, in the above case, when the tenant pleaded that *A.* infeoffed him, he would add further, *that the plaintiff claiming by colour of a deed of feoffment made by the said feoffor, before the feoffment made to the said tenant (by which deed no right passed) entered, upon whom the said tenant entered;* and then he would pray judgment if the assize should pass: and because, in this case, it might appear doubtful in the minds of unlettered men, whether anything did or did not pass by the first infeoffment, as suggested, the law allowed that special matter to constitute a plea in bar sufficient to call upon the judges to decide whether the prior feoffment had really such effect or not.[3]

[1] 37 Hen. VI., 5. [2] *Vide ante*, c. xiv. [3] Doct. and Stud., 295.

This idea of giving colour was further refined upon; for besides suggesting that the plaintiff claiming by colour of a deed of feoffment made by a stranger (where nothing really passed), entered upon the freehold; they used to add, *upon whom A. B. entered, upon whom the tenant entered;* whereas there was no more an entry by *A. B.* than there was a feoffment to the plaintiff. The reason for this manner of pleading was, to protect the defendant from the construction that might be raised to his disadvantage upon the first of these pleas; for if the tenant by that pleading confessed an immediate entry upon the plaintiff, or an immediate ouster of the plaintiff, the consequence would be, that should the title be afterwards found for the plaintiff, the tenant would be convicted of the disseisin by his own confession: and because the tenant, though he had no right to the land, might yet be no disseisor, it was usual to adopt the style of pleading last mentioned for his protection.[1]

This is the general idea upon which pleading *colourably* was first resorted to and allowed by the courts. When this manner of pleading had once established itself, several rules obtained for the government of it, which, in some measure, restrained the fancy of counsel in the choice of such fictitious circumstances as were to be suggested in this colourable way. The principal of these rules, and indeed that which seemed to be of the essence of colour, was, that it should consist of some matter of law, or other difficulty to the lay-gents. For example, if I bring an assize against you, and you plead that you leased the same land to *A.* for his life, and then granted the reversion to me, and afterwards *A.* died, and I claiming the land by virtue of this grant to which the tenant never atturned, entered: or, if a tenant pleaded that he leased to the plaintiff, and afterwards the plaintiff surrendered such lease: in the first of these cases, the lay-gents were not capable of deciding that the grant was defective without attornment; nor in the second, that a surrender might be made by parol. Again, if the tenant said that the father of the plaintiff leased to him for the life of another, and afterwards released to him, and the plaintiff, supposing that the father died seised of the reversion, ousted him after the death of the *cestui qui vie;* this would be a good colourable plea, because the lay-gents could not determine how the release enured, whether by way of feoffment, enlargement, confirmation, or extinguishment of estate. Again, if the tenant pleaded, that the father of the plaintiff infeoffed him, and he suffered the father to hold and occupy the land at will; or if he pleaded that the plaintiff claimed as bastard and eldest son; these were points of difficulty which should properly be decided by the court, and therefore were good colourable suggestions. But if the tenant said that he was seised till the plaintiff disseised him, upon whom he entered, it was ill; because all men, however nnlearned, know, that in such

[1] Dr. and Stud., 201.

a case the tenant was no disseisor: the same if he said that the plaintiff claimed as younger son, because every one knows the younger son cannot inherit before the elder. Such, therefore, as cases perfectly intelligible to the unlettered, were adjudged by law improper to be sent to the jury on the general issue.[1].

Another rule respecting the matter pleaded *colourably* was, that it should give to the plaintiff a fair pretence on which to support his action. Thus, in trespass for goods, it was necessary to give a possession to the plaintiff, though without title, because that was a good ground for an action of trespass; as to say, that the defendant being in possession of the goods as executor, the plaintiff took them, and the defendant retook them.[2] In trespass for taking goods, the defendant said, that before the plaintiff had the goods, he was possessed of them as his own property, and bailed them to *A*. to be rebailed to him; and that *A*. gave them to the plaintiff, who supposing the property to be in *A*. took them, and the defendant retook them.[3] A third rule in pleading colourably was, that it should always be given by the defendant to the plaintiff, and always in a plea in bar.[4] Such were the principal rules by which these fictitious suggestions were measured; and provided these, and some others of less consequence, were adhered to, the defendant was at liberty to state whatever happened to strike his mind; colours being as various as the possible ways in which the subject in question might be transferred and possessed.

It seems not to have been quite clear, in what cases the defendant was required to give colour, and in what the special matter of itself constituted a good bar. To form a judgment of this, we must content ourselves with some few determinations, without attempting to discover the reasons upon which they were decided. It is said, that where such matter was pleaded as bound the *possession* only, the defendant should give colour; as in case of a dying seised, and descent to the defendant.[5] But where the *right* was bound, as by feoffment with warranty, by fine, and the like, there no colour need be given. Again, if a defendant pleaded *liberum tenementum*, he need not give colour, nor where he justified as servant to one who had the freehold:[6] the same where one justified for a distress: because, says the book, where no property was claimed, there no colour need be given.[7] It was held, at one time, that in justification for taking as wreck, or as the goods of felons, the defendant should give colour:[8] but afterwards it was laid down, that in those cases, and also in justification for tithes, for waif and stray, or as a purchase in market overt, no colour need be given;[9] though, in the case of goods sold in market overt, they made this distinction: If the defendant said simply, that *A*. sold them to him, he need not give colour; but if he had said, that

[1] 19 Hen. VI., 21. [2] 7 Hen. VI., 35. [3] 7 Hen. VI., 3.
[4] 19 Hen. VI., 32. [5] 22 Hen. VI., 18. [6] 21 Edw. IV., 15; 18 Edw. IV., 3.
[7] 2 Edw. IV., 12. [8] 59 Hen. IV., 2; 9 Edw. IV., 22.
[9] 21 Edw. IV., 18, 65.

A. was possessed of goods *as of his proper goods*, and sold them to him, colour should be given: because, in this latter case, he fully stated, that no property was in the plaintiff, and therefore that he had no colour of an action; but in the former, there might be still a property in the plaintiff;[1] which distinction seems analogous to that of the two cases before mentioned, where the *right*, and where the *possession* only was bound. For the same reason, where a defendant pleaded wardship through a stranger, he was to give colour.[2] If the plea was founded on an act of parliament, no colour need be given;[3] because, says the book, an act of parliament bound all parties.

It would be unnecessary to enter further into discussion on this obsolete piece of learning, which in a subsequent period was reduced to a more simple form, and at length went quite out of use. In the time of which we are now writing, this was a very prevailing fashion of pleading; and the reasons that were advanced to give it authority, were thought to be well founded: a time came, when these were less considered, and the device of *colour* appeared to pleaders not so indispensably necessary. How this change in opinions operated, will be seen hereafter.

Instead of taking upon himself the defence of the action, the defendant, as we have seen, might call in the assistance of another person to protect him in his defence. One way in which a defendant might protect himself was by *voucher*, which was allowed only in real actions. This is as ancient as anything in the practice of our courts, and has already been so fully explained,[4] as to need no recapitulation. The present practice stood upon the law in Bracton's time, and the few alterations which had been made by statute in the reign of Edward I. and since; and to add anything to the much that has already been said, might be thought an unnecessary repetition.

It is not so with *ad prier*, which bears some affinity with vouching to warranty, and probably was first suggested by it.

Aid prayer.

When an action was brought against a person, who, though in possession of the thing in question, had not the complete and entire property; and if judgment passed against him, another person who had right would be injured; the tenant or defendant might pray to have the aid of such person to defend the suit. Thus a tenant for life, by the courtesy, or the like, might *pray aid* of him in reversion or remainder, to plead for him and defend the inheritance. The entry of *aid prier* was thus: *Et prædictus tenens per attornatum suum venit, et dicit quòd, &c.* (then the cause of aid prayer was alleged). *Et sic prædictus tenens dicit quòd ipse tenet, et die impetrationis brevis originalis prædicti querentis tenuit tenementum prædictum pro termino vitæ suæ remanere cuidum præfato B. et hæredibus masculis de corpore*

[1] 12 Edw. IV., 5 b.
[2] 2 Edw. IV., 27.
[3] 3 Edw. IV., 2.
[4] *Vide ante*, vol. i. c. viii.

suo exeuntibus, sine quo idem tenens non potest tenementum prædictum cum pertenentiis in placitum deducere, neq ; præfato querenti inde respondere. Et PETIT AUXILIUM *de ipso B. &c. Et ei conceditur, &c. Ideo præceptum est vice comiti quòd summoneat per bonos summonitores prædictum B. quòd sit hic a die Paschæ, &c., ad jugendum cum præfato tenente simul, &c., in respondendo præfato querenti de præfato placito si, &c., idem dies datus est partibus prædictus, &c.*[1] Upon demand of aid, and the prayer being granted, a judicial writ was sued out by the tenant, called a summons *ad auxiliandum;* at the return of which, if the prayee did not appear or essoin, if he after made default, judgment was entered, *quòd tenens ad narrationem prædicti querentis sine præfato B. respondeat.*

A tenant for life had his option, either to vouch the reversioner, or pray him in aid.[2] If the remainder in fee was to the tenant for life and another, he should have aid of that other.[3] A tenant might have aid of a remainderman in fee, without showing a deed; for the feoffment might be without deed.[4] If aid was prayed of a reversioner, who took the reversion as conusee of a fine, this amounted to an attornment of the prayor.[5] Aid of the reversioner might be had in a writ of entry, in nature of an assize, though not in an assize ;[6] because the tenant was supposed to be in by reason of his own tortious act.

We find instances of aid granted in personal actions, as in replevin, trespass, debt, and annuity ; in a *scire facias*, in attaint ravishment of ward, and ejectment of ward. If another person was interested in the thing claimed of the defendant, there was the same reason as in real actions that he should have the aid of such person to protect his present possession, or title. Thus, if a writ of annuity, or debt for arrears of an annuity, issuing out of a benefice, was brought against the parson, he might have aid of the patron and ordinary ; the two persons who should have concurred in such a grant, if any was made, and who at least were interested that the benefice should not be charged with such a demand after the death of the present incumbent :[7] if, therefore, such annuity was upon the parson's own deed, as this only bound him, he could not have their aid.[8] Thus in a replevin, a tenant for life of seignory might pray aid of the reversioner ;[9] and a plaintiff in replevin, being a termor, might have aid of the reversioner ;[10] because in both these cases the reversioner would be charged with the event of the suit. Where a defendant in trespass justified by commandment of one who had the freehold, he might have aid of such freeholder.[11] In general, in personal actions, it was a rule that no aid prayer should be had before issue joined ; but this was liable to many exceptions, and it was a point of much controversy

[1] Rast. *Aid. prier.* [2] 9 Hen. VI., 3. [3] 33 Hen. VI., 6. [4] 22 Hen. VI., 1.
[5] 57 Hen. VI., 5. [6] 14 Hen. VI., 22 ; 4 Edw. IV., 14 ; 21 Edw. IV., 15.
[7] 2 Hen. VI., 8. [8] 2 Hen. VI., 12. [9] 9 Hen. VI., 26. [10] 6 Edw. IV., 2.
[11] 7 Hen. VI., 71.

when aid should be allowed before issue joined, and when not.[1]

Aid *of the king* was a piece of learning depending upon considerations somewhat different from those which governed the prayer of aid in the case of common persons. In the first place, as the king could not be vouched, a tenant was driven to pray aid of the king in all instances where, from the nature of his estate, he would be entitled to vouch a common person, or to have warranty of charters;[2] and in such case, if he lost, he would, as in case of voucher, be entitled to recovery in value by petition.[3] Aid of the king was therefore of two kinds; it was either upon a warranty, and was for the purpose of recovery in value, and then it corresponded with voucher; or it was founded on the feebleness of the tenant's estate, and then it corresponded with the *aid prier*, of which we have just been speaking. On this, as well as other accounts, there were several material differences between the practice of praying aid of a common person, and of the king. Thus, in the former case, if it was in an action of trespass, it could not be till after issue joined; in the latter, it must be before;[4] because the king should not be put to support an issue that was joined by a common person.[5]

By aid and voucher, a third person was introduced into the action, through the solicitude of the tenant to defend the subject in dispute. If the tenant took another part, and appeared to defend faintly or collusively, or made default, the person in reversion or remainder, or any one otherwise interested, by authority of certain statutes passed in the reign of Edward I., and extended in subsequent reigns,[6] might *pray to be received*, and defend his freehold or inheritance. The entry in such case was as follows: *Super quo venit quidam A. hic in curiâ in propriâ personâ, et dicit quòd diu ante diem im petrationis brevis originalis, &c.* Then the record set forth the seisin in fee of *A.* who leased to the tenant for life, the reversion in fee continuing in *A.*, and then it went on: *Et dicit quòd pro eo quòd prædictus tenens, &c., in brevi prædicto non petiverunt auxilium de ipso A. neq; ipsum vocaverunt ad warrantizandum, &c., sed per fraudem et collusionem inter ipsos querentum et tenentem, intentione ad faciendum ipsum A. amitere inde jus suum fictè placitverunt, et hoc paratus est verificare; unde ex quo idem A. venit ante judicium redditum paratus præfato querenti respondere, et jus suum defendere, petit quòd* ADMITTATUR *ad defensionem juris sui.*[7]

The time of praying to be received was when judgment was about to be given for the demandant without further process. Upon the receipt of the reversioner, the demandant might count against him *de novo;* for by the receipt the former count was

[1] 7 Edw. IV., 2; *Ibid*, 24. [2] 9 Hen. VI., 56. [3] 9 Hen. VI., 3.
[4] 35 Hen. VI., 56. [5] 7 Edw. IV., 8. [6] *Vide ante*, c. ix.
[7] Rast., 530.

waived, and no advantage could be taken of any defect therein.[1] The persons received might plead almost all pleas, and take all advantages which the tenant might, such as voucher, aid, age, and the like;[2] but he could not imparle: and if he made default it was peremptory, and judgment was entered against the tenant, without taking any notice of the tenant by receipt; because the tenant by receipt having alleged that he was *paratus petenti respondere*, he ought always to be present in court.[3] Receipt was only allowed in real actions; but it had been extended beyond the actions mentioned in the statutes of Edward I. as to waste, *quem reditum redit*, and many others.

To all the foregoing prayers the demandant or plaintiff might, by way of counterplea, allege such matter as would take away the prayer of the tenant or defendant; and the vouchee besides might counterplead the warranty, and show that he was not bound to warrant the land.

The common counterplea to aid and receipt was, that the prayee had nothing in the reversion the day of the writ purchased. It used to be common for a tenant, after the writ was brought, to convey the estate in fee, and take back an estate for life, so as to baffle the demandant: when a tenant who had so acted, pleaded that he was only tenant for life, this used to be replied, and would oust him of his aid; and if replied to the prayer of receipt, it would oust such collusive reversioner of his receipt.[4] The common counterpleas to voucher of warranty were such as are given by the statutes of Edward I.[5]

Another way in which a defendant might relieve himself from the burthen of contesting singly with the plaintiff, was by *garnishment* and *interpleader*. The former of these was allowed only in the action of detinue; the latter, though more frequently used in detinue, might likewise be resorted to in some other actions.

Of garnishment.

The practice of depositing deeds in the hands of a third person to await the performance of covenants, or the doing of some act, upon which they were to be re-delivered to one or other of the parties, still continued,[6] and gave occasion to many actions of detinue, which were brought against the depositary of such writings, whenever the crisis happened for their being demandable, according to the terms of the agreement on which they were deposited. It was in these actions that the defendant would find himself driven to call in the other party to the agreement and deposit, that the re-delivery might be made to the persons who had a legal right to call for it from the defendant. Thus in an action of detinue for such deeds delivered by the plaintiff to the defendant to be re-delivered, the defendant would plead that they were delivered by the plaintiff *and one J. N.* upon certain conditions, and

1 33 Hen. VI., 53.
2 21 Hen. VI., 28.
3 21 Hen. VI., 48.
4 21 Hen. VI., 13; 4 Edw. IV., 14.
5 *Vide ante*, c. xiii.
6 *Vide ante*, c. xiv.

he did not know whether the conditions were performed, therefore he prayed *garnishment* (as it was called) against *J. N.;* that is, that *J. N.* might be summoned to show whether they were: upon this a *scire facias* would issue against *J. N.*, who under the name of *garnishee* became defendant to the suit, the first defendant being considered as out of court by the garnishment.

The entry upon the record stood thus: *Et prædictus defendens in propriâ personâ venit, &c. Et proferendo hìc in curiâ cartam, &c., paratus ad deliberandum cui vel quibus curia domini regis concederet, dicit quòd carta illa die anno et loco supradictis, eidem defendenti tam per prædictum querentem quàm quendam I. N., ùnanimi eorum assensu et consensu, æquâ manu liberata fuit sub certis conditionibus custodiendis, et eidem querenti et I. N., aut eorum alteri sub conditionibus illis reliberandam, sed utrùm conditionis illæ ex parte prædicte I. N., ad impletæ sunt necene, dicit quòd ipse omnino ignorat. Et petit quòd prædictus I. N., inde* PRÆMUNIATUR *et ei conceditur, &c. Ideo præceptum est vicecomiti, quòd per probos, &c., scire faciat præfato I. N., quòd sit hic in, octabis, &c., ostensurus, &c., quare carta prædicta præfato querenti, liberari non debeat si, &c. Idem dies datus est partibus prædictis, hic, &c.*[1]

When the garnishee appeared, he was to plead; and many questions arose upon what the garnishee might plead, and what not. It was very early settled that he should not plead a misnomer of himself in the *scire facias;*[2] nor should he plead in abatement of the writ of detinue, because it was in effect his own writ, he being a party to the bailment;[3] and yet he was allowed to plead excommunication of the plaintiff,[4] or release of all actions.[5] He was not to have oyer of the declaration unless he appeared at the first day, and he was not to be declared against afresh, nor could plead to the writ or declaration, if admitted by the defendant.[6] He might not plead foreign matter but only in cases apparent, as *amicus curiæ.*[7] If the defendant had stated what the conditions were on which the deed was to be delivered, or he admitted those alleged by the plaintiff, the garnishee could not vary from them and allege different conditions; but if the defendant alleged *certain conditions* generally, then the garnishee might show them specially.[8] The remedy for the garnishee, if he conceived the conditions to be different, was to bring a new action against the defendant, and then the conditions might be contested between the two plaintiffs by interpleading, as will be shown presently.[9]

If the plaintiff succeeded in his action, the judgment against the defendant was to recover the deed, which had remained in the custody of the court to abide the decision of the suit, and against the garnishee for damages in the delay occasioned by his plea: if

[1] Rast., 212.
[2] 3 Hen. VI., 37.
[3] *Ibid.*, 40.
[4] *Ibid.*
[5] 20 Hen. VI., 28.
[6] 3 Hen. VI., 50.
[7] 9 Hen. VI., 38, 39.
[8] 21 Hen. VI., 35.
[9] 20 Edw. IV., 13.

he failed, the garnishee would have damages against him.[1] The execution of the garnishee was only of his goods, chattels, and land, and not of the body, because he was not a party to the original writ.[2] If the plaintiff replied to the defendant's prayer, that the deed was delivered by himself alone, and traversed the delivery by him and the stranger, this would prevent the garnishment.[3] The plaintiff might reply to the plea of the garnishee but not the defendant, as he was out of court.[4] Garnishment might be had against executors, as well as the principal who made the bailment. It could not be had against a mere stranger, but must always be preceded by an allegation of privity to the bailment.[5]

If the two parties who concurred in the bailment to the defendant brought several actions for the deed, then the resource of the defendant was in praying that the two plaintiffs might *interplead*. This was upon allegations similar to those made in the case of garnishment; and the entry was thus: *Et prædictus defendens per attornatum suum venit, et tam ad sectam prædicti A, quàm ad sectam prædicti B. defendit vim et injuriam quando, &c. Et proferendo hic in curiâ prædictum scriptum obligatorium paratus ad deliberandum cui prædictorum A. et B. curia hic concederet, dicit quòd scriptum illud est idem scriptum quod uterq; prædictorum A. et B. versus eum exigit, et quòd, &c.*, as in the former precedent. *Et petit, quòd prædictus A. et B. super liberatione scriptorum prædictorum inter eos* INTERPLACITENT, *&c. Ideo consideratum est, quòd prædictus A. et B. super liberatione scriptorum prædictorum habendâ interplacitent, &c. Et dictum est per curiam præfato B. quòd præfato A. ad breve et narrationem suam, de eo quod idem A. inde priùs narravit, respondeat, &c.*[6] It was held, upon such interpleader, that the person whose writ was of the prior date should be the plaintiff, and the other plaintiff should answer his writ and declaration, and so become defendant.[7] If they were of the same date, then he who first came and demanded an answer, or he whom the court pleased to assign, became plaintiff.[8]

Of interpleader.

It was reasonable, where the defendant was a mere depositary of a deed, in which the two persons who agreed in making him the trustee were interested, that he should not be harassed by both, but be allowed to call on the court to award, that they should contest the points in dispute between themselves (*a*). But there were cases where a person possessed of a deed might be liable to the actions of two or more persons for the detinue; and where it was argued with some show of reason, at least as far as topics of a legal and technical nature might be urged, that the defendant should

(*a*) And it is curious that, when this procedure became obsolete, the same principle was carried out in courts of equity; and, in our own time, the jurisdiction was restored to courts of law by the interpleader act of 1 *Will. IV.*, c. v., s. 5.

[1] 1 Edw. V., 3; 27 Hen. VI., 2.
[2] 7 Hen. VI., 45.
[3] 3 Hen. VI., 50.
[4] 14 Hen. VI., 11.
[5] 3 Hen. VI., 44.
[6] Rast., 208.
[7] 3 Hen. VI., 20.
[8] 19 Hen. VI., 3.

not have this privilege, but ought to remain in the situation of defendant to both their actions, and defend himself as well as he could against both the claims to which he was liable, whether by choice or otherwise. Thus a writ of detinue was brought by A., and the plaintiff declared on a bailment made by I. G. to the defendant to rebail to the plaintiff; and I. G. also brought another writ, and declared of a bailment made by himself to the defendant to rebail to the said I. G., and this was pleaded to the former writ. It was argued, that the defendant could not have garnishment against I. G. (if I. G. had not brought his action), because he had alleged no privity, and therefore that A. should not call upon the plaintiff to interplead. But it was said that there needed no privity of bailment, the possession merely, and not the bailment, being the cause of action; for if the defendant had found the deed, and had pleaded that to the action, then it was long settled that they should interplead: so in this case the defendant was properly liable to none but the person who had right, and yet he had no legal defence, and therefore must refer it to an interpleader; for should they both recover, and a writ issue for the delivery of the deed, to whom should it be delivered? On account of all these inconveniences, it was held that the two plaintiffs should interplead.[1]

Some of these considerations arose on the occasion of two actions of detinue for a box of charters; one by the heir who was entitled to the land, and one by the bailor upon a bailment to re-deliver to him. It was there urged that the defendant should not have an interpleader, because he was liable to both the plaintiffs; to the tenant of the land, because he had a right to the charters; and to the bailor, by reason of the bailment; and if he was a sufferer by this double charge, it was his own act, and he must not complain. And it was laid down for law, if a man bails a thing to me to be rebailed, and I afterwards deliver this to another, and he bails it to me to be rebailed, I am chargeable at the suit of both: and in the case at bar it was contended, should the plaintiff who had the land recover the charters, this would be no plea for the defendant to discharge him as against the bailor, although it would be otherwise in the case of executors, or where the thing came to the defendant by a *finding*; for there it would be sufficient if he restored it to the right owner.

This was arguing upon the special manner in which they used to declare in detinue, and seems wholly conformable with the old ideas upon which this action and the pleading in it used to turn; this being the ground upon which the bailment was held to be traversable. But in opposition to this it was answered, as on the former occasion, that the bailment was nothing to the purpose; that the detinue was the point and git of the action; and that the bailment was only the conveyance to it: that in this case, if the bailor should recover, the person who had the land might have

[1] 3 Hen. VI., 43.

detinue against him, as he alone was entitled to the deeds; which circuity would be avoided by an interpleader: to avoid therefore multiplicity of suits, as well as for the other reasons, they were inclined to award an interpleader.[1]

It is not improbable that such opinions as these led to an alteration in the manner of declaring upon a writ of detinue; for if it was settled that a man should not be bound by a special bailment, but that the person who had right should recover, that sort of declaration became futile and unnecessary; and the purpose was equally answered by a general allegation of a *devenerunt ad manus*, or a *trover*. These opinions, however, had not yet grown to be established law. For in 19 Henry VI. we find two several writs of detinue were brought against the same person, and they counted of several bailments. There it was held, that the parties should not interplead, unless the defendant could allege a privity of bailment, or that he found the deeds; for if he chose to charge himself with several bailments, it was his folly, says the court, and he must abide by it: the defendant then pleaded that the two plaintiffs joined in the bailments, and he traversed the several bailments; upon which the court suffered the defendant to have an interpleader,[2] because he now alleged a privity between them. Thus the court would, if possible, get rid of the conclusion that arose upon the special bailment, and enable the defendant to get justice done between the two plaintiffs.

If a defendant had prayed garnishment, and afterwards the garnishee counted against them, it was once held he might have an interpleader between the two plainliffs;[3] though, on a later occasion, it was refused on the notion of the defendant being out of court by the garnishment.[4]

If the two writs were brought in different counties, it was held at one time, that the plaintiffs might still interplead:[5] it seems afterwards to have been held that they should not:[6] the same if the bailments were alleged in different counties.[7] But afterwards (as the above notion began to prevail) it was agreed that the plaintiffs should notwithstanding interplead, upon the idea that the detinue, and not the bailment, was the point of the action.[8]

The interpleading which has hitherto been mentioned is confined to the action of detinue, being that with which this style of pleading was most connected: this expedient, however, was allowed in some few other actions. We find, where two writs of *quare impedit* were brought for the same avoidance, the second plaintiff was awarded to interplead to the elder of the two writs;[9] it was likewise allowed where two writs of ward were brought for the same wardship; but not in ravishment of ward.[10] If a person was found by office to be heir of a tenant to the king in one county, and

[1] 9 Hen. VI., 17. [2] 19 Hen. VI., 3. [3] 8 Hen. VI., 30. [4] 11 Edw. IV., 11. [5] 38 Hen. VI., 2. [6] 8 Hen. VI., 30. [7] 14 Hen. VI., 2. [8] 5 Edw. IV., 25. [9] 19 Hen. VI., 68. [10] 9 Hen. VI., 17.

another was found such in another county, it was the practice for them to interplead before either had livery.[1] There is an instance of three writs of detinue, where, after much argument, the three plaintiffs were awarded to interplead.[2]

Among the pleas that might be pleaded in different actions, there are some few which recurred so frequently, and were so often the subject of discussion in court, that they cannot be passed over without some observation in this place. These were the pleas of *hors de son fee*, of disclaimer, of nontenure, of joint-tenancy, and the common replication of *de son tort demesne.*

Plea of *hors de son fee.*

When a person claimed a seignory, and distrained and avowed for the rent, or brought an action for the disseisin, the tenant might plead *hors de son fee*, that is, that he held nothing of the person who claimed the seignory. By the form of this plea it is apparent, it would not hold in such actions as stated a trifle with certainty: it was: *actionem suam prædictum versus eum habere non debet, quia dicit quòd messuagium prædictum cum pertinentiis est extra fœdum et dominium ipsius A. unde petit judicium si prædictus A. absq; speciali titulo hic ostendendo actionem suam prædictum de reditu prædicto habere debeat, &c.*[3] Such a plea was construed as an admission of the tenancy. In a writ of entry on a disseisin of rent, brought by an abbot on a disseisin made to his predecessor, the writ merely alleged generally, *quam clamat esse jus ecclesiæ suæ, &c.*, of which the tenant disseised his predecessor; and he declared accordingly of the seisin of such a person his predecessor in right of his church. To this was pleaded *hors de son fee;* but it was urged this was not a proper plea, because the seisin and disseisin of the predecessor being laid in the count, this was sufficient title. In answer to this, it was held by the whole court, and resolved, that the plea was good; for the allegation of the predecessor's disseisin could not be said to be a title to anybody, nor could any allegation of seisin, without the title by which that seisin was gained. Further, they said that in formedon, *hors de son fee* was no plea, because sufficient title was comprised in the writ; namely, that such a gift of the rent was made in tail, or for life. So here, if a formedon had been brought in the reverter of the rent, stating a gift in tail to one, and on default of issue a reverter to the demandant; or a writ of intrusion, or other writ of a demise to another for term of life, who died, and the defendant intruded, and that it ought to revert to the demandant; in these cases, *hors de son fee* would not be a good plea, because sufficient title was comprised in the writ to acquaint the terre-tenant what rent was demanded.

But of all these the terre-tenant, in the present case, was ignorant, as the demandant might have several other rents in the same vill. Again, the demandant here claimed in right of his church, and was in by succession, and not by his predecessor; so that it

[1] 9 Hen. VI., 17. [2] 5 Edw. IV., 9. [3] Rast., 128.

was in the nature of a writ of entry for rent and a disseisin done to the demandant himself, in which it was agreed that *hors de son fee* was a good plea, the same as in assize. But where an heir, who claimed by an ancestor, and who was *in* by him, brought a writ of entry *sur disseisin* done to his ancestor, or of mortauncestor, or of cosinage of rent, there seemed more colour that *hors de son fee* should not be a plea; because the writ contained, in some manner, a title, by giving the tenant notice of the rent demanded. And yet it seemed hard that the seisin or disseisin of an ancestor should be construed such a title in the heir as to oust the tenant of this plea, when he really saw no such certainty in the demand as there was in a formedon: and therefore, some of the court held, that it would be a good plea both in mortauncestor and cosinage, or a writ of entry *sur disseisin* done to the ancestor; because dying seised of a rent did not give so strong a title to an heir or successor, as the dying seised of land; for a dying seised would take away the entry of the disseisee, which was giving a sort of title to the heir; but not so of a rent, which might be reseised, or reclaimed, or distrained for (all which were in lieu of an entry), notwithstanding the descent; much more therefore in the case of an abbot, who was not in as heir but by succession.[1]

It was said, that the tenant in replevin should not plead *hors de son fee*, because he might, if he pleased, disclaim; and besides, the issue of *hors de son fee* would be peremptory for the lord and not for the tenant, which was unreasonable.[2] It was likewise held, that *hors de son fee* was a good plea in rescous;[3] but it was afterwards laid down not to be good either in rescous or trespass, but the defendant should show of whom the tenure was, and then he might conclude *issint hors de son fee*;[4] which was making it a plea of *special nontenure*, one of a very different sort from the original form of it, and that upon which all the above discussion arose. The plea of special nontenure was allowed in some cases where the general plea of nontenure was not, as in *scire facias*.[5]

Of disclaimer.

A person on whom a claim was made in a judicial proceeding, whether to recover a seignory or a tenancy, might *disclaim*. Thus the plaintiff in replevin might plead to the avowry, *non tenent de eodem, &c., sed easdem acras terræ de eodem tenere omnino deadvocat, et disclamat, &c.*[6] And in the like way might the tenant in a *præcipe quòd reddat*, or any other writ which demanded the land, or a rent issuing out of the land, disclaim. The effect of this disclaimer in all writs for recovery of land was, that the demandant might enter upon it and take possession; but in a replevin, the avowant, instead of entering, was obliged to bring his writ of right *sur disclaimer;* the replevin not being an action for the recovery of the land itself. In this writ of right, the demandant in his count stated the whole proceedings in

[1] Long., 5 Edw. IV., 91.
[2] 5 Edw. IV., 2.
[3] Long., 5 Edw. IV., 88.
[4] 6 Edw. IV., 4.
[5] 7 Hen VI., 25.
[6] Rast., Disclaimer.

the replevin, with the disclaimer, and then went on, *per quas quidem disclamationem et disadvocationem accrevit jus, &c., ad petendum, &c., in dominico suo ut de fœdo, &c. Et quòd tale sit jus suum petit recognitionem fieri per magnam assisam, &c.*[1] Thus the replevin and disclaimer therein became the ground of the writ of right, which corresponds with the manner of proceeding stated in the time of Henry III. from Bracton.[2]

Upon this subject of disclaimer there was much nicety and refinement, which made it a considerable title in the science of pleading, especially when accompanied, as it sometimes was, with the plea of nontenure and joint-tenancy, which will be considered presently. If the demandant might enter upon the tenant disclaiming, it was nothing more than consistent that the disclaimer should completely estop him, if he brought his assize for such an entry. If the writ was brought against two tenants, and one disclaimed, the whole tenancy rested in the other; so as upon his making default, the demandant had judgment to recover the whole:[3] the same if one of the tenants pleaded nontenure.[4] If a lord paramount distrained upon the tenant paravaile, and in replevin avowed upon him, he could not disclaim, because he did, in truth, hold of him, though *per medium;* but he should state the special matter.[5] None could disclaim but those who were seised in demesne;[6] and therefore it was a good replication to a disclaimer in replevin, that he was not tenant of the freehold at the time of the disclaimer,[7] for he who had nothing could forfeit nothing. If the defendant in replevin justified instead of avowing, it was held, the plaintiff could not disclaim;[8] and the reason of this difference seems to be, that, upon a justification, the defendant was not entitled to any return. As to a disclaimer in one action being pleaded to another action, there seemed to be a difference between actions where damages were recoverable and where they were not. Thus in replevin, where the plaintiff pleaded that he had before disclaimed, it was overruled, and he was obliged to plead his disclaimer again.[9] As a tenant might disclaim, so likewise might a lord. Thus where a tenant by homage ancestral vouched his lord, and the lord had not received the homage, he might disclaim the seignory, and so oust the tenant of his warranty.[10]

The plea of disclaimer was an abatement of the writ, so was that of *nontenure* and *joint-tenancy*. By the plea of nontenure, the tenant said *quòd ipse tenementa prædicta, &c., præfato W. J. reddere non potest, quia dicit quòd ipse* NON EST TENENS *eorudem tenementorum, ut de libero tenemento, nec fuit die impretationis brevis originalis prædicti, &c.* This was no plea in replevin as the former was, nor in *nuper obiit*, and some other writs; but it was good in all the writs for recovery of land, as well as in

Of nontenure.

[1] Rast., 220. [2] *Vide ante*, c. ix. [3] 33 Hen. VI., 53.
[4] 36 Hen. VI., 28. [5] 9 Hen. VI., 27. [6] 21 Edw. IV., 47.
[7] 12 Edw. IV., 13. [8] 15 Edw. IV., 29. [9] 27 Hen. VI., 2.
[10] 28 Hen. VI., 10.

attaint, and in a *scire facias*. This plea had a very different effect from a disclaimer as to the question of property contended for by the demandant; for so far from being entitled to enter, as upon a disclaimer, the demandant by this plea was often entirely disappointed of his remedy; for if he could not find a person who was in such seisin of the land as to be a legal tenant to his writ, all judicial redress was at an end. This effect of the plea of *nontenure* was probably the parent of feoffments in trust, and gave rise to those fraudulent practices which were meant to be checked by the statutes of pernors of profits. Since those acts, it had been usual for the demandant to reply to the plea of nontenure in maintenance of the writ, and state such matter as came within the provisions of those acts, which if proved would make the tenant liable.

The reply to nontenure, under these statutes, was usually this, or the like: That he himself was seised till he was disseised by the said tenant, who made a feoffment to persons unknown, in order to defraud the demandant of his land: with an averment, that the tenant ever since the disseisin had taken the profits. In order that the tenant might not fly from the main point in the action, he was held down to traverse the pernancy of the profits and not the feoffment.[1]

Of joint-tenancy.

The plea of joint-tenancy—namely, that the tenant was seised of the land as joint-tenant with A., and not solely, was applied to the same purpose of protecting a feoffment that had been fraudulently made; and it had been held that this plea was within the equity of the statutes, and therefore that the demandant might reply in maintenance of the writ, as in the former case.[2] Upon argument it was determined, that to a plea of disclaimer there could not be a similar reply, because it was neither within the words nor equity of the statutes:[3] nor indeed, as we have before seen, was there any need of these statutes to assist the demandant in such a case; for he might immediately enter on the land.

If the plea of joint-tenancy went only to part of the land in question, the demandant might get rid of that obstacle by *abridging*, as it was called, his demand as to that, and going on for the remainder. *Abridgment* was an expedient that was allowed only in actions that were particularly circumstanced. Thus, in assize, where the writ was *de libero tenemento;* in dower, where the writ was for the *rationabilis dos;* in ward, where it was *pro custodiâ terræ et hæredis;* and in cases similar to these, the demandant might abridge his plaint or demand, because the writ would still continue to justify the proceeding. But in *præcipe quòd reddat*, where a certain number of acres are demanded, no abridgment was allowed, because the demandant by so doing would falsify his own writ; and where a writ was admitted to be false in part, it abated for the whole. And so in assize *de libero tenemento* in A. and B. the plain-

[1] 1 Edw. IV., 2. [2] 9 Hen. VI., 14. [3] Long., 5 Edw. IV., 44.

tiff could not abridge in B., because his writ would then be false.[1] So if it was pleaded that certain acres extended into the manor of A., the demandant could not abridge those acres.[2] An abridgment of the plaint might be made so late as after the jury had been sworn, and were gone out to consider of their verdict.[3] Thus the demandant, if he thought his proofs not sufficient to maintain his plaint, was at liberty to abridge such part as appeared doubtful at any stage of the proceedings, when it seemed most expedient or necessary.

De son tort demesne.

The common replication to a justification in trespass was *de son tort demesne*, or, as it was generally called, *de injuriâ suâ propriâ*. This was either general or special; it was a denial that the defendant had such cause as he alleged for doing the trespass, and it maintained that he did it of his own wrong. The general replication was, *quoad prædictum placitum prædicti B. &c., in barram placitatum, dicit quòd ipse, &c., precludi non debet, quia dicit quòd, &c., vi et armis, &c., de injuriâ suâ propriâ et absq ; causâ, &c., in eodem placito superiùs allegatâ, &c., in ipsum A. insultum fecit, &c.* If it was special, it went on with a traverse of some of the matter alleged in the bar; as, *absq ; hoc, quòd prædicta acra terræ cum pertinentiis, &c., prout prædictus B. superiùs allegavit.* The former concluded to the country, the latter with a *paratus est verificare ;* which, indeed, was the true reason why it was necessary that it should be ascertained when the one or the other was the proper replication.

Notwithstanding some differences of opinion respecting this point, we find rules laid down for the government of pleaders. Thus, where the justification rested wholly upon a matter of fact, there the replication might be general; but where it consisted of a matter of record or title, or authority of law, in such cases it was required to be special. If a sheriff justified under a writ, the replication must be special; but if a person justified under a sheriff's warrant, this was only matter *in pais*, and the general replication would do.[4] If a defendant pleaded freehold in himself, the replication must be special; but if in another, and he justified by the command of such freeholder, the replication might be general, because, in the latter case, nothing was in issue but the command, and not the freehold.[5]

If the justification was for imprisonment under the warrant of a justice of peace,[6] for apprehending the plaintiff in the attempt to commit a robbery,[7] or to burn a house,[8] or for apprehending one suspected of felony; to all these it was sufficient to reply, *de injuriâ suâ propriâ absq ; tali causâ.* But if it was under an authority from the plaintiff himself, as by a licence, a gift, a lease, or the like; or, in many cases, under the sanction of law, as to view waste,

[1] 14 Hen. VI., 4.
[2] 33 Hen. VI., 4.
[3] *Ibid.*, 18.
[4] 19 Hen. VI., 7.
[5] 8 Hen. VI., 34.
[6] 9 Edw. IV., 31.
[7] *Ibid.*, 27.
[8] 22 Edw. IV., 45.

going into a tavern for victuals, and the like;[1] if a prescription was alleged;[2] if he justified for rent under a lease to the plaintiff;[3] in such cases the general replication would not be sufficient, but he should traverse the special matter of the bar, *absq; hoc* that he leased, and the like; and sometimes he should make a title.

Where two or more persons were equally invested with a right, as executors, parceners, and the like, and any of them declined engaging in a suit that was thought necessary to be brought, the course the others were to take was by *summons* and *severance.* This might be done in any stage of the proceedings, whether at the return of the writ, after issue joined, at *nisi prius*, or at the day in bank, as the case might happen. As soon as either of the plaintiffs made default, the other prayed a summons to be issued against him, requiring him to carry on the suit with the other plaintiff. This writ was called a *summons ad sequendum simul;* and if he did not appear, there was an award, that the other plaintiff might go on without him; the entry of all which upon the record was thus: *Et modò venet* (one of the plaintiffs) *per attornatum suum, et prædictus* (the other plaintiff) *quarto die placiti solenniter exactus non prosecutus est breve suum prædictum; ideo summonitus est quòd sit hìc in octabis, &c., ad sequendum versus, &c., simul cum prædicto, &c. &c., ad quem diem, &c., non venit, &c. Ideo concessum est quòd prædictus* (the one plaintiff) *sequatur solus sine ipso* (the other plaintiff).[4] Summons and severance lay in writs of ward, detinue of charters, and other personal actions of the same kind; in debt, or account by executors; in attaint also, if it lay in the primary action; and it lay in formedon, and other real writs; but not in trespass, conspiracy, and other personal actions founded upon torts: for in these, if an action was brought in the name of two, and one of them declined going on, they were both nonsuited.[5]

Summons and severance.

There still remain many forms of pleading, of which we have not yet treated: these consist in the formal lauguage and manner in which the substantial and effective part of a plea was stated (*a*). It was impossible that a set form of expression could be designed for every matter that might become the subject of a declaration or plea. But many modes and circumstances of property recurred so often in judicial inquiries, as to obtain apt and stated forms of description and allegation, which were established by long usage; the experience of them having

Forms of pleading.

(*a*) One species of pleading was entirely overlooked by our author, and that was pleading by way of estoppel, which is of importance as involving the whole subject of regular procedure, and especially records. For records, as Lord Coke said, were for the avoiding of infiniteness of litigation, and the principle of estoppel was that a man was concluded by his confession or admission, or by verdict found against him in a former suit on the same subject-matter, so that he could not be allowed to set up the contrary (*Year-book*, 7 *Hen. VI.*, 9); a principle, however, which only applied as between the parties to the former suit, or their "privies" in law (*Year-book*, 33

[1] 12 Edw. IV., 10. [2] 28 Hen. VI., 9. [3] 10 Hen. VI., 3.
[4] Rast., 311. [5] 34 Hen. VI., 53.

shown them preferable to all others. These, therefore, were adhered to by pleaders; and the nicety with which they were conceived, is a strong mark of the refinement and curiosity with which this part of our law was cultivated. To give some idea of this, we shall select such specimens as seem most likely to leave an impression on the reader.

When a defendant justified a taking, as for tithes, he being parson at the time of the trespass, this was held to be ill pleaded; because he should say that he was parson at the time of severance, as well as at the time of the taking. So where a sheriff justified an arrest under a *capias*, he ought to say he was sheriff as well at the time of the arrest, as at the time of receiving the writ.[1] In alleging a disseisin, it was not sufficient to say that he was seised till such a one *entered*, and made the feoffment in question; but he should say he was seised till disseised by such a one, or till such a one intruded, for the word entry might be understood of a lawful entry.[2] A person who claimed by tenant for life, tenant in tail, or the parson of a church, or others who were particular tenants, should aver the life of the particular tenant in his pleading.[3] But in trespass where nothing was to be recovered but damages, there the plaintiff in his replication need not aver the life of such particular tenant, especially where he alleged seisin or possession, for this proved the estate to have continuance.[4]

In a justification under a warrant from the sheriff, the defendant ought to state he had returned it to the sheriff; if not, he must show the warrant itself.[5] If an estate was made to two, and the heirs of one, the pleading should be that they were seised, *scilicet*, one *in dominico suo, ut de fœdo*, the other *in dominico suo, ut de libero tenemento*, expressing the distinct estates.[6] A tenant at will must, in pleading, show how he was tenant, whether by demise, as a copyholder, by sufferance or otherwise.[7] In declaring on a judgment it was held, at one time, that the party pleading must commence from the original writ, and go through the whole record.[8] So, in pleading an outlawry, it was held not sufficient to say process was continued till outlawry, but every *capias* must be mentioned, and the whole record in certain.[9] Yet afterwards it seems to have been agreed, that in a plea of outlawry it was enough, if in the same court, to begin at the exigent; and in all cases of debt on a

Hen. VI., 7). It was a fundamental principle that estoppel should be mutual, and hence Prisot, J. in that case, said that no man could set up a record as an estoppel who would not be estopped by it. Hence the records only bound the parties, or their "privies," as their "privies in state." Thus the heir would be bound by a recovery against his ancestor as between himself and the recoverer (*Ibid.*) But the heir could not set up a record between his guardian and another, for he was a stranger to the record (30 *Assize*, 46). It was only when the parties were the same in both suits that there was an estoppel (3 *Hen. VI.*, 15). So if in a suit or deed the defendant had in a former suit of the same party set up that it was his deed (9 *Hen. VI.* 59).

[1] 35 Hen. VI., 48.
[2] 22 Hen. VI., 43.
[3] 19 Hen. VI., 73.
[4] 10 Edw. IV., 18.
[5] 21 Edw. IV., 66.
[6] 37 Hen. VI., 24.
[7] 5 Edw. IV., 12.
[8] 36 Hen. VI., 5.
[9] 11 Hen. VI., 15.

judgment, the declaration might commence at the judgment or the original, at the option of the plaintiff.[1] A particular statute must be specially set forth in pleading, the same as a particular custom, otherwise the party could not avail himself of it as of a general statute.[2]

Nothing can better display the curious nicety with which pleaders attended to this science, than the distinction observed between the forms of pleading the same thing under different circumstances, or in different parts of the record. The reason of such distinctions is not always apparent, nor is often given by the lawyers of these days. It is not, however, to be supposed they had none to give, or that these varieties in form were not, in a technical light, extremely apt and necessary. Of this the reader may judge from the following specimens.

Of differences between declarations and pleas. It was laid down as a rule, that in a bar, and where a title was to be pleaded, it was not sufficient to say that such a one made a lease or gift to the defendant, but it should be stated that such a one was seised, and being so seised, he made the lease or gift; yet in a writ, or declaration, it was enough to say that he made the lease or gift, without suggesting that he was seised.[3] The same if a feoffment or fine, or release, or quit-claim, was pleaded, seisin must be alleged in the feoffer, or conusor, at the time of the feoffment or fine, or release, or quit-claim made; which was not at all necessary in a writ or declaration.[4]

It was held, that if a deed was alleged in a count or avowry, where anything was to be recovered, or a return had, then the place and county where the deed was made must be shown, on account of the venue; and it would be a good plea to say, *nul tiel lieu.* But where a deed was pleaded in bar, and nothing was to be recovered, there was no need to show the place and county where it was made. An avowry was considered in the nature of a declaration, if a return was prayed, otherwise it was treated only as a plea in bar.[5]

Of differences between pleas. If a man was under an obligation to make a feoffment of a certain manor, and he pleaded that he had made the feoffment, he should show where the manor was, because, said they, the feoffment could not be made except on the land. On the other hand, if he was bound to make a release, he need not show where the manor was.[6] If a man justified by special title, as descent, or feoffment, he was required to show the quantity; as that the place contained so many acres of land, and then he was to allege his title; but if he only pleaded that the *locus in quo* was his freehold, there he need not show the quantity.[7] If a man pleaded a lease for years, he was required to show the

[1] 21 Edw. IV., 52. [2] *Ibid.*, 56. [3] 34 Hen. VI., 48.
[4] 2 Hen. VI., 15; 10 Hen. VI., 21. [5] 6 Edw. IV., 11.
[6] 15 Edw. IV., 14. [7] 22 Hen. VI., 24.

place in certain, but not so in a lease for life; because, said they, this was taken to be conveyed by livery, which must be on the land.[1]

In trespass, if a person justified under the command of a stranger, he was required to show the place where the command was given; but if he justified as servant under the command of a master, he need not show the place.[2] One who justified under a sale in market overt, need not show to whom the market belonged; but it was required of a person who justified by reason of a leet, right of common, and the like, to show to whom they belonged, because the former went with the land, the latter not.[3] When a record was pleaded, the defendant was not to say that the writ was returnable before Sir John Prisot and his companions, justices of the common bench, but that it was returnable before the justices of the common bench, without naming them. Yet when the return of a sheriff was to be pleaded, there the plea should allege that A. B., sheriff, returned the writ before Sir John Prisot and others, his companions, justices of the common bench.[4] When a record of the court of king's bench was pleaded, it must show *where* the court then sat; not so of the common-pleas, because that court was by Magna Charta to sit in a certain place; but the other was *coram rege ubicuncq; tunc fuerit in Angliâ.*[5] Similar to these were the differences respecting the allegations of the same facts in a declaration, in different actions. Thus it was held, that in accompt, or in an avowry for an amercement in a court, it was not necessary to show the names of the presentors; but that in debt for such an amercement, the names of the presentors should be specially stated.[6]

It was not only in the wording, but likewise in the degree of perspicuity and intelligence, that a difference was made between declarations and pleas, and between pleas of a different kind. Though certainty was one great object of the refinement in pleading, a difference was made between the degrees of certainty; and these gradations were expressed by terms that sufficiently indicate the subtlety of the distinction, but perhaps do not make it quite intelligible. It was held, that pleas to the writ, and other dilatory pleas, should be good to *every common intent*, because they were to create delay; and so if they might be taken two ways, they should be taken in that which was most against the party pleading them. But it was sufficient for a plea in bar, if it was good to a *common intent;* a declaration was required to be good to *every intent.*[7] Such were the quaint measures of certainty laid down by the pleaders of these times.

Of demurrer.

If the pleading was defective in any of the foregoing requisites, either of substance or form, the adverse party might demur; that is, according to the words of the entry, *dicit quòd ipse ad prædictum placitum prædicti A. modo et formâ*

[1] 3 Edw. IV., 27. [2] 12 Edw. IV., 10. [3] *Ibid.*, 9. [4] 37 Hen. VI., 33. [5] 34 Hen. VI., 27; 5 Edw. IV., 8. [6] 9 Edw. IV., 41. [7] 32 Hen. VI., 12.

superiùs placitatum necesse non habet, nec per legem terræ tenetur respondere, unde pro defectu sufficientis responsionis prædicti A. in hâc parte petit judicium et damna suâ occasione transgressionis prædictæ sibi adjudicari, &c.; or if the demurrer was to a declaration, *dicit quòd prædicta materia in narratione prædictâ contenta non est sufficiens in lege ad actionem prædictam manutenendam unde petit judicium, quòd idem B. ab actione prædictâ habendâ præcludatur, &c.*[1] Thus the conclusion of a demurrer varied according as it belonged to the plaintiff or defendant in the action.

In some cases they used to state some special matter, and then conclude with a demurrer, making the special matter the cause of the demurrer. This in many cases was optional, but in others it was required: thus, in a demurrer to a double plea, it was necessary expressly to demur for the doubleness; for such a plea might not be *insufficient*, as the general form of demurrer always stated a plea to be; but inconvenient only, as part of it might be found for and part against the party pleading it.[2]

If an insufficient plea was not demurred to, but the adverse party replied or rejoined, as the case might be, advantage might still be had of this defect, when the cause stood ready for judgment, by stating such matter as a reason why the *judgment* should be *arrested;* and if that occasion was let pass, it would still remain such a blemish as would make the judgment erroneous, and might therefore be discussed in *a writ of error.* If such errors turned upon a point of law, the decision in either of these stages was peremptory; but if they consisted in the form of pleading, they were called *jeofailes*, and might be set right, by the court taking upon it officially to *amend* the *jeofail*, either by virtue of their authority at common law, or under the statutes that had been passed for that purpose; or, if they felt they had no such authority, by awarding the parties to set it right themselves by *repleading.* The learning of *jeofail* and *amendment*, and of *repleader*, constituted an important appendage to the science of pleading, and deserves a proportionate consideration in the history of this branch of our law.

The before-mentioned statutes of amendment had laid down a rule, by which the judges were to govern themselves in the amendments they made in records:[3] they were thereby authorised to amend what appeared to them to be misprisions of the clerks. As an auxiliary, and in support of this, they had adopted two other considerations which used to weigh with them in the amendments they made; one was, whether there was anything by which they might be guided in their amendment; the other was, whether the amendment was proposed to be made in the same term in which the jeofail happened, or in a subsequent one. How far these operated will be seen by reviewing some few decisions on this subject.

Of jeofail and amendments.

[1] Rast., 146. [2] 22 Edw. IV., 50; 37 Hen. VI., 6. [3] *Vide ante*, c. xvi.

Where an original writ was brought against J. N., but the *capias* and other process, including the *exigent*, were against R. N., it was determined, over and over again, that the *capias* and other process might be amended,[1] but not the *exigent*, because then J. N. would be outlawed, though he had never been proclaimed.[2] Where a juror was omitted in the *habeas corpora*, and the other process, they would not allow the *venire facias* to be amended; but all the process after the *venire facias* was held void.[3] Yet where, on the return of the distress, three jurors, who were before returned, were omitted upon examination of the sheriff and the jurors; it appeared to be an omission of the sheriff, and they were really summoned: this was amended as a misprision of the sheriff's clerk, and so within the statute. The same where the sheriff returned A. B. on the venire, and J. B. on the distress; if A. B. was really summoned, it would be amended: so of a return of *octo tales*, on a writ of *decem tales*, the writ should be returned to the sheriff to amend.[4] But it was different if a tales was returned without manucaptors, for the manucaptors should be found by the parties; and it was their misprision and not that of the sheriff.[5]

These were misprisions of the clerk, when there was already an existing writ, which he ought to have pursued correctly in making out the process issuing out of it. It was otherwise with the original writ, which being the ground of the whole proceeding, and being drawn upon the information of the party himself, was not amendable by the judges; as if a writ run in the *debet, et detinet* where it should be in the *detinet* only; or if it was *vi et armis*, or in any other form that was not so warranted by law.[6] Yet where a writ was grounded upon an obligation or an indenture, then any variance between them was amendable, because it was the misprision of the clerk in chancery, who ought to follow the specialty in making out the writ.[7] But these amendments were not of course; for it seems they used to send for the clerk, and if it appeared upon examination of him, that he had the deed before him at the time, then the original was amendable, as a clear misprision of his:[8] and from hence it may be collected, that should it have turned out that he had made the writ from false instructions, it would not have been amended in this, any more than in the common case, where a writ was made on the information of the party himself.[9] Thus, again, if it appeared that the clerk was rightly informed, but, making a wrong conclusion, drew the writ wrong, this was amendable; as where a writ stated the baron and feme to be tenants in tail, instead of the baron singly.[10] It was under the idea of a clerical mistake, that false Latin in an original was amendable.[11]

1 4 Hen. VI., ; 7 Hen. VI., 27. 2 20 Hen. VI., 18; 38 Hen. VI., 3.
3 34 Hen. VI., 60. 4 37 Hen. VI., 12. 5 9 Edw. IV., 14.
6 10 Edw. IV., 11, 12; 22 Edw. IV., 20; 34 Hen. VI., 26.
7 21 Hen. VI., 7; 22 Hen. VI., 43. 8 11 Edw. IV., 2.
9 18 Edw. IV., 13; 20 Edw. IV., 6. 10 35 Hen. VI., 10 and 13.
11 11 Hen. VI., 2.

We have before seen that the process issuing from an original might be amended if there was any variance. Again, if the entry on the roll varied from the original, it might be amended as well at common law as by the statute.[1] Some variations of the declaration from the writ might be amended. Thus, where the writ was *arbores succidit cepit et asportavit,* in the declaration *succidit* was left out:[2] and it was held a clerical misprision and amendable by the statute: on the same idea it was laid down that many things in the writ, if left out of the declaration might be amended.[3] But where a writ of annuity was for a sum of money, and the declaration was for a less sum, it was held not amendable; and then the court declared it to be no misprision of the clerk, but the act of the party or his counsel.[4] It was a rule that whatever was the act of the party or his counsel, could not be amended. If a plea was pleaded without concluding *et hoc paratus est verificare,* this was held a slip of the party or his counsel, and not amendable.[5]

Some of these amendments might be made by the judges at any time; others could not be made after the term. Thus the judges could not in another term amend any default of their own in giving judgment;[6] and they refused to amend a declaration that varied from a writ, because it was a declaration of a preceding term,[7] which could not be amended but by the assent of parties. In this respect they made a distinction between the roll and record. Thus it was laid down that the record was during the term in the breast of the justices, and not in the roll, which might be amended during the term; but after the term the roll became the actual record.[8] It was held, though the writ of *nisi prius* might be amended by the roll, that being the warrant for it,[9] yet the *nisi prius* record should not. This was in a case where the roll contained the words *die brevis*, and the record of *nisi prius* did not contain them, but the verdict was as if they were in: the reason given for this was, because the justices of *nisi prius* had no warrant for such a verdict.[10]

Of repleader.

As *amendments* wholly applied to those defects which arose from the misprisions of clerks, *repleader* was the remedy for those which were committed by the party himself or his counsel. These being such as he would be allowed to correct at the time, if he had declared "*jeofail,*" or, in other words, "I have failed in my plea, and pray leave to plead it over again;" any default whatsoever apparent upon the record, where the rules of pleading above laid down where violated by either party, might be made a reason for a repleader. For instance, if to a plea of no award it was replied that there was, this was a jeofail, because he ought to show in certain what award was made, and where, and that it was the defendant's fault in not performing

[1] 7 Hen. VI., 45. [2] *Ibid.*, 26. [3] 33 Hen. VI., 2. [4] 9 Edw. IV., 51.
[5] 27 Hen. VI., 10. [6] 9 Edw. IV., 3. [7] 35 Hen. VI., 37. [8] 7 Hen. VI., 29.
[9] 7 Edw. IV., 15. [10] 11 Hen. VI., 11.

it; and a repleader was awarded:[1] the same if a traverse was wrong taken, an issue misjoined, a trial in a wrong county, in short, if there was any defect that would prevent the merits of the cause from being tried and decided upon the then state of the pleadings.

A repleader might be awarded after issue joined; and it was not uncommon, when the jury were ready to give their verdict, if any jeofail appeared to discharge them and give the parties time to replead.[2] This was a short way of doing substantial justice, and there are many instances of it in the reports of this time; but it is probable this was confined to the Middlesex causes, which used to be tried at the bar of the courts at Westminster; for it should seem a judge at *nisi prius* would hardly interfere in questions that were entirely foreign to the issue to be tried. As a repleader was awarded after an issue, so, for the same reason, was it after a demurrer.[3] When a repleader was awarded, they always went back to the part of the record that was defective. Thus, if the bar was good, and the replication bad, they began to replead at the replication. If the bar was bad, and the replication good, then they begun the repleader at the bar, and the plaintiff was to reply *de novo*.[4]

Sometimes a vicious plea might be made good by the replication, and so preclude the necessity of a repleader; as where a release was pleaded without naming a venue, if the plaintiff replied *non est factum*, this cured the defect of the plea: in like manner a declaration might be made good by the plea.[5] As a jeofail might be cured by the subsequent pleading, so it might by a verdict. Thus a bad issue, as a negative pregnant, a double plea, and the like, if found by verdict for the party pleading it, it was held to be cured; not so if found for the adverse party.[6] So if a reversioner prayed to be received, and the demandant counterpleaded that he had nothing in the reversion the day of the writ purchased, it was a *jeofail*; for he should add, nor any time since: yet if it was found in the affirmative for the prayor, it was cured by the verdict: otherwise, if it had been found for the demandant in the negative; for then it might have been that he had the reversion by descent or purchase pending the writ, though he had not had it the day of the writ purchased; which would have clearly manifested the jeofail.[7]

The entry of an award of repleader might be as follows: *Postea continuato inde processu, &c., &c. Et super hoc visis præmissis, et per justitiarios hìc plenè intellectis, satis constat, quòd prædictum placitum, in præclusionem actionis prædictæ placitatum, minùs sufficiens in lege existit, et exitus inde subsequens minùs aptè junctus, per quod dictum est partibus prædictis, quòd replacitent, videlicet, quòd prædictus R. respondeat ad narrationem prædictam, et quòd prædictus S. replicet, et quòd prædictus R. rejungat, quousq;*

[1] 5 Edw. IV., 108. [2] 7 Edw. IV., 1. [3] 9 Hen. VI., 35. [4] 22 Hen. VI., 19.
[5] 18 Edw. IV., 17. [6] 12 Edw. IV., 6. [7] 21 Hen. VI., 14.

novum exitum sive no vos exitus inde bene junxerint, vel in judicium placitaverint. Et prædictus R. petit licentiam interloquendi, &c.[1]

Thus have we laid before the reader such an account of the principal points in pleading as the nature of our historical inquiry would allow. Pleading is a branch of our law that consists of so many unconnected particulars, that it is less capable, perhaps, than any other of being reduced to the compass of a historical narration. The curiosity of pleaders in these reigns had made it so complex that it called for the most laborious attention in the student, and the most vigilant circumspection in the practiser.

When so much anxiety was discovered in cultivating this branch of study it was impossible almost to avoid some of the faults which were before complained of in the lawyers of Edward the Third's time. It cannot be denied that the pleaders of these times gave in to much refinement, raising debates about verbal formalities as points of the greatest moment; and such was the humour of the age that this captiousness was not discountenanced by the bench. When the philosophy of the times was a war of words, it is not to be wondered that a learned profession should pay too great a regard to laborious trifles. The calamity has been that after other branches of knowledge took a more liberal turn, the minutiæ of pleading continued still to be respected with a sort of religious deference.

While we acknowledge ourselves indebted to the practisers of these times for reducing to some method the plain and sensible logic of maintaining and defending a suit in a legal form, it cannot but be lamented that they suffered to creep into it, at the same time, certain technical peculiarities so abstruse and problematical as to give the *science of good pleading* too much an air of mystery (*a*).

The king and government.

There is no mention that the king whose reign we are now reviewing took any personal concern in providing for the improvement of our law, or showed any reasonable regard for it.

Upon the whole the law was left to itself to maintain its ground as it could, amidst the convulsions which the nation underwent during great part of this period. During the reign of Richard II. the dignity of the law, together with the honour of the kingdom,

(*a*) It was held that if a defendant pleaded no such arbitrament *made or delivered* to him, it was "double" (*Year-book*, 10 *Edw. IV.*, fol. 6; 5 *Hen. VII.*, fol. 7; 15 *Hen. VII.*, fol. 10); a mere technicality, because an award was not "made" until it was delivered, as would be the case with any deed. It is to be observed, however, that technicalities were comparatively harmless in parole pleading when the defect could be instantly amended, but became very serious when pleadings were in "writing." The necessity for pleading was based upon the injustice of allowing a party to succeed at the trial on evidence of a defence of which he had given the other no notice (22 *Hen. VI.*, 33; 21 *Hen. VI.*, 6).

[1] Rast., 505.

through the weakness of that prince, and the difficulties occurring in his government, seemed somewhat to decline. When the law had taken this unfavourable turn, it required every encouragement from the settled state of things in the reigns of Hen. IV. and V. to recover itself. This it effectually did, and, having gathered strength, it began to flourish in a manner which enabled it to withstand all shocks from the political world.

In the latter part of the reign of Henry VI., while the nation was in arms, and the throne was overturned by successive revolutions, the courts of law enjoyed an entire peace, and justice was administered with a precision, learning, and effect that was not surpassed in any times before or since. Both this reign and next abounded with eminent lawyers.

Judicature in parliament.

Though the commons in the reign of Henry IV.[1] were checked in their attempt to partake in the judicial authority of the king and lords, and the letter of the resolution then passed stood on record against them; yet such a solemn declaration that their assent was necessary to all *statutes*, joined to some reasoning on the question, at length led to the establishment of this legislative right. The king and lords, however, went on making awards on petitions during the reign of Henry IV. and those that followed; till at last it became too clear that all these, as alterations, in that particular instance of the law, could no longer with propriety be called judgments or awards, but were to all intents and purposes legislative acts, and as such should be assented to by the whole parliament. We shall presently see the steps which led to establish the practice conformably with this opinion.

The criminal part of the original judicature in parliament was exercised in numberless instances during this period, and frequently assisted the reigning party in destroying their enemies, when the common tribunals (summary as even they were) could not, consistently with the colour of legal formality, completely execute their vengeance. We have no intimation that the commons were at all desirous of taking any part in these judgments. In a former reign,[2] the lords temporal, with the king's assent, adjudged that several lords, two knights, and others, who had been taken and beheaded as traitors and rebels, should forfeit all their lands in fee which they had such a day, with all their goods and chattels; to which judgment all the lords present put their names.[3] This could not be considered as a judgment *secundum legem et consuetudinem Angliæ*, as it gave, contrary to the common law, a forfeiture of lands *after* the death of the parties, and that, too, where some of them were commoners. This could only operate as a legislative act.

Sir John Mortimer having been committed to the Tower on suspicion of high-treason, had escaped, and was in 2 Hen. VI. indicted for that escape: being again apprehended, he was brought before

[1] *Vide ante.* [2] Hen. IV. [3] *Parl. Hist.*, vol. ii., 64.

parliament, and judgment was given against him upon the indictment. This was a judicial act of the legislative kind, if it may be so called, which it does not appear the commons had any share in, nor did they make any protestation in support of their pretension. These are selected out of many cases of the like kind during the period of which we are now writing.

Though the house of commons had acquired great weight in the constitution during these reigns, particularly under the house of Lancaster, there is no mention of their having concerned themselves in these parliamentary judgments of life and death.

Richard II. raised money upon the subject without consent of parliament, a stretch of prerogative which neither Henry IV., V., nor VI. ever attempted. It is remarked of the house of Lancaster, that its princes always paid a regard to the rights of the people, a policy to which they adhered probably to avoid exciting any spirit to question their title to the throne. This temper in the crown contributed to raise the house of commons into great consideration during these reigns; they became more jealous of their rank in the state than ever, and particularly on this subject of taxation. It is to be attributed to this, that when Edward IV. invented a new method of raising money without assent of parliament, it was thought prudent to give it the gentle name of *benevolence.*

There happened in 31 Hen. VI. a fact which greatly infringed the privileges of this rising part of the legislature. Their speaker, Thomas Thorpe, was taken in execution in an action of trespass *de bonis asportatis,* at the suit of the duke of York, then president of the parliament. The commons made a representation of this to the king and lords, and they consulted the judges, who were of opinion, that if a member of parliament was arrested for any cause but treason, felony, or surety of the peace, or for a judgment had before parliament, it was usual for such person to be discharged from the arrest. But, notwithstanding this direct and express opinion, the lords came to a resolution, that the speaker should continue in custody, notwithstanding his privilege of member and speaker.[1] The commons acquiesced in this resolution, and chose another speaker in his place. This temper in the commons can only be accounted for from the prevailing prejudice in favour of that great pretender to the throne.

There seems to be the same irregularity in criminal proceedings as in the former periods. Even in a time of tranquillity, and under the administration of the good duke of Gloucester, in the reign of Henry VI. a state-criminal was sentenced without any trial. Sir John Mortimer had been committed to prison, and, having escaped, was indicted for that escape: the indictment was removed into the house of lords, where he was adjudged guilty, and was executed. However, here had been an examination by the jury at least who

[1] Cotton, 651; *Parl. Hist.*, vol. ii., 287.

found the bill; and we have seen that, in the early ages of our law, that was the utmost which a prisoner was entitled to.[1]

In 27 Henry VI. we find a very singular proceeding against the duke of Suffolk. This nobleman was impeached by the commons. The duke upon his knees denied the whole charge before the lords. At length the king sent for all the lords spiritual and temporal then in town to his chamber. There the chancellor put the question to the duke, which way he would be tried: to this the duke answered by referring to his former denial of the charge; and, protesting his innocence, put himself entirely on the king's mercy and award. Then the chancellor, by the king's command, pronounced this sentence: "That, since the duke did not put himself on his peerage, the king as to the articles of treason was doubtful; and as to the articles of misprision, the king, *not as judge by the advice of the lords*, but as one to whose order the duke had submitted himself, did banish him the realm and other his dominions for five years." After this, the lord high-constable stood up on behalf of the bishops and lords, and required it to be enrolled, that the said judgment was by the king's own rule, and not by their assent; and also required, that neither they nor their heirs should by this example be barred of their peerage and privileges.[2]

The statutes.

The memorials of the law during this period consist in the statutes, rolls of parliament, the year-books, and some law treatises. Many inconveniences still arose from the ancient method of making the statutes from the petition and answer on the parliament roll. To remedy these, about the end of the reign of Henry VI. or beginning of Edward IV. the practice was introduced of putting the provisions intended to be made into the full and complete form of an act of parliament, in the first instance, which was the identical instrument that received the king's assent. To this they used to prefix this title: *Item quædam petitio exhibita fuit in hoc parliamento* FORMAM ACTUS *in se continens*, a title which imported in the terms of it a remembrance of the ancient method of preferring a petition. This title is now disused; but, excepting that circumstance, this is the present way of passing acts of parliament. The language of the statutes during the reigns of Henry VI. and Edward IV. was sometimes English, but more usually French.

Reports.

Of the year-books of Henry VI. and his successors it may be said, that both the matter and style of them are more suited to the reading of a modern lawyer than any of the former; so that they are much more worthy of notice than those of the preceding reigns. They contain a fuller account of what passed in court; questions of law are more thoroughly debated, and the opinions of the judges given more at length. The second part of Henry VI. and the whole of Edward IV., particularly the long *Quint*, as it is called, are full of excellent learning.

[1] *Vide ante*, c. ix.

[2] *Parl. Hist.*, vol. ii., 273.

The first part of Henry VI. is pronounced by a great lawyer to be more barren, spending itself in much learning of little moment, and long since out of use.[1]

The other productions of the lawyers of this period which have come down to us, are some law treatises. One of these is Fortescue's book, *De Laudibus Legum Angliæ;* the other is Littleton's *Tenures;* to which may be added Statham's *Abridgment.*

Fortescue.

Sir John Fortescue, who had been some time chief justice of the king's bench, is said to have written this work, *De Laudibus Legum Angliæ*, while he was enduring an exile with the prince of Wales, and others of the Lancastrian party, in France. Sir John was then made chancellor, and in that character he supposes himself holding a conversation with the young prince on the nature and excellence of the laws of England, compared with the civil law, and the laws of other countries. He considers at length the mode of trying matters of fact by jury, and shows how it excels that by witnesses. He informs us, that some of our princes wished to introduce the civil law merely for the sake of governing[2] in the arbitrary way allowed by that law, which declares, *quod principi placuit, legis habet vigorem.* He then proceeds to examine some other points of difference between the civil and common law, always deciding in favour of our own, particularly in the following instances: the bastardising the issue born before wedlock, *partus non sequitur ventrem sed sequitur patrem;* guardianship committed to those who could not by law succeed to the inheritance; and in the punishment of theft, no regard paid to a distinction between *factum manifestum et non manifestum.* He concludes his book with a short account of the societies where the law of England was studied, the degrees and ranks in the profession, and with the manner in which they were conferred; to these are subjoined some short remarks on the conduct and delay of suits.

This treatise seems to be intended as an introduction to some more particular work on the English law, the object of it being rather to take off the discredit which some civilians had endeavoured to throw on it, and to promote a more general acquaintance with it among persons who did not study it professionally. It displays sentiments upon liberty and limited government which one would hardly expect to find in a writer of this period. There runs through the whole an air of probity and piety that concentrates the attention of the reader. This is the principal work of our author, to whom we are indebted for some others of less note.

Miscellaneous facts.

The flourishing state of the law during this period may be collected from a short account of the law societies, and some circumstances relating to their members. We are told that in the reign of Henry VI. there were ten lesser inns, which were called Inns of Chancery, each containing at least one

[1] Hale's *Hist.*, 176.

[2] Chap. 34–36.

hundred students, and some a great many more. These were designed as places for elementary studies. Here they learned the nature of original and judicial writs, which were then considered as the first principles of the law, and for this reason these inns were denominated from the chancery. When young men had made some progress here, and were more advanced in years, then they were admitted into the inns of court. Of these there were four in number, which we have before mentioned in the reigns of Edward II. and III.[1] The least of these, it is said, contained two hundred students.[2]

We are informed by a writer of this time, that a student could not reside in the inns of court for less than £28 per annum, and proportionably more if he had a servant, as most of them had. For this reason, the students of the law were generally sons of persons of quality. Knights, barons, and the greatest nobility of the kingdom often placed their children here, not so much to make the laws their study, as to form their manners, and preserve them from the contagion of vicious habits: for, says the same author, *all vice was there discountenanced and banished, and everything good and virtuous was taught there; music, dancing, singing, history sacred and profane, and other accomplishments.*[3]

The degree of serjeant-at-law was considered in a very respectable light: none could be a judge in the king's bench or common-pleas, but one who had been first a serjeant; nor was a person to be called to the degree of serjeant till he had been in the general study of the law above mentioned at least for sixteen years, which probably meant from his first entrance at an inn of chancery. The ceremony and expense attending a call of serjeants was at this time very great: in general, about seven or eight were called at a time; and on that occasion, says our author, there were revels and feasting for seven days together, *as at a coronation.* The expense each serjeant was at seldom fell short of £260, out of which one-sixth was usually expended on rings. Sir John Fortescue, to whom we are obliged for all this information, says, that it cost him £50 in rings: we may conjecture from this what the profits of practice must have been.[4] They were generally called the *king's serjeants*, because they were called to this honour by the king's writ; and they had a salary from the crown, as well as the king's attorney.

It seems that learned apprentices were not always ambitious of the state and degree of a serjeant; but, on the contrary, when called thereto, some of them had tried all ways to avoid it. There is an instance of this in the fifth year of Henry V., in John Martin, William Rabington, William Pole, William Westbury, John June, and Thomas Rolfe, six grave and famous apprentices, who, having writs delivered to them to take the state and degree of serjeant, returnable in Michaelmas term, and having in vain tried all means

[1] *Vide ante*, c. xiv., xv.

[2] Fortesc. *de Laud.*, c. 49.

[3] *Ibid.*

[4] *Ibid.*, c. 50.

of evading the direction of the writ, upon the return thereof in chancery made an absolute refusal. Upon this they were called before the parliament, that was then sitting, and there charged to take upon them the state and degree of serjeants, which at length they consented to do.[1]

There were usually in the court of common pleas five judges, sometimes six, but never more; in the king's bench there were sometimes four, sometimes five. It is said that they did not sit above three hours a day in court, and that was from eight in the morning to eleven. The courts were not open in the afternoon; but that time, says our author, was left unoccupied, for suitors to consult with their counsel at home.[2] The same writer speaks of the qualifications of a judge as not to be attained but *per viginti annorum lucubrationes.*

The salaries of the judges in the time of Henry IV., were as follow:—The chief baron and other barons had 40 marks per annum; the chief of the king's bench and of the common pleas, £40 per annum; the other justices in either court, 40 marks.[3] But the gains of the practisers had become so great, that they could hardly be tempted to accept a place on the bench with such low salaries: therefore, in 18 Henry VI., the judges of all the courts at Westminster, together with the king's attorney and serjeants, exhibited a petition in parliament concerning the regular payment of their salaries, and perquisites of robes. The king assented to their request, and order was taken for increasing their income, which afterwards became larger, and more fixed: this consisted of a salary, and an allowance for robes. In 1 Edward IV., Markham, the chief justice of the king's bench, had 170 marks per annum pension, £5, 6s. 6d. for his winter robes, and the same for his Whitsuntide robes; *juxta formam* (says the record) *cujusdam actûs in parliamento* 18 Henry VI.[4] Most of the judges had the honour of knighthood; some of them were knights-banneret, and some had the order of the Bath.[5]

The following is the state of the *Hospitia*, or inns, for the residence of professors of the law in the time of Henry VI.

Part of Serjeant's Inn, in Chancery Lane, was inhabited by some serjeants in the time of Henry IV., when it was called Faryndon's Inn: the inheritance of it belonged to the bishops of Ely. In the reign of Henry V., the whole house was demised to the judges and apprentices of the law, as appears by sums accounted for to the bishop. In 9 Henry VI., it obtained the name of *Hospitium Justitiariorum.* In 2 Richard III., there is a lease of it under the name of *Hospitium vocatum Serjeant's Inn;* this demise is at £4 per annum. It appears in 21 Henry VI., that the serjeants then, if not before, held Serjeant's Inn, in Fleet Street, under a demise from the dean and chapter of York, at the rent of ten marks per

[1] *Rot. Parl.*, An. 5 Hen. V., 2 Inst., 24.
[2] Fortesc. *de Laud.*, c. 51.
[3] *Dugd. Orig.*, 105.
[4] *Ibid.*, 109.
[5] *Ibid.*, 103.

annum.[1] There was also Scrope's Inn, inhabited by serjeants, which was sometimes called Serjeant's Inn. This was an inn during the reign of Richard III., and was next to Ely House, opposite St Andrew's Church, in Holborn.[2]

The *inns of court* were the four which have already been mentioned.[3] The ten *inns of chancery* in the reign of Henry VI., were the following:—Clifford's Inn, which was an inn of chancery as early as the reign of Henry V., and had the sign of the black lion. Clement's Inn was a residence for students in the reign of Henry IV., if not before. New Inn had been a common inn for travellers, and, from the sign of the Virgin Mary, it was sometimes called Our Lady's Inn. This house was inhabited by the students who removed from an old inn of chancery, called George's Inn, near St Sepulchre's Church, without Newgate. The Strand Inn, otherwise Chester Inn, from its neighbourhood to the Bishop of Chester's house. This inn, together with the church of St Mary le Strand, was pulled down in Edward VI.'s time, to make room for building Somerset House. Thavies Inn, we have seen, was a residence for students in the reign of Edward III. It was granted in fee to the benchers of Lincoln's Inn in Edward VI.'s time. Furnival's Inn, which once belonged to the Lords Furnival, was an inn of chancery in 9 Henry IV. The students held it under a lease: in the time of Edward VI., the inheritance was in the then Lord Shrewsbury, who sold it to the society of Lincoln's Inn, under whom the society of Furnival's Inn were afterwards tenants. Staple Inn was an inn of chancery in the reign of Henry V. The inheritance of it was granted in 20 Henry VIII. to the society of Gray's Inn. Barnard's Inn was a law society in the time of Henry VI. The tenth was perhaps George's Inn, before mentioned. These inns of chancery became all of them appendages to one or other of the inns of court, and seven only are now subsisting.

[1] *Dudg. Orig.*, 326. [2] *Ibid.* [3] *Vide ante.*

END OF VOL. II.

PRINTED BY BALLANTYNE AND COMPANY, PAUL'S WORK, EDINBURGH.